Overcoming inequality: why governance matters

Overcoming inequality: why governance matters

UNESCO Publishing

United Nations
Educational, Scientific and
Cultural Organization

OXFORD
UNIVERSITY PRESS

This Report is an independent publication commissioned by UNESCO on behalf of the international community. It is the product of a collaborative effort involving members of the Report Team and many other people, agencies, institutions and governments.

The designations employed and the presentation of the material in this publication do not imply the expression of any opinion whatsoever on the part of UNESCO concerning the legal status of any country, territory, city or area, or of its authorities, or concerning the delimitation of its frontiers or boundaries.

The EFA Global Monitoring Report Team is responsible for the choice and the presentation of the facts contained in this book and for the opinions expressed therein, which are not necessarily those of UNESCO and do not commit the Organization.

OXFORD
UNIVERSITY PRESS

Great Clarendon Street, Oxford OX2 6DP
Oxford University Press is a department of the University of Oxford.
It furthers the University's objective of excellence in research, scholarship, and education by publishing worldwide in Oxford New York Auckland Cape Town Dar es Salaam Hong Kong (China) Karachi Kuala Lumpur Madrid Melbourne Mexico City Nairobi New Delhi Shanghai Taipei Toronto With offices in Argentina Austria Brazil Chile Czech Republic France Greece Guatemala Hungary Italy Japan Poland Portugal Republic of Korea Singapore Switzerland Thailand Turkey Ukraine Viet Nam
Oxford is a registered trade mark of Oxford University Press in the UK and in certain other countries.

Published jointly by the United Nations Educational, Scientific and Cultural Organization (UNESCO), 7, Place de Fontenoy, 75352 Paris 07 SP, France and Oxford University Press, Great Clarendon Street, Oxford OX2 6DP, United Kingdom.

© UNESCO, 2009
All rights reserved
Second, revised printing
First published 2008
Published in 2009 by the United Nations Educational, Scientific and Cultural Organization
7, Place de Fontenoy, 75352 Paris 07 SP, France

Graphic design by Sylvaine Baeyens
Layout: Sylvaine Baeyens and Hélène Borel

Library of Congress Cataloging in Publication Data
Data available
Typeset by UNESCO
Printed on acid-free paper by Rotolito Lombarda SpA
OUP ISBN 978-0-19-954419-6
UNESCO ISBN 978-92-3-104089-4

Foreword

When a majority of the world's countries committed at the turn of the new century to achieve Education for All (EFA) by 2015, they did so with the confidence that the EFA goals would stand the test of time.

They are making a difference. Remarkable gains have been registered in many of the world's poorest countries towards universal primary education and gender parity. But we still have a long way to go. Progress has been too slow and too uneven in many countries. There is now a clear and present danger that some key goals will not be achieved. Averting that danger is vital, not just because education is a basic human right, but also because it is crucial for improving child and maternal health, individual incomes, environmental sustainability and economic growth, and for driving progress towards all the Millennium Development Goals.

This seventh edition of the *EFA Global Monitoring Report* offers a warning to governments, donors and the international community. On current trends universal primary education will not be achieved by 2015. Too many children are receiving an education of such poor quality that they leave school without basic literacy and numeracy skills. Finally, deep and persistent disparities based on wealth, gender, location, ethnicity and other markers for disadvantage are acting as a major barrier to progress in education. If the world's governments are serious about Education for All, they must get more serious about tackling inequality.

This Report persuasively argues that equity must be at the centre of the EFA agenda, to offset rising inequalities. Financing and governance reforms have an important role to play. Developing countries are not spending enough on basic education and donors have not lived up to their commitments. Stagnating aid to education is a serious concern for educational prospects in a large number of low-income countries. This clearly has to change in order to achieve EFA. But increased financing without equity will not benefit the most vulnerable and disadvantaged groups. A pro-poor approach to education policy is imperative for the goals to have meaning for the world's out-of-school children and 776 million adult illiterates.

The Report presents some of the public policy and governance reforms that can break the cycle of disadvantage, improve access, raise quality, and enhance participation and accountability.

At the September 2008 United Nations High-Level Event on the Millennium Development Goals, world leaders and a broad range of partners stressed the key role of education for achieving anti-poverty targets and pledged additional resources. It is crucial that governments and donors do not renege on these commitments if education is going to become a reality for all the world's children.

This Report, which tracks progress annually towards the EFA goals, offers a comprehensive overview of the state of education in the world today. It provides national and international policy-makers with the analysis of complex issues, lessons learned and recommendations to provide equal chances in learning for all children, youth and adults. We are now more than halfway to 2015. The diagnosis is clear; so are the most effective strategies for addressing the most pressing educational challenges. By publishing this authoritative annual report, UNESCO, as lead United Nations agency charged with coordinating efforts towards EFA, aims to inform and to influence policy in order to steer the right course to 2015.

Koïchiro Matsuura

Acknowledgements

This report is the product of a cooperative effort. It has been researched and written by the Global Monitoring Report team with the support of many people and organizations worldwide.

The team owes a special debt of gratitude to the members of the International Editorial Board and its chair, Marcela Gajardo. Nicholas Burnett, the former director of the team and now Assistant Director-General for Education at UNESCO, provided constant support and guidance.

The Report depends greatly on the work and expertise of the UNESCO Institute for Statistics (UIS). We thank its director, Hendrik van der Pol, along with Claude Apkabie, Saïd Belkachla, Georges Boade, Michael Bruneforth, Brian Buffet, Weixin Lu, Adriano Miele, Albert Motivans, Juan Cruz Persua, José Pessoa, Pascale Ratovondrahona, Ioulia Sementchouk, Saïd Ould Voffal and Yanhong Zhang. The UIS team made important contributions in many areas, particularly in the preparation of Chapter 2 and the statistical tables. Thanks also to Amy Otchet for helping disseminate the findings of the Report.

The analysis in the Report is informed by commissioned background papers from eminent researchers. We thank all the authors who prepared background papers for this year's Report: Rashid Ahmed, Samer Al-Samarrai, Nadir Altinok, Massimo Amadio, Vaidyanatha Ayyar, Masooda Bano, Elisabet Jané Camacho, Sergio Cardenas, Ketevan Chachakhiani, Luis A. Crouch, Anton De Grauwe, Nader Fergany, Hanspeter Geisseler, Alec Ian Gershberg, Katharine Giffard-Lindsay, Gabriele Göttelmann-Duret, Pablo González, Christine Harris-Van Keuren, Ken Harttgen, Janine Huisman, Ulla Kahla, Jackie Kirk, Stephan Klasen, Karine Kruijff, Xin Ma, Athena Maikish, Ben Mead, Mark Misselhorn, Mario Mouzinho, Karen Mundy, Juan-Enrique Opazo Marmentini, Supote Prasertsri, Claude Sauvageot, Yusuf Sayed, Ai Shoraku, Iveta Silova, Jeroen Smits, Devi Sridhar, Gita Steiner-Khamsi, Eszter Szucs, Tuomas Takala, Barbara Tournier and Paul Vachon.

Tragically, Jacqueline Kirk, one of our background paper authors, died in August 2008 during a mission to Afghanistan. Jackie was a passionate advocate for education in conflict and post-conflict situations, as well as a great scholar. Over the years she made important contributions to the Report in many areas. Her courage, commitment and insights will be greatly missed.

Many colleagues at UNESCO supported the work of the Global Monitoring Report team. We are indebted to numerous individuals within divisions and units of UNESCO's Education Sector, the International Institute for Educational Planning, the International Bureau of Education and the UNESCO Institute for Lifelong Learning. UNESCO regional bureaux provided helpful advice on country-level activities and helped facilitate commissioned studies.

We are grateful to the Education Policy and Data Center at the Academy for Educational Development, and particularly to Karima Barrow, Ania Chaluda, Joseph Goodfriend, George Ingram, HyeJin Kim, Sarah Oliver, Ben Sylla and Annababette Wills for their valuable contribution and data for Chapter 2.

We are also grateful to Desmond Bermingham and Luc-Charles Gacougnolle of the Fast Track Initiative Secretariat and to Julia Benn, Valérie Gaveau, Cecile Sangare and Simon Scott of the Development Assistance Committee (DAC) of the Organisation for Economic Co-operation and Development (OECD) for their continuing support and helpful advice on international cooperation and aid data.

Special thanks to Paul Bennell, Vittoria Cavicchioni, Louis Crouch, Rob Jenkins, Thomas Kellaghan, Marlene Lockheed, Albert Motivans, Steve Packer and Abby Riddell, all of whom provided valuable comments on draft chapters.

We would like to thank François Leclercq for his contribution to the development of the financing section in Chapter 3.

The production of the Report benefited greatly from the editorial expertise of Rebecca Brite and Wenda McNevin as well as from the support of Anaïs Loizillon, who assisted in developing graphic material and the governance mapping Annex. We wish to acknowledge the work of Jan Worall, who prepared the Report's comprehensive index. We also thank our colleagues Fouzia Belhami, Lotfi Ben Khelifa and Judith Roca of the UNESCO Education Knowledge Management Service for their help.

Nino Muñoz Gomez, Sue Williams and the staff of UNESCO's Bureau of Public Information have provided constant support in bringing the report to global media attention and giving advice in matters relating to web, audiovisual and print publication.

The EFA Global Monitoring Report Team

Director
Kevin Watkins

Samer Al-Samarrai, Nicole Bella, Aaron Benavot, Philip Marc Boua Liebnitz, Mariela Buonomo, Fadila Caillaud, Alison Clayson, Cynthia Guttman, Anna Haas, Julia Heiss, Keith Hinchliffe, Diederick de Jongh, Leila Loupis, Isabelle Merkoviç, Patrick Montjourides, Claudine Mukizwa, Ulrika Peppler Barry, Paula Razquin, Pauline Rose, Suhad Varin.

For more information about the Report, please contact:
The Director
EFA Global Monitoring Report Team
c/o UNESCO
7, place de Fontenoy, 75352 Paris 07 SP, France
e-mail: efareport@unesco.org
Tel.: +33 1 45 68 10 36
Fax: +33 1 45 68 56 41
www.efareport.unesco.org

Previous EFA Global Monitoring Reports
2008. Education for All by 2015 – Will we make it?
2007. Strong foundations – Early childhood care and education
2006. Literacy for life
2005. Education for All – The quality imperative
2003/4. Gender and Education for All – The leap to equality
2002. Education for All – Is the world on track?

Any errors or omissions found subsequent to printing will be corrected in the online version at www.efareport.unesco.org

Contents

List of figures, tables, text boxes and map

Figures

Tables

Text boxes

- Children from poor households, rural areas, slums and other disadvantaged groups face major obstacles in access to a good quality education. While children from the wealthiest 20% of households have already achieved universal primary school attendance in most countries, those from the poorest 20% have a long way to go.

- Trends in primary education are susceptible to public policy. Ethiopia and the United Republic of Tanzania are making remarkable progress in increasing enrolment and reaching the poor, thanks to policies such as the abolition of school fees, the construction of schools in underserved areas and increased teacher recruitment. In Nigeria and Pakistan, poor education governance is holding back progress and keeping millions of children out of school.

- In 2006, some 513 million students worldwide – or 58% of the relevant school-age population – were enrolled in secondary school, an increase of nearly 76 million since 1999. Despite progress, access remains limited for most of the world's young people. In sub-Saharan Africa, 75% of secondary-school-age children are not enrolled in secondary school.

Goal 3 – Meeting the lifelong learning needs of youth and adults

- Governments are not giving priority to youth and adult learning needs in their education policies. Meeting the lifelong needs of youth and adults needs stronger political commitment and more public funding. It will also require more clearly defined concepts and better data for effective monitoring.

Goal 4 – Adult literacy

- An estimated 776 million adults – or 16% of the world's adult population – lack basic literacy skills. About two-thirds are women. Most countries have made little progress in recent years. If current trends continue, there will be over 700 million adults lacking literacy skills in 2015.

- Between 1985–1994 and 2000–2006, the global adult literacy rate increased from 76% to 84%. However, forty-five countries have adult literacy rates below the developing country average of 79%, mostly in sub-Saharan Africa, and South and West Asia. Nearly all of them are off track to meet the adult literacy target by 2015. Nineteen of these countries have literacy rates of less than 55%.

- Major disparities in literacy levels within countries are often linked with poverty and other forms of disadvantage. In seven sub-Saharan African countries with low overall adult literacy rates, the literacy gap between the poorest and wealthiest households is more than forty percentage points.

Goal 5 – Gender

- In 2006, of the 176 countries with data, 59 had achieved gender parity in both primary and secondary education – 20 countries more than in 1999. At the primary level, about two-thirds of countries had achieved parity. However, more than half the countries in sub-Saharan Africa, South and West Asia and the Arab States had not reached the target. Only 37% of countries worldwide had achieved gender parity at secondary level.

- There is a confirmed trend towards more female than male enrolments in tertiary education worldwide, in particular in more developed regions and in the Caribbean and Pacific.

- Poverty and other forms of social disadvantage magnify gender disparities. For example, in Mali girls from poor households are four times less likely to attend primary school than those from rich households, rising to eight times at secondary level.

- Once girls are in school, their progress is often hampered by teacher attitudes and gender-biased textbooks that reinforce negative gender stereotypes. These school-based factors interact with wider social and economic factors that influence school performance along gender lines.

Goal 6 – Quality

- International assessments highlight large achievement gaps between students in rich and poor countries. Within countries too, inequality exists between regions, communities, schools and classrooms. These disparities have important implications not just in education but for the wider distribution of opportunities in society.

- In developing countries there are substantially higher proportions of low learning achievement. In a recent Southern and Eastern Africa Consortium for Monitoring Educational Quality assessment (SACMEC II) in sub-Saharan Africa, fewer than 25% of grade 6 pupils reached a desirable level of reading in four countries and only 10% in six others.

- Student background, the organization of the education system and the school environment explain learning disparities within each country. Many essential resources taken for granted in developed countries remain scarce in developing countries – including basic infrastructure such as electricity, seats and textbooks.

- More than 27 million teachers work in the world's primary schools, 80% of them in developing countries. Total primary school staff increased by 5% between 1999 and 2006. In sub-Saharan Africa alone, 1.6 million new teacher posts must be created and teachers recruited by 2015 to achieve UPE, rising to 3.8 million if retirement, resignations and losses (due to HIV/AIDs, for example) are taken into account.

- There are large national and regional disparities in pupil/teacher ratios, with marked teacher shortages in South and West Asia, and sub-Saharan Africa. But it is within countries that the greatest disparities exist, with teachers unevenly distributed across regions.

Financing education

National finance

- In the majority of countries with data, national spending on education has increased since Dakar. In some countries, increased spending has been associated with substantial progress on the EFA goals. However, the share of national income devoted to education decreased in 40 of the 105 countries with data between 1999 and 2006.

- Low-income countries are still spending significantly less on education than are other countries. In sub-Saharan Africa, eleven out of the twenty-one low-income countries with data spend less than 4% of their GNP. In South Asia, several high-population countries continue to spend under or only just over 3% of their GNP on education. This appears to reflect low political commitment to education.

- Global wealth inequalities are mirrored by inequalities in education spending. In 2004, North America and Western Europe alone accounted for 55% of the world's spending on education but only 10% of the population aged 5 to 25. Sub-Saharan Africa accounts for 15% of 5- to 25-year-olds but just 2% of global spending. South and West Asia represents over one-quarter of the population and just 7% of spending.

International aid

- Commitments to basic education are stagnating. In 2006, for developing countries, they amounted to US$5.1 billion, a little below the 2004 level. Half of all commitments to basic education came from just a handful of donors.

- Total aid for basic education for low-income countries in 2006 was US$3.8 billion. The amount will have to be tripled to reach the estimated US$11 billion required annually to finance a narrow range of goals in low-income countries.

- The Fast Track Initiative (FTI) is failing to galvanize additional bilateral donor support for EFA. Current commitments to its Catalytic Fund fall short of those required to meet financing requests in the pipeline. By 2010, countries with plans approved by the FTI could be facing a financing shortfall of US$2.2 billion.

- An ambitious new agenda governing aid hopes to make aid more efficient and effective. To date progress is mixed: though some donors are willing to encourage national ownership, work through national systems and cooperate with other donors, others are more reticent.

Top policy recommendations

Meeting the EFA goals

Early childhood care and education

- **Strengthen the links** between education planning and child health provision, using cash transfer programmes, targeted health interventions and more equitable public spending in health sectors.

- **Prioritize early childhood education and care** in planning for all children, with incentives provided to include those who are vulnerable and disadvantaged.

- **Strengthen wider anti-poverty commitments** by tackling child malnutrition and improving public health systems, using innovative social welfare programmes which target poor households.

Universal primary education

- **Fix ambitious long-term goals** supported by realistic planning and sufficient medium- to long-term budgetary allocations to ensure progress in access, participation and completion in primary education.

- **Support equity** for girls, disadvantaged groups and underserved regions by setting clear targets for reducing disparities, backed by practical strategies for achieving more equitable outcomes.

- **Raise quality while expanding access** by focusing on smooth progression though school and better learning outcomes, increasing textbook supply and quality, strengthening teacher training and support, and ensuring that class sizes are conducive to learning.

Education quality

- **Strengthen policy commitments** to quality education and create effective learning environments for all students, including adequate facilities, well-trained teachers, relevant curricula and clearly identified learning outcomes. A focus on teachers and learning should be at the heart of this commitment.

- Ensure that all children attending primary school for at least four to five years **acquire the basic literacy and numeracy skills** that they need to develop their potential.

- Develop the capacity to **measure, monitor and assess education quality,** in areas that affect learning conditions (infrastructure, textbooks, class sizes), processes (language, instructional time) and outcomes.

- Revise existing policies and regulations to ensure that children have **sufficient instructional time** and that all schools minimize the gap between intended and actual instructional time.

- Participate in comparative regional and international **learning assessments** and translate lessons learned into national policy, and develop national assessments that best reflect each country's particular needs and goals.

Overcoming inequality – lessons for national governance reforms

- **Commit to the reduction of disparities** based on wealth, location, ethnicity, gender and other indicators for disadvantage. Governments should develop well-defined targets for reducing disparities and monitor progress towards their achievement.

- **Sustain political leadership** to reach education targets and tackle inequality through clear policy objectives and improved coordination within government through active engagement with civil society, the private sector and marginalized groups.

- **Strengthen policies for reducing poverty** and deep social inequalities that hinder progress towards education for all. Governments should integrate education planning into wider poverty-reduction strategies.

- **Raise quality standards** in education and work to ensure that disparities in learning achievement between regions, communities and schools are reduced.

- **Increase national education spending,** especially in developing countries that chronically underinvest in education.

- **Put equity at the centre** of financing strategies, in order to reach disadvantaged children, with more accurate estimates of the costs of reducing disparities and the development of incentives for reaching the most marginalized.

- **Ensure that decentralization** has an inbuilt commitment to equity through financing formulas that link resources to levels of poverty and deprivation in education.

- **Recognize that school competition and choice,** and private-public partnerships have their limits. If a public education system works poorly, the priority must be to fix it.

- **Strengthen the recruitment, deployment and motivation of teachers** to ensure that there are enough qualified teachers in all regions and schools, especially in remote and underserved communities.

Aid donors – delivering on commitments

- **Increase aid for basic education,** especially to low-income countries, by providing around US$7 billion to cover current financing gaps in priority EFA areas.

- **Enlarge the group of donor countries** committed to providing aid to basic education, in order to ensure that the financial support for the EFA goals is sustainable.

- **Commit to equity in aid for education** by providing more funds to basic education in low-income countries. Several donors – including France and Germany – should urgently review their current aid allocations.

- **Get behind the Fast Track Initiative** and close the projected financing gap – estimated at US$2.2 billion for 2010 – for countries with approved plans.

- **Improve aid effectiveness** and reduce transaction costs, as set out in the Paris Declaration, through greater alignment of aid behind national priorities, better coordination, increased use of national financial management systems and greater predictability in aid flows. ■

Overview

Eight years have passed since representatives of more than 160 governments gathered at the World Education Forum in Dakar, Senegal, to adopt an ambitious Framework for Action aimed at expanding learning opportunities for children, youth and adults. At the heart of the Framework is a pledge to achieve six Education for All (EFA) goals. The Dakar promise extends from early childhood care and education (ECCE) and universal primary education (UPE) to gender equality, the spread of adult literacy, the expansion of skills programmes for youth and adults, and improvements in the quality of education. Underpinning the Framework is a commitment to inclusive and equitable education provision and opportunity for all the world's citizens.

This edition of the *EFA Global Monitoring Report* comes at a critical moment. With the 2015 deadline for some key goals just over the horizon, there are worrying signs of a large-scale shortfall. Remarkable gains have been registered in many of the world's poorest countries,[1] but the distance remaining is great. Governments and aid donors have to act with a renewed sense of urgency and shared commitment to deliver on the pledges they made in 2000. These promises cannot wait and time is running out.

The Report, titled *Overcoming Inequality: Why Governance Matters*, identifies deep and persistent disparities based on income, gender, location, ethnicity and other markers for disadvantage as a major barrier to progress in education. Inequity in education is linked to wider disparities in the distribution of power, wealth and opportunity. And it is perpetuated by policies that either tolerate or actively exacerbate an unfair distribution of life chances – policies that fuel the transmission of poverty across generations.

Inequalities in education of the magnitude observed in many countries are unacceptable. The circumstances into which children are born, their gender, the wealth of their parents, their language and the colour of their skin should not define their educational opportunities. Apart from being inequitable, large disparities in education are inefficient: they hold back economic growth and progress in other areas. Governments and aid donors can do a great deal to equalize opportunity in education, working with civil society and local movements for change. The starting point is to put equity squarely at the centre of the EFA agenda.

Extreme inequalities in education are linked to wider disparities in society. Overcoming these inequalities requires effective and committed government leadership and a public sector with the human and financial resources to break down disadvantage. More than that, it requires good governance. In its broadest sense, governance is about the processes, policies and institutional arrangements that connect the many actors in education. It defines the responsibilities of national and subnational governments in areas such as finance, management and regulation. Governance rules stipulate who decides what, from the national finance or education ministry down to the classroom and community. Good governance practices can help foster development of more inclusive, more responsive education systems that address the real needs of the marginalized. Bad governance practices have the opposite effect.

Education has been at the forefront of a wider governance reform agenda. Outcomes to date have not been encouraging, especially when it comes to equity. Approaches to financial decentralization, choice and competition in school management, and the integration of education planning with wider strategies for poverty reduction have not given the required impetus to EFA. One reason is that equity considerations have typically been bolted onto governance reforms as an afterthought.

Government responsibility for acting on the Dakar Framework extends to international aid partnerships. Having signed up for the Framework, donors in rich countries have underperformed. Aid flows are falling far short of the required levels, calling into question donors' commitment to ensure that no developing country would fail in its planning for EFA for want of finance. Donors are also falling short of commitments to increase aid by 2010. Besides keeping their promises on aid, donors need to address governance problems that are undermining the quality and effectiveness of development assistance.

1. Throughout the Report, the word 'countries' should generally be understood as meaning 'countries and territories'.

Chapter 1
Education for all: human right and catalyst for development

The EFA agenda is rooted in a commitment to human rights and social justice. It recognizes that expanding and equalizing opportunities for education are development goals in their own right. But the Dakar Framework for Action also defines a public policy agenda linking education to wider development goals. Progress towards equitable education can act as a powerful catalyst for progress in other areas, including public health, poverty reduction, gender equality, participation and democratization.

The Millennium Development Goals (MDGs), also adopted in 2000, are the world's time-bound and quantitative targets for addressing extreme human deprivation in its many dimensions. The targets range from halving extreme poverty to cutting child and maternal death rates and reducing malnutrition. Education is part of the MDG framework. However, the MDG targets for education are far less ambitious and more restrictive than the EFA agenda. The MDG project is at a watershed. While there has been progress in many areas, it has been uneven and too slow to achieve the targets. In September 2008, governments from around the world met at a United Nations summit in New York to reaffirm their MDG commitments – but reaffirmation alone does not bring the targets within reach.

Accelerated progress in education could play an important role in getting the world on track to achieve the wider MDG goals. Recent research has reinforced earlier evidence on the key role of education as a catalyst for human development. The links run two ways. Progress in education can unlock progress in health, nutrition and poverty reduction, and vice versa. This has important implications in areas where the MDG outcomes are lagging far behind target levels:

- **Halving extreme poverty.** Broad-based and equitable economic growth is the key to cutting income poverty. There is strong evidence linking education to higher growth and productivity. The increasing importance of knowledge for economic growth may be strengthening the links. When educational opportunities are broadly shared, with marginalized groups participating, prospects for shared economic growth are strengthened.

- **Child mortality and nutrition.** In many countries, having a mother with secondary or higher education more than halves the risk of child mortality, relative to mothers with no education. Controlling for other factors, when a Bangladeshi mother has completed primary education, it cuts the risk of child stunting by 20%. These outcomes reflect the empowering effects of education in expanding access to information and to health service use. The case for gender equality in education is important in its own right. It is also true that no country can afford the prohibitive human, social and economic costs that come with gender inequality.

The potential benefits of the EFA agenda extend far beyond the MDGs. Recent evidence from sub-Saharan Africa points to the important role of education in building support for multiparty democracy and in challenging autocracy. As the latest learning assessment by the Organisation for Economic Co-operation and Development's Programme for International Student Assessment (OECD-PISA) shows, education also equips children with the learning skills they need to understand complex environmental problems – including climate change – and to hold political leaders to account for resolving them.

Chapter 2
The Dakar goals: monitoring progress and inequality

Monitoring of progress towards the EFA goals serves many purposes. It provides global, regional and national measures of how close the Dakar Framework is to being fulfilled. Effective monitoring can also pick up early warning signals, alerting governments and the international community to potential failures. And it is an essential element for holding governments to account for their actions and performance.

Building on the previous Report's systematic midterm assessment of progress towards EFA, the *EFA Global Monitoring Report 2009* draws on data for the school year ending in 2006. It highlights the extraordinary progress made in many areas, notably by some of the poorest countries. That progress bears testimony to the fact that the EFA goals are attainable. With strong political commitment, the right public policies and sufficient financial commitment, all countries have the potential to move rapidly towards meeting the six goals. The bad news is that the world is not on track for achieving several key targets, including UPE by 2015. Changing this picture requires urgent action. It takes time to build classrooms, train teachers and put in place policies to remove barriers facing the disadvantaged – and time is running out.

Goal 1: Early childhood care and education

ECCE is the foundation of the EFA agenda. The health and nutritional status of children, especially during the first two years of life, has a profound influence on their cognitive development and learning achievements in school. Early childhood malnutrition affects brain development and diminishes prospects for success in school and beyond. Pre-primary education and health provision can counter early childhood disadvantage. Good-quality ECCE programmes have a strong track record in reducing dropout rates in primary school, improving learning achievements and narrowing inequalities.

Childhood malnutrition and poor health are two of the greatest barriers to EFA. Progress in both areas has lagged far behind progress in getting children into school. The upshot is that millions of children entering school have had their brains, their cognitive development and their education potential permanently damaged by hunger and ill health. This runs counter to the commitments made in the Dakar Framework for Action: filling classrooms with malnourished and sick children is not what UPE is about. The facts of childhood deprivation make their own case for a strengthened focus on early childhood:

- **Child mortality.** Around 10 million children a year die in developing countries before their fifth birthday. Survival prospects are improving – but far too slowly. Estimates for 2015 based on current trends show that the gap between the MDG target of a two-thirds reduction in child deaths and actual outcomes will amount to 4.3 million deaths. Already significant inequalities in child death rates between rich and poor are widening in many countries.

- **Stunting and low birth weight.** Around one in three children under 5 – 193 million in total – suffer moderate to severe stunting. The vast majority of these children live in South Asia, where almost half of all children are affected, and in sub-Saharan Africa. Low birth weight is a risk factor for ill-health and stunting and an indicator for poor maternal health. Some 16% of children in developing countries were delivered with low birth weight in 2006, rising to 29% in South Asia.

- **Vitamin and mineral deficiencies.** Millions of children are affected by micronutrient deficiency. Iron deficiency anaemia, which affects around half of pre-school children in developing countries, impairs cognitive development and increases vulnerability to infectious diseases.

More rapid economic growth alone will not overcome these deficits. Over the past two decades, India has been among the world's fastest-growing economies. By contrast, child health and nutrition have been improving very slowly. Rising food prices could undermine international efforts to counteract malnutrition in many countries, with damaging consequences for the EFA goals.

The record on pre-school provision is discouraging. Enrolments are increasing but the vast majority of the world's children continue to lack access to quality pre-schools. Gross enrolment ratios (GERs) in 2006 averaged 79% in developed countries and 36% in developing countries. Of the thirty-five countries in sub-Saharan Africa for which data are available, seventeen had coverage rates below 10%. Coverage rates are lowest for precisely those children who stand to gain the most: namely, the poor and disadvantaged.

Weak public policies in ECCE are holding back accelerated progress towards wider EFA goals and reinforcing education disparities. Evidence from several countries demonstrates what can be achieved. Countries such as Bangladesh, Ethiopia, Nepal and the United Republic of Tanzania have made rapid progress in reducing child mortality and improving child health. In the Philippines an integrated ECCE programme has registered strong improvements in cognitive development. In Mexico a conditional cash transfer programme linked to early childhood health and education has achieved tangible gains in primary school progression and learning achievement.

It is not just developing countries that face problems in ECCE. While most developed countries have high levels of early childhood provision, this is not the case in the United States, which has relatively low and highly unequal levels of coverage. The evidence suggests that inequalities in early childhood education are an important source of disparities in primary and secondary school.

Goal 2: Universal primary education

UPE is not just about getting children into school at an appropriate age. It is also about ensuring that they stay in school to complete a full cycle of quality basic education. The report card is mixed.

Some impressive gains have been registered. The net enrolment ratio (NER) for developing countries as a group increased between 1999 and 2006 at twice the rate of the 1990s. In sub-Saharan Africa, it increased from 54% to 70%. This is six times the rate of the 1990s – and it was achieved despite rapid population growth. In South and West Asia the NER climbed from 75% to 86%. Behind these regional figures are some remarkable achievements:

- Ethiopia more than doubled its NER to 71%.
- The NERs for Benin and the United Republic of Tanzania moved from around 50% to more than 80%.
- In the midst of a civil conflict, Nepal increased its NER from 65% to 79% (in 2004).
- Among the Arab States, Djibouti, Mauritania, Morocco and Yemen registered strong gains.

Post-Dakar progress is also reflected in a decline in the number of children out of school. There were 28 million fewer out-of-school children in 2006 than when governments met in Dakar in 2000. In sub-Saharan Africa, the number of primary-school-age children not in school dropped by 10 million while the population in that age group increased by 17 million. South and West Asia more than halved its out-of-school population, from 37 million to 18 million.

These figures can be traced to political leadership and effective public policies. Increased public investment, ambitious school construction programmes, the abolition of school fees, measures to strengthen quality and – critically – the targeting of disadvantaged groups have all played a role. So have increased recruitment and training of teachers.

The distance travelled towards the EFA goals since 1999 should not obscure the distance that remains. The yardstick is not the record of the 1990s but the target of UPE by 2015. On current trends, it will be missed:

- In 2006 some 75 million children of primary school age were not in school. This is 12% of the developing world's primary-school-age population. In sub-Saharan Africa, nearly one-third of that age group is out of school. At the start of the twenty-first century, in an increasingly prosperous, knowledge-based global economy, millions of children do not even have a foot on the first rung of the EFA ladder.
- Girls still account for the majority of the world's out-of-school children (55%). Importantly, out-of-school girls are also more likely never to have been to school than boys.

This Report provides a partial projection for the out-of-school population in 2015. It is partial because, for reasons of data limitation, it covers countries that are home to just two-thirds of out-of-school children in the relevant age group. Countries that are not covered include Sudan and the Democratic Republic of the Congo, both of which have large populations affected. Even with the exemptions, a business-as-usual trajectory suggests that there will still be 29 million children out of school in 2015. Slow progress towards UPE in Nigeria and Pakistan is pushing these countries towards the top of the out-of-school league table. By 2015, more than 10 million children could be out of school in these two countries alone.

Out-of-school figures and projections capture just one aspect of the challenge that has to be addressed to bring UPE within reach by 2015. In many countries, primary school students are locked into cycles of repetition and early dropout. In Malawi, just over six in ten children enter primary school at the official age – and half of them either drop out or repeat grade 1. Of the thirty-one countries in sub-Saharan Africa with data, eleven have grade 1 and 2 repetition rates in excess of 20%. The problem is also widespread in Latin America. This year's Report highlights the inefficiencies and inequalities associated with grade repetition.

Combining data on enrolment and completion highlights the scale of global inequality in education. Children in Britain or France are more likely to enter tertiary education than children in the Niger or Senegal are to complete primary school. Such inequalities in the international distribution of opportunity for education have important implications for future patterns of globalization. Today's inequalities in education are tomorrow's inequalities in the distribution of wealth and wider opportunities for human development.

Inequality as a barrier to progress

Inequalities within countries are also marked. When it comes to primary school attendance, children from rich and poor households move in different worlds. National averages can obscure this point. If the richest 20% in countries including Bangladesh, Bolivia, Ghana, India and Nigeria were a country, they would almost have achieved UPE. The poor have a long way to go.

Simple UPE arithmetic points to a strong case for greater focus on equity. In countries with school attendance rates above 80%, children from poor households are heavily over-represented among out-of-school children. They account for more than 40% of the non-attending school population in countries from Cameroon and Kenya to Indonesia and Nicaragua. Even in countries with lower levels of attendance reported in household surveys, such as Ghana, India, Mozambique, Nigeria and Zambia, the poorest quintile accounts for 30% to 40% of the out-of-school population.

Income-based disparities intersect with wider inequalities. Rural children in many developing countries are less likely to attend school and more likely to drop out. In Senegal, children in urban areas are twice as likely as those in rural areas to be in school. Slum dwellers face a distinctive set of challenges, with high levels of poverty, ill health and limited provision restricting access. Socio-cultural inequalities linked to ethnicity and language are also important. Disadvantage in each of these areas is related to, and compounded by, poverty and income-based inequalities – but they are also important in their own right.

Other barriers to UPE also have to be removed if the 2015 targets are to be achieved. Child labour is one of the most formidable. There are around 218 million child labourers in developing countries, and numbers are coming down slowly in sub-Saharan Africa and parts of Asia. Ill health and malnutrition undermine school attendance and learning capacity for millions of children. And childhood disability is strongly associated with inequalities in participation, reflecting a widespread failure to implement policies for inclusive education.

Post-primary education

Increasing participation in secondary education is part of the Dakar commitment. Progress in this area is vital. Expanded access to secondary school is needed to absorb the increase in numbers of children emerging from primary schools, to create incentives for primary school completion and to train teachers. Secondary and post-secondary education is also important for the development of skills needed in an increasingly knowledge-based global economy.

There are large regional disparities in participation in secondary schools. At one end of the spectrum, most developed and transition economies are nearing universal secondary education. At the other, the secondary NER for sub-Saharan Africa is just 25%, implying that nearly 78 million children of the relevant age group are not enrolled in secondary school. The transition point from primary to secondary is marked by high levels of dropout in many countries. As at primary level, progression through the secondary school system is characterized by rising inequalities. In Latin America, 88% of children from the wealthiest decile move steadily through the secondary school system without repetition or dropout – twice the share for the poorest decile.

Global disparities are strongly apparent at tertiary level. The global tertiary GER is around 25%. Regional GERs, however, range from 70% in North America and Western Europe to 32% in Latin America and 5% in sub-Saharan Africa. Beyond the quantitative gaps are large qualitative disparities fuelled by differences in financing capacity. In equivalent dollar terms, France spends sixteen times as much per university student as Peru. In 2005, the top American universities spent over twenty-five times as much per student as Dar-es-Salaam University in the United Republic of Tanzania.

Tertiary education is the point at which the cumulative effects of disparities at the primary and secondary level become apparent. In Brazil, the university participation for black people is 6% – just under one-third of the rate for white Brazilians.

Goals 3 and 4: Lifelong learning and literacy

Achieving UPE would establish a basis for lifelong learning and literacy for future generations. But there is an immense backlog of unmet need. Millions of teenagers have never attended primary school and millions more leave without the skills they need. Limited access to educational opportunities in the past has also left 776 million adults –two-thirds of them women – lacking basic literacy skills.

Many governments have paid insufficient attention to youth and adult learning needs. Public funding remains inadequate and provision highly unequal. The fact that some of the goals in the Dakar Framework were vaguely worded may have contributed to a lack of urgency. The sixth International Conference on Adult Education, scheduled for 2009, provides an important opportunity to change this picture.

Illiteracy continues to receive inadequate attention from policy-makers. Although there were 95 million fewer illiterates worldwide in 2000–2006 than in 1985–1994, absolute numbers have increased in sub-Saharan Africa and the Arab States. On current trends there will still be over 700 million adult illiterates in 2015.

Many factors contribute to low literacy levels, including gender disparities, poverty, location and ethnicity. The problem is not restricted to developing countries. Many OECD countries also record high levels of literacy problems: 1 million native Dutch speakers in the Netherlands are classified as functionally illiterate, for example. In metropolitan France, some 10% of the population aged 18 to 65 – more than 3 million people – lacks basic reading, writing, arithmetic and other fundamental skills despite having attended French schools.

Goal 5: Gender disparities and inequalities in education

The Dakar Framework sets out an ambitious two-part agenda on gender equity. The first part aims at gender parity in school participation and the second at wider progress towards equality between girls and boys in educational opportunities and outcomes.

The world has made sustained progress towards gender parity, but deficits remain large. Of the 176 countries in 2006 with data, 59 had achieved gender parity in both primary and secondary education. Over half the countries of sub-Saharan Africa, South and West Asia, and the Arab States have yet to achieve parity at primary level.

There are large regional variations in progress towards gender parity. Advances in sub-Saharan Africa have been slow and uneven. The regional gender parity index (GPI), which measures the ratio of girls to boys primary GER, rose from 0.85 in 1999 to 0.89 in 2006, though several countries – including Ghana and the United Republic of Tanzania – have achieved parity. The GPI for South and West Asia rose from 0.84 to 0.95. However, Pakistan still enrols only 80 girls for every 100 boys in primary school.

Expansion of secondary school enrolment has led to reductions in gender disparities in most regions. However, gender disparities remain larger in secondary education than in primary. In many countries in sub-Saharan Africa, and South and West Asia, participation rates for girls remain low and disparities high. One major exception is Bangladesh, which has achieved gender parity. Public policy, notably the creation of financial incentives through stipend programmes, has played a key role. Underparticipation by boys is marked in many countries, especially in Latin America.

Gender disparities are unequally distributed across societies. Being born into a household that is poor, rural or indigenous, or speaks a minority language, reinforces gender disadvantage in many countries. In Mali, the GPI for the poorest 20% of households was 0.60 in 2001, whereas many more girls in the richest 20% were attending primary school. The secondary GPI is 0.50 for the poorest households and 0.96 for the wealthiest. Such facts demonstrate how poverty often magnifies the effects of gender disparities.

Gender equality is more difficult to measure than parity. Learning achievements provide one benchmark. Four broad themes emerge from international assessments. First, girls often outperform boys in reading and literacy. Second, boys outperform girls in mathematics, though the gap is closing. Third, boys maintain a small advantage in science. Fourth, at the tertiary level women remain under-represented in science and engineering and 'over-represented' in areas such as education and health.

Goal 6: Education quality and learning achievements

The ultimate goal of education is to equip children with the knowledge, skills and opportunities they need to realize their potential and to participate in social and political life. Many education systems are failing to achieve this goal.

Progress in quantitative headcount indicators has masked problems in qualitative learning achievement. In many developing countries, absolute levels of average learning are exceptionally low. International learning assessments draw attention to the very large disparities between rich and poor countries. Within countries, too, there are often large differences in test scores based on socio-economic status, school performance and other variables.

Getting children into school and through a full cycle of basic education remains a major priority. But evidence from many countries suggests that, once in school, many children are acquiring only the most rudimentary skills, as the following examples demonstrate:

- One recent assessment in the Punjab province of Pakistan found that over two-thirds of grade 3 students could not write a sentence in Urdu and a similar proportion could not solve a simple subtraction problem.

- In India, a large-scale assessment found that 45% of children in standard 3 could not read a text designed for standard 1 students.

- Results from the Southern and Eastern Africa Consortium for Monitoring Educational Quality (SACMEQ) II assessment in Africa indicated that the share of grade 6 children reaching the 'desirable' level of literacy was less than 25% in Botswana, Kenya and South Africa, and less than 10% in Malawi, Mozambique, Uganda and Zambia.

- A recent assessment in Peru found that as few as 30% of children in grade 1, and 50% in grade 2, could read a simple passage from a grade 1 textbook.

These examples, which could be multiplied many times over, draw attention to the sheer scale of the learning achievement deficit in many countries.

International assessments reinforce this picture. They draw attention to the low average level of learning in many developing countries relative to developed countries. To take one illustration from the PISA 2001 assessment, the median scores for students in Brazil, Indonesia and Peru would be situated in the lowest 20% of the distribution in France or the United States. PISA 2006 showed that over 60% of students from Brazil and Indonesia scored at or below the lowest level in science, compared with fewer than 10% in Canada or Finland. Other international assessments confirm the scale of global inequalities.

Real learning divides are larger than those captured in international assessments. This is because assessments measure learning outcomes among children in school and do not include children who are currently or permanently out of school. Given that out-of-school children would be expected to score at lower levels than children in school, the real national averages may be well below those indicated.

Within-country inequalities in outcomes often mirror global disparities in scale. In countries including Morocco and South Africa, the top 5% of pupils covered in the Progress in International Reading Literacy Survey (PIRLS) assessment registered scores comparable to those of the best pupils in high-achieving countries. But the scores of the bottom 5% were less than one-fifth of those for top performers. Research in the Indian states of Rajasthan and Orissa also points to extremely large learning disparities.

Many factors influence learning achievement levels. Student characteristics play a significant role. Socio-economic status, family size and composition, immigrant status and home language are all important variables. System-level variables, such as access to early childhood provision, selection and the social composition of schools, are also influential.

School-based factors have a strong effect on learning. Insufficient instructional time is one source of underachievement. A study in Bangladesh found that 10% of government schools provided fewer than 500 hours of instruction, compared with 860 hours at the other end of the spectrum. In many cases, children and teachers lack access to basic learning materials. SACMEQ II found that over half of grade 6 pupils in many countries – including Malawi, Mozambique, Uganda and Zambia – did not have a single book. A poor learning environment can exacerbate social disparities.

The state of a nation's schools can have an important bearing on prospects for success in education. Dilapidated school buildings, overcrowded and under-resourced classrooms, and an inadequate supply of teaching materials can all hurt learning prospects – and dilapidation is widespread. One of the most comprehensive recent surveys of the state of primary schools, overseen by the UNESCO Institute for Statistics, found that more than one-third of students in India, Peru and the Philippines attended schools with insufficient toilets. More than half the school heads in some countries surveyed felt their schools needed complete rebuilding. As in other areas, the poor bear the brunt. Evidence from Latin America shows that badly equipped schools are disproportionately attended by children from the poorest households.

Teachers are the front-line providers in education. Delivery of quality education is critically dependent on having a sufficient supply of properly trained and motivated teachers. How teachers are deployed also has an important bearing on equity and learning outcomes.

Acute teacher shortages remain a problem in many countries. If the world is to achieve UPE by 2015, it will need to recruit an estimated 18 million additional teachers. In sub-Saharan Africa, an additional 145,000 recruitments are needed annually – 77% above the observed increase between 1999 and 2006. South and West Asia will need an additional 3.6 million teachers.

National pupil/teacher ratios (PTRs) sometimes mask very large disparities. There are large variations in ratios within countries, often reflecting differences between rich and poor, rural and urban, and indigenous and non-indigenous areas. Inequalities in access to trained teachers reinforce these differences. In India, the majority of untrained teachers are concentrated in rural areas. In Ghana, they are concentrated in the north, the poorest part of the country.

Reported PTRs are often a misleading indicator for what happens in schools. Teacher absenteeism has an important bearing on learning in many countries. In a recent study covering six developing countries, absenteeism rates averaged 19%, rising to 25% for India. Absenteeism was more pronounced in poorer and rural areas – and it disproportionately affected children from low socio-economic backgrounds. Low teacher morale and weak motivation, linked to inadequate pay, poor conditions of service and weak support systems, are systemic problems in many countries.

Chapter 3
Raising quality and strengthening equity: why governance matters

Education governance is not an abstract concept. It is something that affects the lives of parents, the school experience of children, and the efficiency and equity of education provision. If the precise meaning of 'good governance' can be debated, the consequences of bad governance are readily observable. They include chronically underfinanced schools, service providers and government agencies that are unresponsive to local needs and unaccountable to parents, large disparities in school access, participation and completion, and low levels of learning achievement.

Governance reform is a prominent part of the EFA agenda. Within the vast array of country experience, several themes recur. Many governments have moved towards decentralized provision, shifting the locus of decision-making from central to local level. The umbrella category of decentralization, however, covers multiple patterns. The Report maps decision-making in a large group of countries (see annex on education decision-making), revealing a variety of possible arrangements.

Many of the central currents in governance reform span the developed and developing world. School-based management, which aims at giving schools and communities more autonomy in decision-making, is one illustration. Another is the growth of education provision models emphasizing the virtues of choice and competition, either within the state sector or through an expanded role for the private sector. In many developing countries, low-fee private schools are emerging as another source of choice and competition, often outside government regulation. In teacher management, governance issues focus on concerns over pay and policies for allocating teachers to different areas.

Other governance issues have received less attention. One striking example is the integration of education planning with broader poverty reduction strategies. This is a key issue for the Dakar Framework for Action. Many of the most entrenched barriers to EFA are rooted beyond the school in underlying structures of poverty and social disadvantage. Effective education governance can make some difference. But ultimately, sustained progress towards EFA depends on the effective integration of education planning in wider poverty reduction strategies, for an obvious reason: poverty, poor nutrition and ill health are formidable barriers to success in education.

Governance reform has delivered highly variable results. While the progress achieved in some countries has to be acknowledged, overall outcomes have been disappointing. One reason is that governance reforms have often been designed with scant regard for their impact on the most disadvantaged people and regions. Choice and competition have their merits – but also their limits, notably for the poor. Governance reform design problems have sometimes been compounded by a tendency to embrace fixed blueprints, many of them originating in developed countries.

The Report explores four central themes in national governance reform, principally as they relate to basic education:

- financing;
- 'voice', participation and choice;
- governance of teachers and monitoring of learning;
- integration of EFA and poverty reduction strategies.

Financing for basic education

It costs nothing to set ambitious goals in education. However, achieving those goals requires financial resources, along with policies that maximize efficiency and equity in the management of those resources. While many of the issues appear technical, financial governance has a critical bearing on prospects for achieving EFA.

Countries vary enormously in their capacity to finance education. Increased public spending is not guaranteed to improve access, equity or learning outcomes. But chronic and sustained underfinancing is a sure route to limited, poor-quality provision.

Most countries have increased the share of national income allocated to education since 1999. In some cases, such as those of Ethiopia, Kenya, Mozambique and Senegal, the share has climbed sharply. In others, as in India and Pakistan, it has stagnated at a relatively low 3% of gross national product or less. While cross-regional comparisons have to be treated with caution, spending patterns in South and West Asia would appear to indicate a limited public spending commitment to education.

Global wealth inequalities are mirrored by inequalities in education spending. In 2006, per-student expenditure for primary school (expressed in constant dollars) ranged from less than US$300 in much of sub-Saharan Africa to over US$5,000 in most developed countries. As a region sub-Saharan Africa accounts for 15% of 5- to 25-year-olds but just 2% of global spending on their education. South and West Asia represent over one-quarter of the population and 7% of spending.

As in any area of public financing, efficiency is an important determinant of outcomes. Technical efficiency provides a crude indicator of the cost associated with turning finance into quantitative and qualitative outcomes. In many countries, corruption is a major source of both inefficiency and inequity – the former because it means more public money provides fewer inputs and the latter because the costs of corruption invariably fall most heavily on the poor.

Public spending on education has the potential to redress inequalities but often reinforces them instead. Wealthier regions and advantaged groups often attract more financing than poorer regions and disadvantaged groups. Public spending is often not pro-poor. Governments have developed various approaches aimed at strengthening equity, including school grants and formula funding linked to need – with mixed outcomes.

Financial decentralization has important implications for equity. There is nothing intrinsically equitable or inequitable about reforms in this area: outcomes depend on the rules governing issues such as revenue raising and resource transfer. One obvious danger is that, in the absence of redistributive transfers from richer to poorer areas, decentralization will widen financing gaps in education, with damaging consequences for equity. Another is that subnational governments will seek to mobilize revenue through charges on local services, including education.

Evidence from many countries highlights the risks associated with financial decentralization. In China, Indonesia and the Philippines, decentralization appears to have exacerbated inequalities. In Nigeria, financial decentralization has consolidated large disparities in education financing, often to the detriment of the states facing the most serious problems. However, countries including South Africa, Uganda and Viet Nam have developed models aimed at greater equity, with rules on financial decentralization geared towards the attainment of national goals in education and other areas.

'Voice', participation and choice in school governance

Schools are on the front line of the campaign to bring high-quality education to all children. They are also at the centre of debates on education governance in which choice, competition, participation and 'voice' are buzzwords. Behind these terms are crucial questions about the role of governments, parents, communities and private providers in managing and financing schools.

Many countries with poorly performing education systems suffer from institutional problems. The Dakar Framework does not set out a blueprint for resolving these problems. But it does call on governments to 'develop responsive, participatory and accountable systems of educational governance and management'. Translating these widely shared objectives into practical strategies that tackle institutional weaknesses, expand access, raise quality and strengthen equity is far from straightforward.

The Report focuses on three broad reform currents in school governance. School-based management, the first current, aspires to anchor education in the social fabric of communities. Transferring authority to front-line providers is presented as a vehicle for increasing parental influence in decisions affecting children's education – and for ensuring that schools reflect local priorities and values.

The second reform current focuses on choice and competition. Expanding parental choice in the selection of schools is widely viewed as a key to driving up standards, with competition creating powerful incentives for improved performance. In some countries, public-private partnerships are seen as a route to enlarged choice. Governments are using vouchers and other instruments to facilitate transfers from public to private providers, or contracting out the management of government schools to private providers.

The locus for the third thematic area is outside the public education system. Low-fee private schools have spread rapidly in many countries. Some commentators see these schools as a vehicle for improving access and quality for poor households.

Proponents of all three approaches claim various benefits from governance reform. These range from gains in efficiency to increases in participation, accountability and equity. There is a widely shared underlying assumption that devolution of authority, competition and the growth of low-fee private schools will strengthen the voices of the poor and increase their choices. Are the claims and assumptions backed by evidence?

There are no simple answers to that question. In some cases, school-based management reforms have improved learning achievements and strengthened equity. The EDUCO schools in El Salvador are an example. More widely, though, there is limited evidence either of systematic benefits in learning outcomes or of changes in teaching practices. Effects on 'voice' are also ambiguous. More localized decision-making may bring authority closer to parents and communities, but it does not follow that this will overcome wider disadvantages. An obvious danger is that local power structures associated with poverty and social inequality will limit the real influence of the poor and marginalized.

Choice and competition are at the centre of sometimes polarized debates in both developed and developing countries. Underlying these debates are strongly held views about the role and responsibilities of government. The idea that increased parental choice leads to improved learning outcomes and greater equity may have intuitive appeal. But once again the evidence is not clear cut. Evidence from PISA data does not point to strong effects of school competition on learning outcomes. In the United States, neither the still limited recourse to voucher programmes nor the more expansive development of charter schools has unambiguously raised academic achievement standards or tackled disparities.

Evidence from Chile is also instructive. Over more than two decades, Chile has introduced education governance reforms, aimed at increasing choice, that are broader and deeper than in most countries. Yet private schools with state subsidies do not register any advantage over municipal schools once adjustments are made for socio-economic status. Overall improvements in education quality have been limited – as has progress towards greater equity. While Chile is widely cited as a model governance reformer, it is not clear from the outcomes that it merits this description.

Others countries have a stronger claim to successful governance reform. Sweden is a case in point. Since the mid-1990s it has allowed parents to choose non-public education providers and take state funding with them. There is a broad consensus in Sweden behind the reforms. However, the exportability of the Swedish model is unproven. Increased competition in this case was introduced against the backdrop of a public education system that meets high achievement standards, with relatively low inequality and a highly developed institutional capacity for regulation. These are not the prevailing conditions in most countries, developed or developing.

Serious questions have to be asked about current approaches to school-based management. Parental participation is important and, under the right conditions, choice and competition can help raise standards and equalize opportunity. But the overwhelming priority, especially in the poorest countries, is to ensure that a properly financed public education system is available to all citizens.

The rapid emergence of low-fee private schools raises a different set of concerns. In many countries, these schools are outside state auspices. There is no question that low-fee private schools are catering for real demand. Countries as diverse as Ghana, India, Kenya, Nigeria and Pakistan have experienced increases in enrolment in such schools. But to what extent have they raised standards and enhanced equity?

While international evidence remains patchy, it offers little cause for optimism. In many countries, parents select private schools not as a positive choice but as a negative response to perceived – and usually real – failures of the public system. In the case of slum areas, as in Nairobi, public schools often simply do not exist. In India evidence does not suggest that poor parents are more actively involved in decision-making in low-fee schools, or that teachers are less likely to be absent. While the fact that parents meet school charges may be taken as evidence of willingness to pay, the costs impose a considerable burden on household budgets. Efforts to integrate low-fee private schools into private-public partnerships through voucher-type programmes, as advocated by some, do not appear to offer a short cut to greater equity.

The rapid growth of low-fee private schools is in large measure a symptom of state failure. Chronic underfinancing, often combined with weak accountability, low levels of responsiveness and poor quality of provision, has led millions of poor households to vote with their feet – and their income – to exit public provision. This is not a prescription either for equity or for accelerated progress towards EFA.

Basic education is a fundamental human right, not a tradable commodity. It follows that provision must be available to all, regardless of ability to pay. Moreover, the public sector must govern provision, underwriting finance, providing management and setting a clear policy framework.

Public sector leadership does not mean that actors such as non-government organizations and the private sector have no role or responsibilities. In the right conditions, properly regulated choice and competition can strengthen standards, especially at secondary level. However, there are acute dangers for equity. Where government failure leads to creeping commercialization through the low-fee private sector, it poses the risk of rising inequity, and the fragmentation of services and standards. The real challenge for governments with basic education systems that are broken is to fix the system.

Governance of teachers – improving motivation and monitoring

The effectiveness of any school is heavily influenced by the quality of teaching, and the skills, motivation and commitment of its teachers. Ensuring that children – including the most disadvantaged – have access to enough trained and motivated teachers is vital to the delivery of good and equitable education. The effectiveness and equity of school systems are also linked to national monitoring of standards. Good monitoring systems can help inform policy and so raise quality and enhance equity. Weak systems have the opposite effect.

The governance of teachers raises issues that go far beyond administrative technicalities. One recent assessment of teacher morale in sub-Saharan Africa concludes that school systems catering for tens of millions of children face a 'teacher motivation crisis' over issues ranging from employment conditions to training and support. How teachers are distributed within countries has profound implications for equity and access: deployment patterns in many countries reinforce disparities.

Teacher salaries are at the centre of polarized exchanges in public policy debate. Some commentators say salary levels in many countries are too high and crowd out spending on other aspects of education. Apart from cost factors, hiring teachers centrally on permanent civil service contracts is also viewed as a source of weak accountability and poor performance. The problem with these perspectives is that they overlook wider issues. These include the low absolute salary levels of many teachers. In Malawi, average teacher salaries are too low to meet basic needs. There, and in many other countries, teachers often have to supplement their income with a second job, with damaging consequences for the quality of their teaching.

Teacher recruitment to reduce PTRs and address shortages confronts governments with tough choices. Some governments have attempted to contain costs by recruiting teachers on contract outside the civil service pay structure. Hiring contract teachers can expand access to basic education at lower cost, often benefiting areas that might otherwise not have enough teachers, as in parts of India.

On the other side of the coin are potential threats to quality and equity. Seeking to reduce recruitment costs through contract arrangements can weaken quality by lowering the standard of new entrants or reducing teacher morale. In Togo, expanded use of contract teachers is associated with reduced learning achievement. And if contract teachers are deployed principally in poor and marginalized areas, it can also weaken equity. There are no easy answers, but it is important for governments to be aware of potentially damaging trade-offs between lower-cost recruitment and wider education goals with respect to equity and quality.

Teacher deployment is often inequitable within countries, which can exacerbate disparities. The rural-urban divide is particularly marked. In Uganda, two-thirds of urban teachers are qualified, compared with 40% in rural areas. Urban bias in deployment reflects many teachers' aversion to working in hard-to-reach, remote, rural and sparsely populated areas, often for both professional and personal reasons.

Public policies can overcome inequalities in deployment. In Brazil, central government redistribution of financial resources has been used to support teacher recruitment and training in poor states. In Cambodia and the Lao People's Democratic Republic, institutional incentives encourage the recruitment of teachers from marginalized areas and groups; a lesson from their experience is that very strong incentives may be needed.

One symptom of poor teacher motivation is absenteeism. In many developing countries absenteeism is endemic (see Chapter 2). Motivation is not always the culprit: in parts of Africa HIV-related health problems are heavily implicated. Some governments see performance-related pay as a strategy to address motivation problems and so raise quality. But there is little evidence from cross-country experience that performance-related pay produces positive results – and some evidence that it creates perverse incentives for teachers to focus on the best-performing students.

The importance of monitoring in raising quality standards and addressing equity concerns is widely overlooked. Information is one of the keys to improved learning outcomes – and the flow of information is increasing. Between 2000 and 2006, around half the world's countries conducted at least one national learning assessment. Regional assessments have also expanded: thirty-seven sub-Saharan African countries and sixteen Latin American countries now participate in major regional assessments.

While large gaps in coverage remain, many governments have access to more national and international learning assessment information than their predecessors had in the 1990s. Many of these assessments are 'high stakes' – so called because they have direct consequences for student progression, and sometimes for teachers and schools. Others are 'low stake' exercises that provide information, with no direct consequences for students, teachers or schools. The value of 'high stakes' assessment as a vehicle for holding schools and teachers to account is widely contested. In the United States, the No Child Left Behind Act offers a particularly high-profile example of high stakes testing – and one with a mixed record in terms of its effects on achievement.

How information is used is as important as the flow of information. Education authorities in many developing countries increasingly use assessments to inform policy design. In Kenya, SACMEQ results were a basis for benchmarks on minimum classroom facilities. In Senegal, data from a PASEC assessment showed that grade repetition imposed high costs on school systems with no tangible benefits for learning outcomes – a finding that prompted a prohibition on repetition for some primary grades. Viet Nam has used learning assessments to identify disparities in achievement and guide the framing of regulations aimed at raising input provision for disadvantaged groups and areas. Uruguay has applied carefully designed national assessment programmes to strengthen pedagogical management. Learning outcomes improved in some grades by as much as 30% in six years.

These positive examples are the exception rather than the rule. In many cases, the findings from assessments have no influence on resource allocation or teacher support programmes. Even where good assessment systems are in place, their effects are often limited. The reason, in many cases, is weak institutional capacity. Thus, Bolivia has a first-rate assessment system and strong expertise, but they have had limited impact on policy design or what happens in the classroom.

Integrated planning to advance EFA

Progress in education is contingent on wider social conditions influencing inequalities based on income, gender, ethnicity and location. The Dakar Framework for Action calls for EFA policies to be promoted 'within a sustainable and well-integrated sector framework clearly linked to poverty elimination and development strategies'. While education planning has been strengthened, a failure to join education strategies to general poverty reduction strategies, along with high levels of fragmentation and weak coordination, continues to hamper progress.

Education planning within the framework of sector-wide approaches (SWAps) has been instrumental in clarifying priorities, broadening the EFA agenda and allowing governments to develop longer-term planning horizons. However, many education SWAps suffer from continued weaknesses. Financial costing is often inadequate, education targets are not reflected in national budgets and there is a tendency to adopt blueprint models.

Even more serious is the widespread tendency to delink education planning from wider strategies for overcoming poverty and inequality. Poverty reduction strategy papers (PRSPs) provide a vehicle for addressing this problem. Fifty-four countries – just over half of them in sub-Saharan Africa – have operational PRSPs. While PRSPs are 'nationally owned' documents, they also set out the terms of the aid partnership with donors. PRSPs have brought poverty closer to the centre of the development agenda but they are not yet facilitating effective integration in education planning, for at least four reasons:

- **Weak linkage to the EFA agenda.** The point of reference for PRSPs is the MDGs. One consequence is an overwhelming emphasis on quantitative targets related to primary education, often to the exclusion of wider EFA goals. When wider goals are considered, they are typically not linked to a broader poverty reduction agenda. For example, in a review of eighteen recent PRSPs the Report finds that ECCE is regarded primarily as a mechanism for increasing primary school enrolment rather than as a strategy to improve the health and nutrition of young children.

- **Poor targeting and limited consideration of equity in target-setting.** Targets rarely include the narrowing of equity gaps, with the partial exception of gender parity goals; they invariably address access rather than learning achievement.

- **No link between education and broader governance reforms.** PRSPs often incorporate national commitments to wide-ranging governance reforms. However, the implications of the reforms for equity in education are seldom considered in any detail, even where the reforms have potentially significant consequences. Decentralization is one prominent example. More generally, few PRSPs set out practical strategies for ensuring that governance reforms strengthen the link between education planning and wider poverty reduction efforts.

- **Poor integration of cross-sectoral policies.** As Chapter 2 notes, there are deep and persistent inequalities in education linked to poverty, gender, nutrition, health, disability and other forms of marginalization. Addressing these inequalities requires policies that extend far beyond the education sector. Evidence from PRSPs suggests that education strategies are often disconnected from such policies.

While PRSPs have thus far seldom provided an integrated framework, there are positive experiences to draw upon. Social protection programmes are making a strong contribution to education by addressing problems in health, nutrition and child labour. Targeted cash transfers in Latin America have been particularly successful – so much so that one has been adopted on a pilot basis in New York City. There are strong grounds for considering an increase in public investment and aid for cross-sectoral programmes of this kind in other contexts.

Planning is not just about technical documents. It is also about the political process through which priorities are set. Consultation processes are a central part of PRSPs. They provide opportunities for civil society organizations to participate in policy discussions. They also help ensure that education figures in debates over national poverty strategies. The challenge is to extend participation to ensure that the voices of the poor and vulnerable are heard. This in turn will help focus more attention on ECCE, adult literacy and skills development. It will also inform policy-makers about factors beyond the education sector that are holding back progress towards equitable education. Sustained political commitment is crucial for priorities set out in consultation processes to become reality.

Chapter 4
Increasing aid and improving governance

The Dakar Framework for Action is based on an international partnership. Developing countries pledged to strengthen national education planning, tackle inequalities and enhance accountability. Rich countries also made an important commitment, pledging that no credible national plan would be allowed to fail for want of finance. Increased and more effective aid is vital to achieving the goals and targets set at Dakar. Are donors delivering on their promises?

Not in the area of financing. On a highly conservative estimate, the aid financing required for a narrow range of basic education goals in low-income countries is around US$11 billion annually. In 2006, aid in support of basic education to these countries was just one-third of the estimated requirement, leaving a financing gap of around US$7 billion.

These large aid deficits are holding back progress. Debates over the achievements and effectiveness of development assistance continue. Pessimists claim aid has had a modest impact at best, and a negative effect in many cases. Evidence in education does not support this view. In the United Republic of Tanzania aid has supported a national education strategy that has cut the number of out-of-school children by 3 million since 1999. In Cambodia, Kenya, Mozambique and Zambia, aid helped finance the abolition of school fees, extending educational opportunities to previously excluded children. In Bangladesh and Nepal, aid supported national strategies providing incentives for girls and disadvantaged groups. Development assistance is not a panacea or a corrective for bad policy – but it makes a difference.

Aid levels for education are linked to overall development assistance flows. In 2005 donors made a number of important commitments to increase aid flows, notably at the Gleneagles summit of the Group of Eight (G8) and at a European Council meeting. This was a backdrop to the United Nations 'Millennium +5' summit. Delivery on these commitments would lead to an increase of around US$50 billion in development assistance by 2010 (at 2004 prices), with around half going to sub-Saharan Africa.

Prospects for delivery, however, are not encouraging. As a group, donors are not on track to meet their commitments. Taking into account increased aid and programmed commitments to 2010, there is a shortfall of US$30 billion against the pledges made in 2005 (again in 2004 prices). The aid gap for sub-Saharan Africa is US$14 billion – a financing shortfall that has damaging implications for progress towards the MDGs and EFA. Most individual donor countries are not on track to meet their Gleneagles commitments and two G8 countries – the United States and Japan – continue to invest a very low share of gross national income in development assistance.

Commitments to education have followed the overall trend. The average annual aid commitments in 2005–2006 were below the level for 2003–2004, and there is a real danger that this will be reflected in slower growth of disbursements, or even stagnation.

Donors have a mixed record on aid for basic education. In 2006, half of all aid commitments for basic education came from just three sources – the Netherlands, the United Kingdom and the World Bank's International Development Association. These sources accounted for 85% of the overall increase in aid commitments to basic education in 2006. However, the combined effort of a few committed donors could not counteract an overall fall in aid commitments from 2004.

The profile of donor aid commitments varies widely. Some countries, such as Canada, the Netherlands and the United Kingdom, allocate more than three-quarters of their education aid to low income countries – and at least half to basic education. By contrast, France and Germany, both major donors to education, attach less weight to basic education in the poorest countries. Only 12% of French aid and 7% of German aid is devoted to basic education in low income countries. Both countries put greater priority on subsidizing attendance at their universities by foreign students, mostly from middle income developing countries, than on supporting basic education in low income countries. In France two-thirds of education aid is absorbed by imputed costs for students studying at French tertiary institutions.

The continued aid financing gap in education raises important questions about the future of the Fast Track Initiative (FTI). Established in 2002, the FTI was seen as a multilateral mechanism to encourage broad donor support for EFA and, through the Catalytic Fund begun in 2003, an element of financing. Unfortunately, the FTI has not developed a sufficiently deep donor base and it faces an uncertain future. In mid-2008, the thirty-five countries with endorsed FTI plans faced a financing gap of US$640 million. Factoring in the eight countries with plans in the pipeline would push that figure up to around US$1 billion. By the end of 2009, the financing deficit for countries with approved FTI plans could be as high as US$2.2 billion. Assuming that the Catalytic Fund might be expected to cover around 40% to 50% of the deficit, around US$1 billion would still have to be mobilized.

Current aid financing trends do not augur well for achieving the goals and targets in the Dakar Framework. Yet there are some positive signs. In 2007, the G8 reaffirmed its pledge that no national strategy would fail for want of finance. It also promised to meet shortfalls in FTI-endorsed plans. In June 2008, the European Council also reaffirmed its support for EFA. However, reaffirmations of long-standing commitments do not put children into school or deliver a good-quality education. If donors are serious about their pledges to education, they cannot afford more years of underperformance.

Increased aid is just part of the equation. Ultimately, the case for increased commitments will be accepted only if aid is perceived to deliver real results. Much depends on governance in developing countries. But the governance and management of aid are also important. In 2005, donors and developing country governments pledged to strengthen the effectiveness of development assistance. That promise, in the Paris Declaration, envisages the harmonization and alignment of donor practices behind nationally owned development strategies. The approach signals a shift in emphasis away from project-based support and towards programme support – a shift already strongly evident in education. Targets were set for 2010 to measure progress.

It is too early to fully assess the extent to which new aid principles are being translated into practice. In terms of financial commitment, there has been a strong push away from projects towards programme-based support. Best estimates suggest that just over half of all aid is now delivered through education sector programmes – up from around one-third in 1999–2000.

Preliminary assessment suggests that some Paris Declaration targets will be hard to achieve. Monitoring results for fifty-four countries accounting for half of all aid are not entirely encouraging. Use of national systems remains limited, with only 45% of aid channelled through national public financial management systems (the 2010 target is 80%). In some cases, donors are not using national systems even when they have been strengthened. Donor coordination is often still rudimentary. In 2007, the fifty-four countries received more than 14,000 donor missions, of which only 20% were jointly coordinated.

Progress towards greater coordination has been more evident in education than many other areas. Even so, the rate of progress has been both erratic and uneven – and far more needs to be done. In Cambodia, only 39% of donor missions in education in 2007 were jointly conducted, raising transaction costs for the host government.

While all donors stress their commitment to the alignment of aid with national priorities and the use of national systems, outcomes have been variable. Progress has proved far from straightforward, with frustrations and concerns on both sides. Donors often point to worries over corruption and weak capacity. For their part, many aid recipients complain about what they see as unrealistic donor demands and onerous reporting requirements.

Emerging aid modalities have the potential to resolve these problems. In the best cases, improved national management systems, greater sector coherence, better oversight and coordination of donor activity, and more innovative approaches to finance are coming to the fore. Important achievements have already been made in some countries, including Burkina Faso, Cambodia, India and Mozambique. Successful implementation of the Paris agenda will require commitment and flexibility on both sides, with donors avoiding the use of financial support to leverage change.

Chapter 5
Conclusions and recommendations

Delivering on the pledges set out in the Dakar Framework for Action will require strong political leadership, a sense of urgency and practical strategies. The final chapter of this Report sets out some of the key priorities. While avoiding blueprints, it identifies principles for good practice, including the following:

- **Get serious about equity.** Many governments have not given sufficient weight to policies aimed at overcoming inequalities in education. Setting time-bound 'equity targets' aimed at reducing disparities based on wealth, gender, language and other markers for disadvantage, and carefully monitoring progress, would help to focus political attention. At the same time, education planning has to put far higher priority on pro-poor public spending and the development of incentives targeted at the poorest and most disadvantaged.

- Strengthen the **links between education planning and poverty reduction** strategies. Education policies can make an important difference in equalizing opportunity and reducing disadvantage. However, progress in education depends critically on progress in other areas, including poverty reduction, nutrition and public health. While education sector planning has become stronger, it remains weakly integrated with wider poverty reduction strategies.

- Reinforce the commitment to **quality education** for all. Progress on expanded access to schools is outstripping improvements in quality. Policy-makers should renew and strengthen the Dakar commitment to quality in education and put in place the infrastructure, teacher support and monitoring programmes needed to deliver results.

- Act on the commitment to **equity in financing**. Many governments have failed to develop pro-poor public spending patterns and decentralization reforms have often exacerbated inequalities in education. Looking to the future, it is important for governments to develop approaches that avoid these outcomes. Central government needs to retain its capacity for redistribution from wealthier to poorer regions and subnational bodies need to ensure that spending plans reflect a national commitment to EFA.

- Recognize the **limits to choice and competition**. The development of quasi-markets in education and the rapid emergence of low-fee private providers are not resolving underlying problems in access, equity or quality. While many actors have a role to play in education provision, there is no substitute for a properly financed and effectively managed state education system, especially at primary level.

- Deliver on **aid commitments**. The donor community needs to recognize the wide-ranging benefits of accelerated progress towards EFA and to close the aid financing gap. At a conservative estimate, this means increasing aid to basic education by around US$7 billion annually and acting on the commitments undertaken in 2005. Closing the projected 2010 financing gap of US$2.2 billion in countries with plans approved by the Fast Track Initiative is another priority. Strengthening the commitment of some key donors to equity in aid allocations would help to cut the financing deficits. ■

Planting the seeds for success: teaching young children about healthy eating, in Zimbabwe

© Giacomo Pirozzi/PANOS

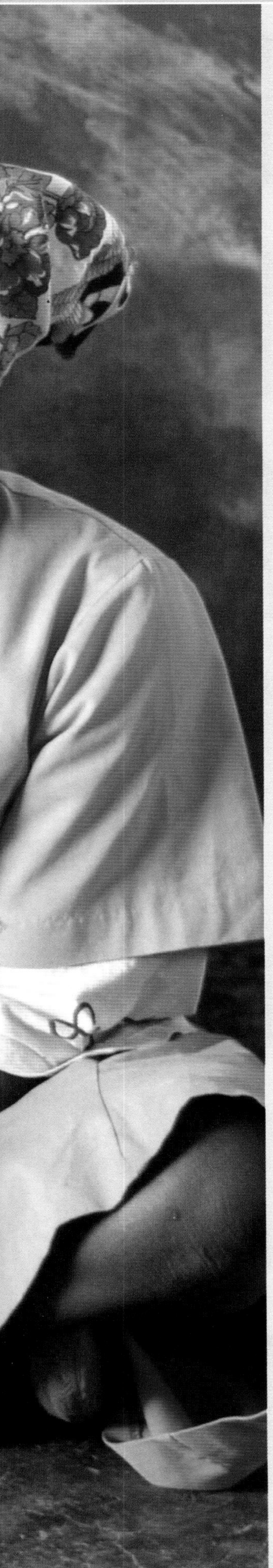

Chapter 1

Education for all: human right and catalyst for development

The international community has adopted ambitious targets for human development. Objectives set under the Millennium Development Goals (MDGs) include the halving of extreme poverty, a two-thirds reduction in child mortality, universal primary education and greater gender equality. The deadline for delivering results is 2015. On current trends, most of the targets will be missed. Accelerated progress towards Education for All, with a strengthened focus on equity, could change this picture. But governments must act with a renewed sense of urgency and political commitment. This chapter looks at the issues at stake.

Introduction

Almost two decades have passed since governments gathered at the World Conference on Education for All (EFA) in Jomtien, Thailand, to reaffirm the human right to education. They set bold targets – but outcomes fell far short of ambition. In 2000, the 164 governments assembled at the World Education Forum in Dakar, Senegal, adopted another set of ambitious goals on education. The Dakar Framework for Action pledges to expand learning opportunities for every child, youth and adult, and to meet targets in six areas by 2015. With the deadline now just six years away, will it be different this time around?

Accelerating progress towards education for all is one of the defining development challenges of the early twenty-first century. The right to education is a basic human right. Like any human right, it should be protected and extended as an end in itself. But education is also a means to wider ends. Prospects for reducing poverty, narrowing extreme inequalities and improving public health are heavily influenced by what happens in education. Progress towards the equalization of opportunity in education is one of the most important conditions for overcoming social injustice and reducing social disparities in any country. It is also a condition for strengthening economic growth and efficiency: no country can afford the inefficiencies that arise when people are denied opportunities for education because they are poor, female or members of a particular social group. And what is true at a national level also applies internationally. Prospects for achieving more equitable patterns of globalization are heavily influenced by developments in education. In an increasingly interconnected and knowledge-based world economy, the distribution of opportunities for education will inevitably have an important bearing on future patterns of international wealth distribution.

Some benefits of education are less tangible and harder to quantify than others. Schools are not just institutions for imparting information. They are a place where children can acquire social skills and self-confidence, where they learn about their countries, their cultures and the world they live in, and where they gain the tools they need to broaden their horizons and ask questions. People denied an opportunity for achieving literacy and wider education skills are less equipped to participate in societies and influence decisions that affect their lives. That is why broad-based education is one of the foundations for democracy and government accountability, and why it is such a vital input for informed public debate in areas – such as environmental sustainability and climate change – that will have a bearing on the well-being of future generations.

The Dakar Framework is not the only pledge on the international development agenda. At the United Nations Millennium Summit, also in 2000, world leaders adopted eight Millennium Development Goals (MDGs). These wide-ranging goals extend from the reduction of extreme poverty and child mortality to improved access to water and sanitation, progress in cutting infectious diseases and strengthened gender equality. The goals are linked to the achievement of specific targets by 2015. In the area of education, the MDGs offer a highly restricted version of the goals adopted at Dakar. They include a commitment to achieve universal primary school completion and gender parity at all levels of schooling by 2015.

At one level the MDG framework is too narrow. EFA means more than five or six years in primary school and more than gender parity, vital as both goals are. The quality of education and learning achievement, access to secondary and post-secondary opportunities, literacy and gender equality, in a broader sense, are all important as well. Yet the Dakar Framework targets and the MDGs are complementary. Progress in education depends on advances in other areas, including the reduction of extreme poverty, the achievement of gender equity and improvements in child health. The links in this direction are obvious but often forgotten. Children whose lives are blighted by hunger, poverty and disease are clearly not equipped to realize their potential in education. Without advances across the broad front of MDG targets, the ambition of education for all cannot be realized. By the same token, progress towards many of the MDG targets depends critically on progress in education. Halving poverty or cutting child mortality by two-thirds by 2015 is not a serious proposition in a situation of slow and unequal progress towards the policy objectives set out at Dakar. The goals adopted by the international community are mutually interdependent – failure in any one area increases the likelihood of failure in all areas.

The interdependence between the MDGs and the Dakar Framework has taken on a new importance. In 2008 the world entered the second half of the commitment period for both undertakings. Now just seven years remain before the 2015 deadline – and the world is off track on many of the targets. On current trends, the goal of universal primary education (UPE) by 2015 will not be achieved and the pledges made at Dakar will be broken. Using a partial projection covering countries that account for just two-thirds of the 75 million primary school age children out of school today, this Report estimates that the countries will still have 29 million out of school in 2015. That number has consequences for the children and countries most immediately affected. But it also has consequences for the entire MDG project. Bluntly stated, the targets set for cutting child and maternal death, reversing the spread of infectious disease and reducing poverty will not be achieved unless governments act decisively on education. Conversely, accelerated progress on the wider MDGs would strengthen prospects in education by lessening the poverty, nutrition and health handicaps that millions of children take with them into school.

Children whose lives are blighted by hunger, poverty and disease are clearly not equipped to realize their potential in education

In September 2008, governments from around the world gathered at a United Nations summit in New York to reaffirm their commitment to the MDGs. The summit was prompted by a recognition that, without fundamental change, the development goals will not be achieved. Averting that outcome and restoring the momentum behind international partnerships for development will require more than encouraging communiqués. What is needed is a sense of urgency, political leadership and practical strategies.

Strengthening the commitment to the education goals set out in the Dakar Framework for Action is one of the most pressing priorities. Much has been achieved since 2000. Indeed, education has a strong claim to being counted as an MDG success story. Progress towards UPE and gender parity has been far more rapid than advances in other areas, such as nutrition or child and maternal mortality. One of the problems for EFA identified in Chapter 2 is precisely the failure of many countries to move more rapidly towards the MDG targets in these areas. But the relative success of education should not deflect attention from the size of the potential 2015 shortfalls in UPE. Making up these shortfalls would act as a powerful catalyst for accelerated progress towards the MDGs.

The backdrop for the September 2008 MDG summit was an unprecedented crisis in international financial markets. The fallout from that crisis remains uncertain. Governments are taking far-reaching measures to stabilize banking systems. The scale and urgency of their actions were guided by a recognition that, when financial markets fail, the contagion effects can spread rapidly across all aspects of society and the real economy. Analogies with education system failure are inexact but instructive. When education systems fail to reach large sections of the population, when children are denied opportunities by virtue of their gender, the income of their parents, their ethnicity or where they happen to live, or when schools deliver chronically substandard learning outcomes, there are also contagion effects. Those effects are not reflected in highly visible bank collapses, fluctuating share prices or mortgage failures. But there are real human, social and economic consequences. Education system failures weaken the real economy, holding back productivity and growth. They undermine efforts to reduce child and maternal mortality, contributing to loss of life and increased health risks. And they contribute to social polarization and the weakening of democracy. Yet despite the high stakes and the costs of inaction, few governments treat the crisis in education as an urgent priority – in stark contrast to their response to financial market problems. This is an area in which national and international leadership is needed to place education firmly at the centre of the political agenda.

Few governments treat the crisis in education as an urgent priority, in stark contrast to their response to financial market problems

The *EFA Global Monitoring Report* was first published in 2002 to track progress towards the six EFA goals enshrined in the Dakar Framework for Action. Since its inception it has covered each of the goals. This year the Report looks beyond the goals to a range of issues in education governance, finance and management. It focuses on the critical importance of equity in educational opportunity because equity should be an overarching public policy goal – and because deep inequalities in education threaten to undermine progress towards both the EFA goals and the MDGs. □

Educational opportunity: highly polarized

The distribution of educational opportunity plays a key role in shaping human development prospects. Within countries, governments and people increasingly recognize that unequal opportunities for education are linked to inequalities in income, health and wider life chances. And what is true within countries is true also between countries. Large global disparities in education reinforce the extreme divides between rich and poor nations in income, health and other aspects of human development.

The full extent of the gulf in opportunities for education is not widely appreciated. Education is a universal human right. However, enjoyment of that right is heavily conditioned by the lottery of birth and inherited circumstance. Opportunities for education are heavily influenced by where one is born and by other factors over which children have no control, including parental income, gender and ethnicity.

From a global perspective, being born in a developing country is a strong indicator for reduced opportunity. School attainment, measured in terms of the average number of years or grade reached in education, is one (admittedly limited) measure of global inequality. While almost all member countries of the Organisation for Economic Co-operation and Development (OECD) have achieved universal school attainment to grade 9, most countries in developing regions are far from this position. Age-specific school attendance pyramids that plot the distribution of age and grades graphically illustrate the contrast in average life-chances for education associated with being born in the OECD countries or in sub-Saharan Africa (Figure 1.1). By age 7, almost all children in the OECD countries are in primary school, compared with 40% for sub-Saharan Africa. At age 16, over 80% of the population of the OECD countries is in secondary school while one-quarter of sub-Saharan Africa's population is still in primary school. Four years later, at age 20, around 30% of the OECD population is in post-secondary education. The figure for sub-Saharan Africa is 2%.

Stark as they are, these figures tell only part of the story. One way of thinking about unequal opportunity is to consider the chance that a child born in one country has of achieving a given level of education relative to a child born somewhere else. Chapter 2 draws on international data to compare educational opportunities across countries. The results are striking. They show that children in countries such as Mali and Mozambique have less chance of completing a full *primary* cycle than children in France or the United Kingdom have of reaching *tertiary* education. The gulf in attainment is not restricted to sub-Saharan Africa. Around one in five pupils entering primary school in Latin America and in South and West Asia does not survive to the last primary grade.

Global inequalities in education mirror inequalities in income. The association is not coincidental. While the relationship between education and wealth creation is complex, knowledge is an important driver for economic growth and productivity (see below). In an increasingly knowledge-based international economy, disparities in education are taking on more importance. There is a growing sense in which today's inequalities in education can be seen as a predictor for tomorrow's inequalities in the global distribution of wealth, and in opportunities for health and employment. The fact that in half the countries of sub-Saharan Africa the survival rate to the last grade of primary school is 67% or less is not irrelevant to prospects for overcoming the region's marginalization in the global economy.

Inequalities within countries create an even starker picture of disparities in opportunity. Data on national average life chances in education have the effect of masking the distribution of life chances across different groups in society. When within-country distribution is superimposed on cross-country disparity, the effect is to magnify the scale of inequality.

To illustrate this point the *EFA Global Monitoring Report 2009* has created a composite regional picture of the distribution of attainment across income groups using national household survey data. Figure 1.2 presents attainment curves at the polar ends of the distribution for the richest and poorest 20%. Once again the results are striking. They show that only around half of the poorest 20% in sub-Saharan Africa, and South and West Asia progress to grade 5, compared with over 80% for the wealthiest quintile. Being born into the poorest 20% of the wealth distribution in sub-Saharan Africa, or in South and West Asia, more than halves

Figure 1.1: Age-specific attendance rates by level in OECD countries and sub-Saharan Africa, 2000-2006[1]

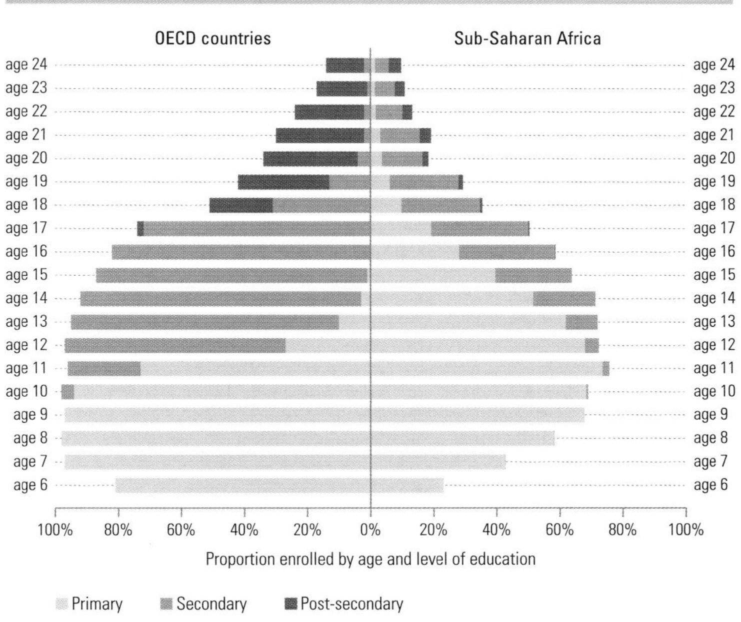

1. Weighted averages. Data are for the most recent year available during the period.
Sources: Calculations based on OECD (2008*b*); World Bank (2008*b*).

Figure 1.2: Grade attainment among 10- to 19-year-olds in Latin America and the Caribbean, South and West Asia, and sub-Saharan Africa, 2000-2006[1]

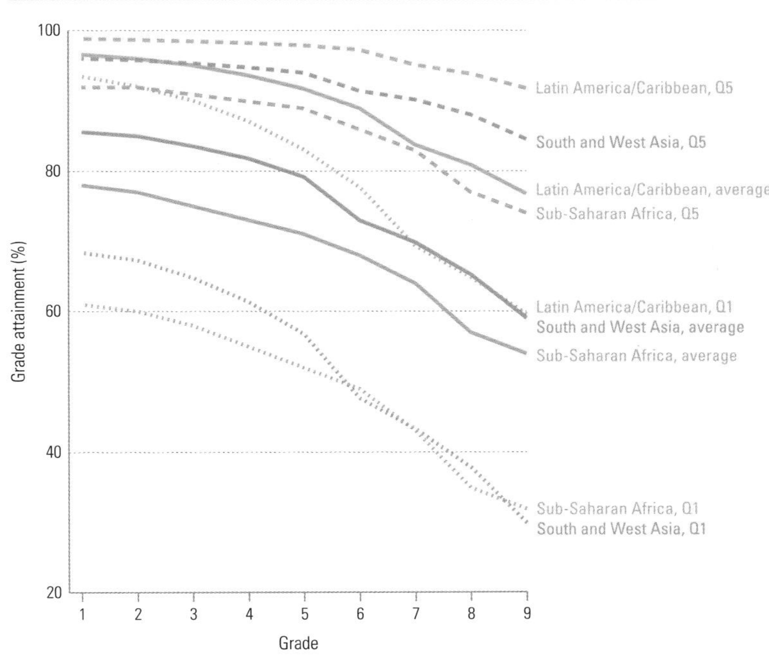

Note: Q1 is the poorest quintile, Q5 the richest.
1. Weighted averages. Data are for the most recent year available during the period.
Source: World Bank (2008*b*).

the chance of school attendance at grade 9. While the wealthiest 20% in Latin America achieve attendance levels close to those in the OECD countries at grade 9, the poorest 20% are closer to the average for sub-Saharan Africa. These income-based disparities are mirrored in differences in average years of education attained by the people aged 17 to 22. In Mozambique, someone in the poorest 20% has on average 1.9 years of education, compared with 5 years for someone from the richest 20%. In Peru, the gap between rich and poor is 4.6 years of schooling, rising to 6.7 years in India (Table 1.1).

Income-based disparities such as those charted above are not the only type of disparity in education. Inherited disadvantages linked to gender, ethnicity, location and other factors are also important. These disadvantages intersect with income-based differences, restricting opportunity and transmitting educational disadvantage and poverty across generations. One of the central messages of this Report is that national governments and international development agencies need to strengthen the focus on equity in order to achieve the core goals in the Dakar Framework for Action.

The human costs of economic, social and educational inequalities are cumulative and cross-generational

Unequal distribution of education has wider consequences. Income-based gaps in educational opportunity reinforce income inequalities and the social divisions that come with them. They also mean the benefits associated with education in areas such as public health, employment and participation in society are unequally distributed. The human costs of these inequalities are cumulative and cross-generational. For example, the fact that women account for the majority of illiterate people in the world today is a reflection of historical gender disparities in access to education. But when women who have been denied an education become mothers, their children also inherit diminished life chances: they are less likely to survive, more likely to experience ill health and less likely to go to school than the children of mothers who have education.

Quality counts

Some inequalities are easier to measure than others. Headcount indicators covering the number of children in school or completing grades allow for relatively straightforward comparisons from country to country. Learning achievement indicators and comparisons pose more of a problem. Although global and regional learning assessments are expanding to cover more countries, information remains sparse and insufficiently available in forms that allow for straightforward global comparisons. Put differently, quantity is easier to measure than quality – yet in the last analysis, it is quality that counts. Ultimately, what matters is the degree to which schooling supports cognitive development, facilitates skills acquisition and enriches children's lives.

Table 1.1: Average years of education for poorest and richest 20% of 17- to 22-year-olds, selected countries, most recent year

	Poorest 20%	Richest 20%
	(years)	
Bangladesh, 2004	3.7	8.1
Burkina Faso, 2003	0.8	5.6
Ethiopia, 2005	1.6	7.4
Ghana, 2003	3.2	9.2
Guatemala, 1999	1.9	8.3
India, 2005	4.4	11.1
Mali, 2001	0.4	4.8
Mozambique, 2003	1.9	5.0
Nicaragua, 2001	2.5	9.2
Nigeria, 2003	3.9	9.9
Peru, 2000	6.5	11.1
Philippines, 2003	6.3	11.0
U.R. Tanzania, 2004	3.9	8.1
Zambia, 2001	4.0	9.0

Source: Demographic and Health Surveys, calculations by Harttgen et al. (2008).

Qualitative inequalities are probably narrowing far more slowly than quantitative gaps. Large though it remains, basic headcount inequality is falling at the primary and secondary levels. Convergence is the order of the day. Developing countries are catching up on enrolment, attendance and completion, albeit unevenly and often from a low base. One reason for this is obvious: rich countries cannot exceed universal coverage at the primary and secondary levels, so any gain by developing countries narrows the gap. However, school attainment has to be adjusted for the quality of education. When it comes to learning achievements and outcomes, an average school year in Zambia is clearly not the same as an average school year in, say, Japan or Finland. There is compelling international evidence (discussed further in Chapter 2) that completing six or even nine years of schooling in developing countries does not assure the development of basic cognitive skills or even functional literacy and numeracy (Filmer et al., 2006; Pritchett, 2004*a*).

International assessment tests provide a pointer to the scale of global inequalities in learning achievement. To take one example, the OECD Programme for International Student Assessment (PISA) survey of reading and literacy skills places the median achievement in developing countries such as Brazil and Peru in the lowest 20% of the distribution for many OECD countries. One recent study of basic educational achievement found very high levels of functional illiteracy in mathematics and science among secondary school students in many developing countries. In Brazil, Ghana, Morocco, Peru and South Africa, fewer than 60% of children in school reached basic competency thresholds (Hanushek and Wößmann, 2007). Factoring in children out of school would be expected to lower the average performance. At primary level, recent surveys in Ghana and Zambia have found that fewer than 60% of young women who completed six years of primary school could read a simple sentence in their own language. Similarly, assessment exercises in countries including India and Pakistan found that over two-thirds of pupils at grade 3 level were unable to write a simple sentence in Urdu. Incorporating data on qualitative achievement magnifies the inequalities associated with quantitative attainment.

Education quality is important both in understanding the distribution of life chances in society and in charting the scale of global inequality in education. The bottom line is that EFA cannot be interpreted, as the MDGs sometimes are, as a simple matter of getting all children into school. It goes without saying that this is important. But it is what children get out of school that will shape their life chances. □

Unlocking the wider benefits of education

There are many good reasons for governments committed to the MDGs to renew their commitment to the Dakar Framework for Action. First and foremost, education is a human right and an important goal in its own right. It is central to the development of human capabilities – people's potential to choose lives that they value (Sen, 1999). Beyond this intrinsic importance, there are strong two-way links between education and progress in areas where the world is off track on the MDG targets.

It is what children get out of school that will shape their life chances

None of this is to imply that the links between education and social or economic benefits are automatic. The impact of education is strongly conditioned by other factors, from macroeconomic and labour market conditions to the state of public health provision and levels of inequality based on wealth, gender and other factors. The benefits of education are likely to be greatest in contexts marked by broad-based economic growth, a strong political commitment to poverty reduction, high levels of equity in access to basic services, and a commitment to democratic and accountable governance.

Economic growth, poverty reduction and equity

The links between education and economic growth, income distribution and poverty reduction are well established. Education equips people with the knowledge and skills they need to increase income and expand opportunities for employment. This is true for households and for national economies. Levels of productivity, economic growth and patterns of income distribution are intimately linked to the state of education and the distribution of educational opportunity. Increasing global economic interdependence and the growing importance of knowledge-based processes in economic growth have raised both the premium on education and the cost associated with education deficits.

All this has important implications for the international development goal of halving extreme poverty (MDG 1). The rate of poverty reduction is a function of two variables: the overall rate of economic growth and the share of any increment in growth that is captured by the poor (Bourguignon, 2000). Education has a bearing on both sides of the equation. Improved access to good quality learning opportunities can strengthen economic growth by raising productivity, supporting innovation and facilitating the adoption of new technology. And broad-based access to good quality basic education is one of the foundations for broad-based growth, since it enables poor households to increase their productivity and secure a greater stake in national prosperity. Recent research, discussed in the following subsections, confirms earlier findings on the key role of education in poverty reduction and highlights the critical importance of quality.

Economic growth

No country has ever reduced poverty over the medium term without sustained economic growth. Education plays a critical role in producing the learning and skills needed to generate the productivity gains that fuel growth. One recent research exercise draws attention to the importance for economic growth of both years in school and learning outcomes. Modelling the impact of attainment in fifty countries between 1960 and 2000, the study found that an additional year of schooling lifted average annual gross domestic product (GDP) growth by 0.37%. The impact of improved cognitive skills was considerably larger, with the combined effect adding, on average, a full percentage point to GDP growth (Hanushek et al., 2008; Hanushek and Wößmann, 2007). There is also some evidence that the impact of gains in education quality on cognitive skills may be larger in developing than in developed countries.

Broad-based access to good quality basic education is one of the foundations for broad-based growth

Education quality has a significant impact on economic returns for households as well. Research in fifteen countries participating in the International Adult Literacy Survey (IALS) found that a standard deviation in literacy (an indicator for quality) had a larger effect on wages than an additional year of schooling – confirmation that it is outcomes which count (Denny et al., 2003).

Individual earnings. A large body of evidence points to high returns on investment in education. The scale of these returns is a matter for debate. One cross-country exercise found each additional year of education increasing earnings by 10%, with variations that reflect underlying conditions: returns are higher for low-income countries, for lower levels of schooling and for women (Psacharopolous and Patrinos, 2004). Other research has generated different results both overall and by level of education (Bennell, 1998). As these differences indicate, findings on returns to education are influenced both by methodological factors, and by economic conditions. Broadly, as countries move towards UPE, returns at the primary level tend to fall as the national skills deficit shifts to the secondary and tertiary levels – a phenomenon widely observed in Latin America (Behrman et al., 2003). In terms of public policy, there are limits to relevance of rate of return analysis. The case for investment in basic education is rooted in human rights and ideas about citizenship, not in monetary calculation. That said, there is compelling evidence that private and public rates of return to education at the primary and secondary levels are sufficiently high to mark this out as a good investment for society. In the agricultural sector, increases in education are strongly associated with higher wages, agricultural income and productivity – all critical indicators for poverty reduction (Appleton and Balihuta, 1996). In contrast to these potential benefits, education inequalities based on gender and other factors inflict real economic costs. In Kenya it was found that increasing the education and input levels of female farmers to those of male farmers could increase yields by as much as 22% (Quisumbing, 1996).

Income distribution. The distribution of educational opportunity is strongly associated with income distribution, though the underlying relationship is highly variable and complex. This has important implications for poverty reduction and the MDGs. Economic growth matters because it raises average income. The rate at which growth is converted into poverty reduction depends on the share of any increment to national income going to people living in poverty. By raising the productivity of the poor, more equitable education can increase overall growth *and* the share of growth that accrues to those below the poverty line.

Less equitable education can have an equal and opposite effect. Evidence from the developed world points towards inequality in education as a cause of wider income inequalities. For example, over the past three decades, growing wage differentials between secondary school graduates and secondary school dropouts has been a major source of rising inequality and social polarization in the United States (Heckman, 2008). With a greater proportion of young Americans graduating from college and a greater proportion dropping out of secondary school, the skills gap is fuelling inequality.

Patterns of income inequality are conditioned by private returns from different levels of education, which in turn reflect developments in labour markets. Rapid increase in demand for people with higher skills in countries with limited secondary school completion and restricted access to tertiary education can lead to pronounced increases in inequality. In India, Indonesia, the Philippines and Viet Nam rising wage inequalities are closely linked to widening wage gaps between people with tertiary education and those at lower attainment levels (Asian Development Bank, 2007). Similarly, evidence from Latin America suggests that returns to secondary and tertiary education are rising more rapidly than those to primary education (Behrman et al., 2003).

Prevailing patterns of income distribution reinforce the case for progress towards equalization of educational opportunity. At global level, the poorest 40% of the world's population, living on less than US$2 a day, accounts for 5% of world income – and the poorest 20% (living on less than US$1 a day) for 1.5% (Dikhanov, 2005). Even small shifts in the share of global income going to the world's poor could have very significant effects for poverty reduction. Measured in financial terms, it would take around US$300 billion – less than 1% of world GDP – to lift the billion people surviving on less than US$1 a day above the poverty line (UNDP, 2005). Given the prevailing level of global inequality, this would represent a modest degree of redistribution for a large impact on poverty. Greater equity in the distribution of educational opportunity could facilitate that redistribution. What appears clear is that more equitable patterns of global integration cannot be built on the vast educational disparities in evidence today.

The same broad conclusion holds true at the national level. Over the past two decades there has been a clear trend towards rising income inequality within countries. Of the seventy-three countries for which data are available, inequality has risen in fifty-three, which account for 80% of the world population. Many factors are involved, with inequality in education linked to technological change and wider forces. But the importance of inequality in education as a driver of wider inequality is increasingly recognized. When education is broadly shared and reaches the poor, women and marginalized groups, it holds out the prospect that economic growth will be broadly shared. Greater equity in education can help fuel a virtuous cycle of increased growth and accelerated poverty reduction, with benefits for the poor and for society as a whole.

The relationship between education on the one side and economic growth and poverty reduction on the other illustrates the importance of context. Schools and education systems are not guarantors of faster growth or greater equity. Problems in macroeconomic management and other policy spheres may reduce the benefits of education. In the Arab States, to take a case in point, regional evidence points to a weak association between the expansion of education and productivity (World Bank, 2008*d*). Increasing the supply of skilled labour in an economy marked by low productivity, stagnation and rising unemployment markedly diminishes the private returns to schooling. It can also give rise to large populations of educated unemployed youths and graduates. In Egypt, adults with secondary education account for 42% of the population but 80% of the unemployed (World Bank, 2008*d*).

Other labour market factors are also important. Education can benefit individuals by facilitating entry into higher-earning occupations and raising earnings within an occupation. To the extent that these two benefits accrue equally to women and men, education can help promote gender equality in earnings. However, discrimination and distortions in the labour market based on gender can negate the equalizing effects of education. In Pakistan, women lag far behind men in labour force participation, are concentrated in a much narrower set of occupations, perform mostly unskilled jobs and have substantially lower earnings. While women's earnings are lower than men's at all levels of education, the economic returns to education and skills defined in terms of the earnings increment from an extra year of schooling are greater for Pakistani women than for men in all occupations (except agriculture), so that education is associated with reduced gender gaps in earnings. But women's participation in the labour market increases only after ten years of education – and only about 10% of Pakistani women have had ten or more years of education (as of the early 2000s). Thus gender barriers to labour market entry, the narrowness of female occupations and limited opportunities for education are diluting the equality-promoting benefits of education in Pakistan (Aslam et al., forthcoming).

Discrimination in the labour market based on gender can negate the equalizing effects of education

Many factors can weaken the relationship between more education on the one side and faster, broader-based growth on the other. An increase in the average number of years in school is not always a good proxy for human capital formation. Where education quality is poor and levels of learning achievement are low, the real skills base of the economy may not increase. Rising enrolment and school completion can have a marginal bearing on human capital. Similarly, increases in the average number of years spent in education will not result in more equitable income distribution if large sections of the population are left behind. What matters in this context is the degree to which the poor are catching up in education with the non-poor. The bottom line is that average years in school is an important indicator of human capital but not the only indicator. Quality and equity are also critical.

Improved education is associated with lower levels of child mortality and better nutrition and health

It is important to recognize the limits to the current state of knowledge on the emerging relationship between education on the one side and economic growth and poverty reduction on the other. Economic modelling exercises can tell us something important about this relationship on the basis of past evidence. The future is always uncertain – but it will not look like the past. Globalization and the increased weight of knowledge-based factors in driving economic growth have important consequences for wealth distribution and poverty reduction nationally and internationally. If knowledge is increasingly recognized as the key to competitiveness, employment and long-term growth prospects, learning endowments become ever more important. In the context of rapidly changing national and international economic structures, there is a premium on the acquisition of transferable skills and knowledge.

Lifelong learning, a core EFA goal, is the critical condition for adjustment to knowledge-based economic life. People and countries need formal education systems that give them opportunities to build their learning skills. And they need opportunities to continually renew their skills and competencies. While literacy and numeracy remain the foundations for all education systems, human development and prosperity in the twenty-first century will rest increasingly on the spread of secondary and post-secondary learning opportunities.

Public health and child mortality: both linked to education

The links between education and public health are well established. Improved education is associated with lower levels of child mortality and better nutrition and health, even when controlling for factors such as income. The transmission mechanisms from education to benefits in these areas are often complex and imperfectly understood. However, empowerment effects are important. Education can equip people with the skills to access and process information, and with the confidence to demand entitlements and hold service providers to account. Whatever the precise channels of influence, there are compelling grounds for placing EFA at the centre of strategies for getting the world on track towards achieving the health-related MDGs.

Child mortality. One of the international development targets is to reduce the child mortality rate by two-thirds (MDG 4). The developing world is so far off track that very deep cuts in death rates will be required to bring the 2015 goal within reach. At current rates of progress, many countries in sub-Saharan Africa and South Asia will not achieve the target until 2050 or later. Failure to close the gap between existing trends and the target will cost lives: the projected gap for 2015 is equivalent to 4.7 million deaths (see Chapter 2). Overcoming gender gaps and getting young girls into school, an imperative in itself, is also one of the most effective strategies for closing the gap.

The association between maternal education and child mortality is irregular. Having a mother with primary education reduces child death rates by almost half in the Philippines and by around one-third in Bolivia. In other countries, such as Ghana and the Niger, primary education has more modest effects. The strongest effects are at post-primary level (Figure 1.3). Having a mother with secondary education or higher dramatically reduces the risk of child death in almost all countries, often far more so than having a mother with just primary schooling. This reinforces the argument for education and gender equity goals that look beyond the primary level. Leaving aside rights-based arguments and the efficiency case for expanded female access to secondary school, it is increasingly clear that failure to expand opportunity in this area will have grave consequences for public health – and for progress towards the targets identified in the MDGs.

What are the reasons behind lower death rates for children of more educated women? Transmission mechanisms vary by country, but they include nutrition, birth spacing and the use of preventive health interventions (Malhotra and Schuler, 2005). To take one illustration, levels of education are

Figure 1.3: Under-5 mortality rate by mother's level of education, selected countries, most recent year

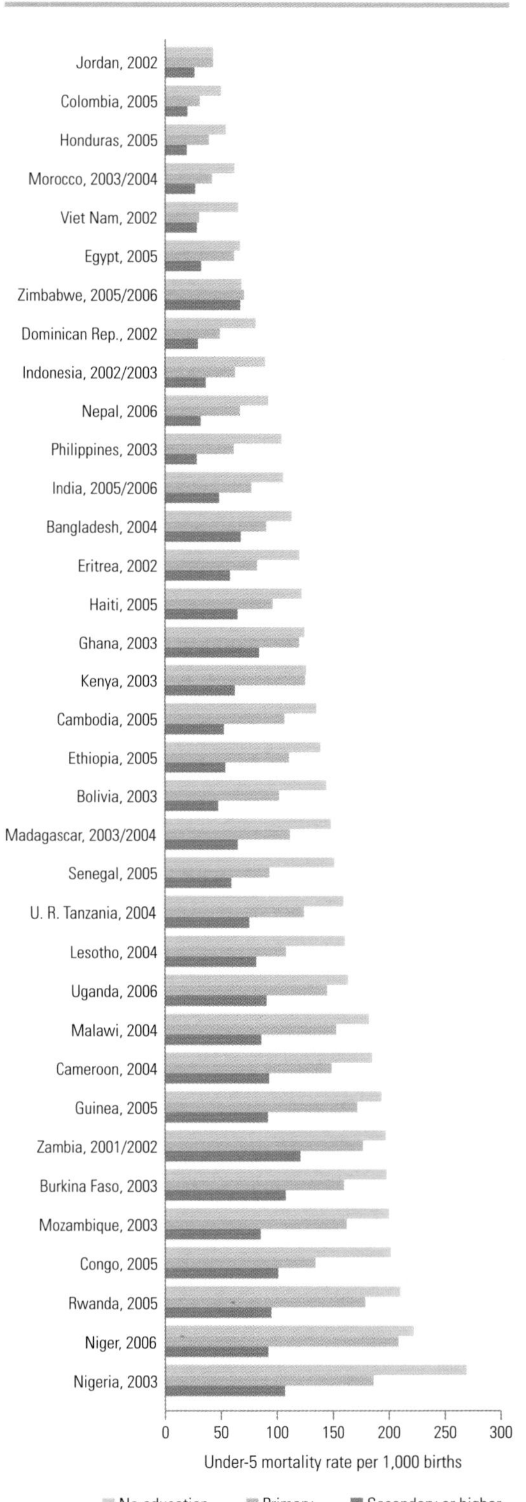

Source: Macro International Inc. (2008).

positively associated in many countries with vaccination levels among children (Figure 1.4).

Maternal mortality. Levels of education also have an important bearing on maternal mortality. Complications in pregnancy and childbirth are a leading cause of death and disability among women of productive age, claiming over 500,000 lives a year. Trend analysis in maternal mortality is problematic because of large margins of uncertainty around the estimates. Nevertheless, the best estimates for 1990–2005 show that mortality rates are falling at a pace far below that needed to achieve the target (MDG 5) of a 75% reduction (WHO et al., 2007). Risk factors include poor nutrition, anaemia and malaria.

The developing world is off track for cutting child deaths and maternal mortality

Figure 1.4: Child vaccination and mother's level of education, selected countries, most recent year (% of 1-year-olds having received selected vaccines by the time of the survey)

Note: 'All vaccinations' = BCG (tuberculosis), measles and three doses of DPT and polio (excluding polio 0).
Source: Macro International Inc. (2008).

Around one-third of children under age 5 are stunted, with damaging consequences for cognitive development and health

Good antenatal care can significantly reduce risk. Apart from the direct benefits of pregnancy monitoring, women who receive antenatal care are more likely to use other health services, opt for institutional delivery and seek professional advice for post-delivery health complications (Ram and Singh, 2006). It should be emphasized that the relationship between antenatal care and maternal welfare is heavily influenced by the quality of the care, but effective provision can sharply reduce both maternal and infant mortality (Carolli et al., 2001; Osungbade et al 2008). Education is important because it is positively associated with recourse to antenatal services. This is true for both primary and secondary education, though once again some of the most pronounced effects are to be found at secondary level (Figure 1.5). The benefits of education are transmitted through channels that range from access to information to empowerment effects and demand for entitlements. As in other areas, the point to be stressed is not that improved access to antenatal care justifies a strong public policy emphasis on female education. The case for gender equity is rooted in the fundamental human right to education and not in incidental benefits. But any country with a concern for accelerated progress in child and maternal well-being should view the evidence in Figure 1.5 as a useful measure of some of the hidden costs of gender disparity in education.

Nutrition. Around one-third of children under 5 are stunted, with damaging consequences for cognitive development and health, and often fatal consequences for life (Chapter 2). Stunting is one proxy for hunger, which the development goals aim to halve by 2015 (MDG 1). Here, too, the world is off track, and sub-Saharan Africa and South Asia, the regions with the highest rates of stunting, have made the least progress. Cross-country evidence suggests education is powerful protection against stunting. Recent research using household survey data found that having a mother who had completed primary education reduced the risk of stunting by 22% in Bangladesh and 26% in Indonesia (Semba et al., 2008). This was after controlling for factors such as household wealth, location and family size. Higher levels of parental education in both countries are associated with greater uptake of a range of health inputs, including childhood immunization, Vitamin A intake and use of iodized salt.

Other empowering effects mediating between maternal education and the physical growth of children have been observed. One potential pathway involves the association between increased maternal education and the decision-making authority of mothers in claiming resources within the household. In many contexts, mothers are more likely than fathers to allocate household resources in ways that promote child nutrition (Huq and

Figure 1.5: Antenatal care by mother's level of education, selected countries, most recent year

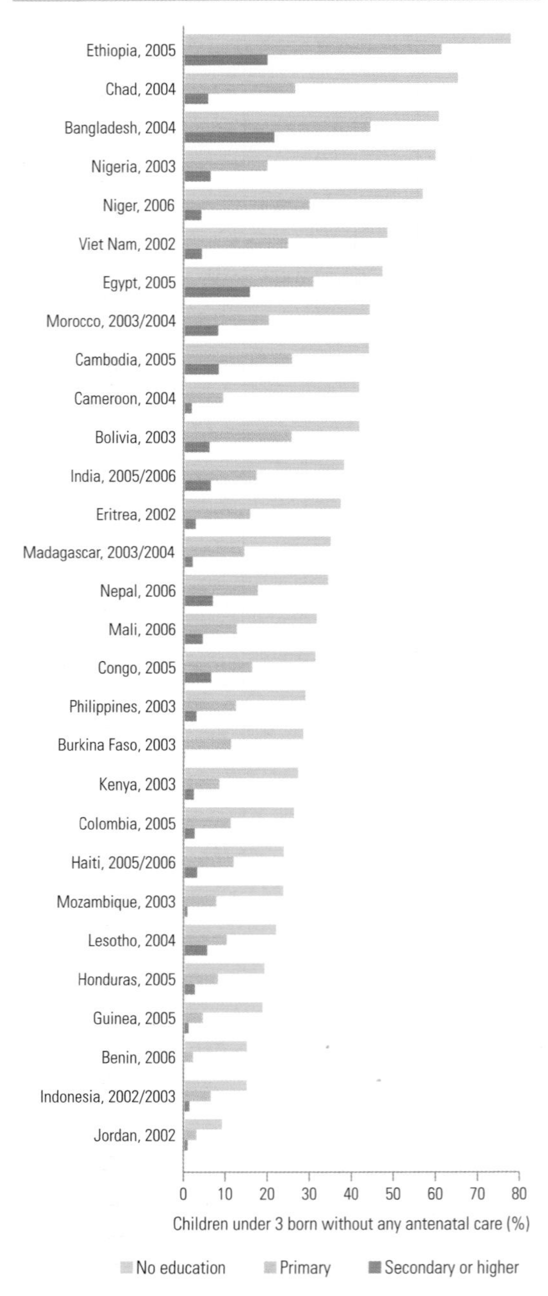

Source: Macro International Inc. (2008).

Tasnin, 2008). As Figure 1.6 shows, the inverse relationship between stunting and maternal education holds across a large group of countries and all developing regions.

HIV/AIDS. The development goals call for countries to 'halt and begin to reverse the spread of HIV/AIDS' (MDG 6). There is strong evidence that primary education has a significant positive impact on knowledge of HIV prevention, with secondary education having an even stronger impact (Herz and Sperling, 2004). One study, covering thirty-two countries, found that women with post-primary education were five times more likely than illiterate women to know about HIV/AIDS (Vandemoortele and Delmonica, 2000). Education systems could play a far more active and effective role in combating HIV/AIDS through teaching and awareness-raising about risky behaviour.

Each of the areas considered above illustrates the potential for education to accelerate progress towards the MDG targets. In important respects, though, static pictures of the potential benefits hide some of the dynamic gains over time. For example, increased female access to education generates cumulative benefits linked to cross-generational effects because the level of maternal education is one of the strongest determinants of whether daughters enrol in school (Alderman and King, 1998; UN Millennium Project, 2005*a*). Unfortunately, costs are also cumulative. Just as the world today would have far lower levels of child mortality and stunting had there been greater progress in education during the 1990s, so the education deficits of today will result in human costs in the future. Improving educational opportunity, especially for girls, is not only a priority in its own right but also essential for improving educational outcomes in the next generation – and for reaching wider goals in public health and nutrition.

Democracy and citizenship – from local to global

Education is about much more than what happens in schools. Through education, societies inculcate their values and ideas, and equip their citizens with skills. This year's Report focuses on education governance. Yet education itself is intimately linked to wider governance issues in society – and to the empowerment of people. As Nelson Mandela has put it: 'Education is the most powerful weapon which you can use to change the world.'

Figure 1.6: Severe stunting among children under 3 by mother's level of education, selected countries, most recent year

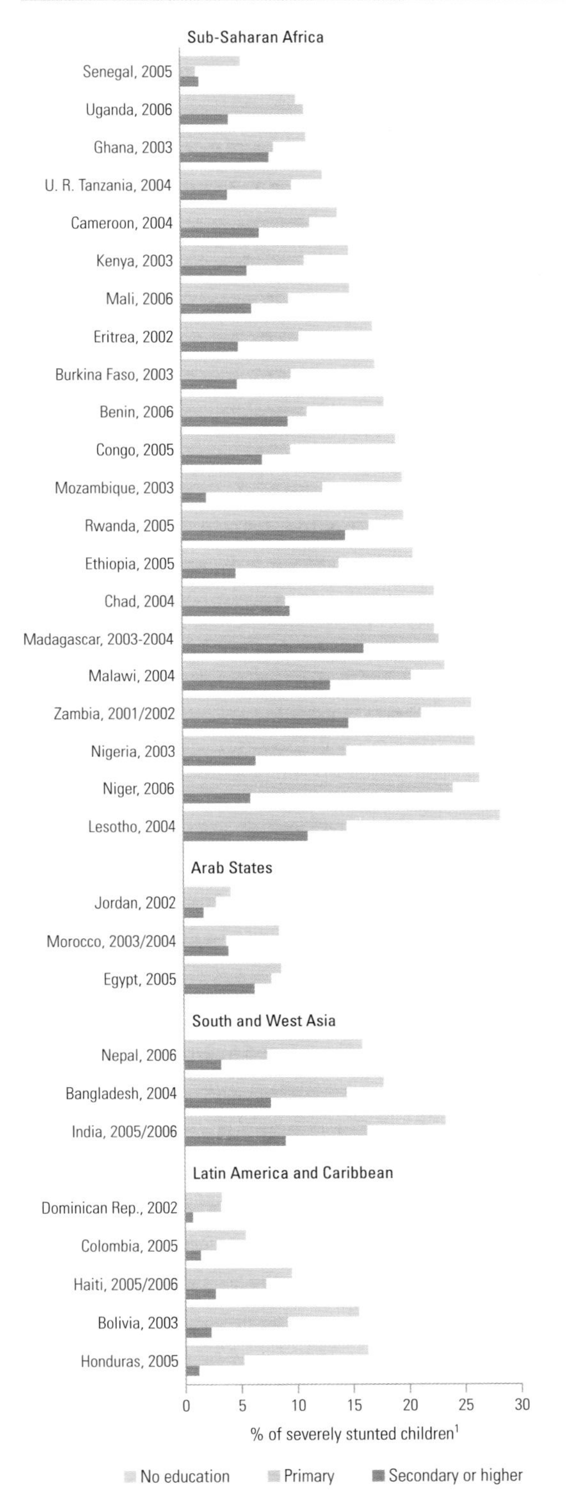

1. Severe stunting is defined as a height-for-age score below minus 3 standard deviations from the reference median (see glossary).
Source: Macro International Inc. (2008).

The education deficits of today will result in human costs in the future

Some of the most powerful effects of education operate through the channels of democracy and participation. History provides plenty of evidence that the effects are neither universal nor straightforward. There are numerous examples, past and present, of societies with a well-educated citizenry that might not be considered model democracies. And there are countries with relatively low levels of education, as measured by indicators for literacy and average years in school, that have a well-developed democratic tradition. India is an example. Yet education is conducive to democracy. It has the potential to equip people with the skills, attitudes and norms needed to hold governments to account, to challenge autocracy and to assess policies that affect their lives (Glaeser et al., 2006). At an individual level, education is a crucial determinant of whether people have the capabilities – the literacy, the confidence, the attitudes – that they need to participate in society (Sen, 1999). As a concrete example, when poor and marginalized people are educated, they are often more likely to participate in meetings of local political bodies and devolved bodies managing education, health and water resources (Alsop and Kurey, 2005).

There are strong links between education, citizenship and informed decision-making

It is not just education that matters for democracy. Cross-country research has drawn attention to the importance both of the average level of education and the education attained by the majority of society in creating the conditions for democracy (Castello-Climent, 2006). Recent evidence from sub-Saharan Africa is instructive. Analysis of national survey data in Malawi found that even primary schooling promotes citizen endorsement of democracy and rejection of non-democratic alternatives (Evans and Rose, 2007*b*). Research into relationships between education and democratic attitudes in eighteen countries of sub-Saharan Africa strongly reinforces this finding (Evans and Rose, 2007*a*). Controlling for a wide range of factors, including religion, age, gender and political preference, schooling emerged as by far the strongest social factor explaining adherence to democratic attitudes. Moreover, the education effects increase in a linear form with the levels of education attained. People of voting age with a primary education are 1.5 times more likely to support democracy than people with no education, rising to three times more likely for someone with secondary education. Here, too, the democratizing effects of education appear to operate through the channels of participation and information: more education is significantly associated with increased political discussion, political knowledge and access to political information from the media.

Due caution has to be exercised in extrapolating lessons from research in a group of countries in one region and applying them to other regions. There is no one model for democratic governance, let alone a universal blueprint for the development of democratic institutions. Even so, the evidence for Africa strongly suggests that investment in education of good quality may be among the most effective antidotes to autocracy and unaccountable governance.

Links between education and citizenship go beyond public attitudes towards democracy. One reason education is conducive to democracy is that it can facilitate the development of informed judgements about issues that have to be addressed through national policies. In any country, public debate and scrutiny can help strengthen policy-making. And once again, what is true at national level applies internationally as well. One feature of global integration is that governments and populations worldwide face problems – in finance, trade, security, environmental sustainability – that do not respect national borders. Education has a key role to play in fostering national and international support for the multilateral governance needed to address such problems.

Climate change provides an illustration. The role of science in developing the skills and technologies on which productivity, employment and prosperity increasingly depend is well known. Less attention has been paid to the role of scientific education in increasing children's awareness of the great environmental challenges their generation faces. Climate change poses a particularly stark set of threats for humanity, in general over the long term and for the poor in particular over the medium term. Understanding the causes of climate change is difficult because of the complex processes that influence the build-up of greenhouse gases in the atmosphere. Evaluating the effects is even more challenging because of the time horizon involved and the uncertainties about when and where effects will be felt and how ecosystems will respond. Similarly, any evaluation of policy responses at national or international level has to grapple with issues that range from energy policy to approaches to burden-sharing in any multilateral agreement.

Understanding the science behind climate change is a vital first step in raising the awareness needed to drive political solutions to the threat. This is true both technically speaking and in terms of people having a sufficient grasp of evidence to assess the action – or inaction – of their governments. The PISA 2006 assessment of scientific literacy among 15-year-old students offers some important lessons (OECD, 2007*b*). When the assessment was published, international attention focused on the ranking of countries. Less emphasis was placed on an innovative survey of the relationship between scientific literacy and global environmental problems. The results of that survey point to:

- A strong association between student levels of environmental awareness and science performance, in all participating countries. On average, an increase of one unit on the PISA composite index of environmental awareness was associated with a performance difference of forty-four score points.
- A significant relationship between science knowledge and environmental awareness on the part of the general public. The majority of citizens in countries with a mean score in science below the basic literacy threshold (of 450 score points) were less aware of environmental issues.
- An association, in all OECD countries surveyed, between higher science performance and a stronger sense of responsibility for sustainable development. That is, students demonstrating higher science knowledge reported feeling more responsible for the environment.

These findings point to the potential for a double dividend. Strong performance in science and awareness of global environmental problems tend to go hand in hand, and both are associated with a sense of responsibility supporting sustainable environmental management. Conversely, weak performance in science is associated with lower awareness of environmental problems. Failure in scientific education will mean less widespread – and less informed – public debate on issues such as climate change and wider environmental problems. This in turn will reduce the pressure on governments to act. In facing up to the challenge of global warming and wider problems, EFA is a vital part of the toolkit for national and international change. □

Conclusion

Much has been achieved since governments signed the Dakar Framework for Action. Perhaps more than in any other area, progress in education bears testimony to the fact that international commitments can make a difference. That does not diminish the case for a greater sense of urgency and stronger political leadership. The bottom line is that 'business as usual' will leave the world far short of reaching the commitments made. And as this chapter shows, shortfalls in education come at a high price.

Accelerated progress towards EFA requires a stronger commitment by countries and donors to equity in education

Breaking with business as usual will require change at many levels. Equity has to be put at the centre of the EFA agenda. As Chapter 2 demonstrates, inequalities in opportunity for education represent a formidable barrier to the achievement of the Dakar goals. Removing that barrier will require political leadership and practical strategies that tackle the underlying causes of disadvantage.

Governance is a central concern. The aim of good governance in education, as in other areas, is to strengthen accountability and give people a voice in decisions that affect their lives so as to enable the delivery of good-quality services. Good governance is also about social justice and fairness. Education for all, as the term itself makes clear, is about all citizens enjoying an equal right to quality education. Translating good governance principles into practice involves reforms in institutional arrangements that link children and parents to schools, local education bodies and national ministries. Unfortunately, the design of governance reform is often guided by blueprints that produce limited benefits, especially from the perspective of the poor, the marginalized and the disadvantaged.

Accelerated progress towards EFA and the goals set in the Dakar Framework for Action is a condition for accelerated progress towards the MDGs. More than that, it is a condition for the development of more equitable and more sustainable patterns of globalization. But accelerated progress towards EFA cannot take place without a far stronger commitment on the part of national governments and international donors to equity in education. Inequality has to be brought to the centre of the EFA agenda. This Report explores why equity matters, and what can be done nationally and internationally to overcome disparities. ■

A nutritious meal, in Lesotho

© Gideon Mendel/Corbis

Signing up for literacy classes, in Honduras

© Neil Cooper/PANOS

Support and encouragement from a primary school teacher, in Djibouti

© Giacomo Pirozzi/PANOS

© Gideon Mendel/Corbis

A disabled child joins the game, in the United Kingdom

Chapter 2

The Dakar goals: monitoring progress and inequality

This chapter provides an overview of progress towards the six Education for All (EFA) goals as set out in the 2000 Dakar Framework for Action. Using the most recent international data, it measures performance against targets, compares the state of education across countries and identifies trends. Looking beyond national averages, the chapter turns the spotlight on inequalities based on wealth, gender, location and other markers for disadvantage. Overcoming inequality would accelerate progress towards the goals, unlocking wider benefits for societies in the process.

Introduction

The maxim 'to improve something, first measure it' encapsulates the importance of monitoring progress towards the EFA goals. Effective measurement can serve as a guide to policy, focusing attention on the targets, giving early warning of failure, stimulating debate, informing advocacy and strengthening accountability. At the international level, cross-country monitoring can help to identify areas of good practice and cases of underperformance. Above all, EFA monitoring is important because it charts progress towards goals that are ultimately about improving the quality of people's lives, extending opportunity and overcoming inequalities.

Monitoring has a special role to play when it comes to international goals. Too often in the past governments have convened high-level summits on development, adopted bold sounding targets and then failed to deliver. Education is no exception to the rule. A decade before the Dakar World Education Forum, the World Conference on Education for All held in Jomtien, Thailand, adopted the target of attaining universal primary education (UPE) by 2000, along with a wider range of similarly impressive goals. Results were less impressive than the targets. National governments and donors fell far short of their commitments, but did so in the absence of intense scrutiny. One of the differences between the commitments made at Jomtien and those undertaken at Dakar is that the latter have been subject to close monitoring since 2002 by the EFA Global Monitoring Report.

In this year's Report we identify areas of progress and offer an early warning of impending failure. As the 2015 deadline for achieving some of the Dakar goals draws nearer, the urgency of breaking with business-as-usual approaches becomes starker.

One of the most important time-bound targets in the Dakar Framework is the commitment to achieve UPE by 2015 – a commitment restated in the Millennium Development Goals (MDGs). The present Report argues that progress towards this goal has been hampered by a systematic failure to place equity at the heart of the EFA agenda and by problems in improving the quality of education. The Report focuses on four areas that are central to achieving EFA by 2015:

- **Early childhood care and education (ECCE).** What happens in the years between birth and primary school is crucial. In this area the Report makes for bleak reading. Around one in three children in developing countries enter primary school with their cognitive development damaged, often irreparably, by malnutrition or disease. This is not a viable foundation for UPE. Most governments are failing to act with sufficient urgency to break the link between child malnutrition and lost educational opportunity. Progress towards high-quality pre-school provision and care, a vital condition for lifelong learning and enhanced equity, remains slow and uneven. And those with most to gain from ECCE programmes are the least likely to have access.

- **Universal primary enrolment and completion.** Progress towards UPE has accelerated since Dakar. Sub-Saharan Africa has made particularly impressive strides, with many governments increasing the priority attached to basic education. Numbers of out-of-school children are coming down. Ultimately, though, progress has to be measured against the benchmark established in Dakar of achieving UPE by 2015. Under a business-as-usual scenario, that target will be missed. The *EFA Global Monitoring Report 2008* has developed projections for 134 countries that accounted in 2006 for 64% of out-of-school children of primary school age. The results indicate that some 29 million will still be out of school in 2015 in these countries alone. Importantly, the projection does not cover countries such as the Democratic Republic of the Congo or the Sudan because of data limitations. While trends can be changed, the current trajectory is worrying. If the targets are to be achieved, governments must attach greater urgency to meeting the triple challenge of getting all children into school, ensuring that they do not drop out and providing the support needed for them to complete the cycle. Several of the world's poorest countries have demonstrated that rapid progress is possible. But deep-rooted and persistent inequalities in opportunity, based on wealth, gender, location, language and other markers for disadvantage, constitute a formidable barrier to UPE. For countries that are close to UPE, going the final mile will require practical strategies for reaching the most marginalized. A strengthened focus on equity will accelerate progress in all countries.

- **The quality imperative.** The ultimate aim of EFA is to ensure that children receive an education that enriches their lives, expands their opportunities and empowers them to participate in society. Much of what currently passes for education fails to meet these criteria. Despite serious data constraints in cross-country monitoring of education quality, the scale of the problem is increasingly apparent. Absolute learning levels are so low in many developing countries that millions of children complete primary school without acquiring basic literacy and numeracy skills. International learning assessments point to very large gaps between developed and developing countries. These gaps are mirrored by large within-country disparities in learning achievements. Education quality problems are often exacerbated by the dilapidated physical state of schools in many countries and by severe shortages of teachers.

- **Progress towards gender parity.** There has been impressive progress towards gender parity at primary and secondary levels. Yet many countries failed to achieve the goal of parity by 2005. Countries in South Asia and sub-Saharan Africa feature strongly in this group. Gender gaps in education are often reinforced by other markers for disadvantage, such as poverty and ethnicity, but country experience suggests that parity can be achieved given strong national commitment accompanied by policies targeting the main constraints.

The decision to focus on four priority areas does not detract from the importance of the larger EFA package. Indeed, a defining feature of the EFA agenda is that it treats the six goals as part of a single comprehensive, integrated framework. In this respect, the Dakar Framework is far broader than the Millennium Development Goal framework, which addresses only UPE and gender parity – an unduly restrictive approach. This chapter also looks at post-secondary education, youth learning opportunities and adult literacy. In addition, its final section updates the EFA Development Index (EDI), a composite measure of overall progress. □

Partial projections indicate that well over 29 million children of primary school age will still be out of school in 2015

Early childhood care and education: a long way to go

Goal 1: Expanding and improving comprehensive early childhood care and education, especially for the most vulnerable and disadvantaged children.

The path towards Education for All starts long before primary school. Adequate nutrition, good health and an emotionally secure, language-rich home environment during the earliest years are vital for later success in education and life. Yet millions of children lack these advantages and are locked at an early age into long-term cycles of deprivation. Failure to deliver on the early childhood goal is hampering overall progress towards the EFA targets set in Dakar.

Well-designed early childhood care and education policies are a powerful antidote to inherited disadvantages. Monitoring evidence suggests, however, that many governments are failing to apply that antidote in two key areas.

The first is child health. One in three children below the age of 6 in the developing world will start primary school with their bodies, brains and long-term learning prospects permanently damaged by malnutrition and ill health. This has important but widely ignored implications for education. Getting children into primary school is an important part of the Dakar promise. When so many of the children entering school have had their lives blighted by sickness and hunger, improved access alone is not a secure foundation for education for all. That is why governments urgently need to strengthen the link between child health and education.

Malnutrition or micronutrient deficiency in the first two years of life can impair brain development, with irreversible consequences

The second area of concern is pre-school provision. While coverage rates are increasing worldwide, early childhood services of good quality remain inaccessible to the majority of the world's children. This is especially true for children in the poorest countries – and for the most disadvantaged among them. The upshot is a perverse outcome for equity: those with the most to gain from ECCE are least likely to participate.

This section builds on the comprehensive analysis set out in the *EFA Global Monitoring Report 2007* on ECCE. It is divided into three parts. After a brief overview of childhood development stages, the second subsection looks at child health and nutrition, two foundations for early childhood development and lifelong learning. Using the MDGs as a benchmark for assessing performance, a stark message emerges: governments are failing children on an international scale. The third subsection focuses on ECCE delivery and provision.

The crucial early years

Child development starts in the womb, where it is affected by the state of the mother's health and nutrition. The period between birth and age 3 is one of rapid cognitive, linguistic, emotional and motor development, with explosive growth in vocabulary starting around 15 to 18 months. Development from age 3 is marked by the emergence of increasingly complex social behaviour, problem-solving and pre-literacy skills that build on earlier achievements (Harvard University Center on the Developing Child, 2007; National Scientific Council on the Developing Child, 2007). This is a critical period for acquisition of the cognitive skills that will carry children through school and influence their life chances in adulthood.

Many factors affect cognitive development. Genetic factors interact with social and environmental influences in shaping the physiological processes through which neurons in the brain form sensing pathways which in turn shape cognitive development and behaviour (Abadzi, 2006). Neurological research continues to shed light on the processes at work. Physiological factors are important. Malnutrition or micronutrient deficiency in the first two years of life can impair brain development and the functioning of the central nervous system, with irreversible consequences (Grantham-McGregor and Baker-Henningham, 2005; *The Lancet*, 2008). Other processes are linked to the quality of the home environment, including care provision and cognitive stimulation. Childhood poverty is one of the most powerful negative influences on the home environment (Farah et al., 2005; Noble et al., 2007). Its impact is cumulative, with poor cognitive development leading to weaker academic outcomes and more limited life chances.

The simple message to emerge from the complex field of neurocognitive research is that early experience is critical. There are no rapid-rewind buttons through which deprivation can be offset and no quick fixes for the injury to cognitive development. Early childhood cognitive damage is for life.

Damage prevention is better than cure for reasons of both equity and efficiency. It is unfair for children to be held back in life because of circumstances – such as having poor parents – over which they have no control. The efficiency argument for ECCE is backed by evidence pointing to high private and social returns: not just improved academic performance, higher productivity and higher income, but also improved health and reduced crime. As the Nobel Prize-winning economist James Heckman has put it: 'Early interventions in children from disadvantaged environments raise no efficiency-equity trade-offs; they raise the productivity of individuals, the workforce and society at large, and reduce lifetime inequality by helping to eliminate the accident of birth' (Heckman and Masterov, 2004, p. 5).

Child health and nutrition: slow and uneven progress

Rapid progress towards UPE cannot be sustained as long as progress in tackling child health problems remains slow. High levels of child mortality and malnutrition represent a formidable development challenge in their own right. They are also symptoms of wider problems that directly affect education.

There is good news: most indicators for child welfare are improving in most countries. In some cases the rate of progress has been impressive:

- *Child survival:* In 2006, there were 3 million fewer deaths of children under age 5 than in 1990 – a decline of one-quarter. In 1990, one South Asian child in every eight died before their fifth birthday. The figure is now one in twelve. Bangladesh, Ethiopia, Mozambique and Nepal are among countries having reduced under-5 mortality by 40% or more (UNICEF, 2007).

- *Vaccination:* Increased immunization is saving lives. World Health Organization projections for 2007 indicated that 75% of children in the seventy-three countries covered by the GAVI Alliance (formerly the Global Alliance for Vaccines and Immunisation) had been immunized with three doses of the diphtheria, pertussis and tetanus vaccine (DPT3) – up from 64% in 2000 (GAVI Alliance, 2008). Vaccination against measles is estimated to have cut deaths worldwide by 60% and in sub-Saharan Africa by 75% (UNICEF, 2007).

- *HIV/AIDS.* At the end of 2007, some 3 million people in developing countries were receiving antiretroviral therapy, up from 30,000 in 2002. Improved access to drugs intended to prevent mother-to-child transmission – a major cause of the 370,000 annual new cases of HIV/AIDS among children – is starting to have an impact (UNAIDS, 2008).

In each of these areas strong national policies backed by global initiatives are making a difference. One example is the Global Fund to Fight AIDS, Tuberculosis and Malaria, established in 2002. As of mid-2008, it was providing 1.75 million people with antiretroviral treatment (a 59% increase in one year) and 59 million antimalarial bed nets (doubling provision over the course of the year) (Global Fund to Fight AIDS, Tuberculosis and Malaria, 2008). While many targets have been missed and insufficient attention has been paid to strengthening national health systems, these are real achievements.

The bad news is that current efforts fall far short of what is required. Notwithstanding the ready availability and affordability of interventions with proven effectiveness, key targets set under the MDGs for child health will be missed.

Child mortality: slow progress and large inequalities

Child mortality is one of the most sensitive barometers of well-being for children under 5. While the measure itself captures premature death, it also provides an insight into the health and nutritional condition of the next generation of primary school-age children.

Each year around 10 million children die before they reach the starting age for primary school (UNICEF, 2007). The vast majority of these deaths result from poverty-related infectious diseases and inadequate access to basic services, such as clean water and sanitation. Around 1.8 million children die annually in developing countries for want of these latter two commodities that people in rich countries take for granted (UNDP, 2006). Sub-Saharan Africa accounts for half of all under-5 deaths, and its share is growing. South Asia accounts for one-third of such deaths.

Childhood mortality figures represent the tip of an iceberg. The diseases that account for the bulk of child deaths, such as pneumonia (19% of the total),

Around 1.8 million children die annually in developing countries for want of basic services, such as clean water and sanitation

diarrhoeal infections (17%), malaria (8%) and measles (4%), inflict far wider and often lasting damage on children's development prospects (Patrinos, 2007; WHO, 2008). For example, diarrhoea is both a cause and a consequence of micronutrient deficiency. Pneumonia not only claims the lives of some 2 million children a year but is also a major opportunistic infection associated with diphtheria, whooping cough and measles (Simoes et al., 2006). Maternal malaria is a significant cause of intrauterine growth retardation and low birth weight, and, in Africa, of childhood anaemia (Breman et al., 2006). The major diseases implicated in child mortality also have consequences for education through long-term effects on nutrition and cognitive development, as well as on school attendance and learning.

In many countries being poor and rural dramatically reduces the prospect of surviving to the fifth birthday

In the MDGs the world's governments have pledged to cut under-5 deaths by two-thirds, from 1990 levels, by 2015. Without a greatly intensified effort, that goal will be missed by a wide margin (Figure 2.1). The situation in sub-Saharan Africa is particularly worrying. The region as a whole has been reducing child mortality at one-quarter the required rate and only three out of forty-six countries are on track for the MDG target. In South Asia, the observed rate of decline for 1990–2006 is around one-third what is required to achieve the MDG. These are large statistical deficits, with large associated human costs. At global level, the projected gap between the MDG target and outcome in 2015 can be measured in terms of the 4.3 million child deaths that would be averted if the goals were achieved (UNICEF, 2007).

Childhood health and survival, and their effects on cognitive development and education, are heavily influenced by patterns of inequality. In many countries being poor and rural dramatically reduces the prospect of surviving to the fifth birthday. For example, in Bolivia and Nigeria, child death rates among the poorest quintile are over three times those of the wealthiest 20% (Figure 2.2). These disparities reflect underlying inequalities in nutrition, vulnerability and access to health services.

Reducing health disparities would deliver a high pay-off in terms of lives saved. Cutting child death rates among the poorest quintile of households to the levels prevailing among the richest 20% would reduce overall deaths by some 40% (UNICEF, 2007). Unfortunately, mortality data suggest that many countries are moving in the wrong direction (Figure 2.3). Disaggregating child mortality data for twenty-two countries for which household survey data by income quintile are available shows that:

- In nine of the seventeen countries that have made progress in reducing child deaths, the mortality gap between the richest and poorest quintiles has widened. In Nicaragua, the Philippines and Zambia the rate of improvement for the poorest 20% fell far behind that for the richest.

Figure 2.1: Rates of decline in under-5 mortality in 1990–2006 and required rates for 2007–2015 to meet the MDG

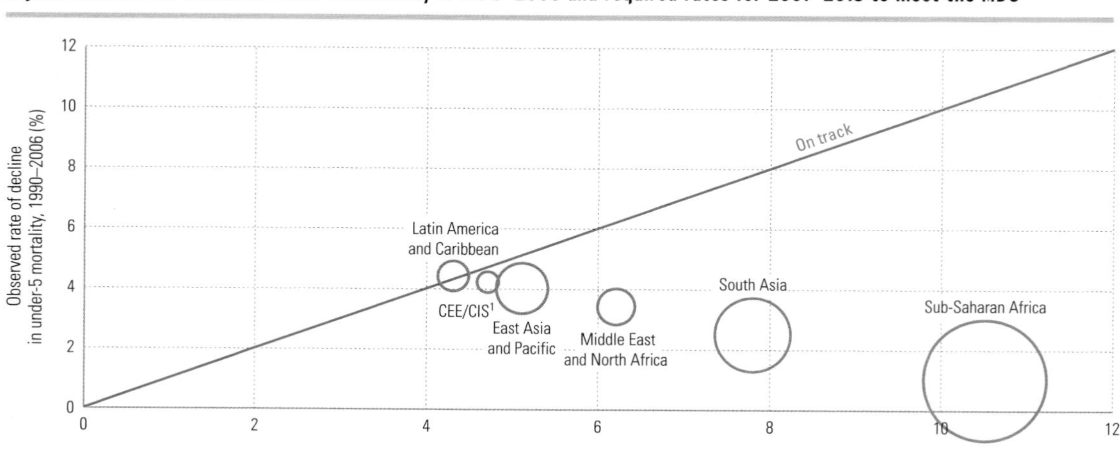

Notes: The area of each circle represents the relative number of current under-5 deaths. The closer the circle is to the on-track line, the closer it is to meeting the MDG. Regions presented are those used by UNICEF, which differ to some extent from the EFA regions.
1. Central and Eastern Europe, and the Commonwealth of Independent States.
Source: UNICEF (2007).

Figure 2.2: Under-5 mortality rates by location and income group, selected countries, most recent year

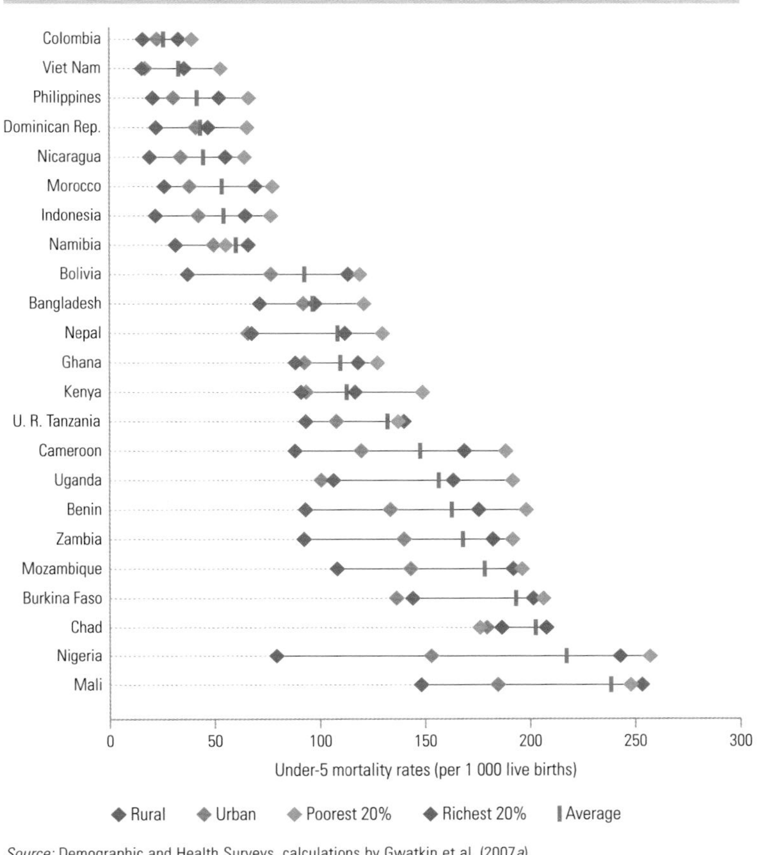

Source: Demographic and Health Surveys, calculations by Gwatkin et al. (2007*a*).

Figure 2.3: Ratio of under-5 mortality rates of the richest 20% compared with those of the poorest 20% of households, selected countries, most recent year

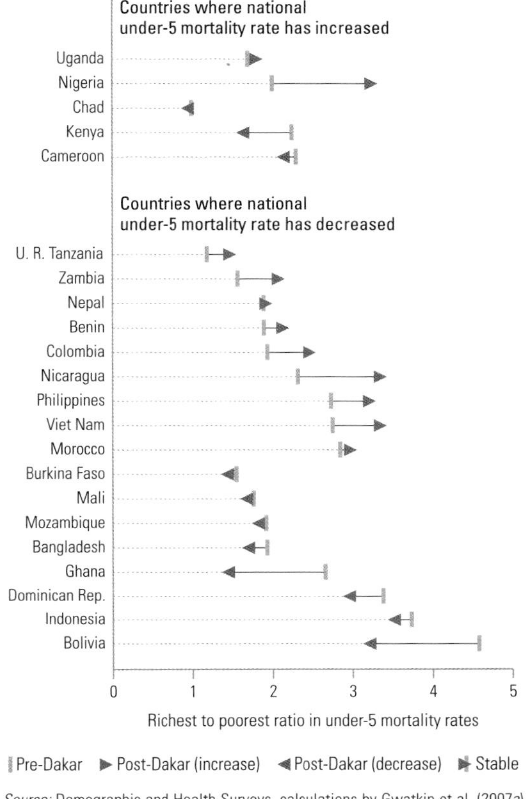

Source: Demographic and Health Surveys, calculations by Gwatkin et al. (2007*a*).

- Among the five countries in which child mortality has increased, the gap between rich and poor widened in Nigeria and Uganda.

The trends in child mortality point in a worrying direction for education on two counts. First, there is a widening disjuncture between the rapid progress in primary school enrolment and the slow progress on child mortality. The implication: childhood diseases will corrode the potential benefits of improved access to education. Second, to the extent that child mortality disparities mirror wider health status, there is a danger that child health inequalities will reinforce the other educational disadvantages facing children from poor rural households once they enter school.

Child malnutrition undermines potential and impedes progress

Malnutrition is the world's most serious health epidemic and one of the biggest barriers to UPE. The epidemic affects one-third of children less than 5 years old. It also accounts for around one-third of the global disease burden for the age group and some 3.5 million child deaths annually (Black et al., 2008). Yet its importance is understated – not least in relation to education.

In 2006, around 193 million children under 5 suffered moderate to severe stunting. By the time they enter primary school, malnutrition will have damaged the brains and cognitive development of many of these children. There is compelling evidence that poor nutrition in early childhood affects cognitive development, fine motor skills, learning acquisition and behaviour. Even moderate malnutrition results in altered behaviour, including lower activity levels, greater apathy and less enthusiasm for play and exploration (Grantham-McGregor, 1995; Grantham-McGregor et al., 2007). Of particular importance is the period between birth and 24 months, during which nutritional

Even moderate malnutrition results in altered behaviour, including lower activity levels, greater apathy and less enthusiasm for play and exploration

India accounts for one in three malnourished children in the world

deficits can have irreversible physical and cognitive effects (*The Lancet,* 2008). Malnourished children are less likely to start school at the official age and less equipped to learn. Research in the Philippines found that malnourished children performed more poorly in school, partly as a result of delayed entry and resultant loss of learning time and partly because of diminished learning capacity (Glewwe et al., 2001). The impact of malnutrition persists into adult life. In Guatemala early stunting is associated with deficits in literacy, numeracy and educational attainment at age 18 (Maluccio et al., 2006).

The scale of malnutrition can be captured in three key indicators:

Low birth weight: The nutrition crisis starts in the womb and is linked to the health status of women. In much of sub-Saharan Africa and South Asia women suffer poor nutrition before and during pregnancy in near epidemic proportions. Low birth weight is a proxy measure for this phenomenon. In 2006, around 16% of children in developing countries – some 19 million – were born underweight and the share reached 29% in South Asia. Such children are twenty times more likely to die in infancy and those who survive are more susceptible to infectious disease. Around 42% of pregnant women in developing countries are anaemic, a primary cause of low birth weight (UNICEF, 2007).

Child stunting: Moderate and severe stunting are indicators of persistent undernutrition.[1] For all developing countries, around one child in three suffers from moderate or severe stunting (*The Lancet,* 2008). The vast majority of these children live in South Asia and sub-Saharan Africa. Almost half of all children in South Asia and one-third in sub-Saharan Africa are affected by stunting. These regional averages mask large differences between countries. Over 40% of the children living in Angola, Burundi, Chad, Ethiopia and Malawi will reach primary school entry age having suffered the debilitating effects of stunting (Figure 2.4). Of the twenty-two countries with a child stunting prevalence of 40% or more, thirteen are in sub-Saharan Africa, six in Asia and two in the Arab States. Many observational studies have shown associations between child stunting or low weight for age, and poor mental and motor development later in life (Grantham-McGregor and Baker-Henningham, 2005).

Micronutrient deficiency: Damage caused by insufficient calorie intake is compounded by nutrient deficiency. Micronutrients such as iodine, iron and vitamin A have a profound effect on a child's development. For example, clinical deficiency of iodine is the single greatest cause of mental retardation. It restricts development of the central nervous system, leading to an average loss of around thirteen IQ points. Iron deficiency anaemia, which affects 47% of pre-school children, impairs concentration and increases vulnerability to infectious disease (Black et al., 2008; Grantham-McGregor et al., 2007).

Measured against internationally agreed benchmarks, progress in reducing child malnutrition has been limited. The MDG target is to halve undernutrition (from 1990 levels) by 2015. Fewer than one-quarter of the 143 countries for which data are available, and only three of the twenty countries that account for 80% of global malnutrition, are on track (*The Lancet,* 2008). In many countries the situation is deteriorating. Malnutrition rates have increased in twenty-six countries, half of them in sub-Saharan Africa. By one estimate, the number of undernourished people in the region increased from 169 million to 206 million between 1990 and 2003 (World Bank, 2006*b*). Much of South Asia is also off track for the MDG target, including countries with high rates of economic growth. The experience of India, which accounts for one in three malnourished children in the world, is instructive and disconcerting in equal measure. For two decades, the country has been in the fast lane of globalization, registering one of the world's highest economic growth rates. Yet this economic breakthrough has not translated into similar progress in tackling child malnutrition (Box 2.1).

The international food crisis could dramatically worsen prospects for achieving the MDGs. In many countries people living on less than US$1 a day spend over 60% of their income on food, leaving them highly vulnerable to even modest price increases (Minot, 2008). Over the past year, international price changes have been anything but modest. Grain prices have doubled since 2006, with prices of other staples increasing even more – by a factor of three in the case of rice (Minot, 2008). Vulnerable households are already suffering the consequences. In Yemen, for instance, rising food prices have reduced the real income of the poorest 20% of households by 12% (World Bank, 2008*a*).

1. Children are classified as suffering from stunting if their height for their age is between two and three standard deviations (moderate stunting) or three or more standard deviations (severe stunting) below the reference median (see glossary).

Figure 2.4: Low birth weight and moderate and severe stunting worldwide[1]

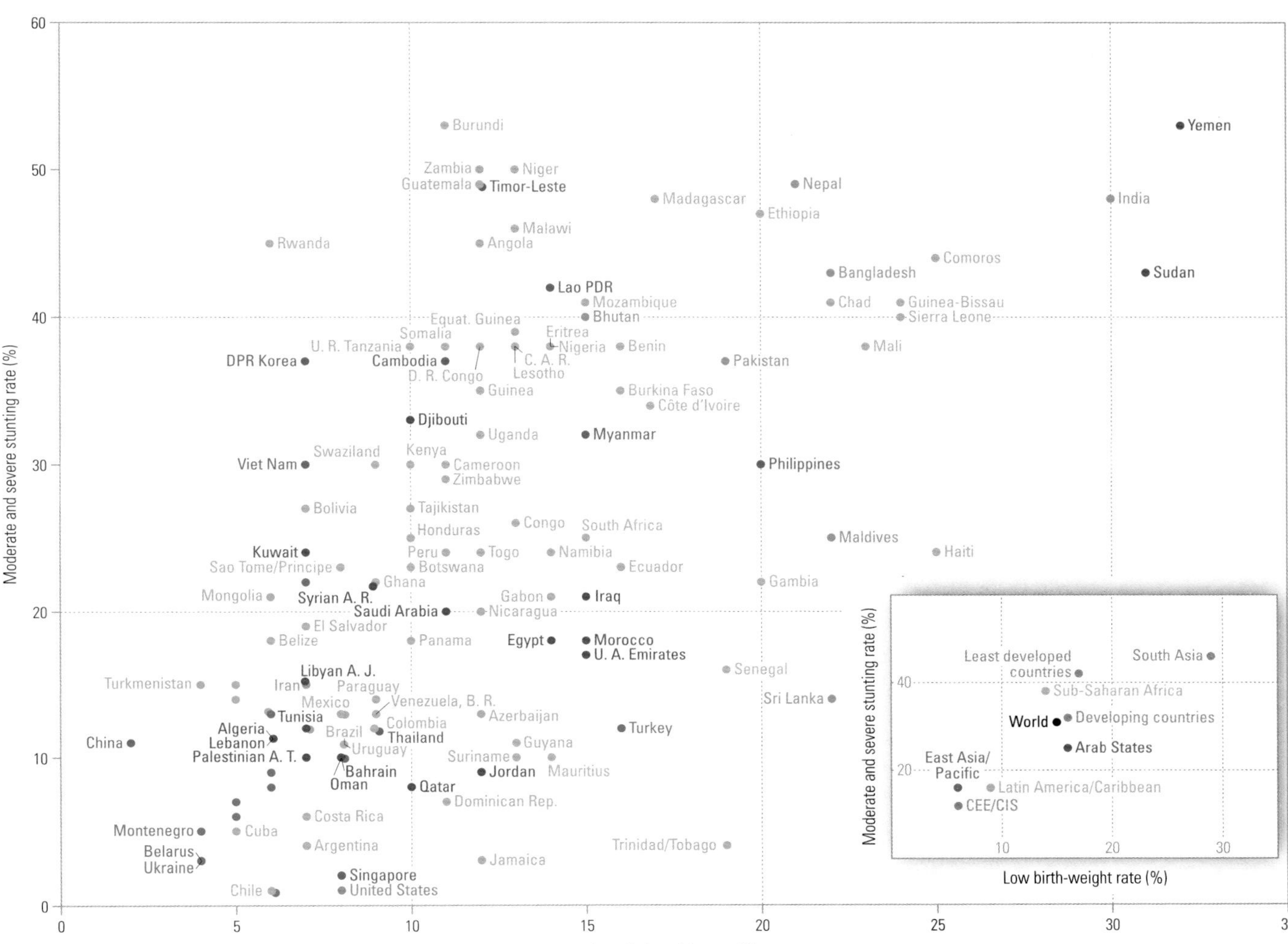

Note: Regions shown are those used by UNICEF, which differ to some extent from the EFA regions. For example, UNICEF includes the Islamic Republic of Iran in the Arab States region, rather than South and West Asia. Data points for countries in Central and Eastern Europe are shown in green, in Central Asia in cyan and in South and West Asia in orange.

1. Data are for the most recent year available.

Sources: Annex, Statistical Table 3A; UNICEF (2007).

On one estimate, food price inflation could push 105 million more people below the poverty line, 30 million of them in sub-Saharan Africa (Wodon et al., 2008).

The slow progress on child well-being indicators is difficult to justify. Priority interventions for child health are well known, effective and affordable. Detailed stategies drawn up by the African Union suggest that additional financing of US$2-3 per capita could cut child death by 30% and maternal mortality by 15%. Expanded immunization, treatment for diarrhoea and pneumonia, use of anti-mosquito bed nets and preventive drugs for malaria, distribution of key micronutrients and measures to prevent mother-to-child HIV transmission could dramatically cut child sickness and death. In rural parts of the United Republic of Tanzania, the incidence of underweight children was reduced by 7% between 1999 and 2004 through integrated maternal and child health interventions, including improved water and sanitation provision, mass immunization and malaria prevention (Alderman et al., 2005). Ethiopia has embarked on a major programme to extend antenatal care and to ensure that essential drugs and vaccines are

Additional financing of US$2-3 per capita could cut child death by 30% and maternal mortality by 15% in sub-Saharan Africa

Box 2.1: Malnutrition compromises India's progress in primary school enrolment

In recent years India has made impressive progress towards universal enrolment in primary school. Progress on child health indicators is less impressive. While India has sustained one of the world's highest economic growth rates for two decades, social indicators for child mortality, nutrition and child health lag far behind:

- Child mortality has been falling at around one-third the rate required for India to achieve the MDG target. Bangladesh and Nepal, with lower levels of income and economic growth, have both outperformed India on this key indicator of child welfare. If India had reduced child mortality to Bangladesh levels, it would have had 200,000 fewer deaths in 2006.
- Rising average income has done little to enhance child nutrition. According to the 2005-2006 National Family Health Survey, the prevalence of underweight children was 46% in 2005, the same level as in 1998.
- Micronutrient deficiencies are pervasive. Iodine deficiency in pregnant women causes congenital mental impairment in an estimated 6.6 million children annually. One-third of all children in the world born with mental damage related to iodine deficiency live in India. In addition, around 75% of pre-school children in India suffer iron deficiency anaemia and 60% have subclinical vitamin A deficiency.
- Health provision is lacking in many areas. More than one-quarter of children with diarrhoea are never treated. Around 45% of children do not receive the full DPT3 vaccination, the same share as in 1998. Vaccination coverage has dropped in ten states since 1998.

This marked disconnect between success in the economy and failure in child nutrition is the product of deep inequalities linked to income, caste, gender and state – and of wide-ranging public policy failures. The Integrated Child Development Services (ICDS) programme is the institutional spearhead of India's efforts to combat child malnutrition. However, its effectiveness is undermined by serious problems in targeting. The five states with the highest prevalence of malnutrition have the lowest level of coverage from the ICDS. In addition, older children (aged 3 to 6) participate much more than younger ones, so the crucial window of opportunity for tackling malnutrition is being missed. Many children from the poorest households are not covered. And the programme fails to preferentially target girls, children from lower castes and the poor, all of whom face higher risks of malnutrition.

The Government of India's publicly declared aspiration is to create a world-class education system that delivers good-quality schooling for all its children. Achieving that goal will require stronger political leadership and practical policies that link the EFA agenda with policies to improve public health and enhance equity.

Sources: Deaton and Drèze (2008); Gragnolati et al. (2006); International Institute for Population Sciences and Macro International Inc. (2007).

Children's achievement in school is affected by what happens to them before they even get to school

available at primary health clinics. To underpin the plan, the government is training and deploying 30,000 female health extension workers recruited from the communities they will serve (UNICEF, 2007). Box 2.2 illustrates the case for such interventions.

Unfortunately, decisive action is the exception rather than the rule. Nutritional security seldom figures among key development priorities and is rarely well integrated into national poverty reduction strategies. A review of malnutrition policy carried out by the medical journal *The Lancet* recently concluded that 'leadership is absent, resources are too few, capacity is fragile, and emergency response systems are fragmentary' (*The Lancet*, 2008, p. 179).

Good-quality ECCE provision: a foundation for equity

Two children are born in Ecuador on the same day. One is born into a household in the top 20% of the wealth distribution in the country, the other into the bottom 20%. At age 3 both score at roughly equivalent levels in tests of vocabulary recognition. By age 5 the child from the richest household is scoring around 40% higher. When they enter primary school, children from the poorest households are so far behind that they are unlikely to ever catch up. This story summarizes the findings of an important study of cognitive development in Ecuador (Paxson and Schady, 2005). It illustrates that what children achieve in education is profoundly affected by what happens to them before they even get to school.

Box 2.2: Country evidence: health and nutrition interventions can enhance cognitive development

Exploiting the window of opportunity for combating malnutrition can deliver high returns. Programmes in many countries make a powerful case for early intervention. For example:

In the **Philippines**, a pilot child nutrition programme focused investments on a wide range of nutrition and preventive health interventions. For children aged 2 to 3, exposure to the programme for seventeen months was associated with significantly higher expressive and receptive language skills (0.92 to 1.80 standard deviations higher), as well as higher weight-for-height scores. Children under 4 also recorded significant lowering of worm infestation and diarrhoea incidence.

Bolivia's Integrated Project for Child Development provides 70% of recommended nutrient inputs and systematic learning environments for poor urban children aged 6 months to 6 years. Controlled comparisons point to large positive effects on cognitive development and language skills, as well as improved weight for height in children under 3.

The Oportunidades programme in **Mexico** provides some of the most compelling evidence for the effectiveness of health interventions. Because the programme has been progressively implemented, it has been possible to conduct a randomized evaluation looking at a range of outcomes. Among the findings:

- Reduced prevalence of stunting. At age 2, children in the programme had a 1-cm height advantage over non-participants.
- Enhanced school attendance and progression. Those who participated between birth and 6 months were more likely to enter school on time, progress steadily through the system and acquire more years in school. Enrolment rates at secondary level increased from 67% to 75% for girls and from 73% to around 78% for boys.
- Strengthened cognitive development. A recent study using administrative data to look at the cumulative benefits of cash and nutrition transfers on health, cognitive development and motor skills found that a doubling of cash transfers was associated with better height-for-age scores and higher scores on three scales of cognitive development and receptive language. Two of the cognitive development domains positively associated with cash transfers – short-term working memory and language – are among the most sensitive to social and economic status.

Sources: Armecin et al. (2006); Behrman and Hoddinott (2005); Behrman et al. (2004); Fernald et al. (2008); Schady (2006).

Research from a large group of countries points to very high returns from investing in good quality ECCE

Provision for under-3s: exploiting the window of opportunity

Institutional arrangements, capacity and quality of service for children under the age of 3 vary enormously. In most developed countries, provision includes regular health visits, immunization, nutritional advice and universal access to child care services. However, there are important exceptions to this rule – and poor children often have the most limited access. In developing countries, interventions are usually far more limited and poorly coordinated.

Households act as the frontline carer in developing countries, although government agencies also have child well-being remits. Maternal and child health services typically fall under the authority of health ministries or dedicated child development services. In Latin America day care centres are widely used to deliver nutritional support to vulnerable households. Governments in the region have also expanded social protection programmes with early childhood components. Sometimes these programmes provide conditional cash transfers: eligible households receive payments if they meet conditions such as presenting their children for growth monitoring and vaccinations, and assuring their attendance in school. The largest such programme is Oportunidades in Mexico, which in 2007 had a budget of US$3.7 billion and reached 5 million families (Fernald et al., 2008). Other social protection programmes provide unconditional cash transfers. An example is Ecuador's Bono de Desarrollo Humano, which provides a cash transfer to women designated as eligible solely on the basis of a composite deprivation index (Paxson and Schady, 2007).

Research from a large group of countries points to very high returns from investing in good quality ECCE. Evaluations of the Bono de Desarrollo Humano programme have identified a range of positive effects on fine motor control, long-term memory and physical well-being. Children of participants in the poorest quartile measure 25% higher in cognitive outcomes than the average for a control group. For the poorest half of these families, the transfer – amounting to US$15 per month –

increases school enrolment from 75% to 85% and reduces child labour by seventeen percentage points (Oosterbeek et al., 2008; Schady and Aranjo, 2006). Other evaluations demonstrate cumulative benefits over time in the form of improved indicators for achievement and learning.

ECCE coverage is lowest in sub-Saharan Africa and the Arab States

Such experiences confirm that ECCE has the potential to make a big difference. Cross-country research suggests there are three conditions for unlocking that potential (Armecin et al., 2006; Grantham-McGregor and Baker-Henningham, 2005; Schady, 2006):

- **Start early.** Effective exploitation of the narrow window of opportunity up to the third birthday diminishes vulnerability to stunting and enhances cognitive development.

- **Operate long term.** Intervention needs to be continuous and to take a variety of forms determined by circumstances, with nutritional, health and behavioural interventions all playing a role.

- **Undertake multiple actions.** For example, feeding programmes that incorporate cognitive stimulation, as in Bolivia and the Philippines, are more effective than either nutrition or stimulation alone.

Formal pre-school access from age 3: uneven expansion, deep inequalities

Around thirty countries have laws making at least one year of pre-school compulsory though few are stringently enforced. In most cases, ministries of education oversee national provision.

Good-quality ECCE provision can equip children with cognitive, behavioural and social skills that generate large benefits in terms of access to primary school, progression through school and learning outcomes (Box 2.3). There is no simple template for determining what constitutes good quality. International research points to the importance of class or group size, the adult/child ratio, the quality of teaching and the availability of materials and curriculum. Interaction among children, carers and teachers is probably the key determinant of quality (Young and Richardson, 2007).

Worldwide access to pre-school facilities has been steadily increasing. Some 139 million children were in ECCE programmes in 2006, up from 112 million in 1999. The global pre-primary gross enrolment ratio (GER) in 2006 averaged 79% in developed countries and 36% in developing countries (Table 2.1). Coverage was lowest in sub-Saharan Africa and the Arab States. Of the thirty-five

Box 2.3: Pre-school benefits for equity and efficiency

Improved access to pre-school can enhance both education outcomes and equity. Much of the evidence comes from extensively researched pilot programmes in the United States, where outcomes included higher test scores, better secondary school graduation rates and increased college enrolment. Two programmes that targeted African-American children provide examples: the Perry Preschool Program was associated with 44% higher pre-school graduation and the Abecedarian Project achieved an increase of one grade in reading and mathematics achievement.

Research from developing countries is more limited but no less compelling:

- In **Argentina** pre-school attendance from age 3 to age 5 increased performance in language and mathematics (by 0.23 to 0.33 standard deviation). Measured through third-grade test scores, the effect was twice as large for students from poor backgrounds.
- In **Uruguay**, pre-school attendance had a positive effect on completed years of schooling, repetition rates and age-grade distortion. By age 10, children who had attended pre-school had an advantage of about one-third of a year over children who had not attended. By age 16, they had accumulated 1.1 additional years of schooling and were 27% more likely to be in school.
- Household survey data in **Cambodia** showed that the availability of pre-school facilities increased the probability of successful school completion from 43% to 54%. The strongest impact was found for remote rural areas and the two poorest income quintiles. Probability of cohort graduation at Grade 6 increased by 13% for the poorest – almost double the increase for the richest cohort.
- A programme in **India's** Haryana state resulted in a 46% decline in dropout among lower-caste children, though it did not significantly change the dropout rate for children from higher castes. Wider evidence from India covering eight states and based on tracking of cohorts found significantly higher rates of retention for children who had been enrolled in ECCE.

Sources: Berlinski et al. (2006); Nores et al. (2005); Schweinhart et al. (2005); UNESCO (2006); Vegas and Petrow (2007).

countries in sub-Saharan Africa for which data are available for 2006, seventeen had coverage rates below 10%. Out of eighteen Arab States with data, six had coverage rates below 10% and three others below 20%.

Participation in pre-primary education tends to rise with income, although the association is not clear-cut. Several high-income Arab States have lower coverage than low-income countries including Ghana, Kenya and Nepal. Further afield, the Philippines provides lower levels of pre-primary education access than does Nicaragua and Bolivia has a higher pre-school GER than wealthier Colombia (Figure 2.5). These comparisons underline the importance of public policy choices. While provision in low-income countries is of course constrained by resource availability, often it is also limited by government neglect – notably with respect to the poor. Aid donors' priorities reinforce such neglect: ECCE accounts for just 5% of total aid for education. This share is hard to justify given the enormous potential benefits of ECCE for primary education goals and the MDGs. The very low level of provision and high level of need in sub-Saharan Africa in particular suggest a strong case for placing a higher priority on ECCE in education strategies (Jaramillo and Mingat, 2008).

Within-country disparities in pre-school attendance. There are marked disparities in pre-primary education provision within countries. Although vulnerable children from poor households stand to benefit most from ECCE interventions that counteract home disadvantage, international evidence points to an inverse relationship between need and provision. Preliminary analysis of data from the latest round of Multiple Indicator Cluster Surveys (MICS3) for seventeen countries points to large gaps in pre-school attendance, with children who are poor and rural at the bottom of the distribution range (Figure 2.7).

Attendance rates for children from poor households fall far below those for children from wealthy households. In the Syrian Arab Republic the attendance rate for the wealthiest 20% is five times the level for the poorest 20% (Figure 2.7). Wealth disparities go beyond attendance indicators. In Brazil, where the average enrolment rate in pre-school is 29% for the poorest households and above 50% for the richest, children from wealthier homes overwhelmingly attend better-resourced private facilities (Azevedo de Aguiar et al., 2007). Research in Rio de Janeiro suggests that average spending per child in private pre-schools is twelve times that in government pre-schools.

ECCE accounts for just 5% of total aid for education. This share is hard to justify

Table 2.1: Pre-primary enrolment and gross enrolment ratios by region, 1999 and 2006

	Total enrolment			Gross enrolment ratios		
	School year ending in 1999	School year ending in 2006	Change between 1999 and 2006	School year ending in 1999	School year ending in 2006	Change between 1999 and 2006
	(millions)	(millions)	(%)	(%)	(%)	(%)
World	112	139	24	33	41	26
Developing countries	80	106	32	27	36	32
Developed countries	25	26	3	73	79	9
Countries in transition	7	7	2	46	62	36
Sub-Saharan Africa	5	9	73	9	14	49
Arab States	2	3	26	15	18	22
Central Asia	1	1	8	21	28	38
East Asia and the Pacific	37	37	-1	40	45	12
East Asia	37	36	-1	40	44	11
Pacific	0.4	1	24	61	74	22
South and West Asia	21	39	81	21	39	84
Latin America and the Caribbean	16	20	24	56	65	16
Caribbean	1	1	18	65	79	21
Latin America	16	20	24	55	64	16
North America and Western Europe	19	20	4	75	81	7
Central and Eastern Europe	9	10	1	49	62	26

Note: Change is computed using non-rounded figures.
Source: Annex, Statistical Table 3B.

Figure 2.5: Change in pre-primary gross enrolment ratios between 1999 and 2006 in countries with GERs below 90% in 2006[1]

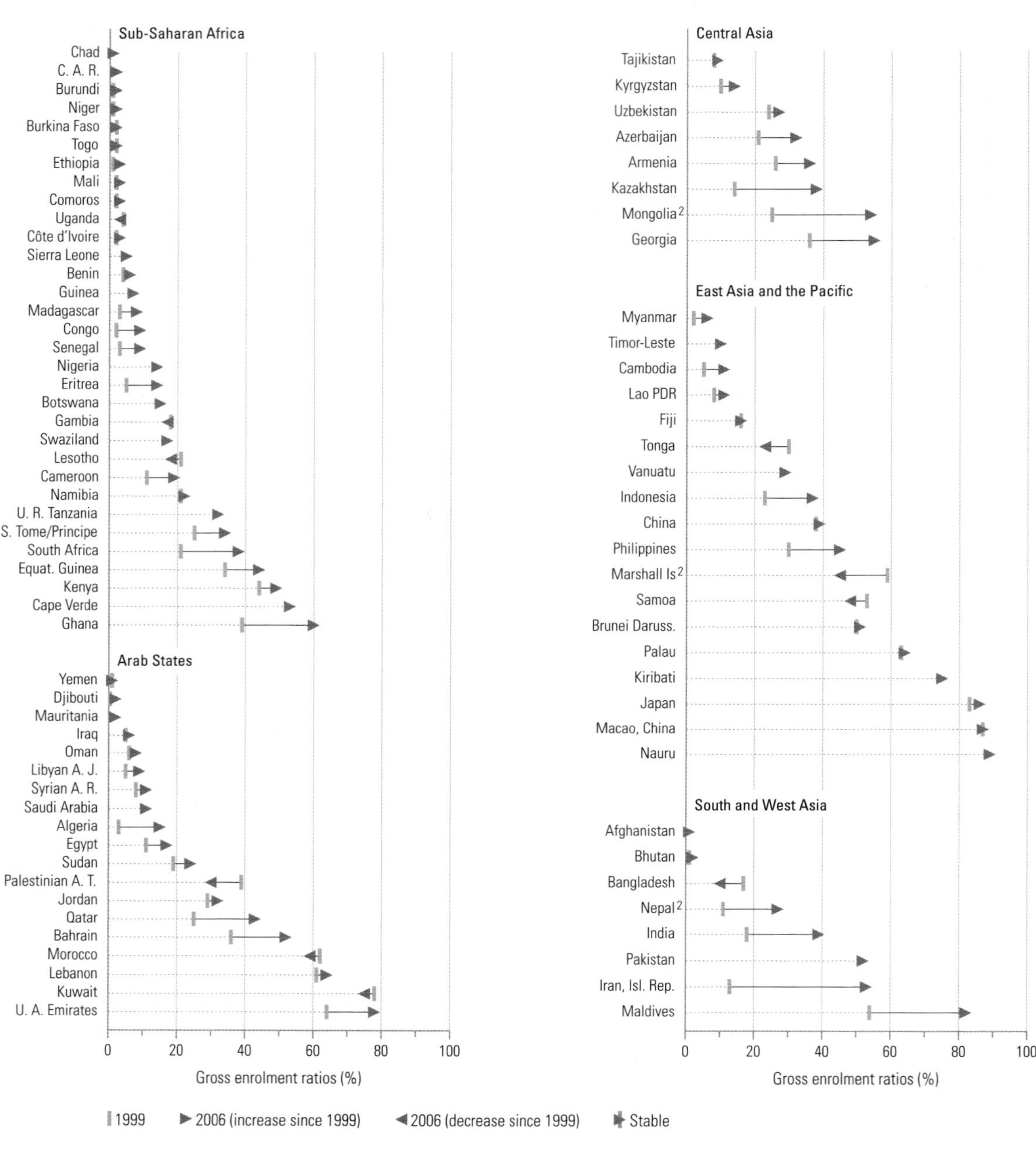

Notes: The apparent decrease in the United Kingdom is due to the reclassification into primary of some programmes formerly considered as pre-primary. See source table for detailed country notes.

1. The GER is 90% or above in forty-one countries or territories: ten in Latin America and the Caribbean, fourteen in Western Europe, nine in East Asia and the Pacific, five in Central and Eastern Europe and three in sub-Saharan Africa.

2. Change in duration between 1999 and 2006. Compared to 1999, pre-primary duration is reported to be one year shorter in Mongolia, Nepal, Nicaragua and Slovenia; one year longer in Chile, Costa Rica and the Marshall Islands and two years longer in Guatemala.

Source: Annex, Statistical Table 3B.

Rural-urban gaps and other geographic disparities are also marked in many countries. For example, in Côte d'Ivoire attendance rates range from less than 1% in the remote north-west to 19% in the capital city, Abidjan. Viet Nam's Red River delta region, with the country's highest average income, has a pre-primary attendance rate of 80%, compared with 40% for the Mekong River delta region, which has some of the worst social indicators. In Bangladesh, slum dwellers are at the bottom end of the distribution for access to ECCE (Figure 2.7).

Factors such as language, ethnicity and religious associations play a part in shaping the distribution as well. In several countries of the former Soviet Union, attendance rates are higher for Russian

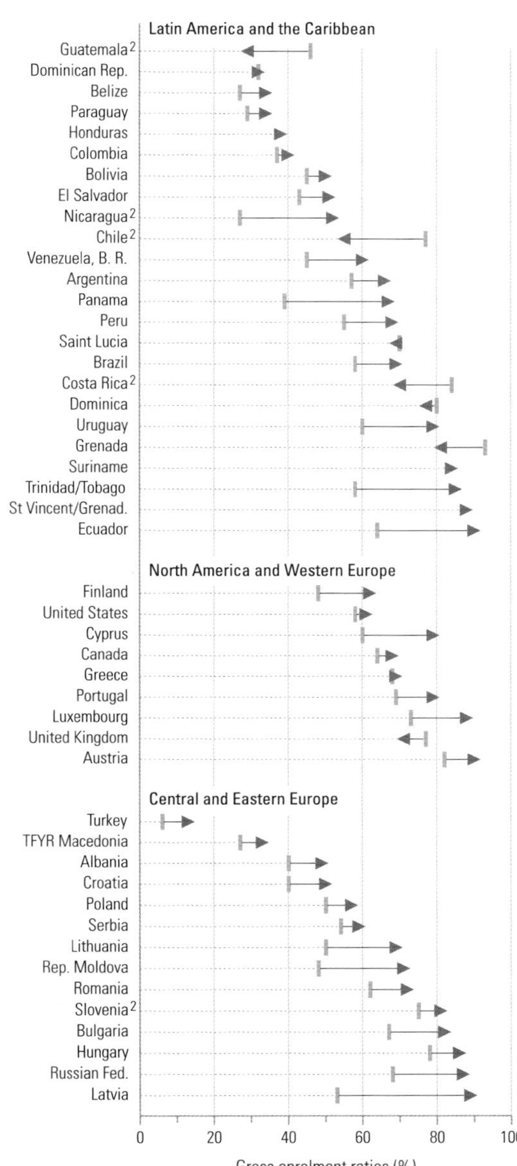

speakers. Roma people living in Serbia have participation levels less than one-sixth of those for Serb nationals in pre-school programmes (Figure 2.7).

Why are children from poor households less likely to go to pre-school? The answer varies by country (see Box 2.4 for one example). In some cases it is because there are no local facilities. In others it is because of cost, or because parents believe the quality is inadequate. Detailed household surveys from Egypt provide an insight into the barriers facing disadvantaged households, highlighting the importance of cost (see Box 2.4).

Box 2.4: In Egypt, national progress but the poor are being left behind

Egypt has embarked on an ambitious programme to expand pre-school provision, focusing on children aged 4 and 5. The increase in coverage has been impressive, but has not significantly reduced pre-school disparities that threaten to aggravate inequalities at the primary level and beyond.

The GER for pre-primary education increased from 11% in 1999 to 17% in 2007. However, the 2005–2006 Egypt Household Education Survey revealed that only 4% of children from the poorest 40% of households ever attended pre-school (Figure 2.6). By contrast, 43% of children from the richest quintile had completed two years in kindergarten.

Two factors stand out as barriers to enhanced and more equitable access. First, for parents in the poorest three quintiles, lack of access is the most commonly cited reason for not sending children to pre-school. Second, around one-third of parents in the poorest 40% cite affordability as a major problem.

Achieving greater equity will require public policy action on several fronts. Providing kindergartens in the poorer districts of cities, small towns and rural areas is an urgent priority. Removing cost barriers will require either targeted transfers to poor households or free provision, or some combination of both. Free school meals could provide another incentive: only 10% of 4- and 5-year-olds in kindergarten receive free food at school.

Source: El-Zanaty and Gorin (2007).

Figure 2.6: Percentage of children aged 4 and 5 in Egypt attending kindergarten, by place of residence and wealth quintile, 2005–2006

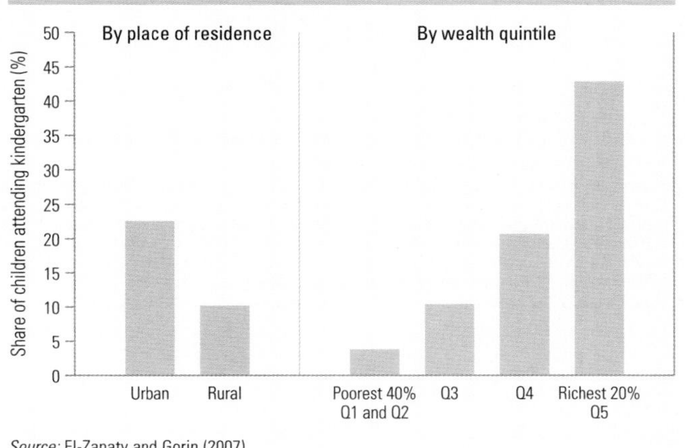

Source: El-Zanaty and Gorin (2007).

Figure 2.7: Disparities in pre-school attendance of 3- and 4-year-olds, selected countries, most recent year

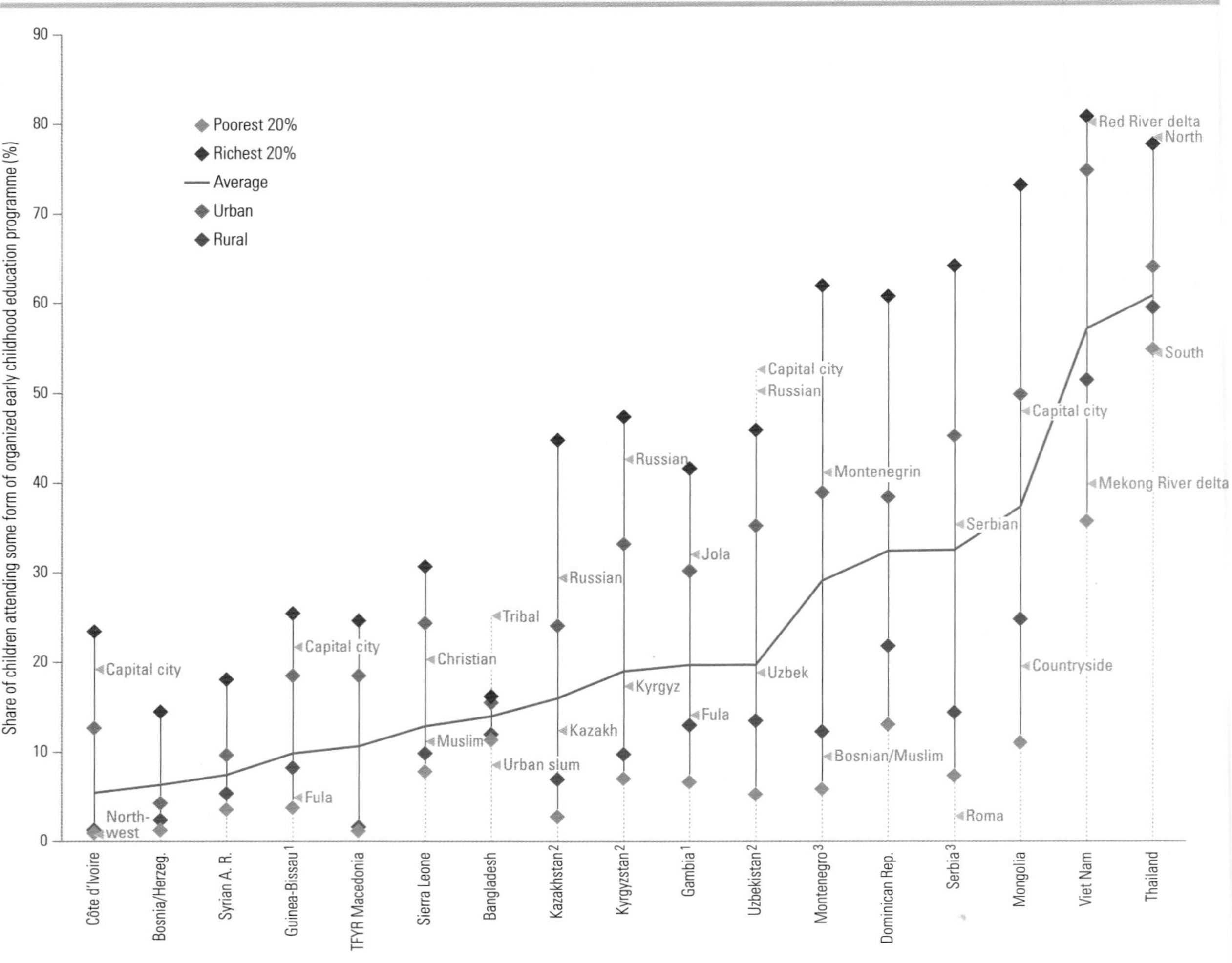

1. The Fula markers refer to the ethnic group.
2. In Kazakhstan, Kyrgyzstan and Uzbekistan, all markers except capital city refer to languages.
3. In Montenegro and Serbia, markers refer to ethnic groups.

Sources: Bangladesh Bureau of Statistics and UNICEF (2007); Bosnia and Herzegovina Directorate for Economic Planning et al. (2007); Côte d'Ivoire National Institute of Statistics (2007); Dominican Republic Secretary of State for Economy, Planning and Development (2008); Gambia Bureau of Statistics (2007); Guinea-Bissau Ministry of Economy (2006); Kyrgyz Republic National Statistical Committee and UNICEF (2007); Macedonia State Statistical Office (2007); Mongolia National Statistical Office and UNICEF (2007); Montenegro Statistical Office and Strategic Marketing Research Agency (2006); Serbia Statistical Office and Strategic Marketing Research Agency (2007); Sierra Leone Statistics and UNICEF (2007); Syrian Arab Republic Central Bureau of Statistics (2008); Thailand National Statistical Office (2006); UNICEF and Agency of the Republic of Kazakhstan on Statistics (2007); UNICEF and State Statistical Committee of the Republic of Uzbekistan (2007); Viet Nam General Statistics Office (2006).

There are large disparities in pre-school provision among rich countries

Rich countries have a mixed record on equity. Developing countries are not the only ones struggling to make ECCE more equitable. There are large disparities in pre-school provision among Organisation for Economic Co-operation and Development (OECD) countries.

While France and Scandinavian countries (except Finland) have achieved near-universal pre-school enrolment, the pre-primary GER of the United States is 61% (see annex, Statistical Table 3A). And within the United States, the disadvantaged lag behind the national average.

Unlike most rich countries, the United States has no national standard or regulatory structure for ECCE. Provision is left to individual states, and both coverage and quality vary widely among and within states. Federal programmes targeting the poor have a mixed record. The largest such programme is Head Start, begun in the mid-1960s under President Johnson's 'War on Poverty' legislation as an effort to break the link between poverty and educational disadvantage. Operated through local agencies, with funds supplied directly by the federal government, it reaches around 11% of children aged 3 and 4. Eligibility is determined by poverty, but not all eligible children take part, and quality indicators are discouraging (Belfield, 2007). Compared with other pre-school programmes, Head Start is modest in terms of absolute size and relative impact – a finding that points to its low value added (Haskins, 2008). While many wider factors drive education inequalities in the United States, disparities in access to good-quality pre-school provision contributes to a persistent school readiness gap between disadvantaged and other children. That gap widens as children progress through the education system (Magnuson and Waldfogel, 2005) (Box 2.5). □

Unlike most rich countries, the United States has no national standard or regulatory structure for ECCE

Box 2.5: The equity gap in early childhood provision in the United States

Almost one in five American children lives in poverty – twice the OECD average. One in eight lives in overcrowded housing and one in ten in households lacking health insurance. This social backdrop is closely related to high levels of inequality in educational outcomes.

Early childhood interventions have the potential to weaken the link between social deprivation and education inequality. However, current programmes appear to be failing on several counts. Measured in terms of equity, they are often failing to reach those in greatest need. In 2008, the *American Human Development Report* examined inequalities in pre-school enrolment by social group, ethnic background, state and congressional district. It found a striking disparity between levels of need as reflected in a human development index (HDI) (a composite indicator for health, education and income) and provision:

- Only 45% of 3- to 5-year-olds in low-income families are enrolled in pre-school, compared with 75% among high-income families.
- There are marked ethnic disparities. The enrolment ratio for Hispanic and Latino children is 45%, compared with 62% for white children.
- For the twenty congressional districts with the highest HDI scores, the average pre-school enrolment rate was 76%, compared with 50% in the bottom twenty.
- Of the top twenty HDI districts, only two had pre-school enrolment rates below 60%, while only three of the bottom twenty had rates above 60%.

The quality of ECCE programmes is also a cause for concern. In the absence of a well-defined federal framework and regulatory structure, management and quality control are highly variable. Another problem is the lack of coherence across programmes covering child poverty and social welfare. The Committee on Education and Labor of the House of Representatives has identified fragmentation in this area as a major problem in most states, counties and cities. Another concern is that the overall level of investment under Head Start is around one-third lower per pupil than in the best performing programmes.

Sources: Burd-Sharps et al. (2008); Haskins (2008); Maghnuson and Waldfogel (2005); UNICEF (2007).

Progress towards UPE: nations at the crossroads

Goal 2: Ensuring that by 2015 all children, particularly girls, children in difficult circumstances and those belonging to ethnic minorities, have access to and complete, free and compulsory primary education of good quality.

More children are entering primary school, but too many fail to complete the cycle

With only seven years to the target date, will governments fulfil their pledge to achieve UPE by 2015? Not if they continue on a business-as-usual trajectory. Some 75 million children of primary school age are still out of school, and their numbers are coming down too slowly and too unevenly to achieve the 2015 target. The twin challenge is to accelerate increases in access and to strengthen retention so that all children enter school and complete a full primary cycle.

Since its inception the *EFA Global Monitoring Report* has charted progress towards UPE and the wider goals adopted at Dakar. If there is one central message to emerge from the reporting set out below it is that this is a make-or-break moment for the commitments to achieve UPE by 2015. Without an urgent drive to get children into school, increase survival and completion rates and strengthen quality, the promise made at Dakar will be broken.

Access and participation: increasing, but a long way to go

The numbers of children entering primary school have climbed sharply since Dakar. In 2006, just over 135 million children stepped through a classroom door for the first time – an increase of about 5 million over the level in 1999. The developing country gross intake rate (GIR), which registers the number of new entrants regardless of age, has increased by just under eight percentage points over the period, with the Arab States, South and West Asia, and sub-Saharan Africa registering the biggest increases (Table 2.2). Some regions have seen their intake levels stagnate or even decline, as in East Asia and the Pacific, Latin America, and North America and Western Europe. This typically reflects a combination of demographic change and a better match between school starting age and progression through the system in countries that started with high GIRs.

Table 2.2: New entrants to grade 1 and gross intake rates by region, 1999 and 2006

	New entrants			Gross intake rates		
	School year ending in		Change between 1999 and 2006	School year ending in		Change between 1999 and 2006
	1999	2006		1999	2006	
	(000)	(000)	(%)	(%)	(%)	(percentage points)
World	130 195	135 340	4	104	111	7
Developing countries	113 366	120 589	6	105	112	8
Developed countries	12 380	11 575	-6	102	102	-0.2
Countries in transition	4 449	3 175	-29	99	100	1
Sub-Saharan Africa	16 397	23 230	42	90	111	22
Arab States	6 297	7 191	14	90	100	10
Central Asia	1 795	1 416	-21	101	102	1
East Asia and the Pacific	37 045	31 830	-14	103	98	-5
East Asia	36 513	31 288	-14	103	98	-5
Pacific	533	542	2	102	101	-1
South and West Asia	40 522	44 823	11	114	127	13
Latin America and the Caribbean	13 176	13 142	-0.3	119	119	-0.1
Caribbean	565	585	4	156	157	1
Latin America	12 612	12 557	-0.4	118	118	-0.2
North America and Western Europe	9 328	8 932	-4	103	103	-0.2
Central and Eastern Europe	5 635	4 370	-22	97	98	0.3

Note: Changes are computed using non-rounded figures.
Source: Annex, Statistical Table 4.

As intake rates have risen, so has overall enrolment. Worldwide, some 40 million more children were in primary school in 2006 than in 1999 (Table 2.3). Sub-Saharan Africa, and South and West Asia accounted for the bulk of the increase, with enrolment in the former increasing by 42% and in the latter by 22%. Elsewhere, total enrolment fell slightly, owing in part to declining school age populations.

Demographic trends: a key factor in education planning

For some regions, slower growth or even contraction of the primary school-age cohort creates an opportunity to increase per capita financing. For others, continued increases in the primary school-age population mean incremental pressure on financial, physical and human resources. East Asia and the Pacific will have some 15 million fewer children of primary school age in 2015; in sub-Saharan Africa the cohort will grow by 26 million, and in the Arab States by 4 million (Figure 2.8). One consequence of such demographic pressure is that governments have to work harder to maintain existing gains. Sub-Saharan Africa, for example, has to expand participation by over two percentage points a year just to stand still in terms of enrolment ratios.

Figure 2.8: School-age population in 2006 and 2015 as a percentage of school-age population in 1995, by region

Source: UIS database.

Where there is demographic pressure, governments have to work harder to maintain existing gains

Table 2.3: Primary enrolment by region, 1991, 1999 and 2006

	Total enrolment					Gross enrolment ratios					Net enrolment ratios				
	School year ending in			Change between 1991 and 1999	Change between 1999 and 2006	School year ending in			Change between 1991 and 1999	Change between 1999 and 2006	School year ending in			Change between 1991 and 1999	Change between 1999 and 2006
	1991	1999	2006			1991	1999	2006			1991	1999	2006		
	(millions)			(% per year)[1]		(%)	(%)	(%)	(percentage points per year)		(%)	(%)	(%)	(percentage points per year)	
World	598	648	688	1.0	0.8	98	99	105	0.1	1.0	81	82	86	0.2	0.6
Developing countries	508	561	609	1.3	1.0	97	99	106	0.1	1.2	78	81	85	0.3	0.7
Developed countries	73	70	66	-0.4	-0.7	102	102	101	0.0	-0.2	96	97	95	0.1	-0.2
Countries in transition	18	16	13	-0.9	-2.8	97	104	99	0.9	-0.9	89	88	90	-0.1	0.3
Sub-Saharan Africa	63	82	116	3.3	4.5	72	78	95	0.7	2.9	54	56	70	0.3	2.0
Arab States	31	35	40	1.9	1.6	84	90	97	0.8	1.3	73	78	84	0.6	0.9
Central Asia	5	7	6	3.1	-1.8	90	98	100	1.1	0.3	84	87	89	0.3	0.3
East Asia and the Pacific	207	218	192	0.6	-1.5	118	112	109	-0.7	-0.5	97	96	93	-0.1	-0.3
East Asia	204	214	189	0.6	-1.6	118	113	110	-0.7	-0.5	97	96	94	-0.1	-0.3
Pacific	3	3	3	2.3	-0.1	98	95	91	-0.4	-0.8	91	90	84	0.0	-0.9
South and West Asia	135	158	192	1.9	2.5	89	90	108	0.2	3.0	70	75	86	0.6	1.5
Latin America/Caribbean	75	70	69	-0.9	-0.3	103	121	118	2.2	-0.6	86	92	94	0.8	0.2
Caribbean	1	3	2	7.1	-0.4	70	112	108	5.3	-0.7	51	75	72	2.9	-0.4
Latin America	74	68	66	-1.1	-0.3	104	122	118	2.1	-0.6	87	93	95	0.8	0.3
N. America/W. Europe	50	53	51	0.7	-0.4	104	103	101	-0.1	-0.2	96	97	95	0.0	-0.2
Central/Eastern Europe	31	26	22	-2.3	-2.2	98	102	97	0.5	-0.9	91	91	92	0.1	0.0

1. Average annual growth rate based on compound growth.

Sources: Annex, Statistical Table 5; UIS database.

Net enrolment ratio: a benchmark for UPE

The net enrolment ratio (NER) is one of the most robust instruments for measuring distance from UPE. It captures the share of primary school age children officially enrolled in school. Countries that consistently register NERs of around 97% or more have effectively achieved UPE since it means that all children of the appropriate age are in primary school and are likely to complete the cycle.

Sub-Saharan Africa has made remarkable advances towards UPE

Post-Dakar progress on NERs has mirrored advances in other areas (Table 2.3). The NER for developing countries as a group has increased since 1999 at double the average annual rate registered in the 1990s. This is a remarkable achievement. Particularly remarkable by recent historical standards has been the progress of sub-Saharan Africa. During the 1990s the region's NER increased at an average of 0.3 percentage points a year to 56% at the end of the decade. In 2006 it stood at 70% – an average annual increase of two percentage points, or six times the rate of the pre-Dakar decade. South and West Asia also recorded an impressive increase in NER, from 75% to 86%. The sharp rise of enrolment rates despite rapid population growth reflects the higher priority being attached to primary education in many countries.

These achievements prove that rapid progress towards UPE is possible, even under difficult circumstances. Several countries in sub-Saharan Africa have registered some particularly impressive progress. For example, Benin, Madagascar, the United Republic of Tanzania and Zambia have moved since 1999 from NERs of between 50% and 70% to levels in excess of 80%. Starting from an even lower baseline, Ethiopia has doubled its NER, reaching 71% (Box 2.6). While the country still has a long way

Box 2.6: Ethiopia – moving into the UPE fast lane

Ethiopia faces daunting development challenges, including high levels of poverty, chronic malnutrition and recurrent drought. Yet the country has sustained an impressive push towards UPE.

The push started in 1997 with the adoption of the first Education Sector Development Plan (ESDP I), which prioritized increased access, greater equity and improved quality. Through the subsequent ESDP II and III, overall enrolment has increased from 3.7 million to 12 million in 2007. Ethiopia has registered one of the fastest NER increases in sub-Saharan Africa. It has cut the number of out-of-school children by over 3 million. Efforts to improve equity have also produced results. The GER in rural areas increased from 45% to 67% between 2000-2001 and 2004-2005. Secondary education has expanded too with numbers doubling since ESDP I.

What are the policy factors behind Ethiopia's success? The priority attached to education in public spending has increased steadily since 1999: the education budget grew from 3.6% of GNP to 6%. Within the education budget, more weight has been attached to the primary sector. It accounts for 55% of spending under ESDP III compared with 46% under ESDP I. International aid accounts for around 17% of projected spending to 2010.

A key target for increased public spending in education has been rural school construction. Of the nearly 6,000 schools built since 1997, 85% are in rural areas. This has reduced distance to school and unlocked demand for education, especially for girls (distance being a significant barrier to girls' participation in education). Textbook distribution has improved and contents revised to enhance quality and relevance: schoolbooks are now published in twenty-two local languages.

Much remains to be done if Ethiopia is to achieve the target of UPE by 2015. Old problems persist – and success has brought new challenges. Regional variations in access remain wide. The two predominantly pastoral regions, Afar and Somali, have GERs of less than 20%. While gender disparities are falling they remain large. And the country still has more than 3 million children out of school.

The substantial expansion of enrolment has created systemwide pressures. Instead of going down as planned, the average pupil/teacher ratio (PTR) increased from 42:1 in 1997 to 65:1 in 2006. A national learning assessment conducted in 2004 recorded no improvement in quality. Dropout rates remain high, with nearly one in four students leaving school before grade 2. Households' contributions to financing are high, both for school construction and recurrent costs, leading to concerns that this could further foster inequality.

Ambitious targets and strategies have been adopted to address these problems. Goals for 2010 include a GER of 109%, a GPI of the GER at 0.94 and a 64% primary school completion rate. Classroom construction is being scaled up, with an emphasis on building near marginalized communities in areas with large out-of-school populations. Financial incentives for girls' education are being strengthened, with targeted interventions in areas where gender gaps are wide. Ethiopia envisages recruiting almost 300,000 teachers by 2010 to bring down PTRs while accelerating progress towards UPE.

Sources: Annex, Statistical Table 5; Ethiopia Ministry of Finance and Economic Development (2006, 2007).

to go to UPE, it has made dramatic advances in improving access and tackling inequalities. One important factor has been an ambitious school construction programme in rural areas, which has spurred demand by reducing the distance to school and addressing security concerns for girls.

There are other striking success stories. Amidst a destabilizing civil conflict, Nepal has increased its NER from 65% to 79% since 1999. Governance reforms involving transfer of resources and authority to local communities and incentives aimed at overcoming gender and caste inequalities played an important role in improving access (Box 2.7). Among the Arab States, Djibouti, Mauritania, Morocco and Yemen, with the region's four lowest NERs, have all registered strong progress (Figure 2.9).

The policies behind increases in NER vary by country but some consistent features emerge. While there are no blueprints, there are some useful guides to good practice. In several countries across sub-Saharan Africa – including Ethiopia, Kenya, Lesotho, the United Republic of Tanzania and Zambia – the elimination of school fees has propelled enrolment rates upwards. This was also a factor in Nepal.

Increased public spending and investment in schools, teachers and teaching materials has been critical. So has an increased focus on equity through measures to remove barriers and create incentives aimed at overcoming disadvantages based on wealth, gender, social standing or caste. International aid partnerships have played an important role in some of the best performing countries, including Ethiopia, Nepal and the United Republic of Tanzania. Consistent and predictable financial support for nationally-owned strategies has made an important difference. The important contribution that aid has made in many countries casts into sharp relief the high costs associated with the collective failure of donors to honour the pledges undertaken at Dakar (see Chapter 4).

Nepal has succeeded in increasing enrolment in the face of civil conflict

Out-of-school children: still a long way to go

In 2006 there were 28 million fewer out-of-school children than when governments met in Dakar in 2000. Viewed against the backdrop of the 1990s, when out of school numbers were rising in some regions, progress has been dramatic. In sub-Saharan Africa the number of primary school-age

Box 2.7: Nepal – also on fast-forward towards UPE

In recent years Nepal has registered rapid progress towards UPE. The NER for 2004 stood at 79% – up from 65% in just five years. Numbers of children out of school have fallen from 1 million to 700,000. And survival to grade 5 has increased from 58% to 79%. The fact that this progress was sustained during a civil conflict that ended only in 2006 points to a remarkable achievement.

Nepal's experience demonstrates that even the most deeply-rooted problems and inequalities are susceptible to public policies. Reforms in the following areas have been particularly important:

- **Strengthened local accountability.** In 2001, reforms were initiated to increase school accountability and strengthen community management. Devolution of authority to district and community level insulated education from a general breakdown in centralized planning and service provision, and from the impact of civil conflict. Around 13% of public schools have been transferred to school management committees. Each committee is provided with a start-up grant. Schools receive salary grants to help them recruit teachers. A shift to financing linked to enrolment diluted political influence over resource allocation.
- **Improved equity.** Reforms have scaled up scholarship programmes for girls, Dalits and disabled children at primary and secondary level. The number of scholarship recipients increased to 1.7 million and the aim is to reach 7 million by 2009. Progress towards greater equity is reflected in a shrinking gender gap: the GPI of the primary GER has increased from 0.77 in 1999 to 0.95 in 2006. And enrolment and survival rates for low-caste groups are increasing.
- **Infrastructure expansion and a focus on quality.** The country has embarked on an ambitious programme to increase the number of schools and classrooms, expand teacher recruitment and improve the supply of textbooks.
- **Effective donor support.** Nepal has been at the forefront of efforts to improve donor governance. Aid harmonization began in 1999, with five donors pooling resources to finance a primary education subsector programme. Building on this, a sector-wide approach was developed to support the 2004-2009 Education for All Programme. Its success resulted in a steady increase in the share of pooled aid finance, reducing transaction costs and enhancing predictability.

Sources: Annex, Statistical Tables 5 and 7; Nepal Ministry of Education and Sports (2006); World Bank (2007*d*).

Figure 2.9: Change in primary net enrolment ratios in countries with NERs below 97% in 1999 or 2006[1]

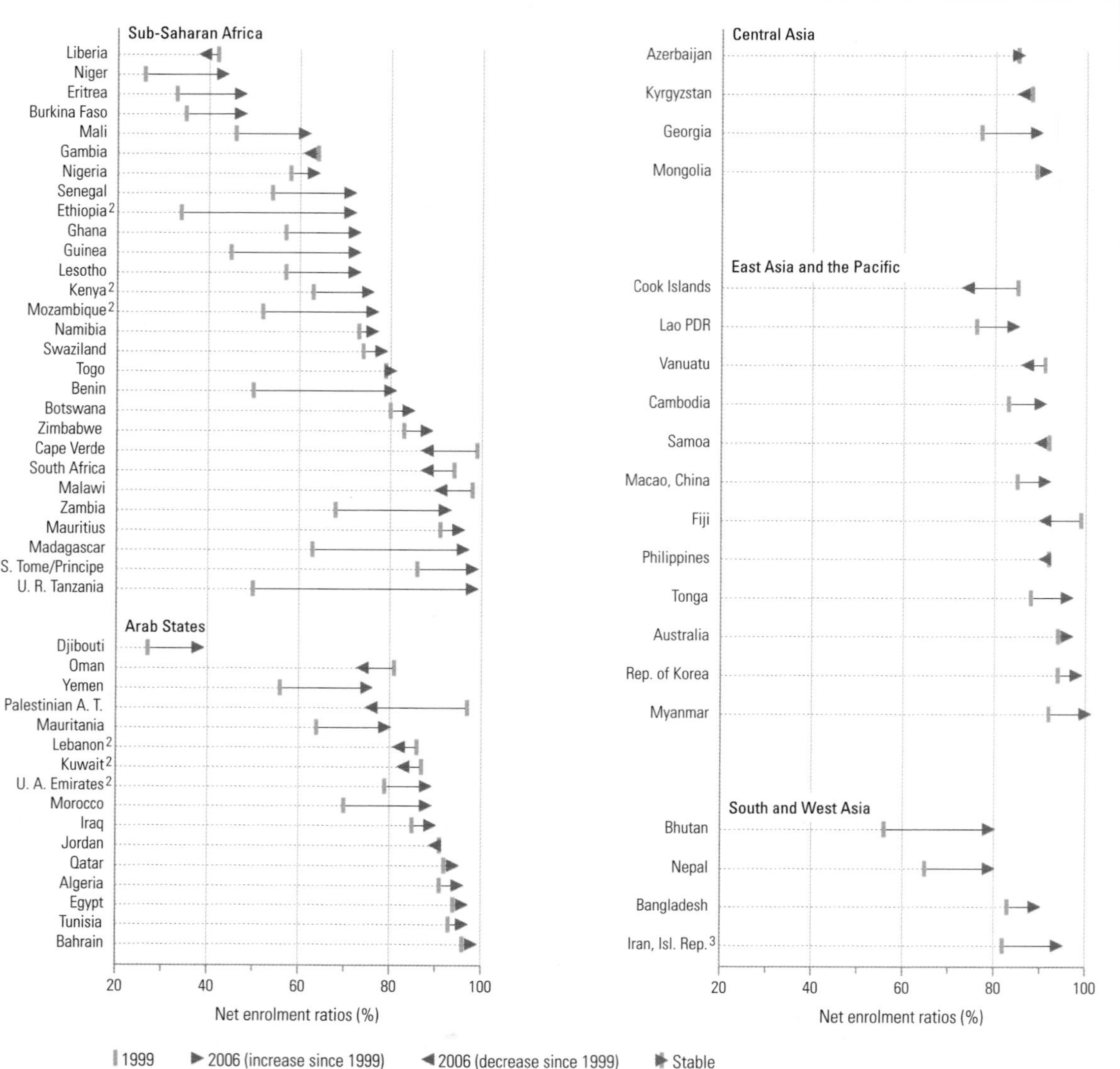

Note: See source table for detailed country notes.
1. The NER exceeded 97% in both years in sixteen countries: nine in Western Europe, three in Latin America and the Caribbean, three in East Asia and the Pacific, and one in South and West Asia.
2. Countries where the duration of primary education changed between 1999 and 2006.
3. The increase in the Islamic Republic of Iran is due to the recent inclusion of literacy programmes.
Source: Annex, Statistical Table 5.

children not in school has fallen by 10 million since 1999, while the population in that age bracket has increased by 17 million. Over the same time-frame, South and West Asia almost halved its out-of-school population, from 37 million to 18 million. Encouraging as these trends may be there is a long way to go. Some 75 million children of primary school age are still not in school – and on current trends the 2015 target will not be achieved.[2]
The circumstances and characteristics of out-of-school children vary. Over four out of five live in rural areas, mostly in South and West Asia, and sub-Saharan Africa. The vast majority are poor and many are the victims of a cross-generational transfer of deprivation. Having a mother with no education doubles the probability of a child's being out of school (UIS, 2005).

Measured in terms of scale and impact on life chances, the out-of-school problem represents a crucial human development challenge. More than that, it represents an indictment of national and international policy failures. In an increasingly knowledge-based global economy, where national and individual prosperity is linked more and more to education, 12% of the developing world's primary-school-age population is not in school. In sub-Saharan Africa the share is almost one in three.

2. The UNESCO Institute for Statistics (UIS) has revised the out-of-school population series using more up-to-date population estimates from the United Nations Population Division. The revisions show that in 2005 there were 77 million children out of school.

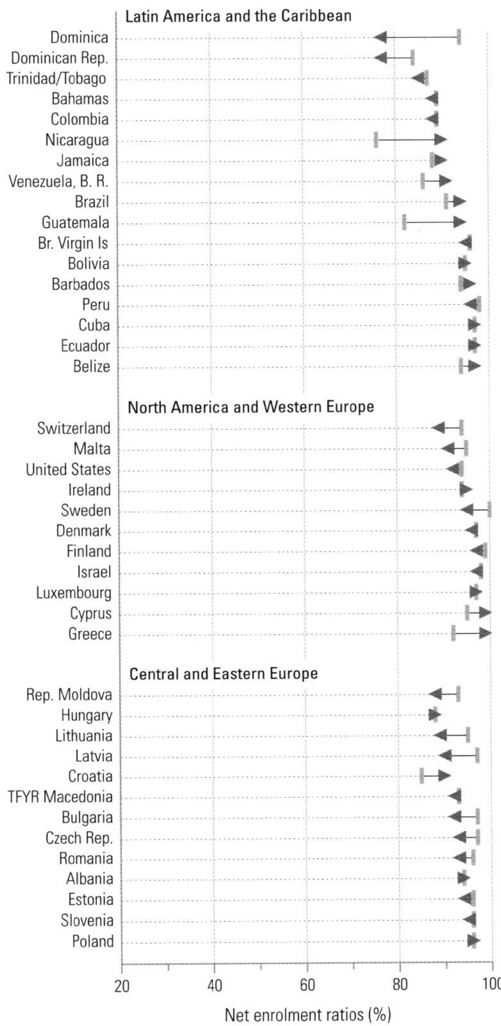

These children are being deprived of the opportunity to get their foot on the first rung of a ladder that could give them the skills and knowledge to climb out of poverty and break the transmission of disadvantage across generations. While the initial costs are borne most directly by those affected, slow progress in getting children into school has wider and longer-term consequences. The loss of human potential behind the out-of-school numbers undermines economic growth, deepens social divisions, slows progress in public health, and weakens the foundations for social participation and democracy – and these are costs borne by society as a whole.

Table 2.4: Estimated number of out-of-school children by region, 1999 and 2006

	1999			2006		
	Total (000)	% by region	% female	Total (000)	% by region	% female
World	103 223	100	58	75 177	100	55
Developing countries	99 877	97	58	71 911	96	55
Developed countries	1 791	2	50	2 368	3	43
Countries in transition	1 555	2	51	899	1	49
Sub-Saharan Africa	45 021	44	54	35 156	47	54
Arab States	7 980	8	59	5 708	8	61
Central Asia	548	1	51	352	0.5	53
East Asia and the Pacific	6 079	6	51	9 535	13	49
East Asia	5 760	6	51	8 988	12	49
Pacific	318	0.3	54	546	1	52
South and West Asia	36 618	35	64	18 203	24	59
Latin America/Caribbean	3 522	3	54	2 631	3	47
Caribbean	493	0.5	50	617	1	51
Latin America	3 029	3	55	2 014	3	46
N. America/W. Europe	1 420	1	50	1 981	3	43
Central/Eastern Europe	2 036	2	59	1 611	2	52

Note: The UIS has revised out-of-school numbers using new United Nations Population Division estimates. The revisions increased estimates of the number of out-of-school children, so figures for 1999 reported here are higher than those in the 2008 Report (UNESCO, 2007*a*).
Source: Annex, Statistical Table 5.

The out-of-school population is heavily concentrated geographically (Table 2.4). With around 19% of the world's primary school-age population, sub-Saharan Africa accounts for 47% of out-of-school children worldwide – a stark reminder of the scale of global inequalities in the distribution of opportunities for education. South and West Asia account for a further one-quarter of the out-of-school population. Within regions there is a heavy concentration by country. Eight countries have more than 1 million out-of-school children each – and four in ten children not in school live in these countries (Figure 2.10).

Eight countries have more than 1 million out-of-school children each

The post-1999 record of countries with large out-of-school populations is mixed. Some have failed to make a dent in the numbers. This group includes Nigeria – with more out-of-school than any other country – along with Burkina Faso, Mali and the Niger. Trends in Nigeria are cause for global concern. The country accounts for around one in nine of the world's out-of-school children (Box 2.8). And there is little evidence to suggest that, on current policies, the country is set for an early breakthrough.

In other countries with large out-of-school populations in 1999, the picture is more encouraging. For example, Bangladesh, Ethiopia,

Box 2.8: Nigeria off track – the price of weak governance

Nigeria had 8 million children out of school in 2005 – 23% of the total for sub-Saharan Africa – and is not on track to achieve UPE by 2015. Its NER increased slowly between 1999 and 2005, from 58% to 63%, well below the regional average. To change this picture the government will have to renew its commitment to equity by addressing the following inequalities head-on:

- **Wide geographical differences** in primary school enrolment. In the south-west, the average primary NER was 82% in 2006, compared with 42% in the poorer north-west.
- **Substantial gender gaps** in primary school, particularly in the north. Only 40% of primary school-age girls are enrolled in some northern states, compared with 80% in the south-east.
- **Major income inequalities** in school access. Children who have never attended primary school come mainly from the poorest households. In Kaduna state, 48% of girls from the poorest 20% of households have never attended, compared with 14% in the richest quintile.

Low enrolment and attendance rates among disadvantaged groups have many causes. Cost is a significant barrier for many. Primary education in Nigeria is supposed to be free, but about half of parents report paying formal or informal fees. Average education-related costs represent about 12% of average household expenditure, a burden especially great on poor households. Other demand-side barriers are less tangible. Cultural attitudes, such as perceptions that girls' education is of lesser value than that of boys, have a powerful bearing on the distribution of opportunity, especially in the north. Parents in northern states often prefer schools offering Islamic education, which do not all teach the core subjects of the national curriculum.

Supply-side factors are also important. Serious quality deficits in education exist across Nigeria. An assessment of fifth-grade students in 2003 found that only 25% knew the answer to more than a quarter of the test questions in core subjects. Average class size ranges from 145 pupils in the northern state of Borno to 32 in the southern state of Lagos. The national ratio of students to core textbooks is 2.3 to 1, the ratio of students to toilets 292 to 1. A significant proportion of teachers lack the minimum requirement of three years of post-secondary education. Many have limited mastery of the subjects they teach.

The Nigerian Government has been forthright about the scale of the challenge it faces, calling for 'nothing less than major renewal of all systems and institutions' (World Bank, 2008e, p. 1). Top priorities include improved quality, intensified efforts to recruit and deploy teachers, strengthened budget management and the development of financing mechanisms that can help allocate resources more equitably. Rapid improvement along these lines will be needed if Nigeria is to achieve UPE by 2015.

Sources: Annex, Statistical Table 5; World Bank (2008e; 2008f).

Figure 2.10: Number of out-of-school children in selected countries,[1] 1999 and 2006

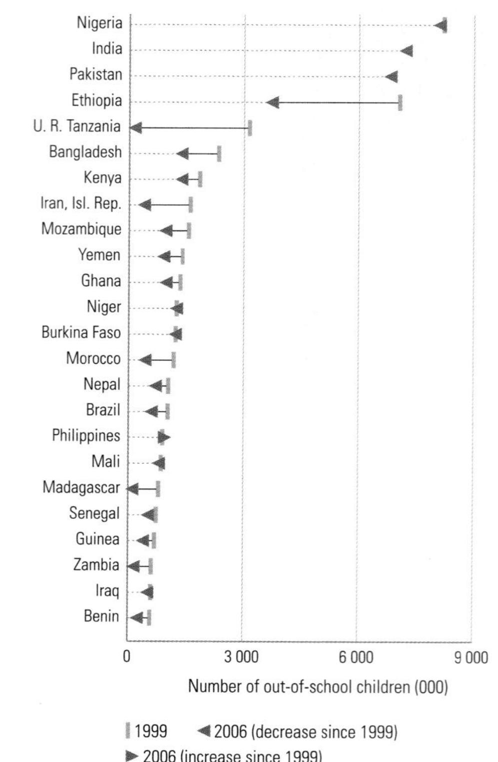

Note: Estimates are for 2006 or the most recent year available. Data for India and Pakistan for 1999 are not available.
1. Countries listed had more than 500,000 out-of-school children in 1999 or 2006.
Source: Annex, Statistical Table 5.

Ghana, Kenya, Nepal and the United Republic of Tanzania have all been making rapid progress towards UPE. The performance of the United Republic of Tanzania is particularly striking. Since 1999 the country has reduced its out-of-school population from over 3 million to less than 150,000 through policy interventions including the abolition of primary school fees in 2001, increased public investment and measures to enhance education quality (Box 2.9).

This Report's data on out-of-school children come with some important caveats. In some countries with large school-age populations (e.g. China, the Sudan, Uganda), data are not available or publishable for 2006. Estimates for these countries are an approximation of the real picture. There are also questions in some cases about the size of the school-age population and the accuracy of administrative data on enrolment.

Box 2.9: United Republic of Tanzania – remarkable progress

A strong partnership of government, donors and civil society has been instrumental in the rapid improvement in access to and completion of primary education in the United Republic of Tanzania since Dakar. In 2001 the government abolished primary school fees and launched a programme to simultaneously improve access and quality at the primary level. The main components of the programme were:

- **Increased spending** on education, with a focus on primary education. Public education spending rose from 3% of GDP in 2000 to 4.5% in 2005.
- **School construction and rehabilitation** through school development grants. Between 2002 and 2004 some 30,000 new classrooms were built.
- **Introduction of double shifts.** Splitting shifts made it possible to accommodate the large, rapid enrolment increases after fee abolition.
- **Recruitment of teachers and upgrading of current staff.** An additional 32,000 primary school teachers were recruited between 2002 and 2004.
- **Introduction of school capitation grants.** At school level, grants have paid for teaching and learning materials, including textbooks, to help defray school operating expenses and to support teachers' professional development.

Between 1999 and 2006 the number of out-of-school children of primary school age decreased dramatically, from over 3 million to under 150,000. The primary NER went from 50% in 1999, before the programme, to 98% in 2006. Completion rates also improved rapidly, partly due to improved teacher training and increased availability of teaching and learning materials. With the introduction of school capitation grants, non-salary spending at school level increased from just 4% of the primary education budget to 27% in 2004. This significantly improved the availability of teaching and learning materials in schools, though pupil/textbook ratios remain high.

Sources: Annex, Statistical Table 5; HakiElimu (2005); United Republic of Tanzania Ministry of Education and Vocational Training (2007); United Republic of Tanzania Research and Analysis Working Group (2007); United Republic of Tanzania Vice President's Office (2005); World Bank (2005e).

Between 1999 and 2006 the number of out-of-school children fell by over 3 million in the United Republic of Tanzania

Reporting systems themselves often provide an imperfect measure of the out-of-school population. This is especially true of countries marked by civil conflict or going through post-conflict recovery (Box 2.10) – as in the Democratic Republic of the Congo. Acknowleging those limitations and omissions, the Report brings together the best of currently available data.

Characteristics of the 'missing' schoolchildren

'Out-of-school children' is a blanket category with a complex underlying story. Not all children in the category are in the same position.

Analysis of enrolment data by age suggests that around 31% of the world's out-of-school population may eventually enrol as late entrants (Figure 2.11). A further 24% were previously enrolled but dropped out. This means that nearly half the children currently out of school have never had any formal education and are unlikely to enrol unless new policies and additional incentives are put in place.

Figure 2.11: Distribution of out-of-school children by school exposure, by region, 2006

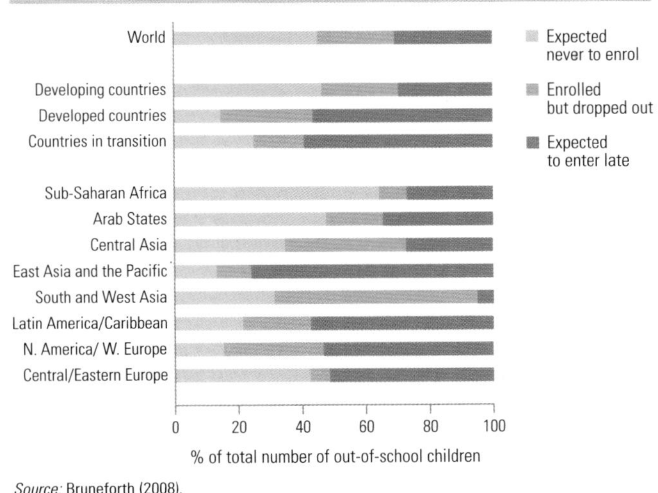

Source: Bruneforth (2008).

Here, too, the regional variations are wide. In sub-Saharan Africa about two-thirds of the out-of-school population is expected never to enrol. In South and West Asia a similar share has enrolled but dropped out. In Latin America and in East Asia, the overwhelming majority of out-of-school children have entered late or dropped out early. As these contrasting experiences suggest, tackling the out-of-school problem requires policy responses that address specific structures of disadvantage.

Box 2.10: Rebuilding statistical capacity in the Democratic Republic of the Congo

After many years of conflict, the Democratic Republic of the Congo has begun an important process of political, social and economic reconstruction. Information on the education system was urgently needed to help decision-makers in planning. With the help of the African Development Bank, the country revitalized its education management information system so that reliable information can be regularly produced. After a pilot phase, data collection was extended countrywide in the 2006-2007 school year. Information was gathered from about 90% of all education institutions and statistical yearbooks were produced. Data collection and analysis continued in 2007-2008. While progress has been impressive, a population census is needed so that important education indicators such as enrolment ratios and completion rates can be computed more accurately.

Source: Sauvageot (2008).

Only integrated approaches can remove the structural barriers that keep children out of school

Gender also has a bearing on the profile of out-of-school children. In 2006, girls accounted for 55% of the world's out-of-school children. In addition, they are far more likely than boys never to enrol. Globally, 53% of out-of-school girls have never been to school, compared with 36% of out-of-school boys. Just over half the girls who were not enrolled in school in 2006, in other words, had never been enrolled and might never go to school without additional incentives. On the other hand, 25% of girls who are out of school may enter late – a lower share than for boys (38%) – and 22% have dropped out (26% for boys). Significant regional and national differences characterize each of these areas:

- Girls' limited access to school is of particular concern in sub-Saharan Africa, where 72% of those not in school have never been enrolled, compared with 55% for boys.

- Dropout seems to be the main reason children are not in school in South and West Asia, with boys particularly affected: 79% of out-of-school boys in the region have dropped out, compared with 53% of girls.

- In East Asia and in Latin America, most out-of-school children, but particularly boys, may eventually enrol late: 88% of boys in East Asia and 76% in Latin America, compared with 67% and 71% of girls, respectively.

- Girls' access to school remains a big issue in India, Nigeria and Pakistan. These countries have very wide gender gaps in the out-of-school population profile. For example, in Nigeria 31% of out-of school boys are unlikely ever to enrol, compared with 69% of out-of-school girls (Figure 2.12). Similar if somewhat smaller gender differences (about twenty percentage points or more) are found in Burundi, Guinea and Yemen.

If the goal of UPE is to be achieved by 2015, many countries will have to strengthen their focus on out-of-school children. There is more to UPE than getting children into school: retention, completion and learning outcomes are also critical. But universal access is the first step. This is an area in which a strengthened commitment to equity is vital. Public investment has to be targeted and distributed to bring education of good quality to marginalized populations and rural areas. For the hardest to reach, free education may not be enough, given the large indirect costs often associated with school attendance: paying for transport, uniforms, books and other items may remain an obstacle. And clearing the backlog of out-of-school children will require more than education policies. The majority of those out of school face disadvantages associated with chronic poverty, gender, ethnicity and disability. Overcoming these disadvantages will require integrated policy approaches aimed at removing the structural barriers that keep children out of school.

The gender profile of out-of-school children highlights areas of great concern for UPE and the 2015 gender parity goals. The fact that out-of-school girls are far more likely never to enrol underscores the resilience of gender disadvantage. Given that the social and economic background of out-of-school girls and boys is broadly similar, it would appear that the low social value ascribed to women's education is at the heart of the problem. If attitudes are part of the problem, part of the solution has to be changing attitudes – an area where political leadership and public campaigning can make a difference. That is a long-term project, but in the meantime governments can lower other gender barriers by providing incentives for girls' education and addressing parental fears for their daughters' safety by building schools in local communities (as the Ethiopian case above shows) and by providing adequate sanitation.

Projections for 2015 – heading towards a broken promise

A year is a long time in politics and seven years is a lifetime when it comes to assessing education scenarios. Someone looking at the United Republic

Figure 2.12: Percentage of out-of-school children unlikely to enrol, by gender, 2006

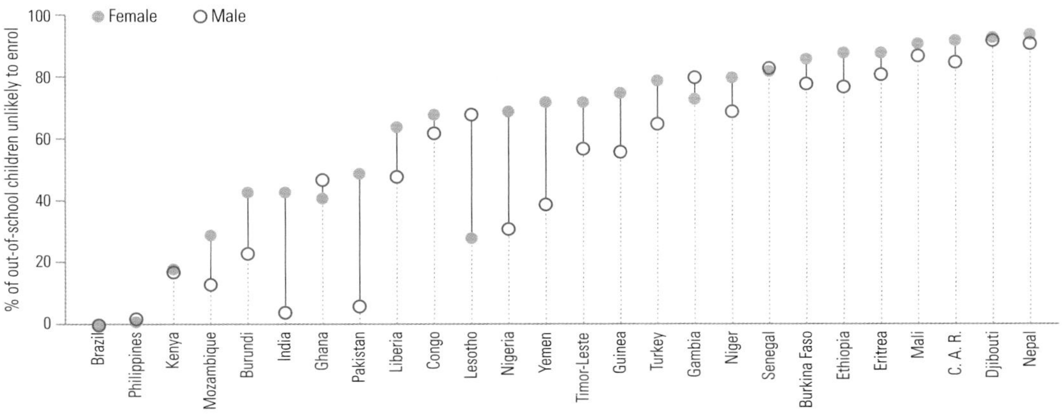

Note: Countries are sorted by the highest percentage, independent of gender.
Source: Bruneforth (2008).

of Tanzania in 1999 on the basis of education performance since 1990 would have been justified in acute pessimism. Projecting trends of that decade to 2015 would have led to the overwhelming conclusion that millions of children would still be out of school and that UPE was a Utopian dream. Re-running the projection on the basis of data from 1999 would produce a very different set of conclusions – and UPE is now very much within reach. As the United Republic of Tanzania has demonstrated, governments have the option of altering their course and choosing a different future.

Any projection to 2015 has to start by acknowledging uncertainty and recognizing that change is possible. Trend-based projections simply draw attention to one possible outcome among many. They do not define a country's destiny. Changes in public policy can dramatically change trends in education. Any global projection is also highly sensitive to data quality and coverage. Data constraints mean that projections regarding children out of school can provide only a partial picture.

With these caveats in mind, research updating trend analysis carried out for the 2008 Report has been used to develop an out-of-school projection. The projection uses data from 1999 through to 2006 to derive out-of-school populations for 2015 on the basis of (i) predicted school-age populations and (ii) total primary net enrolment ratios (TNERs) derived from trend projections (Education Policy and Data Center, 2008*a*). Data availability limited the projection of out-of-school children to 134 countries.

While the list is partial, these countries were home to 48 million children, or 64% of the out-of-school population in 2006. It also includes all but one of the countries in Figure 2.10 with out-of-school populations in excess of 500,000 in 1999 or 2006. However, countries not covered include the Sudan and the Democratic Republic of the Congo.

The results point in a direction that should set alarm bells ringing for all governments that signed the Dakar Framework for Action (Table 2.5). Projections for 2015 provide a clear early warning sign of impending deficits. The main findings are:

- Some 29 million children will be out of school in the countries covered.
- Nigeria will have the largest out-of-school population (7.6 million), followed by Pakistan (3.7 million), Burkina Faso (1.1 million), Ethiopia (1.1 million), the Niger (0.9 million) and Kenya (0.9 million).
- Of these children, 20 million (71% of the total) will be in the seventeen countries that had more than 500,000 children out of school in 2006.
- Just three of these seventeen countries – Bangladesh, Brazil and India – are on track to achieve TNERs in excess of 97% by 2015. The projection highlights the very different trends associated with current policies and outcomes in this key country grouping, and the large gap separating weak and strong performers.

The largest projected out-of-school populations are in Nigeria, followed by Pakistan, Burkina Faso, Ethiopia, the Niger and Kenya

Table 2.5: Projections of out-of-school populations in 2015 for countries with more than 500,000 children out of school in 2006

	TNER for latest year (2004–2007)	Children out-of-school in 2004–2007 (000)	Projected TNER (2015)	Estimated out-of-school children in 2015 (000)	Average annual change in out-of-school population (%)
On track to achieve UPE in 2015					
India	94	7 208	99	626	-24
Bangladesh	92	1 371	98	322	-15
Brazil	96	597	98	248	-9
Not on track to achieve UPE in 2015					
Nigeria	65	8 097	73	7 605	-1
Pakistan	66	6 821	81	3 707	-7
Burkina Faso	48	1 215	64	1 062	-1
Ethiopia	72	3 721	93	1 053	-13
Philippines	92	953	93	919	-0.4
Niger	44	1 245	72	873	-4
Kenya	76	1 371	89	859	-5
Ghana	65	967	81	712	-3
Turkey	91	729	91	710	-0.3
Mali	61	793	76	628	-3
Mozambique	76	954	94	289	-12
Yemen	75	906	94	265	-13
Iraq	89	508	95	246	-8
Senegal	72	513	90	228	-9
Subtotal	–	**37 969**	–	**20 352**	–
Remaining 117 countries included in projection	–	10 387	–	8 341	–
Total	–	**48 356**	–	**28 693**	–

Notes: Countries are included if available information indicates they had out-of-school populations of over 500,000 in 2006. Countries are ranked according to the size of their estimated out-of-school populations in 2015. See Annex, Statistical Table 5, for detailed country notes.
Sources: TNER projections: Education Policy and Data Center (2008*a*); population projections: UIS database.

- Another three of these seventeen countries – Ethiopia, Mozambique and Yemen – also perform strongly in terms of projected percentage declines in out-of-school populations, with annual declines of over 10%. However these countries will not achieve the 2015 target without increased effort.

- The remaining eleven out of seventeen countries reduce out-of-school numbers by less than 10% annually and will miss the 2015 target.

What of countries not covered in the projection? In terms of population, the major absent players are China, the Democratic Republic of the Congo and the Sudan. China is well placed to ensure that all children are in school by 2015. Prospects for the two others are less certain, but hardly encouraging. The Democratic Republic of the Congo had about 10 million children of primary school age in 2005. Using the latest information on primary school enrolment, a conservative estimate would put the number out of school at 3.5 million.[3] The limited data on enrolment expansion between 1999 and 2003 suggest that progress has been slow and the country is unlikely to meet the 2015 goal.[4] A similar pattern emerges in the Sudan, which in 2005 had around 6 million children of primary school age. Extrapolation from GERs would suggest that about 2 million of these children were out of school. While the Sudan has made steady progress since 1999 the country is not on course to enrol all primary school aged children by 2015. Without additional effort approximately 1.3 million children would still be out of school by 2015.[5] In both the Democratic Republic of the Congo and the Sudan, three of the most vital requirements for changing the current trajectory are peace, stability and reconstruction.

3. These figures are intended to demonstrate the likely magnitude of the out-of-school population and are not as precise as those in Table 2.5. They are calculated using GERs, which underestimate the out-of-school population of primary school age because GERs include enrolled children outside the official age range.

4. Primary gross enrolment ratios increased from 48% to 61% between 1999 and 2003.

5. Between 1999 and 2006 the GER in the Sudan rose from 49% to 66%. Estimates for 2015 are based on a linear projection of all GER information between 1999 and 2006.

Out-of-school trends and the projections to 2015 highlight once again the importance of public policies. On average, the percentage of children out of school in developing countries is inversely related to income: as wealth rises, the incidence of children not in school declines. But income is not an absolute constraint. Nigeria is far wealthier than Ethiopia and has access to large revenue flows from oil exports, yet Ethiopia is greatly outperforming Nigeria in progress towards UPE and reduction of out-of-school numbers. Similarly, Pakistan is wealthier than the United Republic of Tanzania or Nepal, yet its slow progress towards UPE will leave it second only to Nigeria in terms of projected out-of-school population in 2015. While the underlying causes of variable performance are complex, governance figures prominently. Ethiopia, Nepal and the United Republic of Tanzania have increased overall investment in education and strengthened their commitment to equity. Nigeria and Pakistan combine weak governance with high levels of inequity in finance and provision (see Chapter 3).

Progression through school: dropout, repetition and low survival rates

Getting children into school is a necessary condition for achieving UPE, but not a sufficient one. What counts is completion of a full cycle. Depending on the length of the primary or basic education cycle, this means all children must be in school by around 2009 at an appropriate age, and progress smoothly through the system, to make the 2015 goal. Even getting within range of this objective will require rapid and far-reaching change.

In many developing countries, students are locked into cycles of repetition and dropout

In many developing countries smooth progression through the primary school system is the exception rather than the rule. Students are locked into cycles of repetition and dropout. The cycles are mutually reinforcing because repetition is often a prelude to dropout. Tracking cohorts through primary school serves to demonstrate the scale of the problem (Figure 2.13). Take the case of Malawi. Just over 60% of children enter primary school at the official age. Around half of these drop out or repeat grade 1

Figure 2.13: Primary school progression without repetition or dropout, selected countries, 2006

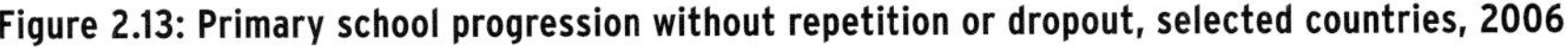

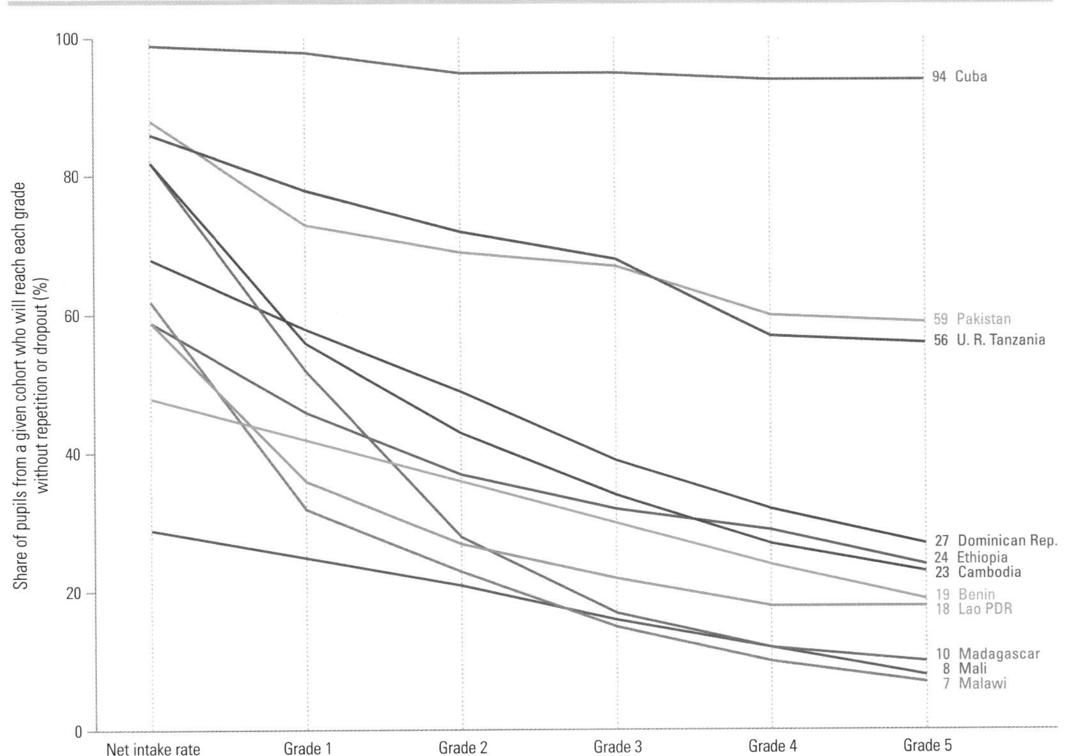

Notes: Primary school progression is calculated using net intake and grade-specific drop-out and repetition rates.
Source: Annex, Statistical Tables 4, 6 and 7.

Grade repetition is costly, and a source of inefficiency and inequity

and only 7% progress smoothly to grade 5. Country patterns for progression through the primary school system vary: some countries, including Cambodia, the Lao People's Democratic Republic and Madagascar, follow the Malawi model in registering very high levels of interruption in the early grades. In others, among them Benin, the pattern is more uniform, with disruption occurring on a more regular basis through the system. At the other end of the scale, 94% of Cuban children progress smoothly through the system. Cohort tracking is an important tool because it can help policy-makers to identify stress points in the primary cycle.

Figure 2.14: Percentage of pupils relative to the official primary-school age group, most recent year

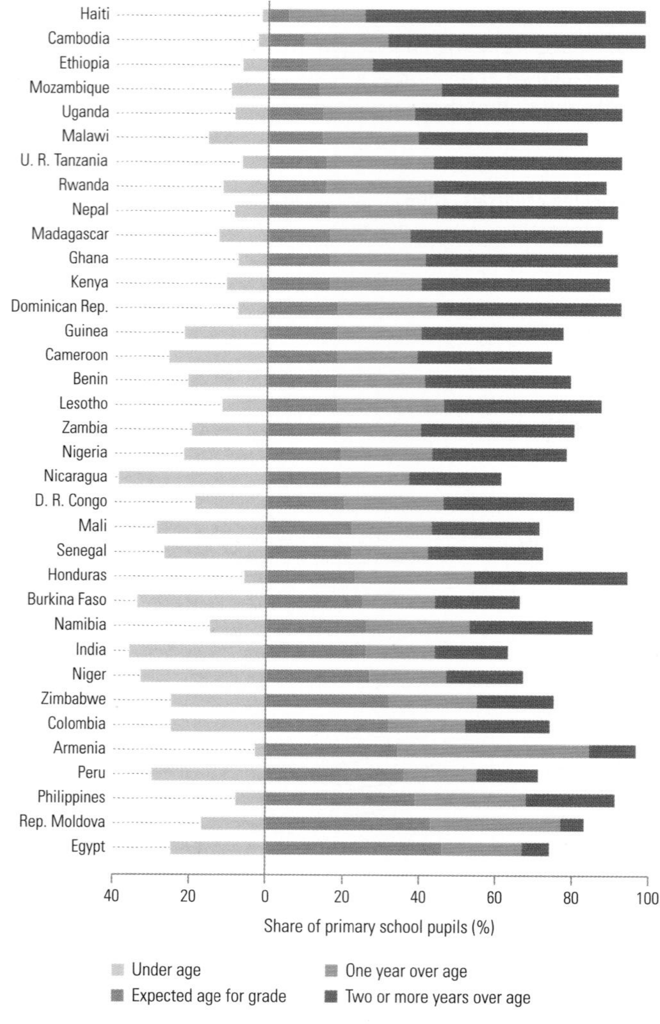

Source: Demographic and Health Surveys, calculations by Education Policy and Data Center (2008*b*).

High repetition rates are endemic in many countries. Educationists are divided on approaches to repetition. Some see it as a necessary device for improved learning and greater resilience at higher grades. Others see grade repetition as an over-used tool with limited education benefits. Much depends on national and local education contexts. But it is clear that high levels of repetition are a major barrier to UPE. Of the countries in sub-Saharan Africa with data available, eleven have grade 1 and nine have grade 2 repetition rates over 20%. In Burundi and Cameroon repetition rates in grade 1 exceed 30%. Several countries in Latin America and the Caribbean have repetition rates in grade 1 above 10%, including Brazil, El Salvador, Guatemala, Honduras and Nicaragua. In South and West Asia, grade 1 repetition rates are below 10% for all countries except Nepal, where they exceed 30% (Annex, Statistical Table 6).

Apart from its damaging consequences for UPE, grade repetition is a source of inefficiency and inequity. Efficiency losses are associated with the costs of repetition. The financing required to provide additional school places for repeaters can be substantial. Repetition consumes an estimated 12% of the education budget in Mozambique and 16% in Burundi (UIS, 2007). High costs are also reported for other regions. Governments in Latin America and the Caribbean spend an estimated US$12 billion annually as a result of grade repetition (UN Economic Commission for Latin America and the Caribbean, 2007). Repetition is a source of inequity: it imposes an increased burden on households in terms of direct financial costs and opportunity costs. As the burden is heaviest for the poorest households, it is more likely to result in dropout.

Late school entry and grade repetition means that only a small proportion of children actually attend the appropriate class for their age in many developing countries (Figure 2.14). Household surveys in thirty-five countries demonstrate the point: for many countries – including Cambodia, Ethiopia, Ghana, Honduras, Mozambique and the United Republic of Tanzania – over 60% of children in primary school are over the expected age for their grade. The presence of over-age children tends to increase by grade as repetition's negative effects are strengthened. At the other end of the spectrum, many countries have a large number of under-age children in primary school. They represent more than 20% of primary school pupils in Egypt, India, Nicaragua, the Niger and Peru.

Why do age profiles for primary school matter? Figure 2.15 provides part of the answer: it shows that over-age children are far less likely to survive through to grade 9. In countries such as India, Mozambique, Peru and the Philippines, being two years over age more than halves the chances of survival. For the thirty-five countries examined, the pattern confirms a well-established trend: over-age children are far more likely to drop out, especially in the later grades.

Less attention has been paid in policy debate to under-age children. The survey evidence suggests this may be a mistake. In many countries, under-age children are far more likely to repeat early grades – an outcome with important implications for class size and education quality. In Cameroon and Uganda, under-age pupils represent a large share of grade 1 pupils and have high repetition rates. Under-age pupils account for the bulk of repeaters in countries with low repetition rates, including India, the Niger and Nigeria (Figure 2.16).

The overall pattern to emerge from monitoring evidence is that being over age strongly predisposes children to drop out, while being under age makes repetition more likely. The prevalence of under-age children in many countries has important implications for education planning. It suggests that, in many countries, parents are using the first primary grade to make up for inadequate pre-school provision. Expanding pre-school participation in such cases could reduce repetition in the early primary grades, with important efficiency and equity benefits.

Under-age children tend to repeat, while over-age children tend to drop out

Figure 2.15: Survival rates to grade 9 for three age groups: expected age for grade, one year over age and two or more years over age, most recent year

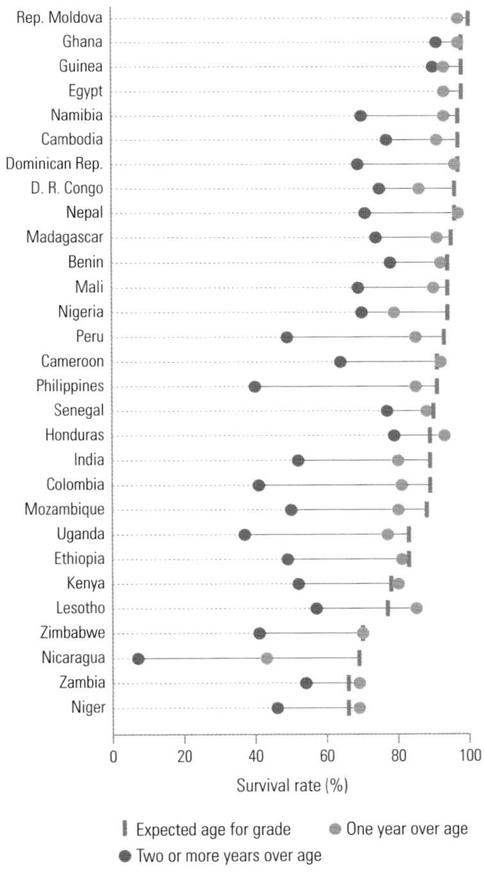

Expected age for grade · One year over age · Two or more years over age

Source: Demographic and Health Surveys, calculations by Education Policy and Data Center (2008*b*).

Figure 2.16: Under-age pupils as a percentage of grade 1 enrolment, total repetition rate and under-age repetition rate for grade 1, most recent year

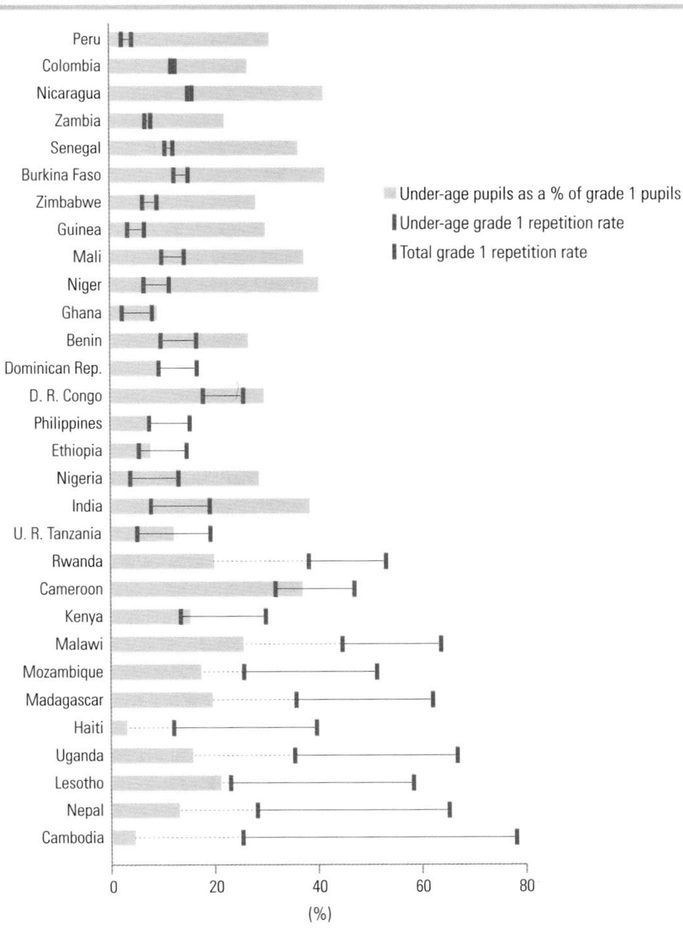

Source: Demographic and Health Surveys, calculations by Education Policy and Data Center (2008*b*).

High dropout rates for over-age pupils point to a wider set of policy problems. Some are linked to education quality: dropout is more likely when children fail grades. Non-school factors are also important. In higher grades over-age pupils may face growing pressure to get a job, to take over household work or, in the case of girls, to marry. To the extent that such pressure is linked to poverty, social protection programmes and financial incentives to keep children in school can make a difference.

A full cycle of primary education is essential for equipping children with the skills they need

Mixed patterns of access and survival

The rate of progress to UPE is a function of advances – or setbacks – on two fronts: enrolment and completion. Enrolment matters for a very obvious reason: being in school is a requirement for receiving a primary education. But getting through a full cycle of primary education is a necessary, though far from sufficient, condition for achieving the level of learning needed to equip children with the skills they need.

The relationship between enrolment and completion is not clear cut. Figure 2.17 illustrates four broad patterns that can be identified using international data. It locates countries on the basis of their NER and survival rates to the last grade of primary school.

1) *Low enrolment, low survival:* this group has the furthest to travel to UPE. It comprises twenty countries, all but three of them in sub-Saharan Africa.

2) *Low enrolment, high survival:* only a small group of countries fit into this category. This group includes Kenya and the Palestinian Autonomous Territories.

3) *High enrolment, low survival:* this category covers twenty-one countries, from Malawi in sub-Saharan Africa to Nicaragua and Guatemala in Latin America and Cambodia and the Philippines in East Asia.

4) *High enrolment, high survival:* this group includes a diverse array of countries that have achieved or are close to achieving UPE.

Countries in groups 1 and 3 face overlapping but distinctive challenges. For group 1, the twin priority is to increase enrolment rapidly while improving retention levels. In Rwanda, one in five primary school-age children were out of school in 2005. Of those in school only around one-third make it through to the last grade. To varying degrees, countries in group 3 have succeeded in raising NER levels but face problems in survival. For example, Madagascar, Malawi and Nicaragua have achieved NERs of 90% and above, but fewer than half of those who enrol survive to the last grade of primary school.

Experience since Dakar powerfully demonstrates that past trends do not dictate destiny. Some countries have moved a long way since 1999, as the experiences of Burundi, Ethiopia, Mozambique and the United Republic of Tanzania demonstrate (Figure 2.18). Each has dramatically increased primary net enrolment. Performance in improving survival to the last grade has been more mixed, with limited progress in Ethiopia and Mozambique but more striking advances in Burundi and, from a higher starting point, the United Republic of Tanzania. The experience of Nepal is also encouraging.

Unfortunately, experience since 1999 also demonstrates that less favourable outcomes are possible. As Figure 2.18 shows, Malawi rapidly increased NER levels in the 1990s, then failed to improve survival rates. The Philippines has sustained high enrolment levels but experienced a decline in survival. Madagascar has registered dramatic progress towards universal enrolment with an equally dramatic decline in survival to the last grade.

In one important respect Figure 2.18 understates the distance to UPE. Survival to the last grade is not the same as completion of the last grade. Many children reaching the final grade prove unable to negotiate the last hurdle. In Burundi, Mauritania, Nepal and Senegal, for instance, only about half the children who survive to the last grade actually complete it (see annex, Statistical Table 7). What that means in Senegal is that only 30% of primary school-age children complete the full primary cycle.

The global gulf in educational opportunity

Progress towards UPE should not deflect attention from the vast disparities in opportunity that divide rich and poor nations. If UPE is a first rung on the ladder, progression up the ladder is heavily influenced not by innate ability but by where a child is born.

Figure 2.17: Primary net enrolment ratios and survival rates to the last grade of primary education, 2005 and 2006[1]

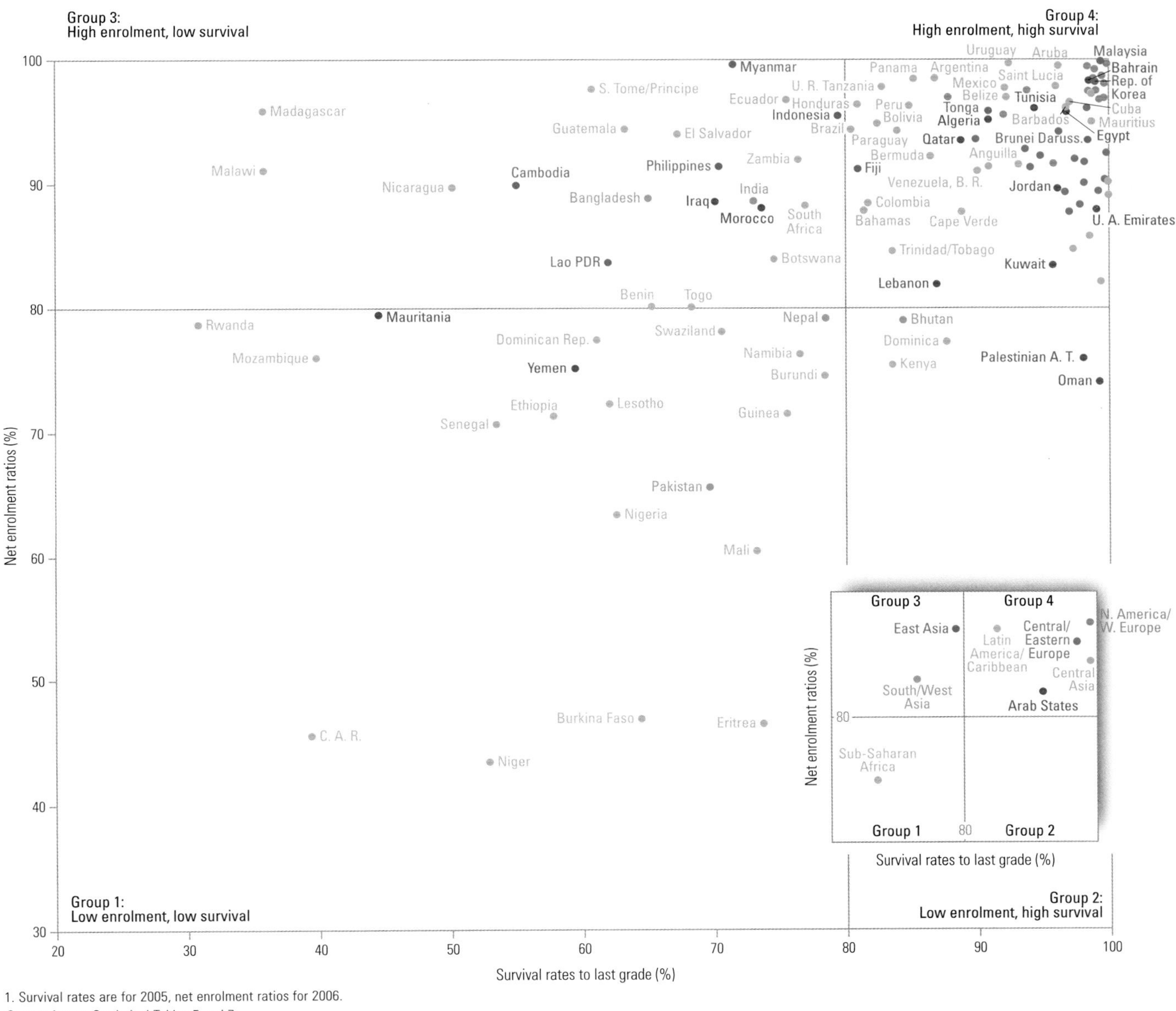

1. Survival rates are for 2005, net enrolment ratios for 2006.
Source: Annex, Statistical Tables 5 and 7.

Consider the education prospects of an average child born in a developed country compared with those for a child born in selected developing countries shown in Figure 2.19. These two children are moving on very different tracks. While one transits smoothly from primary to secondary school with a strong chance of reaching tertiary education, the other is marked by high levels of attrition from primary school on. Simple enrolment and school attendance data do not capture the full extent of the resulting inequalities. But attainment rates and cohort completion data can be used to measure the opportunity gap that divides children in some of the world's richest and poorest countries:

- In rich countries such as Canada and Japan, over half the population aged 25 to 34 reaches university level. Some 40% to 50% of the children in poor countries such as Bangladesh and Guatemala will not even complete primary school.

In rich countries, such as Canada and Japan, over half the population aged 25 to 34 reaches university level

Figure 2.18: Changes in net enrolment ratios and survival rates in primary education, selected countries[1]

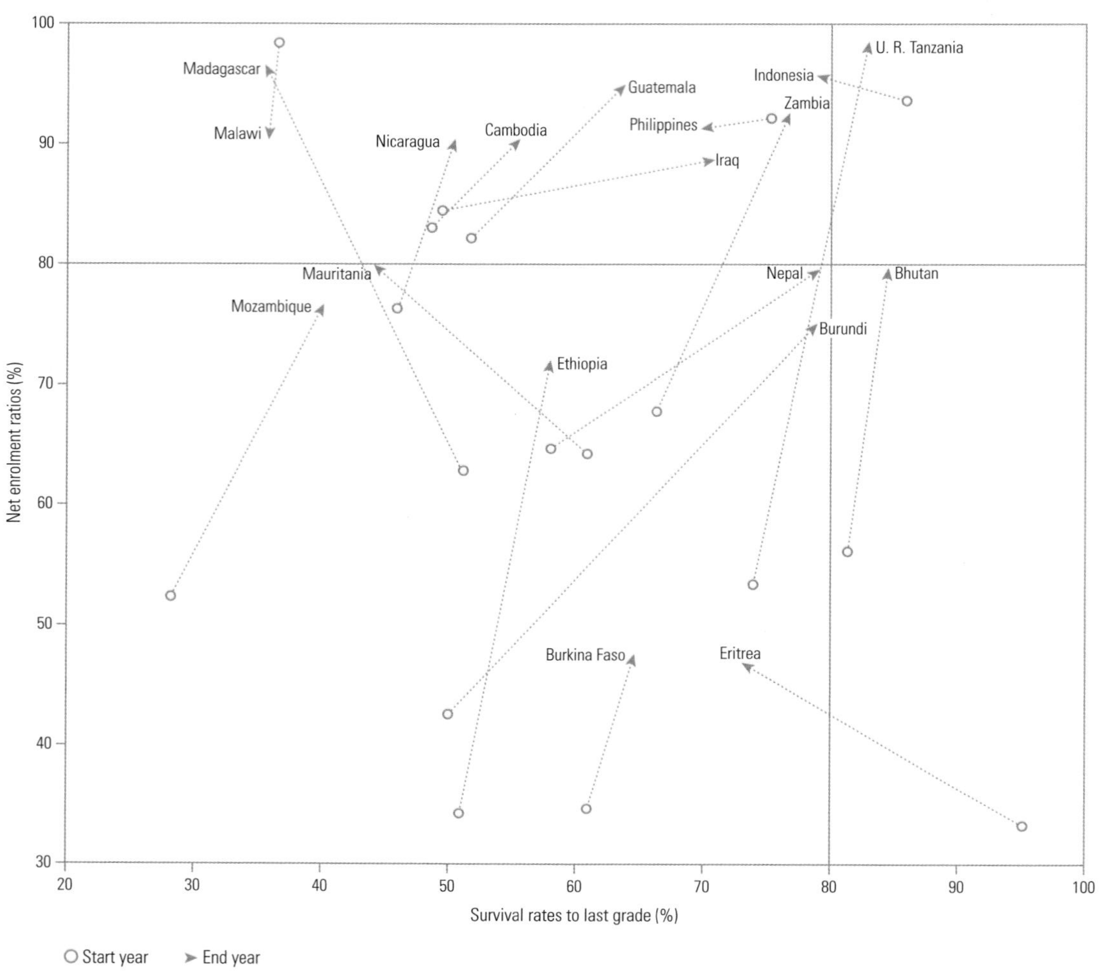

1. The start year is 1999 for all countries except Burundi and the United Republic of Tanzania, where it is 2000. The end year is 2005 for survival rates and 2006 for net enrolment ratios.
Source: Annex, Statistical Tables 5 and 7.

- Children in France are twice as likely to enter tertiary education as children in Benin or the Niger are to complete primary school.
- Children in the United Kingdom have a greater probability of entering tertiary education than their counterparts in countries such as Mozambique, Senegal or Uganda have of completing primary education.

There are limitations to the use of probability indicators for measuring disparity. One limitation is that they heavily understate the scale of the problem, as they measure only quantitative gaps. Introducing quality-adjusted indicators that factor in the level of provision, state of infrastructure and learning outcomes would reveal much larger inequalities.

Disparities within countries: a barrier to EFA

Children do not select the wealth of the households they are born into, or choose their race, language, ethnic group or gender. Yet these predetermined circumstances powerfully influence the distribution of opportunity for education within countries.

In the Dakar Framework countries pledged to try to reach the most disadvantaged and equalize opportunity. Underpinning this commitment to equity are two central ideas: first, that equal opportunity is a hallmark of fairness and social justice; and, second, that equity is central to avoiding deprivation and abject poverty. Greater equity in education, valuable for its own sake, also matters because unequal opportunity in education is linked to the transmission of inequalities and deprivation in other areas, including health, employment, gender disparities and participation in society.

Many countries with high levels of absolute deprivation in education are also marked by extraordinary inequalities of opportunity. This subsection charts the scale of those inequalities in primary education. The picture it provides is partial and limited in important respects. Because cross-country data from Demographic and Health Surveys provide comprehensive information on inequalities linked to wealth, this domain is highlighted. Economic inequalities, however, are only part of the story. They operate alongside, and intersect with, inequalities based on other inherited characteristics which play a role in predetermining life chances.

Why does inequality matter? Unequal opportunities in education, especially those of an extreme nature, are problematic for at least three reasons. First, they are intrinsically unfair. They run counter to basic precepts about what a socially just society should look like – and they violate the idea of education as a basic, universal human right. Second, inequalities in education are undermining progress towards Education for All and the specific goal of UPE by 2015. Third, and apart from considerations of fairness, equity and compliance with global development commitments, extreme inequalities in education are inefficient. They contribute to reduced opportunities for social and economic progress in many areas, as underlined in Chapter 1. In short, overcoming inequality in education is not just the right thing to do, it is also the smart thing to do.

Wealth-based inequalities: one country, several worlds

When it comes to UPE, rich and poor live in different worlds. National data reveal the average distance a country must travel to achieve universal primary education, but averages conceal large wealth-based disparities. In many of the world's poorest countries the richest households already enjoy UPE while the poor lag far behind.

Figure 2.19: Opportunity gaps: population reaching tertiary education in OECD countries and chances of primary school completion in developing countries

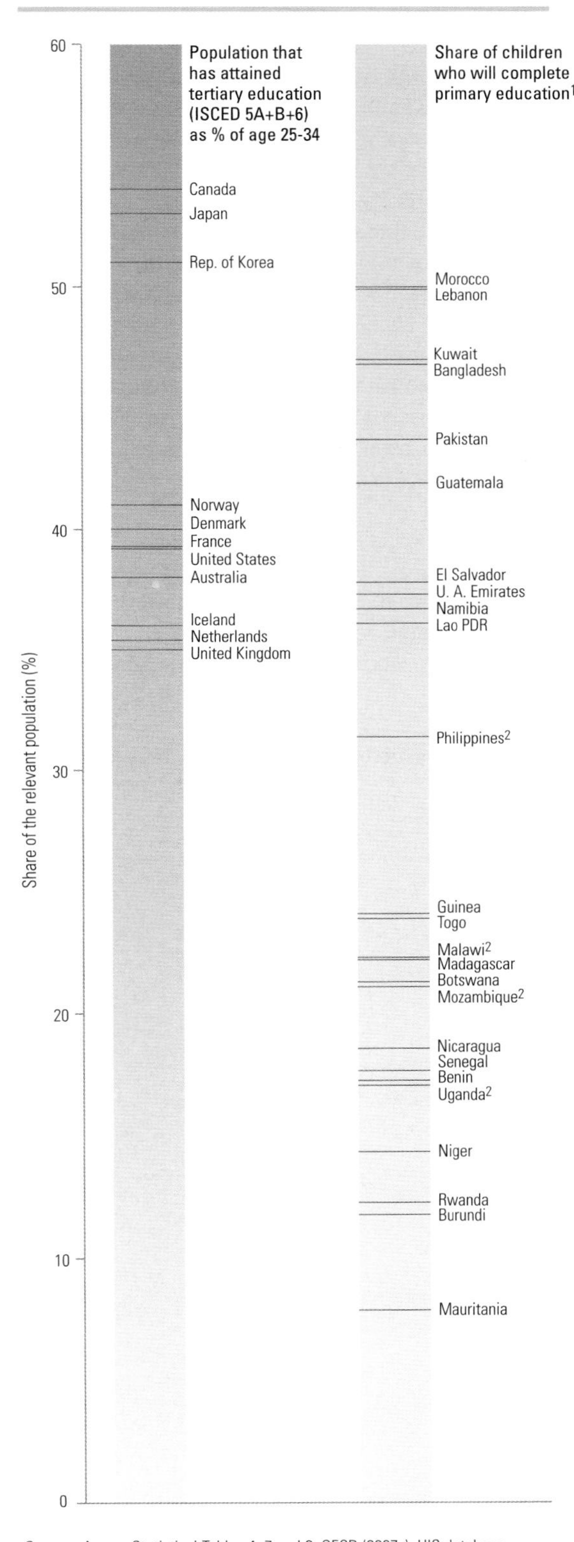

1. The share of children who will complete primary education is calculated by combining net intake and cohort completion rates (or survival to last grade).
2. Data for these countries refer to the survival rate to the last grade of primary school, which will always be greater than or equal to the completion rate.

Sources: Annex, Statistical Tables 4, 7 and 8; OECD (2007*a*); UIS database.

Children in France are twice as likely to enter tertiary education as children in Benin or the Niger are to complete primary school

Figure 2.20 traces the border separating the worlds of rich and poor using household survey data for primary school attendance.[6] While their nations may have a long way to go to UPE, the wealthiest 20% in countries such as Bangladesh, Ghana, India and Nigeria do not: most have already arrived. The wealth gaps reflected in attendance data are often very large. In Bolivia, Burkina Faso, Chad, Ethiopia, Mali and the Niger, children from the richest 20% are two to three times more likely to attend school than children from the poorest quintile. A striking feature to emerge from the data is that, irrespective of the overall wealth position of their country, children born into the richest quintile in all of these countries have similar attendance and attainment rates. For example, attendance rates for the richest quintile in India and Nigeria are the same, even though Nigeria's average attendance rate is far lower.

6. Attendance rates recorded in household surveys are used to look at participation in school, and attainment levels to look at levels of education among people likely to have completed their education. Households are ranked using an index of household assets, then grouped into quintiles according to their level of wealth.

Patterns of inequality are conditioned by attendance levels (Figure 2.21). Disparities tend to be far larger in countries with low average attendance rates, for statistical reasons. As countries progress towards 100% attendance at the top end of the distribution, any average increase in attendance narrows inequalities and produces convergence by definition. Thus, attendance inequalities are far higher in Côte d'Ivoire, for instance, than in Uganda. However, the relationship is not uniform. There are some marked differences between countries at a considerable distance from UPE. To take one example, Nigeria has far wider inequalities in attendance than Senegal, despite having higher average attendance rates. This is an outcome that points to problems of extreme marginalization. The poorest 20% in Nigeria have attendance levels far below those that might be predicted given the national average attendance rate – an indication that some groups or regions are being left far behind.

One word of caution has to be applied to wealth-based cross-country comparisons. The poorest 20% denotes a position in the national distribution and not a common level of income. The poorest 20% in, say, Viet Nam, have higher levels of average income than the poorest 20% in Burkina Faso. The incidence and depth of poverty within the

Figure 2.20: Primary net attendance and primary attainment rates for poorest and richest, selected countries, most recent year

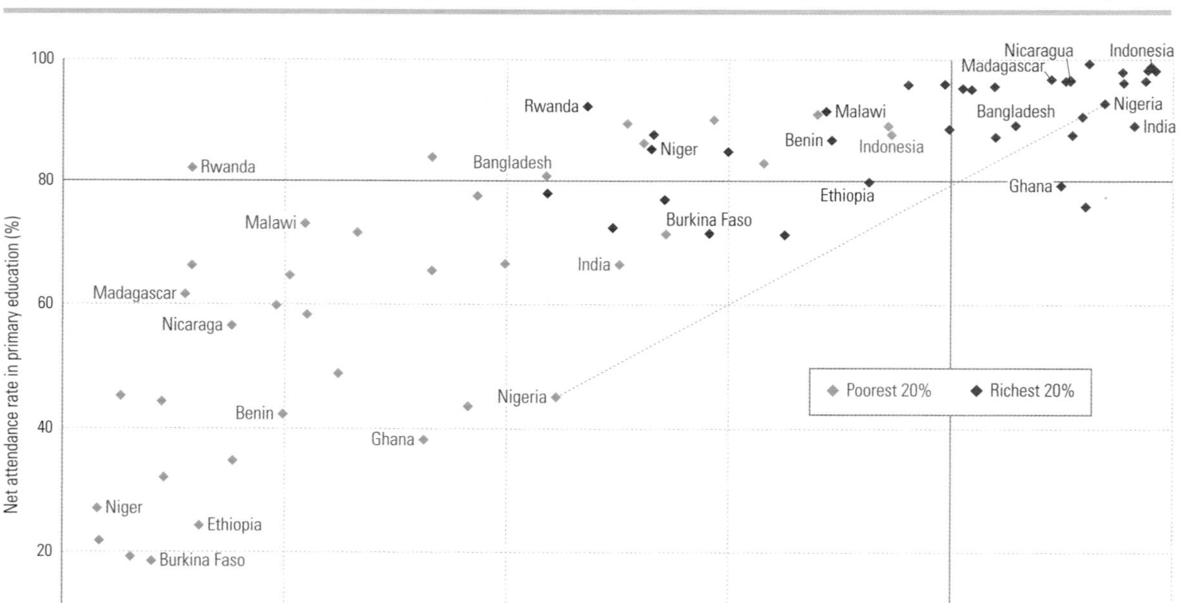

Source: Demographic and Health Surveys, calculations by Harttgen et al. (2008).

poorest 20% also varies with average income and income distribution. Nevertheless, cross-country comparison raises some important questions. Why, for example, does Côte d'Ivoire have a lower attendance rate and higher inequality in attendance than Mozambique despite having a higher average income and lower level of poverty? At the other end of the scale, why does Viet Nam (average income PPP$202) register higher attendance and greater equity than the Philippines (average income PPP$352)? The answers would require detailed cross-country analysis. But the disparities draw attention to the fact that the national income does not dictate education outcomes and that public policy plays a role in shaping the distribution of opportunity.

The most immediate reason that inequality matters for the Dakar target of achieving UPE by 2015 is that the distribution of children not attending school is skewed towards the poor. Table 2.6 illustrates this point for thirty-five countries. The corollary of a higher non-attendance incidence among the poor is that, other things being equal, progress in raising school attendance among the poor has a greater impact on national attendance than progress among other groups.

The UPE arithmetic in favour of greater equity is most starkly apparent for countries at higher attendance levels. Table 2.6 includes data for eighteen countries with average attendance equal to or over 80%. For many of them – including Cameroon, Colombia, Indonesia, Madagascar, Kenya, Nepal, Nicaragua, the Philippines and Uganda – the share of out-of-school children from the poorest quintile is above 40%, rising to 51% in Indonesia and 60% in Viet Nam. Reaching UPE in these countries will require the development of policies targeting the very poor. This is a population that generally includes many hard-to-reach households – in remote rural areas, for instance, and urban slums – facing multiple disadvantages, including chronic poverty, high mortality, and poor health and nutritional status.

For countries that are further from universal primary attendance, the concentration of disadvantage is less marked – but still significant. In all seventeen countries with average attendance rates below 80%, the poorest quintile still accounts for a disproportionate share of non-attendance. Conversely, in none of these countries does the richest quintile account for more than 10% of non-attendance. In several countries with very high non-attendance levels – including Burkina Faso, Ethiopia and Mali – the problem is broadly distributed across the four bottom quintiles. However, this does not imply that equity is unimportant. The poorest quintile accounts for 30% to 40% of non-attendance in many countries with low overall attendance, including Cambodia, Ghana, India, Mozambique, Nigeria and Zambia. The challenge here is to increase participation across society but with a strengthened focus on the poorest groups. This has potential implications

Both national income and public policy shape the distribution of education opportunity

Figure 2.21: Primary net attendance rates by wealth quintile, selected countries, most recent year

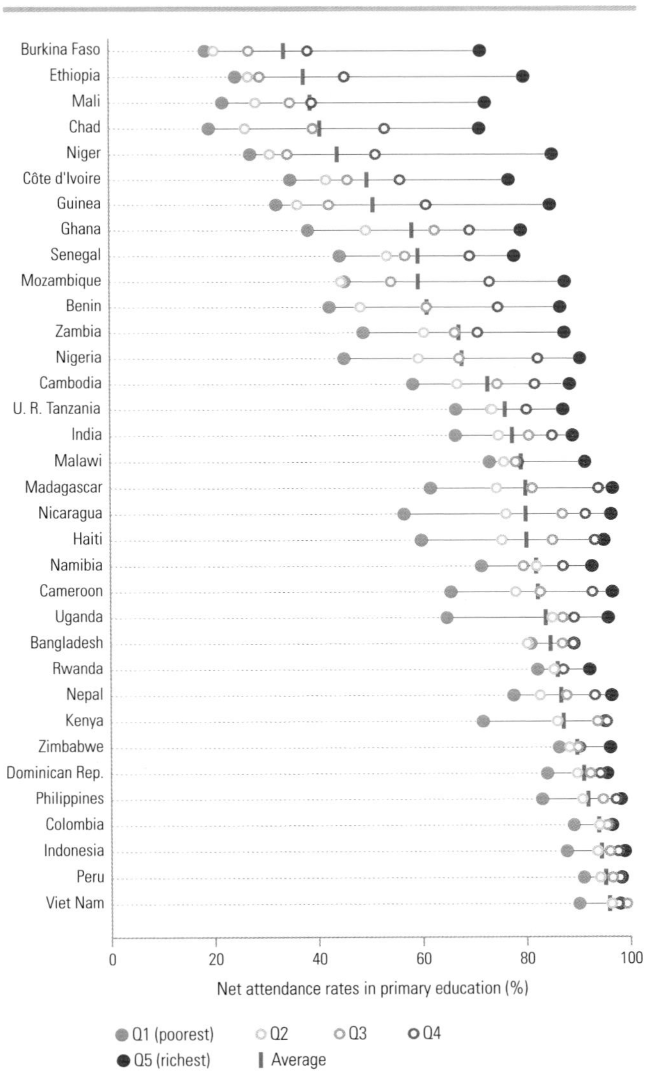

Source: Demographic and Health Surveys, calculations by Harttgen et al. (2008).

Table 2.6: Distribution across wealth quintiles of children not attending primary school

Country	Survey year	Net attendance rate (%)	% of primary school-age group not attending	Distribution of those not attending primary school (%)				
				Q1 poorest quintile	Q2	Q3	Q4	Q5 richest quintile
High primary school attendance (NAR greater than or equal to 80%)								
Viet Nam	2002	96	4	60	19	4	9	7
Peru	2000	95	5	43	28	16	8	5
Indonesia	2003	94	6	51	23	14	8	4
Colombia	2005	94	6	42	21	15	13	10
Philippines	2003	92	8	52	26	13	6	3
Dominican Rep.	2002	91	9	37	23	17	13	10
Zimbabwe	2006	90	10	31	26	21	16	6
Kenya	2003	87	13	53	25	10	6	5
Nepal	2006	87	13	40	28	18	9	4
Rwanda	2005	86	14	27	22	22	19	10
Bangladesh	2004	85	15	30	30	17	13	11
Uganda	2006	84	16	47	20	16	14	4
Cameroon	2004	82	18	42	27	21	7	3
Guatemala	1999	82	18	41	26	20	9	4
Namibia	2000	82	18	36	23	21	12	7
Haiti	2005	80	20	47	27	16	6	4
Nicaragua	2001	80	20	50	26	13	8	3
Madagascar	2004	80	20	45	29	19	6	3
Low primary school attendance (NAR less than 80%)								
Malawi	2004	79	21	28	23	21	20	8
India	2005	77	23	40	25	17	11	7
U. R. Tanzania	2004	76	24	28	22	23	17	10
Cambodia	2005	73	27	35	26	20	13	6
Nigeria	2003	68	32	37	27	20	10	5
Zambia	2001	67	33	30	24	19	18	8
Benin	2006	61	39	31	29	21	13	6
Mozambique	2003	59	41	30	29	24	12	5
Senegal	2005	59	41	30	24	22	14	9
Ghana	2003	58	42	33	27	19	13	8
Guinea	2005	51	49	27	27	24	17	6
Côte d'Ivoire	2004	50	50	30	23	22	17	8
Niger	2006	44	56	28	26	25	16	5
Chad	2004	41	59	30	26	20	15	9
Mali	2001	39	61	25	23	23	21	8
Ethiopia	2005	37	63	27	26	25	18	4
Burkina Faso	2003	34	66	25	25	23	19	7

Source: Data for calculations from Harttgen et al. (2008). See Filmer and Pritchett (1999) for a similar analysis of attainment rates.

for financing and planning. It cannot be assumed that the future marginal costs of reaching children from the poorest households will reflect the past average costs of getting children into school – nor that business-as-usual policy design will suffice. New incentive structures, and stronger integration of education into wider strategies for reducing poverty and inequality, may be required. Box 2.11 outlines key lessons learned from countries that have moved strongly towards UPE.

Household wealth also has a marked bearing on how far children progress in education. Grade survival indicators provide insight into the ways inequalities constrain progress towards UPE. In looking at countries with low survival rates, two broad patterns can be identified (Figure 2.22). For those with low attendance such as Senegal, gaps between wealth groups tend to remain relatively constant as children progress through the primary cycle. This implies that dropout rates are not markedly widening inequalities. Countries including Chad, Ethiopia, Mali and the Niger

Box 2.11: Achieving UPE – lessons from strong performers

There is no blueprint for accelerating progress towards UPE. Countries have differing problems and constraints – and differing financial, institutional and human resources. Blueprints in any case are no substitute for practical policies. Still, five broad thematic lessons can be drawn from the experience of strong performers.

- **Set ambitious targets** – and back them with strong political commitment and effective planning. Political leadership is vital in placing education squarely at the centre of the national policy agenda and the international aid agenda. Successful governments have fixed ambitious long-term goals supported by clear medium-term 'stepping stone' targets. They have underpinned the targets with strengthened pubic spending commitments and a predictable budget framework. Realistic planning requires targets to be reflected in resource allocation decisions and linked to policies for classroom construction, teacher recruitment, textbook provision and other factors.
- **Get serious about equity.** Disparities in education are holding back progress towards UPE. Ensuring that all children participate in education advancement requires practical measures to overcome structural inequalities. Reducing the cost of education for poor households by abolishing fees and wider charges is one strategy for enhancing equity. Another is creating financial incentives for the education of girls and children from disadvantaged backgrounds. More equitable public spending patterns are also critical, to ensure that schools, teachers and resources are skewed towards those with greatest need rather than those with the greatest wealth.
- **Raise quality while expanding access.** Improving the quality of education is one of the most effective strategies for strengthening demand. Enhanced quality requires a focus on smooth progression and learning outcomes, rather than pupil headcounts. Increasing textbook supply and quality, strengthening teacher training and support, and ensuring that class size is conducive to learning and that children are taught in an appropriate language are key elements in raising quality.
- **Strengthen wider anti-poverty commitments.** More efficient and more equitable school systems can only do so much if wider structures perpetuate disadvantage. Eradicating child malnutrition and strengthening public health systems are conditions for accelerated progress towards UPE. Social welfare programmes and cash transfers can shield poor households from economic pressures that force children out of school and into labour markets.
- **Develop an agenda for equitable governance.** 'Good governance' is an imperative that goes beyond UPE. While developing more accountable, transparent and participative education systems is important in its own right, successful governments have also strengthened governance more generally and addressed equity concerns. Ensuring that decentralization does not widen disparities in finance requires a commitment to redistributive public spending. It is now clear that devolving authority does not automatically strengthen equity or participation by the poor – and, in fact, can weaken them.

General principles provide a framework that individual countries must adapt to their own circumstances

Figure 2.22: Grade survival in primary school for 10- to 19-year-olds, by wealth quintile, Cambodia and Senegal, 2005

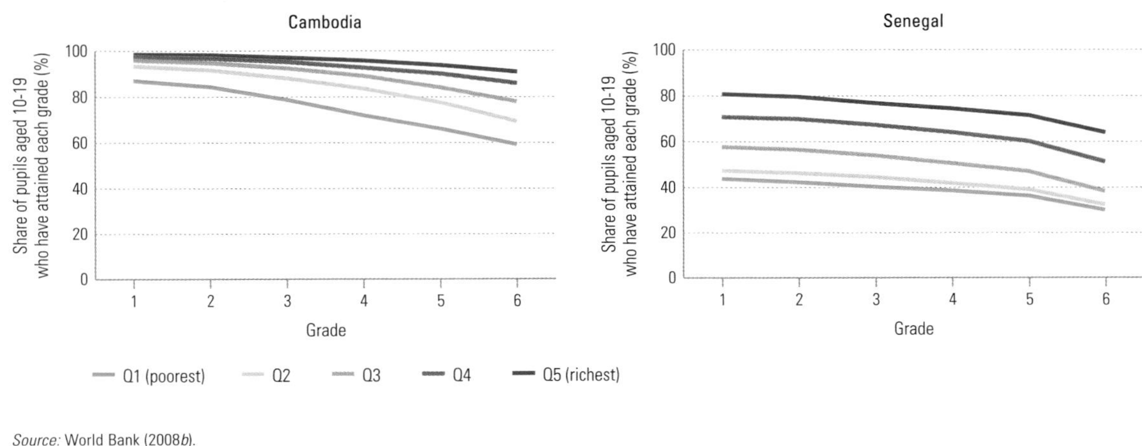

Source: World Bank (2008*b*).

broadly conform to this pattern. The second pattern emerges in countries with high attendance, where children from poor households are often almost as likely to start school as their richer counterparts but far more likely to drop out. Inequalities widen progressively as children progress through the system, as in Cambodia. While the extent of divergence differs, Benin, India, Malawi, Myanmar and Togo broadly conform to this pattern.

Wealth-based inequalities interact with wider disparities

Disparities based on wealth do not exist in isolation. They interact with wider inequalities and markers for disadvantage related to gender, location, language and other factors. Breaking down these inequalities is a key to accelerated progress towards UPE.

There are many benefits to using the child's mother tongue as the medium of instruction during the early years

Rural-urban inequalities. In many countries living in a rural area carries a marked handicap in terms of opportunities for education. Rural children are less likely to attend school, and more likely to drop out, than their urban counterparts. In Senegal, children in urban areas are twice as likely to be in school as their counterparts in rural areas. Poverty provides part of the explanation: some two-thirds of the rural population live in poverty, compared to around half of urban households (IMF, 2006). In addition, correlates of poverty such as the prevalence of child labour and malnutrition are often much higher in rural areas. Demand for different types of schooling may also vary between more traditional rural areas and less traditional urban districts. In Senegal, instruction in Arabic is important for many rural communities, potentially limiting demand for government schools, where the medium of instruction is French (IMF, 2006).

Disparities faced by slum dwellers. Slums are typically characterized by high levels of poverty, poor child health status and limited participation in education. UN-HABITAT recently analysed primary school attendance rates for slums in cities of eighteen countries (UN-HABITAT, 2006). In Benin and Nigeria, children who live in slums had attendance rates some twenty percentage points lower than those of other city children. In six countries, including Bangladesh and Guatemala, attendance rates for the children of slum dwellers were lower even than average rates in rural areas.

Socio-cultural inequalities. Cultural factors such as religion and ethnicity can affect both the demand for schooling and its supply. On the demand side, households from various religious backgrounds may attach differing weight to education, or they may demand schools and curricula different from those provided through the formal education system. In north-western Nigeria, some 15% of children aged between 6 and 16 were not in formal school because their parents preferred them to attend Quranic schools (Nigeria National Population Commission and ORC Macro, 2004).

Language-based disparities. There are large differences in school attendance and completion among linguistic groups. Analysis of household data for 22 countries and over 160 linguistic groups has attempted to identify the weight of different factors behind disparities. It is estimated that socio-economic factors such as household wealth and location account for less than half of observed differences in education outcomes among linguistic groups. So what factors account for the balance of the disparities? The medium of instruction had statistically significant effects: if at least half of schools offer the opportunity to learn in a home language, attendance rises by approximately 10% (Smits et al., 2008). Children living in rural areas were found to be at a particular disadvantage if they did not have access to school instruction in their mother tongue. These results add further weight to the growing body of evidence on the benefits of using the mother tongue in schools, at least in the early years.

Household survey data make it possible to observe and measure inequalities in education as if they fit into neat compartments. In the real world, disparities in educational opportunity and other areas combine, interact and are reproduced through dynamic political and socio-cultural processes that involve complex and unequal power relationships. Disadvantage spans many dimensions. Being poor is a universal marker for restricted opportunity in education. Being rural and poor represents a double disadvantage in many countries. Being poor, rural and female is a triple barrier to equal opportunity. Figure 2.23 captures the multidimensional scale of disadvantage by locating where groups stand in the distribution of educational opportunity, as measured by school attendance.

Three barriers to UPE: child labour, ill health and disability

Every country faces its own distinctive set of challenges in achieving UPE, but high levels of poverty and low average incomes are pervasive in most of the countries furthest from the target. So are the three barriers to UPE considered in this subsection: child labour, ill health and disability.

Child labour

Progress towards universal enrolment and completion of primary education is inextricably bound up with the progressive elimination of child labour. Not all economic activity carried out by children is a barrier to education. But activity that keeps children out of school, limits their mental and physical development or exposes them to hazardous conditions violates children's right to education, along with international conventions.

There were around 218 million child labourers in 2004, of whom 166 million were aged between 5 and 14. In this younger age group, around 74 million were engaged in hazardous work (ILO, 2006).[7] The reported number of child labourers globally has fallen by 11% since 2000 – and by 33% in the hazardous category. However, progress has been uneven. It has been most rapid in Latin America and the Caribbean and slowest in sub-Saharan Africa. Around one-quarter of the region's 5- to 14-year-olds are engaged in child labour. Because population growth has increased faster than child labour rates have fallen, there were some 1 million more child labourers in 2004 than in 2000. In absolute terms, most child labourers – 122 million in total – live in Asia and the Pacific. Here, too, progress towards elimination has been slow, with a decline from 19.2% to 18.8% between 2000 and 2004 (ILO, 2006).

School attendance figures provide stark evidence of the trade-off between child labour and UPE. The Understanding Children's Work programme has used household survey data to examine school attendance in some sixty countries (Guarcello et al., 2006). Its findings indicate that working children face an attendance disadvantage of at least 10%

7. The concept of 'child labour' is based on the ILO Minimum Age Convention of 1973. It excludes children aged 12 and older who work a few hours a week in permitted light work, and those aged 15 or over whose work is not categorized as hazardous. 'Economic activity', a broader concept sometimes used in discussions of child labour, refers to any labour lasting more than one hour per day during a seven-day reference period.

Figure 2.23: Primary net attendance rates by location, wealth quintile and gender, selected countries, most recent year

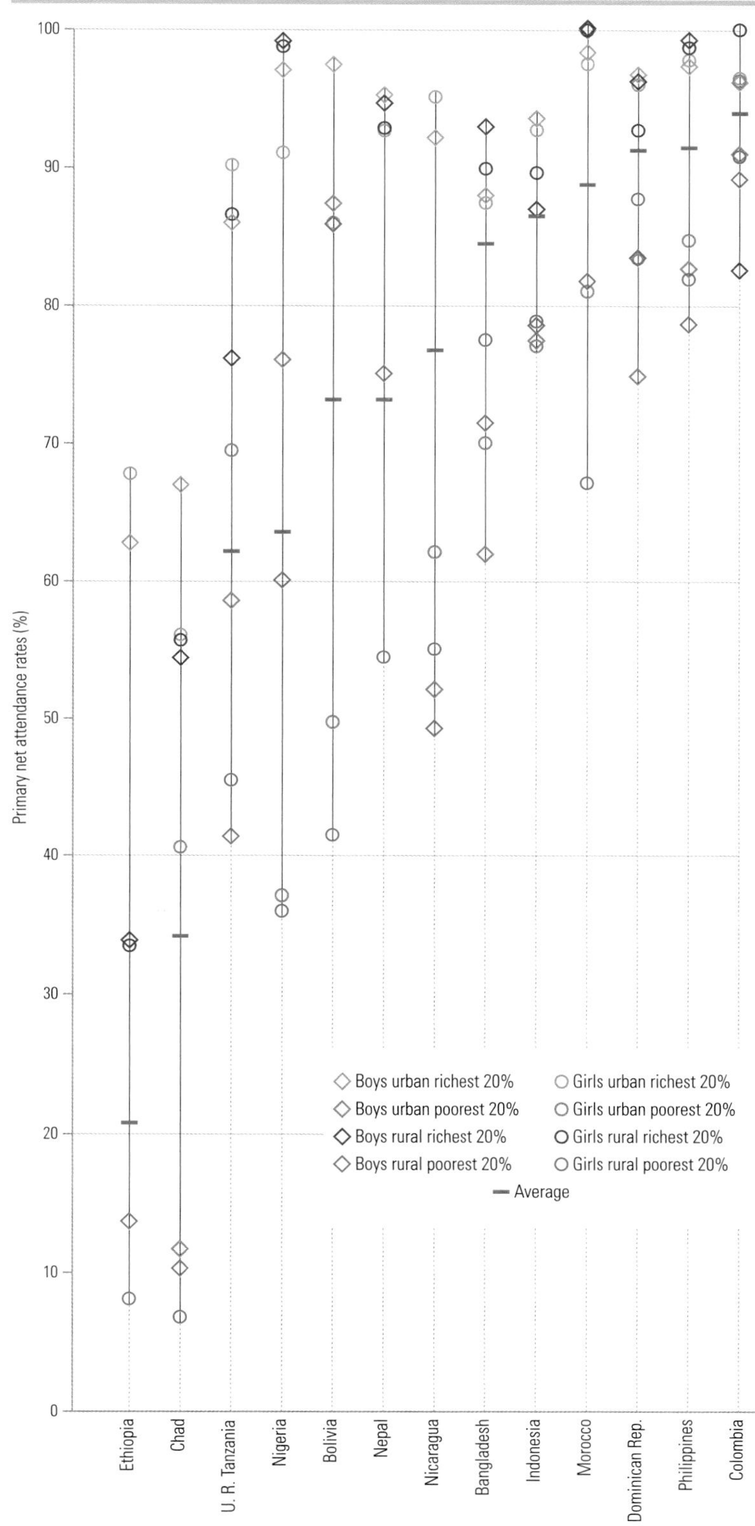

Sources: Demographic and Health Surveys, calculations by Gwatkin et al. (2007*a*, 2007*b*, 2007*c*, 2007*d*, 2007*e*, 2007*f*, 2007*g*, 2007*h*, 2007*i*, 2007*j*, 2007*k*, 2007*l*, 2007*m*, 2007*n*); Macro International Inc. (2008).

in twenty-eight countries, at least 20% in fifteen countries and at least 30% in nine countries (Figure 2.24). Child labour is also associated with delayed school entry. In Cambodia, for example, a working child is 17% less likely to enter school at the official age and thus runs a higher risk of dropout.

While the trade-off between child labour and primary eduction is clear cut, there is wide cross-country variation in the relationship. Moreover, evidence of trade-offs says little about the direction of influence: association is not causation. Are children not attending school because they are working, or are they working because they are not in school? The answer varies among and within countries. When schools are unavailable or distant, when the cost of schooling is high and the perceived quality low, disincentives to send children to school may push them into work. In other cases, household poverty and associated labour demands 'pull' children into labour markets: that is, they are not in school because they are working. These 'pull' factors are often triggered by inability to cope with a crisis, such as a drought. Household survey evidence from Pakistan shows that for around 10% of poor households, withdrawing children from school is a deliberate coping strategy in times of economic and environmental shock (World Bank, 2007c).

Offering school meals and cash incentives can tilt the balance between school and work

How should governments tackle the trade-off between school and work that is slowing progress towards UPE? Practical measures are needed, first to reduce the pressures that force poor households to augment income or labour supply through child work and, second, to strengthen incentives for sending children to school. Removing formal and informal fees and strengthening education quality are first steps. In many countries, including Cameroon, Ghana, Kenya and the United Republic of Tanzania, abolishing school fees has helped reduce child labour. Other interventions, such as school meal programmes, financial incentives for disadvantaged groups, social protection measures to better enable vulnerable households to manage risk, and conditional cash transfer programmes can also play an important role (see Chapter 3).

Health barriers to UPE

The early childhood section of this chapter highlights health handicaps that can affect children from birth to age 5. Such handicaps do not disappear after entry to primary school. Inadequate nutrition and poor health continue to track children

Figure 2.24: School attendance disadvantage for economically active children

Note: The school attendance disadvantage index is the school attendance rate of economically active children expressed as a ratio of the school attendance rate of children who are not economically active. The smaller the index value, the higher the disadvantage.

Source: Guarcello et al. (2006).

after they enter school, trapping them in a vicious cycle of cumulative disadvantage. Reversing this cycle requires public health interventions, some of which can be initiated through schools.

Getting more children into school is an important indicator for progress in education. In many countries, though, it has to be deflated to take into account the consequences of hunger, micronutrient deficiency and infection. On one estimate, as many as 60 million school-age children have iodine deficiency, which limits cognitive development. Some 200 million are anaemic, which affects concentration levels (Pridmore, 2007). Water-related infectious diseases impose an enormous toll on health and learning, costing an estimated 443 million school days per year in absenteeism (UNDP, 2006). Almost half these days are lost as a result of intestinal helminths, such as roundworm, hookworm and whipworm. Over 400 million children are infected with parasitic worms that leave them anaemic, listless and often unable to concentrate (Miguel and Kremer, 2004). Observational studies in the Philippines and the United Republic of Tanzania found a strong negative association between helminth infection and cognitive domains including learning and memory (Ezeamama et al., 2005; Jukes et al., 2002).

Schools can make a difference in all these areas. Of course, they cannot fully compensate for damage caused in early childhood, but they can provide some level of protection. In India, school meal programmes have been used in some states, such as Tamil Nadu, to improve pupils' nutritional status (Sridhar, 2008). Public health programmes can use schools to deliver vaccinations, vitamins and treatment for infectious diseases. In Kenya, a randomized evaluation of a school-based mass treatment campaign for intestinal helminths found marked reductions in infection rates (Edward and Michael, 2004; Kremer and Miguel, 2007). The programme also reduced school absenteeism by one-quarter. This meant children who attended primary school and underwent regular deworming every six months ended up with the equivalent of an extra year of education. School-based treatment costs were very low – around US$0.50 per child – and returns very high: for every dollar spent on deworming Kenya gained an estimated US$30 through the higher income associated with more education.

Linking health and education policies can yield high returns. In the United Republic of Tanzania, the rapid drive towards UPE has been supported by a public health programme aimed at tackling the debilitating effects of helminth infection among schoolchildren. In an initiative launched in 2005, the ministries of health and education undertook a joint risk-mapping exercise, identifying eleven regions as having the highest burden of infection. Teachers from every school in selected districts were trained to identify symptoms, advise parents on causes of infection and deliver medicine with local health workers. As part of the campaign, which is supported by aid donors, free drugs are reaching 5 million children annually. In this example, regional and district school health coordinators have played a pivotal role in facilitating progress in education (Schistosomiasis Control Initiative, 2008).

Investing in public health and using schools to deliver vaccinations, vitamins and treatment for infectious diseases is one of the most cost-effective ways to increase school participation

Investments in public health offer some of the most cost-effective routes to increased school participation. Conversely, failure to invest in health can have large hidden costs for education. Malaria provides a particularly striking example.

Exposure to malaria has grave implications for achievement in school. After controlling for other factors, researchers have found that endemically intensive malaria cuts school completion rates by around 29% and increases repetition by 9% (Thuilliez, 2007). In Sri Lanka another research exercise found that children aged 6 to 14 who had more than five bouts of malaria in a year scored 15% lower in language tests than children who had fewer than three, controlling for factors such as income and location (Fernando et al., 2003). Simple preventive measures in the form of insecticide-treated bed nets and low-cost treatment can dramatically reduce the incidence of malaria. Yet coverage remains limited. Fewer than one in ten children living in malarial areas of sub-Saharan Africa have access to insecticide-treated bed nets, for example. This is one area in which scaled-up global initiatives and strengthened national health systems have the potential to deliver rapid results in education.

HIV/AIDS prevention is another. Previous Reports have documented in detail the devastating impact of the disease on education in areas ranging from teacher attrition to child health. The pandemic is stabilizing, but at very high levels, and progress is uneven. Globally, an estimated 33 million people live with the disease, two-thirds of them (and almost three-quarters of deaths) in sub-Saharan Africa. Beyond the immediate human costs, the HIV/AIDS crisis represents a formidable obstacle to UPE. Around 1.9 million children under 15 in sub-Saharan Africa live with HIV/AIDS and some 9% of the region's children have lost one or both parents to the disease. While the evidence is mixed, there is evidence from several countries – including Kenya, Rwanda and the United Republic of Tanzania – that HIV/AIDS orphans enter school later and are more likely to repeat grades (Bicego et al., 2003; Siaens et al., 2003).[8] In fifty-six countries from which recent household survey data are available, orphans who had lost both parents were 12% less likely to be in school (UNAIDS, 2008) More broadly, the grief, trauma, isolation and depression that can accompany the death of parents also have a destructive impact on education (Kelly, 2004; Pridmore and Yates, 2005).

Children with disabilities are among the most marginalized and least likely to go to school

Progress in combating HIV/AIDS will have powerful spin-off benefits for education. Beyond prevention, the most immediate challenge is to improve access to antiretroviral drugs. Household-level research in western Kenya has documented significant increases in weekly hours of school attendance by children from households affected by HIV/AIDS when the parents have access to medicine. In the six months after treatment is initiated, attendance increases by 20% with no significant drop-off thereafter (Thirumurthy et al., 2007). This is just one example, but it highlights the costs associated with current treatment deficits. While the number of people receiving antiretroviral medicine has increased tenfold in the past six years to 3 million, 30 million are still untreated. Similarly, although mother-to-child transmission rates are falling with an increase in antiretroviral drug coverage, two-thirds of HIV-positive pregnant women are not covered by antiretroviral programmes (UNAIDS, 2008).

Links between public health and education operate in both directions. Strengthened health systems can enhance equity and opportunity in education; progress in education can act as a catalyst for gains in public health (see Chapter 1). From a public policy perspective the important lesson is that planning frameworks have to avoid compartmentalized approaches and integrate a wide range of interventions.

Disabled learners

The promise of EFA, as the phrase implies, applies to all children. It does not differentiate between able-bodied and disabled children. The Convention on the Rights of Persons with Disabilities, adopted by the United Nations General Assembly in December 2006 and in force since May 2008, is the latest legal tool supporting integration of disabled people and the most recent reaffirmation of the human rights of disabled learners. It recognizes a clear link between inclusive education and the right to education. Yet children with disabilities are still among the most marginalized and least likely to go to school.

Data constraints make cross-country comparison of the impact of disability difficult. There is no internationally agreed definition of 'disability',[9] and few governments closely monitor the impact of disability on school attendance. However, evidence from household surveys indicates that disabled children have lower rates of school participation. Figure 2.25 shows the proportions of children with and without disabilities at primary school age (6 to 11) in thirteen countries. The difference in primary school attendance rates between children with disabilities and those with none ranges from ten percentage points in India to almost sixty in Indonesia.

The barriers for disabled children vary. Physical distance to school, the layout and design of school facilities, and shortages of trained teachers all play

8. See Bennell (2005*a*) for a counterargument.

9. Although no satisfactory international working definition of 'disability' exists, the consensus is that any eventual definition must (i) be broad, to encompass the complexity of disability in all its visible and non-visible forms; (ii) be based on the World Health Organization's International Classification of Functioning, Disability and Health; and (iii) reflect the social, rather than medical, model of disability.

Figure 2.25: Proportion of children aged 6 to 11 with and without disabilities who are in school

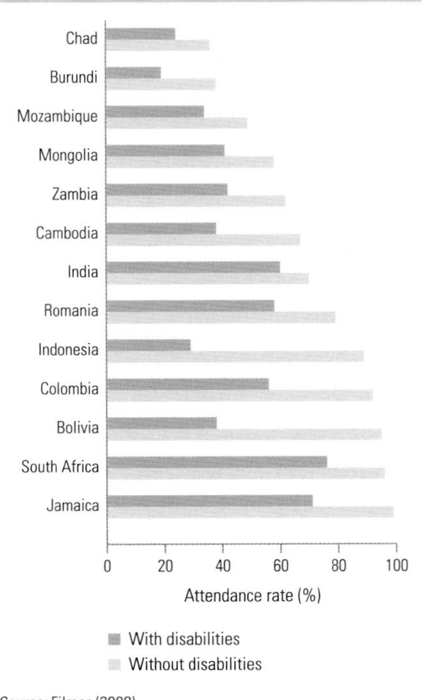

Source: Filmer (2008).

a role. Among the most serious obstacles, however, are negative attitudes towards the disabled, which affect both the school participation and the self-confidence of disabled children (Dutch Coalition on Disability and Development, 2006).

Speeding up progress towards UPE will require a far stronger focus on public policy facilitating access for the disabled – and on political leadership to change public attitudes (Box 2.12). The starting point is that disabled children should be treated as an integral part of the learning community rather than as a 'special' group requiring separate classes or institutions. □

Box 2.12: Uganda's good example of integrating disabled students

In Uganda the human rights of disabled people are enshrined in the Constitution and sign language is recognized as an official language. Deaf children attend their local schools, with appropriate support, such as sign language interpreters, to enable them to learn (Rustemier, 2002).

The Uganda National Institute of Special Education has been training teachers in inclusive and special needs education since 1991. It received legal status and parliamentary recognition as an educational institution in 1996. It is involved in research, community service, and development of educational materials and adaptive devices for learners with special needs. It makes a graphic design/illustration and desktop publishing facility available and offers distance learning opportunities, leading to a certificate or a diploma, open to teachers, parents, social workers, community development personnel, health workers, caregivers and law enforcement personnel. Uganda has also employed media successfully to advocate for the needs of persons with disabilities and to spread awareness of educational opportunities.

Source: The Communication Initiative Network (2002).

The 2006 Convention on the Rights of Persons with Disabilities recognizes the disabled learner's right to education

Secondary education and beyond: some gains

Increasing participation in secondary education is an explicit part of the Dakar commitment to EFA and of the MDG on gender parity and equality. Secondary education is also important for wider reasons. Where opportunities for secondary education are scarce, parents may see less reason to ensure that their children complete primary school, undermining progress towards UPE. There is another link between primary and secondary schools: namely, secondary school graduates represent the primary school teachers of the future. Secondary school is of value for personal development and civic participation as well, and it is a stepping stone to tertiary education. Expanded access to both these levels is essential to equip young people with the skills, know-how and training they and their countries need to succeed in an increasingly integrated and knowledge-based global economy.

Post-primary education is often too academic and removed from social and economic realities

While participation in post-primary education is expanding, access remains limited for most of the world's young people. Disparities in opportunity reinforce persistent inequalities in society. And problems go beyond access to school because many post-primary programmes do not meet real needs. Too often they are overly-academic, selective, stratified and disconnected from social and economic realities (World Bank, 2005*c*). This section reports on recent developments in secondary and tertiary education while emphasizing global, regional and national disparities at these levels.

Assuring the transition from primary to secondary education

Most governments today are committed to providing universal access to basic education, which includes lower secondary as well as primary education.[10] It follows that universal basic education requires completion of primary school and a successful transition to lower secondary. Enforcement of compulsory schooling laws and elimination of primary school-leaving examinations are just two of the measures being taken to improve transition rates. All developed countries, some countries in transition and most countries in Latin America and the Caribbean, and in East Asia and the Pacific consider primary and lower secondary education part of compulsory schooling (UIS, 2006*a*).[11]

Prolonging compulsory schooling has increased access to, and participation in, secondary education. The median transition rate from primary to secondary is above 90% in all regions except South and West Asia, and sub-Saharan Africa. Transition rates remain especially low (70% or less) in twenty-two countries, nineteen of them in sub-Saharan Africa (see annex, Statistical Table 8).

Expanding enrolment in secondary education

Enrolment in secondary education is rising. In 2006, some 513 million students worldwide were enrolled in secondary school, an increase of nearly 76 million since 1999. However, enrolment ratios vary enormously by region (Table 2.7). Worldwide, the average net enrolment ratio (NER) in secondary education increased from 52% in 1999 to 58% in 2006. Developed countries and most transition countries are moving closer to universal enrolment, but developing regions much less so. In sub-Saharan Africa, for example, the secondary NER was just 25% in 2006. This implies that nearly 78 million of the region's secondary school-age children are not enrolled in secondary school.

Regional figures conceal significant differences between countries. In the Arab States, secondary NERs ranged from less than 22% in Djibouti and Mauritania to nearly 90% or more in Bahrain, the Palestinian Autonomous Territories and Qatar in 2006. In South and West Asia they ranged from 30% in Pakistan to 77% in the Islamic Republic of Iran. Secondary NER levels in sub-Saharan Africa were less than 20% in Burkina Faso, Madagascar, Mozambique, the Niger and Uganda, but over 80% in Mauritius and Seychelles (see annex, Statistical Table 8).

10. By international convention, primary and lower secondary education are the first two stages of basic education (UNESCO, 1997). While most countries organize basic education according to the international definition, a significant number define it differently. In twenty-two countries, basic education includes at least one year of pre-primary education, in fifteen countries it consists exclusively of primary education and in twelve countries it includes lower secondary and part of upper secondary education (UNESCO, 2007*a*; UNESCO-IBE, 2007).

11. Some countries, including Bahrain, Malaysia, Mauritius, Oman and Tokelau, have achieved near universal participation in lower secondary education (GERs of at least 90%) even without compulsory school laws (see annex, Statistical Tables 4 and 8).

Table 2.7: Rates of transition to, and participation in, secondary education, 1999 and 2006, worldwide and by region

	Transition rates from primary to secondary education (median)			Secondary education			
				Gross enrolment ratios		Net enrolment ratios	
	School year ending in 2005			School year ending in		School year ending in	
				1999	2006	1999	2006
	Total (%)	Male (%)	Female (%)	(%)	(%)	(%)	(%)
World	93	92	94	60	66	52	58
Developing countries	88	93	83	52	60	45	53
Developed countries	99	…	…	100	101	88	91
Countries in transition	100	100	99	90	89	83	82
Sub-Saharan Africa	62	66	57	24	32	18	25
Arab States	92	90	93	60	68	52	59
Central Asia	99	99	99	83	91	78	83
East Asia and the Pacific	…	…	…	65	75	61	69
East Asia	91	…	…	64	75	61	69
Pacific	…	…	…	111	107	70	66
South and West Asia	87	90	83	45	51	39	45
Latin America and the Caribbean	93	…	…	80	89	59	70
Caribbean	94	…	…	53	57	44	40
Latin America	92	92	92	81	91	59	71
North America and Western Europe	99	99	99	100	101	88	91
Central and Eastern Europe	98	98	99	87	88	80	81

Source: Annex, Statistical Table 8.

Secondary-school enrolment has risen by nearly 76 million since 1999

Between 1999 and 2006, secondary GERs increased in 118 of the 148 countries with data available. Fourteen of the countries that started with enrolment ratios of less than 80% made significant progress with increases of at least fifteen percentage points.[12] In many Western European countries, GERs in secondary education declined as systems became more age-standardized, with fewer under- and over-age students.

Technical and vocational education and training (TVET) occupy an important position in secondary education. Of the more than 513 million students enrolled in secondary schools worldwide in 2006, 10% were in TVET programmes (Table 2.8), mainly at upper secondary level (UNESCO-UNEVOC/UIS, 2006).[13] The percentage had declined slightly since 1999. The relative shares of secondary-level TVET enrolment were highest in Central and Eastern Europe, North America and Western Europe, and the Pacific, and lowest in South and West Asia, the Caribbean and sub-Saharan Africa.

Table 2.8: Percentage of technical and vocational education and training in secondary education, 1999 and 2006

	Enrolment in technical and vocational education % of total secondary	
	School year ending in	
	1999	2006
World	11	10
Developing countries	9	9
Developed countries	18	16
Countries in transition	9	12
Sub-Saharan Africa	6	6
Arab States	15	12
Central Asia	6	10
East Asia and the Pacific	14	13
East Asia	14	13
Pacific	36	33
South and West Asia	2	2
Latin America and the Caribbean	10	10
Caribbean	3	3
Latin America	10	10
North America and Western Europe	15	14
Central and Eastern Europe	18	19

Source: Annex, Statistical Table 8.

12. Cambodia, Costa Rica, Cuba, Ethiopia, Guatemala, Guinea, Macao (China), the Maldives, Mexico, Mongolia, Morocco, Saint Lucia, the Syrian Arab Republic and the Bolivarian Republic of Venezuela.

13. In some countries TVET programmes are post-secondary non-tertiary education (ISCED level 4).

Transition to upper secondary – a dropout point

Countries increasingly make the distinction between lower secondary education (ISCED level 2) and upper secondary education (ISCED level 3) (UNESCO, 1997). The former is frequently part of a compulsory basic education cycle, whereas the onset of the latter typically marks the end of compulsory schooling and consists of diverse programmes and more specialized instruction (UIS, 2006*a*).

The transition from lower to upper secondary is a dropout point in many education systems. At a global level, the average GER in 2006 was much higher in lower secondary education (78%) than in upper (53%) (Table 2.9). Differences in the participation rates between the two levels are especially prominent in East Asia,[14] Latin America and the Caribbean, the Arab States and sub-Saharan Africa (where rates are relatively low at both levels). By contrast, participation levels in lower and upper secondary education are quite similar in North America and Western Europe, Central and Eastern Europe, and Central Asia.

14. In the Pacific subregion, however, the rates are uncertain because the small population base makes it difficult to estimate population reliably.

15. The secondary attainment rate is the percentage of a population that has participated in secondary education though not necessarily completed a full cycle.

Disparities in secondary education attainment

Household surveys help capture the scale of international inequalities at the post-primary level. They provide evidence that, while global primary education disparities may be narrowing, inequalities at the secondary level remain large (Barro and Lee, 2000; Bloom, 2006).

Regional disparities are particularly marked. The average secondary education attainment rate[15] in developed countries is 70% among the population aged 25 or more, but just 40% in East Asia and the Pacific and around 20% in sub-Saharan Africa (Figure 2.26). Attainment rates among the group aged 15 to 24 are higher, pointing to improved access and reduced inequality over time. The exception is sub-Saharan Africa. This is the only region in which 15- to 24-year-olds were less likely to have attended secondary school, indicating a need for urgent action to close the gap with the rest of the world.

Detailed attainment figures broken down by grade level help pinpoint where students face critical transition hurdles. Several patterns

Table 2.9: Gross enrolment ratios in lower and upper secondary education, 1999 and 2006

	Gross enrolment ratios (%)			
	Lower secondary		Upper secondary	
	School year ending in		School year ending in	
	1999	2006	1999	2006
World	73	78	46	53
Developing countries	67	75	37	46
Developed countries	102	103	98	99
Countries in transition	91	89	87	88
Sub-Saharan Africa	27	38	19	24
Arab States	73	81	47	54
Central Asia	85	95	80	84
East Asia and the Pacific	80	92	46	58
East Asia	80	92	45	57
Pacific	92	89	146	139
South and West Asia	62	66	31	39
Latin America and the Caribbean	96	102	62	74
Caribbean	67	72	39	43
Latin America	97	103	63	76
North America and Western Europe	102	103	98	98
Central and Eastern Europe	93	89	80	85

Source: Annex, Statistical Table 8.

Figure 2.26: Secondary attainment rates among adults and youth, by region, circa 2000

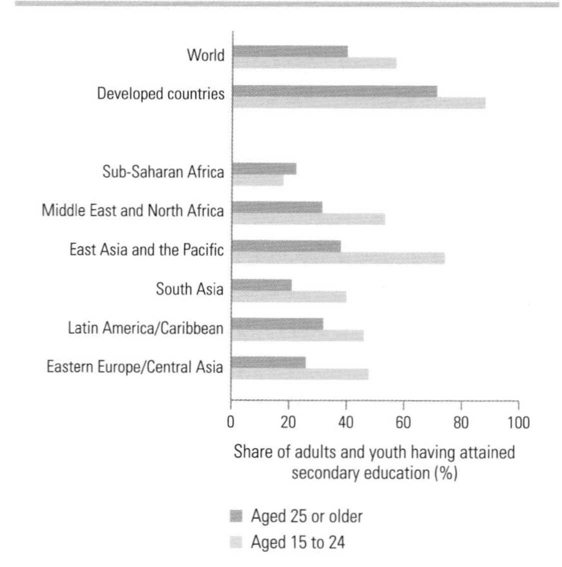

Note: The regional classification in this figure follows that used by the World Bank, which differs to some extent from the EFA classification used in this Report. Developed countries include OECD countries and other high income countries, such as Bahrain, Cyprus, Israel and Kuwait.
Source: Barro and Lee (2000), as reported in Bloom (2006).

emerge from comparing survival rates to the end of secondary education (Figure 2.27).[16] The profile for Armenia, where almost all students complete eight years of schooling (roughly the end of lower secondary education) and only begin to drop out during the upper secondary grades, is typical for most developed and transition countries. For these countries, inequalities in grade attainment become more marked in the post-compulsory years.[17]

Patterns in low-income developing countries look very different. Some countries register steep declines at specific grades, as in the United Republic of Tanzania (grade 7) and Ghana (grade 9). In other cases, such as Malawi and Nicaragua, survival rates decline more gradually, with secondary education marking a broad continuation of the pattern established at the primary level. Finally, some countries, such as Mali, maintain a consistent level of survival at a low level of attainment. Grade-specific attendance data of this

Inequalities at the secondary level remain large

Figure 2.27: Survival rates to each grade of primary and secondary education, by gender, selected countries, most recent year

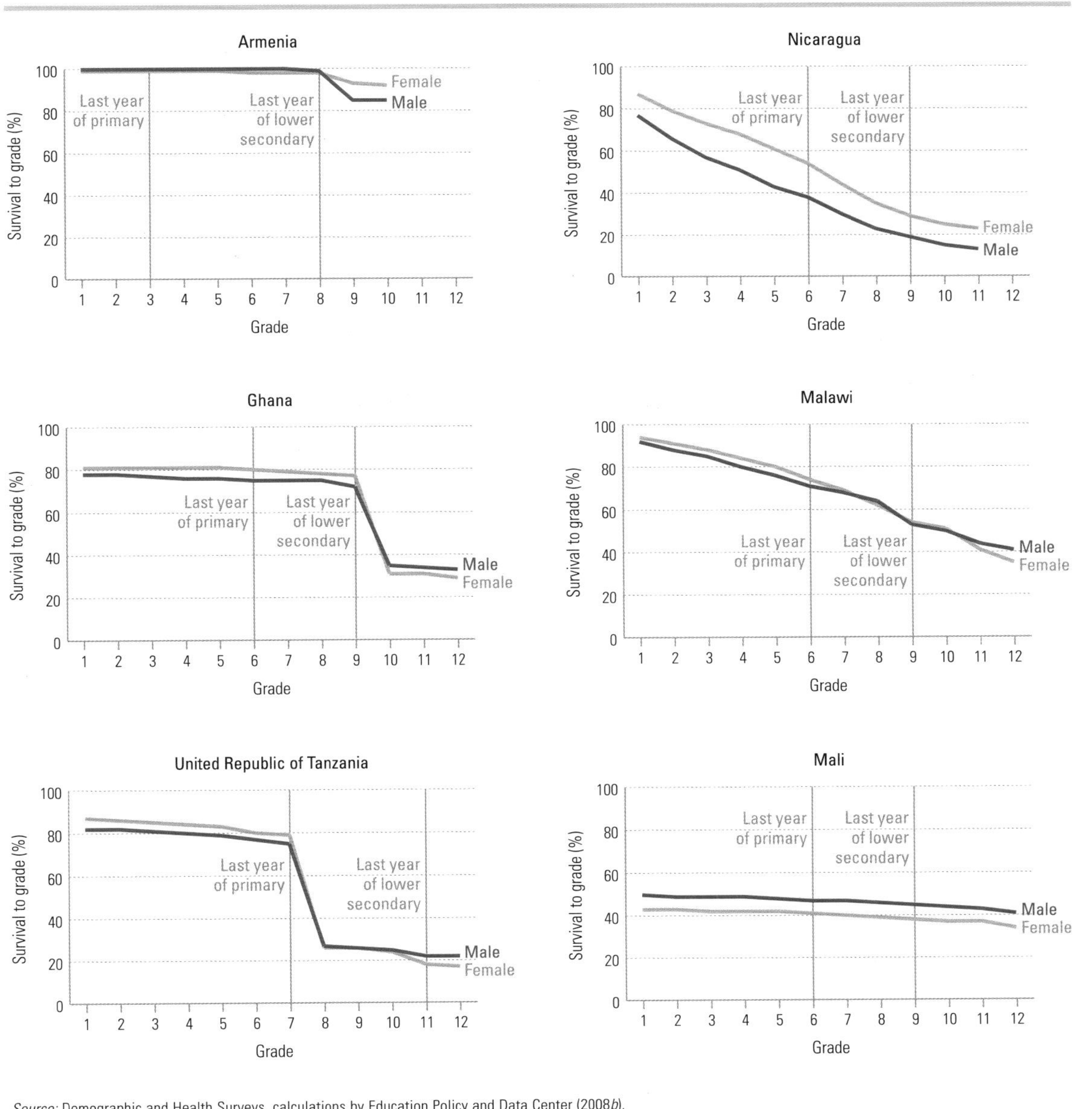

Source: Demographic and Health Surveys, calculations by Education Policy and Data Center (2008*b*).

16. Survival rates by grade portray pupils' ability to progress through the school system and reach higher grades, which is largely determined by cumulative dropout rates. The reported survival rates were calculated based on promotion, repetition and dropout rates for primary- and secondary-age pupils who were currently in school. They are different from the survival rates of cohorts of pupils who start school in a particular age group.

17. Using a different methodology, the World Bank has constructed national profiles of attainment by grade level that indicate the proportion of people aged 15 to 19 who successfully reach each grade of primary and secondary education. These profiles reflect similar patterns to those discussed here. (Both methods use data from household surveys.) See the World Bank Educational Attainment and Enrolment around the World database (World Bank, 2008*b*) and Pritchett (2004*b*).

type are important because they help identify critical moments for public policy intervention.

Disparities within countries are greater than those among countries

Within-country inequalities in secondary education are often more marked than inequalities between countries. This is another area in which wealth matters for the distribution of opportunity.

As Figure 2.28 shows, in many developing countries, secondary attendance rates are significantly lower among poorer households than among richer ones. As at primary level, wealth-based inequalities contract as attendance rates rise to 80% or above. More surprising is the extent to which wealth-based inequalities in secondary attendance vary among countries with similar average attendance. For example, Bangladesh, Benin, Nicaragua and Zambia all have secondary attendance rates of about 60%. Yet the ratios of attendance rates between the richest and poorest households range from 1.4 in Bangladesh to 2.4 in Nicaragua (Benin is at 1.8 and Zambia at 1.7). This cannot be explained by differences in poverty levels or average income: Bangladesh has a higher incidence of extreme poverty and a lower average income than Nicaragua. The evidence from this comparison would suggest that public policies in Nicaragua could be doing far more to narrow disparities. The same would apply to Indonesia and Ghana.

Figure 2.28: Net attendance rates in secondary education, by wealth quintile, selected countries, most recent year

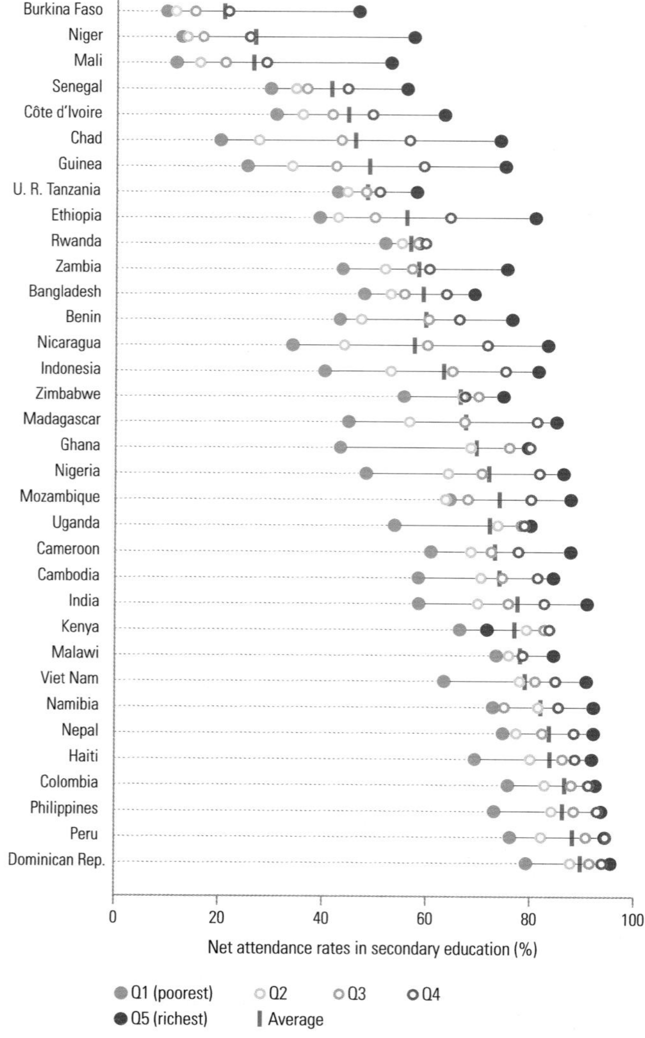

Source: Demographic and Health Surveys, calculations by Harttgen et al. (2008).

Analysis of the relationship between household wealth and survival rates by grade level reveals a number of patterns (Figure 2.29). A dominant one is exemplified by Colombia and India, where the relationship between household wealth and survival rates is fairly muted in the early grades of primary education but much more salient in the upper grades of secondary education. Lesotho, Peru and the Philippines also follow this pattern. In another common pattern, illustrated by Benin and Cambodia, the relationship between household wealth and survival rates remains fairly consistent throughout primary and secondary education (EPDC, 2008*b*).

In some regions there has been a displacement effect with greater equity at the primary level shifting disparities to the secondary level. The experience of Latin America is instructive. Household surveys taken between 1990 and 2005 show a steady increase in the percentage of students achieving timely promotion through the education system at both primary and secondary level. The overall percentage of students aged 15 to 19 having achieved timely promotion at the primary level increased from 43% to 66%. Advances for the cohort aged 10 to 14 were proportionately more beneficial for low-income students, with the rich-poor gap narrowing. Convergence is much less evident at the secondary level. In 2005, some 88% of children in the richest decile moved steadily through school without interruption, compared with 44% of the poorest decile (UN Economic Commission for Latin America and the Caribbean, 2007).

Figure 2.29: Survival rates to each grade of primary and secondary education, by wealth quintile, selected countries, most recent year

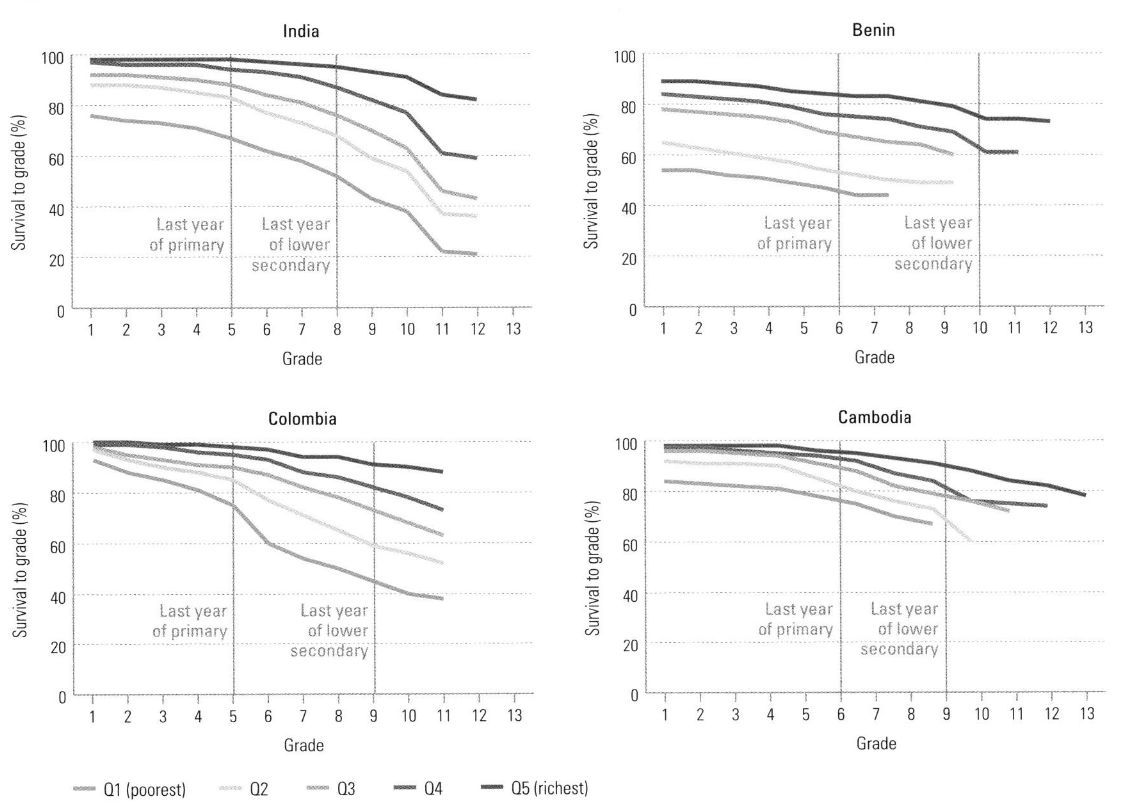

Note: Survival rates for some quintiles and grades could not be calculated because too few observations were available.
Source: Demographic and Health Survey, calculations by Education Policy and Data Center (2008*b*).

The relationship between household wealth and survival rates is most apparent in the post-primary years

Disadvantages based on characteristics other than household wealth also cross the divide between primary and secondary school. Speaking an indigenous or non-official language remains a core marker for disadvantage. When home language and official national language differ, the chances of completing at least one grade of secondary school are reduced. For example, in Mozambique, 43% of people aged 16 to 49 who speak Portuguese (the language of instruction) have at least one grade of secondary schooling; among speakers of Lomwe, Makhuwa, Sena and Tsonga, the shares range from 6% to 16%. In Bolivia, 68% of Spanish speakers aged 16 to 49 have completed some secondary education while one-third or fewer of Aymara, Guaraní and Quechua speakers have done so; in Turkey the corresponding shares are 45% for Turkish speakers and below 21% for Arabic and Kurdish speakers (Smits et al., 2008).

Tertiary education: global patterns of inequality

Tertiary education has expanded rapidly since the Dakar Forum. Worldwide, some 144 million students were enrolled in tertiary education in 2006 – 51 million more than in 1999. Over the same period, the global tertiary GER increased from 18% to 25%. A large majority of the new places in tertiary institutions were created in developing countries, where the total number of tertiary students rose from 47 million in 1999 to 85 million in 2006 (see annex, Statistical Table 9).

Even with rapid growth in tertiary education in developing countries, global disparities remain large (Table 2.10). Tertiary GERs range from 70% in North America and Western Europe to 32% in Latin America, 22% in the Arab States and 5% in sub-Saharan Africa. These disparities capture just

At global level there are huge gaps in spending per student and in university enrolment rates

Table 2.10: Change in tertiary gross enrolment ratios between 1999 and 2006

	Gross enrolment ratios in tertiary education (%) School year ending in 1999	2006
World	18	25
Developing countries	11	17
Developed countries	55	67
Countries in transition	39	57
Sub-Saharan Africa	4	5
Arab States	19	22
Central Asia	18	25
East Asia and the Pacific	14	25
East Asia	13	24
Pacific	47	52
South and West Asia	7	11
Latin America and the Caribbean	21	31
Caribbean	6	6
Latin America	22	32
North America and Western Europe	61	70
Central and Eastern Europe	38	60

Source: Annex, Statistical Table 9A.

the quantitative side of the equation. Qualitative gaps are also important. In equivalent dollar terms, France spent over sixteen times as much per university student in 2004 as did Indonesia and Peru. In 2005, top private universities in the United States, such as Harvard, Princeton and Yale, spent US$100,000 or more per student; the equivalent figure for a student at Dar-es-Salaam University was US$3,239 (Kapur and Crowley, 2008).
Of course, spending per student is not the only indicator for quality at the tertiary level, any more than it is at the primary level. But financing gaps on this scale have implications for disparities in learning opportunities and the provision of teaching materials.

Global inequalities are often magnified at national level. It is at the entry point to tertiary education, that the compound effects of inequalities in access to and completion of basic education, and progression through secondary education, become most visible. Brazil's universities provide a microcosm of a wider problem. The university participation rate for black Brazilians aged 19 to 24 is 6%, compared with 19% for white Brazilians (Paixão and Carvano, 2008). In other words, being born with black skin in Brazil reduces your chance of reaching university by a factor of three.
This is the culmination of disadvantage rooted in poverty, social discrimination and the filtering effect of inequality at lower levels of the education system. □

Meeting the lifelong learning needs of youth and adults

Goal 3: Ensuring that the learning needs of all young people and adults are met through equitable access to appropriate learning and life-skills programmes.

Goal 4: Achieving a 50 per cent improvement in levels of adult literacy by 2015, especially for women, and ***equitable access to basic and continuing education for all adults.***

Fixing early childhood provision, achieving UPE and expanding post-primary education will create the conditions under which future generations can realize their potential. But what of people who have been failed by current systems?

This Report highlights the fact that governments across the world have to address an immense backlog of unmet need. Millions of teenagers have never attended primary school and many millions more have left school lacking the skills they need to earn a livelihood and participate fully in society. To this constituency can be added about 776 million adults who lack basic literacy skills and many others without access to adult education or skills training. To take one priority area, whole sections of the adult population in some countries have no access to the information and communication technology that is pervasive in today's knowledge economy.

Systematic monitoring of EFA goal 3 and the latter part of goal 4 has been stymied by problems of definition and lack of data.[18] There is little agreement about how to define the notions of 'adult learning' and 'life skills', and which learning activities to include (Ellis, 2006; Hargreaves and Shaw, 2006; Hoffmann and Olson, 2006; King and Palmer, 2008; Merle, 2004). 'Life skills' and 'livelihood skills', both aspects of adult learning, have taken on different meanings in different countries (Maurer, 2005). At Dakar 'livelihood skills' was thought to be subsumed within the broader concept of 'life skills.'

Adult learning activities are found in a myriad of formal, informal and non-formal programmes and institutions. In some cases they involve programmes aimed at youth or adults who wish to return to school – that is, equivalency education or second-chance programmes.

Many governments have given little if any priority to youth's and adults' learning needs in their education strategies and policies. Inadequate public funding hampers provision and inadequate monitoring obscures other problems (Hoppers, 2007; UNESCO, 2004). The fact that no clear quantitative targets were established at Dakar, apart from the main literacy target, may have contributed to a lack of urgency. In addition, the language of the commitment is ambiguous. Some read goal 3 as calling for universal access to learning and life-skills programmes, but others, including the drafters of the Dakar Framework, understand no such intent.[19]

The *EFA Global Monitoring Report 2008* explored a range of issues in non-formal education, where much adult learning activity takes place.[20] It found evidence in several countries of significant disparities in provision by location, age group and socio-economic status (UNESCO, 2007). It also found that national history heavily influenced approaches to provision. While Mexico, Nepal and Senegal, for instance, see non-formal provision principally in terms of adult education, Bangladesh and Indonesia take a broader view, stressing flexibility and programme diversity to complement formal education. Burkina Faso, Ghana, Kenya, Nigeria, the Philippines, the United Republic of Tanzania and Zambia, meanwhile, largely conceive of non-formal education as any structured learning activity outside the formal education system.

Lifelong learning needs are great, but rarely reflected in national education strategies and policies

There is a strong case to be made for clarifying the purpose of lifelong learning provision, improving data flows and, critically, strengthening political commitment in this area. As a first step towards more effective monitoring, improved information is needed in the following areas:

- **National conceptions and commitment:** How do government agencies understand the learning needs of out-of-school youth and adults? To what extent do authorities address these needs by articulating a clear vision, setting policy priorities, providing for resource mobilization and allocation, and enabling partnerships with non-government and international organizations? How long do various adult learning programmes last? To what extent are specific lifelong learning opportunities put in place?

18. A future *EFA Global Monitoring Report* will examine these issues as part of an overarching theme.

19. Based on exchanges with Steve Packer and Sheldon Shaeffer, who helped draft the EFA goals.

20. UNESCO's working definition of non-formal education states that it 'may cover education programmes to impart adult literacy, basic education for out-of-school children, life skills, work skills and general culture' (UNESCO, 1997, p. 41).

- **Demand:** What is the demand for youth and adult learning programmes, which populations are involved and how has demand changed over time?

- **Nature of provision:** What are the character and focus of existing youth and adult learning programmes? Do they include frameworks oriented towards re-entry into formal education? Basic literacy programmes (reading, writing and numeracy)? Literacy programmes to promote life skills or livelihood skills? Other skills development programmes (especially related to labour market participation)? Rural development?

Effective monitoring of lifelong learning provision requires better information

- **Target groups:** Which groups do existing youth and adult learning programmes target? Which target groups do the biggest, most established adult learning programmes serve? To what extent does existing provision create or worsen disparities based on age, gender, educational attainment, wealth, residence, ethnicity or language?

- **Flexibility and diversification:** Are youth and adult learning programmes highly standardized, or do they incorporate flexibility so as to better address the learning needs of diverse groups?

- **Sustainability:** How long have youth and adult learning programmes been in existence? Which agencies and stakeholders provide funding? Has funding been constant and/or increasing over time? How long have educator/ facilitator training frameworks existed?

An important and potentially rich source of information is the Sixth International Conference on Adult Education (CONFINTEA VI), scheduled for May 2009 in Belém, Brazil. Its overall aim is 'to draw attention to the relation and contribution of adult learning and education to sustainable development, conceived comprehensively as comprising a social, economic, ecological and cultural dimension.' Five regional preparatory conferences will have examined policies, structures and financing for adult learning and education; inclusion and participation; the quality of adult learning and education; literacy and other key competencies; and poverty eradication. □

Adult literacy: still neglected

Overcoming inequalities in literacy's reach

Goal 4: ***Achieving a 50 per cent improvement in levels of adult literacy by 2015, especially for women,*** *and equitable access to basic and continuing education for all adults.*

Reading and writing are essential skills for today's world. Literacy expands people's choices, gives them more control over their lives, increases their ability to participate in society and enhances self-esteem. It is a key to education that also opens the way to better health, improved employment opportunities and lower child mortality. Despite these advantages for individuals, and the wider benefits in terms of broader social and economic development, literacy remains a neglected goal. As the *EFA Global Monitoring Report 2008* noted: 'Illiteracy is receiving minimal political attention and remains a global disgrace, keeping one in five adults (one in four women) on the margins of society' (UNESCO, 2007*a*, p.1).

Multiple barriers restrict the achievement of widespread literacy. They include insufficient access to quality education, weak support for young people exiting the education system, poorly funded and administratively fragmented literacy programmes, and limited opportunities for adult learning. Many of these barriers disproportionately affect marginal and vulnerable groups, and exacerbate socio-economic inequalities. In developing countries in particular, lower literacy levels are commonly associated with poverty, low socio-economic status, gender discrimination, ill health, immigration, cultural marginalization and disabilities (UNESCO, 2005). Even in highly literate and schooled societies significant pockets of illiteracy and low literacy remain, leaving those affected marginalized and with diminished life chances.

The global literacy progress report is not encouraging. Some 776 million adults – 16% of the world's adult population – are unable to read or write with understanding

Illiteracy in global perspective

An estimated 776 million adults – 16% of the world's adult population – are unable to read and/or write, with understanding, a simple statement in a national or official language (Table 2.11).[21] Most live in South and West Asia, East Asia and sub-Saharan Africa, and nearly two in every three are women.

The global progress report on literacy is not encouraging. Between 1985–1994 and 2000–2006, the number of adults lacking literacy skills fell by almost 100 million, primarily due to a marked

Table 2.11: Estimated number of adult illiterates (age 15+) in 1985-1994 and 2000-2006, with projections to 2015, by region

	1985–1994[1]		2000–2006[1]		2015		Percentage change	
	Total (000)	Female (%)	Total (000)	Female (%)	Total (000)	Female (%)	1985–1994 to 2000–2006	2000–2006 to 2015
World	871 096	63	775 894	64	706 130	64	-11	-9
Developing countries	858 680	63	766 716	64	698 332	64	-11	-9
Developed countries	8 686	64	7 660	62	7 047	59	-12	-8
Countries in transition	3 730	84	1 519	71	752	59	-59	-51
Sub-Saharan Africa	133 013	61	161 088	62	147 669	60	21	-8
Arab States	55 311	63	57 798	67	53 339	69	4	-9
Central Asia	960	74	784	68	328	50	-18	-58
East Asia and the Pacific	229 172	69	112 637	71	81 398	71	-51	-28
East Asia	227 859	69	110 859	71	79 420	71	-51	-28
Pacific	1 313	56	1 778	55	1 979	52	35	11
South and West Asia	394 719	61	392 725	63	380 256	63	-1	-3
Latin America and the Caribbean	39 575	55	36 946	55	31 225	54	-7	-15
Caribbean	2 870	50	2 803	48	2 749	45	-2	-2
Latin America	36 705	55	34 142	56	28 476	55	-7	-17
North America and Western Europe	6 400	63	5 682	61	5 115	59	-11	-10
Central and Eastern Europe	11 945	78	8 235	80	6 801	79	-31	-17

1. Data are for the most recent year available. See the web version of the introduction to the statistical tables in the annex for explanations of national literacy definitions, assessment methods, sources and years of data.
Source: Annex, Statistical Table 2A.

21. This figure is based on conventional approaches that define and measure literacy in dichotomous terms using indirect measurement methods. Other approaches conceive of literacy as a multidimensional phenomenon, embracing a variety of skill domains that need to be directly assessed using wider scales. In general, direct assessments show that conventional approaches understate actual literacy levels, especially in poor countries (UNESCO, 2005).

reduction in East Asia, especially China.[22] The net effect obscures large regional variation. In sub-Saharan Africa, the Arab States and the Pacific, absolute numbers of illiterates increased, reflecting continued population growth. Moreover, global progress has slowed in recent years. The upshot is that, on current trends, over 700 million adults will still lack basic literacy skills in 2015.[23] Changing this picture will require a renewed sense of urgency, on the part of national governments and the international community, particularly in highly populous developing countries.

On current trends, over 700 million adults will still lack basic literacy skills in 2015

In terms of absolute numbers, adult illiteracy is heavily concentrated in a relatively small group of countries. Some 80% of those affected worldwide live in twenty countries (Figure 2.30), with Bangladesh, China, India and Pakistan accounting for over half of the total. While significant reductions have occurred in Algeria, China, Egypt, India, Indonesia, the Islamic Republic of Iran and Turkey since 1985–1994, progress elsewhere has been less promising.

Figure 2.30: Countries with the greatest numbers of adult illiterates (age 15+) as of 2000–2006[1]

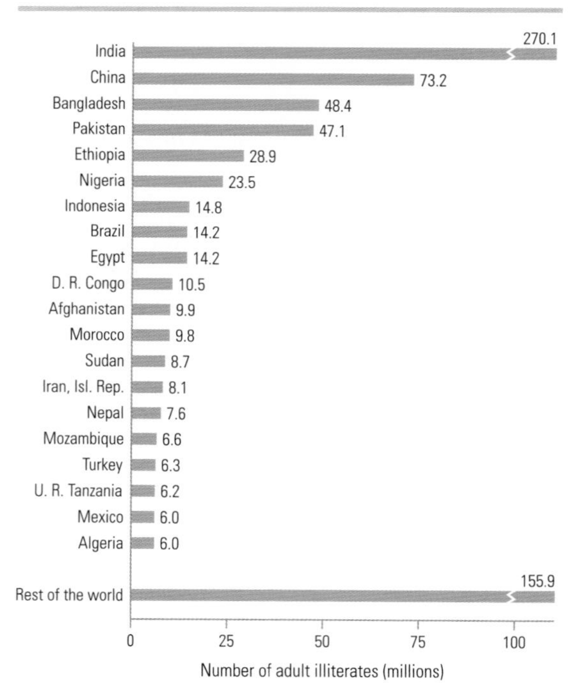

Notes: See source table for detailed country notes.
1. Data are for the most recent year available. See the web version of the introduction to the statistical tables in the annex for explanations of national literacy definitions, assessment methods, sources and years of data.
Source: Annex, Statistical Table 2A.

Adult literacy rates

Between 1985–1994 and 2000–2006, the global adult literacy rate[24] increased from 76% to 84% (Table 2.12). Progress was especially marked in the developing countries as a group, where the average adult literacy rate increased from 68% to 79%. During the period adult literacy levels improved in almost all regions, though not sufficiently in some to cut the number of those lacking literacy skills. Regional adult literacy rates remained below the world average in sub-Saharan Africa, South and West Asia, the Arab States and the Caribbean.

In 45 countries out of 135, mostly in sub-Saharan Africa, and South and West Asia, adult literacy rates are below the developing country average of 79% (see annex, Statistical Table 2A). The most populous countries in this group include Bangladesh, Ethiopia, India, Nigeria and Pakistan. Nineteen countries in the group have very low literacy rates, less than 55%;[25] thirteen are low-income countries in which severe poverty prevails – that is, where 75% or more of the population lives on less than US$2 per day.[26] Current projections indicate a large proportion of countries in the group will not meet the adult literacy goal by 2015.

Youth literacy

Adult illiteracy is the product of past exclusion from educational opportunities. Tomorrow's illiteracy figures will reflect current patterns of access to learning. With the continued expansion of formal education, the global number of youth illiterates (aged 15 to 24) declined from 167 million in 1985–1994 to 130 million in 2000–2006 (see annex, Statistical Table 2A). Declines occurred in most regions, but in sub-Saharan Africa the number of youth lacking basic literacy skills increased by 7 million due to continuing high population growth and low school participation and completion rates. There were also relatively small increases in Central Asia, the Pacific, and North America and Western Europe, partly due to changing population estimates.

The global youth literacy rate also improved during the period, from 84% to 89%, most notably in South and West Asia, sub-Saharan Africa, the Caribbean and the Arab States. Low youth literacy rates (under 80%) were recorded in sub-Saharan Africa, and South and West Asia.

22. China experienced a dramatic increase in numbers of adult literates between 1985–1994 and 2000–2006 and its adult literacy rate rose from 78% to 93%, due to the combined impact of mass literacy campaigns organized in previous decades, expansion of primary education and the spread of text-laden literate environments (UNESCO, 2005).

23. The projection in this Report of 706 million illiterate adults in 2015 is more optimistic than the estimate of 725 million published in the 2008 Report.

24. The number of literate persons expressed as a percentage of the total population aged 15 and over.

25. Afghanistan, Bangladesh, Benin, Bhutan, Burkina Faso, the Central African Republic, Chad, Côte d'Ivoire, Ethiopia, Guinea, Liberia, Mali, Morocco, Mozambique, Niger, Pakistan, Senegal, Sierra Leone and Togo.

26. Bangladesh, Burundi, Cambodia, the Central African Republic, Ethiopia, Ghana, India, Madagascar, Niger, Nigeria, Rwanda, the United Republic of Tanzania and Zambia.

Table 2.12: Estimated adult literacy rates (age 15+) in 1985-1994 and 2000-2006, with projections to 2015, by region

	1985–1994[1]		2000–2006[1]		Projected 2015	
	Literacy rates (%)	GPI	Literacy rates (%)	GPI	Literacy rates (%)	GPI
	Total	(F/M)	Total	(F/M)	Total	(F/M)
World	76	0.85	84	0.89	87	0.92
Developing countries	68	0.77	79	0.85	84	0.90
Developed countries	99	0.99	99	1.00	99	0.99
Countries in transition	98	0.98	99	1.00	100	1.00
Sub-Saharan Africa	53	0.71	62	0.75	72	0.86
Arab States	58	0.66	72	0.75	79	0.81
Central Asia	98	0.98	99	0.99	99	1.00
East Asia and the Pacific	82	0.84	93	0.94	95	0.96
East Asia	82	0.84	93	0.94	96	0.96
Pacific	94	0.99	93	0.99	93	1.00
South and West Asia	48	0.57	64	0.71	71	0.78
Latin America and the Caribbean	87	0.98	91	0.98	93	0.99
Caribbean	66	1.02	74	1.05	78	1.07
Latin America	87	0.97	91	0.98	94	0.99
North America and Western Europe	99	0.99	99	1.00	99	1.00
Central and Eastern Europe	96	0.96	97	0.97	98	0.98

1. Data are for the most recent year available. See the introduction to the statistical tables in the annex for explanations of national literacy definitions, assessment methods, sources and years of data.
Source: Annex, Statistical Tables 2A and 12.

Literacy, inequality and exclusion

National literacy rates conceal major disparities in literacy levels within countries. These disparities are linked to gender, poverty, place of residence, ethnicity, language and disabilities. Age is another important dimension: younger adults tend to have higher literacy rates than older adults.[27]

Gender disparities in adult literacy are widespread, especially in the countries facing the greatest literacy challenge. Worldwide, women account for 64% of the adults who cannot read and write, with understanding, a simple statement from their everyday life. This share is virtually unchanged from the 63% recorded during 1985–1994 (Table 2.11). The global literacy rate is lower for women than men, as reflected in the global GPI of 0.89 in 2000–2006, up from 0.85 in the previous period. Gender disparities to the disadvantage of women are especially marked in South and West Asia, the Arab States and sub-Saharan Africa. Gender disparities in these regions improved between the two periods (Table 2.12). Gender and poverty often interact in relation to literacy: for example, in the Gambia, literacy rates ranged from 12% among extremely poor women to 53% for non-poor men (Caillods and Hallak, 2004).

The close link between **poverty** and illiteracy is observed not only from one country to another but also among regions and households within a country. In India, for example, literacy levels are lower in the poorest states. Evidence from thirty developing countries indicates that literacy levels are substantially lower in the poorest households than in the wealthiest (UNESCO, 2005). In seven sub-Saharan African countries with particularly low overall adult literacy rates, the literacy gap between the poorest and wealthiest households is more than forty percentage points.[28]

Literacy rates also vary by **place of residence**. They are almost always lower in rural areas than in urban areas. Countries where overall literacy rates are comparatively low show large regional disparities: Pakistan census figures report adult literacy rates of 72% in the Islamabad Capital Territory but 44% in rural Balochistan and Sindh (Choudhry, 2005). In Ethiopia regional disparities in literacy rates range from 83% in the Addis Ababa region to 25% in the Amhara region (Shenkut, 2005). Pastoralists and nomads, who number in the tens of millions across the African drylands, the Middle East and parts of Asia, have lower literacy levels than other rural populations (UNESCO, 2005). In the Afar region of Ethiopia,

In seven countries in sub-Saharan Africa, the literacy gap between the poorest and the wealthiest households is more than forty percentage points

27. The relationship between age and literacy rates is sometimes curvilinear; see UNESCO (2005).

28. The countries are Côte d'Ivoire, Guinea-Bissau, Rwanda, Senegal, Sierra Leone, Sudan and Togo.

for example, the literacy rate for adults was 25% in 1999, but in pastoralist areas it was only 8%.

Official literacy figures generally understate the problem in rich and poor countries alike

Indigenous populations, many of them characterized by proficiency in non-official languages, tend to have lower literacy rates than non-indigenous populations. The national literacy rate in Ecuador, for example, was 91% in 2001 but that of indigenous groups was 72%; in Viet Nam the rates in 2000 were 87% nationally, 17% for ethnic minorities and merely 5% for some indigenous groups. Nepal's Dalit population has a significantly lower adult literacy rate than the rest of the population. The Roma in Central Europe also have lower literacy levels than those of majority populations (UNESCO, 2005).

The household surveys and censuses used in determining literacy rates often overlook **other excluded groups** and individuals (Carr-Hill, 2005). People who are homeless, institutionalized in prisons or care homes, or unregistered may not figure. In developing countries, refugees or internally displaced persons often go uncounted. The same is true for street children. In all these cases, official literacy figures are likely to understate the scale of the problem.

Pockets of illiteracy and low literacy in developed countries

In highly schooled countries that achieved UPE some time ago, illiteracy is considered a problem of the past. Yet international and national literacy surveys often reveal substantial pockets of illiteracy and low literacy. International assessments show that many OECD countries have large groups with low levels on key literacy indicators:

- An assessment in Canada (2003) established that 9 million Canadians of working age (42% of people aged 16 to 65) scored at level 2 or below on the prose literacy scale, a figure that had changed little since the previous assessment in 1994 (Grenier et al., 2008).[29]
- A 2004–2005 assessment in metropolitan France found that 3.1 million French adults of working age, some 59% of them men, faced literacy problems. (National Agency to Fight Illiteracy, 2007). Older French adults were more affected than younger ones, with the rates of low literacy being 14% among 46- to 65-year-olds but about 5% for those aged 18 to 35.
- In the Netherlands some 1.5 million adults, of whom roughly 1 million are native Dutch speakers, are classified as functionally illiterate. One-quarter of these native Dutch speakers are almost completely illiterate. In addition, one in ten Dutch-speaking adults functions at the lowest level of literacy. Among employed people, 6%, or one in fifteen workers, have great difficulty reading and writing (Reading and Writing Foundation, 2008, drawing on the 1998 International Adult Literacy Survey).

As these examples suggest, illiteracy and low literacy are not confined to poor countries. Incomplete formal education, high unemployment or underemployment and lack of access to adult education all contribute to a weakening of literacy skills. While largely hidden, low literacy affects sizable populations in rich countries, acting as a barrier to greater social mobility and equality. □

29. The International Adult Literacy and Skills Survey defined levels 1 and 2 as low proficiency and levels 3, 4 and 5 as medium to high proficiency.

Assessing gender disparities and inequalities in education

Goal 5: Eliminating gender disparities in primary and secondary education by 2005, and achieving gender equality in education by 2015, with a focus on ensuring girls' full and equal access to and achievement in basic education of good quality.

The Dakar Framework for Action sets out an ambitious two-part agenda on gender equity. Achieving gender parity in school participation is one part. The other is progress towards gender equality in educational opportunities and outcomes. The combination of the two makes the Dakar Framework far broader in scope than other international development targets, including the MDGs (Colclough, 2007).

How is the world performing against these Dakar benchmarks? The record is mixed. There has been sustained progress towards parity as captured by the gender parity index (GPI), the ratio of male to female enrolment rates. However, the 2005 target for eliminating gender disparities was missed in many countries. Ensuring that the same fate does not befall the 2015 targets will require renewed urgency and commitment. Although progress towards equality is inherently more difficult to measure, clearly much remains to be done.

Gender disparities: still deeply entrenched

The world has made continued progress towards gender parity but many countries still have a long way to travel. In 2006, only 59 of the 176 countries with data available had achieved gender parity (defined as a GPI of GER ranging from 0.97 to 1.03) in both primary and secondary education. That is twenty more than in 1999. But the fact that over half the countries have not achieved gender parity is a source of concern.

About two-thirds of the countries with data available had achieved gender parity at the primary level by 2006. However, more than half the countries in sub-Saharan Africa, South and West Asia, and the Arab States had yet to achieve gender parity. These three regions also account for most of the countries furthest away from achieving the goal (Table 2.13).

At the secondary level many more countries have failed to achieve gender parity. In 2006, only 37% of countries with data, mostly in North America and Europe, had achieved parity. Gender gaps in secondary schools existed in almost all the countries in sub-Saharan Africa, and South and West Asia, in three-quarters of the countries in East Asia and the Pacific, and in half the countries in Latin America and the Caribbean. Worldwide there are about as many countries with gender disparities at the expense of girls (fifty-eight) as at the expense of boys (fifty-three). Countries in the first group are mostly from less developed regions, including sub-Saharan Africa, and South and West Asia. Boys' underparticipation, particularly in upper secondary education, is increasingly marked in Latin America and the Caribbean.

At the tertiary level only a handful of the countries for which data are available have achieved gender parity. In around two-thirds of countries, female enrolment tended to be higher than male enrolment, particularly in the more developed regions (e.g. North America and Western Europe, and Central and Eastern Europe) and in the Caribbean and Pacific. In sub-Saharan Africa, and South and West Asia, the majority of countries have enrolment gaps favouring male students.

The 2005 target for eliminating gender disparities was missed in many countries

Primary education: substantial progress but more effort needed to reach gender parity

Globally, most of the seventy-one countries with data that had not achieved gender parity in primary education by 2006 had nonetheless made progress since 1999 (Figure 2.31). On a less positive note, some countries were moving in the wrong direction. For example, the Dominican Republic, the Libyan Arab Jamahiriya, Mauritania, Niue and Saint Lucia registered gender parity in 1999 but not 2006. In the Congo, gender disparities increased significantly.

Though some countries in South and West Asia failed to meet the gender parity goal, there has been significant progress since Dakar. The region's average GPI rose from 0.84 to 0.95 between 1999 and 2006. Bhutan, India and Nepal have all achieved gender parity in primary education since Dakar, or are close. However, Pakistan, with a large overall school-age population (see the UPE section) still enrols only eighty girls for every hundred boys at primary level.

Table 2.13: Distribution of countries according to their distance from the gender parity goal in primary, secondary and tertiary education, 2006

	Disparities in favour of boys/men			Parity	Disparities in favour of girls/women			
	Far from the goal: GPI below 0.80	Intermediate position: GPI between 0.80 and 0.94	Close to the goal: GPI between 0.95 and 0.96	Goal achieved: GPI between 0.97 and 1.03	Close to the goal: GPI between 1.04 and 1.05	Intermediate position: GPI between 1.06 and 1.25	Far from the goal: GPI above 1.25	Number of countries in the sample
Primary education								
Sub-Saharan Africa	5	16	3	15	1	1		41
Arab States	1	6	2	9	1			19
Central Asia			2	5	1			8
East Asia and the Pacific		6	4	19			1	30
South and West Asia	2		3	3			1	9
Latin America and the Caribbean		4	5	25	2	1		37
North America and Western Europe			1	23				24
Central and Eastern Europe			2	17				19
Total	**8**	**32**	**22**	**116**	**5**	**2**	**2**	**187**
Secondary education								
Sub-Saharan Africa	15	11		3	1	4	1	35
Arab States	3	3	2	3	2	5		18
Central Asia		1	1	4	1	1		8
East Asia and the Pacific	2	5		7	4	8		26
South and West Asia	2	4		2		1		9
Latin America and the Caribbean		2	1	16	4	12	2	37
North America and Western Europe		1	2	15	3	3		24
Central and Eastern Europe		1	2	15	1			19
Total	**22**	**28**	**8**	**65**	**16**	**34**	**3**	**176**
Tertiary education								
Sub-Saharan Africa	20	2		2		4		28
Arab States	5				1	3	6	15
Central Asia	2	1				2	3	8
East Asia and the Pacific	4	2		1		3	5	15
South and West Asia	5	1				1		7
Latin America and the Caribbean		2		1		4	15	22
North America and Western Europe		1			1	8	13	23
Central and Eastern Europe	1					4	13	18
Total	**37**	**9**	**0**	**4**	**2**	**29**	**55**	**136**

Source: Annex, Statistical Tables 9A and 12.

Progress towards gender parity in sub-Saharan Africa has been slow and uneven. The mean regional GPI rose from 0.85 in 1999 to 0.89 in 2006. But the Central African Republic, Chad, Côte d'Ivoire, Mali and the Niger had fewer than eighty girls enrolled in primary school for every hundred boys in 2006. On the other hand, parity has been achieved in many other countries, including Ghana, Kenya and the United Republic of Tanzania.[30] These outcomes demonstrate that gender differences in education can be overcome through public policy action and changes in attitude.

30. The full list of countries having achieved gender parity in primary education in the region: Botswana, Gabon, Ghana, Kenya, Lesotho, Mauritius, Namibia, Rwanda, Sao Tome and Principe, Senegal, Seychelles, Uganda, the United Republic of Tanzania, Zambia and Zimbabwe.

Access to school: where gender disparities begin

Disparities at the entry point to formal education run counter to the principles of human rights. One of the characteristics of universal rights is that they do not differentiate between children on the basis of their gender – and education is a universal right. Beyond the issues raised by basic rights provision, gender disparities at school entry are reflected in future disparities as children progress through school.

Intake disparities and trends broadly mirror those for total enrolment (Figure 2.32). Gaps are widest in South and West Asia, and sub-Saharan Africa

Figure 2.31: Changes in gender disparities in primary gross enrolment ratios between 1999 and 2006

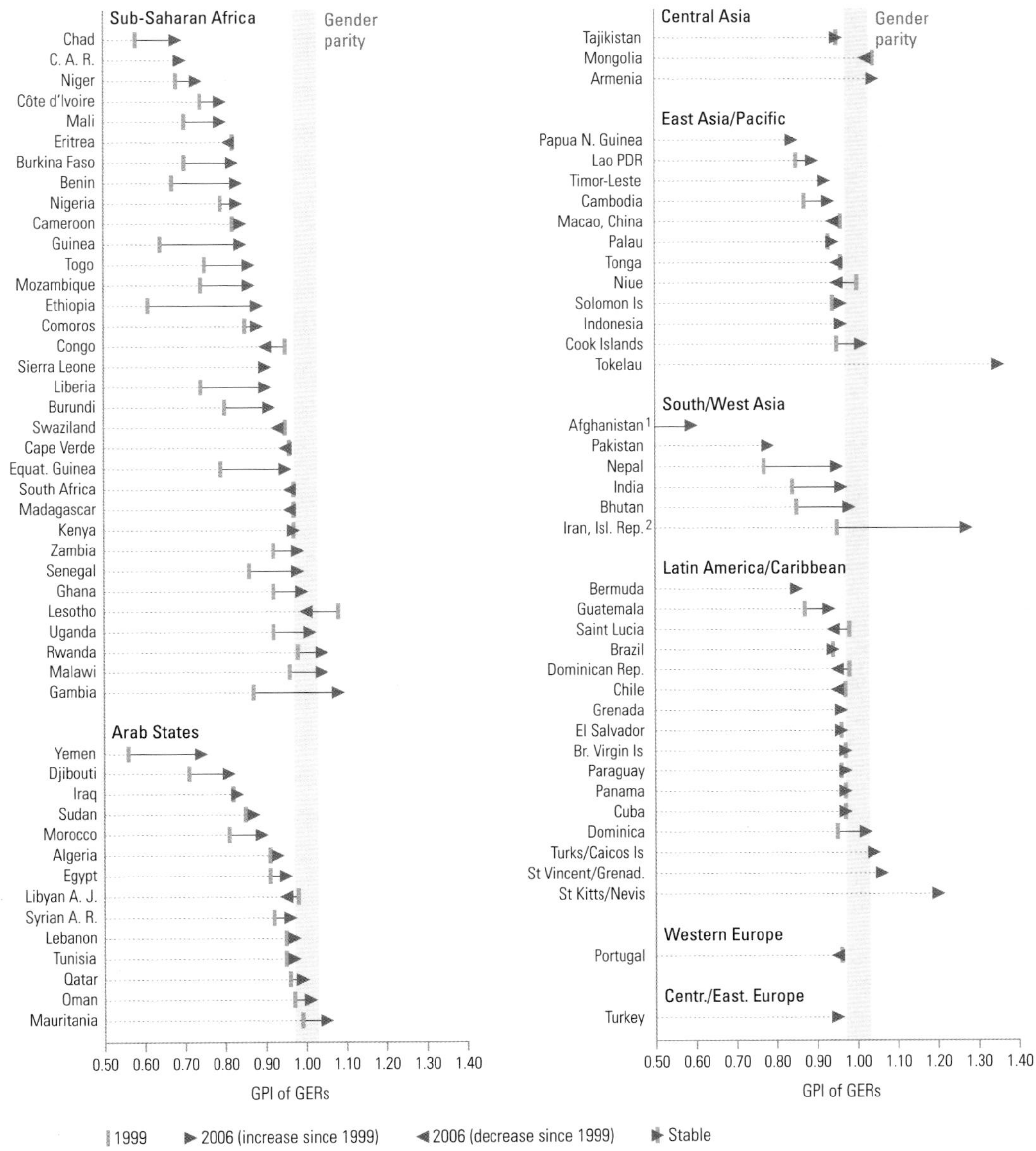

Notes: Excludes countries with GPI between 0.97 and 1.03 in both years. See source table for detailed country notes.
1. In 1999, the GPI for Afghanistan was 0.08.
2. The high increase in female enrolment in the Islamic Republic of Iran is due to recent inclusion in enrolment statistics of literacy programmes in which women are overrepresented.
Source: Annex, Statistical Table 5.

GPIs for Ethiopia, Liberia and Nepal increased by 30% between 1999 and 2006

(average GPIs of 0.94 and 0.92, respectively, in 2006). On a more positive note, in South and West Asia the GPI registered an 11% gain between 1999 and 2006. Some countries in the region reported spectacular progress. For example, the GPI for Nepal increased by 30% and the country achieved gender parity. While overall progress in sub-Saharan Africa has been less marked, Ethiopia and Liberia each achieved a 30% increase in GPI. Burundi had attained gender parity in school access by 2006 (see annex, Statistical Table 4).

School progression

In many countries, girls are less likely to repeat grades, have a greater chance of reaching the final grade and are more likely to complete the primary school cycle.

Grade repetition. In 114 of the 146 countries with data for 2006, girls repeated less than boys (see annex, Statistical Table 6). However, lower repetition rates for girls are not necessarily related to progress in gender parity in enrolment.

Figure 2.32: Changes in gender disparities in access to primary education between 1999 and 2006, by region

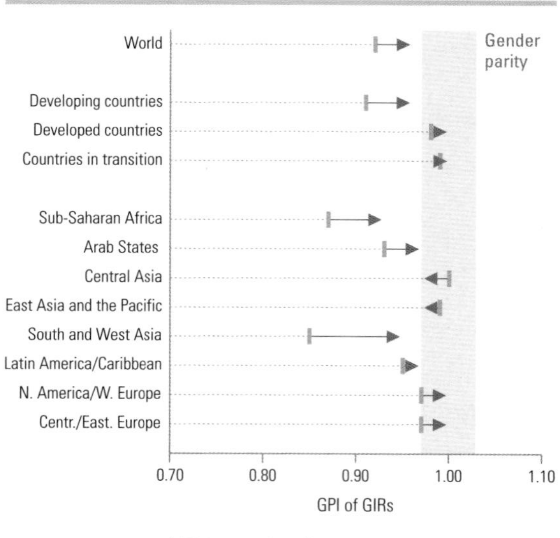

Source: Annex, Statistical Table 4.

In Afghanistan, which had fewer than seventy girls per hundred boys entering school in 2005, the percentage of primary school repeaters was 14% among girls but 18% for boys. Most of the small number of countries where the percentage of female primary-school repeaters was higher were in sub-Saharan Africa. Their ranks included Chad, Guinea, Liberia, Mali, the Niger, Nigeria and Sierra Leone.

School retention. In 63 countries out of the 115 with data, there was gender parity in survival rates to the last grade of primary education in 2005 (again defined as GPI between 0.97 and 1.03). In 36 of the other 52 countries where gender disparities remained, the GPI for the survival rate to the last grade favoured girls – in some cases by a wide margin (Table 2.14). On the other hand, girls' survival rates to the last grade were much lower than boys' in the Central African Republic, Chad, Iraq and Togo.

Gender disparities narrowed in more than half of the 142 countries with data

Table 2.14: Gender disparities in survival rates to last grade, 1999 and 2005

Higher survival for boys (16 countries)

	GPI 1999	GPI 2005
Sub-Saharan Africa		
C. A. R.	...	0.81
Togo	...	0.83
Chad	0.82	0.85
Niger	...	0.90
Eritrea	0.95	0.90
Guinea	...	0.92
Zambia	0.88	0.93
Mali	0.93	0.93
Benin	...	0.93
Mozambique	0.82	0.96
Arab States		
Iraq	0.92	0.78
Yemen	...	0.93
Mauritania	...	0.93
Morocco	1.01	0.95
Central Asia		
Azerbaijan	1.02	0.94
Latin America/Caribbean		
Guatemala	1.08	0.96

Higher survival for girls (36 countries)

	GPI 1999	GPI 2005
Sub-Saharan Africa		
Ethiopia	1.09	1.04
Nigeria	...	1.04
Madagascar	1.02	1.05
Burkina Faso	1.07	1.05
U. R. Tanzania	...	1.05
South Africa	0.96	1.06
Cape Verde	...	1.06
Comoros	...	1.07
Rwanda	...	1.08
Botswana	1.09	1.10
Namibia	1.06	1.10
Burundi	...	1.12
Swaziland	1.06	1.13
S. Tome/Principe	...	1.29
Lesotho	1.32	1.32
Arab States		
Lebanon	1.07	1.09
East Asia/Pacific		
Indonesia	...	1.05
Cambodia	0.87	1.06
Philippines	...	1.14
Kiribati	...	1.18

	GPI 1999	GPI 2005
South/West Asia		
Pakistan	...	1.07
Bangladesh	1.16	1.07
Bhutan	1.10	1.08
Nepal	1.10	1.10
Latin America/Caribbean		
El Salvador	0.99	1.07
Uruguay	...	1.04
Argentina	1.01	1.04
Paraguay	1.06	1.06
Venezuela, B. R.	1.09	1.07
Bahamas	...	1.07
Trinidad/Tobago	...	1.09
Honduras	...	1.09
Colombia	1.08	1.10
Dominican Rep.	1.13	1.12
Nicaragua	1.20	1.18
N. America/W. Europe		
Luxembourg	1.11	1.04

Notes: Excludes countries with GPIs between 0.97 and 1.03 in 2005. Countries with the highest disparities (GPI below 0.90 and above 1.10 in 2005) are highlighted. See source table for detailed country notes.
Source: Annex, Statistical Table 7.

Gender disparities in secondary education: different scales, different patterns

Figure 2.33 documents global progress on gender parity at secondary level. Developed and transition countries had generally achieved gender parity in secondary education by 2006, while the average GPI for developing countries was 0.94, below the world average. Among the developing regions, the Arab States, South and West Asia, and sub-Saharan Africa combined low participation with low GPIs. In several countries in these regions – including Afghanistan, Benin, Eritrea, Ethiopia, Iraq, Mali, the Niger and Yemen – the secondary GERs for girls were less than 70% of those for boys (see annex, Statistical Table 8). Conversely, in many countries in Latin America and the Caribbean, more girls were enrolled than boys at secondary level. Socio-economic context, occupational practices and gender identity in school all appear to play a role in keeping boys away from school. Particularly among disadvantaged and excluded groups, boys are more likely to leave school early to earn a living, opting for shorter and less academic secondary education programmes that do not offer the chance to continue to the tertiary level (UNESCO, 2007*a*).

Expansion of secondary school enrolment has led to reductions in gender disparities in almost all regions. Several countries in South and West Asia have registered rapid progress. Many factors have contributed, including increased primary enrolment and completion for girls, rising average incomes and falling poverty rates. Public policy has also played a key role. In Bangladesh, which has transformed patterns of gender disparity within a decade or so, the creation of financial incentives for girls' education has been critical (Box 2.13). The notable exception to the generally improving situation with respect to gender parity is sub-Saharan Africa, where the GPIs of secondary GERs fell slightly in 2006 (Figure 2.33).

The overall positive trend towards gender parity is also evident at country level. Gender disparities narrowed in more than half of the 142 countries with data (see annex, Statistical Table 8). Progress was striking in many countries, particularly those where gender disparities were still substantial in 1999 (Figure 2.34; see countries above the line). GPIs rose by more than 20% in Benin, Cambodia, Chad, the Gambia, Guinea, Nepal, Togo, Uganda and Yemen. While girls' secondary school participation has worsened in several countries,[31] gender disparities at the expense of boys have increased in some, including Argentina, El Salvador, Georgia, the Republic of Moldova and Tunisia.

Figure 2.33: Change in gender disparities in secondary gross enrolment ratios between 1999 and 2006, by region

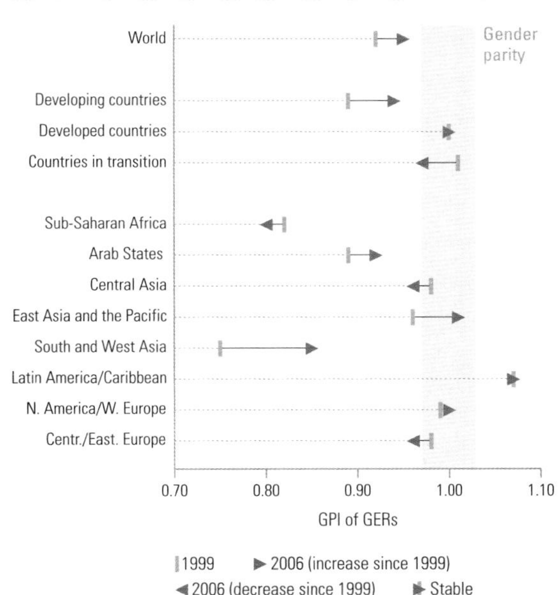

Source: Annex, Statistical Table 8.

The Arab States, South and West Asia, and sub-Saharan Africa combined low participation with low GPIs

Gender disparities in tertiary education: large differences between regions

The world GPI of the tertiary GER rose from 0.96 in 1999 to 1.06 in 2006 (Figure 2.36). This shows that more women than men are enrolled in tertiary education worldwide. However, there are large differences among regions. More women are enrolled in developed and transition countries (GPIs of 1.28 and 1.29, respectively, in 2006), while on average men retain an advantage in developing countries (0.93). The situation of developing regions varies, with higher rates of female participation in the Caribbean (1.69) and the Pacific (1.31), and far fewer female students in tertiary education in South and West Asia (0.76), and sub-Saharan Africa (0.67). In some countries, including Afghanistan, the Central African Republic, Chad, Eritrea, the Gambia, Guinea and the Niger, fewer than thirty women were enrolled for every hundred men in 2006.

31. Azerbaijan, Cameroon, the Comoros, Djibouti, Eritrea, Kenya, Mozambique, Nigeria, Oman, Rwanda and Tajikistan.

Figure 2.34: Changes in gender disparities in secondary gross enrolment ratios between 1999 and 2006

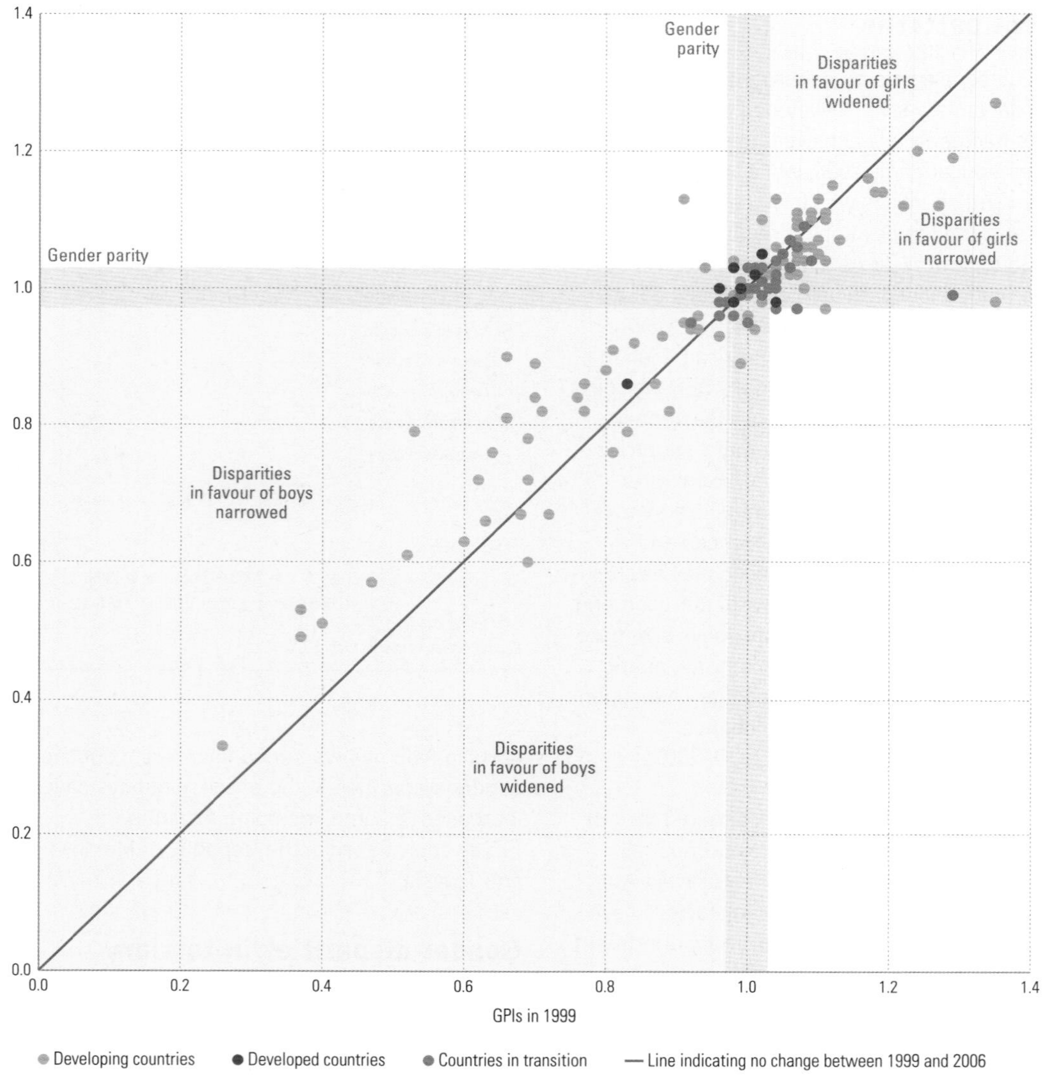

Source: Annex, Statistical Table 8.

There is a strong association between poverty and gender inequalities in education

Gender disparities within countries

Global and regional data provide an insight into the position of the average girl or woman. But, as in other areas highlighted in this chapter, averages can conceal as much as they reveal. Within countries, some girls face greater disadvantage than others. Being born into a poor household, living in a rural area or being a member of a particular ethnic or language group can multiply and reinforce disadvantages that come with gender.

Gender parity and poverty

Cross-national research using household survey data carried out for this Report underlines the strong association between poverty and gender inequalities in education (Harttgen et al., 2008). Children in poor households are less likely to attend school than their wealthier counterparts, irrespective of whether they are boys or girls. Cutting across the wealth divide is an important gender dynamic. Gender disparities are inversely related to wealth: they rise for girls born into the poorest households. This disadvantage also tends to be greater at the secondary level than at the

Box 2.13: Bangladesh's triumph: achieving gender parity by 2005

Bangladesh is one of the few countries in the world to have met the Dakar and MDG target of achieving gender parity in primary and secondary education by 2005 – and it did so ahead of schedule.

At the start of the 1990s, boys in Bangladesh were three times more likely to get to secondary school than girls. By the end of the decade, that immense gap had been closed. Bangladesh is the only country besides Sri Lanka in South and West Asia to have achieved the EFA gender parity goal (Figure 2.35).

Good governance has played a major role, with public policies helping create an enabling environment for gender parity. Programmes aimed at creating incentives for girls' education have been particularly important. In the mid-1990s, rural girls entering secondary school were exempted from tuition fees and given a small stipend or scholarship. Successive reforms strengthened the programme. To keep receiving the benefits, girls must demonstrate attendance rates of 75% or above, pass twice-yearly exams and remain unmarried. Funding for schools also is conditional upon the participation of girls in the stipend programme. Thus the incentives extend from the home to the school.

The impact of the stipend programme reaches well beyond education. Improved levels of secondary education among girls are associated with declines in child mortality, better nutrition, expanded employment opportunities and a narrowing of the gender gap in wages (Al-Samarrai, 2007; World Bank, 2005g).

Bangladesh's success provides important lessons for countries making slower progress towards gender parity. Nevertheless, important challenges remain. Only one child in five who start secondary school will successfully pass the school certificate exam, and girls still lag behind boys on this indicator.

Source: Bangladesh Bureau of Educational Information and Statistics (2006).

Figure 2.35: Gender parity index of secondary school enrolment, Bangladesh

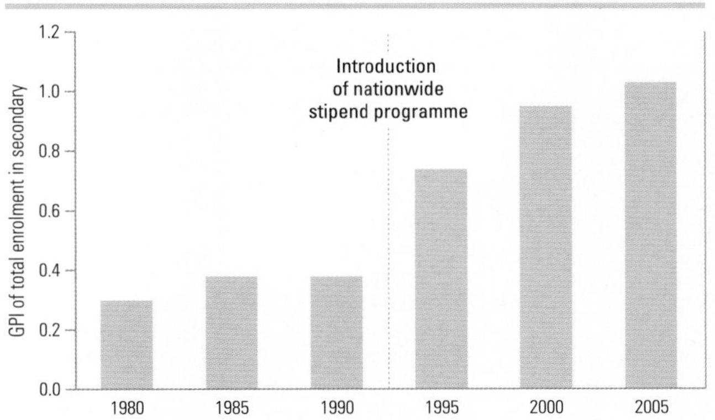

Note: The GPI calculations include general secondary schools and madrasas.
Source: Bangladesh Bureau of Educational Information and Statistics (2006).

primary level (Figure 2.37). While the transmission mechanisms are often complex, poverty has a generalized effect of exacerbating gender inequality.

As for the wealth-based disparities affecting girls, gender differences in net attendance rates tend to be wider for poorer households in countries with relatively low levels of school attendance. Countries such as Burkina Faso, Chad, Guinea, Mali, Nepal, the Niger and Zambia illustrate this point (Figure 2.37). In Mali, the GPI of the primary school net attendance rate in 2001 was only 0.60 for the poorest quintile, whereas many more girls in the richest 20% of households were attending primary school. If these findings were placed on a global scale, Mali's poorest households would rank at the bottom of the international league table. The gap is even more striking at the secondary level, with the GPI about 0.50 for the bottom quintile compared with an average value of 0.96 for the richest group. In some countries where average net attendance rates are higher for girls than boys, the relationship between poverty and gender disparities works the other way.[32] For example, in the Philippines the GPI

Figure 2.36: Change in gender disparities in tertiary gross enrolment ratio by region between 1999 and 2006

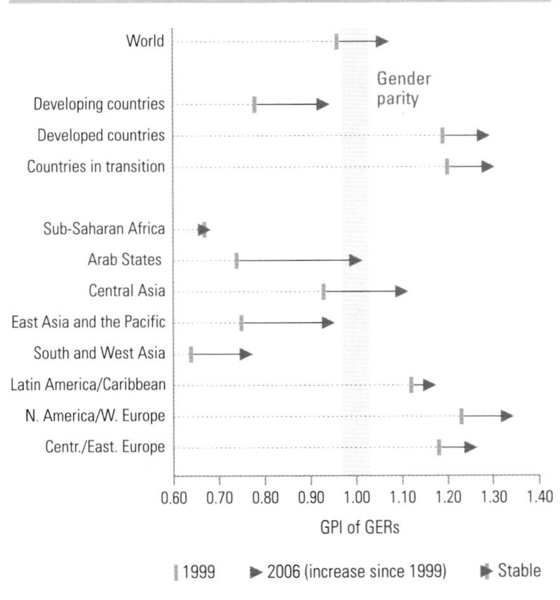

Source: Annex, Statistical Table 9A.

32. This is the case in primary education for Cambodia, Haiti, Madagascar, Malawi, Rwanda and Senegal; in secondary education for Colombia and the Philippines; and at both levels in Ghana and Nicaragua.

Figure 2.37: Gender parity index of net attendance rates, by education level and wealth quintile, selected countries, most recent year

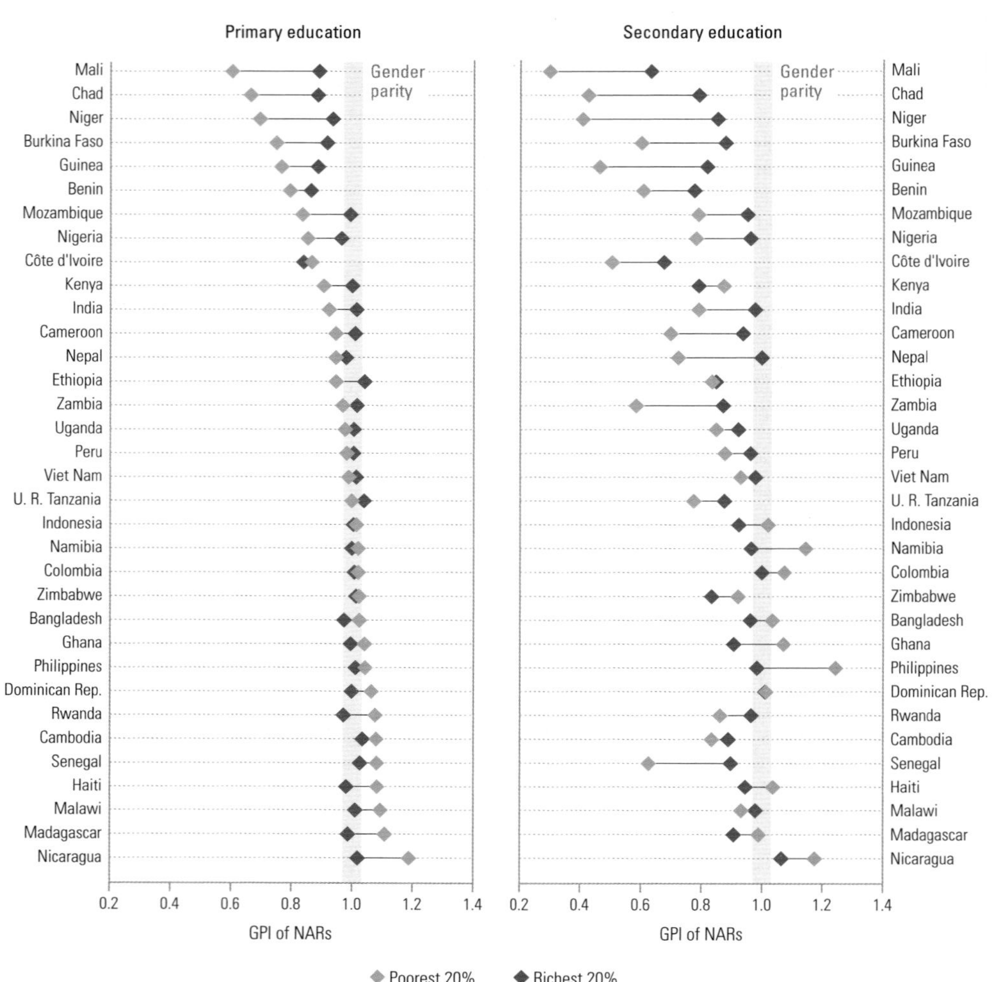

Source: Demographic and Health Surveys, calculations by Harttgen et al. (2008).

School proximity has a positive effect on attendance, especially for girls

of the secondary school net attendance rate for the poorest quintile was 1.24 compared with 0.98 for the richest.

When it comes to school attendance, poverty weighs more heavily on girls than boys. In some cases it weighs far more heavily. The attendance disparity ratios of the richest to poorest quintile are significantly higher for girls than for boys in Burkina Faso, Chad, Guinea, Mali and the Niger. These ratios say something important about the unequal distribution of opportunity. For example, in Mali girls from the richest households are four times more likely to be attending primary school than the poorest girls, an advantage rising to eight times at the secondary level.

Other drivers of gender disadvantages

Wealth disparities interact with wider social, economic and cultural factors to disadvantage girls. As an important cross-country research exercise shows, being born into a group that is indigenous, a linguistic minority, low caste or geographically isolated can magnify disadvantage (Lewis and Lockheed, 2008):

- Indigenous girls in Guatemala are less likely to be enrolled than other demographic groups (Hallman et al., 2007). At age 7, only 54% of indigenous girls are in school, compared with 71% of indigenous boys and 75% of non-indigenous girls. By age 16, only one-quarter of indigenous girls are enrolled, compared with

45% of boys. Poverty has a magnifying effect, with only 4% of 'extremely poor' indigenous girls aged 16 attending school, compared with 45% of their 'non-poor' counterparts.

- India's caste system has a major effect on participation, with 37% of girls aged 7 to 14 belonging to scheduled castes or tribes not attending school, compared with 26% of girls from the majority Hindu group (Lewis and Lockheed, 2006).

- Poor rural girls in Pakistan are among the most deprived in the country. Girls in urban areas and from the highest income group are almost as likely as their male counterparts to attend school or complete the five primary grades (Lloyd et al., 2007). By contrast, one girl for every three boys attends school among the poorest rural households.

- In the Lao People's Democratic Republic, poor rural non-Lao-Tai girls aged between 6 and 12 have the lowest attendance rate of any group. In 2002/2003 their attendance rate was 46%, compared with 55% for poor non-Lao-Tai boys and 70% among poor rural Lao-Tai girls. Poverty and the need to work seem to be the main reasons children do not go to school or drop out early (King and van de Walle, 2007).

Cultural attitudes and practices that promote early marriage, enforce seclusion of young girls or attach more value to boys' education can form a powerful set of barriers to gender parity. In Nepal, 40% of girls are married by age 15 – a barrier to school completion. Norms that keep girls at home during the menses reduce their time in school and lower their school performance (Lewis and Lockheed, 2006). Distance from school is also associated with strong gender disparity effects, especially in rural areas (UN Millennium Project, 2005*b*). In the Lao People's Democratic Republic, distance to school is negatively related to enrolment (King and van de Walle, 2007). Similarly, research in Pakistan reports that having a state school in a village has a strong positive effect on the probability that girls aged 10 to 14 will be enrolled (Lloyd et al., 2007).

Public policy and governance initiatives can help overcome gender inequalities. Removing fees and providing incentives for girls to be in school can counteract financial pressures on households. Building schools close to rural communities and recruiting local teachers can help narrow gender disparities in rural areas. Removing cultural barriers to equity is more difficult. It requires long-term public education, committed political leadership and legislation enforcing the equal rights of girls.

Gender equality in education: more difficult to achieve

In addition to the target of eliminating gender disparities in primary and secondary education by 2005, the EFA gender goal calls for achieving gender equality in education by 2015, with a focus on ensuring girls full and equal access to and achievement in basic education of good quality. That part of the goal is more challenging, as this Report's monitoring of learning outcomes and school practices reveals.

Learning outcomes and subject choice: gender differences persist

Girls and boys achieve very different outcomes in school, not just in overall performance but also by subject. Features of education systems and classroom practices partly explain these differences, but such school-based factors interact with wider social, cultural and economic forces that structure expectations, aspirations and performance along gender lines.

Student assessment results show large gender differences

Student assessment results show wide-ranging gender differences. While the disparities vary, four distinctive patterns emerge:

- **Girls continue to outperform boys in reading literacy and language arts.** This effect holds across a diverse group of countries, including those with significant gender disparities in school participation, such as Burkina Faso in sub-Saharan Africa and Morocco in the Arab States (UNESCO, 2007*a*). In one of the most recent international student assessments, the 2006 Progress in International Reading Literacy Study (PIRLS), average scores on the combined reading literacy scale were significantly higher for girls than for boys in forty-three of the forty-five countries participating (Mullis et al., 2007). Girls' average score across all forty-five countries was seventeen points higher than that for boys, although variations by country were wide. Elsewhere, the 2006 Segundo Estudio Regional Comparativo y Explicativo (SERCE) conducted in Latin America found that girls did significantly better than boys in reading achievement in grades 3 and 6 in half of the sixteen countries participating (UNESCO-OREALC, 2008).[33]

Girls are outperforming boys in mathematics in a growing number of countries

- **Historically, boys have outperformed girls in mathematics in all grades of primary and secondary education – but that picture is changing.** Girls increasingly perform at levels equal to or better than those of boys (Ma, 2007). For example, in Francophone Africa, among students tested in the Programme d'analyse des systèmes éducatifs de la CONFEMEN (PASEC), there were no appreciable gender differences in mathematics achievement at second-grade level; in the fifth grade, small gender differences in favour of boys were reported in half of the eight participating countries (Michaelowa, 2004*b*).[34] Among sixth graders tested in fourteen countries or territories by the Southern and Eastern Africa Consortium for Monitoring Educational Quality (in SACMEQ II, 2000–2003), significant male advantages in mathematics were present in Kenya, Mozambique, the United Republic of Tanzania, Zambia and Zanzibar. In the recent SERCE assessment, eight countries[35] demonstrated gender differences, most of them small, in favour of boys in grade 3 (UNESCO-OREALC, 2008). Moreover, girls are outperforming boys in mathematics in a growing number of countries, including Seychelles (SACMEQ II); Cuba (2006 SERCE); Armenia, the Philippines and the Republic of Moldova (grade 4, in the 2003 Trends in International Mathematics and Science Study, or TIMSS); Bahrain and Jordan (eighth grade, TIMSS, 2003); and Iceland (2003, in the OECD-sponsored Programme for International Student Assessment, or PISA). In TIMSS 2003, as many countries showed gender differences in favour of girls as in favour of boys (Ma, 2007).

- **The science gap is often small, though boys tend to maintain an advantage.** Recent science assessments continue to report cases in which boys hold an advantage over girls, but more often than not the difference is statistically insignificant (Ma, 2007). In Latin America, sixth-grade boys outperformed girls in science in Colombia, El Salvador and Peru. In the remaining countries (Argentina, Cuba, the Dominican Republic, Panama, Paraguay and Uruguay) gender differences were mixed and not statistically significant (UNESCO-OREALC, 2008). In TIMSS 2003 boys outperformed girls in some countries while the reverse was true of a smaller group of countries. The evidence indicates a slightly greater male advantage in the higher grade levels: boys outperformed girls in proportionally more countries in grade 8 than in grade 4. In PISA 2006, which tested reading, mathematics and science, gender differences in science were the smallest among the three (OECD, 2007*b*).

- **Subject choice in tertiary education is still marked by strong gender selection effects.** Despite the increase in female participation, some subject areas remain male domains. Globally, women's median share of tertiary science enrolment in 2006 was 29% and their share in engineering was lower still at 16%. On the other hand, in half the countries with the relevant data women accounted for more than two-thirds of students in fields long considered 'feminine', such as education, health and welfare (see annex, Statistical Table 9B). Social scientists have long sought to understand the forces underlying women's under-representation in scientific fields. Recent studies indicate socialization processes may influence girls' orientation to specific disciplines; examples include poor career counselling, lack of role models, negative attitudes from families, fear of mathematics and fear of being in the minority (Morley, 2005). Course and stream selection in upper secondary is also important.

Why do girls perform differently in achievement tests?

The scope and magnitude of the differences point to a conditioning environment that extends from school policies and classroom practices to ascribed gender roles and perceptions in society (UNESCO, 2007*a*).

Social conditioning and gender stereotyping can limit ambition and create self-fulfilling expectations of disparities in outcomes. Recent research underlines a strong association between the degree of gender equality in society at large and the size of gender gaps in mathematics achievement (Guiso et al., 2008). How children are taught is important not just in relaying knowledge, but also in moulding expectations and building self-confidence. Teacher attitudes and practices that translate into different treatment of boys and girls can affect cognitive development and reinforce gender stereotyping (Carr et al., 1999; Tiedemann, 2000). So can textbooks. Content analyses of textbooks in many

33. The eight countries concerned were Argentina, Brazil, Cuba, the Dominican Republic, Mexico, Panama, Paraguay and Uruguay. In addition there was a statistically significant female advantage among sixth graders in Chile.

34. This was the case in Burkina Faso, Mali, the Niger and Senegal. The four other countries participating were Cameroon, Chad, Côte d'Ivoire and Madagascar.

35. Brazil, Chile, Colombia, Costa Rica, El Salvador, Guatemala, Nicaragua and Peru.

countries continue to reveal gender biases, with girls and women under-represented. Despite the general movement towards gender equality, both sexes continue to be shown in highly stereotyped household and occupational roles, with stereotyped actions, attitudes and traits (UNESCO, 2007*a*). Progress towards eliminating gender bias in textbooks seems very slow. While unrefined examples of sexism have largely disappeared, unbalanced and inappropriate learning material remains prevalent (Blumberg, 2007).

Female teachers can serve as role models for young girls, potentially countering gender stereotypes. Globally, female teachers are overrepresented in lower levels of education while the reverse is true at higher levels (Figure 2.38). In many countries, particularly in the developing world, female teachers tend to be clustered in

Figure 2.38: Percentage of female teachers by level of education and by region, 2006

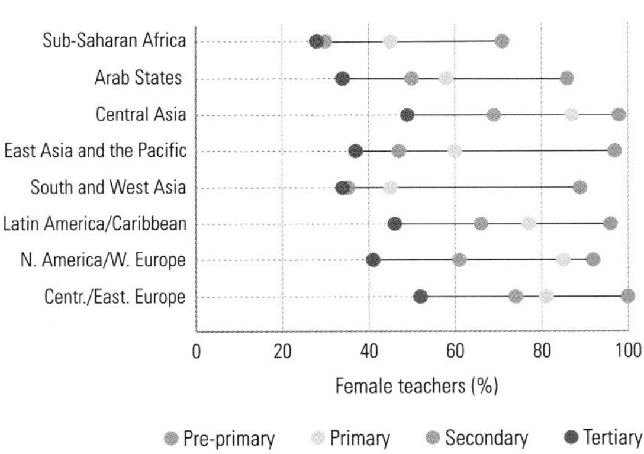

Source: Annex, Statistical Tables 10A and 10B.

urban schools. A recent survey in eleven middle-income countries shows that pupils in rural primary schools are more likely than urban pupils to be taught by male teachers. This is particularly the case in India, Paraguay, Peru and Tunisia (Zhang et al., 2008; see the section on quality below for further survey results and the full list of countries). Rural girls thus have less chance of contact with female role models who might raise their expectations and self-confidence.

The presence of female teachers may also help increase girls' access to school in countries where high gender disparities prevail. Yet it does not always guarantee gender equality in socialization and learning processes (UNESCO, 2007*a*). Teachers of either sex may discriminate informally, reinforcing gender disparities and undermining learning outcomes for disadvantaged groups. Such behaviour can affect learning opportunities if, for example, girls or minority students are seated far from the teacher, do not receive textbooks or are not called on in class. In Yemen, researchers observed that primary school girls were typically seated at the rear of the classroom – an arrangement not conducive to effective participation (Lewis and Lockheed, 2006, pp. 70-1; World Bank, 2003). Greater attention to gender training for teachers would help, but in many countries the gender dimension in teacher training takes a back seat to the teaching of reading and mathematics when it comes to efforts to improve classroom and teacher practices (UNESCO, 2007*a*). □

Progress towards eliminating gender bias in textbooks is slow

Ensuring both equity and the quality of learning

Many children graduate from primary school without acquiring minimum literacy and numeracy skills

Getting all children through a full basic education cycle and into secondary school is an important goal. But the ultimate purpose of schooling is to provide children with an education that equips them with the skills, knowledge and wider perspectives they need to participate fully in the social, economic and political lives of their countries. Education quality is harder to measure than quantitative indicators – but quality and learning is what counts.

Evidence from many developing countries paints a worrying picture on learning achievement. Recent progress in quantitative indicators of school participation has distracted attention from the glaring need to improve education quality at the same time. Many children attend primary school, and even graduate, without ever acquiring a minimum toolkit of literacy and numeracy skills. It would be a Pyrrhic victory for EFA if countries achieved UPE but failed to give children real opportunities to learn. Clearly, then, assuring quality in education – as manifested by the design, scope and depth of learning experiences children encounter in school – is vital, going to the heart of what constitutes good governance in education.

National 'average' learning levels and global disparities

A primary education of good quality should enable children to acquire at a minimum basic skills in language and mathematics, and to aspire to continued learning (Box 2.14). But what level of knowledge and skills do children actually attain in school?

While international assessments consistently spark intense political debate, less attention is paid to the absolute level of learning, especially in developing countries. Recent studies, many based on national assessments, point to deep deficits in student knowledge in many developing countries.

What do learners learn?

In many countries children are acquiring only the most rudimentary skills in school. A recent

Box 2.14: How to measure quality in education?

Measuring quality in education is fraught with difficulty. While indicators exist to measure enrolment, grade attainment and school completion, there is no ready-made yardstick for quality and no globally agreed benchmark for measuring progress.

Participants at the Dakar Forum identified several elements as necessary for quality in education, among them: well-nourished, motivated students; well-trained teachers using active learning techniques; adequate facilities and materials; a relevant, local language curriculum that builds on teachers' and learners' knowledge and experience; a welcoming, gender-sensitive, healthy, safe environment that encourages learning; and a clear definition and accurate assessment of learning outcomes (UNESCO, 2000).

Until recently, monitoring of quality primarily meant tracking input measures, such as educational expenditure, and teacher supply and qualifications. Now, however, with the growth of learning assessments, monitoring increasingly focuses on learning outcomes.[1] Still, as measures of observed teaching and learning remain few and are rarely examined,[2] the bias towards measuring inputs continues (Alexander, 2008).

Another measurement issue concerns equity. Improved quality is typically equated with higher average achievement levels. Student knowledge and competencies are ranked in content domains (e.g. language, mathematics, sciences) based on reported country mean scores on standardized tests. Information about the uneven dispersion of learning across regions, households, ethnic groups and, most importantly, schools and classrooms often goes under-reported.[3]

1. In theory, learning outcomes include subject-based knowledge, broader skills and competencies, social attitudes, moral values and behaviours. In practice, student learning is mainly assessed in terms of either cognitive understanding or skills and competencies. In the past, most international assessments involved high-income countries and a few middle-income ones. Since Dakar more middle- and low-income countries have participated in international and regional assessments. At the same time more national assessments are being conducted, in all regions (Benavot and Tanner, 2007).

2. Studies based on teacher self-reports of teaching processes are more common than those based on classroom observation. See, for example, Anderson et al. (1989).

3. Gender disparities are the exception, having received considerable attention. Disparities based on poverty, ethnicity, language, race, caste, residence and religion are less examined.

assessment in Punjab, Pakistan, demonstrates the point: more than two-thirds of grade 3 students could not form a sentence in Urdu and a similar percentage was unable to subtract three-digit numbers (Das et al., 2006). While most children could recognize and write the English alphabet, large percentages found it difficult to place a word like 'ball' near a picture of a ball. Complicated words and sentences were beyond the reach of the vast majority.

South Asia's problems in education achievement are not confined to Pakistan. Learning assessments in India also point to low levels of literacy and numeracy. Since 2005 a large-scale, non-government initiative has carried out household surveys of rural Indian children to determine their school enrolment status and assess their abilities in reading, arithmetic and English (Pratham Resource Center, 2008). The most recent survey (2007) found that fewer than half the children in standard 3 could read a text designed for standard 1 students, and only about 45% of standard 4 students could read simple words or sentences in English.[36] Just 58% of the students in standard 3 and 38% in standard 4 could subtract or divide. Another recent school-based assessment in India involving over 20,000 students in the states of Andhra Pradesh, Madhya Pradesh, Orissa, Rajasthan and Tamil Nadu confirmed the low level of learning in many primary schools. Many students in standards 3, 4 and 5 were found to lack basic reading, writing and arithmetic skills (Table 2.15).[37]

Assessment exercises elsewhere in the developing world suggest that the situation in Pakistan and India may be less the exception than the rule.

Table 2.15: Percentage of Indian students in standards 3, 4 and 5 who successfully demonstrated basic skills

% of students who can:	Standard 3	Standard 4	Standard 5
Read	59	62	71
Write	47	47	60
Add	52	53	67
Subtract	45	47	59
Multiply	30	40	54
Divide	12	28	41

Note: In reading, children were expected to read ten short, simple sentences at standard 2 level. In writing, they were expected to write ten words and five short, simple sentences of standard 2 difficulty. In arithmetic, they were given five problems each in addition, subtraction, multiplication and division and were defined as competent if they received a score of seventy or above.
Source: Aide et Action (2008).

Research indicates many countries face an immense challenge in helping children acquire minimum language skills:

- In Cambodia a grade 3 assessment of the Khmer language involving almost 7,000 students found that 60% had 'poor' or 'very poor' skills in reading (e.g. as regards pronunciation and word recall) and writing (e.g. punctuation and sentence structure) (Cambodia Education Sector Support Project, 2006).
- In the Dominican Republic, Ecuador and Guatemala half or more of grade 3 students were found to have very low reading levels: they could not recognize the addressee of a family letter or decipher the meaning of a simple text in Spanish (UNESCO-OREALC, 2008).
- A recent assessment in Peru found that as few as 30% of children in grade 1 and only about half in grade 2 could read simple passages from a grade 1 textbook (Crouch, 2006).
- Results from SACMEQ II indicate that fewer than 25% of grade 6 children reached the 'desirable' level of reading literacy in Botswana, Kenya, South Africa and Swaziland, and fewer than 10% in Lesotho, Malawi, Mozambique, Namibia, Uganda and Zambia.

The sheer scale of the quality challenge in education is daunting

These examples draw attention to the sheer scale of the quality challenge in education. Millions of children in the developing world attend primary schools, many for several years, without mastering basic skills. Assessments of more complex abilities, such as conceptualizing, critical thinking and problem-solving, are equally disturbing. For example, in Egypt close to 10,000 fourth grade students in seven governorates were assessed in Arabic, mathematics and science. In all three subjects only one-quarter to one-fifth of students demonstrated an ability to answer questions involving critical thinking and problem-solving (Table 2.16).

Overall, deep learning deficits are too common among schooled children in many developing countries. The policy challenge is clear: creating school systems in which a significant segment of each school-age cohort reaches a minimal learning threshold (Filmer et al., 2006).

36. Standards 1 through 5 are equivalent to primary grades 1 through 5. The 2007 assessment indicated a slight improvement over earlier tests in reading and no change in mathematics. English is introduced by standard 3 in all states except Gujarat; it is the medium of instruction in Jammu and Kashmir State, and Nagaland State.

37. The Children's Competency Assessment tested students in standards 2 through 5.

Table 2.16: Achievement among grade 4 students in Egypt, by cognitive level and content domain, 2006

% of students who correctly answered items assessing:	Arabic	Mathematics	Science
Factual knowledge	50	36	60
Conceptual understanding	43	31	34
Critical thinking and problem-solving	21	17	27

Source: Egypt Ministry of Education (2006).

Figure 2.39: Percentage of low performing students (at or below level 1) in science literacy, PISA 2006

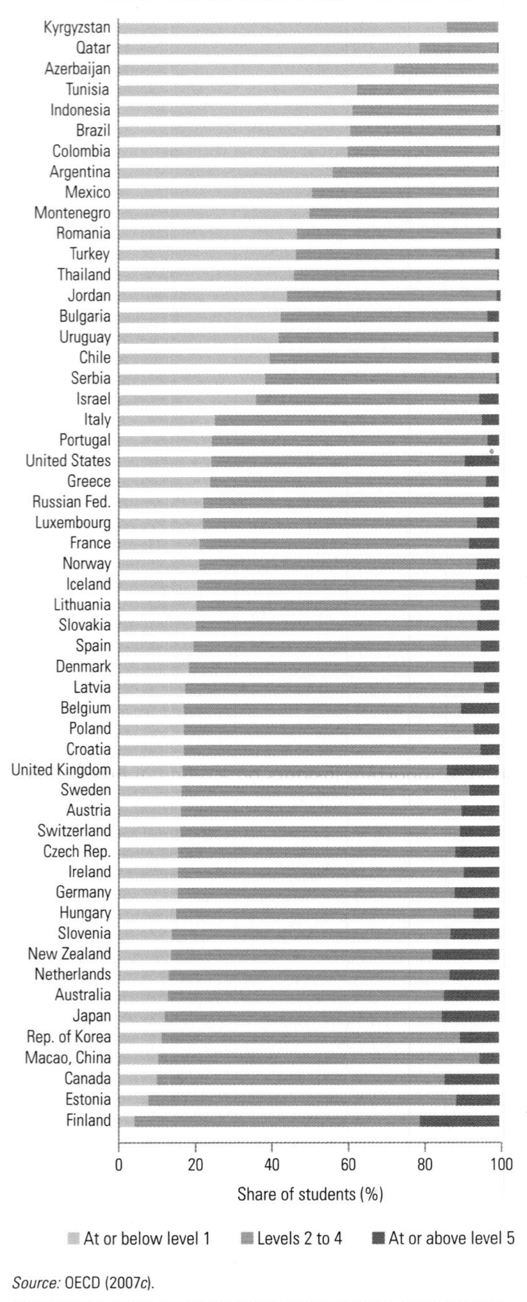

Source: OECD (2007c).

The international divide in learning outcomes

Beyond the concern about low learning levels based on national surveys, international assessments show most developing countries still far behind developed countries. In an increasingly integrated, knowledge-based world economy, these disparities have important implications for development prospects – and for future patterns of globalization.

With more developing countries participating in international assessments over the past twenty years, two consistent findings have emerged. First, there are glaring gaps in achievement between developed and developing country students at similar levels of schooling. Second, the gaps are only partially associated with differences in per capita income.[38] Other differences – linked to school quality, teaching policies and system-wide governance – are also significant.

There are glaring gaps in student achievement between developed and developing country students

International assessments illustrate the extent of low learning levels among 'average' students in participating countries. Results from PISA, which tests 15-year-old students in several competencies, are instructive because they include many non-OECD countries. They highlight striking disparities. The median PISA 2001 scores of Brazilian, Indonesian and Peruvian students, placed on a scale alongside those of students from Denmark, France and the United States, are situated in the lowest 20% of the latter countries' distribution (Filmer et al., 2006). PISA 2006 science results show students from developing countries being much more likely to figure in the lowest achievement levels (Figure 2.39). Over 60% of students from Brazil, Indonesia and Tunisia, but fewer than 10% in Canada and Finland, scored at or below level 1, the lowest level in the PISA science ranking. And fewer than 2% to 3% of students from developing countries attained proficiency levels 5 and 6, whereas 15% or more did so in several OECD countries.

Other international assessments point in a similar direction. In the 2003 TIMSS, half of all grade 8 students achieved the intermediate benchmark (475), but only 17% from the nine participating Arab States[39] did so (UNDP Arab TIMSS Regional Office, 2003). The 2006 PIRLS, testing fourth graders in reading, revealed large disparities between

38. The association is stronger at the lower end of the income scale than at the upper end. In TIMSS 1999, the association between per capita GNP and scores in mathematics and science was about 0.60 (Barber, 2006).

39. Bahrain, Egypt, Jordan, Lebanon, Morocco, the Palestinian Autonomous Territories, Saudi Arabia, the Syrian Arab Republic and Tunisia.

developed and developing countries. The five middle- and low-income countries outside Europe[40] achieved a mean score of 377 – almost 125 achievement points below the international mean (500).[41] Box 2.15 discusses more findings.

While the number of developing countries participating in international assessments has increased, many gaps remain, limiting the scope for cross-country comparison. Exploratory research for this Report attempts to address the problem by standardizing national achievement data in primary education from different assessments to place countries on a single international scale.[42] The exercise shows the achievement scores of many developing countries clustered far below those of developed and transition countries (Figure 2.40).[43] It also suggests that the learning gaps tend to be more pronounced in science than in mathematics and reading (Altinok, 2008).

International assessments can understate the divide between developed and developing countries since they assess learning outcomes only among children in school. They do not include similarly aged children who are currently – or permanently – out of school. Especially in countries where school participation rates are low and dropout rates high, exclusion of out-of-school children can distort national learning profiles. In rural India, for example, when out-of-school children were tested they were half as likely as in-school children to listen to and answer a subtraction problem (Pratham Resource Center, 2008). Similarly, in Ghana, Indonesia and Mexico, tests of language and mathematics among out-of-school youth found lower achievement levels than among enrolled students (Filmer et al., 2006).

Within-country differences in achievement by location and gender are often marked

Box 2.15: New international evidence on learning outcomes: what it reveals about quality

Since the release of the *EFA Global Monitoring Report 2008* (UNESCO, 2007*a*), results from three major international assessments have been published. They provide important insights on a range of qualitative indicators of education performance.

PIRLS 2006 measured grade 4 reading skills. The percentage of students demonstrating basic reading ability – i.e. reaching level 1, the lowest international benchmark – varied from 22% in South Africa and 26% in Morocco to more than 95% in most of North America and Western Europe. The share of students performing at or above the intermediate benchmark, level 2, was over 75% in most OECD countries but less than 20% in developing countries including Indonesia, Morocco and South Africa (Mullis et al., 2007).[1]

PISA 2006 tested 15-year-olds in science, mathematics and reading (OECD, 2007*b*). Twenty of the thirty participating OECD countries had science scores within twenty-five points of the OECD average of 500. Among countries scoring significantly below the OECD average, the variation was considerably greater, from a low of 322 in Kyrgyzstan to a high of 493 in Croatia. PISA 2006 results can be compared with those from 2000 in reading and from 2003 in science and mathematics. For most countries with comparable data, average scores changed relatively little – despite increases in national investment in education (OECD, 2007*b*).

In Latin America the 2006 Segundo Estudio Regional Comparativo y Explicativo (SERCE) assessed reading and mathematics in grade 3, and reading, mathematics and science in grade 6 (UNESCO-OREALC, 2008).[2] Overall, countries fell into four categories: 1) Cuban students outperformed those from other countries in almost all subjects and grade levels; 2) a small group of other consistently high performing countries included Chile, Costa Rica and Uruguay; 3) a large group of relatively poor performing countries included the Dominican Republic, Ecuador, El Salvador, Guatemala, Nicaragua, Panama, Paraguay and Peru; and 4) in countries in the middle – Argentina, Brazil, Colombia and Mexico – pupil achievements varied by subject and grade. For the last three groups, within-country differences in achievement by location and gender were often marked. For example, among poor-performing countries, rural-urban differences were considerably more pronounced in El Salvador, Guatemala and Peru than in the Dominican Republic, Nicaragua and Panama.

1. Of the twenty-seven countries and territories with reading achievement data for both PIRLS 2001 and 2006, eight showed significant gains: Germany, Hong Kong (China), Hungary, Italy, the Russian Federation, Singapore, Slovenia and Slovakia. In Germany, the Russian Federation and Slovakia, improvements in reading achievement were at the expense of equity: gains were made among higher-performing students but not lower-performing ones. Average reading levels declined over time in England (United Kingdom), Lithuania, Morocco, the Netherlands, Romania and Sweden.

2. Sixteen Latin American countries took part in SERCE. The number of countries participating in learning assessments varies: there were forty countries in PIRLS 2006, fifty-seven countries and territories in PISA 2006.

40. Indonesia, the Islamic Republic of Iran, Morocco, South Africa, and Trinidad and Tobago.

41. In addition, two high-income Arab States, Kuwait and Qatar, scored below 350.

42. Another study of this type is Hanushek et al. (2008).

43. Achievement scores for some countries in sub-Saharan Africa, and South and West Asia were excluded due to data limitations.

Figure 2.40: Disparities in mean learning achievement in primary education among developed countries, developing countries and countries

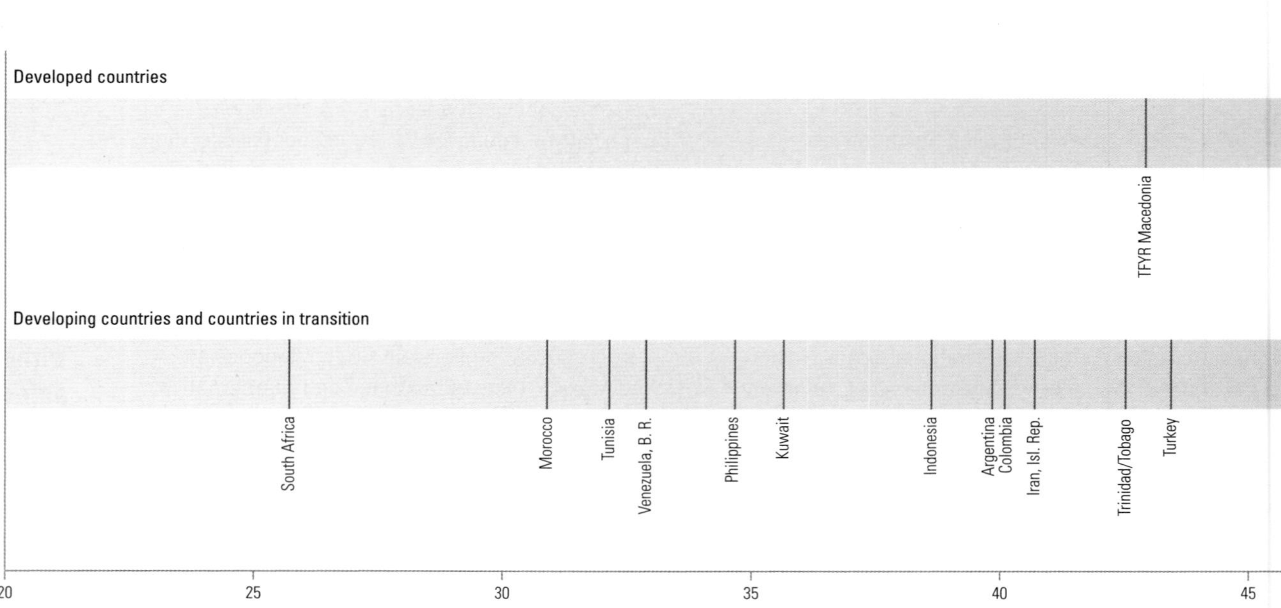

Note: The composite achievement score is the arithmetic mean of all scores of a given country on international assessments between 1995 and 2006. Standardized with a mean of 50 and a standard deviation of 10, it ranges from 0 to 100. Achievement data are only compiled from international and regional assessments, and not from national assessments.
Source: Altinok (2008).

Beyond national averages – huge inequalities in achievement

Unequal learning outcomes, typically related to socio-economic status and other indicators for disadvantage, are most pronounced within countries. They exist at every level: between regions, communities, schools and classrooms. Such unequal outcomes are a source of intense political debate. Parents, policy-makers and often children themselves perceive such disparities as evidence of an unfair and inequitable education system. Improving and equalizing the provision of education of good quality is at the core of the wider EFA governance challenge.

Unequal learning outcomes are most pronounced within countries

Among the huge within-country differences that learning assessments continue to document:

- Reading scores of fourth graders from developing countries varied widely in PIRLS 2006. The gap between the top 5% and bottom 5% was 454 scale points (562 minus 108) in South Africa, 359 points in Morocco and 340 points in Trinidad and Tobago. In all three, high-scoring pupils reached reading levels comparable to some of the best pupils in high-achieving countries (Mullis et al., 2007).
- In SERCE, third-grade reading scores varied extensively in both high- and low-performing countries. In Cuba the point difference between students in the top 10% and bottom 10% of the distribution was 295 scale points (779 minus 484). Most other countries in the region had smaller differences, among them Argentina (236 points), Costa Rica (231), El Salvador (219) and Paraguay (241) (UNESCO-OREALC, 2008).
- Using items based on the 2005 TIMSS, tests were administered to 6,000 ninth-grade students in the Indian states of Rajasthan and Orissa. Not only were average scores very low, with 30% to 40% of the children unable to reach a low international benchmark, but the score distribution was highly unequal: the difference between the top 5% and bottom 5% was among the highest in the world. Students in the top 5% scored higher than the top students in other low-performing countries, and higher than the median students in all but the best-performing countries (Das and Zajonc, 2008; Wu et al., 2007).

in transition, 1995-2006

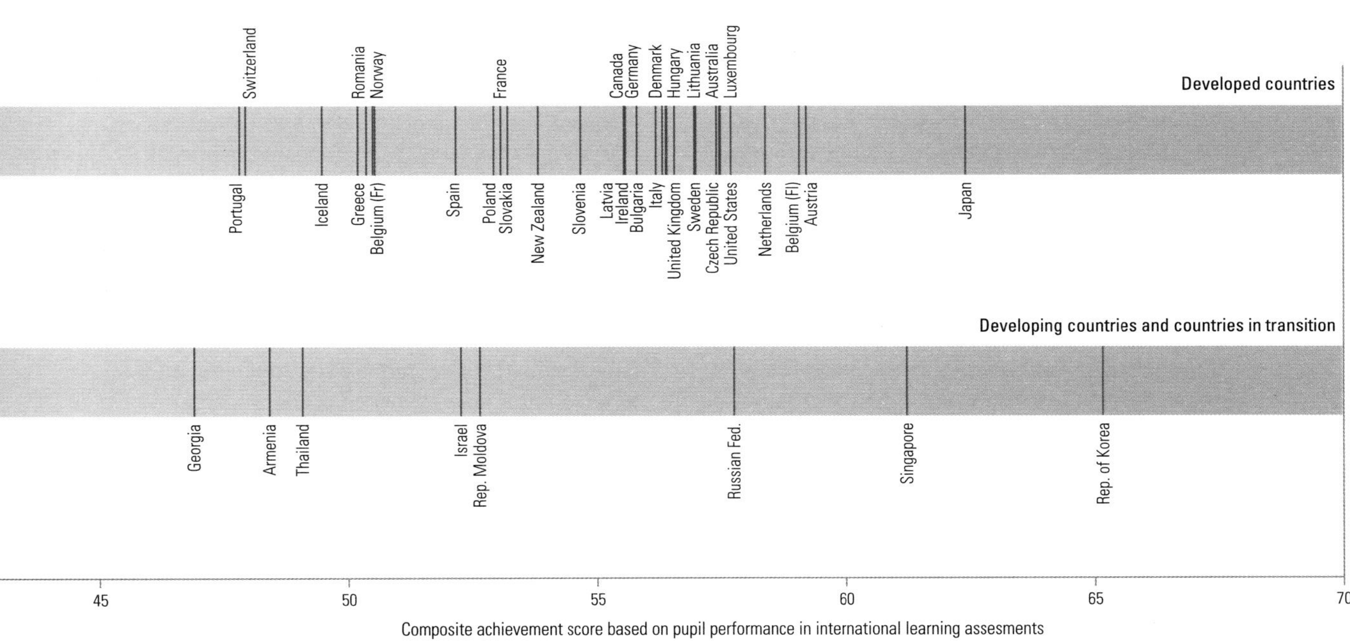

The underlying causes of inequality in learning outcomes are enormously varied. However, research drawing on data from international, regional and national assessments identifies three sets of key factors influencing within-country disparities: student background, school context and system-level characteristics.[44]

Student-related factors

What students bring with them to school influences how well they perform. Some student endowments, such as ability, are inherent and randomly distributed. Others are the product of social, economic and cultural circumstances, such as parents' education, occupation and income; gender (see previous section); home language; and other family characteristics.

Socio-economic-related gaps in achievement are a dominant, recurring theme in national and international research. Students of lower socio-economic status generally score lower than students from more advantaged backgrounds. The level and slope of the socio-economic gradient of learning vary considerably among countries – a key fact, as it shows the influence of public policies in this area (Ma, 2008; Willms, 2006). Interestingly, recent assessments suggest that larger performance gaps linked to socio-economic status exist in Central and Eastern Europe and in North America and Western Europe than in developing countries (Ma, 2008).[45] Research for this Report attempted to clarify the degrees to which occupation, parents' education, family income/ household wealth and 'home literacy' were each associated with pupil achievement in various countries (Ma, 2008). Occupation was found to be the most important socio-economic status component in North America and Europe, while household wealth (family possessions) was the most important in East Asia and the Pacific, and in Latin America and the Caribbean.[46] Parental education, while significant, was found to have less impact. 'Home literacy', defined as the possession of over ten books, had strong positive effects on learning outcomes in most middle- and low-income countries.

Family size and composition also influence learning achievement. Recent research confirms that children with fewer siblings tend to outperform those with more siblings (Dronkers and Robert,

44. See, for example, Fuller (1987), Fuller and Clarke (1994), Keeves (1995), Lockheed and Verspoor (1991), Michaelowa (2004*a*), Mullis et al. (2000), Mullis et al. (2003), Postlethwaite (2004), Riddell (2008), Scheerens (2004) and Wößmann (2003).

45. PISA, employing an index of economic, social and cultural status, found few differences in its effects among the different subject domains: reading, mathematics and science.

46. The author argues that, when it comes to student learning outcomes, in more developed regions social capital at home outweighs material resources at home, whereas in less developed regions the opposite is the case.

Extensive early childhood education boosts equity and helps overcome disadvantage

2008; Park, 2008).[47] Rapid changes in family structure due to divorce, separation, parental death or migration are equally influential. The PISA 2003 mathematics assessment found that in twenty countries with relevant information, students from two-parent homes performed best, on average – a result that held even after controlling for socio-economic status (Hampden-Thompson and Johnston, 2006).[48]

Immigrant status influences learning in many countries. Results from PISA 2003 indicated that first-generation immigrant students (those born abroad) and second-generation students (those whose parents were born abroad) scored lower in reading, mathematics and science than their native counterparts, except in Canada (OECD, 2006*b*).[49] As language proficiencies in the host country improve, achievement disparities among second-generation immigrants decline (Schnepf, 2008). Characteristics of immigrant children's countries of origin and destination also influence achievement (de Heus et al., 2008; Levels et al., 2007). First-generation children from countries where compulsory education lasted longer performed better in science (OECD, 2007*a*) than other, similar children (de Heus et al., 2008). With migration flows increasing worldwide, closing immigration-related inequalities is important not just for achieving equity in education, but also for addressing concerns over social cohesion (International Organization for Migration, 2005; OECD, 2006*b*).

Home language is related to classroom success. In eighteen of the twenty OECD countries participating in PISA 2003, students whose home language differed from the language of instruction had significantly lower scores in mathematics than those who spoke the test language at home (Hampden-Thompson and Johnston, 2006).[50] In many Latin American countries, including Bolivia, Chile, Ecuador, Guatemala, Mexico and Peru, children from households where indigenous languages were spoken scored significantly lower in reading and mathematics than those from non-indigenous households (Flores-Crespo, 2007; Lewis and Lockheed, 2006; McEwan, 2004; McEwan, forthcoming; McEwan and Trowbridge, 2007).[51] In most studies the impact of language remained after adjusting for factors such as poverty, location and other home background indicators.

System-level factors

The way an education system is organized can have a significant bearing on learning outcomes. Rules on promotion between grades, school-leaving exams, institutional differentiation (between different types of school) and instructional differentiation (through ability grouping, streaming, multigrade teaching) all have an impact on learning outcomes. While the impact varies by context, some broad findings emerge from international research (Fuchs and Wößmann, forthcoming; OECD, 2007*a*):

- Sorting students into non-equivalent tracks or streams is associated with reduced equity (unequal learning outcomes) and sometimes lower learning levels. Education systems with very selective academic streams are associated with larger gender gaps in mathematics and science at both primary and secondary level (Bedard and Cho, 2007).

- Extensive early childhood education (of longer duration and higher enrolment coverage) increases equity in education for children from dissimilar family backgrounds (Schütz et al., 2005).

- Public policies and attitudes towards immigration, residency, gender and language are associated with differences in educational opportunities. Where measures encouraging gender equality have been taken, gender gaps in mathematics tend to be smaller (Baker and Jones, 1993; Guiso et al., 2008; Marks, 2008).

47. See also results from national assessments in Cambodia, Ethiopia, Madagascar and Mongolia (Cambodia Education Sector Support Project, 2006; Academy for Education Development and USAID Ethiopia, 2004; Madagascar Ministry of National Education & Scientific Research and UNESCO, 2004; Mongolia Ministry of Education, Culture and Science and UNICEF, 2008).

48. See also Bradshaw and Finch (2002), Downey (1994), Duncan and Brooks-Gunn (1997), Hampden-Thompson and Pong (2005), Haveman et al. (1991), McLanahan and Sandefur (1994) and Pong et al. (2003).

49. This study focused on seventeen countries or territories with large immigrant populations: Australia, Austria, Belgium, Canada, Denmark, France, Germany, Luxembourg, the Netherlands, New Zealand, Norway, Sweden, Switzerland and the United States, among OECD countries, and three non-OECD PISA participants: the Russian Federation, Hong Kong (China) and Macao (China).

50. More recently, poor language achievement by third- and sixth-grade children in the Dominican Republic, Ecuador, Guatemala, Nicaragua, Panama, Paraguay and Peru was reported in SERCE, further illustrating the influence of home language (UNESCO-OREALC, 2008).

51. The 'effect size' of belonging to an indigenous household was, on average, over one-third of a standard deviation; i.e. indigenous children's scores were one-third of a standard deviation lower in Spanish and mathematics than those of non-indigenous children. The indigenous disadvantage was higher for language scores than in mathematics.

- Policies governing the group composition of schools significantly affect learning. The mix of students attending a school – in terms of socio-economic status, ethnicity or race – affects learning not only independently but also indirectly through managerial, pedagogical and psycho-social processes (Dumay and Dupriez, 2007).

- Systems with more privately funded and academically selective schools tend to attain higher learning outcomes, but the achievement advantages tend to be reduced once student background factors are taken into account (OECD, 2007*a*).

- In some assessments, learning outcomes are related to the extent to which schools in a system have autonomy over teacher appointments, budget formulation and allocation, and/or instructional content (see Chapter 3). Evidence from PISA 2006 indicates that learning outcomes tend to be higher in countries that encourage public posting of student performance.

School-based factors

Properly resourced schools, effective teachers and dynamic classrooms are crucial for learning. Even after adjustments for student background and other factors, international research consistently points to large school-based differences in learning outcomes (Willms, 2006). Inequalities in school context and quality are especially pronounced in developing countries and typically account for considerable variation in learning outcomes (Baker et al., 2002; Heyneman and Loxley, 1983).

What makes for an effective learning environment? Dynamic processes are important. Professional leadership, shared vision and goals, teachers who motivate students, and the use of monitoring and evaluation to improve performance are considered key ingredients of 'effective' schools (Creemers, 1997; Reynolds et al., 2002).[52] Sufficient instructional time is also vital (Box 2.16). Dilapidated buildings, overcrowded and under-resourced classrooms, and inadequate supplies of textbooks and workbooks are not conducive to learning. More students from rich families attend well-equipped schools (Table 2.17). The poor state of the school environment in many countries is

Learning gaps in many countries are linked to inadequate and unequal provision of instructional time

Box 2.16: Unequal learning time, unequal outcomes

Learning gaps in many countries are linked to inadequate and unequal provision of instructional time. While almost all countries set official guidelines and rules on the amount of time children should be in school, actual time varies enormously within and among countries (Abadzi, 2007).*

Many factors influence the delivery of instructional time. Armed conflict, ethnic violence, natural disasters and inclement weather can affect the number of days schools are open in some regions and communities and not others (Abadzi, 2007; O'Malley, 2007). Teacher absenteeism and lateness significantly reduce time available for teaching and learning (Abadzi, 2007). The PASEC and SACMEQ surveys report that teacher turnover and late teacher postings leave many African schools unable to follow the official school year (Bonnet, 2007).

Significant disparities in instructional time between schools are reported. An in-depth study of Bangladesh's government primary schools and registered non-government primary schools found large disparities in annual lesson time (Financial Management Reform Programme, 2006*b*). The bottom 10% of government schools provided fewer than 500 lesson hours per year in classes 3, 4 and 5 whereas the top 10% provided more than 860; the equivalent range at the non-government schools was 470 to 700 hours.

In several developing countries school heads report that village schools operate fewer days a year than town/city schools. Similarly, despite uniform countrywide guidelines, grade 4 teachers in village schools in Paraguay, the Philippines and, to a lesser extent, Brazil, Malaysia and Tunisia report teaching significantly fewer annual hours of mathematics and reading than teachers in city/town schools. In some countries the most instructed 10% of pupils receive 50% more instructional time per year than the least instructed 10% (Zhang et al., 2008). In PIRLS 2006 grade 4 teachers also report considerable in-country differences in weekly hours spent on reading (Mullis et al., 2007).

* International agencies recommend 850 to 1,000 hours per year, or about 200 days on a five-day school week (Lockheed and Verspoor, 1991; UNESCO, 2004; World Bank, 2004). In many countries even the official instructional time falls short of this (UNESCO, 2007*a*). Use of double, triple or split shifts significantly reduces yearly instructional time (Abadzi, 2007).

52. Alexander (2008) argues, on the other hand, that the 'effective school' approach aggregates findings from studies conducted by differing methods, at different times and places; inadequately addresses deeper cultural differences having to do with the aims and purposes of each education system; presents teaching as value-neutral, content-free and entirely devoid of the dilemmas of ideal and circumstance; and employs rather arbitrary variables to describe effective schools.

Table 2.17: Percentage of students in grade 10 in well-equipped schools, by parental socio-occupational status[1]

	% of students from highest quartile who attend well-equipped schools	% of students from lowest quartile who attend well-equipped schools
Argentina	61	25
Brazil	64	38
Chile	64	38
Mexico	47	23
Peru	39	10
Latin American countries	59	32
OECD countries[2]	65	58

1. Schools were divided into two groups on the basis of how well they were equipped with libraries, multimedia tools, computer laboratories, chemistry laboratories, etc.
2. Data are for twenty-seven OECD countries, not including Mexico. Regional totals are weighted.
Source: UN Economic Commission for Latin America and the Caribbean (2007).

linked to insufficient financing. Of course, increased spending does not automatically lead to enhanced quality (Hanushek and Luque, 2003).

Many schools lack sufficient toilets, drinking water, desks and books

Research in developing countries in recent years underlines the importance of the school environment. Learning assessments in Madagascar and the Niger found that having electricity in the school significantly improved outcomes (Fomba, 2006; Madagascar Ministry of National Education & Scientific Research and UNESCO, 2004). In Guinea, access to books was shown to significantly improve learning (Blondiaux et al., 2006).

The parlous state of the education infrastructure, documented in past Reports (UNESCO, 2004; UNESCO, 2007*a*), is still of concern. For example, poor and unequal provision of school resources is endemic in sub-Saharan Africa:

- SACMEQ II found that over half the grade 6 students in Kenya, Malawi, Mozambique, Uganda, the United Republic of Tanzania and Zambia attended classrooms that did not have a single book (UNESCO, 2005).
- In these and other countries, 25% to 40% of teachers did not possess a manual in the subjects they taught (Bonnet, 2007).
- Significant percentages of Nigerian students in grades 4 and 6 reported lacking textbooks: 30% in English, 50% in mathematics, 65% in social studies and 75% in science (Nigeria Federal Ministry of Education et al., 2005).

Under such circumstances teachers spend much class time writing lessons and problems on the board while students copy them into exercise books – if they have any.

Poor school infrastructure is also widespread in Latin America. Ecuador, Guatemala, Nicaragua, Panama, Paraguay and Peru have many primary schools lacking several or all of the following: sufficient toilets, potable water, libraries, books and computer rooms (UNESCO- OREALC, 2008). Poorly equipped schools tend to be attended by children from poorer households, exacerbating underlying inequalities in opportunity.

Recent monitoring work underlines the appalling and unequal state of education infrastructure and quality in eleven developing countries (Zhang et al., 2008).[53] Chile, Malaysia and Uruguay were found to have the best-resourced schools, and India, Peru and Sri Lanka the worst. Among key findings:

- School resources are unequally distributed within countries. Schools in cities and towns have significantly more resources (from a list of thirty-one items) than schools in villages and rural areas. Schools attended by more socially advantaged students also have greater resources and private primary schools are better resourced than public sector schools.
- Many schools and classrooms are in a state of disrepair. In Peru, the Philippines and Sri Lanka, half or more of school heads say that the 'school needs complete rebuilding' or 'some classrooms need major repairs'. In all countries except Malaysia, village schools are reported to be in greater need of repair than city/town schools. In India, Peru, the Philippines, Sri Lanka and Tunisia, one-third or more of students attend schools with insufficient toilets.
- Distance and student well-being are serious problems. In the Philippines, Sri Lanka and Tunisia, teachers report that one in seven children has to walk more than 5 kilometres to attend school. Teachers in all countries report that at least 9% of children come to school with an empty stomach, and in some countries the share is as high as 18%.

53. Argentina, Brazil, Chile, India (in the states of Assam, Madya Pradesh, Rajasthan and Tamil Nadu), Malaysia, Paraguay, Peru, the Philippines, Sri Lanka, Tunisia and Uruguay. The response rate in parts of Sri Lanka was low because of armed conflicts and the 2004 tsunami, so results should be interpreted with caution.

- Many countries and schools lack fundamental resources for learning. India, Peru, the Philippines and Sri Lanka suffer an acute shortage of seating. Nearly half of students in Paraguay, the Philippines, Sri Lanka and Tunisia attend schools with no libraries; in Argentina, Chile, Malaysia and Uruguay the share is down to 20% or less. Pupil access to a classroom book corner varies considerably within countries.

- Textbook provision and content remain problems. About 15% to 20% of grade 4 pupils do not have a textbook or have to share one. In Argentina, Paraguay and the Philippines the percentage is higher. Schools in Asian countries and Tunisia rely on materials focusing on basic decoding skills, though most schools in Latin America use more challenging continuous texts (e.g. fables), and imaginary and real-life narrative texts. In general the difficulty and appropriateness of grade 4 texts, and the frequency of their use, varied greatly within and among countries.

Overall, such student, school and system characteristics affect learning outcomes in all countries, with the relative weight of each category varying according to context. New multilevel analyses of student achievement that mostly involve developed and transition countries underscore the overriding importance of student-level factors, followed by school- and system-related factors (Riddell, 2008). Analyses of learning outcomes in developing countries emphasize school resources and teacher-related factors. Clearly governance decisions concerning school infrastructure, classroom processes, and the recruitment, deployment and effectiveness of teachers, as well as the student composition of schools, matter a great deal for learning.

Teacher supply and quality

Delivery of good-quality education is ultimately contingent on what happens in the classroom, and teachers are in the front line of service. To improve student outcomes, having enough teachers and reasonable pupil/teacher ratios (PTRs) is not sufficient: the teachers need to be well trained and motivated. The profile of teachers, and the governance systems through which they are recruited, trained and deployed, have a critical bearing on learning outcomes and on equity.

Numbers and needs worldwide

Good-quality education depends in part on reasonable class sizes. Pupils in large classes have fewer opportunities for participation and interaction with teachers, and generally less access to instructional materials.

More than 27 million teachers were working in primary education institutions worldwide in 2006, 80% of them in developing countries (Table 2.18 and annex, Statistical Table 10A).[54] Total primary teaching staff increased by 5% between 1999 and 2006. The largest increases occurred in sub-Saharan Africa. Teacher numbers also increased in Latin America and the Caribbean. The number of secondary school teachers increased by 5 million over the period, to 29 million. While these increases are impressive, achieving EFA will still require vast efforts in terms of teacher recruitment (Box 2.17).

PTRs are a more useful benchmark for measuring teacher provision than global and regional numbers. There is a broad consensus that a PTR of 40:1 is an approximate ceiling for a primary school learning environment of good quality.[55] Very low ratios point to inefficient allocation of teachers. As secondary education is often organized by subject units, more teachers are needed than in primary school, so global benchmarks are less easily established and compared for this level.

Regional and national PTRs show marked variation and little change. There are large regional and national disparities in PTRs, with marked teacher shortages in South and West Asia, and sub-Saharan Africa (see annex, Statistical Table 10A). In Afghanistan, Chad, Mozambique and Rwanda, national primary PTRs exceed 60:1. In sub-Saharan Africa, and South and West Asia, the supply of new teachers has failed to keep pace with increases in primary school enrolment. Particularly sharp increases in PTRs are evident in some countries, including Afghanistan, Kenya, Rwanda and the United Republic of Tanzania. By contrast, PTRs in Latin America and the Caribbean, and in North America and Western Europe have declined as enrolment decreased and/or teacher numbers increased. In secondary education, the highest PTRs are again observed in sub-Saharan Africa, and South and West Asia. Eritrea, Nigeria and Pakistan, for instance, have ratios above 40:1 (see annex, Statistical Table 10B). As in primary education, there has been no discernible shift in secondary PTRs since 1999.

The most acute teacher shortages are in South and West Asia, and sub-Saharan Africa

54. More than a third of teachers worldwide are in East Asia and the Pacific (mostly in China) and a further fourth are in the most populous countries in other regions: Bangladesh, Brazil, Egypt, India, the Islamic Republic of Iran, Mexico, Nigeria, Pakistan, the Russian Federation and the United States.

55. The PTR is a rough measure of class size because it is calculated by taking the total number of teachers (including some who may not be in classrooms) and dividing it by the total number of pupils enrolled, including those not attending classes. As the indicator is based on teacher headcounts, it does not reflect part-time teaching or double-shifting.

Table 2.18: Teaching staff and pupil/teacher ratios in primary and secondary education, by region, 1999 and 2006

	Primary education						Secondary education					
	Teaching staff School year ending in		Change between 1999 and 2006 (%)	Pupil/teacher ratio[1] School year ending in		Change between 1999 and 2006 (%)	Teaching staff School year ending in		Change between 1999 and 2006 (%)	Pupil/teacher ratio[1] School year ending in		Change between 1999 and 2006 (%)
	1999 (000)	2006 (000)		1999	2006		1999 (000)	2006 (000)		1999	2006	
World	25 795	27 192	5	25	25	1	24 180	28 906	20	18	18	-2
Developing countries	20 466	21 811	7	27	28	2	15 109	19 637	30	21	20	-4
Developed countries	4 485	4 633	3	16	14	-9	6 286	6 595	5	13	13	-5
Countries in transition	843	748	-11	20	18	-10	2 785	2 674	-4	11	10	-10
Sub-Saharan Africa	2 004	2 581	29	41	45	10	872	1 238	42	24	27	13
Arab States	1 554	1 832	18	23	22	-4	1 387	1 776	28	16	16	-3
Central Asia	332	319	-4	21	19	-10	873	923	6	11	12	11
East Asia and the Pacific	10 094	9 671	-4	22	20	-8	7 702	9 415	22	17	17	-1
East Asia	9 938	9 502	-4	22	20	-8	7 476	9 166	23	17	17	-1
Pacific	156	169	8	20	19	-8	226	249	10	14	14	-3
South and West Asia	4 301	4 859	13	37	40	8	2 956	4 138	40	33	30	-10
Latin America/Caribbean	2 684	3 016	12	26	23	-13	2 746	3 594	31	19	16	-15
Caribbean	104	111	7	24	22	-10	53	66	26	22	19	-12
Latin America	2 580	2 905	13	26	23	-13	2 693	3 527	31	19	16	-15
N. America/W. Europe	3 443	3 687	7	15	14	-9	4 487	4 851	8	14	13	-4
Central/Eastern Europe	1 384	1 226	-11	19	18	-6	3 158	2 971	-6	13	11	-10

1. Based on headcounts of pupils and teachers.
Source: Annex, Statistical Tables 10A and 10B.

Box 2.17: How many teachers are needed to achieve EFA?

The 2008 Report (UNESCO, 2007*a*) emphasized that national governments had to recruit and train teachers on a vast scale to achieve the EFA goals. It is estimated that the world will need approximately 18 million additional primary teachers by 2015.[1]

The most pressing need is in sub-Saharan Africa, where an estimated 1.6 million additional posts must be created and teachers recruited by 2015 (on the basis of 2004 data) if UPE is to be achieved. Taking teacher retirement, resignations and losses into account pushes that figure up to 3.8 million. This represents about 145,500 posts and teachers annually, 77% higher than the annual increase observed between 1999 and 2006. In Ethiopia and Nigeria the annual requirement for new posts is more than 11,000. Burkina Faso, the Congo, Chad, Mali and the Niger all need to increase posts and teachers by more than 10% a year.

East Asia and the Pacific will need an estimated 4 million teachers by 2015 and South and West Asia 3.6 million, with the largest increases required in China, India and Indonesia. Teacher needs in these regions, however, are mostly to fill posts left by retiring or otherwise departing teachers.

These estimates do not take account of additional investments (e.g. for teacher training) required to ensure that teaching is effective. Moreover, comprehensive estimates of teacher needs are available only at primary level. Factoring in the number of teachers and other staff needed to meet all the EFA goals increases still further the scale of necessary investment in teacher recruitment and training:

- A study for Senegal, for example, shows that non-formal education will need an additional 1,900 instructors yearly between 2008 and 2010, nearly as many additional posts as are required at primary level.
- Projections in Ghana, Kenya, Malawi, Senegal, Uganda and Zambia[2] show that 321,561 new lower-secondary teachers would be needed between 2006 and 2015 to reduce student dropout and repetition at all levels by 25% and increase primary to lower-secondary transition rates by 25%. Kenya and Malawi, for example, would have to double teacher numbers to meet these goals.

1. Estimated on the basis of 2004 teacher supply and PTRs.
2. Based on constant PTRs at 2006 levels, not disaggregated by subject.
Sources: Diagne (2008); Schuh Moore et al. (2008); UIS (2006*b*).

Trained teachers are in short supply in many countries. While differences in teacher training limit the scope for simple cross-country comparisons,[56] large regional variations are apparent. In primary education, the median shares of trained teachers in the total teaching force range from 68% in South and West Asia to 100% in the Arab States (see annex, Statistical Table 10A). Variations by country are also marked. In Lebanon, for example, just 13% are trained, for an average of one trained teacher per 110 students (Figure 2.41). In Mozambique the percentage of trained teachers is higher (65%) but because the total number is insufficient the ratio of pupils to trained teachers is very high, 104:1. Nearly half the forty countries with data for both 1999 and 2006 increased the presence of trained teachers (see annex, Statistical Table 10A), in some cases by considerable margins. The Bahamas, Myanmar, Namibia and Rwanda raised the proportion of trained primary school teachers by more than 50%.[57] However, more than a third of countries, including Bangladesh, Nepal and the Niger, moved in the opposite direction, with percentages of trained primary school teachers declining.

Excessive PTRs, shortages of trained teachers and questions about teachers' skills point to wide-ranging problems in governance. Teacher shortages often result from inadequate investment in education and questionable incentive structures for teacher recruitment and retention. At the primary level in particular, teacher training is often fragmented and incomplete – in some cases non-existent. Many countries have had trouble increasing the number of primary education teachers because they have not yet expanded secondary education sufficiently to produce enough candidates for teacher-training programmes.

Within-country disparities

The total number of teachers and the national PTR shed some light on the state of a given education system, but they can obscure disparities in teacher assignment associated with location, income and school type. These disparities affect the extent to which a country truly gives everyone the opportunity to receive an education of good quality. In many countries teachers are unevenly distributed, resulting in major disparities in PTRs. In Nepal in 2005, the PTR in the Dhanusa district, in the central region, was 82:1 – double the national average (Sherman and Poirier, 2007). Among the country's seventy-five districts, nearly half had ratios at or above 40:1 while the rest were well staffed,

Figure 2.41: Comparison of PTRs with ratios of pupils to trained teachers in primary education, 2006

Source: UIS database.

providing very small class sizes in some cases. Similarly, PTRs in the Nigerian state of Bayelsa were five times higher than in Lagos. Large variations in PTRs can exist even within local administrative areas: a 2004 survey of 10 of the 493 *upazilas* (subdistricts) in Bangladesh found

Many countries have had trouble increasing the number of primary education teachers because they have not yet expanded secondary education sufficiently

56. Wide variations exist in the institutional quality of pre-service education, programme selectivity and professional development opportunities and requirements.

57. Myanmar's Basic Education Long-term Development Plan (2001/02–2030/31) focused for the first five years on reducing the number of uncertified teachers and expanding teacher-training colleges. It introduced two-year pre-service training programmes and increased the intake of primary and lower secondary teachers to in-service teacher training in twenty education colleges. Also during this period Myanmar's two Institutes of Education, in Yangon and Sagaing, provided more teacher-training programmes for the upper secondary level.

ratios ranging from 36:1 to 93:1 (Ahmed et al., 2007). Geographic disparities in teacher distribution often coincide with socio-economic variation in the populations served. Compared with poorer pupils, wealthier children often attend schools with better PTRs and larger shares of trained teachers.

While urban PTRs tend to be higher than in rural areas, untrained teachers are often concentrated in poor rural areas. Lower PTRs in rural areas reflect many factors, from population dispersal to lower demand for education. They do not necessarily indicate greater equity, as a more detailed look at the composition of the teaching force shows:

Schools attended by wealthier children tend to have smaller classes and more trained teachers than those attended by poorer children

- In Bolivia many teachers are *interinos*, hired on contract. They need not have a teaching degree or even any teaching experience. *Interinos* make up 19% of the total teaching force but 56% of all teachers in rural areas (World Bank, 2006*a*).

- In Ghana untrained teachers are concentrated in the Northern region, which has the lowest economic development and the most out-of-school children. In 2004–2005, the percentage of trained teachers was a third lower in the forty most deprived districts of the country than in other districts (Akyeampong et al., 2007).

- In India the majority of untrained or undertrained teachers are concentrated in rural areas and cater to the poorest and most deprived children (Govinda and Bandyopadhyay, 2008).

PTRs also depend on whether schools are publicly funded. Many countries show a marked gap between government and non-government providers. In Bangladesh average ratios are 64:1 in government schools, 40:1 in non-government ones. Public sector school teachers in Djibouti and Rwanda work in classes that on average are more than two and a half times the size of classes in private schools (Figure 2.42). Because children from poorer households are more likely to attend government schools, unequal PTRs both reflect and reinforce wider inequalities.

The PTR offers an important, if deceptive, headcount indicator showing teacher distribution countrywide. For children in the classroom, however, other factors also affect the quality of teaching and learning. Thus, even favourable headcount indicators can obscure wider problems.

Other factors affecting the quality of teaching and learning

Teacher absenteeism. Teacher counts in employment statistics do not guarantee their presence in the classroom. In a recent study of six countries, teacher absenteeism rates in primary schools averaged 19% and ran as high as 25% in India and 27% in Uganda (Chaudhury et al., 2006).

Figure 2.42: Public-to-private sector disparities in primary PTRs, 2006

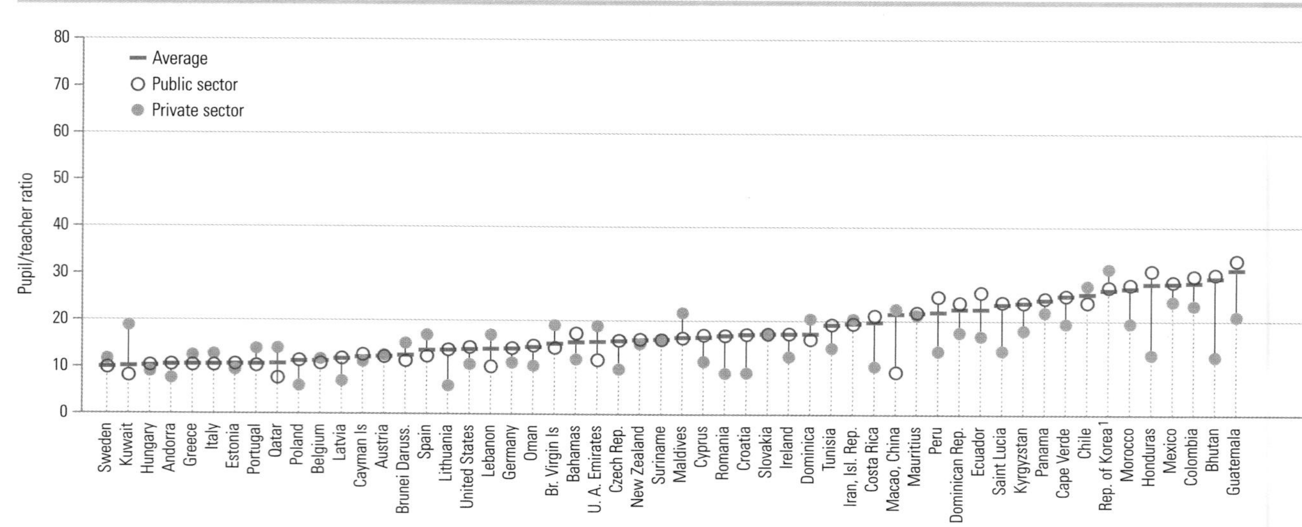

1. Data are for the school year ending in 2007.
Source: UIS database.

Data for Ghana, India, South Africa and the United Republic of Tanzania suggest that teacher absenteeism is more pronounced in public sector schools, in schools with poorer infrastructure, in rural areas, in poorer states and in schools serving children from lower socio-economic backgrounds (Kremer et al., 2005; Sumra, 2006; van der Berg and Louw, 2007; World Bank, 2004). High levels of teacher absenteeism directly affect learning time and outcomes as well as national education costs and spending. In countries participating in SACMEQ II, teacher absenteeism was shown to have significant negative effects on mathematics tests (van der Berg and Louw, 2007). In Peru the economic costs of teacher absenteeism represent 10% of current expenditure in primary education; in Uganda the figure is 24%. A recent study put the cost of absenteeism in India at around US$2 billion per year (Patrinos and Kagia, 2007).

HIV/AIDS. Although teacher mortality rates due to HIV/AIDS are decreasing or are reasonably stable (Bennell, 2006), the epidemic continues to damage lives and education systems. In South Africa, HIV prevalence among teachers was 13% in 2004; projections show it declining slightly by 2015 (Bennell, 2005*b*). In Kenya, where 14,500 teachers are estimated to be HIV positive, between four and six teachers die each day due to AIDS (Bennell, 2005*b*; UNESCO, 2007*b*). In Mozambique, HIV/AIDS kills 1,000 teachers a year: it is estimated that 19,200 teachers and 100 education officials will have died during the current decade (Reuters, 2007). Teachers suffering from HIV/AIDS are more likely to be absent or transferred (particularly in rural areas further from medical facilities) as a result of opportunistic infections.

In Mozambique, HIV/AIDS kills 1,000 teachers a year

Poor morale and weak motivation undermine teacher effectiveness. Teacher retention and absenteeism and the quality of teaching are heavily influenced by whether teachers are motivated and their level of job satisfaction. Evidence suggests many countries face a crisis in teacher morale that is mostly related to poor salaries, working conditions and limited opportunities for professional development (Bennell and Akyeampong, 2007; DFID and VSO, 2008). The surveys in eleven developing countries discussed above (see pp. 116-7) found professional satisfaction among grade 4 teachers to be low. In some cases, salary concerns were paramount: in Argentina, Brazil, Peru, the Philippines and Uruguay, for example, fewer than a third of fourth graders had teachers who thought their pay was adequate (Zhang et al., 2008). Motivation tends to be lower among teachers with large classes and in schools that are poorly resourced or attended by disadvantaged pupils. Issues raised in this section are at the heart of education governement challenges. The recruitment, training, allocation and motivation of teachers are issues that we turn to in Chapter 3. □

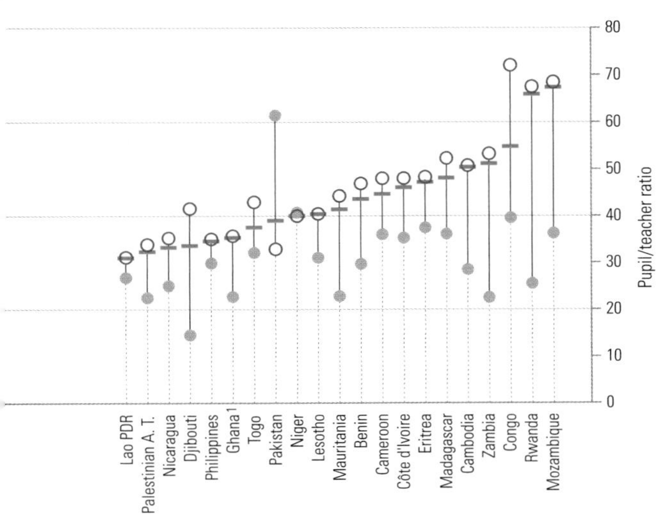

Education for All: measuring composite achievement

The EFA goals represent more than the sum of their parts. While each is important in its own right, what ultimately matters is progress on all fronts. Achieving UPE without advancing policies to strengthen early childhood development, gender parity in post-primary education or progress in adult literacy would put overall EFA achievement at risk. Advancing on all fronts generates cumulative, mutually reinforcing benefits. By contrast, slow progress in one area can erode the benefits of strong performance in others.

While each EFA goal is important in its own right, what ultimately matters is progress on all fronts

The EFA Development Index

The EFA Development Index (EDI) is a composite measure that captures overall progress. Ideally, it should reflect all six Dakar goals, but there are serious data constraints. Reliable and comparable data relating to goal 1 (ECCE) are not available for most countries and progress on goal 3 (learning needs of youth and adults) is not easy to measure or monitor. The EDI thus focuses only on the four most easily quantifiable EFA goals, attaching equal weight to each measure:

- UPE (goal 2) is proxied by the total primary NER.[58]
- Adult literacy (goal 4) is proxied by the literacy rate for those aged 15 and above.[59]
- Gender parity and equality (goal 5) are proxied by the gender-specific EFA index (GEI), an average of the GPIs of primary and secondary GERs, and of the adult literacy rate.
- Quality of education (goal 6) is proxied by the survival rate to grade 5.[60]

The EDI value for a given country is the arithmetic mean of the four proxy indicators. It falls between 0 and 1, with 1 representing full EFA achievement.[61] For the school year ending in 2006 it was possible to calculate values for 129 countries. Coverage varies substantially by region, ranging from fewer than 40% of countries in East Asia and the Pacific to about 80% or more in Central and Eastern Europe, and North America and Western Europe (Table 2.19). Data limitations preclude a global look at overall EFA achievement. Many countries are excluded, among them a majority of what the OECD identifies as fragile states,[62] including those in conflict or post-conflict situations.

Of the 129 countries for which the EDI could be calculated for 2006:

- Fifty-six – five more than in 2005 – have either achieved the four most easily quantifiable EFA goals or are close to doing so, with EDI values averaging 0.95 or above. Most of these high-achieving countries are in more developed regions. With a few exceptions,[63] they have achieved balanced progress on the four EFA goals included in the index.
- Forty-four countries, mostly in Latin America and the Caribbean, the Arab States and sub-Saharan Africa, are midway to achieving EFA as a whole, with EDI values ranging from 0.80 to 0.94. Most of these countries show uneven progress. Participation in primary education is often high, with deficits in other areas, such as adult literacy (Algeria, Belize, Egypt, Kenya, Swaziland, Tunisia, Zambia) education quality as measured by the survival rate to grade 5 (Ecuador, El Salvador, the Dominican Republic, Myanmar, the Philippines, Sao Tome and Principe), or both (Guatemala).
- Twenty-nine countries, more than a fifth of those in the EDI sample, are lagging behind with EDI values below 0.80. Sub-Saharan Africa is overrepresented in this group, with EDI values below 0.60 in Burkina Faso, Chad, Ethiopia, Mali and the Niger. Countries in other regions, including four Arab States and five out

58. The total primary NER measures the proportion of children of primary school age who are enrolled in either primary or secondary education.

59. The literacy data used are based on conventional assessment methods – either self- and third-party declarations or educational attainment proxies – and thus should be interpreted with caution; they are not based on any test and may overestimate actual literacy levels.

60. For countries where primary education lasts fewer than five years, the survival rate to the last grade of primary is used.

61. For further explanation of the EDI rationale and methodology, see The EFA Development Index in the annex, which also includes detailed values and rankings for 2006.

62. The fragile states not included are Afghanistan, Angola, the Central African Republic, the Comoros, the Congo, Côte d'Ivoire, the Democratic Republic of the Congo, the Gambia, Guinea-Bissau, Haiti, Kiribati, Liberia, Papua New Guinea, Sierra Leone, the Solomon Islands, Somalia, the Sudan, Timor-Leste, Uzbekistan and Vanuatu.

63. The total primary NER remains around 90% in Armenia, Belarus and Georgia, as does the average adult literacy rate in the United Arab Emirates.

Table 2.19: Distribution of countries by EDI scores and region, 2006

	Far from EFA: EDI below 0.80	Intermediate position: EDI between 0.80 and 0.94	Close to EFA: EDI between 0.95 and 0.96	EFA achieved: EDI between 0.97 and 1.00	Subtotal sample	Total number of countries
Sub-Saharan Africa	17	9		1	27	45
Arab States	4	9	2		15	20
Central Asia		1	2	4	7	9
East Asia and the Pacific	2	5	2	4	13	33
South and West Asia	5		1		6	9
Latin America and the Caribbean	1	18	3	2	24	41
North America and Western Europe			2	19	21	26
Central and Eastern Europe		2	4	10	16	21
Total	**29**	**44**	**16**	**40**	**129**	**204**

Source: Annex, The EFA Development Index, Table 1.

of six South Asian countries, are also in this category. Except in a few cases where participation of primary school-age children is relatively high (e.g. Bangladesh, Cambodia, India, Madagascar, Malawi, Nicaragua), these low EDI countries face multiple challenges: low education participation, widespread adult illiteracy, gender inequalities and poor education quality.

Progress towards EFA as a whole

Analysis of changes in the EDI between 1999 and 2006 could be carried out for only forty-five countries. Thirty-one of these recorded increases – significant ones, in several cases (Figure 2.43). Though absolute EDI values remained low in Ethiopia, Mozambique and Nepal, they increased by more than 20%. The EDI decreased in fourteen countries. Chad experienced the largest fall: it was in last place in 2006, well behind the others.

Increased school participation was the primary driver of progress in the EDI. The total primary NER increased on average by 7.3% across the forty-five countries. In Ethiopia, the level of participation in school more than doubled, from 35% in 1999 to 72% in 2006. Ethiopia also experienced gains in adult literacy (+35%) and school retention (+14%). In Yemen, significant increases in the total primary NER, adult literacy, and gender parity and equality more than compensated for a large drop in the survival rate to grade 5 (-24%), leading to overall EDI improvement of 10%. For most of the fourteen countries where the EDI declined between 1999 and 2006, the education quality component was an important factor.

Overall EFA achievement: inequalities within countries remain the rule

The EDI provides a snapshot based on national averages. But progress towards EFA, as the word 'all' implies, should be shared equally across the whole of society. One drawback of the standard EDI is that it does not capture variation based on wealth and other indicators of disadvantage. To address this shortcoming, an EFA Inequality Index for Income Groups (EIIIG) was constructed for thirty-five developing countries, using household survey data (Harttgen et al., 2008). The EIIIG uses a different set of indicators to provide a measure similar to the EDI, showing distribution of overall EFA achievement within countries by wealth and by rural/urban location.[64]

Increased school participation was the main driver of progress in the EDI

The EIIIG shows large disparities in overall EFA achievement between wealth groups in most of the thirty-five countries. These gaps are almost as large as those between nations (Figure 2.44). They are particularly wide in Benin, Burkina Faso, Chad, Ethiopia, Mali, Mozambique and the Niger: the EIIIG for the richest group in those countries is more than twice that of the poorest group. In Ethiopia, which had the widest inequality in overall EFA achievement, the EIIIG for the highest wealth quintile was 0.873 in 2003, compared with 0.344 for the lowest quintile. Disparities within income groups were less pronounced in seven countries,

64. The EIIIG differs from the EDI in three main ways. The total primary net attendance rate is used rather than the total primary NER. As many household surveys do not include literacy rates, this EIIIG component is based on the proportion of 15- to 25-year-olds with five or more years of education. Finally, the survival rate for the EIIIG is defined as the proportion of 17- to 27-year-olds who report having at least five years of education among those who reported having at least one year of education.

Figure 2.43: EDI in 2006 and change since 1999

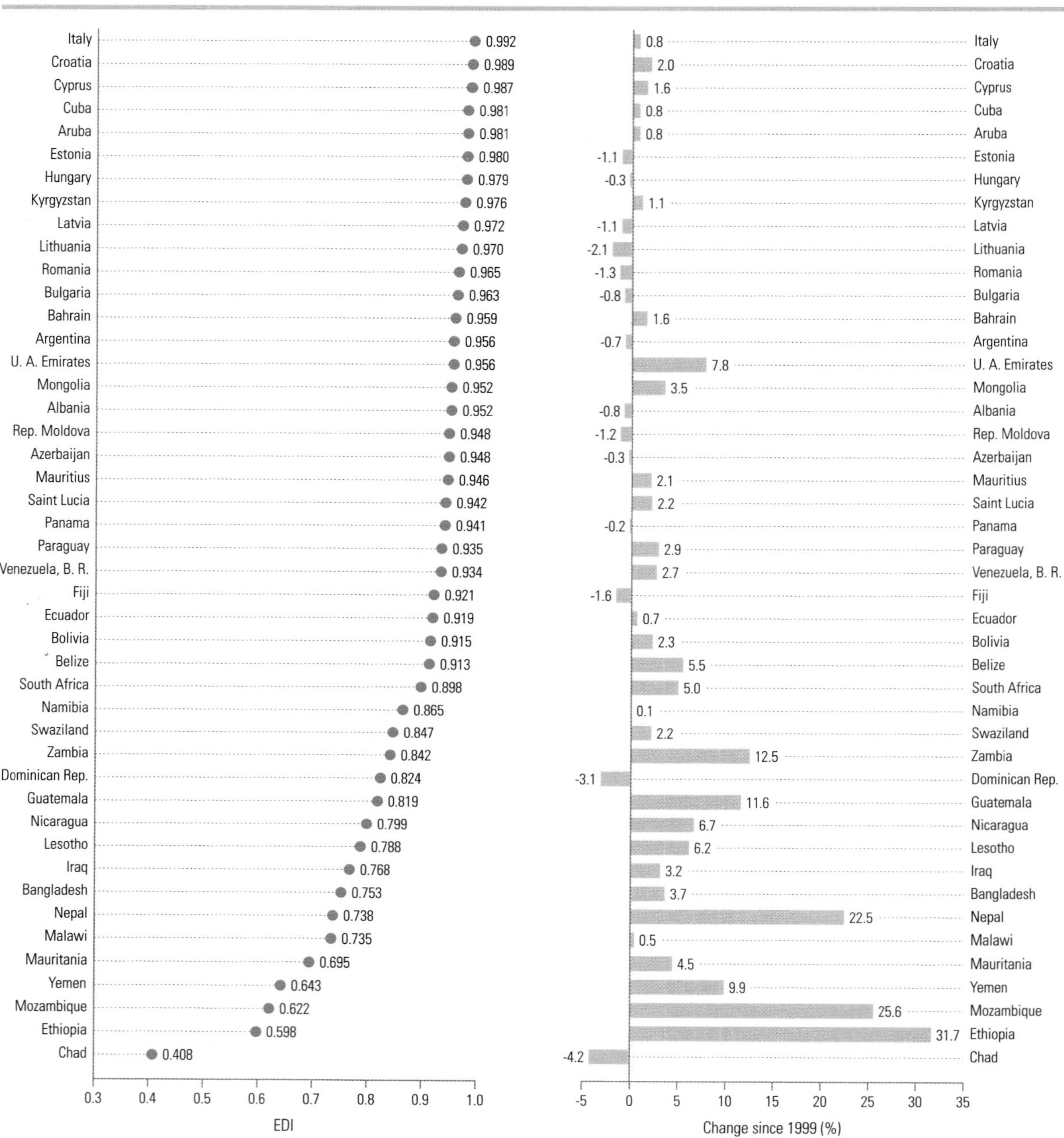

Note: Only countries with EDI values for both 1999 and 2006 are included.
Source: Annex, The EFA Development Index, Table 3.

Figure 2.44: EFA Inequality Index by wealth quintile, selected countries, most recent year

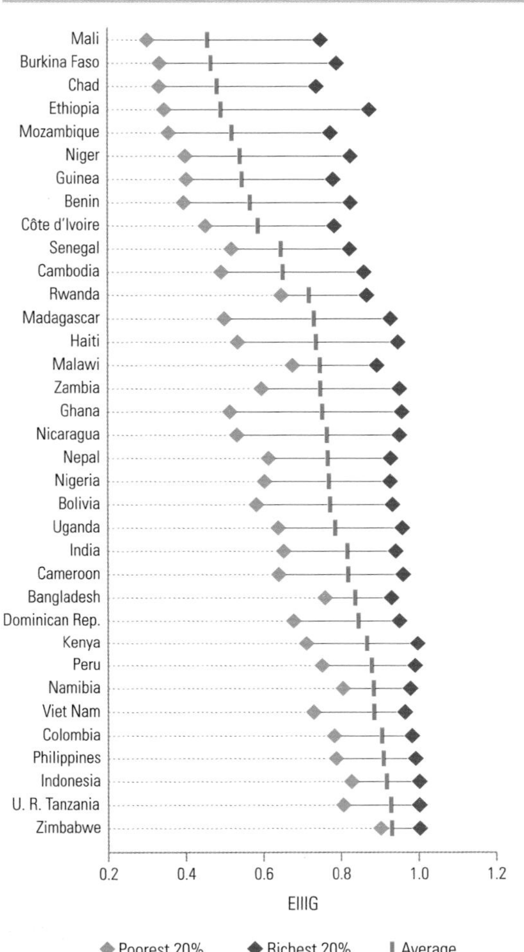

Source: Demographic and Health Surveys, calculations by Harttgen et al. (2008).

including Colombia, Indonesia, the Philippines, the United Republic of Tanzania and Zimbabwe. In these best-performing countries the richest quintile achieved the maximum EIIIG score of 1.00.

The higher the average EIIIG, the fewer the education inequalities. Although cross-country inequalities by income group are highly variable, a general trend is visible: countries with better-functioning education systems have not only higher overall EFA achievement as measured by the EIIIG, but also fewer inequalities.

Progress towards overall EFA achievement has benefited the poorest in most countries. The EIIIG ratio of the richest to poorest population quintile decreased in about three-quarters of the thirty-five countries in the sample. The reductions were particularly significant in Benin, Ethiopia, India and Nepal, with declines of 15% or more. On the other hand, inequalities in overall EFA achievement between the poorest and the richest households increased in the remaining countries, particularly Kenya and Nigeria, where the mean EIIIG decreased slightly.

Education inequality between wealth groups tends to be higher in rural than in urban areas in about two-thirds of the thirty-five countries

Overall EFA achievement is greater in urban than in rural areas, whatever the wealth group. Rural residents are particularly disadvantaged in Burkina Faso, Chad, Ethiopia and Mali, where the ratio of urban to rural EIIIG is about 2 or more. A close look at the interaction between wealth and place of residence highlights the impact of poverty in rural areas. Education inequality between wealth groups as measured by the EIIIG ratio of richest to poorest quintile tends to be higher in rural areas than urban in about two-thirds of the thirty-five countries. In Chad, Ghana, Haiti and Nicaragua the ratio of richest to poorest is close to 2 in rural areas. In other countries, however, including Benin, Cambodia and Mozambique, the urban poor are more disadvantaged. ■

© Gurinder Osan/AP/SIPA

Going their separate ways: school girls and street children in New Delhi

Chapter 3

Raising quality and strengthening equity: why governance matters

Many countries have introduced far-reaching governance reforms in education. This chapter looks at governance problems and reform measures in four important areas: finance, school management, teacher recruitment and allocation, and education planning. Two key findings emerge. The first is that there is no blueprint for good governance: each country has to develop national and local strategies. The second finding is that governments across the world have attached insufficient weight to equity in the design of governance reforms.

Introduction

Governance is a word that conjures up an image of abstract political, administrative and management processes. It is easy to lose sight of the real impact that governance practices in education can have on the lives of ordinary people, the hopes and aspirations of parents and children, and the human development prospects of nations.

To understand why good governance matters in education, consider the alternative. Bad governance leaves parents and communities facing education provision that is unaccountable and unresponsive to their needs. It contributes to education systems that are ineffective in raising learning achievements. It leaves communities and regions with children sitting in classrooms lacking basic teaching materials, and in the charge of untrained and demotivated teachers. In some cases, bad governance also means that financial resources allocated to schools do not arrive.

Poor governance practices in education affect the whole of society. But invariably it is the poor who bear the brunt. Good governance implies not just transparency and accountability, but also a commitment to equal opportunity for all citizens. Unlike the wealthy, who can opt for private provision, poor households depend on governments to deliver education services. When those services are of poor quality, inaccessible or unaffordable, it is the poor who lose. Indicators for bad education governance include large financing gaps between rich and poor areas, provision that is unaffordable for the poor and a lack of attention to strategies for reaching the disadvantaged. Failure to tackle corruption, another hallmark of bad governance, has particularly damaging consequences for poor households. When resources do not reach schools, or when schools levy unauthorized fees, it is the poor who are least able to pay.

The good governance agenda

Governance describes the institutions, rules and norms through which policies are developed and implemented – and through which accountability is enforced. Governance reform in its broadest sense is concerned with changing the rules of the game – that is, changing the processes through which decisions are made and implemented on behalf of members of an organization or a society (Rodrik, 2008). However, governance is not just about abstract institutional processes or formal rules. It is also about power relationships in society. At its most basic level, governance systems define who decides on policies, how resources are distributed across society and how governments are held accountable.

Good governance is now a central part of the international development agenda. Beyond education, it is seen as a condition for increased economic growth, accelerated poverty reduction and improved service provision. The most widely used data on governance indicators show that objectives range from strengthening multiparty democracy to reducing corruption, strengthening the rule of law, increasing the accountability of public institutions and enhancing the participation and voice of citizens (Kaufmann et al., 2007).

Few people would take issue with the intrinsic importance of improving governance in these various dimensions – and most would argue that progress is intrinsically important to development (Rodrik, 2008). As one set of commentators put it: 'Good governance is an ideal in which political processes translate the will of the people into public policies and establish the rules that efficiently and effectively deliver services to all members of society' (Crouch and Winkler, 2007, p. 1). More controversy surrounds the choice of policies to achieve the desired end of good governance. Achieving good governance may require far-reaching political reforms and the reordering of institutional arrangements. This has often been forgotten by donors, who sometimes present their aid partners with lengthy shopping lists for good governance reform, with little regard for prioritization or political feasibility (Grindle, 2004). More broadly, the good governance narrative is often silent on the power relationships and vested interests that may be affected by governance reform.

There has been a parallel failure to acknowledge that national and local contexts are important. When it comes to governance reform, what works in one setting may not work in another. And there is no guarantee that progress towards good governance, as measured by the standard indicators, will resolve wider problems in development.

Education governance: the Dakar Framework and beyond

Education governance is not simply the system of administration and management of education in a country. In its broadest sense, it is concerned with the formal and informal processes by which policies are formulated, priorities identified, resources allocated, and reforms implemented and monitored. Governance is an issue not only for central government but also for every level of the system, from the education ministry down to the classroom and community. It is ultimately concerned with the distribution of power in decision-making at all levels.

Bad governance affects the whole of society, but invariably the poor bear the brunt

As with any service, education provision is affected by wider governance conditions. When democracy, transparency and respect for the rule of law is weak, accountability and participation suffer. Within the education sector, governance structures link many actors and define the terms of their interactions. The ability of parents to participate in school decisions, hold schools and teachers to account, and secure access to information is conditioned by the allocation of rights and responsibilities under governance systems. Governance rules also define the terms on which governments recruit, allocate and train teachers. They have an important bearing on the skills and motivation that teachers bring to the classroom. Beyond the classroom, governance systems shape the relationship between school bodies, local government and central government. They define who sets priorities and makes decisions in key areas ranging from the curriculum to teacher management, and the monitoring and supervision of schools. In the area of finance, education governance is about how priorities are set and how resources are mobilized, allocated and managed.

As this non-exhaustive list suggests, governance involves a broad array of actors and many layers of government, affecting virtually all decisions made in education. Within any country, the relationships between actors and government agencies can be enormously complex and varied. Similarly, change in governance can mean very different things in different contexts. For example, decentralization might reallocate authority in one area (say, teacher recruitment) but not in another (say, teacher pay or curriculum design). It might devolve political authority but keep financial responsibility highly centralized.

The Dakar Framework for Action did not set out a comprehensive agenda on governance reform. However, it did define some broad principles. It committed governments to 'develop responsive, participatory and accountable systems of educational governance and management'. Apart from being intrinsically important, progress in these areas was identified as a strategy for ensuring that governments 'can respond more effectively to the diverse and continuously changing needs of learners' (Unesco, 2000, Expanded Commentary, para. 55). While the Dakar Framework stops well short of offering a blueprint for good governance, it does advocate moving towards 'more decentralized and participatory decision-making, implementation and monitoring at lower levels of accountability'.

Education is often inaccessible, inefficient, unaffordable and of questionable quality

Much of this is consistent with central themes in wider governance debates. The development of more accountable and participatory systems for delivering services has been a broad goal in public service reform. Decentralization – the transfer of political, administrative and fiscal authority to lower levels of government – is one of the most pervasive governance reforms of the past two decades. While decentralization has often been driven by fiscal motives, governments invariably present it as an exercise in bringing decision-making closer to the people affected.

An underlying assumption in approaches to governance reform involving devolution of authority is that they are intrinsically beneficial for equity. Making service providers more accountable to the communities they serve, and giving those communities a greater role in decision-making, is widely presented as a source of empowerment. The widely held conviction is that moving decision-making away from remote government agencies, and making the process more localized and transparent will change incentive structures, prompting education service providers to be more responsive to the needs and concerns of the poor.

After some two decades of far-reaching governance reform in education the jury is still out on the results. Despite continuing enthusiasm, there is surprisingly little evidence that governance policies implemented thus far have actually improved education quality and led to greater equity. This is true not just of countries that have introduced reform on a piecemeal basis, but also of such widely cited models of radical governance reform as undertaken in Chile, South Africa and Uganda (Crouch and Winkler, 2007).

Evaluation of governance reform is a difficult exercise. The EFA Global Monitoring Report team has examined the locus of decision-making in 184 countries, looking at areas ranging from curriculum design and school infrastructure to teacher recruitment and pay to finance and resource allocation (see mapping exercise in annex, p. 252). The sheer complexity of governance systems makes the mapping of decision-making in these areas difficult, even within one country. Cross-country comparison is an even more hazardous enterprise. Nevertheless, despite the complexity of layers of decision-making, some broad patterns emerge. One of the most striking is that, notwithstanding frequent government declarations in favour of decentralization, many decisions in education are still taken by central government authorities.

While governance systems across the world vary, many have one thing in common. They are delivering education services that are often inaccessible, inefficient, unaffordable and of questionable quality. Changing such systems is crucial if countries are to accelerate progress towards the goals set out in the Dakar Framework for Action. Some countries have demonstrated what is possible, but current approaches to governance reform are often failing.

Why have outcomes to date been so disappointing? No generalized answer is possible, as every country faces different constraints and problems in governance reform. Two broad problems can be identified nonetheless.

First, there has been a tendency in many developing countries to apply governance reform 'blueprints' borrowed uncritically from rich countries – a practice that some donors have encouraged – and to extend wider public service reforms to education without paying sufficient attention to their appropriateness for education, or to real institutional constraints and local context for reform.

Second, many governments have failed to place poverty reduction and equity at the centre of governance reform. Too often the interests of the poor have been a rhetorical afterthought.

If there is one clear lesson from experience with governance reform, it is that changes in administrative processes and shifts in the locus of decision-making do not automatically generate 'pro-poor' outcomes. Tackling the root causes of educational disadvantage requires political commitment and policy processes that take account of the problems and priorities of the poor and vulnerable. It also calls for an integrated, cross-sectoral approach to planning.

This chapter does not attempt to cover all aspects of education governance. It focuses selectively on some of the most important currents in governance reform and on themes neglected in wider education reform debates. It is divided into four sections.

1. **Financing strategies for closing the equity gap.** Many governments have increased their public finance commitment to education since Dakar. But many could – and should – be doing much more. Governance reforms have focused on improving efficiency, with scant regard for equity. Decentralization is a case in point. Devolving revenue mobilization in countries marked by large regional wealth gaps can lead to increased inequality in education financing. In many cases, decentralization has reinforced and magnified disparities in education. *The lesson: while decentralization is important, central government should retain a strong role in equalizing the distribution of education finance.*

2. **Choice, competition and voice.** Choice and competition are central themes in education governance reform. The idea is that competition drives gains in efficiency, with wide-ranging advantages for learning achievement and equity. Weak evidence of presumed benefits has not diminished the enthusiasm of many reformers for public-private partnerships involving an enlarged role for private schools and voucher systems to allocate public finance to such schools. 'School-based management', or the devolution of authority to school and community level, has been another powerful reform current. Its stated aim is to make education providers more responsive to local needs. Meanwhile, low-fee private schools are seen by some as a viable alternative to state provision. Positive outcomes associated with reforms in these areas have been muted. Public-private partnerships have a mixed and modest record on learning achievements and equity. And low-fee private schools are a symptom of failure in public provision, not a solution to the problem. *The lesson: transferring responsibility to communities, parents and private providers is not a substitute for fixing public-sector education systems.*

3. **Teacher governance and monitoring.** Teachers have figured prominently on the governance reform agenda. Problems to be addressed range from recruitment to motivation and deployment. Low teacher morale, often linked to poor pay and working conditions, is a major impediment to high-quality learning. In many countries, problems in teacher recruitment are compounded by large disparities in access to well-qualified teachers, with children from poor households and remote rural areas losing out. Monitoring of learning achievements can play an important role in informing policy design – but institutional capacity for effective monitoring is often limited. *The lessons: improve teacher recruitment, deployment and motivation through appropriate incentives and accountability mechanisms to improve learning and enhance equity; and strengthen the use of regional, national and school-level assessments to support policy design aimed at these same ends.*

4. **An integrated approach to education and poverty reduction.** The planning processes through which priorities are set are a key aspect of governance reform. Education-sector planning in developing countries has been strengthened in recent years, reflecting increased political and financial commitment. However, progress towards greater equity in education requires governance reform beyond the education sector itself. Broader strategies are needed to remove barriers to EFA associated with disparities based on wealth, gender, ethnicity and other factors. Coordination across sectors is needed to influence health, nutrition and livelihood opportunities. Poverty reduction strategy papers have potential in this effort, but most are not delivering. *The lesson: integrate education with wider strategies for overcoming poverty and inequality.* □

Tackling the root causes of educational disadvantage requires political commitment and policy processes that take account of the poor and vulnerable

Financing education for equity

Introduction

In the Dakar Framework for Action governments promise to 'enhance significantly investment in basic education' (UNESCO, 2000, para. 8). Implicit in this pledge is the conviction that additional financing is needed if the world is to achieve UPE and the wider EFA goals. But resource mobilization is just one part of a broader set of governance challenges. How governments mobilize, distribute and manage investment in education has a crucial bearing on the efficiency and equity of their school systems.

Countries vary enormously in their capacities for financing education. Differences in wealth contribute to vast disparities in spending per student, which in turn fuel the global inequalities in access and quality discussed in Chapter 2. These inequalities have important implications not just for education, but also for the future distribution of wealth and opportunity in an increasingly integrated global economy.

Failure to tackle corruption reduces efficiency and erodes equity

While low average incomes and high levels of poverty impose obvious budget constraints, patterns of spending on education also reflect political choices. Some governments are far more committed to financing education than others. This has important consequences: higher spending does not lead automatically to improved or more equitable education outcomes, but sustained and chronic underfinancing is definitely not conducive either to the development of high-quality education systems or to equity.

Financial management figures prominently in debates on education governance. The issues at stake have important consequences for equity. Rules governing allocation of funds between students, schools and regions can determine whether the disadvantaged receive more or less financing than the more advantaged. Governance practices also affect the efficiency of government spending, strongly influencing the availability of classrooms, teachers and teaching materials. Failure to tackle corruption, a key governance concern, imposes a double economic burden on education: it penalizes efficiency and, because the burden of corruption falls disproportionately on the poor, it erodes equity.

Decentralization has been widely advocated and adopted as a governance reform. The main argument for decentralization is that it brings decisions closer to people. By devolving decision-making and financial management to local government agencies, the argument runs, decentralized structures offer greater accountability and responsiveness to local problems. However, decentralization can also weaken education provision and widen inequalities. Outcomes depend on the design of decentralization strategies and the commitment of central government to equalizing opportunity.

Government spending on education

In recent years, two contrasting viewpoints have emerged on the importance of increased financing for achieving the EFA goals. Some commentators treat increased spending on education as an automatic indicator of progress. Others point to the harsh lesson provided by analysis of cross-country data: namely, that the relationship between education spending and student performance is weak at best and sometimes non-existent (Hanushek, 2003; Pritchett, 2004; Wößmann, 2003). The latter group has stressed the importance of improving efficiency, viewing it as the best way to progress towards the goals.

Reality is less clear-cut. Dismal learning outcomes and high levels of inequality are possible at low, medium and high levels of spending. Rapid increases in spending do not necessarily lead to improved achievement levels. Yet financing thresholds are important. Students need access to a minimum level of resources and materials. Schools have to be built and buildings maintained. Teachers have to be recruited and paid. Even with improved efficiency, chronic financing gaps in many countries contribute to inadequate access, poor quality, insufficient teacher recruitment and low teacher morale.

Underfinancing is not neutral in its effects. Middle- and high-income groups can compensate for inadequate state provision. They can send their children to private schools and hire private tutors. They can also buy supplementary textbooks and teaching materials. Low-income households are likely to find these choices impossible. For the poorest groups, public investment and provision constitute the only viable route to an education that meets basic quality standards.

Patterns and trends in public spending around the world

Any country's public investment in education is linked to four factors: national wealth, the share of wealth converted into budget revenue, the proportion of public expenditure dedicated to education, and external support. In addition, the distribution of spending on the various education levels has important implications for equity within countries. This subsection provides a brief snapshot of global, regional and national financing for education.

Table 3.1: Total public expenditure on education as a percentage of GNP, by region and income group, 2006

	Minimum	Median	Maximum	Countries with data (%)
World	1.2	4.9	10.8	68
Developing countries	1.4	4.4	10.8	64
Developed countries	1.2	5.3	8.3	82
Countries in transition	2.4	3.9	6.6	75
Sub-Saharan Africa	1.4	4.4	10.8	73
Arab States	1.6	4.6	7.7	50
Central Asia	2.4	3.4	5.3	67
East Asia and the Pacific	1.8	...	10.0	42
South and West Asia	2.6	3.3	8.3	78
Latin America/Caribbean	1.2	4.1	10.8	73
N. America/W. Europe	2.3	5.5	8.3	88
Central and Eastern Europe	3.6	5.3	6.6	76
Income group				
Low income countries	1.4	3.5	6.9	60
Lower middle income countries	2.3	5.6	10.8	67
Upper middle income countries	1.4	4.7	10.8	84
High income countries	1.2	5.3	8.3	76

Note: Country groupings in the first part of this table follow the classification used in the statistical tables in the Report's annex. The income classification in the second part of the table follows that used by the World Bank.
Source: Annex, Statistical Table 11.

Education spending and national income: an irregular association. The share of national income devoted to education differs substantially among regions and income groupings (Table 3.1). On average, the share increases with national wealth, largely because tax revenue collection rises with per capita national income. Low-income countries in sub-Saharan Africa, and South and West Asia, where some 80% of the world's out-of-school children live, tend to invest the smallest proportion of GNP in education. In sub-Saharan Africa, about half of all low-income countries (eleven of the twenty-one with relevant data) spend less than 4% of their national income on education. In South Asia, Bangladesh devotes only 2.6% of its national income to education and Pakistan 2.7% (see annex, Statistical Table 11). More surprisingly, India invests a smaller share of GNP in education – around 3.3% – than the sub-Saharan Africa median, even though average incomes are around one-third higher. While low income countries spend significantly less on education than others, large differences exist within this group. For example, the Central African Republic allocates 1.4% of GNP to education while Ethiopia devotes 6%.

Public spending is rising, but not across the board. In the majority of countries with data, public spending on education as a share of GNP has increased since Dakar (Figure 3.1). Large increases in spending have been associated in some countries with substantial progress on EFA goals (though association is not causation). For example, Ethiopia, Kenya, Mozambique and Senegal have sharply increased the share of GNP invested in education and all have seen significant declines in numbers of out-of-school children (see Chapter 2, Figure 2.10). On a more negative note, the share of national income devoted to education decreased between 1999 and 2006 in 40 of the 105 countries with data. In twelve of them it dropped by more than a percentage point. Worryingly for prospects of achieving UPE by 2015, this group includes several countries with relatively large out-of-school populations, low levels of participation, or both, including the Congo (-3.5 percentage points), Eritrea (-2.9) and India (-1.3). The lack of significant change in Pakistan and Bangladesh, and in some sub-Saharan African countries, is equally worrying. These countries need simultaneously to increase the level, efficiency and equity of public spending on education.

The large share of teacher remuneration in education financing is not an indicator that teachers are overpaid

National commitment to education varies. To the extent that budget priorities reflect political priorities, how governments allocate resources says something important about their ordering of concerns.[1] The share of education in total public expenditure is a more direct measure of government commitment to education than the share in GNP. The median share of government spending on education in sub-Saharan Africa is among the highest for any region (Table 3.2). On the other hand, South and West Asia devotes a smaller share of government resources to education than countries in the Arab States and sub-Saharan Africa. Whatever their resource constraints, many

1. The share of national income devoted to education depends on governments' ability to collect revenue. To devote the same share of GNP to education, a country with a higher revenue share in overall GNP can allocate a smaller share of government resources to education compared with a country with the same national income but a lower revenue share.

Figure 3.1: Change in total public expenditure on education as a percentage of GNP between 1999 and 2006 (percentage points)

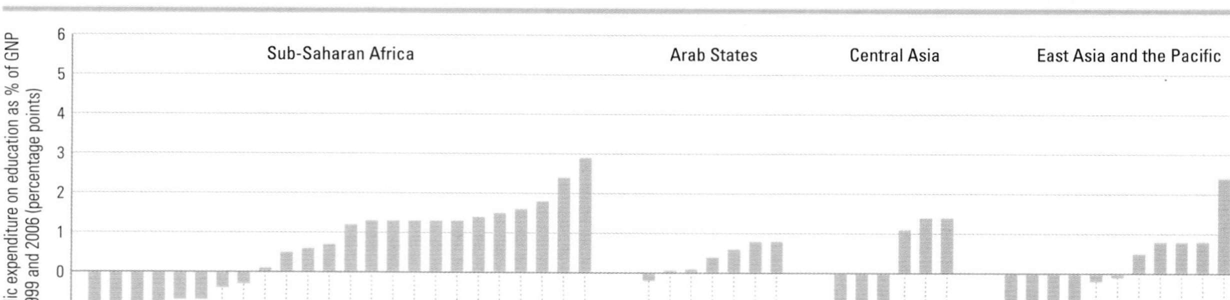

Source: Annex, Statistical Table 11.

Table 3.2: Total public expenditure on education as a percentage of total government expenditure, by region and income group, 2006

	Minimum	Median	Maximum	Countries with data (%)
World	4	15	31	57
Developing countries	4	16	31	52
Developed countries	6	12	17	73
Countries in transition	9	17	20	58
Sub-Saharan Africa	4	18	30	51
Arab States	10	21	31	55
Central Asia	9	…	19	33
East Asia and the Pacific	9	…	25	36
South and West Asia	11	15	19	78
Latin America/Caribbean	9	15	26	59
N. America/W. Europe	9	12	17	81
Central and Eastern Europe	6	13	20	71
Income group				
Low income countries	10	17	26	40
Lower middle income countries	4	13	31	74
Upper middle income countries	8	16	30	53
High income countries	9	13	28	69

Note: Country groupings in the first part of this table follow the classification used in the statistical tables in the Report's annex. The income classification in the second part of the table follows that used by the World Bank.
Source: Annex, Statistical Table 11.

countries in South and West Asia would appear to suffer from a lack of political commitment to education. Once again, regional averages hide large differences across countries. For example, in sub-Saharan Africa, Madagascar devotes 25% of its government budget to education compared to only 10% in Chad (see annex, Statistical Table 11).

Allocation of education finance

Overall resource mobilization patterns are just one side of the financing equation. How governments allocate resources within the education sector is also important. The selection of priorities often says something important about education governance.

Allocations to primary education vary with enrolment patterns. The allocation of funds to a particular education level is influenced by enrolment patterns. Countries with low levels of post-primary enrolment tend to have higher proportions of their overall budget allocated to primary. In thirteen of the twenty-nine sub-Saharan African countries with data, the proportion of government spending allocated to primary education is over 50% (Figure 3.2). Countries in other regions with low post-primary participation rates – Guatemala, Mauritania and the Philippines are examples – demonstrate a similar concentration of resources towards primary education (see annex, Statistical Table 11). The lowest allocations to primary education are

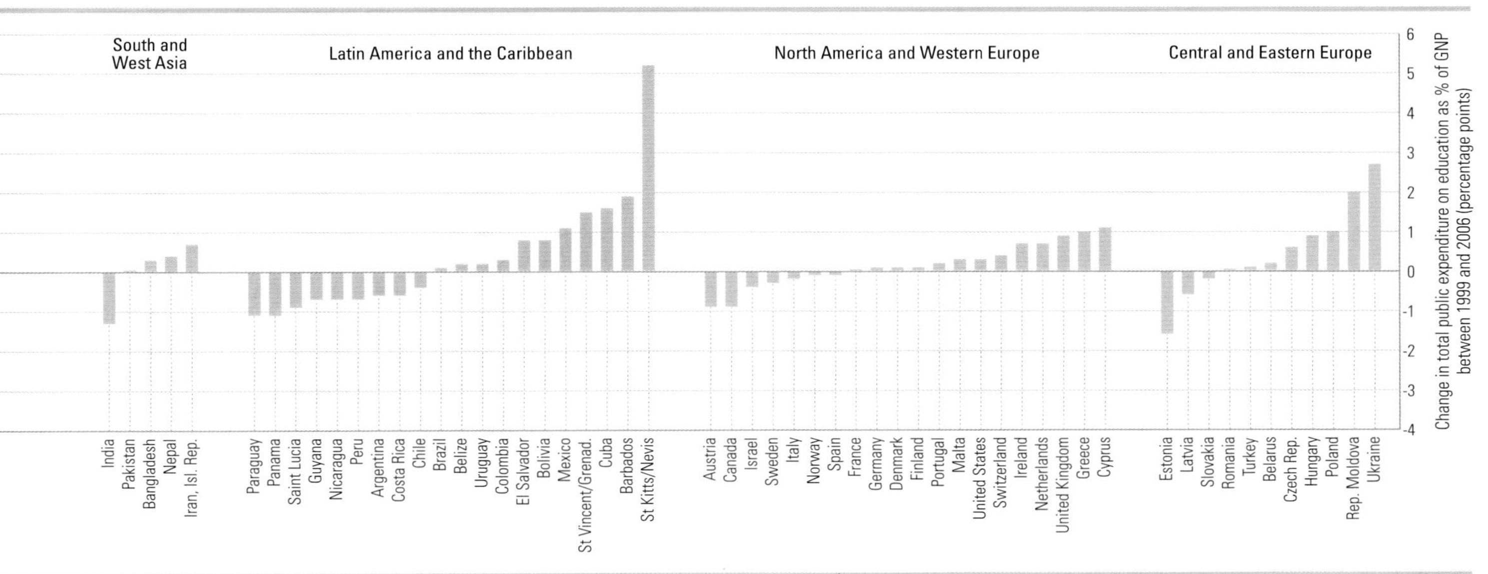

found in countries and regions where secondary enrolment is almost universal and tertiary enrolment high. As always, averages obscure important variations: of the 108 countries with data in all regions, 60 spend more on secondary education than on primary education.

Spending on teachers dominates, especially in the poorest countries. About half the countries with data for 2006 spent more than three-quarters of their primary education recurrent budgets on teacher remuneration in public institutions (see annex, Statistical Table 11). The share of teachers in budget allocations sometimes leaves little space for the financing of other inputs, including learning materials and the professional development of teachers. In Zambia, 93% of the primary recurrent budget goes to teacher salaries and less than 4% to textbooks, and other teaching and learning materials – and this example is no anomaly. The large share of teacher remuneration in education financing is not, as is sometimes assumed, an indicator that teachers are overpaid; many have salary levels close to the poverty line (see section below on teachers and monitoring). Rather, it indicates that the primary education sector is under-resourced, suggesting a need for increased commitment from governments and aid donors.

Weak commitment and inequitable allocation have consequences. Financial governance decisions reflected in resource mobilization and allocation

Figure 3.2: Distribution of public current expenditure on education by level, sub-Saharan Africa, 2006

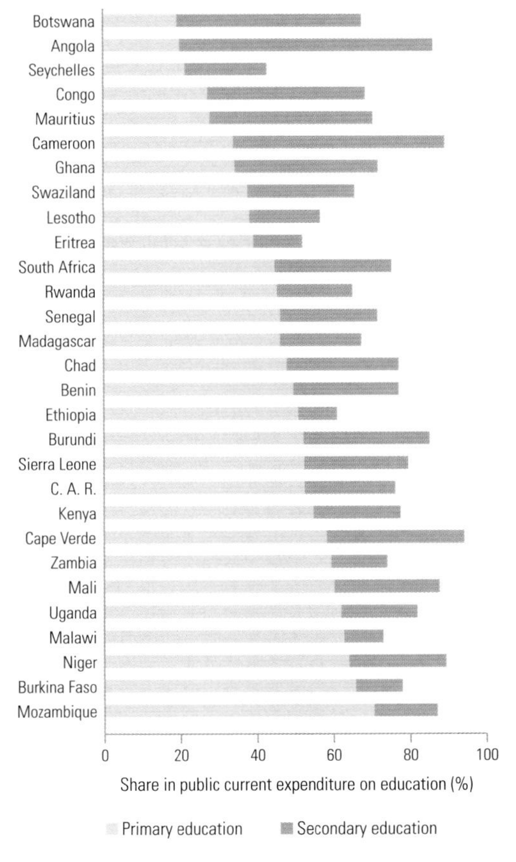

Source: Annex, Statistical Table 11.

In Zambia, 93% of the primary education budget goes to teacher salaries

matter for the experiences of children in classrooms. The case of Nigeria is illustrative. In 2005 between 3.5% and 4.2% of GDP was allocated to education.[2] However, education represents only 11% to 13% of total government spending, which compares unfavourably with the regional average for sub-Saharan Africa (World Bank, 2007*b*, 2008*f*, Table 3.2). The consequences of underfunding are powerfully captured in the following assessment: 'Spending on essential inputs, such as textbooks, instructional materials, in-service teacher training, and operations and maintenance are inadequate. About half of primary schools require major rehabilitation, with an additional 251,000 classrooms needed countrywide' (World Bank, 2008*e*, p. 15). Raising government spending on education in Nigeria to the regional average would release substantial additional resources to address the many difficulties the sector faces.

Low spending can lead to dilapidated schools and poor outcomes

Global and regional inequalities in the distribution of public education expenditure

Wealth inequalities among countries are mirrored by disparities in education spending. These disparities are closely associated with the large global differences in opportunity for education documented in Chapter 1. The links between national wealth and education financing operate in both directions. Differences in national wealth reflect the impact of education attainment and quality on growth and productivity. And differences in education attainment and quality reflect the financing capacities of countries with different levels of national wealth.

Huge gaps in per-student spending between developed and developing countries. In terms of spending per student, children in developed and developing countries live in different worlds. In 2006, per-student expenditure in primary education varied between US$39 in the Congo and US$9,953 in Luxembourg, at purchasing power parity (PPP) in constant 2005 dollars (Figure 3.3). While the transmission mechanisms between education spending and education quality are complex, the very low absolute spending in many developing countries is implicated in the abysmal learning outcomes and dilapidated school infrastructure that Chapter 2 documents. When per-pupil spending is less than PPP US$300 a year and largely absorbed by teacher salaries, the consequences are registered in classrooms with leaking roofs, no books and no chairs.

Global public expenditure on education is highly skewed. Differences in per-student spending translate into an extremely uneven global distribution of public expenditure on education (Figures 3.4 and 3.5). In 2004, North America and

Figure 3.3: Inequality among countries in public expenditure per primary school pupil, 2006

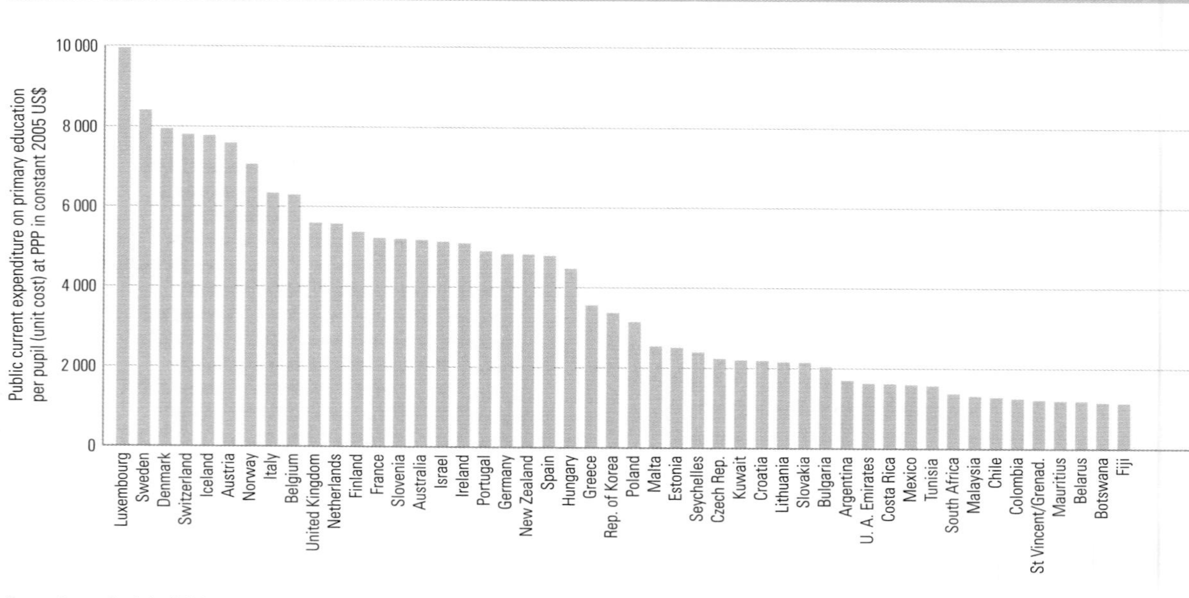

Source: Annex, Statistical Table 11.

2. A range is provided because results differ depending on the estimating technique used. See World Bank (2008*f*) for details.

Western Europe alone accounted for 55% of the world's spending on education but only 10% of the population aged 5 to 25. At the other extreme, sub-Saharan Africa was home to 15% of 5- to 25-year-olds but accounted for just 2% of global spending, and South and West Asia for 28% of the age group but 7% of the spending (UIS, 2007). For the poorest countries, increased aid flows could play an important role in reducing the public education expenditure gap (see Chapter 4).

Both finance and governance matter

Governance reforms can unlock efficiency gains that can expand access and improve quality. The previous subsection showed the wide variation by country in education financing. The extent to which differences in levels of financing explain disparities in outcomes such as those outlined in Chapter 2 is partly determined by education system efficiency. Raising efficiency to increase the flow of benefits,

Differences in per-student spending translate into an extremely uneven global distribution of public expenditure on education

Figure 3.4: Distribution of global public education expenditure by region, 2004

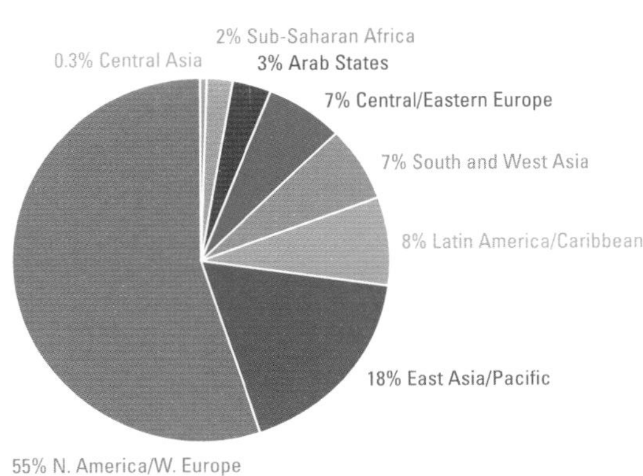

Note: Distribution is calculated using PPP US$.
Source: UIS (2007, Figure 1, p. 11).

Figure 3.5: Distribution of global public education expenditure by country, 2004

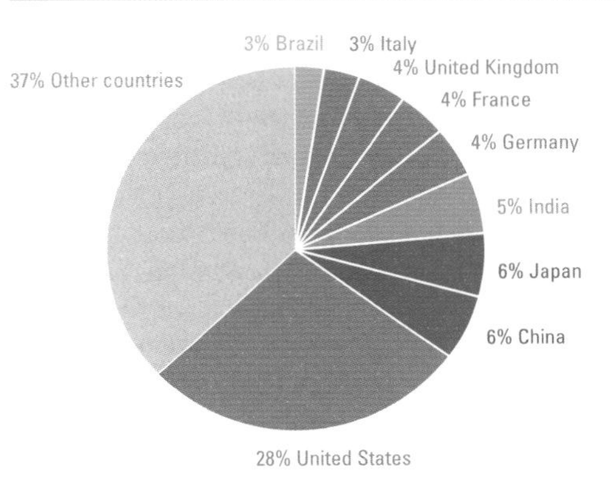

Note: Distribution is calculated using PPP US$.
Source: UIS (2007, Figure 1, p. 11).

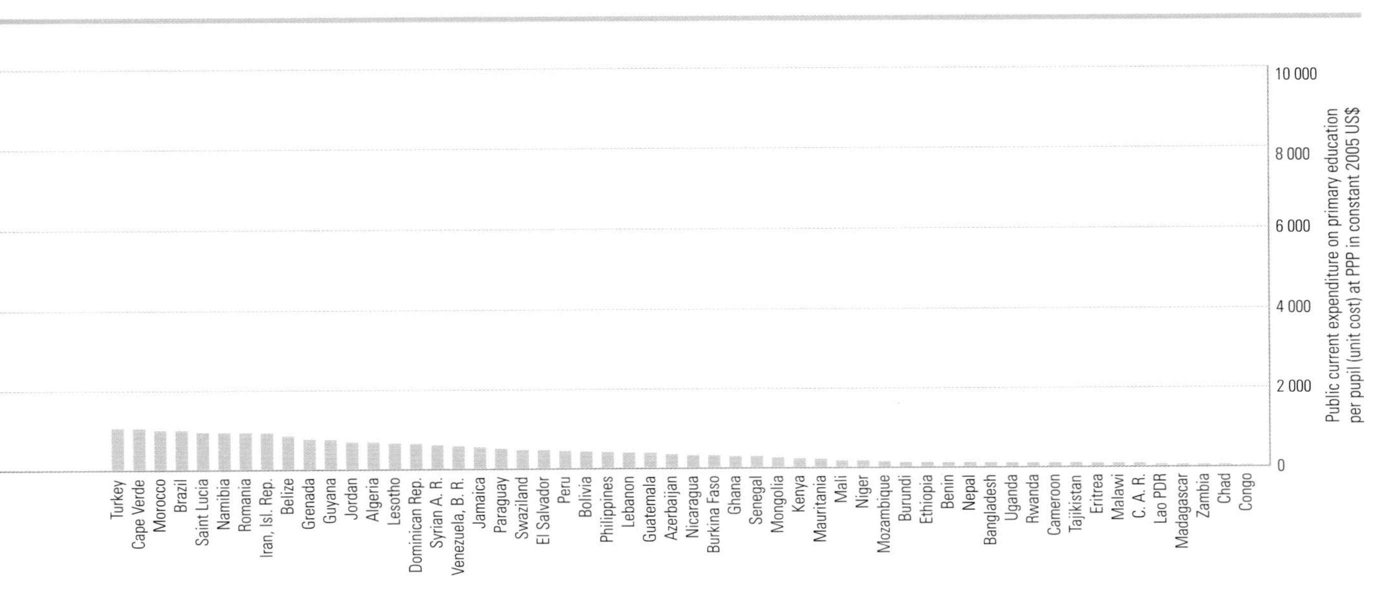

measured in terms of access, attainment and quality, is an important public policy goal.

Improving efficiency and reducing corruption

Efficiency in public spending is about how effectively governments use revenue to advance social welfare. Defining efficiency is not straightforward. Education outcomes cannot be measured simply in terms of numbers, whether of children in classrooms, books or teachers. Qualitative indicators are critical. There are also important questions about how much weight should be attached to equity-related goals. Should an additional year in education for a high-income child in secondary school count for the same as an additional year in primary school for a low-income child? There are no simple answers – but no government can afford to neglect efficiency.

Governments can stretch limited resources by being more efficient

Technical efficiency, at its most basic level, can be thought of in terms of rates of conversion. What level of financing is associated with a specific output? Consider the following example. Senegal and Ethiopia both had primary NERs of 71% in 2006 and 2007, respectively. However, Senegal spent PPP US$299 per primary pupil, compared with Ethiopia's PPP US$130 (2005 dollars). On this simple indicator, Ethiopia's education system is more efficient in translating resources into school places. If the costs of a school place were similar in the two countries, Senegal could easily provide sufficient school places for all primary school-age children with its current levels of public spending. In this comparison differences in efficiency may be driven by many factors, including teacher salary levels and class size. Higher levels of efficiency on the narrow technical indicator of an expenditure/enrolment ratio may not indicate better quality provision. The real question for policy-makers, therefore, is whether better qualitative outcomes (e.g. attainment of basic literacy) can be achieved for less.

Classroom construction provides an example of where efficiency gains can make a big difference. In the Nigerian state of Kano the average building cost per classroom in 2007 was US$14,000, while the average cost estimated by the World Bank for Africa was US$10,000 (FTI Secretariat, 2006; Kano State Ministry of Education, 2008).[3] If improvements in efficiency could reduce the cost in Kano to the average for Africa, an additional 40 classrooms could be built for every 100 currently being constructed. The efficiency saving could result in more school places and reduced overcrowding, within current levels of education spending.

Comparisons of this type do not provide grounds for sweeping conclusions. Classroom construction costs may vary across countries in sub-Saharan Africa and other regions for many reasons. These include the cost of materials, wage levels and the quality of the classrooms constructed. Even so, it would be wrong to understate the critical importance of efficiency. In low-income countries facing tight budget constraints and with large deficits in classroom availability, efficiency is one of the most critical requirements for expanded access to education and enhanced equity. Cross-country evidence can provide education planners with insights into policies for achieving the central goal of maximizing the number of good-quality classrooms available, within their resource envelope.

Improving efficiency is not just an issue for the very poorest countries. Nor is it just about infrastructure and inputs. Efficiency gains can also be reflected in learning achievement indicators. A recent study explored differences in public education spending efficiency across regions in Argentina and Mexico. The study used NERs and test scores as output indicators. It measured efficiency after controlling for levels of regional income, literacy rates and education spending per capita. For Mexico, the analysis estimated that improvements in efficiency alone could increase the primary NER by five percentage points and the secondary NER by fifteen percentage points. For Argentina, it estimated that improving efficiency had the potential to increase mathematics scores by seven percentage points in primary school and by nine percentage points in secondary (Jayasuriya and Wodon, 2007).

Corruption is a source of inefficiency and inequality. Analysis of public education expenditure accounts provides insights into the official picture of resource flows. It reveals the level of resource mobilization and the flow of funds through national budgets to lower levels of government and down to schools. In some countries there is a gap between budget provision and delivery of real inputs to education. Corruption is often implicated.

Tackling corruption in education is important for the sector and for society in a broader sense. Education receives a large share of total public expenditure – in most countries it is the largest

3. The average for Africa was taken from an average based on World Bank projects. The original figure, US$8,000 in constant 2000 prices, was inflated to 2007 prices using the US GDP deflator.

single area of government activity and the largest public employer. Efforts to limit corruption in general are unlikely to succeed if they do not address the education sector in particular. Moreover, 'lack of integrity and unethical behaviour within the education sector is inconsistent with one of the main purposes of education itself, which is to produce "good citizens" respectful of the law, of human rights and of fairness. It is also incompatible with any strategy that considers education as one of the principal means of fighting corruption' (Hallak and Poisson, 2004, p.7).

Corruption is difficult to measure and its effects are hard to evaluate. Because it is illegal it is not recorded in official data and, with government agencies often implicated, its full extent may be hidden. Corruption has adverse consequences for efficiency and equity. Efficiency suffers because corrupt practices mean part of the benefit of public investment is captured in the form of private rent. Equity suffers because corruption acts as a regressive tax that hurts the poor the most.

Notwithstanding the problems with monitoring corruption, cross-country and within-country research has provided interesting insights. One example comes from Nicaragua. Monitoring of six major school upgrade and repair projects that were undertaken by the education ministry demonstrates how corrupt practices diminish resource flows to education (Transparency International, 2005). Comparison of the buildings before and after project completion revealed widespread irregularities. Substandard materials and overpricing contributed to substantial financial losses.

In Brazil, the otherwise highly effective FUNDEF programme (Fundo de Manutenção e Desenvolvimento do Ensino Fundamental e de Valorização do Magistério) was affected in the past by illegal appropriation of funds meant for teacher salaries and training (Transparency International, 2005).[4] On average, around 13% of the total was lost in the course of transfer from the federal budget to municipal bank accounts, rising to 55% for some municipalities. The governance problem was linked to the inability of local councils charged with monitoring the grants to ensure that they were properly received and used.

Measuring cross-country corruption is intrinsically difficult. However, one study using a data set of fifty-seven countries reached a conclusion that has important implications for EFA. It found that increased public spending on education was associated with a significant increase in primary education completion rates *only* in the least corrupt countries and those with better-quality bureaucracies (Rajkumar and Swaroop, 2008).

Corruption is rooted in political cultures of non-accountability

Corruption creates setbacks for equity because the efficiency losses linked to corruption are not distributed equally across society. The greatest burden falls on the poor and disadvantaged, for three reasons. First, the poor tend to be more reliant on public services. Lacking financial resources, they may not have the luxury of responding to corruption by opting out of the public system and putting their children into private schools. Second, the poor are more likely to be susceptible to corrupt practices because they have limited recourse to formal or informal channels through which to seek redress and they often lack a strong enough voice to hold service providers to account. Third, when informal payments are required to secure access to education, the cost is likely to represent a higher proportion of household income for the poor, making it difficult for them to send children to school. In Mexico, every two years the National Survey on Corruption and Good Governance records informal payments by households for thirty-eight public services in all thirty-two federal states, making it possible to quantify what amounts to a tax (Transparency International, 2005). Estimates based on the survey indicate that households pay almost US$10 million in bribes to secure access to public education, which is legally free. In 2003 households paid an average of US$30 each to meet illegal demands from service providers. In a country where around one-quarter of the population was living on less than $2 per day, this is a significant financial burden. There are also indications that informal payments for access to basic services may be charged more frequently to poorer households.

Tackling corruption through information, institutional reform and monitoring. Because corruption represents a regressive transfer of public funds away from the poor and powerless, reducing it is intrinsically good for equity – in the education sector and elsewhere. In rich and poor countries alike, corruption is rooted in political cultures of non-accountability. Rooting out corruption may be a long-term process, but rapid progress is possible in the short term.

4. In 2007 the law governing FUNDEF was amended to add coverage of pre-school and secondary education and to rename the programme FUNDEB – Fundo de Manutenção e Desenvolvimento do Ensino Básico e de Valorização do Magistério (Fund for the Maintenance and Development of Basic Education and Valorization of Teachers).

Governments acting with resolve can put policies in place that make an immediate difference.

An important first step is to acknowledge the scale of the problem and develop a commensurate institutional response. Information has a key role to play because governments and the public alike are often insufficiently aware of the scale of the corruption problem. A recent study in Bangladesh provides a detailed tracking analysis of the flow of resources through the system – an approach that other countries could usefully follow (Box 3.1). The analysis reveals a broadly positive picture while identifying areas requiring greater scrutiny.

In Indonesia, public availability of monitoring reports transformed corruption in the education system from a well-hidden activity to a highly visible subject for public debate

Box 3.1: Tracking public expenditure in Bangladesh

In 2005 a public expenditure tracking and quantitative service delivery survey was conducted to assess the primary education sector in Bangladesh. Among the key findings:

- Records for allocation and expenditure were fairly consistent among various sources, both at national level and at lower levels.
- The teacher payment system appeared to be robust, with no evidence that resources for the payment of teacher salaries were leaking between the centre and local offices, or between local offices and schools.
- Textbook leakage varied, with 98% of allocated books reaching children in government and registered non-government schools compared with 76% in madrasas.
- Poor record-keeping by schools made it hard to track contingency payments and expenditure on small repairs and construction, though no major leakage of funds was found.
- Nearly 20% of stipend payments were misallocated due to exaggerated attendance figures and payments to ineligible children; 5% of stipend resources were unaccounted for.

While the results point to a relatively effective financial management system, some serious problems were identified. For example, informal payments to local education offices were reported by 16% of recently transferred teachers and about 40% of head teachers. Around one in ten households reported making informal payments to get their children into the primary school stipend programme.

Source: Financial Management Reform Programme (2006*a*).

Another positive example comes from Indonesia. Here the School Improvement Grant Programme (SIGP) provided cash grants to primary and junior secondary schools between 2000 and 2004, targeting in particular those in the poorest districts and with large populations of children from households displaced by conflict or natural disaster. A large programme, it covered some 8,000 schools in 130 districts and had a budget of around US$60 million, of which 70% was for physical rehabilitation of school buildings. Recognizing that corruption was a systemic problem, government and donors created an institutional structure aimed at strengthening governance. Among the central features:

- Decision-making was decentralized: district and local committees including non-government representatives selected beneficiary schools.
- School committees were involved in determining needs and construction work involved local people.
- Details of block grants were announced publicly and finance was directly transferred through the banking system, thus avoiding interference from intermediaries.
- Comprehensive guidelines were issued for programme procedures.
- The programme was independently monitored through a Central Independent Monitoring Unit (CIMU).

The monitoring report of the CIMU, which was publicly released, sparked an intense national debate on corruption. It documented forty apparent cases of corruption, from construction consultants illegally charging for services to diversion of funds by local government officers, attempted bribery and collusion on prices between officials and building contractors or textbook suppliers. Measured against past practices, overall levels of corruption in the SIGP were modest – institutionalized transparency made a clear difference. The CIMU report transformed corruption in the education system from a well-hidden activity to a highly visible subject for public debate (Baines, 2005).

Institutionalized public-expenditure tracking is one of the most effective anti-corruption devices. Monitoring real delivery of funds compared with budget provisions can turn a spotlight on problem areas. Since the mid-1990s the World Bank and other donors have conducted Public Expenditure Tracking Surveys (PETS) to evaluate the effectiveness of financial management systems and identify where leakage occurs between ministries and the classroom (Reinikka and Smith, 2004; Winkler, 2005). Building on an exercise undertaken initially in the mid-1990s in Uganda, PETS are now a widely used monitoring tool (Box 3.2). Their impact is strengthened when it is combined with improved public access to information – a point illustrated by the experiences of Indonesia and Uganda.

Not all public expenditure tracking exercises have been successful. When corruption is deeply entrenched and political leaders do not create conditions for strengthened accountability, such exercises can deliver limited results. The PETS on education conducted in Peru in 2002 is an example. Opaque budget planning made it impossible to establish real allocation levels, providing extensive opportunities for corruption. Over 90% of the resources earmarked for education were devoted to payroll, but data lapses on teacher numbers limited the scope for assessing delivery (Reinikka and Smith, 2004).

As Transparency International puts it: 'in many countries, anti-corruption laws and regulation have been in place for years, but citizens do not know about them – often because they are rarely applied. With no visible sanctions, people are inclined to believe that corruption cannot be resisted and therefore will not report it' (Transparency International, 2005, p. 14). Part of the problem is that those who benefit from corruption have much to lose from information campaigns and much to gain from the maintenance of reporting systems that lack transparency. On the other hand, most citizens – particularly the poor and parents with children in school – stand to lose a great deal from failure to act.

Without visible sanctions corruption often goes unreported

Box 3.2: Public expenditure tracking, information campaigns and the fight against corruption in Uganda

Public information and budget monitoring are two of the most powerful antidotes for corruption. Uganda's experience illustrates their effectiveness in strengthening public financial management systems.

In the mid-1990s official budget records were a weak guide to the financing of education in Uganda. In 1996, the World Bank conducted a PETS in 250 schools located in 19 districts. It showed that, according to school records, only 13% of central government capitation grants actually reached schools. Most schools reported having received no funds, and most teachers and parents were unaware that the grants existed. Financing earmarked for education was diverted to other sectors, used for political activities or stolen.

When Uganda introduced free primary education in 1997, donor support was required to replace parental contributions with public spending. Aid partners made support conditional on implementation of an anti-corruption programme, including measures to raise awareness about leakage and give parents a voice. Schools were instructed to publicly post detailed information about funds received from local government. Several national and regional newspapers published information about grant transfers from central to local government, including dates and amounts.

Institutional changes were also introduced. Instead of transferring funds for education and other sectors to districts as a single block grant, the government decided to transfer them as twenty-two separate conditional grants with payments linked to specific actions. A second PETS in 2002 showed that schools were receiving on average 80% of their capitation grant, and that all schools were receiving at least part of the grant.

Evaluations of the Uganda experience have provided some important insights. Detailed statistical analysis indicates that the reduction in grant leakage was greatest in schools that were closest to newspaper outlets – an indication that information had the effect of empowering communities. However, the benefits of information campaigns were not equitably distributed. Their impact was less marked in communities with the lowest literacy levels, thus underlining yet again the importance of education – and literacy skills in particular – to help people make informed choices and to create an enabling environment for responsible and accountable governance.

Sources: Crouch and Winkler (2007); Hubbard (2007).

Unequal spending reinforces disparities

Resource mobilization, efficiency and measures to tackle corruption have system-wide benefits for education. That is why governance in these areas is of such importance for achieving EFA. Equity also matters. Overcoming the disadvantages and disparities documented in Chapter 2 requires financing strategies that aim explicitly at equalizing opportunity, with public financing being used to counteract social deprivation.

In many countries public education spending tends to benefit the relatively well-off

Equitable financing is not an easy concept to define. It clearly means something more than equal per-student financing. Providing equivalent support to children in very unequal circumstances is not the same as equalizing opportunity. Children who are disabled, who lack home advantages associated with parental literacy, who are poor or are disadvantaged by virtue of their gender or ethnicity are not competing on a level playing field. For children in cases like these, achieving a particular outcome in education is likely to entail higher costs than for children from social groups that are not disadvantaged.

Whatever the precise definition of equity, government spending patterns around the world are often highly inequitable. Analysis of the distribution of benefits from public spending across populations suggests inequity is the rule, not the exception. A study of countries in sub-Saharan Africa, Asia and the Pacific, the Middle East and North Africa, and countries in transition, discussed in the 2008 Report, found that total expenditure on education was not pro-poor in any region. In many cases public spending was strongly 'pro-rich', with pro-poor expenditure on primary education outweighed by a bias towards higher income groups in secondary and tertiary education.

National data broadly confirm this picture. In some cases, public financing allocations fail to counteract poverty-related disadvantage. One illustration comes from Indonesia, where per-capita expenditure on education in the poorest 20% of districts amounts to only 54% of expenditure in the richest 20%. The gap in per-student expenditure is smaller because enrolment is lower in the poorest districts (Table 3.3). In a more equitable system the poorest districts, which face the most severe deprivation in education, would receive the highest per-student allocations. In some cases, the contours of unequal financing follow ethnic lines. In the former Yugoslav Republic of Macedonia, schools whose students are of Albanian ethnicity receive almost 20% less in per-student funding than the national average. In rural areas they receive almost 37% less than schools whose students are of Macedonian ethnicity (Table 3.4). In China, per student spending at the primary level varies by a factor of ten between the lowest spending and highest spending provinces, broadly reflecting differences in provincial wealth (Tsang, 2002).

Spending patterns are not fixed in stone. They change with patterns of enrolment and as a result of public policy decisions. During the 1990s, Brazil had one of the world's most inequitable patterns of public spending. Per-student spending in the poorest states of the north-east averaged around half the level in the wealthier states of the south-east. More recently, redistributive financing programmes have significantly changed this picture. Many governments are attempting to redress social inequalities in education directly through new approaches to financial resource allocation, attaching more weight in allocation formulas to disadvantaged groups and regions, or to special programmes. Targeted interventions focused on specific inputs have also been used. For example, spending on free textbook programmes targeting the disadvantaged in three Central American countries was found to successfully redirect resources to the poor (Table 3.5).

Many factors determine how governments allocate resources in education. Technical financing formulas can be useful, but the real drivers of distribution patterns lie elsewhere. Governments with a weak commitment to equity in general are unlikely to attach a great deal of weight to the interests of disadvantaged groups or regions in

Table 3.3: Poverty and public education expenditure in Indonesia, 2004

	Total district education expenditure (Constant 2006US$)	
District quintile	Per capita	Per public school student
Quintile 1 (poorest)	53	147
Quintile 2	75	132
Quintile 3	63	125
Quintile 4	71	151
Quintile 5 (richest)	98	169

Source: Calculations based on Arze del Granado et al. (2007, Table 10, p. 17).

education. Similarly, in situations where the educationally disadvantaged have a weak political voice, they are unlikely to exercise a strong claim on public financial resources. Political leadership can make an enormous difference. For example, in Senegal, Uganda, the United Republic of Tanzania and Zambia the decision of political leaders to abolish user fees in education while increasing spending at the primary level has strengthened equity in public spending and had important positive effects on enrolment.

Strategies for greater equity in financing

There are no ready-made formulas for equitable financing in education. Any strategy aimed at equalizing opportunity has to take into account specific patterns of disadvantage. Some of these patterns might be rooted in regional disparities. Others will involve factors such as the incidence and depth of poverty, or disadvantage based on gender, ethnicity and language. In an equitable system, allocation of education finance would be inversely related to current outcomes, with those in greatest need receiving the most support. Moving from statements of principle to practical measures raises multiple challenges for government.

Table 3.4: Ethnicity and public education expenditure in the former Yugoslav Republic of Macedonia, 2005

School ethnicity type	Municipality type				
	Rural	Small city	Large city	Skopje (capital)	Total
	(Constant 2006 US$)				
Albanian	289	263	261	255	274
Dominant Albanian	341	367	298	238	301
Macedonian	457	347	364	290	359
Dominant Macedonian	467	386	295	360	372
Other	454	…	375	296	395
Total	391	352	332	285	342

Source: Calculations based on World Bank (2008*c*, Table 2.7, p. 24).

Table 3.5: Free textbooks distributed by governments in selected Central American countries, percentage per income quintile, 2000–2004

Country	Quintile 1 (poorest)	Quintile 2	Quintile 3	Quintile 4	Quintile 5 (richest)
	(% of total free textbooks)				
El Salvador	29	26	24	14	7
Guatemala	29	27	21	16	8
Nicaragua	29	23	26	15	8

Source: Porta Pallais and Laguna (2007).

For all the egalitarian rhetoric of public policy discourse on education, it is relatively rare to find a clear link between student needs, as determined by equity criteria, and per-student expenditure. Governance rules for resource allocation vary enormously. Most countries have funding formulas for allocating money, teachers and teaching materials across education systems. These formulas can include a per-student component, a fixed capital cost component and compensatory elements aimed at redressing disadvantage. Compensatory finance can address wide-ranging sources and types of inequality, such as:

- disadvantage associated with racial, ethnic, caste and other characteristics where cultural norms, political disenfranchisement and systemic discrimination hold back achievement;
- problems facing linguistic minorities or students whose native language is not the national or official language of instruction;
- restricted opportunities facing children from poor households whose parents may lack the resources to keep them out of the labour force, to finance transportation to school or to buy school supplies, textbooks, uniforms and school meals;
- lack of provision for students in remote schools, where small class sizes, transport problems, boarding and dormitory costs, and problems in attracting and retaining teachers restrict opportunity;
- the additional financing and specialized teaching that may be required to assist students who are disabled or have special needs.

The link between student needs and per-student expenditure is often weak

One common application of formula funding in developing countries has been the introduction of school grants. Such grants represent a transfer of resources and spending authority from central, regional or district education authorities to local communities and schools (Fredriksen, 2007). They can address a wide range of equity-related goals. On the supply side, grants can be used to increase finance and the flow of teaching materials to schools in areas marked by high concentrations of poverty or with large numbers of disadvantaged students. On the demand side, they can be used to reduce barriers to access. Compensating schools for the loss of revenue that occurs when user charges are withdrawn is an example, as illustrated by Ghana's Capitation Grant Scheme (Box 3.3).

Other countries have also introduced school grants into education financing. In Kenya, the government established a school grant of US$14 per student to enable schools to cover losses from the withdrawal of student fees and to increase spending on materials, maintenance and operations. The programme has improved availability of textbooks and other materials. It has also been used to fund boarding schools to improve access for children living in sparsely populated areas (Fredriksen, 2007). Similarly, the United Republic of Tanzania introduced school grants soon after abolishing fees in 2001. In 2002 its capitation grants for primary schools amounted to about US$10 per pupil for textbooks, teaching and learning materials, school operations and administration, and teacher training (Fredriksen, 2007).[5]

In Ghana, a government grant enables schools to cover losses from the withdrawal of student fees

Formula funding and school grant design are often viewed as narrowly technical matters. They seldom figure in public debate or political programmes.

Box 3.3: Supporting school fee abolition: school grants in Ghana

Under the Free Compulsory Universal Basic Education policy introduced in 1996, Ghana officially eliminated tuition fees for grades 1 to 9. Five years later, the policy had not had its intended effect on enrolment and retention. Policy reviews identified part of the problem as a substitution effect: faced with a loss of revenue, communities and parent-teacher associations authorized the introduction of informal fees.

School grants were introduced in 2004/2005 as a response. They targeted schools in the forty most deprived districts and were linked to school improvement plans. Intended to cover the cost of fee abolition, they were calculated based on student numbers, with a higher per-student grant for girls (the grants were equivalent to US$2.70 per boy and US$3.88 per girl per year). Central government funds were channelled through dedicated bank accounts in each district and then on to individual school bank accounts. Complaints and extensive lobbying from other districts led to the programme being extended to all primary schools from 2005/2006.

How successful has it been? Enrolment figures covering the school years 2002/2003 to 2006/2007 point to sharp increases in overall enrolment ratios (Figure 3.6). For example, the primary NER for girls living in deprived districts increased by twenty-four percentage points over this five year period. While these improvements have been impressive, it is too early to tell whether the programme will have an impact on two central problems facing education in Ghana: high dropout rates and low rates of transition to secondary school.

Figure 3.6: Trends in primary net enrolment ratios in Ghana before and after introduction of the Capitation Grant Scheme

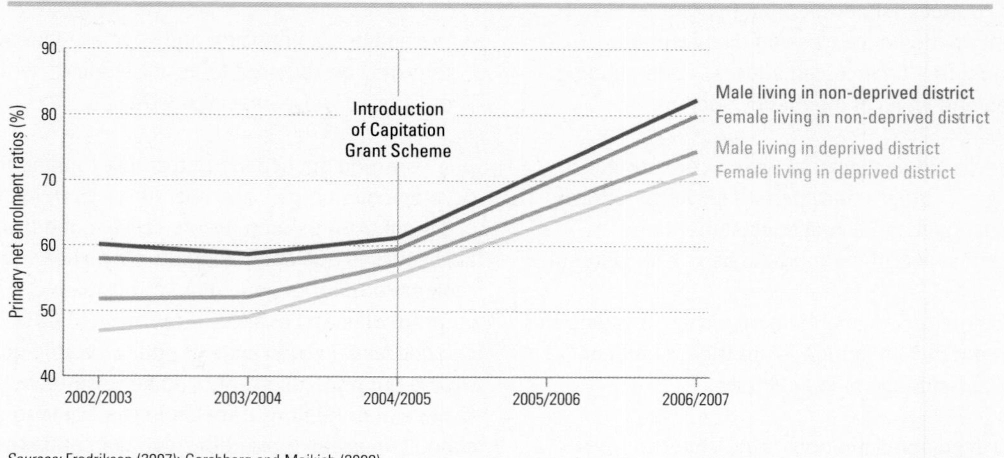

Sources: Fredriksen (2007); Gershberg and Maikish (2008).

5. Other sub-Saharan African countries experimenting with school grants include Ethiopia, Madagascar, Mozambique and Uganda.

This is unhelpful. Financial resource management is complex, but that does not mean it should be the sole preserve of technocrats and administrators. Formula funding design provides a strong indicator of whether governments are intent on translating commitments on equity into practical policies. Chapter 2 suggests that governments could attach more weight to the mapping and monitoring of disparities in education. Approaches to formula funding should be evaluated in the light of this exercise, with governments providing full public disclosure not just of the formula used but also of the equity rationale for its selection.

Decentralization: a potential driver of inequality

The decentralization of public services to local government control has been a major feature of governance reform worldwide. Arguments for decentralization extend from efficiency to equity. Bringing decisions closer to the people affected, and devolving authority to local governments they elect, is seen as a route to more responsive service provision.

Education has figured prominently in decentralization reform. In the developing world, a growing number of countries have transferred responsibility for education to lower levels of government, typically as part of wider public service reform. Decentralization in education redistributes authority not only from central to local government but also from political authorities to school providers (King and Cordeiro Guerra, 2005).

What this means in practice varies by country. Governments seldom devolve power wholesale and devolved education systems operate through multilayered governance structures that link many actors and agencies. Central governments may transfer authority in some areas and either retain authority in others or set rules putting limits on local government choice. Despite widespread advocacy for decentralization, central governments often retain high levels of control, as the governance mapping exercise in this Report's annex shows. Patterns of financial decentralization are particularly complex and have important implications for education provision. The rules and policies governing fiscal decentralization also shape the ways in which it affects education. Any assessment has to take account of three key areas:

- *the assignment of spending authority,* which defines the level of government responsible for making decisions on spending;
- *the assignment of revenue-raising authority,* which defines the powers of the various levels of government to impose taxes and charges;
- *formulas for intergovernment resource transfers,* which determine how revenue is allocated among regions and sectors.

Policies in each of these areas can have an important impact on equity. It cannot be taken as axiomatic that the impact will be positive. The devolution of revenue-raising authority, for example, can give local government greater autonomy but also lead to the introduction of user charges and taxes that may hurt the poor. In Viet Nam, fiscal decentralization has gone a long way but central government controls revenue mobilization and transfers to local government (see below). The only form of revenue autonomy for district and commune governments is in the introduction of fees in areas such as education and health. User charges have been increased in both areas, with damaging implications for equity (Huong, 2006).

Despite widespread advocacy for decentralization, central governments often retain high levels of control

The experience in Viet Nam epitomizes some of the tensions inherent in decentralization. Part of the rationale for decentralization is to improve efficiency and strengthen autonomy by devolving real authority. But devolving revenue mobilization in countries with high levels of inequality comes with grave risks for equity. Governments can mitigate those risks by ensuring that intergovernment resource transfers equalize opportunity. The formulas used by governments in designing these transfers are highly technical – and highly political. The following cases are instructive because equity has been a primary concern in each:

- **Viet Nam:** Provincial governments now have extensive tax collection powers in areas such as land and property, and responsibility for transfers to communes. However, transfers from central government remain the largest revenue stream. Transfers are determined by a formula based on population, but with weighting for poverty, remoteness, health and education norms, and the presence of disadvantaged populations. A 2003 law recalculated the education norm on the basis of all children, rather than in-school children. Since the shares of school-age children enrolled are lower in poorer provinces, this has increased equity. Similarly, the education norm for a child living in mountainous areas (which have the worst education indicators) is 1.7 times that of an urban child. The commitment to equity is reflected in spending: richer regions such as the Red River Delta have some twenty-five times the income of the poorest regions such as the North West, but budget spending per capita is roughly equivalent, reflecting large transfers from rich to poor regions (Adams, 2005; Huong, 2006).

Decentralization is a highly political process

- **Uganda:** Decentralization reforms in Uganda have been among the most ambitious in sub-Saharan Africa. However, decentralized governance has proceeded faster in the sphere of service management and delivery than in finance. While district authorities are allowed to collect local taxes, they are not entitled to charge fees for basic services such as education. They are also constrained in defining spending priorities. Around 90% of revenue in most years comes from central government. Over two-thirds of the funding transferred is a conditional grant, linked to achievement of goals from the national poverty reduction strategy, including UPE, secondary education and teacher recruitment. Most of the rest is an unconditional grant calculated on the basis of population and land area. In addition, a small equalization grant is aimed at reducing the gap between richer and poorer districts (Obwona et al., 2000; Steiner, 2006; Uganda Local Government Finance Commission, 2000).

- **South Africa:** The end of apartheid in 1994 brought a new democratic government and a radical move towards decentralization, with provincial and local governments taking on extensive new responsibilities in areas such as health, education and housing. The financing formula for fiscal decentralization incorporated a strong redistributive component aimed at overcoming inequalities inherited from the apartheid era. Around 95% of provincial government expenditure comes from central government. The largest component is known as an equitable share transfer, weighted to reflect levels of poverty and the costs of achieving minimum national norms in areas such as health and education. In education, financing is based on student numbers, with some additional weight given to poor and rural provinces. Provincial authorities are also required to rank schools by a poverty index, which is used to allocate funding for non-personnel inputs (Gershberg and Winkler, 2003; Momoniat, 2003). As a consequence of these reforms, resource allocations to schools have become more equitable (Crouch and Winkler, 2007).

- **Colombia:** Decentralization of government finance in the 1990s significantly improved equity of intergovernment transfers. Before decentralization, transfers from central government were based on historic transfers – an arrangement that favoured wealthier provinces. Under the reforms, historic allocations were replaced by a formula allocating resources on the basis of population, with adjustments for health and education provision (Bossert et al., 2003).

The motivation for financial decentralization can be important. Where reform is prompted by fiscal pressures on central government, it can result in reduced central government financing. In these circumstances local governments, communities and schools are likely to seek supplementary funding from parents. This is broadly what happened in China in the 1990s (King and Cordeiro Guerra, 2005).

It is sometimes forgotten that decentralization is a highly political process. It is one thing to devolve authority in countries characterized by high levels of national cohesion, strong national, regional and local government institutions, and well-defined processes for conflict resolution. It is quite another to shift the locus of decision-making in countries marked by weak governance systems and high levels of tension. In a country such as Nigeria – where public confidence in institutions is weak, political relationships between regions are tense and democracy is still under construction – decentralization is a fraught political exercise (World Bank, 2008*f*).

Decentralized finance in education

In education, as in other areas, decentralization has to be evaluated on its outcomes. However, in the context of financing EFA, two broad dangers can be identified. First, devolution of finance can act as a powerful driver for disparities in provision. Decentralization with equity requires central governments to retain a strong role in redistributing finance, with a commitment to equalizing opportunity. Second, financial and political devolution to weak local governance structures can have negative consequences for the coverage and quality of education, again with damaging consequences for equity. Here too, successful decentralization requires an active role for central government in building capacity.

China's experience with fiscal decentralization provides a cautionary tale for education equity. During the 1990s the central government reduced its share in overall education financing, giving more responsibility to local governments, schools and communities. This decentralization effort had unintended consequences. Overall resource mobilization for education lagged behind economic growth, leading to a decline in the share of GDP allocated to education from 2.9% in 1991 to 2.2% in 1997. Decentralization also generated major geographic and income-based disparities in per-student spending. The ratio of highest-spending to lowest-spending province in per-student expenditure in primary education almost doubled from 5 to 9 (Table 3.6). Many schools and local authorities resorted to formal and informal household charges, so equity suffered: in effect, fiscal decentralization acted as a regressive education tax on the poor (King and Cordeiro Guerra, 2005; Tsang, 2002).

Recognition that the lack of a strategy to equalize financing has compromised equity and the quality of education in poorer areas has prompted the Chinese Government to rethink its initial strategy. It has removed some tax powers from local government, continued to finance teacher salaries and maintained responsibility for parts of the capital budget. Concerns over inequality are cited as a primary motivation. However, these efforts have met with limited success. While the central government formally prohibits the charging of fees, still many local governments informally encourage it (Wang, 2004) and large gaps in the quality of provision remain. More fundamentally, China still lacks a system of transfers between provinces, and between rich and poor areas within provinces, consistent with a more equitable pattern of expenditure while preserving the principle of decentralized decision-making.

Tensions between the goals of equity and political decentralization are not limited to China. In the Philippines, where education financing has

Table 3.6: Inequality in per-student education expenditure in China following decentralization

	Primary education (constant 2006 US$)			Lower secondary education (constant 2006 US$)		
	1989	1997	2000	1989	1997	2000
Highest-spending province	157	357	419	314	520	424
Mean	66	90	75	141	166	103
Lowest-spending province	30	39	40	69	75	64
Ratio of highest-spending to lowest-spending province	5	9	11	5	7	7

Source: Calculations based on Tsang (2002, Tables 1-3, p. 19).

remained less decentralized, local authorities are permitted to raise revenue for education through a Special Education Fund (SEF) tax on property (King and Cordeiro Guerra, 2005). Spending per student from the SEF in the poorest municipalities with the lowest property values is only 13% of the levels in the richest municipalities and 3% of that in the richest cities. Here too, the absence of a strong formula for redistributive public finance has hampered efforts to strengthen equity.

Decentralization can generate major geographical and income-based disparities in per-student spending

In Indonesia, decentralization has gone hand in hand with a large increase in the share of GNP allocated to education, from less than 2% before decentralization to over 4% today (King and Cordeiro Guerra, 2005). It transfers resources from central to local government via a block grant system incorporating a strong equity component, with the poorer districts receiving the largest transfers. However, central government also requires local districts to mobilize their own resources – and it has devolved tax raising authority. This has an inbuilt danger for equity: in the richest provinces, such as Jakarta, per-capita GDP is some nine times greater than in the poorest provinces, such as South Sulawesi. Enrolment ratios at junior secondary level range from 68% in South Sulawesi to 93% in Jakarta.

The lesson from East Asia is that governments need to plan for equity. The push towards financial devolution has brought a risk of widening disparities between regions, with attendant dangers for the inequalities outlined in Chapter 2. Central government resource transfers hold the key to making financial decentralization work for the poor.

Evidence from Latin America is also instructive. The decentralization of education from federal to provincial governments was an important feature of institutional reform in the region during the 1990s. In Argentina, the transfer of responsibility for secondary schools from federal to provincial level was accompanied by a system of federal tax transfers. Detailed evaluations of the decentralization process have identified many benefits. Nationally, decentralization appears to have improved local participation, strengthened monitoring and improved learning standards. However, the results have not been uniform. Test scores point to a widening gap between wealthier provinces with strong government capacity and poorer provinces with low administrative and institutional capacity; the latter performed worse under decentralization. National efficiency has improved, but at the expense of equity (Galiani et al., forthcoming; Rhoten, 2000).

Central transfer mechanisms and targeted redistribution have proved helpful in redressing education inequalities

Experience in other regions is more limited. In sub-Saharan Africa, financial decentralization is less advanced than political decentralization. Some governments have integrated equity into decentralized financing (as in Uganda). In other cases, fiscal decentralization appears to have had damaging consequences for education equity. This is demonstrated by the experience of Nigeria, whose financial governance system combines a 'worst of two worlds' approach: low overall commitment and highly unequal financing (Box 3.4). In marked contrast, decentralization policies in Ethiopia attach far more weight to equity. Apart from highlighting innovative pro-poor financing approaches in education, Ethiopia's experience demonstrates the importance of flexible policy responses to unanticipated problems (Box 3.5).

Many governments now recognize the importance of central transfer mechanisms to redress education inequalities arising from decentralization. These mechanisms can take various forms. The primary one is often the block grant. Its size can be linked to levels of deprivation, as in Uganda. Central governments can introduce a conditional element into such grants, requiring local governments to meet specified standards for overall sector financing and equity. In other cases, financing can be linked to specified inputs. Two examples from Latin America illustrate the scope for redistribution:

- *Colombia – the use of compensatory financing.* In 2004 Colombia introduced allocation rules using a funding formula based on the number of students enrolled, with a basic cost component (covering teacher salaries and administrative costs per student) supplemented by a compensatory component which includes weighting for geographic dispersion, poverty and the share of rural households in the population. In 2006 the seven poorest and most rural departments received extra funding amounting to between 39% and 112% of the average basic cost. In addition, legislation provides for teachers in rural and remote areas to receive 15% more than the base salary (Meade and Gershberg, 2008). Preliminary evidence, while less than clear-cut, suggests that the move has strengthened equity on some indicators. Transfers to Bogotá, the capital, have increased at a rate below the national average. Meanwhile, in 2006 two of the poorest departments, Chocó and La Guajira, received 30% more than Antioquia, one of the most urban and developed departments (Meade and Gershberg, 2008).

- *Brazil – targeted redistribution through FUNDEF.* When Brazil devolved authority from a highly centralized system to states and municipalities in the mid-1990s, it created FUNDEF to reduce the large national inequalities in per-student spending (de Mello and Hoppe, 2005; Gordon and Vegas, 2005). State and municipal governments were required to transfer a proportion of their tax revenue to FUNDEF, which redistributed it to state and municipal governments that could not meet specified minimum levels of per-student expenditure. FUNDEF has not prevented wealthier regions from increasing their overall spending more rapidly than poorer regions, but it has played a highly redistributive role. It has also increased both the absolute level of spending and the predictability of transfers, notably for poor states and municipalities in the north and north-east. There is strong evidence that FUNDEF has been instrumental in reducing class size, improving the supply and quality of teachers, and expanding enrolment. At municipal level, data show that the 20% of municipalities receiving the most funds from FUNDEF were able to double per-pupil expenditure between 1996 and 2002 in real terms (Gordon and Vegas, 2005).

Are there rules of good practice in decentralization that can be derived from experience to date? As in many other areas of governance, the diversity of country experience militates against drawing simple lessons with universal application.

Box 3.4: Fiscal decentralization in Nigeria – reinforcing regional disparities

Improved governance and the return of democracy to Nigeria have done little to narrow inequalities in education. One reason is that insufficient attention has been paid to the development of a more equitable financing system.

Primary net attendance rates (NARs) in Nigeria range from 85% in Anambra and Ondo states to less than 30% in Jigawa and Zamfara states (Map 3.1). These disparities are linked to substantial differences in poverty rates. In 2004 the poverty headcount ratio in Anambra was 20%, compared with 95% in Jigawa.

Under an equitable financing system more resources would be allocated to states with low levels of participation and high rates of poverty. In Nigeria the equity principle is turned upside down: the wealthiest states and regions with the highest education participation secure the lion's share of federal resources. For example, Lagos receives around five times as much as Jigawa, which has attendance rates less than half of those in the commercial capital.

Fiscal decentralization has reinforced regional disparities in education. Since the return to multiparty democracy in 1999, an increasing share of federal revenue (predominantly from oil and gas) has been allocated to state and local governments. Since 2002 about half the federal budget has been allocated to states and local government areas (LGAs). Of this share, a third is reserved for the four oil-producing states in the Niger delta and the remainder is distributed under a complex formula that produces a simple result: large financing inequalities.

In 2005, Kano, a poor state with a low primary NAR and limited revenue-generating capacity, received 20% less in federation account revenue than Enugu state, with similar revenue raising capacity, lower poverty rates and a higher primary NAR. Unlike most states that depend on federal allocations, Lagos generates two-thirds of its revenue from local sources – an arrangement that reinforces regional financing gaps.

Not all the problems in Nigeria's education financing can be traced to unequal fiscal decentralization. National planning is also weak. No statutory accountability mechanisms exist to ensure that state and LGA plans, where they exist, are aligned with national goals in education. As a result, the priority that LGAs give to primary education varies enormously, even within states. In Kano, 28% of the Dala local government budget was allocated to primary education, compared with 12% in Bichi.

Recognizing the need for additional financing in education, the federal government created the Universal Basic Education Commission (UBEC) intervention fund, which channels federal resources directly to basic education. Between 2005 and early 2008 about US$750 million was made available to states through the fund. Unfortunately, this has done little to enhance equity or efficiency:

Map 3.1: Net attendance rates and education spending per primary school-age child, Nigeria, most recent year

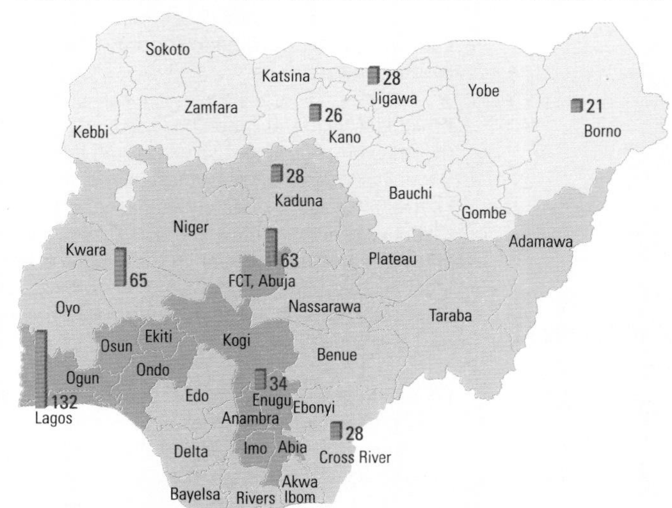

Public spending per primary school-age child (constant 2006 US$)

Primary net attendance rate

- Less than 50%
- 50% - 79%
- 80% and above

The boundaries and names shown and the designations used on this map do not imply official endorsement or acceptance by UNESCO. Based on United Nations map.

Sources: Calculations based on Kano State Ministry of Education (2008); Nigeria National Bureau of Statistics (2006*a*).

- **Equal allocations lead to unequal effect.** Some 70% of available resources are allocated equally across states without regard for differences in need. Only 9% of resources are directed to the most disadvantaged states and to activities promoting education for physically and mentally challenged children.
- **Disbursements have been much lower than expected.** Only 60% of allocated funds had been disbursed by mid-2007. Problems range from inadequate policy coordination to complex bureaucratic procedures and weak capacity in state education bodies.
- **Use of funds is inflexible.** The UBEC has strict guidelines on the proportion of funds that can be spent on pre-primary, primary and junior secondary education, as well as the type of expenditure. For example, 70% of funds must be spent on construction, regardless of need. This makes it more difficult to use resources effectively to support state plans for the development of basic education.

Sources: Adediran et al. (2008); Bennell et al. (2007); Kano State Ministry of Education (2008); Nigeria National Bureau of Statistics (2006*a*, 2006*b*); World Bank (2007*b*, 2008*f*).

Box 3.5: Financial decentralization with equity in Ethiopia

Since the late 1990s Ethiopia has witnessed rapid improvement in education outcomes. The country has also been implementing far-reaching education reform, including radical decentralization, in the context of wider governance reform. Equity is a central concern.

Ethiopia's decentralization has involved a radical overhaul of government structures. In the first phase, a four-tier governance structure was created: the centre, the regions (nine ethnic-based states plus the cities of Addis Ababa and Dire Dawa), the zones and the *woredas* (districts). In the second phase, legal, fiscal and administrative reforms devolved responsibility for management of social services to the *woredas*.

Education is now financed through a two-step process. The first involves fiscal transfers from the federal government to the regions and the second from regional governments to *woredas*, which now manage about 45% of regional public expenditure. Most transfers operate through large federal block grants which regional and *woreda* governments may allocate freely. A 'three parameter' formula for grant allocation to the regions takes into account population size, poverty and development levels, along with an index of revenue effort and sector performance.
While funding formulas have an equity component, they have tended to produce strong biases in favour of regions with smaller populations, even though they are not necessarily the poorest.

Most regional governments use the three-parameter formula to allocate their grants to *woredas*, but there is sufficient flexibility for them to experiment with other approaches. The Southern Nations, Nationalities and Peoples Region, one of the country's poorest, has taken advantage of that flexibility to develop innovative new approaches. Between 2003/2004 and 2006/2007, authorities have experimented with a unit cost approach that distinguishes between recurrent and capital expenditure. Reduced to its essentials, it allocates higher per capita funding for recurrent expenditure to the *woredas* with the more developed social services, so those services can be adequately staffed and function effectively. Meanwhile, higher per capita funding for capital expenditure is allocated to *woredas* having less developed social services so they can expand infrastructure and reduce the gap with the other *woredas*.

Data on education expenditure suggest that the unit cost approach had equalizing effects between *woredas*. For instance, mean per-student recurrent expenditure on primary education increased by 18% between 2001 and 2004, per-student funding became more equal among *woredas*, the mean *woreda*-level primary GER increased from 63% to 73% and enrolment gaps between *woredas* narrowed.

Decentralization in the region seems to have disproportionately favoured remote, food-insecure and pastoral *woredas* (Table 3.7). Despite these outcomes, the unit cost approach has led to some *woredas* receiving lower funding, prompting demands for further reform.

Table 3.7: Ethiopia's Southern Nations, Nationalities and Peoples Region: *woreda*-level spending on education before and after decentralization

Type of *woreda* (district)	Total education		
	2001	2004	Change between 2001 and 2004
	Constant 2006 US$		(%)
Remote (more than 50 km from a zone head city)	266	361	36
Non-remote	516	530	3
Food insecure	431	528	22
Food secure	288	320	11
Pastoral	126	221	75
Non-pastoral	389	453	16

Source: Calculations based on World Bank (2007*b*, Table 4.3, p. 43).

Much depends on how governments use financing arrangements to improve service in poor areas

Decentralization has been described as a process rather than a destination (Bird and Smart, 2001). The way the process unfolds is heavily influenced by public policy choices, institutional capacity and government commitment to deal with poverty issues. In the case of education, much depends on how governments use financing arrangements to equalize opportunity and improve service provision in poor areas. From an equity perspective, the important question would seem to be not whether to decentralize, but how and what to decentralize. Four broad rules would appear to be of particular importance for progress towards EFA.

First, **revenue-raising powers** for local government should be clearly defined. Subnational authorities should not be permitted to mobilize budget resources through user charges in basic education, which have regressive and damaging effects on the poor.

Second, central government should retain **redistributive capacity**. Intergovernment transfers are needed to prevent the growth of regional financing inequalities and the widening gaps in opportunity that can result.

Third, **equity goals** should be built into intergovernment financing formulas. Transfers should be weighted to provide larger per-capita transfers to regions marked by high levels of poverty and marginalization, with education indicators as a central part of the formula. In addition, national rules need to provide a framework for ensuring that lower levels of government prioritize equity in delivery of financing.

Finally, central governments should carefully assess the implications of decentralization for the achievement of **national goals in education**. Ensuring that local governments have the resources and capacity to manage progress towards inclusive education is critical.

Conclusion

Approaches to education finance will continue to exercise a critical influence over prospects for achieving the goals set out in the Dakar Framework for Action. Increased financing is not a sufficient condition for delivering on the commitment to education for all – but in many countries it is a necessary condition. In some cases, national governments are not demonstrating sufficient levels of commitment either to resource mobilization or to equity. Much of South and West Asia falls into this category. In other cases, stronger national commitment will need to be accompanied by scaled-up donor support.

Financial governance challenges vary enormously across regions and countries. Improving efficiency and facing up to corruption are two immediate priorities for many governments. It is also important for governments to take stock of the experience of decentralization. While the case for avoiding overly centralized decision-making and for devolving political authority under appropriate conditions remains strong, decentralization is not a panacea. In the area of financing, there is an urgent need to place equity at the centre of the decentralization agenda. That means central government retaining a strongly redistributive role consistent with commitments to inclusive education and equal opportunity for education. □

Central government should retain a strongly redistributive role consistent with commitments to equal opportunity for education

Choice, competition and voice: school governance reform and EFA

Introduction

Governments around the world repeatedly emphasize their commitment to providing good-quality schooling for all citizens. Outcomes often fall short of the commitment. Persistent problems with education equity and quality, even in countries with high levels of coverage and strong public spending, have brought the management of school systems to the centre of education governance debates.

The evident failure of current education strategies to provide high-quality school systems accessible to all in many countries has prompted calls for wide-ranging reforms. This section looks at some of the central currents in approaches to school governance reforms, with a focus on school-based management and reforms to promote choice in education through public policies. Looking beyond the formal public policy framework, the section also explores the implications of the growth of low-fee private schools for EFA.

Debates over school governance go to the heart of wider questions about the role of government in education

'Voice', 'participation', 'competition' and 'choice' are buzzwords in debates on education governance worldwide. Devolving authority away from central government and towards schools – the core principle behind school-based management – is seen as a means of holding providers to account and increasing participation. Giving parents an opportunity to choose among education providers is widely portrayed as a way to strengthen education provision, with competition acting as a spur to improved quality. While no government treats the education sector as a pure market, many have introduced what have been called 'quasi-market' principles into provision. For some commentators, the entry of low-fee private providers into the education marketplace is important precisely because it provides an impetus towards greater accountability and competition (Tooley, 2007). The motivation behind quasi-market reform has been to raise standards rather than to address inequality. However, advocates for reform often attach to their arguments claims of wide-ranging benefits for equity.

There is a bewildering array of approaches to school governance reform. Countries at very different levels of development have taken up the mantle of reform. The design, scope and depth of reform also come in a multitude of variations. Evaluating outcomes against this backdrop is inherently difficult. Even so, two broad conclusions emerge from the evidence presented in this section.

The first is that context matters. Governance debates are frequently characterized by bold assertions on the presumed benefits of school management reform for learning outcomes and for equity. Evidence to back these assertions is often lacking. Moreover, there is a widespread tendency to generalize findings and to assume that a policy that works in one context will deliver the same results elsewhere. Looking ahead, it is important that policy-makers develop more evidence-based approaches. It is also important that they identify the broader institutional conditions and enabling factors needed to strengthen education quality and equity.

The second conclusion is that competition and choice have the potential to reinforce inequality. Choice is important in education, as in other areas. The Universal Declaration of Human Rights (Article 26) enshrines the right of parents 'to choose the kind of education that shall be given to their children.' Under certain conditions, competition can act as a force to drive up standards and improve efficiency. But choice and competition are not abstract concepts. For people living in chronic poverty, choice is often constrained by a lack of purchasing power, limited access to information and, in many cases, by an absence of responsive providers. Introducing choice and competition into an environment characterized by high levels of inequality without effective public action to equalize opportunity is a prescription for widening disparities. As in many other areas, markets – and quasi-markets – in education are unlikely to prove effective in strengthening equity in the absence of pro-poor regulation.

The issues raised in debates over school governance go to the heart of wider questions about the role of government in education. To what extent should governments finance *and* provide education services? If private providers are to play an expanded role, how should governments manage and regulate their operations? The answers to these questions will vary across countries and across levels of the education system, with a distinction drawn between primary and post-primary education. The critical issue facing policy-makers is to work out strategies through which competition, incentives and accountability can be harnessed to enhance overall quality *and* equity.

The bottom line is that governments have the ultimate responsibility to ensure that everyone has access to basic education systems of acceptable quality. Discharging that responsibility effectively means different things in different places, but it invariably requires placing a premium on the equalization of opportunity across the education system.

School-based management: a broad spectrum of approaches and outcomes

Conventional education governance structures allow schools little control over their affairs. Principals, teachers, parents and even local education bodies have been bound by centralized rules and procedures, leaving them limited scope for influence over staff selection, teaching methods and wider practices. School-based management reforms are challenging this model.

School-based management in its broadest sense aims at increasing school autonomy and empowering teachers and parents to make decisions. It aims to strengthen incentives for schools to deliver services that are responsive to the needs of the communities they serve, and to address problems facing disadvantaged groups (Caldwell, 2005).

Advocates of school-based management point to a wide range of potential benefits. They argue that the devolution of decision-making authority to schools can facilitate and enhance participation – a core strategy in the Dakar Framework for Action. A stronger parental voice and more participation in school management, the argument runs, will lead to greater incentives for education providers to offer more efficient services (World Bank, 2007*f*). Moving decisions away from remote planners and closer to those who know the most about the learners and their educational needs, as well as about local values and realities, is seen as a route to a more responsive system. Equity is another important benefit cited for school-based management. It is assumed that poor households will have a stronger and more effective voice on school management committees and in local community institutions than under more remote centralized systems, empowering them to play a role in framing priorities and in holding school providers to account (World Bank, 2007*f*).

School-based management aims to move decisions closer to those who know more about learners, local values and realities

School-based management is not a recent innovation. Its origins can be traced to the United States in the 1980s and Australia, Canada and the United Kingdom in the 1990s. School-based management programmes have also been adopted in some developing countries. Most of these programmes are in Latin America and South Asia, though sub-Saharan Africa also figures with increasing prominence. While much of the reform impetus in developing countries is home grown, aid donors have played an important role. For example, some 11% of all education projects supported by the World Bank between 2000 and 2006 included school-based management components. These programmes represent around US$1.74 billion in education financing, or just under one-quarter of the World Bank's education portfolio (World Bank, 2007*f*).

School-based management reform is an umbrella description for a diverse range of country experiences. In some countries the schools involved have broad coverage. El Salvador's Educación con Participación de la Comunidad (EDUCO) schools are an example. They account for half of enrolment in public rural pre-schools and 37% in rural basic education. EDUCO is the main schooling option for about 80% of the municipalities with extreme poverty in El Salvador (Meza et al., 2006). In other contexts, the reforms operate on a smaller scale. In some cases, authority is delegated to principals and teachers, with weak community participation included as part of the design. In other cases, decision-making authority is also given to parents or school committees. Similarly, while some programmes transfer authority for hiring and firing teachers, others do not. Variations are found in the degree of devolution of budgetary authority as well. The experience of three Latin American countries with school-based management reform illustrates this diversity (Table 3.8).

The context in which community schools are formed is important. In some cases, the move towards school-based management has been driven from below. In Bolivia, indigenous schools emerged in the 1980s in the context of an intense political struggle over national education policies. The decision of the Quechua communities in some

Education for All Global Monitoring Report 2009

Table 3.8: Functions transferred to schools in three Latin American programmes

	El Salvador EDUCO[1]	Mexico PEC[2]	Nicaragua autonomous schools[3]
Personnel management			
Paying staff salaries	√		√
Hiring/firing teaching staff	√		√
Supervising and evaluating teachers	√		√
Pedagogy			
Setting school calendar, classroom hours			√
Selecting some textbooks/curriculum			√
Method of instruction			
Maintenance and infrastructure			
Building/maintaining school	√	√	√
Buying school materials	√	√	√
Budget			
Oversight	√		√
Allocation			√

1. EDUCO - Educación con Participación de la Comunidad.
2. PEC - Programa Escuelas de Calidad.
3. The policy ended in 2007.
Note: Empty cells indicate that the function was not transferred to schools.
Source: World Bank (2007*f*).

areas to withdraw their children from state schools started out as a protest against teacher absenteeism but rapidly became part of a movement against the imposition of the dominant 'Criollo' culture (the culture and language of the Creole Spanish descendents). Communities themselves took over the running of schools and recruitment of teachers, and they initiated a curriculum for indigenous language teaching. Under the 1994 Education Act and subsequent legislation, indigenous communities have been given greater autonomy within the state system and indigenous language teaching has been brought to the centre of the national curriculum (Albó and Anaya, 2003; Regalsky and Laurie, 2007).

In Latin America and East Asia, school-based management has not greatly affected teaching practices

Learning achievement: a mixed record

Assessing the impact of school-based management reforms on learning outcomes presents serious methodological problems. Cross-country comparisons are of limited relevance and within-country assessments point in various directions. In some cases positive results have been registered but the association between school-based management and improved education quality is weak.

Several factors contribute to the difficulty in extrapolating clear lessons for education quality. Diversity of context is one obvious factor. More broadly, it is difficult to identify or isolate the 'school-based management effect' in achievement, not least because school-based management is usually part of a broader package of political, administrative or educational change. Selection bias is another problem. Schools and communities either self-select into school-based management programmes or are selected to participate by government authorities, often on the basis of specific characteristics that differentiate them from others. This makes it difficult to tell how, or whether, school autonomy in particular had an influence on outcomes.

Most detailed school-based management evaluations come from Latin America. The regional evidence points to some positive effects on attainment. Some studies have found an association between delegation of management functions and reduction of school repetition and dropout (Gertler et al., 2006; Jimenez and Sawada, 2003; Murnane et al., 2006; Paes de Barros and Mendonça, 1998; Skoufias and Shapiro, 2006; World Bank, 2007*e*). Learning outcomes are more variable, with marked differences among countries. A study of mathematics and language performance among grade 3 students found that EDUCO schools in El Salvador scored lower than traditional schools. However, after controlling for background, the differences disappeared and EDUCO pupils actually scored slightly higher in language tests, on average (Jimenez and Sawada, 1999). On the other hand, evaluations in Honduras of schools in the Programa Hondureño de Educación Comunitaria (PROHECO) concluded that the delegation of decision-making was not associated with significant changes in learning achievement (Di Gropello and Marshall, 2005).

Autonomy and pedagogy: a loose connection. An important assumption behind school-based managment is that greater autonomy will permit more flexible, responsive and innovative teaching. That assumption is not strongly backed by evidence.

Findings from Latin America show that school-based management reforms can result in improved teacher motivation. Reduced absenteeism, more time meeting with parents and more hours spent at school are among the key indicators for improved motivation (Di Gropello, 2006; Sawada and Ragatz, 2005). However, evidence from a wide range of country experiences suggests that teaching practices in schools with more autonomy do not differ significantly from those in other schools (Di Gropello and Marshall, 2005; Fuller and Rivarola, 1998; Gunnarsson et al., 2004; Jimenez and Sawada, 1999; King and Ozler, 1988; Parker, 2005). Why has improved motivation not led to new teaching practices?

Once again the explanation varies by country and context. An important factor is that school-based management reforms do not always increase the autonomy of schools and teachers in areas such as pedagogy, as Table 3.8 shows. Even where reforms do provide for greater flexibility, schools and teachers often have not had an opportunity to acquire the capacity and skills to introduce innovative practices. This is borne out by evidence from East Asia. In Indonesia, legislation allows schools to devote 20% of instruction to locally designed subject matter. In Thailand, 30% of the curriculum in basic education can be locally determined. Yet these windows of opportunity for greater flexibility are not fully exploited in either country, partly because teachers have no training or experience in developing innovative approaches to instruction and curriculum design (Bjork, 2004; Shoraku, 2008).

Enabling environments are important

Devolving authority to schools shifts the locus of decision-making and transfers new responsibilities to parents, teachers and principals. Such governance reforms can change incentives and influence relationships between key actors in the delivery of education. Under what circumstances is devolved authority likely to produce positive results? Outcomes invariably depend on local factors but case studies have identified four broad conditions influencing equity and efficiency (Cárdenas, 2008):

- voluntary participation of the school and the surrounding community;
- organizational and technical capacity in, or available to, the school;
- strong and committed school leadership;
- support from upper levels of government.

Voluntary participation. Public-sector schools managed by communities need the motivation and capacity to generate demand for schooling. School-based management initiatives are likely to be most successful when they are driven by demand from below. However, community participation can be a double-edged sword from an equity perspective, especially when it involves competition for resources. Schools with committed principals and organized communities are in a stronger position to exploit opportunities. Evidence from Mexico's Programa Escuelas de Calidad (PEC) illustrates the point: voluntary participation by itself resulted in a selection of schools that were neither located in the poorest communities nor among the lowest performers (Cárdenas, 2008). An important lesson is that voluntary participation has to be supported by measures that strengthen equity.

Successful devolution to schools requires strong school leadership and high-level government support

Organizational and technical capacity of schools. Schools must have sufficient financial and human resources to take on new responsibilities. Drawing up school plans, budgets, and requests for financial and material inputs from central government may require new skills. Evidence suggests that technical capacity of this kind on the part of the head teacher and staff is an important condition for overall school improvement (Abu-Duhou, 1999; Briggs and Wohlstetter, 2003; UNESCO, 2004). The delegation of management functions to schools in Central Asian countries in recent years has been hampered by a lack of programmes to develop school staff capacity for the additional responsibilities involved (Chapman et al., 2005). One danger for equity that comes with school-based management derives from the unequal capacities of schools. In some cases, schools that select themselves for school-based management may have stronger planning capacity than other schools and thus be better able to secure access to resources (Cárdenas, 2008; Reimers and Cárdenas, 2007). The upshot is that schools with weak capacity and the greatest needs may fall further behind.

Strong and committed school leadership. The *EFA Global Monitoring Report 2005* argued that strong school leadership was a prerequisite for creating a culture of school improvement (UNESCO, 2004). Because school-based management increases their responsibilities, head teachers often end up spending more time on administration than on leadership to support pedagogical initiatives and quality improvements. In Nicaragua a common feature of autonomous schools that succeeded in reducing school failure and improving learning outcomes was the principal's leadership abilities (PREAL and Foro Educativo Nicaragüense EDUQUEMOS, 2008). Skilled head teachers can take advantage of the opportunities autonomy provides rather than getting buried in administrative burdens. But the skills needed to maintain a balance between such responsibilities are often lacking, pointing to a need for any move towards school autonomy to be accompanied by training of head teachers for their new roles.

School grants need to be predictable, timely and adequately funded

Sustained support from upper levels of government. If the goal is to reduce disparities in learning, upper levels of government need to focus their efforts on schools with disadvantaged learners. This means strengthening the schools' institutional and technical capacity and ensuring that teachers use their increased autonomy effectively. There should be feedback mechanisms that link monitoring through school supervision to the provision of pedagogical support, including staff training (an issue discussed in the section below on governance of teachers and monitoring).

Building financial capacity: the role of school grants

Autonomy without financial capacity is a general prescription for weak governance. To be effective, schools taking on new responsibilities need sufficient financial and human resources to meet those responsibilities.

Some countries have attempted to build school capacity through school grant programmes. Disbursed and allocated in a variety of ways, grants can be used to achieve a wide range of goals in areas such as education quality and equity. In some cases disbursement is tied to development of a strategic plan to achieve agreed goals in areas such as quality (Espínola, 2000; Nielsen, 2007). In others, grants are geared towards the provision of specific services and inputs.

Uses for school grants range from upgrading infrastructure to contracting additional teachers. Grants provided under the PEC in Mexico have been used mainly for improving infrastructure and acquiring school materials rather than changing teaching practices or working with parents (Yoshikawa et al., 2007). Participation in the programme is associated with overall improvement in school progression although differences in capacity have contributed to inequalities (Skoufias and Shapiro, 2006; Box 3.6). In Brazil there is evidence that the School Development Plan and School Improvement Projects under the Fundo

Box 3.6: Planning for strengthened school autonomy in Mexico

Introducing school-based management in an environment marked by deep capacity inequalities between schools is unlikely to enhance equity. The Programa Escuelas de Calidad (PEC) in Mexico has attempted to strengthen support for its most disadvantaged areas, but has encountered problems linked to weak capacity.

The PEC aims to increase school autonomy and strengthen performance. Schools compete for grants, which are provided for up to five years to improve pedagogical practices, encourage collaborative work between teachers, parents and school authorities, and improve planning in pre-schools and primary schools.

Though the intent is to encourage participation by disadvantaged schools, in practice the initial allocations were skewed against the poorest communities and the worst-performing schools. The schools were often the least equipped to make successful applications, even though they were in greatest need of support.

To apply to the PEC, a school must prepare a Strategic Transformation Plan. This requires a level of organizational capacity often lacking in schools with many disadvantaged students. Differences in the priorities set out in school plans also have important implications for outcomes. Rural and indigenous schools participating in the programme are likely to use the funds for infrastructure and materials instead of pedagogical improvement. As a result, the quantity and quality of physical inputs and materials have generally improved more than the quality of the education process.

The overall record of the PEC remains problematic. While it has made available technical and supervisory support that has improved quality in participating schools, the support has been greater in wealthier states and at more advantaged schools. Instead of reducing gaps between less and more advantaged children, the initiative risks amplifying inequalities.

Sources: Bracho (2006); Murnane et al. (2006); Reimers and Cárdenas (2007); Yoshikawa et al. (2007).

de Fortalecimento da Escola (FUNDESCOLA) are associated with increased availability of learning materials. For schools in FUNDESCOLA that have managed to increase spending, evidence indicates some improvement in learning outcomes (Carnoy et al., 2008).

School grants do not automatically produce positive results. To be effective, they need to be predictable, timely and large enough to cover the activities in the strategic plan. These conditions are not always in place. In Nepal, a school improvement plan is a condition for the release of government block grants, but funds are very limited. Inadequate grant transfers can have adverse implications for equity. In the case of Nepal, there is evidence that underfinancing has led to parents being asked for the funds to recruit teachers and meet other basic needs (Vaux et al., 2006).

Involving parents and communities in school management

In the Dakar Framework for Action, governments pledge to 'develop responsive, participatory and accountable systems of educational governance and management.' The devolution of authority to schools and local communities is seen by many as a means to this end. Whatever the intrinsic merits of devolution, its implications for parental and community participation are not straightforward.

Moves towards greater school autonomy are often accompanied by the creation of formal structures, such as school committees, village education committees and parent-teacher associations, to facilitate parental and community involvement in school management. The terms of engagement and the distribution of authority between schools and parents vary, with important implications for decision-making structures. But whatever the arrangements, formal devolution does not override deeply entrenched imbalances in power linked to wealth, gender and other factors.

The transfer of decision-making responsibility from central governments to 'user groups' has been a recurrent theme in areas such as health and water provision as well as school management. Numerous development programmes have aimed to empower the poor by transferring authority to village-level associations. In many cases, the effect has been to concentrate power in the hands of affluent and powerful members of society, with local elites dominating decision-making and capturing the lion's share of resources (Mosse, 2004). Education has not been immune to the effects of 'elite capture'.

Parental participation: some voices are louder than others

While schools may officially have formal structures designed to facilitate community and parental involvement, there is often a large gap between intent and outcome. Membership of these bodies may or may not be representative. And they may or may not facilitate influence over decision-making.

To the extent that cross-country evidence is available, it suggests that in both developed and developing countries the direct involvement of parents in school affairs is limited (OECD, 2007*b*; Zhang et al., 2008). Even when parents nominally participate in school management, they may have a limited say. In some contexts 'participation' is confined to raising money, with limited influence over how it is used. Research in some West African countries is instructive. It shows that parent associations have only nominal control over the use of financial resources – much of which they have contributed – because they lack the capacity to exercise control (Lugaz and De Grauwe, 2006).

Transferring decision-making to village-level associations often concentrates power in the hands of local elites

Evidence from Cambodia points in a similar direction. There the devolution of authority to schools is backed by the creation of local school support committees. Comprising community members and the school principal, the committees are charged with monitoring children's progress, increasing enrolment, developing school improvement plans and monitoring the management of operational budgets allocated by the Priority Action Programme. However, a Public Expenditure Tracking Survey reveals that the committees have not been effective, that few parents know about the funds and that parental representation is limited (Shoraku, 2008; World Bank, 2005*a*).

Representation is an important component of participation. Having a voice on a school management committee implies either a direct presence or the delegation of authority through a democratic process. In practice, community representation is often just one of the considerations shaping the committee profile. Formal and informal eligibility rules can create a barrier to equitable representation. In Pakistan's

Punjab province, membership of school councils for rural public-sector elementary schools is divided along socio-economic status and gender lines: most members are men of high socio-economic status, even for girls' schools. Members of school management councils are meant to be elected, but they are often appointed by principals, who choose people with relatively high education, wealth or social status, partly because of the social networks they can bring to benefit the schools (Khan, 2007).

Poor, illiterate parents may lack the expertise and confidence to evaluate approaches to teaching or curriculum design

If participation is to enhance equity, the poor, marginalized and disadvantaged need to be not just adequately represented but actively engaged. They have to be able to articulate their concerns and to influence decisions. In many cases this implies a change in power relationships. It also requires the design of governance structures that empower poor households. Unfortunately, school-based management reforms seldom address this issue of 'voice' explicitly. Programme design often just assumes that devolved authority is inherently more equitable.

Evidence from several countries suggests that far more attention needs to be paid to the conditions for participation. Many factors influence 'voice', including parental socio-economic status, education level, race, caste and gender (Dunne et al., 2007; Educational Research Network for West and Central Africa and USAID, 2002; Khan, 2007; OECD, 2006*a*). For example, people who are chronically poor, of low caste or from an indigenous minority may have little experience of articulating concerns in a forum including wealthier community members. A study in India of participatory decision-making in local government found landless labourers far less likely than others to participate in meetings (Alsop and Kurey, 2005). Two factors were critical in weakening their voice. First, economic dependence on landed groups, combined with their low caste, was seen as a constraint on dissent. Second, education and access to information were significantly associated with participation. On a constructed scale of participation, someone with ten years of education was 27% more active than someone with no education.

The terms of dialogue on school management boards can reinforce the marginalization of the poor. One study reviewing parental participation in the management of rural schools in South Africa found that the language employed, the use of technical jargon and ways of addressing the parents all affected participation. This might explain why a survey in Gauteng province found that, despite a general view that parental participation had increased, real participation remained limited: only 10% of parents had voted in elections for the boards (Naidoo, 2005).

Any assessment of the role of participation has to start by asking what is being assessed. Participation is viewed by many as a goal in its own right. But for most parents the ultimate aim of any involvement in school management is to improve children's education. Formal participation and consultative arrangements may not facilitate achievement of this goal. Participants may have limited knowledge about issues under discussion, such as school performance and teaching practices. Parents may lack the expertise or confidence to appraise approaches to pedagogy or curriculum effectively. Poor, illiterate parents with limited school experience are at a particular disadvantage. One possible approach, when many parents lack the time and basic literacy skills to participate effectively, is to train community volunteers to support children's learning (Box 3.7).

If real participation, rather than the creation of formal participatory structures, is the ultimate aim of policy, then many current approaches to school

Box 3.7: Community involvement in Uttar Pradesh

The Sarva Shiksha Abhiyan (Universal Elementary Education) programme in India gives a prominent role to village education committees. Each committee comprises three parents, the principal of the village school and the head of local government. Its tasks include monitoring school performance. Despite the committees' prominence in education policy, most parents are either unaware that the committees exist or do not realize that they can be involved in school affairs. Furthermore, many committee members are not aware of the options they have to improve school quality.

Would improved access to information make a difference in their effectiveness? A project by the Indian NGO Pratham in Uttar Pradesh suggests that information is only part of the story. Pratham carried out interventions aimed at encouraging greater participation by village members in the monitoring and improvement of education. It reported, however, that even mobilizing communities, spreading information about the village committees and informing people about their potential to improve the quality of schooling, were not enough to induce effective participation and improve children's learning. Far more effective was the training of volunteers to conduct reading classes for village children.

Sources: Banerjee et al. (2006); Banerjee et al. (2008); Pritchett and Pande (2006).

management have to be rethought. The idea that the devolution of authority to parents, schools and communities is inherently pro-poor is not well grounded. One of the defining characteristics of poverty and marginalization in many contexts is precisely that those affected lack an effective voice. That is why central and local governments should ensure that moves towards devolution are backed by measures aimed at facilitating real participation. Such measures might include affirmative action in areas such as representation of, say, women or people of low caste. At the same time government agencies should manage devolution to ensure that powerful groups with a strong voice do not introduce policies – on school fees, for example – that might have damaging implications for equity.

Choice and competition in education provision

In standard economic theory, choice and competition are two of the most powerful drivers of efficiency, with the spur of the market acting to raise productivity and enhance welfare. Few people see education provision as directly comparable with the production of market goods and services. But competition and its corollary, choice, are increasingly viewed as antidotes for the failings of public education systems in relation to learning standards and equity gaps.

This theme is at the centre of some of the most heated controversies about education governance reform. In the United States, much of Europe and parts of the developing world, the topic divides political parties and can generate polarized debates. Underlying the debates are strongly held views and questions about the proper role of government in education provision, the place of non-state providers and the rights of parents to choose.

What do choice and competition in education mean in practice? In almost all countries, the ultimate responsibility for school systems resides with the state. Governments set policy, curriculum and standards, and are responsible for assessment and the regulation of the system as a whole. Within this framework, however, many approaches are possible. In broad terms, education service delivery can be broken down into four types, depending on who owns and manages schools, and who finances them (Table 3.9).

Governments play a key role in defining the parameters of choice. They can provide financial support to private providers, either directly or in the form of financing arrangements that allow parents to send children to private schools. Since the early 1990s Sweden has used a voucher-type system to give parents the right to take children out of state schools, put them in independent schools and take state funding with them. In some states in the United States, authorities distribute vouchers to parents who can use them to finance the transition of their children to private schools. Another approach is to contract the management of government provision to the non-state sector. For example, other American states have sought to increase competition by encouraging the development of charter schools. Several European Union countries, including parts of the United Kingdom, also follow this model, in effect substituting private management for state management while retaining public finance.

Competition and choice are increasingly viewed as antidotes for the failings of public education systems

In all these cases, governments have developed public-private partnerships to facilitate choice and competition. Not all competition involves such partnerships (see the discussion below of low-fee private schools that operate independently of state control or support), but they are a powerful force in governance reform. To what extent is this good news in terms of improving the overall quality of education and enhancing equity?

As in the case of school-based management, there is no simple answer. Experiences and outcomes have varied. Once again, context is important. It is one thing to introduce vouchers in Sweden, which offers high-quality public education for all, and quite another in Pakistan, which does not. What makes sense in Chile may be entirely inappropriate for Burkina Faso. Institutional capacity, levels of

Table 3.9: Responsibilities of the public and private sectors in provision and financing of education service delivery

Public provision	Private provision
Public finance	
Purely government schooling	• Vouchers to parents • Subsidies to private schools • Contracting management to private operators (e.g. charter schools)
Private finance	
User fees for government schooling	• Purely private schooling: low-fee to elite

Source: Adapted from Patrinos and Sosale (2007).

inequality and the effectiveness of education planning all play an important role in defining governance reform options.

One problem with the current debate on education governance is that insufficient attention is paid to evidence and context. There is a widespread tendency to draw far-reaching public policy conclusions from a weak evidence base (Lubienski, 2008). The importance of national circumstance is often forgotten. Advocacy for increased competition and choice in the developing world makes repeated reference to programmes in high-income and some middle-income countries – voucher systems, charter schools and other public-private partnership arrangements (Patrinos and Sosale, 2007). Quite apart from the fact that such governance reforms have been highly contentious in rich countries and that the evidence on their impact is uncertain, little attention is paid to key questions of institutional capacity in poor countries.

School choice and achievement – strong claims, weak association

The idea that increased parental choice leads to improved learning outcomes has intuitive appeal but is not well supported by evidence. While there may be good reasons to allow parents greater flexibility in selecting schools, the assumption that this will raise standards is questionable.

Advocacy for increased competition and choice in the developing world makes repeated reference to programmes in high-income countries

The evidence in favour of public-private partnerships is not clear-cut even in the developed world. One study using data from thirty-five countries claimed that private providers using public funding delivered the largest gains in learning outcomes (Wößmann, 2006). However, interpretation of this exercise is open to question since the results were largely driven by scores in just a few countries, notably Belgium, Denmark and the Netherlands.

Another study, based on analysis of data from the PISA 2006 assessment, found that around 60% of students in mainly OECD countries had a choice between two or more schools. Results of a modelling exercise showed that students at the schools competing with other schools in the same area did perform better in terms of average test scores. The effect disappeared when demographic and socio-economic factors were accounted for, however; and effects on both equity and quality were muted. As the PISA analysis puts it: 'Whether students are in competitive schools or not does not matter for their performance when socio-economic factors are accounted for. ... None of the factors related to parent's pressure and choice were found to have a statistically significant association with educational equity' (OECD, 2007*b*, p. 236). One of the most detailed reviews of the impact of choice and competition for part of the United Kingdom reaches a broadly similar conclusion. Focusing on primary schools in the South-East of England, the study assessed test scores on the basis of parental choice (defined in terms of location) and school competition for a fixed pool of students. It found that neither choice nor competition had a bearing on test results (Gibbons et al., 2006).

Some of the most detailed evidence on school competition and learning achievement comes from the United States and Chile. Both countries have been in the forefront of governance reforms aimed at expanding choice. Measured in terms of learning achievements, the outcomes have been mixed.

Assessing these learning achievements is difficult. Consider first the charter school experience in the United States. Such schools represent a hybrid approach to provision in which the public sector gives funds to private organizations to establish and manage schools independently of state administration while meeting certain conditions set by the state (Lubienski, 2008). During the 2004/2005 school year charter schools served around 1 million students in forty states and the District of Columbia (Education Commission of the States, 2008; US Department of Education, National Center for Education Statistics, 2007), or just over 2% of total American public-sector school enrolment (Center for Education Reform, cited in Lubienski, 2008). The broad aim is to improve performance by removing many of the rules binding regular public-sector schools and by introducing competition. Because the schools' characteristics are determined by state law, the diversity of arrangements is immense – making comparison far from straightforward. Although charter schools cater disproportionately for African-American students in several states, the percentage of those from better-off households is also higher than in regular public-sector schools.

Evaluations of the impact of programmes aimed at increasing choice, including through charter schools, have found widely disparate results. Some commentators have identified positive effects on learning in some states (Hoxby and Murarka, 2008). Other research finds little benefit.

Using a national data set to examine mathematics achievement at grade 4, one evaluation found charter school students to be performing significantly below their public-sector school counterparts (Lubienski and Lubienski, 2006, cited in Lubienski, 2008). Another study found similar results for reading (Braun et al. 2006, cited in Lubienski, 2008). Still another found the overall charter school effect on African-American students to be negative (Carnoy et al., 2005). To the extent that any conclusion can be drawn, it is that generalizations are not warranted on the basis of the available evidence. Findings are heavily influenced by localized contexts and by the evaluation methodology used.

Flagship programmes aimed at expanding choice have also produced little compelling evidence that choice makes a difference. The 2001 No Child Left Behind Act (see section below on teachers and monitoring) contains a federal mandate in favour of school choice: parents can transfer their children from schools that repeatedly fail to meet targets of academic progress to non-failing public-sector schools in the same district. Students who opted to change schools under this provision showed no significant gains after two or more years (Zimmer et al., 2007).

The United States experience with school vouchers is also ambiguous. Research has identified positive effects on student achievement in some subjects after children switched schools, but not in others, with effects usually emerging after some time (Molnar, 1999; Rouse, 1998). Meanwhile, small private voucher programmes introduced in Dayton (Ohio), New York City and Washington, DC, in the late 1990s resulted in improved test scores for African-American students but not for other groups (Peterson and Howell, 2006).[6] One review of the Washington, DC, district-wide voucher programme, conducted two years after its initiation, found no significant impact on the academic achievement of public schools (Winters and Greene, 2007).

It might be argued that the outcomes of small voucher programmes are sensitive to levels of competition and to time horizons. Such programmes could generate small initial effects, with benefits increasing with the level of competition and over time. Evidence from the Milwaukee Parental Choice Programme, the longest-running voucher scheme in the country, lends some weight to the proposition that there are long-run competition effects. In this case, there is some evidence that public-sector schools with high levels of student eligibility for vouchers have raised their standards – an outcome interpreted by some as evidence that the risk of losing students has created incentives for more efficient teaching (Chakrabarti, 2007; Hoxby, 2003). Evidence from other states, however, is inconclusive: partly positive in Florida, negative in Michigan, insignificant in California, North Carolina and Texas (Arsen and Ni, 2008; Miron et al., 2008; Ni, 2007). At best, the overall results are muted. As one commentator put it: 'If any general finding is available it is that advantages to academic outcomes stemming from voucher programmes are at most notably modest, and also certainly do not rise to the level anticipated by the early optimistic assumptions' (Lubienski, 2008).

Flagship programmes aimed at expanding choice have produced little compelling evidence that choice makes a difference

In the developing world Chile is often viewed as a standard-bearer for choice-based governance reform. It has had a nationwide system of school vouchers for over two decades. Yet here, too, the results have been disappointing (Box 3.8).

The United States and Chilean experiences provide no definitive evidence in favour of choice and competition. Experience in Sweden has been more positive (Box 3.9). There, increased choice and competition have led to expansion of independent private schools, albeit from a low base. Importantly, though, reform in Sweden was not prompted by a chronically underperforming public system. Moreover, it was introduced in a country with relatively low levels of inequality and strong regulatory institutions. While the Swedish model provides useful insights and lessons, there are limits to its exportability to developed countries with greater social polarization and failing public education systems – and even stronger limits to its relevance for developing countries.

Choice, competition and inequality

Choice and competition are often presented in education governance debates as drivers not only of efficiency improvements but also of enhanced equity. The fact that competition by its nature creates losers as well as winners is sometimes forgotten. This has specific consequences in education where losers are students remaining in underperforming schools while the winners are those with parents who have the motivation, information, resources or connections to secure transfers to schools of better quality (Arsen and Ni, 2008). One obvious question that arises is whether

6. Other studies have shown that the results are sensitive to the way race and ethnicity are measured and to how the sample for the baseline data is constructed (Krueger and Zhu, 2002).

Box 3.8: Chile's experience with choice and competition: no advertisement for the governance reform blueprint

Increased competition between schools has been just one element in Chile's education governance reforms. A partial list of wider measures includes devolution to municipal level in many areas of management, increased use of exams and assessment to monitor performance, increased funding (since the return of democracy in 1990), performance-related incentives for teachers and the lengthening of the school day. The reforms have led to large gains in education coverage, especially at secondary level, and they have made Chile a widely-cited 'model' for governance reform.

Outcomes for learning achievement and equity have been far from impressive. Private schools with public subsidies do register an advantage over municipal schools on the yardstick provided by fourth-grade standardized tests. However, the findings are reversed when the socio-economic characteristics of schools are taken into account. In other words, there is no equalizing effect. Municipal schools do a better job than private schools of lifting the achievement of students in the lowest group. Only among students in the middle socio-economic group do private subsidized schools have higher associated test scores.

Analysis of international assessment data over time also calls into question Chile's credentials as a governance success story. Governance reforms have certainly done little to close the gap between Chile and the developed world. For example, while the PISA reading assessment shows 32% of 15-year-old students in OECD countries scoring in the top two levels, only 6% of students in Chile do so. National standardized achievement tests show little improvement over time, even in primary education, where enrolment has been near universal since the early 1970s. The TIMSS assessment of 2003 told roughly the same story of poor performance as in 1999, with Chile failing to catch up with countries such as Egypt and Thailand – neither of which has been in the front rank of reformers. And Chile retains some of the starkest education disparities in Latin America, with large gaps in test scores persisting between students in municipal schools, which serve students primarily from socio-economically disadvantaged backgrounds, and private school students.

While Chile's experience with education governance reform is often held up as a model, Chileans themselves have been more circumspect. The government is embarking on a new wave of reforms with a more explicit focus on equity. Secondary school students have responded not with enthusiasm for past governance reforms, but with street protests over poor quality and highly unequal education provision. After more than fifteen years of education reform under a democratic government and ten years before that under the military government, Chile remains a weak advertisement for the governance reform blueprint favoured by many governments and aid donors.

Sources: Bellei (2005); Contreras (2001); Crouch and Winkler (2007); González (2008); Mizala and Romaguera (2000); Mizala et al. (1998); Sapelli and Vial (2002); Tokman Ramos (2002); World Bank (2007*a*).

governments should allow choice to be exercised on terms that leave many behind. Governance reform that aims to expand school choice without building in protection for equity carries an inherent risk of school systems becoming sources of widening disparities.

School choice can exacerbate inequalities in many ways. If high-performing schools are allowed to select students on the basis of measured ability at a given age, disadvantages linked to income or ethnic background are magnified. Students with high levels of inherited disadvantage end up concentrated in the worst-performing schools. The same thing can happen if high-performing schools are allowed to select students when total applications exceed places (Epple et al., 2004). Evidence from the OECD is instructive: cross-country research shows that countries with highest levels of school choice tend to be more socially segmented (OECD, 2007*b*). In Chile too, the student composition of schools is marked by rigid divides. Municipal schools largely enrol students from lower socio-economic groups, while private independent schools draw pupils almost entirely from higher ones (González, 2008). Parent surveys show that active choice in school selection is strongly associated with higher socio-economic status and that parents making active choices tend to choose schools with a more homogeneous demographic composition (Elacqua, 2004).

Inequalities associated with school choice interact with wider inequalities in society. People who are poor, marginalized or illiterate may lack access to information to enable them to make choices. Research in the United States shows that parents with wider social networks and more access to information are more likely to take advantage of choice policies and that they are better able to ensure that their children enter the higher-quality schools they select (Goldring and Rowley, 2006; Lacireno-Paquet and Brantley, 2008).

Where private school enrolment is expanding and attracting a large share of children from the middle class, which can include many of the most motivated students and most active parents, public education stands to lose a powerful constituency with a strong political voice in claiming financial resources. The economist Albert Hirschman identified the phenomenon of middle-class exit from public education systems as a threat to school quality and equity as a major problem some four

Box 3.9: Swedish lessons in competition: not readily exportable

The Swedish school system is marked by strong achievement in international learning assessments and high levels of equity. Since the early 1990s, the country has introduced radical and wide-ranging education governance reforms, with more extensive power devolved to the local level as a core objective. The 'Swedish model' is frequently held up as a blueprint for others to follow. Is this justified?

Expanded parental choice is a central pillar of reform in Sweden. Since the early 1990s parents have had the right to send their children to independent schools. Public funding follows the children. Independent schools are closely regulated: they cannot select pupils by ability or charge fees and they follow national curricula.

Independent schools have been spreading in some parts of the country. By 2007 there were nearly 1,000 of them, providing for about 9% of children aged 7 to 16 and 17% of those aged 16-plus. At lower levels, many of these schools provide for children with learning difficulties. Higher-level schools often provide vocational training. Initially a source of intense political controversy, independent schools today enjoy broad support.

Private school providers have clearly responded to parental demands in important areas of education. Evaluation results on the standard academic curriculum suggest that growth in independent school enrolment has been associated with improved achievement in mathematics. The impact on equity is less clear-cut. Positive achievement effects have not been observed for students with less educated parents, or for foreign-born students.

The Swedish experience of governance reform provides valuable insights and lessons. There have clearly been important benefits. However, none of this means that the 'Swedish model' is an exportable blueprint, or that the model itself is as far-reaching as is sometimes assumed.

Despite the incentives for the private sector provided by the reforms, independent schools still cover only a minority of students and their presence varies widely by municipality. Many municipalities have no independent schools; their presence is most visible in urban centres. The transferability of the reforms is questionable. Sweden has relatively low levels of inequality: an emphasis on equality is deeply embedded in society. Governance reform and competition were not introduced in the context of a national crisis in public education but rather were driven by a desire for diversity in the school system. Public schools continue to offer all children the option of a good education. The country also has a highly developed institutional capacity for regulation and oversight of private providers at the central level. Many of these conditions are absent in other developed countries, let alone much of the developing world.

Sources: Björklund et al. (2004); Böhlmark and Lindahl (2007); Sandström and Bergström (2005); Swedish National Agency for Education (2008).

There is a real danger that an enlarged role for choice and competition will leave public education systems in a downward spiral of under-investment, poor quality and widening inequalities

decades ago (Hirschman, 1970). Evidence from many countries suggests that he was right. Today there is a real danger in many countries that poorly managed 'quasi-markets' in education with an enlarged role for choice and competition will leave public education systems trapped in a downward spiral of underinvestment, poor quality of provision and widening inequalities.

There are important respects in which choice and competition have enjoyed an exaggerated press. In most countries, governments continue overwhelmingly to dominate education provision, finance and management, especially at the primary level. However, advocates of choice and competition continue to exercise a marked influence on education governance reform debates in the developed world and – increasingly – the developing world.

The evidence and issues at stake need to be carefully weighed up. While analogies with markets may have some effect in the context of political debate, their relevance to the real world of education is questionable. Schools are not allowed to go 'bankrupt' and no government can allow schools to fail – the social, economic and political stakes are too high. Similarly, no government with a concern to protect basic citizenship rights can allow disadvantaged children to be further marginalized through competitive choice. Assertions to the effect that school competition creates 'a rising tide that lifts all boats' (Hoxby, 2003, p. 288) are not substantiated by cross-country evidence. Simultaneously raising achievement and strengthening equity needs good governance supported by strong institutional arrangements – and it requires political leadership in tackling poverty and inequality.

Low-fee private schools: symptom of state failure

Debate over the role of public-private partnerships can divert attention from pressing concerns. Unplanned growth in private schooling for the poor in some parts of the world is symptomatic of an underlying malaise: underperformance, or outright failure, of public providers.

The previous subsection looked at choice within the formal education governance structure. In developing countries, however, millions of households are exercising choice outside that structure. While private schools affordable only to middle-class and high-income groups continue to play an important role, new patterns of private provision are emerging.

Even a cursory observation of education provision in slums from Hyderabad to Nairobi demonstrates that private provision in some developing countries is no longer the sole preserve of the rich. Private primary schools charging modest fees and operating as small businesses, often with neither regulation nor support from government, are changing the education landscape. Whatever the formal education policy may be, a growing marketplace in education provision is appearing by default. The rapid emergence of low-fee private schools is reflected in wider education governance debates.

In some developing countries, low-fee private schools are changing the education landscape

Some observers see the growth in this sector as a potentially powerful force for greater equity and expanded opportunity. Guidelines written for USAID to inform its investment in private primary schooling provide an illustration: 'The private sector... has played a critical role in meeting the needs of disadvantaged groups and has the potential to further increase access and equity. Private provision of education is more effective in terms of student achievement on standardized tests and is an effective alternative to publicly provided education' (Chandani et al., 2007, p. 6).

In a similar vein, the World Bank's 2006 *Education Sector Strategy Update* signals a commitment to promote an enlarged role for the private sector in reaching the poor: 'Increased competition among public and private education institutions (for example, through new methods of public finance that shift education decisions to private households) is providing more incentives to improve quality. The Bank can help countries investigate the market for education, develop an enabling environment for private participation and competition, and align private provision whenever possible with equity principles laid out in national education strategies' (World Bank, 2005*b*, p. 34). Some advocates of more radical privatization options have called on governments and donors to use public financing, vouchers and other public-private partnership arrangements to open the door to a large-scale exit from public provision (Tooley, 2007).

As in other areas, sweeping recommendations have been weakly grounded in evidence. Clearly, unplanned growth in low-fee private primary schools is responding to real demand. Many poor people are voting with their feet and their meagre incomes to leave public provision. The important question for public policy is whether governments should use financial resources to accelerate that trend, or resolve the underlying problem driving it: namely, the failure of public education systems to meet the needs of the poor. Given that nine out of ten primary school children in developing countries attend public-sector schools, the overwhelming priority should be to improve their standards and accessibility rather than to channel public finance into the private sector.

Provision expanding but difficult to measure

Estimating the size of the low-fee private sector is intrinsically difficult because documentation is poor, institutions are typically unregistered and national administrative data provide only a very partial account. Even so, observation and anecdotal evidence suggest the sector is growing rapidly in many developing countries.

The extent of its expansion varies. Evidence from countries as diverse as Ghana, India, Kenya, Nigeria and Pakistan points to rapid growth. In urban India, around 96% of the total increase in primary enrolment between 1993 and 2002 is estimated to be due to growth in private schools unaided by government. While growth in private enrolment was slower in rural India, it still accounted for 24% of the increase in rural areas (Kingdon, 2006). In Pakistan's Punjab province, one in every three children enrolled in primary school studies in a private school (Andrabi et al., 2006). Nigeria has also witnessed prolific growth in low-fee private schooling. It is estimated that in parts of Lagos state, three-quarters of the children in school are enrolled in registered and unregistered private schools. According to one (admittedly speculative) study, incorporating students enrolled in unregistered private schools into administrative data would reduce the proportion of those out of school from 50% to 26% (Tooley and Dixon, 2007).

These figures should be interpreted with caution. The fact that a country has many low-fee private school providers in slums is not a sound basis for extrapolation to rural areas with more dispersed, and often much poorer, populations. National averages can also give a distorted picture of coverage. One study in India finds that 28% of rural people have access to a private school in their village, and that half of the schools are unrecognized. Variation among states, however, is considerable: fewer than 1% of villages have a private school in rural Gujarat and Maharashtra, compared with over 50% in Rajasthan, Bihar, Uttar Pradesh, Punjab and Haryana. In general, richer states are more likely to have rural private schools (Muralidharan and Kremer, 2006).

Questions of quality, accountability and affordability

Whatever the precise dimensions of the phenomenon, low-fee private schools are clearly an important element in education provision for many poor households. And the sector is expanding. Advocates of a bigger role for the private sector see in these two observations evidence that such schools are cost-effective, affordable, less prone to teacher absenteeism than public schools, better equipped to provide a good-quality education and more accountable to parents (Tooley and Dixon, 2007).[7] Evidence to support these wide-ranging claims is less emphatic than the claims themselves. Available data does not provide a robust base for meaningful large-scale comparisons across or even within countries. The findings of the most credible assessments point to large grey areas in which parental motivation, perceptions of quality and the availability of alternative providers intersect to inform choice.

Parental perceptions and motivations. Parents clearly would not pay to send children to private schools if they believed government providers offered better provision at an equivalent or lower price, let alone for free. Parents send their children to low-fee private schools because they perceive an advantage, whether in the form of reduced teacher absenteeism, greater pupil and teacher discipline, and smaller class sizes.

These are not the only attractions, however. The choice of low-fee private schools may also be associated with aspirations for social mobility, especially if the schools use English as the medium of instruction (Rose, 2006; Srivastava, 2007). Detailed work on attitudes in Uttar Pradesh state, India, shows parental motivation to be complex (Box 3.10). Other research in the same state finds that recourse to private providers is not

In India, some families seek access to a low-fee private school in order to distinguish themselves from others within their community

Box 3.10: Why poor households choose low-fee schools in an Indian district

Why do low-income households, many with children who are first-generation learners, choose for-profit, low-fee private schools even where a less costly state alternative exists?

The reasons are complex, according to a qualitative study on low-fee private schools in Lucknow District of Uttar Pradesh state in India. Not all parents, particularly in rural areas, are convinced of the quality at low-fee private schools. While such schools are seen as a better option than government provision, they were not necessarily seen as being of acceptable quality. Rather than basing choice on the quality of education provided, however, some families seek access to a low-fee private school in order to distinguish themselves from others within their communities. Lalita Bai, a rural migrant and wife of a labourer, whose family belongs to a scheduled caste, explained why she sent her daughters and sons to a low-fee private school: 'Only those who are absolutely penniless, the lowest of the low in society, can send their children to government schools. Most people cannot bring themselves to send them there.' Some higher-caste families had a similar explanation for why they found low-fee private schooling important. Rambha Devi, a rural grandmother of four, said: 'Only low-caste children attend government schools so no real schooling takes place there.'

The concerns expressed in these views are revealing. They point to a disconcerting lack of confidence in public provision on the part of the poor, coupled with a concern to maintain social divides on the part of some households. The overall findings suggest that there is an urgent need to examine more closely the role of low-fee private schools in the context of achieving India's EFA goals, including the wider social impact of household choices within increasingly socially and economically segmented schooling arenas.

Source: Srivastava (2006, 2008).

7. Teachers in low-fee private schools are usually recruited under conditions similar to those of contract teachers in government schools, for whom similar arguments are made regarding accountability. See the section on teachers and monitoring.

the same as trust, or an indicator for preferences between providers. Interviews with parents reveal a high level of mistrust of the private sector. The most widely stated parental preference in this case was for a properly functioning government system; parents resorted to private school because they felt they had no alternative (Härmä, 2008).

Assessing quality. Do low-fee private schools offer an efficient route to improved education quality? Data constraints rule out a general answer to the question, but country evidence suggests that caution is in order. There is evidence that in many contexts private schools are outperforming state schools. In parts of India and Pakistan, children enrolled in low-fee private schools perform better, on average, than those in government schools, once adjustments are made for socio-economic status and other variables (Andrabi et al., 2008; Aslam, 2007; Das et al., 2006; Muralidharan and Kremer, 2006; Schagen and Shamsen, 2007). This does not mean government provision is *necessarily* worse than private provision across the board. Even in Pakistan, where the poor condition of government education in general is widely recognized, the top-performing public-sector providers outperform private schools. The problem is that there are many more poorly performing government schools, in which learning outcomes are considerably lower than in the worst private schools. As one study concludes: 'The only reason the private schools look so good is that the poorly performing public schools are so disastrous: if at some future date, children actually started demanding something more than the most rudimentary education, the semi-educated teachers in the private schools would actually find it hard to cope' (Andrabi et al., 2008, p. xiii).

Even low fees are a burden for poor families

Teacher accountability and parental participation. It is widely argued that dependence on parental finance makes low-fee private schools and their teachers more accountable. Available evidence does not lend clear support to this view. In Pakistan, a survey in Punjab has suggested that teacher absenteeism (one indicator for accountability) is less of a problem in private schools than in government schools. The study found that head teachers reported 13% absenteeism in the former and 8% in the latter. By contrast, a more rigorous analysis of teacher absenteeism in rural India, based on data collected during unannounced visits to schools, reported very little difference in teacher absenteeism – around one-quarter of teachers were absent from both types of school (Muralidharan and Kremer, 2006). In addition, a qualitative study in Lucknow District of Uttar Pradesh, India, found low parental participation and interest in the private schools, which proprietors and households attributed to parents' low education levels and inexperience with schooling. Interaction with the school was limited to fee-related complaints rather than dealing with concerns to do with education (Srivastava, 2007).

Affordability in perspective. Advocates for low-fee private schools claim that they are affordable to the poor. However, affordability is not a straightforward concept. When poor households pay for education, they divert income from other areas, including nutrition, health, shelter and savings for emergencies. Education expenditure by poor households for low-fee private schools can be viewed, as it is by some, as a market preference freely expressed. Alternatively, it can be seen, with more credibility, as an entry charge to education paid by vulnerable households with two options: paying for education through severe sacrifices in other areas, or accepting that their children have no opportunity for an education meeting minimum quality standards. Evidence from a variety of contexts illustrates the real trade-offs facing poor households when they have to pay low-fee providers:

- In Hyderabad, India, a city with a fast growing market for low-fee private primary schools, it is estimated that a family living on the minimum wage would have to spend roughly one-quarter of its income to put three children through such a school, even before taking account of additional related costs for nutrition and other household needs (Watkins, 2004).

- In rural Uttar Pradesh, India, one survey puts the total cost of educating four children (the average family size) in a low-fee school at half the mean annual salary for households in the lowest two income quintiles. Unsurprisingly, most of these households send their children to government schools. Choice is limited to better-off households. Those in the richest 20% of the sample were almost eleven times more likely to choose private schooling than families in the poorest 20% (Härmä, 2008).

- In urban Malawi, even the relatively modest fees cited by owners of low-fee private schools (around US$3 per term in 2004) are beyond the reach of poor households, even before taking other costs of education into account. For the two-thirds of the population living below the poverty line, fees at this level would translate to over one-third of available resources per person per household (Kadzamira et al., 2004).

- In Ghana's capital, Accra, around 17% of total enrolment in primary education is in the private sector. But households in the rural north and other areas where enrolment is already low are far less likely to opt for private schools, since school costs are already the major reason their children are out of school. While private schools are spreading in rural Ghana, it is mainly in areas where fishing and trading are the main occupations, not areas dependent on subsistence farming (Akyeampong, 2008). Households with livelihoods in the latter area tend to be poorer.

Access and equity. Recourse to private schools on the part of the poor is not an indicator for equitable access. As noted, chronically poor households may not be able to finance even relatively low fees without suffering adverse consequences. Locality is also a limitation on equity. By definition, low-fee private schools will be established only where enough parents are willing to pay fees. As such markets are far more likely in high-density urban areas than remote rural areas, the schools could exacerbate the rural-urban divide. In addition, significant gender disparities have been observed with low-fee private schooling. Parents lacking the resources to send all their children to private school often choose to send only some of them. Studies in India and Pakistan find significant pro-male bias in this choice (Aslam, 2007; Härmä, 2008; Mehrotra and Panchamukhi, 2007). In India's Bihar state, 10% of all enrolled scheduled-caste girls are in private schools that receive no public funds, compared with 21% of upper-caste girls. In Uttar Pradesh the respective shares are 16% and 37% (Mehrotra and Panchamukhi, 2007).

Where there is no choice. While many poor households are rejecting public provision by switching to private providers, the extent of choice is often exaggerated. People in some slums of the Kenyan capital, Nairobi, do not have the option of sending their children to government schools for a very simple reason: there are none. The residents of these informal settlements lack formal property rights, so the government provides no basic services in education (Box 3.11). State failure in education provision in slum areas across many countries has created a strong impetus for the development of private school markets. Even where children can travel to a school in a neighbouring area, they often cannot enrol as they lack the

Box 3.11: Government schools for the rich, private schools for the poor in Kenya's slums

Does the high incidence of low-fee private schools in slum areas reflect the power of choice in a competitive market? Not in the Kenyan capital, Nairobi.

Over 60% of Nairobi's population lives in slums. This population is crowded into just 5% of the residential area of the city. Slums are marked by high levels of poverty and deprivation, and are not at first sight an obvious location for private education provision. Yet a longitudinal study covering two slum and two non-slum areas, with a total sample of over 13,000 children, finds that children living in slum areas are more likely to attend private school. Conversely, children of higher socio-economic status were more likely to attend a government school: the richest 20% of households were more than twice as likely as the poorest to send their children to a government school.

The Kenyan study suggests that government schools are the preferred choice for richer, non-slum residents, while private providers are the only viable option for the poor. From the perspective of the poor, however, the choice is highly constrained. There are no government providers in some slums. Where there are government schools on the periphery of the slums, they require an official residency title for entry. Because most slum dwellers lack legal property status, their children are excluded.

In this context, 'choice' is an inappropriate description of the parameters for decision-making. Parents 'choose' low-fee private providers because there is no alternative. It is not a positive choice based on an assessment of the relative merits of different providers. Indeed, household surveys show that parents complain about the private schools, with staff shortages, congested classrooms and lack of teaching materials identified as common problems.

Source: Mugisha et al. (2008).

People in some slums of Nairobi do not have the option of sending their children to government schools for a very simple reason: there are none

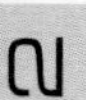

necessary paperwork and residential eligibility. Thus poor slum dwellers may find the only schooling available to them is a low-fee private school, while richer households have the choice of attending a government school.

Governing low-fee private schools

The bottom-line obligation for all governments is to develop publicly financed and operated primary schooling of good quality for all children

Low-fee private schools are the subject of an often polarized debate. Some advocates of increased competition and of an expanded role in education for the private sector see them as an alternative to publicly financed and delivered provision. Critics see them as a symptom of state failure. Whatever the perspective, it is clear that the low-fee private school sector is a response to demand and that it is unlikely to shrink rapidly, let alone disappear, in the foreseeable future. Governance of the sector to advance the EFA goals is therefore a priority.

In many countries low-fee private schools currently operate as a governance-free zone. The schools have increased in number far faster than the capacity of regulatory and management regimes to ensure that their activity is aligned with national policies. Malawi has only one person in the education ministry responsible for school registration, so small private schools effectively remain outside the system (Kadzamira et al., 2004). In India, compliance of low-fee private schools with the rules and norms governing teacher qualifications, teaching practices, the curriculum and infrastructure is haphazard at best, non-existent at worst (Kingdon, 2006). Even where governments do regulate low-fee private providers, the focus is often on assessment at the time of school registration rather than regular monitoring of performance and outcomes.

More effective management and regulation are easier to advocate in principle than to deliver in practice. Low-fee private providers tend to expand most rapidly in areas where many government schools are struggling to meet standards and levels of poverty are often high. Nigeria, for example, has stringent legislation on private-sector regulation, including fines and even imprisonment if providers do not comply with regulations. Yet the states in which private provision is most prevalent, such as Lagos, find it almost impossible to enforce the legislation, not least given the government failure to provide alternatives for children whose schools would be closed (Rose and Adelabu, 2007).

Public-private partnerships offer another regulatory option. In principle, education authorities can use financing and other measures to generate incentives and enforce rules while addressing concerns over equity. Pakistan's programme of public-private partnership is an example. The government, with support of donors, has embarked on a range of public-private partnership projects aimed at addressing long-standing problems in access and equity. The problems are acute: Pakistan's NER is 73% for boys and 57% for girls. Not only are overall enrolment levels lower than in poorer countries such as Nepal and the United Republic of Tanzania, but Pakistan is near the bottom of the international league table for gender parity. Large disparities between states, between urban and rural areas and between richer and poorer households are at the heart of Pakistan's slow progress in basic education. Low-fee private providers are widely presented as a dynamic force for change, though experience and evidence point to the case for a more cautious appraisal (Box 3.12).

Countries with more developed institutional capabilities might be well placed to oversee effective partnerships with low-fee private schools. But the countries in which such schools are flourishing are those with weaker institutional capacity and tighter financial constraints. For these countries, it is not obvious that public-private partnerships involving management relationships with large numbers of small private providers will deliver progress towards a national system based on uniform standards and equal access for all. The question remains: why are governments not using their capabilities to deliver equitable and affordable public education?

There is no 'one-size-fits-all' model for effective governance of low-fee private schools. The overarching challenge for governments is to develop strong national strategies for achieving EFA and to ensure that all providers operate within these strategies. The bottom-line obligation of all governments, especially at the primary school level, is to develop a publicly financed and operated education system that offers the option of good-quality, free education to all citizens.

Box 3.12: In Pakistan, a questionable public-private partnership

The Government of Pakistan, with support of aid donors, has made public-private partnerships the 'anchor' of its strategy to address the challenges of education access, quality and equity. A 2004 policy paper spelled out the premise underpinning the current policy framework: 'Government has officially recognized that the public sector on its own lacks all the necessary resources and expertise to effectively address and rectify low education indicators.'

Low-fee private schools figure prominently in this strategy. Such schools are expanding rapidly in parts of Pakistan. Coverage is variable: there are more of the schools in the relatively prosperous Punjab province (where enrolment is already higher) than in rural Sindh or Balochistan, which have the lowest enrolment rates overall and particularly wide gender gaps (Figure 3.7). Although equity concerns have figured in the design of public-private partnerships, experience in Punjab illustrates just how difficult it can be to achieve more equitable outcomes.

The Punjab Education Foundation has been running two different but overlapping public-private partnership models. Under an education voucher programme for selected slums, parents can use state funding for entry to low-fee private schools. Meanwhile, a Foundation Assisted Schools programme provides a per-child subsidy for children enrolled directly in private schools in selected high-priority areas. While there is some initial evidence of positive influence on enrolment and learning outcomes, serious problems have been identified:

- *Fragmented authority and inequality of financing.* Responsibility for running public-private partnerships rests not within the Ministry of Education but with semi-autonomous education foundations that depend on their ability to raise external funds. Provinces such as the Punjab that are already in a stronger position in terms of education can benefit more because they have the possibility to recruit qualified staff, have more potential NGO and private sector partners, and are a priority client for most donors.
- *Financial sustainability.* Public-private partnership models have been an important component of education-sector World Bank loans in Punjab and Sindh. Their continuation and expansion is contingent on sustained donor support, as the Ministry of Education has so far not decided to mainstream the models. That support cannot be taken for granted.
- *Limited scope.* Notwithstanding the international attention Pakistan's public-private partnership programme is receiving as a potential model for other countries to follow, the school voucher programme reaches only 10,000 students and the Foundation Assisted Schools programme only 50,000 (Punjab Education Foundation, 2008). This is in a country with 2.7 million boys and 4.1 million girls out of school.

Whatever the course of public-private partnership projects, the majority of children from poor households in Pakistan rely on government provision – and will continue to do so. Reaching children who are not in school will require expansion of the public education system, with a far stronger focus on wealth, gender and regional inequalities. Chronic underfinancing of education is an immediate problem, with just 2.7% of GNP (12% of total government expenditure) allocated to education.

Sources: Andarabi et al. (2006, 2008); Aslam (2007); Bano (2008).

Figure 3.7: Primary gross enrolment ratios in Pakistan by location and gender, 2004/2005

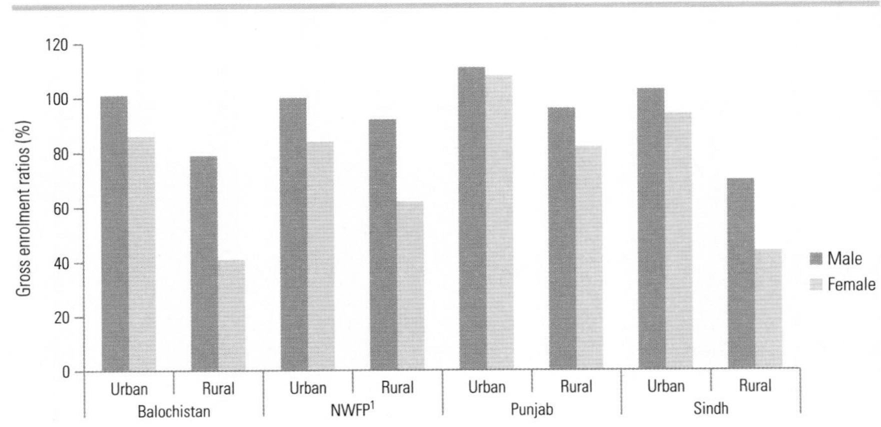

1. North West Frontier Province.
Source: Pakistan Ministry of Education (2006).

Conclusion

Governance reform in school management has been widely cited as a positive force promoting a wide range of important goals in basic education, including improved quality and enhanced equity. Strengthened choice, competition between schools, devolved authority and increased public participation have all been identified as drivers of more accountable education provision. Disadvantaged households are commonly presented as first among equals in the list of beneficiaries.

For marginalized, vulnerable and impoverished households, choice remains highly constrained

Evidence presented in this section calls into question some of the more optimistic assessments of school governance reform, particularly with regard to the ability to promote free, good-quality, equitable education for all citizens. Increasing accountability and participation are important ends in themselves in the design of education policy. But devolving authority to schools does not automatically confer increased voice in school management on parents or communities, especially if they are poor and marginalized. Similarly, while choice and competition between providers may have the potential to play a role in improving education quality, there is little evidence of that potential being realized on a significant scale. For marginalized, vulnerable and impoverished households, choice remains highly constrained – and access to basic education remains contingent on public education provision. The rapid emergence of low-fee private schools may be a response to real demand, but there is little evidence to suggest that low-fee providers offer a genuine choice of affordable, accessible, quality education.

All this points to a strong case for governments to focus their energies and resources on public provision of quality basic education for everyone. Private finance and private providers have a role to play, and governments need to ensure that they are integrated into properly managed national strategies. However, transferring responsibility to schools, parents, communities and private providers will not address the underlying problems faced by education systems in providing equitable opportunities for quality education. These will only be revealed through governance systems that combine strong institutional arrangements with a commitment to equity. □

Strengthening teacher governance and monitoring

Introduction

Getting children into school, through a full primary education cycle and into secondary school is a priority for public policy. But education is about more than putting bodies in classrooms. It is about engaging minds, expanding horizons and ensuring that students have access to real opportunities for learning. The ultimate aim of any education system is to ensure that children develop their cognitive, emotional and social capacities – and that they acquire the skills they need to realize their potential (UNESCO, 2004). Schools are the primary institution for achieving this aim. And teachers are on the front line of delivery.

Chapter 2 documents serious problems in the quality of education. In many countries absolute levels of learning are so low as to raise questions about the value of primary schooling. There is disconcerting evidence that the gap in average performance between rich and poor countries may be widening. Moreover, that average gap obscures large disparities in learning achievement within countries. In short, many school systems are failing to deliver services that meet even the most basic standards for quality and equity.

Improved governance in teacher management is vital for changing this picture. Education systems need to attract qualified people into the teaching profession, retain them, provide the skills and knowledge they need, and ensure that they are motivated. But how should poor countries with limited financial resources set about achieving these goals? And what mechanisms are available to ensure that disadvantaged children living in marginalized areas have access to good teachers?

This section addresses these questions. It also looks at the crucial role of monitoring as a vehicle for raising standards. In the absence of effective monitoring, problems relating to education quality and equity often remain invisible to the public and policy-makers alike. When integrated into policy formulation, monitoring can play a key role in raising quality and strengthening equity.

Recruitment, deployment and motivation

If the world's poorest countries are to achieve UPE by 2015, millions of additional teachers have to be recruited, trained and deployed, the majority of them in marginalized areas characterized by high levels of poverty. The problem is not just a quantitative one of recruitment. A recent cross-country survey on teacher motivation in sub-Saharan Africa and South Asia concludes: '[V]ery sizeable proportions of primary school teachers, particularly in sub-Saharan Africa, have low levels of job satisfaction and are poorly motivated. Many tens of millions of children are not being taught properly and are not receiving even a minimally acceptable education. ... [T]he unavoidable conclusion is that most schooling systems are faced with what amounts to a teacher motivation crisis' (Bennell and Akyeampong, 2007, p. 25).

Many school systems are faced with a teacher motivation crisis

Increasing recruitment, strengthening motivation and improving qualifications are issues at the heart of the teacher governance challenge. Equity concerns are also paramount. The distribution of more experienced, better-qualified teachers is often skewed towards the best performing schools and students from higher socio-economic backgrounds. Marginal rural areas and low-income urban settlements are more likely to attract unqualified teachers or to experience large deficits in teaching staff. This subsection looks at four important governance themes relating to teachers:

- salaries and living standards;
- recruitment and contract teachers;
- deployment patterns;
- motivation and performance-related pay.

Salaries and living standards

Teacher salaries figure prominently in education governance debates. This is for good reason. Remuneration for teachers absorbs the lion's share of education budgets, especially in low-income countries. Pay levels also influence recruitment. Salary has an important bearing on the number of people entering the profession and their qualifications. Higher salary levels are likely to be positively associated with levels of recruitment, experience and morale. By the same token, the higher the recruitment costs, the fewer teachers can be recruited within a fixed budget.

Poor training, poor pay and poor working conditions contribute to teacher discontent

There is no simple formula for determining an appropriate level for teacher salaries. As in any labour market, costs are determined partly by supply and demand, and partly by political factors. Decisions on recruitment levels, qualification requirements, and pay and conditions are all important. Average teacher wages as a multiple of GNP tend to decline as a country develops economically (Bruns et al., 2003). But the ratio of teacher salaries to GNP is of questionable relevance in determining what salary corresponds to the attainment of specified goals in areas such as recruitment and motivation. In any country, policies on teacher pay and recruitment have to take into account average incomes, relative pay with comparable professions and wider labour market conditions.

Whatever the national ratio of pay to GNP, it is clear that many teachers in developing countries have very low income levels. In some countries pay levels do not cover basic living costs and this is a major factor in the teacher motivation crisis. In much of sub-Saharan Africa and South Asia teacher pay levels are perilously near, or even below, the poverty line (Bennell and Akyeampong, 2007; Benveniste et al., 2008; Sinyolo, 2007). In some cases salaries have fallen precipitously. In Malawi, average teacher salaries were 30% lower in real terms in 2004 than in 1992. At the equivalent of just US$3.50 per day, a teacher's average pay is below the amount needed to cover the most immediate household needs (Kadzamira, 2006). Late payment, a widespread problem in many countries, adds to the pressures associated with low salaries (Benveniste et al., 2008; Sherry, 2008; VSO, 2007).

It is not just absolute salary levels that are important. Relative pay matters in terms of both recruitment and morale. In Latin America, teacher salaries are generally well above the poverty threshold but compare unfavourably with pay in other professional and technical occupations (Morduchowicz and Duro, 2007). Similarly, teacher salaries in much of Central Asia are considered unattractive. This is true even in countries such as Armenia and Tajikistan where teacher salaries increased markedly between 2003 and 2007 (Steiner-Khamsi et al., 2008). One consequence of low relative pay in Central Asia has been an increase in the number of teachers seeking to supplement their income through a second job – a phenomenon that has been extensively documented in most Central Asian countries (Education Support Program, 2006). This practice can have damaging consequences for the quality of education, with some teachers withholding curriculum to pressure students into private tutoring (Bray, 2003). The students least able to pay for private tutoring stand to lose the most.

Debates over teacher pay have to be viewed in a broader context. Governance reforms have often increased teachers' level of responsibility and workload. In many countries teachers are being asked to use demanding new 'learner-centred' curricula which entail major changes in teaching practice, and frequently increased preparation and marking time. Yet these new responsibilities are seldom reflected in pay and conditions, helping explain why many teachers lack enthusiasm for reform efforts (Bennell and Akyeampong, 2007).

Contract teachers: increasing recruitment at the expense of quality and equity?

All governments operate under real budget constraints in education. The constraints are particularly severe in many of the poorest countries. The fact that these countries need to increase recruitment on a large scale poses an obvious public spending problem: namely, how to increase the supply of teachers within a sustainable budget framework. Many governments have attempted to resolve the problem by increasing the recruitment of contract teachers.

Teachers have traditionally been recruited as civil servants. This influences the structure of their pay and benefits – and the costs of recruitment. Recruiting teachers on a contract basis, outside the civil service scale, has the potential to reduce costs. It also gives education authorities greater flexibility with respect to hiring and firing. One feature of civil service employment in many countries is that teachers have a high level of immunity when it comes to being fired. According to one study in India, only one in 3,000 head teachers surveyed has ever fired a teacher (Chaudhury et al., 2006). Such findings confirm that education authorities have trouble dismissing tenured teachers for substandard performance. This is seen by some as a factor in the high levels of absenteeism in many countries noted in Chapter 2. Contract teaching arrangements are seen by some as a vehicle for greater flexibility. While civil service employment is a long-term arrangement, contracts are time-bound and can be revoked swiftly. Increasing the opportunity for communities and head teachers to hire and fire teachers is widely cited as a governance benefit of private schools, discussed earlier in this chapter.

Recruitment on a contract basis has increased the supply of teachers in many countries. This is particularly the case in West Africa (Göttelmann-Duret and Tournier, 2008). Over a third of teachers in Guinea, the Niger and Togo are contract teachers (UNESCO, 2007*a*). Many other countries have also stepped up recruitment of contract teachers, among them Cambodia, China, India, Nepal, Nicaragua, Pakistan and Sri Lanka (Duthilleul, 2005; Göttelmann-Duret and Tournier, 2008; Govinda and Josephine, 2004). To what extent has this enabled governments to achieve EFA goals?

The evidence on contract teachers is mixed. The increase in the supply of contract teachers has enabled governments to reduce pupil/teacher ratios (PTRs) in many countries. However, that superficially positive outcome has to be weighed against concerns that there may be a trade-off between the supply of contract teachers and overall education quality. For example, contract teachers in Togo appear to provide lower-quality education. That is not entirely surprising since they have less experience and training than civil service teachers (Box 3.13). There is also evidence from West Africa that recourse to contract teaching may in some cases compound problems of teacher morale. The testimony of one contract teacher in Cameroon provides an eloquent account of the impact of contract teaching arrangements on self-esteem in one particular context (Box 3.14). The broader concern with contract teaching is that what might appear as an advantage from one perspective (more flexibility and reduced cost) might be seen from another perspective as a threat to livelihood security and a source of low morale.

Evidence from other regions also varies. In some cases, increased recruitment of contract teachers can have positive effects on equity. This is especially true where contract teachers are recruited from regions and communities that are not well served. There is also some evidence – admittedly mixed – that contract teachers are less likely to be absent. This appears to be the case in India, where the practice of employing contract teachers has expanded rapidly since 2002 (Box 3.15). Most contract teachers in the country work in rural areas, often teaching in schools used by very poor communities. However, even here the implications for equity are ambiguous. An obvious concern is that contract teaching arrangements will leave some of India's most marginalized children to be taught by its least qualified and experienced teachers.

Box 3.13: Weighing the costs of lower teacher wages in Togo

Public sector reforms in Togo in the 1980s and 1990s resulted in pay and recruitment freezes for teachers, leading to a sharp rise in PTRs. The country responded by recruiting contract teachers. One-half of public primary school teachers are now contract teachers. Their wages are some 60% below those on the civil service salary scale, and they are not entitled to promotion, pension rights or other non-wage benefits. While contract recruits often receive teacher training and may have as many years of general education as civil service teachers, they tend to have fewer years of teaching experience.

What difference has the introduction of more flexible contracts made to accountability and quality? An analysis of data from the PASEC achievement survey found no difference in absenteeism between contract and civil service teachers. The threat of not having a contract renewed does not appear to have changed teachers' behaviour, probably because the threat is seldom acted upon. However, the analysis did find that, controlling for student background and for teacher education and experience, students in classes taught by contract teachers performed worse than those taught by civil service teachers. In other words, low-wage contracts do appear to have attracted a needed pool of teachers, as intended, but with the unintended consequence of potentially long-term detrimental effects on education quality.

Source: Vegas and De Laat (2003).

There is a potential trade-off between the recruitment of contract teachers and education quality

The issues raised by contract teaching are far from straightforward. All governments need to assess carefully the potential risks, in terms of equity and education quality, of a recruitment strategy that lowers the standards for recruited teachers. From an EFA perspective, increasing teacher supply while lowering quality standards is a false economy. The first objective of teacher governance should be raising learning achievement. At the same time, governments have to operate within a defined resource envelope. In the poorest countries, increased national effort and increased aid to meet recurrent costs in education may be needed for meeting recruitment goals.

One way of reducing the pressure for recruitment is to strengthen teacher retention. In many countries, large numbers of teachers are leaving the profession not just because of poor pay and conditions, but also because of inadequate support,

In Cameroon, recruitment of contract teachers is allowing an expansion in enrolment at the expense of teacher morale

Box 3.14: 'Marginal and frustrated': a contract teacher's view from Cameroon

In Cameroon, contract teachers make up more than half of the teaching staff at primary level. The experience of one teacher, Mr Bikono, who works in a government school in Yaounde, illustrates the potential trade-off between teacher supply on the one hand and teacher morale on the other.

Unable to get a job after qualifying as a lawyer, Mr Bikono took the qualifying exam to enter the teaching profession. After eight years of experience as a substitute teacher, he achieved contract teacher status. Being a contract teacher in Cameroon makes Mr Bikono 'feel marginal and frustrated'. His monthly salary amounts to 99,000 CFA francs (about US$158), a long way from the starting salary of 140,000 CFA francs for a teacher with a civil service job. He also lacks benefits attached to civil service posts, such as a pension. Mr Bikono sees it as discrimination. 'We're doing the same job and we have the same amount of work. In fact, contractors are sometimes better qualified than civil servants.' He is indignant about his paltry salary, which forces him to live in his father's home. His wife has left him, tired of waiting for a 'supposed improvement of the situation'.

The mass recruitment of contract teachers has provided a short cut to expanding the teaching force. This is in a national context where one-third of teachers are untrained and there is a need to more than double teacher numbers to achieve UPE by 2015. While the recruitment of contract teachers is allowing an expansion in enrolment, the effect on the morale of teachers such as Mr Bikono is damaging. The danger is that contract teaching will lead to further deterioration of quality, which in turn would have worrying implications for the number of children successfully completing the primary cycle.

Sources: Ekwè (2007); UIS (2006*b*).

Box 3.15: Contract teaching in India: reaching the underserved

The recruitment of contract teachers in India aims to address the dual challenges of teacher shortages and high absenteeism in some states. Outcomes for access, equity and quality have been mixed.

Contract teachers have been a feature of the education system in several Indian states since the 1990s. The practice has expanded rapidly since 2002, when states were permitted to recruit such teachers through central government grants. By 2004 half a million contract teachers had been hired. Their recruitment is aimed at reaching villages not served by regular government schools and increasing the number of teachers in single-teacher schools. Most contract teachers, accordingly, work in remote rural schools, particularly in the states of Madhya Pradesh (which accounts for 46% of all contract teachers) and Rajasthan (21%); contract teachers make up half the teaching force in the former and a third in the latter. Their pay averages around one-fifth to half of what civil service teachers make. The least qualified, lowest-paid contract teachers are concentrated in rural tribal areas serving deprived children.

What impact has the increased recruitment of contract teachers had on education? There is insufficient evidence to provide a clear answer to that question. Contract teachers are often recruited from marginalized communities, increasing the supply of teachers in areas where civil service teachers often do not want to work. Indeed, the policy of hiring teachers under contract has been supported in some cases by civil service teachers, who benefit by not having to transfer to less attractive areas. Clearly, many children being taught by contract teachers would not otherwise receive an education. The fact that these teachers may be of a similar background to the children they are teaching may help to address problems of caste stigma. There is also some evidence that contract teachers are less likely to be absent, thus helping schools open more regularly and for longer hours; and that learning outcomes are at least as good for children taught by contract teachers as for those taught by civil service teachers.

From a broader public policy perspective the questions facing India are similar to those raised elsewhere. While contract teachers have brought real benefits for many communities, increased the equity of teacher deployment and cut average recruitment costs, they are often less qualified and experienced than civil service teachers. The obvious danger is that children who are poor, low caste and living in remote rural areas will be taught by lower-quality teachers – an outcome that will reinforce wider inequalities in India.

Sources: Govinda and Josephine (2004); Muralidharan and Sundaraman (2006); Pandey (2006).

large class sizes and low job status. Reducing the outflow requires an approach that looks beyond pay to the wider factors affecting the morale of teachers who, it must be remembered, provide a critical public service.

Tackling equity gaps in teacher deployment

Average PTRs can mask serious problems in deployment of teachers within a country. Areas that are remote, poor and home to disadvantaged ethnic, racial or caste groups are often underserved, especially in having their share of experienced teachers. This is not surprising: where teachers have a choice, they may be unwilling to work in hard-to-reach locations offering poor housing, no water or electricity and few public services, especially if they must also be separated from their spouses. But the skewed allocation of teachers is a factor in the large equity gaps in access and learning outcomes discussed in Chapter 2.

Urban bias is a systemic problem. In countries where most teachers come from urban areas and there are few recruits from disadvantaged groups, filling posts serving rural areas and minority groups is often difficult. Most teachers want to be posted to urban schools for both professional and personal reasons, including the education of their own children. But the effect in many countries is to reinforce the rural-urban gulf in educational opportunity. In Pakistan, lack of transport, security problems and poor housing in remote rural areas form a major deterrent to equitable deployment of teachers, especially women (Khan, 2007). In Namibia, 40% of teachers in rural schools in the north are qualified, compared with 92% in the capital. Two-thirds of urban teachers in Uganda are qualified, but only half of rural teachers (Bennell and Akyeampong, 2007).

Public policies can create incentives that weaken the urban bias. One strategy is to change recruitment patterns so that more teachers from underserved areas join the profession. Another is to provide special incentive packages, such as accelerated career advancement, eligibility for study leave and better housing aimed at drawing teachers towards underserved areas. Giving teachers bonuses for accepting rural postings is another incentive that can change location preferences. All these measures are widely, if haphazardly, used in sub-Saharan Africa. The problem is that the incentives are usually insufficient to outweigh the perceived disadvantages of living in isolated areas (Bennell and Akyeampong, 2007).

Recruitment of teachers from under-represented groups offers several potential benefits. Most immediately, it helps target increases in teacher supply on the areas where it is most needed. There are also motivational benefits. Some evidence suggests that locally recruited teachers in sub-Saharan Africa and South Asia tend to be more satisfied with their jobs, which should help reduce attrition (Bennell and Akyeampong, 2007). In addition locally recruited teachers are more likely to be familiar with the cultural context in which they are working, with potential benefits for the quality and relevance of their teaching. Where teachers are part of the community, there is also greater opportunity for closer monitoring by parents, which can increase teacher effort and reduce absenteeism. In El Salvador, for example, parental oversight of teacher attendance and working hours resulted in increases in the time teachers spent on work (Di Gropello, 2006).

Areas that are remote, poor and home to disadvantaged ethnic, racial or caste groups often lack experienced teachers

Various strategies have been developed to create incentives for the recruitment of teachers from under-represented groups. Some countries have set teacher training quotas, including for women and people from ethnic minorities or low castes. Further incentives can be generated by waiving fees for entry to training on condition that candidates agree to teach for a stipulated period in their local areas. Devolving authority for teacher hiring to communities or regional and district governments can also facilitate the recruitment of teachers from under-represented groups.

None of this implies that increased local recruitment is straightforward. Locally recruited teachers are often untrained initially and may have less education than other teachers – some may have completed only primary school. Increasing the cohort of secondary-school graduates in underserved areas is often a first step in ensuring that teachers from under-represented groups meet required national standards. This may be difficult in educationally disadvantaged areas, however. Experience in the Lao People's Democratic Republic and Cambodia demonstrates the problems that governments face (Box 3.16). Both countries have succeeded in getting more teachers from ethnic minority groups into teacher training, partly by reducing eligibility requirements. However,

Box 3.16: Recruiting ethnic minority teachers in the Lao People's Democratic Republic and Cambodia

The Lao People's Democratic Republic and Cambodia are accelerating progress towards UPE, but teacher shortages in remote areas are holding back their efforts to expand access and overcome marked regional disparities. In response, authorities in both countries are trying to recruit teachers from ethnic minority groups.

In the Lao People's Democratic Republic initiatives emerged as a response to the failure of incentives to increase teacher supply in remote, mountainous areas. Under a previous policy, the government offered supplements equivalent to between 15% and 20% of salary, but these proved insufficient to outweigh teacher preferences for urban postings.

The emphasis has now shifted to a programme aimed at recruiting ethnic minorities into teacher training. Entry requirements have been adjusted and financial inducements provided. Numbers passing through the programme have increased. However, serious administrative problems have been identified. Some of the students recruited do not actually come from targeted villages but are enrolling to receive the benefits offered. Language problems in teacher training have resulted in high dropout levels for indigenous minorities. And many of the students who graduate do not go back to teach in their home area, suggesting that the pull of urban employment is stronger than the incentives on offer to return to the local area to teach.

Public policy in Cambodia has followed a similar trajectory. In the past, transferring teachers into areas of high need, coupled with incentives for rural hardship postings, met with limited success. Salaries were too low to support the transfer of teachers lacking an extended family, housing or land in the area. Special resettlement allowances also proved insufficient. There has also been an increased emphasis on local recruitment.

Entry requirements for teacher training (set at grade 12 for national recruitment) have been waived in districts and provinces where secondary education is not widely available. This has opened the door to students from those areas who have only a lower secondary education. Teacher training scholarships for students from poor and ethnic minority (non-Khmer) backgrounds have helped. Affirmative action targets have been set for the recruitment of minority students into teacher-training colleges, with one in four places reserved for non-Khmer students.

Evidence suggests that the strategy may be starting to pay dividends, although problems remain. Teaching posts in many remote areas remain unfilled. Moreover, it has not been possible either to fill all quota places with ethnic minority students or to prevent abuse of the quota system. Even so, local recruitment has helped rapidly expand the supply of teachers to isolated rural areas.

Source: Benveniste et al. (2008).

In Cambodia, local recruitment of ethnic minority teachers is helping tackle shortages in remote areas

they have faced problems in ensuring that trained teachers return to teach in their home areas. Cambodia's approach, combining quotas for such groups in teacher training with local recruitment, has been more promising.

Some countries have developed national programmes aimed at overcoming disparities in teacher allocation through financing mechanisms to support teacher recruitment in underserved areas. One particularly striking example comes from Brazil. During the 1990s, high levels of inequality in education attainment and achievement in the country were linked to deep disparities in teacher allocation. The FUNDEF programme used national education financing strategies to change this picture. Under FUNDEF, a share of subnational tax revenue was pooled and used to supplement spending per student in poor states. Around 60% of these resources were used to hire and train teachers or to increase teacher salaries. The highest salary increases were in the poorer states of the north-east with the greatest education needs. After FUNDEF began in 1998, the percentage of teachers having completed more than a primary education rose sharply, especially in poor areas such as the north-east. The programme has been associated with sharp increases in school attendance, particularly in the upper grades of basic education (Gordon and Vegas, 2005).

Fragile states affected by conflict face particularly acute problems in teacher allocation. Restoring education systems is a critical part of post-conflict reconstruction. Yet teachers may have good reasons for wishing to avoid placement in areas recently or currently affected by security problems. The experience of Afghanistan is instructive. The country is showing signs of success in its programmes to improve school access, but large disparities in teacher allocation remain. Now that the governance system is being rebuilt, the country must ensure that qualified teachers are deployed to the areas where they are most needed. Bringing community-recruited teachers into the system is one response (Box 3.17).

Local recruitment is not a quick fix for inequalities in teacher deployment. Training and support programmes also have to be developed and made accessible. Several countries are using teacher resource centres[8] to address this challenge and to break the isolation of teachers in rural areas. Teacher resource centres offer an alternative to central or regional teacher training, enabling teachers to develop their capacity while remaining in the community. In India, Kenya, Malawi, Mali and Uganda, teacher resource centres have been an important mechanism for rapid teacher upgrading, accreditation and professional development, and for generating local solutions to local problems (Giordano, 2008; Global March Against Child Labour and International Center on Child Labor and Education, 2006).

According to one review, teachers participating in teacher resource centres report increased professional dialogue and commitment, increased awareness of child-centred teaching methods and increased access to materials and resources. There is also some evidence of wider benefits, with teacher resource centres reportedly having helped to narrow the achievement gap between urban and rural schools (Chile and Kenya) and to reduce repetition and improve retention (Cambodia). Nevertheless, teacher resource centres are not universally effective. In the worst cases, they reproduce many of the problems of national teacher-training programmes. Often they are underfinanced and training is disconnected from teachers' and pupils' real classroom needs (Giordano, 2008).

Teacher deployment patterns are not just a reflection of incentives and teacher preferences. Weak management capacity and corruption also play a role. Bribery of politicians and officials by teachers to secure favoured postings is reported to be common in some countries (Hallak and Poisson, 2007). In a study in Bangladesh, for example, over 40% of secondary school teachers believed that teacher appointment procedures were unfair and that informal payments were needed to secure a post. Many head teachers also saw promotion and transfer procedures for government teachers as unfair and reported that informal payments were commonly required to secure a transfer (Financial Management Reform Programme, 2005). Contrary to some widely held views, devolution of authority to parent-teacher associations is not an automatic cure for such practices. For example, there is evidence in West Africa of school principals and parent-teacher association chairs appointing relatives or friends as teachers (De Grauwe et al., 2005). In Rajasthan, India, local recruitment combined with a lack of performance or duty incentives encourages teachers to network with political leaders and local bureaucrats to secure posts and awards (Ramachandran et al., 2005). As both these cases demonstrate, governance problems associated with teacher recruitment and deployment seldom have simple solutions.

Box 3.17: Teacher deployment in a fragile state: the experience of Afghanistan

Given the massive increases in student enrolment taking place in Afghanistan since 2002 and the high numbers of school-age children who remain out of school, rapid teacher training, recruitment and targeted deployment are critical.

The government took the important step of deciding to build a comprehensive system of thirty-eight teacher training colleges in a context where schools have long relied on teachers with little or no professional training. However, training is a route to increased supply rather than equitable deployment. Over 20% of teacher-training students – and almost 40% of women students – are in Kabul, the capital.

One way to redress the imbalance is by integrating community schools into the government system and improving their status. Under the Ministry of Education's Community-based Education Policy, teachers previously paid by communities on a largely ad hoc basis, often with small cash or in-kind contributions, are being brought onto the government payroll. Achieving the transition has been a major undertaking. In collaboration with provincial Ministry of Education officers, a partnership of four non-government organizations called PACE-A (Partnership for Advancing Community Education in Afghanistan) has been collecting from teachers the signatures and photos needed to include them on the payroll.

Source: Kirk (2008).

Teacher resource centres can help to make training accessible and break the isolation of teachers in rural areas

The limits to performance-related pay

Teacher pay in most countries is tied not to learning outcomes but to qualifications and years of experience. The weakness of the link between pay and student learning achievement has prompted some to advocate a shift towards performance-related pay. Paying teachers for what they deliver rather than their qualifications and years of experience, the argument runs, could create new incentives that might significantly raise learning outcomes while improving motivation and retention among the best teachers (Sander, 2008).

The ideas behind performance-related pay are not new. Nor are they restricted to education.

8. Also known as teacher development centres.

The concept has been widely applied in a variety of public sector reforms. The broad idea is that less weight should be attached to the fixed salary component of teacher pay (usually linked to qualifications and experience) and more to actual teacher performance payments (linked to student or school results). The issues at stake are highly contentious, with teacher unions frequently opposing what they see as market-based incentives that are inappropriate to education (Umansky, 2005).

Linking teacher pay to performance can create perverse incentives, including teachers focussing on the best-performing students

Despite the controversy and the enthusiasm for performance-related pay in some quarters, evidence of the benefits claimed is limited. One reason is that the measurement issues involved are enormously complex. Measuring performance is challenging for many reasons, not least because of the difficulty in separating teacher performance from the multitude of other home-based factors, school-based factors and random events that influence learning outcomes. Another problem with performance-related pay systems is their potential for producing perverse outcomes in at least two areas. First, they can lead to a focus on the development of a narrow range of subjects and skills needed to pass tests, at the expense of creative thinking. Second, they can encourage teachers and schools to exclude from tests the children who are least likely to do well (Glewwe et al., 2003).

Box 3.18: Problems in Mongolia's teacher bonus system

Introducing performance-related pay is not a simple administrative matter. In Mongolia, large bonuses, up to 25% of annual salary or three months' pay, were introduced in 2006 with the aim of acknowledging outstanding teacher performance. In the first year of the reform, schools received central funding with which to give bonuses to selected teachers. In subsequent years schools were to raise their own funds or deduct money from salary supplements for some teachers to reward others. The idea of bonuses was abandoned a year after its inception, for several reasons:

- a strongly held belief in social redistribution that prohibits rewarding a few at the expense of others;
- concerns that the plan would emphasize a hierarchical structure between those who are monitored (teachers) and those who monitor (head teachers);
- the heavy load of documentation and paperwork that resulted from close and continuous monitoring over the course of a year.

Source: Steiner-Khamsi et al. (2008).

Relatively few countries have introduced performance-related pay on a large scale. Moreover, the different contexts in which pilot programmes have been introduced make meaningful cross-country comparison difficult. In many cases the evidence is inconclusive. For example, extensive evaluations of experience in the United States and other developed countries do not indicate a clear cause-effect relationship between performance-related pay and teacher performance (Umansky, 2005).

Evidence of perverse incentives comes from several countries. In Chile a national performance-related pay system, the Sistema Nacional de Evaluación del Desempeño, awards the schools that show the greatest progress in student achievement, giving them a financial bonus for teachers equivalent to about half a month's salary. Schools are stratified within regions by socio-economic status and other external factors that affect school performance. This ensures that competition is among comparable establishments. However, the design has some inherent flaws. It rewards schools that are already doing well rather than those that are improving yet still need to do better (Carnoy et al., 2007). Similar problems have emerged in Mexico. In this case, a long-standing programme, the Carrera Magisterial, allows teachers to move up a pay level based on assessment of a range of criteria, including their students' performance. The approach encourages teachers to focus on the best-performing students (Vegas and Petrow, 2007).

The experience of Chile and Mexico is instructive in a wider sense. While the introduction of performance-related pay was highly controversial in both countries, the impact of the pay incentives on learning achievement has been minimal. This is partly because only a small minority of teachers has any real likelihood of receiving a reward in the form of a bonus in Chile or promotion in Mexico (Vegas and Petrow, 2007). Salary increments for performance have emerged as a popular governance reform in a number of post-socialist countries in Central Asia. Political and administrative obstacles, however, have often prevented their effective implementation, as Mongolia's experience demonstrates (Box 3.18).

There is even less experience with performance-related pay in poor countries with very low teacher pay. Some small-scale randomized experiments have been conducted, mainly through NGOs, with indeterminate results. Studies in the Indian state of Andhra Pradesh and in Kenya found that student test results were better in schools exposed to performance-related pay than in others. Both programmes gave teachers a financial bonus if students achieved higher-than-average scores on standardized tests. However, a key factor behind improved results in both countries was a tendency of teachers to train students for the test, often excluding other aspects of the curriculum. In Kenya the learning achievement improvement was found to be short-lived – an outcome that raises questions about sustainability. In addition, teachers receiving incentives were as likely to be absent from school as those receiving none, raising further questions about the strength of incentive effects associated with performance-related pay (Glewwe et al., 2003; Muralidharan and Sundararaman, 2006). By contrast, evidence from another randomized experiment in India found a positive effect on teacher attendance and learning outcomes. In this case, what appears to have been important is a mix of close monitoring and financial incentives (Box 3.19). Monitoring of the intensity carried out in this case, however, is neither feasible nor desirable on a national scale.

Box 3.19: Incentives to reduce absenteeism in India: a randomized experiment

Combining teacher incentives with close monitoring of teachers can reduce absenteeism and enhance quality, a randomized experiment in India has shown. The project selected 60 one-teacher non-formal education centres from among 120 operated by an NGO in villages. The other centres served as a control group. Instructors were given a camera with a tamper-proof time and date function, which children were asked to use at the beginning and the end of each school day. The teacher's salary was linked to proven hours in school. Absenteeism fell immediately, from 44% to 24%, in the schools supplied with cameras, while staying the same in the other schools. The programme also resulted in higher test scores and, one year after the experiment, higher rates of student transition into regular schools.

Source: Duflo et al. (2007).

The idea that teacher earnings should reward good teaching and not just qualifications and seniority has intuitive appeal. Yet learning processes are very complex and so is the attribution of improvement in student performance to teachers alone. This makes it extremely difficult to develop a policy framework that links pay to improved learning outcomes. Another problem with some performance-related pay proposals is that they take a highly reductionist view of teacher motivation. Factors such as job satisfaction, status, an ethos of public service and work conditions may have as much bearing on teacher motivation as monetary incentives (Bennell and Akyeampong, 2007).

Monitoring education systems for enhanced quality and equity

Broad-based learning and the acquisition of skills defined in national curricula are the ultimate education policy objectives. Monitoring these qualitative outcomes is more difficult than counting heads. Yet it is vital for policy-makers on four counts: to chart progress and identify disparities in learning; to influence and monitor policy measures aimed at improving learning (related to teacher training, curriculum development and textbook revision, for example); to determine the allocation of resources to support poorly performing schools; and to provide information to parents and policy-makers, ensuring that schools are held to account for student performance.[9]

From classroom to system level, the weakness of existing monitoring mechanisms in many countries undermines efforts to address the learning needs of the most disadvantaged schools and students. Two strategies have been adopted to address this problem: more extensive use of large-scale learning assessments and reform of school supervision services.[10] A key motive for large-scale assessments has been to track performance of education systems as a whole, while supervision reforms have aimed to improve monitoring and support quality at school level. This subsection discusses the role of these two strategies for improving quality and equity.

Recent growth in the number of large-scale learning assessments indicates an increased emphasis on learning outcomes

Learning assessments: more coverage, but weak links to planning

Recent growth in the number of large-scale learning assessments indicates the increased emphasis on learning outcomes. Between 2000 and 2006, around half of all countries conducted at least one national learning assessment (UNESCO, 2007*a*). In addition, an increasing number of developing countries are participating in international learning assessments primarily designed for OECD countries, although their involvement remains limited (three sub-Saharan

9. Monitoring is also important in building public confidence in the education system, and giving parents and communities an opportunity to hold schools to account – aspects of which are reviewed earlier in this chapter.

10. The terms 'school inspection' and 'inspectorate' are used in many countries.

African countries participated in the most recent round of the PIRLS, PISA or TIMSS assessments – Botswana, Ghana and South Africa). Regional learning assessments, more explicitly designed to address concerns in developing countries, have expanded. Thirty-seven African countries participate in SACMEQ and PASEC, and sixteen Latin American countries in LLECE (Lockheed, 2008).[11] The limits to assessment have to be recognized: many developing countries have never carried out a countrywide learning assessment and many other have only recently done so (Benavot and Tanner, 2007). But there has been an exponential increase in the flow of information on learning outcomes.

How countries use information from different types of assessments varies greatly. At one extreme, yearly census-based test results in Chile are widely disseminated. Public access to information is seen as a mechanism for holding schools and municipalities to account, informing parental choice and creating competition between schools. By contrast, in Uruguay assessment results from individual schools are not made public and there are no school rankings. The government's stated policy is to use assessments not to create competition in the education system but to inform policies and resource allocation, and guide the targeting of support to teachers (Benveniste, 2002). These differing approaches are rooted partly in different governance agendas. Some countries see testing as a mechanism for promoting an agenda that emphasizes competition, choice and public information to hold service providers to account. Others view testing results as an input to public policy design. The optimal design is to combine both.

Translating lessons from assessments into policy design and implementation remains a pressing challenge

Even where data from assessments are available, it does not follow that they are widely used. For example, South Africa has seen a proliferation of national and international assessments generated through large investments of human and financial resources. These assessments have provided a better understanding of how learning occurs by developing some key indicators. But the use of test results remains limited. Education authorities seldom use them to inform approaches to equity in addressing the learning needs of students from disadvantaged backgrounds. Reporting of information to schools as part of a strategy to improve their performance also remains uncommon (Kanjee, forthcoming).

11. Chapter 2 gives fuller description of learning outcomes from these assessments.

South Africa's experience is a microcosm of a common problem. While education policy-makers are equipped with an increasing amount of information, learning assessment data often have a relatively weak impact on policy design. One reason is weak institutional capacity, reinforced in some cases by institutional segmentation between assessment agencies and education planning. While the need for information on achievement is widely recognized, translating the lessons that emerge from assessments into policy design and implementation remains a pressing challenge (Postlethwaite and Kellaghan, Forthcoming).

High-stakes testing

Most recent national, regional and international learning assessments have been conducted to measure the performance of education systems as a whole. These sample-based assessments are often described as 'low-stakes' because they are not directly linked with incentives for participants (students or schools) to perform well, or with sanctions for those performing badly. In 'high-stakes' assessments, measured outcomes have direct consequences, most commonly for the pupil. Tests can also serve as accountability measures for schools and teachers, and the results used as the basis for rewards and sanctions.

High-stakes assessment is most frequently associated with consequences for student progression and certification. It is also used in some cases to inform approaches to performance-related pay for teachers (see above). Cross-country evidence on the implications for student learning is limited. Standardized exit examinations at the end of secondary school are the most studied accountability measure. Findings suggest that students perform significantly better in countries with such exams than in countries lacking them. On the other hand, this association is variable: taking demographic and socio-economic factors into account, exit exams are positively associated with an increase in average scores for students from both poor and rich households, but students from rich households improve their scores by a greater amount (Schütz et al., 2007). One implication, then, is that high-stakes testing may reinforce inequalities in learning achievement. Another problem is that high-stakes testing can have unintended consequences for the quality of education and for weaker students. Recent evidence on the impact of England's rigorous testing system shows that the overall rise in test scores since the mid-1990s has been achieved at the price of a narrowed curriculum and extensive time devoted to test preparation. Particularly worrying is the finding by some researchers that the intensified focus on passing tests has lowered the self-esteem of poorly performing students (Harlen, 2007; Wyse et al., 2008).

Most developing countries have long-standing traditions of high-stakes testing through public examinations. Results are primarily used for student certification and selection. Here, too, there have been unintended effects for efficiency and equity. In some developing countries, such exams have contributed to increased grade repetition and lower levels of transition from primary to secondary school (Kellaghan and Greaney, 2004; N'tchougan-Sonou, 2001). A study in Kenya, for example, found that the transition rate from grade 6 to grade 7 was reduced partly because poor-performing pupils were discouraged from taking the final primary examination. The reason: schools' average scores were made public in league tables and school officials did not want the poorer pupils to pull down their average (Ackers et al., 2001).

As a mechanism for holding schools and teachers to account, high-stakes testing has strengths and weaknesses. The strengths include the generation of simple and comparable results. The weaknesses are also results-related. The assumption is that teachers and schools strive harder when they can work towards standardized goals, with incentives attached to meeting specified targets. But if the driving concern is to maximize average school scores, underperformers or hard-to-teach children may be viewed as potential liabilities (as in Kenya). There will be incentives in this case to support the students who are most likely to pass the tests and devote less time to their weaker classmates. Moreover, where selection to schools is related to socio-economic status, which in turn is closely correlated with performance, rewarding schools for test scores can be tantamount to penalizing the schools that enrol less wealthy students.

In the United States, high-stakes testing has yielded uncertain outcomes

Recent international debate on high-stakes testing has been heavily influenced by experience in the United States. The 2001 No Child Left Behind Act, which was introduced expressly to close equity gaps in learning achievement, uses high-stakes testing as a device aimed at strengthening accountability, extending choice and improving school management (Box 3.20). There is a great deal

Box 3.20: No Child Left Behind in the United States: the jury is still out

The No Child Left Behind Act has given a push to high-stakes testing in the United States. Legislation now requires all states to put in place accountability systems, including mandatory testing in mathematics and reading, annually for all pupils in grades 3 through to 8 (corresponding roughly to ages 8 to 13) and once in secondary school. Test results are used as the basis for decisions on a range of important questions, such as whether to adopt special improvement measures for a school or district and whether pupils receive subsidized tutoring. Sustained low performance can result in interventions that range from the replacement of teaching staff to the contracting out of school management to a private operator.

There are obvious difficulties associated with evaluating outcomes at this relatively early stage. One of the most comprehensive studies so far concludes that average learning achievements in mathematics and reading improved between 2002-2006. However, it notes that changes in this area cannot be directly attributed to the 2001 legislation because implementation has coincided with other national and state level programmes.

The study finds that achievement gaps between ethnic groups have narrowed in some states, though once again stopping short of attribution. Moreover, in twenty-four of thirty-eight states with comparable data, differences in reading test scores remained unchanged between white and African-American pupils. Given that closing equity gaps is one of the reform's key objectives, this evidence suggests that it may be under-performing.

The No Child Left Behind legislation has generated extensive debate in the United States. For instance, 144 major education and labour organizations in 2008 together called for major corrections to make the Act fairer and more effective. They questioned the overwhelming reliance on standardized test and advocated for wider measures to hold states and school districts accountable. More broadly, critics of the Act suggest that the tests are too narrowly focused, encourage 'teaching to the test' and exclude low-scoring children to boost test results. They also say implementation of the Act is underfunded.

Sources: Center on Education Policy (2007); Forum on Educational Accountability (2008).

of controversy surrounding the record to date. However, the evidence does not suggest that the legislation has been an unequivocal success story.

Using monitoring to improve policy-making

Whatever the problems associated with high-stakes testing, information from learning assessments can play a critical role in informing policy design. The following examples identify some key areas:

In Viet Nam, using information from learning assessments has helped to reduce quality gaps between the poorest and the richest districts

- **Defining minimum learning standards.** In Lesotho and Sri Lanka, national learning assessments have been used to establish minimum learning standards against which pupils' achievements are monitored (Greaney and Kellaghan, 2008). Kenya has used SACMEQ results to set benchmarks for classroom facilities, such as textbooks and desks per pupil (Nzomo and Makuwa, 2006).

- **Informing curriculum reform.** An evaluation of the value of participating in PIRLS and TIMSS found that twenty out of twenty-four low- and middle-income countries participating indicated that taking part in the assessments had influenced changes in curriculum. In Romania, for instance, poor results in TIMSS were a 'wake-up call' spurring curriculum changes. Topics were added to the mathematics curriculum, an integrated science curriculum was approved, new teacher guides in science were developed for some grades, and several new chemistry and mathematics textbooks were written (Gilmore, 2005).

- **Reviewing policy.** High repetition rates have been cause for concern in Senegal. Data from the PASEC learning assessments from 1995 to 2000 were used to shed light on the effects of grade repetition for primary school outcomes. The results consistently showed that, on average, Senegalese students who repeated a grade did not perform better than those who did not repeat, taking aspects such as family background, school environment and initial achievement levels into account. This gave further weight to the education ministry's desire to reduce repetition. As a result, the government has prohibited repetition for some primary grades since 2003 (Bernard and Michaelowa, 2006).

- **Contributing to education planning and reform.** Results from the SACMEQ cross-national learning assessments in sub-Saharan Africa have been used in national reviews and commissions on the status of the education systems in Mauritius, Namibia, Zambia, Zanzibar (United Republic of Tanzania) and Zimbabwe. These analyses of learning conditions have played a role in formulation of sector or subsector reform programmes (Greaney and Kellaghan, 2008).

Information from learning assessments can also play an important role in addressing equity goals. One example comes from Viet Nam. In 2001 the country conducted a national grade 5 learning assessment in mathematics and reading. The results provided a basis for understanding the problems and identifying ways to improve education quality in some of the country's most deprived areas. After controlling for socio-economic background and school location, the assessment showed strong correlations between pupil achievements and both teacher qualifications and availability of school resources. In 2003 Viet Nam adopted new regulations for primary schools, specifying minimum levels for several education inputs, including learning materials, school infrastructure, teacher qualifications and in-service training. By 2005 the concerted efforts to raise the quality of the learning environment had begun to show results, with reduced gaps in quality inputs between the poorest and richest districts (Swinkels and Turk, 2006; World Bank, 2005*f*).

The experience in Viet Nam demonstrates a strong link between assessment and policy design. Such linkage is not always evident. By definition, 'low-stakes' assessments generate weak incentives to change. A survey covering Ethiopia, Malawi, the Niger, Nigeria, South Africa and Uganda showed that only one country had used the findings from assessment exercises as a basis for allocating resources to schools and only two had undertaken campaigns to inform teachers or schools about the assessment process (Kellaghan and Greaney, 2004). Limited public awareness is one factor that may have weakened incentives in these cases: nowhere were the assessment results subject to parliamentary debate.

Good quality assessment systems are no guarantee of effective integration into public policy. Institutional structures and capacity are also important. Bolivia, for example, has an evaluation system called SIMECAL that is of very high standard. It uses nationally developed test items that reflect Bolivia's culture in both Spanish and indigenous languages. The SIMECAL staff has high levels of expertise. Yet despite the technical excellence, inadequate funding has resulted in sporadic and irregular testing. Moreover, weak links between SIMECAL evaluations and policy management units in the education ministry has meant that policy development in several critical areas, from pedagogy to curriculum development and teacher training, has not been tied to assessment results (World Bank, 2006*a*).

What conditions can facilitate better use of assessment results? An environment promoting close interaction between the various actors in the education system is important. So is an overall focus on supporting teachers' professional development. Recent practices in Uruguay are instructive (Box 3.21).

Box 3.21: Assessments inform teacher support in Uruguay's schools

Uruguay has managed to improve learning outcomes rapidly in recent years. Its quality improvement efforts have been informed by sample-based assessments aimed at strengthening pedagogical management in schools.

By combining the assessments with cluster-based teacher training and support, spread over the whole school year, education authorities have turned information into policy practice. Evidence suggests that learning outcomes improved in certain grades by 30% over six years. Special measures have been taken to improve the functioning of weaker schools. Important moves to redress learning disparities have included targeting financial resources primarily on the basis of poverty rather than test results and using test results to provide targeted support to teachers in weaker schools and districts.

Sources: Crouch and Winkler (2007); Ravela (2005).

As concern has shifted towards the poor quality of education in many countries, monitoring is emerging as a central governance theme. The experiences of two countries at the forefront of education reform are instructive. In post-apartheid South Africa, the school management and public financing systems have been transformed to expand access and address equity concerns. Yet the record on quality gains has been disappointing. A national assessment in 2004 revealed that learner performance on grade 6 tasks was worse than that on grade 3 tasks in 2001 and that proficiency levels were low in absolute terms (only 40% of answers were correct). In Chile, sweeping reforms during the 1990s produced disappointing outcomes with respect to quality. National assessments point to a very slow rate of improvement and international assessments suggest that Chile has not overtaken developing countries with more centralized systems. One key problem identified in both countries has been the lack of an effective pedagogical management system – extending from the setting of curriculum standards to supervision, information management, school inspection and support, and in-service training – to address problems identified in monitoring exercises (Crouch and Winkler, 2007).

Combining national assessment with school-level monitoring

To understand the realities facing schools, information from international, regional and national assessments needs to be combined with monitoring at school level. School supervision is an essential aspect of monitoring, not only to check teacher and school performance but also to identify and support needed quality improvements.

External assessment can be reinforced by school-level assessment as part of broader quality improvement strategies. This is an area in which South Africa's District Development Support Programme has been attempting to strengthen national commitment to equity. The programme aims to improve education quality in grades 1 to 9 at the weakest schools. Since its inception in 2000, the programme has focused on improving classroom learning, and school and district management. To improve classroom assessment practices, resource materials have been developed, and extensive training and support provided to teachers. External supervision and learning assessments further underpin these school-level efforts. Evaluations of the programme are largely positive. They suggest that a gain in learning achievements between 2000 and 2003 resulted partly from the increased supervisory support available to schools and teachers, and partly from increased use of classroom assessments (Schollar, 2006).[12]

Linking classrooms and education ministries, school supervision plays a crucial role in education system management

As the only direct institutional link between classrooms and education ministries, school supervision plays a crucial role in education system management. School visits can allow supervisors not only to support and monitor implementation of official policies but also to bring school realities to

12. The District Development Support Programme ended in 2003, and was succeeded by the Integrated Education Programme.

the attention of policy-makers. School supervision systems in developing countries are under-researched, though anecdotal evidence suggests they are overstretched. With demanding mandates, and limited human and financial resources, few developing countries have supervision services that are fit for the task at hand. However, in their quest for quality education, many countries have changed and clarified the role and structure of supervision in recent years (De Grauwe, 2008). The experience of Uganda shows that supervision can be used to foster more cooperative approaches aimed at raising learning achievement and reducing inequality (Box 3.22).

What weak schools need is not just inspection but also consistent pedagogical support

The very large gaps in learning outcomes between schools in many developing countries mirror other inequalities in education and in society at large. Supervision has a key role to play in closing these gaps. What weak schools need is not just inspection but also consistent pedagogical support, including regular visits by support-oriented supervisors. This implies radical institutional change, with supervisors finding the right balance between allowing schools sufficient autonomy and intervening to identify performance problems (De Grauwe, 2008).

Box 3.22: Reforming school supervision in Uganda

Uganda's recent strides towards improving the quality of education have included a strengthened inspection service. After a slow start, the Education Standards Agency began operating in 2001, replacing an outdated inspectorate in the education ministry. Efforts have been made to tailor the service to what is feasible with limited resources. Where the former body covered such disparate areas as policy, curriculum development, exams, troubleshooting, staff development and independent school registration, the new one focuses on school visits.

The inspection service reform drew on experience in Masindi, one of Uganda's poorest districts, with many internally displaced families from conflict-affected northern Uganda and refugees from neighbouring countries. In 2000 Masindi scored among the lowest districts in the national primary-school leaving exam. An extensive district-based programme of school improvement, combining internal school evaluation and external district-based supervision, produced remarkable results: Masindi went from one of the poorest-performing districts in 2000 to one of the top five in 2007. Know-how from Masindi was fed into the revised national inspection approach, which was subject to a national consultation in 2005.

Sources: Penny et al. (2008); Roebuck (2007).

One model based on a more collaborative and supportive approach has been developed in Chile, where each supervisor visits a limited number of carefully selected schools, giving priority to the weakest ones. To improve teaching and school functioning, school plans and projects are developed in collaboration with the supervisor. Learning assessments allow the education ministry and the supervision service to know which schools to focus on. The most intricate challenge has been changing the culture of the supervision service from one of control over many schools to one of supporting a few selected schools. That challenge has been addressed through training, new job descriptions with removal of all control functions and the elaboration of new working tools. Supervisors have found it difficult nonetheless to abandon their tradition of control and to adopt a support-oriented approach (De Grauwe, 2008).

Conclusion

Delivering high-quality education for all will require far-reaching governance reforms in the areas covered by this section. There are no ready-made solutions to the problems identified. Clearly, governments need to recognize that declines in teacher pay and conditions have the potential to damage morale, quite apart from reducing quality in recruitment and the quantity of applicants seeking to join the profession. It is important that governments recognize the potential risks for equity and education quality of scaling-up contract teacher recruitment. In the case of teacher allocation, far more emphasis has to be placed on the development of incentives for greater equity, in some cases through a stronger commitment to the training and local recruitment of teachers from marginalized groups and areas.

Learning assessments provide a valuable and increasing flow of information. That information could – and should – be used to identify the factors behind low levels of learning achievement and to map disparities in achievement. The limits of high-stakes testing in strengthening accountability, performance and equity have to be recognized. At the same time, it is important for governments to reinforce the institutional links between assessment exercises, on the one hand, and public policy development, monitoring practices and school supervision on the other. □

An integrated approach to education and poverty reduction: the missing link

Introduction

Accelerated progress towards EFA requires more than increased public investment, more and better equipped schools, and an increase in the number of well-trained and motivated teachers. It also requires progress towards poverty reduction and a reduction in social disparities. Education reforms can make an important contribution in both areas. But good policies in the education sector cannot compensate for weak policies on poverty reduction or for the failure of political leaders to tackle extreme inequality. Achieving EFA requires an integrated approach to planning for education and poverty reduction.

When they met in Dakar, governments recognized that their ambition could not be achieved through education reform alone. That is why they called for EFA policies to be promoted within 'a sustainable and well-integrated sector framework clearly linked to poverty elimination and development strategies'. The engagement and participation of civil society in the formulation, implementation and monitoring of strategies was seen as an important means to this end.

This section asks whether governments have acted on their Dakar commitment. More specifically, it examines how education has been integrated into wider strategies for overcoming poverty and inequality. The issues involved are highly political. They relate directly to the power relationships that sustain social inequities. Chapter 2 documents the barriers to EFA created by disparities based on wealth, gender, ethnicity and wider disadvantages. In principle, the Dakar Framework commits governments to rapid removal of these barriers. Yet the disparities themselves indicate past and present failure to address the underlying causes of unequal educational opportunities. In short, government tolerance of extreme inequality has been, and remains, part of the problem.

This section explores the link between education planning and wider policies for combating poverty and inequality. It focuses on the treatment of education within poverty reduction strategy papers (PRSPs). These documents set out governments' broad development priorities and provide a framework for international cooperation. Clearly, PRSPs are not the only measure of policy coherence. But they do reveal something important about the degree to which education is being integrated into the wider public policies that shape prospects for attaining the Dakar goals. PRSPs are a vital link in the governance chain for education. Apart from providing a broad framework for poverty reduction policies, they represent a vehicle for dialogue between a wide range of actors.

Planning is about more than producing technical documents. National plans provide an opportunity for governments to set out their goals and their strategies for achieving them. They define a purpose against which governments can be held to account. Hence, plans – and planning processes – are a vital part of the governance architecture. The stated intent is to give civil society opportunities to shape priorities and strategies, in the expectation that this will assure greater responsiveness to the marginalized. But have PRSPs provided a coherent framework and facilitated real dialogue?

Education remains poorly integrated into poverty reduction planning

The central message of this section is that education remains poorly integrated into poverty reduction planning. With some exceptions, governments have not acted on their commitments. PRSPs in general fail to articulate clear strategies either for overcoming poverty-related barriers to education or for reducing inequalities. Most take a narrow and reductionist approach to education, rarely reflecting the broad EFA agenda. There are promising experiences that PRSPs could draw on. The development of integrated social protection programmes in several countries shows that interventions aimed at tackling social inequality and reducing vulnerability have large potential benefits for education. The record on participation in planning processes is more encouraging: PRSPs have widened the space for dialogue with civil society. However, participation and 'voice' are not the same as influence and outcome – and there have been distinct limits to the policy influence of the poor and marginalized.

Education planning: stronger, but still not strong enough

Since the Dakar Forum many countries have strengthened their education planning capabilities. The 2008 Report provided an overview of achievements in this area. It highlighted the greater clarity evident in many national education plans with respect to the formulation of clear objectives and time-bound targets. Strategic priorities are also more apparent: UPE is a well-defined core priority and there is a strengthened focus on gender parity.

The development of sector-wide approaches (SWAps) has played an important role in strengthening national education planning. Experience with SWAps over the past decade indicates they are potentially more effective than previous planning approaches in addressing education quality and equity problems. Sri Lanka provides an illustration (Box 3.23).[13]

Cross-sectoral planning is characterized by fragmentation and weak political leadership

While much has been achieved in education planning, continued systemic challenges remain in three areas. One of these is finance. Education plans may set out medium-term targets but they rarely include plausible cost estimates for achieving them. That partly explains why education goals are commonly absent from the medium-term financial frameworks that shape real budget allocations (FTI Secretariat, 2007*b*). One lesson from the lengthy and not particularly encouraging history of goal-setting in development is that targets that are not backed by finance are seldom attained.

Another weakness has been the tendency of planning documents to follow a highly generalized blueprint. One recent assessment of forty-five national education plans found remarkable similarity in policy approach, with limited attention paid to social and political context or to the constraints faced by marginalized groups (UNESCO-IIEP, 2006). This is unhelpful because overcoming marginalization requires the delineation of practical strategies within a particular context.

Cross-sectoral planning weaknesses constitute another area for concern. Education planners know they are not operating in an insulated sector; they recognize the enormous importance of poverty, public health, child nutrition, social marginalization and other factors in shaping prospects for education. Yet the cross-sectoral planning processes needed to address these problems continue to be characterized by high levels of fragmentation and weak political leadership. The standard education-plan blueprint also tends to downplay the importance of progress in some key areas. For example, early childhood education, literacy and non-formal education are often EFA 'orphans' (UNESCO, 2007*a*).

Poverty reduction strategies: new generation, old problems

When they were launched in 2000, PRSPs were seen as a bold innovation in development cooperation. The aim was to provide a comprehensive integrated framework for placing poverty reduction strategies at the centre of macroeconomic policy. Each country was expected to identify clear goals, which would be reflected in short-term budget allocations and long-term financial planning. In line with a broader shift away

Box 3.23: Strengthening equity through sector-wide approaches: Sri Lanka's experience

Sri Lanka has a long-standing commitment to equity in education planning. Even so, persistent widespread poverty (estimated to affect one-quarter of the population) and the impact of ethnic conflict in the north and east remain challenges. The devastating effects of the 2004 tsunami are also still being felt.

The development of the Education Sector Development Framework and Programme for 2006–2010 has helped strengthen Sri Lanka's approach to tackling inequality. This SWAp recognizes that equity is a matter not just of access but also of quality and resourcing, and it attempts to mainstream various aspects of equity from the outset. It provides a clear strategic approach and monitoring framework, linked to a medium-term budgetary framework allowing resources to be aimed at the most disadvantaged schools.

One important aspect is that the SWAp also sets quantifiable goals for reducing disparities. Equity-based targets extend from the number of disabled students enrolled in regular schools, the number of special education centres and centres for street children, and the presence of professionally qualified teachers in difficult schools to learning outcomes by school, district, urban/rural area and gender.

Source: Jayaweera and Gunawardena (2007).

13. Boxes on Ethiopia, Nepal and the United Republic of Tanzania in Chapter 2 further illustrate the benefits of SWAps in addressing equity challenges.

from loan conditionality and project-based approaches, PRSPs defined a new set of core principles. They were to be country owned, developed through dialogue with civil society, results oriented, long term, and comprehensive and multidimensional in their approach to poverty.

PRSPs remain a core poverty reduction planning document. While some commentators downplay their importance in public policy, PRSPs play a key role in setting and reflecting national priorities and strategies. They also define the terms and broad goals of the 'aid partnership' between developing country governments and aid donors – an issue explored in Chapter 4. Fifty-four countries now have operational PRSPs. Most are low-income countries, twenty-eight of them in sub-Saharan Africa.
It would be a mistake to overstate the significance of PRSPs or to exaggerate the level of country ownership they imply. Donors retain a strong influence in framing PRSP priorities in many countries. However, given their scope and the intensity of the dialogue surrounding their development, PRSPs provide important insights into the place of education in national poverty reduction processes.

Box 3.24: Building capacity for pro-poor reform in the United Republic of Tanzania

The relationship between education and poverty has been a policy focus in the United Republic of Tanzania since independence. It was central to President Nyerere's policy of Education for Self-Reliance. The PRSP process has built on this existing political commitment to strengthen institutional capacity for pro-poor reform.

The country's first PRSP in 2000 was relatively narrow, focusing on macroeconomic policy and key social investments. However, as implementation unfolded, the strategy was steadily broadened. Sector strategies were further developed and incorporated into the overall development agenda. With the second PRSP, the 2005 National Strategy for Growth and Reduction of Poverty, the medium-term development programme was clearly articulated across a broad range of sectors, incorporated cross-cutting issues and was linked to medium-term countrywide goals. Attention within the education sector has also broadened: while the first plan focused on primary schooling, the second PRSP includes attention to secondary education, in accordance with priorities set in the country's Secondary Education Sector Development Plan.

Source: Wedgwood (2007); World Bank and IMF (2005).

The implementation period for second-generation PRSPs is now well advanced. Have the lessons of the first generation been absorbed? Has there been a significant improvement in quality? In some countries both these questions can be answered in the affirmative. In Uganda, the first country to adopt a PRSP, the PRSP built on the existing Poverty Eradication Action Plan to set out well-defined goals and budget commitments aimed at accelerating progress in health, education and the development of rural infrastructure, with positive results (see Chapter 4). These strong foundations have been built upon, facilitating a marked increase in programme-based aid from many donors. Moreover, in countries with well-developed education sector plans, there is evidence that education planning and poverty reduction strategies are mutually supportive. For example, the United Republic of Tanzania has steadily strengthened its institutional capacity, resulting in better integration of education within a poverty reduction framework (Box 3.24).

Wider experience is less encouraging. Cross-country evidence suggests that second-generation PRSPs suffer from many of the same problems as their predecessors. They continue to focus on a narrow range of education goals and targets, often limited to those associated with the MDGs. Attainment of UPE heavily outweighs wider education goals in priority-setting. Moreover, surprisingly little attention has been paid to the interaction between deprivation in education and other areas in explaining the intergenerational transmission of poverty. Detailed evidence relating to the types of policies that might break the vicious cycle of education deprivation and poverty is in similarly short supply (Rose and Dyer, 2006). As a result, many PRSPs fail in their core purpose. There is also little evidence to suggest that the development of second-generation PRSPs has helped break down the fragmentation in planning between education and other line ministries. Such fragmentation has real consequences for poor and vulnerable people – and for progress towards the goals set in the Dakar Framework for Action.

In exploring the link between education planning and poverty reduction, this *EFA Global Monitoring Report* has carried out a detailed review of eighteen second-generation PRSPs.[14] Part of the aim was to examine whether there has been a change from the approaches set out in the first PRSPs. In particular, the review considered whether the latest PRSPs

14. The eighteen countries with two PRSPs included in the review are: Burkina Faso, Cambodia, Ethiopia, the Gambia, Ghana, Guinea, Madagascar, Malawi, Mali, Mauritania, Mozambique, Nicaragua, Rwanda, Senegal, the United Republic of Tanzania, Uganda, Viet Nam and Zambia. Table 3.10 at the end of this Chapter presents a selected summary of this review.

were less prone to blueprint approaches and more geared towards addressing the underlying causes of disparity in education. Table 3.10, at the end of this chapter, summarizes some of the key findings. The conclusions to emerge from the review are not encouraging. They point to a broad failure on the part of governments and donors to articulate a more integrated approach to education planning. With some exceptions, PRSPs also downplay the issues raised by extreme inequalities in opportunity. Four areas stand out as meriting an urgent rethink of current approaches:

- the weak link with the EFA agenda;
- problems in defining credible equity-based targets;
- the separation of education from broader governance reforms;
- limited attention to wider drivers of education disadvantage.

Weak link to the EFA agenda

The point of reference for most first-generation PRSPs was the MDGs and associated targets for 2015 (Caillods and Hallak, 2004). This focus appears to have strengthened over time. One practical consequence is that most PRSPs attach far more weight to the quantitative target of UPE by 2015 than to other EFA goals. Where education equity is identified as needing attention, it is almost exclusively associated with strategies for improving access to primary schooling.

While UPE is undeniably important, this is a highly limited approach. The need for particular attention to disadvantaged learners is rarely recognized in PRSPs. Meanwhile, wider EFA goals are either downplayed or separated from a broader poverty reduction agenda. To the extent that the eighteen second-generation PRSPs mention ECCE at all, it is still frequently seen as a means of improving learning in primary schools rather than as a source of progress in child health, nutrition and cognitive development with potential benefits for primary and secondary education – and for wider opportunities (see Chapter 2). Strategies concerning technical and vocational education and training (TVET) and skills development are often considered principally in relation to the role of the private sector. The distribution of benefits in TVET provision is rarely considered – and the linkage to poverty reduction is often vague. Other intersectoral links between education and employment strategies are barely visible. Literacy is another part of the EFA agenda for which vital intersectoral links are absent.

The narrow focus on primary education has eclipsed other EFA goals and the broader development agenda

This is surprising in view of the critical role of literacy in overcoming poverty, inequality and political marginalization.

One consequence of the overwhelming weight attached to primary education is the neglect of secondary schooling. This is counterproductive at many levels. As primary school completion rates increase, demand for secondary school places will grow. Indeed, improving access to secondary school is one of the conditions in many countries for creating incentives to complete primary education. Some recent PRSPs pay more attention to equity considerations at secondary level, although the focus is primarily on building schools (Table 3.10). The barriers facing poor households in getting children into and through secondary school seldom figure in PRSPs. This is despite the fact that public policies in this area can have a powerful impact on gender equity – as witnessed by the experience of Bangladesh (see Chapter 2).

Fragmentation is at the heart of many of these problems. To take one example, progress in literacy requires coordination across a wide range of government bodies. PRSPs rarely acknowledge this, even though most successful policies explicitly address the problem of institutional fragmentation. Madagascar's programme on non-formal education is an example. It is based on cooperation between different parts of government and various United Nations agencies, and integrates literacy into several specialized areas of development. The programme is noted for contributing to a 'strong literacy lens' in the national PRSP (UNESCO, 2008, p. 10, cited in Robinson-Pant, 2008). Such experience is, however, extremely rare.

Problems in target-setting

For targets to be meaningful guides to policy, they must be both credible and consistent. Those set in many PRSPs are neither. For example, Senegal aims to achieve a primary school NER of 90% according to an MDG follow-up document, while its PRSP puts the objective for this indicator at 98%; the United Republic of Tanzania sets a target of primary school NER at 99% by 2010, but aims for only 30% of orphans and vulnerable children enrolled or having completed primary education by that year (UNESCO-IIEP, 2006). Such inconsistencies send confused signals to budget planners and other policy-makers involved in the development of national strategies.

Another concern is that few countries provide specific targets to enable monitoring of equity in education (Figure 3.8). Among the eighteen countries with two PRSPs, only Nicaragua, in its first PRSP, included a poverty-disaggregated education indicator; the United Republic of Tanzania includes a focus on orphans and vulnerable children in its second PRSP; and, most unusually, both PRSPs of Viet Nam include an indicator related to ethnicity, linked with the attention to strategies to provide support within the education sector and beyond. Target-setting is stronger with respect to gender (see below). This may be due to the attention generated by virtue of the MDGs. Even so, six of the eighteen countries still do not include gender-disaggregated targets in their second PRSP. Where equity targets are set, they invariably address access rather than learning, revealing a limited focus on education quality. There is no discernible improvement between the first and second PRSPs in this area.

Figure 3.8: Education equity-associated targets in eighteen PRSPs

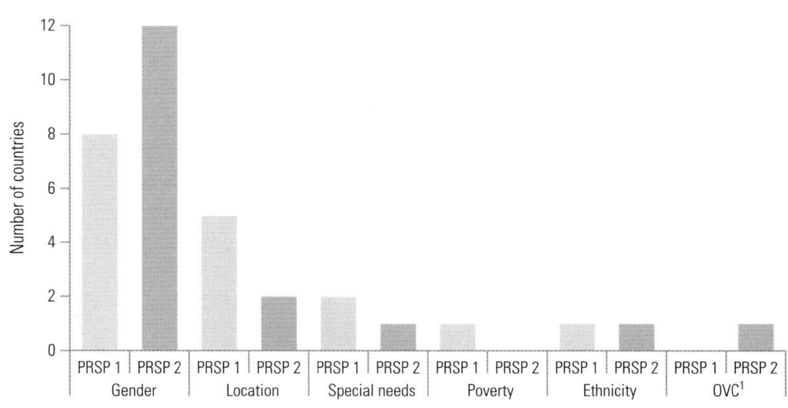

1. Orphans and vulnerable children.
Sources: See Table 3.10.

The mismatch between targets, strategies and financing commitments is another area in which progress has been limited. One detailed review of four second-generation PRSPs identified problems at several levels. In Ghana and Nepal budgets were not aligned with planned activities. Cambodia and Ethiopia manifested a clear mismatch between stated planning intentions and budgetary feasibility; a World Bank-IMF assessment found that in Ethiopia the assumptions of economic growth underpinning national financing projections were unrealistic (Giffard-Lindsay, 2008).

A separation between education strategies and governance reform

Many PRSPs emphasize the importance of governance reform, often presenting it as a separate pillar of poverty reduction. Governance reform has also become increasingly prominent in education sector planning, where it commonly reflects strategies on the broader governance agenda, particularly decentralization and participation.

Since governance strategies, such as decentralization, usually originate outside the education sector, PRSPs provide an opportunity to strengthen the linkage between education and broader governance reform. Governance reform is seldom neutral in its implications for people who are poor, marginalized and disadvantaged in education. In principle, the PRSP process could be used to look at how emerging approaches to governance might help – or hinder – efforts to reduce disparities in education. In practice, the opportunity for strengthening coherence is rarely pursued. One evaluation of seventeen PRSPs identified a marked bias towards technocratic planning approaches (Grant and Marcus, 2006). One consequence – ironically, given the nature of the documents – is that the implications of governance reform for distribution and poverty reduction are largely ignored (Grindle, 2004).

Many PRSPs tend to be technocratic blueprints that separate education from broader governance reform

The treatment of governance suffers from wider problems. One aim of PRSPs was to move away from development blueprints and focus on country-specific problems. Yet many PRSPs reflect a blueprint approach to governance. This is apparent from the education governance agenda set out in the eighteen second-generation PRSPs reviewed by this Report. The review identified decentralization and participation as common PRSP themes in education. However, the governance reforms in education were typically delinked from the wider governance agenda, with scant regard directed to their implications for equity in education. As shown earlier in this chapter, financial decentralization can have a major impact on equity. Yet PRSPs seldom consider the potentially negative outcomes of devolving finance to subnational government.

In terms of the education sector itself, the governance priorities in PRSPs closely resemble those frequently provided in education planning documents. A recent review of forty-five education plans identifies three recurring themes. First, decentralization, accompanied by aspirations for grass-roots participation, features prominently in thirty-six plans, including all those in Latin America and in South and West Asia, and all but one in sub-Saharan Africa (Zimbabwe being the exception). The second theme, school-based management and school autonomy, figures in seventeen plans, most notably in Latin America. The third theme, appearing in thirty plans, is increased recourse to and support for private providers, particularly in South and West Asia and in sub-Saharan Africa (UNESCO-IIEP, 2006).

Apart from this striking uniformity, some obvious equity-related questions arise from the governance content of PRSPs. How will decentralization be pursued without widening financing gaps between richer and poorer regions? If authority is devolved to regional and local governments and schools, what measures will be taken to facilitate participation by marginalized groups? If the private sector is to play an expanded role, what regulatory measures will be put in place to prevent the development of a two-tier system and to keep poor households from being priced out of provision? How will the education ministry fulfil its mandate of assuring EFA if it lacks control over a wide variety of private providers and no institutional mechanism for monitoring them exists? These are some of the challenges raised in earlier sections of the chapter that PRSPs have the potential to address – but they are not doing so.

Real progress in education depends on addressing the underlying causes of poverty and inequality outside the school

The experience of Nepal draws attention to the importance of country-specific circumstances. As Chapter 2 notes, Nepal has made great strides in education planning within a sector-wide framework, resulting in improvements in access and equity. However, governance challenges remain. Drawing up uniform 'good governance' blueprints is a simple enough exercise but, under the conditions prevailing in Nepal, decentralization and devolution can have adverse consequences linked to a lack of capacity or imbalances in political power and can as a result have the effect of disadvantaging certain groups (Box 3.25).

Box 3.25: Decentralization in Nepal: a difficult journey

Central to the education strategies in Nepal's PRSP (which corresponds to its tenth national plan, 2002-2007), and education planning in the country more generally, is the devolution of school management, including teacher recruitment, to communities. Initiatives are being funded through District Development Councils but implementation has not been straightforward for a number of reasons:

- Line ministries' reluctance to relinquish control of budgets and programmes is stalling the process.
- Political uncertainty, resistance from some groups, security constraints and weak monitoring have also hampered implementation.
- Many schools lack the necessary financial and technical capacity.
- Parents have trouble judging school quality and influencing government decisions, which affects school management committee activities and weakens accountability by government decision-makers.
- Because the central government handed down a fixed programme framework and budget allocation, communities feel burdened rather than empowered.

Sources: Acharya (2007); International Development Association and IMF (2006); Nepal National Planning Commission (2005).

Education missing in cross-sectoral approaches

Recognition that poverty is multidimensional is at the heart of the PRSP concept. Yet strategies for tackling multidimensional poverty are often conspicuous by their absence. An earlier review of PRSPs carried out in 2003 found that the education component was little more than a 'copy-summary' of education ministry plans. More broadly, education sector planning was weakly integrated into poverty reduction strategy formulation and, to an even greater degree, into budget planning (Caillods and Hallak, 2004). One more recent review finds that PRSPs continue to present a summary of education plans (Giffard-Lindsay, 2008). While this has the advantage of ensuring that priorities developed in the education sector are aligned with those in PRSPs, it means the potential of PRSPs to address causes of education disadvantage originating outside the sector is not being realized. This is arguably the most serious of all PRSP failings. While education policy can make a real difference in extending opportunity, progress in education depends critically on addressing the underlying causes of poverty and inequality outside of the school.

The problem can be illustrated by reference to six areas highlighted in Chapter 2, in which initiatives outside education are critical to EFA progress:

- tackling gender equality;
- reducing child malnutrition;
- responding to HIV/AIDS;
- addressing disability;
- overcoming marginalization;
- responding to problems associated with conflict.

Gender equality features less prominently than gender parity. Gender is more visible in PRSPs than other dimensions of education inequity. Attention to gender parity has been growing: twelve of the eighteen countries in this Report's analysis have a second PRSP that includes gender-disaggregated targets (Figure 3.8). There are also promising signs that some of these countries' strategies now go beyond targeting headcount parity in school and are seeking to address wider issues of inequality, such as violence and abuse in schools (Table 3.10).

Nevertheless, gender equity in PRSPs focuses on improving girls' access to education. This narrow approach can be traced to education plans and, to some degree, the MDG framework. A review of twenty-eight education plans by the EFA Fast Track Initiative (FTI) showed that half lacked a strategy for girls' education. Where 'strategies' were included, they took the form of a list of unprioritized interventions (FTI Secretariat, 2007*b*).

Restricted approaches to gender have important analytical and wider policy consequences. Consider the interface between female education and the position of women in labour markets. In Bangladesh, a range of education policies – including increased spending, stipends for girls' secondary education and recruitment of more female teachers – have played an important role in strengthening gender parity. However, one of the most critical drivers of change has been the income and empowerment effects associated with mass female employment in the garment industry (Hossain, 2007; Schuler, 2007). In this context, it could be argued that change in education has been driven to a large degree by changes in employment and labour markets. From a policy perspective, one conclusion might be that education planning should consider the potential benefits of policy interventions in areas that shape women's lives and aspirations, including the strengthening of employment rights and minimum wage provision. The relevant conclusion that can be drawn for PRSPs is that what happens in employment is an education issue.

Malnourished children. EFA cannot be achieved while mass childhood malnutrition continues at current levels (Chapter 2). In countries where stunting affects 30% to 40% of the population, the goal of UPE by 2015 is out of reach. This is a challenge that cannot be addressed through compartmentalized policies. Achieving breakthroughs requires secure access to adequate food, a sanitary environment, adequate health services and education. It also requires political commitment from a variety of sectors, including agriculture, local government, health, water and sanitation, environment, public works and education, as well as links with finance, economic planning and justice.

Achieving breakthroughs in childhood nutrition requires political commitment from a variety of sectors

Most PRSPs point to a combination of neglect and highly fragmented approaches to malnutrition (Grant and Marcus, 2006; Shekar and Lee, 2006). The neglect is related to the insufficient attention that has been directed towards malnutrition under the MDG framework, which often guides priorities in PRSPs. In turn, this problem can be traced to the absence of a visible constituency in a position to put malnutrition on the political agenda (Benson, 2004). The malnourished are not just widely dispersed – they are overwhelmingly poor and marginalized. Yet the neglect of policy options associated with nutrition affects the lives of young children and the educational opportunities of those who survive. This neglect was captured in a recent review of forty PRSPs for countries where malnutrition is particularly acute:

- Only thirteen countries included activities to address vitamin A deficiency and anaemia, despite recognition that they are public health problems in the vast majority of the forty countries.

- Only 35% of the PRSPs allocated budget resources specifically for nutrition. Yet more than 90% mentioned food security interventions, even when food security was not necessarily the main problem (Shekar and Lee, 2006).

PRSPs often identify malnutrition as an important symptom of poverty yet fail to include actions or budgets for improving nutrition. Where budgets are included, they may cover only micronutrient programmes or specific interventions. School feeding is one common intervention, although such programmes are not always found to have much impact on nutrition – particularly for children who are too ill to attend school in the first place (Shekar and Lee, 2006).

There are exceptions to this picture of fragmentation. Nutrition is among the six pillars of Bangladesh's PRSP, which has helped institutionalize nutrition in the country's development agenda, building on the earlier Bangladesh Integrated Nutrition Project and National Nutrition Project. In Madagascar nutrition is being mainstreamed and scaled up after project experience. The Ethiopian government has developed a national nutrition strategy with coordinated support from development partners (Shekar and Lee, 2006). Nevertheless, the more common institutionalized failure of PRSPs to address the crisis in malnutrition points to a deeper obstacle to progress towards EFA.

There is slow progress in integrating HIV/AIDS and children with disabilities into multisectoral planning

HIV/AIDS: the high price of uncoordinated responses. The devastating impact of HIV/AIDS on education systems in highly affected countries has been extensively documented. Yet many of these countries have not developed an effective planning response to prevent new infections and to limit the effect of HIV/AIDS on families, communities and schools. In many cases the focus has been on curriculum reform in education to include teaching on HIV/AIDS prevention rather than an integrated response aimed at addressing the multiple disadvantages faced by children affected by HIV/AIDS (Table 3.10). There are exceptions to this rule, as the experience of Cambodia shows (Box 3.26).

The approach to HIV/AIDS and education in PRSPs is closely associated with wider failures in education planning. A review of twelve FTI-endorsed education plans found considerable variability in how HIV/AIDS was addressed: five made no mention of it and only four had specific cost estimates (Clark and Bundy, 2004). Follow-up research found that the FTI appraisal and endorsement process was still uneven despite amendments to the guidelines following the first report (Clark and Bundy, 2006). Three of the eight plans endorsed had no HIV/AIDS component, even though two of the countries involved have a generalized HIV epidemic (HIV prevalence above 1% in the general adult population); and two had only a limited set of interventions. More promisingly, the other three – Ethiopia, Kenya and Lesotho – were moving towards a comprehensive response and provided good examples of what could be achieved.

Disabled children: little evidence of inclusive approaches. Disability is a significant source of inequality and marginalization in education (see Chapter 2). If governments are to get the remaining out-of-school children into school, removing barriers facing disabled children is one priority. Another is the creation of inclusive education systems that respond to varying needs. A shift towards more inclusive systems is supported by the Convention on the Rights of Persons with Disabilities, which came into force in May 2008. It not only recognizes that inclusive education is a right, but calls for an improved educational environment for the disabled and measures to break down barriers and stereotypes related to disability (United Nations, 2006).

Progress in recognizing disability as an area needing policy attention has been limited. Only ten of the twenty-eight education plans endorsed by the

Box 3.26: Intersectoral planning on HIV/AIDS and education in Cambodia

Cambodia's Ministry of Education, Youth and Sports (MOEYS) established an Interdepartmental Committee on HIV/AIDS in 1999 to coordinate mainstreaming of HIV/AIDS issues in the education sector. The committee, chaired by the MOEYS secretary of state, comprises representatives of fifteen departments and institutes. It has ensured that priority is given to HIV/AIDS, which since 2001 has been referred to as a key cross-cutting priority in Education Strategic Plans (2001-2005 and 2006-2010), in the annual Education Sector Support Programme and in the PRSP (the National Strategic Development Plan, 2006-2010). In terms of the curriculum, HIV/AIDS is integrated as a regular topic in primary and secondary schools, and in non-formal education settings, and is part of pre- and in-service teacher training. MOEYS has a strategic plan on HIV/AIDS (2008-2012) and recently became the first Cambodian ministry to adopt a workplace policy on the issue. Political commitment is reported to have contributed to a rapid decline in the prevalence of HIV, from 3% in 1997 to 1.9% in 2005.

Source: Cambodia Ministry of Education, Youth and Sports, and Interdepartmental Committee on HIV/AIDS (2007).

FTI between 2002 and 2006 included a strategy for children affected by disability. While thirteen others mention disability, there is little detail of strategies for the inclusion of disabled children in education, and five make no mention at all (World Vision, 2007).

Ensuring that disabled children receive an inclusive education demands a multisector approach. PRSPs could play an important role in coordinating health and social welfare issues that affect educational opportunities and outcomes for disabled children, such as nutrition, access to health services, early childhood care and social assistance. The United Republic of Tanzania, with its 2003 National Policy on Disability, is a rare example of a country that includes targets and strategies aimed at increasing educational opportunities for children with disabilities in its second PRSP (Figure 3.8) (World Vision, 2007). PRSPs that include strategies aimed at supporting children with disabilities tend to focus on school infrastructure and sometimes curriculum relevance (Table 3.10). Few PRSPs and education plans address the interlocking forms of social exclusion that children with disabilities often face.

The 'invisible' marginalized. Chapter 2 shows that simply living in a particular part of a country can reinforce disadvantage in educational opportunities. An Oxfam review of first-generation PRSPs found that only a few had education strategies for the special needs of marginalized or impoverished areas of countries (Oxfam International, 2004). Second-generation PRSPs continue to pay sparse attention to geographic factors limiting the visibility of particular groups (Table 3.10) (Chronic Poverty Research Centre, 2008). Uniform strategies are commonly identified, with insufficient attention to the ways in which forms of disadvantage vary for different population groups geographically; targets are usually not differentiated by location (Figure 3.8).

Where PRSPs do address geographic imbalances, they usually focus on disadvantaged rural areas, often failing to recognize the plight of slum dwellers (Chronic Poverty Research Centre, 2008). There is, moreover, almost no mention in recent PRSPs of the educational needs of child migrants (whether with their families or alone) (Black, 2004). Given that children of both domestic migrants and, in many cases, cross-border migrants are among the most disadvantaged in education, this is a serious omission. Similarly, children living on the street are seldom considered as a distinctive group facing disadvantage.

Also neglected are ethnic minorities. Where they do appear in PRSPs, the main strategy aimed at overcoming inequalities is associated with educational access (Grant and Marcus, 2006). But children from minority groups face exclusion beyond the school environment. Kenya provides a rare illustration of an integrated approach to the needs of marginalized people with its Pastoralist Thematic Group, which influenced the PRSP (Box 3.27). Attention to religious minorities is rarer still – none of the eighteen second-generation PRSPs refers to education of religious minority groups (Table 3.10).

Children from marginalized or impoverished areas and ethnic minorities need greater visibility in planning

Children in conflict-affected states are too often an absent constituency. Many of the world's children without any opportunity to attend school live in fragile states. In some cases, their lives are directly affected by violence and civil conflict. In others, their countries are undergoing post-conflict reconstruction. Either way, with weak institutions, limited resources and often restricted government authority, fragile states face distinctive problems in planning for education and poverty reduction.

Box 3.27: Getting pastoralist concerns onto the PRSP agenda in Kenya

The pastoralists of Kenya's arid and semi-arid regions make up about a quarter of the total population. In 2000 only 20% of their children had the opportunity to attend school. Yet the interim PRSP totally neglected pastoralist issues.

This picture started to change from early 2001 when a Pastoralist Thematic Group was included in PRSP consultations. There was wide-ranging discussion on whether to present these concerns as a cross-cutting theme in a separate chapter or fit them to each ministry's priorities. In the final PRSP (Investment Programme for the Economic Recovery Strategy for Wealth and Employment Creation, 2003-2007), pastoralist issues were discussed under the theme of human resource development. The discussion combined a number of interlinked aspects, including closing the gap with the rest of the country by developing a creative schooling programme for pastoralist children, strengthening community-based health care systems and preventive medicine, and improving food security through community-based early warning systems. A target of increasing primary enrolment among pastoralists to 40% was adopted.

Source: Abkula (2002).

Many lack the technical capacity to develop plans. Political commitment is often constrained and likely to result in particular groups being ignored in the planning process. Recent experiences with PRSPs developed in Afghanistan and the Democratic Republic of the Congo show nonetheless that, even in particularly challenging contexts, it is possible to develop conflict-sensitive education strategies, to varying degrees of success.

Afghanistan demonstrates the importance of developing an education plan that can provide the basis for conflict-sensitive strategies in the PRSP. The development of the country's Education Strategic Plan under the leadership of the education minister is a considerable achievement associated with a series of key changes in management of the sector. The plan is incorporated under Social and Economic Development in the 2008 Afghanistan National Development Strategy, the country's PRSP. Given the technical work already undertaken for the sector strategy, the education sector was well advanced for inclusion in the national development strategy.

Afghanistan has shown political commitment to developing conflict-sensitive education strategies

Conflict and reconstruction define the context for education planning. Afghanistan faces some of the world's highest estimated rates of disability and gender inequality. It is estimated that half the school-age population is out of school; thus, the government's aim to achieve primary NERs of at least 60% for girls and 75% for boys by 2010 is laudable. However, as the PRSP notes: 'threats to schools, destruction of school buildings, killing and maiming of students and teachers is increasing, particularly in the southern provinces'. Schools are not always considered safe, a fact affecting the enrolment of girls in particular. Against this backdrop, Afghanistan still has far to go to achieve EFA and to narrow the gender gap. While the Education Strategic Plan and PRSP provide a clear basis for moving in the right direction, along with clear signals of political commitment, some commentators have pointed to the need for greater consideration to be given to strategies that can address the impact of security issues on the education sector (Greeley, 2007*a*).

The specific challenges posed for education by conflict vary across countries. In the Democratic Republic of the Congo, education is at the heart of a reform process whose urgency is underscored by recognition that broader state legitimization depends in large measure on the perceived strength of government commitment to improving education provision (Greeley, 2007*b*). As a marker of such commitment, the government elected in 2006 has developed a PRSP, the Poverty Reduction and Growth Strategy Paper. Education appears under the pillar of improving access to social services and reducing vulnerability. The paper identifies core problems in the sector, including deterioration in the primary GER from 92% in 1972 to 64% in 2002 and a stagnant secondary GER at 30%. However, while there are some similarities to Afghanistan in terms of the formal PRSP approach, the substantive differences are also marked. In contrast to Afghanistan, the government has not yet developed a more detailed education sector strategy that takes into account the realities in the country. Thus the PRSP deals with governance, provision of free education and equity issues, but lacks details of how to achieve the goals set out. Given the devastating impact of conflict on nutrition, health, poverty and security, there is an urgent need for policies that address the real problems facing the Democratic Republic of the Congo.

Integrated social protection for the poor and vulnerable

The compartmentalized approach to planning evident in many PRSPs contrasts strongly with emerging approaches to tackling poverty and inequality. One example is social protection. Many of these approaches place an emphasis on linkages between education, health and employment – and on policy integration across sectors. They also stress the importance of equipping poor households with the capabilities they need to break the cross-generational transmission of poverty.

Recognizing that poverty is multidimensional, many governments are introducing programmes that target reductions in risk and vulnerability at several levels in health, nutrition, education and employment. 'Social protection' describes a broad set of policies that can help poor and vulnerable households manage risk through transfers of cash, food or entitlements to key services during critical periods (Marcus, 2007). For households lacking assets or insurance, a drought, a flood, a shift in labour market conditions or an illness can give rise to coping strategies that lead to long-run cycles of deprivation. For example, in East Africa drought is often the catalyst for reduced nutrition and withdrawal of children from school. Poor households may also withdraw children from school in difficult times, partly to save on schooling costs but also to send them to work.

Successful programmes in several Latin American countries combine social protection and enhancement of investments in children's education and health with alleviation of pressure to send children to work. The objective is to go beyond traditional social welfare transfers by equipping vulnerable households with assets that will break the cycle of poverty. Cash transfer has played an important role in the design of social protection programmes, some of which now operate on a national scale. For example, the Bolsa Família programme in Brazil reaches around 11 million families. It provides a cash transfer of up to US$35 per month to poor families with children, conditional on their keeping the children in school and taking them for regular health checks (Lindert et al., 2007).

Social protection programmes have far-reaching aims. Rather than responding to poverty through welfare payments, they aim to meet immediate needs and break the intergeneration transmission of poverty through their impact on education and child health. Evaluations point to some positive results. A recent study of targeted social protection programmes in Honduras, Mexico and Nicaragua found them effective not only at increasing school attendance and but also at keeping poor children in school when households faced shocks to their livelihoods (de Janvry et al., 2006*b*). They have also had significant positive effects on children's health and nutritional status, particularly in the early years (Gertler, 2004). In Nicaragua, the Red de Proteción Social programme increased visits to health centres and improved diet, resulting in a five percentage point decline in the stunting of children under 5 compared with control areas (Maluccio and Flores, 2004).[15]

The Oportunidades programme in Mexico, which provides poor households with a cash transfer of up to US$55 per month if they send their children to school and visit nutrition monitoring centres regularly, is often held up as a successful cross-sectoral social protection programme. A recent study showed that unemployment or illness of the household head reduced the chances of poor children enrolling in school by some two percentage points. For Oportunidades beneficiaries, however, the drop was almost completely non-existent (de Janvry et al., 2006*a*).

Social protection programmes are also having an impact on child labour. The employment of children is both a consequence of poverty and a cause of restricted opportunity in education. Few PRSPs pay explicit attention to the trade-off between education and child labour (World Bank, 2005*d*). Yet social protection programmes have demonstrated that the links between poverty and child labour can be broken. Bono de Desarrollo Humano in Ecuador illustrates what can be achieved. Under this programme, households identified as extremely poor receive a cash transfer of US$15 per month. Unlike Oportunidades, the programme does not make the transfer conditional on changes in household behaviour. A recent evaluation based on an experimental research design found that the programme had a large positive impact on school enrolment (by about 10%) and a large negative impact on child labour (a reduction of around 17%) (Schady and Araujo, 2006).

Social protection programmes in Latin America show positive impacts on poverty, health and education

Other programmes that provide unconditional cash support targeting families of poor children have also led to marked improvement in the children's educational and nutritional status. For example, a recent study of the child support grant in South Africa found that children who had been in the programme for a large part of their childhood had significantly higher height-for-age ratios, a measure of improved nutrition (Agüero et al., 2006). The programme has also had a significant impact on school enrolment (Case et al., 2005).

Part of the success of social protection programmes in improving educational outcomes for the poor and disadvantaged comes from their effectiveness at channelling resources to target groups. A recent study on programmes in Brazil (Bolsa Família), Chile (Solidario) and Mexico (Oportunidades) found that about 60% of transfer funds flowed to the poorest 20% of the population. Conditional cash transfers have materially increased equity in the income distribution (Soares et al., 2007). The success of social protection programmes is increasingly recognized. Mexico's Oportunidades programme even offers a rare example of policy transfer from a developing country to a developed country (Box 3.28).

These examples provide a practical demonstration of how integrated approaches to reducing vulnerability benefit education. The good news is that social protection has emerged as a greater

15. Stunting is defined as a height-for-age z-score two or more standard deviations below the reference median (see glossary).

Box 3.28: New York City is learning lessons from Mexico's Oportunidades programme

Ideas for combating extreme deprivation in education usually travel a one-way street, from North to South. Now one of the most successful programmes is moving in the opposite direction, from Mexico to the United States.

In an effort to help some of its most deprived people escape poverty traps that cross generations, New York City is experimenting with a model based on Mexico's Oportunidades programme.

The Opportunity NYC programme was introduced in late 2007 after the city's mayor led a team of officials to Mexico to study Oportunidades. While its Mexican counterpart covers 25 million people, Opportunity NYC is currently a small pilot programme covering just over 5,000 families in parts of the Bronx, Harlem and Brooklyn. The districts included are marked by high levels of social deprivation. Poverty rates average around 40%, compared with a 21% average for the city as a whole; and unemployment rates are 19%, compared with 5% for the city.

Families covered by the programme are drawn mainly from the Latino and African-American communities. They can receive as much as US$4,000 to US$6,000 per year in transfers every two months, as long as they meet conditions in health (including regular medical and dental visits), job training and education. Education targets include regular school attendance, parental attendance at parent-teacher conferences and the obtaining of a library card. Improvements in test scores and secondary school graduation attract additional bonuses.

The overall approach is to provide financial transfers not just to address immediate hardship, but to create incentives that will induce behavioural change. Opportunity NYC is an innovative attempt to apply this model. The two-year, US$53 million programme is privately funded by the Rockefeller Foundation and other donors. Will it succeed? It is too early to tell: the first payments were made at the end of 2007. Half the families covered will be part of a control group and implementation is designed to facilitate a random assignment evaluation. By building evaluation into the implementation of the project from the outset, policy-makers should have access to a steady flow of data and information that can inform future policy design.

Whatever the outcome in New York, there is sufficient evidence from programmes of this kind to draw two broad conclusions for education. The first is that integrated poverty reduction planning is far more effective than the compartmentalized models evident in many PRSPs. The second is that, if governments are serious about achieving the goals in the Dakar Framework and the MDGs, they are heavily underinvesting in cash transfer programmes.

Sources: Jack (2008); MDRC (2007); Seedco (2007).

Mexico's Oportunidades programme offers a rare example of policy transfer from a developing country to a developed country

priority and is increasingly forming part of the PRSP agenda. One review of eighteen recent PRSPs found that seventeen included sections on social protection and those of Bolivia, Nepal, Pakistan and Senegal made it a core pillar. However, formal endorsement in PRSPs for social protection sometimes obscures what remains a piecemeal, project-based approach (Grant and Marcus, 2006). Pakistan's experience demonstrates the point: social protection is used as an umbrella for a wide range of unconnected strategies, to limited effect (Box 3.29).

Positive lessons from the more successful social protection programmes include the importance of sustained political commitment, large-scale programmes with allocation of significant and predictable resources, careful targeting and the coordination of planning across sectors. Social protection is not a panacea for the poverty and inequality that are holding back progress towards EFA. Outcomes depend on policy design, financing and implementation. By focusing on the development of a policy framework that integrates health, education, employment and wider concerns, social protection has facilitated more effective, integrated planning of the type envisaged – but not delivered – under the Dakar Framework for Action.

Strengthening participatory planning for the most vulnerable

The Dakar Framework calls on governments to engage in consultation on policy with 'learners, teachers, parents, communities, non-governmental organizations and other bodies representing civil society' (UNESCO 2000, Expanded Commentary, para. 53). PRSPs are widely seen as having made a positive contribution in this area by extending consultation to civil society organizations and coalitions, some of which explicitly aim to represent the disadvantaged (Chronic Poverty Research Centre, 2008).

Box 3.29: Social protection in Pakistan's poverty reduction strategy: the effects of fragmentation

Pakistan's 2003 PRSP, called Accelerating Economic Growth and Reducing Poverty: The Road Ahead, reflects the growing importance of vulnerability in poverty analyses. Social protection is identified as a central priority, but programme implementation has been dogged by institutional fragmentation, inadequate financing and poor targeting.

Why is this relevant to Pakistan's efforts to achieve EFA? First, the children are highly vulnerable as a result of high levels of poverty. Second, ill health, unemployment and natural disaster are a recurring theme in the lives of the poor, often leading to children being taken out of school. Around 10% of poor households in one study reported taking children out of school and putting them to work during such crises. Because poor households have fewer resources to support coping strategies, crises tend to widen social and economic disparities.

In response, Pakistan has established a range of social protection initiatives, including microfinance, public works, pensions and various social safety nets. Such measures are intended to protect the households at greatest risk and help them regarding income in times of financial crisis so they may eventually escape poverty. Some initiatives are directly linked to education while others have an indirect impact. Examples specific to education include:

- central government stipends to girls in middle school from poor districts;
- provincial stipend programmes, such as one in Punjab;
- free textbooks for poor students who attend government schools;
- a pilot child support programme in five districts (since 2006/2007);
- the Tawana Pakistan Project, a school-feeding programme aimed at improving health, nutrition and enrolment;
- non-formal education provision for vulnerable children, such as child labourers.

The list is impressive, but it also highlights a series of problems:

- Programmes overlap in their intended scope, with uncoordinated financing and delivery modes (e.g. via federal or provincial government, quasi-government and non-government organizations).
- Coordination is lacking among bodies responsible for implementation, including the ministries of education, labour, social welfare and special education, and science and technology, along with the National Technical and Vocational Education Commission.
- Many initiatives are experiments or relatively small in scale.
- In a context where government commitment to education and other social sector spending is already low (education spending amounts to just 2.7% of GDP), measures often depend on external resources and so are unlikely to be sustainable.
- Targeted stipend programmes are extremely limited in scale, fail to pay beneficiaries regularly and do not show a positive impact on schooling.

Sources: Bano (2007, 2008); World Bank (2007c).

Whether consultation translates into action depends on political actors' willingness to listen and respond, which is affected in turn by the influence of the electorate on political priorities and by the extent of support from elites. A convergence of interests among a range of stakeholders on access to primary schooling has helped keep this topic high on the agenda in many countries. In some contexts, concerns about the need to develop a skilled workforce have also raised awareness of the stakes. However, where priorities are set according to whose voices are heard, other areas of the EFA agenda are at risk of being further sidelined.

Amplifying the voice of civil society including the unheard poor

As the *EFA Global Monitoring Report 2008* noted, civil society organizations are increasingly influential in the formulation of national education plans, a trend further strengthened by the formation of national coalitions of such organizations since 2000 in many countries, in response to commitments made at Dakar. However, as the Report observed, challenges remain:

- Opportunities to participate systematically in agenda-setting and final drafting remain limited.
- New concerns have arisen as a result of broadening consultation, including rising

Whether consultation translates into action depends on political actors' willingness to listen and respond

stakeholder expectations that plans will reflect their concerns more prominently.

- Some civil society organizations lack the analytical capacity to engage in consultation productively and confidently.
- Consultation can serve to validate decisions already taken rather than to facilitate genuine engagement.

PRSP consultation exercises have led to engagement with civil society organizations on a large scale

As in any process of political dialogue and consultation, issues of representation are important in education planning. A detailed analysis of civil society participation in Burkina Faso, Kenya, Mali and the United Republic of Tanzania identified a wide range of actors interested in participating, including national and international non-government organizations, faith-based groups, national parent-teacher associations, teachers' unions, private provider groups and research networks. The analysis found a lack of transparency in the processes for selecting which actors to invite to the policy dialogue table. Those most likely to represent critical viewpoints are excluded. Teachers' unions, many of which oppose education reforms that affect employment and pay conditions, are often not invited to participate in policy dialogue (Mundy et al., 2007).

The shortcomings of participation in education sector planning are also evident in PRSP consultations, with participation by civil society organizations and coalitions working on education remaining restricted (Commonwealth Education Fund, 2007).

Despite the important role of civil society organizations and coalitions in mobilizing public concern over the policy decisions most likely to affect the disadvantaged, such groups do not usually include the voices of the poor directly. To address this deficiency, participatory poverty assessments have been undertaken in many countries as part of the PRSP consultation process. There have also been attempts to involve the marginalized more directly in consultation.

These are laudable aims. There have also been some important results. National participatory poverty assessments have given new insights into the underlying causes of poverty and vulnerability. In some cases – Uganda is an example – the evidence collected has had a direct bearing on the framing of national poverty reduction priorities. Efforts have been made to increase the accessibility of PRSP documents (for example, by making them available in national languages). And there have been efforts to extend consultation. Nepal's recent PRSP process provided opportunities for extensive consultation in the fragile economic and political context of an ethnically, geographically and linguistically diverse country emerging from years of conflict between government and Maoist forces. It went far beyond the consultation process for education plans, which has been top-down with little real involvement of minority rights groups (Giffard-Lindsay, 2008; Vaux et al., 2006).

For all these advances, the limits to consultation have to be acknowledged. Some of the limits relate to representation. PRSP consultation exercises have led to engagement with national and civil society organizations on a very large scale. Engagement with organizations of the poor, as distinct from organizations claiming to speak on their behalf, has been far more limited. Marginalized groups face many barriers to meaningful engagement, including lack of time, literacy and organizational capacity. Even when their views seem to be invited, information asymmetry can mean that they remain weakly involved (Goetz and Jenkins, 2005). Marginalized groups may simply lack access to the information they need to develop policy inputs. There is also a wider point to be made. PRSPs do not override everyday political realities that perpetuate deep inequalities in society. Governments that turn a deaf ear to the concerns of the poor in everyday public policy formulation are unlikely to undergo political transformation as a result of PRSP exercises. Tackling poverty and reducing inequality require policies and public spending priorities that are likely to call into question prevailing power relationships in many countries. That is precisely why many political elites prefer to ensure that PRSPs are pitched at a very high level of generality with a restricted process of dialogue and consultation.

PRSPs are part of a wider process of public policy development and political debate – a process that involves donors as well as national governments and political constituencies. Outcomes will be shaped by the interactions and power relationships between actors. In many cases,

PRSPs may give rise to tensions. Take the twin commitment to national ownership and equity. These goals might be attainable. But what if national governments are not committed to equity, or if they are less committed than sections of their society – or aid donors – might desire? (Booth and Curran, 2005).

Priorities in poverty reduction strategies are not set in a political vacuum. They are formulated by governments that assess constraints, opportunities and political pay-off. Experience in education is instructive. Undertaking highly visible reforms such as the abolition of user fees often generates a high and fast political return. The Kenyan Government announced the abolition of secondary school fees at a moment that coincided with the controversy surrounding the 2008 election. In Burundi, school fees were abolished in 2005 following a controversial one-party election. Elsewhere, too, user-fee abolition has been seen as a quick route to enhanced political legitimacy (Rose and Brown, 2004).

Interventions in other areas with a longer payback period have been less enthusiastically taken up. For example, the development of strategic policy frameworks to strengthen education standards and monitoring has not received a great deal of prominence in political discourse (Giffard-Lindsay, 2008). The same is true in areas that are likely to raise questions of social division, such as the narrowing of regional inequalities or transfers from higher-income to lower-income groups and areas. Reforms that have less immediately visible outcomes, such as improvements to education quality, or ones that might challenge political authority and patronage systems, such as those supporting girls' education, might gain less popularity in election processes (Rose and Brown, 2004).

Moving towards integrated and more equitable education planning poses challenges at many levels. Potentially, many of the issues involved are highly divisive. This is especially the case in societies marked by high levels of social polarization. Part of the challenge is to create a political discourse that looks beyond narrow self-interest to national interest and to shared goals – including the goals of equal citizenship and shared opportunity. One reason Bangladesh has progressed so rapidly in primary enrolment is that the return of multiparty democracy in the 1990s was marked by a broad-based consensus in favour of education. Another important factor was a recognition by national elites of the benefits of education for poverty reduction and development (Hossain, 2007).

The starting point for political consensus is a shared recognition that greater equity in education is not a zero-sum game. No section of society has to lose out – and society as a whole stands to gain from progress towards UPE and wider education goals. As Chapter 1 argues, equitable education is a powerful force for economic growth and rising living standards, as well as gains in other areas. Viewed from a different perspective, large-scale disparities are a source of inefficiency. This can also hamper advances in areas such as public health and fuel social polarization.

Conclusion

There is evidence that education planning has improved since Dakar. Education planning within a sector-wide framework is leading to greater coherence in priority-setting. However, serious problems remain. Far more has to be done to integrate education planning into wider poverty reduction strategies and to back priorities with budget commitments. Particular attention has to be paid to the interlocking disadvantages that are holding back progress towards EFA. Social protection programmes provide important lessons. They demonstrate that broad-based strategies for reducing poverty and vulnerability can generate important gains for education, creating new opportunities for the poor. Achieving this outcome will require the development of high-level political commitment, supported by strong national consensus, in favour of education for all. ■

Far more has to be done to integrate education planning into wider poverty reduction strategies and to back priorities with budget commitments

Table 3.10: Strategies to address education inequity in eighteen PRSPs

	Primary education											
	Curriculum relevance		School building/ infrastructure		Stipends		Community sensitization		School feeding		Fee abolition	
Type of inequity	PRSP1	PRSP2	PRSP1	PRSP2	PRSP1	PRSP2	PRSP1	PRSP2	PRSP1	PRSP2	PRSP1	PRSP2
Gender	2	5	2	3	1	3	2	4	1	0	0	0
Poor/vulnerable	0	0	1	1	6	6	1	1	3	4	5	2
HIV/AIDS	8	8	0	0	0	1	2	1	0	1	0	0
Disabled/special education needs	1	1	6	5	2	0	1	0	0	0	0	0
Geographic (e.g. region)	1	0	5	3	0	1	1	0	2	1	0	0
Conflict-affected areas	0	3	0	0	0	0	0	0	0	0	0	0
Ethnicity	1	0	0	0	0	1	0	0	0	0	0	0
Out-of-school children	0	0	0	0	0	1	1	0	0	0	0	0
Rural/urban	0	0	4	1	1	0	0	0	0	0	0	0
Religion	0	0	0	0	0	0	0	0	0	0	0	0
Not specified	0	0	0	0	1	0	0	1	0	1	2	3
Total number of strategies	13	17	18	13	11	13	8	7	6	7	7	5

	Secondary education											
	School building/ infrastructure		Curriculum relevance		Stipends		Quotas		Counselling		Total secondary	
Type of inequity	PRSP1	PRSP2	PRSP1	PRSP2	PRSP1	PRSP2	PRSP1	PRSP2	PRSP1	PRSP2	PRSP1	PRSP2
Gender	0	4	1	3	0	2	0	1	1	0	4	12
Poor/vulnerable	0	2	0	0	3	1	1	0	0	0	4	5
HIV/AIDS	0	0	0	2	0	0	0	0	0	0	0	4
Disabled/special education needs	0	2	0	0	1	1	0	0	0	0	1	6
Geographic (e.g. region)	1	1	0	1	1	0	0	0	0	0	7	3
Conflict-affected areas	0	0	0	0	0	0	0	0	0	0	0	0
Ethnicity	0	0	0	1	0	0	0	0	0	0	0	1
Out-of-school children	0	0	0	0	0	0	0	0	0	0	6	2
Rural/urban	1	2	0	0	0	0	0	0	0	0	2	3
Religion	0	0	0	0	0	0	0	0	0	0	0	0
Not specified	0	1	0	0	0	0	0	0	0	0	2	3
Total number of strategies	2	12	1	7	5	4	1	1	1	0	26	39

Table 3.10 presents information on PRSPs for the eighteen countries that have prepared two plans. Most of the first PRSPs were prepared around 2000, with the second prepared in most cases between 2004 and 2007. Based on the information provided in the PRSPs, the table indicates the number of countries that propose strategies aimed at addressing educational inequalities in the areas of ECCE, primary and secondary education, TVET and adult literacy, as well as the forms of disadvantage addressed.

The table identifies ten broad sources of inequality identified in PRSPs. It then summarizes the number of plans with proposed actions, comparing the first- and second-generation PRSPs. The broad headline message is that PRSPs pay insufficient attention to addressing educational inequalities and the change between the first- and second-generation PRSPs was limited. Among the findings to emerge from an analysis of the information in the table:

- Attention to primary education strategies aimed at tackling disparities increased slightly between the first- and second-generation PRSPs, with a total of seventy-one strategies presented in the first and eighty in the second.
- This increase is due to the inclusion of a wider range of strategies aimed at achieving gender parity and equality. In total, twenty-five gender-related strategies are mentioned in the more recent PRSPs, compared with eleven in the early ones. Encouragingly, this is due in part to a focus on strategies aimed at addressing gender inequality within the school environment (including recruitment of female teachers and addressing gender abuse in schools) – an area that did not appear in early PRSPs.

Primary education												
Female teachers		Teacher sensivity training		Addressing abuse in school		Water and sanitation		Language of instruction		Total primary		
PRSP1	PRSP2	PRSP1	PRSP2	PRSP1	PRSP2	PRSP1	PRSP2	PRSP1	PRSP2	PRSP1	PRSP2	Type of inequity
0	4	1	2	0	2	1	2	1	0	11	25	Gender
0	0	0	0	0	0	0	0	0	0	16	14	Poor/vulnerable
0	0	1	1	0	0	0	0	0	0	11	12	HIV/AIDS
0	0	0	1	0	0	0	1	0	0	10	8	Disabled/special education needs
0	0	0	0	0	0	0	0	1	0	10	5	Geographic (e.g. region)
0	0	0	0	0	0	0	0	0	0	0	3	Conflict-affected areas
0	0	0	0	0	0	0	0	2	1	3	2	Ethnicity
0	0	0	0	0	0	0	0	0	0	1	1	Out-of-school children
0	0	0	0	0	0	0	0	0	0	5	1	Rural/urban
0	0	0	0	0	0	0	0	0	0	0	0	Religion
1	1	0	0	0	2	0	0	0	1	4	9	Not specified
1	5	2	4	0	4	1	3	4	2	71	80	Total number of strategies

	ECCE		TVET				Adult literacy	
			Relevance		Non formal			
Type of inequity	PRSP1	PRSP2	PRSP1	PRSP2	PRSP1	PRSP2	PRSP1	PRSP2
Gender	0	0	1	2	1	0	4	3
Poor/vulnerable	1	3	0	2	0	0	0	1
HIV/AIDS	0	1	0	1	0	1	0	0
Disabled/special education needs	0	1	0	3	0	0	0	0
Geographic (e.g. region)	1	1	3	0	2	1	0	0
Conflict-affected areas	0	0	0	0	0	0	0	0
Ethnicity	0	0	0	0	0	0	0	0
Out-of-school children	0	0	2	1	4	1	1	1
Rural/urban	1	2	1	1	0	0	1	1
Religion	0	0	0	0	0	0	1	0
Not specified	7	7	1	0	1	2	1	1
Total number of strategies	10	15	8	10	8	5	8	7

Note: 'Not specified' indicates that the strategy included in the PRSP does not specify the type of disparity that is being targeted.

Sources: Burkina Faso Ministry of Economy and Development (2004); Burkina Faso Ministry of Economy and Finance (2000); Cambodia Council for Social Development (2002); Cambodia Government (2005); Ethiopia Ministry of Finance and Economic Development (2002, 2006); Gambia Department of State for Finance and Economic Affairs (2002, 2006); Ghana National Development Planning Commission (2003, 2005); Guinea Government (2002); Guinea Ministry of the Economy, Finances and Planning (2007); Madagascar Government (2003, 2007); Malawi Government (2002, 2006); Mali Government (2006); Mali Ministry of Economy and Finance (2002); Mauritania Government (2000, 2006); Mozambique Government (2001, 2006); Nicaragua Government (2001, 2005); Rwanda Ministry of Finance and Economic Planning (2002, 2007); Senegal Government (2002, 2006); Uganda Ministry of Finance, Planning and Economic Development (2000, 2004); United Republic of Tanzania Government (2000, 2005); Viet Nam Government (2003, 2006); Zambia Government (2006); Zambia Ministry of Finance and National Planning (2002).

- Some countries include strategies in both first- and second-generation PRSPs to increase participation by poor and vulnerable households, notably through stipends and school feeding programmes. Given the potential of such strategies in supporting educational opportunities, the number of countries including them remains low. For example, stipends for the poor and vulnerable are mentioned in only six of the eighteen PRSPs. Moreover, there is limited emphasis on fee abolition (five of the eighteen second-generation PRSPs mention it as a strategy), even though informal fees continue to be an important barrier to enrolment of poor and vulnerable children.
- Approaches to supporting children with disabilities are mainly focused on improving accessibility of school infrastructure rather than paying attention to curriculum reform.
- Strategies aimed at tackling regional and rural-urban marginalization have declined, mainly because less attention is given to school construction. Strategies aimed at supporting ethnic or religious minorities remain extremely limited.
- More positively, greater attention is being given to education strategies aimed at overcoming inequalities at secondary level. As with primary schooling, the focus is on school infrastructure and curriculum relevance.
- Inequality in ECCE continues to receive limited attention. Even where strategies are mentioned, they often do not specify how they intend to address particular forms of disadvantage.
- Similarly, there is limited attention in PRSPs to addressing inequalities in TVET and adult literacy (the main focus of the latter is on women's literacy).

© Ami Vitale/PANOS

Empowering local communities: low caste women meet to exchange information and voice their concerns, in Uttar Pradesh, India

Chapter 4

Increasing aid and improving governance

Increased and more effective aid is vital to achieving the EFA goals. At the 2000 World Education Forum in Dakar, rich countries pledged that no credible national plan would be allowed to fail for want of finance. The pledge has yet to be honored. This chapter examines the most recent evidence on aid flows. That evidence points to continued shortfalls in development assistance – and to worrying signs that promises made in 2005 are not being met. The chapter also explores the significant shift in approaches to aid governance under the 2005 Paris Declaration on Aid Effectiveness. Drawing on recent evidence, it asks whether the strengthened focus on country ownership, sector-wide approaches and harmonization is creating an enabling environment for more effective aid.

Introduction

The Dakar Framework for Action is built on a compact between developing countries and rich countries. Like any compact, it involves two-way responsibilities and obligations. Developing countries pledged to strengthen national education plans, tackle inequality and enhance accountability to their citizens. Governments of developed countries pledged to provide the aid needed to ensure that no credible strategy in the poorest countries would fail for want of finance. Since Dakar, both groups of countries have reinforced these pledges on numerous occasions.

As Chapters 2 and 3 show, the record of developing countries in translating their pledges into actions has been mixed. The record of donors is also mixed, but it is one of collective failure. As a group, donors have failed to act on their commitments – and they have failed to close a large financing gap. On conservative estimates, US$11 billion of aid is needed annually in low income countries to achieve three of the targets set in the Dakar Framework for Action: universal primary education (UPE), early childhood programmes and literacy. In 2006 aid in support of basic education in low income countries was just one-third of the estimated requirement. Several major donors appear to have almost abandoned support for Education for All in spite of explicit promises. During 2005, the Gleneagles summit of the Group of Eight (G8) and commitments made by donors outside this group raised expectations of a sharp increase in aid by 2010 to achieve the Millennium Development Goals (MDGs). There is now a clear danger that donors will not deliver and current trends point in the direction of a large shortfall against the target.

All of this has grave implications for progress towards the goals set at Dakar. Having been encouraged to draw up ambitious national plans, many developing countries will be left without the resources required for their full implementation. Changing this picture is an urgent priority because of the time lag between investment and outcome. If countries are to achieve UPE by 2015, they cannot wait to put in place the financing needed to build schools, recruit and train teachers, and provide incentives needed to reach marginalized social groups. More broadly, progress in education is contingent on delivery of the aid needed to achieve the MDGs in areas such as child health, water and sanitation, and the reduction of extreme poverty.

The bottom line message is that time is running out. While developing country governments have to redouble their efforts, in the absence of a concerted drive by donors to close the gap between aid pledges and aid delivery, the targets set at Dakar will not be achieved in many countries.

Both donors and the governments receiving aid have recognized that there are serious problems in aid governance. Too often, national ownership is weak, transaction costs are high and development assistance is delivered in ways that erode, rather than build, the institutional capacity of aid recipients. New approaches to aid governance are emerging, slowly. The emphasis is shifting away from aid projects to support for sector programmes and national budgets – and education is in the forefront of this transition. In addition, donors have taken on other important commitments to enhance aid effectiveness and cut transaction costs. All of these commitments have quantifiable targets for 2010. Early monitoring suggests that, while some progress has been made, without acceleration most of the 2010 targets will be missed. There are also concerns that the agenda may turn out to be a double-edged sword, if stronger collective action on the part of donors leads to a weakening of national ownership.

Good governance is at the heart of the emerging aid dialogue in education. Commitment by governments to accountability, transparency, participation and equity is vital for achieving the targets set under the Dakar Framework for Action. These are intrinsically important goals in their own right, as well as a means to education progress. Unfortunately, as Chapter 3 shows, too many governments have not taken this commitment seriously enough. As for donors, there is a danger they might seek to advance a good governance blueprint geared towards a narrow set of policies of questionable relevance to the needs of developing countries.

This chapter is divided into two parts. The first provides a monitoring overview of developments in the level of aid. Looking beyond current trends in commitments and disbursements, it also explores issues of equity in aid distribution. The second part turns to the evolving agenda concerning the delivery of aid. It examines how the strengthened donor commitment to supporting sector programmes is playing out in the education sector. It also looks at what donors understand by 'good governance' in education and the types of programmes they and governments are developing together to achieve it. □

Aid for education

International aid is at the centre of an increasingly polarized debate. Most governments in rich countries, backed by United Nations agencies and international financial organizations, and prompted by non-government organizations, see increased development assistance as a condition for achieving the MDGs and wider development goals. Aid 'pessimists' respond with the claim that big increases in aid have achieved small results at best and that at worst aid is a barrier to progress.

In reality, the situation is more complex than either view suggests. No amount of international aid will override the consequences of widespread corruption, inefficient service delivery or inequitable patterns of public spending. And how donors provide aid is also important. The benefits of development assistance are certainly contingent on good governance, not only in the receiving country but also on the part of the donor community. That being said, aid can – and does – make a large difference. And it makes the biggest difference when it is aligned behind nationally owned country strategies. In the case of EFA, international aid has played a crucial role in supporting policies that have improved access to education, enhanced equity and addressed the quality issue. While disentangling the precise effects of aid is difficult, it seems clear that many countries that have achieved rapid progress towards some or all of the Dakar goals would have progressed more slowly without aid, as the following examples illustrate:

As a group, donors have failed to act on their commitments to close a large financing gap

- In Cambodia, Ghana, Kenya, Mozambique, the United Republic of Tanzania and Zambia, the increase in international aid has facilitated the abolition of primary school tuition fees, leading to a large expansion of primary school enrolment. While the main responsibility for financing basic education lies with governments, external assistance can make a difference (Box 4.1).

- In the case of the United Republic of Tanzania, aid has supported an education sector strategy that has cut the number of out-of-school children by 3 million since 1999.

- In Ethiopia, education's share of the budget increased from 3.6% of gross national product (GNP) to 6% between 1999 and 2006. International aid was a critical component of overall financing.

Box 4.1: Aid supports the abolition of school fees in Kenya

In 2003, a new government in Kenya abolished primary school tuition fees, resulting in 1.3 million additional pupils pouring into the country's schools, overwhelming school infrastructure and catching ill-prepared teachers by surprise. Schools in slums found it especially difficult to cope with the large numbers. The government disbursed US$6.8 million in emergency grants to provide for basic items such as chalk and exercise books. But this was insufficient to meet the overwhelming need for extra textbooks, classrooms, and water and sanitation facilities. In the following year grants totalling US$109 million were made by the Organization of the Petroleum Exporting Countries, Sweden, UNICEF, the United Kingdom, the World Bank and the World Food Programme.

Bolstered by this support, the decision to scrap primary school tuition fees has advanced Kenya's quest to provide free primary education for all children. Between 2002 and 2006, enrolment increased by 25%, repetition rates tumbled and more pupils completed school. Despite this progress, however, challenges remain. In some areas there are as many as 100 pupils for every teacher.

Source: Chinyama (2006).

The number of out-of-school children dropped from 7 million to 3.7 million over the same period.

- International aid has played a central role in stipend programmes for girls in secondary education in Bangladesh. One effect has been to stimulate a parallel programme in primary education for girls from poor families. Taken together, these programmes have pushed Bangladesh rapidly towards gender parity in school participation at primary and secondary levels.

- Donors in Nepal have pooled financial support for an education strategy that has empowered local communities to expand access while scaling up teacher recruitment, school construction and targeted incentive programmes aimed at children from low-caste backgrounds. As a result, the out-of-school population fell from 1.0 million in 1999 to 0.7 million in 2004.

In the absence of aid, many more children would be out of school or sitting in even more overcrowded classrooms

It is hard to escape the conclusion that, in the absence of aid, many more children would be out of school or sitting in even more overcrowded classrooms, without books or desks. Yet, none of these examples owes its success to aid alone. The case for increased aid remains dependent on recipients' ability to deliver positive results. That outcome, in turn, ultimately depends on enhanced capacity, strengthened systems and the integration of education into wider strategies for tackling poverty and extreme inequality.

The remainder of this section focuses on aid as a source of finance for accelerated progress towards the Dakar goals. The amount available for basic education is a function of the overall mobilization of development assistance, the share of aid allocated to education and the distribution of aid within the education sector.

Total aid flows: donors are not delivering on their commitments

The overall levels of aid, as well as the trends, directly affect the degree of progress made towards the Dakar targets and goals, on two accounts. First, the education sector is vulnerable to shifts in aid availability. Second, more rapid and more equitable progress towards EFA is intricately linked with developments in other areas in which aid plays an important role – especially efforts to combat child mortality and infectious diseases, improve access to clean water and sanitation, and reduce extreme poverty. It is in this wider context that aid trends point in a worrying direction, with most donors falling far short of their commitments. In 2005 at the Gleneagles G8 meeting and the UN 'Millennium +5' and European Union summits, the donor community undertook to increase aid. Combining the pledges, the Development Assistance Committee of the Organisation for Economic Co-operation and Development (OECD-DAC) estimated that meeting these commitments would increase official development assistance (ODA) from US$80 billion in 2004 to US$130 billion by 2010, at 2004 prices (OECD-DAC, 2008*d*). Half the increase was earmarked for sub-Saharan Africa. The commitments were made at a time when aid was on a rising trend. Total net disbursements of ODA increased significantly between 1999 and 2005, from US$64 billion to US$110 billion, or 8% per year. Much of this growth was driven by debt relief. Total ODA then fell for two consecutive years to less than US$97 billion, with a decline of 8.4% in 2007 (Figure 4.1).[1] As a share of OECD gross national income (GNI), ODA declined from 0.33% in 2005 to 0.28% in 2007.

The OECD recently completed its first comprehensive survey of donors' spending plans (OECD-DAC, 2008*d*). It reports that of the promised increase in programme aid of US$50 billion by 2010, about US$5 billion was delivered in 2005 and an additional US$16 billion was either committed by donors to the multilateral development agencies or included in their own spending plans for 2010. Almost US$30 billion (in 2004 prices) remains to be committed if the overall promise on aid is to be met.

Behind the overall deficit are wide variations in donor performance. They relate to current disbursements measured as a share of GNI, and to both initial promises and progress to date (Figure 4.2). Between 2005 and 2007, Denmark, Luxembourg, the Netherlands, Norway and Sweden each maintained a level of aid above 0.8% of GNI. At the other end of the scale, Japan and the United States allocated a very low share of GNI and made only modest commitments in 2005 to increase this. Having set the bar low, both countries are likely to achieve their targets. All countries in the European Union have set the bar higher and in many cases, particularly those of Greece, Italy, Portugal and Spain, achieving the target level will take a sustained increase in aid. Only Ireland and Spain significantly increased their share of national income devoted to aid between 2005 and 2007. Overall, most donors are not on track to fulfil their promises and will need to make unprecedented increases to meet the targets they have set themselves for 2010 (OECD-DAC, 2008*d*).

Global trends in aid financing give serious cause for concern not just for education but for a wide range of development goals: donor performance in 2006 and 2007 may reflect weakening commitment to the Gleneagles pledges and, by extension, to the MDGs. With economic growth slowing in many OECD countries and governments facing mounting fiscal pressure, there is additional danger that aid budgets will be cut still further.

Figure 4.1: Total ODA net disbursements, 1999–2007

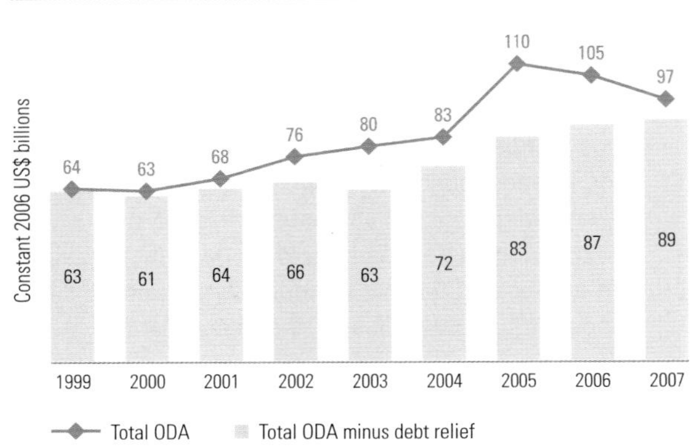

Source: OECD-DAC (2008*c*).

Figure 4.2: Aid as a percentage of GNI, net disbursements, 2005–2010

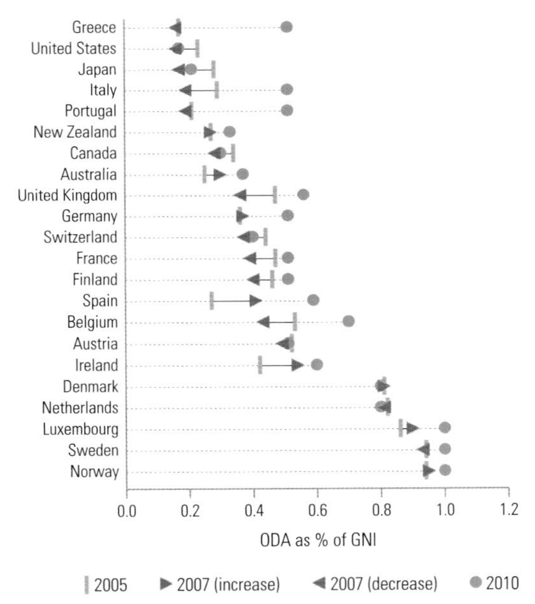

Sources: OECD-DAC (2008*b*, 2008*c*).

Almost US$30 billion remains to be committed if the overall promise on aid is to be met

Aid to education is stagnating

Domestic resource mobilization is the key to sustainable financing for EFA. Even in the poorest countries, national finance is far more important than aid. Nonetheless, for a significant number of low income countries, external assistance is needed to help them reach the Dakar goals. Millions of children from poor backgrounds and rural communities are still deprived of access

1. These figures refer to contributions made by OECD-DAC countries either directly (bilateral aid) or indirectly through multilateral organizations (multilateral aid). Other donors are increasing their ODA but information remains sketchy. Contributions from donors other than DAC members and from private foundations are discussed later in the chapter.

to primary education because many governments cannot make adequate provision and continue to charge school tuition fees or impose other costs on primary school attendance. In most low income countries, early childhood programmes remain largely underdeveloped and illiteracy is still widespread, especially for women. Challenges also remain in increasing access to post-primary education as well as in improving education quality and addressing threats to education systems from pandemics, natural disasters and civil conflict.

Aid to basic education in 2006 was below 2004 levels

The Dakar Framework for Action sets ambitious targets and goals in all these areas. It also incorporates an important commitment. When developed countries signed on to the Framework, they affirmed that 'no countries seriously committed to education for all will be thwarted in their achievement of this goal by a lack of resources' (UNESCO, 2000). The G8 reaffirmed this at its 2007 summit in Heiligendamm, Germany (Group of 8, 2007). Two years earlier at Gleneagles, G8 leaders declared: 'We support our African partners' commitment to ensure that by 2015 all children have access to and complete free and compulsory primary education' (Group of 8, 2005). To what extent are donors acting on their promises?

The *EFA Global Monitoring Report 2007* estimated that an annual US$11 billion of aid was required for low income countries to achieve UPE, make significant gains in reducing adult illiteracy and expand early childhood programmes (UNESCO, 2006). For the full set of EFA goals, including providing basic life skills for all youth and adults and reaching the literacy goal, the requirement would be higher. Aid commitments to the education sector have broadly followed overall aid trends. The period between 1999 and 2004 was marked by a significant increase, from US$7.3 billion to US$11.0 billion. However, commitments fell by 23% in 2005 to US$8.5 billion (Figure 4.3). Commitments to basic education followed the same pattern, increasing to US$5.2 billion by 2004 and then falling to US$3.7 billion in 2005. (Box 4.2 details the assumptions made to compute aid to education and to basic education.) Overall commitments increased again in 2006, but only to a level slightly above that of 2004 – and aid to basic education did not regain even its 2004 level. Annual variability alone does not explain the pattern. The slowdown in the growth of aid for education, and even more so for basic education, is confirmed by calculating two-year averages to reduce the effect of volatility in year-on-year commitments. As Figure 4.3 shows, the average annual aid commitments in 2005 and 2006 were below those made in 2003 and 2004 for both education and basic education.

The shares of education and basic education in total ODA are indicators of the priority they receive. There has been little change. Table 4.1 shows that education's share in total aid remained broadly stable at around 9% between 2000 and 2006, with the exception of a fall in 2005. The share for basic education was also maintained at around 4%, suggesting that its position within the education sector remained about the same. In other words, all the growth in aid commitments to both

Figure 4.3: Total aid commitments to education and basic education, 1999-2006

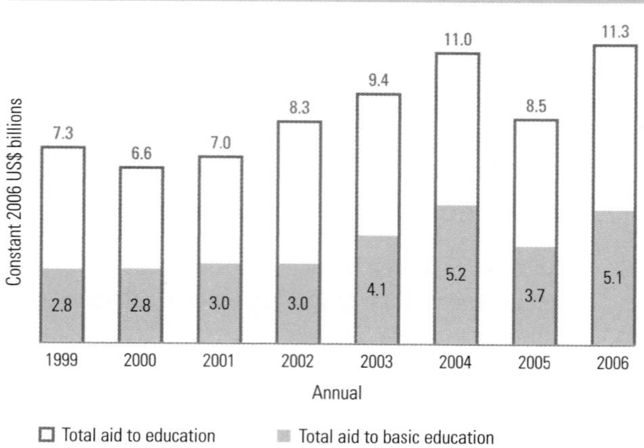

Source: OECD-DAC (2008*c*).

Box 4.2: Assessing the amount of total aid to the education sector

The OECD-DAC statistical reporting system distinguishes three main levels of education: basic, secondary and post-secondary. Aid to basic education is divided into early childhood education, primary education and basic life skills for youth and adults, including literacy. However, not all aid for education is specified as going to a particular level of education. Since 2006, the *EFA Global Monitoring Report* and the Secretariat of the EFA Fast Track Initiative (FTI) have assumed that half of 'level unspecified' aid for education benefits basic education. In addition, the education sector receives aid as part of general budget support. It is assumed that one-fifth of this is allocated to education, with half of that benefiting basic education.* Hence:

- Total aid to the education sector = direct aid to education + 20% of general budget support.
- Total aid to basic education = direct aid to basic education + 50% of 'level unspecified' aid to education + 10% of general budget support.

Figure 4.4 shows the components of total aid commitments and disbursements to education and to basic education in 2006 for all recipient countries.

* A review of World Bank Poverty Reduction Support Credits suggests that between 15% and 25% of general budget support typically benefits the education sector (FTI Secretariat, 2006).

Figure 4.4: Components of aid to education and to basic education, 2006

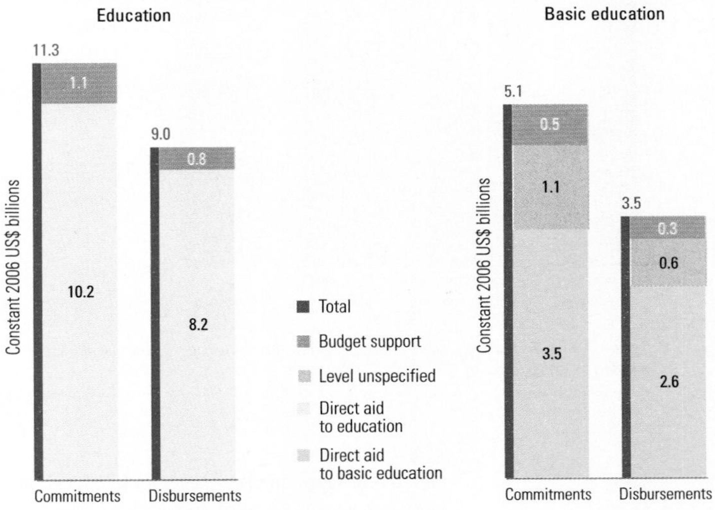

Source: OECD-DAC (2008*c*).

education and basic education over this period resulted from the general increase in aid commitments rather than from any shifts in priority.

How has the education sector fared in comparison with other social sectors? Increased commitments from multilateral agencies and the growth of global funds led to a rise in the share of health and population programmes in total aid commitments from 7% to 9% between 1999–2000 and 2005–2006 (Figure 4.5). The share for water and sanitation remained at 5%. Overall, the share of total ODA allocated to these social sectors (education, health, population programmes, and water and sanitation), which are at the heart of the MDGs, remained constant at 21% between 1999–2000 and 2005–2006.

Discussion so far has centred on aid commitments. These are important since they reflect current priorities given to aid in general and to individual sectors. However, the aid committed in a given year is usually disbursed over several years. Disbursements reflect the amount of aid actually made available to countries in any given year.

Table 4.1: Share of education and basic education in aid commitments, 2000–2006

	2000	2001	2002	2003	2004	2005	2006
Education as a share of total ODA	9%	9%	10%	9%	10%	7%	9%
Basic education as a share of total aid to education	42%	43%	36%	43%	48%	44%	45%
Basic education as a share of total ODA	4%	4%	3%	4%	5%	3%	4%

Source: OECD-DAC (2008*c*).

Because of the time lag between the decision to commit aid and its disbursement, total disbursements reflect commitments in previous years. Figure 4.6 shows total aid disbursements to education and to basic education between 2002 (the first year for which the data are available) and 2006, pointing to a continual increase. Disbursements for education reached US$9.0 billion in 2006, up from US$5.5 billion in 2002 – an average increase of 11% per year. Aid disbursements for basic education grew at the same rate, reaching US$3.5 billion in 2006 compared with US$2.1 billion in 2002.

Figure 4.5: Share of social sectors in total aid commitments, 1999-2006

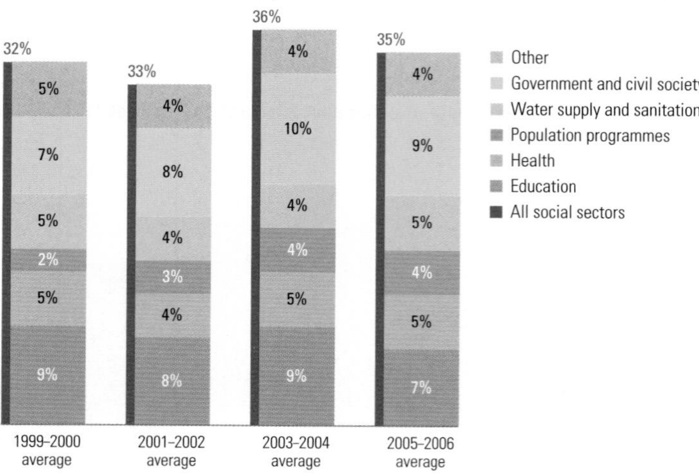

Note: This figure shows only direct contribution to sectors. It excludes general budget support.
Source: OECD-DAC (2008*c*).

Figure 4.6: Total aid disbursements to education and basic education, 2002-2006

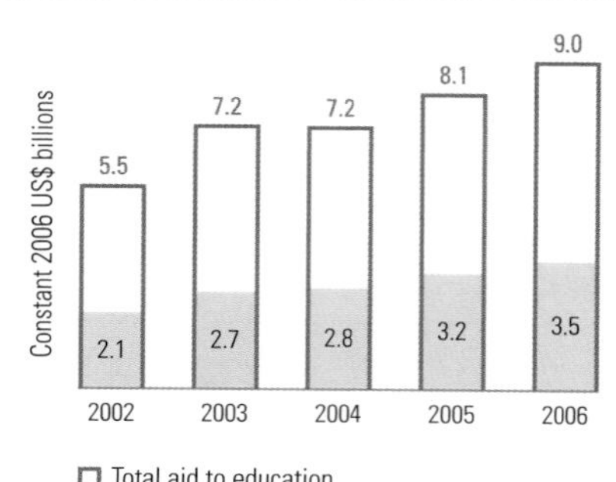

Note: The European Commission was the only multilateral agency reporting data on disbursements to the OECD-DAC Secretariat, although the IDA provided unofficial data.
Source: OECD-DAC (2008*c*).

There is a risk that the slowdown in growth in commitments since 2004 will soon be reflected in slower growth of disbursements

If commitments increase year on year, disbursements will tend to be lower than commitments in any given year. Provided the commitment/disbursement ratio remains roughly constant, education planners can expect an increased flow of real funding. The opposite also holds: any contraction of commitments signals shrinkage in future flows. In the current aid context, there is a risk that the slowdown in growth in commitments since 2004 will soon be reflected in slower growth, or even stagnation, of disbursements.

Allocating aid to those in greatest need: is equity improving?

As financial aid is scarce, its distribution is important. Achieving maximum impact and reaching those in greatest need are twin imperatives, but combining efficiency with equity is often a difficult balancing act: there is no guarantee that aid to those in greatest need will achieve the greatest impact. While there is no formula for determining the right balance, increasing attention is being paid to how aid is distributed, especially given the slowdown in the growth of aid commitments for education and basic education since 2004. Previous *EFA Global Monitoring Reports*, particularly the 2008 Report, have described in detail the amounts of aid received by individual countries and changes since 1999. In the aid tables of the annex to this year's report, monitoring information has been updated for 2006. This subsection goes beyond descriptions of aid levels by country. It attempts to evaluate the degree to which allocations are equitable, as defined by indicators for need, and whether they are related to progress towards EFA. The analysis draws on data for total aid committed to education and basic education in 2006 across sixty-eight low income countries.

What share of aid to education goes to the poorest countries?

Aid for education was allocated to 147 countries in 2006. The OECD-DAC defines seventy-nine of these as middle income developing countries and sixty-eight as low income developing countries (OECD-DAC, 2007*a*). The latter group includes fifty countries categorized as least developed. In 2006, the low income countries received US$6.4 billion in aid to education, slightly below the amount received in 2004 but higher than in earlier years (Figure 4.7). Their share of total aid to education in 2006 was 57%. While this aid share may appear relatively low, it is higher than for any year since 2000 apart from 2004. Low income countries received a higher share of overall aid to basic education: 75% in 2006. Again, apart from 2004, this was higher than in any other recent year, and almost ten percentage points higher than during 2001–2003. These positive trends notwithstanding, middle income developing countries received over two-fifths of aid to education and a quarter of aid to basic education in 2006. Given their Dakar and G8 commitments, donors may need to ask themselves whether this allocation is consistent with distributional equity and the achievement of the Dakar goals.

Figure 4.7: Aid to education and basic education by income group, commitments

Year	Education: low income countries (Constant 2006 US$ billions)	Education: least developed countries	Basic education: low income countries	Basic education: least developed countries
1999	3.4	1.9	1.6	0.9
2000	3.7	2.4	2.0	1.2
2001	3.7	2.2	1.9	1.3
2002	4.1	2.7	2.0	1.4
2003	4.6	3.0	2.7	1.8
2004	6.5	4.1	4.1	2.6
2005	4.6	3.2	2.5	1.7
2006	6.4	3.8	3.8	2.2

Year	Education: low income countries (Share in total)	Education: least developed countries	Basic education: low income countries	Basic education: least developed countries
1999	46%	23%	59%	34%
2000	57%	36%	72%	45%
2001	53%	31%	65%	42%
2002	49%	33%	65%	48%
2003	49%	32%	67%	44%
2004	60%	37%	79%	49%
2005	55%	38%	69%	46%
2006	57%	34%	75%	43%

Source: OECD-DAC (2008*c*).

Since 2000, there has been very little increase in the share of aid for education, including basic education, directed to the fifty least developed countries. With per capita income below US$900, these are the world's poorest countries. From 2000 to 2005 their share of overall aid to education increased slightly, from an average of 33% in 2000–2002 to almost 36% in 2003–2005. During the same period, their share in total aid to basic education barely increased, from 45% to 46% (Figure 4.7). The data for 2006 are uncertain since two donors made relatively large commitments of aid for basic education through the Fast Track Initiative (FTI) in that year, but the amounts that least developed countries will receive are not yet known.

Allocation across low income countries remains inconsistent

Aid allocations to individual low income countries are inevitably influenced by historical and political factors. But to what extent are allocations also shaped by a country's relative need and proven ability to use aid effectively? The evidence is mixed.

The low income group itself is diverse. These sixty-eight countries range from Kenya and Viet Nam, which are close to reaching at least some EFA goals, to Chad, the Niger and Pakistan, which have a long way to go. There are also significant differences in per capita income, which affects countries' potential ability to finance EFA programmes. Recent performance indicators vary as well. Diversity of country characteristics and outcomes points to a need for caution in cross-country comparisons. Nevertheless, such comparisons can provide useful insights into aid efficiency and equity. This subsection looks first at the relationship between aid levels and the scale of education challenges as measured by the number of children out of school. It then examines the relationship between aid and progress in moving towards the EFA goals.

While need can be measured in many ways, the number of out-of-school children might be considered a useful first approximation. Accordingly, if aid flows reflect need, aid levels

Since 2000, there has been very little increase in the share of overall aid allocated to education, including basic education to the least developed countries

should rise with the number of out-of-school children and countries with similar numbers of out-of-school children should receive broadly similar amounts. Yet Figure 4.8 suggests that the relationship between the level of aid and the number of out-of-school children is not consistent. For example, prior to Dakar, Ethiopia had twice as many out-of-school children as the United Republic of Tanzania but received three-fifths of the amount of aid for basic education. Similarly, while the number of out-of-school children in Kenya was over three times as high as that in Zambia, the latter received twice as much aid. In 2006, Kenya still received a small amount of aid to basic education relative to the number of out-of-school children compared with countries such as Mozambique and the United Republic of Tanzania. However, while the relationship between aid and number of out-of-school children is weak, simple regression analysis indicates there is some movement towards needs-based provision. Aid to basic education was more concentrated on the countries with the highest number of out-of-school children in 2006 than in 2000.

Countries making more progress received, on average, slightly more aid

If the average association between aid and out-of-school children is positive but weak, did poorer countries receive more aid than countries with similar numbers of out-of-school children but higher per capita incomes? The answer appears to be negative. For example, while the per capita income of Bangladesh was three times that of the Niger, it received five times as much aid for basic education, though both countries had around 1.3 million children out of school (see annex, aid tables and Statistical Table 5). While donors have increasingly allocated more aid for basic education to countries with more out-of-school children, there is no evidence that they have given greater priority to the poorest countries.

Figure 4.8: Total aid to basic education (commitments) and out-of-school children of primary-school age, 1999-2000 and 2005-2006

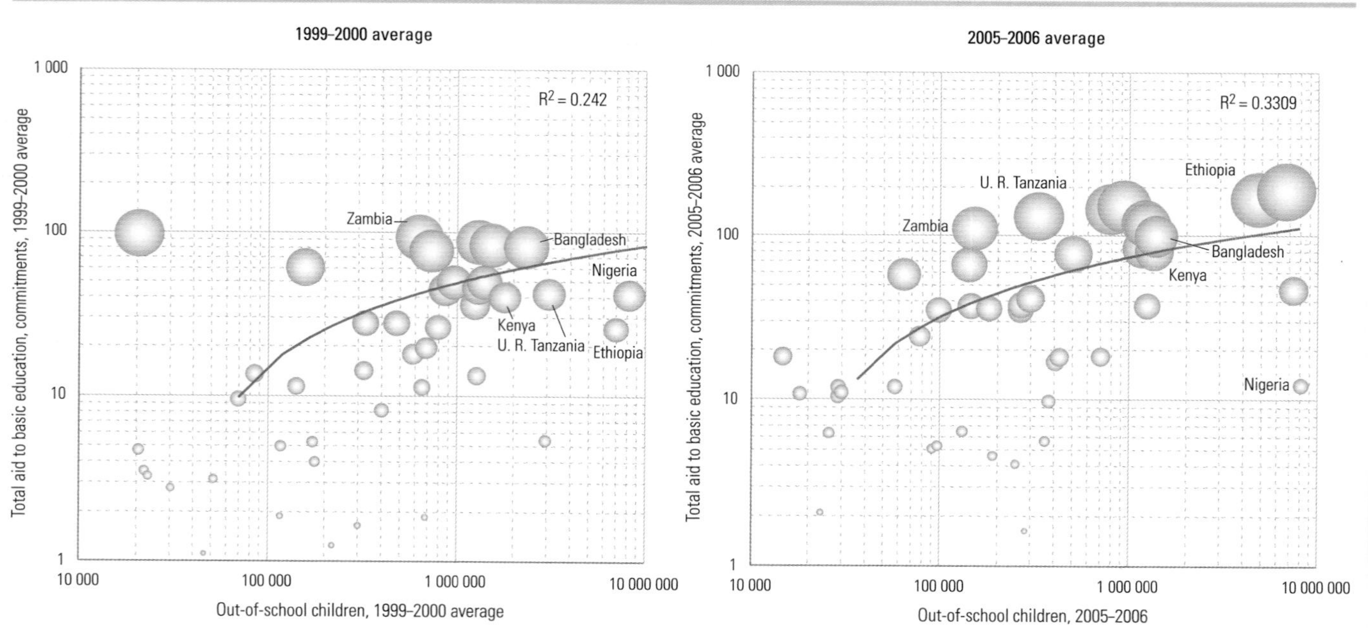

	1999–2000 average					
	Bangladesh	Ethiopia	Kenya	Nigeria	U. R. Tanzania	Zambia
Total aid to basic education, US$ millions	82	26	40	42	42	93
Out-of-school children, millions	2.3	7.0	1.8	8.1	3.1	0.6

	2005–2006 average					
	Bangladesh	Ethiopia	Kenya	Nigeria	U. R. Tanzania	Zambia
Total aid to basic education, US$ millions	101	169	81	12	133	111
Out-of-school children, millions	1.4	4.8	1.3	8.0	0.3	0.2

Notes: Logarithmic scale. Size of bubbles reflects total aid to basic education (commitments).
Sources: Annex, Statistical Table 5; OECD-DAC (2008*c*).

Is a country's recent performance in educational development reflected in the allocation of aid? Figure 4.9 plots the amount of aid committed to basic education per primary school-age child in 2005–2006 against the change in net enrolment ratios since Dakar in forty-one countries. The relationship overall is positive but weak. Countries making more progress (shown towards the right side of the figure) received, on average, slightly more aid. The relationship, however, is far from perfect. Countries including Ethiopia and the United Republic of Tanzania, where enrolment rates have almost doubled since Dakar, received less aid per capita than Burkina Faso, Mali, Senegal and Zambia, where progress was slower. Overall, progress in increasing enrolment explained only about 15% of the variance in the distribution of the amounts of aid to basic education per child.

Measured against common indicators of progress, the aid distribution reveals some apparently arbitrary outcomes. For example, if aid is partly intended to reflect strong performance on shared goals, it is not clear why Malawi received somewhat more aid than Ethiopia, since the enrolment rate fell in the former and doubled in the latter. Clearly, donor perceptions of countries' capacity to absorb increased aid are important, although this would appear to provide a limited explanation. The Niger, for instance, has a stronger record than Burkina Faso on getting children into school, but received only one-third the amount of aid per primary school-age child.

Fragile states are a distinctive subset of countries. By almost any standard they have high need relative to domestic financing capacity. Many also face tight constraints in terms of institutional capacity. Is it possible to judge whether donors are giving sufficient attention to such countries? In 2006, the thirty-five countries that the OECD-DAC defines as fragile received US$1.6 billion in aid to education, of which US$0.9 billion was allocated to basic education.[2] These amounts represented 14% of all education aid and 17% of aid to basic education, only slightly higher than the share of fragile states in the combined population of all developing countries. Given the low levels of access to education, low completion rates and severe problems in education quality in the fragile states, combined with their domestic financing and capacity constraints, these aid levels would appear to reflect a very limited commitment to needs-based aid financing.

Figure 4.9: Aid to basic education (commitments) and progress towards UPE

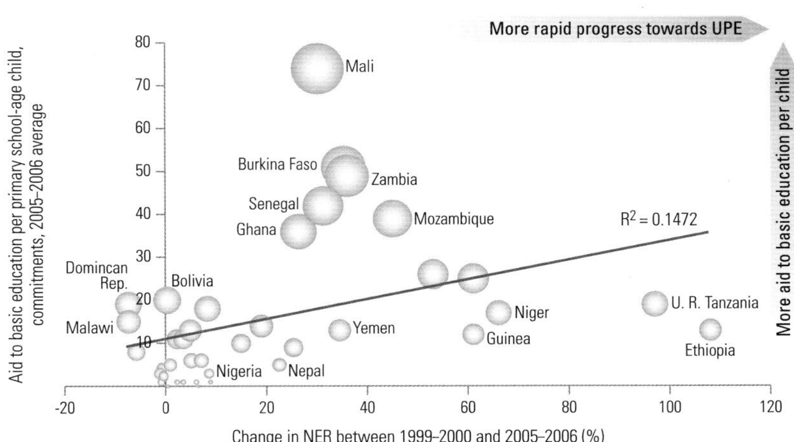

	Total aid to basic education per primary school-age child (Constant 2006 US$)	Out-of-primary school children (000)	Change in net enrolment ratios between 1999-2000 and 2005-2006
	2005-2006 average	2005-2006 average	(%)
Dominican Rep.	19	239	-7
Malawi	15	180	-7
Bolivia	20	52	0
Nigeria	1	8 097	9
Nepal	5	702	22
Ghana	36	1 200	26
Mali	74	795	30
Senegal	42	500	31
Yemen	13	906	34
Burkina Faso	51	1 237	35
Zambia	49	150	36
Mozambique	39	928	45
Guinea	12	403	61
Niger	17	1 238	66
U. R. Tanzania	19	329	97
Ethiopia	13	4 782	108

Note: Size of bubbles reflects total aid to basic education per primary school-age child (commitments).
Sources: Annex, Statistical Table 5; OECD-DAC (2008*c*).

The overall record can be briefly summarized. In recent years there has been a slight shift towards targeting aid to basic education in the countries most in need. Low income countries' share of total aid to education marginally increased, though within this group the share going to the least developed countries remained constant. Within the low income country group there is a weak but positive trend in aid commitments towards the countries with the greatest educational needs, as defined by the size of their out-of-school population. There is also some evidence – albeit limited and inconsistent – that countries that have performed

2. The education sectors of fragile states also received 2% of all emergency aid allocations (Save the Children, 2008*b*).

relatively well in expanding access to basic education have been rewarded with aid. Yet none of this points to any overarching commitment to greater efficiency or equity in aid flows.

Financing to education is dominated by a small core of donors

It is important to exercise caution in interpreting these results. The concept of need is broad and can be measured in various ways. Similarly, there is no single yardstick for progress towards EFA. Nevertheless, there appear to be strong grounds for strengthening both the focus on equity and the level of aid commitments to those countries registering progress.

Donor performance: a mixed record

In their dialogue with developing countries, donors have strongly emphasized the importance of equity in public spending. The share of basic education in overall spending is widely used as an indicator for equity. Were they to apply the same standards to themselves, many donors would regard their own aid programmes as highly inequitable. Few give high priority to supporting the EFA goals, either through their own programmes or in contributions to the Fast Track Initiative Catalytic Fund.

Although several countries have made significant aid contributions to education relative to the size of their economies (e.g. Canada, Denmark, Ireland, Luxembourg), overall financing to education is dominated by a small core of donors. In 2006, France was the largest (US$1.9 billion), followed by Germany (US$1.4 billion), the Netherlands (US$1.4 billion), the United Kingdom (US$1.2 billion) and the International Development Association (IDA) of the World Bank (US$1.0 billion) (Figure 4.10). Apart from Japan, the European Commission and the United States, no other donor committed more than US$300 million to education. Because of its relatively small economy, the performance of the Netherlands stands out.

When it comes to distribution among different levels of education, large donors have a mixed record. For example, in 2006 France directed only 17% of total aid to education to the basic levels and Germany only 11%. Both countries' education aid is skewed towards tertiary education. In contrast, the Netherlands allocated 83% of its total education aid to basic education and the United Kingdom 71%. The Netherlands was the largest donor to basic education in 2006 at US$1.1 billion, almost one-

Figure 4.10: Total aid to education and basic education (commitments), by donor, 2006

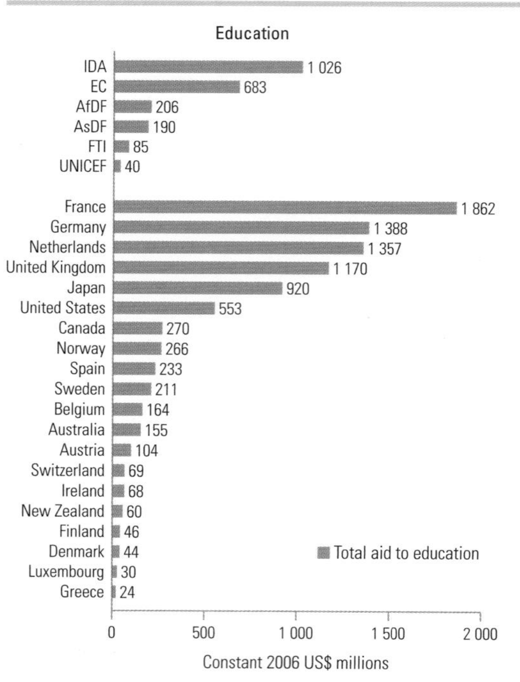

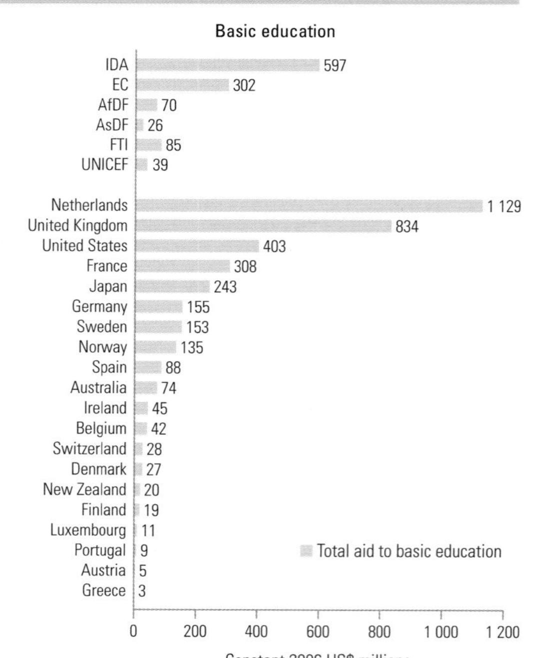

Note: Italy did not report aid data in 2006.
Source: OECD-DAC (2008*c*).

quarter of the total. Other major donors were the United Kingdom (US$843 million), IDA (US$597 million), the United States (US$403 million), France (US$308 million) and the European Commission (US$302 million). Half of all aid commitments to basic education came from just three donors – the Netherlands, the United Kingdom and IDA. These three were also responsible for 60% of all aid for basic education to low income countries, a situation which poses troubling questions about the commitment of many individual donors to EFA.

A majority of bilateral donors increased their overall aid to education in 2006 (Figure 4.11). The largest increase was by the United Kingdom, which almost tripled its aid to education that year. German aid to education also nearly tripled, though this might be explained in part by an under-reporting of tertiary education costs in 2005. The Netherlands more than doubled its aid to education, as did Switzerland. Other bilateral donors marginally increased their aid to education, while Denmark, Finland, Greece, Luxembourg, New Zealand, Portugal and the United States actually reduced theirs. Among the multilateral agencies, IDA and the African Development Bank increased commitments to education while some other agencies decreased them.

Figure 4.11: Change in aid to education and basic education between 2005 and 2006, by donor, commitments

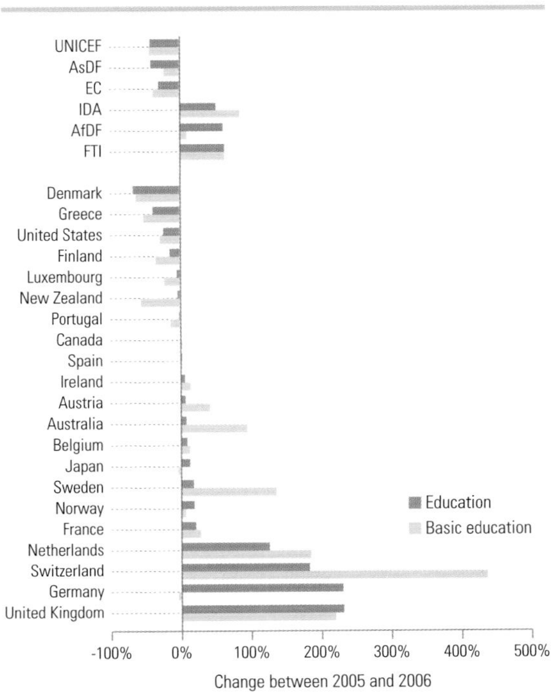

Note: Italy did not report aid data in 2006.
Source: OECD-DAC (2008*c*).

The picture for basic education is more mixed. Only seven of twenty-one OECD-DAC bilateral donors significantly increased[3] their aid for basic education in 2006 (Australia, France, the Netherlands, Norway, Sweden, Switzerland and the United Kingdom), while significant decreases were recorded in six countries (Denmark, Finland, Germany, Japan, New Zealand and the United States). In the remaining eight countries, there was no significant change. Aid to basic education was lower in 2006 than in 2005 for UNICEF, the Asian Development Bank and the European Commission. Ultimately, what matters is the overall level of aid for basic education and its distribution among developing countries, rather than the performance of individual donors. However, when growth is driven by a handful of donors, there is a greater danger of a sudden reduction in aid, with damaging consequences for progress towards EFA.

The Netherlands, the United Kingdom and IDA were responsible for 60% of all aid for basic education to low income countries

To summarize the balance sheet for 2005–2006:

- The overall growth in aid to basic education was more the result of action by a very few donors than of a broad-based effort by the international community.
- Twelve donor countries and agencies decreased their aid (by US$0.49 billion) while fifteen increased it (by US$1.86 billion). The Netherlands, the United Kingdom and IDA were responsible for 85% of the increase in aid to basic education.
- The increased effort of a small number of donors in 2006 was insufficient to counteract the large fall in commitments in 2005, so total aid to basic education was still lower in 2006 than in 2004 (Figure 4.3).

Fast Track Initiative: not meeting expectations

The continued aid financing gap in education raises important questions about the future of a major post-Dakar multilateral initiative. The FTI was created in 2002 as a mechanism to encourage broad donor support for EFA and, in late 2003, the Catalytic Fund was established (see the 2008 Report for a detailed description). At the centre of the FTI are governments' education sector plans,

3. Change was considered significant when its absolute value was more than US$10 million.

whose endorsement by local donor representatives serves as an indicator of readiness for scaled-up aid. The Catalytic Fund is not intended as a first call for aid for basic education – bilateral and multilateral agency programmes continue to play that role. The Fund's initial purpose was to provide short-term support to countries without bilateral programmes. The rules for eligibility and length of support have since been expanded. Currently, thirty-five country plans have been endorsed, eight others were expected to be by the end of 2008 and a further thirteen during 2009. While the FTI's central role is to leverage bilateral programmes, several countries see its Catalytic Fund as an important source of finance in its own right.

Looking to the future, the Fast Track Initiative's Catalytic Fund faces a large and imminent shortfall

The balance sheet raises some important questions about the current and prospective role of the Catalytic Fund. One concerns the failure to develop a deep donor support base. Pledges to the Fund for 2004–2011 amount to US$1.3 billion from seventeen donors. Pledges for 2007 and 2008 were below those for 2006 (US$265 million and US$383 million, against US$439 million). So far the Netherlands has pledged 43% of the total and the United Kingdom 21%. Together with the European Commission and Spain, these donors are responsible for 79% of all pledges. Eight of the sixteen bilateral donors that are members of the FTI and regularly take part in its meetings have so far pledged less than US$20 million each. This suggests either a low level of commitment or a low level of confidence in the Catalytic Fund, or both.

When measured in terms of overall financing, the Catalytic Fund is of limited relevance. Of the US$1.3 billion pledged, US$1.1 billion has been notionally allocated but not all of it has been transferred yet. Agreements totalling just US$329 million have been made with countries, with total disbursements by the end of February 2008 amounting to US$270 million. Eighteen countries have received grants; the largest amounts went, in descending order, to Kenya, Yemen, Madagascar, Ghana and Nicaragua. No other country has received above US$10 million. Of the total commitments of aid to basic education in low income countries in 2006, the Catalytic Fund accounted for just over 2%. Looking to the future, the Fund faces a large and imminent shortfall. For 2008, the projected needs for endorsed programmes are estimated at US$1.0 billion. By 2010, the estimated financing gap for the fifty-six countries expected to have had their plans endorsed is US$2.2 billion per year. Without more pledges, projected needs will not be met. Some countries receiving support from the Catalytic Fund will see it interrupted while those with newly endorsed plans will not be able to get support from the fund at all.

Non-DAC and other kinds of aid

The data on aid presented so far are those reported by bilateral and multilateral agencies to the OECD-DAC Secretariat. Non-DAC bilateral donors also support education in developing countries. For instance, the number of African students on government scholarships in China is expected to double from 2,000 in 2006 to at least 4,000 by 2009. China has also agreed to train 15,000 African professionals between 2007 and 2009 in several technical, scientific and administrative fields, and to construct 100 rural schools (Forum on China-Africa Cooperation, 2006).

Private foundations increasingly provide support for basic education. In 2006 the Hewlett and Gates foundations announced they would provide a series of grants totalling US$60 million to improve the quality of primary and secondary school education in developing countries (William and Flora Hewlett Foundation, 2006). In 2007 they allocated US$9.1 million over three years to the Indian non-government organization (NGO) Pratham for its Read India programme, which works to improve reading skills across 100 districts in India (William and Flora Hewlett Foundation, 2007). Another significant initiative in 2007 was the launch of Dubai Cares. This foundation has raised nearly US$1 billion from individuals and businesses in Dubai and entered a partnership with UNICEF to educate 1 million children (UNICEF, 2008). The first activities of this partnership are a programme in Djibouti to build and rehabilitate primary schools to benefit 30,000 children and to improve the quality of education. In addition, the foundation has allocated US$16.6 million to Save the Children to support education in Sudan (Save the Children, 2008*a*).

As well as providing ODA through grants and concessional loans, several multilateral agencies provide non-concessional loans for education. The World Bank is the largest source of such loans. It provided US$1.3 billion a year on average between 1999 and 2006 to support education development, mainly in middle income countries, including about US$700 million for basic education, which is slightly above the amount of aid allocated to basic education through IDA. Around 60% of the loans were made to Latin American countries in 2005 and 2006, the largest recipients being Brazil, Colombia, Mexico and the Bolivarian Republic of Venezuela (plus the Philippines). Regional development banks are also active. Over 1999–2006, the African Development Bank committed US$16 million a year, the Asian Development Bank US$83 million a year and the Inter-American Development Bank about US$283 million a year, on average (Figure 4.12). About half these loans were specifically for basic education.

Figure 4.12: Non-concessional loans for education, 1999-2006, commitments

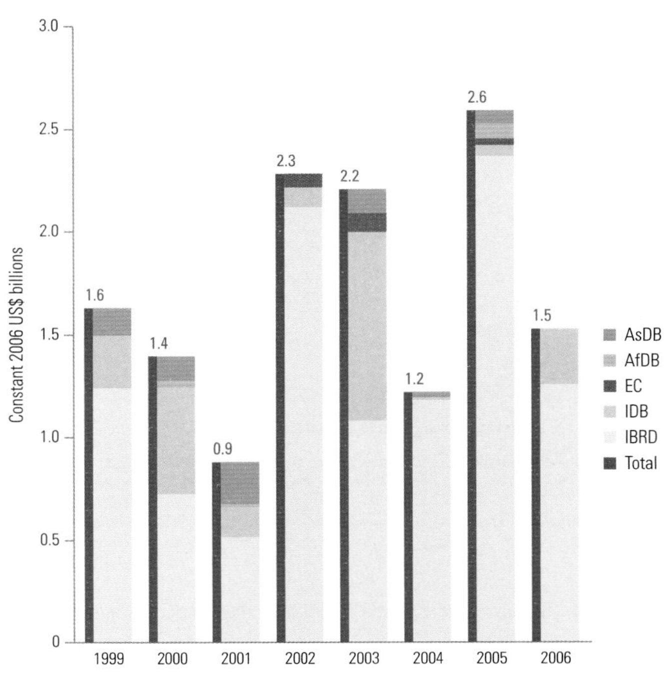

Source: OECD-DAC (2008*c*).

Are donors adequately supporting EFA in low income countries?

International aid for education is at a watershed. As Chapter 2 shows, achieving the goals and targets of the Dakar Framework for Action will require a significant increase in momentum. National policies will determine prospects for success. But if donors do not renew their commitment to act on their Dakar pledge that no country should fail in its efforts to achieve EFA for want of resources, the UPE goal will not be reached.

An earlier section cites the estimate of US$11 billion needed annually to achieve a subset of basic education goals in low income countries. Achieving all the EFA goals requires more than that. To close the financing gap, overall aid to basic education in low income countries will have to rise by a factor of three from the current level of US$3.8 billion a year. Whether this is done through an increase in total aid or redistribution of total aid to education, or both, it is clear that current practices have to change – and soon. The Dakar UPE commitment is time-bound. To achieve UPE by 2015, governments need to put the long-term plans in place today for building schools, recruiting and training teachers, and providing incentives for marginalized groups.

In reality, it does not make sense to talk of 'the donors' for basic education in aggregate, because there are vast differences among the countries and organizations supporting EFA. Some are clearly giving it high priority – increasing overall aid for education, focusing on the poorest countries and allocating a high share to the basic levels – and some are not (Figure 4.13).

- In 2005 and 2006, Canada, IDA, the Netherlands and the United Kingdom each allocated, on average, more than three-quarters of their education aid to low income countries and basic education made up at least half of their total aid to education. To a lesser degree, Norway and Sweden have demonstrated similar priorities.
- Several other major donors are falling short on one or more counts. France, Germany and Japan have shown a relative neglect of basic education and low income countries. France and Germany maintain aid programmes that are weakly aligned with their international commitments to the Dakar Framework for Action and the education MDGs. Both give greater weight to subsidizing the entry into their universities of foreign students, mainly from middle income developing countries, than to supporting basic education in low income countries (Box 4.3). The recent commitment by the French Government to work with the United Kingdom in a partnership aimed at getting 16 million sub-Saharan African children into school by 2015 is welcome if it signals a more thoroughgoing reassessment of aid priorities (France Ministry of External and European Affairs, 2008).

France, Germany and Japan have shown a relative neglect of basic education and low income countries

Figure 4.13: Donor priority to low income countries and to basic education, aid commitments, 2005-2006 annual average

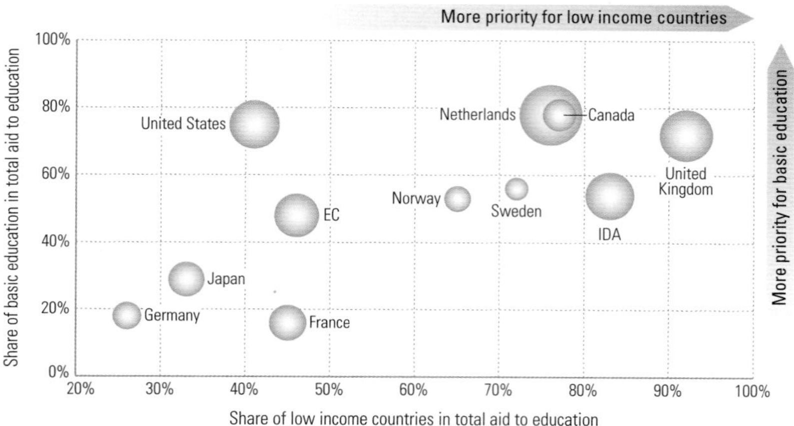

Notes: Size of bubbles reflects total aid for basic education to low income countries, 2005–2006 average (commitments). Only donors with education aid above US$100 million on average in 2005 and 2006 are shown.
Source: OECD-DAC (2008c).

- Some donors have a strong record on prioritizing aid to basic education but a weak record on targeting low income countries. For example, the United States and the European Commission allocate less than half their education aid to low income countries.

Missed opportunities, collective underperformance and a weak voice for EFA

Current trends in aid raise serious concerns about prospects for delivering on the promises made at Dakar. Commitments to education were no higher in 2006 than in 2004 – and in basic education they were a little lower. Distribution remains a serious concern: less than half of aid for basic education was allocated to the fifty least developed countries.

It is not just the level of aid that is less than what is needed – and what was promised. Central parts of the post-Dakar aid architecture are falling short. The FTI was created to support the development of the credible EFA plans called for in the Dakar Framework, to harmonize donor efforts in basic education and to encourage more bilateral aid. The subsequent creation of the Catalytic Fund, initially for countries not linked with bilateral donors but later expanded to others, was an important addition. Yet, having created these institutions, donors are failing to deliver. Bilateral support for basic education is stalling and, unless the Catalytic Fund is replenished sufficiently, its credibility and that of the FTI itself will be diminished.

Box 4.3: France and Germany focus on aid to post-secondary education

In 2005 and 2006, France's aid to education averaged US$1.7 billion annually and Germany's US$0.9 billion, making them the largest and third-largest donors to the sector (Figure 4.14). However, only 12% of France's aid to education supported basic education in low income countries, while for Germany the share was 7%. They allocated a large share of their overall education aid to the imputed cost of students from developing countries studying in their tertiary education institutions. Imputed student costs accounted for 62% of France's aid to education and 50% of Germany's.

Imputed student costs were a significant share of all aid to education for some recipient countries. In Algeria, for example, they accounted for 80% and in Tunisia for 40%. In Morocco, where the net enrolment ratio was below 90% in 2006 and the adult literacy rate was just over 50%, two-thirds of all aid to education took the form of imputed student costs while only 7% supported the EFA goals.

Figure 4.14: Distribution of aid to education by level, France and Germany, commitments, 2005-2006 annual average

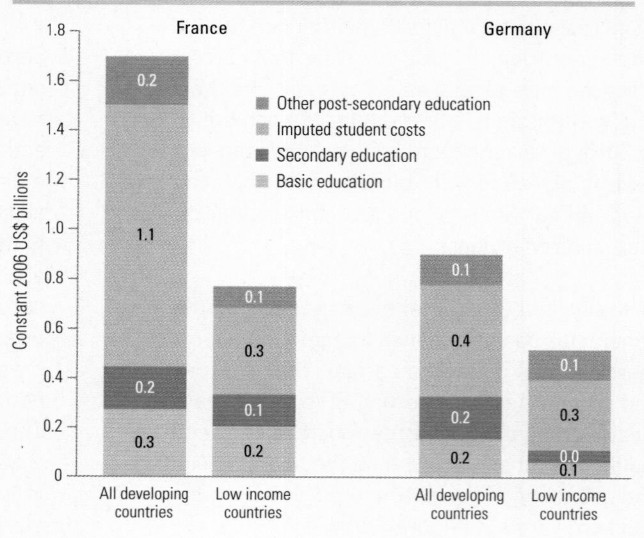

Source: OECD-DAC (2008c).

An opportunity to help galvanize donors as a whole behind the EFA agenda will have been lost.

Set against this discouraging background are some positive signs. The reaffirmation in the 2007 G8 communiqué of the Dakar commitment to ensure that lack of resources does not undermine national EFA efforts was encouraging (Group of 8, 2007). So was the promise to work 'to meet shortfalls in all FTI-endorsed countries', repeated in 2008 in Hokkaido. In June 2008, the European Council reaffirmed its support for EFA and pledged an increase in education aid of €4.3 billion by 2010 (Council of the European Union, 2008).

But promises are only as good as their realization. If donors are serious, they cannot afford another two years of collective underperformance. Accelerated progress towards EFA will not be possible without a strengthened international commitment to increase overall aid to the levels pledged in 2005. In the current international environment, that commitment will require renewed international leadership – part of which must come from the education sector itself. The most obvious source of guidance is the High-Level Group on Education for All, the intent of which is to bring together heads of state or government, ministers of education and of international cooperation, heads of development agencies, and representatives of civil society and the private sector. Its role is to reinforce political will in order to accelerate progress towards EFA, strengthen partnerships, identify priorities and highlight the resources to be mobilized.

Meetings of the High-Level Group have so far failed to drive the Dakar Framework forward and to galvanize international action, partly because they have not attracted sufficient ministerial attendance from donor countries. The broader problem is that, with the notable exception of a few bilateral donors, EFA has lacked a strong and consistent voice to keep it at the centre of the international development agenda. An important challenge for the High-Level Group meeting in 2008, and for UNESCO, is to provide that voice and to lay the base for reinvigorating donor support to EFA. □

Governance and aid effectiveness

Increased aid is one part of the equation for delivering on the commitments made at Dakar. More effective aid is the other. Ultimately, the case for more aid will be won only if it is perceived as delivering positive results. Whether aid is effective is partly a function of governance in developing countries. High levels of corruption, low levels of transparency and accountability, and an absence of effective development strategies add up to an environment not conducive to effective aid. The governance of aid itself is also important. Ensuring that development assistance builds, rather than erodes, national capacity to deliver change, that it is predictable and that it supports national strategies for achieving well-defined goals is critical to its effectiveness.

EFA has lacked a strong and consistent voice to keep it at the centre of the international development agenda

Recent years have witnessed a growing concern to address problems in aid quality. Some of that concern originates with aid recipients. Developing country governments point to the high transaction costs, undue donor influence in policy design and a failure to use national systems as problems that reduce aid effectiveness. For their part, donors have recognized that traditional aid delivery systems are flawed. Increasingly, developed country governments have acknowledged that aid conditionality is less effective in delivering results than national ownership of development strategies. Wider problems in aid governance have also been recognized. These include the channelling of aid through stand-alone projects rather than through national budgets, financial systems and programmes; weak coordination between donors; and unpredictable aid financing.

Accordingly, in 2005 donors set out a new vision for the governance of development assistance in the Paris Declaration on Aid Effectiveness (OECD-DAC, 2005). In it, rich countries resolve 'to take far-reaching and monitorable actions to reform the ways we deliver and manage aid'. The watchwords of the new approach are harmonization, alignment and national ownership. Specific commitments have been undertaken in the form of targets for enhancing aid predictability, using national institutions and financial systems, and cutting transaction costs through improved donor coordination.

Is the new governance model delivering results? In some cases, changes in aid delivery mechanisms are lowering transaction costs and reducing fragmentation. In others, new delivery mechanisms have not been able to overcome existing problems. The emerging aid governance system is struggling to produce benign outcomes, partly because genuine national ownership requires a real capacity to develop, implement and evaluate strategies, which has not yet emerged in all countries; and partly because some old donor habits die hard and many donors find it difficult to remain at arms length. One example, touched on at the end of this section, is that donors tend to develop their own positions on what constitutes 'good governance' in the education sector and elsewhere. This may be giving rise to a rather narrowly defined range of good governance measures that governments perceive as necessary to attract donor support.

The Paris Declaration marks an important acknowledgement by donors of real failings in their performance

In the rest of this section the emerging aid governance agenda is examined to see what difference, if any, it has made to the quality and effectiveness of aid to education. The recent approach of donors to education governance in developing countries is also described.

Improving the quality of aid

Viewed from one perspective, the importance of international aid is exaggerated. In the case of the Dakar commitments, as in other areas, real progress ultimately depends on whether goverments address problems, mobilize domestic resources and tackle inequalities in their education systems. But as this chapter has made clear, for many countries aid matters: even the best plans will not deliver UPE and wider goals by 2015 in the poorest countries without a large increase in development assistance.

How aid is delivered can be as important as how much aid is delivered. Unpredictable flows do not provide a secure foundation for long-term investment in schools, teacher recruitment and training, and targeted support for marginal groups. Similarly, when donors provide aid in ways that bypass national systems and overstretch national management capacity, the outcomes are seldom sustainable.

The new aid paradigm is intended to address governance problems in aid delivery and highlight government responsibility. Few people would contest the objectives. Respect for national ownership and the pursuit of greater efficiency in donors' contributions to poverty reduction are intrinsically laudable. In practice, though, it is more difficult to change procedures than it is to change the language of aid governance.

The Paris Declaration marks an important acknowledgement by donors of real failings in their performance. Donor proliferation, the use of projects to bypass government structures, weak coordination and disparate reporting systems are hallmarks of poor aid governance that have left a deep imprint on many countries. Consequences have included weakened policy-making and budgeting processes, fragmentation of service delivery, and erosion of capacity and national institutions. The OECD-DAC, in its 2008 survey of aid practices in fifty-four countries, revealed the scale of the problem. Only 43% of donor-supported projects and programmes evaluated were using partner country procurement systems. The Niger hosted over 600 donor missions in 2007, fewer than 100 of which were joint missions (OECD-DAC, 2008*a*).

OECD-DAC members have adopted indicators to measure progress towards more effective aid. Goals include quantified reductions in the share of aid not reported or included in national budgets, and targets for increasing joint missions. There is also a commitment to increase the share of aid delivered through programme-based, rather than project-based, approaches to two-thirds of the total. Recognizing that short- as well as medium-term aid predictability is central to sound public finances, the Paris agenda includes a commitment to halve the proportion of aid not disbursed in the fiscal year for which it was scheduled.

Despite good intentions, progress in all these areas has been variable (Box 4.4). Of course, not all the problems and shortfalls can be attributed to donor failings. It makes little sense, for instance, to channel resources through national budgets in countries where egregious corruption is known to exist. Still, donors' performance against their own benchmarks raises important governance questions. Donors can hold aid recipients to account for good governance by simply restricting aid flows, but how might aid recipients who have delivered on their side of the compact hold donors to account? Do any incentives exist to encourage good behaviour by donors?

Monitoring the Paris agenda commitments is an important step towards genuinely shared accountability. Yet monitoring exercises are only as effective as their follow-up. The 2008 OECD-DAC survey provides clear evidence of serious problems in aid partnerships. National ownership remains weak, transaction costs are high, donor commitment to national systems is still lacking and donor coordination remains rudimentary. If aid is scaled up while governance arrangements remain largely the same, transaction costs can be expected to rise without a commensurate increase in aid effectiveness, as measured in real development results.

The following subsections examine what the emerging agenda on the governance of aid has meant for aid to education and for prospects of achieving the goals and targets set under the Dakar Framework for Action. Four areas are considered:

- the shift from projects to programmes;
- action on ownership;
- alignment of aid with national priorities and systems;
- donor coordination.

Shifting from projects to programmes

One benchmark used to assess progress on the new approach to delivering aid is the level of donor commitment to programme-based aid. Project-based support is widely perceived as an underlying cause of fragmentation, involving high transaction costs and, especially where projects are administered and evaluated through separate units, potentially undermining efforts to strengthen national capacity. The criteria for measuring commitment to programme-based aid include growth in the share of aid provided as pooled funding and budget support. The target is to provide two-thirds of the total by 2010. There has been a particularly strong trend towards the adoption of sector-wide approaches (SWAps) in social sectors, with education figuring prominently. The trend has been driven by a conviction that coordinated provision of aid from all donors to support broad sector programmes will strengthen national ownership and improve development results. Experience to date suggests that this view is broadly justified, with some important caveats.

In terms of financial commitment, there has been a strong push towards programme-based support in education. Although the data represent only a rough guide because of definition problems, the best estimate suggests that the share of aid delivered through sector programmes increased from 31% in 1999–2000 to 54% in 2005–2006 (Figure 4.15). Examples of education sector programmes developed and implemented in five countries over the past decade are summarized in Figure 4.16. From a narrow base, the number of donors involved in these programmes has increased. However, some major donors, including Japan and the United States, as yet provide no financial support directly through SWAps.

Box 4.4: Aid effectiveness – falling short of the 2010 targets

The Paris Declaration marked a departure for aid governance. For the first time, donors and recipient governments set targets for 2010 for measuring aid effectiveness. Early monitoring results from fifty-four developing countries and twenty-seven donors, accounting for half of all aid delivered in 2007, suggest that the targets will not be achieved in most countries and that progress has been slow and uneven:

- *Country ownership remains weak.* Fewer than one-quarter of the surveyed countries have national development strategies that are clearly linked to the national budget. This is up from 17% in 2005, but far short of the 2010 target of 75%.
- *Monitoring capacity is limited.* Fewer than 10% of the aid recipients covered are assessed as having systems capable of monitoring development results – a slight increase from 7% in 2005, but the 2010 target is 35%.
- *Progress on aligning aid with government programmes has been minimal.* 46% of all aid was delivered through common aid delivery arrangements such as SWAps. This is roughly the same proportion as in 2005. The target for 2010 is 66%.
- *Use of national systems remains limited.* Only 45% of aid is channelled through national public financial management systems. This is not a major increase over the 40% level registered in 2005 and is only just over halfway towards the 2010 target of 80%. Even in countries with good systems, donors are not necessarily making more use of them, indicating that quality is not the only factor influencing donor choices. For example, although Mongolia's financial management system was ranked one of the highest among the fifty-four countries monitored, only 17% of all aid to the country is managed through its national system.
- *Donor coordination is still rudimentary.* In 2007, the fifty-four countries received more than 14,000 donor missions, of which only one in five was coordinated on a joint-donor basis. The 2010 target is 40%.

Source: OECD-DAC (2008*a*).

There has been a strong push towards programme-based support in education

Figure 4.15: Categories of aid to basic education, 1999-2006, commitments

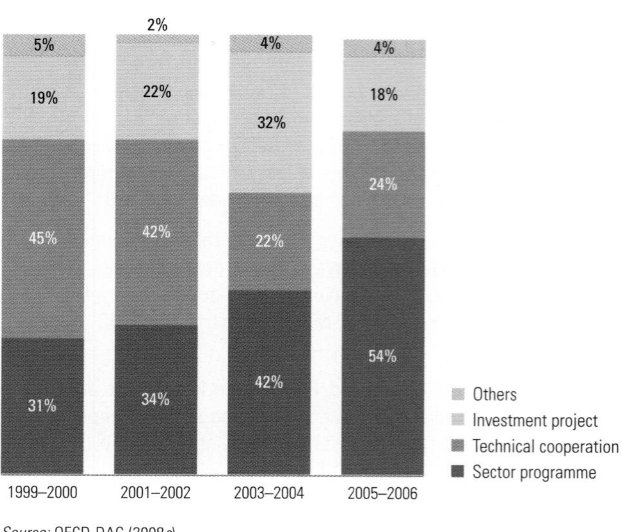

Source: OECD-DAC (2008*c*).

The strength of the momentum towards programme-based support varies. In broad terms, it has been strongest in low income, more aid dependent countries. While it was initially driven largely by donors, governments in these countries expect that programme-based support will allow for greater flexibility, more predictability and reduced transaction costs, and that national priorities will dictate programme content. In contrast, governments in middle income countries, which tend to have fewer donors and are less aid dependent, often prefer to negotiate with donors separately rather than with a coordinated group. Coordinated aid to education sector programmes is also uncommon in fragile states, mainly because of the lack of government capacity to lead the process.

Sector-wide approaches can weaken aid recipients' negotiating position and strengthen donors' policy leverage

Acting on ownership

One aim of programme-based support is to strengthen national ownership. In the language of the new aid governance paradigm, country ownership requires governments to 'exercise leadership in developing and implementing their national development strategies through broad consultative processes' and donors to 'respect partner country leadership and help strengthen the capacity to exercise it' (OECD-DAC, 2005). Is this happening in education?

In the education sector as in other areas, SWAps are widely presented as a vehicle for strengthened ownership. In a world of good governance, education sector plans would be developed by governments, with clear priorities reflected in national budgets and wider strategies, and they would be supported through coordinated donor actions. Early SWAps did not conform to this model. Most governments lacked capacity to develop effective SWAps, and donor influence weighed heavily in design and implementation. Over time, ownership and government leadership have strengthened, but progress has been neither universal nor uniform.

An obvious dilemma for aid dependent countries is that donors control the purse strings and have a 'right of last refusal'. Paradoxically, SWAps can weaken aid recipients' negotiating position and strengthen donors' policy leverage. Project-based aid, whatever its wider limitations, was based on a bilateral relationship between recipients and individual donors. The strength of any donor was contingent on the size of its financial commitment or strategic role. With programme-based aid, donors act collectively, effectively pooling their resources in national budgets. Collective action in this context can increase the negotiating strength of the donor community in SWAp discussions. The prospect of increased donor power may be one reason why some governments continue to prefer projects. Programme aid might offer a textbook route to greater efficiency, but it can also entail greater intrusion into national policy. As one commentator puts it, 'recipients now face a more intimate supervision of all aspects of national planning, budgeting and development programme implementation than at any time since independence' (Fraser, 2006).

Governments vary, of course, in their ability to take responsibility for education sector programme development, to lead the dialogue with donors and to restrict donor influence. Countries face different types of problems, and governments have different levels of policy-making, administrative and financial capacity. How these differences affect the relationships that frame the development and implementation of SWAps is a complex matter. The contrasting experiences of India and Mozambique illustrate the point and provide a pointer to some conditions for more effective government leadership.

The Government of India's current programme to achieve UPE is Sarva Shiksha Abhiyan (SSA).

Figure 4.16: Donor involvement in education sector programmes in five countries

	1997	1998	1999	2000	2001	2002	2003	2004	2005	2006	2007	2008	2009	2010	2011
Mali					**2001-2005: PISE I** Launch of Mali's 10-year education sector plan PRODEC in 2000, accompanied by the SWAp PISE I in 2001, with pooled funding from three donors (the Netherlands, Sweden and the World Bank) and non-pooled funding from ten donors. A Partnership Framework sets the principles for donor coordination with rotating lead donor and joint review missions.					**2006-2009: PISE II** Second phase of PRODEC/PISE supported by fourteen donors through sector budget support from six donors and eight donors financing specific components of the sector plan through projects. Joint Financial Arrangement signed by the six budget support donors.					
Nepal			**1999-2003: BPEP II** Donor harmonization started with pooled financing from five donors (Denmark, EC, Finland, Norway and the World Bank) to the Second Basic and Primary Education Programme. Use of IDA management procedures.					**2004-2009: National EFA programme** Supported by a SWAp including pooled financing from seven donors and three non-pooled donors. Joint Financial Arrangement signed by the pooled donors, specifying use of the government's management procedures. Code of Conduct sets principles for all donor coordination and alignment. The government, all donors and NGO representatives participate in annual joint review missions of the national EFA programme.							
Nicaragua								**2004-2008: PCT** The Common Work Plan (PCT) was adopted by the Ministry of Education as a sector programme and accepted as a SWAp by all donors. Funded by a majority of aid regardless of aid modality. Budget support from the European Commission and a pooled fund with support from three donors introduced in 2005. Sector-wide committee monitors implementation.							
United Republic of Tanzania	**1997-2001: ESDP** Launch of the government's Basic Education Master Plan in 1997, with the supporting Education Sector Development Programme, including non-pooled support from eighteen donors. Intensive government-donor consultations and sector analysis to move towards programme aid. Donor group formed under an appointed lead donor.				**2001-2006: PEDP I** The government's Primary Education Development Programme launched in 2001, accompanied by a subsector SWAp, including pooled funding from nine donors governed by a Memorandum of Understanding (MoU). The PEDP steered by a committee, with attached technical working groups.						**2007-2011: ESDP** SWAp covering the whole education sector. All previous donors contributing to the pooled fund moved to budget support. Launch of the Joint Assistance Strategy for the United Republic of Tanzania in 2006, stating government's preference for general budget support and concerns about pooled funds as parallel mechanisms.				
Zambia			**1999-2002: BESSIP I** Launch of the Basic Education Sub-Sector Investment Programme, with pooled aid from four donors (Ireland, the Netherlands, Norway and the United Kingdom). By the end of BESSIP, fourteen donors involved in the SWAp.				**2003-2007: MoESP** The government's second education plan, covering the whole education sector. Nine donors and the government signed a MoU to specify the principles of government-donor interaction and pooled financing. The Joint Assistance Strategy for Zambia to coordinate all aid to the country was launched in 2007, indicating the government's preference for general budget support. At the end of MoESP, four donors left the pool to move to general budget support.								

Launched in 2001, it received donor support two years later and has become the world's largest SWAp in basic education. While donors have a large stake in absolute financial terms, they represent a relatively small part of the overall financing envelope: 4% of the total cost. Evaluations of SSA leave little doubt that it is country led, with the government firmly in control of priority-setting and implementation.

SSA developed out of a long process of national policy development and donor dialogue, and its origins can be traced to the success of the District Primary Education Programme (DPEP), which began in 1994 and was developed under strong government leadership, including strict national management of donor participation (Box 4.5). Negotiating authority was delegated to the federal department of education, which brought together the relevant national organizations to forge

Box 4.5: India's education aid: standing firm in negotiations

India's District Primary Education Programme is in many respects a prototype of what sector programmes aim to achieve. It was unique at the time of its inception, not only in its design, which emphasized participatory planning and outcomes, but also because of the level of government leadership.

From the outset, the central government adopted a firm position on limiting donor influence. Agreement on aid was reached only after donors had given clear assurances that they accepted the programme's goals and approach, and that the federal government alone had the right to develop and oversee its implementation in the states. To manage the donors, DPEP pioneered common financial procedures, joint reporting and joint review mechanisms. Prolonged negotiations were required on the scope and composition of review missions and the participation of the federal government as an equal partner. Late in 1994, agreement was reached on modalities and on the limited areas of implementation donors could assess. Two years after DPEP was scaled up and relaunched as the SSA in 2001, DFID, the European Commission and the World Bank provided support within all existing parameters.

Source: Ayyar (2008).

agreement on the framework of the programme. Intense negotiations between the central and state governments reconciled divergent interests and perceptions prior to discussions with donors. Capacity-building was identified early on as a major priority, with many national institutes mobilized to provide support programmes.

The Mozambique experience shows that ownership can develop over time

The situation in Mozambique has been less conducive to government leadership in the aid relationship. Even so, its experience shows that ownership can develop over time. Twenty-two multilateral and bilateral donor agencies and around a hundred NGOs are involved in the education sector, making aid effectiveness a daily preoccupation. Some 42% of the education budget is provided externally. Since 1998 most of this assistance has been given in the context of SWAps, first focusing mainly on primary education (to 2005) and then adopting more comprehensive coverage (2006–2011).

Preparation of the current plan took more than three years. It tested the ability of the government and donors to come to agreement. On several occasions, including the sensitive area of teachers' pay and conditions, donors collectively challenged government positions. However, an assessment of the relationship suggests that donors have primarily pressed for clarity and more dialogue on priorities, rather than exerting direct pressure on policies and strategies (Takala, 2008). With regard to implementation, despite an agreement in 1998 to follow the national planning cycle, donors initially continued to bypass planning and budgeting procedures, and to micro-manage the activities they funded. However, in 2003, fifteen donors collectively recognized the negative effects of their behaviour and agreed to change it. This resulted in an increase in the government's ability to take charge of the programme (Takala, 2008).

The Indian example shows it is possible for a recipient government to lead the aid relationship. Low levels of aid dependence, high levels of government capacity and strong national institutions for capacity development enabled India to engage with donors on its own terms. In addition, the federal government had a clearly defined strategy for education and it instigated domestic political processes through which differences among states, and between the states and the central government were resolved before negotiations with donors began. Mozambique faced a very different set of circumstances, having emerged from a protracted civil war with very weak capacity in key areas of administration, a collapsed education system and high dependence on donors. Inevitably, donors had considerable policy leverage capacity. However, the picture changed over time, with government capacity strengthening and donor confidence in national systems increasing.

Aligning aid with national priorities and using government systems

The Paris Declaration envisages an aid relationship in which donors support the strategies, institutions and procedures of their partner governments. This vision reflects a belief that when aid is aligned with country priorities and systems it is likely to be more effective than when aid is donor driven, fragmented and administered through donor systems. As with ownership, assessing alignment of aid in this broad sense is difficult.

While many statements have been made in support of aligning aid with government priorities and practices, donor behaviours vary. They range from very loose support to fully shared acceptance. Progress towards alignment has proved far from straightforward, with frustrations on both sides. The issues involved raise complex questions. Using national procedures to channel aid makes donors much more dependent on national systems. Being answerable to their citizens and legislative bodies for ensuring that aid is used effectively, donors are very concerned about corruption and the speed of delivery. For their part, many aid recipients complain about the administrative and reporting requirements of programme aid.

Such challenges notwithstanding, efforts to align aid to education sector programmes and national management systems can have positive outcomes. Greater sector coherence is one example. Closer collaboration in areas such as joint planning and monitoring can provide better oversight of donor activities, averting fragmented service delivery. Programme aid, including budget support and pooled funds, can also help increase flexibility. Traditionally, aid for the education sector funded development expenditure such as classroom construction. Yet much of the incremental cost of expanding the education system and improving its quality requires increased recurrent expenditure, notably for teacher salaries. Programme aid has the advantage of being able to cover both development and recurrent costs. Millions of additional primary school teachers are needed to achieve UPE by 2015 and it will be difficult for aid dependent governments to finance them without relying on more, and more flexible, external aid (Foster, 2008).

Some countries have indeed increased the proportion of programme aid to the education sector with positive results. In Uganda, for example, an initial surge in primary school enrolments after the withdrawal of tuition fees severely compromised aid effectiveness. The government responded by developing the Education Strategic Investment Plan, which reflected a strong national commitment to education, enshrined in the national poverty reduction strategy. The plan, covering the whole education sector, became a central tool for more strategic decision-making. The government integrated aid flows into sector-wide planning. Donor support enabled Uganda to strengthen its public finance management system, which in turn encouraged donors to channel aid through it. From a donor perspective, the key factor enabling the effective use of aid to the education sector was the government's capacity for strategic decision-making, which provided a basis for reduced fragmentation and increased flexibility of aid. The stability and predictability of funding was enhanced by a medium-term budget framework guaranteeing the availability of budget funds to the sector (Ward et al., 2006).

While donors and aid recipients may share a commitment to alignment in their policy pronouncements, differences do arise. The complex history of aid to Rwanda is a case in point. Today, almost half the national recurrent budget and over 95% of the development budget for the education sector come from external resources. The past fifteen years have seen an extraordinary evolution of the aid relationship, from a huge number of emergency aid and relief projects in the mid-1990s to a sector-wide approach. The transition has not been without tension. Donors have attached overwhelming priority to primary and lower secondary education, whereas the government has also wanted to expand tertiary education. Several donors put pressure on Rwanda to lower its allocation to tertiary education (from 37%) and give higher priority to basic education. The result has been a package of cost savings at tertiary level, including higher charges for boarding facilities (Hayman, 2007).

Project-based aid is often a response to a negative risk assessment. However, it is possible to strengthen alignment, at least in policy areas, through project aid provided a strong sector plan is in place. The experience of Cambodia is instructive. The introduction of the Education Strategic Plan in 2001 marked the beginning of closer government-donor cooperation. The plan has given the government more focus internally and has gradually become the key reference for almost all donor support to primary education. With sixty separate basic education projects from fourteen donors in 2007, national planning and monitoring remain complex. Yet the Ministry of Education's leadership within the education reform process has strengthened, and ministry officials report that the increased importance given to the plan by donors has helped improve the ministry's knowledge of, and influence on, donor actions (Pirnay, 2007; Prasertsri, 2008).

In addition to governments developing strong sector programmes, donor support for improving national management systems and efforts to increase aid predictability are two key conditions for successful alignment.

Progress towards alignment has not been straightforward, with frustrations on both sides

Developing management systems. The new aid agenda assumes that increased recourse to national management systems will create incentives for their improvement and that, rather than circumventing national systems to facilitate rapid delivery of aid, many donors will recognize that effective aid ultimately depends on improved institutionalized capacity for its delivery.

Progress on aid predictability has been limited, and many donors have been slow to improve their own institutional practices

The overall record of progress on the use of national systems is mixed, as Box 4.4 showed. Their use is also arbitrary. The 2008 OECD-DAC survey of aid practices reported that donor policies on the use of national systems are often very slow to respond to successful reforms. Even when countries register improvement in their capacity for financial management, many donors still prefer their own systems. Others are sending more consistent signals. In Burkina Faso, for example, Canada, the Netherlands and the World Bank have worked with the Ministry of Basic Education to improve government management structures so as to disburse funds through them. As a result, the predictability of external funds has improved and the number of donors accepting common funding arrangements has increased. In 2007, 57% of the country's total aid to basic education was disbursed through such arrangements (Vachon, 2007).

Not all donors agree on the benefits of channelling aid through government management systems. A group including Canada, the Netherlands and the United Kingdom has been willing to use deficient systems while supporting efforts to strengthen them. Most of these donors share the view that aligned aid delivery stands a better chance of developing sustainable institutions and that administering aid flows through continued reliance on parallel project implementation units is ineffective and unsustainable. Another group of donors takes the more cautious position that systems have to function better before they are ready to channel aid through them. Australia, Portugal and the United States are prominent in this group.

Increasing aid predictability. Unpredictable aid flows make national planning in education a hazardous affair. Hiring teachers has financial implications over several years. In dialogue with the OECD-DAC, aid recipients have stressed the importance of aid predictability in making their budget management and planning more effective (OECD-DAC, 2007*b*).

Programme aid is not an automatic route to greater medium-term predictability. A recent survey of donor support to fourteen countries for 2006 showed that 94% of committed sector budget support was delivered within the year (Strategic Partnership with Africa, 2008). However, while commitments for 2007 had been made for 90% of the budget support programmes, the share fell to 68% for 2008 and to 47% for 2009. While short-term predictability of sector budget support is high, medium- to long-term predictability still tends to be low.

Progress on aid predictability has been limited. Some of the reasons can be traced to developing country governance practices. It is clearly legitimate for donors to withhold support when faced with systematic underperformance. But many donors have been slow to address weaknesses in their own institutional practices. Bilateral donors often use an annual funding cycle linked to their budgeting processes. National legislation may prevent them from signing binding medium- or long-term financing agreements, thus precluding predictable multiyear provision. Recent initiatives have started to address this problem. The European Commission's MDG contracts, the United Kingdom's ten year memoranda of understanding and the United States Millennium Challenge Corporation all provide for multiyear commitments. The MDG contracts become operational in 2008, with the aim of committing general budget support for six years. Monitoring will mainly focus on outcomes in the education and health sectors. The initial contracts will be made with countries that have shown good performance in managing budget support and strong commitment to achieving the MDGs.

Cross-country evidence on efforts to strengthen national leadership and improve alignment points to the importance of several enabling conditions:

- Recipient governments' political will to lead the education agenda is fundamental – and the development of well-structured education sector plans can facilitate their task.

- National commitment to improve public management, especially financial management, is a prerequisite for increasing donor confidence in national systems and procedures, though donors can do much to create incentives and provide support.

- For aid alignment to be effective, donors must be willing and able to adapt to country circumstances and to set aside many of their own agendas.
- Mutual trust is another key ingredient. For SWAps and programme aid to be sustained over time, governments must be confident of donors' commitment and donors must have a degree of trust in government policy direction and management capacities.
- Tailoring the new aid agenda to national realities is critical. Countries vary widely in institutional capacity to meet donor standards. Fragile states in particular face deeply entrenched problems (Box 4.6).

Improving coordination among donors

For countries with a narrow base of skilled administrators, inefficient time allocation has high costs. One source of inefficiency is the management of donors. When multiple donors arrive separately to assess performance in the same programmes, or local donor representatives require separate meetings with government, the transaction costs of aid and the opportunity costs associated with the diversion of human resources are high. Better management and coordination of donors can reduce these costs.

Having to service multiple missions when a single joint mission might suffice is one source of inefficiency. The Paris agenda sets targets for increasing the number of joint missions. While donors vary in their preference for joint missions, collectively they are far short of the target level. In 2007 only 20% of missions were conducted on a joint basis, while the target is 40% (OECD-DAC, 2008*a*). Education is widely cited as the sector in which donors have made the most progress on this count. For instance, a recent survey by the FTI Secretariat (2008) showed that in Honduras, 73% of education donor missions in 2007 were conducted jointly, and in Ethiopia 55%. However, just 20% of donor analytic work on Nicaragua's education sector was undertaken in joint exercises. Some aid recipients are beginning to cut transaction costs and manage the flow of demands from donors. Several have introduced 'mission-free' periods. Ghana, for instance, does not accommodate missions during the one-month period when it finalizes the national budget.

Box 4.6: Fragile states and the new aid agenda

Fragile states present particularly challenging environments for aid. In some states, such as Sudan and Afghanistan, violent conflict continues to hold back development. In others, post-conflict reconstruction confronts governments with enormous political challenges. Two common features link all fragile states: limited institutional capacity and vast unmet needs. In education, such states are dealing not just with a backlog of deprivation but also with school systems that fail to reach many citizens. In Somalia, for instance, two generations have reached adulthood with practically no access to education (Netherlands Ministry of Foreign Affairs, 2006).

Few fragile states are in a position to meet the demands of the new aid agenda, with its emphasis on country ownership, donor alignment with education sector plans and the use of national systems. Most lack the capacity to plan, implement and report through national systems. Emergency assistance and project aid thus continue to play an important role, and the road from emergency aid to development aid is not straightforward. The FTI has encountered difficulty, for example, in supporting fragile states. Its endorsement process requires credible education sector plans, which many fragile states are unprepared to develop.

Where government capacity is weak, early engagement by donors is crucial to a managed transition to long-term development aid. Afghanistan is an example. In 2002, the Afghanistan Reconstruction Trust Fund (ARTF) was established as a coordinated aid mechanism, pooling contributions from twenty-five donors. By mid-2007 the ARTF had mobilized US$1.45 billion to finance the government's recurrent budget and priority reconstruction projects (Berry, 2007). In the education sector, the ARTF pays the salaries of around 100,000 teachers and provides financial support to community initiatives to build and renovate schools. The priority given to external financing of recurrent salary expenditure is seen as crucial to strengthening the country's long-term effort to reconstruct its public service delivery system. Although the Ministry of Education's capacity is weak, it has shown some willingness and ability to engage with and coordinate donors to rebuild the education system. Bridging emergency and development aid requires such qualities.

The emergence of new donor coordination practices across the education sector could play an important role in lowering transaction costs. In many countries donor groups are being formed with appointed lead donors. Among the countries which had received funds from the FTI Catalytic Fund by the end of 2007, all but the Republic of Moldova had such arrangements (FTI Secretariat, 2007*a*). These donor groups have considerable responsibility, for instance in managing appraisals of education sector plans. Some are more effective than others, however, and capacities vary among countries. Donors move at different speeds, and some groups are restricted to general information sharing rather than joint aid management.

Ghana does not accommodate donor missions when it finalizes the national budget

Duplication frequently persists, notably in textbook provision and classroom construction. The Netherlands, the United Kingdom and some Scandinavian countries have taken the lead in harmonizing their donor procedures; others, including Japan and the United States, prefer to continue working through parallel structures. In some cases, the incentive systems for donor staff are holding back progress. Pressure for tangible and visible results, rigid administrations and lack of support for staff members' coordination of work across agencies have limited their interest (De Renzio et al., 2005).

The aid system has become increasingly complex, with ever more donors and financing mechanisms

A large number of donors each providing small amounts of aid is a prescription for higher than necessary transaction costs. The Paris Declaration stresses the need to reduce this kind of fragmentation, for good reason: in 2006, fourteen countries each had to deal with at least twelve donors for basic education.[4] To look at it the other way round: on average, each OECD-DAC donor had aid programmes in basic education with thirty-three countries (counting only programmes of at least US$100,000). France topped the list with programmes in seventy-two countries.

As the aid system has become increasingly complex, with ever more donors and financing mechanisms, donors are beginning to recognize the need to rationalize their delivery of aid. However, progress has been limited. Between 2002 and 2006, fourteen out of twenty-one major donors increased the number of countries to which they provided aid for basic education. The largest increases were for the European Commission, Greece, Japan and the United States. While most of these fourteen donors also increased their total aid to basic education during the period, several – including Austria, Greece, Ireland, Japan and Spain – increased recipient countries more rapidly than aid levels, thereby reducing the average amount of aid per country. In sharp contrast, five donors reduced the number of recipient countries while increasing aid, thereby raising the amount of aid per country. In particular, the two largest bilateral donors to basic education, the Netherlands and the United Kingdom, more than doubled total disbursements to basic education while each reduced the number of recipient countries by five.

In 2007 the European Union adopted a code of conduct to address skewed aid distribution. The code encourages a division of labour among donors. Where appropriate, one donor may provide resources to another to administer alongside its own aid programme. The code also encourages more equitable distribution of donors among countries. The European Commission, after surveying donors on the challenges of applying the code in the education sector, indicated that Denmark, Finland, Ireland, the Netherlands, Norway and Spain, along with the Commission itself, would withdraw from active participation in some countries. The decisions resulted partly from exercises analysing the division of labour within countries and partly from limited capacity in the field. Finland, Ireland and Norway reported that they had withdrawn direct support to education but secured continued aid for the sector through general budget support. Denmark and the Netherlands similarly chose to redirect some of their education aid through the FTI Catalytic Fund (European Commission, 2007*b*).

Donors are not alone in addressing fragmentation. Some governments in 'donor-dense' developing countries are attempting to rationalize the assistance they receive. For example, the Government of Afghanistan has introduced a rule to reduce the number of donors in each sector, including education. A donor wishing to provide funding to more than three sectors must contribute at least US$30 million per sector (Rocha Menocal and Mulley, 2006). In the United Republic of Tanzania, one aim of the Joint Assistance Strategy is to develop a more effective division of labour among donors. Among its eighteen donors in education, Finland, Ireland, the Netherlands and Norway recently decided to withdraw following consultations with government and other donors on overall financing. Similarly, after the Joint Assistance Strategy in Zambia reviewed the involvement of donors in education, two left the sector and four moved to general budget support. In India the government is strongly selective, accepting aid for the SSA programme from only three donors.

Most efforts towards more effective division of labour among donors are very recent and it is too early to evaluate their impact on the quality and quantity of aid to education. Again, though, recent work by the OECD-DAC points to the importance of government leadership in low income countries (OECD-DAC, 2008*d*).

4. This understates the problem as it includes only OECD-DAC donors.

Looking ahead

Sector-wide approaches have driven the new model of aid emphasizing country ownership and leadership, alignment and harmonization. The Paris agenda in turn has further reinforced SWAps as the default model of aid to education in many low income countries. That model can point to significant achievements, including large enrolment increases in several countries having sector-wide programmes, such as Burkina Faso, Ethiopia, India, Nepal, Uganda, the United Republic of Tanzania and Zambia.

Yet SWAps are far from straightforward and major challenges remain. Recipient government leadership stands out as the most critical determinant of success. Strong education plans cannot be carried through with weak political leadership. Nor can they be managed by governments lacking capacity. Where education ministries remain unconvinced of their advantages or unable to develop capacity to take the lead, SWAps have not facilitated education reform.

The new modalities face common tensions in country level aid management. The tensions are not new but have become more explicit through increased harmonization and alignment. Among them:

- *Long-term capacity-building versus short-term impact:* SWAps typically emphasize long-term institutional capacity development, mainly through more extensive use of national management systems. The argument is sometimes made that investment in these areas of capacity-building, mainly channelled as programme aid, comes at the expense of short-term effects, for instance in terms of numbers of schools built and textbooks distributed. Others see short-term achievements through project aid as undermining efforts to build and sustain national capacity. While the trade-off between short-term delivery and long-term capacity may be overstated, it is important to consider whether countries are best served by adopting one model rather than a mix of models.

- *Sector coherence versus donor influence on national policies:* SWAps have potentially opened recipients' doors to increased donor influence. Sector analysis and government-donor discussions on sector policies and strategies have undeniably contributed to more coherent thinking and implementation of education activities. Yet at the same time programme support has provided opportunities for donors to strengthen their collective influence over strategic decisions. Differences between donors may counteract this effect to some degree by giving rise to 'lowest common denominator' positions. But a government in a very poor, highly aid dependent country is unlikely to risk a breach with a group of major donors. Does collective action by donors weaken the potential for real national ownership? To prevent such trade-offs, donors must exercise a high level of self-restraint when policy differences arise.

- *Process-oriented consensus building versus the drive for results:* At country level, much energy goes into coordination and consultation. These are clearly important, as making SWAps effective requires substantial 'process' work. However, without a firm managerial hand and a focus on results, SWAp processes can become ends in themselves, absorbing large amounts of technical assistance and diverting government resources. The focus on results, though, carries its own risks because of a growing tendency to assess performance on the basis of common sets of key indicators – an approach that can reduce complex processes to static and reductionist yardsticks.

Recipient government leadership stands out as the most critical determinant of success

More aid for better governance

The restructuring of aid relationships is leading to less direct involvement of donors in designing programmes and monitoring implementation. Recourse to aid conditionality as a lever for reform is also more limited. However, 'aid dialogue' remains a source of donor influence. Increasingly central to that dialogue are issues of good governance. Donors advocate their own approaches to governance reform, in terms of what areas are important and what policies are effective, and may use aid programmes to leverage change. The question is whether donors' approaches to governance are consistent with the needs of poor countries and the spirit of the Paris agenda.

Governance is climbing the aid agenda

Financial flows provide one indicator of the growing profile of governance issues in aid programmes. The share of all sector-allocable ODA supporting projects and programmes in the 'governance and civil society' category was 9% in 2006 – the highest share of any single sector (Figure 4.5). This does not include programmes in other sectors, such as education and health, that have governance components.

Donors have invested heavily in developing their approaches to governance reform. In 2006 and 2007 several major donors (including the European Commission, France, the Netherlands, the United Nations Development Programme, the United Kingdom, the United States and the World Bank) adopted new strategies on governance. A 2006 United Kingdom white paper on aid policy captures the emerging mood by committing the government to '[p]ut support for good governance at the centre of what we do, focusing on state capability, responsiveness and accountability' (DFID, 2006). The European Commission and the World Bank have been particularly active in promoting good governance through their aid programmes. The broad governance agenda covers a multitude of areas ranging from public financial management, decentralization, transparency and accountability (linked to corruption) to participation and reform of public sector employment, to mention a few. Donors have also developed quantitative and qualitative tools to measure the status of a country's governance arrangements (Advisory Board for Irish Aid, 2008). DFID produces Country Governance Analyses, the European Commission prepares Governance Profiles for its main partner countries, the Netherlands carries out Strategic Governance and Anti-Corruption Assessments, and the World Bank is piloting a Governance and Anti-Corruption Assessment instrument. Increasingly, these measures are being used to inform decisions on aid allocation and assessment. They also play an important role by highlighting donor concerns and priorities that governments must bear in mind when developing programmes they hope donors will support.

The European Commission and the World Bank are promoting a broad good-governance agenda through their aid programmes

Education figures prominently in governance reforms. Any broad public sector reform, whether in employment conditions, budget management or financial management, affects education because the sector accounts for a large share of public expenditure and a commensurately large share of the public sector wage bill. Donors have also supported governance reforms in the education sector directly through specific projects and SWAps. The most recent World Bank Education Sector Strategy Update sends a clear institutional signal on key elements of good governance to be included in projects and programmes. In a section on maximizing the effectiveness of education aid, it calls for more support to decentralized local authorities, increased devolution of power to schools and more public-private partnerships, as part of a strategy for integrating education into a broader policy framework (World Bank, 2005*b*). The emphasis on governance reform is stronger in the update than in its 1999 predecessor. Most bilateral donors have also followed this trend.

How has increased interest in governance among donors influenced policies and practices in the education sector in recipient countries? This is not a simple question to answer. In a traditional project almost wholly funded by a donor, it is reasonable to assume that the donor strongly influences the design and that implementation is closely monitored. With programme support, influence is more difficult to untangle because it is embedded in complex processes of dialogue and bargaining. However, by examining the components of recently prepared projects and programmes supported by donors, it is possible to discern the contours of a distinctive governance agenda.

The EFA Global Monitoring Report team reviewed eighteen projects or programmes in basic education supported by the World Bank since 2006. The focus was on activities relating to governance and on loan conditions. Thirteen of the operations are relatively conventional arrangements in which financial support is provided for specific activities. However, reflecting the change in aid modalities, these are generally components of the government's sector plan. Four of the operations provide budget support for sector programmes. The remaining one is an example of the treatment of education sector reform in a recent programme of general budget support. Table 4.2 describes the components of each operation. The World Bank was chosen partly because it is one of the largest sources of development assistance for education, especially in the poorest countries, partly because it makes more information available than most donors, and partly because the terms and conditions of its operations reflect and inform the views of the wider donor community. Other donors are involved in several of the sector programmes being supported.

What broad conclusions about approaches to governance can be drawn from these eighteen operations? In the thirteen that can be categorized as conventional projects, seven cover governance as a peripheral issue, their main focus being on direct financial support for school buildings, learning materials and teacher training. These seven projects are in Afghanistan, Burundi, the Democratic Republic of the Congo, the Gambia, Haiti, Mali and Nigeria; all but Mali are categorized as fragile states. Improvements in governance are sought largely through capacity development in the Ministry of Education and through

Table 4.2: Governance components of recent education projects and programmes supported by the World Bank

Conventional basic education projects

Burundi 2007: Education Reconstruction Project	Components: expansion of primary enrolment by financing school buildings; support for teaching and learning through in-service training programmes, provision of textbooks for all primary and lower secondary students, and measurement of reading adequacy; and *capacity-building in policy and planning in the ministry.*
Democratic Republic of the Congo 2007: Education Sector Project	Components: increasing access and equity in primary schooling through the rehabilitation of school infrastructure and support for eliminating school fees; improving quality through the provision of textbooks; and *building capacity to assess learning achievement and strengthening institutional capacity in the education system by preparing policies for teacher training, and strengthening education sector policy making and planning, and the project management unit.*
Nigeria 2007: State Education Sector Project	Components: school development grants to improve the quality of teaching and learning; development of model 'whole' schools through infrastructure and furniture grants plus basic teaching inputs to a small selection of schools; *institutional development of state and local government authorities particularly via the EMIS and the Inspectorate plus project management and monitoring, and evaluation support to all states.*
Mali 2006: Second Education Sector Investment Programme Project	Components: improving the quality of basic education through establishing reading areas in classrooms and providing libraries in teacher-training colleges, funding schemes to purchase school supplies, and providing in-service and accelerated training programmes for teachers; increasing access to education through financing new classrooms in basic education and one new secondary school; *strengthening institutional management capacity in the education sector in human resources, EMIS, budgetary and financial management, and programme coordination.*
Haiti 2007: First Phase of the Education for All Project	Components: improving access and equity in primary education; *operationalizing partnerships between public and non-public sectors;* and *building capacity to assess learning outcomes.*
Gambia 2006: Third Education Phase Two Sector Programme	Components: construction/rehabilitation of urban and multigrade classrooms; support for in-service teacher training and mentoring; developing monitoring tools for tracking instructional time, observations of classroom instruction, attendance of school personnel and students, and parental involvement; *technical assistance for functional analysis of the education ministry and for the development of management and teacher in-service training modules, monitoring and evaluation,* and *support to the project coordination unit.*
Afghanistan 2008: Second Education Quality Improvement Programme	Components: quality enhancement and social awareness; teacher training and increases in female teachers; *school grants for infrastructure;* and *project management, monitoring and evaluation.*
Uzbekistan 2006: Basic Education Project	Components: providing modern, low-cost learning materials in selected schools to improve learning; *strengthening community participation in school decision-making; building capacity in the education sector for budget planning and formulation, and management and accounting; enhancing the capacity of line units in the ministry to implement the project and, in doing so, to strengthen capacity overall.*
Philippines 2006: National Program Support for Basic Education Project	Components: *develop and strengthen school-based management; improve teacher effectiveness through refining teacher competency standards and using them for appraisal, training needs and promotion, and through a more equitable distribution of teachers across schools; increase equity and quality by applying a standards-based approach to address growing disparities in inputs and outcomes; improve budget planning and management in the education department.*
Pakistan 2006: Balochistan Education Support Project	Components: *establish community schools in rural areas; support private schools;* and *provide capacity-building activities for education NGO staff, members of parent education committees and teachers including through training, school monitoring and supervision.*
Indonesia 2007: Better Education through Reformed Management and Universal Teacher Upgrading	Components: reform teacher pre-service training; *strengthen structures for teacher improvement at the local level; reform teacher accountability and incentive systems for performance appraisal and career advancement;* and *monitoring and evaluation, including the development of a teacher data base.*
Honduras 2008: Education Quality, Governance and Institutional Strengthening	Components: scale up interventions in pre-school and primary schools in poor areas; *increase community participation within a new integrated school management system; governance and institutional strengthening of the ministry;* and *project administration.*
Colombia 2008: Rural Education Project	Components: *improve the capacity of a set of departmental and municipality secretariats to deliver rural education; strengthening rural education at the school level in these municipalities;* and *strengthening the Ministry of Education in the area of rural education.*

Improvements in governance are sought through capacity development in the Ministry of Education

Table 4.2 (continued)

Education sector/subsector-wide plan

Kenya 2006: Education Sector Support Project	Support for the government's programme to provide basic education and improve the quality of education for all children through twenty-three investment programmes in four areas; equity of access to basic education; improving quality and learning achievement; providing opportunities for post-primary education and training; and strengthening education sector management. *'All of the investment programmes emphasise information dissemination, transparency, accountability and addressing corruption, within the context of the sector's strategy for good governance.'*
Bangladesh 2007: Third Education Sector Development Support Project	This loan directly focuses on governance and a general sector reform progammme which 'attempts to address systemic governance issues in order to raise the quality and cost effectiveness of service delivery'. The reform agenda focuses on *accountability and systemic improvement through enforcing the criteria for establishing new schools, linking school grants to measures of school performance and strengthening school management committees; building administrative capacity through further development of oversight measures and devolving more responsibility to lower levels of government; improving monitoring and evaluation through expenditure tracking surveys and impact evaluations plus greater dissemination of information on examination outcomes, school performance and programme effectiveness; increasing teacher quality through the establishment of an autonomous teacher registration and accreditation authority; and improving the efficiency of textbook production and curriculum development through production being opened up to competition and transparent textbook evaluation and approval mechanisms.* Triggers for the loan are in areas related to *accountability and systemic improvements in school financing, teacher effectiveness and textbook production.*
Pakistan 2007: Fourth Punjab Education Development Policy Credit Project	The reform programme being supported has three pillars – improve fiscal sustainability and the fiduciary environment through ensuring increases in education expenditure *and increasing transparency of financial management and procurement practices;* improve equitable access to primary education *through participation of the private sector* and its quality through better teaching practices and textbooks, and a credible examination system; and *improve public education sector governance and management through strengthening district departments and expanding school-based management and the monitoring of schools by communities.* Triggers include *performance formulae for school grants, a draft law for establishing a procurement regulatory authority, approval of policy and implementation modalities to scale up government financial support to private schools, textbooks printed and published through open competitive bidding, and a performance monitoring index, including for teacher absenteeism, approved with quarterly ranking of districts against the indicators.*
Pakistan 2007: First Sindh Education Sector Development Policy Credit Project	The reform programme being supported has four components: improving fiscal sustainability and the effectiveness of public expenditures in education, partly through *improving financial management and procurement reforms to increase credibility, transparency and accountability of public resources;* improving education sector management through *reforms to strengthen the functioning, capacity and accountability of provincial and district management in line with devolution objectives and to strengthen the role of school management committees;* improving access to quality education with a focus on rural areas and girls through infrastructure and *reducing implementation bottlenecks of incentive programmes (free textbooks and stipends)* and by *launching partnerships with the non-government/private sector;* and improving the quality of teaching and learning through *merit-based recruitment of teachers and improved accountability and through a competency-based system of teacher education and continuous professional development.*

General budget support and the education sector

India 2007: First Bihar Development Policy Loan/Credit	This loan is part of a wider framework of support to India's poorest and second largest state by the World Bank, DFID, the Asian Development Bank and Japan. *The overall objective is to 'support the implementation of critical fiscal, governance, administrative and service delivery reforms'.* Bihar's Eleventh Plan (2007) emphasizes three pillars – increasing public investment and *strengthening public financial management and governance;* raising economic growth through agriculture, investment climate reforms and infrastructure; and *improving public service delivery in the social services.* The last of these focuses strongly on teachers. Huge numbers of teachers are required to move towards universal primary and elementary schooling. The plan emphasizes the need to *refine recruitment criteria for teachers, selection processes, contracting terms and the overall management.* The current situation is summed up as 'Lack of comprehensive data on teachers leads to problems such as corruption and political manoeuvring in teacher recruitment, irrational deployment and transfer of teachers, high teacher absenteeism and ineffective overall management'. Prior actions for the release of the first tranche of the loan include devolution to *panchayats* (local governments) of the responsibility for all new teacher hiring, with a first round of approximately 100,000 teachers hired. Conditions for the release of the second tranche include hiring the second round of 100,000 teachers, *incorporating lessons learned in terms of standardization of recruitment criteria, increased transparency of candidate review process with proper registries and third party monitoring of selection processes and sample-based evaluation of the recruitment process by an independent agency.* Indicative triggers for a potential follow-up loan include the development and piloting of a *teacher competence assessment tool* and an assessment of the 100,000 new teacher hirings in basic education levels and pedagogical skills plus the development and implementation of a *monitoring system to record and improve teacher attendance in both primary and secondary schools.*

Note: Governance components are displayed in italics.

the strengthening of monitoring and evaluation units. A deeper governance agenda is nonetheless discernible in the components for school autonomy in Afghanistan and public-private partnerships in Haiti.

In the remaining conventional projects, governance issues are predominant. This is reflected in support for community participation in the running of schools (Honduras, the province of Balochistan in Pakistan and Uzbekistan), school-based management (the Philippines), development of formulas for school funding (the Philippines), teacher recruitment, deployment and monitoring (Indonesia, the Philippines), support for private schooling (Balochistan) and significant efforts to improve overall administration and governance across the sector (all countries, but particularly Colombia).

The education sector programmes being supported are associated with the promotion of a yet more ambitious governance agenda. Programmes in Bangladesh, Kenya and the provinces of Punjab and Sindh in Pakistan set wide-ranging goals. They include accountability, transparency, decentralization, school autonomy, information sharing, reforms of teacher recruitment and placement, teacher performance monitoring, and private sector involvement in schools and textbook production. In addition, there is a common focus on improving broad aspects of public financial management. Triggers for the loans include government actions intended to improve criteria for school financing, teacher effectiveness and textbook production, and to provide support to private schools. In the case of general budget support to the state of Bihar in India, required actions concern the rules for hiring teachers and monitoring teacher performance.

This examination reveals some patterns. Traditional education projects focusing on activities directly aimed at expanding access (such as through provision of school buildings) and improving the quality of schooling (such as through provision of learning materials and support for pre-service and in-service teacher training) are typical in countries with weak governments or bureaucracies. In other countries where aid is still tied to specific activities, the focus has shifted towards improving education service delivery, accountability and transparency. When it comes to SWAps, the governance agenda dominates even more strongly. The initial government-donor negotiations on the grant or loan, and the triggers required for the release of financing tranches, provide mechanisms for leveraging reform. Sector plans give a great deal of emphasis to teachers, including recruitment, terms of service, lines of accountability, transfers and absenteeism. Measures to support greater community participation in schools through village or school education committees, and the auditing of school funds, are also common. So, too, is the encouragement of private sector participation, both through private schools – often supported by public funds – and expansion of the private sector in producing, printing and distributing learning materials.

What conclusions can be drawn from this exercise? Clearly, caution has to be exercised in deriving general lessons from these particular projects and programmes. Yet even with this caveat, there is compelling evidence that governance now figures prominently in aid dialogues on education, as well as strong grounds for predicting it will figure even more prominently in the future. At one level, this is entirely justified. The need for good governance in the education sector cannot be contested. Indeed, it is a condition for achieving the goals and targets set in the Dakar Framework for Action. Furthermore, as aid is increasingly directed towards broad sector programmes rather than specific activities, and more of it is managed through government systems, it is not surprising if donors pay greater attention to the broad governance framework. At the same time, donors have no monopoly on insights into what constitutes good governance for education. There is a risk that policies reflecting particular currents of education policy debates in rich countries – such as shifting powers from local authorities to schools, expansion of voucher programmes, performance-related pay for teachers, and an increased role for private sector provision – will become routinely promoted. As Chapter 3 shows, the evidence for their relevance in poor countries is not always strong. ■

Donors have no monopoly on insights into what constitutes good governance for education

© Abbie Trayler-Smith/PANOS

The long road to education: walking through the desert to get to school, in Yemen

Chapter 5

Policy conclusions and recommendations

Inequality is one of the major barriers to the goals set out in the Dakar Framework for Action. Governments across the world need to act with far greater resolve to reduce the disparities that restrict opportunity in education. One of the central lessons to emerge from this Report is that there is no quick fix for enhanced equity, or for accelerated progress towards education for all. However, it is possible to identify some of the broad principles and approaches needed to guide policy. This chapter sets out key priorities for national governments, donors and civil society.

What governments can do

Every country faces a different set of constraints and challenges in education. That is why effective national planning is the starting point for governance reform and for the development of national strategies to accelerate progress towards EFA.

With the 2015 target date for key EFA goals drawing closer, the early warning indicators for failure are clearly visible. Particularly disconcerting is the fact that, on current trends, the goal of universal primary education (UPE) will not be achieved. Governments need to act with far greater urgency in tackling the inequalities holding back progress in this area. Simultaneously, education quality and learning achievement must be brought to the centre of national education planning at the primary level and beyond. In taking forward the EFA agenda, eight broad thematic lessons can be drawn from the experience of strong national performances.

1 Get serious about equity

Education planners need to ensure that the benefits of expanded provision are shared by disadvantaged groups and underserved regions. Practical strategies for strengthening equity include the removal of user fees, the introduction of financial incentives for the education of girls and children from disadvantaged backgrounds, targeted support to keep children in school and the deployment of well-trained teachers proficient in local languages. More equitable public spending patterns are also critical to ensure that schools, teachers and resources are skewed towards those with the greatest need rather than those with the greatest wealth.

Setting clear equity targets is one of the most important things governments can do in rethinking planning approaches. Current EFA targets, such as those in the Millennium Development Goals (MDGs), are set in terms of national average goals. The problem, as Chapter 2 shows, is that national averages can mask deep underlying disparities. Average progress that leaves whole sections of society behind is not consistent with the spirit of the Dakar Framework for Action: the EFA goals are for everyone. Going beyond national average targeting to identify well-defined equity goals would make a difference at a number of levels. Even taking the political decision to adopt equity goals in education and monitor progress towards them would send an important signal. It would place inequality of opportunity where it deserves to be: at the centre of the political agenda. Concrete targets for reducing disparities could also provide a benchmark for holding political leaders to account.

Equity goals in education need to be well-defined. As in other areas discussed in this Report, there are no blueprints. The starting point is an assessment of current disparities. For purposes of illustration, the overall commitment to UPE by 2015 could be supported by interim 2010–2012 targets for, say, halving the school attendance gap between the richest and poorest 20%, or between rural and urban areas, or majority and minority ethnic populations. Specific targets could be set for particularly marginalized groups or regions with high concentrations of deprivation. Progress towards the equity targets could be monitored through household surveys and education reporting systems.

Equity targets could also play a role in informing approaches to national planning. Meaningful targets would have to be backed by financing and wider policy commitments. Particular attention would have to be paid to estimating the cost of reaching disadvantaged groups and areas, not least since the marginal costs are likely to be far higher than average costs. Similarly, extending opportunity to children from households marked by poverty, ill-health and acute vulnerability might require higher levels of per capita spending than for children from more advantaged households. This is an area that continues to receive insufficient consideration in education planning. An important priority for EFA is for governments and donors to develop estimates of the costs of reaching the marginalized and reducing disparities – and to make provisions for these costs in national budgets. Moreover, strategies for achieving equity targets in education would have to consider not just school-based policies, but also wider strategies on nutrition, health and poverty. The targets themselves could provide an opportunity to develop the type of integrated approach to education planning and poverty reduction set out in Chapter 3.

The commitment to equity has to start before primary school – and continue afterwards. Good-quality early childhood care and education (ECCE) strengthens cognitive development and helps prepare children for school. The benefits are reflected in improved attainment and achievement levels in school. Progress towards ECCE has been disappointing and highly unequal, both among and within countries. National governments should prioritize ECCE in planning, with incentives provided to improve coverage of disadvantaged children. Similarly, it is increasingly apparent that progress in many EFA areas – and towards many of the MDGs – depends on a rapid scaling up of opportunities for good-quality secondary education.

2 Provide leadership, set ambitious targets and forge effective partnerships

International evidence provides insights into the specific policies that can accelerate progress towards EFA. But the crucial ingredient for success is leadership. There is no substitute for sustained political commitment. Political leaders need to put education at the centre of national development strategies and use their influence to make equity a shared goal throughout society. They also need to reach beyond government agencies to involve civil society, the voluntary and private sectors, and groups representing the poor in policy processes. Ensuring that the voices of the poor and marginalized are heard in policy formulation is a condition for strengthened equity.

Strategies for achieving equity targets in education should also consider wider constraints linked to nutrition, health and poverty

Setting clear policy objectives is crucial. Successful governments have fixed ambitious long-term goals that are supported by clear medium-term 'stepping stone' targets and backed by commitments on inputs ranging from classroom construction to teacher recruitment and textbook supply. Governments with less successful track records have often set ambitious goals but failed to underpin them either with coherent strategies for delivery or with predictable budget commitments.

Another crucial condition for progress in education is ensuring that the policies of departments whose work affects education are complementary rather than contradictory. Many countries have improved policy coherence within the education sector and between education and other line ministries. Sector-wide approaches have played an important role in this regard. Even so, problems remain. Education targets are often weakly integrated in national budgets and financing strategies.

3 Strengthen wider anti-poverty commitments

It is a widely overlooked fact that sustained progress in education cannot be built on the foundations of mass poverty and deep social inequality. One in three pre-school children has what amounts to brain damage as a result of malnutrition, which constitutes a formidable obstacle to UPE. The associated facts that 10 million children die before the age of 5 and that tens of millions more suffer life-threatening diseases represent further limitations on the human right to education.

Conditional cash transfer programmes in Brazil and Mexico have demonstrated that strategies for tackling child labour, poor health and weak nutrition can yield large benefits for education

National governments should strengthen policies for combating the poverty, inequality and wider structural factors that produce such outcomes. Cash transfer programmes, targeted health interventions and more equitable public spending in health service provision all have a role to play. Child malnutrition must also be accorded a far higher priority. The bottom line is that progress in education is being held back by the failings of current national strategies for poverty reduction.

The Dakar Framework envisages the integration of education planning within effective national poverty reduction strategies. This is an important goal because many of the most insurmountable barriers to access and learning are located beyond the school. Unfortunately, progress towards coherent national strategies linking education and poverty reduction has been limited. Many countries urgently need poverty reduction strategies to address the health, nutrition and wider poverty-related constraints on progress towards EFA. Conditional cash transfer programmes in countries such as Brazil and Mexico have demonstrated that strategies for tackling child labour, poor health and weak nutrition can yield large benefits for education. All governments and donors should actively explore the potential for strengthening and expanding social protection as part of the strategy for advancing the EFA agenda. Within the education sector, far more weight should be attached to targeted interventions such as incentive programmes for children who are disadvantaged as a consequence of poverty, gender, caste, ethnicity or location. Ensuring that schools and classroom are built and teachers allocated so they are within reach of marginalized communities is also important.

4 Raise quality standards

Senior policy-makers should renew and strengthen the Dakar pledge on education quality. Policies should emphasize new approaches to teaching and learning, improved provision of learning materials and strong incentives to raise standards. National authorities, community officials and local school leaders must work together to ensure that every school becomes an effective learning environment. Such an environment requires well-nourished and motivated students, well-trained teachers using adequate facilities and instructional materials, a relevant, local-language curriculum, and a welcoming, gender-sensitive, healthy, safe environment that encourages learning. This must be accompanied by a clear definition and accurate assessment of learning outcomes. It is also important that students receive the threshold international benchmark of 850 hours per year in instructional time. These are all areas in which clear norms and policy rules have to be defined and enforced.

5 Strengthen capacity to measure, monitor and assess education quality, and inform parents and policy-makers

The methods used and the information collected in monitoring and assessment exercises should be transparent and accessible to diverse education stakeholders. Successful monitoring is not just about generating information. It is also about creating institutional mechanisms through which monitoring can inform the development and implementation of policy.

The monitoring of education quality should include three dimensions: (i) input or enabling conditions for learning (from infrastructure and learning materials to qualified, trained teachers and adequate budgets); (ii) pedagogy and the learning process, including an appropriate language of instruction, and learning time; and (iii) learning outcomes. Official reporting in these areas can be supplemented by monitoring undertaken by civil society organizations.

6 Scale up education financing with a commitment to equity

High levels of education financing do not guarantee universal access or strong learning achievements.

Nevertheless, sustained underfinancing is unequivocally bad for efficiency, equity and education quality. Many developing countries, especially (though not exclusively) in South Asia, chronically underinvest in education. Under-financing is not consistent with a commitment to EFA or the targets set in the Dakar Framework for Action. To make matters worse, current spending patterns are often pro-rich rather than pro-poor.

Decentralization, under the right conditions, can help foster political accountability, but it is not a panacea for inequality. On the contrary, financial decentralization can widen disparities to the detriment of poor regions and disadvantaged communities. Avoiding this outcome requires a built-in commitment to equity in the financing formulas adopted for decentralization. It is important for central government to retain a strong redistributive role, facilitating the transfer of resources from richer to poorer subnational regions. In developing rules for transfers to subnational authorities, central governments must also attach sufficient weight to equity indicators – such as poverty levels, health status and children out of school – in allocating transfers. The guiding principle should be that those in greatest need receive the most per capita support. Too often the inverse is the case, with the wealthiest regions receiving the highest levels of per capita public spending in education. While one aim of decentralization is the devolution of authority, in the area of finance governments should recognize the limits to fiscal autonomy. In particular, fiscal autonomy for local governments should not mean authority to mobilize revenue through user charges in basic education. As Chapter 3 suggests, the real issue raised by decentralization is not *whether* to do it, but *how* to do it. And the starting point has to be a commitment to decentralization with equity.

7 Recognize the limits to competition and choice

Under the right conditions, competition and choice can support EFA goals. At the same time, policy-makers need to recognize that education provision cannot be reduced to oversimplified market principles. Imperfect and asymmetric information, time and distance constraints, and institutional capacity failings all impose limits on competition. Meanwhile, poverty and social disadvantage limit choice. Public-private partnership models aim to expand choice by separating education finance and management. Voucher programmes, state funding for private schools and the development of independent schools are all public-private partnership strategies – and each has a limited record of success, even in the developed world. Private schools in Sweden are one exception to this rule – but the 'Swedish model' is not readily transferable to other developed countries, let alone developing ones.

Choice and competition are often presented as a solution to the failings of public provision. Some commentators view low-fee private schools in the same light. The failings of public provision are strongly evident in many countries. And millions of poor households are voting with their feet, switching to low-fee private providers. However, the vast majority of the world's children – especially those from poor and disadvantaged households – will depend on public provision for the foreseeable future. Low-fee private schools will continue to play a role, but they are symptoms of state failure and the entry costs impose a considerable burden on poor households. Introducing choice and competition into a system in which all parents have the option of sending their children to a good-quality public provider is one thing. Using private providers to compensate for state failure is quite another – and in most cases will not be the best option when it comes to efficiency and equity. The bottom line, for governments in countries where public-sector basic education is failing the poor, is to fix the system first and consider options for competition between providers second.

Policy-makers need to recognize that education provision cannot be reduced to oversimplified market principles

8 Strengthen the recruitment, deployment and motivation of teachers

An adequate supply of motivated, qualified and properly trained teachers is a foundation of good-quality education for all. All countries have to assess remuneration levels consistent with building that foundation. Poverty-level wages and poor conditions, moreover, are not consistent with strong motivation. Improving the teaching environment through the provision of learning materials, training and support is vital for raising morale.

Hiring contract teachers can reduce the marginal costs of recruitment and thereby release resources for investment in other areas. But it can also reduce the quality of recruited teachers and weaken motivation, with damaging consequences for children in classrooms. There is a case for recourse to contract teacher recruitment as a strategy for reaching marginalized groups and underserved areas. However, it is important for governments to recognize the potential trade-off between teacher quantity and quality that can come with contract teaching. Other strategies for reaching marginalized groups include incentives for teachers to locate in underserved areas and measures to increase recruitment from disadvantaged communities.

Performance-related pay for teachers is a popular topic in discussions of governance. In practice, however, it is difficult to implement and unlikely to create incentives for improved learning achievement. It may also have damaging consequences for equity as schools and teachers focus on the students most likely to attain high scores.

In some countries, especially in sub-Saharan Africa, expanding teacher recruitment is an urgent priority. UPE by 2015 will not be attainable without a marked increase in the rate of recruitment and retention. In many cases, donors will need to increase support to achieve these goals. If teacher retirement is taken into account, sub-Saharan Africa alone will need to recruit around 3.8 million teachers by 2015. □

The role of aid donors

Donors need to increase aid for basic education to at least US$11 billion annually

National governments carry the main responsibility for achieving the EFA goals. Many of the developing countries that are most off track are highly dependent on aid, and will remain so for the foreseeable future. Developed countries can support progressive strategies by increasing their level of financial commitment, improving aid practices and ensuring that aid is used to support national priorities.

UPE will not be achieved without effective aid partnerships. What is needed is the renewal and the realization of the compact embodied in the Dakar Framework for Action. There are responsibilities and obligations on both sides. But donors need to demonstrate a far greater level of resolve and political leadership. This Report proposes action in four areas.

Delivering on commitments and expanding the donor base

Donors pledged in 2005 to 'double aid to halve poverty'. Since then they have instead cut development assistance. Debt relief explains only part of the reduction. Meeting the 2005 commitment requires an additional US$30 billion (at 2004 prices) – some three times the increases currently set out in aid spending plans. The shortfall for sub-Saharan Africa is around US$14 billion (2004 prices).

Failure to act on the Gleneagles commitment will hamper global poverty reduction efforts, with damaging consequences for education. More detailed national and international efforts to update estimates of education financing gaps are required; however, having promised that no national strategy would fail for want of finance, donors need to increase aid for basic education to at least US$11 billion annually. In 2006, commitments to basic education in low-income countries totalled US$3.8 billion – around a third of the level required. The two year average for 2005 and 2006 points unmistakably towards a reduction in commitments for basic education, compared with the previous two years. This is true for developing countries in general and the poorest countries in particular. Failure to reverse the trend will adversely affect future disbursements. As an immediate priority, donors should commit to an increase of US$7 billion annually in aid financing for basic education.

Aid flows to basic education are heavily concentrated in a small group of donors. Just three donors – the Netherlands, the United Kingdom and the International Development Association – accounted for half of all aid commitments and 85% of the increase in disbursements in 2006. The narrowness of the donor base is a source of underfinancing. It is also a source of potential instability and unpredictability in aid.

Strengthening the commitment to equity

Several donors appear to attach a low priority to equity in their education aid. France, Germany and Japan, for example, have shown neglect for basic education and low-income countries. Calculations for this Report suggest that France and Germany devote far more aid to bringing students to study in their domestic tertiary education systems than they spend on aid to basic education. If developing country governments followed this practice and allocated well over half their education budget to the tertiary level, they would – justifiably – stand accused of questionable governance practices. To avoid potential double standards, it is important for donors to consider whether their aid allocation patterns are consistent with a commitment to equity and to the spirit of the Dakar Framework for Action.

Getting behind the Fast Track Initiative

The balance sheet of the Fast Track Initiative (FTI) is a source of growing concern. In mid-2008, there were thirty-five countries with plans endorsed by the FTI, entailing programme costs estimated at US$8 billion and external financing needs of US$2 billion. The gap between current aid pledges and external financing requirements was around US$640 million. With eight countries expected to join the FTI by the end of the year, that gap could climb to US$1 billion. Another thirteen countries are scheduled to join in 2009, which means the total annual financing gap could reach US$2.2 billion. Closing that gap is the responsibility of a wide range of bilateral and multilateral donors. However, working on an assumption that the Catalytic Fund of the FTI might be expected to cover around 40% to 50%, a prospective 2010 financing gap of around US$1 billion will remain. These looming shortfalls pose a real and imminent threat to efforts to achieve the targets set in the Dakar Framework for Action. They also call into question donors' commitments to ensure that no viable plan for achieving UPE and wider education goals would be allowed to fail for want of financial support. Addressing the FTI deficit is an urgent priority. At the same time, it is important for the FTI to broaden its currently narrow base of donor support.

Delivering on the Paris agenda

Progress towards the goals set in the Paris Declaration for improved aid quality has been limited and uneven. Donors could do far more to reduce transaction costs and improve aid effectiveness through greater alignment of aid behind national priorities, better coordination, increased use of national financial management systems and improved predictability in aid flows. Increased emphasis on programme-based aid creates opportunities and threats. The opportunities lie in the potential for more effective national planning and donor alignment behind national priorities. The threats derive from donors' ability to use collective action through programme aid to assert their priorities. There are no easy answers – but donors must engage in genuine dialogue. □

The role of non-government actors

This Report has emphasized the central importance of government leadership and public policy. That is not to minimize the responsibilities and capacities of other actors. Achieving EFA requires partnerships at many levels – between schools and parents, between civil society organizations and governments, between state and non-state education providers.

Governance reform provides an opportunity to strengthen the voice and effectiveness of civil society organizations, and to enhance participation and accountability

Civil society has a critical role to play in strengthening equity in education. Organizations of the marginalized – slum dwellers, child labourers, members of low castes, indigenous people – have been in the forefront of international efforts to extend education to all, often in the face of government indifference or outright hostility. National and international non-government organizations have also emerged as key EFA actors, holding governments to account, supporting provision and building capacity. Governance reform provides an opportunity to strengthen the voice and effectiveness of civil society organizations and to enhance participation and accountability.

Governance in education cannot be treated in isolation from wider governance issues. Democracy, transparency and the rule of law are enabling conditions for effective participation and accountability. When citizens lack a voice in choosing their government, or when they face arbitrary laws, they are unlikely to have an effective voice in framing education priorities. Within the education sector, governance reforms can play a role in devolving authority to parents and communities. Yet devolution is not an automatic ticket to empowerment; there is a danger that poor and marginalized communities will lack the capacities and resources needed for effective management. To ensure that devolved responsibilities do not result in a further widening of equity gaps, schools that are in disadvantaged areas or serving disadvantaged groups need to be provided with extra resources and support. ■

© Crispin Hughes/PANOS

A committed teacher opens young minds to the excitement and benefits of education, in rural Mali

Annex

The Education for All Development Index

Global and regional patterns in education decision-making 252

Statistical tables

Aid tables

The Education For All Development Index

Introduction

The EFA goals represent more than the sum of their individual parts. While each is individually important, it is also useful to have a means of indicating achievement of EFA as a whole. The EFA Development Index (EDI), a composite of relevant indicators, provides one way of doing so. Ideally, it should reflect all six EFA goals but, due to data constraints, it currently focuses only on the four most easily quantifiable EFA goals: universal primary education (UPE), adult literacy, the quality of education and gender parity. The two goals not yet included in the EDI are goals 1 and 3. Neither has a quantitative target for 2015. Goal 1 (early childhood care and education) is multidimensional and covers both the care and education aspects. The indicators currently available on this goal cannot easily be incorporated in the EDI because national data are insufficiently standardized and reliable, and comparable data are not available for most countries (see Chapter 2 and *EFA Global Monitoring Report 2007)*. Goal 3 (learning needs of youth and adults) has not yet been sufficiently defined for quantitative measurement (see Chapter 2).

In accordance with the principle of considering each goal to be equally important, one indicator is used as a proxy measure for each of the four EDI components[1] and each component is assigned equal weight in the overall index. The EDI value for a particular country is thus the arithmetic mean of the observed values for each component. Since the components are all expressed as percentages, the EDI value can vary from 0 to 100% or, when expressed as a ratio, from 0 to 1. The closer a country's EDI value is to the maximum, the greater the extent of its overall EFA achievement and the nearer the country is to the EFA goal as a whole.

Choice of indicators as proxy measures of EDI components

In selecting indicators, relevance has to be balanced with data availability.

1. The EDI's gender component is itself a composite index.

Universal primary education

The UPE goal includes both universal access to and universal completion of primary education. However, while both access and participation at this level are relatively easy to measure, there is a lack of consensus on the definition of primary school completion. Therefore, the indicator selected to measure UPE achievement (goal 2) in the EDI is the total primary net enrolment ratio (NER), which reflects the percentage of primary school-age children who are enrolled in either primary or secondary school. Its value varies from 0 to 100%. A NER of 100% means all eligible children are enrolled in school in a given school year, even though some of them may not complete it. However, if the NER is at 100% for many consecutive years, it may imply that all children enrolled do complete school.

Adult literacy

The adult literacy rate is used as a proxy to measure progress towards the first part of goal 4.[2] This has its limitations. First, the adult literacy indicator, being a statement about the stock of human capital, is slow to change and thus it could be argued that it is not a good 'leading indicator' of year-by-year progress. Second, the existing data on literacy are not entirely satisfactory. Most of them are based on 'conventional' non-tested methods that usually overestimate the level of literacy among individuals.[3] New methodologies, based on tests and on the definition of literacy as a continuum of skills, are being developed and applied in some countries to improve the quality of literacy data. Providing a new data series of good quality for even a majority of countries will take many years, however. The literacy rates now used are the best currently available internationally.

2. The first part of goal 4 is: 'Achieving a 50 per cent improvement in levels of adult literacy by 2015, especially for women'. To enable progress towards this target to be monitored for all countries, whatever their current adult literacy level, it was decided as of the *EFA Global Monitoring Report 2006* to interpret it in terms of a reduction in the adult illiteracy rate.

3. In most countries, particularly developing countries, current literacy data are derived from methods of self-declaration or third-party reporting (e.g. a household head responding on behalf of other household members) used in censuses or household surveys. In other cases, particularly as regards developed countries, they are based on education attainment proxies as measured in labour force surveys. Neither method is based on any test, and both are subject to bias (overestimation of literacy), which affects the quality and accuracy of literacy data.

Quality of education

There is considerable debate about the concept of quality and how it should be measured. Several proxy indicators are generally used to measure quality of education, among them measures of students' learning outcomes, which are widely used for this purpose, particularly among countries at similar levels of development. However, measures of learning achievement are incomplete, as they are often limited to basic skills (reading, numeracy, science) and do not include values, capacities and other non-cognitive skills that are also important aims of education (UNESCO, 2004, pp. 43-4). They also tell nothing about the cognitive value added by schooling (as opposed to home background) or the distribution of ability among children enrolled in school.[4] Despite these drawbacks, learning outcomes would likely be the most appropriate single proxy for the average quality of education, but as comparable data are not yet available for a large number of countries, it is not yet possible to use them in the EDI.

Among the feasible proxy indicators available for a large number of countries, the survival rate to grade 5 seems to be the best available for the quality of education component of the EDI.[5] Figures 1, 2 and 3 show that there is a clear positive link between such survival rates and learning achievement across various regional and international assessments. The coefficient of correlation (R^2) between survival rates and learning outcomes in reading is 37% (Figure 1). Education systems capable of retaining a larger proportion of their pupils to grade 5 tend to perform better, on average, in student assessment tests. The survival rate to grade 5 is associated even more strongly with learning outcomes in mathematics (with a coefficient of 45%; Figure 2) and science (42%; Figure 3).

Another possible proxy indicator for quality is the pupil/teacher ratio (PTR). Among Latin American countries participating in the 2006 Segundo Estudio Regional Comparativo y Explicativo (SERCE) assessment, the association between this indicator and learning outcomes in mathematics is strong (45%), about the same as for the survival rate to grade 5. Many other studies, however, produce much more ambiguous evidence of the relationship between PTRs and learning outcomes (UNESCO, 2004). In a multivariate context, PTRs are associated with higher learning outcomes in some studies, but not in many others. In addition,

Figure 1: Survival rates to grade 5 and learning outcomes in reading at lower secondary level, 2006

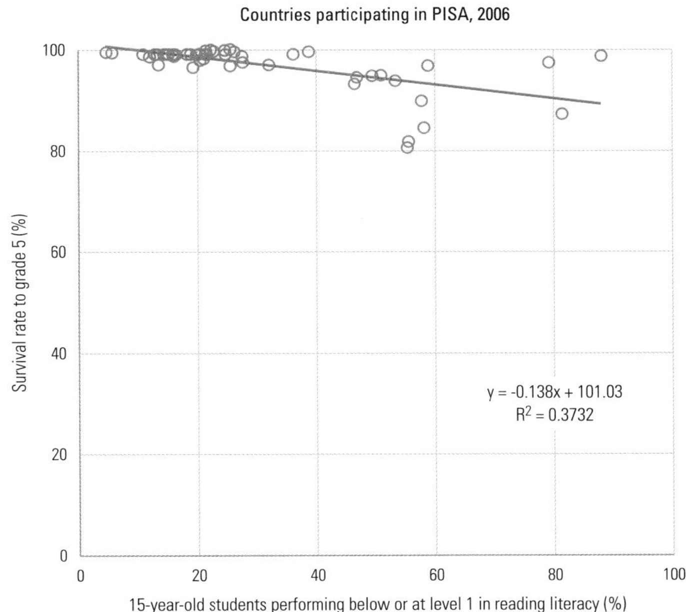

Sources: Annex, Statistical Table 7; OECD (2007*b*).

Figure 2: Survival rates to grade 5 and learning outcomes in mathematics at primary level, 2006

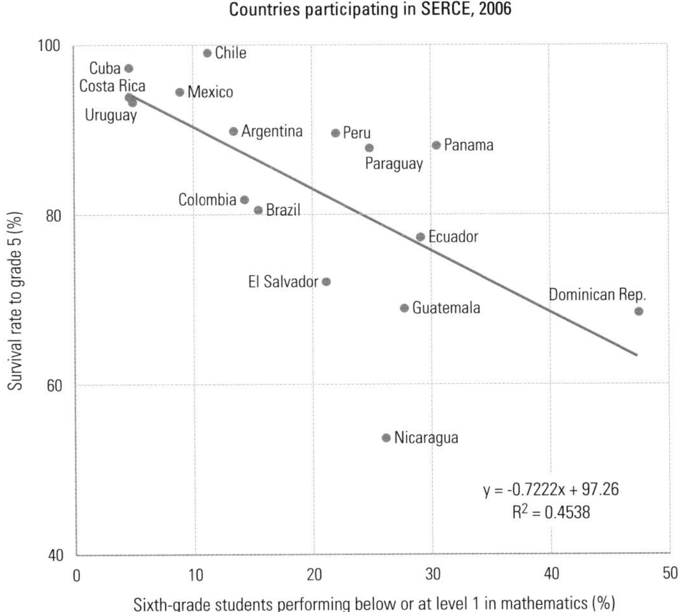

Sources: Annex, Statistical Table 7; UNESCO-OREALC (2008).

4. Strictly speaking, it would be necessary to compare average levels of cognitive achievement for pupils completing a given school grade across countries with similar levels and distributions of income, and with similar levels of NER, so as to account for home background and ability cohort effects.

5. See *EFA Global Monitoring Report 2003/4*, Appendix 2, for background.

Figure 3: Survival rates to grade 5 and learning outcomes in science at lower secondary level, 2006

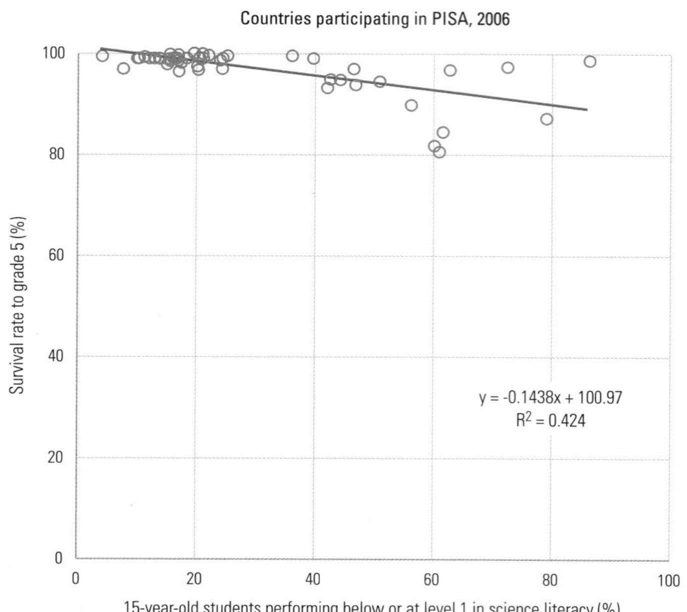

Sources: Annex, Statistical Table 7; OECD (2007*b*).

the relationship seems to vary by the level of mean test scores. For low levels of test scores, a decrease in the number of pupils per teacher has a positive impact on learning outcomes, but for higher levels of test scores, additional teachers, which leads to lower PTRs, have only limited impact. For these reasons, the survival rate is used as a safer proxy for learning outcomes and hence for the education quality component of the EDI.[6]

Gender

The fourth EDI component is measured by a composite index, the gender-specific EFA index (GEI). Ideally, the GEI should reflect the whole gender-related EFA goal, which calls for 'eliminating gender disparities in primary and secondary education by 2005, and achieving gender equality in education by 2015, with a focus on ensuring girls' full and equal access to and achievement in basic education of good quality'. There are thus two subgoals: gender parity (achieving equal participation of girls and boys in primary and secondary education) and gender equality (ensuring that educational equality exists between boys and girls).

The first subgoal is measured by the gender parity indexes (GPIs) of the gross enrolment ratios (GERs) at primary and secondary levels. Defining, measuring and monitoring gender equality in education is difficult, as it includes both quantitative and qualitative aspects (see Chapter 2; UNESCO, 2003). Essentially, measures of outcomes, which are also part of gender equality, are needed for a range of educational levels, disaggregated by sex. No such measures are available on an internationally comparable basis. As a step in that direction, however, the GEI includes the gender parity measure for adult literacy. Thus, the GEI is calculated as a simple average of three GPIs: for the GER in primary education, for the GER in secondary education and for the adult literacy rate. This means the GEI does not fully reflect the equality aspect of the EFA gender goal.

The GPI, when expressed as the ratio of female to male enrolment ratios or literacy rates, can exceed unity when more girls/women than boys/men are enrolled or literate. For the purposes of the GEI the standard F/M formula is inverted to M/F in cases where the GPI is higher than 1. This solves mathematically the problem of including the GEI in the EDI (where all components have a theoretical limit of 1, or 100%) while maintaining the GEI's ability to show gender disparity. Figure 4 shows how 'transformed' GPIs are arrived at to highlight gender disparities that disadvantage males. Once all three GPI values have been calculated, and converted into 'transformed' GPIs (from 0 to 1) where needed, the composite GEI is obtained by calculating a simple average of the three GPIs, with each being weighted equally.

Figure 5 illustrates the calculation for Uruguay, using data for the school year ending in 2006. The GPIs in primary education, secondary education and adult literacy were 0.973, 1.161 and 1.007, respectively, resulting in a GEI of 0.943.

GEI = 1/3 (primary GPI)
 + 1/3 (transformed secondary GPI)
 + 1/3 (transformed adult literacy GPI)
GEI = 1/3 (0.973) + 1/3 (0.862) + 1/3 (0.993) = 0.943

Calculating the EDI

The EDI is the arithmetic mean of its four components: total primary NER, adult literacy rate, GEI and survival rate to grade 5. As a simple average, the EDI may mask important variations among its components: for example, results for goals on which a country has made less progress can offset its advances on others. Since all the EFA goals are equally important, a synthetic indicator such as the EDI is thus very useful to inform the policy

6. Another reason is that survival rates, like the other EDI components, but unlike PTRs, range from 0% to 100%. Therefore, the use of the survival rate to grade 5 in the EDI avoids a need to rescale the data.

Figure 4: Calculating the 'transformed' GPI

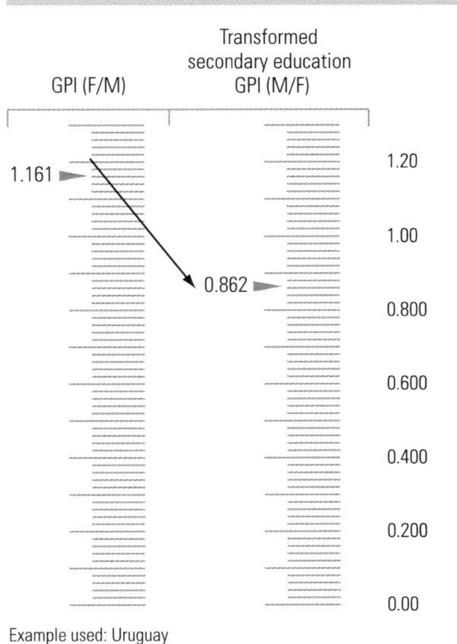

Example used: Uruguay

Figure 5: Calculating the GEI

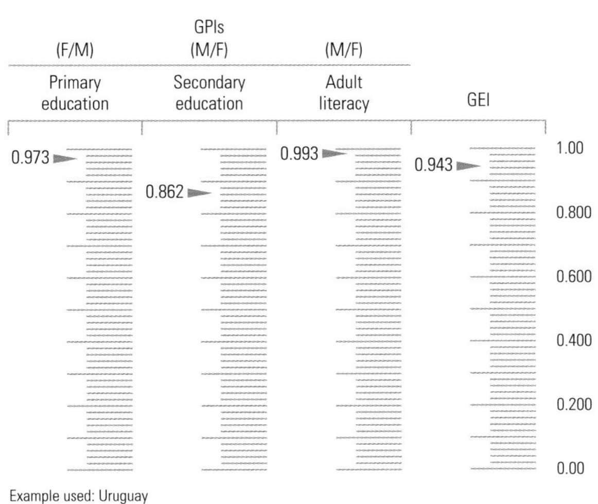

Example used: Uruguay

debate on the prominence of all the EFA goals and to highlight the synergy among them.

Figure 6 illustrates the calculation of the EDI, again using Uruguay as an example. The total primary NER, adult literacy rate and GEI are for 2006 while the survival rate to grade 5 is for 2005. Their values were 1.00, 0.978, 0.943 and 0.931, respectively, resulting in an EDI of 0.963.

EDI = 1/4 (total primary NER)
+ 1/4 (adult literacy rate)
+ 1/4 (GEI)
+ 1/4 (survival rate to grade 5)
EDI = 1/4 (1.00) + 1/4 (0.978) + 1/4 (0.943) + 1/4 (0.931)
= 0.963

Figure 6: Calculating the EDI

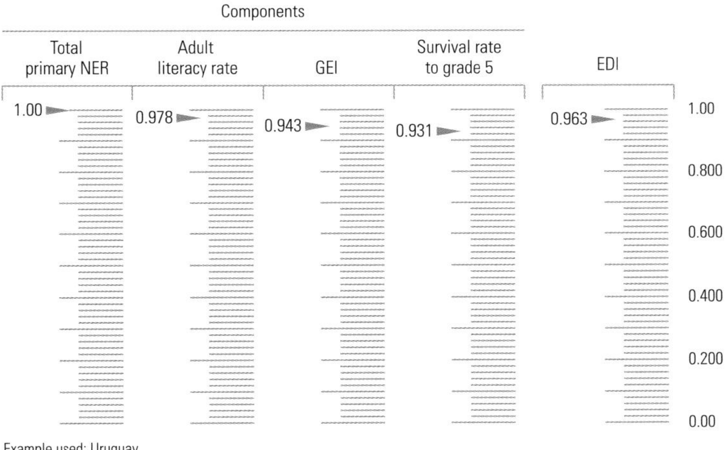

Example used: Uruguay

Data sources and country coverage

All data used to calculate the EDI for the school year ending in 2006 are from the statistical tables in this annex and the UNESCO Institute for Statistics (UIS) database, with one exception. Adult literacy data for some OECD countries that did not answer the annual UIS literacy survey are based on European Labour Force Survey data.

Only the 129 countries with a complete set of the indicators required to calculate the EDI are included in this analysis. Many countries thus are not included in the EDI, among them a number of fragile states and countries with weak education statistical systems. This fact, coupled with the exclusion of goal 1 and 3, means the EDI does not yet provide a fully comprehensive global overview of EFA achievement.

Table 1: The EFA Development Index (EDI) and its components, 2006

Ranking according to level of EDI	Countries/Territories	EDI	Total primary NER[1]	Adult literacy rate	Gender-specific EFA index (GEI)	Survival rate to grade 5
High EDI						
1	Kazakhstan	0.995	0.990	0.996	0.993	1.000
2	Japan[3]	0.994	0.998	0.992	0.998	0.990
3	Germany[2]	0.994	0.996	1.000	0.992	0.989
4	Norway[2]	0.994	0.981	1.000	0.996	0.999
5	United Kingdom[2]	0.993	0.996	0.998	0.989	0.990
6	Italy	0.992	0.994	0.988	0.991	0.995
7	Denmark[2]	0.992	0.986	1.000	0.991	0.990
8	France[2]	0.991	0.993	0.988	0.995	0.990
9	Luxembourg[2]	0.989	0.987	0.990	0.983	0.996
10	Croatia	0.989	0.989	0.986	0.983	0.997
11	New Zealand[3]	0.989	0.995	0.988	0.982	0.990
12	Iceland[2]	0.988	0.976	1.000	0.987	0.991
13	Slovenia	0.988	0.968	0.997	0.997	0.989
14	Finland[2]	0.987	0.970	1.000	0.985	0.994
15	Austria2	0.987	0.974	1.000	0.985	0.990
16	Cyprus[2]	0.987	0.995	0.976	0.985	0.991
17	Netherlands[2]	0.986	0.982	0.987	0.985	0.990
18	Spain	0.985	0.997	0.974	0.969	1.000
19	Sweden[2]	0.984	0.949	1.000	0.997	0.990
20	Republic of Korea[3]	0.984	0.985	0.991	0.967	0.993
21	Greece	0.984	0.997	0.970	0.982	0.986
22	Cuba	0.981	0.970	0.998	0.986	0.972
23	Aruba	0.981	0.995	0.981	0.980	0.967
24	Poland[2]	0.981	0.963	0.983	0.990	0.986
25	Estonia	0.980	0.969	0.998	0.985	0.969
26	Israel[2]	0.980	0.970	0.971	0.984	0.995
27	Belgium[2]	0.979	0.975	0.990	0.987	0.964
28	Hungary[2]	0.979	0.946	1.000	0.993	0.978
29	Czech Republic[2]	0.979	0.925	0.999	0.993	0.998
30	Switzerland[2]	0.976	0.935	1.000	0.980	0.990
31	TFYR Macedonia	0.976	0.972	0.968	0.981	0.982
32	Kyrgyzstan	0.976	0.935	0.993	0.990	0.986
33	Ireland[2]	0.976	0.949	0.994	0.975	0.985
34	Seychelles	0.974	0.995	0.918	0.991	0.990
35	Latvia	0.972	0.922	0.998	0.986	0.981
36	Brunei Darussalam	0.972	0.974	0.946	0.970	0.998
37	Tajikistan	0.971	0.973	0.996	0.927	0.987
38	Slovakia[2]	0.971	0.921	0.996	0.991	0.974
39	Lithuania	0.970	0.920	0.997	0.996	0.967
40	Georgia[3]	0.970	0.903	0.998	0.977	1.000
41	Belarus	0.969	0.899	0.997	0.987	0.992
42	Portugal	0.969	0.992	0.946	0.947	0.990
43	Armenia	0.967	0.907	0.995	0.974	0.994
44	Tonga	0.967	0.984	0.992	0.970	0.921
45	Malaysia	0.965	0.999	0.915	0.952	0.993
46	Romania	0.965	0.955	0.976	0.991	0.937
47	Uruguay	0.963	1.000	0.978	0.943	0.931
48	Bulgaria	0.963	0.938	0.983	0.981	0.948
49	Maldives	0.959	0.980	0.970	0.966	0.921
50	Bahrain	0.959	0.994	0.883	0.971	0.989
51	Argentina	0.956	0.991	0.976	0.961	0.897
52	United Arab Emirates	0.956	0.951	0.898	0.984	0.991
53	Mexico	0.956	0.994	0.917	0.969	0.944
54	Malta	0.955	0.935	0.914	0.980	0.990
55	Mongolia	0.952	0.972	0.974	0.954	0.909
56	Albania	0.952	0.936	0.990	0.981	0.899
Medium EDI						
57	Republic of Moldova	0.948	0.852	0.992	0.979	0.970
58	Azerbaijan	0.948	0.854	0.993	0.972	0.973
59	Macao, China	0.947	0.913	0.929	0.955	0.990
60	Mauritius	0.946	0.950	0.870	0.975	0.989
61	Barbados[3]	0.943	0.962	0.884	0.980	0.946
62	Jordan	0.943	0.937	0.927	0.960	0.947
63	Saint Lucia[2]	0.942	0.988	0.901	0.921	0.959
64	Trinidad and Tobago	0.941	0.894	0.986	0.974	0.910
65	Panama	0.941	0.991	0.932	0.960	0.880

Table 1 (continued)

Ranking according to level of EDI	Countries/Territories	EDI	Total primary NER[1]	Adult literacy rate	Gender-specific EFA index (GEI)	Survival rate to grade 5
Medium EDI						
66	Kuwait	0.935	0.885	0.933	0.966	0.958
67	Qatar	0.935	0.982	0.898	0.988	0.871
68	Paraguay	0.935	0.949	0.936	0.977	0.877
69	Venezuela, B. R.	0.934	0.932	0.930	0.954	0.920
70	Peru	0.931	0.990	0.887	0.951	0.895
71	Indonesia	0.925	0.984	0.910	0.963	0.844
72	Fiji[3]	0.921	0.942	0.929	0.953	0.860
73	Bahamas[3]	0.921	0.884	0.958	0.990	0.850
74	Ecuador	0.919	0.994	0.924	0.986	0.773
75	Bolivia	0.915	0.963	0.898	0.950	0.848
76	Belize[3]	0.913	0.991	0.769	0.970	0.922
77	Palestinian A. T.	0.913	0.798	0.924	0.949	0.981
78	Turkey	0.909	0.914	0.881	0.873	0.969
79	Colombia	0.905	0.920	0.923	0.962	0.817
80	Brazil	0.901	0.956	0.896	0.948	0.805
81	St Vincent/Grenad.[2]	0.901	0.925	0.881	0.917	0.880
82	Tunisia	0.900	0.974	0.769	0.891	0.967
83	South Africa	0.898	0.934	0.876	0.958	0.824
84	Myanmar	0.895	0.996	0.899	0.969	0.715
85	Algeria	0.888	0.977	0.746	0.880	0.952
86	Philippines	0.888	0.920	0.933	0.960	0.740
87	Lebanon[3]	0.887	0.830	0.883	0.924	0.909
88	Honduras	0.887	0.970	0.826	0.916	0.834
89	Oman	0.885	0.765	0.837	0.938	1.000
90	Cape Verde	0.883	0.884	0.830	0.898	0.919
91	Egypt	0.877	0.960	0.714	0.867	0.968
92	Botswana	0.867	0.841	0.821	0.980	0.825
93	El Salvador	0.867	0.957	0.836	0.954	0.721
94	Namibia	0.865	0.764	0.876	0.951	0.868
95	Sao Tome and Principe	0.857	0.977	0.875	0.935	0.641
96	Swaziland	0.847	0.785	0.796	0.966	0.841
97	Zambia	0.842	0.935	0.680	0.861	0.893
98	Dominican Republic	0.824	0.797	0.888	0.925	0.684
99	Guatemala	0.819	0.961	0.725	0.901	0.689
100	Kenya	0.816	0.762	0.736	0.937	0.829
Low EDI						
101	Nicaragua	0.799	0.914	0.801	0.946	0.537
102	India	0.794	0.961	0.652	0.834	0.730
103	Lesotho	0.788	0.727	0.822	0.866	0.737
104	Cambodia	0.778	0.899	0.756	0.833	0.622
105	Bhutan	0.777	0.799	0.543	0.833	0.932
106	Iraq	0.768	0.774	0.741	0.750	0.806
107	Burundi	0.757	0.748	0.593	0.808	0.879
108	Lao PDR	0.753	0.837	0.725	0.830	0.620
109	Bangladesh	0.753	0.921	0.525	0.914	0.651
110	Nepal	0.738	0.801	0.552	0.815	0.785
111	Madagascar	0.737	0.960	0.707	0.921	0.358
112	Malawi	0.735	0.918	0.709	0.870	0.442
113	Nigeria	0.725	0.650	0.710	0.815	0.726
114	Rwanda	0.712	0.841	0.649	0.898	0.458
115	Mauritania	0.695	0.799	0.552	0.856	0.574
116	Togo	0.686	0.827	0.532	0.641	0.746
117	Djibouti[3]	0.684	0.383	0.703	0.750	0.899
118	Pakistan	0.652	0.656	0.542	0.714	0.697
119	Senegal	0.643	0.722	0.420	0.779	0.650
120	Benin	0.643	0.822	0.397	0.637	0.715
121	Yemen	0.643	0.754	0.573	0.581	0.663
122	Mozambique	0.622	0.760	0.438	0.713	0.576
123	Eritrea[3]	0.621	0.475	0.576	0.695	0.737
124	Guinea	0.608	0.727	0.295	0.600	0.809
125	Ethiopia	0.598	0.723	0.359	0.667	0.644
126	Mali	0.570	0.605	0.229	0.633	0.812
127	Burkina Faso	0.538	0.478	0.260	0.688	0.725
128	Niger	0.470	0.441	0.298	0.575	0.565
129	Chad	0.408	0.604	0.257	0.440	0.332

Notes: Data in blue indicate that gender disparities are at the expense of boys or men, particularly at secondary level.

1. Total primary NER includes children of primary school age who are enrolled in either primary or secondary schools.
2. The adult literacy rate is a proxy measure based on educational attainment; that is, the proportion of the adult population with at least a complete primary education.
3. Adult literacy rates are unofficial UIS estimates.

Sources: Annex, Statistical Tables 2, 5, 7 and 8; UIS database; European Commission (2007*a*) for proxy literacy measure for European countries.

Table 2: Countries ranked according to value of EDI and components, 2006

Countries/ Territories	EDI	Total primary NER[1]	Adult literacy rate	Gender-specific EFA index (GEI)	Survival rate to grade 5
High EDI					
Kazakhstan	1	23	21	7	3
Japan[3]	2	7	1	10	33
Germany[2]	3	3	28	1	20
Norway[2]	4	33	1	4	5
United Kingdom[2]	5	8	14	19	20
Italy	6	15	34	12	11
Denmark[2]	7	27	1	13	20
France[2]	8	17	35	6	20
Luxembourg[2]	9	26	31	34	9
Croatia	10	24	37	35	8
New Zealand[3]	11	11	33	36	20
Iceland[2]	12	37	1	23	17
Slovenia	13	50	18	2	35
Finland[2]	14	47	1	27	12
Austria[2]	15	41	1	29	20
Cyprus[2]	16	10	45	31	19
Netherlands[2]	17	31	36	28	20
Spain	18	5	47	60	4
Sweden[2]	19	63	1	3	20
Republic of Korea[3]	20	28	29	61	15
Greece	21	4	49	37	39
Cuba	22	48	11	25	48
Aruba	23	9	41	44	53
Poland[2]	24	51	39	18	38
Estonia	25	49	12	30	51
Israel[2]	26	46	48	32	10
Belgium[2]	27	38	32	21	56
Hungary[2]	28	66	1	8	45
Czech Republic[2]	29	78	10	9	6
Switzerland[2]	30	73	1	42	20
TFYR Macedonia	31	44	51	38	42
Kyrgyzstan	32	72	25	16	40
Ireland[2]	33	65	23	50	41
Seychelles	34	12	66	11	20
Latvia	35	79	13	24	43
Brunei Darussalam	36	40	54	56	7
Tajikistan	37	42	20	89	37
Slovakia[2]	38	81	19	15	46
Lithuania	39	84	17	5	55
Georgia[3]	40	90	15	47	1
Belarus	41	92	16	22	16
Portugal	42	18	53	83	20
Armenia	43	89	22	52	13
Tonga	44	29	26	57	69
Malaysia	45	2	68	77	14
Romania	46	60	44	14	64
Uruguay	47	1	42	85	66
Bulgaria	48	68	40	40	60
Maldives	49	34	50	63	68
Bahrain	50	13	81	54	36
Argentina	51	19	43	67	77
United Arab Emirates	52	61	73	33	18
Mexico	53	14	67	59	63
Malta	54	71	69	41	20
Mongolia	55	43	46	74	73
Albania	56	70	30	39	75
Medium EDI					
Republic of Moldova	57	98	27	46	49
Azerbaijan	58	97	24	53	47
Macao, China	59	88	61	72	20
Mauritius	60	62	87	49	34
Barbados[3]	61	53	79	43	62
Jordan	62	69	62	69	61
Saint Lucia[2]	63	25	71	92	57
Trinidad and Tobago	64	93	38	51	72
Panama	65	21	58	68	80
Medium EDI					
Kuwait	66	94	57	64	58
Qatar	67	32	74	20	84
Paraguay	68	64	55	48	83
Venezuela, B. R.	69	76	59	75	70
Peru	70	22	78	79	78
Indonesia	71	30	70	65	89
Fiji[3]	72	67	60	76	86
Bahamas[3]	73	96	52	17	87
Ecuador	74	16	63	26	101
Bolivia	75	52	75	80	88
Belize[3]	76	20	96	55	67
Palestinian A. T.	77	108	64	81	44
Turkey	78	87	82	102	50
Colombia	79	83	65	66	95
Brazil	80	59	76	82	99
St Vincent/Grenad.[2]	81	77	83	94	81
Tunisia	82	39	97	100	54
South Africa	83	75	85	71	94
Myanmar	84	6	72	58	111
Algeria	85	35	99	101	59
Philippines	86	82	56	70	103
Lebanon[3]	87	102	80	91	74
Honduras	88	45	91	95	91
Oman	89	112	88	86	2
Cape Verde	90	95	90	99	71
Egypt	91	57	104	104	52
Botswana	92	100	93	45	93
El Salvador	93	58	89	73	109
Namibia	94	113	84	78	85
Sao Tome/Principe	95	36	86	88	119
Swaziland	96	110	95	62	90
Zambia	97	74	109	106	79
Dominican Republic	98	109	77	90	114
Guatemala	99	54	102	97	113
Kenya	100	114	101	87	92
Low EDI					
Nicaragua	101	86	94	84	125
India	102	55	110	108	106
Lesotho	103	119	92	105	104
Cambodia	104	91	98	110	120
Bhutan	105	106	117	109	65
Iraq	106	111	100	117	98
Burundi	107	117	112	114	82
Lao PDR	108	101	103	111	121
Bangladesh	109	80	120	96	116
Nepal	110	105	115	112	100
Madagascar	111	56	107	93	128
Malawi	112	85	106	103	127
Nigeria	113	123	105	113	107
Rwanda	114	99	111	98	126
Mauritania	115	107	116	107	123
Togo	116	103	119	123	102
Djibouti[3]	117	129	108	116	76
Pakistan	118	122	118	118	112
Senegal	119	121	122	115	117
Benin	120	104	123	124	110
Yemen	121	116	114	127	115
Mozambique	122	115	121	119	122
Eritrea[3]	123	127	113	120	105
Guinea	124	118	126	126	97
Ethiopia	125	120	124	122	118
Mali	126	124	129	125	96
Burkina Faso	127	126	127	121	108
Niger	128	128	125	128	124
Chad	129	125	128	129	129

Notes:

1. Total primary NER includes children of primary school age who are enrolled in either primary or secondary schools.
2. The adult literacy rate is a proxy measure based on educational attainment; that is, the proportion of the adult population with at least a complete primary education.
3. Adult literacy rates are unofficial UIS estimates.

Sources: Annex, Statistical Tables 2, 5, 7 and 8; UIS database; European Commission (2007*a*) for proxy literacy measure for European countries.

Table 3: Change in EDI and its components between 1999 and 2006

Countries/ Territories	EFA Development Index		Variation 1999–2006 (in relative terms)	Change in EDI components between 1999 and 2006 (% in relative terms)			
	1999	2006		Total primary NER[1]	Adult literacy rate	Gender-specific EFA index (GEI)	Survival rate to grade 5
Italy	0.984	0.992	0.8	-0.4	0.4	0.1	3.0
Croatia	0.970	0.989	2.0	7.6	0.5	0.2	0.0
Cyprus[2]	0.971	0.987	1.6	1.6	0.8	0.8	3.1
Cuba	0.974	0.981	0.8	-2.2	0.0	1.9	3.7
Aruba	0.974	0.981	0.8	1.6	0.8	0.7	-0.1
Estonia	0.991	0.980	-1.1	-3.0	0.0	1.0	-2.2
Hungary[2]	0.982	0.979	-0.3	-2.5	0.0	0.4	1.1
Kyrgyzstan	0.965	0.976	1.1	-0.8	0.6	0.5	4.3
Latvia	0.983	0.972	-1.1	-6.4	0.0	0.6	1.2
Lithuania	0.991	0.970	-2.1	-6.2	0.0	0.4	-2.6
Romania	0.978	0.965	-1.3	-4.4	0.3	0.9	-2.1
Bulgaria	0.971	0.963	-0.8	-5.1	0.1	-0.2	2.0
Bahrain	0.944	0.959	1.6	0.8	2.0	2.0	1.5
Argentina	0.963	0.956	-0.7	-0.6	0.4	-1.7	-0.6
United Arab Emirates	0.887	0.956	7.8	16.6	6.9	1.6	7.3
Mongolia	0.920	0.952	3.5	6.4	-0.4	4.1	4.2
Albania	0.960	0.952	-0.8	-0.9	0.3	-0.2	-2.7
Republic of Moldova	0.960	0.948	-1.2	-6.7	0.7	-0.8	1.7
Azerbaijan	0.951	0.948	-0.3	-0.1	0.6	-2.3	0.8
Mauritius	0.927	0.946	2.1	4.9	3.2	1.3	-0.6
Saint Lucia	0.922	0.942	2.2	1.6	0.0	0.7	6.5
Panama	0.942	0.941	-0.2	2.2	1.5	-0.2	-4.3
Paraguay	0.909	0.935	2.9	-1.7	1.5	1.0	12.3
Venezuela, B. R.	0.910	0.934	2.7	7.1	0.0	2.5	1.4
Fiji[3]	0.936	0.921	-1.6	-4.6	0.0	-0.1	-1.7
Ecuador	0.913	0.919	0.7	0.4	1.6	0.5	0.4
Bolivia	0.894	0.915	2.3	0.4	3.5	2.4	3.1
Belize	0.866	0.913	5.5	3.8	0.0	0.8	18.6
South Africa	0.855	0.898	5.0	-5.3	3.8	1.4	27.3
Namibia	0.864	0.865	0.1	4.1	3.0	0.1	-5.9
Swaziland	0.829	0.847	2.2	5.0	0.0	-0.6	5.2
Zambia	0.748	0.842	12.5	37.1	0.0	4.2	10.8
Dominican Republic	0.850	0.824	-3.1	-6.3	2.1	-0.2	-8.8
Guatemala	0.734	0.819	11.6	15.1	4.9	6.1	23.1
Nicaragua	0.749	0.799	6.7	14.2	4.4	0.2	10.8
Lesotho	0.742	0.788	6.2	26.0	0.0	4.6	-0.4
Iraq	0.744	0.768	3.2	-8.4	0.0	2.0	22.9
Bangladesh	0.725	0.753	3.7	6.7	10.5	0.0	0.2
Nepal	0.603	0.738	22.5	19.7	13.6	20.6	35.3
Malawi	0.731	0.735	0.5	-7.2	9.0	9.4	-9.6
Mauritania	0.666	0.695	4.5	24.3	7.8	3.3	-15.4
Yemen	0.585	0.643	9.9	34.0	24.3	32.0	-24.2
Mozambique	0.495	0.622	25.6	45.1	10.3	12.8	35.0
Ethiopia	0.454	0.598	31.7	107.9	35.1	4.4	14.0
Chad	0.426	0.408	-4.2	18.1	0.0	14.0	-39.7

Notes:

1. Total primary NER includes children of primary school age who are enrolled in either primary or secondary schools.
2. The adult literacy rate is a proxy measure based on educational attainment; that is, the proportion of the adult population with at least a complete primary education.
3. Adult literacy rates are unofficial UIS estimates.

Sources: Annex, Statistical Tables 2, 5, 7 and 8; UIS database; European Commission (2007*a*) for proxy literacy measure for European countries.

Global and regional patterns in education decision-making

Governance reforms in education involve the reallocation of decision-making authority across levels of government. These arrangements affect the roles of parents, teachers, civil servants and politicians at local and national levels. The issues at stake range from financing to school supervision, curriculum development, and teacher recruitment and management.

Decentralization has been a dominant theme in governance reforms. What does this mean in practice for the locus of decision-making? A mapping of 184 countries, described in the accompanying box, finds that some broad patterns in levels of decision-making are discernable, as Table 1 shows. One prominent finding is that, even in nominally decentralized structures, central government continues to play a key role in various areas of education service delivery – notably in designing curricula and instructional materials, in teacher governance and management, and in financing arrangements. Other actors – including local government, schools and communities – play a highly variable role. The following are among the findings to emerge:

- In most countries, the central government continues to take overall responsibility for curriculum development and the design of instructional materials. In two-thirds of countries in Central and Eastern Europe, and North America and Western Europe, the curriculum is jointly developed by schools and teachers based on a general framework established by the central government.

- The central government remains strong in many aspects of teacher governance and management, especially with regard to training standards, salary levels and conditions of service. Teacher training is organized and run by the central government in sixty-eight of the seventy-six countries with the relevant information.

- When teacher recruitment, appointment and deployment are not centralized, as in around half the cases covered, this administrative role is usually undertaken by a mix of provincial or municipal governments. In one-quarter of Latin America and Caribbean countries, decisions in this area are shared among various government levels. Generally, schools have little control over teacher management.

- With respect to infrastructure, school mapping and other decisions regarding the opening and closing of schools occur at all levels of government. The decisions may originate at one government level and the budget to implement them at another. In Croatia, Ethiopia, the Gambia, Latvia, Nepal and the Syrian Arab Republic, for example, the largest source of capital funds is the central government, while school infrastructure decisions are taken at municipal or provincial levels.

- School inspection and supervision occurs at either national or municipal level in most countries.

- The central government is the main source of funding for primary schools in more than three-quarters of the countries surveyed. Although financial responsibility in some countries is located at the level of provinces (7% of cases) or municipalities (13%), this does not preclude high levels of central government involvement. Municipalities are responsible for operating expenditure in one-third of the countries surveyed, mostly developed countries or countries in transition.

- Parental involvement in school governance and management tends to be limited in most countries to providing additional funding and, particularly in sub-Saharan Africa, supporting school construction.

While these broad patterns are informative, there is a need to understand in more detail how decisions are made, by whom and for what purpose, within a given context. Decisions are sometimes made at more than one level and patterns are not static – countries that have decentralized aspects of service delivery may later recentralize them. Of particular concern for this Report, as Chapter 3 highlights, is that the ways in which decisions are made within a particular context can significantly affect educational opportunities available to the poor.

Box 1: Mapping levels of decision-making in primary education

UNESCO's International Bureau of Education (UNESCO-IBE) has compiled data for 184 countries on governance, management and financing of formal education, focusing on who makes key decisions. The regional compilations of country reports, commissioned for this Report and available online (www.efareport.unesco.org), were used to develop a database of levels of decision-making and responsibility for primary education in six key areas:

- curriculum and learning materials;
- teacher training, management and employment conditions;
- school infrastructure;
- school supervision and inspection;
- financing arrangements;
- administration/management.

For each function, the database identifies the level at which decisions are made, including whether decision-making is shared by multiple levels. Five levels of decision-making authority are identified: central government; subnational government (state, province, region or governorate); local government (district, municipality or other locality); school boards or other school authorities; and non-state (including the private sector, non-government organizations, communities and aid donors). Table 1 presented in this Annex presents a summary of some indicators available in the database.

UNESCO-IBE compiled the information for the database from an array of sources, including its own 2006/2007 World Data on Education database and 2004 series of National Reports, as well as sources such as websites of ministries of education, World Bank public expenditure reviews, regional development bank reports and education reports by various international organizations.

Table 1: Levels of decision-making in primary education, by function and region, circa 2006/2007

	Central government	Subnational government[1]	Local government[2]	School[3]	Joint responsibility	Non-state[4]	Number of countries in the sample
Curriculum and learning materials							
Curriculum development/revision							
Arab States (20)	14	0	0	0	0	0	14
Central and Eastern Europe (20)	4	1	0	0	9	0	14
Central Asia (9)	3	1	0	0	2	0	6
East Asia and the Pacific (33)	11	2	0	0	2	0	15
Latin America and the Caribbean (41)	17	0	0	0	5	0	22
North America and Western Europe (26)	5	1	0	0	11	0	17
South and West Asia (9)	8	0	0	0	0	0	8
Sub-Saharan Africa (45)	28	1	0	0	0	0	29
Total	**90**	**6**	**0**	**0**	**29**	**0**	**125**
Development of instructional materials							
Arab States (20)	15	0	0	0	0	0	15
Central and Eastern Europe (20)	2	0	0	0	0	0	2
Central Asia (9)	5	0	0	0	0	0	5
East Asia and the Pacific (33)	7	0	1	0	0	0	8
Latin America and the Caribbean (41)	6	0	0	0	0	0	6
North America and Western Europe (26)	4	0	0	0	0	0	4
South and West Asia (9)	7	0	0	0	0	0	7
Sub-Saharan Africa (45)	15	0	0	0	0	0	15
Total	**61**	**0**	**1**	**0**	**0**	**0**	**62**

Table 1 (continued)

	Central government	Subnational government[1]	Local government[2]	School[3]	Joint responsibility	Non-state[4]	Number of countries in the sample
Teachers							
Teacher training							
Arab States (20)	7	0	0	0	0	0	7
Central and Eastern Europe (20)	7	0	0	0	0	0	7
Central Asia (9)	4	0	1	0	0	0	5
East Asia and the Pacific (33)	9	1	0	0	0	0	10
Latin America and the Caribbean (41)	17	0	0	0	2	0	19
North America and Western Europe (26)	3	2	0	0	0	0	5
South and West Asia (9)	5	0	0	0	0	0	5
Sub-Saharan Africa (45)	16	2	0	0	0	0	18
Total	**68**	**5**	**1**	**0**	**2**	**0**	**76**
In-service training							
Arab States (20)	9	0	0	0	0	0	9
Central and Eastern Europe (20)	6	0	0	0	1	0	7
Central Asia (9)	2	0	1	0	0	0	3
East Asia and the Pacific (33)	3	0	1	0	0	0	4
Latin America and the Caribbean (41)	7	1	0	1	0	0	9
North America and Western Europe (26)	4	2	1	0	1	0	8
South and West Asia (9)	2	0	0	0	0	0	2
Sub-Saharan Africa (45)	15	4	0	0	0	0	19
Total	**48**	**7**	**3**	**1**	**2**	**0**	**61**
Teacher management (recruitment, appointment, dismissal, deployment, promotion, transfer, discipline)							
Arab States (20)	0	3	0	0	0	0	3
Central and Eastern Europe (20)	0	0	0	1	0	0	1
Central Asia (9)	0	0	0	0	0	0	0
East Asia and the Pacific (33)	1	0	1	2	0	0	4
Latin America and the Caribbean (41)	10	1	1	0	4	0	16
North America and Western Europe (26)	2	2	4	0	0	0	8
South and West Asia (9)	2	0	1	0	0	0	3
Sub-Saharan Africa (45)	11	1	2	0	2	0	16
Total	**26**	**7**	**9**	**3**	**6**	**0**	**51**
Establishment of teacher salary levels and other conditions of service (allowances, vacations, promotions)							
Arab States (20)	3	0	0	0	0	0	3
Central and Eastern Europe (20)	4	0	0	0	2	0	6
Central Asia (9)	0	0	0	0	1	0	1
East Asia and the Pacific (33)	1	1	0	0	0	0	2
Latin America and the Caribbean (41)	12	0	1	0	0	0	13
North America and Western Europe (26)	6	2	0	0	0	0	8
South and West Asia (9)	1	1	0	0	0	0	2
Sub-Saharan Africa (45)	9	0	0	0	0	0	9
Total	**36**	**4**	**1**	**0**	**3**	**0**	**44**

	Central government	Subnational government[1]	Local government[2]	School[3]	Joint responsibility	Non-state[4]	Number of countries in the sample
Infrastructure							
Establishment/opening and closure of schools, school mapping							
Arab States (20)	5	2	2	0	0	0	9
Central and Eastern Europe (20)	0	0	7	0	0	0	7
Central Asia (9)	0	0	2	0	0	0	2
East Asia and the Pacific (33)	1	0	2	0	0	0	3
Latin America and the Caribbean (41)	4	1	5	0	0	0	10
North America and Western Europe (26)	0	2	7	0	0	0	9
South and West Asia (9)	0	0	1	0	0	0	1
Sub-Saharan Africa (45)	3	2	3	0	0	0	8
Total	**13**	**7**	**29**	**0**	**0**	**0**	**49**

Table 1 (continued)

	Central government	Subnational government[1]	Local government[2]	School[3]	Joint responsibility	Non-state[4]	Number of countries in the sample
Supervision							
School supervision/inspection practices							
Arab States (20)	2	1	6	0	0	0	9
Central and Eastern Europe (20)	5	0	5	0	0	0	10
Central Asia (9)	0	0	0	0	0	0	0
East Asia and the Pacific (33)	2	0	2	0	0	0	4
Latin America and the Caribbean (41)	11	0	2	0	0	0	13
North America and Western Europe (26)	3	1	3	0	0	0	7
South and West Asia (9)	0	1	1	0	0	0	2
Sub-Saharan Africa (45)	9	2	8	0	1	0	20
Total	**32**	**5**	**27**	**0**	**1**	**0**	**65**

	Central government	Subnational government[1]	Local government[2]	School[3]	Joint responsibility	Non-state[4]	Number of countries in the sample
Financing arrangements[5]							
General							
Arab States (20)	15	0	0	0	0	0	15
Central and Eastern Europe (20)	9	1	6	0	0	0	16
Central Asia (9)	2	0	6	0	0	0	8
East Asia and the Pacific (33)	14	2	0	0	0	1	17
Latin America and the Caribbean (41)	20	1	0	0	1	0	22
North America and Western Europe (26)	11	4	4	0	0	0	19
South and West Asia (9)	4	1	0	0	0	0	5
Sub-Saharan Africa (45)	24	0	0	0	0	0	24
Total	**99**	**9**	**16**	**0**	**1**	**1**	**126**
Capital expenditure							
Arab States (20)	6	0	1	0	0	0	7
Central and Eastern Europe (20)	2	0	3	0	0	0	5
Central Asia (9)	0	0	0	0	0	0	0
East Asia and the Pacific (33)	1	0	2	3	0	1	7
Latin America and the Caribbean (41)	6	0	0	0	2	0	8
North America and Western Europe (26)	2	0	8	0	0	0	10
South and West Asia (9)	2	1	0	0	0	1	4
Sub-Saharan Africa (45)	6	0	0	0	0	5	11
Total	**25**	**1**	**14**	**3**	**2**	**7**	**52**
Personnel expenditure							
Arab States (20)	5	0	0	0	0	0	5
Central and Eastern Europe (20)	8	0	1	0	0	0	9
Central Asia (9)	0	0	0	0	0	0	0
East Asia and the Pacific (33)	4	1	0	0	0	0	5
Latin America and the Caribbean (41)	16	1	0	0	0	0	17
North America and Western Europe (26)	6	4	1	1	0	0	12
South and West Asia (9)	3	1	0	0	0	0	4
Sub-Saharan Africa (45)	22	0	1	0	0	0	23
Total	**64**	**7**	**3**	**1**	**0**	**0**	**75**
Current or operating expenditure							
Arab States (20)	5	0	1	0	0	0	6
Central and Eastern Europe (20)	1	0	8	0	0	0	9
Central Asia (9)	0	0	0	0	0	0	0
East Asia and the Pacific (33)	1	0	1	3	0	0	5
Latin America and the Caribbean (41)	10	0	1	0	0	0	11
North America and Western Europe (26)	2	0	6	1	0	0	9
South and West Asia (9)	0	1	0	0	0	0	1
Sub-Saharan Africa (45)	10	0	0	0	0	2	12
Total	**29**	**1**	**17**	**4**	**0**	**2**	**53**

Note: Figures in parenthesis following the names of the regions refer to the number of countries in the EFA regions described in the Introduction to the Statistical Tables.

1. State, province, region or governorate.
2. District, municipality, local or zoning area.
3. School authorities or school boards.
4. Private sector, non-government organizations, communities, aid donors and other non-state entities.
5. Indicates the level providing the largest share of funding.

Sources: UNESCO-IBE (2008*a*, 2008*b*, 2008*c*, 2008*d*, 2008*e*, 2008*f*, 2008*g*, 2008*h*).

Statistical tables*

Introduction

The most recent data on pupils, students, teachers and expenditure presented in these statistical tables are for the school year ending in 2006.[1] They are based on survey results reported to and processed by the UNESCO Institute for Statistics (UIS) before the end of May 2008. Data received and processed after this date will be used in the next *EFA Global Monitoring Report*. A small number of countries[2] submitted data for the school year ending in 2007, presented in bold in the statistical tables.

These statistics refer to all formal schools, both public and private, by level of education. They are supplemented by demographic and economic statistics collected or produced by other international organizations, including the United Nations Development Programme (UNDP), the United Nations Children's Fund (UNICEF), the United Nations Population Division (UNPD) and the World Bank.

A total of 204 countries and territories are listed in the statistical tables.[3] Most of them report their data to the UIS using standard questionnaires issued by the Institute. For some countries, however, education data are collected via surveys carried out under the auspices of the World Education Indicators (WEI) or are provided by the Organisation for Economic Co-operation and Development (OECD) and the Statistical Office of the European Communities (Eurostat).

Population

The indicators on school access and participation in the statistical tables were calculated using the 2006 revision of population estimates produced by the UNPD. Because of possible differences between national population estimates and those of the United Nations, these indicators may differ from those published by individual countries or by other organizations.[4] The UNPD does not provide data by single year of age for countries with a total population of fewer than 80,000. Where no UNPD estimates exist, national population figures, when available, or estimates from the UIS were used to calculate enrolment ratios.

ISCED classification

Education data reported to the UIS are in conformity with the 1997 revision of the International Standard Classification of Education (ISCED). In some cases, data have been adjusted to comply with the ISCED97 classification. Data for the school year ending in 1991 may conform to the previous version of the classification, ISCED76, and therefore may not be comparable in some countries with those for years after 1997. ISCED is used to harmonize data and introduce more international comparability among national education systems. Countries may have their own definitions of education levels that do not correspond to ISCED. Some differences between nationally and internationally reported enrolment ratios may be due, therefore, to the use of these nationally defined education levels rather than the ISCED standard, in addition to the population issue raised above.

Adult participation in basic education

ISCED does not classify education programmes by participants' age. For example, any programme with a content equivalent to primary education, or ISCED 1, may be classed as ISCED 1 even if provided to adults. The guidance the UIS provides for respondents to its regular annual education survey, on the other hand, asks countries to exclude 'data on programmes designed for people beyond regular school age'. As for the guidance for the UIS/OECD/Eurostat (UOE) and WEI questionnaires, until 2005 it stated that 'activities classified as "continuing", "adult" or "non-formal" education should be included' if they 'involve studies with subject content similar to regular educational programmes' or if 'the underlying

1. This means 2005/2006 for countries with a school year that overlaps two calendar years and 2006 for those with a calendar school year.

2. Egypt, Ethiopia, Ghana, Kazakhstan, the Marshall Islands, the Federated States of Micronesia, Nauru, the Republic of Korea, Saint Kitts and Nevis, Saint Vincent and the Grenadines, Sao Tome and Principe, Serbia, Seychelles, Sierra Leone, the United Republic of Tanzania, Uzbekistan and Vanuatu.

3. Serbia and Montenegro are now presented separately as two independent entities.

4. Where obvious inconsistencies exist between enrolment reported by countries and the United Nations population data, the UIS may decide to not calculate or publish the enrolment ratios. This is the case, for example, with China, publication of whose NER is suspended pending further review of the population data.

* For more detailed statistics and indicators, please consult the website: www.efareport.unesco.org

programmes lead to similar potential qualifications' as do the regular programmes. Since 2005, however, the countries involved in the UOE/WEI survey have been requested to report data for such programmes separately so that the UIS can exclude them when calculating internationally comparable indicators. Despite the UIS instructions, data from countries in the annual survey may still include pupils who are substantially above the official age for basic education.

Literacy data

UNESCO has long defined literacy as the ability to read and write, with understanding, a short simple statement related to one's daily life. However, a parallel definition arose with the introduction in 1978 of the notion of functional literacy. A definition approved in the UNESCO General Conference that year stated that a person was considered functionally literate who could engage in all activities in which literacy is required for effective functioning of his or her group and community, and also for enabling him or her to continue to use reading, writing and calculation for his or her own and the community's development.

In many cases, the current UIS literacy statistics rely on the first definition and are largely based on data sources that use a 'self-declaration' method: respondents are asked whether they and the members of their household are literate, as opposed to being asked a more comprehensive question or to demonstrate the skill. Some countries assume that persons who complete a certain level of education are literate.[5] As definitions and methodologies used for data collection differ by country, data need to be used with caution.

Literacy data in this report cover adults aged 15 and over as well as youth aged 15 to 24. They refer to two periods, 1985–1994 and 2000–2006. Data for the first period are mostly based on observed information obtained from national censuses and surveys taken during that period. For the second period, most of the literacy data in the table are UIS estimates. They refer to 2006 and are based on the most recent observed national data. For countries indicated with an asterisk (*), for which estimates could not be made, national observed literacy data are used. The reference years and literacy definitions for each country are presented in a longer version of this introduction, posted on the *EFA Global Monitoring Report* website. Both UIS estimates and projections to 2015 presented in the literacy statistical table are produced using the Global Age-specific Literacy Projections Model. For a description of the projection methodology, see p. 261 of the *EFA Global Monitoring Report 2006*, as well as *Global Age-specific Literacy Projections Model (GALP): Rationale, Methodology and Software*, available at www.uis.unesco.org/TEMPLATE/pdf/Literacy/GALP.pdf.

5. For reliability and consistency reasons, the UIS has decided no longer to publish literacy data based on educational attainment proxies. Only data reported by countries based on the 'self-declaration method' and 'household declaration' are included in the statistical tables. However, in the absence of such data, educational attainment proxies are used to calculate the EDI for some countries, particularly developed ones.

In many countries, interest in assessing the literacy skills of the population is growing. In response to this interest, the UIS has developed a methodology and data collection instrument called the Literacy Assessment and Monitoring Programme (LAMP). Following the example of the International Adult Literacy Survey (IALS), LAMP is based on the actual, functional assessment of literacy skills. It aims to provide literacy data of higher quality and is based on the concept of a continuum of literacy skills rather than the common literate/illiterate dichotomy.

Estimates and missing data

Both actual and estimated education data are presented throughout the statistical tables. When data are not reported to the UIS using the standard questionnaires, estimates are often necessary. Wherever possible, the UIS encourages countries to make their own estimates, which are presented as national estimates. Where this does not happen, the UIS may make its own estimates if sufficient supplementary information is available. Gaps in the tables may also arise where data submitted by a country are found to be inconsistent. The UIS makes every attempt to resolve such problems with the countries concerned, but reserves the final decision to omit data it regards as problematic.

To fill the gaps in the statistical tables, data for previous school years were included when information for the school year ending in 2006 was not available. Such cases are indicated by a footnote.

Data processing timetable

The timetable for collection and publication of data used in this report was as follows.

- June 2006 (or December 2006 for some countries with a calendar school year): the final school year in the data collection period ended.
- November 2006 and June 2007: questionnaires were sent to countries whose data are collected directly either by the UIS or through the WEI and UOE questionnaires, with data submission deadlines of 31 March 2007, 1 August 2007 and 30 September 2007, respectively.

- June 2007: after sending reminders by e-mail, fax, phone and/or post, the UIS began to process data and calculate indicators.
- September 2007: estimation was done for missing data.
- October 2007: provisional statistical tables were produced and draft indicators sent to member states for their review.
- End February 2008: the first draft of statistical tables was produced for the *EFA Global Monitoring Report*.
- April 2008: the final statistical tables were sent to the Report team.

Regional averages

Regional figures for literacy rates, gross intake rates, gross and net enrolment ratios, school life expectancy and pupil/teacher ratios are weighted averages, taking into account the relative size of the relevant population of each country in each region. The averages are derived from both published data and broad estimates for countries for which no reliable publishable data are available.

The figures for the countries with larger populations thus have a proportionately greater influence on the regional aggregates. Where not enough reliable data are available to produce an overall weighted mean, a median figure is calculated for countries with available data only.

Capped figures

There are cases where an indicator theoretically should not exceed 100 (the NER, for example), but data inconsistencies may have resulted nonetheless in the indicator exceeding the theoretical limit. In these cases the indicator is 'capped' at 100 but the gender balance is maintained: the higher value, whether for male or female, is set equal to 100 and the other two values – the lower of male or female plus the figure for both sexes – are then recalculated so that the gender parity index for the capped figures is the same as that for the uncapped figures.

Footnotes to the tables, along with the glossary following the statistical tables, provide additional help in interpreting the data and information.

Symbols used in the statistical tables (printed and web versions)

* National estimate

** UIS estimate

... Missing data

– Magnitude nil or negligible

. Category not applicable

./. Data included under another category

Composition of regions

World classification[6]

- Countries in transition (12):
  Countries of the Commonwealth of Independent States, including 4 in Central and Eastern Europe (Belarus, Republic of Moldova, Russian Federation[w], Ukraine) and the countries of Central Asia minus Mongolia.

- Developed countries (44):
  North America and Western Europe (minus Cyprus[o] and Israel[o]); Central and Eastern Europe (minus Belarus, the Republic of Moldova, the Russian Federation[w], Turkey[o] and Ukraine); Australia[o], Bermuda, Japan[o] and New Zealand[o].

- Developing countries (148):
  Arab States; East Asia and the Pacific (minus Australia[o], Japan[o] and New Zealand[o]); Latin America and the Caribbean (minus Bermuda); South and West Asia; sub-Saharan Africa; Cyprus[o], Israel[o], Mongolia and Turkey[o].

EFA regions

- Arab States (20 countries/territories)
  Algeria, Bahrain, Djibouti, Egypt[w], Iraq, Jordan[w], Kuwait, Lebanon, Libyan Arab Jamahiriya, Mauritania, Morocco, Oman, Palestinian Autonomous Territories, Qatar, Saudi Arabia, Sudan, Syrian Arab Republic, Tunisia[w], United Arab Emirates and Yemen.

- Central and Eastern Europe (21 countries)
  Albania[o], Belarus, Bosnia and Herzegovina[o], Bulgaria[o], Croatia, Czech Republic[o], Estonia[o], Hungary[o], Latvia[o], Lithuania[o], Montenegro, Poland[o], Republic of Moldova, Romania[o], Russian Federation[w], Serbia, Slovakia, Slovenia[o], The former Yugoslav Republic of Macedonia[o], Turkey[o] and Ukraine.

6. This is a United Nations Statistical Division country classification revised in 2004.

- Central Asia (9 countries)
Armenia, Azerbaijan, Georgia, Kazakhstan, Kyrgyzstan, Mongolia, Tajikistan, Turkmenistan and Uzbekistan.

- East Asia and the Pacific (33 countries/ territories)
Australia[o], Brunei Darussalam, Cambodia, China[w], Cook Islands, Democratic People's Republic of Korea, Fiji, Indonesia[w], Japan[o], Kiribati, Lao People's Democratic Republic, Macao (China), Malaysia[w], Marshall Islands, Micronesia (Federated States of), Myanmar, Nauru, New Zealand[o], Niue, Palau, Papua New Guinea, Philippines[w], Republic of Korea[o], Samoa, Singapore, Solomon Islands, Thailand[w], Timor-Leste, Tokelau, Tonga, Tuvalu, Vanuatu and Viet Nam.

- East Asia (16 countries/territories)
Brunei Darussalam, Cambodia, China[w], Democratic People's Republic of Korea, Indonesia[w], Japan[o], Lao People's Democratic Republic, Macao (China), Malaysia[w], Myanmar, Philippines[w], Republic of Korea[o], Singapore, Thailand[w], Timor-Leste and Viet Nam.

- Pacific (17 countries/territories)
Australia[o], Cook Islands, Fiji, Kiribati, Marshall Islands, Micronesia (Federated States of), Nauru, New Zealand[o], Niue, Palau, Papua New Guinea, Samoa, Solomon Islands, Tokelau, Tonga, Tuvalu and Vanuatu.

- Latin America and the Caribbean (41 countries/territories)
Anguilla, Antigua and Barbuda, Argentina[w], Aruba, Bahamas, Barbados, Belize, Bermuda, Bolivia, Brazil[w], British Virgin Islands, Cayman Islands, Chile[w], Colombia, Costa Rica, Cuba, Dominica, Dominican Republic, Ecuador, El Salvador, Grenada, Guatemala, Guyana, Haiti, Honduras, Jamaica[w], Mexico[o], Montserrat, Netherlands Antilles, Nicaragua, Panama, Paraguay[w], Peru[w], Saint Kitts and Nevis, Saint Lucia, Saint Vincent and the Grenadines, Suriname, Trinidad and Tobago, Turks and Caicos Islands, Uruguay[w] and the Bolivarian Republic of Venezuela.

- Caribbean (22 countries/territories)
Anguilla, Antigua and Barbuda, Aruba, Bahamas, Barbados, Belize, Bermuda, British Virgin Islands, Cayman Islands, Dominica, Grenada, Guyana, Haiti, Jamaica[w], Montserrat, Netherlands Antilles, Saint Kitts and Nevis, Saint Lucia, Saint Vincent and the Grenadines, Suriname, Trinidad and Tobago, and Turks and Caicos Islands.

- Latin America (19 countries)
Argentina[w], Bolivia, Brazil[w], Chile[w], Colombia, Costa Rica, Cuba, Dominican Republic, Ecuador, El Salvador, Guatemala, Honduras, Mexico[o], Nicaragua, Panama, Paraguay[w], Peru[w], Uruguay[w] and the Bolivarian Republic of Venezuela.

- North America and Western Europe (26 countries/territories)
Andorra, Austria[o], Belgium[o], Canada[o], Cyprus[o], Denmark[o], Finland[o], France[o], Germany[o], Greece[o], Iceland[o], Ireland[o], Israel[o], Italy[o], Luxembourg[o], Malta[o], Monaco, Netherlands[o], Norway[o], Portugal[o], San Marino, Spain[o], Sweden[o], Switzerland[o], United Kingdom[o] and United States[o].

- South and West Asia (9 countries)
Afghanistan, Bangladesh, Bhutan, India[w], Islamic Republic of Iran, Maldives, Nepal, Pakistan and Sri Lanka[w].

- Sub-Saharan Africa (45 countries)
Angola, Benin, Botswana, Burkina Faso, Burundi, Cameroon, Cape Verde, Central African Republic, Chad, Comoros, Congo, Côte d'Ivoire, Democratic Republic of the Congo, Equatorial Guinea, Eritrea, Ethiopia, Gabon, Gambia, Ghana, Guinea, Guinea-Bissau, Kenya, Lesotho, Liberia, Madagascar, Malawi, Mali, Mauritius, Mozambique, Namibia, Niger, Nigeria, Rwanda, Sao Tome and Principe, Senegal, Seychelles, Sierra Leone, Somalia, South Africa, Swaziland, Togo, Uganda, United Republic of Tanzania, Zambia and Zimbabwe[w].

o Countries whose education data are collected through UOE questionnaires

w WEI project countries

- Least developed countries (50 countries)[7]
Afghanistan, Angola, Bangladesh, Benin, Bhutan, Burkina Faso, Burundi, Cambodia, Cape Verde, Central African Republic, Chad, Comoros, Democratic Republic of the Congo, Djibouti, Equatorial Guinea, Eritrea, Ethiopia, Gambia, Guinea, Guinea-Bissau, Haiti, Kiribati, Lao People's Democratic Republic, Lesotho, Liberia, Madagascar, Malawi, Maldives, Mali, Mauritania, Mozambique, Myanmar, Nepal, Niger, Rwanda, Samoa, Sao Tome and Principe, Senegal, Sierra Leone, Solomon Islands, Somalia, Sudan, Timor-Leste, Togo, Tuvalu, Uganda, United Republic of Tanzania, Vanuatu, Yemen and Zambia.

7. Fifty countries are currently designated by the United Nations as 'least developed countries' (LDCs). The list of LDCs is reviewed every three years by the Economic and Social Council of the United Nations, in the light of recommendations made by the Committee for Development Policy. The LDCs grouping is not presented in the statistical tables but is discussed in the main text.

Table 1
Background statistics

Country or territory	DEMOGRAPHY[1]							HIV/AIDS[2]		
	Total population (000)	Average annual growth rate (%) total population	Average annual growth rate (%) age 0-4 population	Life expectancy at birth (years)			Total fertility rate (children per woman)	HIV prevalence rate (%) in adults (15-49)	% of women among people (age 15+) living with HIV	Orphans due to AIDS (000)
	2006	2005-2010	2005-2010	2005-2010			2005-2010	2007	2007	2007
				Total	Male	Female		Total		
Arab States										
Algeria	33 351	1.5	1.7	72	71	74	2.4	0.1	29	…
Bahrain	739	1.8	-0.4	76	74	77	2.3	…	…	…
Djibouti	819	1.7	0.3	55	54	56	3.9	3.1	58	5
Egypt	74 166	1.8	0.9	71	69	74	2.9	…	29	…
Iraq	28 506	1.8	0.0	60	58	61	4.3	…	…	…
Jordan	5 729	3.0	1.6	73	71	74	3.1	…	…	…
Kuwait	2 779	2.4	2.3	78	76	80	2.2	…	…	…
Lebanon	4 055	1.1	0.0	72	70	74	2.2	0.1	<33	…
Libyan Arab Jamahiriya	6 039	2.0	1.5	74	72	77	2.7	…	…	…
Mauritania	3 044	2.5	1.2	64	62	66	4.4	0.8	28	3
Morocco	30 853	1.2	1.0	71	69	73	2.4	0.1	28	…
Oman	2 546	2.0	1.2	76	74	77	3.0	…	…	…
Palestinian A. T.	3 889	3.2	1.7	73	72	75	5.1	…	…	…
Qatar	821	2.1	1.6	76	75	76	2.7	…	…	…
Saudi Arabia	24 175	2.2	1.4	73	71	75	3.4	…	…	…
Sudan	37 707	2.2	0.8	59	57	60	4.2	1.4	59	…
Syrian Arab Republic	19 408	2.5	1.6	74	72	76	3.1	…	…	…
Tunisia	10 215	1.1	0.8	74	72	76	1.9	0.1	28	…
United Arab Emirates	4 248	2.8	3.4	79	77	81	2.3	…	…	…
Yemen	21 732	3.0	2.7	63	61	64	5.5	…	…	…
Central and Eastern Europe										
Albania	3 172	0.6	0.0	76	73	80	2.1	…	…	…
Belarus	9 742	-0.6	-0.3	69	63	75	1.2	0.2	30	…
Bosnia and Herzegovina	3 926	0.1	-3.1	75	72	77	1.2	<0.1	…	…
Bulgaria	7 693	-0.7	-0.4	73	69	77	1.3	…	…	…
Croatia	4 556	-0.1	-0.2	76	72	79	1.3	<0.1	…	…
Czech Republic	10 189	0.0	0.4	76	73	80	1.2	…	<33	…
Estonia	1 340	-0.3	1.7	71	66	77	1.5	1.3	24	…
Hungary	10 058	-0.3	-0.7	73	69	77	1.3	0.1	<30	…
Latvia	2 289	-0.5	0.8	73	67	78	1.3	0.8	27	…
Lithuania	3 408	-0.5	-0.2	73	67	78	1.3	0.1	<45	…
Montenegro	601	-0.3	0.5	75	72	77	1.8	…	…	…
Poland	38 140	-0.2	0.2	76	71	80	1.2	0.1	29	…
Republic of Moldova	3 833	-0.9	-0.8	69	65	72	1.4	0.4	30	…
Romania	21 532	-0.4	-0.8	72	69	76	1.3	0.1	50	…
Russian Federation	143 221	-0.5	1.1	65	59	73	1.3	1.1	26	…
Serbia	9 851	0.1	0.8	74	72	76	1.8	0.1	28	…
Slovakia	5 388	0.0	0.6	75	71	79	1.3	<0.1	…	…
Slovenia	2 001	0.0	0.2	78	74	82	1.3	<0.1	…	…
TFYR Macedonia	2 036	0.1	-1.7	74	72	77	1.4	<0.1	…	…
Turkey	73 922	1.3	0.3	72	69	74	2.1	…	…	…
Ukraine	46 557	-0.8	1.0	68	62	74	1.2	1.6	44	…
Central Asia										
Armenia	3 010	-0.2	2.1	72	68	75	1.4	0.1	<42	…
Azerbaijan	8 406	0.8	3.3	67	64	71	1.8	0.2	17	…
Georgia	4 433	-0.8	-1.5	71	67	75	1.4	0.1	<37	…
Kazakhstan	15 314	0.7	4.2	67	62	72	2.3	0.1	28	…
Kyrgyzstan	5 259	1.1	1.9	66	62	70	2.5	0.1	26	…
Mongolia	2 605	1.0	-0.2	67	64	70	1.9	0.1	<20	…
Tajikistan	6 640	1.5	0.1	67	64	69	3.3	0.3	21	…
Turkmenistan	4 899	1.3	0.5	63	59	68	2.5	<0.1	…	…
Uzbekistan	26 981	1.4	0.6	67	64	70	2.5	0.1	29	…
East Asia and the Pacific										
Australia	20 530	1.0	0.5	81	79	84	1.8	0.2	7	…
Brunei Darussalam	382	2.1	0.3	77	75	80	2.3	…	…	…
Cambodia	14 197	1.7	1.2	60	57	62	3.2	0.8	29	…
China	1 320 864	0.6	-0.1	73	71	75	1.7	0.1	29	…

GNP, AID AND POVERTY							INEQUALITY IN INCOME OR EXPENDITURE[4]				
GNP per capita[3]				Net aid per capita (US$)[4]	Population living on less than US$1 per day[4] (%)	Population living on less than US$2 per day[4] (%)	Share of income or expenditure %		Inequality measure		
Current US$		PPP US$					Poorest 20%	Richest 20%	Richest 20% to poorest 20%[6]	Gini index[7]	
1998	2006	1998	2006	2005	1990-2005[5]	1990-2005[5]	1992-2005[5]	1992-2005[5]	1992-2005[5]	1992-2005[5]	**Country or territory**
											Arab States
1 570	3 030	4 110	5 940	11	...	15	7	43	6	35	Algeria
9 940	...	22 020	...	...	...	...	...	...	...	...	Bahrain
730	1 060	1 590	2 180	99	...	...	...	...	...	...	Djibouti
1 240	1 360	3 360	4 940	13	3	44	9	44	5	34	Egypt
...	...	...	...	...	...	...	...	...	...	...	Iraq
1 590	2 650	2 960	4 820	115	...	7	7	46	7	39	Jordan
17 770	...	40 180	...	...	...	...	...	...	...	...	Kuwait
4 250	5 580	7 330	9 600	68	...	...	...	...	...	...	Lebanon
...	7 290	...	11 630	...	...	...	...	...	...	...	Libyan Arab Jamahiriya
560	760	1 350	1 970	62	26	63	6	46	7	39	Mauritania
1 310	2 160	2 480	3 860	22	...	14	7	47	7	40	Morocco
6 270	...	13 590	...	12	...	...	...	...	...	...	Oman
...	...	...	...	304	...	...	...	...	...	...	Palestinian A. T.
...	...	...	...	...	...	...	...	...	...	...	Qatar
8 030	13 980	17 060	22 300	1	...	...	...	...	...	...	Saudi Arabia
310	800	1 000	1 780	51	...	...	...	...	...	...	Sudan
920	1 560	3 270	4 110	4	...	...	...	...	...	...	Syrian Arab Republic
2 050	2 970	4 070	6 490	38	...	7	6	47	8	40	Tunisia
20 020	...	28 880	...	...	...	...	...	...	...	...	United Arab Emirates
380	760	1 710	2 090	16	16	45	7	41	6	33	Yemen
											Central and Eastern Europe
890	2 930	3 180	6 000	102	...	10	8	40	5	31	Albania
1 550	3 470	4 490	9 700	...	...	...	9	38	5	30	Belarus
1 430	3 230	4 490	6 780	140	...	...	10	36	4	26	Bosnia and Herzegovina
1 270	3 990	5 240	10 270	...	...	6	9	38	4	29	Bulgaria
4 600	9 310	8 600	13 850	28	...	...	8	40	5	29	Croatia
5 580	12 790	13 380	20 920	...	...	...	10	36	4	25	Czech Republic
3 730	11 400	8 370	18 090	...	...	8	7	43	6	36	Estonia
4 320	10 870	9 920	16 970	...	...	...	10	37	4	27	Hungary
2 650	8 100	6 560	14 840	...	...	5	7	45	7	38	Latvia
2 600	7 930	7 060	14 550	...	...	8	7	43	6	36	Lithuania
...	4 130	...	8 930	...	...	...	...	...	...	...	Montenegro
4 300	8 210	8 950	14 250	...	...	...	8	42	6	35	Poland
460	1 080	1 260	2 660	46	...	21	8	41	5	33	Republic of Moldova
1 520	4 830	5 730	10 150	...	...	13	8	39	5	31	Romania
2 140	5 770	6 000	12 740	...	...	12	6	47	8	40	Russian Federation
...	4 030	...	9 320	...	...	...	...	...	...	...	Serbia
4 100	9 610	10 660	17 060	...	...	29	9	35	4	26	Slovakia
10 530	18 660	14 990	23 970	...	...	...	9	36	4	28	Slovenia
1 930	3 070	5 450	7 850	113	...	...	6	46	8	39	TFYR Macedonia
3 070	5 400	5 970	8 410	6	3	19	5	50	9	44	Turkey
850	1 940	2 870	6 110	...	...	5	9	38	4	28	Ukraine
											Central Asia
590	1 920	1 830	4 950	64	...	31	9	43	5	34	Armenia
510	1 840	1 850	5 430	27	4	33	7	45	6	37	Azerbaijan
770	1 580	1 970	3 880	69	7	25	6	46	8	40	Georgia
1 390	3 870	4 000	8 700	15	...	16	7	42	6	34	Kazakhstan
350	500	1 150	1 790	52	...	21	9	39	4	30	Kyrgyzstan
460	1 000	1 700	2 810	83	11	45	8	41	5	33	Mongolia
180	390	760	1 560	37	7	43	8	41	5	33	Tajikistan
560	...	...	...	6	...	...	6	48	8	41	Turkmenistan
620	610	1 320	2 190	7	...	...	7	45	6	37	Uzbekistan
											East Asia and the Pacific
21 890	35 860	24 760	33 940	...	...	...	6	41	7	35	Australia
14 480	26 930	40 260	49 900	...	...	...	...	...	...	...	Brunei Darussalam
280	490	720	1 550	38	34	78	7	50	7	42	Cambodia
790	2 000	1 960	4 660	1	10	35	4	52	12	47	China

Table 1 (continued)

Country or territory	DEMOGRAPHY[1]							HIV/AIDS[2]		
	Total population (000)	Average annual growth rate (%) total population	Average annual growth rate (%) age 0-4 population	Life expectancy at birth (years)			Total fertility rate (children per woman)	HIV prevalence rate (%) in adults (15-49)	% of women among people (age 15+) living with HIV	Orphans due to AIDS (000)
	2006	2005-2010	2005-2010	2005-2010			2005-2010	2007	2007	2007
				Total	Male	Female		Total		
Cook Islands	14	-2.2	…	…	…	…	…	…	…	…
DPR Korea	23 708	0.3	-2.1	67	65	69	1.9	…	…	…
Fiji	833	0.6	-1.1	69	67	71	2.8	0.1	…	…
Indonesia	228 864	1.2	-0.6	71	69	73	2.2	0.2	20	…
Japan	127 953	0.0	-1.4	83	79	86	1.3	…	24	…
Kiribati	94	1.6	…	…	…	…	…	…	…	…
Lao PDR	5 759	1.7	0.8	64	63	66	3.2	0.2	24	…
Macao, China	478	0.7	1.1	81	79	83	0.9	…	…	…
Malaysia	26 114	1.7	-0.1	74	72	77	2.6	0.5	27	…
Marshall Islands	58	2.2	…	…	…	…	…	…	…	…
Micronesia	111	0.5	-1.4	69	68	69	3.7	…	…	…
Myanmar	48 379	0.9	-0.3	62	59	65	2.1	0.7	42	…
Nauru	10	0.3	…	…	…	…	…	…	…	…
New Zealand	4 140	0.9	0.3	80	78	82	2.0	0.1	<36	…
Niue	2	-1.8	…	…	…	…	…	…	…	…
Palau	20	0.4	…	…	…	…	…	…	…	…
Papua New Guinea	6 202	2.0	-0.5	57	55	60	3.8	1.5	40	…
Philippines	86 264	1.9	0.4	72	70	74	3.2	…	27	…
Republic of Korea	48 050	0.3	-1.8	79	75	82	1.2	<0.1	28	…
Samoa	185	0.9	-2.5	71	69	75	3.9	…	…	…
Singapore	4 382	1.2	-3.0	80	78	82	1.3	0.2	29	…
Solomon Islands	484	2.3	0.7	64	63	64	3.9	…	…	…
Thailand	63 444	0.7	0.0	71	66	75	1.9	1.4	42	…
Timor-Leste	1 114	3.5	4.6	61	60	62	6.5	…	…	…
Tokelau	1	0.0	…	…	…	…	…	…	…	…
Tonga	100	0.5	0.9	73	72	74	3.8	…	…	…
Tuvalu	10	0.4	…	…	…	…	…	…	…	…
Vanuatu	221	2.4	1.1	70	68	72	3.7	…	…	…
Viet Nam	86 206	1.3	0.0	74	72	76	2.1	0.5	27	…
Latin America and the Caribbean										
Anguilla	12	1.4	…	…	…	…	…	…	…	…
Antigua and Barbuda	84	1.2	…	…	…	…	…	…	…	…
Argentina	39 134	1.0	0.6	75	72	79	2.3	0.5	27	…
Aruba	104	0.0	-1.7	74	71	77	2.0	…	…	…
Bahamas	327	1.2	-0.1	73	71	76	2.0	3.0	26	…
Barbados	293	0.3	-1.2	77	74	80	1.5	1.2	<45	…
Belize	282	2.1	-0.1	76	73	79	2.9	2.1	59	…
Bermuda	64	0.3	…	…	…	…	…	…	…	…
Bolivia	9 354	1.8	0.1	66	63	68	3.5	0.2	28	…
Brazil	189 323	1.3	0.0	72	69	76	2.2	0.6	34	…
British Virgin Islands	22	1.1	…	…	…	…	…	…	…	…
Cayman Islands	46	1.5	…	…	…	…	…	…	…	…
Chile	16 465	1.0	0.2	79	75	82	1.9	0.3	28	…
Colombia	45 558	1.3	-1.0	73	69	77	2.2	0.6	29	…
Costa Rica	4 399	1.5	0.2	79	76	81	2.1	0.4	28	…
Cuba	11 267	0.0	-2.9	78	76	80	1.5	0.1	29	…
Dominica	68	-0.3	…	…	…	…	…	…	…	…
Dominican Republic	9 615	1.5	0.2	72	69	75	2.8	1.1	51	…
Ecuador	13 202	1.1	-0.8	75	72	78	2.6	0.3	28	…
El Salvador	6 762	1.4	-0.3	72	69	75	2.7	0.8	29	…
Grenada	106	0.0	-3.4	69	67	70	2.3	…	…	…
Guatemala	13 029	2.5	1.2	70	67	74	4.2	0.8	98	…
Guyana	739	-0.2	-4.2	67	64	70	2.3	2.5	59	…
Haiti	9 446	1.6	0.5	61	59	63	3.5	2.2	53	…
Honduras	6 969	1.9	0.5	70	67	74	3.3	0.7	28	…
Jamaica	2 699	0.5	-1.2	73	70	75	2.4	1.6	29	…
Mexico	105 342	1.1	-1.0	76	74	79	2.2	0.3	29	…
Montserrat	6	1.2	…	…	…	…	…	…	…	…
Netherlands Antilles	189	1.3	-1.3	75	71	79	1.9	…	…	…
Nicaragua	5 532	1.3	0.3	73	70	76	2.8	0.2	28	…
Panama	3 288	1.6	0.1	76	73	78	2.6	1.0	29	…

GNP, AID AND POVERTY							INEQUALITY IN INCOME OR EXPENDITURE[4]				
GNP per capita[3]				Net aid per capita (US$)[4]	Population living on less than US$1 per day[4] (%)	Population living on less than US$2 per day[4] (%)	Share of income or expenditure %		Inequality measure		
Current US$		PPP US$					Poorest 20%	Richest 20%	Richest 20% to poorest 20%[6]	Gini index[7]	
1998	2006	1998	2006	2005	1990-2005[5]	1990-2005[5]	1992-2005[5]	1992-2005[5]	1992-2005[5]	1992-2005[5]	**Country or territory**
...	...	...	...	...	...	...	...	...	...	...	Cook Islands
...	...	...	...	...	...	...	...	...	...	...	DPR Korea
2 290	3 720	3 030	4 450	76	...	...	...	...	...	...	Fiji
670	1 420	2 140	3 310	11	8	52	8	43	5	34	Indonesia
32 970	38 630	24 240	32 840	...	...	...	11	36	3	25	Japan
1 150	1 240	5 520	6 230	...	...	...	...	...	...	...	Kiribati
310	500	1 100	1 740	50	27	74	8	43	5	35	Lao PDR
15 260	...	20 880	...	...	...	...	...	...	...	...	Macao, China
3 630	5 620	7 630	12 160	1	...	9	4	54	12	49	Malaysia
2 070	2 980	6 490	8 040	...	...	...	...	...	...	...	Marshall Islands
2 030	2 390	5 020	6 070	...	...	...	...	...	...	...	Micronesia
...	...	410	...	3	...	...	...	...	...	...	Myanmar
...	...	...	...	...	...	...	...	...	...	...	Nauru
15 480	26 750	17 020	25 750	...	...	...	6	44	7	36	New Zealand
...	...	...	...	...	...	...	...	...	...	...	Niue
...	7 990	...	14 340	...	...	...	...	...	...	...	Palau
810	740	1 480	1 630	45	...	...	5	57	13	51	Papua New Guinea
1 080	1 390	2 260	3 430	7	15	43	5	51	9	45	Philippines
9 200	17 690	12 590	22 990	...	...	...	8	38	5	32	Republic of Korea
1 330	2 270	3 300	5 090	238	...	...	...	...	...	...	Samoa
23 490	28 730	28 130	43 300	...	...	...	5	49	10	43	Singapore
870	690	1 880	1 850	415	...	...	...	...	...	...	Solomon Islands
2 120	3 050	4 410	7 440	-3	...	25	6	49	8	42	Thailand
...	840	...	5 100	189	...	...	...	...	...	...	Timor-Leste
...	...	...	...	...	...	...	...	...	...	...	Tokelau
1 720	2 250	3 790	5 470	310	...	...	...	...	...	...	Tonga
...	...	...	...	...	...	...	...	...	...	...	Tuvalu
1 300	1 690	3 270	3 480	187	...	...	...	...	...	...	Vanuatu
350	700	1 220	2 310	23	...	...	9	44	5	34	Viet Nam
											Latin America and the Caribbean
...	...	...	...	...	...	...	...	...	...	...	Anguilla
7 810	11 050	10 490	15 130	89	...	...	...	...	...	...	Antigua and Barbuda
8 020	5 150	9 160	11 670	3	7	17	3	55	18	51	Argentina
...	...	...	...	...	...	...	...	...	...	...	Aruba
12 920	...	...	...	...	...	...	...	...	...	...	Bahamas
7 680	...	...	...	-8	...	...	...	...	...	...	Barbados
2 710	3 740	4 650	7 080	44	...	...	...	...	...	...	Belize
...	...	...	...	...	...	...	...	...	...	...	Bermuda
1 000	1 100	3 000	3 810	64	23	42	2	63	42	60	Bolivia
4 880	4 710	6 540	8 700	1	8	21	3	61	22	57	Brazil
...	...	...	...	...	...	...	...	...	...	...	British Virgin Islands
...	...	...	...	...	...	...	...	...	...	...	Cayman Islands
5 270	6 810	8 700	11 300	9	...	6	4	60	16	55	Chile
2 440	3 120	4 720	6 130	11	7	18	3	63	25	59	Colombia
3 500	4 980	6 180	9 220	7	3	10	4	54	16	50	Costa Rica
...	...	...	...	8	...	...	...	...	...	...	Cuba
3 300	...	5 660	...	211	...	...	...	...	...	...	Dominica
1 770	2 910	3 410	5 550	9	3	16	4	57	14	52	Dominican Republic
1 810	2 910	4 760	6 810	16	18	41	3	58	17	54	Ecuador
1 870	2 680	4 340	5 610	29	19	41	3	56	21	52	El Salvador
3 020	...	6 010	...	421	...	...	...	...	...	...	Grenada
1 670	2 590	4 060	5 120	20	14	32	3	60	20	55	Guatemala
880	1 150	2 420	3 410	182	...	...	...	...	...	...	Guyana
400	430	1 130	1 070	60	54	78	2	63	27	59	Haiti
750	1 270	2 520	3 420	95	15	36	3	58	17	54	Honduras
2 660	3 560	5 590	7 050	14	...	14	5	52	10	46	Jamaica
4 020	7 830	8 440	11 990	2	3	12	4	55	13	46	Mexico
...	...	...	...	...	...	...	...	...	...	...	Montserrat
...	...	...	...	...	...	...	...	...	...	...	Netherlands Antilles
670	930	1 820	2 720	135	45	80	6	49	9	43	Nicaragua
3 550	5 000	5 960	8 690	6	7	18	3	60	24	56	Panama

Table 1 (continued)

Country or territory	DEMOGRAPHY[1] Total population (000) 2006	Average annual growth rate (%) total population 2005-2010	Average annual growth rate (%) age 0-4 population 2005-2010	Life expectancy at birth (years) 2005-2010 Total	Male	Female	Total fertility rate (children per woman) 2005-2010	HIV/AIDS[2] HIV prevalence rate (%) in adults (15-49) 2007 Total	% of women among people (age 15+) living with HIV 2007	Orphans due to AIDS (000) 2007
Paraguay	6 016	1.8	0.3	72	70	74	3.1	0.6	29	…
Peru	27 589	1.2	0.2	71	69	74	2.5	0.5	28	…
Saint Kitts and Nevis	50	1.3	…	…	…	…	…	…	…	…
Saint Lucia	163	1.1	1.1	74	72	76	2.2	…	…	…
St Vincent/Grenad.	120	0.5	-0.1	72	69	74	2.2	…	…	…
Suriname	455	0.6	-1.0	70	67	74	2.4	2.4	28	…
Trinidad and Tobago	1 328	0.4	0.9	70	68	72	1.6	1.5	59	…
Turks and Caicos Islands	25	1.4	…	…	…	…	…	…	…	…
Uruguay	3 331	0.3	-0.8	76	73	80	2.1	0.6	28	…
Venezuela, B. R.	27 191	1.7	0.5	74	71	77	2.5	…	…	…
North America and Western Europe										
Andorra	74	0.4	…	…	…	…	…	…	…	…
Austria	8 327	0.4	-0.3	80	77	83	1.4	0.2	30	…
Belgium	10 430	0.2	-0.5	79	76	82	1.6	0.2	27	…
Canada	32 577	0.9	0.3	81	78	83	1.5	0.4	27	…
Cyprus	846	1.1	1.5	79	76	82	1.6	…	…	…
Denmark	5 430	0.2	-1.1	78	76	81	1.8	0.2	23	…
Finland	5 261	0.3	0.6	79	76	82	1.8	0.1	<42	…
France	61 330	0.5	-0.3	81	77	84	1.9	0.4	27	…
Germany	82 641	-0.1	-1.2	79	77	82	1.4	0.1	29	…
Greece	11 123	0.2	0.2	79	77	82	1.3	0.2	27	…
Iceland	298	0.8	0.6	82	80	83	2.1	0.2	<40	…
Ireland	4 221	1.8	2.2	79	76	81	2.0	0.2	27	…
Israel	6 810	1.7	0.4	81	79	83	2.8	0.1	59	…
Italy	58 779	0.1	-0.1	81	78	83	1.4	0.4	27	…
Luxembourg	461	1.1	0.3	79	76	82	1.7	0.2	…	…
Malta	405	0.4	0.0	79	77	81	1.4	0.1	…	…
Monaco	33	0.3	…	…	…	…	…	…	…	…
Netherlands	16 379	0.2	-2.0	80	78	82	1.7	0.2	27	…
Norway	4 669	0.6	-0.1	80	78	83	1.8	0.1	<33	…
Portugal	10 579	0.4	0.0	78	75	81	1.5	0.5	28	…
San Marino	31	0.8	…	…	…	…	…	…	…	…
Spain	43 887	0.8	1.8	81	78	84	1.4	0.5	20	…
Sweden	9 078	0.4	1.2	81	79	83	1.8	0.1	47	…
Switzerland	7 455	0.4	-0.8	82	79	84	1.4	0.6	37	…
United Kingdom	60 512	0.4	1.0	79	77	82	1.8	0.2	29	…
United States	302 841	1.0	0.8	78	76	81	2.1	0.6	21	…
South and West Asia										
Afghanistan	26 088	3.9	3.6	44	44	44	7.1	…	…	…
Bangladesh	155 991	1.7	-0.3	64	63	65	2.8	…	17	…
Bhutan	649	1.4	-1.6	66	64	67	2.2	0.1	<20	…
India	1 151 751	1.5	-0.1	65	63	66	2.8	0.3	38	…
Iran, Islamic Republic of	70 270	1.4	3.0	71	69	73	2.0	0.2	28	…
Maldives	300	1.8	3.1	68	68	69	2.6	…	…	…
Nepal	27 641	2.0	0.8	64	63	64	3.3	0.5	25	…
Pakistan	160 943	1.8	1.9	65	65	66	3.5	0.1	29	…
Sri Lanka	19 207	0.5	-1.1	72	69	76	1.9	…	38	…
Sub-Saharan Africa										
Angola	16 557	2.8	2.5	43	41	44	6.4	2.1	61	50
Benin	8 760	3.0	2.4	57	56	58	5.4	1.2	63	29
Botswana	1 858	1.2	0.7	51	50	51	2.9	23.9	61	95
Burkina Faso	14 359	2.9	2.4	52	51	54	6.0	1.6	51	100
Burundi	8 173	3.9	5.3	50	48	51	6.8	2.0	59	120
Cameroon	18 175	2.0	0.4	50	50	51	4.3	5.1	60	300
Cape Verde	519	2.2	1.1	72	68	74	3.4	…	…	…
Central African Republic	4 265	1.8	1.0	45	43	46	4.6	6.3	65	72
Chad	10 468	2.9	2.3	51	49	52	6.2	3.5	61	85
Comoros	818	2.5	1.0	65	63	67	4.3	<0.1	<50	<0.1
Congo	3 689	2.1	1.2	55	54	57	4.5	3.5	59	69

GNP, AID AND POVERTY							INEQUALITY IN INCOME OR EXPENDITURE[4]				
GNP per capita[3]				Net aid per capita (US$)[4]	Population living on less than US$1 per day[4] (%)	Population living on less than US$2 per day[4] (%)	Share of income or expenditure %		Inequality measure		
Current US$		PPP US$					Poorest 20%	Richest 20%	Richest 20% to poorest 20%[6]	Gini index[7]	
1998	2006	1998	2006	2005	1990-2005[5]	1990-2005[5]	1992-2005[5]	1992-2005[5]	1992-2005[5]	1992-2005[5]	Country or territory
1 650	1 410	3 480	4 040	8	14	30	2	62	26	58	Paraguay
2 240	2 980	4 630	6 490	14	11	31	4	57	15	52	Peru
6 150	…	9 990	…	73	…	…	…	…	…	…	Saint Kitts and Nevis
3 880	…	6 870	…	67	…	…	…	…	…	…	Saint Lucia
2 620	…	4 670	…	41	…	…	…	…	…	…	St Vincent/Grenad.
2 500	4 210	5 840	7 720	98	…	…	…	…	…	…	Suriname
4 440	12 500	7 610	16 800	- 2	12	39	6	45	8	39	Trinidad and Tobago
…	…	…	…	…	…	…	…	…	…	…	Turks and Caicos Islands
6 610	5 310	7 880	9 940	4	…	6	5	51	10	45	Uruguay
3 360	6 070	8 430	10 970	2	19	40	3	52	16	48	Venezuela, B. R.
											North America and Western Europe
…	…	…	…	…	…	…	…	…	…	…	Andorra
27 250	39 750	25 790	36 040	…	…	…	9	38	4	29	Austria
25 950	38 460	24 580	33 860	…	…	…	9	41	5	33	Belgium
20 310	36 650	24 530	36 280	…	…	…	7	40	6	33	Canada
14 770	23 270	19 260	25 060	…	…	…	…	…	…	…	Cyprus
32 960	52 110	25 620	36 190	…	…	…	8	36	4	25	Denmark
24 910	41 360	20 950	33 170	…	…	…	10	37	4	27	Finland
25 200	36 560	23 620	32 240	…	…	…	7	40	6	33	France
27 170	36 810	23 840	32 680	…	…	…	9	37	4	28	Germany
15 050	27 390	19 600	30 870	…	…	…	7	42	6	34	Greece
28 390	49 960	24 060	33 740	…	…	…	…	…	…	…	Iceland
20 780	44 830	20 640	34 730	…	…	…	7	42	6	34	Ireland
16 880	20 170	16 960	23 840	…	…	…	6	45	8	39	Israel
21 240	31 990	22 220	28 970	…	…	…	7	42	7	36	Italy
43 620	71 240	43 020	60 870	…	…	…	…	…	…	…	Luxembourg
8 790	15 310	15 630	20 990	…	…	…	…	…	…	…	Malta
…	…	…	…	…	…	…	…	…	…	…	Monaco
25 820	43 050	26 340	37 940	…	…	…	8	39	5	31	Netherlands
35 400	68 440	35 710	50 070	…	…	…	10	37	4	26	Norway
11 560	17 850	15 620	19 960	…	…	…	6	46	8	39	Portugal
…	45 130	…	…	…	…	…	…	…	…	…	San Marino
15 220	27 340	19 500	28 200	…	…	…	7	42	6	35	Spain
28 930	43 530	22 470	34 310	…	…	…	9	37	4	25	Sweden
41 560	58 050	30 210	40 840	…	…	…	8	41	6	34	Switzerland
22 860	40 560	23 090	33 650	…	…	…	6	44	7	36	United Kingdom
30 620	44 710	31 650	44 070	…	…	…	5	46	8	41	United States
											South and West Asia
…	…	…	…	…	…	…	…	…	…	…	Afghanistan
340	450	750	1 230	9	41	84	9	43	5	33	Bangladesh
600	1 430	1 910	4 000	98	…	…	…	…	…	…	Bhutan
420	820	1 340	2 460	2	34	80	8	45	6	37	India
1 730	2 930	6 350	9 800	2	…	7	5	50	10	43	Iran, Islamic Republic of
1 930	3 010	2 550	4 740	203	…	…	…	…	…	…	Maldives
210	320	730	1 010	16	24	69	6	55	9	47	Nepal
470	800	1 590	2 410	11	17	74	9	40	4	31	Pakistan
810	1 310	2 250	3 730	61	6	42	7	48	7	40	Sri Lanka
											Sub-Saharan Africa
460	1 970	1 810	3 890	28	…	…	…	…	…	…	Angola
340	530	960	1 250	41	31	74	7	45	6	37	Benin
3 350	5 570	7 640	11 730	40	28	56	3	65	20	61	Botswana
240	440	760	1 130	50	27	72	7	47	7	40	Burkina Faso
140	100	300	320	48	55	88	5	48	10	42	Burundi
630	990	1 470	2 060	25	17	51	6	51	9	45	Cameroon
1 240	2 130	1 700	2 590	317	…	…	…	…	…	…	Cape Verde
280	350	610	690	24	67	84	2	65	33	61	Central African Republic
220	450	820	1 170	39	…	…	…	…	…	…	Chad
420	660	940	1 140	42	…	…	…	…	…	…	Comoros
560	…	1 940	…	362	…	…	…	…	…	…	Congo

Table 1 (continued)

Country or territory	DEMOGRAPHY[1] Total population (000) 2006	Average annual growth rate (%) total population 2005-2010	Average annual growth rate (%) age 0-4 population 2005-2010	Life expectancy at birth (years) 2005-2010 Total	Male	Female	Total fertility rate (children per woman) 2005-2010	HIV/AIDS[2] HIV prevalence rate (%) in adults (15-49) 2007 Total	% of women among people (age 15+) living with HIV 2007	Orphans due to AIDS (000) 2007
Côte d'Ivoire	18 914	1.8	0.8	48	48	49	4.5	3.9	60	420
D. R. Congo	60 644	3.2	3.5	46	45	48	6.7	…	…	…
Equatorial Guinea	496	2.4	2.0	52	50	53	5.4	3.4	60	5
Eritrea	4 692	3.2	3.1	58	56	60	5.0	1.3	60	18
Ethiopia	81 021	2.5	1.6	53	52	54	5.3	2.1	60	650
Gabon	1 311	1.5	0.4	57	56	57	3.1	5.9	59	18
Gambia	1 663	2.6	1.3	59	59	60	4.7	0.9	60	3
Ghana	23 008	2.0	0.6	60	60	60	3.8	1.9	60	160
Guinea	9 181	2.2	1.5	56	54	58	5.4	1.6	59	25
Guinea-Bissau	1 646	3.0	3.1	46	45	48	7.1	1.8	58	6
Kenya	36 553	2.7	2.9	54	53	55	5.0	…	…	…
Lesotho	1 995	0.6	-0.4	43	43	42	3.4	23.2	58	110
Liberia	3 579	4.5	4.7	46	45	47	6.8	1.7	59	15
Madagascar	19 159	2.7	1.5	59	58	61	4.8	0.1	26	3
Malawi	13 571	2.6	1.5	48	48	48	5.6	11.9	58	560
Mali	11 968	3.0	3.2	54	52	57	6.5	1.5	60	44
Mauritius	1 252	0.8	-0.5	73	70	76	1.9	1.7	29	<0.5
Mozambique	20 971	1.9	0.6	42	42	42	5.1	12.5	58	400
Namibia	2 047	1.3	0.4	53	52	53	3.2	15.3	61	66
Niger	13 737	3.5	3.1	57	58	56	7.2	0.8	30	25
Nigeria	144 720	2.3	1.2	47	46	47	5.3	3.1	58	1 200
Rwanda	9 464	2.8	4.0	46	45	48	5.9	2.8	60	220
Sao Tome and Principe	155	1.6	0.3	66	64	67	3.9	…	…	…
Senegal	12 072	2.5	1.3	63	61	65	4.7	1.0	59	8
Seychelles	86	0.5	…	…	…	…	…	…	…	…
Sierra Leone	5 743	2.0	1.9	43	41	44	6.5	1.7	59	16
Somalia	8 445	2.9	2.0	48	47	49	6.0	0.5	28	9
South Africa	48 282	0.6	-0.5	49	49	50	2.6	18.1	59	1 400
Swaziland	1 134	0.6	0.2	40	40	39	3.4	26.1	59	56
Togo	6 410	2.6	1.4	58	57	60	4.8	3.3	58	68
Uganda	29 899	3.2	3.1	52	51	52	6.5	5.4	59	1 200
United Republic of Tanzania	39 459	2.5	1.2	53	51	54	5.2	6.2	58	970
Zambia	11 696	1.9	0.9	42	42	42	5.2	15.2	57	600
Zimbabwe	13 228	1.0	0.3	43	44	43	3.2	15.3	57	1 000
	Sum	Weighted average						Weighted average		
World	6 578 149	1.2	0.5	68.6	66.5	70.8	2.6	0.8	50	15 000
Countries in transition	278 295	-0.1	1.2	66.5	61.0	72.5	1.6	…	…	…
Developed countries	1 015 689	0.4	0.2	79.2	76.2	82.0	1.7	…	…	…
Developing countries	5 284 165	1.4	0.5	66.7	65.1	68.5	2.8	…	…	…
Arab States	314 822	2.0	1.2	68.8	67.0	70.7	3.2	…	…	…
Central and Eastern Europe	403 456	-0.1	0.5	69.9	65.3	74.8	1.5	…	…	…
Central Asia	77 546	1.0	1.5	67.2	63.4	71.0	2.3	…	…	…
East Asia and the Pacific	2 119 172	0.7	-0.2	73.0	71.0	75.1	1.9	…	…	…
East Asia	2 085 044	0.7	-0.2	72.9	70.9	75.1	1.9	0.1	27	…
Pacific	34 128	1.2	0.1	75.7	73.3	78.2	2.3	0.4	30	…
Latin America/Caribbean	559 994	1.2	-0.2	73.4	70.2	76.6	2.2	…	…	…
Caribbean	16 628	1.1	0.0	65.4	63.2	67.6	3.0	1.1	50	…
Latin America	543 365	1.3	-0.2	73.6	70.5	76.8	2.2	0.5	32	…
N. America/W. Europe	744 476	0.6	0.4	79.3	76.6	82.0	1.8	…	…	…
South and West Asia	1 612 841	1.6	0.3	64.7	63.4	66.2	2.9	…	…	…
Sub-Saharan Africa	745 842	2.4	1.8	50.3	49.4	51.2	5.2	5.0	59	11 592

1. UN Population Division (2007), medium variant.
2. UNAIDS (2008).
3. World Bank (2008).
4. UNDP (2007).
5. Data are for the most recent year available during the period specified. For more details see UNDP (2007).

GNP, AID AND POVERTY							INEQUALITY IN INCOME OR EXPENDITURE[4]				
GNP per capita[3]				Net aid per capita (US$)[4]	Population living on less than US$1 per day[4] (%)	Population living on less than US$2 per day[4] (%)	Share of income or expenditure %		Inequality measure		
Current US$		PPP US$					Poorest 20%	Richest 20%	Richest 20% to poorest 20%[6]	Gini index[7]	
1998	2006	1998	2006	2005	1990-2005[5]	1990-2005[5]	1992-2005[5]	1992-2005[5]	1992-2005[5]	1992-2005[5]	Country or territory
730	880	1 520	1 580	7	15	49	5	51	10	45	Côte d'Ivoire
110	130	240	270	32	...	...	...	...	...	...	D. R. Congo
1 120	8 510	5 100	16 620	78	...	...	...	...	...	...	Equatorial Guinea
210	190	750	680	81	...	...	...	...	...	...	Eritrea
130	170	410	630	27	23	78	9	39	4	30	Ethiopia
4 070	5 360	12 240	11 180	39	...	...	...	...	...	...	Gabon
300	290	810	1 110	38	59	83	5	53	11	50	Gambia
370	510	820	1 240	51	45	79	6	47	8	41	Ghana
470	400	840	1 130	19	...	...	7	46	7	39	Guinea
140	190	390	460	50	...	...	5	53	10	47	Guinea-Bissau
440	580	1 140	1 470	22	23	58	6	49	8	43	Kenya
650	980	1 320	1 810	38	36	56	2	67	44	63	Lesotho
130	130	250	260	...	...	...	...	...	...	...	Liberia
250	280	700	870	50	61	85	5	54	11	48	Madagascar
200	230	600	690	45	21	63	7	47	7	39	Malawi
280	460	690	1 000	51	36	72	6	47	8	40	Mali
3 760	5 430	6 740	10 640	26	...	...	...	...	...	...	Mauritius
220	310	400	660	65	36	74	5	54	10	47	Mozambique
2 030	3 210	3 360	4 770	61	35	56	1	79	56	74	Namibia
200	270	540	630	37	61	86	3	53	21	51	Niger
270	620	1 010	1 410	49	71	92	5	49	10	44	Nigeria
260	250	530	730	64	60	88	5	53	10	47	Rwanda
...	800	...	1 490	204	...	...	...	...	...	...	Sao Tome and Principe
510	760	1 140	1 560	59	17	56	7	48	7	41	Senegal
7 320	8 870	12 770	14 360	223	...	...	...	...	...	...	Seychelles
160	240	340	610	62	57	75	1	63	58	63	Sierra Leone
...	...	...	...	...	...	...	...	...	...	...	Somalia
3 280	5 390	6 140	8 900	16	11	34	4	62	18	58	South Africa
1 460	2 400	3 820	4 700	41	48	78	4	56	13	50	Swaziland
300	350	680	770	14	...	...	...	...	...	...	Togo
280	300	600	880	42	...	...	6	53	9	46	Uganda
220	350	630	980	39	58	90	7	42	6	35	United Republic of Tanzania
310	630	800	1 140	81	64	87	4	55	15	51	Zambia
570	...	...	...	28	56	83	5	56	12	50	Zimbabwe

Weighted average							Weighted average				
...	7 448	...	9 209	16	...	...	...	...	...	...	World
...	...	...	...	...	...	...	...	...	...	...	Countries in transition
...	...	...	...	...	...	...	...	...	...	...	Developed countries
...	...	...	...	17	...	...	...	...	...	...	Developing countries
...	...	...	...	94	...	...	...	...	...	...	Arab States
...	...	...	...	...	...	...	...	...	...	...	Central and Eastern Europe
...	...	...	...	...	...	...	...	...	...	...	Central Asia
...	1 856	...	4 359	5	...	...	...	...	...	...	East Asia and the Pacific
...	...	...	...	...	...	...	...	...	...	...	East Asia
...	...	...	...	...	...	...	...	...	...	...	Pacific
...	4 785	...	8 682	11	...	...	...	...	...	...	Latin America/Caribbean
...	...	...	...	...	...	...	...	...	...	...	Caribbean
...	...	...	...	...	...	...	...	...	...	...	Latin America
...	...	...	...	...	...	...	...	...	...	...	N. America/W. Europe
...	...	...	...	...	...	...	...	...	...	...	South and West Asia
...	829	...	1 681	42	...	...	...	...	...	...	Sub-Saharan Africa

6. Data show the ratio of income or expenditure share of the richest group to that of the poorest.
7. A value of 0 represents perfect equality and a value of 100 perfect inequality.

Table 2
Adult and youth literacy

Country or territory	ADULT LITERACY RATE (15 and over) (%)									ADULT ILLITERATES (15 and over)					
	1985-1994[1]			2000-2006[1]			Projected 2015			1985-1994[1]		2000-2006[1]		Projected 2015	
	Total	Male	Female	Total	Male	Female	Total	Male	Female	Total (000)	% Female	Total (000)	% Female	Total (000)	% Female
Arab States															
Algeria	50*	63*	36*	75	84	65	81	88	74	6 572	64*	6 030	68	5 392	68
Bahrain	84*	89*	77*	88	90	86	92	93	90	56	56*	64	49	55	49
Djibouti	…	…	…	…	…	…	…	…	…	…	…	…	…	…	…
Egypt	44*	57*	31*	71	83	60	77	86	68	16 428	62*	14 213	71	13 822	70
Iraq	…	…	…	74*	84*	64*	…	…	…	…	…	4 327	69*	…	…
Jordan	…	…	…	93	96	89	95	98	93	…	…	266	74	215	73
Kuwait	74*	78*	69*	93*	95*	91*	96	96	95	276	48*	145	50*	114	48
Lebanon	…	…	…	…	…	…	…	…	…	…	…	…	…	…	…
Libyan Arab Jamahiriya	76	88	63	86	94	78	91	97	84	685	73	580	78	472	81
Mauritania	…	…	…	55	63	47	61	66	55	…	…	817	59	934	57
Morocco	42*	55*	29*	55	68	42	62	74	51	9 602	62*	9 826	66	9 458	67
Oman	…	…	…	84	89	76	89	93	84	…	…	278	60	242	62
Palestinian A. T.	…	…	…	92	97	88	95	98	93	…	…	161	78	135	76
Qatar	76*	77*	72*	90	90	90	93	93	93	68	30*	66	28	54	30
Saudi Arabia	71*	80*	57*	84	89	78	89	92	85	2 907	59*	2 506	58	2 176	60
Sudan[2]	…	…	…	61*	71*	52*	…	…	…	…	…	8 674	63*	…	…
Syrian Arab Republic	…	…	…	83	89	76	87	92	82	…	…	2 169	69	2 037	70
Tunisia	…	…	…	77	86	68	83	90	76	…	…	1 764	69	1 464	71
United Arab Emirates	71*	72*	69*	90	90	89	94	95	92	473	31*	347	31	259	39
Yemen	37*	57*	17*	57	76	39	70	85	55	4 686	66*	5 076	72	4 961	75
Central and Eastern Europe															
Albania	…	…	…	99	99	99	99	99	99	…	…	24	66	19	59
Belarus	98*	99*	97*	100	100	100	100	100	100	166	87*	25	68	16	50
Bosnia and Herzegovina	…	…	…	97*	99*	94*	…	…	…	…	…	110	86*	…	…
Bulgaria	…	…	…	98	99	98	98	98	98	…	…	114	63	118	58
Croatia	97*	99*	95*	99	99	98	99	100	99	120	82*	52	81	31	74
Czech Republic	…	…	…	…	…	…	…	…	…	…	…	…	…	…	…
Estonia	100*	100*	100*	100	100	100	100	100	100	3	79*	2	50	2	47
Hungary	…	…	…	…	…	…	…	…	…	…	…	…	…	…	…
Latvia	99*	100*	99*	100	100	100	100	100	100	11	80*	4	54	4	51
Lithuania	98*	99*	98*	100	100	100	100	100	100	44	76*	9	52	8	52
Montenegro	…	…	…	…	…	…	…	…	…	…	…	…	…	…	…
Poland	…	…	…	…	…	…	…	…	…	…	…	…	…	…	…
Republic of Moldova	96*	99*	94*	99	100	99	100	100	100	113	82*	26	78	12	63
Romania	97*	99*	95*	98	98	97	98	98	97	589	78*	443	67	394	58
Russian Federation	98*	99*	97*	100	100	99	100	100	100	2 290	88*	604	72	398	61
Serbia	…	…	…	…	…	…	…	…	…	…	…	…	…	…	…
Slovakia	…	…	…	…	…	…	…	…	…	…	…	…	…	…	…
Slovenia	100*	100*	99*	100	100	100	100	100	100	7	60*	6	57	5	57
TFYR Macedonia	94*	97*	91*	97	99	95	98	99	97	87	77*	52	77	36	73
Turkey	79*	90*	69*	88*	96*	80*	91	97	86	7 640	75*	6 285	83*	5 282	84
Ukraine	…	…	…	100	100	100	100	100	100	…	…	129	70	83	58
Central Asia															
Armenia	99*	99*	98*	99	100	99	100	100	100	31	77*	13	73	8	63
Azerbaijan	…	…	…	99	100	99	100	100	100	…	…	42	78	24	76
Georgia	…	…	…	…	…	…	…	…	…	…	…	…	…	…	…
Kazakhstan	98*	99*	96*	100	100	99	100	100	100	278	82*	46	74	34	65
Kyrgyzstan	…	…	…	99	99	99	99	100	99	…	…	27	67	21	55
Mongolia	…	…	…	97	97	98	96	95	98	…	…	49	44	85	32
Tajikistan	98*	99*	97*	100	100	99	100	100	100	68	74*	16	70	11	62
Turkmenistan	…	…	…	99	100	99	100	100	100	…	…	18	71	12	61
Uzbekistan	…	…	…	97*	98*	96*	…	…	…	…	…	565	68*	…	…
East Asia and the Pacific															
Australia	…	…	…	…	…	…	…	…	…	…	…	…	…	…	…
Brunei Darussalam	88*	92*	82*	95	96	93	97	98	96	21	67*	15	65	11	65
Cambodia	…	…	…	76	86	67	81	88	75	…	…	2 188	72	2 146	69
China	78*	87*	68*	93	96	90	96	98	93	184 214	70*	73 232	73	49 848	74
Cook Islands	…	…	…	…	…	…	…	…	…	…	…	…	…	…	…
DPR Korea	…	…	…	…	…	…	…	…	…	…	…	…	…	…	…

YOUTH LITERACY RATE (15-24) (%)									YOUTH ILLITERATES (15-24)						
1985-1994[1]			2000-2006[1]			Projected 2015			1985-1994[1]		2000-2006[1]		Projected 2015		
Total	Male	Female	Total	Male	Female	Total	Male	Female	Total (000)	% Female	Total (000)	% Female	Total (000)	% Female	Country or territory
															Arab States
74*	86*	62*	92	94	90	95	95	95	1 215	73*	593	63	320	48	Algeria
97*	97*	97*	100	100	100	100	100	100	3	53*	0.5	42	0.1	45	Bahrain
…	…	…	…	…	…	…	…	…	…	…	…	…	…	…	Djibouti
63*	71*	54*	85	90	80	91	92	90	3 473	60*	2 238	66	1 435	55	Egypt
…	…	…	85*	89*	80*	…	…	…	…	…	877	63*	…	…	Iraq
…	…	…	99	99	99	99	99	100	…	…	11	45	7	30	Jordan
87*	91*	84*	99*	99*	98*	100	100	100	37	62*	7	45*	0.05	37	Kuwait
…	…	…	…	…	…	…	…	…	…	…	…	…	…	…	Lebanon
95	99	91	99	100	98	100	100	100	55	89	18	88	0.7	67	Libyan Arab Jamahiriya
…	…	…	66	70	62	71	73	70	…	…	207	54	211	52	Mauritania
58*	71*	46*	74	83	64	83	89	78	2 239	65*	1 704	68	1 017	67	Morocco
…	…	…	98	99	98	99	100	99	…	…	10	62	3	63	Oman
…	…	…	99	99	99	99	99	100	…	…	7	52	6	36	Palestinian A. T.
90*	89*	91*	97	96	98	99	99	99	6	31*	3	28	1.05	60	Qatar
88*	94*	81*	97	98	96	99	99	98	369	74*	150	66	75	76	Saudi Arabia
…	…	…	77*	85*	71*	…	…	…	…	…	1 659	64*	…	…	Sudan [2]
…	…	…	93	95	91	96	97	95	…	…	298	63	163	60	Syrian Arab Republic
…	…	…	95	97	94	98	98	97	…	…	100	65	39	57	Tunisia
82*	81*	85*	97	98	96	99	100	98	36	38*	17	60	5	78	United Arab Emirates
60*	83*	35*	79	93	64	90	97	83	1 122	78*	1 003	82	587	87	Yemen
															Central and Eastern Europe
…	…	…	99	99	99	99	99	99	…	…	4	44	4	41	Albania
100*	100*	100*	100	100	100	100	100	100	3	43*	3	37	3	33	Belarus
…	…	…	100*	100*	100*	…	…	…	…	…	1	38*	…	…	Bosnia and Herzegovina
…	…	…	98	98	98	96	96	96	…	…	25	50	28	46	Bulgaria
100*	100*	100*	100	100	100	100	100	100	2	53*	2	48	2	44	Croatia
…	…	…	…	…	…	…	…	…	…	…	…	…	…	…	Czech Republic
100*	100*	100*	100	100	100	100	100	100	0.3	35*	0.4	37	…	…	Estonia
…	…	…	…	…	…	…	…	…	…	…	…	…	20	33	Hungary
100*	100*	100*	100	100	100	100	100	100	0.8	40*	1.0	41	0.8	42	Latvia
100*	100*	100*	100	100	100	100	100	100	2	44*	1	46	0.8	50	Lithuania
…	…	…	…	…	…	…	…	…	…	…	…	…	…	…	Montenegro
…	…	…	…	…	…	…	…	…	…	…	…	…	…	…	Poland
100*	100*	100*	100	100	100	100	100	100	2	48*	2	48	2	49	Republic of Moldova
99*	99*	99*	98	97	98	96	96	97	35	53*	81	47	86	42	Romania
100*	100*	100*	100	100	100	100	100	100	56	44*	72	40	53	36	Russian Federation
…	…	…	…	…	…	…	…	…	…	…	…	…	…	…	Serbia
…	…	…	…	…	…	…	…	…	…	…	…	…	…	…	Slovakia
100*	100*	100*	100	100	100	100	100	100	0.7	44*	0.4	37	0.3	30	Slovenia
99*	99*	99*	99	99	99	99	99	98	4	62*	4	57	4	52	TFYR Macedonia
93*	97*	88*	96*	98*	94*	97	99	96	867	76*	507	78*	388	75	Turkey
…	…	…	100	100	100	100	100	100	…	…	15	41	12	39	Ukraine
															Central Asia
100*	100*	100*	100	100	100	100	100	100	0.5	49*	1	38	1.3	33	Armenia
…	…	…	100	100	100	100	100	100	…	…	1	28	0.6	18	Azerbaijan
…	…	…	…	…	…	…	…	…	…	…	…	…	…	…	Georgia
100*	100*	100*	100	100	100	100	100	100	8	44*	5	38	5	36	Kazakhstan
…	…	…	100	100	100	99	99	100	…	…	4	38	6	31	Kyrgyzstan
…	…	…	96	94	97	91	86	96	…	…	25	30	46	24	Mongolia
100*	100*	100*	100	100	100	100	100	100	3	56*	2	47	2	44	Tajikistan
…	…	…	100	100	100	100	100	100	…	…	2	41	2	33	Turkmenistan
…	…	…	99*	99*	99*	…	…	…	…	…	39	52*	…	…	Uzbekistan
															East Asia and the Pacific
…	…	…	…	…	…	…	…	…	…	…	…	…	…	…	Australia
98*	98*	98*	100	100	99	100	100	100	0.9	49*	0.3	53	0.12	57	Brunei Darussalam
…	…	…	85	89	81	91	93	89	…	…	495	62	313	59	Cambodia
94*	97*	91*	99	99	99	100	100	100	14 352	73*	1 703	58	907	51	China
…	…	…	…	…	…	…	…	…	…	…	…	…	…	…	Cook Islands
…	…	…	…	…	…	…	…	…	…	…	…	…	…	…	DPR Korea

Table 2 (continued)

Country or territory	ADULT LITERACY RATE (15 and over) (%)									ADULT ILLITERATES (15 and over)					
	1985-1994[1]			2000-2006[1]			Projected 2015			1985-1994[1]		2000-2006[1]		Projected 2015	
	Total	Male	Female	Total	Male	Female	Total	Male	Female	Total (000)	% Female	Total (000)	% Female	Total (000)	% Female
Fiji	…	…	…	…	…	…	…	…	…	…	…	…	…	…	…
Indonesia	82*	88*	75*	91	95	87	94	96	92	21 577	68*	14 772	71	11 158	71
Japan	…	…	…	…	…	…	…	…	…	…	…	…	…	…	…
Kiribati	…	…	…	…	…	…	…	…	…	…	…	…	…	…	…
Lao PDR	…	…	…	72	80	66	78	83	73	…	…	967	64	993	62
Macao, China	…	…	…	93	96	90	95	97	93	…	…	28	74	22	73
Malaysia	83*	89*	77*	92	94	89	94	96	93	1 989	66*	1 527	64	1 244	63
Marshall Islands	…	…	…	…	…	…	…	…	…	…	…	…	…	…	…
Micronesia	…	…	…	…	…	…	…	…	…	…	…	…	…	…	…
Myanmar	…	…	…	90*	94*	86*	…	…	…	…	…	3 529	70*	…	…
Nauru	…	…	…	…	…	…	…	…	…	…	…	…	…	…	…
New Zealand	…	…	…	…	…	…	…	…	…	…	…	…	…	…	…
Niue	…	…	…	…	…	…	…	…	…	…	…	…	…	…	…
Palau	…	…	…	…	…	…	…	…	…	…	…	…	…	…	…
Papua New Guinea	…	…	…	57	62	53	61	63	60	…	…	1 579	55	1 831	52
Philippines	94*	94*	93*	93	93	94	94	94	95	2 325	53*	3 711	48	4 073	46
Republic of Korea	…	…	…	…	…	…	…	…	…	…	…	…	…	…	…
Samoa	98*	98*	97*	99	99	98	99	99	99	2	60*	1	58	1	54
Singapore	89*	95*	83*	94	97	91	96	98	94	259	78*	207	76	157	74
Solomon Islands	…	…	…	…	…	…	…	…	…	…	…	…	…	…	…
Thailand	…	…	…	94	96	92	96	97	94	…	…	3 022	66	2 387	65
Timor-Leste	…	…	…	…	…	…	…	…	…	…	…	…	…	…	…
Tokelau	…	…	…	…	…	…	…	…	…	…	…	…	…	…	…
Tonga	…	…	…	99	99	99	99	99	99	…	…	0.5	46	0.4	45
Tuvalu	…	…	…	…	…	…	…	…	…	…	…	…	…	…	…
Vanuatu	…	…	…	…	…	…	84	85	82	…	…	…	…	…	…
Viet Nam	88*	93*	83*	90*	94*	87*	…	…	…	4 789	72*	5 892	69*	…	…
Latin America and the Caribbean															
Anguilla	…	…	…	…	…	…	…	…	…	…	…	…	…	…	…
Antigua and Barbuda	…	…	…	…	…	…	…	…	…	…	…	…	…	…	…
Argentina	96*	96*	96*	98	98	98	98	98	98	889	53*	701	51	602	50
Aruba	…	…	…	98	98	98	98	99	98	…	…	2	54	1	54
Bahamas	…	…	…	…	…	…	…	…	…	…	…	…	…	…	…
Barbados	…	…	…	…	…	…	…	…	…	…	…	…	…	…	…
Belize	70*	70*	70*	…	…	…	…	…	…	32	49*	…	…	…	…
Bermuda	…	…	…	…	…	…	…	…	…	…	…	…	…	…	…
Bolivia	80*	88*	72*	90	95	85	93	97	90	825	71*	597	76	471	77
Brazil	…	…	…	90*	89*	90*	93	92	93	…	…	14 242	50*	11 275	49
British Virgin Islands	…	…	…	…	…	…	…	…	…	…	…	…	…	…	…
Cayman Islands	…	…	…	…	…	…	…	…	…	…	…	…	…	…	…
Chile	94*	95*	94*	96	96	96	97	97	97	547	53*	447	52	367	51
Colombia	81*	81*	81*	92*	92*	92*	95	95	95	4 458	52*	2 461	52*	1 876	51
Costa Rica	…	…	…	96	96	96	97	96	97	…	…	133	47	124	46
Cuba	…	…	…	100	100	100	100	100	100	…	…	19	53	17	54
Dominica	…	…	…	…	…	…	…	…	…	…	…	…	…	…	…
Dominican Republic	…	…	…	89	88	89	92	91	92	…	…	718	49	641	48
Ecuador	88*	90*	86*	92	93	91	94	95	93	731	59*	678	57	636	56
El Salvador	74*	77*	71*	84*	87*	81*	89	91	87	830	58*	729	61*	594	60
Grenada	…	…	…	…	…	…	…	…	…	…	…	…	…	…	…
Guatemala	64*	72*	57*	72	78	67	79	83	74	1 915	61*	2 047	63	2 106	63
Guyana	…	…	…	…	…	…	…	…	…	…	…	…	…	…	…
Haiti	…	…	…	…	…	…	…	…	…	…	…	…	…	…	…
Honduras	…	…	…	83	82	83	86	85	88	…	…	734	49	747	46
Jamaica	…	…	…	85	80	91	89	85	94	…	…	269	33	218	30
Mexico	88*	90*	85*	92*	94*	90*	94	96	93	6 397	62*	6 037	64*	4 880	64
Montserrat	…	…	…	…	…	…	…	…	…	…	…	…	…	…	…
Netherlands Antilles	95*	95*	95*	96	96	96	97	97	97	7	54*	6	55	5	54
Nicaragua	…	…	…	80	79	81	84	82	85	…	…	693	49	685	46
Panama	89*	89*	88*	93	94	93	95	95	94	175	52*	156	55	150	55
Paraguay	90*	92*	89*	94	94	93	95	95	95	255	59*	250	55	242	53
Peru	87*	93*	82*	89*	94*	83*	93	96	90	1 848	72*	2 126	74*	1 578	75
Saint Kitts and Nevis	…	…	…	…	…	…	…	…	…	…	…	…	…	…	…

YOUTH LITERACY RATE (15-24) (%)									YOUTH ILLITERATES (15-24)						
1985-1994[1]			2000-2006[1]			Projected 2015			1985-1994[1]		2000-2006[1]		Projected 2015		
Total	Male	Female	Total	Male	Female	Total	Male	Female	Total (000)	% Female	Total (000)	% Female	Total (000)	% Female	**Country or territory**
...	...	...	...	...	...	...	...	...	...	...	...	...	...	...	Fiji
96*	97*	95*	99	99	99	99	99	99	1 421	65*	506	53	335	42	Indonesia
...	...	...	...	...	...	...	...	...	...	...	...	...	...	...	Japan
...	...	...	...	...	...	...	...	...	...	...	...	...	...	...	Kiribati
...	...	...	82	85	79	87	89	85	...	...	228	58	196	58	Lao PDR
...	...	...	100	100	100	100	100	100	...	...	0.2	37	0.05	22	Macao, China
96*	96*	95*	98	98	98	99	99	99	155	53*	90	47	51	43	Malaysia
...	...	...	...	...	...	...	...	...	...	...	...	...	...	...	Marshall Islands
...	...	...	...	...	...	...	...	...	...	...	...	...	...	...	Micronesia
...	...	...	95*	96*	93*	...	...	...	...	...	509	60*	...	...	Myanmar
...	...	...	...	...	...	...	...	...	...	...	...	...	...	...	Nauru
...	...	...	...	...	...	...	...	...	...	...	...	...	...	...	New Zealand
...	...	...	...	...	...	...	...	...	...	...	...	...	...	...	Niue
...	...	...	...	...	...	...	...	...	...	...	...	...	...	...	Palau
...	...	...	64	63	65	68	63	74	...	...	434	48	490	40	Papua New Guinea
97*	96*	97*	94	94	95	95	94	96	428	45*	950	42	997	38	Philippines
...	...	...	...	...	...	...	...	...	...	...	...	...	...	...	Republic of Korea
99*	99*	99*	99	99	99	100	99	100	0.3	49*	0.2	42	0.2	37	Samoa
99*	99*	99*	100	100	100	100	100	100	6	44*	2	38	1	31	Singapore
...	...	...	...	...	...	...	...	...	...	...	...	...	...	...	Solomon Islands
...	...	...	98	98	98	99	99	99	...	...	187	52	132	49	Thailand
...	...	...	...	...	...	...	...	...	...	...	...	...	...	...	Timor-Leste
...	...	...	...	...	...	...	...	...	...	...	...	...	...	...	Tokelau
...	...	...	100	100	100	100	100	100	...	...	0.1	40	0.1	45	Tonga
...	...	...	...	...	...	...	...	...	...	...	...	...	...	...	Tuvalu
...	...	...	...	...	...	...	...	...	...	...	...	...	...	...	Vanuatu
94*	94*	93*	94*	94*	94*	...	...	...	831	53*	1 771	39*	...	...	Viet Nam
															Latin America and the Caribbean
...	...	...	...	...	...	...	...	...	...	...	...	...	...	...	Anguilla
...	...	...	...	...	...	...	...	...	...	...	...	...	...	...	Antigua and Barbuda
98*	98*	99*	99	99	99	99	99	99	92	43*	60	39	48	37	Argentina
...	...	...	99	99	99	100	99	100	...	...	0.1	44	0.07	40	Aruba
...	...	...	...	...	...	...	...	...	...	...	...	...	...	...	Bahamas
...	...	...	...	...	...	...	...	...	...	...	...	...	...	...	Barbados
76*	76*	77*	...	...	...	...	...	...	9	49*	...	...	...	...	Belize
...	...	...	...	...	...	...	...	...	...	...	...	...	...	...	Bermuda
94*	96*	92*	98	99	98	99	99	99	83	70*	30	68	18	63	Bolivia
...	...	...	98*	97*	98*	99	98	99	...	...	853	33*	375	26	Brazil
...	...	...	...	...	...	...	...	...	...	...	...	...	...	...	British Virgin Islands
...	...	...	...	...	...	...	...	...	...	...	...	...	...	...	Cayman Islands
98*	98*	99*	99	99	99	99	99	100	38	41*	28	41	17	39	Chile
91*	89*	92*	98*	98*	98*	98	98	99	693	43*	181	42*	139	34	Colombia
...	...	...	98	98	98	98	98	99	...	...	18	38	13	35	Costa Rica
...	...	...	100	100	100	100	100	100	...	...	0.4	52	0.2	64	Cuba
...	...	...	...	...	...	...	...	...	...	...	...	...	...	...	Dominica
...	...	...	96	95	97	97	97	98	...	...	76	37	52	34	Dominican Republic
96*	97*	96*	96	96	97	97	96	97	79	54*	89	46	88	41	Ecuador
85*	85*	85*	95*	94*	95*	97	96	98	173	51*	64	45*	45	35	El Salvador
...	...	...	...	...	...	...	...	...	...	...	...	...	...	...	Grenada
76*	82*	71*	85	88	82	89	90	88	462	62*	396	60	362	56	Guatemala
...	...	...	...	...	...	...	...	...	...	...	...	...	...	...	Guyana
...	...	...	...	...	...	...	...	...	...	...	...	...	...	...	Haiti
...	...	...	90	88	93	92	89	95	...	...	146	38	140	31	Honduras
...	...	...	94	90	98	96	94	99	...	...	30	19	20	17	Jamaica
95*	96*	95*	98*	98*	98*	99	99	99	828	56*	402	57*	215	45	Mexico
...	...	...	...	...	...	...	...	...	...	...	...	...	...	...	Montserrat
97*	97*	97*	98	98	98	99	99	99	0.9	44*	0.4	50	0.3	49	Netherlands Antilles
...	...	...	88	85	91	92	88	95	...	...	140	36	109	29	Nicaragua
95*	95*	95*	96	97	96	97	97	97	25	52*	22	52	21	50	Panama
96*	96*	95*	96	96	96	97	97	97	37	52*	47	47	39	44	Paraguay
95*	97*	94*	98*	99*	97*	99	99	98	215	67*	121	67*	79	54	Peru
...	...	...	...	...	...	...	...	...	...	...	...	...	...	...	Saint Kitts and Nevis

Table 2 (continued)

Country or territory	ADULT LITERACY RATE (15 and over) (%)									ADULT ILLITERATES (15 and over)					
	1985-1994[1]			2000-2006[1]			Projected 2015			1985-1994[1]		2000-2006[1]		Projected 2015	
	Total	Male	Female	Total	Male	Female	Total	Male	Female	Total (000)	% Female	Total (000)	% Female	Total (000)	% Female
Saint Lucia	…	…	…	…	…	…	…	…	…	…	…	…	…	…	…
Saint Vincent/Grenad.	…	…	…	…	…	…	…	…	…	…	…	…	…	…	…
Suriname	…	…	…	90	93	88	92	94	91	…	…	32	63	27	62
Trinidad and Tobago	97*	98*	96*	99	99	98	99	99	99	26	70*	14	67	10	62
Turks and Caicos Islands	…	…	…	…	…	…	…	…	…	…	…	…	…	…	…
Uruguay	95*	95*	96*	98*	97*	98*	98	98	99	102	46*	56	45*	45	42
Venezuela, B. R.	90*	91*	89*	93*	93*	93*	…	…	…	1 242	54*	1 318	52*	…	…
North America and Western Europe															
Andorra	…	…	…	…	…	…	…	…	…	…	…	…	…	…	…
Austria	…	…	…	…	…	…	…	…	…	…	…	…	…	…	…
Belgium	…	…	…	…	…	…	…	…	…	…	…	…	…	…	…
Canada	…	…	…	…	…	…	…	…	…	…	…	…	…	…	…
Cyprus	94*	98*	91*	98	99	96	99	99	98	29	81*	17	78	9	75
Denmark	…	…	…	…	…	…	…	…	…	…	…	…	…	…	…
Finland	…	…	…	…	…	…	…	…	…	…	…	…	…	…	…
France	…	…	…	…	…	…	…	…	…	…	…	…	…	…	…
Germany	…	…	…	…	…	…	…	…	…	…	…	…	…	…	…
Greece	93*	96*	89*	97	98	96	98	99	97	615	74*	289	70	200	67
Iceland	…	…	…	…	…	…	…	…	…	…	…	…	…	…	…
Ireland	…	…	…	…	…	…	…	…	…	…	…	…	…	…	…
Israel	…	…	…	…	…	…	…	…	…	…	…	…	…	…	…
Italy	…	…	…	99	99	99	99	99	99	…	…	596	63	386	62
Luxembourg	…	…	…	…	…	…	…	…	…	…	…	…	…	…	…
Malta	88*	88*	88*	91	90	93	93	92	95	31	50*	29	41	24	37
Monaco	…	…	…	…	…	…	…	…	…	…	…	…	…	…	…
Netherlands	…	…	…	…	…	…	…	…	…	…	…	…	…	…	…
Norway	…	…	…	…	…	…	…	…	…	…	…	…	…	…	…
Portugal	88*	92*	85*	95	96	93	97	98	96	965	67*	486	68	268	68
San Marino	…	…	…	…	…	…	…	…	…	…	…	…	…	…	…
Spain	96*	98*	95*	97	99	96	98	99	97	1 103	73*	988	72	787	72
Sweden	…	…	…	…	…	…	…	…	…	…	…	…	…	…	…
Switzerland	…	…	…	…	…	…	…	…	…	…	…	…	…	…	…
United Kingdom	…	…	…	…	…	…	…	…	…	…	…	…	…	…	…
United States	…	…	…	…	…	…	…	…	…	…	…	…	…	…	…
South and West Asia															
Afghanistan	…	…	…	28*	43*	13*	…	…	…	…	…	9 916	59*	…	…
Bangladesh	35*	44*	26*	52	58	47	61	64	58	44 458	56*	48 392	55	48 189	53
Bhutan	…	…	…	54	66	40	64	73	54	…	…	202	60	198	60
India[2]	48*	62*	34*	65	76	53	72	81	62	283 848	61*	270 058	65	261 687	65
Iran, Islamic Republic of	66*	74*	56*	84	89	78	89	93	85	11 124	62*	8 133	67	6 504	69
Maldives	96*	96*	96*	97	97	97	98	97	98	5	47*	6	48	6	46
Nepal	33*	49*	17*	55	69	42	66	77	56	7 619	63*	7 620	67	7 346	67
Pakistan	…	…	…	54*	68*	40*	62	73	49	…	…	47 060	64*	49 588	64
Sri Lanka[2]	…	…	…	91*	93*	89*	93	94	92	…	…	1 339	61*	1 061	59
Sub-Saharan Africa															
Angola	…	…	…	67*	83*	54*	…	…	…	…	…	2 828	74*	…	…
Benin	27*	40*	17*	40	52	27	47	59	35	2 131	59*	2 959	61	3 476	61
Botswana	69*	65*	71*	82	82	82	87	87	88	247	47*	215	51	176	49
Burkina Faso	14*	20*	8*	26	34	18	36	43	30	4 136	55*	5 740	56	6 567	56
Burundi	37*	48*	28*	59*	67*	52*	…	…	…	1 945	61*	1 831	61*	…	…
Cameroon	…	…	…	68*	77*	60*	…	…	…	…	…	3 367	62*	…	…
Cape Verde	63*	75*	53*	83	89	78	89	93	86	70	70*	54	69	45	68
Central African Republic	34*	48*	20*	49*	65*	33*	…	…	…	1 085	63*	1 263	67*	…	…
Chad	12*	…	…	26*	41*	13*	…	…	…	3 177	…	4 133	60*	…	…
Comoros	…	…	…	…	…	…	…	…	…	…	…	…	…	…	…
Congo	74	83	65	86	92	81	92	95	89	404	67	299	70	216	72
Côte d'Ivoire	34*	44*	23*	49*	61*	39*	…	…	…	4 180	55*	5 541	60*	…	…
D. R. Congo	…	…	…	67*	81*	54*	…	…	…	…	…	10 486	71*	…	…
Equatorial Guinea	…	…	…	87*	93*	80*	…	…	…	…	…	38	75*	…	…
Eritrea	…	…	…	…	…	…	…	…	…	…	…	…	…	…	…

YOUTH LITERACY RATE (15-24) (%)									YOUTH ILLITERATES (15-24)						
1985-1994[1]			2000-2006[1]			Projected 2015			1985-1994[1]		2000-2006[1]		Projected 2015		
Total	Male	Female	Total	Male	Female	Total	Male	Female	Total (000)	% Female	Total (000)	% Female	Total (000)	% Female	**Country or territory**
...	...	...	...	...	...	...	...	...	...	...	...	...	...	...	Saint Lucia
...	...	...	...	...	...	...	...	...	...	...	...	...	...	...	Saint Vincent/Grenad.
...	...	...	95	96	94	96	96	96	...	...	4	56	3	53	Suriname
99*	99*	99*	99	99	99	100	100	100	2	50*	1	49	0.8	48	Trinidad and Tobago
...	...	...	...	...	...	...	...	...	...	...	...	...	...	...	Turks and Caicos Islands
99*	98*	99*	99*	98*	99*	99	99	99	6	37*	6	34*	6	30	Uruguay
95*	95*	96*	97*	96*	98*	...	...	...	176	39*	148	34*	...	...	Venezuela, B. R.
															North America and Western Europe
...	...	...	...	...	...	...	...	...	...	...	...	...	...	...	Andorra
...	...	...	...	...	...	...	...	...	...	...	...	...	...	...	Austria
...	...	...	...	...	...	...	...	...	...	...	...	...	...	...	Belgium
...	...	...	...	...	...	...	...	...	...	...	...	...	...	...	Canada
100*	100*	100*	100	100	100	100	100	100	0.4	44*	0.2	37	0.1	36	Cyprus
...	...	...	...	...	...	...	...	...	...	...	...	...	...	...	Denmark
...	...	...	...	...	...	...	...	...	...	...	...	...	...	...	Finland
...	...	...	...	...	...	...	...	...	...	...	...	...	...	...	France
...	...	...	...	...	...	...	...	...	...	...	...	...	...	...	Germany
99*	99*	99*	99	99	99	99	100	99	16	49*	10	50	6.0	56	Greece
...	...	...	...	...	...	...	...	...	...	...	...	...	...	...	Iceland
...	...	...	...	...	...	...	...	...	...	...	...	...	...	...	Ireland
...	...	...	...	...	...	...	...	...	...	...	...	...	...	...	Israel
...	...	...	100	100	100	100	100	100	...	...	7	46	4	46	Italy
...	...	...	...	...	...	...	...	...	...	...	...	...	...	...	Luxembourg
98*	97*	99*	97	96	99	98	97	99	1	26*	2	24	0.9	21	Malta
...	...	...	...	...	...	...	...	...	...	...	...	...	...	...	Monaco
...	...	...	...	...	...	...	...	...	...	...	...	...	...	...	Netherlands
...	...	...	...	...	...	...	...	...	...	...	...	...	...	...	Norway
99*	99*	99*	100	100	100	100	100	100	13	46*	5	44	2	42	Portugal
...	...	...	...	...	...	...	...	...	...	...	...	...	...	...	San Marino
100*	100*	100*	100	100	100	100	100	100	29	47*	17	48	12	50	Spain
...	...	...	...	...	...	...	...	...	...	...	...	...	...	...	Sweden
...	...	...	...	...	...	...	...	...	...	...	...	...	...	...	Switzerland
...	...	...	...	...	...	...	...	...	...	...	...	...	...	...	United Kingdom
...	...	...	...	...	...	...	...	...	...	...	...	...	...	...	United States
															South and West Asia
...	...	...	34*	51*	18*	...	...	...	...	...	3 324	60*	...	...	Afghanistan
45*	52*	38*	71	70	72	83	80	85	12 833	55*	9 175	48	5 908	41	Bangladesh
...	...	...	76	81	70	88	90	87	...	...	36	59	17	55	Bhutan
62*	74*	49*	81	86	76	88	90	86	63 893	64*	41 644	62	29 320	58	India[2]
87*	92*	81*	98	98	97	99	99	99	1 399	70*	423	61	169	52	Iran, Islamic Republic of
98*	98*	98*	98	98	98	98	98	99	1	45*	1	42	1	37	Maldives
50*	68*	33*	78	85	71	88	91	85	1 847	67*	1 228	64	819	60	Nepal
...	...	...	69*	79*	58*	78	83	72	...	...	11 151	65*	8 771	60	Pakistan
...	...	...	97*	97*	98*	99	98	99	...	...	90	40*	43	35	Sri Lanka[2]
															Sub-Saharan Africa
...	...	...	72*	84*	63*	...	...	...	...	...	888	70*	...	...	Angola
40*	55*	27*	51	63	40	60	69	51	612	62*	870	61	895	61	Benin
89*	86*	92*	94	93	95	95	95	96	31	35*	26	39	20	43	Botswana
20*	27*	14*	34	40	28	45	47	43	1 495	54*	1 912	54	2 068	51	Burkina Faso
54*	59*	48*	73*	77*	70*	...	...	...	495	56*	473	56*	...	...	Burundi
...	...	...	...	...	...	...	...	...	...	...	...	...	...	...	Cameroon
88*	90*	86*	97	96	98	99	98	100	8	58*	4	40	1	20	Cape Verde
48*	63*	35*	59*	70*	47*	...	...	...	270	64*	365	65*	...	...	Central African Republic
17*	...	...	38*	56*	23*	...	...	...	1 042	...	1 235	63*	...	...	Chad
...	...	...	...	...	...	...	...	...	...	...	...	...	...	...	Comoros
94	96	91	98	99	97	100	100	100	35	69	14	67	3	60	Congo
49*	60*	38*	61*	71*	52*	...	...	...	1 054	60*	1 587	62*	...	...	Côte d'Ivoire
...	...	...	70*	78*	63*	...	...	...	...	...	3 512	63*	...	...	D. R. Congo
...	...	...	95*	95*	95*	...	...	...	...	...	5	49*	...	...	Equatorial Guinea
...	...	...	...	...	...	...	...	...	...	...	...	...	...	...	Eritrea

Table 2 (continued)

Country or territory	ADULT LITERACY RATE (15 and over) (%) 1985-1994[1] Total	Male	Female	2000-2006[1] Total	Male	Female	Projected 2015 Total	Male	Female	ADULT ILLITERATES (15 and over) 1985-1994[1] Total (000)	% Female	2000-2006[1] Total (000)	% Female	Projected 2015 Total (000)	% Female
Ethiopia	27*	36*	19*	36*	50*	23*	…	…	…	23 045	57*	28 859	64*	…	…
Gabon	72*	79*	65*	85	90	81	91	94	88	165	64*	124	65	92	66
Gambia	…	…	…	…	…	…	…	…	…	…	…	…	…	…	…
Ghana	…	…	…	64	71	57	71	76	66	…	…	5 053	59	5 152	58
Guinea	…	…	…	29*	43*	18*	…	…	…	…	…	3 628	59*	…	…
Guinea-Bissau	…	…	…	…	…	…	…	…	…	…	…	…	…	…	…
Kenya	…	…	…	74*	78*	70*	…	…	…	…	…	5 473	58*	…	…
Lesotho	…	…	…	82*	74*	90*	…	…	…	…	…	205	31*	…	…
Liberia	41	52	30	54	60	49	64	65	64	652	60	865	56	946	51
Madagascar	…	…	…	71*	77*	65*	…	…	…	…	…	3 154	60*	…	…
Malawi	49*	65*	34*	71	79	63	79	83	74	2 197	68*	2 094	64	2 009	61
Mali	…	…	…	23	31	16	27	34	20	…	…	4 832	58	6 146	57
Mauritius	80*	85*	75*	87	90	84	90	92	89	150	63*	124	62	103	60
Mozambique	…	…	…	44	57	32	49	58	41	…	…	6 566	64	7 112	60
Namibia	76*	78*	74*	88	88	87	90	90	91	198	56*	156	54	150	49
Niger	…	…	…	30	44	16	36	48	23	…	…	5 014	60	6 334	60
Nigeria	55*	68*	44*	71	79	63	79	85	74	23 296	64*	23 451	65	21 577	63
Rwanda	58*	…	…	65*	71*	60*	…	…	…	1 468	…	1 871	61*	…	…
Sao Tome and Principe	73*	85*	62*	87	93	82	91	94	88	17	73*	11	74	10	68
Senegal	27*	37*	18*	42	53	32	47	56	38	2 964	56*	4 067	60	4 802	59
Seychelles	88*	87*	89*	92*	91*	92*	…	…	…	…	…	…	…	…	…
Sierra Leone	…	…	…	37	49	26	47	58	37	…	…	2 066	61	2 080	61
Somalia	…	…	…	…	…	…	…	…	…	…	…	…	…	…	…
South Africa	…	…	…	88	88	87	91	92	91	…	…	4 088	55	3 107	55
Swaziland	67*	70*	65*	80*	81*	78*	…	…	…	126	59*	141	56*	…	…
Togo	…	…	…	53*	69*	38*	…	…	…	…	…	1 706	67*	…	…
Uganda	56*	68*	45*	73	81	64	81	86	75	4 185	64*	4 154	66	4 045	64
United Republic of Tanzania	59*	71*	48*	72	79	65	74	79	70	5 217	65*	6 157	63	7 185	59
Zambia	65*	73*	57*	68*	76*	60*	…	…	…	1 541	62*	2 039	63*	…	…
Zimbabwe	84*	89*	79*	91	94	88	94	96	93	990	66*	754	67	532	65

	Weighted average									Sum	% F	Sum	% F	Sum	% F
World	76	82	70	84	88	79	87	90	83	871 096	63	775 894	64	706 130	64
Countries in transition	98	99	97	99	100	99	100	100	100	3 730	84	1 519	71	752	59
Developed countries	99	99	99	99	99	99	99	100	99	8 686	64	7 660	62	7 047	59
Developing countries	68	77	59	79	85	73	84	88	79	858 680	63	766 716	64	698 332	64
Arab States	58	70	46	72	82	61	79	87	71	55 311	63	57 798	67	53 339	69
Central and Eastern Europe	96	98	94	97	99	96	98	99	97	11 945	78	8 235	80	6 801	79
Central Asia	98	99	97	99	99	98	99	99	100	960	74	784	68	328	50
East Asia and the Pacific	82	89	75	93	96	90	95	97	94	229 172	69	112 637	71	81 398	71
East Asia	82	89	75	93	96	90	96	97	94	227 859	69	110 859	71	79 420	71
Pacific	94	94	93	93	93	92	93	93	93	1 313	56	1 778	55	1 979	52
Latin America/Caribbean	87	88	86	91	91	90	93	94	93	39 575	55	36 946	55	31 225	54
Caribbean	66	65	67	74	72	76	78	75	81	2 870	50	2 803	48	2 749	45
Latin America	87	88	86	91	92	90	94	94	93	36 705	55	34 142	56	28 476	55
N. America/W. Europe	99	99	99	99	99	99	99	99	99	6 400	63	5 682	61	5 115	59
South and West Asia	48	60	34	64	74	52	71	79	62	394 719	61	392 725	63	380 256	63
Sub-Saharan Africa	53	63	45	62	71	53	72	78	67	133 013	61	161 088	62	147 669	60

Note: For countries indicated with (*), national observed literacy data are used. For all others, UIS literacy estimates are used. The estimates were generated using the UIS Global Age-specific Literacy Projections model. Those in the most recent period refer to 2006 and are based on the most recent observed data available for each country.

The population used to generate the number of illiterates is from the United Nations Population Division estimates (2007), revision 2006. For countries with national observed literacy data, the population corresponding to the year of the census or survey was used. For countries with UIS estimates, populations used are for 1994 and 2006.

YOUTH LITERACY RATE (15-24) (%)									YOUTH ILLITERATES (15-24)						
1985-1994[1]			2000-2006[1]			Projected 2015			1985-1994[1]		2000-2006[1]		Projected 2015		
Total	Male	Female	Total	Male	Female	Total	Male	Female	Total (000)	% Female	Total (000)	% Female	Total (000)	% Female	**Country or territory**
34*	39*	28*	50*	62*	39*	...	...	...	7 404	54*	8 068	62*	...	...	Ethiopia
93*	94*	92*	97	98	96	98	99	97	13	59*	9	66	5	72	Gabon
...	...	...	...	...	...	...	...	...	...	...	...	...	...	...	Gambia
...	...	...	77	79	75	84	84	84	...	...	1 111	54	867	48	Ghana
...	...	...	47*	59*	34*	...	...	...	...	...	967	61*	...	...	Guinea
...	...	...	...	...	...	...	...	...	...	...	...	...	...	...	Guinea-Bissau
...	...	...	80*	80*	81*	...	...	...	...	...	1 588	49*	...	...	Kenya
...	...	...	...	...	...	...	...	...	...	...	...	...	...	...	Lesotho
51	56	47	70	67	74	80	72	87	196	54	212	44	200	31	Liberia
...	...	...	70*	73*	68*	...	...	...	...	...	1 108	54*	...	...	Madagascar
59*	70*	49*	82	83	81	90	89	91	616	64*	484	53	380	45	Malawi
...	...	...	29	36	22	33	38	27	...	...	1 732	55	2 175	55	Mali
91*	91*	92*	96	95	97	97	96	98	18	46*	8	37	6	31	Mauritius
...	...	...	52	58	46	57	59	56	...	...	1 977	56	2 225	52	Mozambique
88*	86*	90*	93	91	94	94	91	96	35	40*	34	39	34	32	Namibia
...	...	...	38	53	25	46	56	36	...	...	1 493	64	1 884	60	Niger
71*	81*	62*	86	88	84	92	92	91	5 091	67*	4 171	58	3 078	51	Nigeria
75*	...	...	78*	79*	77*	...	...	...	305	...	524	52*	...	...	Rwanda
94*	96*	92*	95	95	95	95	93	96	1	65*	2	48	2	35	Sao Tome and Principe
38*	49*	28*	51	58	43	56	61	51	849	58*	1 224	58	1 322	55	Senegal
99*	98*	99*	99*	99*	99*	...	...	...	...	...	...	...	...	...	Seychelles
...	...	...	52	63	42	67	76	59	...	...	522	61	430	63	Sierra Leone
...	...	...	...	...	...	...	...	...	...	...	...	...	...	...	Somalia
...	...	...	95	94	96	98	97	98	...	...	491	41	218	35	South Africa
84*	83*	84*	88*	87*	90*	...	...	...	24	51*	33	44*	...	...	Swaziland
...	...	...	74*	84*	64*	...	...	...	...	...	346	69*	...	...	Togo
70*	77*	63*	85	88	83	91	92	91	1 061	62*	893	58	711	52	Uganda
82*	86*	78*	78	79	76	77	76	77	831	62*	1 795	53	2 306	49	United Republic of Tanzania
66*	67*	66*	69*	73*	66*	...	...	...	543	51*	758	55*	...	...	Zambia
95*	97*	94*	98	98	98	99	99	100	102	62*	62	41	25	16	Zimbabwe

Weighted average									Sum	% F	Sum	% F	Sum	% F	
84	88	79	89	91	86	92	93	91	166 725	62	130 498	59	92 655	54	World
100	100	100	100	100	100	100	100	100	122	46	149	43	133	33	Countries in transition
99	99	99	99	99	99	99	99	99	752	53	789	52	786	52	Developed countries
80	85	75	87	90	84	91	92	90	165 852	62	129 559	59	91 736	54	Developing countries
76	84	67	86	91	81	93	95	90	10 934	66	8 949	67	5 192	63	Arab States
98	99	97	99	99	98	99	99	98	1 056	71	774	67	643	63	Central and Eastern Europe
100	100	100	99	99	100	99	99	100	58	47	82	43	108	27	Central Asia
95	97	93	98	98	98	99	99	99	19 961	68	6 449	54	3 935	47	East Asia and the Pacific
95	97	93	98	98	98	99	99	99	19 607	69	5 974	54	3 404	47	East Asia
92	93	92	91	90	91	90	89	92	354	54	475	48	531	40	Pacific
94	93	94	97	96	97	98	97	98	5 638	46	3 290	43	2 170	38	Latin America/Caribbean
78	75	81	86	82	90	91	87	95	578	44	462	36	303	26	Caribbean
94	94	95	97	97	97	98	98	99	5 060	46	2 828	45	1 867	40	Latin America
99	100	99	99	100	99	99	100	99	476	52	495	52	497	52	N. America/W. Europe
61	72	49	79	84	74	87	89	85	92 147	62	67 074	60	46 007	56	South and West Asia
64	70	58	71	76	67	81	82	80	36 456	59	43 385	59	34 101	53	Sub-Saharan Africa

1. Data are for the most recent year available during the period specified.
See the web version of the introduction to the statistical tables for a broader explanation of national literacy definitions, assessment methods, and sources and years of data.
2. Literacy data for the most recent year do not include some geographic regions.

Table 3A
Early childhood care and education (ECCE): care

	CHILD SURVIVAL[1]		CHILD WELL-BEING[2]						
				% of children under age 5 suffering from:			% of children who are:		
Country or territory	Infant mortality rate (‰) 2005-2010	Under-5 mortality rate (‰) 2005-2010	Infants with low birth weight (%) 1999-2006[3]	Underweight moderate and severe 2000-2006[3]	Wasting moderate and severe 2000-2006[3]	Stunting moderate and severe 2000-2006[3]	Exclusively breastfed (<6 months) 2000-2006[3]	Breastfed with complementary food (6-9 months) 2000-2006[3]	Still breastfeeding (20-23 months) 2000-2006[3]
Arab States									
Algeria	31	33	6	4	3	11	7	39	22
Bahrain	11	14	8	9	5	10	34	65	41
Djibouti	85	126	10	29	21	33	1	23	18
Egypt	29	34	14	6	4	18	38	67	37
Iraq	82	105	15	8	5	21	25	51	36
Jordan	19	22	12	4	2	9	27	70	12
Kuwait	8	10	7	10	11	24	12	26	9
Lebanon	22	26	6	4	5	11	27	35	11
Libyan Arab Jamahiriya	18	20	7	5	3	15	…	…	23
Mauritania	63	92	…	32	13	35	20	78	57
Morocco	31	36	15	10	9	18	31	66	15
Oman	12	14	8	18	7	10	…	92	73
Palestinian A. T.	18	20	7	3	1	10	27	…	…
Qatar	8	10	10	6	2	8	12	48	21
Saudi Arabia	19	22	11	14	11	20	31	60	30
Sudan	65	105	31	41	16	43	16	47	40
Syrian Arab Republic	16	18	9	10	9	22	29	37	16
Tunisia	20	22	7	4	2	12	47	…	22
United Arab Emirates	8	9	15	14	15	17	34	52	29
Yemen	59	79	32	46	12	53	12	76	…
Central and Eastern Europe									
Albania	19	22	7	8	7	22	2	38	20
Belarus	9	12	4	1	1	3	9	38	4
Bosnia and Herzegovina	12	14	5	2	3	7	18	29	10
Bulgaria	12	14	10	…	…	…	…	…	…
Croatia	6	8	6	1	1	1	23	…	…
Czech Republic	4	5	7	…	…	…	…	…	…
Estonia	7	10	4	…	…	…	…	…	…
Hungary	7	8	9	…	…	…	…	…	…
Latvia	10	14	5	…	…	…	…	…	…
Lithuania	9	11	4	…	…	…	…	…	…
Montenegro	22	24	4	3	3	5	19	35	13
Poland	7	8	6	…	…	…	…	…	…
Republic of Moldova	16	19	6	4	4	8	46	18	2
Romania	15	18	8	3	2	10	16	41	…
Russian Federation	17	21	6	3	4	13	…	…	…
Serbia	12	14	5	2	3	6	15	39	8
Slovakia	7	8	7	…	…	…	…	…	…
Slovenia	5	6	6	…	…	…	…	…	…
TFYR Macedonia	15	17	6	2	2	9	37	8	10
Turkey	28	32	16	4	1	12	21	38	24
Ukraine	13	16	4	1	0	3	6	83	11
Central Asia									
Armenia	29	34	8	4	5	13	33	57	15
Azerbaijan	72	86	12	7	2	13	7	39	16
Georgia	39	41	7	3	2	12	18	12	12
Kazakhstan	24	29	6	4	4	13	17	39	16
Kyrgyzstan	53	64	5	3	4	14	32	49	26
Mongolia	40	54	6	6	2	21	57	57	65
Tajikistan	60	78	10	17	7	27	25	15	34
Turkmenistan	75	95	4	11	6	15	11	54	37
Uzbekistan	55	66	5	5	3	15	26	45	38
East Asia and the Pacific									
Australia[6]	4	6	7	…	…	…	…	…	…
Brunei Darussalam	6	7	10	…	…	…	…	…	…
Cambodia	63	89	11	36	7	37	60	82	54

CHILD WELL-BEING[2]					PROVISION FOR UNDER-3s		WOMEN'S EMPLOYMENT AND MATERNITY LEAVE		
% of 1-year-old children immunized against									
Tuberculosis	Diphtheria, Pertussis, Tetanus	Polio	Measles	Hepatitis B	Official programmes targeting children	Youngest age group targeted in programmes	Female labour force participation rate (age 15 and above)[4]	Duration of paid maternity leave[5]	
Corresponding vaccines:									
BCG	DPT3	Polio3	Measles	HepB3	under age 3	(years)	(%)	(weeks)	
2006	2006	2006	2006	2006	2005	c. 2005	2003	2005-2007[3]	**Country or territory**
									Arab States
99	95	95	91	80	…	…	34	14	Algeria
…	98	98	99	98	Yes	0-2	29	…	Bahrain
88	72	72	67	…	…	…	53	…	Djibouti
99	98	98	98	98	Yes	2-3	21	13	Egypt
91	60	63	60	75	…	…	20	…	Iraq
95	98	98	99	98	Yes	0-3	26	…	Jordan
…	99	99	99	99	No	.	45	…	Kuwait
…	92	92	96	88	Yes	0-2	30	…	Lebanon
99	98	98	98	98	…	…	28	12	Libyan Arab Jamahiriya
86	68	68	62	68	…	…	54	14	Mauritania
95	97	97	95	95	No	.	27	14	Morocco
99	98	98	96	99	No	.	20	…	Oman
99	96	96	99	97	Yes	0-4	…	…	Palestinian A. T.
99	96	95	99	96	…	…	36	…	Qatar
95	96	96	95	96	…	…	17	…	Saudi Arabia
77	78	77	73	60	Yes	0-6	23	0	Sudan
99	99	99	98	98	Yes	0-2	37	…	Syrian Arab Republic
99	99	99	98	99	No	.	27	4	Tunisia
98	94	94	92	92	No	.	36	…	United Arab Emirates
70	85	85	80	85	No	.	29	…	Yemen
									Central and Eastern Europe
98	98	97	97	98	No	.	50	52	Albania
99	99	97	97	98	…	…	53	18	Belarus
97	87	91	90	82	Yes	0-3	55	…	Bosnia and Herzegovina
98	95	96	96	96	No	.	45	19	Bulgaria
98	96	96	96	…	…	…	45	58	Croatia
99	98	98	97	98	No	.	51	28	Czech Republic
99	95	95	96	95	Yes	1-6	53	20	Estonia
99	99	99	99	…	Yes	0-2	43	24	Hungary
99	98	98	95	97	No	.	51	16	Latvia
99	94	94	97	95	No	.	53	18	Lithuania
98	90	90	90	90	…	…	…	…	Montenegro
94	99	99	99	98	…	…	48	16	Poland
99	97	98	96	98	…	…	57	18	Republic of Moldova
99	97	97	95	99	No	.	49	17	Romania
97	99	99	99	98	…	…	54	20	Russian Federation
99	92	97	88	93	…	…	…	…	Serbia
98	99	99	98	99	…	…	53	28	Slovakia
…	97	97	96	…	Yes	1-3	50	15	Slovenia
92	93	92	94	89	No	.	43	…	TFYR Macedonia
88	90	90	98	82	Yes	0-2	27	12	Turkey
97	98	99	98	96	Yes	0-3	51	18	Ukraine
									Central Asia
91	87	87	92	78	Yes	2	50	20	Armenia
99	95	97	96	93	Yes	0-2	60	18	Azerbaijan
95	87	88	95	83	Yes	0-2	57	8	Georgia
99	99	99	99	99	Yes	1-6	64	18	Kazakhstan
99	92	93	97	90	Yes	1-3	55	18	Kyrgyzstan
98	99	98	99	98	Yes	2-3	54	…	Mongolia
94	86	81	87	86	No	.	49	…	Tajikistan
99	98	98	99	98	Yes	0-2	61	16	Turkmenistan
98	95	94	95	97	Yes	2-3	56	18	Uzbekistan
									East Asia and the Pacific
…	92	92	94	94	Yes	1-4	55	52	Australia[6]
96	99	99	97	99	…	…	44	…	Brunei Darussalam
87	80	80	78	80	Yes	0-6	74	…	Cambodia

Table 3A (continued)

Country or territory	CHILD SURVIVAL[1]		CHILD WELL-BEING[2]						
				% of children under age 5 suffering from:			% of children who are:		
	Infant mortality rate (‰)	Under-5 mortality rate (‰)	Infants with low birth weight (%)	Underweight moderate and severe	Wasting moderate and severe	Stunting moderate and severe	Exclusively breastfed (<6 months)	Breastfed with complementary food (6-9 months)	Still breastfeeding (20-23 months)
	2005-2010	2005-2010	1999-2006[3]	2000-2006[3]	2000-2006[3]	2000-2006[3]	2000-2006[3]	2000-2006[3]	2000-2006[3]
China	23	29	2	7	…	11	51	32	15
Cook Islands	…	…	3	10	…	…	19	…	…
DPR Korea	48	62	7	23	7	37	65	31	37
Fiji	20	24	10	…	…	…	47	…	…
Indonesia	27	32	9	28	…	…	40	75	59
Japan	3	4	8	…	…	…	…	…	…
Kiribati	…	…	5	13	…	…	80	…	…
Lao PDR	51	67	14	40	15	42	23	10	47
Macao, China	7	8	…	…	…	…	…	…	…
Malaysia	9	11	9	8	…	…	29	…	12
Marshall Islands	…	…	12	…	…	…	63	…	…
Micronesia	34	42	18	15	…	…	60	…	…
Myanmar	66	97	15	32	9	32	15	66	67
Nauru	…	…	…	…	…	…	…	…	…
New Zealand	5	6	6	…	…	…	…	…	…
Niue	…	…	0	…	…	…	…	…	…
Palau	…	…	9	…	…	…	59	…	…
Papua New Guinea	61	84	11	…	…	…	59	74	66
Philippines	23	27	20	28	6	30	34	58	32
Republic of Korea	4	5	4	…	…	…	…	…	…
Samoa	22	27	4	…	…	…	…	…	…
Singapore	3	4	8	3	2	2	…	…	…
Solomon Islands[7]	55	72	13	…	…	…	65	…	…
Thailand	11	15	9	9	4	12	5	43	19
Timor-Leste	67	92	…	…	…	…	…	…	…
Tokelau	…	…	…	…	…	…	…	…	…
Tonga	19	22	3	…	…	…	62	…	…
Tuvalu	…	…	5	…	…	…	…	…	…
Vanuatu	28	34	6	…	…	…	50	…	…
Viet Nam	20	23	7	25	7	30	17	70	23
Latin America and the Caribbean									
Anguilla	…	…	…	…	…	…	…	…	…
Antigua and Barbuda	…	…	5	…	…	…	…	…	…
Argentina	13	16	7	4	1	4	…	…	…
Aruba	17	20	…	…	…	…	…	…	…
Bahamas	14	17	7	…	…	…	…	…	…
Barbados	10	11	13	…	…	…	…	…	…
Belize	16	20	6	7	1	18	24	54	23
Bermuda	…	…	…	…	…	…	…	…	…
Bolivia	46	61	7	8	1	27	54	74	46
Brazil	24	29	8	6	2	11	…	30	17
British Virgin Islands	…	…	…	…	…	…	…	…	…
Cayman Islands	…	…	…	…	…	…	…	…	…
Chile	7	9	6	1	0	1	63	47	…
Colombia	19	26	9	7	1	12	47	65	32
Costa Rica	10	11	7	5	2	6	35	47	12
Cuba	5	7	5	4	2	5	41	42	9
Dominica	…	…	10	…	…	…	…	…	…
Dominican Republic	30	33	11	5	1	7	4	36	15
Ecuador	21	26	16	9	2	23	40	77	23
El Salvador	22	29	7	10	1	19	24	76	43
Grenada	34	41	9	…	…	…	39	…	…
Guatemala	30	39	12	23	2	49	51	67	47
Guyana	43	57	13	14	11	11	11	42	31
Haiti	49	72	25	22	9	24	41	87	35
Honduras	28	42	10	11	1	25	30	69	48
Jamaica	14	17	12	4	4	3	15	36	24
Mexico	17	20	8	5	2	13	38	36	21
Montserrat	…	…	…	…	…	…	…	…	…
Netherlands Antilles	15	17	…	…	…	…	…	…	…
Nicaragua	21	26	12	10	2	20	31	68	39

CHILD WELL-BEING[2]					PROVISION FOR UNDER-3s		WOMEN'S EMPLOYMENT AND MATERNITY LEAVE		
% of 1-year-old children immunized against									
Tuberculosis	Diphtheria, Pertussis, Tetanus	Polio	Measles	Hepatitis B	Official programmes targeting children	Youngest age group targeted in programmes	Female labour force participation rate (age 15 and above)[4]	Duration of paid maternity leave[5]	
Corresponding vaccines:									
BCG	DPT3	Polio3	Measles	HepB3	under age 3	(years)	(%)	(weeks)	
2006	2006	2006	2006	2006	2005	c. 2005	2003	2005-2007[3]	**Country or territory**
92	93	94	93	91	Yes	0-3	70	13	China
99	99	99	99	99	…	…	…	…	Cook Islands
96	89	98	96	96	Yes	0-3	51	…	DPR Korea
93	81	83	99	81	No	.	50	…	Fiji
82	70	70	72	70	Yes	0-6	51	0	Indonesia
…	99	97	99	…	Yes	0-6	49	14	Japan
99	86	86	61	88	No	.	…	…	Kiribati
61	57	56	48	57	Yes	0-2	54	12	Lao PDR
…	…	…	…	…	No	.	54	…	Macao, China
99	96	96	90	87	Yes	0-3	45	0	Malaysia
92	74	95	96	97	…	…	…	0	Marshall Islands
55	67	81	83	84	…	…	…	…	Micronesia
85	82	82	78	75	…	…	68	12	Myanmar
99	72	45	99	99	…	…	…	…	Nauru
…	89	89	82	87	Yes	0-5	59	14	New Zealand
99	99	99	99	99	…	…	…	…	Niue
…	98	98	98	98	…	…	…	…	Palau
75	75	75	65	70	No	.	72	…	Papua New Guinea
91	88	88	92	77	No	.	52	9	Philippines
98	98	98	99	99	Yes	0-5	49	12	Republic of Korea
84	56	57	54	56	…	…	40	…	Samoa
98	95	95	93	94	Yes	2-6	50	12	Singapore
84	91	91	84	93	No	.	55	0	Solomon Islands[7]
99	98	98	96	96	Yes	0-5	65	13	Thailand
72	67	66	64	…	…	…	54	…	Timor-Leste
…	…	…	…	…	…	…	…	…	Tokelau
99	99	99	99	99	…	…	46	…	Tonga
99	97	97	84	97	…	…	…	…	Tuvalu
92	85	85	99	85	…	…	79	12	Vanuatu
95	94	94	93	93	Yes	0-2	72	17	Viet Nam
									Latin America and the Caribbean
…	…	…	…	…	…	…	…	…	Anguilla
…	99	99	99	99	…	…	…	13	Antigua and Barbuda
99	91	92	97	84	Yes	0-5	52	13	Argentina
…	…	…	…	…	…	…	…	…	Aruba
…	95	94	88	96	…	…	64	13	Bahamas
…	84	85	92	84	Yes	0-2	65	12	Barbados
97	98	98	99	98	…	…	42	14	Belize
…	…	…	…	…	…	…	…	4	Bermuda
93	81	79	81	81	Yes	0-4	63	13	Bolivia
99	99	99	99	97	Yes	0-3	57	17	Brazil
…	…	…	…	…	Yes	0-3	54	13	British Virgin Islands
…	…	…	…	…	…	…	…	…	Cayman Islands
98	94	94	91	94	Yes	0-2	37	18	Chile
88	86	86	88	86	Yes	0-5	60	12	Colombia
88	91	91	89	90	Yes	0-3	42	17	Costa Rica
99	89	99	96	89	Yes	1-6	43	18	Cuba
99	95	88	99	7	…	…	…	12	Dominica
95	81	85	99	74	…	…	44	12	Dominican Republic
99	98	97	97	98	Yes	0-4	54	12	Ecuador
93	96	96	98	96	Yes	0-3	47	12	El Salvador
…	91	91	98	91	Yes	0-2	…	12	Grenada
96	80	81	95	80	Yes	0-6	33	12	Guatemala
96	93	92	90	93	No	.	43	13	Guyana
75	53	52	58	…	Yes	0-3	55	…	Haiti
90	87	87	91	87	Yes	0-3	44	12	Honduras
90	85	86	87	87	No	.	57	8	Jamaica
99	98	98	96	98	Yes	0-3	39	12	Mexico
…	…	…	…	…	…	…	…	…	Montserrat
…	…	…	…	…	…	…	50	…	Netherlands Antilles
99	87	88	99	87	Yes	0-3	36	12	Nicaragua

Table 3A (continued)

Country or territory	CHILD SURVIVAL[1]		CHILD WELL-BEING[2]						
				% of children under age 5 suffering from:			% of children who are:		
	Infant mortality rate (‰) 2005-2010	Under-5 mortality rate (‰) 2005-2010	Infants with low birth weight (%) 1999-2006[3]	Underweight moderate and severe 2000-2006[3]	Wasting moderate and severe 2000-2006[3]	Stunting moderate and severe 2000-2006[3]	Exclusively breastfed (<6 months) 2000-2006[3]	Breastfed with complementary food (6-9 months) 2000-2006[3]	Still breastfeeding (20-23 months) 2000-2006[3]
Panama	18	24	10	8	1	18	25	38	21
Paraguay	32	38	9	5	1	14	22	60	…
Peru	21	29	11	8	1	24	64	81	41
Saint Kitts and Nevis	…	…	9	…	…	…	56	…	…
Saint Lucia	13	16	12	…	…	…	…	…	…
Saint Vincent/Grenad.	23	28	5	…	…	…	…	…	…
Suriname	28	35	13	13	7	10	9	25	11
Trinidad and Tobago	12	18	19	6	4	4	13	43	22
Turks and Caicos Islands	…	…	…	…	…	…	…	…	…
Uruguay	13	16	8	5	2	11	…	…	…
Venezuela, Bolivarian Rep. of	17	22	9	5	4	13	7	50	31
North America and Western Europe									
Andorra	…	…	…	…	…	…	…	…	…
Austria	4	5	7	…	…	…	…	…	…
Belgium	4	5	8	…	…	…	…	…	…
Canada	5	6	6	…	…	…	…	…	…
Cyprus	6	7	…	…	…	…	…	…	…
Denmark	4	6	5	…	…	…	…	…	…
Finland	4	5	4	…	…	…	…	…	…
France	4	5	7	…	…	…	…	…	…
Germany	4	5	7	…	…	…	…	…	…
Greece	7	8	8	…	…	…	…	…	…
Iceland	3	4	4	…	…	…	…	…	…
Ireland	5	6	6	…	…	…	…	…	…
Israel	5	6	8	…	…	…	…	…	…
Italy	5	6	6	…	…	…	…	…	…
Luxembourg	5	7	8	…	…	…	…	…	…
Malta	6	8	6	…	…	…	…	…	…
Monaco	…	…	…	…	…	…	…	…	…
Netherlands	5	6	…	…	…	…	…	…	…
Norway	3	4	5	…	…	…	…	…	…
Portugal	5	7	8	…	…	…	…	…	…
San Marino	…	…	…	…	…	…	…	…	…
Spain	4	5	6	…	…	…	…	…	…
Sweden	3	4	4	…	…	…	…	…	…
Switzerland	4	5	6	…	…	…	…	…	…
United Kingdom	5	6	8	…	…	…	…	…	…
United States[7]	6	8	8	2	0	1	…	…	…
South and West Asia									
Afghanistan	157	235	…	39	7	54	…	29	54
Bangladesh	52	69	22	48	13	43	37	52	89
Bhutan	45	65	15	19	3	40	…	…	…
India	55	79	30	43	20	48	46	56	…
Iran, Islamic Republic of	31	35	7	11	5	15	44	…	0
Maldives	34	42	22	30	13	25	10	85	…
Nepal	54	72	21	39	13	49	53	75	95
Pakistan	67	95	19	38	13	37	16	31	56
Sri Lanka	11	13	22	29	14	14	53	…	73
Sub-Saharan Africa									
Angola	132	231	12	31	6	45	11	77	37
Benin	98	146	16	23	7	38	70	50	57
Botswana	46	68	10	13	5	23	34	57	11
Burkina Faso	104	181	16	37	23	35	7	50	85
Burundi	99	169	11	39	7	53	45	88	…
Cameroon	88	144	11	19	6	30	21	64	21
Cape Verde	25	29	13	…	…	…	57	64	13
Central African Republic	97	163	13	29	10	38	23	55	47
Chad	119	189	22	37	14	41	2	77	65
Comoros	48	63	25	25	8	44	21	34	45

CHILD WELL-BEING[2]					PROVISION FOR UNDER-3s		WOMEN'S EMPLOYMENT AND MATERNITY LEAVE		
% of 1-year-old children immunized against									
Tuberculosis	Diphtheria, Pertussis, Tetanus	Polio	Measles	Hepatitis B	Official programmes targeting children	Youngest age group targeted in programmes	Female labour force participation rate (age 15 and above)[4]	Duration of paid maternity leave[5]	
Corresponding vaccines:									
BCG	DPT3	Polio3	Measles	HepB3	under age 3	(years)	(%)	(weeks)	Country or territory
2006	2006	2006	2006	2006	2005	c. 2005	2003	2005-2007[3]	
99	99	99	94	99	Yes	2-4	47	14	Panama
75	73	72	88	73	Yes	0-4	64	9	Paraguay
99	94	95	99	94	Yes	0-5	58	13	Peru
99	99	99	99	99	...	...	...	13	Saint Kitts and Nevis
94	85	85	94	85	Yes	0-2	52	12	Saint Lucia
99	99	99	99	99	...	...	52	13	Saint Vincent/Grenad.
...	84	84	83	84	...	...	35	...	Suriname
...	92	89	89	89	Yes	0-5	49	13	Trinidad and Tobago
...	...	...	...	...	Yes	2	...	...	Turks and Caicos Islands
99	95	95	94	95	Yes	0-3	55	12	Uruguay
83	71	73	55	71	Yes	0-2	53	24	Venezuela, Bolivarian Rep. of
									North America and Western Europe
...	93	93	91	84	Yes	0-3	...	16	Andorra
...	83	83	80	83	Yes	1-3	50	16	Austria
...	97	97	88	78	Yes	1-3	43	15	Belgium
...	94	94	94	14	Yes	0-6	61	17	Canada
...	97	97	87	93	Yes	0-5	54	16	Cyprus
...	93	93	99	...	Yes	0-2	60	18	Denmark
98	97	97	97	...	Yes	0-6	57	18	Finland
84	98	98	87	29	Yes	0-3	48	16	France
...	90	96	94	86	Yes	0-2	50	14	Germany
88	88	87	88	88	Yes	0-3	41	17	Greece
...	97	97	95	...	Yes	0-6	70	13	Iceland
93	91	91	86	...	Yes	0-5	49	26	Ireland
...	95	93	95	95	Yes	0-4	49	12	Israel
...	96	97	87	96	Yes	0-2	37	21	Italy
...	99	99	95	95	No	...	44	16	Luxembourg
...	85	83	94	86	...	...	30	14	Malta
90	99	99	99	99	...	...	...	16	Monaco
...	98	98	96	...	Yes	0-3	55	16	Netherlands
...	93	93	91	...	Yes	0-5	62	9	Norway
89	93	93	93	94	Yes	0-3	55	17	Portugal
...	95	95	94	95	...	...	...	72	San Marino
...	98	98	97	81	Yes	0-3	44	16	Spain
17	99	99	95	...	Yes	1-6	60	15	Sweden
...	95	94	86	...	Yes	0-5	59	16	Switzerland
...	92	92	85	...	Yes	1-3	55	26	United Kingdom
...	96	92	93	92	Yes	0-4	59	12	United States[7]
									South and West Asia
90	77	77	68	...	...	...	38	12	Afghanistan
96	88	88	81	88	No	.	55	12	Bangladesh
92	95	96	90	95	No	.	39	...	Bhutan
78	55	58	59	6	Yes	0-6	35	12	India
99	99	99	99	99	Yes	0-6	35	16	Iran, Islamic Republic of
99	98	98	97	98	Yes	0-3	40	...	Maldives
93	89	91	85	69	No	.	51	7	Nepal
89	83	83	80	83	Yes	0-6	32	12	Pakistan
99	99	98	99	98	...	...	35	12	Sri Lanka
									Sub-Saharan Africa
65	44	44	48	...	...	...	74	...	Angola
99	93	93	89	93	Yes	2-5	54	14	Benin
99	97	97	90	85	Yes	0-4	48	12	Botswana
99	95	94	88	76	...	...	77	14	Burkina Faso
84	74	64	75	74	...	...	91	12	Burundi
85	81	78	73	81	Yes	1-6	52	14	Cameroon
70	72	72	65	69	...	...	34	6	Cape Verde
70	40	40	35	...	Yes	2-5	71	14	Central African Republic
40	20	36	23	...	...	...	65	14	Chad
84	69	69	66	69	...	...	58	...	Comoros

Table 3A (continued)

Country or territory	CHILD SURVIVAL[1]		CHILD WELL-BEING[2]						
				% of children under age 5 suffering from:			% of children who are:		
	Infant mortality rate (‰)	Under-5 mortality rate (‰)	Infants with low birth weight (%)	Underweight moderate and severe	Wasting moderate and severe	Stunting moderate and severe	Exclusively breastfed (<6 months)	Breastfed with complementary food (6-9 months)	Still breastfeeding (20-23 months)
	2005-2010	2005-2010	1999-2006[3]	2000-2006[3]	2000-2006[3]	2000-2006[3]	2000-2006[3]	2000-2006[3]	2000-2006[3]
Congo	70	102	13	14	7	26	19	78	21
Côte d'Ivoire	117	183	17	20	7	34	4	54	37
D. R. Congo	114	196	12	31	13	38	24	79	52
Equatorial Guinea	92	155	13	19	7	39	24	...	...
Eritrea	55	77	14	40	13	38	52	43	62
Ethiopia	87	145	20	38	11	47	49	54	...
Gabon	54	86	14	12	3	21	6	62	9
Gambia	74	128	20	20	6	22	41	44	53
Ghana	57	90	9	18	5	22	54	58	56
Guinea	103	156	12	26	9	35	27	41	71
Guinea-Bissau	113	195	...	...	...	...	...	...	...
Kenya	64	104	10	20	6	30	13	84	57
Lesotho	65	98	13	20	4	38	36	79	60
Liberia	133	205	...	26	6	39	35	70	45
Madagascar	66	106	17	42	13	48	67	78	64
Malawi	89	132	13	19	3	46	56	89	73
Mali	129	200	23	33	11	38	25	32	69
Mauritius	14	17	14	15	14	10	21	...	...
Mozambique	96	164	15	24	4	41	30	80	65
Namibia	42	66	14	24	9	24	19	57	37
Niger	111	188	13	44	10	50	14	62	62
Nigeria	109	187	14	29	9	38	17	64	34
Rwanda	112	188	6	23	4	45	88	69	77
Sao Tome and Principe	72	95	8	9	8	23	60	60	18
Senegal	66	115	19	17	8	16	34	61	42
Seychelles	...	...	...	...	...	...	...	...	...
Sierra Leone	160	278	24	30	9	40	8	52	57
Somalia	116	193	11	36	11	38	9	15	35
South Africa	45	66	15	12	3	25	7	46	...
Swaziland	71	114	9	10	1	30	24	60	25
Togo	89	126	12	26	14	24	28	35	44
Uganda	77	127	12	20	5	32	60	80	54
United Republic of Tanzania	73	118	10	22	3	38	41	91	55
Zambia	93	157	12	20	6	50	40	87	58
Zimbabwe	58	94	11	17	6	29	22	79	28
	Weighted average		**Weighted average**				**Weighted average**		
World	49	74	15	25	11	31	38	56	39
Countries in transition	31	38	...	...	...	...	...	...	...
Developed countries	6	7	...	...	...	...	...	...	...
Developing countries	54	81	16	26	11	32	38	56	40
Arab States	41	54	16	17	8	25	28	57	25
Central and Eastern Europe	17	21	...	...	...	...	...	...	...
Central Asia	51	62	...	...	...	...	...	...	...
East Asia and the Pacific	24	31	6	14	...	16	43	45	27
East Asia	24	31	...	...	...	...	...	...	...
Pacific	26	36	...	...	...	...	...	...	...
Latin America and the Caribbean	22	27	9	7	2	16	...	...	...
Caribbean	39	56	...	...	...	...	...	...	...
Latin America	21	26	...	...	...	...	...	...	...
N. America/W. Europe	5	7	...	...	...	...	...	...	...
South and West Asia	58	83	...	...	...	...	...	...	...
Sub-Saharan Africa	95	158	14	28	9	38	30	67	50

1. UN Population Division (2007), median variant.
2. UNICEF (2007).
3. Data are for the most recent year available during the period specified.
4. Employed and unemployed women as a share of the working age population, including women with a job but temporarily not at work (e.g. on maternity leave), home employment for the production of goods and services for own household consumption, and domestic and personal services produced by employing paid domestic staff. Data exclude women occupied solely in domestic duties in their own households (ILO, 2008).

CHILD WELL-BEING[2] % of 1-year-old children immunized against: Tuberculosis — Corresponding vaccines: BCG 2006	Diphtheria, Pertussis, Tetanus — DPT3 2006	Polio — Polio3 2006	Measles — Measles 2006	Hepatitis B — HepB3 2006	PROVISION FOR UNDER-3s: Official programmes targeting children under age 3 2005	Youngest age group targeted in programmes (years) c. 2005	WOMEN'S EMPLOYMENT AND MATERNITY LEAVE: Female labour force participation rate (age 15 and above)[4] (%) 2003	Duration of paid maternity leave[5] (weeks) 2005-2007[3]	Country or territory
84	79	79	66	...	...	...	61	15	Congo
77	77	76	73	77	...	...	39	14	Côte d'Ivoire
87	77	78	73	...	...	...	61	14	D. R. Congo
73	33	39	51	...	...	...	50	12	Equatorial Guinea
99	97	96	95	97	Yes	0-6	59	...	Eritrea
72	72	69	63	...	No	.	71	6	Ethiopia
89	38	31	55	38	...	...	61	14	Gabon
99	95	95	95	95	...	...	59	...	Gambia
99	84	84	85	84	Yes	0-2	71	0	Ghana
90	71	70	67	...	Yes	0-3	79	...	Guinea
87	77	74	60	...	...	...	62	...	Guinea-Bissau
92	80	77	77	80	...	...	69	8	Kenya
96	83	80	85	85	No	.	47	...	Lesotho
89	88	87	94	...	Yes	2-6	55	...	Liberia
72	61	63	59	61	Yes	0-3	79	14	Madagascar
99	99	99	85	99	...	...	85	0	Malawi
85	85	83	86	90	Yes	0-3	72	14	Mali
97	97	98	99	97	Yes	0-2	41	12	Mauritius
87	72	70	77	72	...	...	85	...	Mozambique
88	74	74	63	...	Yes	0-1	47	...	Namibia
64	39	55	47	...	Yes	2-6	71	14	Niger
69	54	61	62	41	Yes	0-3	46	12	Nigeria
98	99	99	95	99	...	...	81	8	Rwanda
98	99	97	85	75	...	...	30	9	Sao Tome and Principe
99	89	89	80	89	Yes	0-5	57	14	Senegal
99	99	99	99	99	Yes	0-3	...	10	Seychelles
82	64	64	67	...	No	.	56	0	Sierra Leone
50	35	35	35	...	...	...	59	...	Somalia
97	99	99	85	99	Yes	0-5	47	26	South Africa
78	68	67	57	68	Yes	0-6	31	...	Swaziland
96	87	87	83	...	...	...	51	14	Togo
85	80	81	89	80	...	...	80	...	Uganda
99	90	91	93	90	...	...	86	12	United Republic of Tanzania
94	80	80	84	80	Yes	0-6	66	0	Zambia
99	90	90	90	90	...	...	63	13	Zimbabwe

Weighted average							Median		
87	79	80	80	60	...	...	52	14	World
...	...	...	...	...	...	...	55	18	Countries in transition
...	...	...	...	...	...	...	51	16	Developed countries
86	78	79	78	59	...	...	53	12	Developing countries
92	91	91	89	88	...	...	30	...	Arab States
...	...	...	...	...	...	...	51	19	Central and Eastern Europe
...	...	...	...	...	...	...	55	18	Central Asia
91	89	89	89	86	...	...	55	...	East Asia and the Pacific
...	...	...	...	...	...	...	55	12	East Asia
...	...	...	...	...	...	...	...	...	Pacific
96	92	92	93	89	...	...	54	13	Latin America/Caribbean
...	...	...	...	...	...	...	54	13	Caribbean
...	...	...	...	...	...	...	54	12	Latin America
...	...	...	...	...	...	...	54	16	N. America/W. Europe
...	...	...	...	...	...	...	40	12	South and West Asia
82	72	74	72	48	...	...	60	13	Sub-Saharan Africa

5. Refers to paid employment-protected leave duration for employed women around the time of childbirth.

6. Maternity leave duration refers to unpaid parental leave, as no specific maternity leave policy exists (except for special medical cases).

7. Maternity leave duration refers to unpaid maternity leave.

Sources: For women's maternity leave status, US Social Security Administration (2006, 2007*a*, 2007*b*, 2008); OECD (2008).

Table 3B

Early childhood care and education (ECCE): education

	Country or territory	Age group	ENROLMENT IN PRE-PRIMARY EDUCATION				Enrolment in private institutions as % of total enrolment		GROSS ENROLMENT RATIO (GER) IN PRE-PRIMARY EDUCATION (%)			
			School year ending in				School year ending in		School year ending in			
			1999		2006		1999	2006	1999			
		2006	Total (000)	% F	Total (000)	% F			Total	Male	Female	GPI (F/M)
	Arab States											
1	Algeria	4-5	36	49	166	47	.	45	3	3	3	1.01
2	Bahrain	3-5	14	48	19	48	100	100	36	37	36	0.96
3	Djibouti	4-5	0.2	60	1	47	100	72	0.4	0.3	0.5	1.50
4	Egypt	4-5	328	48	**580**	**47**	54	**30**	11	11	10	0.95
5	Iraq	4-5	68	48	*93*[z]	*49*[z]	.	.[z]	5	5	5	0.98
6	Jordan	4-5	74	46	95	47	100	94	29	30	27	0.91
7	Kuwait	4-5	57	49	67	48	24	40	78	78	79	1.02
8	Lebanon	3-5	143	48	148	48	78	78	61	62	60	0.97
9	Libyan Arab Jamahiriya	4-5	10	*48*	22	48	.	17	5	*5*	*5*	*0.97*
10	Mauritania	3-5	…	…	*5*[z]	…	…	*78*[z]	…	…	…	…
11	Morocco	4-5	805	34	705	40	100	100	62	82	43	0.52
12	Oman	4-5	7	45	10	47	100	100	6	6	6	0.88
13	Palestinian A. T.	4-5	77	48	77	48	100	100	39	40	39	0.96
14	Qatar	3-5	8	48	16	49	100	90	25	25	25	0.98
15	Saudi Arabia	3-5	…	…	…	…	…	…	…	…	…	…
16	Sudan	4-5	366	…	505	49	*90*	70	19	…	…	…
17	Syrian Arab Republic	3-5	108	46	155	47	67	75	8	9	8	0.90
18	Tunisia	3-5	78	47	…	…	88	…	14	14	13	0.95
19	United Arab Emirates	4-5	64	48	90	48	68	77	64	65	63	0.97
20	Yemen	3-5	12	45	18[z]	45[z]	37	49[z]	0.7	0.7	0.6	0.86
	Central and Eastern Europe											
21	Albania	3-5	82	50	80[y]	48[y]	.	5[y]	40	39	41	1.06
22	Belarus	3-5	263	47*	271	48	–	5	75	77*	73*	0.95*
23	Bosnia and Herzegovina	3-5	…	…	…	…	…	…	…	…	…	…
24	Bulgaria	3-6	219	48	206	48	0.1	0.3[z]	67	67	66	0.99
25	Croatia	3-6	81	48	90	48	5	10	40	40	39	0.98
26	Czech Republic	3-5	312	50	284	48	2	1	90	87	93	1.07
27	Estonia	3-6	55	48	45	48	1	2	87	88	87	0.99
28	Hungary	3-6	376	48	327	48	3	5	78	79	77	0.98
29	Latvia	3-6	58	48	65	48	1	3	53	54	51	0.95
30	Lithuania	3-6	94	48	89	48	0.3	0.2	50	50	49	0.97
31	Montenegro	…	…	…	…	…	…	…	…	…	…	…
32	Poland	3-6	958	49	840	49	3	9	50	50	50	1.01
33	Republic of Moldova[1,2]	3-6	103	48	102	48	…	0.2	48	49	48	0.96
34	Romania	3-6	625	49	648	49	1	1	62	61	63	1.02
35	Russian Federation	3-6	4 379	…	4 530	47	…	2	68	…	…	…
36	Serbia[1]	3-6	175	46	**173**	**49**	…	**0.1**	*54*	*57*	*51*	*0.90*
37	Slovakia	3-5	169	…	145	48	0.4	2	82	…	…	…
38	Slovenia	3-5	59	46	43	48	1	2	75	78	71	0.91
39	TFYR Macedonia	3-6	33	49	33[z]	49[z]	.	.[z]	27	27	28	1.01
40	Turkey	3-5	261	47	550	48	6	9	6	6	6	0.94
41	Ukraine	3-5	1 103	48	1 032	48	0.04	3	50	50	49	0.98
	Central Asia											
42	Armenia	3-6	57	…	49	51	–	2	26	…	…	…
43	Azerbaijan	3-5	111	46	109	47	–	0.1	21	22	20	0.89
44	Georgia	3-5	74	48	76	46	0.1	–	36	36	36	1.00
45	Kazakhstan	3-6	165	48	**331**	**48**	10	**5**	14	15	14	0.96
46	Kyrgyzstan	3-6	48	43	57	49	1	1	10	11	9	0.80
47	Mongolia	3-6	74	54	95	52	4	1[z]	25	23	27	1.21
48	Tajikistan	3-6	56	42	62	46	.	.	8	9	7	0.76
49	Turkmenistan	3-6	…	…	…	…	…	…	…	…	…	…
50	Uzbekistan	3-6	616	47	**562**	**48**	…	**4**	24	24	23	0.94
	East Asia and the Pacific											
51	Australia	4-4	…	…	263	48	…	67	…	…	…	…
52	Brunei Darussalam	3-5	11	49	12	48	66	66	50	49	51	1.04
53	Cambodia	3-5	*58*	*50*	106	51	*22*	29	*5*	*5*	*5*	*1.03*
54	China	4-6	24 030	46	21 790	45	…	31	38	38	37	0.97

GROSS ENROLMENT RATIO (GER) IN PRE-PRIMARY EDUCATION (%)				NET ENROLMENT RATIO (NER) IN PRE-PRIMARY EDUCATION (%)				GROSS ENROLMENT RATIO (GER) IN PRE-PRIMARY AND OTHER ECCE PROGRAMMES (%)				NEW ENTRANTS TO THE FIRST GRADE OF PRIMARY EDUCATION WITH ECCE EXPERIENCE (%)			
School year ending in 2006				School year ending in 2006				School year ending in 2006				School year ending in 2006			
Total	Male	Female	GPI (F/M)	Total	Male	Female	GPI (F/M)	Total	Male	Female	GPI (F/M)	Total	Male	Female	
														Arab States	
15	15	14	0.93	6[z]	6[z]	6[z]	0.96[z]	…	…	…	…	4	4	4	1
52	52	51	0.98	51	51	50	0.98	55	56	54	0.97	82	83	81	2
2	2	2	0.92	*1*	*1*	*1*	*0.99*	2	2	2	0.92	2	2	2	3
17	**18**	**17**	**0.94**	**16**	**17**	**16**	**0.93**	**17**	**18**	**17**	**0.94**	…	…	…	4
6[z]	*6[z]*	*6[z]*	*1.00[z]*	*6[z]*	*6[z]*	*6[z]*	*1.00[z]*	*6[z]*	*6[z]*	*6[z]*	*1.00[z]*	…	…	…	5
32	33	31	0.94	*30*	*31*	*29*	*0.95*	32	33	31	0.94	50	52	49	6
75	76	73	0.96	50	50	49	0.98	75	76	73	0.96	87	87	87	7
64	65	63	0.97	62	63	61	0.97	64	65	63	0.97	95	95	95	8
9	9	9	0.97	8	8	7	0.96	…	…	…	…	…	…	…	9
2[z]	…	…	…	…	…	…	…	…	…	…	…	50	52	48	10
59	70	48	0.69	52	62	43	0.70	59	70	48	0.69	…	…	…	11
8	9	8	0.94	7	7	7	0.95	8	9	8	0.94	…	…	…	12
30	31	30	0.98	25	25	25	0.98	30	31	30	0.98	…	…	…	13
43	43	43	1.00	40	39	40	1.02	43	43	43	1.00	…	…	…	14
…	…	…	…	…	…	…	…	…	…	…	…	…	…	…	15
24	24	24	1.00	*24[z]*	*24[z]*	*24[z]*	*1.00[z]*	24	24	24	1.00	51	47	55	16
11	11	11	0.93	11	11	10	0.93	11	11	11	0.93	12[z]	12[z]	12[z]	17
…	…	…	…	…	…	…	…	…	…	…	…	…	…	…	18
78	79	77	0.98	56	57	56	0.98	78	79	77	0.98	83	83	83	19
0.9[z]	1.0[z]	0.8[z]	0.85[z]	…	…	…	…	…	…	…	…	…	…	…	20
														Central and Eastern Europe	
49[y]	49[y]	49[y]	1.00[y]	47[y]	47[y]	47[y]	1.00[y]	49[y]	49[y]	49[y]	1.00[y]	…	…	…	21
103	104	102	0.98	90	90	89	0.99	120	122	119	0.98	…	…	…	22
…	…	…	…	…	…	…	…	…	…	…	…	…	…	…	23
82	82	82	0.99	79	79	78	0.99	82	82	82	0.99	…	…	…	24
50	50	49	0.98	50	50	49	0.98	50	50	49	0.98	…	…	…	25
114	116	112	0.96	…	…	…	…	114	116	112	0.96	…	…	…	26
93	93	92	0.99	88	88	88	1.00	…	…	…	…	…	…	…	27
86	87	86	0.99	85	86	85	1.00	86	87	86	0.99	…	…	…	28
89	90	88	0.98	87	87	86	0.99	89	90	88	0.98	…	…	…	29
69	70	68	0.98	68	68	67	0.98	69	70	68	0.98	…	…	…	30
…	…	…	…	…	…	…	…	…	…	…	…	…	…	…	31
57	57	58	1.01	56	55	56	1.01	57	57	58	1.01	…	…	…	32
71	71	70	0.99	69	69	68	0.99	71	71	70	0.99	…	…	…	33
72	72	73	1.01	71	71	72	1.02	72	72	73	1.01	…	…	…	34
87	90	85	0.95	70[y]	…	…	…	…	…	…	…	…	…	…	35
59	**59**	**59**	**1.00**	…	…	…	…	…	…	…	…	…	…	…	36
93	95	92	0.97	*86[z]*	*88[z]*	*85[z]*	*0.96[z]*	93	95	92	0.97	…	…	…	37
81	82	80	0.97	79	79	78	0.98	81	82	80	0.97	…	…	…	38
33[z]	33[z]	34[z]	1.03[z]	32[z]	31[z]	32[z]	1.02[z]	…	…	…	…	…	…	…	39
13	14	13	0.96	13	14	13	0.96	…	…	…	…	…	…	…	40
90	91	88	0.97	68	*69*	*67*	*0.97*	90	91	88	0.97	…	…	…	41
														Central Asia	
36	33	40	1.21	26*	24*	29*	1.20*	36	33	40	1.21	…	…	…	42
32	32	32	1.02	22	22	23	1.04	32	32	33	1.02	7	7	7	43
55	56	54	0.96	39	40	38	0.95	55	56	54	0.96	2[y]	2[y]	2[y]	44
38	**38**	**38**	**0.98**	**38**	**38**	**37**	**0.98**	…	…	…	…	…	…	…	45
14	14	14	1.00	11	11	11	1.00	14	14	14	1.00	13	13	13	46
54	51	57	1.13	47	…	…	…	…	…	…	…	…	…	…	47
9	10	9	0.88	7	7	7	0.91	…	…	…	…	…	…	…	48
…	…	…	…	…	…	…	…	…	…	…	…	…	…	…	49
27	**27**	**26**	**0.94**	21	…	…	…	…	…	…	…	…	…	…	50
														East Asia and the Pacific	
104	106	103	0.97	63	63	62	0.97	104	106	103	0.97	…	…	…	51
51	51	51	1.00	46	45	46	1.02	55	55	55	1.01	*99*	*99*	*99*	52
11	11	11	1.06	*10*	*10*	*10*	*1.07*	12	12	13	1.06	16	15	17	53
39	40	38	0.95	…	…	…	…	39	40	38	0.95	…	…	…	54

Table 3B (continued)

	Country or territory	Age group 2006	ENROLMENT IN PRE-PRIMARY EDUCATION, School year ending in 1999: Total (000)	1999: % F	2006: Total (000)	2006: % F	Enrolment in private institutions as % of total enrolment, School year ending in 1999	2006	GROSS ENROLMENT RATIO (GER) IN PRE-PRIMARY EDUCATION (%), School year ending in 1999: Total	Male	Female	GPI (F/M)
55	Cook Islands[1]	4-4	0.4	47	0.5[z]	45[z]	25	19[z]	86	87	85	0.98
56	DPR Korea	4-5	…	…	…	…	…	…	…	…	…	…
57	Fiji	3-5	9	49	9	49	…	*100*[z]	16	16	16	1.02
58	Indonesia	5-6	*1 981*	*49*	3 143	50	*99*	99	*23*	*23*	*23*	*1.01*
59	Japan	3-5	2 962	*49*	3 073	…	65	67	83	*82*	*84*	*1.02*
60	Kiribati	3-5	…	…	*5*[y]	…	…	…	…	…	…	…
61	Lao PDR	3-5	37	52	49	51	18	30	8	7	8	1.11
62	Macao, China	3-5	17	47	10	49	94	95	87	89	85	0.95
63	Malaysia	5-5	572	50	668[z]	51[z]	49	43[z]	108	105	110	1.04
64	Marshall Islands[1]	4-5	2	50	**1**	**48**	19	…	*59*	*57*	*60*	*1.04*
65	Micronesia	3-5	3	…	…	…	…	…	37	…	…	…
66	Myanmar	3-4	41	…	93	50	90	50	2	…	…	…
67	Nauru	3-5	…	…	**1**	**49**	…	…	…	…	…	…
68	New Zealand	3-4	101	49	102	49	…	98	85	85	85	1.00
69	Niue[1]	4-4	0.1	44	0.03[z]	58[z]	.	…	154	159	147	0.93
70	Palau[1]	3-5	0.7	54	*1*[z]	*53*[z]	24	*20*[z]	63	56	69	1.23
71	Papua New Guinea	6-6	…	…	…	…	…	…	…	…	…	…
72	Philippines	5-5	593	50	912	49	47	43	30	30	31	1.05
73	Republic of Korea	5-5	535	47	**547**	**48**	75	**78**	80	83	77	0.92
74	Samoa	3-4	*5*	*53*	*5*[y]	*54*[y]	*100*	…	*53*	*48*	*58*	*1.21*
75	Singapore[3]	3-5	*99*	*32*	…	…	…	…	…	…	…	…
76	Solomon Islands	3-5	*13*	*48*	…	…	…	…	*35*	*35*	*35*	*1.02*
77	Thailand	3-5	2 745	49	2 462	49	19	21	97	96	97	1.01
78	Timor-Leste	4-5	…	…	7[z]	51[z]	…	…	…	…	…	…
79	Tokelau[1]	3-4	…	…	*0.1*[y]	*48*[y]	…	…	…	…	…	…
80	Tonga	3-4	2	53	*1*[z]	*56*[z]	…	12[y]	30	27	33	1.24
81	Tuvalu[1]	3-5	…	…	0.7	52	…	…	…	…	…	…
82	Vanuatu	3-5	…	…	**5**	**48**	…	**83**	…	…	…	…
83	Viet Nam	3-5	2 179	48	2 713	48	49	61	39	41	38	0.94
	Latin America and the Caribbean											
84	Anguilla	3-4	0.5	52	0.5	49	100	100	…	…	…	…
85	Antigua and Barbuda	3-4	…	…	…	…	…	…	…	…	…	…
86	Argentina	3-5	1 191	50	1 334[z]	50[z]	28	30[z]	57	56	57	1.02
87	Aruba	4-5	3	49	3	49	83	75	99	99	99	1.00
88	Bahamas	3-4	1	51	…	…	…	…	12	11	12	1.09
89	Barbados	3-4	6	49	6	49	…	16	74	75	73	0.98
90	Belize	3-4	4	50	5	52	…	81	27	27	27	1.03
91	Bermuda	4-4	…	…	…	…	…	…	…	…	…	…
92	Bolivia	4-5	208	49	241	49	…	10	45	44	45	1.01
93	Brazil	4-6	5 733	49	7 298[z]	49[z]	28	29[y]	58	58	58	1.00
94	British Virgin Islands[1]	3-4	0.5	53	0.7	52	100	100	62	57	66	1.16
95	Cayman Islands[3]	4-4	0.5	48	0.7	52	88	92	…	…	…	…
96	Chile	3-5	450	49	402	50	45	52	77	77	76	0.99
97	Colombia	3-5	1 034	50	1 084	49	45	39	37	37	38	1.02
98	Costa Rica	4-5	70	49	110	49	10	11	84	84	85	1.01
99	Cuba	3-5	484	50	465	48	.	.	109	107	111	1.04
100	Dominica[1]	3-4	3	52	2[z]	50[z]	100	100[z]	80	76	85	1.11
101	Dominican Republic	3-5	195	49	212	49	45	44	32	31	32	1.01
102	Ecuador	5-5	181	50	261	49	39	43	64	63	66	1.04
103	El Salvador	4-6	194	49	240	50	*22*	18	43	42	43	1.01
104	Grenada[1]	3-4	4	50	*3*[z]	*52*[z]	…	…	93	93	93	1.01
105	Guatemala	3-6	308	49	451	50	22	20	46	46	45	0.97
106	Guyana	4-5	37	49	*33*	*49*	1	*8*	124	125	124	0.99
107	Haiti	3-5	…	…	…	…	…	…	…	…	…	…
108	Honduras	3-5	…	…	211	50	…	14	…	…	…	…
109	Jamaica	3-5	138	51	154[z]	50[z]	88	91[z]	78	75	81	1.08
110	Mexico	4-5	3 361	50	4 463	49	9	15	74	73	75	1.02
111	Montserrat	3-4	0.1	52	0.1	56	.	–	…	…	…	…
112	Netherlands Antilles	4-5	7	50	…	…	75	…	111	110	112	1.02
113	Nicaragua	3-5	161	50	210	49	17	16	27	27	28	1.04
114	Panama	4-5	49	49	92	49	23	17	39	39	40	1.01

GROSS ENROLMENT RATIO (GER) IN PRE-PRIMARY EDUCATION (%) School year ending in 2006				NET ENROLMENT RATIO (NER) IN PRE-PRIMARY EDUCATION (%) School year ending in 2006				GROSS ENROLMENT RATIO (GER) IN PRE-PRIMARY AND OTHER ECCE PROGRAMMES (%) School year ending in 2006				NEW ENTRANTS TO THE FIRST GRADE OF PRIMARY EDUCATION WITH ECCE EXPERIENCE (%) School year ending in 2006			
Total	Male	Female	GPI (F/M)	Total	Male	Female	GPI (F/M)	Total	Male	Female	GPI (F/M)	Total	Male	Female	
94[z]	99[z]	89[z]	0.90[z]	88[z]	92[z]	83[z]	0.91[z]	94[z]	99[z]	89[z]	0.90[z]	100[z]	100[z]	100[z]	55
...	...	...	...	...	...	...	...	...	...	...	...	...	...	...	56
16	16	16	1.01	15	15	15	1.01	16	16	16	1.01	...	...	...	57
37	36	38	1.03	26	26	27	1.03	37	36	38	1.03	42	42	42	58
86	...	...	...	85	...	...	...	101	...	...	...	...	...	...	59
75[y]	...	...	...	...	...	...	...	75[y]	...	...	...	...	...	...	60
11	11	12	1.06	11	10	11	1.07	11	11	12	1.06	10	9	10	61
87	87	86	0.99	82	82	81	0.99	87	87	86	0.99	97	97	97	62
125[z]	120[z]	131[z]	1.10[z]	74[z]	73[z]	77[z]	1.05[z]	125[z]	120[z]	131[z]	1.10[z]	76[z]	74[z]	79[z]	63
45	**45**	**45**	**1.00**	**9**	**9**	**10**	**1.05**	**45**	**45**	**45**	**1.00**	...	...	...	64
...	...	...	...	...	...	...	...	...	...	...	...	...	...	...	65
6	5	6	1.02	6	5	6	1.02	...	...	...	...	11	11	11	66
89	**89**	**88**	**0.99**	...	...	...	...	...	...	...	...	...	...	...	67
92	91	93	1.02	91	89	92	1.02	...	...	...	...	...	...	...	68
119[z]	108[z]	129[z]	1.19[z]	...	...	...	...	119[z]	108[z]	129[z]	1.19[z]	...	...	...	69
64[z]	59[z]	68[z]	1.16[z]	...	...	...	...	64[z]	59[z]	68[z]	1.16[z]	...	...	...	70
...	...	...	...	...	...	...	...	...	...	...	...	...	...	...	71
45	44	45	1.02	35	36	35	0.96	45	44	45	1.02	58	57	60	72
101	**100**	**103**	**1.03**	**54**	**54**	**55**	**1.03**	**101**	**100**	**103**	**1.03**	...	...	...	73
48[y]	43[y]	54[y]	1.26[y]	...	...	...	...	48[y]	43[y]	54[y]	1.26[y]	...	...	...	74
...	...	...	...	...	...	...	...	...	...	...	...	...	...	...	75
...	...	...	...	...	...	...	...	...	...	...	...	...	...	...	76
92	91	92	1.01	84	84	85	1.01	...	...	...	...	...	...	...	77
10[z]	10[z]	11[z]	1.09[z]	...	...	...	...	10[z]	10[z]	11[z]	1.09[z]	...	...	...	78
125[y]	126[y]	125[y]	1.00[y]	...	...	...	...	125[y]	126[y]	125[y]	1.00[y]	...	...	...	79
23[z]	19[z]	26[z]	1.37[z]	...	...	...	...	23[z]	19[z]	26[z]	1.37[z]	...	...	...	80
107	98	116	1.18	92	84	100	1.19	...	...	...	...	...	...	...	81
29	**29**	**29**	**0.98**	**20**	**20**	**20**	**1.02**	**29**	**29**	**29**	**0.98**	...	...	...	82
...	...	...	...	...	...	...	...	...	...	...	...	...	...	...	83
												Latin America and the Caribbean			
103	110	97	0.88	93	100	87	0.87	103	110	97	0.88	100	100	100	84
...	...	...	...	...	...	...	...	...	...	...	...	...	...	...	85
66[z]	65[z]	66[z]	1.02[z]	65[z]	65[z]	66[z]	1.02[z]	66[z]	65[z]	66[z]	1.02[z]	94[z]	94[z]	94[z]	86
99	99	98	1.00	96	96	97	1.00	99	99	98	1.00	90[z]	90[z]	90[z]	87
...	...	...	...	...	...	...	...	...	...	...	...	...	...	...	88
94	94	94	1.00	83	82	83	1.01	94	94	94	1.00	100	100	100	89
34	32	35	1.09	32	31	34	1.10	34	32	35	1.09	.	.	.	90
...	...	...	...	...	...	...	...	...	...	...	...	...	...	...	91
50	50	51	1.01	42	41	42	1.02	50	50	51	1.01	66	66	66	92
69[z]	69[z]	68[z]	0.98[z]	53[z]	53[z]	53[z]	1.00[z]	...	...	...	...	...	...	...	93
93	88	97	1.11	84	80	88	1.10	166	158	175	1.11	99	102	97	94
...	...	...	...	...	...	...	...	...	...	...	...	90*	90*	90*	95
55	54	55	1.03	...	...	...	...	55	54	55	1.03	...	...	...	96
40	41	40	0.99	35	35	35	1.00	40	41	40	0.99	...	...	...	97
70	70	70	1.00	...	...	...	...	74	74	74	1.00	86	86	86	98
113	113	113	1.00	100	99	100	1.01	193	193	193	1.00	99	99	99	99
77[z]	72[z]	82[z]	1.13[z]	...	...	...	...	77[z]	72[z]	82[z]	1.13[z]	100[y]	100[y]	100[y]	100
32	32	32	1.00	28	28	28	1.02	...	...	...	...	...	...	...	101
90	89	90	1.02	74	74	75	1.01	193	187	200	1.07	58	57	59	102
51	51	52	1.03	45	44	46	1.05	51	51	52	1.03	68	66	69	103
81[z]	77[z]	84[z]	1.09[z]	80[y]	76[y]	83[y]	1.09[y]	81[z]	77[z]	84[z]	1.09[z]	...	...	...	104
29	29	29	1.01	27	27	27	1.01	29	29	29	1.01	...	...	...	105
99	99	100	1.01	84	83	84	1.00	99	99	100	1.01	...	...	...	106
...	...	...	...	...	...	...	...	...	...	...	...	...	...	...	107
38	37	39	1.05	28	27	28	1.04	44	43	45	1.05	...	...	...	108
92[z]	91[z]	94[z]	1.03[z]	91[z]	90[z]	93[z]	1.04[z]	92[z]	91[z]	94[z]	1.03[z]	...	...	...	109
106	106	106	1.00	93	93	93	1.00	106	106	106	1.00	...	...	...	110
91	76	108	1.42	79	65	95	1.47	91	76	108	1.42	78[z]	114[z]	48[z]	111
...	...	...	...	...	...	...	...	...	...	...	...	...	...	...	112
52	52	53	1.02	52	52	53	1.02	74	...	...	...	42	42	43	113
67	67	67	1.01	60	59	60	1.01	67	67	67	1.01	69	68	70	114

Table 3B (continued)

	Country or territory	Age group 2006	ENROLMENT IN PRE-PRIMARY EDUCATION, School year ending in 1999: Total (000)	1999: % F	2006: Total (000)	2006: % F	Enrolment in private institutions as % of total enrolment, School year ending in 1999	2006	GROSS ENROLMENT RATIO (GER) IN PRE-PRIMARY EDUCATION (%), School year ending in 1999: Total	Male	Female	GPI (F/M)
115	Paraguay	3-5	123	50	148[z]	49[z]	29	28[z]	29	29	30	1.03
116	Peru	3-5	1 017	50	1 131	49	15	22	55	54	56	1.02
117	Saint Kitts and Nevis	3-4	…	…	**2**	**52**	…	**68**	…	…	…	…
118	Saint Lucia	3-4	*4*	*50*	4	50	…	100	*70*	*69*	*71*	*1.03*
119	Saint Vincent/Grenad.	3-4	…	…	*4[z]*	*49[z]*	…	*100[z]*	…	…	…	…
120	Suriname	4-5	…	…	16	47	…	48	…	…	…	…
121	Trinidad and Tobago	3-4	*23*	*50*	30[*,z]	49[*,z]	*100*	100[*,z]	*58*	*57*	*58*	*1.01*
122	Turks and Caicos Islands	4-5	0.8	54	1[z]	47[z]	47	65[z]	…	…	…	…
123	Uruguay	3-5	100	49	122	49	…	*43*	60	59	60	1.02
124	Venezuela, Bolivarian Rep. of	3-5	738	50	1 011	49	20	19	45	44	45	1.03
	North America and Western Europe											
125	Andorra[1]	3-5	…	…	3	47	…	2	…	…	…	…
126	Austria	3-5	225	49	217	48	25	27	82	82	82	0.99
127	Belgium	3-5	399	49	412	49	56	53	111	112	110	0.99
128	Canada	4-5	512	49	*494[y]*	*49[y]*	8	…	64	64	64	0.99
129	Cyprus[1]	3-5	19	49	20	48	54	50	60	59	60	1.02
130	Denmark	3-6	251	49	253	49	27	…	90	90	90	1.00
131	Finland	3-6	125	49	140	49	10	9	48	49	48	0.99
132	France[4]	3-5	2 393	49	2 628	49	13	13	112	112	112	1.00
133	Germany	3-5	2 333	48	2 418	48	54	63	94	94	93	0.98
134	Greece	4-5	143	49	143	49	3	3	68	67	68	1.01
135	Iceland	3-5	12	48	12	49	*5*	8	88	88	87	0.99
136	Ireland	3-3	…	…	…	…	…	…	…	…	…	…
137	Israel	3-5	355	48	362	49	7	3	105	106	105	0.98
138	Italy	3-5	1 578	48	1 662	48	30	30	95	96	95	0.98
139	Luxembourg	3-5	12	49	15	48	5	7	73	73	73	1.00
140	Malta	3-4	10	48	9[z]	50[z]	37	39[z]	103	103	102	0.99
141	Monaco[3]	3-5	0.9	52	1[y]	…	26	19[y]	…	…	…	…
142	Netherlands	4-5	390	49	355	49	69	70[y]	97	98	97	0.99
143	Norway	3-5	139	50	159	…	40	44	75	73	77	1.06
144	Portugal	3-5	220	49	262	49	52	47	69	69	69	0.99
145	San Marino[3]	3-5	…	…	1[y]	…	…	.[y]	…	…	…	…
146	Spain	3-5	1 131	49	1 490	49	32	35	100	100	100	1.00
147	Sweden	3-6	360	49	333	50	10	12	76	76	76	1.01
148	Switzerland	5-6	158	48	156	48	6	9	89	89	88	0.99
149	United Kingdom[5]	3-4	1 155	49	990	50	6	29	77	77	77	1.00
150	United States	3-5	7 183	48	7 342	49	34	37	58	59	57	0.97
	South and West Asia											
151	Afghanistan	3-6	…	…	*25[y]*	*43[y]*	…	…	…	…	…	…
152	Bangladesh	3-5	1 825	50	1 109[y]	49[y]	…	52[y]	17	17	17	1.04
153	Bhutan	4-5	0.3	48	*0.4*	*47*	100	*100*	1	1	1	0.93
154	India	3-5	13 869	48	29 254[z]	49[z]	…	…	18	18	19	1.02
155	Iran, Islamic Republic of[6]	5-5	220	50	549	51	…	8	13	13	14	1.05
156	Maldives	3-5	12	48	14	49	30	38[z]	54	54	54	1.00
157	Nepal	3-4	*238*	*41*	392	46	…	…	*11*	*13*	*10*	*0.73*
158	Pakistan	3-4	…	…	4 075[z]	46[z]	…	…	…	…	…	…
159	Sri Lanka	4-4	…	…	…	…	…	…	…	…	…	…
	Sub-Saharan Africa											
160	Angola	3-5	…	…	…	…	…	…	…	…	…	…
161	Benin	4-5	18	48	31	50	20	37[z]	4	4	4	0.97
162	Botswana	3-5	…	…	20[z]	50[z]	…	96[z]	…	…	…	…
163	Burkina Faso	4-6	20	50	27	48	34	…	2	2	2	1.04
164	Burundi	4-6	5	50	12	52	49	54	0.8	0.8	0.8	1.01
165	Cameroon	4-5	104	48	195	50	57	62	11	11	11	0.95
166	Cape Verde	3-5	…	…	21	50	…	–	…	…	…	…
167	Central African Republic	3-5	…	…	*6[y]*	*51[y]*	…	…	…	…	…	…
168	Chad	3-5	…	…	*8[z]*	*33[z]*	…	47[y]	…	…	…	…
169	Comoros	3-5	1	51	*2[z]*	*48[z]*	100	*62[z]*	2	2	2	1.07
170	Congo	3-5	6	61	28	52	85	79	2	2	3	1.59

GROSS ENROLMENT RATIO (GER) IN PRE-PRIMARY EDUCATION (%)				NET ENROLMENT RATIO (NER) IN PRE-PRIMARY EDUCATION (%)				GROSS ENROLMENT RATIO (GER) IN PRE-PRIMARY AND OTHER ECCE PROGRAMMES (%)				NEW ENTRANTS TO THE FIRST GRADE OF PRIMARY EDUCATION WITH ECCE EXPERIENCE (%)			
School year ending in 2006				School year ending in 2006				School year ending in 2006				School year ending in 2006			
Total	Male	Female	GPI (F/M)	Total	Male	Female	GPI (F/M)	Total	Male	Female	GPI (F/M)	Total	Male	Female	
34[z]	34[z]	34[z]	1.01[z]	30[z]	30[z]	31[z]	1.03[z]	34[z]	34[z]	34[z]	1.01[z]	75[y]	74[y]	76[y]	115
68	67	68	1.02	67	66	68	1.02	68	67	68	1.02	61	61	62	116
99	**91**	**107**	**1.18**	...	...	...	...	**143**	**133**	**153**	**1.15**	...	...	...	117
69	67	70	1.05	53	53	54	1.03	...	...	...	...	...	...	...	118
88[z]	*89[z]*	*86[z]*	*0.97[z]*	...	...	...	...	*88[z]*	*89[z]*	*86[z]*	*0.97[z]*	*100[z]*	*100[z]*	*100[z]*	119
84	87	80	0.93	*83[z]*	*82[z]*	*84[z]*	*1.02[z]*	...	...	...	...	100	100	100	120
85[*,z]	86[*,z]	84[*,z]	0.97[*,z]	68[*,z]	68[*,z]	67[*,z]	1.00[*,z]	85[*,z]	86[*,z]	84[*,z]	0.97[*,z]	81[*,y]	80[*,y]	82[*,y]	121
118[z]	*132[z]*	*106[z]*	*0.80[z]*	*73[z]*	*80[z]*	*68[z]*	*0.85[z]*	*118[z]*	*132[z]*	*106[z]*	*0.80[z]*	100[z]	101[z]	100[z]	122
79	79	80	1.01	79	79	80	1.01	94	94	95	1.02	96	96	96	123
60	60	60	1.01	54	54	54	1.02	80	80	80	1.01	75	74	76	124
North America and Western Europe															
102	102	102	1.00	86	86	87	1.00	102	102	102	1.00	...	...	...	125
90	90	89	0.99	*87*	*87*	*86*	*0.99*	90	90	89	0.99	...	...	...	126
121	122	121	0.99	100	100	100	1.00	121	122	121	0.99	...	...	...	127
68[y]	*68[y]*	*68[y]*	*1.00[y]*	...	...	...	...	...	...	...	...	...	...	...	128
79	80	78	0.98	71	72	70	0.98	79	80	78	0.98	...	...	...	129
95	95	96	1.01	92	90	93	1.04	95	95	96	1.01	...	...	...	130
62	62	62	0.99	61	61	61	1.00	62	62	62	0.99	...	...	...	131
116	116	115	1.00	100[y]	100[y]	100[y]	1.00[y]	116	116	115	1.00	...	...	...	132
105	106	105	0.99	...	...	...	...	105	106	105	0.99	...	...	...	133
69	68	70	1.02	69	68	70	1.02	69	68	70	1.02	...	...	...	134
96	96	96	1.00	96	96	96	1.00	96	96	96	1.00	...	...	...	135
...	...	...	...	...	...	...	...	...	...	...	...	...	...	...	136
91	91	91	1.00	86	85	87	1.02	91	91	91	1.00	...	...	...	137
104	105	104	0.98	99	100	98	0.98	104	105	104	0.98	...	...	...	138
88	88	88	1.00	86	86	86	1.01	88	88	88	1.00	...	...	...	139
97[z]	95[z]	100[z]	1.05[z]	83[z]	82[z]	85[z]	1.04[z]	97[z]	95[z]	100[z]	1.05[z]	...	...	...	140
...	...	...	...	...	...	...	...	...	...	...	...	...	...	...	141
90	90	90	0.99	90	90	90	0.99	90	90	90	0.99	...	...	...	142
90	...	...	...	90	...	...	...	90	...	...	...	...	...	...	143
79	79	80	1.01	78	78	79	1.02	79	79	80	1.01	...	...	...	144
...	...	...	...	...	...	...	...	...	...	...	...	...	...	...	145
121	121	120	1.00	100	100	100	1.00	...	...	...	...	...	...	...	146
95	93	98	1.05	95	92	98	1.06	95	93	98	1.05	...	...	...	147
99	99	98	1.00	74	74	74	0.99	99	99	98	1.00	...	...	...	148
72	71	73	1.03	67	67	68	1.03	72	71	73	1.03	...	...	...	149
61	61	61	1.00	56	56	57	1.02	61	61	61	1.00	...	...	...	150
South and West Asia															
0.8[y]	*0.9[y]*	*0.7[y]*	*0.80[y]*	...	...	...	...	*0.8[y]*	*0.9[y]*	*0.7[y]*	*0.80[y]*	...	...	...	151
10[y]	10[y]	10[y]	1.01[y]	9[y]	9[y]	9[y]	1.01[y]	...	...	...	...	...	...	...	152
2	*2*	*2*	*0.93*	...	...	...	...	*1.6*	*1.7*	*1.5*	*0.93*	...	...	...	153
39[z]	38[z]	40[z]	1.04[z]	...	...	...	...	39[z]	38[z]	40[z]	1.04[z]	...	...	...	154
53	50	56	1.11	...	...	...	...	53	50	56	1.11	31[z]	34[z]	29[z]	155
82	82	82	1.00	69	69	69	0.99	82	82	82	1.00	94	94	93	156
27	28	26	0.91	...	...	...	...	27	28	26	0.91	19[z]	19[z]	18[z]	157
52[z]	55[z]	50[z]	0.90[z]	43[z]	45[z]	40[z]	0.89[z]	...	...	...	...	57[z]	52[z]	63[z]	158
...	...	...	...	...	...	...	...	...	...	...	...	...	...	...	159
Sub-Saharan Africa															
...	...	...	...	...	...	...	...	...	...	...	...	...	...	...	160
6	6	6	1.05	*3[z]*	*3[z]*	*3[z]*	*1.03[z]*	...	...	...	...	...	...	...	161
15[z]	15[z]	15[z]	1.00[z]	11[z]	11[z]	11[z]	1.01[z]	15.4[z]	15.4[z]	15.3[z]	1.00[z]	...	...	...	162
2	2	2	0.97	...	...	...	...	2	2	2	0.97	3[y]	3[y]	3[y]	163
2	2	2	1.09	...	...	...	...	2	2	2	1.09	1	1	1	164
19	19	19	1.01	...	...	...	...	19	19	19	1.01	...	...	...	165
53	53	53	1.00	50	49	50	1.01	53	53	53	1.00	85	84	86	166
2[y]	*2[y]*	*2[y]*	*1.05[y]*	*2[y]*	*2[y]*	*2[y]*	*1.05[y]*	*2[y]*	*2[y]*	*2[y]*	*1.05[y]*	...	...	...	167
0.8[z]	*1.1[z]*	*0.5[z]*	*0.49[z]*	...	...	...	...	...	...	...	...	...	...	...	168
3[z]	*3[z]*	*3[z]*	*0.96[z]*	...	...	...	...	...	...	...	...	...	...	...	169
9	8	9	1.11	9	8	9	1.11	9	8	9	1.11	12[z]	11[z]	13[z]	170

Table 3B (continued)

	Country or territory	Age group 2006	ENROLMENT IN PRE-PRIMARY EDUCATION, School year ending in 1999: Total (000)	1999: % F	2006: Total (000)	2006: % F	Enrolment in private institutions as % of total enrolment, School year ending in 1999	2006	GROSS ENROLMENT RATIO (GER) IN PRE-PRIMARY EDUCATION (%), School year ending in 1999: Total	Male	Female	GPI (F/M)
171	Côte d'Ivoire	3-5	36	49	54	50	46	53	2	2	2	0.96
172	D. R. Congo	3-5	…	…	…	…	…	…	…	…	…	…
173	Equatorial Guinea	3-6	17	51	25[z]	45[z]	37	49[z]	34	33	34	1.04
174	Eritrea	5-6	12	47	36	50	97	44	5	6	5	0.89
175	Ethiopia	4-6	90	49	**219**	**49**	100	**95**	1	1	1	0.97
176	Gabon	3-5	…	…	…	…	…	…	…	…	…	…
177	Gambia	3-6	29	47	*30*[y]	*50*[y]	…	*100*[y]	18	19	17	0.91
178	Ghana	3-5	*667*	*49*	**1 105**	**50**	*33*	**19**	*39*	*39*	*39*	*1.02*
179	Guinea	3-6	…	…	80	49	…	84	…	…	…	…
180	Guinea-Bissau	4-6	*4*	*51*	…	…	*62*	…	*3*	*3*	*3*	*1.05*
181	Kenya	3-5	1 188	50	1 672	48	10	31[z]	44	44	43	1.00
182	Lesotho	3-5	*33*	*52*	30	64	*100*	100	*21*	*20*	*22*	*1.08*
183	Liberia	3-5	112	42	358	51	39	32	41	47	35	0.74
184	Madagascar	3-5	*50*	*51*	146	51	*93*	94	*3*	*3*	*3*	*1.02*
185	Malawi	3-5	…	…	…	…	…	…	…	…	…	…
186	Mali	3-6	21	51	51	*49*	…	…	2	2	2	1.06
187	Mauritius	3-4	42	50	37	50	85	83	96	95	97	1.02
188	Mozambique	3-5	…	…	…	…	…	…	…	…	…	…
189	Namibia	3-5	35	53	33	50	100	*100*[y]	21	19	22	1.15
190	Niger	4-6	12	50	24	51	33	31	1	1	1	1.04
191	Nigeria	3-5	…	…	1 753[y]	49[y]	…	…	…	…	…	…
192	Rwanda	4-6	…	…	…	…	…	…	…	…	…	…
193	Sao Tome and Principe	3-6	4	52	**6**	**51**	–	–[z]	25	24	26	1.12
194	Senegal	4-6	24	50	95	52	68	76	3	3	3	1.00
195	Seychelles[1]	4-5	3	49	**3**	**48**	5	**6**	109	107	111	1.04
196	Sierra Leone	3-5	…	…	**25**	**52**	…	**50**	…	…	…	…
197	Somalia	3-5	…	…	…	…	…	…	…	…	…	…
198	South Africa	6-6	207	50	387[y]	50[y]	26	7[y]	21	20	21	1.01
199	Swaziland	3-5	…	…	*15*[z]	*49*[z]	…	.[z]	…	…	…	…
200	Togo	3-5	11	50	*13*[y]	*50*[y]	53	*59*[y]	2	2	2	0.99
201	Uganda	4-5	*66*	*50*	69	50	*100*	100	*4*	*4*	*4*	*1.00*
202	United Republic of Tanzania	5-6	…	…	**795**	**51**	…	**2**	…	…	…	…
203	Zambia	3-6	…	…	…	…	…	…	…	…	…	…
204	Zimbabwe	3-5	*439*	*51*	…	…	…	…	*41*	*40*	*41*	*1.03*

			Sum	% F	Sum	% F	Median		Weighted average			
I	World	…	112 367	48	138 895	48	30	34	33	33	32	0.97
II	Countries in transition	…	7 139	47	7 316	47	0.02	2	46	47	44	0.94
III	Developed countries	…	25 376	49	26 049	49	6	9	73	73	73	0.99
IV	Developing countries	…	79 851	47	105 529	48	47	49	27	28	26	0.96
V	Arab States	…	2 441	43	3 078	46	83	76	15	17	13	0.77
VI	Central and Eastern Europe	…	9 455	48	9 597	48	0.7	2	49	50	49	0.97
VII	Central Asia	…	1 365	47	1 476	48	0.1	1	21	21	20	0.92
VIII	East Asia and the Pacific	…	37 027	47	36 833	47	49	55	40	40	39	0.98
IX	East Asia	…	36 615	47	36 323	47	57	50	40	40	39	0.98
X	Pacific	…	412	49	510	48	…	…	61	61	61	1.00
XI	Latin America and the Caribbean	…	16 392	49	20 335	49	29	39	56	55	56	1.02
XII	Caribbean	…	672	50	792	51	88	86	65	64	67	1.05
XIII	Latin America	…	15 720	49	19 544	49	23	20	55	55	56	1.01
XIV	North America and Western Europe	…	19 133	48	19 881	49	26	27	75	76	74	0.98
XV	South and West Asia	…	21 425	46	38 807	48	…	…	21	22	20	0.94
XVI	Sub-Saharan Africa	…	5 129	49	8 887	49	53	53	9	10	9	0.98

1. National population data were used to calculate enrolment ratios.
2. Enrolment and population data exclude Transnistria.
3. Enrolment ratios were not calculated due to lack of United Nations population data by age.
4. Data include French overseas departments and territories (DOM-TOM).
5. The decline in enrolment is essentially due to a reclassification of programmes. From 2004, it was decided to include children categorized as being aged '4 rising 5' in primary education enrolment rather than pre-primary enrolment even if they started the school year at the latter level. Such children typically (though not always) start primary school reception classes in the second or third term of the school year.

GROSS ENROLMENT RATIO (GER) IN PRE-PRIMARY EDUCATION (%)				NET ENROLMENT RATIO (NER) IN PRE-PRIMARY EDUCATION (%)				GROSS ENROLMENT RATIO (GER) IN PRE-PRIMARY AND OTHER ECCE PROGRAMMES (%)				NEW ENTRANTS TO THE FIRST GRADE OF PRIMARY EDUCATION WITH ECCE EXPERIENCE (%)			
School year ending in 2006				School year ending in 2006				School year ending in 2006				School year ending in 2006			
Total	Male	Female	GPI (F/M)	Total	Male	Female	GPI (F/M)	Total	Male	Female	GPI (F/M)	Total	Male	Female	
3	3	3	0.99	…	…	…	…	3	3	3	0.99	…	…	…	*171*
…	…	…	…	…	…	…	…	…	…	…	…	…	…	…	*172*
44[z]	48[z]	40[z]	0.83[z]	…	…	…	…	44[z]	48[z]	40[z]	0.83[z]	70[z]	67[z]	72[z]	*173*
14	13	14	1.03	7	7	7	1.01	18	17	18	1.06	…	…	…	*174*
3	**3**	**3**	**0.96**	**2**	**2**	**2**	**0.96**	**3**	**3**	**3**	**0.96**	…	…	…	*175*
…	…	…	…	…	…	…	…	…	…	…	…	…	…	…	*176*
17[y]	*16[y]*	*17[y]*	*1.04[y]*	…	…	…	…	…	…	…	…	…	…	…	*177*
60	**59**	**62**	**1.04**	**42**	**41**	**43**	**1.05**	…	…	…	…	…	…	…	*178*
7	7	7	1.01	7	7	7	1.01	7	7	7	1.01	17[z]	17[z]	18[z]	*179*
…	…	…	…	…	…	…	…	…	…	…	…	…	…	…	*180*
49	51	48	0.94	27	27	27	0.98	…	…	…	…	…	…	…	*181*
18	13	23	1.79	12	7	16	2.19	…	…	…	…	…	…	…	*182*
100	97	102	1.05	35	34	36	1.08	…	…	…	…	…	…	…	*183*
8	8	8	1.04	8	7	8	1.05	8	8	8	1.04	…	…	…	*184*
…	…	…	…	…	…	…	…	…	…	…	…	…	…	…	*185*
3	*3*	*3*	*0.99*	…	…	…	…	3	*3*	*3*	*0.99*	3	0.4	7	*186*
101	100	101	1.02	90	89	91	1.02	101	100	101	1.02	100	100	100	*187*
…	…	…	…	…	…	…	…	…	…	…	…	…	…	…	*188*
22	22	22	1.01	…	…	…	…	…	…	…	…	.[y]	.[y]	.[y]	*189*
2	2	2	1.10	1	1	2	1.09	2	2	2	1.10	…	…	…	*190*
14[y]	14[y]	13[y]	0.98[y]	10[y]	10[y]	10[y]	0.95[y]	…	…	…	…	…	…	…	*191*
…	…	…	…	…	…	…	…	…	…	…	…	…	…	…	*192*
34	**33**	**35**	**1.07**	**34**	**32**	**35**	**1.08**	…	…	…	…	**42**	**42**	**43**	*193*
9	9	10	1.11	6	6	7	1.12	…	…	…	…	4[y]	4[y]	5[y]	*194*
109	**110**	**107**	**0.97**	**95**	**97**	**92**	**0.95**	**109**	**110**	**107**	**0.97**	…	…	…	*195*
5	**4**	**5**	**1.07**	**4**	**4**	**4**	**1.07**	…	…	…	…	…	…	…	*196*
…	…	…	…	…	…	…	…	…	…	…	…	…	…	…	*197*
38[y]	37[y]	38[y]	1.02[y]	…	…	…	…	58[y]	…	…	…	…	…	…	*198*
17[z]	*17[z]*	*17[z]*	*0.99[z]*	11[y]	11[y]	11[y]	0.99[y]	*17[z]*	*17[z]*	*17[z]*	*0.99[z]*	…	…	…	*199*
2[y]	*2[y]*	*2[y]*	*0.98[y]*	*2[y]*	*2[y]*	*2[y]*	*0.98[y]*	*2[y]*	*2[y]*	*2[y]*	*0.98[y]*	…	…	…	*200*
3	3	3	1.03	2	2	2	1.01	…	…	…	…	…	…	…	*201*
32	**31**	**33**	**1.07**	**32**	**31**	**33**	**1.07**	**32**	**31**	**33**	**1.07**	…	…	…	*202*
…	…	…	…	…	…	…	…	…	…	…	…	17	16	17	*203*
…	…	…	…	…	…	…	…	…	…	…	…	…	…	…	*204*
Weighted average				Weighted average				Weighted average				Median			
41	41	40	0.98	…	…	…	…	…	…	…	…	…	…	…	*I*
62	64	61	0.95	…	…	…	…	…	…	…	…	…	…	…	*II*
79	79	79	1.00	…	…	…	…	…	…	…	…	…	…	…	*III*
36	36	35	0.98	…	…	…	…	…	…	…	…	…	…	…	*IV*
18	19	17	0.89	…	…	…	…	…	…	…	…	…	…	…	*V*
62	63	61	0.96	…	…	…	…	…	…	…	…	…	…	…	*VI*
28	29	28	0.96	…	…	…	…	…	…	…	…	…	…	…	*VII*
45	45	44	0.97	…	…	…	…	…	…	…	…	…	…	…	*VIII*
44	45	44	0.97	…	…	…	…	…	…	…	…	…	…	…	*IX*
74	75	73	0.98	…	…	…	…	…	…	…	…	…	…	…	*X*
65	65	65	1.00	…	…	…	…	…	…	…	…	…	…	…	*XI*
79	77	82	1.06	…	…	…	…	…	…	…	…	…	…	…	*XII*
64	64	64	1.00	…	…	…	…	…	…	…	…	…	…	…	*XIII*
81	81	81	1.00	…	…	…	…	…	…	…	…	…	…	…	*XIV*
39	39	39	1.01	…	…	…	…	…	…	…	…	…	…	…	*XV*
14	14	14	0.97	…	…	…	…	…	…	…	…	…	…	…	*XVI*

6. The apparent increase in the gender parity index (GPI) is due to the recent inclusion in enrolment statistics of literacy programmes in which 80% of participants are women.
Data in italic are UIS estimates.
Data in bold are for the school year ending in 2007.

(z) Data are for the school year ending in 2005.
(y) Data are for the school year ending in 2004.
(*) National estimate.

Table 4
Access to primary education

Country or territory	Compulsory education (age group)	Legal guarantees of free education[1]	New entrants (000) School year ending in		GROSS INTAKE RATE (GIR) IN PRIMARY EDUCATION (%) School year ending in							
			1999	2006	1999				2006			
					Total	Male	Female	GPI (F/M)	Total	Male	Female	GPI (F/M)
Arab States												
Algeria[2]	6-14	Yes	745	569	101	102	100	0.98	98	99	97	0.98
Bahrain	6-15	Yes	13	15	105	103	107	1.04	125	124	126	1.02
Djibouti	6-15	No	6	11	29	33	25	0.74	52	57	48	0.85
Egypt[3]	6-14	Yes	*1 451*	**1 702**	*92*	*94*	*91*	*0.96*	**103**	**105**	**102**	**0.97**
Iraq	6-11	Yes	*709*	*844*[z]	*102*	*109*	*95*	*0.88*	*108*[z]	*111*[z]	*105*[z]	*0.94*[z]
Jordan[2]	6-15	Yes	126	131	101	100	101	1.00	90	89	90	1.01
Kuwait[2]	6-14	Yes	35	41	97	97	98	1.01	94	96	93	0.97
Lebanon[2,3]	6-15	Yes	71	68	93	97	90	0.92	86	86	86	0.99
Libyan Arab Jamahiriya[2]	6-14	Yes	…	…	…	…	…	…	…	…	…	…
Mauritania[3]	6-14	Yes	…	103	…	…	…	…	127	124	129	1.04
Morocco	6-14	Yes	731	615	112	115	108	0.94	102	104	100	0.96
Oman	6-15	Yes	52	44	87	87	87	1.00	76	76	76	1.01
Palestinian A. T.	6-15	…	95	95	103	103	104	1.01	78	78	78	1.01
Qatar[3]	6-17	Yes	*11*	13	*108*	*109*	*107*	*0.98*	108	107	109	1.02
Saudi Arabia	6-11	Yes	…	…	…	…	…	…	…	…	…	…
Sudan[3]	6-13	Yes	…	795	…	…	…	…	77	83	72	0.87
Syrian Arab Republic[2]	6-14	Yes	466	568	106	109	103	0.94	123	125	122	0.97
Tunisia	6-16	Yes	204	158	100	100	100	1.00	98	97	100	1.02
United Arab Emirates[3]	6-14	Yes	47	56	93	95	92	0.97	102	103	101	0.99
Yemen[3]	6-14	Yes	440	*730*	76	88	63	0.71	*112*	*122*	*102*	*0.83*
Central and Eastern Europe												
Albania[3]	6-13	Yes	*67*	56[y]	*96*	*97*	*95*	*0.98*	99[y]	100[y]	99[y]	0.99[y]
Belarus[3]	6-15	Yes	173	91	131	132	131	0.99	101	102	100	0.98
Bosnia and Herzegovina[3]	…	Yes	…	…	…	…	…	…	…	…	…	…
Bulgaria[2,3]	7-14	Yes	93	64	101	102	100	0.98	100	100	100	1.00
Croatia[3]	7-14	Yes	50	46	94	95	93	0.98	97	97	97	1.00
Czech Republic	6-15	Yes	124	92	100	101	99	0.98	109	109	108	1.00
Estonia	7-15	Yes	18	12	100	101	100	0.99	96	96	95	0.99
Hungary	7-16	Yes	127	97	102	104	101	0.97	97	97	96	1.00
Latvia[3]	7-15	Yes	32	18	98	*99*	*98*	*1.00*	95	95	95	1.00
Lithuania[2]	7-15	Yes	54	35	104	105	104	0.99	96	98	94	0.96
Montenegro	…	…	…	…	…	…	…	…	…	…	…	…
Poland[2,4]	7-15	Yes	535	386	101	*101*	*100*	*0.99*	97	*97*	*98*	*1.00*
Republic of Moldova[3,5,6]	7-15	Yes	62	40	105	*105*	*104*	*1.00*	98	98	97	0.99
Romania[3]	7-14	Yes	269	217	94	95	94	0.99	97	97	97	1.00
Russian Federation[3]	6-15	Yes	1 866	1 288	96	…	…	…	100	*101*	*100*	*0.99*
Serbia	7-14	Yes	…	…	…	…	…	…	…	…	…	…
Slovakia[2]	6-15	Yes	75	56	102	102	101	0.99	101	102	101	0.99
Slovenia[2]	6-14	Yes	21	17	98	98	97	0.99	96	95	96	1.00
TFYR Macedonia[2,3]	7-14	Yes	32	26[z]	102	102	102	1.00	99[z]	99[z]	99[z]	1.01[z]
Turkey[3]	6-14	Yes	…	*1 311*	…	…	…	…	*94*	*95*	*92*	*0.97*
Ukraine[3]	6-17	Yes	623	395*	97	97	97	1.00	99*	99*	99*	1.00*
Central Asia												
Armenia[3]	7-14	Yes	…	40	…	…	…	…	104	102	106	1.05
Azerbaijan[3]	6-16	Yes	175	124	94	94	95	1.01	98	99	97	0.98
Georgia[3]	6-14	Yes	74	49	99	99	100	1.02	100	97	103	1.06
Kazakhstan	7-17	Yes	…	**235**	…	…	…	…	**110**	**110**	**110**	**1.00**
Kyrgyzstan[3]	7-15	Yes	120*	103	100*	99*	100*	1.02*	97	98	97	0.99
Mongolia[3]	7-15	Yes	70	56	109	109	109	1.00	122	122	122	1.00
Tajikistan[3]	7-15	Yes	177	173	99	102	96	0.95	101	103	99	0.95
Turkmenistan[3]	7-15	Yes	…	…	…	…	…	…	…	…	…	…
Uzbekistan[3]	7-15	Yes	677	**505**	102	…	…	…	**93**	**95**	**92**	**0.97**
East Asia and the Pacific												
Australia	5-15	Yes	…	*269*[z]	…	…	…	…	*106*[z]	*106*[z]	*105*[z]	*1.00*[z]
Brunei Darussalam	5-16	No	8	8	107	107	106	0.99	105	105	105	1.00
Cambodia[3]	…	Yes	*404*	435	*109*	*112*	*106*	*0.95*	131	135	127	0.94
China[3,7]	6-14	Yes	…	16 764	…	…	…	…	88	88	87	0.99

NET INTAKE RATE (NIR) IN PRIMARY EDUCATION (%)								SCHOOL LIFE EXPECTANCY (expected number of years of formal schooling from primary to tertiary education)						
School year ending in								School year ending in						
1999				2006				1999			2006			
Total	Male	Female	GPI (F/M)	Total	Male	Female	GPI (F/M)	Total	Male	Female	Total	Male	Female	Country or territory
														Arab States
77	79	76	0.97	85	86	84	0.98	…	…	…	13[z]	13[z]	13[z]	Algeria[2]
89	86	91	1.06	99	99	100	1.01	13	13	14	15	14	16	Bahrain
21	24	18	0.75	37	41	33	0.81	3	4	3	4	5	4	Djibouti
…	…	…	…	93[y]	93[y]	92[y]	0.99[y]	13	…	…	12[y]	…	…	Egypt[3]
79	83	74	0.90	83[z]	86[z]	79[z]	0.92[z]	8	9	7	10[z]	11[z]	8[z]	Iraq
67	67	68	1.02	62[y]	63[y]	62[y]	0.99[y]	…	…	…	13	13	13	Jordan[2]
62	63	61	0.97	55[z]	54[z]	55[z]	1.01[z]	14	13	14	13	12	13	Kuwait[2]
69	70	67	0.95	60	61	59	0.97	12	12	12	13	13	13	Lebanon[2,3]
…	…	…	…	…	…	…	…	…	…	…	…	…	…	Libyan Arab Jamahiriya[2]
…	…	…	…	38	38	39	1.04	7	…	…	8	8	8	Mauritania[3]
51	53	48	0.92	84	86	82	0.96	8	9	7	10	…	…	Morocco
70	70	71	1.01	54	53	54	1.01	…	…	…	12	12	11	Oman
…	…	…	…	58	58	58	0.99	12	12	12	14	13	14	Palestinian A. T.
…	…	…	…	…	…	…	…	13	12	14	13	13	14	Qatar[3]
…	…	…	…	…	…	…	…	…	…	…	…	…	…	Saudi Arabia
…	…	…	…	…	…	…	…	5	…	…	…	…	…	Sudan[3]
60	60	59	0.98	52	52	52	1.00	…	…	…	…	…	…	Syrian Arab Republic[2]
…	…	…	…	88	88	89	1.02	13	13	13	14	13	14	Tunisia
49	49	49	1.00	38	39	37	0.94	11	10	11	…	…	…	United Arab Emirates[3]
25	30	20	0.68	…	…	…	…	8	10	5	9	11	7	Yemen[3]
														Central and Eastern Europe
…	…	…	…	…	…	…	…	11	11	11	11[y]	11[y]	11[y]	Albania[3]
76	77	76	0.99	84	85	83	0.98	14	13	14	15	14	15	Belarus[3]
…	…	…	…	…	…	…	…	…	…	…	…	…	…	Bosnia and Herzegovina[3]
…	…	…	…	…	…	…	…	13	13	13	14	13	14	Bulgaria[2,3]
68	69	66	0.97	…	…	…	…	12	12	12	14	13	14	Croatia[3]
…	…	…	…	…	…	…	…	13	13	13	15	15	15	Czech Republic
…	…	…	…	…	…	…	…	14	14	15	16	15	17	Estonia
…	…	…	…	65[z]	67[z]	63[z]	0.94[z]	14	14	14	15	15	16	Hungary
…	…	…	…	…	…	…	…	14	13	14	16	14	17	Latvia[3]
…	…	…	…	…	…	…	…	14	13	14	16	15	17	Lithuania[2]
…	…	…	…	…	…	…	…	…	…	…	…	…	…	Montenegro
…	…	…	…	…	…	…	…	15	14	15	15	15	16	Poland[2,4]
…	…	…	…	71	71	71	1.00	11	11	12	12	12	13	Republic of Moldova[3,5,6]
…	…	…	…	…	…	…	…	12	12	12	14	14	14	Romania[3]
…	…	…	…	…	…	…	…	…	…	…	14	13	14	Russian Federation[3]
…	…	…	…	…	…	…	…	…	…	…	…	…	…	Serbia
…	…	…	…	…	…	…	…	13	13	13	15	14	15	Slovakia[2]
…	…	…	…	…	…	…	…	15	14	15	17	16	17	Slovenia[2]
…	…	…	…	…	…	…	…	12	12	12	12[z]	12[z]	12[z]	TFYR Macedonia[2,3]
…	…	…	…	74[z]	75[z]	73[z]	0.97[z]	…	…	…	11	12	11	Turkey[3]
69	…	…	…	75*	75*	75*	1.00*	13	13	13	14	14*	15*	Ukraine[3]
														Central Asia
…	…	…	…	55	53	58	1.08	11	…	…	11	11	12	Armenia[3]
…	…	…	…	70	71	69	0.98	10	10	10	11	11	11	Azerbaijan[3]
69	68	69	1.02	74	73	76	1.05	12	12	12	12	12	13	Georgia[3]
…	…	…	…	**59**	**61**	**57**	**0.93**	12	12	12	**15**	**15**	**16**	Kazakhstan
58*	59*	58*	0.99*	59	60	58	0.96	11	11	12	12	12	13	Kyrgyzstan[3]
81	81	81	0.99	79	79	79	1.00	9	8	10	13	12	14	Mongolia[3]
93	95	90	0.95	98	100	95	0.95	10	11	9	11	12	10	Tajikistan[3]
…	…	…	…	…	…	…	…	…	…	…	…	…	…	Turkmenistan[3]
…	…	…	…	77	…	…	…	11	11	10	**11**	**12**	**11**	Uzbekistan[3]
														East Asia and the Pacific
…	…	…	…	72[z]	69[z]	75[z]	1.08[z]	20	20	20	20	20	21	Australia
…	…	…	…	68	67	69	1.03	14	13	14	14	14	14	Brunei Darussalam
64	65	63	0.97	82	83	82	1.00	…	…	…	10	10	9	Cambodia[3]
…	…	…	…	…	…	…	…	…	…	…	11	11	11	China[3,7]

Table 4 (continued)

Country or territory	Compulsory education (age group)	Legal guarantees of free education[1]	New entrants (000) School year ending in 1999	New entrants (000) School year ending in 2006	GROSS INTAKE RATE (GIR) IN PRIMARY EDUCATION (%) School year ending in 1999 Total	1999 Male	1999 Female	1999 GPI (F/M)	2006 Total	2006 Male	2006 Female	2006 GPI (F/M)
Cook Islands[5]	5-15	…	0.6	0.3[z]	131	…	…	…	*68[z]*	*67[z]*	*70[z]*	*1.04[z]*
DPR Korea	6-15	Yes	…	…	…	…	…	…	…	…	…	…
Fiji	6-15	No	…	18	…	…	…	…	96	96	96	1.00
Indonesia	7-15	No	…	5 122	…	…	…	…	121	123	119	0.96
Japan[4]	6-15	Yes	1 222	1 205	101	102	101	1.00	99	99	99	1.01
Kiribati[5]	6-15	No	3	*3[z]*	109	106	113	1.06	*120[z]*	*119[z]*	*121[z]*	*1.02[z]*
Lao PDR	6-10	No	180	186	114	121	108	0.89	124	129	120	0.93
Macao, China	5-14	…	6	4	88	88	89	1.02	95	94	96	1.02
Malaysia	…	No	…	520[z]	…	…	…	…	98[z]	98[z]	98[z]	0.99[z]
Marshall Islands[2,5]	6-14	No	1	**1.6**	*123*	*122*	*123*	*1.01*	**100**	**105**	**96**	**0.91**
Micronesia	6-13	No	…	…	…	…	…	…	…	…	…	…
Myanmar[3]	5-9	Yes	1 226	1 173	132	130	133	1.03	138	139	136	0.98
Nauru	…	No	…	**0.2**	…	…	…	…	***71***	***65***	***77***	***1.19***
New Zealand[4]	5-16	Yes	…	*58[z]*	…	…	…	…	*104[z]*	*105[z]*	*104[z]*	*1.00[z]*
Niue[5]	5-16	…	0.05	*0.02[z]*	105	79	137	1.73	*81[z]*	*69[z]*	*93[z]*	*1.34[z]*
Palau[2,5]	6-14	Yes	*0.4*	0.3[y]	*118*	*120*	*115*	*0.96*	*87[y]*	…	…	…
Papua New Guinea	6-14	No	…	…	…	…	…	…	…	…	…	…
Philippines[3]	6-12	Yes	2 551	2 547	133	136	129	0.95	126	131	121	0.93
Republic of Korea[2,4]	6-14	Yes	711	**606**	106	109	103	0.94	**107**	**106**	**109**	**1.02**
Samoa	5-14	No	5	*6[y]*	105	106	104	0.98	*101[y]*	*101[y]*	*101[y]*	*1.00[y]*
Singapore	6-16	No	…	…	…	…	…	…	…	…	…	…
Solomon Islands	…	No	…	…	…	…	…	…	…	…	…	…
Thailand	6-14	Yes	*1 037*	…	*110*	*111*	*107*	*0.96*	…	…	…	…
Timor-Leste[3]	7-15	Yes	…	37[z]	…	…	…	…	112[z]	118[z]	105[z]	0.89[z]
Tokelau[5]	…	…	…	*0.04[y]*	…	…	…	…	*78[y]*	*48[y]*	*109[y]*	*2.28[y]*
Tonga	6-14	No	3	3	104	107	100	0.94	116	118	114	0.97
Tuvalu[5]	7-14	No	*0.2*	0.3	*89*	*94*	*83*	*0.89*	112	120	104	0.86
Vanuatu	6-12	No	*6*	7[y]	*109*	*109*	*109*	*1.00*	120[y]	122[y]	117[y]	0.96[y]
Viet Nam[3]	6-14	Yes	2 035	*1 355*	106	110	103	0.93	…	…	…	…
Latin America and the Caribbean												
Anguilla[3]	5-17	Yes	0.2	0.2	…	…	…	…	*116*	*101*	*137*	*1.36*
Antigua and Barbuda	5-16	Yes	…	…	…	…	…	…	…	…	…	…
Argentina[2,3]	5-14	Yes	781	743[z]	112	111	112	1.00	109[z]	109[z]	108[z]	0.99[z]
Aruba[5]	6-16	…	1	1	109	112	106	0.94	98	93	103	1.10
Bahamas	5-16	No	7	6	116	122	111	0.91	107	106	108	1.01
Barbados	5-16	Yes	4	4	99	99	98	0.99	111	112	109	0.97
Belize	5-14	Yes	8	9	128	129	126	0.98	123	122	124	1.02
Bermuda[5]	5-16	…	…	1	…	…	…	…	103	…	…	…
Bolivia[3]	6-13	Yes	282	287	124	124	125	1.01	122	122	122	1.00
Brazil[3]	7-14	Yes	…	4 323[z]	…	…	…	…	125[z]	…	…	…
British Virgin Islands[5]	5-16	…	0.4	0.4	106	109	103	0.95	113	110	115	1.04*
Cayman Islands[8]	5-16	…	1	1	…	…	…	…	…	…	…	…
Chile[2,3]	6-13	Yes	284	252	95	95	94	0.99	99	100	99	0.98
Colombia[2]	5-14	No	1 267	1 129	137	140	134	0.96	125	127	123	0.97
Costa Rica[3]	6-15	Yes	87	86	104	104	105	1.01	108	108	108	1.00
Cuba	6-14	Yes	164	145	106	109	104	0.95	103	102	104	1.02
Dominica[5]	5-16	No	2	1	111	118	104	0.88	82	79	85	1.07
Dominican Republic[3]	5-13	Yes	267	217	132	137	128	0.94	101	102	100	0.98
Ecuador[3]	5-14	Yes	374	399	134	134	134	1.00	137	138	137	0.99
El Salvador[3]	7-15	Yes	*196*	183	*134*	*138*	*129*	*0.94*	119	121	116	0.96
Grenada[5]	5-16	No	…	*2[z]*	…	…	…	…	*100[z]*	*102[z]*	*99[z]*	*0.96[z]*
Guatemala[3]	7-15	Yes	425	460	131	135	127	0.94	124	125	122	0.98
Guyana[3]	6-15	Yes	18	*20[y]*	126	123	128	1.05	*126[y]*	*126[y]*	*127[y]*	*1.02[y]*
Haiti	6-11	No	…	…	…	…	…	…	…	…	…	…
Honduras[2,3]	6-11	Yes	…	252	…	…	…	…	137	139	134	0.96
Jamaica	6-11	No	…	*52[z]*	…	…	…	…	*93[z]*	*94[z]*	*92[z]*	*0.98[z]*
Mexico[3]	6-15	Yes	2 509	2 355	111	111	111	1.00	111	112	110	0.98
Montserrat	5-16	…	0.1	0.1	…	…	…	…	*110*	*108*	*113*	*1.04*
Netherlands Antilles	6-15	…	*4*	…	*112*	*109*	*115*	*1.06*	…	…	…	…
Nicaragua[3]	6-12	Yes	203	228	141	144	137	0.95	168	173	163	0.94
Panama[3]	6-11	Yes	69	78	112	113	111	0.99	115	116	114	0.98

NET INTAKE RATE (NIR) IN PRIMARY EDUCATION (%)								SCHOOL LIFE EXPECTANCY (expected number of years of formal schooling from primary to tertiary education)						
School year ending in								School year ending in						
1999				2006				1999			2006			
Total	Male	Female	GPI (F/M)	Total	Male	Female	GPI (F/M)	Total	Male	Female	Total	Male	Female	**Country or territory**
…	…	…	…	51[z]	49[z]	53[z]	1.08[z]	11	11	11	10[z]	10[z]	10[z]	Cook Islands[5]
…	…	…	…	…	…	…	…	…	…	…	…	…	…	DPR Korea
…	…	…	…	70[z]	70[z]	70[z]	1.00[z]	…	…	…	13[z]	13[z]	13[z]	Fiji
…	…	…	…	41	42	41	0.97	…	…	…	12	…	…	Indonesia
…	…	…	…	…	…	…	…	14	15	14	15	15	15	Japan[4]
…	…	…	…	…	…	…	…	12	11	12	12[z]	12[z]	13[z]	Kiribati[5]
52	53	51	0.96	66	66	66	1.00	8	9	7	9	10	8	Lao PDR
63	61	65	1.07	78	78	79	1.02	12	12	12	15	16	14	Macao, China
…	…	…	…	…	…	…	…	12	12	12	13[z]	12[z]	13[z]	Malaysia
…	…	…	…	…	…	…	…	…	…	…	…	…	…	Marshall Islands[2,5]
…	…	…	…	…	…	…	…	…	…	…	…	…	…	Micronesia
90	…	…	…	…	…	…	…	8	7	8	…	…	…	Myanmar[3]
…	…	…	…	…	…	…	…	…	…	…	8*	8*	9*	Nauru
…	…	…	…	100[z]	100[z]	100[z]	1.00[z]	17	17	18	19	19	20	New Zealand[4]
…	…	…	…	…	…	…	…	12	12	12	12[z]	12[z]	12[z]	Niue[5]
…	…	…	…	…	…	…	…	…	…	…	…	…	…	Palau[2,5]
…	…	…	…	…	…	…	…	…	…	…	…	…	…	Papua New Guinea
46	47	45	0.95	45	42	47	1.12	12	11	12	12	11	12	Philippines[3]
97	100	94	0.94	**98**	**97**	**100**	**1.04**	15	16	14	**17**	**18**	**15**	Republic of Korea[2,4]
77	77	77	1.00	…	…	…	…	12	12	13	…	…	…	Samoa
…	…	…	…	…	…	…	…	…	…	…	…	…	…	Singapore
…	…	…	…	…	…	…	…	7	8	7	8[z]	9[z]	8[z]	Solomon Islands
…	…	…	…	…	…	…	…	…	…	…	14	13	14	Thailand
…	…	…	…	39[z]	39[z]	38[z]	0.97[z]	…	…	…	…	…	…	Timor-Leste[3]
…	…	…	…	…	…	…	…	…	…	…	11[y]	10[y]	11[y]	Tokelau[5]
48	50	47	0.94	…	…	…	…	13	13	14	13[y]	13[y]	13[y]	Tonga
…	…	…	…	…	…	…	…	…	…	…	…	…	…	Tuvalu[5]
…	…	…	…	55[y]	56[y]	54[y]	0.97[y]	9	…	…	10[y]	11[y]	10[y]	Vanuatu
79	…	…	…	…	…	…	…	10	11	10	…	…	…	Viet Nam[3]
														Latin America and the Caribbean
…	…	…	…	78[z]	…	…	…	…	…	…	11	11	11	Anguilla[3]
…	…	…	…	…	…	…	…	…	…	…	…	…	…	Antigua and Barbuda
…	…	…	…	98[z]	100[z]	97[z]	0.97[z]	15	14	16	15[z]	14[z]	16[z]	Argentina[2,3]
90	91	89	0.98	81[z]	80[z]	82[z]	1.02[z]	13	13	14	14	13	14	Aruba[5]
84	85	82	0.96	70	67	73	1.09	…	…	…	…	…	…	Bahamas
77	77	76	0.99	87	87	87	1.00	13	13	14	…	…	…	Barbados
78	80	76	0.95	68	68	68	1.00	…	…	…	13[y]	13[y]	13[y]	Belize
…	…	…	…	…	…	…	…	…	…	…	13[z]	13[z]	14[z]	Bermuda[5]
69	68	69	1.03	71	71	72	1.01	13	…	…	…	…	…	Bolivia[3]
…	…	…	…	…	…	…	…	14	14	14	14[z]	14[z]	15[z]	Brazil[3]
73	70	76	1.09	70[z]	66[z]	74[z]	1.12[z]	16	15	17	17[z]	15[z]	19[z]	British Virgin Islands[5]
…	…	…	…	…	…	…	…	…	…	…	…	…	…	Cayman Islands[8]
…	…	…	…	…	…	…	…	13	13	13	14	14	14	Chile[2,3]
60	61	59	0.96	…	…	…	…	11	11	11	12	12	13	Colombia[2]
…	…	…	…	…	…	…	…	10	10	10	12[z]	12[z]	12[z]	Costa Rica[3]
98	…	…	…	99	98	100	1.02	12	12	13	16	15	17	Cuba
80	83	78	0.94	46[y]	46[y]	46[y]	1.01[y]	12	12	13	13[z]	13[z]	14[z]	Dominica[5]
58	58	58	1.00	68[z]	68[z]	68[z]	1.00[z]	…	…	…	12[y]	12[y]	13[y]	Dominican Republic[3]
84	83	84	1.01	89	89	89	1.00	…	…	…	…	…	…	Ecuador[3]
…	…	…	…	60	60	61	1.01	11	11	11	12	12	12	El Salvador[3]
…	…	…	…	…	…	…	…	…	…	…	12[z]	12[z]	12[z]	Grenada[5]
56	58	54	0.92	71	72	70	0.97	…	…	…	10	11	10	Guatemala[3]
91	90	93	1.03	…	…	…	…	…	…	…	13[z]	13[z]	14[z]	Guyana[3]
…	…	…	…	…	…	…	…	…	…	…	…	…	…	Haiti
…	…	…	…	70	69	72	1.05	…	…	…	11[y]	11[y]	12[y]	Honduras[2,3]
…	…	…	…	75[z]	74[z]	76[z]	1.03[z]	…	…	…	…	…	…	Jamaica
89	89	89	1.01	90[y]	90[y]	89[y]	0.99[y]	12	12	12	13	14	13	Mexico[3]
…	…	…	…	56[z]	42[z]	73[z]	1.76[z]	…	…	…	16	15	16	Montserrat
77	72	82	1.14	…	…	…	…	15	14	15	…	…	…	Netherlands Antilles
39	40	38	0.95	67	66	68	1.04	…	…	…	…	…	…	Nicaragua[3]
84	84	84	1.00	88[y]	87[y]	89[y]	1.02[y]	13	12	13	13	13	14	Panama[3]

Table 4 (continued)

Country or territory	Compulsory education (age group)	Legal guarantees of free education[1]	New entrants (000) School year ending in 1999	New entrants (000) School year ending in 2006	GROSS INTAKE RATE (GIR) IN PRIMARY EDUCATION (%) School year ending in 1999 Total	1999 Male	1999 Female	1999 GPI (F/M)	2006 Total	2006 Male	2006 Female	2006 GPI (F/M)
Paraguay[3]	6-14	Yes	*179*	158[z]	*131*	*134*	*128*	*0.96*	111[z]	113[z]	110[z]	0.97[z]
Peru[3]	6-16	Yes	676	615	110	110	110	1.00	109	109	110	1.01
Saint Kitts and Nevis[5]	5-16	No	…	0.9[z]	…	…	…	…	95[z]	92[z]	99[z]	1.08[z]
Saint Lucia	5-15	No	*4*	3	*107*	*109*	*106*	*0.97*	107	104	110	1.05
Saint Vincent/Grenad.	5-15	No	…	*2*[z]	…	…	…	…	*95*[z]	*101*[z]	*90*[z]	*0.89*[z]
Suriname[3]	6-12	Yes	…	11	…	…	…	…	113	115	111	0.97
Trinidad and Tobago[2,3]	5-11	Yes	20	17[*,z]	94	94	93	0.98	94[*,z]	96[*,z]	92[*,z]	0.96[*,z]
Turks and Caicos Islands	4-16	…	*0.3*	0.4[z]	…	…	…	…	*83*[z]	*83*[z]	*84*[z]	*1.01*[z]
Uruguay[3]	6-15	Yes	60	52	107	107	107	1.00	101	100	101	1.01
Venezuela, B. R.[3]	6-15	Yes	537	561	98	99	97	0.98	101	102	99	0.97
North America and Western Europe												
Andorra[2,5]	6-16	…	…	1	…	…	…	…	96	96	96	1.01
Austria[2,4]	6-14	Yes	100	*87*[z]	106	107	105	0.98	*101*[z]	*102*[z]	*100*[z]	*0.98*[z]
Belgium[4]	6-18	Yes	…	114	…	…	…	…	99	98	99	1.02
Canada	6-16	Yes	…	*362*[y]	…	…	…	…	*96*[y]	*97*[y]	*95*[y]	*0.99*[y]
Cyprus[2,5]	6-14	Yes	…	9	…	…	…	…	106	108	105	0.97
Denmark	7-16	Yes	66	67	100	100	100	1.00	98	97	98	1.01
Finland	7-16	Yes	65	57	100	100	100	1.00	96	97	96	1.00
France[9]	6-16	Yes	736	…	102	*103*	*101*	*0.98*	…	…	…	…
Germany	6-18	Yes	869	820	100	101	100	1.00	104	104	103	0.99
Greece[2]	6-14	Yes	113	104	106	107	105	0.98	100	100	99	0.99
Iceland	6-16	Yes	4	4	99	101	97	0.96	98	96	99	1.03
Ireland	6-15	Yes	51	57	100	101	99	0.98	98	97	99	1.02
Israel[3]	5-15	Yes	…	124	…	…	…	…	96	95	98	1.03
Italy[2]	6-14	Yes	558	555	100	101	99	0.99	105	105	104	0.99
Luxembourg	6-15	Yes	5	6	97	…	…	…	99	97	100	1.03
Malta[2]	5-15	Yes	5	4[z]	102	103	102	0.99	94[z]	93[z]	95[z]	1.02[z]
Monaco[2,8]	6-15	No	…	0.4[y]	…	…	…	…	…	…	…	…
Netherlands[2,4]	5-17	Yes	199	202	99	100	99	0.99	102	103	101	0.98
Norway	6-16	Yes	61	60	100	100	99	0.99	100	100	100	1.00
Portugal[2]	6-14	Yes	…	119	…	…	…	…	109	108	109	1.01
San Marino[2,8]	6-16	No	…	0.3[y]	…	…	…	…	…	…	…	…
Spain	6-16	Yes	*403*	*414*	*104*	*104*	*104*	*1.00*	*104*	*104*	*104*	*1.00*
Sweden	7-16	Yes	127	*93*[z]	104	105	103	0.98	*95*[z]	*96*[z]	*95*[z]	*0.99*[z]
Switzerland	7-15	Yes	82	74	93	91	95	1.04	90	88	92	1.04
United Kingdom	5-16	Yes	…	…	…	…	…	…	…	…	…	…
United States	6-17	No	4 322	4 142	104	107	101	0.95	104	105	102	0.97
South and West Asia												
Afghanistan[3]	6-15	Yes	…	742[z]	…	…	…	…	96[z]	113[z]	79[z]	0.70[z]
Bangladesh[3]	6-10	Yes	4 005	4 318[y]	113	115	112	0.98	123[y]	122[y]	124[y]	1.02[y]
Bhutan[3]	6-16	Yes	12	16	79	83	75	0.90	118	119	117	0.98
India[3]	6-14	Yes	29 639	32 366	120	129	111	0.86	130	133	126	0.95
Iran, Islamic Republic of[3,10]	6-10	Yes	1 563	*1 400*	91	91	91	0.99	*130*	*112*	*150*	*1.35*
Maldives	6-12	No	8	6	102	101	102	1.01	100	100	99	0.99
Nepal[3]	5-9	Yes	879	1 155*	132	150	113	0.76	160*	160*	160*	1.00*
Pakistan	5-9	No	…	4 425	…	…	…	…	113	125	100	0.80
Sri Lanka[2]	5-13	No	…	*324*[z]	…	…	…	…	*109*[z]	*109*[z]	*109*[z]	*1.00*[z]
Sub-Saharan Africa												
Angola[2]	6-9	No	…	…	…	…	…	…	…	…	…	…
Benin	6-11	No	…	291	…	…	…	…	115	122	108	0.89
Botswana	6-15	No	50	53[z]	114	115	113	0.99	122[z]	124[z]	120[z]	0.97[z]
Burkina Faso	6-16	No	154	306	45	52	37	0.72	73	79	67	0.85
Burundi	7-12	No	*146*	366	*71*	*78*	*64*	*0.83*	164	164	164	1.00
Cameroon	6-11	No	*335*	517	*74*	*82*	*67*	*0.81*	107	114	100	0.88
Cape Verde[2]	6-11	No	*13*	11	*101*	*102*	*100*	*0.98*	86	86	85	0.99
Central African Republic	6-15	No	…	74	…	…	…	…	61	70	52	0.73
Chad[2,3]	6-11	Yes	175	287[z]	72	84	60	0.71	94[z]	109[z]	79[z]	0.73[z]
Comoros[2]	6-13	No	13	*16*[z]	70	76	64	0.84	*70*[z]	*74*[z]	*66*[z]	*0.89*[z]
Congo[3]	6-16	Yes	32	91	37	36	37	1.02	90	92	87	0.94

NET INTAKE RATE (NIR) IN PRIMARY EDUCATION (%)								SCHOOL LIFE EXPECTANCY (expected number of years of formal schooling from primary to tertiary education)						
School year ending in								School year ending in						
1999				2006				1999			2006			
Total	Male	Female	GPI (F/M)	Total	Male	Female	GPI (F/M)	Total	Male	Female	Total	Male	Female	Country or territory
…	…	…	…	69[z]	68[z]	70[z]	1.04[z]	11	11	11	12[z]	12[z]	12[z]	Paraguay [3]
79	79	79	1.00	82	81	82	1.02	…	…	…	14	14	14	Peru [3]
…	…	…	…	66[y]	66[y]	67[y]	1.00[y]	…	…	…	12[z]	12[z]	13[z]	Saint Kitts and Nevis [5]
76	76	75	0.99	75	73	77	1.05	…	…	…	14	13	14	Saint Lucia
…	…	…	…	62[z]	66[z]	58[z]	0.88[z]	…	…	…	12[z]	12[z]	12[z]	Saint Vincent/Grenad.
…	…	…	…	86	86	86	1.00	…	…	…	…	…	…	Suriname [3]
67	66	67	1.02	65[z]	64[z]	66[z]	1.03[z]	11	11	12	11[z]	11[z]	11[z]	Trinidad and Tobago [2,3]
…	…	…	…	54[z]	57[z]	51[z]	0.90[z]	…	…	…	11[z]	11[z]	12[z]	Turks and Caicos Islands
…	…	…	…	…	…	…	…	14	13	15	15	14	16	Uruguay [3]
60	60	60	1.01	65	65	65	1.00	…	…	…	13	…	…	Venezuela, B. R. [3]
														North America and Western Europe
…	…	…	…	47[z]	48[z]	46[z]	0.97[z]	…	…	…	11	11	11	Andorra [2,5]
…	…	…	…	…	…	…	…	15	15	15	15	15	16	Austria [2,4]
…	…	…	…	…	…	…	…	18	18	18	16	16	16	Belgium [4]
…	…	…	…	…	…	…	…	…	…	…	17[y]	17[y]	17[y]	Canada
…	…	…	…	…	…	…	…	13	12	13	14	13	14	Cyprus [2,5]
…	…	…	…	73[z]	69[z]	77[z]	1.11[z]	16	16	17	17	16	17	Denmark
…	…	…	…	93[z]	91[z]	95[z]	1.04[z]	17	17	18	17	17	18	Finland
…	…	…	…	…	…	…	…	16	15	16	16	16	17	France [9]
…	…	…	…	…	…	…	…	16	16	16	16	16	16	Germany
97	97	96	0.99	94[z]	93[z]	94[z]	1.00[z]	14	13	14	17	17	17	Greece [2]
98	100	96	0.97	96[z]	98[z]	95[z]	0.97[z]	17	16	17	18	17	19	Iceland
…	…	…	…	…	…	…	…	16	16	17	18	17	18	Ireland
…	…	…	…	…	…	…	…	15	15	15	15	15	16	Israel [3]
…	…	…	…	…	…	…	…	15	15	15	16	16	17	Italy [2]
…	…	…	…	…	…	…	…	14	13	14	14	13	14	Luxembourg
…	…	…	…	…	…	…	…	…	…	…	15[z]	15[z]	15[z]	Malta [2]
…	…	…	…	…	…	…	…	…	…	…	…	…	…	Monaco [2,8]
…	…	…	…	…	…	…	…	16	17	16	16	17	16	Netherlands [2,4]
…	…	…	…	…	…	…	…	17	17	18	17	17	18	Norway
…	…	…	…	…	…	…	…	16	15	16	15	15	16	Portugal [2]
…	…	…	…	…	…	…	…	…	…	…	…	…	…	San Marino [2,8]
…	…	…	…	…	…	…	…	16	15	16	16	16	17	Spain
…	…	…	…	…	…	…	…	19	17	20	16	15	17	Sweden
…	…	…	…	…	…	…	…	15	15	14	15	15	15	Switzerland
…	…	…	…	…	…	…	…	16	16	16	16	16	17	United Kingdom
…	…	…	…	70[z]	69[z]	72[z]	1.03[z]	16	…	…	16	15	16	United States
														South and West Asia
…	…	…	…	…	…	…	…	…	…	…	8[y]	11[y]	4[y]	Afghanistan [3]
74	74	74	1.00	86[y]	83[y]	88[y]	1.07[y]	8	9	8	8[y]	8[y]	8[y]	Bangladesh [3]
20	21	19	0.91	43	44	42	0.95	7	8	7	10	11	10	Bhutan [3]
…	…	…	…	…	…	…	…	…	…	…	10[z]	11[z]	9[z]	India [3]
44	45	43	0.97	94[z]	…	…	…	12	12	11	13[z]	13[z]	13[z]	Iran, Islamic Republic of [3,10]
87	86	87	1.01	78	78	79	1.01	12	12	12	12	12	12	Maldives
…	…	…	…	…	…	…	…	…	…	…	…	…	…	Nepal [3]
…	…	…	…	88	97	78	0.80	…	…	…	7	7	6	Pakistan
…	…	…	…	97[y]	…	…	…	…	…	…	…	…	…	Sri Lanka [2]
														Sub-Saharan Africa
…	…	…	…	…	…	…	…	4	4	3	…	…	…	Angola [2]
…	…	…	…	48[z]	51[z]	45[z]	0.89[z]	6	8	5	8[z]	…	…	Benin
23	21	25	1.20	31[z]	28[z]	34[z]	1.22[z]	11	11	12	12[z]	12[z]	12[z]	Botswana
19	22	16	0.71	27	30	25	0.83	3	4	3	5	5	4	Burkina Faso
…	…	…	…	54	54	55	1.02	…	…	…	7	8	7	Burundi
…	…	…	…	…	…	…	…	7	…	…	9	10	8	Cameroon
65	64	66	1.03	70	70	71	1.01	…	…	…	12	11	12	Cape Verde [2]
…	…	…	…	…	…	…	…	…	…	…	…	…	…	Central African Republic
22	25	18	0.72	…	…	…	…	…	…	…	6[z]	7[z]	4[z]	Chad [2,3]
16	18	13	0.70	…	…	…	…	7	7	6	8[y]	9[y]	7[y]	Comoros [2]
…	…	…	…	53	54	52	0.96	…	…	…	…	…	…	Congo [3]

Table 4 (continued)

Country or territory	Compulsory education (age group)	Legal guarantees of free education[1]	New entrants (000) School year ending in 1999	New entrants (000) School year ending in 2006	GROSS INTAKE RATE (GIR) IN PRIMARY EDUCATION (%) School year ending in 1999 Total	1999 Male	1999 Female	1999 GPI (F/M)	2006 Total	2006 Male	2006 Female	2006 GPI (F/M)
Côte d'Ivoire	6-15	No	309	344	64	71	57	0.80	67	73	61	0.83
D. R. Congo[3]	6-13	Yes	767	…	50	49	52	1.07	…	…	…	…
Equatorial Guinea	7-11	Yes	…	15[z]	…	…	…	…	112[z]	116[z]	107[z]	0.92[z]
Eritrea	7-14	No	57	61	54	60	49	0.81	49	53	46	0.86
Ethiopia	7-12	No	1 537	**3 221**	78	92	63	0.69	**136**	**144**	**128**	**0.89**
Gabon	6-16	Yes	…	…	…	…	…	…	…	…	…	…
Gambia[3]	7-12	Yes	28	30	78	80	76	0.95	68	65	71	1.09
Ghana[2,3]	6-14	Yes	469	*627*	85	87	83	0.96	*107*	*105*	*110*	*1.05*
Guinea	7-12	No	119	231	52	58	46	0.80	91	94	87	0.92
Guinea-Bissau[3]	7-12	Yes	*35*	…	*92*	*106*	*79*	*0.74*	…	…	…	…
Kenya	6-13	No	892	*1 113[z]*	102	104	101	0.97	*110[z]*	*112[z]*	*108[z]*	*0.96[z]*
Lesotho	6-12	No	51	56	99	99	100	1.01	102	105	99	0.94
Liberia[2]	5-11	No	50	117	60	73	46	0.63	108	109	106	0.98
Madagascar[3]	6-10	Yes	495	1 000	107	108	106	0.98	178	181	176	0.97
Malawi	6-13	No	616	664	175	174	177	1.02	150	145	156	1.07
Mali[3]	7-15	Yes	*171*	301	*58*	*67*	*50*	*0.75*	83	89	76	0.85
Mauritius[3]	6-11	Yes	22	19	98	96	99	1.04	104	104	104	1.00
Mozambique	6-12	No	536	930	104	112	95	0.84	148	153	143	0.93
Namibia[3]	6-15	Yes	54	53	97	96	98	1.02	104	104	105	1.01
Niger[3]	7-12	Yes	133	279	43	50	35	0.71	68	76	59	0.78
Nigeria[3]	6-14	Yes	3 714	4 431[z]	102	114	89	0.79	108[z]	116[z]	99[z]	0.85[z]
Rwanda[3]	7-12	Yes	295	527	127	129	126	0.97	208	209	206	0.99
Sao Tome and Principe	7-12	Yes	4	**5**	106	108	105	0.97	**114**	**113**	**114**	**1.01**
Senegal[3]	7-12	Yes	190	313	66	*68*	*65*	*0.96*	97	95	98	1.03
Seychelles[5]	6-15	Yes	2	**1**	117	116	118	1.02	**127**	**131**	**124**	**0.94**
Sierra Leone	6-12	No	…	**296**	…	…	…	…	**180**	**188**	**172**	**0.92**
Somalia	…	No	…	…	…	…	…	…	…	…	…	…
South Africa	7-15	No	1 157	1 173[y]	115	117	114	0.97	115[y]	118[y]	112[y]	0.95[y]
Swaziland	6-12	Yes	31	31[z]	99	101	97	0.96	107[z]	111[z]	103[z]	0.92[z]
Togo	6-15	No	139	178	91	97	86	0.88	98	101	95	0.94
Uganda	6-12	No	…	1 448	…	…	…	…	146	145	147	1.02
United Republic of Tanzania[3]	7-13	No	714	***1 267***	75	75	74	0.99	***107***	***108***	***106***	***0.99***
Zambia	7-13	No	252	435	84	84	84	1.01	122	119	125	1.05
Zimbabwe	6-12	No	398	…	111	113	109	0.97	…	…	…	…
			Sum	**Sum**	**Weighted average**							
World	…	…	130 195	135 340	104	109	100	0.92	111	114	108	0.95
Countries in transition	…	…	4 449	3 175	99	100	99	0.99	100	101	100	0.99
Developed countries	…	…	12 380	11 575	102	103	101	0.98	102	103	101	0.99
Developing countries	…	…	113 366	120 589	105	110	100	0.91	112	115	109	0.95
Arab States	…	…	6 297	7 191	90	93	87	0.93	100	102	98	0.96
Central and Eastern Europe	…	…	5 635	4 370	97	99	96	0.97	98	98	97	0.99
Central Asia	…	…	1 795	1 416	101	101	101	1.00	102	103	100	0.98
East Asia and the Pacific	…	…	37 045	31 830	103	103	102	0.99	98	99	97	0.98
East Asia	…	…	36 513	31 288	103	103	102	0.99	98	99	97	0.98
Pacific	…	…	533	542	102	104	101	0.97	101	103	99	0.96
Latin America/Caribbean	…	…	13 176	13 142	119	122	116	0.95	119	122	117	0.96
Caribbean	…	…	565	585	156	153	159	1.04	157	157	156	0.99
Latin America	…	…	12 612	12 557	118	121	115	0.95	118	120	115	0.96
N. America/W. Europe	…	…	9 328	8 932	103	104	101	0.97	103	103	102	0.99
South and West Asia	…	…	40 522	44 823	114	123	104	0.85	127	130	123	0.94
Sub-Saharan Africa	…	…	16 397	23 637	90	96	84	0.87	111	116	106	0.92

1. *Source:* Tomasevski (2006).
2. Information on compulsory education comes from the Reports under the United Nations Human Rights Treaties.
3. Some primary school fees continue to be charged despite the legal guarantee of free education (Bentaouet-Kattan, 2005; Tomasevski, 2006; World Bank, 2002).
4. No tuition fees are charged but some direct costs have been reported (Bentaouet-Kattan, 2005; Tomasevski, 2006; World Bank, 2002).
5. National population data were used to calculate enrolment ratios.
6. Enrolment and population data exclude Transnistria.
7. Children can enter primary school at age 6 or 7.
8. Enrolment ratios were not calculated due to lack of United Nations population data by age.

NET INTAKE RATE (NIR) IN PRIMARY EDUCATION (%)								SCHOOL LIFE EXPECTANCY (expected number of years of formal schooling from primary to tertiary education)						
School year ending in								School year ending in						
1999				2006				1999			2006			
Total	Male	Female	GPI (F/M)	Total	Male	Female	GPI (F/M)	Total	Male	Female	Total	Male	Female	Country or territory
26	29	23	0.79	...	...	...	...	*6*	*7*	*5*	...	...	...	Côte d'Ivoire
23	22	24	1.09	...	...	...	...	*4*	...	...	...	...	...	D. R. Congo[3]
...	...	...	...	...	...	...	...	...	...	...	...	...	...	Equatorial Guinea
17	18	16	0.89	22	23	21	0.91	*4*	*5*	*3*	*5*^{y}	*6*^{y}	*4*^{y}	Eritrea
20	23	18	0.80	**59**	**61**	**57**	**0.94**	*4*	*5*	*3*	***8***	***8***	***7***	Ethiopia
...	...	...	...	...	...	...	...	*13*	*14*	*13*	...	...	...	Gabon
46	*47*	*45*	*0.97*	38	36	40	1.09	*7*	*8*	*6*	*7*^{y}	*7*^{y}	*7*^{y}	Gambia[3]
29	*29*	*29*	*1.00*	*33*	*32*	*34*	*1.06*	...	...	...	***9***	***10***	***9***	Ghana[2,3]
20	21	18	0.87	40	41	40	0.98	...	...	...	8	10	7	Guinea
...	...	...	...	...	...	...	...	...	...	...	...	...	...	Guinea-Bissau[3]
30	*29*	*31*	*1.05*	...	...	...	...	...	...	...	*10*^{y}	*10*^{y}	*9*^{y}	Kenya
26	25	27	1.06	48^{z}	48^{z}	49^{z}	1.01^{z}	9	9	10	10	10	10	Lesotho
...	...	...	...	...	...	...	...	*8*	*10*	*7*	...	...	...	Liberia[2]
...	...	...	...	82	82	82	1.01	...	...	...	9	10	9	Madagascar[3]
...	...	...	...	62	60	65	1.09	*11*	*12*	*10*	*9*^{y}	*10*^{y}	*9*^{y}	Malawi
...	...	...	...	29	32	26	0.83	*5*	*6*	*4*	*7*	...	...	Mali[3]
72	71	73	1.03	91	91	91	1.00	*12*	*12*	*12*	*14*^{z}	*14*^{z}	*13*^{z}	Mauritius[3]
18	19	17	0.93	53	53	53	0.99	*5*	...	...	*8*^{z}	*9*^{z}	*7*^{z}	Mozambique
55	*54*	*57*	*1.06*	59	58	61	1.05	...	...	...	*11*	*11*	*11*	Namibia[3]
27	32	22	0.68	45	51	39	0.76	...	...	...	*4*	*5*	*3*	Niger[3]
...	...	...	...	*67*^{y}	*73*^{y}	*61*^{y}	*0.85*^{y}	*7*	*8*	*7*	*8*^{y}	*9*^{y}	*7*^{y}	Nigeria[3]
...	...	...	...	96	97	95	0.99	*6*	...	...	*9*^{z}	*8*^{z}	*9*^{z}	Rwanda[3]
...	...	...	...	**45**	**44**	**46**	**1.04**	...	...	...	*10*	*10*	*10*	Sao Tome and Principe
37	*38*	*36*	*0.96*	59	58	59	1.02	*5*	...	...	*7*^{z}	...	...	Senegal[3]
75	74	77	1.03	96	97	94	0.97	14	14	14	**15**	**14**	**15**	Seychelles[5]
...	...	...	...	...	...	...	...	...	...	...	...	...	...	Sierra Leone
...	...	...	...	...	...	...	...	...	...	...	...	...	...	Somalia
44	45	43	0.95	52^{y}	53^{y}	51^{y}	0.98^{y}	*13*	*13*	*14*	*13*^{y}	*13*^{y}	*13*^{y}	South Africa
42	40	43	1.06	48^{z}	48^{z}	47^{z}	0.99^{z}	*10*	*10*	*9*	*10*^{z}	*10*^{z}	*10*^{z}	Swaziland
37	40	35	0.87	42	44	41	0.94	*9*	*11*	*7*	...	...	...	Togo
...	...	...	...	62	62	63	1.02	*10*	*11*	*9*	*10*^{y}	*11*^{y}	*10*^{y}	Uganda
14	13	15	1.16	86	86	87	1.01	*5*	*5*	*5*	...	...	...	United Republic of Tanzania[3]
37	36	38	1.07	44	43	46	1.08	*7*	*7*	*6*	...	...	...	Zambia
...	...	...	...	...	...	...	...	*10*	...	...	...	...	...	Zimbabwe

Median								Weighted average						
...	...	...	...	68	67	68	1.01	10	10	9	11	11	11	World
...	...	...	...	...	...	...	...	12	12	12	13	13	13	Countries in transition
...	...	...	...	...	...	...	...	15	15	16	16	15	16	Developed countries
...	...	...	...	66	66	67	1.00	9	10	8	10	11	10	Developing countries
65	65	64	0.99	60	61	59	0.97	10	11	9	11	11	10	Arab States
...	...	...	...	...	...	...	...	12	12	12	13	13	13	Central and Eastern Europe
...	...	...	...	72	72	73	1.02	11	11	11	12	12	12	Central Asia
...	...	...	...	...	...	...	...	10	11	10	12	12	12	East Asia and the Pacific
...	...	...	...	67	66	67	1.01	10	11	10	12	12	11	East Asia
...	...	...	...	...	...	...	...	15	15	15	14	14	14	Pacific
77	72	82	1.14	70	66	74	1.12	13	12	13	13	13	14	Latin America/Caribbean
...	...	...	...	70	67	73	1.09	11	11	11	11	11	11	Caribbean
69	68	69	1.03	71	72	71	0.99	13	12	13	13	13	14	Latin America
...	...	...	...	...	...	...	...	16	15	16	16	15	16	N. America/W. Europe
...	...	...	...	87	90	83	0.92	8	9	7	9	10	9	South and West Asia
27	29	27	0.92	52	53	51	0.98	7	7	6	8	9	8	Sub-Saharan Africa

9. Data include French overseas departments and territories (DOM-TOM).

10. The apparent increase in the gender parity index (GPI) is due to the recent inclusion in enrolment statistics of literacy programmes in which 80% of participants are women.

Data in italic are UIS estimates.

Data in bold are for the school year ending in 2007.

(z) Data are for the school year ending in 2005.

(y) Data are for the school year ending in 2004.

(*) National estimate.

Table 5
Participation in primary education

	Country or territory	Age group	School-age population[1] (000)	ENROLMENT IN PRIMARY EDUCATION				Enrolment in private institutions as % of total enrolment		GROSS ENROLMENT RATIO (GER) IN PRIMARY EDUCATION (%)			
				School year ending in				School year ending in		School year ending in			
				1999		2006		1999	2006	1999			
		2006	2005	Total (000)	% F	Total (000)	% F			Total	Male	Female	GPI (F/M)
	Arab States												
1	Algeria	6-11	3 799	4 779	47	4 197	47	.	–	105	110	100	0.91
2	Bahrain	6-11	75	76	49	90	49	19	25	107	106	108	1.01
3	Djibouti	6-11	122	38	41	54	44	9	13	33	39	28	0.71
4	Egypt	6-11	9 466	*8 086*	*47*	**9 988**	**48**	...	**8**	*102*	*106*	*97*	*0.91*
5	Iraq	6-11	4 535	3 604	44	*4 430[z]*	*44[z]*	.	.[z]	92	101	83	0.82
6	Jordan	6-11	833	706	49	805	49	29	31	98	98	98	1.00
7	Kuwait	6-10	211	140	49	203	49	32	34	100	99	101	1.01
8	Lebanon	6-11	475	395	48	448	48	66	67	105	108	103	0.95
9	Libyan Arab Jamahiriya	6-11	684	822	48	755	48	.	5	120	121	118	0.98
10	Mauritania	6-11	458	346	48	466	50	2	7	89	89	88	0.99
11	Morocco	6-11	3 720	3 462	44	3 944	46	4	7	86	95	77	0.81
12	Oman	6-11	349	316	48	288	49	5	5	91	93	89	0.97
13	Palestinian A. T.	6-9	463	368	49	382	49	9	9	105	105	106	1.01
14	Qatar	6-11	68	61	48	71	49	37	63	102	104	100	0.96
15	Saudi Arabia	6-11	3 220	...	...	...	...	...	...	...	...	...	...
16	Sudan	6-11	5 878	*2 513*	*45*	3 881	46	*2*	5[z]	*49*	*53*	*45*	*0.85*
17	Syrian Arab Republic	6-9	1 806	2 738	47	2 280	48	4	4	102	107	98	0.92
18	Tunisia	6-11	1 048	1 443	47	1 134	48	0.7	1	113	116	111	0.95
19	United Arab Emirates	6-10	262	270	48	272	49	44	65	90	92	89	0.97
20	Yemen	6-11	3 747	2 303	35	3 220[z]	42[z]	1	2[z]	71	91	51	0.56
	Central and Eastern Europe												
21	Albania	6-9	217	292	48	250[y]	48[y]	.	4[y]	103	104	102	0.98
22	Belarus	6-9	383	632	48	368	48	0.1	0.1	111	111	110	0.99
23	Bosnia and Herzegovina	6-9	198	...	...	...	...	...	...	...	...	...	...
24	Bulgaria	7-10	272	412	48	273	48	0.3	0.4[z]	106	108	105	0.98
25	Croatia	7-10	197	203	49	195	49	0.1	0.2	92	93	92	0.98
26	Czech Republic	6-10	474	655	49	473	48	0.8	1	103	104	103	0.99
27	Estonia	7-12	80	127	48	80	48	1	3	102	103	100	0.97
28	Hungary	7-10	428	503	48	416	48	5	7	102	103	101	0.98
29	Latvia	7-10	83	141	48	79	48	1	1	100	101	99	0.98
30	Lithuania	7-10	159	220	48	150	48	0.4	0.5	102	103	101	0.98
31	Montenegro	...	...	...	...	...	...	...	...	...	...	...	...
32	Poland	7-12	2 666	3 434	48	2 602	49	...	2	98	99	97	0.98
33	Republic of Moldova[3,4]	7-10	...	262	49	171	49	...	0.9	100	100	100	1.00
34	Romania	7-10	895	1 285	49	938	48	.	0.2	105	106	104	0.98
35	Russian Federation[5]	7-10	5 381	6 743	49	5 165	49	...	0.6	108	109	107	0.98
36	Serbia[3]	7-10	...	*387*	*49*	**297**	**49**	...	...	*112*	*112*	*111*	*0.99*
37	Slovakia	6-9	235	317	49	235	48	4	5	103	103	102	0.99
38	Slovenia	6-10	93	92	48	93	48	0.1	0.1	100	100	99	0.99
39	TFYR Macedonia	7-10	109	130	48	110[z]	48[z]	.	.[z]	101	102	100	0.98
40	Turkey	6-11	8 438	...	...	*7 950*	*48*	...	*2*	...	...	...	...
41	Ukraine	6-9	1 717	2 200	49	1 754	49	0.3	0.5	109	110	109	0.99
	Central Asia												
42	Armenia	7-9	124	255	...	121	48	...	2	100	...	...	...
43	Azerbaijan	6-9	559	707	49	538	47	–	0.2	94	94	94	1.00
44	Georgia	6-11	341	302	49	327	49	0.5	6	98	98	98	1.00
45	Kazakhstan	7-10	932	1 249	49	**948**	**49**	0.5	**0.8**	97	97	98	1.01
46	Kyrgyzstan	7-10	438	470	49	424	49	0.2	0.6	98	98	97	0.99
47	Mongolia	7-11	248	251	50	250	50	0.5	3[z]	97	96	99	1.04
48	Tajikistan	7-10	686	690	48	688	48	.	.	98	101	96	0.95
49	Turkmenistan	7-9	295	...	...	...	...	...	...	...	...	...	...
50	Uzbekistan	7-10	2 313	2 570	49	**2 165**	**49**	...	.	98	99	98	1.00
	East Asia and the Pacific												
51	Australia	5-11	1 849	1 885	49	1 939	49	27	29	100	100	100	1.00
52	Brunei Darussalam	6-11	43	46	47	46	48	36	36	114	115	112	0.97
53	Cambodia	6-11	2 113	2 127	46	2 582	47	2	0.9	97	104	90	0.87
54	China[6]	7-11	97 931	...	...	108 925	47	...	4	...	...	...	...

GROSS ENROLMENT RATIO (GER) IN PRIMARY EDUCATION (%)				NET ENROLMENT RATIO (NER) IN PRIMARY EDUCATION (%)								OUT-OF-SCHOOL CHILDREN (000)[2]				
School year ending in				School year ending in								School year ending in				
2006				1999				2006				1999		2006		
Total	Male	Female	GPI (F/M)	Total	Male	Female	GPI (F/M)	Total	Male	Female	GPI (F/M)	Total (000)	% F	Total (000)	% F	
														Arab States		
110	114	106	0.93	91	93	89	0.96	95	96	94	0.98	357	61	88	70	1
120	120	119	1.00	96	95	97	1.03	98[z]	98[z]	98[z]	1.00[z]	1.0	6	0.4[z]	33[z]	2
44	49	39	0.81	27	32	23	0.73	38	42	34	0.82	83	53	75	53	3
105	**107**	**102**	**0.95**	*94*	*97*	*90*	*0.93*	***96***	***98***	***94***	***0.96***	*285*	*97*	***232***	***96***	4
99[z]	*109[z]*	*90[z]*	*0.83[z]*	85	91	78	0.85	*89[z]*	*95[z]*	*82[z]*	*0.86[z]*	605	71	*508[z]*	*78[z]*	5
97	96	98	1.02	91	91	91	1.01	90	89	90	1.02	40	46	53	42	6
96	97	96	0.99	87	86	87	1.01	83	84	83	0.99	10	46	24	50	7
94	96	93	0.97	*86*	*88*	*85*	*0.96*	82	82	82	0.99	*44*	*55*	81	50	8
110	113	108	0.95	...	...	...	...	...	...	...	...	...	...	...	...	9
102	99	104	1.05	64	65	64	0.99	79	78	82	1.05	139	49	92	44	10
106	112	100	0.89	70	76	65	0.85	88	91	85	0.94	1 183	59	429	61	11
82	82	83	1.01	81	81	81	1.00	74	73	75	1.02	61	48	82	47	12
83	82	83	1.00	97	97	97	1.00	76	76	76	1.00	4	31	94	49	13
105	105	104	0.99	92	92	92	1.01	94	93	94	1.01	1.9	50	1.2	35	14
...	...	...	...	...	...	...	...	...	...	...	...	...	...	...	...	15
66	71	61	0.87	...	...	...	...	...	...	...	...	...	...	...	...	16
126	129	123	0.96	*92*	*95*	*88*	*0.93*	...	...	...	...	*139*	*84*	...	...	17
108	110	107	0.97	93	94	92	0.98	96	96	97	1.01	82	55	27	34	18
104	104	103	0.99	79	80	79	0.99	88	88	88	1.00	55	50	13	47	19
87[z]	100[z]	74[z]	0.74[z]	56	70	41	0.59	75[z]	85[z]	65[z]	0.76[z]	1 410	65	906[z]	70[z]	20
														Central and Eastern Europe		
105[y]	106[y]	105[y]	0.99[y]	*94*	*95*	*94*	*0.98*	94[y]	94[y]	93[y]	0.99[y]	*16*	*55*	15[y]	51[y]	21
96	97	95	0.98	...	...	...	...	89	*90*	*88*	*0.98*	...	...	39	*53*	22
...	...	...	...	...	...	...	...	...	...	...	...	...	...	...	...	23
100	101	99	0.99	97	98	96	0.98	92	93	92	0.99	4	77	17	51	24
99	99	99	1.00	85	86	85	0.98	90	91	90	0.99	18	52	2	7	25
100	100	100	0.99	*97*	*96*	*97*	*1.00*	*93[z]*	*91[z]*	*94[z]*	*1.03[z]*	*21*	*46*	*37[z]*	*41[z]*	26
99	100	98	0.98	*96*	*96*	*95*	*0.98*	94	95	94	0.99	*0.1*	*66*	2	46	27
97	98	96	0.98	88	88	88	0.99	88	89	88	0.99	15	46	23	48	28
95	96	93	0.96	*97*	*98*	*96*	*0.98*	*90[z]*	*89[z]*	*92[z]*	*1.03[z]*	*2*	*56*	*7[z]*	*37[z]*	29
95	95	94	0.99	95	96	95	0.99	89	90	89	0.99	4	44	13	48	30
...	...	...	...	...	...	...	...	...	...	...	...	...	...	...	...	31
98	98	97	1.00	96	96	96	1.00	96	96	96	1.01	133	48	100	45	32
97	97	96	0.99	*93*	...	...	...	88	88	88	1.00	*11*	...	17	48	33
105	105	104	0.99	96	...	...	...	93	93	93	1.00	2	...	40	47	34
96	96	96	1.00	...	...	...	...	91	91	91	1.00	...	...	337	44	35
97	**97**	**97**	**1.00**	...	...	...	...	**95**	**95**	**95**	**1.00**	...	...	**15**	**48**	36
100	101	99	0.98	...	...	...	...	*92[z]*	*92[z]*	*92[z]*	*1.01[z]*	...	...	*19[z]*	*47[z]*	37
100	100	100	0.99	96	97	95	0.99	95	96	95	1.00	1.7	58	3	48	38
98[z]	98[z]	98[z]	1.00[z]	93	94	92	0.98	92[z]	92[z]	92[z]	1.00[z]	1.4	95	3[z]	45[z]	39
94	*96*	*92*	*0.95*	...	...	...	...	91	93	89	0.96	...	...	729	60	40
102	102	102	1.00	...	...	...	...	90	90*	90*	1.00*	...	...	161	49*	41
														Central Asia		
98	96	100	1.04	...	...	...	...	82	80	84	1.05	...	...	12	3	42
96	98	95	0.97	85	85	86	1.01	85	86	83	0.97	109	47	82	53	43
96	94	97	1.03	77*	77*	77*	1.00*	89	88	91	1.03	70*	49*	33	41	44
105	**105**	**105**	**1.00**	...	...	...	...	**90**	**90**	**90**	**1.00**	...	...	**9**	**29**	45
97	97	96	0.99	88*	89*	87*	0.99*	86	86	85	0.99	28*	50*	29	49	46
101	99	102	1.02	89	87	90	1.04	91	90	93	1.02	22	38	7	15	47
100	103	98	0.95	...	...	...	...	97	99	95	0.96	...	...	19	89	48
...	...	...	...	...	...	...	...	...	...	...	...	...	...	...	...	49
95	**97**	**94**	**0.97**	...	...	...	...	...	...	...	...	...	...	...	...	50
														East Asia and the Pacific		
105	105	105	1.00	94	94	94	1.01	96	96	97	1.01	108	46	63	44	51
107	107	106	0.99	...	...	...	...	94	94	94	1.00	...	...	1.1	42	52
122	126	118	0.93	*83*	*87*	*79*	*0.91*	90	91	89	0.98	*366*	*61*	213	54	53
111	112	111	0.99	...	...	...	...	...	...	...	...	...	...	...	...	54

Table 5 (continued)

	Country or territory	Age group	School-age population[1] (000)	ENROLMENT IN PRIMARY EDUCATION				Enrolment in private institutions as % of total enrolment		GROSS ENROLMENT RATIO (GER) IN PRIMARY EDUCATION (%)			
				School year ending in				School year ending in		School year ending in			
				1999		2006		1999	2006	1999			
		2006	2005	Total (000)	% F	Total (000)	% F			Total	Male	Female	GPI (F/M)
55	Cook Islands[3]	5-10	…	3	46	2[z]	48[z]	15	20[z]	96	99	94	0.95
56	DPR Korea	6-9	1 602	…	…	…	…	…	…	…	…	…	…
57	Fiji	6-11	110	116	48	110	48	…	*99*[z]	109	109	108	0.99
58	Indonesia	7-12	25 394	…	…	28 983	48	…	16	…	…	…	…
59	Japan	6-11	7 231	7 692	49	7 229	49	0.9	1	101	101	101	1.00
60	Kiribati[3]	6-11	…	14	49	16[z]	49[z]	…	…	104	104	105	1.01
61	Lao PDR	6-10	769	828	45	892	46	2	3	111	120	102	0.85
62	Macao, China	6-11	33	47	47	35	47	*95*	97	100	102	97	0.96
63	Malaysia	6-11	3 201	3 040	48	3 202[z]	49[z]	…	0.8[z]	98	99	97	0.98
64	Marshall Islands[3]	6-11	…	8	48	**8**	**48**	25	…	*101*	*102*	*100*	*0.98*
65	Micronesia	6-11	17	…	…	**19**	**49**	…	***8***	…	…	…	…
66	Myanmar[7]	5-9	4 342	4 733	49	4 969	50	.	.	100	101	100	0.99
67	Nauru	6-11	…	…	…	**1**	**49**	…	…	…	…	…	…
68	New Zealand	5-10	345	361	49	351	49	…	12	100	100	100	1.00
69	Niue[3]	5-10	…	0.3	46	0.2[z]	51[z]	.	…	99	99	98	1.00
70	Palau[3]	6-10	…	2	47	*2*[z]	*48*[z]	18	*21*[z]	114	118	109	0.93
71	Papua New Guinea	7-12	965	…	…	532	44	…	…	…	…	…	…
72	Philippines	6-11	11 877	12 503	49	13 007	49	8	8	113	113	113	1.00
73	Republic of Korea	6-11	3 857	3 845	47	**3 933**	**47**	2	**1**	95	97	94	0.97
74	Samoa	5-10	32	27	48	*32*[z]	*48*[z]	16	*17*[z]	99	99	98	0.98
75	Singapore	6-11	…	300	48	285	48	…	…	…	…	…	…
76	Solomon Islands	6-11	76	58	46	75[z]	47[z]	…	…	88	91	86	0.94
77	Thailand	6-11	5 417	6 120	48	5 844	48	13	17	106	107	105	0.99
78	Timor-Leste	6-11	186	…	…	178[z]	47[z]	…	…	…	…	…	…
79	Tokelau[3]	5-10	…	…	…	*0.2*[y]	*57*[y]	…	…	…	…	…	…
80	Tonga	5-10	15	17	46	17	47	7	9[y]	108	110	106	0.96
81	Tuvalu[3]	6-11	…	1	48	1	48	…	…	98	97	99	1.02
82	Vanuatu	6-11	34	34	48	**38**	**48**	…	**27**	111	112	110	0.98
83	Viet Nam	6-10	…	10 250	47	7 318	48	0.3	0.5	108	112	104	0.93
	Latin America and the Caribbean												
84	Anguilla	5-11	…	2	50	2	49	5	8	…	…	…	…
85	Antigua and Barbuda	5-11	…	…	…	…	…	…	…	…	…	…	…
86	Argentina[8]	6-11	4 119	4 821	49	4 651[z]	49[z]	20	22[z]	117	116	117	1.00
87	Aruba	6-11	9	9	49	10	49	83	79	114	114	114	0.99
88	Bahamas	5-10	37	34	49	36	49	…	26	95	96	94	0.98
89	Barbados	5-10	22	25	49	22	49	…	12	98	99	98	0.98
90	Belize	5-10	42	44	48	51	49	…	83	118	120	116	0.97
91	Bermuda[3]	5-10	…	…	…	5	46	…	35	…	…	…	…
92	Bolivia	6-11	1 386	1 445	49	1 508	49	…	8	113	114	112	0.98
93	Brazil	7-10	13 752	20 939	48	18 661[z]	48[z]	8	10[y]	154	159	150	0.94
94	British Virgin Islands[3]	5-11	…	3	49	3	48	13	23	112	113	110	0.97
95	Cayman Islands[9]	5-10	…	3	47	3	48	36	35	…	…	…	…
96	Chile	6-11	1 624	1 805	48	1 695	48	45	53	101	102	99	0.97
97	Colombia	6-10	4 568	5 162	49	5 296	49	20	19	114	114	114	1.00
98	Costa Rica	6-11	491	552	48	547	48	7	7	108	109	107	0.98
99	Cuba	6-11	880	1 074	48	890	48	.	.	111	113	109	0.97
100	Dominica[3]	5-11	…	12	48	9	49	24	31	104	107	102	0.95
101	Dominican Republic	6-11	1 257	1 315	49	1 234	48	*14*	17	113	114	111	0.98
102	Ecuador	6-11	1 717	1 899	49	2 006	49	21	29	114	114	114	1.00
103	El Salvador	7-12	908	940	48	1 035	48	*11*	10	112	114	109	0.96
104	Grenada[3]	5-11	…	…	…	*16*[z]	*49*[z]	…	…	…	…	…	…
105	Guatemala	7-12	2 117	1 824	46	2 405	48	15	11	101	108	94	0.87
106	Guyana	6-11	96	107	49	117[z]	49[z]	1	2[z]	121	122	120	0.98
107	Haiti	6-11	1 389	…	…	…	…	…	…	…	…	…	…
108	Honduras	6-11	1 094	…	…	1 293	49	…	7	…	…	…	…
109	Jamaica	6-11	342	*316*	*49*	326[z]	49[z]	*4*	8[z]	*92*	*93*	*92*	*1.00*
110	Mexico	6-11	12 951	14 698	49	14 595	49	7	8	111	112	109	0.98
111	Montserrat	5-11	…	0.4	44	0.5	46	38	34	…	…	…	…
112	Netherlands Antilles	6-11	17	25	48	…	…	74	…	131	135	127	0.95
113	Nicaragua	6-11	834	830	49	966	48	16	15	100	100	101	1.01
114	Panama	6-11	392	393	48	437	48	10	11	108	110	106	0.97

GROSS ENROLMENT RATIO (GER) IN PRIMARY EDUCATION (%)				NET ENROLMENT RATIO (NER) IN PRIMARY EDUCATION (%)								OUT-OF-SCHOOL CHILDREN (000)[2]				
School year ending in				School year ending in								School year ending in				
2006				1999				2006				1999		2006		
Total	Male	Female	GPI (F/M)	Total	Male	Female	GPI (F/M)	Total	Male	Female	GPI (F/M)	Total (000)	% F	Total (000)	% F	
80[z]	*79[z]*	*80[z]*	*1.01[z]*	85	87	83	0.96	*74[z]*	*73[z]*	*75[z]*	*1.03[z]*	0.4	54	*0.7[z]*	*45[z]*	55
...	...	...	...	...	...	...	...	...	...	...	...	...	...	...	...	56
100	100	99	0.98	99	98	99	1.01	91	91	91	1.00	1.4	30	6	47	57
114	116	112	0.96	...	...	...	...	96	...	...	...	...	...	418	...	58
100	100	100	1.00	100	...	...	...	100	...	...	...	3	...	16	...	59
113[z]	112[z]	114[z]	1.01[z]	*97*	*96*	*98*	*1.01*	...	...	...	...	*0.1*	...	...	...	60
116	123	109	0.89	76	79	73	0.92	84	86	81	0.94	178	56	125	57	61
106	109	102	0.94	85	84	85	1.01	91	92	90	0.98	7	47	2.9	55	62
100[z]	101[z]	100[z]	1.00[z]	98	...	...	...	100[z]	100[z]	100[z]	1.00[z]	70	...	4[z]	100[z]	63
93	**94**	**92**	**0.97**	...	...	...	...	**66**	**67**	**66**	**0.99**	...	...	**3**	**49**	64
110	**109**	**110**	**1.01**	...	...	...	...	...	...	...	...	...	...	...	...	65
114	114	115	1.01	*92*	*92*	*91*	*0.99*	100	...	...	...	*387*	*51*	16	...	66
79	***78***	***80***	***1.03***	...	...	...	...	...	...	...	...	...	...	...	...	67
102	102	102	1.00	99	99	99	1.00	99	99	99	1.00	2.0	45	2	44	68
105[z]	107[z]	102[z]	0.95[z]	99	99	98	1.00	...	...	...	...	0.0	50	...	...	69
104[z]	*107[z]*	*101[z]*	*0.94[z]*	*97*	*99*	*94*	*0.94*	...	...	...	...	*0.05*	*91*	...	...	70
55	60	50	0.84	...	...	...	...	...	...	...	...	...	...	...	...	71
110	110	109	0.99	92	92	92	1.00	91	90	92	1.02	895	48	953	42	72
105	**107**	**103**	**0.97**	94	96	93	0.97	**98**	...	...	...	215	62	**57**	...	73
100[z]	*100[z]*	*100[z]*	*1.00[z]*	92	92	91	0.99	*90[y]*	...	...	...	1.6	50	*0.3[y]*	...	74
...	...	...	...	...	...	...	...	...	...	...	...	...	...	...	...	75
101[z]	102[z]	98[z]	0.96[z]	...	...	...	...	62[z]	62[z]	61[z]	0.99[z]	...	...	29[z]	48[z]	76
108	108	108	1.00	...	...	...	...	94	...	...	...	...	...	0.9	...	77
99[z]	103[z]	95[z]	0.92[z]	...	...	...	...	*68[z]*	*70[z]*	*67[z]*	*0.96[z]*	...	...	*57[z]*	*51[z]*	78
93[y]	*79[y]*	*107[y]*	*1.35[y]*	...	...	...	...	...	...	...	...	...	...	...	...	79
113	116	110	0.95	88	90	86	0.96	96[z]	...	...	...	1.8	56	0.2[z]	...	80
106	106	105	0.99	...	...	...	...	...	...	...	...	...	...	...	...	81
108	**110**	**106**	**0.97**	91	92	91	0.99	**87**	**88**	**86**	**0.99**	2.5	51	**4**	**51**	82
...	...	...	...	95	...	...	...	...	...	...	...	447	...	...	...	83
Latin America and the Caribbean																
93	*94*	*92*	*0.99*	...	...	...	...	*92*	*92*	*91*	*1.00*	...	...	*0.1*	*48*	84
...	...	...	...	...	...	...	...	...	...	...	...	...	...	...	...	85
112[z]	113[z]	112[z]	0.99[z]	99*	99*	99*	1.00*	99[z]	99[z]	98[z]	0.99[z]	10*	52*	36[z]	86[z]	86
115	116	113	0.98	98	97	100	1.03	100	99	100	1.00	0.1	7	0.04	24	87
98	98	98	1.00	89	90	89	0.99	88	87	89	1.03	4	50	4	43	88
103	104	102	0.98	*94*	*94*	*94*	*0.99*	96	97	96	0.99	*1.6*	*51*	0.8	54	89
123	125	121	0.97	*94*	*94*	*94*	*0.99*	97	97	97	1.01	*1.7*	*49*	0.4	12	90
100	108	92	0.85	...	...	...	...	*92*	...	...	...	...	...	*0.3*	...	91
109	109	109	1.00	95	95	95	1.00	95	94	95	1.01	52	51	52	43	92
137[z]	141[z]	133[z]	0.94[z]	91	...	...	...	94[z]	93[z]	95[z]	1.02[z]	1 033	...	597[z]	36[z]	93
112	114	110	0.97	*96*	*95*	*97*	*1.02*	*95*	*95*	*95*	*1.00*	*0.04*	*42*	*0.1*	*46*	94
...	...	...	...	...	...	...	...	...	...	...	...	...	...	...	...	95
104	107	102	0.95	...	...	...	...	...	...	...	...	...	...	...	...	96
116	117	115	0.99	89	*89*	*90*	*1.01*	88	89	88	1.00	369	*46*	367	48	97
111	112	111	0.99	...	...	...	...	...	...	...	...	...	...	...	...	98
101	102	100	0.97	97	...	...	...	97	96	97	1.01	9	...	27	44	99
86	85	87	1.02	*94*	*95*	*93*	*0.98*	77	75	79	1.06	*0.4*	*61*	1.9	39	100
98	101	96	0.95	84	83	84	1.01	77	76	78	1.03	174	47	255	45	101
117	117	117	1.00	97	97	98	1.01	97	...	...	...	17	16	11	...	102
114	116	112	0.96	...	...	...	...	94	94	94	1.00	...	...	39	45	103
93[z]	*94[z]*	*91[z]*	*0.96[z]*	...	...	...	...	*84[z]*	*84[z]*	*83[z]*	*0.99[z]*	...	...	*2[z]*	*49[z]*	104
114	118	109	0.93	82	86	78	0.91	94	96	92	0.96	299	61	82	75	105
124[z]	125[z]	124[z]	0.99[z]	...	...	...	...	...	...	...	...	...	...	...	...	106
...	...	...	...	...	...	...	...	...	...	...	...	...	...	...	...	107
118	119	118	0.99	...	...	...	...	96	96	97	1.02	...	...	33	35	108
95[z]	95[z]	95[z]	1.00[z]	*88*	*87*	*88*	*1.00*	*90[z]*	*90[z]*	*90[z]*	*1.00[z]*	*38*	*49*	*31[z]*	*48[z]*	109
113	114	111	0.97	97	97	97	1.00	98	98	97	0.99	55	17	73	84	110
114	*114*	*114*	*1.00*	...	...	...	...	*99*	...	...	...	...	...	*0.0*	...	111
...	...	...	...	...	...	...	...	...	...	...	...	...	...	...	...	112
116	117	114	0.98	76	76	77	1.01	90	90	90	1.00	165	47	72	47	113
112	113	110	0.97	96	96	96	0.99	98	99	98	0.99	11	53	3.7	60	114

Table 5 (continued)

	Country or territory	Age group	School-age population[1] (000)	ENROLMENT IN PRIMARY EDUCATION				Enrolment in private institutions as % of total enrolment		GROSS ENROLMENT RATIO (GER) IN PRIMARY EDUCATION (%)			
				School year ending in				School year ending in		School year ending in			
				1999		2006		1999	2006	1999			
		2006	2005	Total (000)	% F	Total (000)	% F			Total	Male	Female	GPI (F/M)
115	Paraguay	6-11	844	*951*	*48*	934^{z}	48^{z}	*15*	17^{z}	*119*	*121*	*116*	*0.96*
116	Peru	6-11	3 459	4 350	49	4 026	49	13	18	122	123	121	0.99
117	Saint Kitts and Nevis	5-11	...	...	...	**6**	**54**	...	**20**	...	...	...	...
118	Saint Lucia	5-11	20	26	49	24	48	*2*	3	109	110	108	0.98
119	Saint Vincent/Grenad.	5-11	16	...	...	**15**	**51**	...	**4**	...	...	...	...
120	Suriname	6-11	55	...	...	66	48	...	47	...	...	...	...
121	Trinidad and Tobago	5-11	133	172	49	130^{*,z}	49^{*,z}	*72*	*70*^{z}	96	96	95	1.00
122	Turks and Caicos Islands	6-11	...	2	49	2^{z}	51^{z}	18	30^{z}	...	...	...	...
123	Uruguay	6-11	318	366	49	365	48	...	14	111	112	111	0.99
124	Venezuela, Bolivarian Rep. of	6-11	3 309	3 261	49	3 452	48	15	14	100	101	99	0.98
	North America and Western Europe												
125	Andorra[3]	6-11	...	...	...	4	47	...	2	...	...	...	...
126	Austria	6-9	349	389	48	355	49	4	5	103	103	102	0.99
127	Belgium	6-11	718	763	49	733	49	55	54	105	105	105	0.99
128	Canada	6-11	2 329	2 429	49	*2 389*^{y}	*49*^{y}	6	...	99	99	99	1.00
129	Cyprus[3]	6-11	...	64	48	60	49	4	6	97*	98*	97*	1.00*
130	Denmark	7-12	421	372	49	416	49	11	12	101	102	101	1.00
131	Finland	7-12	379	383	49	372	49	1	1	99	99	99	1.00
132	France[10]	6-10	3 690	3 944	49	4 052	48	15	15	107	107	106	0.99
133	Germany	6-9	3 224	3 767	49	3 329	49	2	3	106	106	105	0.99
134	Greece	6-11	634	646	48	645	49	7	7	94	94	95	1.00
135	Iceland	6-12	31	30	48	30	49	1	1	99	100	98	0.98
136	Ireland	4-11	446	457	49	462	48	0.9	1	104	104	103	0.99
137	Israel	6-11	730	722	49	803	49	...	.	112	112	111	0.99
138	Italy	6-10	2 697	2 876	48	2 790	48	7	7	103	103	102	0.99
139	Luxembourg	6-11	35	31	49	35	49	7	7	101	100	102	1.02
140	Malta	5-10	29	35	49	30^{z}	48^{z}	36	38^{z}	107	106	107	1.01
141	Monaco[9]	6-10	...	2	50	2^{y}	...	31	26^{y}	...	...	...	...
142	Netherlands	6-11	1 199	1 268	48	1 277	48.2	68	69^{y}	108	109	107	0.98
143	Norway	6-12	438	412	49	430	48.8	1	2^{z}	101	101	101	1.00
144	Portugal	6-11	652	815	48	750	48	9	11	123	126	121	0.96
145	San Marino[9]	6-10	...	...	...	1^{y}	...	...	.^{y}	...	...	...	...
146	Spain	6-11	2 388	2 580	48	2 501	48	33	33	106	106	105	0.99
147	Sweden	7-12	656	763	49	627	49	3	7	110	108	111	1.03
148	Switzerland	7-12	531	530	49	517	49	3	4	102	102	102	1.00
149	United Kingdom	5-10	4 293	4 661	49	4 518	49	5	5	101	101	101	1.00
150	United States	6-11	24 767	24 938	49	24 319	49	12	10	101	100	102	1.03
	South and West Asia												
151	Afghanistan	7-12	4 430	957	7	4 319^{z}	36^{z}	...	...	28	51	4	0.08
152	Bangladesh	6-10	17 649	17 622	49	17 953^{y}	50^{y}	37	42^{y}	102	102	102	0.99
153	Bhutan	6-12	101	81	46	102	49	2	2	75	81	69	0.85
154	India	6-10	124 357	110 986	43	139 170	47	...	...	93	100	85	0.84
155	Iran, Islamic Republic of[11]	6-10	6 176	8 667	47	7 274	55	...	5	96	99	94	0.95
156	Maldives	6-12	47	74	49	55	48	3	2	134	134	135	1.01
157	Nepal	5-9	3 571	3 588	42	4 503	47	...	15^{z}	114	128	98	0.77
158	Pakistan	5-9	19 837	...	...	16 688	42	...	34	...	...	...	...
159	Sri Lanka	5-9	1 491	...	...	*1 635*^{z}	*49*^{z}	...	*2*^{z}	...	...	...	...
	Sub-Saharan Africa												
160	Angola	6-9	1 913	*1 057*	*46*	...	...	*5*	...	*64*	*69*	*59*	*0.86*
161	Benin	6-11	1 415	872	39	1 357	44	7	13	74	89	59	0.67
162	Botswana	6-12	304	322	50	327^{z}	49^{z}	5	5^{y}	104	104	104	1.00
163	Burkina Faso	7-12	2 327	816	40	1 391	44	11	14	43	51	36	0.70
164	Burundi	7-12	1 283	*702*	*44*	1 325	48	*1*	1	*60*	*67*	*54*	*0.80*
165	Cameroon	6-11	2 796	2 134	45	2 998	45	28	23	84	92	75	0.82
166	Cape Verde	6-11	77	92	49	81	49	–	0.3	119	122	116	0.96
167	Central African Republic	6-11	691	...	...	419	41	...	10^{z}	...	...	...	...
168	Chad	6-11	1 730	840	37	1 262^{z}	40^{z}	25	31^{z}	63	79	46	0.58
169	Comoros	6-11	128	83	45	*107*^{z}	*46*^{z}	12	*10*^{z}	76	82	69	0.85
170	Congo	6-11	573	276	49	617	47	10	38	56	58	55	0.95

GROSS ENROLMENT RATIO (GER) IN PRIMARY EDUCATION (%)				NET ENROLMENT RATIO (NER) IN PRIMARY EDUCATION (%)								OUT-OF-SCHOOL CHILDREN (000)[2]				
School year ending in				School year ending in								School year ending in				
2006				1999				2006				1999		2006		
Total	Male	Female	GPI (F/M)	Total	Male	Female	GPI (F/M)	Total	Male	Female	GPI (F/M)	Total (000)	% F	Total (000)	% F	
111[z]	113[z]	110[z]	0.97[z]	96	96	96	1.00	94[z]	94[z]	95[z]	1.01[z]	28	46	43[z]	46[z]	*115*
116	116	117	1.01	*98*	…	…	…	96	96	97	1.01	*6*	…	33	9	*116*
94	**86**	**103**	**1.20**	…	…	…	…	**71**	**64**	**78**	**1.22**	…	…	**2**	**35**	*117*
118	121	114	0.94	*96*	*97*	*96*	*0.99*	98	99	97	0.98	*0.7*	*52*	0.2	75	*118*
97	**94**	**100**	**1.06**	…	…	…	…	90[z]	92[z]	88[z]	0.96[z]	…	…	1.2[z]	61[z]	*119*
121	121	121	1.00	…	…	…	…	96	95	98	1.03	…	…	1.9	26	*120*
95[*,z]	96[*,z]	94[*,z]	0.98[*,z]	87	87	88	1.01	85[*,z]	85[*,z]	85[*,z]	1.00[*,z]	16	46	15[*,z]	48[*,z]	*121*
90[z]	*88[z]*	*92[z]*	*1.04[z]*	…	…	…	…	*78[z]*	*75[z]*	*81[z]*	*1.07[z]*	…	…	*0.5[z]*	*42[z]*	*122*
115	117	113	0.97	…	…	…	…	100	…	…	…	…	…	0.1	…	*123*
104	106	103	0.98	86	85	86	1.01	91	91	91	1.00	424	47	226	46	*124*
North America and Western Europe																
90	90	90	1.00	…	…	…	…	83	83	83	1.01	…	…	0.8	46	*125*
102	102	101	0.99	*97*	*97*	*98*	*1.01*	*97*	*97*	*98*	*1.01*	*10*	*38*	*9*	*38*	*126*
102	102	102	0.99	99	99	99	1.00	97	97	97	1.00	6	43	18	47	*127*
100[y]	*100[y]*	*99[y]*	*0.99[y]*	99	99	99	1.00	…	…	…	…	30	42	…	…	*128*
102	103	102	1.00	95	95	95	1.00	99	99	99	1.00	1.3	49	0.3	49	*129*
99	99	99	1.00	97	97	97	1.00	96	95	96	1.01	8	42	16	40	*130*
98	98	98	1.00	99	99	98	1.00	97	97	97	1.00	5	57	11	45	*131*
110	110	109	0.99	99	99	99	1.00	99	98	99	1.00	9	34	27	34	*132*
103	103	103	1.00	…	…	…	…	*98*	…	…	…	…	…	*12*	…	*133*
102	102	102	1.00	92	92	93	1.01	99	100	99	1.00	31	44	1.9	71	*134*
98	98	97	0.99	99	…	…	…	98	98	97	0.99	0.3	…	0.7	63	*135*
104	104	103	0.99	94	93	94	1.01	95	94	95	1.01	28	45	23	44	*136*
110	109	111	1.02	98	98	98	1.00	97	96	97	1.01	15	51	22	40	*137*
103	104	103	0.99	99	…	…	…	99	99	98	0.99	7	…	17	72	*138*
102	101	102	1.01	97	96	98	1.03	97	96	98	1.01	0.6	16	0.4	19	*139*
100[z]	101[z]	99[z]	0.98[z]	95	94	96	1.02	91[z]	92[z]	91[z]	0.99[z]	1.7	41	2.6[z]	51[z]	*140*
…	…	…	…	…	…	…	…	…	…	…	…	…	…	…	…	*141*
107	108	105	0.98	99	100	99	0.99	98	99	97	0.99	6.4	99	21	69	*142*
98	98	98	1.01	100	100	100	1.00	98	98	98	1.01	0.6	60	8	42	*143*
115	118	112	0.95	…	…	…	…	98	98	98	0.99	…	…	5	63	*144*
…	…	…	…	…	…	…	…	…	…	…	…	…	…	…	…	*145*
105	106	104	0.98	100	100	100	1.00	100	100	99	1.00	6	69	7	86	*146*
96	96	95	1.00	100	…	…	…	95	95	95	1.00	2	…	33	50	*147*
97	98	97	0.99	94	94	94	1.00	89	89	89	0.99	10	37	35	48	*148*
105	105	106	1.01	100	100	100	1.00	98	98	99	1.01	2.0	25	16	0.1	*149*
98	98	99	1.01	94	94	94	1.00	92	91	93	1.02	1 215	49	1 683	42	*150*
South and West Asia																
101[z]	126[z]	75[z]	0.59[z]	…	…	…	…	…	…	…	…	…	…	…	…	*151*
103[y]	101[y]	105[y]	1.03[y]	83*	83*	83*	1.00*	89[*,y]	87[*,y]	90[*,y]	1.04[*,y]	2 350*	48*	1 371[*,y]	39[*,y]	*152*
102	103	101	0.98	56	60	53	0.89	79	79	79	1.00	47	53	20	49	*153*
112	114	109	0.96	…	…	…	…	89	90	87	0.96	…	…	7 208	64	*154*
118	104	132	1.27	*82*	*83*	*81*	*0.97*	*94*	…	…	…	*1 616*	*52*	*391*	…	*155*
116	118	114	0.97	98	97	98	1.01	97	97	97	1.00	1.1	41	0.9	46	*156*
126	129	123	0.95	65*	72*	57*	0.79*	*79[y]*	*84[y]*	*74[y]*	*0.87[y]*	1 043*	61*	*702[y]*	*62[y]*	*157*
84	94	73	0.78	…	…	…	…	*66*	*73*	*57*	*0.78*	…	…	*6 821*	*60*	*158*
108[z]	*108[z]*	*108[z]*	*1.00[z]*	…	…	…	…	*97[y]*	…	…	…	…	…	*51[y]*	…	*159*
Sub-Saharan Africa																
…	…	…	…	…	…	…	…	…	…	…	…	…	…	…	…	*160*
96	105	87	0.83	50*	59*	40*	0.68*	80	87	73	0.84	586*	59*	244	71	*161*
107[z]	107[z]	106[z]	0.99[z]	80	79	82	1.04	84[z]	83[z]	85[z]	1.03[z]	55	44	49[z]	45[z]	*162*
60	66	54	0.82	35	41	28	0.70	47	52	42	0.82	1 231	54	1 215	54	*163*
103	108	98	0.91	…	…	…	…	75	76	73	0.97	…	…	324	53	*164*
107	117	98	0.84	…	…	…	…	…	…	…	…	…	…	…	…	*165*
106	108	103	0.95	*99*	*99*	*98*	*0.98*	88	88	87	0.99	*0.8*	*90*	9	52	*166*
61	72	49	0.69	…	…	…	…	46	53	38	0.72	…	…	375	57	*167*
76[z]	90[z]	61[z]	0.68[z]	51	63	39	0.62	…	…	…	…	654	62	…	…	*168*
85[z]	*91[z]*	*80[z]*	*0.88[z]*	49	54	45	0.85	…	…	…	…	53	54	…	…	*169*
108	113	102	0.90	…	…	…	…	55	58	52	0.90	…	…	243	53	*170*

Table 5 (continued)

	Country or territory	Age group 2006	School-age population[1] (000) 2005	ENROLMENT IN PRIMARY EDUCATION, School year ending in 1999: Total (000)	1999: % F	2006: Total (000)	2006: % F	Enrolment in private institutions as % of total enrolment, School year ending in 1999	2006	GROSS ENROLMENT RATIO (GER) IN PRIMARY EDUCATION (%), School year ending in 1999: Total	Male	Female	GPI (F/M)
171	Côte d'Ivoire	6-11	2 993	1 911	43	2 112	44	12	12	69	79	59	0.74
172	D. R. Congo	6-11	10 043	4 022	47	…	…	19	…	48	51	46	0.90
173	Equatorial Guinea	7-11	64	75	44	76[z]	49[z]	33	30[z]	142	159	125	0.79
174	Eritrea	7-11	585	262	45	364	44	11	8	52	57	47	0.82
175	Ethiopia	7-12	13 142	5 168	38	**12 175**	**47**	…	…	48	59	36	0.61
176	Gabon	6-11	184	265	50	*281*[y]	*49*[y]	17	*29*[y]	148	148	148	1.00
177	Gambia	7-12	246	150	46	182	51	*3*	3[y]	77	83	72	0.87
178	Ghana	6-11	3 409	2 377	47	**3 366**	**49**	13	**16**	75	78	72	0.92
179	Guinea	7-12	1 425	727	38	1 258	45	15	22	57	70	45	0.64
180	Guinea-Bissau	7-12	265	*145*	*40*	…	…	*19*	…	*70*	*84*	*56*	*0.67*
181	Kenya	6-11	5 763	4 782	49	6 101	49	…	4[z]	93	94	91	0.97
182	Lesotho	6-12	371	365	52	425	50	…	0.4	102	98	106	1.08
183	Liberia	6-11	588	396	42	538	47	38	…	85	98	73	0.74
184	Madagascar	6-10	2 652	2 012	49	3 699	49	22	19	93	95	92	0.97
185	Malawi	6-11	2 461	2 582	49	2 934	50	…	1	137	140	134	0.96
186	Mali	7-12	2 009	959	41	1 610	44	22	38	59	70	49	0.70
187	Mauritius	5-10	119	133	49	121	49	24	26	105	105	106	1.00
188	Mozambique	6-12	3 983	2 302	43	4 173	46	…	2	70	80	59	0.74
189	Namibia	6-12	376	383	50	403	50	4	4	104	104	105	1.01
190	Niger	7-12	2 226	530	39	1 127	41	4	4	31	37	25	0.68
191	Nigeria[12]	6-11	23 631	17 907	44	22 267[z]	45[z]	*4*	…	88	98	78	0.79
192	Rwanda	7-12	1 443	1 289	50	2 020	51	…	1	92	93	91	0.98
193	Sao Tome and Principe	7-12	24	24	49	**31**	**49**	–	–[z]	108	109	106	0.97
194	Senegal	7-12	1 845	1 034	*46*	1 473	49	12	12	64	*69*	*59*	*0.86*
195	Seychelles[3]	6-11	…	10	49	**9**	**49**	5	**6**	116[y]	117	116	0.99
196	Sierra Leone	6-11	871	…	…	**1 322**	**48**	…	**3**	…	…	…	…
197	Somalia	6-12	1 520	…	…	…	…	…	…	…	…	…	…
198	South Africa	7-13	7 116	7 935	49	7 444[y]	49[y]	2	2[y]	116	117	114	0.97
199	Swaziland	6-12	207	213	49	222[z]	48[z]	–	.[z]	100	102	97	0.95
200	Togo	6-11	1 027	954	43	1 052	46	36	43	112	127	96	0.75
201	Uganda	6-12	6 309	6 288	47	7 364	50	…	9	125	130	119	0.92
202	United Republic of Tanzania	7-13	7 217	4 190	50	**8 317**	**49**	0.2	**1**	67	67	67	1.00
203	Zambia	7-13	2 292	1 556	48	2 679	49	…	3	80	84	77	0.92
204	Zimbabwe	6-12	2 417	2 460	49	2 446	50	88	…	100	101	98	0.97

			Sum	Sum	% F	Sum	% F	Median		Weighted average			
I	World	…	654 297	648 135	47	688 173	47	7	7	99	103	95	0.92
II	Countries in transition	…	13 348	16 469	49	13 165	49	0.2	0.6	104	105	103	0.99
III	Developed countries	…	65 763	70 414	49	66 423	49	4	4	102	102	102	1.00
IV	Developing countries	…	575 186	561 252	46	608 585	47	11	10	99	103	94	0.91
V	Arab States	…	41 219	35 402	46	40 150	47	4	7	90	96	84	0.87
VI	Central and Eastern Europe	…	22 520	26 063	48	21 792	48	0.3	0.7	102	104	100	0.96
VII	Central Asia	…	5 938	6 884	49	5 957	48	0.3	0.7	98	99	98	0.99
VIII	East Asia and the Pacific	…	175 938	217 564	48	192 241	47	8	10	112	113	112	0.99
IX	East Asia	…	172 464	214 392	48	189 096	47	2	3	113	113	112	0.99
X	Pacific	…	3 474	3 172	48	3 145	48	…	20	95	97	94	0.97
XI	Latin America and the Caribbean	…	58 255	70 206	48	68 553	48	15	17	121	123	119	0.97
XII	Caribbean	…	2 236	2 500	49	2 412	49	21	28	112	113	111	0.98
XIII	Latin America	…	56 019	67 705	48	66 141	48	15	14	122	123	120	0.97
XIV	North America and Western Europe	…	50 698	52 882	49	51 377	49	7	7	103	102	103	1.01
XV	South and West Asia	…	177 659	157 510	44	192 040	47	…	5	90	98	82	0.84
XVI	Sub-Saharan Africa	…	122 070	81 625	46	116 063	47	11	8	78	84	71	0.85

1. Data are for 2005 except for countries with a calendar school year, in which case data are for 2006.
2. Data reflect the actual number of children not enrolled at all, derived from the age-specific enrolment ratios of primary school age children, which measures the proportion of those who are enrolled either in primary or in secondary schools (total primary NER).
3. National population data were used to calculate enrolment ratios.
4. Enrolment and population data exclude Transnistria.
5. In the Russian Federation two education structures existed in the past, both starting at age 7. The most common or widespread one lasted three years and was used to calculate indicators; the second one, in which about one-third of primary pupils were enrolled, had four grades. Since 2004, the four-grade structure has been extended all over the country.
6. Children enter primary school at age 6 or 7. Since 7 is the most common entrance age, enrolment ratios were calculated using the 7-11 age group for population.

GROSS ENROLMENT RATIO (GER) IN PRIMARY EDUCATION (%)				NET ENROLMENT RATIO (NER) IN PRIMARY EDUCATION (%)								OUT-OF-SCHOOL CHILDREN (000)[2]				
School year ending in				School year ending in								School year ending in				
2006				1999				2006				1999		2006		
Total	Male	Female	GPI (F/M)	Total	Male	Female	GPI (F/M)	Total	Male	Female	GPI (F/M)	Total (000)	% F	Total (000)	% F	
71	79	62	0.79	52	60	45	0.75	...	...	...	...	1 290	58	...	...	171
...	...	...	...	...	...	...	...	...	...	...	...	...	...	...	...	172
122[z]	125[z]	119[z]	0.95[z]	89	...	...	...	...	...	...	...	6	...	...	...	173
62	69	56	0.81	33	36	31	0.86	47	50	43	0.87	335	52	308	53	174
91	**97**	**85**	**0.88**	34	41	28	0.69	**71**	**74**	**68**	**0.92**	7 069	55	**3 721**	**55**	175
152[y]	*153[y]*	*152[y]*	*0.99[y]*	...	...	...	...	...	...	...	...	...	...	...	...	176
74	71	77	1.08	64	68	61	0.89	62	59	64	1.09	68	55	90	46	177
98	**98**	**97**	**0.99**	*57*	*58*	*55*	*0.96*	**72**	**73**	**71**	**0.97**	*1 349*	*50*	**967**	**51**	178
88	96	81	0.84	45	52	36	0.69	72	77	66	0.86	698	56	389	59	179
...	...	...	...	*45*	*53*	*37*	*0.71*	...	...	...	...	*114*	*57*	...	...	180
106	107	104	0.97	63	63	64	1.01	75	75	76	1.02	1 859	49	1 371	48	181
114	115	114	1.00	57	54	61	1.12	72	71	74	1.04	152	46	101	47	182
91	96	87	0.90	42	47	36	0.77	39	40	39	0.97	268	55	356	50	183
139	142	137	0.96	63	63	63	1.01	96	96	96	1.00	796	50	106	49	184
119	117	121	1.04	98	...	...	...	91	88	94	1.06	20	...	202	33	185
80	90	71	0.79	*46*	*55*	*38*	*0.70*	61	67	54	0.79	*862*	*58*	793	59	186
102	102	102	1.00	91	90	91	1.01	95	94	96	1.02	12	47	6	41	187
105	113	97	0.86	52	58	46	0.79	76	79	73	0.93	1 574	56	954	56	188
107	107	107	1.00	73	71	76	1.07	76	74	79	1.06	98	45	89	45	189
51	58	43	0.73	26	31	21	0.68	43	50	37	0.73	1 255	52	1 245	55	190
96[z]	105[z]	87[z]	0.83[z]	*58*	*64*	*52*	*0.82*	*63[z]*	*68[z]*	*59[z]*	*0.86[z]*	*8 218*	*57*	*8 097[z]*	*56[z]*	191
140	137	142	1.04	...	...	...	...	*79[z]*	*76[z]*	*81[z]*	*1.06[z]*	...	...	*303[z]*	*45[z]*	192
127	**128**	**127**	**1.00**	86	86	85	0.99	**98**	**97**	**98**	**1.01**	2.7	50	**0.6**	**38**	193
80	81	79	0.98	54	*57*	*50*	*0.88*	71	71	70	0.98	740	*54*	513	51	194
125	**126**	**125**	**0.99**	...	...	...	...	99[y]	...	...	...	...	...	0.04[y]	...	195
147	**155**	**139**	**0.90**	...	...	...	...	...	...	...	...	...	...	...	...	196
...	...	...	...	...	...	...	...	...	...	...	...	...	...	...	...	197
106[y]	108[y]	103[y]	0.96[y]	94	93	94	1.01	88[y]	88[y]	88[y]	1.00[y]	97	2	469[y]	44	198
106[z]	110[z]	102[z]	0.93[z]	74	73	75	1.02	78[z]	78[z]	79[z]	1.01[z]	54	48	45[z]	49[z]	199
102	110	95	0.86	79	89	70	0.79	80	86	75	0.87	148	81	176	68	200
117	116	117	1.01	...	...	...	...	...	...	...	...	...	...	...	...	201
112	**113**	**111**	**0.98**	50	49	50	1.04	98	98	97	0.99	3 148	49	143	65	202
117	118	116	0.98	68	69	67	0.96	92	90	94	1.03	616	52	150	36	203
101	102	101	0.99	83	83	83	1.01	88	87	88	1.01	406	49	281	47	204

Weighted average				Weighted average				Weighted average				Sum	% F	Sum	% F	
105	108	102	0.95	82	85	80	0.93	86	88	85	0.97	103 223	58	75 177	55	I
99	99	98	0.99	88	88	87	0.99	90	90	89	0.99	1 555	51	899	49	II
101	101	101	1.00	97	97	97	1.00	95	95	96	1.01	1 791	50	2 368	43	III
106	109	103	0.94	81	84	77	0.92	85	87	84	0.96	99 877	58	71 911	55	IV
97	102	92	0.90	78	82	74	0.90	84	87	81	0.93	7 980	59	5 708	61	V
97	98	96	0.98	91	93	90	0.97	92	92	91	0.98	2 036	59	1 611	52	VI
100	101	99	0.98	87	87	86	0.99	89	90	88	0.98	548	51	352	53	VII
109	110	108	0.99	96	96	96	1.00	93	94	93	1.00	6 079	51	9 535	49	VIII
110	110	109	0.99	96	96	96	1.00	94	94	93	1.00	5 760	51	8 988	49	IX
91	92	89	0.97	90	91	89	0.98	84	85	83	0.97	318	54	546	52	X
118	120	116	0.97	92	93	91	0.98	94	94	94	1.00	3 522	54	2 631	47	XI
108	109	107	0.99	75	76	74	0.97	72	73	70	0.97	493	50	617	51	XII
118	120	116	0.97	93	94	92	0.98	95	95	95	1.00	3 029	55	2 014	46	XIII
101	101	101	1.00	97	97	97	1.00	95	95	95	1.01	1 420	50	1 981	43	XIV
108	111	105	0.95	75	81	69	0.84	86	88	83	0.95	36 618	64	18 203	59	XV
95	101	89	0.89	56	60	53	0.89	70	73	67	0.92	45 021	54	35 156	54	XVI

7. The dramatic increase in primary education NER from 90% in 2005 (figure published in the 2008 GMR) to the nearly 100% figure for 2006 published in this year Report is essentially due to the use of the latest UN population estimates (2006 revision) that indicate a lower primary school age population as compared with the previous estimates (2004 revision). The reported change should not be interpreted as an accurate representation of progress towards UPE as the country own data show.

8. Enrolment ratios were not calculated due to lack of United Nations population data by age.

9. Data include French overseas departments and territories (DOM-TOM).

10. The apparent increase in the gender parity index (GPI) is due to the recent inclusion in enrolment statistics of literacy programmes in which 80% of participants are women.

11. Due to the continuing discrepancy in enrolment by single age, the net enrolment ratio in primary education is estimated using the age distribution of the 2004 DHS data.

Data in italic are UIS estimates.

Data in bold are for the school year ending in 2007.

(z) Data are for the school year ending in 2005.

(y) Data are for the school year ending in 2004.

(*) National estimate.

Table 6

Internal efficiency: repetition in primary education

	Country or territory	Duration[1] of primary education	REPETITION RATES BY GRADE IN PRIMARY EDUCATION (%) — School year ending in 2005											
			Grade 1			Grade 2			Grade 3			Grade 4		
		2006	Total	Male	Female	Total	Male	Female	Total	Male	Female	Total	Male	Female
	Arab States													
1	Algeria	6	12.6	14.6	10.4	10.6	12.9	8.1	5.6	7.1	3.9	10.1	12.8	7.1
2	Bahrain	6	3.0[y]	2.4[y]	3.5[y]	3.2[y]	3.7[y]	2.6[y]	3.4[y]	4.0[y]	2.8[y]	2.5[y]	3.2[y]	1.8[y]
3	Djibouti	6	3.9	4.1	3.5	9.6	9.5	9.7	6.3	6.0	6.8	5.5	5.6	5.4
4	Egypt	6	–	–	–	***1.8***	…	…	***2.5***	…	…	***4.1***	…	…
5	Iraq	6	*9.2[y]*	*10.3[y]*	*7.9[y]*	*7.7[y]*	*8.7[y]*	*6.5[y]*	*6.4[y]*	*7.4[y]*	*5.2[y]*	*7.2[y]*	*8.5[y]*	*5.5[y]*
6	Jordan	6	0.5	…	…	0.4	…	…	0.4	…	…	1.4	…	…
7	Kuwait	5	2.6	2.7	2.5	1.5	1.5	1.6	1.9	2.2	1.5	1.7	2.1	1.3
8	Lebanon	6	5.4	6.4	4.4	6.6	8.1	5.0	6.3	7.8	4.7	16.6	19.0	14.1
9	Libyan Arab Jamahiriya	6	…	…	…	…	…	…	…	…	…	…	…	…
10	Mauritania	6	8.9	9.1	8.7	9.4	9.6	9.3	10.4	10.4	10.5	10.2	10.1	10.3
11	Morocco	6	16.2	17.3	14.9	13.7	15.4	11.8	13.8	16.0	11.2	11.3	13.8	8.4
12	Oman	6	0.3	0.3	0.2	0.1	0.1	0.0	0.1	0.1	0.1	0.0	0.0	0.0
13	Palestinian A. T.	4	0.0[y]	0.0[y]	0.0[y]	0.0[y]	0.0[y]	0.0[y]	0.4[y]	0.4[y]	0.4[y]	2.2[y]	2.4[y]	2.1[y]
14	Qatar	6	1.4	1.9	1.0	1.0	1.3	0.7	1.6	2.2	1.0	0.8	0.8	0.7
15	Saudi Arabia	6	…	…	…	…	…	…	…	…	…	…	…	…
16	Sudan	6	1.4[y]	1.1[y]	1.8[y]	1.6[y]	1.4[y]	1.9[y]	1.8[y]	1.6[y]	2.1[y]	2.1[y]	1.7[y]	2.5[y]
17	Syrian Arab Republic	4	10.7	11.7	9.5	7.3	8.4	6.0	4.3	5.1	3.4	2.8	3.4	2.1
18	Tunisia	6	1.0	1.2	0.9	9.4	10.8	7.9	2.1	2.6	1.6	12.1	14.4	9.4
19	United Arab Emirates	5	2.6	2.5	2.8	1.9	2.0	1.7	1.8	2.0	1.6	2.0	2.8	1.2
20	Yemen	6	*4.3*	*4.3*	*4.3*	…	…	…	…	…	…	…	…	…
	Central and Eastern Europe													
21	Albania	4	3.2[x]	3.7[x]	2.7[x]	2.1[x]	2.5[x]	1.6[x]	1.5[x]	1.9[x]	1.1[x]	1.7[x]	2.0[x]	1.4[x]
22	Belarus	4	0.2	0.2	0.2	0.0	0.0	0.0	0.0	0.0	0.0	0.0	0.0	0.0
23	Bosnia and Herzegovina	4	…	…	…	…	…	…	…	…	…	…	…	…
24	Bulgaria	4	0.8	0.9	0.6	2.8	3.3	2.3	2.3	2.8	1.8	2.7	3.0	2.5
25	Croatia	4	0.7	0.7	0.6	0.3	0.4	0.2	0.2	0.2	0.1	0.1	0.1	0.1
26	Czech Republic	5	1.1	1.3	1.0	0.6	0.7	0.5	0.5	0.6	0.4	0.6	0.7	0.5
27	Estonia	6	1.6	2.0	1.1	1.1	1.4	0.8	1.3	1.8	0.9	1.9	2.5	1.2
28	Hungary	4	3.7	4.1	3.2	1.5	1.7	1.2	1.1	1.3	0.8	1.1	1.4	0.8
29	Latvia	4	4.8	6.4	3.0	2.0	2.7	1.3	1.8	2.4	1.1	2.2	3.0	1.4
30	Lithuania	4	1.2	1.4	0.9	0.6	0.6	0.5	0.4	0.5	0.2	0.3	0.5	0.2
31	Montenegro	…	…	…	…	…	…	…	…	…	…	…	…	…
32	Poland	6	0.8	…	…	0.4	…	…	0.4	…	…	0.9	…	…
33	Republic of Moldova	4	0.5	0.6	0.3	0.1	0.1	0.1	0.1	0.1	0.1	0.1	0.1	0.0
34	Romania	4	4.0	4.5	3.5	1.8	2.2	1.4	1.3	1.6	1.0	1.4	1.8	1.1
35	Russian Federation	4	0.8	*0.8*	*0.8*	…	…	…	…	…	…	…	…	…
36	Serbia	4	…	…	…	…	…	…	…	…	…	…	…	…
37	Slovakia	4	5.0	5.3	4.7	2.3	2.5	2.0	1.6	1.9	1.4	1.9	2.1	1.6
38	Slovenia	5	0.5	0.6	0.4	…	…	…	…	…	…	…	…	…
39	TFYR Macedonia	4	0.3[y]	0.3[y]	0.2[y]	0.2[y]	0.2[y]	0.2[y]	0.1[y]	0.1[y]	0.1[y]	0.2[y]	0.2[y]	0.1[y]
40	Turkey	6	*4.1*	*4.4*	*3.7*	*1.9*	*1.9*	*1.9*	*1.9*	*1.7*	*2.2*	*2.3*	*1.8*	*2.7*
41	Ukraine	4	0.3	0.3*	0.3*	0.1	*0.1*	*0.1*	…	…	…	…	…	…
	Central Asia													
42	Armenia	3	–	–	–	0.3	0.2	0.4	0.2	0.2	0.2	…	…	…
43	Azerbaijan	4	0.3	0.3	0.3	0.3	0.3	0.3	0.2	0.2	0.2	0.3	0.3	0.2
44	Georgia	6	0.4	*0.5*	*0.4*	0.2	…	…	0.2	…	…	0.2	…	…
45	Kazakhstan	4	**0.1**	**0.1**	**0.0**	**0.1**	**0.2**	**0.1**	**0.1**	**0.1**	**0.1**	**0.1**	**0.1**	**0.0**
46	Kyrgyzstan	4	0.2	0.2	0.2	0.1	0.2	0.1	0.1	0.1	0.1	0.1	0.1	0.0
47	Mongolia	5	0.5	0.5	0.4	…	…	…	…	…	…	…	…	…
48	Tajikistan	4	0.0	*0.0*	*0.0*	0.4	*0.4*	*0.3*	0.2	*0.2*	*0.2*	0.2	*0.2*	*0.2*
49	Turkmenistan	3	…	…	…	…	…	…	…	…	…	…	…	…
50	Uzbekistan	4	–	–	–	…	…	…	…	…	…	…	…	…
	East Asia and the Pacific													
51	Australia	7	…	…	…	…	…	…	…	…	…	…	…	…
52	Brunei Darussalam	6	0.5	0.6	0.3	0.5	0.8	0.3	0.3	0.5	0.2	1.5	2.1	0.8
53	Cambodia	6	22.2	23.0	21.3	14.7	15.8	13.3	12.0	13.5	10.3	8.6	9.9	7.3
54	China	5	…	…	…	…	…	…	…	…	…	…	…	…
55	Cook Islands	6	…	…	…	…	…	…	…	…	…	…	…	…
56	DPR Korea	4	…	…	…	…	…	…	…	…	…	…	…	…

REPETITION RATES BY GRADE IN PRIMARY EDUCATION (%)									REPEATERS, ALL GRADES (%)						
School year ending in 2005									School year ending in						
Grade 5			Grade 6			Grade 7			1999			2006			
Total	Male	Female	Total	Male	Female	Total	Male	Female	Total	Male	Female	Total	Male	Female	
														Arab States	
12.1	15.2	8.4	17.3	19.7	14.7	.	.	.	11.9	14.6	8.7	12.0	14.4	9.2	*1*
2.8[y]	3.5[y]	2.1[y]	1.9[y]	3.1[y]	0.8[y]	.	.	.	3.8	4.6	3.1	2.7	3.0	2.3	*2*
…	…	…	…	…	…	.	.	.	16.6	*16.9*	*16.1*	7.5	7.6	7.2	*3*
3.9	…	…	***6.8***	…	…	.	.	.	*6.0*	*7.1*	*4.6*	**3.1**	**3.9**	**2.2**	*4*
13.1[y]	*15.2*[y]	*10.2*[y]	*4.2*[y]	*4.4*[y]	*3.8*[y]	.	.	.	10.0	10.7	9.2	*8.0*[z]	*9.1*[z]	*6.5*[z]	*5*
2.0	…	…	2.1	…	…	.	.	.	0.7	0.7	0.7	1.1	1.1	1.1	*6*
2.7	3.8	1.4	…	…	…	.	.	.	3.3	3.4	3.1	2.1	2.5	1.6	*7*
11.1	12.6	9.4	10.1	11.5	8.8	.	.	.	9.1	10.5	7.7	9.6	11.2	7.9	*8*
…	…	…	…	…	…	.	.	.	…	…	…	…	…	…	*9*
12.3	11.8	12.8	18.2	17.4	19.0	.	.	.	…	…	…	10.2	10.1	10.3	*10*
8.6	10.9	6.0	9.0	11.4	6.2	.	.	.	12.4	14.1	10.2	12.6	14.6	10.2	*11*
1.4	0.9	1.9	1.3	0.8	1.9	.	.	.	8.0	9.5	6.4	0.6	0.4	0.8	*12*
…	…	…	…	…	…	.	.	.	2.1	2.2	2.0	0.7[z]	0.7[z]	0.7[z]	*13*
3.3	4.1	2.5	1.5	2.3	0.6	.	.	.	*2.7*	*3.5*	*1.9*	1.5	2.0	1.0	*14*
…	…	…	…	…	…	.	.	.	…	…	…	…	…	…	*15*
1.8[y]	1.5[y]	2.2[y]	1.9[y]	1.5[y]	2.4[y]	.	.	.	*11.3*	*10.9*	*11.8*	1.7[z]	1.4[z]	2.1[z]	*16*
…	…	…	…	…	…	.	.	.	6.5	7.2	5.6	6.4	7.3	5.4	*17*
2.3	2.8	1.7	7.0	8.5	5.3	.	.	.	18.3	20.0	16.4	6.1	7.3	4.7	*18*
1.8	2.5	1.0	…	…	…	.	.	.	3.5	4.4	2.5	2.0	2.3	1.7	*19*
…	…	…	*5.0*	*5.7*	*3.7*	.	.	.	10.6	11.7*	8.7*	*4.9*	*5.3*	*4.3*	*20*
														Central and Eastern Europe	
.	.	.	.	.	.	.	.	.	*3.9*	*4.6*	*3.2*	2.1[y]	2.6[y]	1.7[y]	*21*
.	.	.	.	.	.	.	.	.	0.5	0.5	0.5	0.1	0.1	0.1	*22*
.	.	.	.	.	.	.	.	.	…	…	…	…	…	…	*23*
.	.	.	.	.	.	.	.	.	3.2	3.7	2.7	2.3	2.6	2.0	*24*
.	.	.	.	.	.	.	.	.	0.4	0.5	0.3	0.3	0.4	0.2	*25*
0.5	0.7	0.4	.	.	.	.	.	.	1.2	1.5	1.0	0.7	0.8	0.6	*26*
2.2	3.0	1.4	3.2	4.7	1.5	.	.	.	2.5	3.5	1.4	2.1	2.9	1.3	*27*
.	.	.	.	.	.	.	.	.	2.2	2.1	2.2	1.9	2.2	1.5	*28*
.	.	.	.	.	.	.	.	.	2.1	*2.7*	*1.3*	2.8	3.8	1.8	*29*
.	.	.	.	.	.	.	.	.	0.9	1.3	0.5	0.6	0.8	0.5	*30*
…	…	…	…	…	…	.	.	.	…	…	…	…	…	…	*31*
0.9	…	…	0.5	…	…	.	.	.	1.2	…	…	0.7	1.0	0.3	*32*
.	.	.	.	.	.	.	.	.	0.9	*0.9*	*0.9*	0.2	0.2	0.1	*33*
.	.	.	.	.	.	.	.	.	3.4	4.1	2.6	2.2	2.6	1.8	*34*
.	.	.	.	.	.	.	.	.	1.4	…	…	0.6	*0.6*	*0.6*	*35*
.	.	.	.	.	.	.	.	.	…	…	…	…	…	…	*36*
.	.	.	.	.	.	.	.	.	2.3	2.6	2.0	2.8	3.0	2.5	*37*
.	.	.	.	.	.	.	.	.	1.0	1.3	0.7	0.5	0.6	0.3	*38*
.	.	.	.	.	.	.	.	.	0.0	0.1	0.0	0.2[z]	0.2[z]	0.2[z]	*39*
…	…	…	…	…	…	.	.	.	…	…	…	*2.9*	*2.7*	*3.1*	*40*
.	.	.	.	.	.	.	.	.	0.8	…	…	0.1	*0.1*	*0.1*	*41*
														Central Asia	
.	.	.	.	.	.	.	.	.	…	…	…	0.2	0.1	0.2	*42*
.	.	.	.	.	.	.	.	.	0.4	0.4	0.4	0.3	0.3	0.3	*43*
0.3	…	…	0.3	*0.4*	*0.2*	.	.	.	0.3	*0.5*	*0.2*	0.3	*0.4*	*0.2*	*44*
.	.	.	.	.	.	.	.	.	0.3	…	…	**0.1**	**0.1**	**0.1**	*45*
.	.	.	.	.	.	.	.	.	0.3	0.4	0.2	0.1	0.1	0.1	*46*
0.2	0.2	0.1	.	.	.	.	.	.	0.9	1.0	0.8	0.3	0.3	0.3	*47*
.	.	.	.	.	.	.	.	.	0.5	*0.5*	*0.6*	0.2	*0.2*	*0.2*	*48*
.	.	.	.	.	.	.	.	.	…	…	…	…	…	…	*49*
.	.	.	.	.	.	.	.	.	0.1	…	…	–	–	–	*50*
														East Asia and the Pacific	
…	…	…	…	…	…	.	.	.	…	…	…	…	…	…	*51*
1.0	1.5	0.5	5.5	7.6	3.3	.	.	.	.	.	.	1.6	2.2	0.9	*52*
5.9	6.8	4.8	2.7	3.1	2.2	.	.	.	*24.6*	*25.4*	*23.5*	12.7	13.8	11.4	*53*
…	…	…	.	.	.	.	.	.	…	…	…	0.3	0.3	0.2	*54*
…	…	…	…	…	…	.	.	.	2.6	…	…	–[z]	–[z]	–[z]	*55*
…	…	…	.	.	.	.	.	.	…	…	…	…	…	…	*56*

Table 6 (continued)

	Country or territory	Duration[1] of primary education 2006	REPETITION RATES BY GRADE IN PRIMARY EDUCATION (%) School year ending in 2005 Grade 1 Total	Grade 1 Male	Grade 1 Female	Grade 2 Total	Grade 2 Male	Grade 2 Female	Grade 3 Total	Grade 3 Male	Grade 3 Female	Grade 4 Total	Grade 4 Male	Grade 4 Female
57	Fiji	6	*4.0*	*4.7*	*3.2*	*2.1*	*2.7*	*1.4*	*1.3*	*1.7*	*0.8*	*1.2*	*1.8*	*0.6*
58	Indonesia	6	*6.5*	*7.5*	*5.4*	*5.0*	*6.1*	*3.7*	*4.2*	*5.2*	*3.2*	*3.1*	*3.7*	*2.4*
59	Japan	6	–	–	–	...	...	...	...	...	...	...	...	...
60	Kiribati	6	.[y]	.[y]	.[y]	.[y]	.[y]	.[y]	...	...	...	...	...	...
61	Lao PDR	5	32.9	33.7	31.9	18.0	19.3	16.5	12.1	13.6	10.4	7.8	9.0	6.3
62	Macao, China	6	2.3	2.7	1.9	2.5	3.4	1.6	4.5	5.7	3.1	...	...	...
63	Malaysia	6	.[y]	.[y]	.[y]	.[y]	.[y]	.[y]	.[y]	.[y]	.[y]	.[y]	.[y]	.[y]
64	Marshall Islands	6	.[x]	.[x]	.[x]	0.0[x]	.[x]	0.0[x]	0.0[x]	.[x]	0.0[x]	0.0[x]	.[x]	0.0[x]
65	Micronesia	6	...	...	...	...	...	...	...	...	...	...	...	...
66	Myanmar	5	0.8	0.8	0.8	0.5	0.6	0.5	0.5	0.6	0.4	0.4	0.7	0.1
67	Nauru	6	...	...	...	...	...	...	...	...	...	...	...	...
68	New Zealand	6	...	...	...	...	...	...	...	...	...	...	...	...
69	Niue	6	...	...	...	...	...	...	...	...	...	...	...	...
70	Palau	5	...	...	...	...	...	...	...	...	...	...	...	...
71	Papua New Guinea	6	...	...	...	...	...	...	...	...	...	...	...	...
72	Philippines	6	5.6	6.6	4.5	3.0	3.9	2.0	2.3	3.0	1.4	1.7	2.4	1.0
73	Republic of Korea	6	**0.0**	**0.0**	**0.0**	**0.0**	**0.0**	**0.0**	**0.0**	**0.0**	**0.0**	**0.0**	**0.0**	**0.0**
74	Samoa	6	*2.6*[x]	*2.9*[x]	*2.2*[x]	...	...	...	...	...	...	...	...	...
75	Singapore	6	...	...	...	...	...	...	...	...	...	...	...	...
76	Solomon Islands	6	...	...	...	...	...	...	...	...	...	...	...	...
77	Thailand	6	...	...	...	...	...	...	...	...	...	...	...	...
78	Timor-Leste	6	...	...	...	...	...	...	...	...	...	...	...	...
79	Tokelau	6	.	.	.	.	.	.	.	.	.	.	.	.
80	Tonga	6	.	.	.	.	.	.	.	.	.	.	.	.
81	Tuvalu	6	.	.	.	...	...	...	...	...	...	...	...	...
82	Vanuatu	6	*13.2*[x]	*13.4*[x]	*13.0*[x]	...	...	...	...	...	...	...	...	...
83	Viet Nam	5	*2.9*	...	...	*0.9*	...	...	*0.7*	...	...	*0.6*	...	...
	Latin America and the Caribbean													
84	Anguilla	7	1.4[y]	3.2[y]	–[y]	–[y]	–[y]	–[y]	0.5[y]	0.9[y]	–[y]	–[y]	–[y]	–[y]
85	Antigua and Barbuda	7	...	...	...	...	...	...	...	...	...	...	...	...
86	Argentina	6	9.8[y]	11.2[y]	8.2[y]	6.7[y]	7.9[y]	5.5[y]	5.9[y]	7.0[y]	4.7[y]	5.8[y]	7.0[y]	4.6[y]
87	Aruba	6	15.5	18.8	12.0	11.8	13.3	10.0	8.5	...	...	8.0	...	...
88	Bahamas	6	–	–	–	–	–	–	–	–	–	–	–	–
89	Barbados	6	.	.	.	.	.	.	.	.	.	.	.	.
90	Belize	6	16.5	19.0	14.0	9.6	10.9	8.3	10.6	11.6	9.5	8.5	9.8	7.1
91	Bermuda	6	.	...	...	.	...	...	.	...	...	.	...	...
92	Bolivia	6	*1.4*[x]	*1.5*[x]	*1.4*[x]	*1.3*[x]	*1.4*[x]	*1.2*[x]	*1.6*[x]	*1.6*[x]	*1.5*[x]	*1.5*[x]	*1.6*[x]	*1.3*[x]
93	Brazil	4	27.3[x]	...	...	20.5[x]	...	...	15.4[x]	...	...	15.4[x]	...	...
94	British Virgin Islands	7	8.3	...	...	4.2	...	...	...	...	...	...	...	...
95	Cayman Islands	6	1.3[y]	2.1[y]	0.4[y]	–[y]	–[y]	–[y]	–[y]	–[y]	–[y]	–[y]	–[y]	–[y]
96	Chile	6	2.5	3.0	2.1	2.2	2.6	1.8	2.0	2.3	1.6	1.8	2.1	1.4
97	Colombia	5	6.6	7.2	5.9	4.1	4.6	3.5	3.2	3.6	2.7	2.5	2.9	2.1
98	Costa Rica	6	13.3	14.9	11.5	8.3	9.5	6.9	7.2	8.3	5.9	8.8	10.3	7.2
99	Cuba	6	–	–	–	1.5	2.0	0.9	–	–	–	0.8	1.1	0.4
100	Dominica	7	12.2	15.8	8.7	3.8	...	...	2.7	...	...	2.6	...	...
101	Dominican Republic	6	6.5	7.8	5.0	8.0	9.8	5.9	12.4	15.3	9.1	7.4	9.6	5.1
102	Ecuador	6	3.1	3.5	2.8	2.0	2.3	1.7	1.4	1.6	1.1	1.0	1.1	0.8
103	El Salvador	6	14.7	16.1	13.1	6.7	7.9	5.5	5.4	6.2	4.6	5.3	6.4	4.2
104	Grenada	7	*1.7*	*2.6*	*0.8*	*3.0*	*3.3*	*2.6*	*2.9*	*3.7*	*2.0*	...	...	...
105	Guatemala	6	24.4	25.7	22.9	13.5	14.6	12.4	10.1	11.0	9.1	7.0	7.8	6.2
106	Guyana	6	*1.1*[y]	*1.2*[y]	*1.0*[y]	...	...	...	...	...	...	...	...	...
107	Haiti	6	...	...	...	...	...	...	...	...	...	...	...	...
108	Honduras	6	16.4	17.6	15.1	9.5	10.8	8.2	6.4	7.2	5.5	4.1	4.6	3.5
109	Jamaica	6	*3.9*[y]	*5.1*[y]	*2.6*[y]	...	...	...	...	...	...	...	...	...
110	Mexico	6	6.7	7.8	5.4	6.6	7.8	5.3	4.5	5.5	3.5	3.7	4.7	2.8
111	Montserrat	7	12.3[y]	...	...	...	...	...	...	...	...	...	...	...
112	Netherlands Antilles	6	...	...	...	...	...	...	...	...	...	...	...	...
113	Nicaragua	6	18.0	19.2	16.5	9.6	10.9	8.2	8.4	9.5	7.2	6.6	7.8	5.3
114	Panama	6	9.5	10.7	8.2	8.2	9.3	7.0	6.0	7.2	4.7	4.4	5.3	3.3
115	Paraguay	6	10.2[y]	11.5[y]	8.7[y]	6.9[y]	8.3[y]	5.5[y]	5.1[y]	6.1[y]	4.0[y]	3.4[y]	4.2[y]	2.5[y]
116	Peru	6	5.1	5.3	4.9	14.0	14.3	13.6	11.2	11.6	10.9	8.4	8.7	8.1
117	Saint Kitts and Nevis	7	.[y]	.[y]	.[y]	.[y]	.[y]	.[y]	...	...	...	...	...	...

REPETITION RATES BY GRADE IN PRIMARY EDUCATION (%)									REPEATERS, ALL GRADES (%)						
School year ending in 2005									School year ending in						
Grade 5			Grade 6			Grade 7			1999			2006			
Total	Male	Female	Total	Male	Female	Total	Male	Female	Total	Male	Female	Total	Male	Female	
1.0	*1.4*	*0.7*	*3.4*	*3.5*	*3.4*	.	.	.	...	...	...	2.2	2.7	1.7	57
2.1	*2.5*	*1.6*	*0.2*	*0.2*	*0.1*	.	.	.	...	...	...	3.7	4.5	2.9	58
...	...	...	...	...	...	.	.	.	...	...	...	...	...	...	59
...	...	...	...	...	...	.	.	.	.	.	.	.^{z}	.^{z}	.^{z}	60
4.5	5.5	3.3	.	.	.	.	.	.	20.9	22.4	19.1	18.2	19.3	17.0	61
...	...	...	...	...	...	.	.	.	6.3	7.3	5.1	5.7	7.0	4.2	62
.^{y}	...	...	.^{y}	...	...	.	.	.	.	.	.	.^{z}	.^{z}	.^{z}	63
0.0^{x}	.^{x}	0.0^{x}	.^{x}	.^{x}	.^{x}	.	.	.	.	.	.	.	.	.	64
...	...	...	...	...	...	.	.	.	...	...	...	...	...	...	65
0.2	0.3	0.2	.	.	.	.	.	.	1.7	*1.7*	*1.7*	0.5	0.6	0.4	66
...	...	...	...	...	...	.	.	.	...	...	...	...	...	...	67
...	...	...	...	...	...	.	.	.	...	...	...	...	...	...	68
...	...	...	...	...	...	.	.	.	.	.	.	.^{z}	.^{z}	.^{z}	69
...	...	...	.	.	.	.	.	.	–	–	–	4.7^{y}	...	...	70
...	...	...	...	...	...	.	.	.	...	...	...	...	...	...	71
1.5	2.1	0.8	0.8	1.1	0.4	.	.	.	1.9	2.4	1.4	2.7	3.5	1.9	72
0.0	**0.0**	**0.0**	**0.0**	**0.0**	**0.0**	.	.	.	–	–	–	**0.0**	**0.0**	**0.0**	73
...	...	...	*0.3*^{x}	*0.4*^{x}	*0.1*^{x}	.	.	.	1.0	1.1	0.9	*0.9*^{y}	*1.1*^{y}	*0.7*^{y}	74
...	...	...	...	...	...	.	.	.	...	...	...	...	...	...	75
...	...	...	...	...	...	.	.	.	...	...	...	...	...	...	76
...	...	...	...	...	...	.	.	.	3.5	3.4	3.5	...	...	...	77
...	...	...	...	...	...	.	.	.	...	...	...	...	...	...	78
.	.	.	...	...	...	.	.	.	...	...	...	.^{y}	.^{y}	.^{y}	79
.	.	.	20.2	22.7	17.3	.	.	.	8.8	8.5	9.2	5.2	5.9	4.4	80
...	...	...	.	.	.	.	.	.	.	.	.	.	.	.	81
...	...	...	*13.5*^{x}	*13.5*^{x}	*13.5*^{x}	.	.	.	*10.6*	*11.1*	*9.9*	10.7^{y}	*11.5*^{y}	*9.7*^{y}	82
0.1	...	...	.	.	.	.	.	.	3.8	4.2	3.2	*1.0*	...	...	83
Latin America and the Caribbean															
–^{y}	...	...	0.5^{y}	...	...	–^{y}	...	...	0.3	0.4	0.3	–	–	–	84
...	...	...	...	...	...	...	...	...	...	...	...	...	...	...	85
5.4^{y}	6.5^{y}	4.2^{y}	4.4^{y}	5.5^{y}	3.4^{y}	.	.	.	6.1	7.1	5.0	6.4^{z}	7.6^{z}	5.2^{z}	86
7.5	...	...	3.9	...	...	.	.	.	7.7	9.5	5.9	8.8	9.8	7.7	87
–	–	–	–	–	–	.	.	.	.	.	.	–	–	–	88
.	...	...	.	...	...	.	.	.	.	.	.	.	.	.	89
9.3	10.0	8.4	7.6	8.7	6.5	.	.	.	9.7	10.8	8.4	10.4	11.7	8.9	90
.	...	...	.	...	...	.	.	.	...	...	...	.	.	.	91
1.4^{x}	*1.6*^{x}	*1.3*^{x}	*2.9*^{x}	*3.3*^{x}	*2.5*^{x}	.	.	.	2.4	2.6	2.3	0.9	0.9	0.8	92
...	...	...	.	.	.	.	.	.	24.0	24.0	24.0	18.7^{z}	...	...	93
...	...	...	...	...	...	...	...	...	*3.8*	*4.1*	*3.6*	6.8	8.5	4.9	94
–^{y}	...	...	–^{y}	...	...	.	.	.	*0.2*	*0.2*	*0.1*	–	–	–	95
...	...	...	...	...	...	.	.	.	2.4	2.9	1.9	2.3	2.8	1.7	96
2.1	2.6	1.7	.	.	.	.	.	.	5.2	5.8	4.6	3.8	4.4	3.3	97
6.4	7.3	5.3	0.7	0.8	0.5	.	.	.	9.2	10.4	7.9	7.3	8.4	6.1	98
0.4	0.5	0.2	0.1	0.2	0.1	.	.	.	1.9	2.6	1.1	0.5	0.7	0.3	99
2.1	...	...	2.3	...	...	0.2	...	...	3.6	3.8	3.5	3.8	4.6	3.0	100
5.4	7.2	3.6	4.3	5.9	2.7	.	.	.	4.1	4.5	3.7	7.8	9.9	5.5	101
0.7	0.8	0.5	0.4	0.4	0.3	.	.	.	2.7	3.0	2.4	1.5	1.7	1.3	102
4.5	5.5	3.6	4.2	5.1	3.3	.	.	.	*7.1*	*7.7*	*6.4*	7.5	8.7	6.3	103
...	...	...	...	...	...	...	...	...	...	...	...	*3.4*^{z}	*4.1*^{z}	*2.8*^{z}	104
4.7	5.2	4.0	1.5	1.7	1.2	.	.	.	14.9	15.8	13.8	12.1	13.0	11.1	105
...	...	...	*0.7*^{y}	*0.8*^{y}	*0.6*^{y}	.	.	.	3.1	3.6	2.5	0.9^{z}	1.1^{z}	0.8^{z}	106
...	...	...	...	...	...	.	.	.	...	...	...	...	...	...	107
2.6	3.1	2.1	0.7	0.9	0.6	.	.	.	...	...	...	7.4	8.3	6.5	108
...	...	...	...	...	...	.	.	.	...	...	...	*2.8*^{z}	*3.3*^{z}	*2.3*^{z}	109
2.6	3.4	1.8	0.6	0.7	0.5	.	.	.	6.6	7.6	5.5	4.2	5.1	3.3	110
...	...	...	...	...	...	...	...	...	0.8	1.4	–	3.1	3.3	3.0	111
...	...	...	...	...	...	.	.	.	*12.0*	*14.5*	*9.3*	...	...	...	112
4.7	5.5	3.9	2.5	3.2	1.9	.	.	.	4.7	5.3	4.1	9.5	10.8	8.2	113
3.1	4.0	2.2	1.3	1.5	1.0	.	.	.	6.4	7.4	5.2	5.6	6.6	4.6	114
2.0^{y}	2.5^{y}	1.4^{y}	1.0^{y}	1.3^{y}	0.7^{y}	.	.	.	7.8	8.8	6.7	5.1^{z}	6.1^{z}	4.1^{z}	115
7.2	7.5	6.9	4.0	4.3	3.7	.	.	.	10.2	10.5	9.9	8.7	9.0	8.4	116
...	...	...	...	...	...	...	...	...	...	...	...	.	.	.	117

Table 6 (continued)

	Country or territory	Duration[1] of primary education 2006	REPETITION RATES BY GRADE IN PRIMARY EDUCATION (%) School year ending in 2005 Grade 1 Total	Grade 1 Male	Grade 1 Female	Grade 2 Total	Grade 2 Male	Grade 2 Female	Grade 3 Total	Grade 3 Male	Grade 3 Female	Grade 4 Total	Grade 4 Male	Grade 4 Female
118	Saint Lucia	7	6.2	7.6	4.8	…	…	…	…	…	…	…	…	…
119	Saint Vincent/Grenad.	7	5.3[y]	6.5[y]	3.9[y]	…	…	…	…	…	…	…	…	…
120	Suriname	6	…	…	…	…	…	…	…	…	…	…	…	…
121	Trinidad and Tobago	7	10.8[*,y]	12.8[*,y]	8.6[*,y]	3.5[*,y]	2.7[*,y]	4.3[*,y]	4.1[*,y]	5.1[*,y]	3.0[*,y]	4.1[*,y]	4.9[*,y]	3.2[*,y]
122	Turks and Caicos Islands	6	0.9[x]	1.8[x]	–[x]	…	…	…	…	…	…	…	…	…
123	Uruguay	6	13.9	16.0	11.6	9.5	10.7	8.3	6.8	8.2	5.5	5.4	6.5	4.2
124	Venezuela, B. R.	6	10.0	11.8	8.0	7.8	9.4	5.9	7.5	9.2	5.5	5.4	6.9	3.9
	North America and Western Europe													
125	Andorra	6	…	…	…	…	…	…	…	…	…	…	…	…
126	Austria	4	1.2[x]	1.4[x]	1.1[x]	1.3[x]	1.5[x]	1.2[x]	1.3[x]	1.5[x]	1.0[x]	1.0[x]	1.1[x]	0.9[x]
127	Belgium	6	6.5	6.9	6.1	4.4	4.4	4.4	…	…	…	2.5	2.7	2.3
128	Canada	6	…	…	…	…	…	…	…	…	…	…	…	…
129	Cyprus	6	1.1	1.4	0.8	0.1	0.2	0.1	0.0	0.0	0.0	0.0	0.0	–
130	Denmark	6	.[y]	.[y]	.[y]	.[y]	.[y]	.[y]	.[y]	.[y]	.[y]	.[y]	.[y]	.[y]
131	Finland	6	0.9	1.1	0.6	0.9	1.1	0.7	0.3	0.4	0.2	0.2	0.2	0.1
132	France	5	…	…	…	…	…	…	…	…	…	…	…	…
133	Germany	4	1.2	1.3	1.1	1.2	1.2	1.1	1.4	1.5	1.3	0.8	0.8	0.7
134	Greece	6	1.3	1.4	1.2	0.7	0.7	0.6	0.5	0.6	0.4	0.4	0.5	0.4
135	Iceland	7	–	–	–	–	–	–	–	–	–	–	–	–
136	Ireland	8	*1.8*	*2.0*	*1.7*	*1.2*	*1.4*	*1.1*	*0.7*	*0.9*	*0.6*	*0.4*	*0.5*	*0.4*
137	Israel	6	1.7	2.1	1.2	0.8	1.0	0.6	0.9	1.2	0.6	1.2	1.5	0.9
138	Italy	5	0.4	0.5	0.3	0.2	0.2	0.1	0.1	0.2	0.1	0.1	0.2	0.1
139	Luxembourg	6	5.4	6.3	4.6	5.2	6.3	4.1	5.1	5.2	5.1	4.0	4.5	3.5
140	Malta	6	0.8[y]	0.8[y]	0.8[y]	0.8[y]	0.9[y]	0.7[y]	…	…	…	…	…	…
141	Monaco	5	–[x]	…	…	–[x]	…	…	–[x]	…	…	–[x]	…	…
142	Netherlands	6	.	.	.	…	…	…	…	…	…	…	…	…
143	Norway	7	–	–	–	–	–	–	–	–	–	–	–	–
144	Portugal	6	–	–	–	…	…	…	…	…	…	…	…	…
145	San Marino	5	…	…	…	…	…	…	…	…	…	…	…	…
146	Spain	6	–	–	–	…	…	…	…	…	…	…	…	…
147	Sweden	6	…	…	…	…	…	…	…	…	…	…	…	…
148	Switzerland	6	…	…	…	…	…	…	…	…	…	…	…	…
149	United Kingdom	6	…	…	…	…	…	…	…	…	…	…	…	…
150	United States	6	–	–	–	–	–	–	–	–	–	–	–	–
	South and West Asia													
151	Afghanistan	6	*8.8*[y]	*8.1*[y]	*10.5*[y]	…	…	…	…	…	…	…	…	…
152	Bangladesh	5	7.1[x]	6.8[x]	7.4[x]	6.7[x]	6.6[x]	6.7[x]	9.2[x]	9.4[x]	8.9[x]	7.7[x]	8.2[x]	7.3[x]
153	Bhutan	7	8.1	8.6	7.5	7.8	8.9	6.6	7.9	8.7	7.1	5.9	6.5	5.4
154	India	5	3.7	3.7	3.7	…	…	…	…	…	…	…	…	…
155	Iran, Islamic Republic of	5	*4.0*	*4.9*	*3.2*	…	…	…	…	…	…	…	…	…
156	Maldives	7	0.5	…	…	0.4	…	…	…	…	…	…	…	…
157	Nepal	5	37.0	36.8*	37.3*	19.3	18.5*	20.1*	15.0	15.0*	15.1*	15.9	15.9*	16.0*
158	Pakistan	5	2.3	2.5	2.1	…	…	…	…	…	…	…	…	…
159	Sri Lanka	5	*0.3*[y]	…	…	*0.7*[y]	…	…	…	…	…	…	…	…
	Sub-Saharan Africa													
160	Angola	4	…	…	…	…	…	…	…	…	…	.	.	.
161	Benin	6	1.4	1.6	1.1	9.3	9.4	9.2	11.2	11.1	11.3	11.5	11.0	12.2
162	Botswana	7	.[y]	.[y]	.[y]	.[y]	.[y]	.[y]	.[y]	.[y]	.[y]	.[y]	.[y]	.[y]
163	Burkina Faso	6	6.4	6.5	6.3	9.6	9.8	9.3	11.9	12.1	11.6	14.0	14.0	13.9
164	Burundi	6	36.5	36.1	37.0	35.1	35.4	34.7	32.7	32.5	32.9	31.8	31.5	32.2
165	Cameroon	6	*31.8*	*33.4*	*29.8*	…	…	…	…	…	…	…	…	…
166	Cape Verde	6	1.4	1.6	1.2	24.8	29.0	19.8	13.4	15.7	11.0	16.8	19.1	14.2
167	Central African Republic	6	29.6	29.8	29.3	23.5	23.9	23.0	31.3	30.3	32.7	27.6	27.1	28.4
168	Chad	6	23.2[y]	22.8[y]	23.7[y]	21.9[y]	21.2[y]	22.7[y]	21.5[y]	19.5[y]	24.7[y]	21.3[y]	20.3[y]	22.8[y]
169	Comoros	6	*33.3*[y]	*35.0*[y]	*31.2*[y]	*28.9*[y]	*27.5*[y]	*30.4*[y]	*28.5*[y]	*30.4*[y]	*26.2*[y]	*24.1*[y]	*26.0*[y]	*21.9*[y]
170	Congo	6	27.7[y]	…	…	…	…	…	…	…	…	…	…	…
171	Côte d'Ivoire	6	…	…	…	…	…	…	…	…	…	…	…	…
172	D. R. Congo	6	…	…	…	…	…	…	…	…	…	…	…	…
173	Equatorial Guinea	5	…	…	…	…	…	…	…	…	…	…	…	…
174	Eritrea	5	13.7	13.9	13.5	14.2	14.4	14.0	13.5	13.8	13.2	14.8	14.8	14.7

REPETITION RATES BY GRADE IN PRIMARY EDUCATION (%)									REPEATERS, ALL GRADES (%)						
School year ending in 2005									School year ending in						
Grade 5			Grade 6			Grade 7			1999			2006			
Total	Male	Female	Total	Male	Female	Total	Male	Female	Total	Male	Female	Total	Male	Female	
...	...	...	...	...	...	...	...	...	*2.4*	*2.8*	*2.0*	2.2	2.6	1.7	118
...	...	...	...	...	...	16.0[y]	21.9[y]	11.2[y]	...	...	...	4.1[z]	5.0[z]	3.0[z]	119
...	...	...	...	...	...	.	.	.	...	...	...	20.3[z]	22.3[z]	18.1[z]	120
4.2[*,y]	5.0[*,y]	3.3[*,y]	5.2[*,y]	6.5[*,y]	4.0[*,y]	3.2[*,y]	2.9[*,y]	3.4[*,y]	4.7	4.9	4.4	5.2[*,z]	6.0[*,z]	4.4[*,z]	121
...	...	...	...	...	...	.	.	.	...	...	...	2.9[z]	3.2[z]	2.6[z]	122
4.2	5.1	3.2	2.0	2.6	1.4	.	.	.	7.9	9.3	6.5	7.0	8.2	5.7	123
3.6	4.6	2.6	1.5	1.9	1.0	.	.	.	*7.0*	*8.5*	*5.5*	6.1	7.5	4.6	124
North America and Western Europe															
...	...	...	...	...	...	.	.	.	...	...	...	–	–	–	125
.	.	.	.	.	.	.	.	.	1.5	1.8	1.3	1.2[y]	1.4[y]	1.1[y]	126
2.5	2.7	2.3	1.1	1.2	1.1	.	.	.	...	...	...	3.2	3.3	3.1	127
...	...	...	...	...	...	.	.	.	...	...	...	...	...	...	128
0.0	–	0.1	0.1	0.1	0.1	.	.	.	0.4	0.5	0.3	0.2	0.3	0.2	129
.[y]	.[y]	.[y]	.[y]	.[y]	.[y]	.	.	.	.	.	.	–	–	–	130
0.2	0.2	0.1	0.2	0.2	0.1	.	.	.	0.4	0.6	0.3	0.4	0.5	0.3	131
...	...	...	...	...	...	.	.	.	4.2	*4.2*	*4.2*	...	...	...	132
.	.	.	.	.	.	.	.	.	1.7	1.9	1.5	1.1	1.2	1.1	133
0.4	0.4	0.3	0.4	0.4	0.3	.	.	.	–	–	–	0.6	0.7	0.5	134
–	–	–	–	–	–	–	–	–	–	–	–	–	–	–	135
0.5	*0.5*	*0.5*	*0.4*	...	...	*0.7*	...	...	1.8	2.1	1.6	0.7	0.8	0.7	136
1.3	1.7	0.9	0.9	1.2	0.7	.	.	.	...	...	...	1.4	1.7	1.0	137
0.3	0.3	0.2	...	...	...	.	.	.	0.4	0.5	0.3	0.2	0.3	0.2	138
3.9	4.7	3.1	0.9	1.0	0.9	.	.	.	...	...	...	4.2	4.8	3.6	139
...	...	...	...	...	...	.	.	.	2.1	2.4	1.8	2.6[z]	2.9[z]	2.2[z]	140
–[x]	...	...	...	...	...	.	.	.	–	–	–	–[y]	...	...	141
...	...	...	...	...	...	.	.	.	.	.	.	.	.	.	142
–	–	–	–	–	–	–	–	–	.	.	.	–	–	–	143
...	...	...	...	...	...	.	.	.	...	...	...	*10.2[z]*	...	...	144
...	...	...	...	...	...	.	.	.	...	...	...	–[y]	...	...	145
...	...	...	...	...	...	.	.	.	...	...	...	*2.3[z]*	*2.6[z]*	*1.9[z]*	146
...	...	...	...	...	...	.	.	.	...	...	...	...	...	...	147
...	...	...	...	...	...	.	.	.	1.8	1.9	1.6	1.4	1.5	1.3	148
...	...	...	...	...	...	.	.	.	–	–	–	–	–	–	149
–	...	...	–	...	...	.	.	.	–	–	–	–	–	–	150
South and West Asia															
...	...	...	...	...	...	.	.	.	...	...	...	16.3[z]	17.6[z]	13.9[z]	151
5.1[x]	5.5[x]	4.7[x]	.	.	.	.	.	.	6.5	6.8	6.2	7.0[y]	7.2[y]	6.9[y]	152
9.1	10.4	7.7	5.8	6.1	5.5	3.5	3.7	3.4	12.1	12.5	11.7	6.9	7.6	6.1	153
4.0	4.1	3.8	.	.	.	.	.	.	4.0	4.0	4.1	3.4	3.4	3.4	154
...	...	...	.	.	.	.	.	.	...	...	...	*2.0*	*2.8*	*1.4*	155
...	...	...	...	...	...	.	.	.	...	...	...	4.7	5.5	3.7	156
12.0	11.8*	12.3*	.	.	.	.	.	.	22.9	22.2	23.8	20.6	20.8*	20.4*	157
2.2	2.4	1.8	.	.	.	.	.	.	...	...	...	2.2	2.4	1.9	158
...	...	...	.	.	.	.	.	.	...	...	...	*0.8[z]*	*0.9[z]*	*0.7[z]*	159
Sub-Saharan Africa															
...	...	...	.	.	.	.	.	.	*29.0*	*29.0*	*29.0*	...	...	...	160
12.2	11.5	13.2	4.4	4.6	4.1	.	.	.	...	...	...	7.8	7.9	7.8	161
.[y]	.[y]	.[y]	.[y]	.[y]	.[y]	.[y]	.[y]	.[y]	3.3	3.9	2.7	.[z]	.[z]	.[z]	162
15.1	14.6	15.8	32.1	31.0	33.4	.	.	.	17.7	17.5	18.0	12.0	12.1	11.8	163
42.2	40.7	44.1	46.3	44.2	48.9	.	.	.	*20.3*	*20.3*	*20.4*	28.8	29.2	28.4	164
...	...	...	*26.0*	*28.7*	*22.5*	.	.	.	*26.7*	*26.8*	*26.5*	25.1	26.8	23.1	165
10.6	12.6	8.7	12.2	13.7	10.8	.	.	.	*11.6*	*12.8*	*10.3*	14.0	16.4	11.5	166
27.3	27.9	26.5	33.7	34.3	32.9	.	.	.	...	...	...	28.2	28.2	28.2	167
22.6[y]	21.1[y]	25.1[y]	23.2[y]	22.9[y]	23.9[y]	.	.	.	25.9	25.7	26.3	22.5[z]	21.8[z]	23.5[z]	168
22.7[y]	*23.6[y]*	*21.7[y]*	*26.2[y]*	*27.9[y]*	*24.3[y]*	.	.	.	26.0	26.4	25.5	*27.1[z]*	*28.2[z]*	*25.9[z]*	169
...	...	...	...	...	...	.	.	.	39.1	40.0	38.2	21.2	21.5	20.9	170
...	...	...	...	...	...	.	.	.	23.7	*22.8*	*24.9*	23.5	23.4	23.7	171
...	...	...	...	...	...	.	.	.	...	...	...	...	...	...	172
...	...	...	.	.	.	.	.	.	11.8	9.3	14.9	25.6[z]	25.5[z]	25.6[z]	173
8.9	9.1	8.7	.	.	.	.	.	.	19.4	18.2	20.8	13.7	13.9	13.5	174

Table 6 (continued)

	Country or territory	Duration[1] of primary education 2006	REPETITION RATES BY GRADE IN PRIMARY EDUCATION (%) School year ending in 2005 — Grade 1 Total	Grade 1 Male	Grade 1 Female	Grade 2 Total	Grade 2 Male	Grade 2 Female	Grade 3 Total	Grade 3 Male	Grade 3 Female	Grade 4 Total	Grade 4 Male	Grade 4 Female
175	Ethiopia	6	**7.1**	**7.4**	**6.8**	**5.2**	**5.6**	**4.8**	**5.8**	**6.4**	**5.1**	**7.6**	**8.2**	**6.8**
176	Gabon	6	...	...	...	...	...	...	...	...	...	...	...	...
177	Gambia	6	...	...	...	...	...	...	...	...	...	...	...	...
178	Ghana	6	9.7[y]	10.1[y]	9.3[y]	...	...	...	...	...	...	...	...	...
179	Guinea	6	3.2	3.2	3.3	12.3	11.9	12.8	4.3	4.0	4.7	13.3	12.5	14.5
180	Guinea-Bissau	6	...	...	...	...	...	...	...	...	...	...	...	...
181	Kenya	6	*6.2[y]*	*6.4[y]*	*5.9[y]*	*5.8[y]*	*6.0[y]*	*5.6[y]*	*6.1[y]*	*6.4[y]*	*5.8[y]*	*6.2[y]*	*6.5[y]*	*5.9[y]*
182	Lesotho	7	28.1	31.5	24.1	24.5	28.2	20.1	21.0	25.0	16.6	21.1	24.9	17.1
183	Liberia	6	...	...	...	...	...	...	...	...	...	...	...	...
184	Madagascar	5	12.5	12.9	12.1	27.8	28.9	26.6	28.4	29.2	27.5	8.2	8.4	8.0
185	Malawi	6	25.7	26.1	25.4	21.6	22.0	21.2	22.6	22.9	22.3	17.3	17.8	16.9
186	Mali	6	12.2	12.1	12.4	11.5	11.1	11.9	18.4	18.0	18.9	20.5	19.5	21.7
187	Mauritius	6	.	.	.	.	.	.	.	.	.	.	.	.
188	Mozambique	7	3.6	3.7	3.5	8.2	8.4	8.0	4.4	4.6	4.1	3.5	3.7	3.3
189	Namibia	7	19.1	21.3	16.7	13.4	16.1	10.6	12.0	14.1	9.8	14.4	17.2	11.5
190	Niger	6	0.2	0.2	0.2	3.0	3.0	3.1	4.7	4.5	4.9	5.6	5.3	6.1
191	Nigeria	6	1.2[y]	1.3[y]	1.2[y]	...	...	...	...	...	...	...	...	...
192	Rwanda	6	*17.7*	*15.8*	*19.4*	...	...	...	...	...	...	...	...	...
193	Sao Tome and Principe	6	***28.0***	***30.4***	***25.5***	***28.7***	***29.9***	***27.5***	***25.5***	***26.3***	***24.7***	***16.6***	***18.5***	***14.5***
194	Senegal	6	5.3	5.4	5.2	9.6	9.7	9.5	9.3	9.4	9.3	11.3	11.1	11.5
195	Seychelles	6	.[y]	.[y]	.[y]	.[y]	.[y]	.[y]	.[y]	.[y]	.[y]	.[y]	.[y]	.[y]
196	Sierra Leone	6	...	...	...	...	...	...	...	...	...	...	...	...
197	Somalia	7	...	...	...	...	...	...	...	...	...	...	...	...
198	South Africa	7	10.2[x]	10.7[x]	9.6[x]	8.0[x]	8.6[x]	7.4[x]	9.1[x]	9.8[x]	8.3[x]	9.5[x]	9.9[x]	8.9[x]
199	Swaziland	7	20.5[y]	22.9[y]	17.9[y]	18.1[y]	21.1[y]	14.6[y]	19.7[y]	22.7[y]	16.4[y]	17.6[y]	19.9[y]	15.1[y]
200	Togo	6	27.6	28.1	27.1	...	...	...	...	...	...	...	...	...
201	Uganda	7	12.3[y]	11.1[y]	13.6[y]	*12.2[y]*	*12.5[y]*	*11.9[y]*	*14.3[y]*	*15.2[y]*	*13.4[y]*	*13.2[y]*	*13.2[y]*	*13.2[y]*
202	United Republic of Tanzania	7	***8.5***	***8.6***	***8.4***	***4.9***	***5.1***	***4.7***	***4.2***	***4.2***	***4.2***	***8.7***	***8.7***	***8.8***
203	Zambia	7	6.4	6.4	6.4	5.9	6.0	5.8	6.0	6.1	5.9	6.8	7.1	6.5
204	Zimbabwe	7	...	...	...	...	...	...	...	...	...	...	...	...
I	World[2]	...	2.9	...	...	2.2	2.6	1.9	2.3	2.9	1.6	2.5	2.9	2.1
II	Countries in transition	...	0.2	0.2	0.2	0.1	0.2	0.1	0.1	0.1	0.1	0.1	0.1	0.0
III	Developed countries	...	0.8	...	...	0.7	0.7	0.6	0.5	0.6	0.4	0.5	0.6	0.4
IV	Developing countries	...	5.4	6.4	4.4	6.3	6.9	5.6	5.1	6.1	4.0	5.4	6.7	4.0
V	Arab States	...	2.8	2.5	3.1	3.2	3.7	2.6	2.5	...	...	2.8	3.4	2.1
VI	Central and Eastern Europe	...	1.0	1.1	0.9	0.8	1.0	0.6	1.1	1.3	0.8	1.1	1.4	0.8
VII	Central Asia	...	0.1	0.1	0.1	0.3	...	...	0.2	...	...	0.2	...	...
VIII	East Asia and the Pacific	...	0.8	0.8	0.8	...	...	...	...	...	...	...	...	...
IX	East Asia	...	2.3	2.7	1.9	1.7	...	...	1.5	...	...	1.5	2.1	0.8
X	Pacific	...	...	...	...	...	...	...	...	...	...	...	...	...
XI	Latin America/Caribbean	...	6.6	7.2	5.9	6.6	7.8	5.3	5.1	6.1	4.0	4.1	4.8	3.4
XII	Caribbean	...	2.8	3.8	1.7	1.5	1.7	1.3	...	...	...	...	...	...
XIII	Latin America	...	9.8	11.2	8.2	7.8	9.4	5.9	6.0	7.2	4.7	5.3	6.4	4.2
XIV	N. America/W. Europe	...	0.8	0.8	0.8	0.7	0.8	0.6	0.2	0.3	0.2	0.2	0.2	0.1
XV	South and West Asia	...	4.0	4.9	3.2	6.7	6.6	6.7	...	...	...	...	...	...
XVI	Sub-Saharan Africa	...	12.2	12.1	12.4	11.8	11.8	11.9	11.9	13.1	10.7	13.2	13.2	13.2

1. Duration in this table is defined according to ISCED97 and may differ from that reported nationally.
2. All values shown are medians.
Data in italic are UIS estimates.
Data in bold are for the school year ending in 2006 for repetition rates by grade, and the school year ending in 2007 for percentage of repeaters (all grades).

(z) Data are for the school year ending in 2005.
(y) Data are for the school year ending in 2004.
(x) Data are for the school year ending in 2003.
(*) National estimate.

REPETITION RATES BY GRADE IN PRIMARY EDUCATION (%)									REPEATERS, ALL GRADES (%)						
School year ending in 2005									School year ending in						
Grade 5			Grade 6			Grade 7			1999			2006			
Total	Male	Female	Total	Male	Female	Total	Male	Female	Total	Male	Female	Total	Male	Female	
9.0	**9.6**	**8.3**	**7.1**	**8.1**	**5.7**	.	.	.	10.6	9.8	11.9	**6.0**	**6.6**	**5.4**	*175*
...	...	...	...	...	...	.	.	.	...	...	...	...	...	...	*176*
...	...	...	...	...	...	.	.	.	12.2	12.1	12.3	6.1	6.3	5.9	*177*
...	...	...	...	...	...	.	.	.	4.2	4.3	4.1	5.8[z]	6.0[z]	5.7[z]	*178*
4.2	3.7	4.8	17.8	16.3	20.0	.	.	.	26.2	25.5	27.4	8.6	8.3	9.0	*179*
...	...	...	...	...	...	.	.	.	*24.0*	*23.6*	*24.5*	...	...	...	*180*
5.9[y]	...	...	*5.5*[y]	...	...	.	.	.	...	...	...	*5.8*[z]	*6.0*[z]	*5.6*[z]	*181*
17.6	20.4	14.9	13.4	15.1	12.1	16.0	14.5	17.1	20.3	22.9	17.9	18.6	21.3	15.8	*182*
...	...	...	...	...	...	.	.	.	...	...	...	5.7	5.6	5.8	*183*
22.1	22.0	22.1	.	.	.	.	.	.	*28.3*	*27.7*	*28.9*	19.7	20.4	19.0	*184*
16.5	16.8	16.1	13.3	13.2	13.4	.	.	.	14.4	14.4	14.4	20.8	21.1	20.4	*185*
25.4	24.3	27.0	25.5	24.4	27.0	.	.	.	17.4	17.2	17.7	17.0	16.7	17.3	*186*
.	.	.	20.1	23.2	16.7	.	.	.	3.8	4.1	3.5	4.4	5.2	3.6	*187*
9.4	9.4	9.4	1.4	1.6	1.2	10.0	10.0	10.1	23.8	23.2	24.7	5.3	5.5	5.1	*188*
22.5	25.6	19.3	15.1	16.8	13.5	16.9	17.5	16.4	12.3	13.9	10.7	16.4	18.6	14.1	*189*
8.0	7.6	8.7	16.8	16.1	18.0	.	.	.	12.2	12.4	11.8	4.9	4.7	5.0	*190*
...	...	...	*1.9*[y]	*1.9*[y]	*1.9*[y]	.	.	.	...	...	...	*2.9*[z]	*2.8*[z]	*3.0*[z]	*191*
...	...	...	...	...	...	.	.	.	29.1	29.2	29.0	14.6	14.6	14.6	*192*
24.7	***24.7***	***24.7***	***33.6***	***33.1***	***34.1***	.	.	.	30.7	32.6	28.7	**25.9**	**27.4**	**24.5**	*193*
12.0	11.8	12.2	22.2	21.8	22.7	.	.	.	14.4	*14.5*	*14.2*	10.6	10.8	10.5	*194*
.[y]	.[y]	.[y]	.[y]	.[y]	.[y]	.	.	.	.	.	.	.	.	.	*195*
...	...	...	...	...	...	.	.	.	...	...	...	**9.9**	**9.7**	**10.2**	*196*
...	...	...	...	...	...	.	.	.	...	...	...	...	...	...	*197*
7.3[x]	7.8[x]	6.7[x]	5.8[x]	5.7[x]	5.8[x]	5.4[x]	5.6[x]	5.3[x]	10.4	11.6	9.2	8.0[y]	8.4[y]	7.5[y]	*198*
18.3[y]	20.0[y]	16.6[y]	16.8[y]	18.0[y]	15.6[y]	7.3[y]	7.7[y]	7.0[y]	17.1	19.5	14.5	17.3[z]	19.5[z]	15.0[z]	*199*
...	...	...	*17.6*	*16.8*	*18.8*	.	.	.	31.2	30.9	31.6	*22.9*	*22.6*	*23.3*	*200*
13.8[y]	*13.7*[y]	*13.9*[y]	*13.2*[y]	*11.9*[y]	*14.5*[y]	*10.2*[y]	*10.8*[y]	*9.5*[y]	...	...	...	*13.1*[z]	*13.0*[z]	*13.3*[z]	*201*
0.1	***0.1***	***0.1***	***0.0***	***0.0***	***0.0***	***0.0***	***0.0***	***0.0***	3.2	3.1	3.2	**4.2**	**4.3**	**4.2**	*202*
6.6	6.8	6.5	7.6	7.8	7.4	12.6	13.2	11.6	*6.1*	*6.4*	*5.8*	6.9	7.2	6.5	*203*
...	...	...	...	...	...	...	...	...	.	.	.	...	...	...	*204*
1.8	1.5	2.2	0.5	...	...	.	.	.	3.8	4.2	3.2	2.9	2.7	3.1	*I*
.	.	.	.	.	.	.	.	.	0.5	0.5	0.5	0.2	0.2	0.1	*II*
.	.	.	.	.	.	.	.	.	1.2	...	...	0.7	1.0	0.3	*III*
4.2	5.1	3.2	1.9	3.1	0.8	.	.	.	6.8	8.1	5.5	5.3	5.5	5.1	*IV*
3.1	3.8	2.3	5.0	5.7	3.7	.	.	.	8.0	9.5	6.4	4.0	4.6	3.3	*V*
...	...	...	...	...	...	.	.	.	1.2	1.5	1.0	0.7	0.9	0.4	*VI*
...	...	...	...	...	...	.	.	.	0.3	0.5	0.2	0.2	0.2	0.2	*VII*
...	...	...	0.0	0.0	0.0	.	.	.	1.7	1.7	1.7	1.0	...	...	*VIII*
1.0	1.5	0.5	0.0	0.0	0.0	.	.	.	2.7	2.9	2.4	1.6	2.2	0.9	*IX*
...	...	...	...	...	...	.	.	.	0.0	0.0	0.0	0.0	0.0	0.0	*X*
2.9	3.7	2.0	1.1	1.4	0.8	.	.	.	4.7	5.3	4.1	4.1	5.1	3.1	*XI*
...	...	...	...	...	...	.	.	.	3.1	3.6	2.5	2.9	3.2	2.6	*XII*
3.6	4.6	2.6	1.4	1.7	1.0	.	.	.	6.5	7.5	5.4	6.4	7.6	5.2	*XIII*
0.0	0.0	0.1	0.1	0.1	0.1	.	.	.	0.4	0.5	0.3	0.4	0.5	0.3	*XIV*
5.1	5.5	4.7	.	.	.	.	.	.	...	...	...	4.7	5.5	3.7	*XV*
12.2	11.5	13.2	13.3	13.2	13.4	.	.	.	17.4	17.2	17.7	13.1	13.0	13.3	*XVI*

Table 7
Internal efficiency: primary education dropout and completion

Country or territory	Duration[1] of primary education	DROPOUT RATES BY GRADE IN PRIMARY EDUCATION (%)														
		School year ending in 2005														
		Grade 1			Grade 2			Grade 3			Grade 4			Grade 5		
	2006	Total	Male	Female	Total	Male	Female	Total	Male	Female	Total	Male	Female	Total	Male	Female
Arab States																
Algeria	6	1.2	1.7	0.6	1.0	0.7	1.4	0.7	0.3	1.2	1.5	1.9	1.0	3.9	4.5	3.3
Bahrain	6	–[y]	–[y]	–[y]	–[y]	–[y]	–[y]	0.0[y]	–[y]	0.4[y]	0.2[y]	–[y]	0.5[y]	0.1[y]	–[y]	0.2[y]
Djibouti	6	4.1	1.5	7.0	2.7	2.7	2.7	2.3	2.0	2.8	0.7	1.0	0.4	...	...	...
Egypt	6	***1.9***	***2.4***	***1.3***	–	...	...	***0.3***	...	...	***3.0***	...	...	–	...	...
Iraq	6	*11.1*[y]	*9.1*[y]	*13.4*[y]	*1.4*[y]	–[y]	*3.7*[y]	*1.1*[y]	–[y]	*2.9*[y]	*5.2*[y]	*3.2*[y]	*7.8*[y]	*11.2*[y]	*8.8*[y]	*14.6*[y]
Jordan	6	–	...	...	0.2	...	...	–	...	...	0.7	...	...	3.6	...	...
Kuwait	5	0.7	1.5	–	–	–	–	–	–	–	4.5	5.3	3.7	...	...	...
Lebanon	6	2.2	2.5	1.8	1.3	1.6	1.1	1.1	1.4	0.6	3.8	4.9	2.5	3.8	5.1	2.4
Libyan Arab Jamahiriya	6	...	...	...	...	...	...	...	...	...	...	...	...	...	...	...
Mauritania	6	7.6	7.7	7.6	8.3	7.7	8.8	13.1	12.1	14.0	17.3	17.0	17.6	19.6	18.9	20.4
Morocco	6	5.4	5.2	5.8	2.7	2.4	3.2	4.3	3.8	4.9	5.9	5.3	6.6	7.5	6.6	8.7
Oman	6	0.2	0.3	0.1	–	–	–	–	–	–	–	–	–	1.9	1.2	2.6
Palestinian A. T.	4	0.9[y]	0.9[y]	0.9[y]	–[y]	–[y]	–[y]	1.2[y]	1.2[y]	1.4[y]	...	...	...	...	...	...
Qatar	6	4.9	5.5	4.3	5.5	6.1	5.0	3.2	0.6	5.9	–	–	–	–	–	–
Saudi Arabia	6	...	...	...	...	...	...	...	...	...	...	...	...	...	...	...
Sudan	6	6.1[y]	6.7[y]	5.3[y]	6.3[y]	5.6[y]	7.1[y]	4.9[y]	4.8[y]	5.0[y]	5.7[y]	6.6[y]	4.6[y]	5.5[y]	5.8[y]	5.0[y]
Syrian Arab Republic	4	4.4	4.1	4.7	1.5	1.7	1.3	1.4	1.7	1.0	...	...	...	...	...	...
Tunisia	6	0.2	0.2	0.3	0.7	0.8	0.6	0.4	0.3	0.4	1.7	1.9	1.4	2.3	2.5	2.2
United Arab Emirates	5	0.8	1.2	0.4	–	–	–	–	–	–	–	–	–	...	...	...
Yemen	6	13.5[y]	15.1[y]	11.5[y]	8.9[y]	8.5[y]	9.4[y]	6.7[y]	5.4[y]	8.5[y]	7.9[y]	6.7[y]	9.9[y]	9.6[y]	8.4[y]	11.7[y]
Central and Eastern Europe																
Albania	4	3.5[x]	4.1[x]	2.8[x]	3.4[x]	3.8[x]	3.1[x]	3.3[x]	3.5[x]	3.0[x]	...	...	...	.	.	.
Belarus	4	0.0	0.2	–	0.2	0.5	–	0.1	0.4	–	...	...	...	.	.	.
Bosnia and Herzegovina	4	...	...	...	...	...	...	...	...	...	...	...	...	.	.	.
Bulgaria	4	2.0	2.0	2.1	1.9	1.8	1.9	1.2	1.1	1.3	...	...	...	.	.	.
Croatia	4	–	–	–	–	–	–	–	–	–	...	...	...	.	.	.
Czech Republic	5	0.5	0.5	0.5	–	–	–	–	–	–	–	–	–	.	.	.
Estonia	6	1.0	1.1	0.8	0.7	0.8	0.5	0.6	0.6	0.5	0.9	0.6	1.3	0.6	1.1	0.1
Hungary	4	1.7	1.9	1.4	0.2	0.2	0.2	*0.2*	*0.3*	*0.1*	...	...	...	.	.	.
Latvia	4	1.4	1.6	1.2	0.3	–	0.8	0.1	0.4	–	...	...	...	.	.	.
Lithuania	4	1.5	1.8	1.2	1.0	0.9	1.0	0.8	0.6	1.0	...	...	...	.	.	.
Montenegro	...	...	...	...	...	...	...	...	...	...	...	...	...	...	...	...
Poland	6	0.6	...	...	0.2	...	...	0.3	...	...	0.3	...	...	0.2	...	...
Republic of Moldova	4	0.7	0.9	0.4	1.3	2.0	0.7	1.0	1.2	0.8	...	...	...	.	.	.
Romania	4	3.1	3.2	3.0	1.7	1.9	1.4	1.5	1.6	1.3	...	...	...	.	.	.
Russian Federation	4	2.7	*3.4*	*2.0*	...	...	...	...	...	...	...	...	...	.	.	.
Serbia	4	...	...	...	...	...	...	...	...	...	...	...	...	.	.	.
Slovakia	4	1.5	1.8	1.3	0.4	0.2	0.5	0.6	0.6	0.5	...	...	...	.	.	.
Slovenia	5	...	...	...	...	...	...	...	...	...	...	...	...	.	.	.
TFYR Macedonia	4	1.0[y]	1.5[y]	0.5[y]	0.1[y]	0.0[y]	0.3[y]	0.6[y]	0.8[y]	0.5[y]	...	...	...	.	.	.
Turkey	6	0.1[y]	0.5[y]	–[y]	0.8[y]	0.7[y]	0.9[y]	1.0[y]	0.9[y]	1.2[y]	1.1[y]	0.6[y]	1.6[y]	2.9[y]	1.9[y]	3.9[y]
Ukraine	4	1.2	*1.4*	*1.0*	0.7	*0.7*	*0.7*	...	...	...	...	...	...	.	.	.
Central Asia																
Armenia	3	1.2	1.1	1.3	–	–	–	...	...	...	.	.	.	.	.	.
Azerbaijan	4	0.5	–	1.6	0.9	0.2	1.6	0.3	–	1.5	...	...	...	.	.	.
Georgia	6	0.3	...	...	–	–	–	–	–	–	0.9	...	...	–	–	–
Kazakhstan	4	–	–	–	**0.3**	**0.2**	**0.3**	–	–	–	...	...	...	.	.	.
Kyrgyzstan	4	0.3	1.0	–	0.5	0.4	0.5	0.6	1.3	–	...	...	...	.	.	.
Mongolia	5	5.6[x]	5.5[x]	5.7[x]	2.0[x]	1.9[x]	2.0[x]	1.7[x]	2.2[x]	1.2[x]	...	...	...	...	...	...
Tajikistan	4	–	–	–	–	–	–	0.6	–	*1.3*	...	...	...	.	.	.
Turkmenistan	3	...	...	...	...	...	...	...	...	...	...	...	...	.	.	.
Uzbekistan	4	0.2	0.7	–	0.7	0.9	0.5	0.4	0.4	0.5	...	...	...	.	.	.
East Asia and the Pacific																
Australia	7	...	...	...	...	...	...	...	...	...	...	...	...	...	...	...
Brunei Darussalam	6	0.3	0.9	–	0.6	0.1	1.2	–	–	–	–	–	–	1.5	1.5	1.5
Cambodia	6	9.4	9.3	9.6	9.5	9.8	9.2	9.2	9.8	8.5	10.1	10.6	9.5	10.8	11.0	10.5
China	5	...	...	...	...	...	...	...	...	...	...	...	...	...	...	...

PRIMARY EDUCATION COMPLETION															
SURVIVAL RATE TO GRADE 5 (%)						SURVIVAL RATE TO LAST GRADE (%)						PRIMARY COHORT COMPLETION RATE (%)			
School year ending in						School year ending in						School year ending in			
1999			2005			1999			2005			2005			
Total	Male	Female	Total	Male	Female	Total	Male	Female	Total	Male	Female	Total	Male	Female	**Country or territory**
															Arab States
95	94	96	95	95	96	91	90	93	91	90	92	86[y]	84[y]	88[y]	Algeria
97	*97*	*98*	99[y]	100[y]	98[y]	*92*	*91*	*93*	99[y]	100[y]	97[y]	…	…	…	Bahrain
77	71	85	90	92	87	…	…	…	…	…	…	…	…	…	Djibouti
99	*99*	*99*	…	…	…	*99*	*99*	*99*	**97**	…	…	…	…	…	Egypt
66	*67*	*63*	*81[y]*	*87[y]*	*73[y]*	*49*	*51*	*47*	*70[y]*	*78[y]*	*61[y]*	*68[y]*	*75[y]*	*60[y]*	Iraq
98	98	97	…	…	…	97	97	97	96	…	…	…	…	…	Jordan
…	…	…	96	95	97	94	93	95	96	95	97	86	83	90	Kuwait
91	88	95	91	88	94	91	88	95	87	83	91	83	78	88	Lebanon
…	…	…	…	…	…	…	…	…	…	…	…	…	…	…	Libyan Arab Jamahiriya
68	*70*	*66*	57	59	56	*61*	…	…	45	46	43	21[y]	21[y]	20[y]	Mauritania
82	82	82	80	82	79	75	75	76	74	76	72	60	63	56	Morocco
94	94	94	100	100	100	92	92	92	99	100	99	98[y]	98[y]	97[y]	Oman
…	…	…	…	…	…	99	100	99	98[y]	99[y]	97[y]	…	…	…	Palestinian A. T.
…	…	…	…	…	…	…	…	…	89	89	89	…	…	…	Qatar
…	…	…	…	…	…	…	…	…	…	…	…	…	…	…	Saudi Arabia
84	*81*	*88*	79[y]	78[y]	79[y]	*77*	*74*	*81*	74[y]	73[y]	75[y]	…	…	…	Sudan
92	92	91	…	…	…	87	87	87	92	92	93	…	…	…	Syrian Arab Republic
92	91	93	97	96	97	87	86	88	94	94	95	…	…	…	Tunisia
92	93	92	99	98	100	90	90	89	99	98	100	98	…	…	United Arab Emirates
87	…	…	66[y]	67[y]	65[y]	*80*	…	…	59[y]	61[y]	57[y]	…	…	…	Yemen
															Central and Eastern Europe
…	…	…	…	…	…	*92*	*90*	*95*	90[x]	89[x]	91[x]	…	…	…	Albania
…	…	…	…	…	…	99	99	99	99	99	100	97	96	100	Belarus
…	…	…	…	…	…	…	…	…	…	…	…	…	…	…	Bosnia and Herzegovina
…	…	…	…	…	…	93	93	93	95	95	95	…	…	…	Bulgaria
…	…	…	…	…	…	100	99	100	100	99	100	…	…	…	Croatia
98	98	99	100	100	100	98	98	99	100	100	100	…	…	…	Czech Republic
99	99	99	97	97	97	99	98	99	96	96	97	…	…	…	Estonia
…	…	…	…	…	…	97	96	98	*98*	*97*	*98*	…	…	…	Hungary
…	…	…	…	…	…	97	97	97	98	98	98	…	…	…	Latvia
…	…	…	…	…	…	99	99	100	97	97	97	…	…	…	Lithuania
…	…	…	…	…	…	…	…	…	…	…	…	…	…	…	Montenegro
99	…	…	99	…	…	98	…	…	98	…	…	…	…	…	Poland
…	…	…	…	…	…	95	…	…	97	96	98	…	…	…	Republic of Moldova
…	…	…	…	…	…	96	95	96	94	93	94	…	…	…	Romania
…	…	…	…	…	…	95	…	…	…	…	…	…	…	…	Russian Federation
…	…	…	…	…	…	…	…	…	…	…	…	…	…	…	Serbia
…	…	…	…	…	…	97	96	98	97	97	98	…	…	…	Slovakia
…	…	…	…	…	…	…	…	…	…	…	…	…	…	…	Slovenia
…	…	…	…	…	…	97	96	99	98[y]	98[y]	99[y]	…	…	…	TFYR Macedonia
…	…	…	97[y]	97[y]	97[y]	…	…	…	94[y]	95[y]	93[y]	…	…	…	Turkey
…	…	…	…	…	…	97	…	…	…	…	…	…	…	…	Ukraine
															Central Asia
…	…	…	…	…	…	…	…	…	99	100	99	…	…	…	Armenia
…	…	…	…	…	…	97	96	98	97	100	94	96	100	93	Azerbaijan
…	…	…	100	…	…	99	99	100	100	…	…	84	…	…	Georgia
…	…	…	…	…	…	…	…	…	**100**	**100**	**100**	99	99	100	Kazakhstan
…	…	…	…	…	…	95*	95*	94*	99	97	100	95	92	97	Kyrgyzstan
…	…	…	…	…	…	87	85	90	91[x]	91[x]	91[x]	…	…	…	Mongolia
…	…	…	…	…	…	97	*100*	*94*	99	*100*	*97*	97[y]	…	…	Tajikistan
…	…	…	…	…	…	…	…	…	…	…	…	…	…	…	Turkmenistan
…	…	…	…	…	…	100	*100*	*99*	99	98	99	…	…	…	Uzbekistan
															East Asia and the Pacific
…	…	…	…	…	…	…	…	…	…	…	…	…	…	…	Australia
…	…	…	100	100	100	…	…	…	98	98	99	83	81	84	Brunei Darussalam
56	*58*	*54*	62	61	64	*49*	*52*	*45*	55	54	57	…	…	…	Cambodia
…	…	…	…	…	…	…	…	…	…	…	…	…	…	…	China

Table 7 (continued)

Country or territory	Duration[1] of primary education 2006	DROPOUT RATES BY GRADE IN PRIMARY EDUCATION (%) School year ending in 2005 Grade 1 Total	Grade 1 Male	Grade 1 Female	Grade 2 Total	Grade 2 Male	Grade 2 Female	Grade 3 Total	Grade 3 Male	Grade 3 Female	Grade 4 Total	Grade 4 Male	Grade 4 Female	Grade 5 Total	Grade 5 Male	Grade 5 Female
Cook Islands	6	…	…	…	…	…	…	…	…	…	…	…	…	…	…	…
DPR Korea	4	…	…	…	…	…	…	…	…	…	…	…	…	…	…	…
Fiji	6	*7.1*	*6.9*	*7.4*	*–*	*–*	*–*	*4.3*	*4.6*	*3.9*	*4.6*	*4.6*	*4.7*	*5.7*	*5.7*	*5.8*
Indonesia	6	*4.1*	*4.7*	*3.5*	*1.6*	*1.8*	*1.4*	*3.0*	*3.6*	*2.2*	*7.0*	*7.4*	*6.7*	*5.7*	*5.9*	*5.6*
Japan	6	…	…	…	…	…	…	…	…	…	…	…	…	…	…	…
Kiribati	6	12.0[x]	11.4[x]	12.5[x]	2.9[x]	4.2[x]	1.6[x]	0.8[x]	1.6[x]	0.1[x]	3.3[x]	8.7[x]	–[x]	0.6[x]	1.5[x]	–[x]
Lao PDR	5	13.0	12.7	13.2	6.8	6.7	6.9	7.7	7.8	7.7	7.2	6.5	8.0	…	…	…
Macao, China	6	–	–	–	–	–	–	–	–	–	…	…	…	…	…	…
Malaysia	6	–[y]	–[y]	–[y]	–[y]	–[y]	–[y]	–[y]	–[y]	–[y]	0.0[y]	0.0[y]	0.0[y]	–[y]	…	…
Marshall Islands	6	…	…	…	…	…	…	…	…	…	…	…	…	…	…	…
Micronesia	6	…	…	…	…	…	…	…	…	…	…	…	…	…	…	…
Myanmar	5	11.3	12.0	10.6	5.9	4.9	6.9	6.7	7.3	6.2	7.9	8.1	7.7	…	…	…
Nauru	6	…	…	…	…	…	…	…	…	…	…	…	…	…	…	…
New Zealand	6	…	…	…	…	…	…	…	…	…	…	…	…	…	…	…
Niue	6	…	…	…	…	…	…	…	…	…	…	…	…	…	…	…
Palau	5	…	…	…	…	…	…	…	…	…	…	…	…	…	…	…
Papua New Guinea	6	…	…	…	…	…	…	…	…	…	…	…	…	…	…	…
Philippines	6	14.4	15.9	12.8	4.9	5.7	4.1	4.0	5.0	2.9	4.0	5.0	2.9	4.7	6.0	3.4
Republic of Korea	6	–	–	–	**0.2**	**0.2**	**0.2**	**0.3**	**0.3**	**0.2**	**0.4**	**0.4**	**0.3**	**0.4**	**0.4**	**0.4**
Samoa	6	…	…	…	…	…	…	…	…	…	…	…	…	…	…	…
Singapore	6	…	…	…	…	…	…	…	…	…	…	…	…	…	…	…
Solomon Islands	6	…	…	…	…	…	…	…	…	…	…	…	…	…	…	…
Thailand	6	…	…	…	…	…	…	…	…	…	…	…	…	…	…	…
Timor-Leste	6	…	…	…	…	…	…	…	…	…	…	…	…	…	…	…
Tokelau	6	…	…	…	…	…	…	…	…	…	…	…	…	…	…	…
Tonga	6	4.2	4.3	4.0	1.6	0.2	3.1	2.8	3.8	1.5	–	–	–	1.3	2.3	0.2
Tuvalu	6	…	…	…	…	…	…	…	…	…	…	…	…	…	…	…
Vanuatu	6	…	…	…	…	…	…	…	…	…	…	…	…	…	…	…
Viet Nam	5	*2.1*	…	…	*1.6*	…	…	*2.0*	…	…	*2.3*	…	…	…	…	…
Latin America and the Caribbean																
Anguilla	7	1.0[y]	3.2[y]	–[y]	–[y]	–[y]	–[y]	0.9[y]	–[y]	1.9[y]	1.0[y]	0.9[y]	1.3[y]	–[y]	…	…
Antigua and Barbuda	7	…	…	…	…	…	…	…	…	…	…	…	…	…	…	…
Argentina	6	3.4[y]	3.7[y]	3.1[y]	1.9[y]	2.2[y]	1.6[y]	1.9[y]	2.2[y]	1.6[y]	2.7[y]	3.0[y]	2.4[y]	3.0[y]	3.7[y]	2.4[y]
Aruba	6	0.2	0.9	–	2.2	2.7	1.6	–	…	…	–	…	…	–	…	…
Bahamas	6	8.7	10.6	6.7	3.0	5.3	0.7	2.0	0.7	3.2	2.0	2.3	1.7	4.3	4.2	4.3
Barbados	6	3.2	1.6	4.8	0.5	1.6	–	0.8	–	1.6	1.0	2.6	–	–	…	…
Belize	6	4.0	2.5	5.6	0.7	0.7	0.7	1.4	3.3	–	0.8	1.3	0.2	–	–	–
Bermuda	6	1.6	…	…	1.4	…	…	9.8	…	…	–	–	–	3.7	…	…
Bolivia	6	*7.9*[x]	*8.2*[x]	*7.7*[x]	*1.6*[x]	*1.5*[x]	*1.6*[x]	*3.8*[x]	*3.6*[x]	*4.0*[x]	*2.6*[x]	*2.4*[x]	*2.8*[x]	*2.7*[x]	*1.7*[x]	*3.8*[x]
Brazil	4	8.4[x]	…	…	2.0[x]	…	…	5.5[x]	…	…	…	…	…	…	…	…
British Virgin Islands	7	1.4	…	…	0.7	…	…	…	…	…	…	…	…	.	.	.
Cayman Islands	6	5.6[y]	4.9[y]	6.3[y]	5.7[y]	1.9[y]	9.9[y]	6.6[y]	7.8[y]	5.4[y]	6.4[y]	9.8[y]	2.0[y]	–[y]	…	…
Chile	6	0.4[x]	0.4[x]	0.5[x]	1.3[x]	1.5[x]	1.1[x]	–[x]	–[x]	–[x]	–[x]	–[x]	–[x]	0.5[x]	0.7[x]	0.3[x]
Colombia	5	10.9	12.0	9.5	3.4	4.4	2.3	4.1	4.9	3.3	–	–	–	…	…	…
Costa Rica	6	2.3	2.5	2.0	0.8	1.3	0.3	0.4	0.2	0.6	2.2	2.3	2.2	3.3	3.7	2.9
Cuba	6	1.4	1.9	1.0	1.3	2.1	0.4	–	–	–	0.1	–	0.3	0.1	0.2	0.1
Dominica	7	4.6	3.5	5.6	–	…	…	3.5	…	…	1.3	…	…	3.5	…	…
Dominican Republic	6	8.0	8.0	8.0	7.1	7.5	6.7	8.9	10.2	7.4	9.0	9.7	8.2	10.1	11.3	8.9
Ecuador	6	13.1	13.2	12.9	3.5	3.5	3.4	3.7	3.8	3.5	3.8	4.2	3.4	2.2	2.1	2.3
El Salvador	6	11.2	11.7	10.7	6.1	6.4	5.7	4.8	5.3	4.3	6.1	6.8	5.4	6.3	6.6	6.1
Grenada	7	…	…	…	…	…	…	…	…	…	…	…	…	…	…	…
Guatemala	6	8.7	8.5	8.8	6.1	5.6	6.6	7.2	6.4	8.1	8.3	7.8	8.8	7.8	7.6	8.0
Guyana	6	…	…	…	…	…	…	…	…	…	…	…	…	…	…	…
Haiti	6	…	…	…	…	…	…	…	…	…	…	…	…	…	…	…
Honduras	6	6.9	8.0	5.7	2.7	3.5	1.9	2.8	3.4	2.3	3.2	3.5	2.9	2.9	3.7	2.1
Jamaica	6	…	…	…	…	…	…	…	…	…	…	…	…	…	…	…
Mexico	6	1.8	2.1	1.6	0.9	1.0	0.8	1.6	1.7	1.4	1.2	1.4	0.9	2.3	2.6	2.0
Montserrat	7	…	…	…	…	…	…	…	…	…	…	…	…	…	…	…
Netherlands Antilles	6	…	…	…	…	…	…	…	…	…	…	…	…	…	…	…
Nicaragua	6	17.1	17.8	16.3	10.0	11.3	8.6	9.1	10.2	7.8	14.4	15.4	13.4	6.1	7.7	4.6
Panama	6	4.5	4.5	4.5	2.3	2.8	1.8	1.9	2.4	1.3	3.0	3.1	2.8	3.0	2.9	3.2

PRIMARY EDUCATION COMPLETION															
SURVIVAL RATE TO GRADE 5 (%)						SURVIVAL RATE TO LAST GRADE (%)						PRIMARY COHORT COMPLETION RATE (%)			
School year ending in						School year ending in						School year ending in			
1999			2005			1999			2005			2005			
Total	Male	Female	Total	Male	Female	Total	Male	Female	Total	Male	Female	Total	Male	Female	Country or territory
...	...	...	...	...	...	...	...	...	...	...	...	...	...	...	Cook Islands
...	...	...	...	...	...	...	...	...	...	...	...	...	...	...	DPR Korea
87	89	86	*86*	*85*	*87*	82	82	82	*81*	*80*	*82*	...	...	...	Fiji
...	...	...	*84*	*83*	*86*	...	...	...	*79*	*78*	*81*	...	...	...	Indonesia
...	...	...	...	...	...	...	...	...	...	...	...	...	...	...	Japan
...	...	...	82[x]	76[x]	88[x]	...	...	...	81[x]	75[x]	89[x]	...	...	...	Kiribati
54	55	54	62	62	62	54	55	54	62	62	62	58[y]	58[y]	57[y]	Lao PDR
...	...	...	...	...	...	...	...	...	...	...	...	...	...	...	Macao, China
...	...	...	99[y]	99[y]	100[y]	...	...	...	99[y]	...	...	...	...	...	Malaysia
...	...	...	...	...	...	...	...	...	...	...	...	...	...	...	Marshall Islands
...	...	...	...	...	...	...	...	...	...	...	...	...	...	...	Micronesia
...	...	...	72	71	72	...	...	...	72	71	72	70[y]	68[y]	71[y]	Myanmar
...	...	...	...	...	...	...	...	...	...	...	...	...	...	...	Nauru
...	...	...	...	...	...	...	...	...	...	...	...	...	...	...	New Zealand
...	...	...	...	...	...	...	...	...	...	...	...	...	...	...	Niue
...	...	...	...	...	...	...	...	...	...	...	...	...	...	...	Palau
...	...	...	...	...	...	...	...	...	...	...	...	...	...	...	Papua New Guinea
...	...	...	74	70	78	...	...	...	70	66	75	...	...	...	Philippines
100	100	100	**99**	**99**	**99**	100	100	100	**99**	**99**	**99**	...	...	...	Republic of Korea
94	91*	96*	...	...	...	92	91*	94*	...	...	...	...	...	...	Samoa
...	...	...	...	...	...	...	...	...	...	...	...	...	...	...	Singapore
...	...	...	...	...	...	...	...	...	...	...	...	...	...	...	Solomon Islands
...	...	...	...	...	...	...	...	...	...	...	...	...	...	...	Thailand
...	...	...	...	...	...	...	...	...	...	...	...	...	...	...	Timor-Leste
...	...	...	...	...	...	...	...	...	...	...	...	...	...	...	Tokelau
...	...	...	92	92	92	...	...	...	91	90	92	...	...	...	Tonga
...	...	...	...	...	...	...	...	...	...	...	...	...	...	...	Tuvalu
72	72	72	...	...	...	69	67	71	...	...	...	...	...	...	Vanuatu
83	80	86	*92*	...	...	83	80	86	*92*	...	...	...	...	...	Viet Nam
															Latin America and the Caribbean
...	...	...	97[y]	94[y]	100[y]	...	...	...	93[y]	...	...	88[y]	...	...	Anguilla
...	...	...	...	...	...	...	...	...	...	...	...	...	...	...	Antigua and Barbuda
90	90	90	90[y]	88[y]	91[y]	89	88	89	87[y]	85[y]	89[y]	...	...	...	Argentina
...	...	...	97	...	...	97	99	95	96	...	...	95[y]	93[y]	97[y]	Aruba
...	...	...	85	82	88	...	...	...	81	79	84	...	...	...	Bahamas
...	...	...	...	...	...	94	95	93	97	...	...	...	...	...	Barbados
78	...	...	92	...	...	77	77	76	92	91	94	...	...	...	Belize
...	...	...	90	...	...	...	...	...	86	...	...	...	...	...	Bermuda
82	83	81	*85*[x]	*85*[x]	*85*[x]	80	82	77	*82*[x]	*83*[x]	*81*[x]	...	...	...	Bolivia
...	...	...	...	...	...	...	...	...	80[x]	...	...	...	...	...	Brazil
...	...	...	...	...	...	...	...	...	...	...	...	...	...	...	British Virgin Islands
74	...	...	...	...	...	...	...	...	78[y]	...	...	...	...	...	Cayman Islands
100	100	100	99[x]	99[x]	99[x]	100	99	100	98[x]	98[x]	98[x]	...	...	...	Chile
67	64	69	82	78	86	67	64	69	82	78	86	75[y]	73[y]	77[y]	Colombia
91	90	93	94	93	95	88	86	89	90	89	92	81	80	83	Costa Rica
94	94	94	97	96	98	93	92	93	97	96	98	...	...	...	Cuba
91	...	...	92	...	...	...	...	...	88	...	...	83[x]	83[x]	83[x]	Dominica
75	71	79	68	66	71	71	66	75	61	58	65	...	...	...	Dominican Republic
77	77	77	77	77	78	75	74	75	76	75	76	*70*[x]	*70*[x]	*71*[x]	Ecuador
65	*64*	*66*	72	70	74	*62*	*63*	*62*	67	65	70	63	60	65	El Salvador
...	...	...	...	...	...	...	...	...	...	...	...	...	...	...	Grenada
56	55	58	69	70	68	52	50	54	63	65	62	61[y]	63[y]	59[y]	Guatemala
95	...	...	...	...	...	93	...	...	...	...	...	...	...	...	Guyana
...	...	...	...	...	...	...	...	...	...	...	...	...	...	...	Haiti
...	...	...	83	80	87	...	...	...	81	77	85	...	...	...	Honduras
...	...	...	...	...	...	...	...	...	...	...	...	...	...	...	Jamaica
89	88	90	94	94	95	87	86	88	92	91	93	...	...	...	Mexico
...	...	...	...	...	...	...	...	...	...	...	...	...	...	...	Montserrat
...	...	...	...	...	...	*84*	*78*	*91*	...	...	...	...	...	...	Netherlands Antilles
48	44	53	54	50	57	46	42	50	50	46	55	47[y]	44[y]	51[y]	Nicaragua
92	92	92	88	87	89	90	90	91	85	84	86	84	...	...	Panama

Table 7 (continued)

Country or territory	Duration[1] of primary education	DROPOUT RATES BY GRADE IN PRIMARY EDUCATION (%)														
		School year ending in 2005														
		Grade 1			Grade 2			Grade 3			Grade 4			Grade 5		
	2006	Total	Male	Female	Total	Male	Female	Total	Male	Female	Total	Male	Female	Total	Male	Female
Paraguay	6	4.9[y]	5.2[y]	4.5[y]	1.7[y]	2.1[y]	1.2[y]	2.0[y]	2.4[y]	1.5[y]	3.4[y]	4.0[y]	2.8[y]	4.2[y]	4.7[y]	3.6[y]
Peru	6	2.6	2.4	2.8	2.5	2.3	2.7	2.4	2.0	2.8	2.4	2.2	2.7	4.7	4.6	4.9
Saint Kitts and Nevis	7	…	…	…	…	…	…	…	…	…	…	…	…	…	…	…
Saint Lucia	7	1.5[y]	1.8[y]	1.1[y]	1.1[y]	–[y]	2.3[y]	0.2[y]	0.1[y]	0.3[y]	1.2[y]	1.8[y]	0.6[y]	2.0[y]	3.3[y]	0.7[y]
Saint Vincent/Grenad.	7	…	…	…	…	…	…	…	…	…	…	…	…	…	…	…
Suriname	6	…	…	…	…	…	…	…	…	…	…	…	…	…	…	…
Trinidad and Tobago	7	–[*,y]	–[*,y]	–[*,y]	3.8[*,y]	5.1[*,y]	2.4[*,y]	3.9[*,y]	4.7[*,y]	3.1[*,y]	1.6[*,y]	1.4[*,y]	1.9[*,y]	4.1[*,y]	4.3[*,y]	3.8[*,y]
Turks and Caicos Islands	6	…	…	…	…	…	…	…	…	…	…	…	…	…	…	…
Uruguay	6	4.2	4.7	3.7	0.4	0.5	0.3	0.5	0.8	0.2	1.0	1.3	0.6	0.7	0.9	0.5
Venezuela, B. R.	6	2.8	3.4	2.1	0.9	1.2	0.5	1.7	2.1	1.1	2.2	2.9	1.5	2.1	2.7	1.4
North America and Western Europe																
Andorra	6	…	…	…	…	…	…	…	…	…	…	…	…	…	…	…
Austria	4	1.4[x]	3.0[x]	–[x]	–[x]	–[x]	–[x]	–[x]	–[x]	–[x]	…	…	…	.	.	.
Belgium	6	1.7	2.1	1.3	0.8	0.8	0.7	0.4	0.4	0.4	0.5	0.6	0.5	2.8	3.1	2.5
Canada	6	…	…	…	…	…	…	…	…	…	…	…	…	…	…	…
Cyprus	6	0.0	–	0.1	–	–	–	0.3	0.5	0.1	0.1	0.3	–	–	–	–
Denmark	6	1.0[y]	0.8[y]	1.3[y]	4.8[y]	4.8[y]	4.9[y]	1.6[y]	1.6[y]	1.6[y]	–[y]	–[y]	–[y]	1.4[y]	1.5[y]	1.3[y]
Finland	6	0.0	0.4	–	–	–	–	–	–	–	–	–	–	–	–	–
France	5	…	…	…	…	…	…	…	…	…	…	…	…	…	…	…
Germany	4	–	–	–	1.2	1.3	1.0	0.6	0.5	0.6	…	…	…	.	.	.
Greece	6	1.8	2.6	0.9	–	–	–	–	–	–	–	–	–	–	–	–
Iceland	7	–	–	–	–	–	–	–	–	–	–	–	–	–	–	–
Ireland	8	*0.4*	*1.5*	–	–	–	–	–	–	–	–	–	–	–	–	–
Israel	6	–	–	–	–	–	–	–	–	–	–	–	–	–	–	–
Italy	5	–	–	–	–	–	–	–	–	–	–	–	–	…	…	…
Luxembourg	6	–	–	–	–	–	–	–	–	–	1.8	2.3	1.3	11.6	12.7	10.3
Malta	6	…	…	…	…	…	…	…	…	…	…	…	…	…	…	…
Monaco	5	…	…	…	…	…	…	…	…	…	…	…	…	…	…	…
Netherlands	6	…	…	…	…	…	…	…	…	…	…	…	…	…	…	…
Norway	7	–	–	–	–	–	–	–	–	–	–	–	–	–	–	–
Portugal	6	…	…	…	…	…	…	…	…	…	…	…	…	…	…	…
San Marino	5	…	…	…	…	…	…	…	…	…	…	…	…	…	…	…
Spain	6	–[y]	–[y]	–[y]	–[y]	–[y]	–[y]	–[y]	–[y]	–[y]	–[y]	–[y]	–[y]	–[y]	–[y]	–[y]
Sweden	6	…	…	…	…	…	…	…	…	…	…	…	…	…	…	…
Switzerland	6	…	…	…	…	…	…	…	…	…	…	…	…	…	…	…
United Kingdom	6	…	…	…	…	…	…	…	…	…	…	…	…	…	…	…
United States	6	2.2	3.7	0.7	0.0	2.0	–	0.8	–	1.8	0.0	–	1.3	–	…	…
South and West Asia																
Afghanistan	6	…	…	…	…	…	…	…	…	…	…	…	…	…	…	…
Bangladesh	5	14.6[x]	17.6[x]	11.2[x]	9.9[x]	11.4[x]	8.3[x]	5.8[x]	5.2[x]	6.4[x]	7.2[x]	5.5[x]	8.9[x]	…	…	…
Bhutan	7	–	–	–	1.8	1.8	1.8	3.1	3.9	2.2	1.5	2.4	0.7	4.4	5.1	3.8
India	5	14.0[y]	14.3[y]	13.6[y]	6.8[y]	6.6[y]	7.0[y]	6.0[y]	6.2[y]	5.9[y]	1.9[y]	1.4[y]	2.4[y]	…	…	…
Iran, Islamic Republic of	5	*1.8*	*4.0*	–	…	…	…	…	…	…	…	…	…	…	…	…
Maldives	7	–	…	…	–	…	…	…	…	…	…	…	…	…	…	…
Nepal	5	10.8	12.2*	9.3*	0.3	1.1*	–*	1.3	1.5*	1.0*	2.1	2.8*	1.4*	…	…	…
Pakistan	5	15.3[y]	15.4[y]	15.1[y]	4.7[y]	6.1[y]	2.5[y]	3.8[y]	4.7[y]	2.5[y]	9.2[y]	9.1[y]	9.4[y]	…	…	…
Sri Lanka	5	…	…	…	…	…	…	…	…	…	…	…	…	…	…	…
Sub-Saharan Africa																
Angola	4	…	…	…	…	…	…	…	…	…	…	…	…	.	.	.
Benin	6	10.0	10.3	9.7	6.6	6.9	6.4	5.0	4.7	5.5	7.9	7.3	8.7	7.6	5.9	10.1
Botswana	7	8.8[y]	9.2[y]	8.3[y]	2.6[y]	2.9[y]	2.4[y]	–[y]	–[y]	–[y]	8.5[y]	10.4[y]	6.4[y]	3.5[y]	3.8[y]	3.1[y]
Burkina Faso	6	9.5	9.4	9.7	5.0	4.7	5.5	8.1	9.0	6.9	5.0	5.7	4.1	9.4	9.9	8.8
Burundi	6	2.8	3.3	2.2	0.1	0.6	–	1.9	2.7	1.0	0.3	1.2	–	2.8	3.9	1.4
Cameroon	6	*10.2*	*8.6*	*12.1*	…	…	…	…	…	…	…	…	…	…	…	…
Cape Verde	6	–	–	–	2.1	2.6	1.6	1.0	1.4	0.7	4.4	5.7	3.0	2.9	3.2	2.7
Central African Republic	6	9.3	7.9	11.2	5.0	3.9	6.7	14.6	14.1	15.2	14.8	14.2	15.8	14.2	12.9	16.2
Chad	6	20.0[y]	18.9[y]	21.6[y]	12.2[y]	11.2[y]	13.5[y]	22.4[y]	25.3[y]	17.8[y]	19.7[y]	18.3[y]	21.9[y]	17.6[y]	15.9[y]	20.3[y]
Comoros	6	*1.4*[y]	*1.7*[y]	*1.2*[y]	*2.2*[y]	*2.3*[y]	*2.2*[y]	*3.2*[y]	*4.1*[y]	*2.3*[y]	*7.0*[y]	*6.1*[y]	*8.2*[y]	*7.4*[y]	*8.8*[y]	*5.9*[y]
Congo	6	…	…	…	…	…	…	…	…	…	…	…	…	…	…	…

PRIMARY EDUCATION COMPLETION															
SURVIVAL RATE TO GRADE 5 (%)						SURVIVAL RATE TO LAST GRADE (%)						PRIMARY COHORT COMPLETION RATE (%)			
School year ending in						School year ending in						School year ending in			
1999			2005			1999			2005			2005			
Total	Male	Female	Total	Male	Female	Total	Male	Female	Total	Male	Female	Total	Male	Female	Country or territory
78	*76*	*80*	88[y]	86[y]	90[y]	*73*	*71*	*76*	84[y]	82[y]	86[y]	…	…	…	Paraguay
87	88	87	89	90	89	83	84	82	85	86	84	…	…	…	Peru
…	…	…	…	…	…	…	…	…	…	…	…	…	…	…	Saint Kitts and Nevis
90	…	…	…	…	…	…	…	…	96[y]	95[y]	97[y]	…	…	…	Saint Lucia
…	…	…	…	…	…	…	…	…	…	…	…	…	…	…	Saint Vincent/Grenad.
…	…	…	…	…	…	…	…	…	…	…	…	…	…	…	Suriname
…	…	…	91[*,y]	90[*,y]	92[*,y]	…	…	…	84[*,y]	80[*,y]	87[*,y]	…	…	…	Trinidad and Tobago
…	…	…	…	…	…	…	…	…	…	…	…	…	…	…	Turks and Caicos Islands
…	…	…	93	92	95	…	…	…	92	91	94	…	…	…	Uruguay
91	88	94	92	90	94	88	84	92	90	87	93	…	…	…	Venezuela, B. R.
															North America and Western Europe
…	…	…	…	…	…	…	…	…	…	…	…	…	…	…	Andorra
…	…	…	…	…	…	…	…	…	98[x]	97[x]	100[x]	…	…	…	Austria
…	…	…	96	96	97	…	…	…	94	93	94	…	…	…	Belgium
…	…	…	…	…	…	…	…	…	…	…	…	…	…	…	Canada
96	95	97	99	98	100	96	95	97	99	98	100	…	…	…	Cyprus
…	…	…	93[y]	93[y]	93[y]	100	100	100	92[y]	92[y]	92[y]	…	…	…	Denmark
…	…	…	99	99	100	100	100	100	99	99	100	…	…	…	Finland
98	*98*	*97*	…	…	…	98	*98*	*97*	…	…	…	…	…	…	France
…	…	…	…	…	…	99	99	100	99	98	99	…	…	…	Germany
…	…	…	99	97	100	…	…	…	98	97	100	…	…	…	Greece
…	…	…	99	98	100	100	…	…	99	98	100	…	…	…	Iceland
95	94	97	*99*	*97*	*100*	…	…	…	…	…	…	…	…	…	Ireland
…	…	…	…	…	…	…	…	…	100	100	99	…	…	…	Israel
97	…	…	100	99	100	97	…	…	100	99	100	…	…	…	Italy
96	*93*	*100*	100	99	100	*89*	*84*	*94*	88	86	90	…	…	…	Luxembourg
99	100	99	…	…	…	99	…	…	…	…	…	…	…	…	Malta
…	…	…	…	…	…	…	…	…	…	…	…	…	…	…	Monaco
100	100	100	…	…	…	100	100	100	…	…	…	…	…	…	Netherlands
…	…	…	100	100	100	100	100	100	100	99	100	…	…	…	Norway
…	…	…	…	…	…	…	…	…	…	…	…	…	…	…	Portugal
…	…	…	…	…	…	…	…	…	…	…	…	…	…	…	San Marino
…	…	…	*100[y]*	*100[y]*	*100[y]*	…	…	…	*100[y]*	*100[y]*	*100[y]*	…	…	…	Spain
…	…	…	…	…	…	…	…	…	…	…	…	…	…	…	Sweden
…	…	…	…	…	…	…	…	…	…	…	…	…	…	…	Switzerland
…	…	…	…	…	…	…	…	…	…	…	…	…	…	…	United Kingdom
94	…	…	97	96	98	92	…	…	96	…	…	…	…	…	United States
															South and West Asia
…	…	…	…	…	…	…	…	…	…	…	…	…	…	…	Afghanistan
65	60	70	65[x]	63[x]	67[x]	65	60	70	65[x]	63[x]	67[x]	55[x]	52[x]	58[x]	Bangladesh
90	89	92	93	91	95	81	78	86	84	81	88	…	…	…	Bhutan
62	63	60	73[y]	73[y]	73[y]	62	63	60	73[y]	73[y]	73[y]	…	…	…	India
…	…	…	…	…	…	…	…	…	…	…	…	…	…	…	Iran, Islamic Republic of
…	…	…	…	…	…	…	…	…	…	…	…	…	…	…	Maldives
58	56	61	79	75*	83*	58	56	61	79	75*	83*	*38.6[y]*	*35.4[y]*	*42.8[y]*	Nepal
…	…	…	70[y]	68[y]	72[y]	…	…	…	70[y]	68[y]	72[y]	48[y]	47[y]	51[y]	Pakistan
…	…	…	…	…	…	…	…	…	…	…	…	…	…	…	Sri Lanka
															Sub-Saharan Africa
…	…	…	…	…	…	…	…	…	…	…	…	…	…	…	Angola
…	…	…	72	72	71	…	…	…	65	67	63	36[y]	38[y]	34[y]	Benin
87	84	89	83[y]	80[y]	85[y]	82	79	86	75[y]	71[y]	78[y]	69[y]	…	…	Botswana
68	67	70	72	71	74	61	59	63	64	63	66	…	…	…	Burkina Faso
…	…	…	88	84	92	…	…	…	78	74	83	36[y]	38[y]	32[y]	Burundi
81	…	…	…	…	…	*78*	…	…	…	…	…	…	…	…	Cameroon
…	…	…	92	89	94	…	…	…	89	86	92	82[y]	…	…	Cape Verde
…	…	…	50	53	45	…	…	…	39	43	35	…	…	…	Central African Republic
55	58	50	33[y]	34[y]	32[y]	47	50	41	26[y]	27[y]	23[y]	…	…	…	Chad
…	…	…	*80[y]*	*79[y]*	*81[y]*	…	…	…	*72[y]*	*69[y]*	*74[y]*	…	…	…	Comoros
…	…	…	…	…	…	…	…	…	…	…	…	…	…	…	Congo

Table 7 (continued)

Country or territory	Duration[1] of primary education 2006	DROPOUT RATES BY GRADE IN PRIMARY EDUCATION (%) School year ending in 2005 Grade 1 Total	Grade 1 Male	Grade 1 Female	Grade 2 Total	Grade 2 Male	Grade 2 Female	Grade 3 Total	Grade 3 Male	Grade 3 Female	Grade 4 Total	Grade 4 Male	Grade 4 Female	Grade 5 Total	Grade 5 Male	Grade 5 Female
Côte d'Ivoire	6	…	…	…	…	…	…	…	…	…	…	…	…	…	…	…
D. R. Congo	6	…	…	…	…	…	…	…	…	…	…	…	…	…	…	…
Equatorial Guinea	5	…	…	…	…	…	…	…	…	…	…	…	…	…	…	…
Eritrea	5	6.9	7.0	6.8	5.3	4.8	5.9	4.9	3.0	7.2	8.2	6.8	10.0	…	…	…
Ethiopia	6	**15.7**	**15.8**	**15.6**	**12.9**	**13.2**	**12.5**	**8.5**	**8.7**	**8.3**	**1.4**	**1.8**	**0.9**	**9.2**	**9.7**	**8.7**
Gabon	6	…	…	…	…	…	…	…	…	…	…	…	…	…	…	…
Gambia	6	…	…	…	…	…	…	…	…	…	…	…	…	…	…	…
Ghana	6	…	…	…	…	…	…	…	…	…	…	…	…	…	…	…
Guinea	6	–	–	–	5.2	3.9	6.8	7.9	7.6	8.2	6.4	6.4	6.5	6.3	5.4	7.5
Guinea-Bissau	6	…	…	…	…	…	…	…	…	…	…	…	…	…	…	…
Kenya	6	*9.1*[y]	*9.9*[y]	*8.3*[y]	*5.9*[y]	*6.6*[y]	*5.1*[y]	–[y]	–[y]	–[y]	*4.0*[y]	*4.2*[y]	*3.8*[y]	–[y]	…	…
Lesotho	7	9.3	9.8	8.8	2.0	2.9	0.9	3.7	4.8	2.5	6.3	7.8	4.7	7.1	9.7	4.6
Liberia	6	…	…	…	…	…	…	…	…	…	…	…	…	…	…	…
Madagascar	5	24.5	24.7	24.3	18.4	18.4	18.4	11.6	11.8	11.3	18.4	18.6	18.1	…	…	…
Malawi	6	22.1	21.7	22.4	6.4	5.7	7.0	14.9	15.3	14.5	12.2	12.5	11.8	15.6	15.3	16.0
Mali	6	2.9	2.9	3.0	3.5	2.9	4.1	5.1	4.7	5.6	5.3	5.0	5.6	7.1	6.3	8.2
Mauritius	6	–	–	–	–	–	–	0.4	0.9	–	0.2	0.3	0.0	1.2	1.3	1.0
Mozambique	7	14.4	13.7	15.3	12.9	12.2	13.6	9.6	9.0	10.3	12.0	11.0	13.2	21.3	21.5	20.9
Namibia	7	5.5	6.4	4.6	1.9	2.3	1.5	2.3	2.8	1.8	1.8	2.2	1.4	6.6	7.8	5.4
Niger	6	16.1	15.2	17.4	18.9	17.9	20.3	8.9	8.4	9.5	7.3	7.0	7.7	5.9	5.1	7.1
Nigeria	6	*8.7*[x]	*9.1*[x]	*8.3*[x]	*2.7*[x]	*3.0*[x]	*2.3*[x]	*7.1*[x]	*7.4*[x]	*6.7*[x]	*11.1*[x]	*12.0*[x]	*9.9*[x]	*13.5*[x]	*13.3*[x]	*13.7*[x]
Rwanda	6	21.0[x]	21.4[x]	20.5[x]	11.7[x]	11.7[x]	11.7[x]	10.8[x]	13.4[x]	8.3[x]	12.4[x]	13.8[x]	11.0[x]	24.9[x]	23.9[x]	25.9[x]
Sao Tome and Principe	6	***11.6***	***10.7***	***12.5***	***4.2***	***7.4***	***0.6***	***3.2***	***7.7***	–	***12.0***	***10.6***	***13.4***	***3.2***	***5.0***	***1.3***
Senegal	6	17.4	17.6	17.2	6.6	6.2	7.0	8.7	8.9	8.6	4.3	4.4	4.1	15.6	15.2	16.2
Seychelles	6	…	…	…	…	…	…	…	…	…	…	…	…	…	…	…
Sierra Leone	6	…	…	…	…	…	…	…	…	…	…	…	…	…	…	…
Somalia	7	…	…	…	…	…	…	…	…	…	…	…	…	…	…	…
South Africa	7	10.0[x]	10.6[x]	9.4[x]	2.9[x]	3.1[x]	2.7[x]	1.7[x]	1.1[x]	2.3[x]	2.2[x]	2.7[x]	1.6[x]	2.6[x]	2.9[x]	2.2[x]
Swaziland	7	5.5[y]	5.7[y]	5.3[y]	0.6[y]	0.8[y]	0.5[y]	4.0[y]	4.8[y]	3.0[y]	3.3[y]	4.3[y]	2.2[y]	5.2[y]	5.8[y]	4.5[y]
Togo	6	6.5[y]	6.0[y]	7.1[y]	2.5[y]	1.7[y]	3.5[y]	6.0[y]	5.2[y]	7.0[y]	5.5[y]	4.1[y]	7.3[y]	6.0[y]	4.0[y]	8.7[y]
Uganda	7	*31.6*[y]	*32.8*[y]	*30.5*[y]	*3.9*[y]	*4.7*[y]	*3.0*[y]	*7.1*[y]	*4.5*[y]	*9.6*[y]	*11.4*[y]	*11.7*[y]	*11.1*[y]	*15.2*[y]	*14.4*[y]	*16.0*[y]
United Republic of Tanzania	7	***1.2***	***2.3***	***0.1***	**2.1**	**2.5**	**1.7**	***1.1***	***2.4***	–	**7.9**	**7.2**	**8.5**	***1.3***	***1.3***	***1.2***
Zambia	7	5.7	5.1	6.3	–	–	–	3.0	2.0	4.0	2.9	2.6	3.2	8.1	7.9	8.3
Zimbabwe	7	…	…	…	…	…	…	…	…	…	…	…	…	…	…	…
World[2]	…	2.6	2.4	2.8	1.4	…	…	1.5	1.7	1.4	2.3	…	…	2.0	2.3	1.6
Countries in transition	…	0.3	1.0	0.0	0.4	0.3	0.4	0.4	0.2	1.0	…	…	…	.	.	.
Developed countries	…	1.0	1.1	0.9	0.1	…	…	0.3	…	…	…	…	…	.	.	.
Developing countries	…	5.2	5.3	5.0	2.1	2.6	1.6	2.8	3.6	1.9	3.3	4.3	2.2	3.5	…	…
Arab States	…	2.0	2.5	1.6	1.2	1.2	1.2	1.1	0.7	1.8	2.3	…	…	3.8	5.1	2.4
Central and Eastern Europe	…	1.2	1.4	1.0	0.5	0.5	0.5	0.6	0.6	0.5	…	…	…	.	.	.
Central Asia	…	0.3	…	…	0.4	0.3	0.4	0.4	0.4	0.5	…	…	…	.	.	.
East Asia and the Pacific	…	…	…	…	…	…	…	…	…	…	…	…	…	…	…	…
East Asia	…	3.1	…	…	1.6	…	…	2.5	…	…	4.0	5.0	2.9	…	…	…
Pacific	…	…	…	…	…	…	…	…	…	…	…	…	…	…	…	…
Latin America/Caribbean	…	4.1	3.6	4.6	1.8	2.1	1.4	2.0	0.7	3.2	2.1	2.3	2.0	2.8	2.7	3.0
Caribbean	…	1.6	…	…	1.1	0.0	2.3	…	…	…	…	…	…	–	…	…
Latin America	…	4.9	5.2	4.5	2.0	…	…	2.4	2.0	2.8	2.6	2.7	2.6	3.0	3.7	2.4
N. America/W.Europe	…	–	–	–	–	–	–	–	–	–	–	–	–	–	–	–
South and West Asia	…	10.8	12.2	9.3	3.2	4.0	2.2	3.8	4.7	2.5	2.1	2.8	1.4	…	…	…
Sub-Saharan Africa	…	9.3	7.9	11.2	4.0	6.1	1.8	5.1	4.7	5.5	6.7	6.6	6.9	7.1	9.7	4.6

1. Duration in this table is defined according to ISCED97 and may differ from that reported nationally.
2. All regional values shown are medians.
Data in italic are UIS estimates.
Data in bold are for the school year ending in 2006.

(y) Data are for the school year ending in 2004.
(x) Data are for the school year ending in 2003.
(*) National estimate.

PRIMARY EDUCATION COMPLETION															
SURVIVAL RATE TO GRADE 5 (%)						SURVIVAL RATE TO LAST GRADE (%)						PRIMARY COHORT COMPLETION RATE (%)			
School year ending in						School year ending in						School year ending in			
1999			2005			1999			2005			2005			
Total	Male	Female	Total	Male	Female	Total	Male	Female	Total	Male	Female	Total	Male	Female	Country or territory
69	73	65	...	...	...	62	67	56	...	...	...	...	...	...	Côte d'Ivoire
...	...	...	...	...	...	...	...	...	...	...	...	...	...	...	D. R. Congo
...	...	...	...	...	...	...	...	...	...	...	...	...	...	...	Equatorial Guinea
95	97	93	74	77	70	95	97	93	74	77	70	...	...	...	Eritrea
56	55	59	**64**	**64**	**65**	51	49	54	**58**	**57**	**59**	...	...	...	Ethiopia
...	...	...	...	...	...	...	...	...	...	...	...	...	...	...	Gabon
...	...	...	...	...	...	...	...	...	...	...	...	...	...	...	Gambia
...	...	...	...	...	...	...	...	...	...	...	...	...	...	...	Ghana
...	...	...	81	83	78	...	...	...	76	79	72	65[x]	69[x]	59[x]	Guinea
...	...	...	...	...	...	...	...	...	...	...	...	...	...	...	Guinea-Bissau
...	...	...	...	...	...	...	...	...	*84*[y]	...	...	*71*[y]	...	...	Kenya
74	67	80	74	68	80	58	50	66	62	53	71	...	...	...	Lesotho
...	...	...	...	...	...	...	...	...	...	...	...	...	...	...	Liberia
51	51	52	36	35	37	51	51	52	36	35	37	27	...	...	Madagascar
49	55	43	44	44	44	37	39	34	36	36	36	...	...	...	Malawi
78	*79*	*77*	81	83	79	*66*	*67*	*63*	73	75	70	...	...	...	Mali
99	100	99	99	98	100	99	100	99	99	97	100	...	...	...	Mauritius
43	47	37	58	60	55	28	31	25	40	41	39	...	...	...	Mozambique
92	92	93	87	84	90	82	79	84	77	73	80	*63*[x]	*59*[x]	*67*[x]	Namibia
...	...	...	56	58	54	...	...	...	53	55	50	39[y]	40[y]	36[y]	Niger
...	...	...	*73*[x]	*71*[x]	*75*[x]	...	...	...	*63*[x]	*61*[x]	*64*[x]	...	...	...	Nigeria
45	...	...	46[x]	43[x]	49[x]	30	...	...	31[x]	30[x]	32[x]	13[x]	15[x]	12[x]	Rwanda
...	...	...	**64**	**58**	**71**	...	...	...	***61***	***54***	***69***	...	...	...	Sao Tome and Principe
...	...	...	65	65	65	...	...	...	53	54	53	30	24	37	Senegal
...	...	...	...	...	...	99	99	100	...	...	...	...	...	...	Seychelles
...	...	...	...	...	...	...	...	...	...	...	...	...	...	...	Sierra Leone
...	...	...	...	...	...	...	...	...	...	...	...	...	...	...	Somalia
65	65	64	82[x]	82[x]	83[x]	57	59	56	77[x]	75[x]	79[x]	...	...	...	South Africa
80	72	88	84[y]	81[y]	87[y]	64	62	66	71[y]	66[y]	75[y]	...	...	...	Swaziland
...	...	...	75[y]	79[y]	70[y]	...	...	...	68[y]	74[y]	62[y]	63[y]	70[y]	55[y]	Togo
...	...	...	*49*[y]	*49*[y]	*49*[y]	...	...	...	*25*[y]	*26*[y]	*25*[y]	...	...	...	Uganda
...	...	...	***87***	***85***	***89***	...	...	...	***83***	***81***	***85***	...	...	...	United Republic of Tanzania
81	83	78	89	92	87	66	70	62	76	79	73	...	...	...	Zambia
...	...	...	...	...	...	...	...	...	...	...	...	...	...	...	Zimbabwe

Total	Male	Female	Total	Male	Female	Total	Male	Female	Total	Male	Female	Total	Male	Female	Country or territory
...	...	...	...	...	...	...	...	...	88	88	89	...	...	...	World[2]
...	...	...	...	...	...	97	...	...	99	100	97	...	...	...	Countries in transition
...	...	...	...	...	...	98	98	99	98	98	98	...	...	...	Developed countries
...	...	...	83	80	87	...	...	...	81	79	83	...	...	...	Developing countries
92	90	93	...	...	...	90	89	92	92	92	93	...	...	...	Arab States
...	...	...	...	...	...	97	96	98	97	97	98	...	...	...	Central and Eastern Europe
...	...	...	...	...	...	97	98	96	99	99	98	...	...	...	Central Asia
...	...	...	...	...	...	...	...	...	...	...	...	...	...	...	East Asia and the Pacific
...	...	...	84	83	86	...	...	...	79	78	81	...	...	...	East Asia
...	...	...	...	...	...	...	...	...	...	...	...	...	...	...	Pacific
87	...	...	90	88	91	84	78	91	85	84	86	...	...	...	Latin America/Caribbean
...	...	...	...	...	...	...	...	...	...	...	...	...	...	...	Caribbean
85	86	84	88	86	90	81	83	80	84	82	86	...	...	...	Latin America
...	...	...	...	...	...	...	...	...	99	98	100	...	...	...	N. America/W. Europe
...	...	...	73	73	73	...	...	...	73	73	73	...	...	...	South and West Asia
...	...	...	74	77	70	...	...	...	67	71	62	...	...	...	Sub-Saharan Africa

Table 8
Participation in secondary education[1]

	Country or territory	TRANSITION FROM PRIMARY TO SECONDARY GENERAL EDUCATION (%) School year ending in 2005 Total	Male	Female	ENROLMENT IN SECONDARY EDUCATION Age group 2006	School-age population[2] (000) 2005	Total enrolment, School year ending in 1999 Total (000)	1999 % F	2006 Total (000)	2006 % F	Enrolment in private institutions as % of total enrolment, School year ending in 2006	Enrolment in technical and vocational education, School year ending in 2006 Total (000)	% F
	Arab States												
1	Algeria	76	74	79	12-17	4 450	…	…	*3 756*[z]	*51*[z]	–[z]	*464*[z]	*39*[z]
2	Bahrain	96	95	98	12-17	72	59	51	74	50	17	15	39
3	Djibouti	73	75	70	12-18	135	16	42	30	40	17	2	37
4	Egypt	*86*[x]	*83*[x]	*89*[x]	12-17	9 457	*7 671*	*47*	*8 330*[y]	*47*[y]	*5*[y]	*2 525*[y]	*44*[y]
5	Iraq	*70*[y]	*73*[y]	*66*[y]	12-17	3 953	1 105	38	*1 751*[z]	*39*[z]	.[z]	*140*[z]	*32*[z]
6	Jordan	96	97	96	12-17	732	579	49	649	49	17	*32*	*35*
7	Kuwait	98	95	100	11-17	267	*235*	*49*	236	50	29	5	8
8	Lebanon	86	83	88	12-17	449	372	52	366	52	55	50	40
9	Libyan Arab Jamahiriya	…	…	…	12-18	783	…	…	733	53	2	…	…
10	Mauritania	48	51	45	12-17	397	*63*	*42*	99*	45*	17*	3*	34*
11	Morocco	77	78	77	12-17	3 930	1 470	43	2 061	…	5	119	…
12	Oman	98	99	98	12-17	338	229	49	299	48	1	.	.
13	Palestinian A. T.	98	98	99	10-17	730	444	50	686	50	4	6	31
14	Qatar	98	96	100	12-17	58	44	50	59	49	32[z]	0.6	–
15	Saudi Arabia	…	…	…	12-17	2 958	…	…	…	…	…	…	…
16	Sudan	97	94	100	12-16	4 281	*965*	…	1 447	48	8	44	47
17	Syrian Arab Republic	96	95	97	10-17	3 541	1 030	47	2 465	48	4	114	42
18	Tunisia	88	86	90	12-18	1 469	1 059	49	1 247	*51*	5	113	*39*
19	United Arab Emirates	99	99	100	11-17	331	202	50	298	49	46	1	.
20	Yemen	83[y]	83[y]	82[y]	12-17	3 281	1 042	26	1 455[z]	32[z]	2[z]	10[z]	6[z]
	Central and Eastern Europe												
21	Albania	*100*[x]	*100*[x]	*99*[x]	10-17	502	364	48	397[y]	48[y]	3[y]	24[y]	34[y]
22	Belarus	100	99	100	10-16	914	978	50	879	49	0.1	6	27
23	Bosnia and Herzegovina	…	…	…	10-17	405	…	…	…	…	…	…	…
24	Bulgaria	96	96	96	11-17	629	700	48	667	48	0.9[z]	203	39
25	Croatia	100	100	100	11-18	434	416	49	396	50	1	151	47
26	Czech Republic	99	99	99	11-18	1 005	928	50	966	49	7	381	46
27	Estonia	98	…	…	13-18	120	116	50	120	49	2	19	34
28	Hungary	*99*	*99*	*99*	11-18	994	1 007	49	949	49	10	129	38
29	Latvia	97	97	97	11-18	262	255	50	258	49	1	38	39
30	Lithuania	98	98	99	11-18	415	407	49	411	49	0.4	38	35
31	Montenegro	…	…	…	…	…	…	…	…	…	…	…	…
32	Poland	*92*	…	…	13-18	3 332	3 984	49	3 317	48	3	779	36
33	Republic of Moldova[3,4]	99	98	99	11-17	…	415	50	382	50	1	38	43
34	Romania	98	98	98	11-18	2 344	2 218	49	2 013	49	0.7	683	44
35	Russian Federation	…	…	…	11-17	13 746	…	…	11 548	48	0.6	1 958	37
36	Serbia[3]	…	…	…	11-18	…	*737*	*49*	**616**	**49**	**0.2**	**220**	**47**
37	Slovakia	98	97	98	10-18	679	674	50	640	49	8	220	46
38	Slovenia	…	…	…	11-18	183	220	49	174	49	1	60	42
39	TFYR Macedonia	100[y]	100[y]	99[y]	11-18	251	219	48	214[z]	48[z]	0.6[z]	58[z]	43[z]
40	Turkey	92[y]	93[y]	90[y]	12-16	6 851	…	…	*5 388*	*44*	*2*	1 112	38
41	Ukraine	…	…	…	10-16	4 171	5 214	50*	3 896	48*	0.4	311	34*
	Central Asia												
42	Armenia	100	100	99	10-16	398	347	…	356	50	1	2	33
43	Azerbaijan	99	100	98	10-16	1 267	929	49	1 052	48	0.4	3	29
44	Georgia	99	*98*	*100*	12-16	370	442	49	314	*50*	4	6	*31*
45	Kazakhstan	**100**	**100**	**100**	11-17	2 091	1 966	49	**1 874**	**49**	**0.8**	**106**	**31**
46	Kyrgyzstan	100	100	100	11-17	832	633	50	719	50	1	29	35
47	Mongolia	97	95	99	12-17	368	205	55	329	52	4[z]	22	46
48	Tajikistan	98	…	…	11-17	1 209	769	46	999	45	.	25	28
49	Turkmenistan	…	…	…	10-16	804	…	…	…	…	…	…	…
50	Uzbekistan	100	100	100	11-17	4 528	3 411	49	**4 598**	**49**	.	**1 075**	**49**
	East Asia and the Pacific												
51	Australia[5]	…	…	…	12-17	1 687	2 491	49	2 537	47	27	1 048	43.6
52	Brunei Darussalam	94	92	96	12-18	47	34	51	46	49	13	3	40
53	Cambodia	81	83	80	12-17	2 162	*318*	*34*	825	43	3	26	43

GROSS ENROLMENT RATIO (GER) IN SECONDARY EDUCATION (%)																NET ENROLMENT RATIO (NER) IN SECONDARY EDUCATION (%)				
Lower secondary				Upper secondary				Total secondary								Total secondary				
School year ending in 2006				School year ending in 2006				School year ending in 1999				School year ending in 2006				School year ending in 2006				
Total	Male	Female	GPI (F/M)	Total	Male	Female	GPI (F/M)	Total	Male	Female	GPI (F/M)	Total	Male	Female	GPI (F/M)	Total	Male	Female	GPI (F/M)	
																Arab States				
108[z]	*111[z]*	*105[z]*	*0.95[z]*	*58[z]*	*50[z]*	*67[z]*	*1.36[z]*	…	…	…	…	*83[z]*	*80[z]*	*86[z]*	*1.08[z]*	*66*	*65[y]*	*68[y]*	*1.06[y]*	1
104	104	104	1.00	100	96	104	1.08	95	91	98	1.08	102	100	104	1.04	93	91	96	1.05	2
27	32	22	0.69	16	20	13	0.63	14	16	12	0.72	22	27	18	0.67	*22[z]*	*26[z]*	*17[z]*	*0.66[z]*	3
98[y]	*102[y]*	*95[y]*	*0.93[y]*	*77[y]*	*79[y]*	*75[y]*	*0.95[y]*	*82*	*86*	*79*	*0.92*	*88[y]*	*91[y]*	*85[y]*	*0.94[y]*	…	…	…	…	4
58[z]	*70[z]*	*45[z]*	*0.64[z]*	*32[z]*	*38[z]*	*26[z]*	*0.70[z]*	34	41	26	0.63	*45[z]*	*54[z]*	*36[z]*	*0.66[z]*	*38[z]*	*45[z]*	*32[z]*	*0.70[z]*	5
94	94	95	1.01	78	75	80	1.06	89	88	90	1.02	89	88	90	1.03	*82*	*81*	*83*	*1.03*	6
91	91	92	1.01	85	80	90	1.12	*98*	*98*	99	*1.02*	89	87	91	1.05	*77*	*75*	*78*	*1.05*	7
88	85	92	1.09	74	70	78	1.12	74	70	77	1.09	81	78	85	1.10	73	70	76	1.10	8
116	117	115	0.99	77	65	91	1.41	…	…	…	…	94	86	101	1.17	…	…	…	…	9
27	29	26	0.88	22*	24*	20*	0.84*	*19*	*21*	*16*	*0.77*	25*	27*	23*	0.86*	*16*	*16*	*15*	*0.90*	10
69	…	…	…	36	…	…	…	37	41	32	0.79	52	…	…	…	…	…	…	…	11
94	96	92	0.95	83	84	82	0.97	75	75	75	1.00	89	90	87	0.96	77	77	77	0.99	12
100	98	102	1.04	73	68	78	1.16	80	79	82	1.04	94	91	97	1.06	90	87	92	1.06	13
101	103	100	0.97	101	103	100	0.97	87	83	92	1.11	101	103	100	0.97	91	91	90	0.99	14
…	…	…	…	…	…	…	…	…	…	…	…	…	…	…	…	…	…	…	…	15
47	49	45	0.92	25	24	25	1.01	*26*	…	…	…	34	34	33	0.96	…	…	…	…	16
92	95	89	0.94	33	33	33	0.99	40	42	38	0.91	70	71	68	0.95	*63*	*64*	*61*	*0.95*	17
107	107	106	1.00	70	*63*	*77*	*1.22*	72	72	73	1.02	85	*81*	*89*	*1.10*	…	…	…	…	18
97	97	96	0.99	81	78	85	1.09	76	74	78	1.06	90	89	91	1.02	79	78	80	1.02	19
51[z]	67[z]	34[z]	0.52[z]	40[z]	54[z]	25[z]	0.46[z]	41	58	22	0.37	46[z]	61[z]	30[z]	0.49[z]	*37[z]*	*48[z]*	*26[z]*	*0.53[z]*	20
																Central and Eastern Europe				
97[y]	98[y]	97[y]	0.98[y]	56[y]	58[y]	53[y]	0.93[y]	71	72	70	0.98	77[y]	78[y]	75[y]	0.96[y]	*73[y]*	*74[y]*	*72[y]*	*0.97[y]*	21
109	111	107	0.97	71	65	77	1.19	85	83	87	1.05	96	95	97	1.02	88	*87*	*89*	*1.02*	22
…	…	…	…	…	…	…	…	…	…	…	…	…	…	…	…	…	…	…	…	23
91	93	88	0.95	123	125	122	0.97	91	92	90	0.98	106	108	104	0.96	89	90	88	0.98	24
98	97	99	1.02	85	83	86	1.04	84	84	85	1.02	91	90	93	1.03	*87*	*86*	*88*	*1.02*	25
100	100	100	1.00	92	91	94	1.03	83	81	84	1.04	96	95	97	1.01	…	…	…	…	26
110	113	107	0.95	92	87	96	1.10	93	91	95	1.04	100	99	101	1.02	91	90	92	1.02	27
97	98	96	0.98	94	94	95	1.00	94	93	94	1.02	96	96	95	0.99	90	90	90	1.00	28
103	104	101	0.97	93	91	96	1.06	88	87	90	1.04	99	98	99	1.00	…	…	…	…	29
100	101	99	0.98	95	93	98	1.06	95	95	96	1.01	99	99	99	1.00	92	92	93	1.01	30
…	…	…	…	…	…	…	…	…	…	…	…	…	…	…	…	…	…	…	…	31
101	102	100	0.98	98	99	98	0.99	99	100	99	0.99	100	100	99	0.99	94	93	94	1.02	32
93	92	93	1.01	82	77	87	1.13	83	84	82	0.98	89	87	91	1.04	81	80	83	1.04	33
98	99	98	0.98	77	76	78	1.03	79	79	80	1.01	86	86	86	1.00	73	74	73	0.98	34
80	80	80	1.00	91	94	88	0.94	…	…	…	…	84	85	83	0.98	…	…	…	…	35
97	**97**	**96**	**0.99**	**80**	**77**	**82**	**1.07**	*93*	*93*	*94*	*1.01*	**88**	**87**	**89**	**1.03**	…	…	…	…	36
96	97	96	0.99	92	91	93	1.03	85	84	86	1.02	94	94	95	1.01	…	…	…	…	37
92	92	92	1.00	98	98	99	1.00	100	98	101	1.03	95	95	95	1.00	90	90	91	1.01	38
94[z]	93[z]	94[z]	1.01[z]	75[z]	77[z]	72[z]	0.95[z]	82	83	81	0.97	84[z]	85[z]	83[z]	0.98[z]	81[z]	82[z]	80[z]	0.98[z]	39
88	*94*	*83*	*0.88*	72	80	63	0.79	…	…	…	…	*79*	*86*	*71*	*0.83*	*69*	*74*	*64*	*0.86*	40
93	93*	93*	1.00*	94	96*	91*	0.95*	98	97*	100*	1.03*	93	94*	93*	0.98*	84	83*	84*	1.01*	41
																Central Asia				
93	93	94	1.02	81	78	85	1.09	91	…	…	…	90	88	91	1.04	86	84	88	1.04	42
90	92	88	0.96	66	68	65	0.95	76	76	76	1.00	83	85	81	0.96	78	79	76	0.96	43
93	92	94	1.03	74	*72*	*76*	*1.06*	79	80	78	0.98	85	*83*	*86*	*1.04*	79	77	81	1.05	44
103	**102**	**103**	**1.00**	**71**	**74**	**69**	**0.94**	92	92	92	1.00	**93**	**93**	**92**	**0.99**	**86**	**86**	**86**	**1.00**	45
91	91	91	1.01	75	74	76	1.03	83	83	84	1.02	86	86	87	1.01	80	80	81	1.02	46
94	90	98	1.09	81	74	88	1.19	58	51	65	1.27	89	84	95	1.12	*82*	*77*	*87*	*1.13*	47
94	99	88	0.89	55	68	42	0.61	74	80	68	0.86	83	90	75	0.83	80	87	74	0.84	48
…	…	…	…	…	…	…	…	…	…	…	…	…	…	…	…	…	…	…	…	49
97	**98**	**96**	**0.98**	**115**	**116**	**114**	**0.98**	86	87	86	0.98	**102**	**103**	**101**	**0.98**	…	…	…	…	50
																East Asia and the Pacific				
114	114	114	0.99	223	234	211	0.90	157	158	157	1.00	150	154	146	0.95	87	87	88	1.02	51
116	118	114	0.96	84	79	90	1.14	85	81	89	1.09	98	96	100	1.04	90	88	92	1.05	52
54	59	49	0.84	21	25	16	0.65	*17*	*22*	*12*	*0.53*	38	43	34	0.79	*31*	*33*	*28*	*0.85*	53

Table 8 (continued)

	Country or territory	TRANSITION FROM PRIMARY TO SECONDARY GENERAL EDUCATION (%)			ENROLMENT IN SECONDARY EDUCATION								
		School year ending in 2005			Age group	School-age population[2] (000)	Total enrolment				Enrolment in private institutions as % of total enrolment	Enrolment in technical and vocational education	
							School year ending in				School year ending in 2006	School year ending in 2006	
							1999		2006				
		Total	Male	Female	2006	2005	Total (000)	% F	Total (000)	% F		Total (000)	% F
54	China	…	…	…	12-17	134 016	77 436	…	101 195	48	7	15 306	51
55	Cook Islands[3]	…	…	…	11-17	…	2	50	2^{z}	49^{z}	14^{z}	.^{z}	.^{z}
56	DPR Korea	…	…	…	10-15	2 456	…	…	…	…	…	…	…
57	Fiji	*99*	*99*	*100*	12-18	119	98	51	100	51	*92*^{z}	2	34
58	Indonesia	*88*	*88*	*89*	13-18	25 575	…	…	16 424	49	44	2 232	42
59	Japan	…	…	…	12-17	7 456	8 959	49	7 561	49	19	961	43
60	Kiribati[3]	…	…	…	12-17	…	9	53	11^{z}	52^{z}	…	–^{z}	–^{z}
61	Lao PDR	*77*	*79*	*75*	11-16	910	240	40	395	43	1	5	35
62	Macao, China	90	87	93	12-17	47	32	51	46	49	95	2	44
63	Malaysia	*100*^{y}	*100*^{y}	*99*^{y}	12-18	3 634	2 177	51	2 489^{z}	51^{z}	3^{z}	146^{z}	43^{z}
64	Marshall Islands[3]	…	…	…	12-17	…	6	50	**5**	**49**	…	**0.2**	**50**
65	Micronesia	…	…	…	12-17	16	…	…	***15***	…	…	…	…
66	Myanmar	74	76	72	10-15	5 503	2 059	50	2 696	49	.	–	–
67	Nauru	…	…	…	12-17	…	…	…	**0.7**	**51**	…	.	.
68	New Zealand	…	…	…	11-17	437	437	50	522	50	21	…	…
69	Niue[3]	…	…	…	11-16	…	0.3	54	0.2^{z}	48^{z}	…	.	.
70	Palau[3]	…	…	…	11-17	…	2	49	*2*^{z}	…	*27*^{z}	…	…
71	Papua New Guinea	…	…	…	13-18	808	…	…	…	…	…	…	…
72	Philippines	99	100	98	12-15	7 582	5 117	51	6 302	52	20	.	.
73	Republic of Korea	**99**	**99**	**99**	12-17	3 958	4 368	48	**3 864**	**47**	**32**	**494**	**46**
74	Samoa	*96*^{x}	*95*^{x}	*97*^{x}	11-17	31	22	50	*24*^{z}	*51*^{z}	*32*^{z}	.^{z}	.^{z}
75	Singapore	…	…	…	12-15	…	172	48	215	48	…	26	36
76	Solomon Islands	…	…	…	12-18	77	17	41	22^{z}	43^{z}	…	.^{z}	.^{z}
77	Thailand	…	…	…	12-17	5 802	…	…	4 530	51	15	703	45
78	Timor-Leste	…	…	…	12-17	147	…	…	75^{z}	49^{z}	…	3^{z}	40^{z}
79	Tokelau[3]	…	…	…	11-15	…	…	…	*0.2*^{y}	*45*^{y}	…	.^{y}	…
80	Tonga	62	62	62	11-16	15	15	50	14	48	…	…	…
81	Tuvalu	…	…	…	12-17	…	…	…	…	…	…	…	…
82	Vanuatu	**64**	**63**	**65**	12-18	36	9	45	14^{y}	45^{y}	…	3^{y}	30^{y}
83	Viet Nam	*93*	…	…	11-17	…	7 401	47	9 975	49	*10*^{z}	500	54
	Latin America and the Caribbean												
84	Anguilla[6]	98^{y}	100^{y}	96^{y}	12-16	…	1	53	1	52	.	…	…
85	Antigua and Barbuda	…	…	…	12-16	…	…	…	…	…	…	…	…
86	Argentina	93^{y}	92^{y}	94^{y}	12-17	4 138	3 722	51	3 476^{z}	52^{z}	28^{z}	1 234^{z}	54^{z}
87	Aruba	99	…	…	12-16	7	6	51	7	50	92	1	38
88	Bahamas	99	99	99	11-16	36	27	49	33	50	28	.	.
89	Barbados	99	100	97	11-15	20	22	51	21	50	5	.	.
90	Belize	86	85	88	11-16	38	22	51	30	51	71	2	40
91	Bermuda[3]	95	…	…	11-17	…	…	…	5	51	42	.	.
92	Bolivia	*90*^{x}	*90*^{x}	*90*^{x}	12-17	1 264	830	48	1 043	48	13	.	.
93	Brazil	81^{x}	…	…	11-17	23 439	24 983	52	24 863^{z}	52^{z}	12^{y}	754^{z}	50^{z}
94	British Virgin Islands[3]	94	100	89	12-16	…	2	47	2	53	11	0.3	58
95	Cayman Islands[7]	…	…	…	11-16	…	2	48	3	49	30	.	.
96	Chile	97^{y}	96^{y}	98^{y}	12-17	1 792	1 305	50	1 634	50	54	395	47
97	Colombia	99	99	100	11-16	5 453	3 589	52	4 484	52	24	254	54
98	Costa Rica	98	100	97	12-16	436	235	51	374	50	10	56	50
99	Cuba	98	98	99	12-17	991	740	50	928	49	.	271	44
100	Dominica[3]	93	…	…	12-16	…	7	57	7	50	32	0.2	67
101	Dominican Republic	84	81	87	12-17	1 150	611	55	794	54	23	35	61
102	Ecuador	78	80	75	12-17	1 633	904	50	1 103	50	33	251	51
103	El Salvador	91	91	92	13-18	820	406	49	529	50	18	107	53
104	Grenada[3]	…	…	…	12-16	…	…	…	14^{*,z}	50^{*,z}	…	0.7^{*,z}	46^{*,z}
105	Guatemala	91	92	90	13-17	1 513	435	45	809	48	74	*239*	*51*
106	Guyana	…	…	…	12-16	68	66	50	*71*	*50*	…	…	…
107	Haiti	…	…	…	12-18	1 512	…	…	…	…	…	…	…
108	Honduras	71	68	74	12-16	854	…	…	635^{z}	56^{z}	33^{z}	241^{z}	58^{z}
109	Jamaica	*99*^{y}	*100*^{y}	*97*^{y}	12-16	285	*231*	*50*	246^{z}	50^{z}	6^{z}	–^{z}	–^{z}
110	Mexico	94	95	93	12-17	12 486	8 722	50	10 883	51	15	1 602	56
111	Montserrat	…	…	…	12-16	…	0.3	47	0.3	46	.	.	.
112	Netherlands Antilles	…	…	…	12-17	17	15	54	…	…	…	…	…
113	Nicaragua	…	…	…	12-16	681	*321*	*54*	448	53	26	23	54

GROSS ENROLMENT RATIO (GER) IN SECONDARY EDUCATION (%)																NET ENROLMENT RATIO (NER) IN SECONDARY EDUCATION (%)				
Lower secondary				Upper secondary				Total secondary								Total secondary				
School year ending in 2006				School year ending in 2006				School year ending in 1999				2006				School year ending in 2006				
Total	Male	Female	GPI (F/M)	Total	Male	Female	GPI (F/M)	Total	Male	Female	GPI (F/M)	Total	Male	Female	GPI (F/M)	Total	Male	Female	GPI (F/M)	
98	98	98	1.00	55	54	56	1.03	62	…	…	…	76	75	76	1.01	…	…	…	…	54
…	…	…	…	…	…	…	…	60	58	63	1.08	72[z]	71[z]	74[z]	1.04[z]	…	…	…	…	55
…	…	…	…	…	…	…	…	…	…	…	…	…	…	…	…	…	…	…	…	56
99	96	102	1.06	63	57	69	1.19	80	76	84	1.11	84	80	88	1.10	79	76	83	1.10	57
78	77	79	1.02	51	51	50	0.97	…	…	…	…	64	64	64	1.00	59	59	59	1.00	58
101	101	101	1.00	102	102	102	1.00	102	101	102	1.01	101	101	101	1.00	99	99	99	1.00	59
112[z]	109[z]	115[z]	1.06[z]	65[z]	57[z]	74[z]	1.30[z]	84	77	91	1.18	88[z]	82[z]	94[z]	1.14[z]	68[z]	65[z]	72[z]	1.11[z]	60
52	58	46	0.80	35	39	29	0.75	33	39	27	0.69	43	49	38	0.78	35	38	32	0.86	61
115	118	113	0.96	83	80	86	1.07	76	73	79	1.08	98	98	98	1.00	77	76	79	1.05	62
90[z]	89[z]	91[z]	1.02[z]	53[z]	48[z]	58[z]	1.22[z]	65	63	68	1.07	69[z]	66[z]	72[z]	1.10[z]	69[z]	66[z]	72[z]	1.10[z]	63
82	82	83	1.01	59	59	60	1.02	72	70	74	1.06	66	66	67	1.02	45	43	47	1.08	64
100	100	99	0.99	…	…	…	…	…	…	…	…	91	…	…	…	…	…	…	…	65
56	56	56	0.99	35	35	36	1.04	36	36	36	1.01	49	49	49	1.00	46	46	46	1.00	66
…	…	…	…	…	…	…	…	…	…	…	…	46	42	50	1.19	…	…	…	…	67
104	104	103	1.00	141	134	148	1.11	113	110	115	1.05	120	117	123	1.05	…	…	…	…	68
…	…	…	…	…	…	…	…	98	93	103	1.10	99[z]	96[z]	102[z]	1.07[z]	…	…	…	…	69
107[z]	…	…	…	97[z]	92[z]	103[z]	1.12[z]	101	98	105	1.07	102[z]	…	…	…	…	…	…	…	70
…	…	…	…	…	…	…	…	…	…	…	…	…	…	…	…	…	…	…	…	71
86	83	90	1.09	73	66	80	1.22	76	72	79	1.09	83	79	88	1.11	60	55	66	1.21	72
101	106	97	0.91	93	94	92	0.97	100	100	100	1.01	98	100	94	0.94	96	99	93	0.94	73
100[z]	100[z]	100[z]	1.00[z]	72[z]	66[z]	79[z]	1.20[z]	79	76	84	1.10	81[z]	76[z]	86[z]	1.13[z]	66[y]	62[y]	70[y]	1.14[y]	74
…	…	…	…	…	…	…	…	…	…	…	…	…	…	…	…	…	…	…	…	75
46[z]	49[z]	44[z]	0.89[z]	17[z]	19[z]	14[z]	0.74[z]	25	28	21	0.76	30[z]	32[z]	27[z]	0.84[z]	…	…	…	…	76
98	96	100	1.04	59	55	64	1.18	…	…	…	…	78	75	82	1.09	71	68	75	1.11	77
68[z]	67[z]	69[z]	1.02[z]	37[z]	38[z]	37[z]	0.96[z]	…	…	…	…	53[z]	53[z]	53[z]	1.00[z]	…	…	…	…	78
…	…	…	…	…	…	…	…	…	…	…	…	101[y]	107[y]	94[y]	0.88[y]	…	…	…	…	79
99	100	99	1.00	81	75	88	1.17	102	97	108	1.11	94	92	96	1.04	60	54	67	1.25	80
…	…	…	…	…	…	…	…	…	…	…	…	…	…	…	…	…	…	…	…	81
46[y]	46[y]	47[y]	1.04[y]	31[y]	39[y]	23[y]	0.58[y]	30	32	28	0.87	40[y]	43[y]	37[y]	0.86[y]	38[y]	41[y]	35[y]	0.87[y]	82
…	…	…	…	…	…	…	…	62	65	58	0.90	…	…	…	…	…	…	…	…	83
Latin America and the Caribbean																				
82	83	81	0.98	84	80	88	1.10	…	…	…	…	83	82	84	1.02	81[z]	83[z]	79[z]	0.96[z]	84
…	…	…	…	…	…	…	…	…	…	…	…	…	…	…	…	…	…	…	…	85
102[z]	99[z]	104[z]	1.05[z]	67[z]	61[z]	73[z]	1.21[z]	94	91	97	1.07	84[z]	80[z]	89[z]	1.11[z]	78[z]	75[z]	82[z]	1.10[z]	86
119	126	111	0.88	88	80	96	1.20	99	96	103	1.07	100	98	102	1.04	74	70	77	1.10	87
95	95	95	0.99	86	85	88	1.03	79	79	78	0.99	91	90	91	1.01	84	83	85	1.02	88
100	101	99	0.99	105	100	111	1.11	100	98	103	1.05	102	100	104	1.04	89	88	89	1.02	89
87	85	89	1.05	61	59	64	1.09	64	62	67	1.08	79	77	81	1.06	67	64	69	1.08	90
91	93	89	0.96	79	74	85	1.15	…	…	…	…	84	82	87	1.06	…	…	…	…	91
93	95	91	0.96	77	78	75	0.96	78	80	75	0.93	82	84	81	0.96	71	72	70	0.98	92
114[z]	111[z]	116[z]	1.05[z]	95[z]	87[z]	103[z]	1.19[z]	99	94	104	1.11	105[z]	100[z]	111[z]	1.10[z]	79[z]	75[z]	83[z]	1.11[z]	93
115	110	121	1.10	93	85	101	1.18	99	103	94	0.91	107	100	113	1.13	88[z]	82[z]	95[z]	1.16[z]	94
…	…	…	…	…	…	…	…	…	…	…	…	…	…	…	…	…	…	…	…	95
99	101	98	0.97	87	85	89	1.05	79	78	81	1.04	91	90	92	1.02	…	…	…	…	96
90	87	94	1.08	66	60	72	1.19	70	67	74	1.11	82	78	87	1.11	65	61	68	1.11	97
104	102	105	1.03	60	56	65	1.15	57	55	60	1.09	86	83	89	1.06	…	…	…	…	98
96	98	95	0.97	91	89	94	1.07	77	75	80	1.07	94	93	94	1.02	87	86	88	1.03	99
125	134	117	0.87	78	68	88	1.29	90	77	104	1.35	106	107	105	0.98	81	77	85	1.10	100
79	74	83	1.13	64	57	71	1.25	57	51	63	1.24	69	63	75	1.20	52	47	57	1.22	101
77	78	76	0.98	58	56	60	1.07	57	56	57	1.03	68	67	68	1.02	57	57	58	1.03	102
80	80	80	1.01	48	46	50	1.10	52	52	51	0.98	65	63	66	1.04	54	53	55	1.05	103
102[z]	104[z]	100[z]	0.96[z]	97[z]	89[z]	104[z]	1.17[z]	…	…	…	…	100[z]	99[z]	102[z]	1.03[z]	79[z]	78[z]	80[z]	1.02[z]	104
58	62	54	0.87	46	46	47	1.01	33	36	30	0.84	53	56	51	0.92	38	40	37	0.92	105
…	…	…	…	68	68	69	1.01	82	82	83	1.02	105	105	104	0.98	…	…	…	…	106
…	…	…	…	…	…	…	…	…	…	…	…	…	…	…	…	…	…	…	…	107
65[z]	60[z]	70[z]	1.18[z]	93[z]	75[z]	110[z]	1.45[z]	…	…	…	…	76[z]	66[z]	86[z]	1.30[z]	…	…	…	…	108
93[z]	93[z]	93[z]	1.00[z]	77[z]	73[z]	81[z]	1.11[z]	88	87	88	1.02	87[z]	86[z]	88[z]	1.03[z]	78[z]	76[z]	80[z]	1.05[z]	109
112	109	114	1.04	61	61	61	1.00	70	69	70	1.01	87	86	88	1.02	70	71	70	0.99	110
131	146	116	0.80	115	98	136	1.39	…	…	…	…	125	127	124	0.98	96[*,y]	…	…	…	111
…	…	…	…	…	…	…	…	92	85	99	1.16	…	…	…	…	…	…	…	…	112
73	71	76	1.07	54	47	61	1.29	52	47	56	1.19	66	62	70	1.14	43	40	47	1.16	113

Table 8 (continued)

	Country or territory	TRANSITION FROM PRIMARY TO SECONDARY GENERAL EDUCATION (%) School year ending in 2005			ENROLMENT IN SECONDARY EDUCATION								
					Age group	School-age population[2] (000)	Total enrolment School year ending in 1999		2006		Enrolment in private institutions as % of total enrolment School year ending in 2006	Enrolment in technical and vocational education School year ending in 2006	
		Total	Male	Female	2006	2005	Total (000)	% F	Total (000)	% F		Total (000)	% F
114	Panama	94	92	95	12-17	368	230	51	257	51	16	48	50
115	Paraguay	89[y]	89[y]	89[y]	12-17	803	425	50	529[z]	50[z]	21[z]	47[z]	47[z]
116	Peru	95	97	94	12-16	2 921	2 278	48	2 760	50	24	220	61
117	Saint Kitts and Nevis	90[x]	…	…	12-16	…	…	…	**5**	**50**	**3**	.	.
118	Saint Lucia	71[y]	63[y]	79[y]	12-16	16	12	56	14	54	4	0.6	37
119	Saint Vincent/Grenad.	84[y]	79[y]	88[y]	12-16	13	…	…	10[z]	55[z]	25[z]	0.4[z]	34[z]
120	Suriname	…	…	…	12-18	60	…	…	47	56	20	20	51
121	Trinidad and Tobago	93[*,y]	94[*,y]	92[*,y]	12-16	121	117	52	97[*,z]	50[*,z]	24[*,z]	0.9[z]	28[z]
122	Turks and Caicos Islands	88[y]	84[y]	92[y]	12-16	…	1	51	2[z]	48[z]	16[z]	0.1[z]	48[z]
123	Uruguay	81	76	87	12-17	320	284	53	323	53	11	50	46
124	Venezuela, B. R.	99	99	99	12-16	2 734	1 439	54	2 105	52	25	115	51
	North America and Western Europe												
125	Andorra[3]	96[x]	95[x]	96[x]	12-17	…	…	…	4	50	4	0.2	50
126	Austria	…	…	…	10-17	768	748	48	783	48	10	303	44
127	Belgium	…	…	…	12-17	749	1 033	51	822	48	68	335	43
128	Canada	…	…	…	12-17	2 592	…	…	2 999[y]	48[y]	…	…	…
129	Cyprus[3]	100	100	100	12-17	…	63	49	65	49	14	4	17
130	Denmark	100[y]	100[y]	99[y]	13-18	388	422	50	464	49	14	124	44
131	Finland	99	98	99	13-18	387	480	51	433	50	7	125	46
132	France[8]	…	…	…	11-17	5 260	5 955	49	5 994	49	25	1 165	42
133	Germany	99	99	99	10-18	8 128	8 185	48	8 185	48	8	1 813	42
134	Greece	99	100	99	12-17	683	771	49	705	48	6	125	37
135	Iceland	100	100	100	13-19	31	32	50	34	49	6	7	41
136	Ireland	99[y]	…	…	12-16	281	346	50	313	51	0	50	54
137	Israel	73	73	72	12-17	665	569	49	613	49	.	124	43
138	Italy	99	100	99	11-18	4 519	4 450	49	4 532	48	5	1 676	40
139	Luxembourg	…	…	…	12-18	38	33	50	37	50	19	12	48
140	Malta	94[y]	93[y]	94[y]	11-17	38	…	…	38[z]	49[z]	28[z]	4[z]	33[z]
141	Monaco[7]	…	…	…	11-17	…	3	51	3[y]	…	23[y]	0.5[y]	…
142	Netherlands	98[x]	96[x]	100[x]	12-17	1 204	1 365	48	1 423	48	83[y]	657	46
143	Norway	100	99	100	13-18	365	378	49	412	49	7[z]	134	43
144	Portugal	…	…	…	12-17	679	848	51	662	51	16	111	42
145	San Marino	…	…	…	11-18	…	…	…	…	…	…	…	…
146	Spain	…	…	…	12-17	2 603	3 299	50	3 091	50	28	482	50
147	Sweden	…	…	…	13-18	727	946	55	751	49	11	210	44
148	Switzerland	100	…	…	13-19	630	544	47	584	47	7	182	40
149	United Kingdom	…	…	…	11-17	5 470	5 192	49	5 358	49	25	976	49
150	United States	…	…	…	12-17	26 149	22 445	…	24 552	49	8	.	.
	South and West Asia												
151	Afghanistan	…	…	…	13-18	3 589	…	…	651[z]	23[z]	…	9[z]	10[z]
152	Bangladesh	89[x]	86[x]	92[x]	11-17	24 010	9 912	49	10 355[y]	50[y]	96[y]	168[y]	27[y]
153	Bhutan	93	92	94	13-18	92	20	44	45	48	8	0.7	36
154	India	85[y]	87[y]	83[y]	11-17	167 545	67 090	39	89 462[z]	43[z]	…	742[z]	15[z]
155	Iran, Islamic Republic of	88	93	83	11-17	11 922	9 727	47	9 942[z]	47[z]	8[z]	876[z]	38[z]
156	Maldives	81	76	85	13-17	39	15	51	33	50	12	…	…
157	Nepal	77[x]	79[x]	74[x]	10-16	4 596	1 265	40	1 984	45	27[z]	22	22
158	Pakistan	72	69	75	10-16	28 057	…	…	8 421	42	32	284	39
159	Sri Lanka	98[y]	…	…	10-17	2 602	…	…	2 332[y]	49[y]	…	…	…
	Sub-Saharan Africa												
160	Angola	…	…	…	10-16	2 915	300	43	…	…	…	…	…
161	Benin	71	72	70	12-18	1 377	213	31	435[z]	35[z]	25[z]	58[z]	43[z]
162	Botswana	97[y]	97[y]	98[y]	13-17	220	158	51	169[z]	51[z]	…	11[z]	38[z]
163	Burkina Faso	44	45	43	13-19	2 203	173	38	320	41	39	23	49
164	Burundi	34	37	31	13-19	1 347	…	…	192	43	11	12	49
165	Cameroon	33	32	34	12-18	2 941	626	45	698	44	28	118	39
166	Cape Verde	84	81	87	12-17	77	…	…	61	53	14	2	42
167	Central African Republic	47	44	51	12-18	690	…	…	…	…	…	…	…
168	Chad	51[y]	56[y]	42[y]	12-18	1 617	123	21	237[z]	25[z]	…	3[z]	41[z]
169	Comoros	63[y]	70[y]	55[y]	12-18	125	29	44	43[z]	43[z]	41[z]	0.2[z]	7[z]

GROSS ENROLMENT RATIO (GER) IN SECONDARY EDUCATION (%)																NET ENROLMENT RATIO (NER) IN SECONDARY EDUCATION (%)				
Lower secondary				Upper secondary				Total secondary								Total secondary				
School year ending in 2006				School year ending in 2006				School year ending in 1999				School year ending in 2006				School year ending in 2006				
Total	Male	Female	GPI (F/M)	Total	Male	Female	GPI (F/M)	Total	Male	Female	GPI (F/M)	Total	Male	Female	GPI (F/M)	Total	Male	Female	GPI (F/M)	
84	83	86	1.03	55	51	60	1.17	67	65	69	1.07	70	67	73	1.09	64	61	67	1.11	114
79[z]	79[z]	80[z]	1.01[z]	53[z]	52[z]	55[z]	1.05[z]	58	57	59	1.04	66[z]	66[z]	67[z]	1.03[z]	57[z]	56[z]	59[z]	1.06[z]	115
109	107	112	1.05	72	73	71	0.97	84	87	81	0.94	94	93	96	1.03	72	72	72	1.00	116
…	…	…	…	…	…	…	…	…	…	…	…	**105**	**110**	**100**	**0.91**	**65**	**70**	**61**	**0.87**	117
94	87	100	1.15	78	69	87	1.26	71	62	79	1.29	87	80	95	1.19	73[z]	65[z]	80[z]	1.24[z]	118
90[z]	83[z]	96[z]	1.16[z]	54[z]	44[z]	64[z]	1.46[z]	…	…	…	…	75[z]	67[z]	83[z]	1.24[z]	64[z]	57[z]	71[z]	1.23[z]	119
96	89	105	1.18	54	36	72	1.97	…	…	…	…	77	66	90	1.37	68[z]	57[z]	79[z]	1.38[z]	120
79[*,z]	78[*,z]	80[*,z]	1.03[*,z]	73[*,z]	70[*,z]	76[*,z]	1.07[*,z]	77	74	81	1.10	76[*,z]	75[*,z]	78[*,z]	1.05[*,z]	65[z]	64[z]	66[z]	1.04[z]	121
86[z]	89[z]	84[z]	0.95[z]	85[z]	89[z]	82[z]	0.92[z]	…	…	…	…	86[z]	89[z]	83[z]	0.94[z]	70[z]	72[z]	69[z]	0.96[z]	122
109	105	113	1.08	93	82	104	1.26	92	84	99	1.17	101	94	109	1.16	…	…	…	…	123
87	84	91	1.08	61	55	68	1.23	56	51	62	1.22	77	73	82	1.12	66	62	71	1.14	124
North America and Western Europe																				
91	92	91	0.99	72	65	78	1.20	…	…	…	…	85	83	87	1.04	74	73	75	1.03	125
103	103	102	0.99	101	104	98	0.94	99	101	97	0.96	102	104	100	0.96	…	…	…	…	126
114	116	111	0.95	108	109	106	0.97	143	138	148	1.07	110	111	108	0.97	87	89	85	0.96	127
100[y]	101[y]	100[y]	0.99[y]	134[y]	137[y]	132[y]	0.97[y]	…	…	…	…	117[y]	119[y]	116[y]	0.97[y]	…	…	…	…	128
96	96	97	1.00	97	95	98	1.03	93	92	95	1.03	97	96	97	1.02	94	93	95	1.02	129
116	115	117	1.02	123	121	126	1.04	125	121	128	1.06	120	118	121	1.03	89	88	90	1.03	130
102	102	102	1.00	121	117	126	1.08	121	116	126	1.09	112	109	114	1.04	96	96	96	1.00	131
112	113	112	0.99	116	115	117	1.02	111	111	111	1.00	114	114	114	1.00	99	98	100	1.02	132
101	101	101	1.00	100	103	96	0.94	98	99	97	0.98	101	102	99	0.98	…	…	…	…	133
101	103	100	0.97	105	106	104	0.98	90	89	92	1.04	103	104	102	0.97	92	92	93	1.01	134
102	103	101	0.98	116	113	120	1.06	110	107	113	1.06	110	108	111	1.03	90	89	91	1.02	135
107	105	108	1.03	119	112	126	1.13	107	104	111	1.06	112	108	116	1.07	87	85	90	1.05	136
76	76	76	1.00	109	109	108	0.99	90	90	90	1.00	92	93	92	0.99	89	88	89	1.00	137
104	106	102	0.97	98	98	98	1.00	92	92	91	0.99	100	101	100	0.99	94	93	94	1.01	138
107	107	108	1.01	88	85	91	1.08	98	96	99	1.04	96	94	98	1.04	84	82	86	1.05	139
104[z]	103[z]	105[z]	1.03[z]	89[z]	92[z]	87[z]	0.94[z]	…	…	…	…	99[z]	99[z]	100[z]	1.00[z]	87[z]	84[z]	90[z]	1.07[z]	140
…	…	…	…	…	…	…	…	…	…	…	…	…	…	…	…	…	…	…	…	141
128	131	125	0.96	108	108	108	1.01	124	126	121	0.96	118	119	117	0.98	88	88	89	1.01	142
100	100	101	1.00	126	127	125	0.99	120	118	121	1.02	113	113	112	0.99	96	96	97	1.01	143
114	114	115	1.01	81	74	89	1.20	106	102	110	1.08	97	94	102	1.09	82	78	86	1.10	144
…	…	…	…	…	…	…	…	…	…	…	…	…	…	…	…	…	…	…	…	145
116	116	117	1.00	123	114	133	1.17	108	105	112	1.07	119	115	122	1.06	94	92	96	1.03	146
104	105	104	0.99	102	103	102	1.00	157	137	177	1.29	103	104	103	0.99	99	99	99	1.00	147
109	108	110	1.03	80	85	75	0.87	94	98	90	0.92	93	95	90	0.95	82	84	80	0.96	148
99	99	100	1.01	97	95	99	1.04	101	101	101	1.00	98	97	99	1.03	92	90	94	1.04	149
100	101	99	0.99	88	88	88	1.00	95	…	…	…	94	94	94	0.99	88	88	88	1.00	150
South and West Asia																				
25[z]	37[z]	13[z]	0.35[z]	12[z]	18[z]	5[z]	0.28[z]	…	…	…	…	19[z]	28[z]	9[z]	0.33[z]	…	…	…	…	151
60[y]	57[y]	63[y]	1.10[y]	31[y]	32[y]	30[y]	0.94[y]	45	45	45	1.01	44[y]	43[y]	45[y]	1.03[y]	41[y]	40[y]	42[y]	1.04[y]	152
59	60	58	0.97	29	34	24	0.70	37	41	33	0.81	49	51	46	0.91	38	38	39	1.01	153
71[z]	75[z]	66[z]	0.88[z]	41[z]	46[z]	35[z]	0.75[z]	44	52	36	0.71	54[z]	59[z]	49[z]	0.82[z]	…	…	…	…	154
86[z]	90[z]	82[z]	0.91[z]	77[z]	79[z]	76[z]	0.96[z]	78	81	75	0.93	81[z]	83[z]	78[z]	0.94[z]	77[z]	79[z]	75[z]	0.94[z]	155
124	117	132	1.13	…	…	…	…	43	42	44	1.07	83	80	86	1.07	67	64	70	1.09	156
66	70	63	0.89	24	26	22	0.87	34	40	28	0.70	43	46	40	0.89	…	…	…	…	157
42	47	36	0.76	21	24	19	0.80	…	…	…	…	30	34	26	0.78	30	33	26	0.77	158
103[y]	100[y]	106[y]	1.05[y]	73[y]	74[y]	72[y]	0.97[y]	…	…	…	…	87[y]	86[y]	88[y]	1.02[y]	…	…	…	…	159
Sub-Saharan Africa																				
…	…	…	…	…	…	…	…	13	15	11	0.76	…	…	…	…	…	…	…	…	160
41[z]	51[z]	30[z]	0.58[z]	20[z]	27[z]	14[z]	0.52[z]	19	26	12	0.47	32[z]	41[z]	23[z]	0.57[z]	…	…	…	…	161
89[z]	86[z]	92[z]	1.07[z]	58[z]	58[z]	58[z]	1.00[z]	74	72	76	1.07	76[z]	75[z]	78[z]	1.05[z]	56[z]	52[z]	60[z]	1.14[z]	162
19	22	17	0.75	7	9	5	0.61	10	12	7	0.62	15	17	12	0.72	12	14	10	0.71	163
19	22	17	0.77	7	9	6	0.64	…	…	…	…	14	16	12	0.74	…	…	…	…	164
30	33	26	0.80	15	17	13	0.78	25	27	23	0.83	24	26	21	0.79	…	…	…	…	165
99	93	104	1.11	61	55	67	1.22	…	…	…	…	80	75	86	1.15	59	56	63	1.13	166
15*	18*	12*	0.68*	…	…	…	…	…	…	…	…	…	…	…	…	…	…	…	…	167
19[z]	28[z]	10[z]	0.36[z]	10[z]	15[z]	4[z]	0.26[z]	10	16	4	0.26	15[z]	23[z]	8[z]	0.33[z]	…	…	…	…	168
41[z]	47[z]	35[z]	0.75[z]	27[z]	30[z]	24[z]	0.78[z]	25	28	22	0.81	35[z]	40[z]	30[z]	0.76[z]	…	…	…	…	169

Table 8 (continued)

	Country or territory	TRANSITION FROM PRIMARY TO SECONDARY GENERAL EDUCATION (%) School year ending in 2005 Total	Male	Female	ENROLMENT IN SECONDARY EDUCATION Age group 2006	School-age population[2] (000) 2005	Total enrolment School year ending in 1999 Total (000)	1999 % F	2006 Total (000)	2006 % F	Enrolment in private institutions as % of total enrolment School year ending in 2006	Enrolment in technical and vocational education School year ending in 2006 Total (000)	% F
170	Congo	*58[y]*	*58[y]*	*58[y]*	12-18	572	…	…	*235[y]*	*46[y]*	*22[y]*	*43[y]*	*48[y]*
171	Côte d'Ivoire	…	…	…	12-18	3 169	*592*	*35*	…	…	…	…	…
172	D. R. Congo	…	…	…	12-17	8 205	1 235	34	…	…	…	…	…
173	Equatorial Guinea	…	…	…	12-18	74	20	27	…	…	…	…	…
174	Eritrea	83	86	79	12-18	733	115	41	228	38	5	2	43
175	Ethiopia	**89**	**90**	**87**	13-18	10 911	1 060	40	**3 430**	**40**	…	**191**	**44**
176	Gabon	…	…	…	12-18	209	87	46	…	…	…	…	…
177	Gambia	…	…	…	13-18	202	50	39	90	47	39[y]	–	–
178	Ghana	…	…	…	12-17	3 171	1 024	44	***1 581***	***46***	13	***32***	***50***
179	Guinea	71	75	66	13-19	1 384	*172*	*26*	483	34	16	4	14
180	Guinea-Bissau	…	…	…	13-17	178	…	…	…	…	…	…	…
181	Kenya	…	…	…	12-17	5 140	1 822	49	2 584	48	*6[z]*	23	62
182	Lesotho	68	68	68	13-17	254	74	57	94	56	3	2	53
183	Liberia	…	…	…	12-17	482	114	39	…	…	…	…	…
184	Madagascar	55	56	54	11-17	3 072	…	…	730	49	43	32	34
185	Malawi	72	74	71	12-17	1 946	556	41	565	45	10	.	.
186	Mali	*57*	*63*	*48*	13-18	1 635	218	34	463	38	24	51	41
187	Mauritius	67	61	72	11-17	146	104	49	*128[z]*	*49[z]*	…	*18[z]*	*31[z]*
188	Mozambique	54	52	56	13-17	2 368	103	41	367	42	13	26	31
189	Namibia	75	72	77	13-17	268	116	53	153	53	5	.	.
190	Niger	60	61	58	13-19	1 939	105	38	217	39	10	6	48
191	Nigeria	…	…	…	12-17	20 204	3 845	47	6 398[z]	45[z]	…	*–[z]*	*–[z]*
192	Rwanda	…	…	…	13-18	1 502	105	51	*204[z]*	*48[z]*	…	*73[z]*	*48[z]*
193	Sao Tome and Principe	***55***	***53***	***56***	13-17	18	…	…	**8**	**51**	–[z]	*0.1*	*18*
194	Senegal	50	52	48	13-19	1 883	237	39	*447*	*43*	23[z]	…	…
195	Seychelles[3]	95[x]	93[x]	97[x]	12-16	…	8	50	**8**	**50**	**6**	.	.
196	Sierra Leone	…	…	…	12-17	738	…	…	**240**	**41**	**7**	**12**	**60**
197	Somalia	…	…	…	13-17	876	…	…	…	…	…	…	…
198	South Africa	90[x]	89[x]	91[x]	14-18	4 886	4 239	53	4 593[y]	52[y]	3[y]	276[y]	40[y]
199	Swaziland	88[y]	88[y]	89[y]	13-17	153	62	50	71[z]	50[z]	.[z]	.[z]	.[z]
200	Togo	*65*	*68*	*61*	12-18	1 014	232	29	*399[z]*	*34[z]*	*28[z]*	*22[z]*	*18[z]*
201	Uganda	43	*42*	*43*	13-18	4 294	*318*	*40*	*760[z]*	*44[z]*	45[y]	*32[z]*	*32[z]*
202	United Republic of Tanzania	*46*	*47*	*45*	14-19	5 252	*271*	*45*	…	…	…	…	…
203	Zambia	54	49	60	14-18	1 377	237	*43*	*409[z]*	*45[z]*	4[y]	*8[z]*	*8[z]*
204	Zimbabwe	…	…	…	13-18	2 080	835	47	831	48	…	.	.

		Median				Sum	Sum	% F	Sum	% F	Median	Sum	% F
I	World	93	92	94	…	782 637	437 287	47	513 261	47	11	51 575	46
II	Countries in transition	100	100	99	…	30 758	31 633	49	27 229	48	0.6	3 389	39
III	Developed countries	99	…	…	…	83 553	84 564	49	84 414	49	8	13 685	43
IV	Developing countries	88	93	83	…	668 325	321 090	46	401 618	47	14	34 502	47
V	Arab States	92	90	93	…	41 613	22 682	46	28 208	47	5	3 449	43
VI	Central and Eastern Europe	98	98	99	…	38 380	39 582	49	33 661	48	1	6 540	39
VII	Central Asia	99	99	99	…	11 868	9 270	49	10 853	48	0.9	1 098	45
VIII	East Asia and the Pacific	…	…	…	…	216 003	133 770	47	162 445	48	19	21 564	49
IX	East Asia	91	…	…	…	212 747	130 498	47	158 963	48	13	20 419	49
X	Pacific	…	…	…	…	3 256	3 272	49	3 482	47	…	1 145	44
XI	Latin America/Caribbean	93	…	…	…	66 038	52 953	51	59 033	51	22	5 964	53
XII	Caribbean	94	…	…	…	2 239	1 151	50	1 270	50	20	40	49
XIII	Latin America	92	92	92	…	63 799	51 802	51	57 764	51	23	5 924	53
XIV	N. America/W. Europe	99	99	99	…	62 429	60 661	49	62 899	49	10	8 619	43
XV	South and West Asia	87	90	83	…	242 452	97 783	41	123 089	44	19	2 336	31
XVI	Sub-Saharan Africa	62	66	57	…	103 854	20 585	45	33 071	44	13	2 006	41

1. Refers to lower and upper secondary education (ISCED levels 2 and 3).
2. Data are for 2005 except for countries with a calendar school year, in which case data are for 2006.
3. National population data were used to calculate enrolment ratios.
4. Enrolment and population data exclude Transnistria.
5. Enrolment data for upper secondary education include adult education (students over age 25), particularly in pre-vocational/vocational programmes, in which males are in the majority. This explains the high level of GER and the relatively low GPI.
6. The apparent decrease in total secondary education enrolment between 1999 and 2005 is essentially due to a change in data reporting. Since 2003, programmes designed for people beyond the regular school age (e.g. adult education) have been excluded from the figures for secondary enrolment, leading to a reported decline in the GER. The secondary NER has increased over the period in question.

GROSS ENROLMENT RATIO (GER) IN SECONDARY EDUCATION (%)																NET ENROLMENT RATIO (NER) IN SECONDARY EDUCATION (%)				
Lower secondary				Upper secondary				Total secondary								Total secondary				
School year ending in 2006				School year ending in 2006				School year ending in 1999				2006				School year ending in 2006				
Total	Male	Female	GPI (F/M)	Total	Male	Female	GPI (F/M)	Total	Male	Female	GPI (F/M)	Total	Male	Female	GPI (F/M)	Total	Male	Female	GPI (F/M)	
57y	60y	53y	0.88y	*23y*	*27y*	*19y*	*0.69y*	…	…	…	…	*43y*	*47y*	*39y*	*0.84y*	…	…	…	…	170
…	…	…	…	…	…	…	…	*22*	*28*	*15*	*0.54*	…	…	…	…	…	…	…	…	171
…	…	…	…	…	…	…	…	18	24	12	0.52	…	…	…	…	…	…	…	…	172
…	…	…	…	…	…	…	…	33	48	18	0.37	…	…	…	…	…	…	…	…	173
46	56	36	0.63	19	25	14	0.54	21	25	17	0.69	31	39	23	0.60	25	30	20	0.67	174
39	**47**	**32**	**0.67**	**11**	**13**	**8**	**0.64**	12	15	10	0.68	**30**	**36**	**24**	**0.67**	*24*	*29*	*19*	*0.64*	175
…	…	…	…	…	…	…	…	49	53	46	0.86	…	…	…	…	…	…	…	…	176
60	62	59	0.95	28	31	25	0.80	32	38	25	0.66	45	47	43	0.90	38	40	37	0.94	177
69	**72**	**66**	**0.91**	***28***	***31***	***26***	***0.82***	37	41	33	0.80	***49***	***52***	***46***	***0.88***	***45***	***47***	***43***	***0.91***	178
43	54	31	0.58	23	32	13	0.42	*14*	*21*	*8*	*0.37*	35	45	24	0.53	28	35	20	0.57	179
…	…	…	…	…	…	…	…	…	…	…	…	…	…	…	…	…	…	…	…	180
89	91	87	0.96	31	32	29	0.91	38	39	37	0.96	50	52	49	0.93	42	43	42	0.97	181
45	40	51	1.29	24	22	27	1.22	31	26	35	1.35	37	33	41	1.27	24	19	29	1.55	182
…	…	…	…	…	…	…	…	29	35	23	0.65	…	…	…	…	…	…	…	…	183
32	33	32	0.96	11	12	11	0.89	…	…	…	…	24	24	23	0.95	*17*	*17*	*18*	*1.04*	184
39	42	36	0.87	17	20	15	0.77	36	42	30	0.70	29	32	27	0.84	24	25	23	0.93	185
39	48	30	0.63	17	21	12	0.56	16	22	11	0.52	28	35	21	0.61	…	…	…	…	186
99z	98z	100z	1.02z	*80z*	*81z*	*78z*	*0.96z*	76	76	75	0.98	*88z*	*89z*	*88z*	*0.99z*	*82z*	*81z*	*82z*	*1.02z*	187
22	25	18	0.72	5	6	4	0.66	5	6	4	0.69	16	18	13	0.72	4	4	4	0.89	188
74	68	79	1.16	30	29	32	1.12	55	52	58	1.12	57	53	61	1.15	35	30	40	1.31	189
15	18	12	0.65	5	6	4	0.61	7	9	5	0.60	11	14	9	0.63	9	12	7	0.63	190
35z	38z	32z	0.84z	30z	33z	26z	0.79z	23	24	22	0.89	32z	36z	29z	0.82z	26z	28z	23z	0.84z	191
18z	*19z*	*17z*	*0.89z*	*10z*	*10z*	*9z*	*0.89z*	9	10	9	0.99	*13z*	*14z*	*13z*	*0.89z*	…	…	…	…	192
70	*65*	*74*	*1.13*	*28*	*28*	*28*	*0.97*	…	…	…	…	*46*	*44*	*47*	*1.07*	33z	31z	34z	1.11z	193
32	36	28	0.78	*12*	*15*	*10*	*0.67*	15	19	12	0.64	*24*	*27*	*20*	*0.76*	20	23	18	0.76	194
116	**111**	**121**	**1.09**	**106**	**96**	**116**	**1.21**	113	111	115	1.04	**112**	**105**	**119**	**1.13**	**94**	…	…	…	195
46	**54**	**37**	**0.69**	**17**	**20**	**14**	**0.69**	…	…	…	…	**32**	**37**	**26**	**0.69**	**23**	**27**	**19**	**0.71**	196
…	…	…	…	…	…	…	…	…	…	…	…	…	…	…	…	…	…	…	…	197
98y	96y	100y	1.05y	92y	89y	96y	1.08y	89	83	94	1.13	95y	92y	98y	1.07y	…	…	…	…	198
56z	55z	56z	1.02z	33z	34z	32z	0.94z	45	45	45	1.00	47z	47z	47z	1.00z	32z	29z	35z	1.21z	199
54z	69z	39z	0.57z	*20z*	*31z*	*10z*	*0.31z*	28	40	16	0.40	*40z*	*54z*	*27z*	*0.51z*	…	…	…	…	200
22z	*24z*	*20z*	*0.84z*	*10z*	*12z*	*8z*	*0.68z*	*10*	*12*	*8*	*0.66*	*18z*	*20z*	*16z*	*0.81z*	*16*	*17*	*15*	*0.91*	201
…	…	…	…	…	…	…	…	*6*	*7*	*5*	*0.82*	…	…	…	…	…	…	…	…	202
47z	50z	44z	0.87z	*18z*	*21z*	*16z*	*0.73z*	20	*23*	*18*	*0.77*	*30z*	*33z*	*27z*	*0.82z*	*28z*	*31z*	*25z*	*0.80z*	203
58	59	58	0.99	31	33	28	0.87	43	46	40	0.88	40	41	38	0.93	37	38	36	0.96	204
Weighted average																Weighted average				
78	80	76	0.95	53	54	51	0.95	60	62	57	0.92	66	67	64	0.95	58	59	57	0.96	I
89	89	88	0.99	88	91	86	0.94	90	90	91	1.01	89	90	87	0.97	82	83	81	0.98	II
103	104	103	0.99	99	99	99	1.00	100	100	100	1.00	101	101	101	1.00	91	90	91	1.01	III
75	77	72	0.94	46	48	45	0.93	52	55	49	0.89	60	62	58	0.94	53	54	51	0.95	IV
81	85	77	0.90	54	55	53	0.97	60	63	57	0.89	68	70	65	0.92	59	61	57	0.94	V
89	90	89	0.98	85	88	83	0.94	87	88	87	0.98	88	89	86	0.96	81	82	80	0.97	VI
95	96	93	0.97	84	87	81	0.93	83	84	82	0.98	91	93	90	0.96	83	85	82	0.97	VII
92	92	92	1.00	58	58	59	1.03	65	66	64	0.96	75	75	76	1.01	69	69	70	1.01	VIII
92	92	92	1.00	57	57	58	1.03	64	65	63	0.96	75	74	75	1.01	69	69	70	1.02	IX
89	91	88	0.97	139	143	135	0.94	111	111	111	0.99	107	109	104	0.96	66	66	65	0.99	X
102	100	104	1.04	74	70	79	1.12	80	78	83	1.07	89	86	93	1.07	70	68	73	1.07	XI
72	71	72	1.02	43	42	44	1.05	53	53	54	1.03	57	56	57	1.03	40	39	42	1.07	XII
103	101	105	1.05	76	71	80	1.13	81	78	84	1.07	91	87	94	1.07	71	69	74	1.07	XIII
103	104	103	0.99	98	98	98	1.00	100	101	100	0.99	101	101	101	1.00	91	90	91	1.01	XIV
66	70	62	0.89	39	43	34	0.80	45	51	38	0.75	51	55	46	0.85	45	48	41	0.86	XV
38	43	34	0.79	24	27	21	0.80	24	26	21	0.82	32	35	28	0.80	25	27	23	0.83	XVI

7. Enrolment ratios were not calculated due to lack of United Nations population data by age.
8. Data include French overseas departments and territories (DOM-TOM).
Data in italic are UIS estimates.
Data in bold are for the school year ending in 2006 for transition rates, and the school year ending in 2007 for enrolment and enrolment ratios.

(z) Data are for the school year ending in 2005.
(y) Data are for the school year ending in 2004.
(x) Data are for the school year ending in 2003.
(*) National estimate.

Table 9A
Participation in tertiary education

Country or territory	ENROLMENT IN TERTIARY EDUCATION											
	Total students enrolled (000)				Gross enrolment ratio (GER) (%)							
	School year ending in				School year ending in							
	1999		2006		1999				2006			
	Total (000)	% F	Total (000)	% F	Total	Male	Female	GPI (F/M)	Total	Male	Female	GPI (F/M)
Arab States												
Algeria	456	…	818	55	14	…	…	…	22	19	24	1.26
Bahrain	11	60	18	68	22	16	28	1.76	32	19	47	2.46
Djibouti	0.2	51	2	40	0.3	0.3	0.3	1.05	2	3	2	0.68
Egypt	2 447	…	2 594[z]	…	37	…	…	…	35[z]	…	…	…
Iraq	272	34	425[z]	36[z]	11	15	8	0.54	16[z]	20[z]	12[z]	0.59[z]
Jordan	…	…	220	52	…	…	…	…	39	37	41	1.11
Kuwait	32	68	38	65	23	14	33	2.40	18	11	26	2.32
Lebanon	113	50	173	53	33	33	33	1.00	48	45	51	1.16
Libyan Arab Jamahiriya	308	49	…	…	50	51	50	0.98	…	…	…	…
Mauritania	13	…	10	26	5	…	…	…	4	5	2	0.36
Morocco	273	42	385	45	9	11	8	0.71	12	13	11	0.81
Oman	…	…	68	50	…	…	…	…	25	25	26	1.04
Palestinian A. T.	66	46	169	54	25	26	23	0.89	48	44	53	1.22
Qatar	9	72	10	68	23	11	41	3.82	19	10	33	3.41
Saudi Arabia	350	57	615	59	20	16	24	1.50	29	23	35	1.50
Sudan	201	47	…	…	6	6	6	0.92	…	…	…	…
Syrian Arab Republic	…	…	…	…	…	…	…	…	…	…	…	…
Tunisia	157	48	325	58	17	17	17	0.97	31	26	37	1.42
United Arab Emirates	40	67	…	…	18	10	29	2.97	…	…	…	…
Yemen	164	21	209	26	10	16	4	0.28	9	14	5	0.37
Central and Eastern Europe												
Albania	39	60	53[y]	62[y]	15	12	17	1.43	19[y]	15[y]	23[y]	1.60[y]
Belarus	387	56	544	57	51	44	58	1.30	66	56	76	1.37
Bosnia and Herzegovina	…	…	…	…	…	…	…	…	…	…	…	…
Bulgaria	270	59	243	53	45	36	55	1.54	46	41	50	1.21
Croatia	96	53	137	54	31	28	33	1.16	44	40	49	1.23
Czech Republic	231	50	338	54	26	26	27	1.03	50	45	55	1.22
Estonia	49	58	68	62	50	42	59	1.40	65	49	82	1.67
Hungary	279	54	439	58	33	30	37	1.24	69	56	82	1.47
Latvia	82	62	131	63	50	38	63	1.65	74	53	95	1.80
Lithuania	107	60	199	60	44	35	53	1.53	76	60	93	1.56
Montenegro	…	…	…	…	…	…	…	…	…	…	…	…
Poland	1 399	57	2 146	57	45	38	52	1.38	66	55	77	1.40
Republic of Moldova[2,3]	104	56	144	57	33	29	37	1.29	39	33	46	1.38
Romania	408	51	835	55	22	21	23	1.09	52	46	59	1.30
Russian Federation	…	…	9 167	57	…	…	…	…	72	61	83	1.36
Serbia	…	…	…	…	…	…	…	…	…	…	…	…
Slovakia	123	52	198	58	26	25	28	1.11	45	38	53	1.42
Slovenia	79	56	115	58	53	45	61	1.36	83	68	99	1.46
TFYR Macedonia	35	55	49[z]	57[z]	22	19	24	1.28	30[z]	25[z]	35[z]	1.38[z]
Turkey	1 465	40	2 343	42	22	25	17	0.68	35	39	30	0.75
Ukraine	1 737	53	2 740	54*	47	44	50	1.15	73	65*	81*	1.23*
Central Asia												
Armenia	61	54	99	55	24	22	25	1.11	32	29	34	1.18
Azerbaijan	108	39	132	47	15	19	12	0.64	15	15	14	0.94
Georgia	130	52	145	52	36	35	37	1.07	38	36	41	1.13
Kazakhstan	324	53	**773**	**58**	24	23	26	1.15	**51**	**42**	**61**	**1.44**
Kyrgyzstan	131	51	233	56	29	28	30	1.04	43	38	48	1.27
Mongolia	65	65	138	61	26	18	34	1.88	47	37	58	1.57
Tajikistan	76	25	133	27	14	20	7	0.35	19	27	10	0.37
Turkmenistan	…	…	…	…	…	…	…	…	…	…	…	…
Uzbekistan	296	45	**289**	**41**	13	14	12	0.82	**10**	**11**	**8**	**0.71**
East Asia and the Pacific												
Australia	846	54	1 040	55	65	59	72	1.22	73	64	82	1.28
Brunei Darussalam	3.7	66	5	66	12	8	16	1.98	15	10	20	1.99
Cambodia	…	…	76	33	…	…	…	…	5	6	3	0.50
China	6 366	…	23 361	47	6	…	…	…	22	22	21	0.98
Cook Islands	.	.	.	.	.	.	.	.	.	.	.	.

DISTRIBUTION OF STUDENTS BY ISCED LEVEL (%)						FOREIGN STUDENTS				
Total students			Percentage of females at each level							
School year ending in			School year ending in			School year ending in				
2006			2006			1999		2006		
Level 5A	Level 5B	Level 6	Level 5A	Level 5B	Level 6	Total (000)	% F	Total (000)	% F	Country or territory
										Arab States
82	13	5	58	36	45	…	…	6	…	Algeria
92	8	0	70	51	–	…	…	0.7	49	Bahrain
68	32	.	37	46	.	–	–	–	–	Djibouti
…	…	…	…	…	…	…	…	…	…	Egypt
78[z]	*17[z]*	*5[z]*	*39[z]*	*22[z]*	*35[z]*	…	…	4[y]	19[y]	Iraq
87	12	1	51	61	31	…	…	22	28	Jordan
97	.	3	66	.	51	…	…	…	…	Kuwait
84	15	1	54	49	38	16	…	17	54	Lebanon
…	…	…	…	…	…	…	…	…	…	Libyan Arab Jamahiriya
97	3	.	26	12	.	…	…	*0.2[y]*	…	Mauritania
75	19	6	46	47	33	4	16	6	26	Morocco
80	20	1	51	46	25	…	…	0.2	…	Oman
90	10	.	54	47	.	3	29	–	–	Palestinian A. T.
97[z]	*3[z]*	1[z]	…	…	…	…	…	2[z]	61[z]	Qatar
84	*14*	*2*	*65*	*21*	*40*	6	25	13[z]	33[z]	Saudi Arabia
…	…	…	…	…	…	…	…	…	…	Sudan
…	…	…	…	…	…	…	…	…	…	Syrian Arab Republic
…	…	…	…	…	…	3[j]	…	2[y]	…	Tunisia
…	…	…	…	…	…	…	…	…	…	United Arab Emirates
…	…	…	…	…	…	…	…	…	…	Yemen
										Central and Eastern Europe
99[y]	1[y]	./.[1,y]	62[y]	73[y]	./.[1,y]	0.8	27	0.5[y]	25[y]	Albania
71	28	1	58	54	54	3	…	4	…	Belarus
…	…	…	…	…	…	…	…	…	…	Bosnia and Herzegovina
88	10	2	54	54	50	8	42	9	41	Bulgaria
66	33	1	55	52	47	0.5[j]	…	3	…	Croatia
84	9	7	53	68	38	5	*41*	21	51	Czech Republic
63	34	3	62	62	53	0.8	58	1	56	Estonia
92	6	2	58	66	47	9[j]	54	14	48	Hungary
85	14	1	64	60	60	2[j]	…	2[z]	…	Latvia
70	29	1	60	59	57	0.5	22	0.9[z]	48[z]	Lithuania
…	…	…	…	…	…	…	…	…	…	Montenegro
97	1	2	57	80	49	6[j]	48	11	52	Poland
89	10	1	58	56	63	2	…	2	35	Republic of Moldova[2,3]
94	3	3	56	58	48	13	40	9	…	Romania
77	21	2	58	53	43	…	…	77	…	Russian Federation
…	…	…	…	…	…	…	…	…	…	Serbia
93	1	5	58	67	43	…	…	2	46	Slovakia
54	45	1	62	54	46	0.7	40	1	54	Slovenia
94[z]	6[z]	–[z]	57[z]	50[z]	–[z]	0.3	43	0.3[z]	49[z]	TFYR Macedonia
69	29	1	43	41	39	18[v]	28	19	32	Turkey
80	18	1	55*	52*	54*	18	…	27	…	Ukraine
										Central Asia
98	.	2	55	.	37	…	…	4	42	Armenia
99	.	1	48	.	27	2	35	3	20	Azerbaijan
99	.	1	52	.	63	0.3	…	0.1	…	Georgia
99	.	**1**	**58**	.	**66**	8	…	**12**	…	Kazakhstan
99	.	1	56	.	60	1	*51*	27	62	Kyrgyzstan
95	3	1	61	66	58	0.3	50	1	50	Mongolia
99	.	1	27	.	36	5	*25*	1	31	Tajikistan
…	…	…	…	…	…	…	…	…	…	Turkmenistan
99	.	**1**	**41**	.	**47**	…	…	0.1	…	Uzbekistan
										East Asia and the Pacific
81	15	4	55	53	50	117	49	207[z]	46[z]	Australia
62	38	0	69	62	19	0.1	53	0.2	54	Brunei Darussalam
100	.	–	33	.	–	0.02	25	0.1	10	Cambodia
…	46	…	…	49	…	…	…	36	45	China
.	.	.	.	.	.	.	.	.	.	Cook Islands

Table 9A (continued)

Country or territory	ENROLMENT IN TERTIARY EDUCATION											
	Total students enrolled (000)				Gross enrolment ratio (GER) (%)							
	School year ending in				School year ending in							
	1999		2006		1999				2006			
	Total (000)	% F	Total (000)	% F	Total	Male	Female	GPI (F/M)	Total	Male	Female	GPI (F/M)
DPR Korea	…	…	…	…	…	…	…	…	…	…	…	…
Fiji	…	…	*13z*	*53z*	…	…	…	…	*15z*	*14z*	*17z*	*1.20z*
Indonesia	…	…	3 657	…	…	…	…	…	17	…	…	…
Japan	3 941	45	4 085	46	45	49	41	0.85	57	61	54	0.88
Kiribati	.	.	.	.	.	.	.	.	.	.	.	.
Lao PDR	12	32	57	40	2	3	2	0.49	9	11	7	0.68
Macao, China	7	46	23	46	28	32	24	0.76	57	64	51	0.81
Malaysia	473	50	697z	56z	23	23	23	1.02	29z	25z	32z	1.29z
Marshall Islands	…	…	…	…	…	…	…	…	…	…	…	…
Micronesia	2	…	…	…	14	…	…	…	…	…	…	…
Myanmar	*335*	*61*	…	…	*7*	*6*	*9*	*1.61*	…	…	…	…
Nauru	.	.	.	.	.	.	.	.	.	.	.	.
New Zealand	167	59	238	59	64	52	77	1.46	80	64	96	1.51
Niue	.	.	.	.	.	.	.	.	.	.	.	.
Palau	…	…	…	…	…	…	…	…	…	…	…	…
Papua New Guinea	*10*	*35*	…	…	*2*	*3*	*1*	*0.55*	…	…	…	…
Philippines	2 209	55	2 484	54	29	25	32	1.26	28	25	32	1.24
Republic of Korea	2 636	35	**3 204**	**37**	66	83	47	0.57	**93**	**111**	**72**	**0.65**
Samoa	1.9	47	…	…	11	11	12	1.04	…	…	…	…
Singapore	…	…	…	…	…	…	…	…	…	…	…	…
Solomon Islands	.	…	.	.	.	.	.	.	.	.	.	.
Thailand	1 814	53	2 339	51	33	31	36	1.16	46	44	47	1.07
Timor-Leste	…	…	…	…	…	…	…	…	…	…	…	…
Tokelau	.	.	.	.	.	.	.	.	.	.	.	.
Tonga	0.4	55	*0.7y*	*60y*	3	3	4	1.29	*6y*	*5y*	*8y*	*1.68y*
Tuvalu	.	…	.	.	.	.	.	.	.	.	.	.
Vanuatu	*0.6*	…	*1y*	*36y*	*4*	…	…	…	*5y*	*6y*	*4y*	*0.59y*
Viet Nam	810	43	1 355z	41z	11	12	9	0.76	…	…	…	…
Latin America and the Caribbean												
Anguilla	.	.	0.05	83	.	.	.	.	*5*	*2*	*8*	4.86
Antigua and Barbuda	.	.	.y	.y	.	.	.	.	.y	.y	.y	.y
Argentina	1 601	62	2 083z	59z	49	37	60	1.63	64z	52z	76z	1.45z
Aruba	1.4	54	2	60	27	25	29	1.19	32	25	39	1.56
Bahamas	…	…	…	…	…	…	…	…	…	…	…	…
Barbados	7	69	…	…	33	20	45	2.28	…	…	…	…
Belize	…	…	0.7y	70y	…	…	…	…	3y	2y	4y	2.43y
Bermuda	…	…	**0.9**	**71**	…	…	…	…	…	…	…	…
Bolivia	253	…	*346y*	…	33	…	…	…	*41y*	…	…	…
Brazil	2 457	…	4 572z	56z	14	13	16	1.26	25z	22z	29z	1.30z
British Virgin Islands[2]	0.9	70	*1z*	*69z*	60	36	86	2.40	*75z*	*46z*	*106z*	*2.28z*
Cayman Islands[4]	*0.4*	*74*	0.6	72	…	…	…	…	…	…	…	…
Chile	451	47	661	49	38	39	36	0.91	47	47	46	1.00
Colombia	878	52	1 315	51	22	21	23	1.11	31	30	32	1.09
Costa Rica	59	53	*111z*	*54z*	16	15	17	1.17	*25z*	*23z*	*28z*	1.26z
Cuba	153	53	682	61	21	19	22	1.19	88	67	110	1.65
Dominica	.	.	.z	.z	.	.	.	.	.z	.z	.z	.z
Dominican Republic	…	…	*294y*	*61y*	…	…	…	…	*35y*	*27y*	*42y*	*1.59y*
Ecuador	…	…	…	…	…	…	…	…	…	…	…	…
El Salvador	118	55	125	55	18	16	20	1.24	21	19	23	1.21
Grenada	.	.	.z	.z	.	.	.	.	.z	.z	.z	.z
Guatemala	…	…	112*	46*	…	…	…	…	9*	10*	8*	0.82
Guyana	…	…	7	69	…	…	…	…	12	7	16	2.17
Haiti	…	…	…	…	…	…	…	…	…	…	…	…
Honduras	*85*	*56*	*123y*	*59y*	*14*	*13*	*16*	*1.24*	*17y*	*14y*	*20y*	*1.41y*
Jamaica	…	…	…	…	…	…	…	…	…	…	…	…
Mexico	1 838	…	2 447	50	18	19	17	0.91	26	27	25	0.93
Montserrat	.	.	.	.	…	…	…	…	.	.	.	.
Netherlands Antilles	2	53	…	…	19	18	20	1.11	…	…	…	…
Nicaragua	…	…	…	…	…	…	…	…	…	…	…	…
Panama	109	61	131	61	41	31	50	1.59	45	35	56	1.61
Paraguay	66	57	*156z*	*52z*	13	11	15	1.38	*26z*	*24z*	*27z*	*1.13z*
Peru	…	…	*952*	*51*	…	…	…	…	*35*	*34*	*36*	*1.06*

DISTRIBUTION OF STUDENTS BY ISCED LEVEL (%)						FOREIGN STUDENTS				
Total students			Percentage of females at each level							
School year ending in			School year ending in			School year ending in				
2006			2006			1999		2006		
Level 5A	Level 5B	Level 6	Level 5A	Level 5B	Level 6	Total (000)	% F	Total (000)	% F	**Country or territory**
...	...	...	...	...	...	...	...	...	...	DPR Korea
86[z]	*12*[z]	*1*[z]	*52*[z]	*63*[z]	*43*[z]	...	...	4[y]	*53*[y]	Fiji
78	...	...	*47*	...	...	0.3	...	0.4[y]	...	Indonesia
74	24	2	41	61	30	57	43	130	49	Japan
.	.	.	.	.	.	.	.	.[y]	.[y]	Kiribati
47	53	.	40	40	.	0.1	14	0.2	28	Lao PDR
85	13	2	44	62	25	...	...	12	34	Macao, China
59[z]	40[z]	1[z]	59[z]	52[z]	38[z]	4	...	40[z]	...	Malaysia
...	...	...	...	...	...	...	...	...	...	Marshall Islands
...	...	...	...	...	...	...	...	...	...	Micronesia
...	...	...	...	...	...	...	...	...	...	Myanmar
.	.	.	.	.	.	.	.	.[y]	.[y]	Nauru
71	27	2	59	59	51	7	51	41[z]	50[z]	New Zealand
.	.	.	.	.	.	.	.	.[y]	.[y]	Niue
...	...	...	...	...	...	...	...	...	...	Palau
...	...	...	...	...	...	*0.3*	*32*	...	...	Papua New Guinea
89	10	0	55	53	61	4	...	5[z]	...	Philippines
62	**37**	**1**	**37**	**38**	**34**	3	38	**22**	**47**	Republic of Korea
...	...	...	...	...	...	0.1	39	...	...	Samoa
...	...	...	...	...	...	...	...	...	...	Singapore
.	.	.	.	.	.	.	.	...	...	Solomon Islands
83	17	0	52	48	54	2[j]	55	...	...	Thailand
...	...	...	...	...	...	...	...	...	...	Timor-Leste
.	.	.	.	.	.	.	.	.[z]	.[z]	Tokelau
30[y]	*42*[y]	*28*[y]	*34*[y]	*95*[y]	*36*[y]	...	...	...	...	Tonga
.	.	.	.	.	.	.	.	.	.	Tuvalu
...	...	...	...	...	...	...	...	...	...	Vanuatu
67[z]	30[z]	3[z]	47[z]	29[z]	28[z]	0.5	15	2[z]	21[z]	Viet Nam
										Latin America and the Caribbean
72	28	.	82	85	.	.	.	–	–	Anguilla
.[y]	.[y]	.[y]	.[y]	.[y]	.[y]	.	.	...	...	Antigua and Barbuda
74[z]	26[z]	0[z]	55[z]	69[z]	56[z]	...	...	...	...	Argentina
31	69	.	74	54	.	...	...	0.2	59	Aruba
...	...	...	...	...	...	...	...	...	...	Bahamas
...	...	...	...	...	...	...	...	...	...	Barbados
100[y]	.[y]	.[y]	70[y]	.[y]	.[y]	...	...	–[y]	–[y]	Belize
.	**100**	.	.	**71**	.	...	...	...	...	Bermuda
...	...	...	...	...	...	...	...	...	...	Bolivia
93[z]	5[z]	3[z]	57[z]	36[z]	55[z]	...	...	1[y]	...	Brazil
67[z]	*33*[z]	.[z]	*75*[z]	*56*[z]	.[z]	.	.	.[y]	.[y]	British Virgin Islands [2]
11	89	.	90	69	.	...	...	0.2	71	Cayman Islands [4]
66	33	0	52	44	41	2	...	2[z]	...	Chile
72	27	0	53	47	34	...	...	...	...	Colombia
...	...	...	...	...	...	...	...	1	...	Costa Rica
99	.	1	61	.	43	...	...	15	...	Cuba
.[z]	.[z]	.[z]	.[z]	.[z]	.[z]	.	.	.[y]	.[y]	Dominica
91[y]	*8*[y]	*1*[y]	*65*[y]	*25*[y]	*40*[y]	...	...	...	...	Dominican Republic
...	...	...	...	...	...	...	...	...	...	Ecuador
87	13	0	55	53	10	...	...	0.6	47	El Salvador
.[z]	.[z]	.[z]	.[z]	.[z]	.[z]	...	...	.[y]	.[y]	Grenada
96*	4*	.*	45*	70*	.*	...	...	...	...	Guatemala
43	57	.	67	70	.	...	...	0.04[z]	51[z]	Guyana
...	...	...	...	...	...	...	...	...	...	Haiti
91[y]	*9*[y]	*0*[y]	*58*[y]	*67*[y]	*33*[y]	...	...	...	...	Honduras
...	...	...	...	...	...	0.6	...	...	...	Jamaica
96	3	1	51	43	41	2	...	...	...	Mexico
.	.	.	.	.	.	.	.	.	.	Montserrat
...	...	...	...	...	...	...	...	...	...	Netherlands Antilles
...	...	...	...	...	...	...	...	...	...	Nicaragua
91	9	0	61	58	63	...	...	...	...	Panama
90[z]	*10*[z]	...	51[z]	66[z]	...	...	...	...	...	Paraguay
60	*40*	...	47	57	...	...	...	...	...	Peru

Table 9A (continued)

Country or territory	ENROLMENT IN TERTIARY EDUCATION											
	Total students enrolled (000)				Gross enrolment ratio (GER) (%)							
	School year ending in				School year ending in							
	1999		2006		1999				2006			
	Total (000)	% F	Total (000)	% F	Total	Male	Female	GPI (F/M)	Total	Male	Female	GPI (F/M)
Saint Kitts and Nevis	.	.	.z	.z	.	.	.	.	.z	.z	.z	.z
Saint Lucia	…	…	1.6	85	…	…	…	…	10	3	16	5.46
Saint Vincent/Grenad.	.	.	.z	.z	.	.	.	.	.z	.z	.z	.z
Suriname	…	…	…	…	…	…	…	…	…	…	…	…
Trinidad and Tobago	7.6	57	*17z*	*56z*	6	5	7	1.38	*11z*	*10z*	*13z*	*1.28z*
Turks and Caicos Islands	.	.	.z	.z	.	.	.	.	.z	.z	.z	.z
Uruguay	*91*	*63*	113	62	*34*	*25*	*44*	*1.76*	46	35	58	1.68
Venezuela, Bolivarian Rep. of	…	…	1 381*	…	…	…	…	…	52*	…	…	…
North America and Western Europe												
Andorra[2]	…	…	0.4	53	…	…	…	…	10	9	11	1.25
Austria	253	50	253	54	54	52	55	1.05	50	45	55	1.21
Belgium	352	53	394	55	57	53	61	1.15	63	56	70	1.25
Canada	1 221	56	*1 327y*	*56y*	60	52	69	1.34	*62y*	*53y*	*72y*	*1.36y*
Cyprus[2]	11	56	21	51	21	19	23	1.25	33	33	34	1.05
Denmark	190	56	229	57	56	48	64	1.33	80	67	93	1.39
Finland	263	54	309	54	82	74	91	1.23	93	84	103	1.22
France[5]	2 012	54	2 201	55	52	47	58	1.24	56	50	63	1.27
Germany	…	…	…	…	…	…	…	…	…	…	…	…
Greece	388	50	653	51	47	45	49	1.11	95	89	101	1.13
Iceland	8	62	16	64	40	30	50	1.69	73	51	96	1.87
Ireland	151	54	186	55	46	42	50	1.20	59	52	66	1.27
Israel	247	58	310	55	48	40	57	1.44	58	51	65	1.29
Italy	1 797	55	2 029	57	47	41	53	1.28	67	56	78	1.38
Luxembourg	2.7	52	3	52	11	10	11	1.10	10	10	11	1.12
Malta	6	51	9z	56z	20	18	21	1.13	32z	27z	36z	1.35z
Monaco	.	.	.	.	.	.	.	.	.	.	.	.
Netherlands	470	49	580	51	49	49	50	1.01	60	58	62	1.08
Norway	187	57	215	60	66	55	77	1.40	78	61	94	1.54
Portugal	357	56	367	55	45	39	51	1.30	55	48	61	1.28
San Marino	…	.	…	…	…	…	…	…	…	…	…	…
Spain	1 787	53	1 789	54	57	52	62	1.18	67	61	74	1.23
Sweden	335	58	423	60	64	53	75	1.41	79	62	96	1.55
Switzerland	156	42	205	47	36	41	30	0.73	46	48	43	0.90
United Kingdom	2 081	53	2 336	57	60	55	64	1.16	59	50	69	1.40
United States	13 769	*56*	17 487	57	73	*63*	*83*	*1.31*	82	68	96	1.41
South and West Asia												
Afghanistan	…	…	28y	20y	…	…	…	…	1y	2y	1y	0.28y
Bangladesh	709	32	912z	33z	5	7	4	0.51	6z	8z	4z	0.53z
Bhutan	*1.5*	*36*	4	33	*3*	*3*	*2*	*0.58*	6	7	4	0.59
India	…	…	12 853	40	…	…	…	…	12	14	10	0.72
Iran, Islamic Republic of	1 308	43	2 399	52	19	21	17	0.80	27	25	28	1.11
Maldives	.	.	–	–	.	.	.	.	–	–	–	–
Nepal	…	…	147y	28y	…	…	…	…	6y	8y	3y	0.40y
Pakistan	…	…	820	45	…	…	…	…	5	5	4	0.85
Sri Lanka	…	…	…	…	…	…	…	…	…	…	…	…
Sub-Saharan Africa												
Angola	8	39	48z	…	0.6	0.7	0.5	0.63	3z	…	…	…
Benin	19	*20*	43	…	3	*5*	*1*	*0.25*	5	…	…	…
Botswana	5.5	44	11z	50z	3	3	3	0.79	5z	5z	5z	1.00z
Burkina Faso	10	23	30	31	0.9	1.4	0.4	0.30	2	3	1	0.46
Burundi	5	30	17	31	1.0	1.4	0.6	0.41	2	3	1	0.43
Cameroon	67	…	120	42	5	…	…	…	7	8	6	0.72
Cape Verde	0.7	…	4.6	52	2	…	…	…	8	8	8	1.09
Central African Republic	6	16	4	22	2	3	0.6	0.18	1	2	0.5	0.28
Chad	…	…	*10z*	*13z*	…	…	…	…	*1z*	*2z*	*0.3z*	*0.14z*
Comoros	0.6	43	*1.8y*	*43y*	1.0	1.1	0.9	0.75	*2y*	*3y*	*2y*	*0.77y*
Congo	11	21	…	…	4	6	1	0.26	…	…	…	…
Côte d'Ivoire	97	26	…	…	6	9	3	0.36	…	…	…	…
D. R. Congo	*60*	…	…	…	*1*	…	…	…	…	…	…	…

DISTRIBUTION OF STUDENTS BY ISCED LEVEL (%)						FOREIGN STUDENTS				
Total students			Percentage of females at each level			School year ending in				
School year ending in 2006			School year ending in 2006			1999		2006		
Level 5A	Level 5B	Level 6	Level 5A	Level 5B	Level 6	Total (000)	% F	Total (000)	% F	Country or territory
.z	.z	.z	.z	.z	.z	.	.	.y	.y	Saint Kitts and Nevis
75	25	.	91	64	.	…	…	0.1	33	Saint Lucia
.z	.z	.z	.z	.z	.z	.	.	.z	.z	Saint Vincent/Grenad.
…	…	…	…	…	…	…	…	…	…	Suriname
51z	34z	…	60z	48z	…	1	46	1.0y	55y	Trinidad and Tobago
.z	.z	.z	.z	.z	.z	.	.	.y	.y	Turks and Caicos Islands
…	…	0	…	…	40	0.9	…	…	…	Uruguay
64*	36*	…	…	…	…	…	…	2y	…	Venezuela, Bolivarian Rep. of
										North America and Western Europe
40	60	.	59	49	.	…	…	…	…	Andorra 2
84	9	7	53	68	46	30	49	39	53	Austria
46	52	2	51	58	41	36	48	25	…	Belgium
73y	24y	3y	58y	52y	46y	115	…	…	…	Canada
22	76	1	73	44	49	2	39	5	24	Cyprus 2
85	12	2	59	46	46	12	61	12	59	Denmark
93	0	7	54	16	52	5	41	12	43	Finland
72	24	3	56	56	46	131±	…	248	49	France 5
…	…	…	48	61	…	178	46	260z	50z	Germany
59	37	3	53	48	44	…	…	17	…	Greece
97	2	1	65	39	58	0.2	72	0.7	64	Iceland
68	29	3	58	49	48	7eo	51	13	51	Ireland
79	18	3	55	55	52	…	…	…	…	Israel
97	1	2	57	60	52	23	50	49	58	Italy
68	…	…	…	…	…	0.7j	…	1	…	Luxembourg
85z	14z	1z	56z	57z	30z	0.3j	53	0.6z	57z	Malta
.	.	.	.	.	.	.	.	.y	.y	Monaco
99	.	1	51	.	41	14	46	27	56	Netherlands
97	1	2	60	57	46	9	53	14	58	Norway
93	1	6	55	57	56	…	…	17	49	Portugal
…	…	…	…	…	…	…	…	…	…	San Marino
82	13	4	54	51	51	33	51	18	54	Spain
90	5	5	61	50	49	24	45	21	48	Sweden
74	17	8	49	42	40	25	44	28	47	Switzerland
74	22	4	55	66	45	233	47	330	48	United Kingdom
77	21	2	57	60	52	452	42	585	…	United States
										South and West Asia
…	…	…	…	…	…	…	…	…	…	Afghanistan
91z	9z	0z	35z	20z	28z	…	…	1z	…	Bangladesh
100	–	.	33	–	.	…	…	–	–	Bhutan
100	–	0	40	–	40	…	…	8y	…	India
69	30	1	56	43	28	…	…	3	28	Iran, Islamic Republic of
–	–	–	–	–	–	.	.	…	…	Maldives
99y	.y	1y	28y	.y	23y	…	…	…	…	Nepal
94	5	1	45	45	27	…	…	…	…	Pakistan
…	…	…	…	…	…	…	…	…	…	Sri Lanka
										Sub-Saharan Africa
100z	.z	–z	…	…	…	…	…	…	…	Angola
…	…	…	…	…	…	…	…	…	…	Benin
94z	6z	–z	52z	16z	–z	…	…	0.7z	…	Botswana
70	30	–	33	27	–	…	…	0.9z	38z	Burkina Faso
35	64	0	39	26	19	0.1	…	…	…	Burundi
87	12	2	…	…	…	…	…	2	…	Cameroon
100	.	–	52	.	–	…	…	…	…	Cape Verde
77	23	.	20	30	.	…	…	0.5	9	Central African Republic
…	…	…	…	…	…	…	…	…	…	Chad
68y	32y	.y	39y	52y	.y	.	.	…	…	Comoros
…	…	…	…	…	…	…	…	0.1y	…	Congo
…	…	…	…	…	…	…	…	…	…	Côte d'Ivoire
…	…	…	…	…	…	…	…	…	…	D. R. Congo

Table 9A (continued)

Country or territory	ENROLMENT IN TERTIARY EDUCATION											
	Total students enrolled (000)				Gross enrolment ratio (GER) (%)							
	School year ending in				School year ending in							
	1999		2006		1999				2006			
	Total (000)	% F	Total (000)	% F	Total	Male	Female	GPI (F/M)	Total	Male	Female	GPI (F/M)
Equatorial Guinea	…	…	…	…	…	…	…	…	…	…	…	…
Eritrea	4.0	14	5[y]	13[y]	1.0	1.7	0.3	0.16	1[y]	2[y]	0.3[y]	0.15[y]
Ethiopia	52	19	**210**	**25**	0.9	1.4	0.3	0.23	**3**	**4**	**1**	**0.34**
Gabon	7.5	36	…	…	7	9	5	0.54	…	…	…	…
Gambia	1.2	23	1.5[y]	19[y]	1	2	0.5	0.30	1[y]	2[y]	0.4[y]	0.24[y]
Ghana	…	…	**140**	**34**	…	…	…	…	**6**	**8**	**4**	**0.54**
Guinea	…	…	43	21	…	…	…	…	5	8	2	0.28
Guinea-Bissau	*0.5*	*16*	…	…	*0.4*	*0.7*	*0.1*	*0.18*	…	…	…	…
Kenya	…	…	103[y]	38[y]	…	…	…	…	3[y]	3[y]	2[y]	0.60[y]
Lesotho	4	64	9	55	2	2	3	1.65	4	3	4	1.19
Liberia	21	19	…	…	8	13	3	0.24	…	…	…	…
Madagascar	31	*46*	50	47	2	*2*	*2*	*0.84*	3	3	3	0.87
Malawi	3	28	5[y]	35[y]	0.3	0.4	0.2	0.37	0.4[y]	0.5[y]	0.3[y]	0.55[y]
Mali	19	32	33[z]	*31*[z]	2	3	1	0.45	3[z]	*4*[z]	*2*[z]	*0.45*[z]
Mauritius	7.6	46	17	53	7	7	6	0.88	17	16	18	1.15
Mozambique	10	…	28[z]	33[z]	0.6	…	…	…	1[z]	2[z]	1[z]	0.49[z]
Namibia	…	…	13	47	…	…	…	…	6	6	5	0.88
Niger	…	…	11	27	…	…	…	…	1	2	0.5	0.29
Nigeria	699	43	1 392[z]	41[z]	6	7	5	0.76	10[z]	12[z]	8[z]	0.69[z]
Rwanda	6	…	*26*[z]	*39*[z]	1	…	…	…	*3*[z]	*3*[z]	*2*[z]	*0.62*[z]
Sao Tome and Principe	.	.	.	.	.	.	.	.	.	.	.	.
Senegal	29	…	59[*,z]	…	3	…	…	…	6[*,z]	…	…	…
Seychelles	.	.	.	.	.	.	.	.	.	.	.	.
Sierra Leone	…	…	…	…	…	…	…	…	…	…	…	…
Somalia	…	…	…	…	…	…	…	…	…	…	…	…
South Africa	633	54	741	55	14	13	15	1.16	15	14	17	1.24
Swaziland	5	48	6	50	5	5	4	0.86	4	4	4	0.98
Togo	15	17	…	…	3	5	1	0.21	…	…	…	…
Uganda	41	*35*	88[y]	38[y]	2	*2*	*1*	*0.53*	3[y]	4[y]	3[y]	0.62[y]
United Republic of Tanzania	19	21	**55**	**32**	0.6	1.0	0.3	0.27	**1**	**2**	**1**	**0.48**
Zambia	*23*	*32*	…	…	*2*	*3*	*1*	*0.46*	…	…	…	…
Zimbabwe	*43*	…	…	…	*3*	…	…	…	…	…	…	…

	Sum	%F	Sum	%F	Weighted average				Weighted average			
World	92 272	48	143 723	50	18	18	17	0.96	25	24	25	1.06
Countries in transition	8 684	54	14 432	56	39	35	42	1.20	57	50	64	1.29
Developed countries	36 358	53	43 961	55	55	51	60	1.19	67	58	75	1.28
Developing countries	47 229	43	85 331	47	11	12	10	0.78	17	18	17	0.93
Arab States	5 165	42	7 038	49	19	22	16	0.74	22	22	22	1.00
Central and Eastern Europe	12 421	53	20 125	55	38	35	41	1.18	60	53	66	1.25
Central Asia	1 223	48	1 974	52	18	19	18	0.93	25	24	26	1.10
East Asia and the Pacific	22 674	42	43 621	47	14	16	12	0.75	25	25	24	0.94
East Asia	21 635	41	42 313	47	13	15	11	0.73	24	25	23	0.94
Pacific	1 039	55	1 308	55	47	42	52	1.24	52	45	59	1.31
Latin America/Caribbean	10 664	53	16 247	54	21	20	23	1.12	31	29	34	1.16
Caribbean	81	57	107	63	6	5	6	1.30	6	5	8	1.69
Latin America	10 583	53	16 140	53	22	21	23	1.12	32	30	34	1.15
N. America/W. Europe	28 230	54	33 742	56	61	55	68	1.23	70	60	80	1.33
South and West Asia	9 758	37	17 253	41	7	9	6	0.64	11	12	9	0.76
Sub-Saharan Africa	2 136	40	3 723	40	4	4	3	0.67	5	6	4	0.67

1. Data are included in ISCED level 5A.
2. National population data were used to calculate enrolment ratios.
3. Enrolment and population data exclude Transnistria.
4. Enrolment ratios were not calculated due to lack of United Nations population data by age.
5. Data include French overseas departments and territories (DOM-TOM).

DISTRIBUTION OF STUDENTS BY ISCED LEVEL (%)						FOREIGN STUDENTS				
Total students			Percentage of females at each level							
School year ending in			School year ending in			School year ending in				
2006			2006			1999		2006		
Level 5A	Level 5B	Level 6	Level 5A	Level 5B	Level 6	Total (000)	% F	Total (000)	% F	**Country or territory**
...	...	...	...	...	...	...	...	...	...	Equatorial Guinea
77^{y}	23^{y}	.^{y}	12^{y}	16^{y}	.^{y}	0.1	16	...	...	Eritrea
100	**.**	**0**	**25**	**.**	**2**	...	...	...	...	Ethiopia
...	...	...	...	...	...	0.4	...	...	...	Gabon
100^{y}	.^{y}	.^{y}	19^{y}	.^{y}	.^{y}	...	...	–^{y}	–^{y}	Gambia
73	**26**	**0**	**35**	**33**	**26**	...	...	**2**	**52**	Ghana
...	...	...	...	...	...	...	...	0.9	26	Guinea
...	...	...	...	...	...	...	...	...	...	Guinea-Bissau
66^{y}	34^{y}	–^{y}	35^{y}	43^{y}	–^{y}	...	...	...	...	Kenya
79	21	.	51	70	.	1	46	0.1	...	Lesotho
...	...	...	...	...	...	...	...	...	...	Liberia
76	19	5	47	45	42	1	...	1	23	Madagascar
100^{y}	.^{y}	.^{y}	35^{y}	.^{y}	.^{y}	...	...	...	...	Malawi
95^{z}	*5^{z}*	.^{z}	*31^{z}*	*51^{z}*	.^{z}	1	...	...	...	Mali
56	43	1	53	54	38	...	...	0.1^{y}	53^{y}	Mauritius
100^{z}	.^{z}	.^{z}	33^{z}	.^{z}	.^{z}	...	...	...	...	Mozambique
61	39	0	43	52	45	...	...	0.2	...	Namibia
80	20	–	22	45	–	...	...	*0.2^{z}*	*25^{z}*	Niger
52^{z}	47^{z}	1^{z}	36^{z}	46^{z}	24^{z}	...	...	...	...	Nigeria
65^{z}	*35^{z}*	.^{z}	*41^{z}*	*35^{z}*	.^{z}	0.1	...	...	...	Rwanda
.	.	.	.	.	.	.	.	.^{z}	.^{z}	Sao Tome and Principe
...	...	...	...	...	...	1	...	...	...	Senegal
.	.	.	.	.	.	.	.	.	.	Seychelles
...	...	...	...	...	...	...	...	...	...	Sierra Leone
...	...	...	...	...	...	...	...	...	...	Somalia
62	36	1	55	56	42	...	...	54	48	South Africa
99	.	1	50	.	50	0.1	...	0.1	...	Swaziland
...	...	...	...	...	...	0.5	33	...	...	Togo
62^{y}	36^{y}	2^{y}	41^{y}	35^{y}	37^{y}	...	...	...	...	Uganda
...	...	...	...	...	...	...	...	0.3^{y}	20^{y}	United Republic of Tanzania
...	...	...	...	...	...	...	...	...	...	Zambia
...	...	...	...	...	...	...	...	...	...	Zimbabwe

Median			Median			Sum	%F	Sum	%F	
78	...	...	52	39	22	...	...	...	...	World
99	.	1	55	.	37	...	...	...	...	Countries in transition
82	13	4	56	57	30	...	...	...	...	Developed countries
75	22	3	45	57	13	...	...	...	...	Developing countries
84	15	1	53	47	31	...	...	...	...	Arab States
84	12	4	58	55	58	...	...	...	...	Central and Eastern Europe
99	–	1	54	–	53	...	...	...	...	Central Asia
62	37	1	40	51	15	...	...	...	...	East Asia and the Pacific
74	24	2	47	29	28	...	...	...	...	East Asia
.	.	.	.	.	.	...	...	...	...	Pacific
66	33	0	55	53	10	...	...	...	...	Latin America/Caribbean
.	.	.	.	.	.	...	...	...	...	Caribbean
90	10	0	55	53	10	...	...	...	...	Latin America
78	19	3	55	61	45	...	...	...	...	N. America/W. Europe
94	5	1	35	20	28	...	...	...	...	South and West Asia
76	21	2	36	23	12	...	...	...	...	Sub-Saharan Africa

(eo) Full-time only.
(j) Data refer to ISCED levels 5A and 6 only.
(v) Data do not include ISCED level 6.

± Partial data.
Data in italic are UIS estimates.
Data in bold are for the school year ending in 2007.

(z) Data are for the school year ending in 2005.
(y) Data are for the school year ending in 2004.
(*) National estimate.

Table 9B. **Tertiary education: distribution of students by field of study and female share in each field, school year ending in 2006**

Country or territory	Total enrolment		PERCENTAGE DISTRIBUTION BY FIELD OF STUDY								
	(000)	% F	Education	Humanities and arts	Social sciences, business and law	Science	Engineering, manufacturing and construction	Agriculture	Health and welfare	Services	Not known or unspecified
Arab States											
Algeria	818	55	1.7	17.5	38.9	8.3	9.9	2.2	6.6	1.0	14.0
Bahrain	18	68	2.1	8.8	51.8	9.2	8.6	.	7.0	3.0	9.6
Djibouti	1.9	40	.	23.3	43.9	22.6	5.9	.	.	4.3	–
Egypt	*2594*[z]	…	…	…	…	…	…	…	…	…	…
Iraq	*425*[z]	*36*[z]	20.1[y]	10.7[y]	21.3[y]	5.2[y]	19.0[y]	4.0[y]	8.1[y]	11.8[y]	–[y]
Jordan	220	52	14.2	15.6	26.0	9.8	12.5	1.7	12.8	0.4	7.1
Kuwait	38	65	27.8	…	…	…	…	.	…	.	4.5
Lebanon	173	53	3.4	16.2	44.5	12.8	11.6	0.3	9.5	1.0	0.6
Libyan Arab Jamahiriya	…	…	…	…	…	…	…	…	…	…	…
Mauritania	10	26	3.6[z]	13.0[z]	19.8[z]	6.2[z]	–[z]	–[z]	–[z]	–[z]	57.4[z]
Morocco	385	45	1.3	17.6	53.0	16.2	5.6	0.6	4.4	1.1	0.2
Oman	68	50	*29.7*[z]	*8.3*[z]	*20.5*[z]	*10.7*[z]	*9.3*[z]	*0.2*[z]	*3.1*[z]	–[z]	*18.2*[z]
Palestinian A.T.	169	54	34.5	10.7	31.7	9.6	6.6	0.6	6.1	0.2	0.0
Qatar	*10*	*68*	12.6[y]	6.4[y]	48.3[y]	14.5[y]	4.7[y]	0.2[y]	3.9[y]	–[y]	9.3[y]
Saudi Arabia	*615*	*59*	23.8[z]	32.4[z]	14.6[z]	14.1[z]	3.3[z]	0.4[z]	5.2[z]	0.1[z]	6.1[z]
Sudan	…	…	…	…	…	…	…	…	…	…	…
Syrian Arab Republic	…	…	…	…	…	…	…	…	…	…	…
Tunisia	325	58	1.0	20.0	17.5	14.8	10.7	2.7	7.7	12.9	12.6
United Arab Emirates	…	…	…	…	…	…	…	…	…	…	…
Yemen	*209*	*26*	…	…	…	…	…	…	…	…	…
Central and Eastern Europe											
Albania	53[y]	62[y]	16.6[y]	13.0[y]	40.2[y]	4.2[y]	8.0[y]	7.6[y]	8.0[y]	1.7[y]	–[y]
Belarus	544	57	12.8	5.5	38.6	2.4	25.4	7.9	4.0	3.3	–
Bosnia and Herzegovina	…	…	…	…	…	…	…	…	…	…	…
Bulgaria	243	53	7.0	7.9	42.5	5.0	21.0	2.5	6.4	7.6	…
Croatia	137	54	4.3	9.9	40.5	7.4	16.3	3.8	7.5	10.2	…
Czech Republic	338	54	14.7[z]	9.5[z]	28.1[z]	9.5[z]	19.7[z]	3.8[z]	9.8[z]	4.5[z]	0.5[z]
Estonia	68	62	7.6	11.6	39.0	10.0	12.3	2.5	8.5	8.5	…
Hungary	439	58	13.4	8.0	41.6	5.2	12.4	2.9	8.2	8.3	…
Latvia	131	63	12.2	7.0	54.2	5.2	10.0	1.2	5.2	4.9	…
Lithuania	199	60	12.3	7.0	41.8	6.1	18.0	2.3	9.2	3.4	…
Montenegro	…	…	…	…	…	…	…	…	…	…	…
Poland	2 146	57	14.5	9.2	40.9	9.7	12.6	2.2	5.7	5.4	…
Republic of Moldova	144	57	…	…	…	…	…	…	…	…	…
Romania	835	55	2.3	10.5	50.0	4.7	18.2	2.9	5.7	3.0	2.8
Russian Federation	9 167	57	…	…	…	…	…	…	…	…	…
Serbia	…	…	…	…	…	…	…	…	…	…	…
Slovakia	198	58	16.5	6.0	28.3	9.0	16.4	2.8	15.2	5.8	–
Slovenia	115	58	8.8	7.5	43.5	5.4	15.6	3.1	7.4	8.7	…
TFYR Macedonia	49[z]	57[z]	13.3[z]	10.9[z]	32.8[z]	7.4[z]	18.1[z]	4.0[z]	9.0[z]	4.5[z]	–[z]
Turkey	2 343	42	12.3	6.9	47.4	7.5	13.3	3.5	5.6	3.5	–
Ukraine	2 740	54*	8.9	5.1	42.2	4.1	22.1	4.6	5.3	6.0	1.7
Central Asia											
Armenia	99	55	19.6	4.6	27.1	0.2	6.2	3.2	6.9	3.4	28.8
Azerbaijan	132	47	…	…	…	…	…	…	…	…	…
Georgia	145	52	2.8	39.1	30.3	4.6	7.4	3.2	9.4	3.2	0.0
Kazakhstan	**773**	**58**	…	…	…	…	…	…	…	…	…
Kyrgyzstan	233	56	23.9	12.8	34.5	8.1	9.7	1.1	3.3	6.7	0.0
Mongolia	138	61	9.3	11.8	39.4	6.5	16.3	2.9	7.8	5.0	1.0
Tajikistan	133	27	7.0	31.2	26.4	13.3	14.4	2.7	3.5	1.5	–
Turkmenistan	…	…	…	…	…	…	…	…	…	…	…
Uzbekistan	**289**	**41**	32.8	12.0	21.0	5.8	15.3	3.8	7.0	2.2	–
East Asia and the Pacific											
Australia	1 040	55	9.0	11.7	37.9	10.6	10.4	1.4	15.4	3.5	…
Brunei Darussalam	5	66	51.8	9.3	13.9	6.8	6.6	.	6.8	.	4.9
Cambodia	76	33	14.6	0.9	52.6	12.2	3.6	3.4	6.0	–	6.7
China	23 361	47	…	…	…	…	…	…	…	…	100.0
Cook Islands	.	.	.	.	.	.	.	.	.	.	.
DPR Korea	…	…	…	…	…	…	…	…	…	…	…

PERCENTAGE FEMALE IN EACH FIELD									
Education	Humanities and arts	Social sciences, business and law	Science	Engineering, manufacturing and construction	Agriculture	Health and welfare	Services	Not known or unspecified	Country or territory
									Arab States
70	74	58	57	31	47	59	26	38	Algeria
51	83	70	75	21	.	85	69	72	Bahrain
.	48	47	22	21	.	.	49	–	Djibouti
...	...	...	...	...	...	...	...	...	Egypt
50[y]	38[y]	33[y]	51[y]	19[y]	30[y]	41[y]	37[y]	–[y]	Iraq
84	66	40	41	27	55	47	54	65	Jordan
80	...	...	...	...	.	...	.	64	Kuwait
95	66	52	49	21	48	66	50	60	Lebanon
...	...	...	...	...	...	...	...	...	Libyan Arab Jamahiriya
17[z]	24[z]	26[z]	21[z]	–[z]	–[z]	–[z]	–[z]	25[z]	Mauritania
41	47	47	40	27	32	66	47	1	Morocco
69[z]	*60*[z]	*41*[z]	*53*[z]	*20*[z]	*25*[z]	*67*[z]	–[z]	*40*[z]	Oman
70	66	40	46	28	18	57	31	40	Palestinian A.T.
89[y]	73[y]	65[y]	75[y]	16[y]	–[y]	100[y]	–[y]	94[y]	Qatar
71[z]	64[z]	43[z]	60[z]	15[z]	0[z]	44[z]	27[z]	45[z]	Saudi Arabia
...	...	...	...	...	...	...	...	...	Sudan
...	...	...	...	...	...	...	...	...	Syrian Arab Republic
...	...	...	...	...	...	...	...	...	Tunisia
...	...	...	...	...	...	...	...	...	United Arab Emirates
...	...	...	...	...	...	...	...	...	Yemen
									Central and Eastern Europe
82[y]	71[y]	60[y]	74[y]	26[y]	39[y]	74[y]	21[y]	–[y]	Albania
78	75	70	51	29	30	81	42	–	Belarus
...	...	...	...	...	...	...	...	...	Bosnia and Herzegovina
68	63	60	49	32	43	67	47	...	Bulgaria
92	71	64	42	25	45	74	26	...	Croatia
74[z]	63[z]	60[z]	36[z]	21[z]	54[z]	75[z]	38[z]	11[z]	Czech Republic
90	75	65	39	27	53	89	51	...	Estonia
73	66	65	31	19	45	76	59	...	Hungary
85	77	67	30	21	49	86	52	...	Latvia
78	73	68	34	25	47	84	43	...	Lithuania
...	...	...	...	...	...	...	...	...	Montenegro
73	70	62	37	27	53	73	49	...	Poland
...	...	...	...	...	...	...	...	...	Republic of Moldova
75	69	62	54	30	37	67	46	47	Romania
...	...	...	...	...	...	...	...	...	Russian Federation
...	...	...	...	...	...	...	...	...	Serbia
75	59	63	36	29	40	81	44	–	Slovakia
80	73	66	33	24	55	80	47	...	Slovenia
74[z]	68[z]	60[z]	55[z]	32[z]	34[z]	74[z]	38[z]	–[z]	TFYR Macedonia
53	46	45	40	19	44	61	31	–	Turkey
...	...	...	...	...	...	...	...	...	Ukraine
									Central Asia
94	55	48	27	30	30	36	13	52	Armenia
...	...	...	...	...	...	...	...	...	Azerbaijan
55	62	44	57	28	33	75	13	22	Georgia
...	...	...	...	...	...	...	...	...	Kazakhstan
83	60	53	48	29	21	50	20	–	Kyrgyzstan
77	71	64	47	39	61	80	36	53	Mongolia
...	...	...	...	...	...	...	...	...	Tajikistan
...	...	...	...	...	...	...	...	...	Turkmenistan
57	63	24	56	12	15	46	30	–	Uzbekistan
									East Asia and the Pacific
74	63	54	35	21	53	76	52[z]	67[z]	Australia
71	59	63	58	37	.	78	.	75	Brunei Darussalam
39	29	40	14	6	24	35	–	10	Cambodia
...	...	...	...	...	...	...	...	47	China
.	.	.	.	.	.	.	.	.	Cook Islands
...	...	...	...	...	...	...	...	...	DPR Korea

Table 9B (continued)

Country or territory	Total enrolment		PERCENTAGE DISTRIBUTION BY FIELD OF STUDY								
	(000)	% F	Education	Humanities and arts	Social sciences, business and law	Science	Engineering, manufacturing and construction	Agriculture	Health and welfare	Services	Not known or unspecified
Fiji	*13*[z]	*53*[z]	…	…	…	…	…	…	…	…	…
Indonesia	3 657	…	…	…	…	…	…	…	…	…	…
Japan	4 085	46	7.2	15.8	29.3	2.9	16.1	2.1	12.2	5.7	8.7
Kiribati	.	.	.	.	.	.	.	.	.	.	.
Lao PDR	57	40	21.6	14.2	15.3	1.9	7.7	6.8	2.0	2.8	27.7
Macao, China	23	46	4.3	6.9	69.3	3.7	2.2	–	5.4	8.3	–
Malaysia	697[z]	56[z]	13.2[z]	9.8[z]	27.1[z]	19.4[z]	18.4[z]	2.9[z]	6.7[z]	2.5[z]	–[z]
Marshall Islands	…	…	…	…	…	…	…	…	…	…	…
Micronesia	…	…	…	…	…	…	…	…	…	…	…
Myanmar	…	…	…	…	…	…	…	…	…	…	…
Nauru	.	.	.	.	.	.	.	.	.	.	.
New Zealand	238	59	10.2	17.5	34.8	13.9	6.6	1.0	12.6	2.7	0.7
Niue	.	.	.	.	.	.	.	.	.	.	.
Palau	…	…	…	…	…	…	…	…	…	…	…
Papua New Guinea	…	…	…	…	…	…	…	…	…	…	…
Philippines	2 484	54	16.9[y]	3.2[y]	28.0[y]	11.8[y]	15.5[y]	3.2[y]	13.2[y]	0.7[y]	7.3[y]
Republic of Korea	**3 204**	**37**	**6.3**	**18.3**	**21.6**	**8.6**	**28.9**	**1.3**	**8.8**	**6.2**	–
Samoa	…	…	…	…	…	…	…	…	…	…	…
Singapore	…	…	…	…	…	…	…	…	…	…	…
Solomon Islands	.	.	.	.	.	.	.	.	.	.	.
Thailand	2 339	51	…	…	…	…	…	…	…	…	100.0
Timor-Leste	…	…	…	…	…	…	…	…	…	…	…
Tokelau	.	.	.	.	.	.	.	.	.	.	.
Tonga	*0.7*[y]	*60*[y]	…	…	…	…	…	…	…	…	…
Tuvalu	.	.	.	.	.	.	.	.	.	.	.
Vanuatu	*1.0*[y]	*36*[y]	…	…	…	…	…	…	…	…	…
Viet Nam	1 355[z]	41[z]	…	…	…	…	…	…	…	…	…
Latin America and the Caribbean											
Anguilla	0.05	83	40.4	.	59.6	.	.	.	.	.	.
Antigua and Barbuda	.[y]	.[y]	…	…	…	…	…	…	…	…	…
Argentina	2 083[z]	59[z]	10.7[z]	12.5[z]	39.6[z]	10.0[z]	8.1[z]	3.5[z]	12.6[z]	2.9[z]	0.2[z]
Aruba	2.1	60	17.9	.	44.2	.	19.5	.	18.5	.	.
Bahamas	…	…	…	…	…	…	…	…	…	…	…
Barbados	…	…	…	…	…	…	…	…	…	…	…
Belize	0.7[y]	70[y]	25.3[y]	3.7[y]	29.4[y]	9.1[y]	0.1[y]	–[y]	8.9[y]	–[y]	23.4[y]
Bermuda	**0.9**	**71**	**4.1**	**9.3**	**33.0**	**12.5**	**6.0**	–	**7.7**	**3.3**	**24.3**
Bolivia	*346*[y]	…	…	…	…	…	…	…	…	…	…
Brazil	4 572[z]	56[z]	19.8[z]	3.4[z]	40.5[z]	8.3[z]	7.5[z]	2.1[z]	13.6[z]	2.1[z]	2.7[z]
British Virgin Islands	*1.2*[z]	*69*[z]	…	…	…	…	…	…	…	…	…
Cayman Islands	0.6	72	.	.	81.0	16.4	.	.	.	.	2.6
Chile	661	49	13.8	7.7	25.7	8.0	18.5	4.5	14.8	7.1	…
Colombia	1 315	51	8.8	4.2	42.8	3.3	32.3	–	8.5	–	–
Costa Rica	*111*[z]	*54*[z]	26.5[y]	4.0[y]	25.7[y]	8.5[y]	14.9[y]	3.0[y]	11.1[y]	3.3[y]	3.0[y]
Cuba	682	61	16.6	1.3	24.0	2.5	2.1	1.0	17.3	6.7	28.5
Dominica	.[z]	.[z]	…	…	…	…	…	…	…	…	…
Dominican Republic	*294*[y]	*61*[y]	…	…	…	…	…	…	…	…	…
Ecuador	…	…	…	…	…	…	…	…	…	…	…
El Salvador	125	55	8.3	4.4	47.1	11.2	11.9	1.1	16.0	0.0	–
Grenada	.[z]	.[z]	.[z]	.[z]	.[z]	.[z]	.[z]	.[z]	.[z]	.[z]	.[z]
Guatemala	112*	46*	13.1*	0.7*	46.0*	2.3*	18.6*	2.9*	7.0*	–*	9.4*
Guyana	7	69	30.5	2.9	41.7	9.9	6.5	2.2	4.9	0.8	0.7
Haiti	…	…	…	…	…	…	…	…	…	…	…
Honduras	*123*[y]	*59*[y]	…	…	…	…	…	…	…	…	…
Jamaica	…	…	…	…	…	…	…	…	…	…	…
Mexico	2 447	50	10.6	4.3	39.6	12.6	18.6	2.5	8.4	2.8	…
Montserrat	.	.	.	.	.	.	.	.	.	.	.
Netherlands Antilles	…	…	…	…	…	…	…	…	…	…	…
Nicaragua	…	…	…	…	…	…	…	…	…	…	…
Panama	131	61	14.9	9.8	39.6	8.0	11.2	1.1	8.0	6.9	0.5
Paraguay	*156*[z]	*52*[z]	…	…	…	…	…	…	…	…	…
Peru	*952*	*51*	*10.3*	…	*5.9*	*6.7*	*0.6*	*1.2*	*9.0*	…	*66.3*
Saint Kitts and Nevis	.[z]	.[z]	…	…	…	…	…	…	…	…	…
Saint Lucia	1.6	85	15.5	0.3	19.1	0.1	.	.	.	.	37.8

PERCENTAGE FEMALE IN EACH FIELD									
Education	Humanities and arts	Social sciences, business and law	Science	Engineering, manufacturing and construction	Agriculture	Health and welfare	Services	Not known or unspecified	Country or territory
...	...	...	...	...	...	...	...	...	Fiji
...	...	...	...	...	...	...	...	...	Indonesia
70	67	35	25	12	39	60	80	49	Japan
.	.	.	.	.	.	.	.	.	Kiribati
49	41	38	40	11	24	57	22	46	Lao PDR
63	74	40	14	14	–	74	66	–	Macao, China
61[z]	55[z]	60[z]	56[z]	39[z]	79[z]	66[z]	70[z]	–[z]	Malaysia
...	...	...	...	...	...	...	...	...	Marshall Islands
...	...	...	...	...	...	...	...	...	Micronesia
...	...	...	...	...	...	...	...	...	Myanmar
.	.	.	.	.	.	.	.	.	Nauru
82	64	56	43	25	58	80	48[z]	63	New Zealand
.	.	.	.	.	.	.	.	.	Niue
...	...	...	...	...	...	...	...	...	Palau
...	...	...	...	...	...	...	...	...	Papua New Guinea
...	...	...	...	...	...	...	...	...	Philippines
70	**56**	**36**	**29**	**16**	**32**	**63**	**31**	–	Republic of Korea
...	...	...	...	...	...	...	...	...	Samoa
...	...	...	...	...	...	...	...	...	Singapore
.	.	.	.	.	.	.	.	.	Solomon Islands
...	...	...	...	...	...	...	...	51	Thailand
...	...	...	...	...	...	...	...	...	Timor-Leste
.	.	.	.	.	.	.	.	.	Tokelau
...	...	...	...	...	...	...	...	...	Tonga
.	.	.	.	.	.	.	.	.	Tuvalu
...	...	...	...	...	...	...	...	...	Vanuatu
...	...	...	...	...	...	...	...	...	Viet Nam
									Latin America and the Caribbean
89	.	79	.	.	.	.	.	.	Anguilla
...	...	...	...	...	...	...	...	...	Antigua and Barbuda
81[z]	65[z]	58[z]	47[z]	31[z]	42[z]	68[z]	57[z]	54[z]	Argentina
79	.	63	.	12	.	87	.	.	Aruba
...	...	...	...	...	...	...	...	...	Bahamas
...	...	...	...	...	...	...	...	...	Barbados
...	...	...	...	–[y]	–[y]	...	–[y]	...	Belize
89	**72**	**78**	**59**	**4**	–	**93**	**62**	**75**	Bermuda
...	...	...	...	...	...	...	...	...	Bolivia
74[z]	60[z]	52[z]	34[z]	26[z]	40[z]	71[z]	66[z]	54[z]	Brazil
...	...	...	...	...	...	...	...	...	British Virgin Islands
.	.	74	60	.	.	.	.	80	Cayman Islands
69	50	52	32	24	47	69	46	...	Chile
66	45	57	49	37	–	71	–	–	Colombia
73[y]	57[y]	57[y]	35[y]	29[y]	41[y]	55[y]	50[y]	61[y]	Costa Rica
71	65	66	45	25	31	78	30	52	Cuba
...	...	...	...	...	...	...	...	...	Dominica
...	...	...	...	...	...	...	...	...	Dominican Republic
...	...	...	...	...	...	...	...	...	Ecuador
75	54	57	37	25	36	73	59	–	El Salvador
.[z]	.[z]	.[z]	.[z]	.[z]	.[z]	.[z]	.[z]	.[z]	Grenada
56*	68*	51*	61*	25*	17*	59*	–	43*	Guatemala
85	75	71	44	16	36	73	68	73	Guyana
...	...	...	...	...	...	...	...	...	Haiti
...	...	...	...	...	...	...	...	...	Honduras
...	...	...	...	...	...	...	...	...	Jamaica
71	56	57	40	25	37	64	59	...	Mexico
.	.	.	.	.	.	.	.	.	Montserrat
...	...	...	...	...	...	...	...	...	Netherlands Antilles
...	...	...	...	...	...	...	...	...	Nicaragua
77	60	65	46	31	24	76	58	58	Panama
...	...	...	...	...	...	...	...	...	Paraguay
63	...	55	42	19	30	80	...	46	Peru
...	...	...	...	...	...	...	...	...	Saint Kitts and Nevis
84	100	75	–	.	.	.	.	67	Saint Lucia

Table 9B (continued)

Country or territory	Total enrolment (000)	Total enrolment % F	Education	Humanities and arts	Social sciences, business and law	Science	Engineering, manufacturing and construction	Agriculture	Health and welfare	Services	Not known or unspecified
			PERCENTAGE DISTRIBUTION BY FIELD OF STUDY								
Saint Vincent/Grenad.	.[z]	.[z]	.[z]	.[z]	.[z]	.[z]	.[z]	.[z]	.[z]	.[z]	.[z]
Suriname	…	…	…	…	…	…	…	…	…	…	…
Trinidad and Tobago	*17*[z]	*56*[z]	4.9[y]	8.4[y]	26.7[y]	13.7[y]	22.6[y]	3.6[y]	9.9[y]	4.2[y]	5.9[y]
Turks and Caicos Islands	.[z]	.[z]	.[y]	.[y]	.[y]	.[y]	.[y]	.[y]	.[y]	.[y]	.[y]
Uruguay	113	62	20.2[z]	4.5[z]	40.0[z]	5.3[z]	11.1[z]	2.9[z]	11.5[z]	0.6[z]	3.6[z]
Venezuela, B. R.	1 381*	…	…	…	…	…	…	…	1.7*	…	98.3*
North America and Western Europe											
Andorra	0.4	53	–	6.7	55.1	24.7	–	–	13.5	–	–
Austria	253	54	12.8	14.9	35.0	12.4	11.8	1.6	9.4	2.1	…
Belgium	394	55	10.2	10.5	27.5	6.9	10.6	2.5	22.1	1.5	…
Canada	*1 327*[y]	*56*[y]	…	…	…	…	…	…	…	…	…
Cyprus	21	51	9.4	8.5	47.4	12.7	6.1	0.1	6.6	9.2	…
Denmark	229	57	11.4	15.0	29.5	8.0	10.1	1.5	22.2	2.3	–
Finland	309	54	5.3	14.5	22.5	11.4	25.9	2.2	13.3	4.8	…
France[1]	2 201	55	3.1	16.5	34.5	12.3	11.5	1.0	14.2	3.5	…
Germany	…	…	7.3	15.6	27.4	15.2	15.7	1.4	14.7	2.5	…
Greece	653	51	6.5[z]	11.6[z]	31.9[z]	15.7[z]	16.5[z]	5.9[z]	6.9[z]	5.0[z]	–[z]
Iceland	16	64	17.4	14.8	38.0	8.0	7.3	0.5	12.4	1.5	…
Ireland	186	55	5.3	15.7	23.1	11.6	10.4	1.2	12.8	4.5	…
Israel	310	55	13.8	11.1	38.7	9.6	17.9	0.6	7.2	.	…
Italy	2 029	57	6.4	15.5	36.5	7.9	15.6	2.3	12.5	2.6	…
Luxembourg	3	52	22.7	8.2	45.2	8.4	15.0	…	0.4	…	…
Malta	*9*[z]	*56*[z]	15.7[z]	13.5[z]	41.6[z]	5.9[z]	7.8[z]	0.8[z]	14.5[z]	0.2[z]	…
Monaco	.	.	.[y]	.[y]	.[y]	.[y]	.[y]	.[y]	.[y]	.[y]	.[y]
Netherlands	580	51	14.6	8.3	37.5	6.6	8.2	1.2	16.2	5.8	1.8
Norway	215	60	14.7[z]	11.5[z]	32.2[z]	9.4[z]	6.9[z]	0.9[z]	19.0[z]	3.8[z]	1.6[z]
Portugal	367	55	7.2	8.6	31.5	7.3	21.9	1.9	16.0	5.6	…
San Marino	…	…	…	…	…	…	…	…	…	…	…
Spain	1 789	54	9.2	10.4	31.9	11.4	17.8	3.4	9.9	5.6	0.5
Sweden	423	60	15.2	12.6	26.2	9.7	16.3	0.9	17.2	1.8	0.2
Switzerland	205	47	10.3	13.0	37.1	10.7	13.4	1.2	10.2	3.8	…
United Kingdom	2 336	57	8.9	17.0	27.0	13.7	8.2	0.9	18.8	0.7	4.9
United States	17 487	57	9.4	10.6	27.3	8.9	6.7	0.6	13.9	5.1	…
South and West Asia											
Afghanistan	28[y]	20[y]	…	…	…	…	…	…	…	…	…
Bangladesh	912[z]	33[z]	2.7[z]	24.2[z]	33.9[z]	15.5[z]	5.0[z]	0.9[z]	2.4[z]	0.2[z]	15.1[z]
Bhutan	4	33	38.3	17.4	14.8	3.2	14.4	6.1	5.8	–	–
India	12 853	40	1.3[z]	36.0[z]	13.5[z]	14.3[z]	5.9[z]	–[z]	2.2[z]	–[z]	26.8[z]
Iran, Islamic Republic of	2 399	52	6.5	12.3	26.9	11.0	30.3	5.3	5.6	2.0	–
Maldives	–	–	…	…	…	…	…	…	…	…	…
Nepal	147[y]	28[y]	…	…	…	…	…	…	…	…	…
Pakistan	820	45	4.6	11.5	18.3	4.6	5.6	1.5	7.5	.	46.3
Sri Lanka	…	…	…	…	…	…	…	…	…	…	…
Sub-Saharan Africa											
Angola	48[z]	…	…	…	…	…	…	…	…	…	…
Benin	43	…	…	…	…	…	…	…	…	…	…
Botswana	11[z]	50[z]	21.4[z]	25.7[z]	24.8[z]	11.8[z]	5.5[z]	–[z]	–[z]	0.3[z]	10.6[z]
Burkina Faso	30	31	1.4	11.5	53.2	19.9	5.6	–	8.2	0.2	–
Burundi	17	31	…	…	…	…	…	…	…	…	…
Cameroon	120	42	0.9	7.7	64.5	19.7	4.9	0.6	1.3	0.4	0.1
Cape Verde	5	52	…	…	…	…	…	…	…	…	…
Central African Republic	4	22	…	…	…	…	…	…	…	…	…
Chad	*10*[z]	*13*[z]	…	…	…	…	…	…	…	…	…
Comoros	*2*[y]	*43*[y]	…	…	…	…	…	…	…	…	…
Congo	…	…	…	…	…	…	…	…	…	…	…
Côte d'Ivoire	…	…	…	…	…	…	…	…	…	…	…
D. R. Congo	…	…	…	…	…	…	…	…	…	…	…
Equatorial Guinea	…	…	…	…	…	…	…	…	…	…	…
Eritrea	5[y]	13[y]	21.9[y]	1.8[y]	23.7[y]	9.3[y]	27.9[y]	9.0[y]	6.5[y]	–[y]	–[y]
Ethiopia	**210**	**25**	**26.8**	**2.9**	**36.9**	**7.0**	**8.0**	**8.5**	**9.1**	**.**	**0.8**

PERCENTAGE FEMALE IN EACH FIELD									
Education	Humanities and arts	Social sciences, business and law	Science	Engineering, manufacturing and construction	Agriculture	Health and welfare	Services	Not known or unspecified	**Country or territory**
.[z]	.[z]	.[z]	.[z]	.[z]	.[z]	.[z]	.[z]	.[z]	Saint Vincent/Grenad.
...	...	...	...	...	...	...	...	...	Suriname
69[y]	78[y]	70[y]	51[y]	21[y]	55[y]	64[y]	66[y]	67[y]	Trinidad and Tobago
.[y]	.[y]	.[y]	.[y]	.[y]	.[y]	.[y]	.[y]	.[y]	Turks and Caicos Islands
78[z]	67[z]	63[z]	49[z]	36[z]	41[z]	72[z]	12[z]	62[z]	Uruguay
...	...	...	...	...	...	...	...	...	Venezuela, Bolivarian Rep. of
									North America and Western Europe
–	78	63	11	–	–	78	–	–	Andorra
75	66	55	34	21	61	67	51	...	Austria
73	56	53	32	24	51	72	45	...	Belgium
...	...	...	...	...	...	...	...	...	Canada
88	76	48	36	14	–	69	39	...	Cyprus
71	62	50	33	33	52	80	22	–	Denmark
81	71	63	40	19	51	84	70	...	Finland
75	69	61	36	23	41	71	40	...	France [1]
69	66	49	35	18	47	74	51	...	Germany
70[z]	73[z]	55[z]	39[z]	28[z]	44[z]	74[z]	44[z]	–[z]	Greece
83	66	59	38	32	43	87	82	...	Iceland
78	64	56	42	16	45	79	48	...	Ireland
83	62	56	40	27	56	76	.	...	Israel
87	72	57	50	28	45	66	48	...	Italy
...	...	...	...	...	...	...	...	...	Luxembourg
72[z]	57[z]	56[z]	35[z]	28[z]	31[z]	67[z]	33[z]	...	Malta
.[y]	.[y]	.[y]	.[y]	.[y]	.[y]	.[y]	.[y]	.[y]	Monaco
74	54	47	16	15	50	74	49	41	Netherlands
75[z]	62[z]	56[z]	32[z]	24[z]	57[z]	81[z]	49[z]	59[z]	Norway
82	61	59	49	26	56	77	49	...	Portugal
...	...	...	...	...	...	...	...	...	San Marino
78	61	59	34	28	54	76	57	45	Spain
76	62	61	43	28	60	81	59	74	Sweden
71	59	46	29	15	49	69	51	...	Switzerland
74	62	55	37	20	61	78	65	62	United Kingdom
79	58	56	39	16	50	80	53	...	United States
									South and West Asia
...	...	...	...	...	...	...	...	...	Afghanistan
36[z]	41[z]	33[z]	26[z]	15[z]	17[z]	38[z]	33[z]	36[z]	Bangladesh
36	37	33	32	20	20	45	–	–	Bhutan
44[z]	44[z]	36[z]	40[z]	24[z]	–[z]	35[z]	–[z]	38[z]	India
71	71	56	70	26	41	76	57	–	Iran, Islamic Republic of
...	...	...	...	...	...	...	...	...	Maldives
...	...	...	...	...	...	...	...	...	Nepal
65	43	22	21	15	16	47	.	58	Pakistan
...	...	...	...	...	...	...	...	...	Sri Lanka
									Sub-Saharan Africa
...	...	...	...	...	...	...	...	...	Angola
...	...	...	...	...	...	...	...	...	Benin
58[z]	62[z]	56[z]	9[z]	12[z]	–[z]	–[z]	87[z]	53[z]	Botswana
20	40	31	23	43	–	31	75	–	Burkina Faso
...	...	...	...	...	...	...	...	...	Burundi
...	...	...	...	...	...	...	...	...	Cameroon
...	...	...	...	...	...	...	...	...	Cape Verde
...	...	...	...	...	...	...	...	...	Central African Republic
...	...	...	...	...	...	...	...	...	Chad
...	...	...	...	...	...	...	...	...	Comoros
...	...	...	...	...	...	...	...	...	Congo
...	...	...	...	...	...	...	...	...	Côte d'Ivoire
...	...	...	...	...	...	...	...	...	D. R. Congo
...	...	...	...	...	...	...	...	...	Equatorial Guinea
9[y]	41[y]	16[y]	21[y]	10[y]	6[y]	20[y]	–[y]	–[y]	Eritrea
24	**32**	**31**	**23**	**15**	**15**	**26**	.	**26**	Ethiopia

Table 9B (continued)

Country or territory	Total enrolment (000)	Total enrolment % F	PERCENTAGE DISTRIBUTION BY FIELD OF STUDY: Education	Humanities and arts	Social sciences, business and law	Science	Engineering, manufacturing and construction	Agriculture	Health and welfare	Services	Not known or unspecified
Gabon	…	…	…	…	…	…	…	…	…	…	…
Gambia	2	19	3.6[y]	34.6[y]	18.8[y]	20.5[y]	.[y]	.[y]	15.1[y]	.[y]	7.4[y]
Ghana	**140**	**34**	11.4[y]	39.1[y]	12.0[y]	14.6[y]	11.6[y]	4.3[y]	3.7[y]	1.8[y]	1.5[y]
Guinea	43	21	4.3	11.1	32.0	19.4	3.9	10.9	7.8	1.1	9.5
Guinea-Bissau	…	…	…	…	…	…	…	…	…	…	…
Kenya	103[y]	38[y]	…	…	…	…	…	…	…	…	…
Lesotho	9	55	17.2	9.0	34.0	10.5	–	4.2	4.2	–	21.0
Liberia	…	…	…	…	…	…	…	…	…	…	…
Madagascar	50	47	2.9	11.2	57.7	12.1	6.0	2.7	7.1	0.1	0.3
Malawi	5[y]	35[y]	…	…	…	…	…	…	…	…	…
Mali	33[z]	*31[z]*	…	…	…	…	…	…	…	…	…
Mauritius	17	53	18.6	19.3	35.2	8.9	15.4	1.9	0.1	0.3	0.4
Mozambique	28[z]	33[z]	7.6[z]	11.1[z]	43.9[z]	13.9[z]	9.9[z]	5.2[z]	5.2[z]	2.7[z]	0.5[z]
Namibia	13	47	…	…	…	…	…	…	…	…	…
Niger	11	27	…	…	…	…	…	…	…	…	…
Nigeria	1 392[z]	41[z]	0.0[z]	0.0[z]	0.2[z]	0.2[z]	0.0[z]	0.0[z]	0.0[z]	0.0[z]	99.5[z]
Rwanda	*26[z]*	*39[z]*	…	…	…	…	…	…	…	…	…
Sao Tome and Principe	.	.	.[z]	.[z]	.[z]	.[z]	.[z]	.[z]	.[z]	.[z]	.[z]
Senegal	59[*,z]	…	…	…	…	…	…	…	…	…	…
Seychelles	.	.	.	.	.	.	.	.	.	.	.
Sierra Leone	…	…	…	…	…	…	…	…	…	…	…
Somalia	…	…	…	…	…	…	…	…	…	…	…
South Africa	741	55	13.3	4.9	52.9	10.4	9.5	1.8	5.9	1.2	0.0
Swaziland	6	50	10.7	21.1	45.5	5.7	3.1	6.1	7.0	0.8	.
Togo	…	…	…	…	…	…	…	…	…	…	…
Uganda	88[y]	38[y]	32.1[y]	5.3[y]	40.3[y]	3.3[y]	7.2[y]	1.6[y]	4.4[y]	3.7[y]	2.1[y]
United Republic of Tanzania	**55**	**32**	*12.9[z]*	*7.1[z]*	*20.2[z]*	*15.2[z]*	*9.0[z]*	*4.7[z]*	*6.6[z]*	*1.7[z]*	*22.4[z]*
Zambia	…	…	…	…	…	…	…	…	…	…	…
Zimbabwe	…	…	…	…	…	…	…	…	…	…	…

	Sum	% F	Median								
World	143 723	50	10	11	27	7	11	2	22	2	…
Countries in transition	14 432	56	13	6	39	2	25	8	4	3	–
Developed countries	43 961	55	9	11	27	9	7	1	14	5	…
Developing countries	85 331	47	10	…	6	7	1	1	9	…	66
Arab States	7 038	49	8	10	34	10	2	0.1	2	.	33
Central and Eastern Europe	20 125	55	12	7	45	7	16	3	7	3	–
Central Asia	1 974	52	14	8	33	3	11	3	7	4	15
East Asia and the Pacific	43 621	47	6	18	22	9	29	1	9	6	–
East Asia	42 313	47	14	5	40	16	11	3	6	1	3
Pacific	1 308	55	.	.	.	.	.	.	.	.	.
Latin America/Caribbean	16 247	54	12	7	43	6	13	3	10	1	5
Caribbean	107	63	4	9	30	13	14	2	9	4	15
Latin America	16 140	53	13	4	36	5	19	4	11	4	…
N. America/W. Europe	33 742	56	9	10	37	11	6	0	10	7	…
South and West Asia	17 253	41	5	12	18	5	6	2	8	.	46
Sub-Saharan Africa	3 723	40	…	…	…	…	…	…	…	…	…

1. Data include French overseas departments and territories (DOM-TOM).
Data in italic are UIS estimates.
Data in bold are for the school year ending in 2007.

(z) Data are for the school year ending in 2005.
(y) Data are for the school year ending in 2004.
(*) National estimate.

PERCENTAGE FEMALE IN EACH FIELD									
Education	Humanities and arts	Social sciences, business and law	Science	Engineering, manufacturing and construction	Agriculture	Health and welfare	Services	Not known or unspecified	**Country or territory**
...	...	...	...	...	...	...	...	...	Gabon
2^{y}	19^{y}	14^{y}	14^{y}	.^{y}	.^{y}	13^{y}	.^{y}	68^{y}	Gambia
36^{y}	37^{y}	42^{y}	27^{y}	8^{y}	20^{y}	37^{y}	22^{y}	33^{y}	Ghana
30	20	24	16	12	17	33	15	20	Guinea
...	...	...	...	...	...	...	...	...	Guinea-Bissau
...	...	...	...	...	...	...	...	...	Kenya
...	...	...	...	...	...	...	...	...	Lesotho
...	...	...	...	...	...	...	...	...	Liberia
40	59	50	34	18	37	51	43	61	Madagascar
...	...	...	...	...	...	...	...	...	Malawi
...	...	...	...	...	...	...	...	...	Mali
57	63	58	47	27	57	21	9	78	Mauritius
33^{z}	36^{z}	41^{z}	21^{z}	10^{z}	27^{z}	54^{z}	21^{z}	23^{z}	Mozambique
...	...	...	...	...	...	...	...	...	Namibia
...	...	...	...	...	...	...	...	...	Niger
49^{z}	38^{z}	31^{z}	4^{z}	11^{z}	23^{z}	33^{z}	29^{z}	41^{z}	Nigeria
...	...	...	...	...	...	...	...	...	Rwanda
.^{z}	.^{z}	.^{z}	.^{z}	.^{z}	.^{z}	.^{z}	.^{z}	.^{z}	Sao Tome and Principe
...	...	...	...	...	...	...	...	...	Senegal
.	.	.	.	.	.	.	.	.	Seychelles
...	...	...	...	...	...	...	...	...	Sierra Leone
...	...	...	...	...	...	...	...	...	Somalia
72	61	57	44	26	43	67	66	50	South Africa
53	63	49	36	9	18	65	62	.	Swaziland
...	...	...	...	...	...	...	...	...	Togo
39^{y}	41^{y}	41^{y}	24^{y}	19^{y}	22^{y}	40^{y}	53^{y}	55^{y}	Uganda
38^{z}	56^{z}	41^{z}	24^{z}	10^{z}	26^{z}	29^{z}	16^{z}	*32*^{z}	United Republic of Tanzania
...	...	...	...	...	...	...	...	...	Zambia
...	...	...	...	...	...	...	...	...	Zimbabwe

Median									
70	56	36	29	16	32	63	31	–	World
...	...	...	...	...	...	...	...	...	Countries in transition
75	66	59	43	27	47	74	48	53	Developed countries
55	66	50	49	17	17	62	31	22	Developing countries
70	74	58	57	31	47	59	26	38	Arab States
75	59	63	36	29	40	81	44	–	Central and Eastern Europe
77	71	64	47	39	61	80	36	53	Central Asia
...	...	...	...	...	...	...	...	...	East Asia and the Pacific
...	...	...	...	...	...	...	...	...	East Asia
.	.	.	.	.	.	.	.	.	Pacific
71	65	66	45	25	31	78	30	52	Latin America/Caribbean
69	78	70	51	21	55	64	66	67	Caribbean
72	61	61	40	27	36	67	40	57	Latin America
75	62	56	32	24	57	81	49	59	N. America/W. Europe
44	44	36	40	24	–	35	–	38	South and West Asia
...	...	...	...	...	...	...	...	...	Sub-Saharan Africa

Table 10A
Teaching staff in pre-primary and primary education

Country or territory	PRE-PRIMARY EDUCATION											
	Teaching staff				Trained teachers (%)[1]						Pupil/teacher ratio[2]	
	School year ending in				School year ending in						School year ending in	
	1999		2006		1999			2006			1999	2006
	Total (000)	% F	Total (000)	% F	Total	Male	Female	Total	Male	Female		
Arab States												
Algeria	1	93	7	69	…	…	…	…	…	…	28	24
Bahrain	0.7	100	1	100	18	–	18	58	100	58	21	16
Djibouti	0.01	100	*0.05*	*45*	…	…	…	100[z]	100[z]	100[z]	29	*16*
Egypt	*14*	*99*	**23**	**99**	…	…	…	…	…	…	*24*	**25**
Iraq	5	100	*6[z]*	*100[z]*	…	…	…	100[y]	.[y]	100[y]	15	*16[z]*
Jordan	3	100	*5*	*99*	…	…	…	…	…	…	22	*20*
Kuwait	4	100	5	100	100	100	100	100	100	100	15	12
Lebanon	11	95	10	99	…	…	…	9	9	9	13	16
Libyan Arab Jamahiriya	1	100	2	96	…	…	…	…	…	…	8	9
Mauritania	…	…	*0.3[z]*	*100[z]*	…	…	…	100[y]	.[y]	100[y]	…	*19[z]*
Morocco	40	40	40	57	…	…	…	100[z]	100[z]	100[z]	20	17
Oman	0.4	100	*0.5*	*100*	93	.	93	*100*	.	*100*	20	*18*
Palestinian A. T.	3	100	3	99	…	…	…	100	100	100	29	26
Qatar	*0.4*	*96*	0.9	99	…	…	…	36	67	35	*21*	18
Saudi Arabia	…	…	…	…	…	…	…	…	…	…	…	…
Sudan	*12*	*84*	17	95	…	…	…	60	60	60	*30*	29
Syrian Arab Republic	5	96	7	96	87	84	87	24	26	24	24	24
Tunisia	4	95	…	…	…	…	…	…	…	…	20	…
United Arab Emirates	3	100	5	100	59	71	59	50[z]	80[z]	50[z]	19	18
Yemen	0.8	93	1[z]	97[z]	…	…	…	…	…	…	17	15[z]
Central and Eastern Europe												
Albania	4	100	*4[y]*	*100[y]*	…	…	…	…	…	…	20	*21[y]*
Belarus	53	…	44	99	…	…	…	64	64	64	5	6
Bosnia and Herzegovina	…	…	…	…	…	…	…	…	…	…	…	…
Bulgaria	19	*100*	18	100	…	…	…	…	…	…	11	11
Croatia	6	100	6	99	76	86	76	…	…	…	13	14
Czech Republic	17	*100*	24	100	…	…	…	…	…	…	18	12
Estonia	7	100	6	100	…	…	…	…	…	…	8	8
Hungary	32	100	31	100	…	…	…	…	…	…	12	11
Latvia	7	99	6	100	…	…	…	…	…	…	9	10
Lithuania	13	99	11	100	…	…	…	…	…	…	7	8
Montenegro	…	…	…	…	…	…	…	…	…	…	…	…
Poland	*77*	…	49	98	…	…	…	…	…	…	*12*	17
Republic of Moldova	13	100	10	100	*92*	.	*92*	90	.	90	8	10
Romania	37	100	36	100	…	…	…	…	…	…	17	18
Russian Federation	642	…	628	100	…	…	…	…	…	…	7	7
Serbia	8	*98*	**10**	**98**	…	…	…	…	…	…	21	**17**
Slovakia	16	100	11	100	…	…	…	…	…	…	10	14
Slovenia	3	*99*	*2*	*100*	…	…	…	…	…	…	18	*18*
TFYR Macedonia	3	99	3[z]	99[z]	…	…	…	…	…	…	10	11[z]
Turkey	17	*99*	21	94	…	…	…	…	…	…	15	26
Ukraine	143	100	124	99	…	…	…	…	…	…	8	8
Central Asia												
Armenia	8	…	5	100	…	…	…	56[y]	20[y]	56[y]	7	9
Azerbaijan	12	100	11	100	78	.	78	90	100	90	9	10
Georgia	6	100	7	100	…	…	…	…	…	…	13	11
Kazakhstan	19	…	**31**	**99**	…	…	…	…	…	…	9	**11**
Kyrgyzstan	3	100	2	100	32	–	32	41	40	41	18	24
Mongolia	3	100	3	99	99	75	99	…	…	…	25	29
Tajikistan	5	100	5	100	…	…	…	82	.	82	11	13
Turkmenistan	…	…	…	…	…	…	…	…	…	…	…	…
Uzbekistan	66	96	**61**	**95**	…	…	…	**100**	**100**	**100**	9	**9**
East Asia and the Pacific												
Australia	…	…	…	…	…	…	…	…	…	…	…	…
Brunei Darussalam	0.6*	83*	0.6	95	…	…	…	69	93	67	20*	19
Cambodia	*2*	*99*	4	96	…	…	…	85	…	…	*27*	24
China	875	94	952	98	…	…	…	…	…	…	27	23

PRIMARY EDUCATION

Teaching staff				Trained teachers (%)[1]						Pupil/teacher ratio[2]		
School year ending in				School year ending in						School year ending in		
1999		2006		1999			2006			1999	2006	
Total (000)	% F	Total (000)	% F	Total	Male	Female	Total	Male	Female			Country or territory
												Arab States
170	46	171	52	94	92	96	99	99	100	28	24	Algeria
...	...	...	...	...	...	...	...	...	...	...	...	Bahrain
1	28	2	27	...	...	...	79	80	77	40	34	Djibouti
346	*52*	***369***	***56***	...	...	...	...	...	...	*23*	***27***	Egypt
141	72	*216[z]*	*72[z]*	...	...	...	100[y]	100[y]	100[y]	25	*21[z]*	Iraq
...	...	...	...	...	...	...	...	...	...	...	...	Jordan
10	73	20	87	100	100	100	100	100	100	13	10	Kuwait
28	82	32	85	15	...	...	13	14	12	14	14	Lebanon
...	...	...	...	...	...	...	...	...	...	...	...	Libyan Arab Jamahiriya
7	26	11	32	...	...	...	100	100	100	47	41	Mauritania
123	39	146	47	...	...	...	100[z]	100[z]	100[z]	28	27	Morocco
12	52	20	65	100	100	99	100	100	100	25	14	Oman
10	54	12	67	100	100	100	100[z]	100[z]	100[z]	38	32	Palestinian A. T.
5	75	7	85	...	...	...	52	51	53	13	11	Qatar
...	...	...	...	...	...	...	...	...	...	...	...	Saudi Arabia
...	...	113	68	...	...	...	59	73	52	...	34	Sudan
110	*65*	...	...	81	...	...	...	...	...	25	...	Syrian Arab Republic
60	50	59	52	...	...	...	...	...	...	24	19	Tunisia
17	73	18	84	...	...	...	60[z]	69[z]	58[z]	16	15	United Arab Emirates
103	*20*	...	...	...	...	...	...	...	...	*22*	...	Yemen
												Central and Eastern Europe
13	*75*	*12[y]*	*76[y]*	...	...	...	...	...	...	*23*	*21[y]*	Albania
32	99	23	99	...	...	...	100	100	100	20	16	Belarus
...	...	...	...	...	...	...	...	...	...	...	...	Bosnia and Herzegovina
23	*91*	17	93	...	...	...	...	...	...	18	16	Bulgaria
11	89	11	90	100	100	100	...	...	...	19	17	Croatia
36	85	30	95	...	...	...	...	...	...	18	16	Czech Republic
8	*86*	8	89	...	...	...	...	...	...	16	11	Estonia
47	85	41	96	...	...	...	...	...	...	11	10	Hungary
9	97	7	97	...	...	...	...	...	...	15	12	Latvia
13	98	11	98	...	...	...	...	...	...	17	14	Lithuania
...	...	...	...	...	...	...	...	...	...	...	...	Montenegro
...	...	232	84	...	...	...	...	...	...	...	11	Poland
12	96	10	97	...	...	...	...	...	...	21	17	Republic of Moldova
69	86	56	87	...	...	...	...	...	...	19	17	Romania
367	98	301	98	...	...	...	...	...	...	18	17	Russian Federation
23	...	***22***	...	...	...	...	...	...	...	*17*	***13***	Serbia
17	93	14	89	...	...	...	...	...	...	19	17	Slovakia
6	96	*6*	*97*	...	...	...	...	...	...	14	*15*	Slovenia
6	66	6[z]	70[z]	...	...	...	...	...	...	22	19[z]	TFYR Macedonia
...	...	...	...	...	...	...	...	...	...	...	...	Turkey
107	98	102	99	...	...	...	100	...	...	20	17	Ukraine
												Central Asia
...	...	6	99	...	...	...	77[z]	22[z]	78[z]	...	21	Armenia
37	83	43	86	100	100	100	100	...	...	19	13	Azerbaijan
17	92	*25[y]*	*95[y]*	...	...	...	...	...	...	17	*15[y]*	Georgia
...	...	**57**	**98**	...	...	...	...	...	...	...	**17**	Kazakhstan
19	95	18	97	48	49	48	61	61	61	24	24	Kyrgyzstan
8	93	8	95	...	...	...	...	...	...	32	33	Mongolia
31	56	31	65	...	...	...	93	...	...	22	22	Tajikistan
...	...	...	...	...	...	...	...	...	...	...	...	Turkmenistan
123	84	**119**	**85**	...	...	...	**100**	**100**	**100**	21	**18**	Uzbekistan
												East Asia and the Pacific
105	...	...	...	...	...	...	...	...	...	*18*	...	Australia
3*	66*	4	73	...	...	...	85	92	82	14*	13	Brunei Darussalam
45	*37*	51	42	...	...	...	98	...	...	*48*	50	Cambodia
...	...	5 968	55	...	...	...	...	...	...	...	18	China

Table 10A (continued)

Country or territory	PRE-PRIMARY EDUCATION											
	Teaching staff				Trained teachers (%)[1]						Pupil/teacher ratio[2]	
	School year ending in				School year ending in						School year ending in	
	1999		2006		1999			2006			1999	2006
	Total (000)	% F	Total (000)	% F	Total	Male	Female	Total	Male	Female		
Cook Islands	0.03	100	0.02z	91z	…	…	…	61z	–z	67z	14	21z
DPR Korea	…	…	…	…	…	…	…	…	…	…	…	…
Fiji	…	…	0.5	…	…	…	…	…	…	…	…	19
Indonesia	*118*	*98*	*202*	…	…	…	…	…	…	…	*17*	*16*
Japan	96	…	107	*98*	…	…	…	…	…	…	31	29
Kiribati	…	…	…	…	…	…	…	…	…	…	…	…
Lao PDR	2	100	3	99	86	100	86	80	36	81	18	16
Macao, China	0.5	100	0.4	100	93	.	93	98	.	98	31	23
Malaysia	21	100	30z	96z	…	…	…	…	…	…	27	23z
Marshall Islands	0.1	…	…	…	…	…	…	…	…	…	11	…
Micronesia	…	…	…	…	…	…	…	…	…	…	…	…
Myanmar	2	…	6	99	…	…	…	50	29	51	22	16
Nauru	…	…	**0.04**	**97**	…	…	…	**82**	–	**84**	…	**18**
New Zealand	7	98	7	99	…	…	…	…	…	…	15	14
Niue	0.01	100	…	…	…	…	…	…	…	…	11	…
Palau	…	…	…	…	…	…	…	…	…	…	…	…
Papua New Guinea	…	…	…	…	…	…	…	…	…	…	…	…
Philippines	18	*92*	28	97	*100*	…	…	…	…	…	33	33
Republic of Korea	23	100	**28**	**99**	…	…	…	…	…	…	24	**20**
Samoa	…	…	*0.1y*	*94y*	…	…	…	…	…	…	…	*42y*
Singapore	…	…	…	…	…	…	…	…	…	…	…	…
Solomon Islands	…	…	…	…	…	…	…	…	…	…	…	…
Thailand	111	79	99	78	…	…	…	…	…	…	25	25
Timor-Leste	…	…	0.2z	97z	…	…	…	…	…	…	…	29z
Tokelau	…	…	*0.01y*	*100y*	…	…	…	…	…	…	…	*14y*
Tonga	0.1	100	…	…	…	…	…	…	…	…	18	…
Tuvalu	…	…	…	…	…	…	…	…	…	…	…	…
Vanuatu	…	…	**0.5**	**91**	…	…	…	…	…	…	…	**11**
Viet Nam	94	100	160	98	44	.	44	71	…	…	23	17
Latin America and the Caribbean												
Anguilla	0.03	100	0.04	98	38	.	38	54	–	55	18	11
Antigua and Barbuda	…	…	…	…	…	…	…	…	…	…	…	…
Argentina	50	96	69z	96z	…	…	…	…	…	…	24	19z
Aruba	0.1	100	0.1	99	100	.	100	100	100	100	26	21
Bahamas	0.2	97	…	…	53	*50*	*53*	…	…	…	9	…
Barbados	*0.3*	*93*	*0.4*	*95*	…	…	…	63z	29z	65z	*18*	*18*
Belize	0.2	98	0.3	99	…	…	…	10	33	9	19	17
Bermuda	…	…	…	…	…	…	…	…	…	…	…	…
Bolivia	5	93	*6z*	*92z*	…	…	…	…	…	…	42	*41z*
Brazil	304	98	396z	97z	…	…	…	…	…	…	19	18z
British Virgin Islands	*0.03*	*100*	0.05	100	*29*	.	*29*	…	…	…	*13*	15
Cayman Islands	0.1	96	0.05	100	92	50	94	100	.	100	9	13
Chile	…	…	20	98	…	…	…	…	…	…	…	20
Colombia	59	94	50	96	…	…	…	.	.	.	18	22
Costa Rica	4	97	7	94	92	…	…	82	66*	83*	19	15
Cuba	26	98	27	100	98	–	100	100	.	100	19	17
Dominica	0.1	100	0.2z	100z	75	.	75	*78y*	*.y*	*78y*	18	14z
Dominican Republic	8	95	8	94	54	59	53	76	69	76	24	26
Ecuador	10	90	15	87	…	…	…	73	61	75	18	17
El Salvador	…	…	7	91	…	…	…	90	62	93	…	33
Grenada	0.2	96	*0.3z*	*99z*	…	…	…	…	…	…	18	*10z*
Guatemala	12	…	18*	91*	…	…	…	…	…	…	26	25*
Guyana	2	99	*2*	*99*	38	41	38	48z	21z	49z	18	*16*
Haiti	…	…	…	…	…	…	…	…	…	…	…	…
Honduras	…	…	8	…	…	…	…	64y	53y	65y	…	26
Jamaica	5	…	*7z*	*98z*	…	…	…	…	…	…	25	*22z*
Mexico	150	94	159	96	…	…	…	…	…	…	22	28
Montserrat	0.01	100	0.01	100	100	.	100	100	.	100	12	11
Netherlands Antilles	0.3	99	…	…	100	100	100	…	…	…	21	…
Nicaragua	6	97	9	92	32	19	33	33	33	33	26	25
Panama	3	98	5	95	36	35	36	45	8	47	19	19

PRIMARY EDUCATION												
Teaching staff				Trained teachers (%)[1]						Pupil/teacher ratio[2]		
School year ending in				School year ending in						School year ending in		
1999		2006		1999			2006			1999	2006	
Total (000)	% F	Total (000)	% F	Total	Male	Female	Total	Male	Female			**Country or territory**
0.1	86	0.1[z]	77[z]	…	…	…	95[z]	…	…	18	16[z]	Cook Islands
…	…	…	…	…	…	…	…	…	…	…	…	DPR Korea
…	…	*4[z]*	*57[z]*	…	…	…	…	…	…	…	*28[z]*	Fiji
…	…	*1428*	…	…	…	…	…	…	…	…	*20*	Indonesia
367	…	386	*65*	…	…	…	…	…	…	21	19	Japan
0.6	62	0.7[z]	75[z]	…	…	…	…	…	…	25	25[z]	Kiribati
27	43	29	46	76	69	85	86	81	91	31	31	Lao PDR
2	87	2	87	81	62	84	89	72	91	31	21	Macao, China
143	66	190[z]	66[z]	…	…	…	…	…	…	21	17[z]	Malaysia
0.6	…	…	…	…	…	…	…	…	…	15	…	Marshall Islands
…	…	***1***	…	…	…	…	…	…	…	…	***17***	Micronesia
155	73	166	82	60	60	60	98	98	98	31	30	Myanmar
…	…	**0.05**	**91**	…	…	…	…	…	…	…	**23**	Nauru
20	82	22	83	…	…	…	…	…	…	18	16	New Zealand
0.02	100	*0.02[z]*	*100[z]*	…	…	…	…	…	…	16	*12[z]*	Niue
0.1	82	*0.2[z]*	…	…	…	…	…	…	…	15	*13[z]*	Palau
…	…	*15*	*43*	…	…	…	…	…	…	…	*36*	Papua New Guinea
360	87	376	87	*100*	…	…	…	…	…	35	35	Philippines
124	64	**148**	**76**	…	…	…	…	…	…	31	**27**	Republic of Korea
1	*71*	*1[y]*	*73[y]*	…	…	…	…	…	…	*24*	*25[y]*	Samoa
11	80	13	83	…	…	…	…	…	…	27	23	Singapore
3	41	…	…	…	…	…	…	…	…	19	…	Solomon Islands
298	63	320	60	…	…	…	…	…	…	21	18	Thailand
…	…	5[z]	31[z]	…	…	…	…	…	…	…	34[z]	Timor-Leste
…	…	*0.04[y]*	*69[y]*	…	…	…	…	…	…	…	*6[y]*	Tokelau
0.8	67	0.8	…	…	…	…	…	…	…	21	22	Tonga
0.1	…	0.1[y]	…	…	…	…	…	…	…	19	19[y]	Tuvalu
1	49	2[y]	54[y]	…	…	…	…	…	…	24	20[y]	Vanuatu
337	78	354	78	78	75	78	96	93	96	30	21	Viet Nam
												Latin America and the Caribbean
0.1	87	0.09	93	76	78	76	64	17	67	22	17	Anguilla
…	…	…	…	…	…	…	…	…	…	…	…	Antigua and Barbuda
221	88	279[z]	88[z]	…	…	…	…	…	…	22	17[z]	Argentina
0.5	78	0.6	82	100	100	100	99	97	100	19	18	Aruba
2	63	2	81	58	*57*	*59*	89	71	93	14	15	Bahamas
1	*76*	*1*	*78*	…	…	…	73[z]	78[z]	72[z]	*18*	*15*	Barbados
2	*64*	2	71	…	…	…	39	37	40	*24*	23	Belize
…	…	0.6	89	…	…	…	100	100	100	…	8	Bermuda
58	*61*	*64[y]*	*61[y]*	…	…	…	…	…	…	*25*	*24[y]*	Bolivia
807	93	887[z]	88[z]	…	…	…	…	…	…	26	21[z]	Brazil
0.2	86	0.2	88	72	55	75	74	30	80	18	15	British Virgin Islands
0.2	89	0.3	88	98	96	98	97	94	98	15	12	Cayman Islands
56	77	66	78	…	…	…	…	…	…	32	26	Chile
215	77	188	76	…	…	…	…	…	…	24	28	Colombia
20	80	28	80	93	…	…	88	88*	88*	27	20	Costa Rica
91	79	89	77	100	100	100	100	100	100	12	10	Cuba
0.6	75	0.5	84	64	46	70	64	44	68	20	17	Dominica
…	…	55	76	…	…	…	88	81	90	…	23	Dominican Republic
71	68	89	70	…	…	…	71	70	71	27	23	Ecuador
…	…	26*	70*	…	…	…	94*	92*	95*	…	40*	El Salvador
…	…	*0.9[z]*	*76[z]*	…	…	…	*67[z]*	*65[z]*	*68[z]*	…	*18[z]*	Grenada
48	…	78*	64*	…	…	…	…	…	…	38	31*	Guatemala
4	86	4[z]	86[z]	52	52	52	57[z]	52[z]	58[z]	27	28[z]	Guyana
…	…	…	…	…	…	…	…	…	…	…	…	Haiti
…	…	46	…	…	…	…	87[y]	86[y]	88[y]	…	28	Honduras
…	…	*12[z]*	*89[z]*	…	…	…	…	…	…	…	*28[z]*	Jamaica
540	62	521	67	…	…	…	…	…	…	27	28	Mexico
0.02	84	0.03	100	100	100	100	77	–	77	21	17	Montserrat
1	86	…	…	100	100	100	…	…	…	20	…	Netherlands Antilles
24	83	29	74	79	63	82	74	59	79	34	33	Nicaragua
15	75	18	76	79	86	77	91	94	90	26	25	Panama

Table 10A (continued)

Country or territory	PRE-PRIMARY EDUCATION											
	Teaching staff				Trained teachers (%)[1]						Pupil/teacher ratio[2]	
	School year ending in				School year ending in						School year ending in	
	1999		2006		1999			2006			1999	2006
	Total (000)	% F	Total (000)	% F	Total	Male	Female	Total	Male	Female		
Paraguay	…	…	*6*[y]	*88*[y]	…	…	…	…	…	…	…	*26*[y]
Peru	…	…	50	96	…	…	…	…	…	…	…	23
Saint Kitts and Nevis	…	…	0.3[z]	100[z]	…	…	…	*46*[z]	.[z]	*46*[z]	…	6[z]
Saint Lucia	*0.3*	*100*	0.3	…	…	…	…	*56*[z]	–[z]	*56*[z]	*13*	11
Saint Vincent/Grenad.	…	…	*0.3*[z]	*100*[z]	…	…	…	*59*[z]	.[z]	*59*[z]	…	*11*[z]
Suriname	…	…	0.5	99	…	…	…	…	…	…	…	31
Trinidad and Tobago	*2*	*100*	2[*,z]	100[*,z]	*20*	–	*20*	*25*[y]	.[y]	*25*[y]	*13*	14[*,z]
Turks and Caicos Islands	*0.1*	*92*	*0.1*[z]	*95*[z]	*61*	*40*	*63*	*76*[z]	*25*[z]	*78*[z]	*13*	*12*[z]
Uruguay	3	*98*	5	…	…	…	…	…	…	…	31	23
Venezuela, Bolivarian Rep. of	…	…	63[z]	94[z]	…	…	…	86[z]	70[z]	87[z]	…	15[z]
North America and Western Europe												
Andorra	…	…	0.2	95	…	…	…	100	100	100	…	12
Austria	14	99	16	99	…	…	…	…	…	…	16	14
Belgium	…	…	29	98	…	…	…	…	…	…	…	14
Canada	30	*68*	…	…	…	…	…	…	…	…	17	…
Cyprus	1	99	1	99	…	…	…	…	…	…	19	18
Denmark	45	92	…	…	…	…	…	…	…	…	6	…
Finland	10	96	*12*	*97*	…	…	…	…	…	…	12	*12*
France	128	78	*142*	*81*	…	…	…	…	…	…	19	*18*
Germany	…	…	208	98	…	…	…	…	…	…	…	12
Greece	9	*100*	12	99	…	…	…	…	…	…	16	12
Iceland	*2*	*98*	2	97	…	…	…	…	…	…	*5*	6
Ireland	…	…	…	…	…	…	…	…	…	…	…	…
Israel	…	…	…	…	…	…	…	…	…	…	…	…
Italy	119	99	134	100	…	…	…	…	…	…	13	12
Luxembourg	…	…	1	98	…	…	…	…	…	…	…	12
Malta	0.9	99	0.9[z]	99[z]	…	…	…	…	…	…	12	10[z]
Monaco	*0.1*	*100*	*0.1*[y]	*100*[y]	…	…	…	…	…	…	*18*	*17*[y]
Netherlands	…	…	…	…	…	…	…	…	…	…	…	…
Norway	…	…	…	…	…	…	…	…	…	…	…	…
Portugal	…	…	17	98	…	…	…	…	…	…	…	15
San Marino	…	…	0.1[y]	…	…	…	…	…	…	…	…	8[y]
Spain	68	93	111	89	…	…	…	…	…	…	17	13
Sweden	…	…	34	96	…	…	…	…	…	…	…	10
Switzerland	…	…	11	98	…	…	…	…	…	…	…	14
United Kingdom	…	…	44	97	…	…	…	…	…	…	…	22
United States	327	95	458	91	…	…	…	…	…	…	22	16
South and West Asia												
Afghanistan	…	…	*4*[y]	*100*[y]	…	…	…	…	…	…	…	*7*[y]
Bangladesh	68	33	33[y]	90[y]	…	…	…	41[y]	50[y]	40[y]	27	34[y]
Bhutan	0.01	31	*0.02*	…	100	100	100	…	…	…	22	*23*
India	…	…	717[z]	100[z]	…	…	…	…	…	…	…	41[z]
Iran, Islamic Republic of	9	98	19[z]	89[z]	…	…	…	…	…	…	23	27[z]
Maldives	0.4	90	0.6	98	47	46	47	45	46	45	31	23
Nepal	*10*	*31*	…	…	–	–	–	…	…	…	*24*	…
Pakistan	…	…	*86*[y]	*45*[y]	…	…	…	…	…	…	…	*41*[y]
Sri Lanka	…	…	…	…	…	…	…	…	…	…	…	…
Sub-Saharan Africa												
Angola	…	…	…	…	…	…	…	…	…	…	…	…
Benin	0.6	61	0.6	78	100	100	100	100[y]	100[y]	100[y]	28	49
Botswana	…	…	0.9[z]	55[z]	…	…	…	50[z]	…	…	…	22[z]
Burkina Faso	…	…	0.9	71	…	…	…	38	96	14	…	29
Burundi	*0.2*	*99*	0.4*	93*	…	…	…	66[y]	25[y]	69[y]	*28*	29*
Cameroon	4	97	9	99	…	…	…	48	51	48	23	21
Cape Verde	…	…	1.0	100	…	…	…	11	.	11	…	22
Central African Republic	…	…	…	…	…	…	…	…	…	…	…	…
Chad	…	…	*0.2*[z]	…	…	…	…	…	…	…	…	*38*[z]
Comoros	*0.1*	*94*	…	…	…	…	…	…	…	…	*26*	…
Congo	0.6	100	1	97	…	…	…	53[z]	–[z]	62[z]	10	19

PRIMARY EDUCATION

Teaching staff: 1999 Total (000)	1999 % F	2006 Total (000)	2006 % F	Trained teachers (%)[1]: 1999 Total	1999 Male	1999 Female	2006 Total	2006 Male	2006 Female	Pupil/teacher ratio[2]: 1999	2006	Country or territory
…	…	*33[y]*	*72[y]*	…	…	…	…	…	…	…	*28[y]*	Paraguay
…	…	184	64	…	…	…	…	…	…	…	22	Peru
…	…	**0.4**	**87**	…	…	…	**64**	…	…	…	**15**	Saint Kitts and Nevis
1	*84*	1	86	…	…	…	80	98	77	22	24	Saint Lucia
…	…	*1[z]*	*73[z]*	…	…	…	*74[z]*	*68[z]*	*76[z]*	…	*18[z]*	Saint Vincent/Grenad.
…	…	4	91	…	…	…	…	…	…	…	16	Suriname
8	76	8[*,z]	72[*,z]	71	74	71	81[*,y]	72[*,y]	84[*,y]	21	17[*,z]	Trinidad and Tobago
0.1	*92*	*0.1[z]*	*89[z]*	*81*	*63*	*82*	*82[z]*	*81[z]*	*83[z]*	*18*	*15[z]*	Turks and Caicos Islands
18	*92*	19	…	…	…	…	…	…	…	20	20	Uruguay
…	…	184[z]	81[z]	…	…	…	84[z]	70[z]	87[z]	…	19[z]	Venezuela, Bolivarian Rep. of
												North America and Western Europe
…	…	0.4	76	…	…	…	100	100	100	…	10	Andorra
29	89	29	89	…	…	…	…	…	…	13	12	Austria
…	…	65	79	…	…	…	…	…	…	…	11	Belgium
141	*68*	…	…	…	…	…	…	…	…	17	…	Canada
4	67	4	83	…	…	…	…	…	…	18	16	Cyprus
37	63	…	…	…	…	…	…	…	…	10	…	Denmark
22	71	*24*	*76*	…	…	…	…	…	…	17	*16*	Finland
209	78	*218*	*82*	…	…	…	…	…	…	19	*19*	France
221	82	238	84	…	…	…	…	…	…	17	14	Germany
48	*57*	61	64	…	…	…	…	…	…	14	11	Greece
3	*76*	*3*	*80*	…	…	…	…	…	…	*11*	*10*	Iceland
21	85	27	85	…	…	…	…	…	…	22	17	Ireland
54	…	60	86	…	…	…	…	…	…	13	13	Israel
254	95	264	96	…	…	…	…	…	…	11	11	Italy
…	…	3	72	…	…	…	…	…	…	…	11	Luxembourg
2	87	3[z]	86[z]	…	…	…	…	…	…	20	12[z]	Malta
0.1	*87*	*0.1[y]*	*80[y]*	…	…	…	…	…	…	*16*	*14[y]*	Monaco
…	…	…	…	…	…	…	…	…	…	…	…	Netherlands
…	…	*41[y]*	*73[y]*	…	…	…	…	…	…	…	*11[y]*	Norway
…	…	71	81	…	…	…	…	…	…	…	11	Portugal
…	…	0.2[y]	…	…	…	…	…	…	…	…	6[y]	San Marino
172	68	184	70	…	…	…	…	…	…	15	14	Spain
62	80	63	81	…	…	…	…	…	…	12	10	Sweden
…	…	41	79	…	…	…	…	…	…	…	13	Switzerland
244	76	250	81	…	…	…	…	…	…	19	18	United Kingdom
1 618	86	1 761	89	…	…	…	…	…	…	15	14	United States
												South and West Asia
26	–	52[z]	*34[z]*	…	…	…	36[z]	…	…	36	83[z]	Afghanistan
312	33	353[y]	34[y]	64	64	64	48[y]	47[y]	52[y]	56	51[y]	Bangladesh
2	32	4	50	100	100	100	92	92	92	42	29	Bhutan
3 135*	33*	*3 388[y]*	*44[y]*	…	…	…	…	…	…	35*	*40[y]*	India
327	53	374	62	…	…	…	100[z]	100[z]	100[z]	27	19	Iran, Islamic Republic of
3	60	3	70	67	70	65	68	70	67	24	16	Maldives
92	23	*113*	*30*	46	50	35	31[z]	32[z]	27[z]	39	*40*	Nepal
…	…	428	45	…	…	…	85	92	75	…	39	Pakistan
…	…	*75[z]*	*79[z]*	…	…	…	…	…	…	…	*22[z]*	Sri Lanka
												Sub-Saharan Africa
…	…	…	…	…	…	…	…	…	…	…	…	Angola
16	23	31	17	58	52	77	72	71	76	53	44	Benin
12	81	13[z]	78[z]	90	81	92	87[z]	89[z]	86[z]	27	24[z]	Botswana
17	25	30	30	…	…	…	87	85	91	49	46	Burkina Faso
12	*54*	24	55	…	…	…	88[z]	83[z]	91[z]	*57*	54	Burundi
41	36	67	40	…	…	…	62*	58*	67*	52	45	Cameroon
3	*62*	3	66	…	…	…	81	77	84	*29*	25	Cape Verde
…	…	…	…	…	…	…	…	…	…	…	…	Central African Republic
12	9	20[z]	12[z]	…	…	…	27[z]	21[z]	70[z]	68	63[z]	Chad
2	26	*3[z]*	*33[z]*	…	…	…	…	…	…	35	*35[z]*	Comoros
5	42	11	47	…	…	…	89	84	95	61	55	Congo

Table 10A (continued)

	PRE-PRIMARY EDUCATION											
	Teaching staff				Trained teachers (%)[1]						Pupil/teacher ratio[2]	
	School year ending in				School year ending in						School year ending in	
	1999		2006		1999			2006			1999	2006
Country or territory	Total (000)	% F	Total (000)	% F	Total	Male	Female	Total	Male	Female		
Côte d'Ivoire	2	96	3	90	...	...	...	...	...	...	23	16
D. R. Congo	...	...	...	...	...	...	...	...	...	...	...	...
Equatorial Guinea	0.4	36	...	...	...	...	...	...	...	...	43	...
Eritrea	0.3	97	1	96	65	22	66	65	54	66	36	35
Ethiopia	2	93	**8**	...	63	37	65	76	...	...	36	**27**
Gabon	...	...	...	...	...	...	...	...	...	...	...	...
Gambia	...	...	*0.8^{y}*	*56^{y}*	...	...	...	...	...	...	...	*38^{y}*
Ghana	*26*	*91*	**34**	...	*24*	*14*	*25*	22^{z}	25^{z}	22^{z}	*25*	**32**
Guinea	...	...	3	50	...	...	...	34	31	38	...	29
Guinea-Bissau	*0.2*	*73*	...	...	...	...	...	...	...	...	*21*	...
Kenya	44	55	75	87	...	...	...	71	55	73	27	22
Lesotho	...	...	2	99	...	...	...	$-^{z}$	$-^{z}$	$-^{z}$	...	19
Liberia	6	19	25	22	...	...	...	...	...	...	18	14
Madagascar	...	...	4	97	...	...	...	13	10	13	...	37
Malawi	...	...	...	...	...	...	...	...	...	...	...	...
Mali	...	...	...	...	...	...	...	...	...	...	...	...
Mauritius	3	100	3	100	100	.	100	88	.	88	16	15
Mozambique	...	...	...	...	...	...	...	...	...	...	...	...
Namibia	1	88	...	...	77	12	86	...	...	...	27	...
Niger	0.6	98	0.9	94	96	91	96	95	...	...	21	27
Nigeria	...	...	...	...	...	...	...	...	...	...	...	...
Rwanda	...	...	...	...	...	...	...	...	...	...	...	...
Sao Tome and Principe	0.1	95	*0*	*48*	...	...	...	...	...	...	28	*23*
Senegal	1	78	*3*	*82*	...	...	...	100^{z}	100^{z}	100^{z}	19	*36*
Seychelles	0.2	100	**0.2**	**100**	86	.	86	...	...	...	16	**15**
Sierra Leone	...	...	**1**	**79**	...	...	...	**52**	**53**	**52**	...	**20**
Somalia	...	...	...	...	...	...	...	...	...	...	...	...
South Africa	*6*	*80*	*11^{y}*	*78^{y}*	...	...	...	...	...	...	*36*	*34^{y}*
Swaziland	...	...	*0.5^{z}*	*75^{z}*	...	...	...	...	...	...	...	*32^{z}*
Togo	0.6	97	*0.7^{y}*	*91^{y}*	...	...	...	...	...	...	20	*18^{y}*
Uganda	*3*	*70*	2	70	...	...	...	...	...	...	*25*	42
United Republic of Tanzania	...	...	**18**	**56**	...	...	...	**14**	**8**	**19**	...	**43**
Zambia	...	...	...	...	...	...	...	...	...	...	...	...
Zimbabwe	...	...	...	...	...	...	...	...	...	...	...	...

	Sum	%F	Sum	%F	Median						Weighted average	
World	5 430	91	6 656	93	...	...	...	...	...	...	21	21
Countries in transition	984	98	941	99	...	...	...	82	.	82	7	8
Developed countries	1 448	94	1 717	93	...	...	...	...	...	...	18	15
Developing countries	2 998	87	3 997	92	...	...	...	...	...	...	27	26
Arab States	117	77	151	86	...	...	...	100	100	100	21	20
Central and Eastern Europe	1 122	99	1 048	100	...	...	...	...	...	...	8	9
Central Asia	136	98	138	98	...	...	...	82	.	82	10	11
East Asia and the Pacific	1 430	94	1 684	97	...	...	...	...	...	...	26	22
East Asia	1 405	94	1 654	97	...	...	...	...	...	...	26	22
Pacific	26	94	29	92	...	...	...	...	...	...	16	17
Latin America and the Caribbean	748	96	968	96	...	...	...	64	53	65	22	21
Caribbean	22	97	25	99	61	40	63	59	.	59	31	31
Latin America	726	96	943	96	...	...	...	75	65	76	22	21
North America and Western Europe	1 100	92	1 388	92	...	...	...	...	...	...	17	14
South and West Asia	601	69	968	89	...	...	...	...	...	...	36	40
Sub-Saharan Africa	177	69	311	71	...	...	...	...	...	...	29	29

1. Data on trained teachers (defined according to national standards) are not collected for countries whose education statistics are gathered through the OECD, Eurostat or the World Education Indicators questionnaires.

2. Based on headcounts of pupils and teachers.

Data in italic are UIS estimates.

Data in bold are for the school year ending in 2007.

(z) Data are for the school year ending in 2005.

(y) Data are for the school year ending in 2004.

(*) National estimate.

PRIMARY EDUCATION

Teaching staff				Trained teachers (%)[1]						Pupil/teacher ratio[2]		
School year ending in				School year ending in						School year ending in		
1999		2006		1999			2006			1999	2006	
Total (000)	% F	Total (000)	% F	Total	Male	Female	Total	Male	Female			**Country or territory**
45	20	46	23	…	…	…	…	…	…	43	46	Côte d'Ivoire
155	21	…	…	…	…	…	…	…	…	26	…	D. R. Congo
1	28	…	…	…	…	…	…	…	…	57	…	Equatorial Guinea
6	35	8	43	73	75	69	88	92	82	47	47	Eritrea
112	28	…	…	…	…	…	…	…	…	46	…	Ethiopia
6	42	*8*[y]	*45*[y]	…	…	…	…	…	…	44	*36*[y]	Gabon
5	29	5*	34*	72	*72*	*72*	76*	75*	78*	33	35*	Gambia
80	32	**95**	**37**	72	64	89	**59**	…	…	30	**35**	Ghana
16	25	28	25	…	…	…	68	65	74	47	44	Guinea
3	*20*	…	…	…	…	…	…	…	…	*44*	…	Guinea-Bissau
148	42	*154*[z]	*45*[z]	…	…	…	99[y]	98[y]	99[y]	32	*40*[z]	Kenya
8	80	11	78	78	68	81	66	49	71	44	40	Lesotho
10	19	28	27	…	…	…	…	…	…	39	19	Liberia
43	58	77	57	…	…	…	36[z]	30[z]	40[z]	47	48	Madagascar
…	…	…	…	…	…	…	…	…	…	…	…	Malawi
15*	23*	29	30	…	…	…	…	…	…	62*	56	Mali
5	54	6	64	100	100	100	100	100	100	26	22	Mauritius
37	25	62	26	…	…	…	65	57	86	61	67	Mozambique
12	67	*13*	*67*	29	27	30	92[z]	83[z]	97[z]	32	*31*	Namibia
13	31	28	40	98	98	98	92	92	92	41	40	Niger
440	*47*	599[z]	51[z]	…	…	…	50[z]	39[z]	60[z]	*41*	37[z]	Nigeria
24	55	31	53	49	52	46	98	98	98	54	66	Rwanda
0.7	…	*1*	*55*	…	…	…	…	…	…	36	*31*	Sao Tome and Principe
21	*23*	38	*25*	…	…	…	100[z]	100[z]	100[z]	49	39	Senegal
0.7	85	**0.7**	**85**	82	76	83	…	…	…	15	**12**	Seychelles
…	…	**30**	**26**	…	…	…	**49**	**45**	**63**	…	**44**	Sierra Leone
…	…	…	…	…	…	…	…	…	…	…	…	Somalia
227	78	*209*[y]	*76*[y]	62	65	61	…	…	…	35	*36*[y]	South Africa
6	75	7[z]	73[z]	91	89	92	91[z]	89[z]	91[z]	33	33[z]	Swaziland
23	13	28	12	…	…	…	37[z]	37[z]	38[z]	41	38	Togo
110	33	150	*39*	…	…	…	85[z]	84[z]	86[z]	57	49	Uganda
104	45	**157**	**49**	…	…	…	**100**	**100**	**100**	40	**53**	United Republic of Tanzania
33	49	52	48	94	93	95	…	…	…	47	51	Zambia
60	47	64	…	…	…	…	…	…	…	41	38	Zimbabwe

Sum	%F	Sum	%F	Median						Weighted average		
25 795	58	27 192	62	…	…	…	…	…	…	25	25	World
843	93	748	94	…	…	…	100	100	100	20	18	Countries in transition
4 485	81	4 633	83	…	…	…	…	…	…	16	14	Developed countries
20 466	52	21 811	57	…	…	…	85	92	79	27	28	Developing countries
1 554	52	1 832	58	…	…	…	100	99	100	23	22	Arab States
1 384	82	1 226	81	…	…	…	…	…	…	19	18	Central and Eastern Europe
332	84	319	87	…	…	…	93	…	…	21	19	Central Asia
10 094	55	9 671	60	…	…	…	…	…	…	22	20	East Asia and the Pacific
9 938	55	9 502	60	…	…	…	…	…	…	22	20	East Asia
156	71	169	75	…	…	…	…	…	…	20	19	Pacific
2 684	76	3 016	77	…	…	…	80	85	81	26	23	Latin America and the Caribbean
104	50	111	57	76	78	76	74	30	80	24	22	Caribbean
2 580	77	2 905	78	…	…	…	88	87	88	26	23	Latin America
3 443	81	3 687	85	…	…	…	…	…	…	15	14	North America and Western Europe
4 301	35	4 859	45	…	…	…	68	70	67	37	40	South and West Asia
2 004	43	2 581	45	…	…	…	85	84	86	41	45	Sub-Saharan Africa

Table 10B
Teaching staff in secondary and tertiary education

Country or territory	SECONDARY EDUCATION															
	Teaching staff												Trained teachers (%)[1]			
	Lower secondary				Upper secondary				Total secondary				Total secondary			
	School year ending in				School year ending in				School year ending in				School year ending in			
	1999		2006		1999		2006		1999		2006		2006			
	Total (000)	% F	Total (000)	% F	Total (000)	% F	Total (000)	% F	Total (000)	% F	Total (000)	% F	Total	Male	Female
Arab States															
Algeria	…	…	113[Y]	51[Y]	…	…	64[Y]	46[Y]	…	…	176[Y]	49[Y]	…	…	…
Bahrain	…	…	…	…	…	…	…	…	…	…	…	…	…	…	…
Djibouti	0.5	24	…	…	0.2	17	…	…	0.7	22	1.0	23	…	…	…
Egypt	207	44	231[Y]	45[Y]	247	38	257[Y]	38[Y]	454	41	488[Y]	41[Y]	…	…	…
Iraq	34	77	61[Z]	59[Z]	23	57	32[Z]	56[Z]	56	69	93[Z]	58[Z]	100[Y]	100[Y]	100[Y]
Jordan	…	…	…	…	10	48	10[Y]	35[Y]	…	…	…	…	…	…	…
Kuwait	11	58	…	…	11	53	…	…	22	56	24	53	100[Z]	100[Z]	100[Z]
Lebanon	27	57	19	61	15	42	22	47	42	51	41	53	12	14	11
Libyan Arab Jamahiriya	…	…	…	…	…	…	74	71	…	…	…	…	…	…	…
Mauritania	1	11	2	11	1	10	2*	11*	2	10	4*	11*	100*	100*	100*
Morocco	53	35	60[Y]	36[Y]	35	29	40[Y]	29[Y]	88	33	100[Y]	33[Y]	…	…	…
Oman	7	48	12	54	5	51	7	48	13	50	19	52	100	100	100
Palestinian A. T.	14	49	19	51	3	38	5	46	18	48	25	50	…	…	…
Qatar	2	56	3	56	2	57	3	57	4	57	6	57	56	45	65
Saudi Arabia	…	…	…	…	…	…	…	…	…	…	…	…	…	…	…
Sudan	…	…	30	67	18	47	36	42	…	…	66	54	80	…	…
Syrian Arab Republic	…	…	…	…	…	…	40	47	54	…	…	…	…	…	…
Tunisia	27	46	33	52	30	35	32	45	56	40	65	49	…	…	…
United Arab Emirates	8	54	13	56	8	55	11	53	16	55	24	55	46[Z]	47[Z]	46[Z]
Yemen	29	20	…	…	19	18	…	…	48	19	…	…	…	…	…
Central and Eastern Europe															
Albania	16	51	…	…	6	54	…	…	22	52	23[Y]	56[Y]	…	…	…
Belarus	…	…	…	…	…	…	…	…	107	77	103	80	…	…	…
Bosnia and Herzegovina	…	…	…	…	…	…	…	…	…	…	…	…	…	…	…
Bulgaria	27	76	24	80	29	70	32	76	56	73	56	77	…	…	…
Croatia	16	67	18	71	18	62	23	64	33	64	41	67	…	…	…
Czech Republic[3]	…	…	43	74	…	…	48	57	…	…	92	65	…	…	…
Estonia	5	85	5	82	6	78	3	81	11	81	8	82	…	…	…
Hungary	47	86	49	78	53	59	41	64	100	71	90	72	…	…	…
Latvia	16	83	15	85	9	76	10	85	25	80	25	85	…	…	…
Lithuania	24	81	39	82	12	76	…	…	36	79	41	81	…	…	…
Montenegro	…	…	…	…	…	…	…	…	…	…	…	…	…	…	…
Poland	…	…	128	73	…	…	134	65	…	…	261	69	…	…	…
Republic of Moldova	25	74	23	77	8	68	8	73	33	72	31	76	…	…	…
Romania	104	67	89	68	73	60	68	65	177	64	157	67	…	…	…
Russian Federation	…	…	…	…	…	…	…	…	…	…	1 284	80	…	…	…
Serbia	24	…	**25**	…	24	…	**27**	**63**	48	…	**52**	…	…	…	…
Slovakia	29	77	27	76	25	66	23	69	54	72	50	73	…	…	…
Slovenia	7	77	…	…	9	62	…	…	17	69	16	71	…	…	…
TFYR Macedonia	8	46	9[Z]	51[Z]	5	53	6[Z]	56[Z]	13	49	15[Z]	53[Z]	…	…	…
Turkey	…	…	…	…	…	…	168	42	…	…	…	…	…	…	…
Ukraine	…	…	…	…	…	…	…	…	400	76	349	79*	…	…	…
Central Asia															
Armenia	…	…	…	…	…	…	…	…	…	…	43	83	…	…	…
Azerbaijan	…	…	…	…	…	…	…	…	118	63	129	66	…	…	…
Georgia	…	…	…	…	…	…	…	…	59	77	34[Y]	82[Y]	…	…	…
Kazakhstan	…	…	…	…	…	…	…	…	…	…	**180**	**85**	…	…	…
Kyrgyzstan	…	…	…	…	…	…	…	…	48	68	53	73	78	76	78
Mongolia	8	69	11	75	3	67	5	70	11	69	16	73	…	…	…
Tajikistan	…	…	…	…	…	…	…	…	47	43	61	47	92[Y]	…	…
Turkmenistan	…	…	…	…	…	…	…	…	…	…	…	…	…	…	…
Uzbekistan	…	…	…	…	…	…	…	…	307	57	**352**	**63**	**100**	**100**	**100**
East Asia and the Pacific															
Australia	…	…	…	…	…	…	…	…	…	…	…	…	…	…	…
Brunei Darussalam	2*	48*	…	…	1*	47*	…	…	3	48	4	59	90	91	90
Cambodia	14	28	21	33	4	24	9	31	18	27	29	32	95	…	…

SECONDARY EDUCATION						TERTIARY EDUCATION				
Pupil/teacher ratio[2]						Teaching staff				
Lower secondary		Upper secondary		Total secondary						
School year ending in		School year ending in		School year ending in		School year ending in				
1999	2006	1999	2006	1999	2006	1999		2006		
						Total (000)	% F	Total (000)	% F	Country or territory
										Arab States
...	*21*[y]	...	*20*[y]	...	*21*[y]	...	...	30	34	Algeria
...	...	...	...	...	...	...	...	*0.8*[z]	*41*[z]	Bahrain
26	...	16	...	23	31	0.02	30	0.1	16	Djibouti
22	*20*[y]	*13*	*14*[y]	*17*	*17*[y]	...	...	*81*[y]	...	Egypt
22	*19*[z]	*16*	*19*[z]	*20*	*19*[z]	12	31	*19*[z]	*35*[z]	Iraq
...	...	17	17[y]	...	...	...	...	*8*	*21*	Jordan
12	...	*9*	...	*11*	*10*	*2*	...	*2*	*27*	Kuwait
9	10	*8*	8	*9*	9	9	28	21	37	Lebanon
...	...	...	5	...	...	12	*13*	...	...	Libyan Arab Jamahiriya
28	28	*24*	24*	*26*	26*	...	...	0.4	4	Mauritania
19	*20*[y]	*14*	*17*[y]	*17*	*19*[y]	16	23	19	*24*	Morocco
19	*13*	16	*20*	18	*16*	...	...	3	34	Oman
26	29	19	22	*24*	28	3	13	6	17	Palestinian A. T.
13	10	*8*	9	*10*	10	*0.7*	*32*	0.7[z]	32[z]	Qatar
...	...	...	...	...	...	20	36	*27*	*33*	Saudi Arabia
...	28	*22*	17	...	22	4	23	...	...	Sudan
...	...	...	11	19	...	...	...	...	...	Syrian Arab Republic
23	20	*15*	19	*19*	19	6	41	17	41	Tunisia
14	14	10	10	12	12	...	...	...	...	United Arab Emirates
22	...	21	...	*22*	...	5	1	*6*[z]	*16*[z]	Yemen
										Central and Eastern Europe
16	...	17	...	*16*	*18*[y]	2	36	*2*[y]	*41*[y]	Albania
...	...	...	...	9	9	30	51	42	56	Belarus
...	...	...	...	...	...	...	...	...	...	Bosnia and Herzegovina
13	12	12	11	13	12	24	*41*	22	46	Bulgaria
14	11	11	8	12	10	7	35	9	41	Croatia
...	11	...	10	...	11	19	*38*	23	38	Czech Republic[3]
11	11	10	19	10	14	6	49	*6*	*48*	Estonia
11	10	9	*12*	10	*11*	21	38	25	39	Hungary
10	10	10	11	10	10	6	52	6	57	Latvia
11	8	*11*	...	*11*	*10*	15	50	13	53	Lithuania
...	...	...	...	...	...	...	...	...	...	Montenegro
...	*13*	...	*13*	...	*13*	*76*	...	98	42	Poland
13	12	12	14	13	12	7	50	8	55	Republic of Moldova
12	11	13	15	13	13	26	37	32	43	Romania
...	...	...	...	...	9	...	...	656	57	Russian Federation
17	***13***	14	**11**	*15*	***12***	...	...	...	...	Serbia
13	13	*12*	13	*13*	13	*11*	*38*	13	42	Slovakia
14	...	13	...	13	*11*	2	21	*5*	*34*	Slovenia
16	14[z]	16	16[z]	16	15[z]	3	42	3[z]	44[z]	TFYR Macedonia
...	...	...	17	...	...	60	35	85	39	Turkey
...	...	...	...	13	11	133	...	192	...	Ukraine
										Central Asia
...	...	...	...	...	8	9	42	13	46	Armenia
...	...	...	...	8	8	13	36	16	41	Azerbaijan
...	...	...	...	8	*9*[y]	14	49	12	39	Georgia
...	...	...	...	...	**10**	27	58	**43**	**63**	Kazakhstan
...	...	...	...	13	14	8	32	13	56	Kyrgyzstan
19	21	17	19	19	20	6	*47*	8	55	Mongolia
...	...	...	...	16	16	6	29	9	32	Tajikistan
...	...	...	...	...	...	...	...	...	...	Turkmenistan
...	...	...	...	11	**13**	17	36	**23**	**36**	Uzbekistan
										East Asia and the Pacific
...	...	...	...	...	...	...	...	...	...	Australia
12*	...	10*	...	11	11	0.5	32	0.6	39	Brunei Darussalam
16	30	*21*	25	*18*	28	1	19	3	11	Cambodia

Table 10B (continued)

	SECONDARY EDUCATION														
	Teaching staff												Trained teachers (%)[1]		
	Lower secondary				Upper secondary				Total secondary				Total secondary		
	School year ending in				School year ending in				School year ending in				School year ending in		
	1999		2006		1999		2006		1999		2006		2006		
Country or territory	Total (000)	% F	Total (000)	% F	Total (000)	% F	Total (000)	% F	Total (000)	% F	Total (000)	% F	Total	Male	Female
China	3 213	*41*	3 649	46	…	…	*2 117*	*43*	…	…	*5 766*	*45*	…	…	…
Cook Islands	…	…	…	…	…	…	…	…	…	…	0.1[z]	61[z]	97[z]	100[z]	95[z]
DPR Korea	…	…	…	…	…	…	…	…	…	…	…	…	…	…	…
Fiji	…	…	3[y]	50[y]	…	…	*2[y]*	*50[y]*	…	…	*5[y]*	*50[y]*	…	…	…
Indonesia	…	…	*748*	…	…	…	*600*	…	…	…	*1 347*	…	…	…	…
Japan	268	…	259	…	362	…	350	…	630	…	610	…	…	…	…
Kiribati	0.2	59	*0.3[z]*	*52[z]*	0.3	38	*0.3[z]*	*42[z]*	0.5	46	0.7[z]	47[z]	…	…	…
Lao PDR	9	40	*10*	*42*	3	40	*6*	*44*	12	40	16	43	95	95	95
Macao, China	0.9	59	1	63	0.5	49	1	54	1	56	2	59	68	55	77
Malaysia	76	65	…	…	…	…	…	…	…	…	147[z]	63[z]	…	…	…
Marshall Islands	0.1	…	…	…	0.2	…	…	…	0.3	…	…	…	…	…	…
Micronesia	…	…	…	…	…	…	…	…	…	…	…	…	…	…	…
Myanmar	54	77	59	84	14	73	20	79	68	76	80	82	95	96	95
Nauru	…	…	…	…	…	…	…	…	…	…	**0.04**	**81**	…	…	…
New Zealand	13	63	17	66	15	54	19	58	28	58	36	61	…	…	…
Niue	0.02	43	…	…	0.0	50	…	…	0.03	44	0.03[z]	68[z]	…	…	…
Palau	0.1	54	…	…	0.1	49	…	…	0.2	51	…	…	…	…	…
Papua New Guinea	…	…	…	…	…	…	…	…	…	…	…	…	…	…	…
Philippines	100	76	118	76	50	76	51	77	150	76	169	76	…	…	…
Republic of Korea	90	54	**100**	**65**	102	27	**114**	**40**	192	40	**214**	**52**	…	…	…
Samoa	*0.3*	*76*	*0.4[y]*	*74[y]*	0.8	49	*0.8[y]*	*53[y]*	*1*	*57*	*1[y]*	*60[y]*	…	…	…
Singapore	…	…	…	…	…	…	…	…	9	65	12	67	…	…	…
Solomon Islands	…	…	…	…	…	…	…	…	1	33	…	…	…	…	…
Thailand	…	…	126	56	…	…	83	53	…	…	209	55	…	…	…
Timor-Leste	…	…	2[z]	*26[z]*	…	…	1[z]	*24[z]*	…	…	3[z]	*25[z]*	…	…	…
Tokelau	…	…	…	…	…	…	…	…	…	…	*0.03[y]*	*44[y]*	…	…	…
Tonga	*0.7*	*49*	…	…	*0.3*	*48*	…	…	*1*	*48*	…	…	…	…	…
Tuvalu	…	…	…	…	…	…	…	…	…	…	…	…	…	…	…
Vanuatu	…	…	…	…	…	…	…	…	0.4	47	…	…	…	…	…
Viet Nam	194	70	306	68	64	51	133	54	258	65	439	64	*98*	…	…
Latin America and the Caribbean															
Anguilla	…	…	…	…	…	…	…	…	*0.07*	*63*	0.1	69	*67[z]*	*71[z]*	*65[z]*
Antigua and Barbuda	…	…	…	…	…	…	…	…	…	…	…	…	…	…	…
Argentina	171	73	120[z]	72[z]	…	…	137[z]	63[z]	…	…	257[z]	68[z]	…	…	…
Aruba	*0.2*	*49*	…	…	*0.2*	*49*	…	…	0.4	49	0.5	54	93	95	92
Bahamas	*0.6*	*73*	1	59	*0.6*	*75*	1	58	*1*	*74*	3	59	90	89	90
Barbados	*0.7*	*58*	…	…	*0.5*	*58*	…	…	*1*	*58*	1	59	57	57	57
Belize	*0.7*	*63*	1	61	*0.2*	*60*	0.5	52	*0.9*	*62*	2	58	36	29	41
Bermuda	…	…	0.4	68	…	…	0.4	67	…	…	0.7	67	100	100	100
Bolivia	*14*	*59*	*19[y]*	*61[y]*	25	48	*25[y]*	*47[y]*	*39*	*52*	*45[y]*	*53[y]*	…	…	…
Brazil	703	84	966[z]	88[z]	401	70	646[z]	70[z]	1 104	79	1 612[z]	81[z]	…	…	…
British Virgin Islands	0.2	64	0.1	67	0.05	57	0.08	68	0.2	63	0.2	67	…	…	…
Cayman Islands	0.1	52	0.1	61	0.1	41	0.2	56	0.2	46	0.3	58	100	99	100
Chile	16	78	23	78	29	54	44	54	45	62	67	63	…	…	…
Colombia	*138*	*50*	…	…	*48*	*50*	…	…	*187*	*50*	165	52	…	…	…
Costa Rica	*9*	*51*	15*	57*	*4*	*54*	6*	59*	*13*	*52*	21*	58*	80*	81*	79*
Cuba	40	68	46	64	25	49	42	48	65	60	89	56	100	100	100
Dominica	*0.3*	*68*	0.2	63	*0.1*	*67*	0.2	65	*0*	*68*	0.5	64	34	29	37
Dominican Republic	…	…	13	76	14	47	20	53	…	…	33	62	80	72	85
Ecuador	*31*	*49*	44	50	*23*	*50*	33*	49*	*54*	*50*	77*	49*	70*	64*	77*
El Salvador	…	…	12*	51*	…	…	7*	44*	…	…	19*	48*	89*	87*	90*
Grenada	…	…	0.6[z]	60[z]	…	…	0.3[z]	57[z]	…	…	0.9[z]	59[z]	35[z]	39[z]	33[z]
Guatemala	20	…	31*	43*	13	…	18*	42*	33	…	50*	43*	…	…	…
Guyana	*3*	*63*	…	…	*0.9*	*63*	*1.0*	*63*	*4*	*63*	*4*	*63*	*55[z]*	*46[z]*	*60[z]*
Haiti	…	…	…	…	…	…	…	…	…	…	…	…	…	…	…
Honduras	…	…	11[y]	56[y]	…	…	5[y]	52[y]	…	…	17[y]	55[y]	64[y]	59[y]	69[y]
Jamaica	…	…	…	…	…	…	…	…	…	…	*13[z]*	*68[z]*	…	…	…
Mexico	321	46	366	49	198	40	245	43	519	44	610	47	…	…	…
Montserrat	*0.0*	*63*	…	…	*0.01*	*60*	…	…	0.03	*62*	0.03	63	52	20	71
Netherlands Antilles	0.7	46	…	…	0.4	66	…	…	1	53	…	…	…	…	…
Nicaragua	7*	56*	9	50	3*	56*	4	58	10*	56*	14	53	53	46	59

SECONDARY EDUCATION						TERTIARY EDUCATION				
Pupil/teacher ratio[2]						Teaching staff				
Lower secondary		Upper secondary		Total secondary						
School year ending in		School year ending in		School year ending in		School year ending in				
1999	2006	1999	2006	1999	2006	1999		2006		
						Total (000)	% F	Total (000)	% F	**Country or territory**
17	17	…	*18*	…	*18*	504	…	1 332	42	China
…	…	…	…	…	16[z]	.	.	.	.	Cook Islands
…	…	…	…	…	…	…	…	…	…	DPR Korea
…	22[y]	…	22[y]	…	22[y]	…	…	…	…	Fiji
…	*13*	…	*11*	…	*12*	…	…	272[z]	*39*[z]	Indonesia
16	14	13	11	14	12	465	…	511	*18*	Japan
21	*21*[z]	19	*13*[z]	20	17[z]	.	.	.	.	Kiribati
20	*23*	22	*27*	20	25	1	31	3	34	Lao PDR
24	23	21	20	23	22	0.7	…	2	32	Macao, China
18	…	…	…	…	17[z]	…	…	45[z]	48[z]	Malaysia
28	…	18	…	22	…	…	…	…	…	Marshall Islands
…	…	…	…	…	…	0.1	…	…	…	Micronesia
28	34	38	32	30	34	*9*	*76*	…	…	Myanmar
…	…	…	…	…	**16**	.	.	.	.	Nauru
18	15	13	14	15	15	11	43	15	50	New Zealand
6	…	21	…	11	8[z]	.	.	.	.	Niue
14	…	12	…	13	…	…	…	…	…	Palau
…	…	…	…	…	…	*1*	*20*	…	…	Papua New Guinea
41	42	21	26	34	37	94	…	*113*[z]	*56*[z]	Philippines
22	**21**	23	**16**	23	**18**	127	25	**193**	**31**	Republic of Korea
26	*25*[y]	17	*19*[y]	*20*	*21*[y]	0.2	41	…	…	Samoa
…	…	…	…	19	18	…	…	…	…	Singapore
…	…	…	…	13	…	.	.	.[z]	.[z]	Solomon Islands
…	22	…	21	…	22	50	53	*70*	*51*	Thailand
…	28[z]	…	18[z]	…	24[z]	…	…	…	…	Timor-Leste
…	…	…	…	…	*7*[y]	.	.	.	.	Tokelau
15	…	*13*	…	*15*	…	0.07	21	…	…	Tonga
…	…	…	…	…	…	.	.	.	.	Tuvalu
…	…	…	…	23	…	…	…	…	…	Vanuatu
29	21	29	27	29	23	28	37	48[z]	40[z]	Viet Nam
										Latin America and the Caribbean
…	…	…	…	*15*	10	.	.	0.02	50	Anguilla
…	…	…	…	…	…	.	.	.[y]	.[y]	Antigua and Barbuda
13	18[z]	…	10[z]	…	14[z]	102	54	*139*[z]	*50*[z]	Argentina
16	…	*16*	…	16	14	0.2	43	0.2	46	Aruba
23	13	*23*	12	*23*	13	…	…	…	…	Bahamas
18	…	*18*	…	*18*	15	*0.6*	*41*	…	…	Barbados
24	18	*23*	15	*24*	17	…	…	0.1[z]	*49*[z]	Belize
…	6	…	6	…	6	…	…	**0.1**	**55**	Bermuda
24	…	20	*24*[y]	*21*	…	13	…	*18*[y]	…	Bolivia
23	16[z]	21	15[z]	23	15[z]	174	41	293[z]	44[z]	Brazil
6	11	10	8	7	10	0.08	49	*0.1*[z]	*55*[z]	British Virgin Islands
11	11	7	7	9	9	0.02	42	0.05	24	Cayman Islands
32	25	27	24	29	24	…	…	…	…	Chile
19	…	*20*	…	*19*	27	86	34	87*	35*	Colombia
18	18*	*18*	17*	*18*	18*	…	…	…	…	Costa Rica
12	10	10	11	11	10	24	48	116	58	Cuba
21	21	*15*	11	*19*	16	.	.	.[z]	.[z]	Dominica
…	24	28	24	…	24	…	…	*11*[y]	*41*[y]	Dominican Republic
17	14	*17*	14*	*17*	14*	…	…	…	…	Ecuador
…	29*	…	26*	…	28*	7	32	9	33	El Salvador
…	*14*[z]	…	18*[,z]	…	15*[,z]	.	.	.[z]	.[z]	Grenada
15	17*	11	14*	13	16*	…	…	4	31	Guatemala
19	…	*19*	*18*	*19*	*18*	…	…	0.5	48	Guyana
…	…	…	…	…	…	…	…	…	…	Haiti
…	28[y]	…	45[y]	…	33[y]	…	…	*7*[y]	*38*[y]	Honduras
…	…	…	…	…	*18*[z]	…	…	…	…	Jamaica
18	20	14	15	17	18	192	…	262	…	Mexico
11	…	*10*	…	10	12	.	.	.	.	Montserrat
12	…	21	…	15	…	*0.2*	*42*	…	…	Netherlands Antilles
31*	33	*31*	32	*31*	33	…	…	…	…	Nicaragua

Table 10B (continued)

Country or territory	SECONDARY EDUCATION – Teaching staff – Lower secondary – 1999 Total (000)	% F	2006 Total (000)	% F	Upper secondary – 1999 Total (000)	% F	2006 Total (000)	% F	Total secondary – 1999 Total (000)	% F	2006 Total (000)	% F	Trained teachers (%)[1] – Total secondary – 2006 Total	Male	Female
Panama	8	55	9	60	6	55	7	54	14	55	16	58	90	88	92
Paraguay	…	…	…	…	…	…	…	…	…	…	*44[y]*	*62[y]*	…	…	…
Peru	…	…	…	…	…	…	…	…	…	…	173	45	…	…	…
Saint Kitts and Nevis	…	…	…	…	…	…	…	…	…	…	**0.4**	**66**	**46**	…	…
Saint Lucia	*0.4*	*65*	0.8	64	*0.3*	*62*	…	…	0.7	*64*	1	64	57	53	59
Saint Vincent/Grenad.	…	…	*0.4[z]*	*58[z]*	…	…	*0.2[z]*	*57[z]*	…	…	*1[z]*	*58[z]*	*55[z]*	*58[z]*	*53[z]*
Suriname	…	…	2	64	…	…	1	52	…	…	3	59	…	…	…
Trinidad and Tobago	*3*	*61*	*3[z]*	*62[z]*	*2*	55	*2[z]*	*62[z]*	*6*	*59*	*6[z]*	*62[z]*	*56[y]*	*58[y]*	*54[y]*
Turks and Caicos Islands	*0.1*	*61*	*0.1[z]*	*61[z]*	*0.05*	*63*	*0.07[z]*	*64[z]*	*0.1*	*62*	*0.2[z]*	*62[z]*	*100[z]*	*100[z]*	*100[z]*
Uruguay	14	75	14	…	5	65	7	…	19	72	21	…	…	…	…
Venezuela, B. R.	…	…	116[z]	65[z]	…	…	72[z]	60[z]	…	…	188[z]	63[z]	83[z]	76[z]	86[z]
North America and Western Europe															
Andorra	…	…	0.4[z]	61[z]	…	…	0.07[z]	51[z]	…	…	0.5[z]	59[z]	…	…	…
Austria	43	64	43	69	30	49	29	51	73	57	72	62	…	…	…
Belgium	…	…	43	60	…	…	…	…	…	…	*82*	*57*	…	…	…
Canada	71	*68*	…	…	68	*68*	…	…	139	*68*	…	…	…	…	…
Cyprus	*2*	*54*	3	68	*2*	*49*	3	55	*5*	*51*	6	61	…	…	…
Denmark	20	63	…	…	24	30	…	…	44	45	…	…	…	…	…
Finland	20	71	21[z]	72[z]	…	…	*14[z]*	*59[z]*	…	…	*35[z]*	*67[z]*	…	…	…
France	255	…	…	…	240	…	…	…	495	57	*524*	*58*	…	…	…
Germany	365	57	412	61	168	39	182	47	533	51	594	57	…	…	…
Greece	37	*64*	42	66	38	*49*	44	48	75	*56*	86	57	…	…	…
Iceland	*1*	*78*	*1*	*80*	1	44	2	53	*3*	*58*	*3*	*65*	…	…	…
Ireland	…	…	…	…	…	…	…	…	…	…	30	62	…	…	…
Israel	19	…	21	79	36	…	30	65	55	…	51	71	…	…	…
Italy	177	73	178	76	245	59	249	60	422	65	427	67	…	…	…
Luxembourg	…	…	…	…	…	…	…	…	…	…	4	47	…	…	…
Malta	3	50	3[z]	60[z]	0.2	31	…	…	4	48	4[z]	57[z]	…	…	…
Monaco	*0.2*	*69*	…	…	*0.2*	*54*	…	…	*0.4*	*61*	*0.4[y]*	*66[y]*	…	…	…
Netherlands	…	…	…	…	…	…	…	…	…	…	107	46	…	…	…
Norway	…	…	*20[y]*	*73[y]*	26	44	*26[y]*	*47[y]*	…	…	*46[y]*	*58[y]*	…	…	…
Portugal	…	…	47	67	…	…	47	65	…	…	94	66	…	…	…
San Marino	…	…	0.1[y]	69[y]	…	…	…	…	…	…	…	…	…	…	…
Spain	…	…	161	62	…	…	121	50	…	…	282	57	…	…	…
Sweden	28	…	40	66	35	50	39	51	63	…	79	59	…	…	…
Switzerland	…	…	32	49	…	…	…	…	…	…	42	47	…	…	…
United Kingdom	142	55	153[z]	61[z]	212	56	235[z]	61[z]	355	56	388[z]	61[z]	…	…	…
United States	764	60	921	68	740	51	758	56	1 504	56	1 680	62	…	…	…
South and West Asia															
Afghanistan	…	…	32[z]	…[z]	…	…	…	…	…	…	…	…	…	…	…
Bangladesh	136	13	186[y]	17[y]	129	13	192[y]	19[y]	265	13	378[y]	18[y]	32[y]	31[y]	35[y]
Bhutan	0.4	32	1	49	0.2	32	0.8	28	0.6	32	2	41	92	92	92
India	…	…	1 312[y]	37[y]	…	…	1 274[y]	31[y]	*1 995*	*34*	2 586[y]	34[y]	…	…	…
Iran, Islamic Republic of	179	45	236[z]	49[z]	143	44	294[z]	47[z]	322	45	530[z]	48[z]	100[z]	100[z]	100[z]
Maldives	0.8	25	3	39	0.05	27	…	…	0.9	25	…	…	…	…	…
Nepal	22	12	30[y]	16[y]	18	7	…	…	40	9	…	…	…	…	…
Pakistan	…	…	…	…	…	…	…	…	…	…	197[*,y]	51[*,y]	…	…	…
Sri Lanka	…	…	*67[y]*	*64[y]*	…	…	*52[y]*	*62[y]*	…	…	*119[y]*	*63[y]*	…	…	…
Sub-Saharan Africa															
Angola	…	…	…	…	…	…	…	…	*16*	*33*	…	…	…	…	…
Benin	*6*	*12*	*10[y]*	*11[y]*	*3*	*14*	*4[y]*	*15[y]*	*9*	*12*	*14[y]*	*12[y]*	…	…	…
Botswana	…	…	…	…	…	…	…	…	9	45	*12[z]*	*54[z]*	…	…	…
Burkina Faso	*5*	…	…	…	*1*	…	…	…	*6*	…	11	17	26	25	30
Burundi	…	…	…	…	…	…	…	…	…	…	*8[y]*	*21[y]*	…	…	…
Cameroon	*13*	*28*	…	…	*13*	*28*	…	…	*26*	*28*	*43*	*26*	…	…	…
Cape Verde	…	…	2	40	…	…	1	36	…	…	3	38	62[z]	60[z]	65[z]
Central African Republic	…	…	…	…	…	…	…	…	…	…	…	…	…	…	…
Chad	2	5	…	…	1	6	…	…	4	5	*7[z]*	…	…	…	…
Comoros	…	…	*2[z]*	*16[z]*	…	…	*1[z]*	*9[z]*	…	…	*3[z]*	*13[z]*	…	…	…

SECONDARY EDUCATION						TERTIARY EDUCATION				
Pupil/teacher ratio[2]						Teaching staff				
Lower secondary		Upper secondary		Total secondary						
School year ending in		School year ending in		School year ending in		School year ending in				
1999	2006	1999	2006	1999	2006	1999		2006		
						Total (000)	% F	Total (000)	% F	Country or territory
17	17	15	15	16	16	8	...	12	46	Panama
...	...	...	...	...	12[y]	...	...	...	...	Paraguay
...	...	...	...	...	16	...	...	...	...	Peru
...	...	...	...	...	**11**	.	.	.[z]	.[z]	Saint Kitts and Nevis
19	11	16	...	18	17	...	...	0.2	47	Saint Lucia
...	18[z]	...	18[z]	...	18[z]	.	.	.[z]	.[z]	Saint Vincent/Grenad.
...	16	...	11	...	14	...	...	...	...	Suriname
22	16[z]	19	16[z]	21	16[z]	0.5	31	2[z]	33[z]	Trinidad and Tobago
9	9[z]	9	9[z]	9	9[z]	.	.	.[z]	.[z]	Turks and Caicos Islands
12	13	23	20	15	15	11	...	14	...	Uruguay
...	12[z]	...	9[z]	...	11[z]	...	...	109*	...	Venezuela, B. R.
										North America and Western Europe
...	7[z]	...	14[z]	...	8[z]	...	...	0.08	40	Andorra
9	9	12	14	10	11	26	...	40	35	Austria
...	7	...	...	...	10	...	...	26	41	Belgium
17	...	...	...	...	...	129	41	...	...	Canada
14	11	12	11	13	11	1	34	2	40	Cyprus
10	...	9	...	10	...	...	...	...	...	Denmark
10	10[z]	...	17[z]	...	12[z]	18	46	19	46	Finland
13	...	11	...	12	11	102	40	136[y]	39[y]	France
15	13	16	16	15	14	272	30	288	35	Germany
10	8	10	8	10	8	17	31	29	35	Greece
11	10	14	12	13	11	1	43	2	44	Iceland
...	...	...	...	...	11	10	33	12	38	Ireland
12	12	9	12	10	12	...	...	...	...	Israel
10	10	11	11	11	11	73	28	100	34	Italy
...	...	...	...	...	10	...	...	...	...	Luxembourg
...	8[z]	...	...	...	10[z]	0.7	25	0.7[z]	23[z]	Malta
10	...	7	...	8	9[y]	.	.	.	.	Monaco
...	...	...	...	...	13	...	...	44	36	Netherlands
...	9[y]	8	8[y]	...	9[y]	14	36	18	40	Norway
...	8	...	6	...	7	...	...	37	43	Portugal
...	6[y]	...	...	...	...	...	...	...	...	San Marino
...	12	...	9	...	11	108	35	146	39	Spain
12	10	18	9	15	9	29	...	36	43	Sweden
...	9	...	...	...	14	8	16	33	31	Switzerland
16	15[z]	14	14[z]	15	15[z]	92	32	126	41	United Kingdom
16	14	14	15	15	15	992	41	1 290	45	United States
										South and West Asia
...	14[z]	...	...	...	...	...	...	2[y]	12[y]	Afghanistan
43	34[y]	32	21[y]	37	27[y]	45	14	52[z]	15[z]	Bangladesh
35	30	27	12	32	23	0.2	...	0.4	...	Bhutan
...	37[y]	...	28[y]	34	33[y]	...	...	539[y]	40[y]	India
30	19[z]	31	19[z]	30	19[z]	65	17	122	20	Iran, Islamic Republic of
18	11	9	...	17	...	.	.	–	–	Maldives
38	40[y]	24	...	32	...	...	...	...	...	Nepal
...	...	...	...	...	42[y]	...	...	45	37	Pakistan
...	20[y]	...	19[y]	...	20[y]	...	...	...	...	Sri Lanka
										Sub-Saharan Africa
...	...	...	...	18	...	0.8	20	...	...	Angola
27	27[y]	15	16[y]	24	24[y]	0.7	9	...	...	Benin
...	...	...	...	18	14[z]	0.5	28	0.5[z]	37[z]	Botswana
29	...	23	...	28	30	0.8	...	1	7	Burkina Faso
...	...	...	...	...	19[y]	0.4	...	0.7[z]	14[z]	Burundi
26	...	21	...	24	16	3	...	3[z]	...	Cameroon
...	21	...	17	...	19	...	...	0.5	43	Cape Verde
...	...	...	...	...	...	0.3	5	...	...	Central African Republic
41	...	23	...	34	34[z]	...	...	1[z]	3[z]	Chad
...	16[z]	...	11[z]	...	14[z]	0.1	10	0.1[y]	15[y]	Comoros

Table 10B (continued)

Country or territory	SECONDARY EDUCATION – Teaching staff – Lower secondary – School year ending in 1999 – Total (000)	1999 % F	2006 Total (000)	2006 % F	Upper secondary – 1999 Total (000)	1999 % F	2006 Total (000)	2006 % F	Total secondary – 1999 Total (000)	1999 % F	2006 Total (000)	2006 % F	Trained teachers (%)[1] – Total secondary – 2006 Total	Male	Female
Congo	…	…	4[y]	15[y]	…	…	*3[y]*	*11[y]*	…	…	*7[y]*	*13[y]*	…	…	…
Côte d'Ivoire	*13*	…	…	…	*7*	*13*	…	…	*20*	…	…	…	…	…	…
D. R. Congo	…	…	…	…	…	…	…	…	89	10	…	…	…	…	…
Equatorial Guinea	0.7	5	…	…	0.1	7	…	…	0.9	5	…	…	…	…	…
Eritrea	1	12	2	10	1	11	2	12	2	12	4	11	49	47	64
Ethiopia	…	…	…	…	…	…	…	…	…	…	…	…	…	…	…
Gabon	*2*	*17*	…	…	*0.7*	*15*	…	…	*3*	*16*	…	…	…	…	…
Gambia	2	16	3*	18*	0.6	12	0.9*	12*	2	15	4*	16*	89*	90*	83*
Ghana	40	24	**67**	**23**	12	16	***18***	***19***	52	22	***85***	***22***	…	…	…
Guinea	4	11	9	5	*1*	*10*	…	…	*6*	*11*	…	…	…	…	…
Guinea-Bissau	…	…	…	…	…	…	…	…	…	…	…	…	…	…	…
Kenya	…	…	…	…	…	…	…	…	…	…	*78[z]*	*38[z]*	…	…	…
Lesotho	*2*	*51*	…	…	*1.0*	*53*	…	…	3	51	4	55	87	78	95
Liberia	4	16	…	…	3	16	…	…	7	16	…	…	…	…	…
Madagascar	…	…	22	…	…	…	8	…	…	…	31	*47*	…	…	…
Malawi	…	…	…	…	…	…	10	18	…	…	…	…	…	…	…
Mali	5*	17*	10	17	3	10	…	…	8*	14*	…	…	…	…	…
Mauritius	…	…	…	…	…	…	…	…	5	47	7[z]	55[z]	…	…	…
Mozambique	…	…	8	16	…	…	2	15	…	…	10	16	64	62	80
Namibia	4	45	…	…	1	49	…	…	5	46	6	*50*	97[z]	…	…
Niger	2	23	5	18	2	12	2	13	4	18	7	17	21	21	20
Nigeria	…	…	…	…	…	…	…	…	…	…	159[z]	36[z]	…	…	…
Rwanda	…	…	…	…	…	…	…	…	…	…	*8[z]*	*20[z]*	…	…	…
Sao Tome and Principe	…	…	…	…	…	…	…	…	…	…	*0.4*	*13*	…	…	…
Senegal	*6*	*14*	…	…	*3*	*13*	…	…	*9*	*14*	*15[z]*	*14[z]*	51[y]	50[y]	55[y]
Seychelles	*0.4*	*54*	…	…	*0.2*	*55*	…	…	0.6	54	**0.6**	**55**	…	…	…
Sierra Leone	…	…	…	…	…	…	…	…	…	…	**10**	**16**	**82**	**81**	**89**
Somalia	…	…	…	…	…	…	…	…	…	…	…	…	…	…	…
South Africa	…	…	…	…	…	…	…	…	145	50	149[y]	52[y]	…	…	…
Swaziland	…	…	…	…	…	…	…	…	…	…	4[z]	46[z]	99[z]	98[z]	99[z]
Togo	5	13	…	…	2	15	…	…	7	13	*13[z]*	*7[z]*	47[y]	47[y]	39[y]
Uganda	…	…	…	…	…	…	…	…	…	…	*36[z]*	*22[z]*	82[y]	81[y]	86[y]
United Republic of Tanzania	…	…	…	…	…	…	…	…	…	…	…	…	…	…	…
Zambia	*4*	*28*	…	…	*6*	*27*	…	…	*10*	*27*	…	…	…	…	…
Zimbabwe	…	…	…	…	…	…	…	…	31	37	…	…	…	…	…

	Sum	% F	Sum	% F	Sum	% F	Sum	% F	Sum	% F	Sum	% F	Median		
World	…	…	…	…	…	…	…	…	24180	52	28906	53	…	…	…
Countries in transition	…	…	…	…	…	…	…	…	2 785	74	2 674	76	…	…	…
Developed countries	…	…	…	…	…	…	…	…	6 286	55	6 595	59	…	…	…
Developing countries	…	…	…	…	…	…	…	…	15 109	47	19 637	48	…	…	…
Arab States	…	…	…	…	…	…	…	…	1 387	46	1 776	50	…	…	…
Central and Eastern Europe	…	…	…	…	…	…	…	…	3 158	72	2 971	74	…	…	…
Central Asia	…	…	…	…	…	…	…	…	873	66	923	69	…	…	…
East Asia and the Pacific	…	…	…	…	…	…	…	…	7 702	46	9 415	47	…	…	…
East Asia	…	…	…	…	…	…	…	…	7 476	46	9 166	46	…	…	…
Pacific	…	…	…	…	…	…	…	…	226	57	249	56	…	…	…
Latin America/Caribbean	…	…	…	…	…	…	…	…	2 746	64	3 594	66	66	65	67
Caribbean	…	…	…	…	…	…	…	…	53	44	66	39	56	56	56
Latin America	…	…	…	…	…	…	…	…	2 693	64	3 527	66	…	…	…
N. America/W. Europe	…	…	…	…	…	…	…	…	4 487	56	4 851	61	…	…	…
South and West Asia	…	…	…	…	…	…	…	…	2 956	35	4 138	35	…	…	…
Sub-Saharan Africa	…	…	…	…	…	…	…	…	872	31	1 238	30	…	…	…

1. Data on trained teachers (defined according to national standards) are not collected for countries whose education statistics are gathered through the OECD, Eurostat or the World Education Indicators questionnaires.

2. Based on headcounts of pupils and teachers.

3. Teaching staff in upper secondary includes full- and part-time teachers.

SECONDARY EDUCATION						TERTIARY EDUCATION				
Pupil/teacher ratio[2]						Teaching staff				
Lower secondary		Upper secondary		Total secondary						
School year ending in		School year ending in		School year ending in		School year ending in				
1999	2006	1999	2006	1999	2006	1999		2006		
						Total (000)	% F	Total (000)	% F	Country or territory
…	45[y]	…	*18*[y]	…	*34*[y]	*0.4*	*5*	…	…	Congo
34	…	*21*	…	*29*	…	…	…	…	…	Côte d'Ivoire
…	…	…	…	14	…	4	6	…	…	D. R. Congo
25	…	15	…	23	…	…	…	…	…	Equatorial Guinea
55	59	45	47	51	54	0.2	13	0.4[y]	14[y]	Eritrea
…	…	…	…	…	…	2	6	**8**	**9**	Ethiopia
28	…	*28*	…	*28*	…	0.6	17	…	…	Gabon
20	23*	25	28*	22	24*	0.1	15	0.1[y]	16[y]	Gambia
20	**17**	19	***25***	20	***19***	*2*	*13*	**4**	**11**	Ghana
31	40	*26*	…	*30*	…	…	…	1	3	Guinea
…	…	…	…	…	…	*0.03*	*18*	…	…	Guinea-Bissau
…	…	…	…	…	*32*[z]	…	…	…	…	Kenya
24	…	*17*	…	22	25	0.4	*45*	0.6	47	Lesotho
17	…	18	…	17	…	0.6	15	…	…	Liberia
…	27	…	16	…	24	1	31	2	28	Madagascar
…	…	…	16	…	…	0.5	25	0.4[y]	32[y]	Malawi
31*	35	24	…	28*	…	1.0	…	*1*[z]	…	Mali
…	…	…	…	20	*17*[z]	*0.6*	*26*	…	…	Mauritius
…	39	…	24	…	36	…	…	3[z]	21[z]	Mozambique
25	…	21	…	24	25	…	…	0.8	42	Namibia
34	33	12	20	24	30	…	…	1	*6*	Niger
…	…	…	…	…	40[z]	52	31	37[y]	17[y]	Nigeria
…	…	…	…	…	*26*[z]	0.4	10	*2*[z]	*12*[z]	Rwanda
…	…	…	…	…	*22*	.	.	.	.	Sao Tome and Principe
29	…	*19*	…	*25*	*26*[z]	…	…	…	…	Senegal
14	…	*14*	…	14	**13**	.	.	.	.	Seychelles
…	…	…	…	…	**24**	…	…	…	…	Sierra Leone
…	…	…	…	…	…	…	…	…	…	Somalia
…	…	…	…	29	31[y]	…	…	44	51	South Africa
…	…	…	…	…	17[z]	0.2	32	0.5	40	Swaziland
40	…	23	…	35	*30*[z]	0.4	10	…	…	Togo
…	…	…	…	…	*21*[z]	2	17	4[y]	19[y]	Uganda
…	…	…	…	…	…	2	14	**3**	**18**	United Republic of Tanzania
29	…	*19*	…	*23*	…	…	…	…	…	Zambia
…	…	…	…	27	…	…	…	…	…	Zimbabwe

Weighted average						Sum	% F	Sum	% F	
…	…	…	…	18	18	6 422	39	9 156	41	World
…	…	…	…	11	10	744	54	1 032	55	Countries in transition
…	…	…	…	13	13	2 784	34	3 414	38	Developed countries
…	…	…	…	21	20	2 893	39	4 711	41	Developing countries
…	…	…	…	16	16	205	33	280	34	Arab States
…	…	…	…	13	11	941	50	1 255	52	Central and Eastern Europe
…	…	…	…	11	12	102	44	142	49	Central Asia
…	…	…	…	17	17	1 608	33	2 701	37	East Asia and the Pacific
…	…	…	…	17	17	1 533	33	2 628	37	East Asia
…	…	…	…	14	14	75	44	73	43	Pacific
…	…	…	…	19	16	832	45	1 249	46	Latin America/Caribbean
…	…	…	…	22	19	6	47	8	50	Caribbean
…	…	…	…	19	16	826	45	1 241	46	Latin America
…	…	…	…	14	13	2 043	38	2 600	41	N. America/W. Europe
…	…	…	…	33	30	573	31	777	35	South and West Asia
…	…	…	…	24	27	116	29	153	28	Sub-Saharan Africa

Data in italic are UIS estimates.
Data in bold are for the school year ending in 2007.

(z) Data are for the school year ending in 2005.
(y) Data are for the school year ending in 2004.
(*) National estimate.

Table 11
Commitment to education: public spending

Country or territory	Total public expenditure on education as % of GNP		Total public expenditure on education as % of total government expenditure		Public current expenditure on education as % of total public expenditure on education		Public current expenditure on primary education as % of public current expenditure on education		Public current expenditure on primary education per pupil (unit cost) at PPP in constant 2005 US$		Public current expenditure on primary education as % of GNP	
	1999	2006	1999	2006	1999	2006	1999	2006	1999	2006	1999	2006
Arab States												
Algeria	…	…	…	…	…	…	…	…	…	*692*[x]	…	*1.6*[x]
Bahrain	…	…	…	…	…	…	…	…	…	…	…	…
Djibouti	7.5	7.6	…	**23**	…	…	…	…	…	…	…	…
Egypt	…	4.2	…	**13**	…	…	…	…	…	…	…	…
Iraq	…	…	…	…	…	…	…	…	…	…	…	…
Jordan	5.0	…	21	…	…	…	…	…	568	695[z]	1.9	1.8[z]
Kuwait	…	*3.4*	…	*13*	…	*92*	…	*21*	…	2 204[z]	…	0.7
Lebanon	2.0	2.8	10	11[z]	…	93	…	*33*[z]	…	*402*[z]	…	*0.9*[z]
Libyan Arab Jamahiriya	…	…	…	…	68	…	*12*	…	…	…	…	…
Mauritania	*2.8*	2.8	…	10	…	99	…	*62*[z]	…	*224*[z]	…	*1.4*[z]
Morocco	6.2	6.8[z]	26	27[z]	91	95[z]	39	45[z]	697	1 005[z]	2.2	2.9[z]
Oman	4.2	5.0	21	31	…	92	…	50[z]	…	…	1.4	1.8[y]
Palestinian A. T.	…	…	…	…	…	…	…	…	…	…	…	…
Qatar	…	…	…	20[z]	…	*88*[y]	…	…	…	…	…	…
Saudi Arabia	7.0	6.7[y]	26	28[y]	…	…	…	…	…	…	…	…
Sudan	…	…	…	…	…	…	…	…	…	…	…	…
Syrian Arab Republic	…	…	…	…	…	…	…	…	349	611	1.7	1.9
Tunisia	7.2	7.7[z]	…	21[z]	…	87[z]	…	*35*[z]	…	*1 581*[z]	…	*2.4*[z]
United Arab Emirates	…	1.6[*,y]	…	*28*[z]	…	…	…	…	1 997	1 636[y]	0.7	0.4[y]
Yemen	…	…	…	…	…	…	…	…	…	…	…	…
Central and Eastern Europe												
Albania	…	…	…	…	…	…	…	…	…	…	…	…
Belarus	6.0	6.2	…	13	…	94	…	*9*	…	*1 196*	…	*0.5*
Bosnia and Herzegovina	…	…	…	…	…	…	…	…	…	…	…	…
Bulgaria	…	4.5[z]	…	6[y]	…	91[z]	…	20[z]	…	2 045[z]	…	0.8[z]
Croatia	…	4.6[y]	…	10[x]	…	95[y]	…	*18*[y]	…	*2 197*[x]	…	*0.8*[y]
Czech Republic	4.1	4.7[y]	10	10[y]	*91*	90[y]	*18*	15[y]	*1 688*	2 242[y]	*0.7*	0.6[y]
Estonia	7.0	5.4[y]	…	15[y]	…	91[y]	…	26[y]	…	2 511[y]	…	1.3[y]
Hungary	5.0	5.8[z]	13	11[z]	*91*	93[z]	*20*	21[z]	*2 339*	4 479[z]	*0.9*	1.1[z]
Latvia	5.8	5.2[y]	…	14[y]	…	…	…	…	…	…	…	…
Lithuania	…	5.3[z]	…	15[z]	…	94[z]	…	15[z]	…	2 166[z]	…	0.7[z]
Montenegro	…	…	…	…	…	…	…	…	…	…	…	…
Poland	4.7	5.7[z]	11	13[y]	*93*	95[z]	…	30[z]	…	3 155[z]	…	1.7[z]
Republic of Moldova	4.6	6.6	16	20	…	86	…	…	…	…	…	…
Romania	*3.6*	3.6[z]	…	9[y]	…	94[z]	…	*14*[z]	…	*941*[z]	…	*0.5*[z]
Russian Federation	…	3.9[z]	…	13[y]	…	…	…	…	…	…	…	…
Serbia	…	…	…	…	…	…	…	…	…	…	…	…
Slovakia	4.2	4.1[z]	14	11[y]	*96*	94[z]	*14*	17[z]	*1 245*	2 149[z]	*0.6*	0.6[z]
Slovenia	…	6.0[z]	…	13[z]	…	93[z]	…	*20*[z]	…	*5 206*[z]	…	*1.1*[z]
TFYR Macedonia	*4.2*	…	…	…	…	…	…	…	…	…	…	…
Turkey	4.0	4.1[y]	…	…	…	90[y]	…	*40*[y]	…	*1 059*[y]	…	*1.5*[y]
Ukraine	3.7	6.4	14	19	…	…	…	…	…	…	…	…
Central Asia												
Armenia	*3.1*	…	…	…	…	…	…	…	…	…	…	…
Azerbaijan	4.3	2.4	24	17	99	98	…	*17*	…	*356*	…	*0.4*
Georgia	2.0	3.2	10	9	…	97[y]	…	…	…	…	…	…
Kazakhstan	4.0	2.5[z]	14	…	…	…	…	…	…	…	…	…
Kyrgyzstan	3.7	5.0[z]	…	…	99	95[z]	…	…	…	…	…	…
Mongolia	6.0	5.3[y]	…	…	…	94[y]	…	24[y]	…	261[y]	…	1.2[y]
Tajikistan	2.2	3.5	12	19	90	88[z]	…	*27*[z]	…	*106*[z]	…	*0.9*[z]
Turkmenistan	…	…	…	…	…	…	…	…	…	…	…	…
Uzbekistan	…	…	…	…	…	…	…	…	…	…	…	…
East Asia and the Pacific												
Australia	4.9	4.7[z]	…	…	*96*	96[z]	*33*	33[z]	*4 637*	5 181[z]	*1.6*	1.5[z]
Brunei Darussalam	…	…	*9*	…	97	…	…	…	…	…	…	…
Cambodia	1.0	1.8[y]	9	…	…	…	…	…	…	…	…	…
China	1.9	…	13	…	*93*	…	*34*	…	…	…	*0.6*	…
Cook Islands	0.4	…	*13*	…	99	…	53	…	…	…	0.2	…
DPR Korea	…	…	…	…	…	…	…	…	…	…	…	…

Public current expenditure on primary education per pupil as % of GNP per capita		Public current expenditure on secondary education as % of public current expenditure on education		Public current expenditure on secondary education per pupil (unit cost) at PPP in constant 2005 US$		Public current expenditure on secondary education as % of GNP		Public current expenditure on secondary education per pupil as % of GNP per capita		Primary teachers' compensation as % of current expenditure on primary education, in public institutions		Country or territory
1999	2006	1999	2006	1999	2006	1999	2006	1999	2006	1999	2006	
												Arab States
…	*11*[x]	…	…	…	*1 049*[x]	…	*1.9*[x]	…	*17*[x]	…	…	Algeria
…	…	…	…	…	…	…	…	…	…	…	…	Bahrain
…	…	…	…	…	…	…	…	…	…	…	…	Djibouti
…	…	…	…	…	…	…	…	…	…	…	…	Egypt
…	…	…	…	…	…	…	…	…	…	…	…	Iraq
13	12[z]	…	…	658	858[z]	1.8	1.7[z]	15	15[z]	78	85[z]	Jordan
…	8	…	*38*	…	3 280[z]	…	1.2	…	13	…	77	Kuwait
…	*8*[z]	…	*30*[z]	…	*449*[z]	…	*0.8*[z]	…	*8*[z]	69	84[z]	Lebanon
…	…	*10*	…	…	…	…	…	…	…	…	…	Libyan Arab Jamahiriya
…	*10*[z]	…	*33*[z]	…	*564*[z]	…	*0.7*[z]	…	*24*[z]	…	…	Mauritania
18	22[z]	44	38[z]	1 830	*1 738*[z]	2.5	2.5[z]	47	*38*[z]	…	…	Morocco
11	15[y]	…	41[z]	…	…	2.0	1.6[y]	21	14[y]	75	91[y]	Oman
…	…	…	…	…	…	…	…	…	…	…	…	Palestinian A. T.
…	…	…	…	…	…	…	…	…	…	…	…	Qatar
…	…	…	…	…	…	…	…	…	…	…	…	Saudi Arabia
…	…	…	…	…	…	…	…	…	…	…	…	Sudan
10	16	…	…	602	…	1.1	…	18	…	…	…	Syrian Arab Republic
…	*20*[z]	…	*43*[z]	…	*1 832*[z]	…	*2.9*[z]	…	*23*[z]	…	…	Tunisia
8	7[y]	…	…	2 605	2 115[y]	0.7	0.6[y]	10	9[y]	…	77[y]	United Arab Emirates
…	…	…	…	…	…	…	…	…	…	…	…	Yemen
												Central and Eastern Europe
…	…	…	…	…	…	…	…	…	…	…	…	Albania
…	*14*	…	*41*	…	*2 247*	…	*2.4*	…	*26*	…	…	Belarus
…	…	…	…	…	…	…	…	…	…	…	…	Bosnia and Herzegovina
…	22[z]	…	46[z]	…	1 955[z]	…	1.9[z]	…	21[z]	…	55[z]	Bulgaria
…	*19*[x]	…	*51*[y]	…	*2 777*[x]	…	*2.2*[y]	…	*24*[x]	…	…	Croatia
10	12[y]	*50*	52[y]	*3 328*	4 221[y]	*1.8*	2.2[y]	*20*	23[y]	45	47[y]	Czech Republic
…	18[y]	…	47[y]	…	3 362[y]	…	2.3[y]	…	25[y]	…	…	Estonia
18	26[z]	*41*	41[z]	*2 435*	3 983[z]	*1.8*	2.2[z]	*19*	23[z]	…	…	Hungary
…	…	…	…	…	…	…	…	…	…	…	…	Latvia
…	16[z]	…	51[z]	…	2 784[z]	…	2.5[z]	…	20[z]	…	…	Lithuania
…	…	…	…	…	…	…	…	…	…	…	…	Montenegro
…	23[z]	…	36[z]	…	2 979[z]	…	2.0[z]	…	22[z]	…	…	Poland
…	…	…	…	…	…	…	…	…	…	…	…	Republic of Moldova
…	*11*[z]	…	*46*[z]	…	*1 407*[z]	…	*1.5*[z]	…	*16*[z]	…	…	Romania
…	…	…	…	…	…	…	…	…	…	…	…	Russian Federation
…	…	…	…	…	…	…	…	…	…	…	…	Serbia
10	14[z]	*56*	50[z]	*2 246*	2 336[z]	*2.2*	1.9[z]	*18*	15[z]	62	54[z]	Slovakia
…	*24*[z]	…	*49*[z]	…	*6 711*[z]	…	*2.7*[z]	…	*30*[z]	…	*41*[z]	Slovenia
…	…	…	…	…	…	…	…	…	…	…	…	TFYR Macedonia
…	*13*[y]	…	*34*[y]	…	*1 313*[y]	…	*1.2*[y]	…	*16*[y]	…	…	Turkey
…	…	…	…	…	…	…	…	…	…	…	…	Ukraine
												Central Asia
…	…	…	…	…	…	…	…	…	…	…	…	Armenia
…	*6*	…	*50*	…	*547*	…	*1.2*	…	*10*	…	…	Azerbaijan
…	…	…	…	…	…	…	…	…	…	…	…	Georgia
…	…	…	…	…	…	…	…	…	…	…	…	Kazakhstan
…	…	…	…	…	…	…	…	…	…	*47*	…	Kyrgyzstan
…	13[y]	…	32[y]	…	241[y]	…	1.6[y]	…	12[y]	…	…	Mongolia
…	*8*[z]	…	*50*[z]	…	*138*[z]	…	*1.6*[z]	…	*11*[z]	…	…	Tajikistan
…	…	…	…	…	…	…	…	…	…	…	…	Turkmenistan
…	…	…	…	…	…	…	…	…	…	…	…	Uzbekistan
												East Asia and the Pacific
16	16[z]	*40*	39[z]	*4 218*	4 675[z]	*1.9*	1.8[z]	*14*	14[z]	60	63[z]	Australia
…	…	…	…	…	…	…	…	…	…	…	…	Brunei Darussalam
…	…	…	…	…	…	…	…	…	…	…	…	Cambodia
…	…	*38*	…	*455*	…	*0.7*	…	*11*	…	…	…	China
2*	…	40	…	…	…	0.2	…	2*	…	…	…	Cook Islands
…	…	…	…	…	…	…	…	…	…	…	…	DPR Korea

Table 11 (continued)

Country or territory	Total public expenditure on education as % of GNP		Total public expenditure on education as % of total government expenditure		Public current expenditure on education as % of total public expenditure on education		Public current expenditure on primary education as % of public current expenditure on education		Public current expenditure on primary education per pupil (unit cost) at PPP in constant 2005 US$		Public current expenditure on primary education as % of GNP	
	1999	2006	1999	2006	1999	2006	1999	2006	1999	2006	1999	2006
Fiji	5.7	6.5^{y}	18	…	…	97^{y}	…	40^{y}	…	1 143^{y}	…	2.5^{y}
Indonesia	…	*3.8*	…	***18***	…	…	…	…	…	…	…	…
Japan	3.6	3.5^{z}	9	9^{z}	…	…	…	…	…	…	…	…
Kiribati	7.7	…	…	…	…	…	…	…	…	…	…	…
Lao PDR	1.0	3.4	…	14	…	37	…	46^{z}	…	61^{z}	…	0.5^{z}
Macao, China	3.6	…	14	14^{z}	…	89^{y}	…	…	…	…	…	…
Malaysia	6.1	6.6^{y}	25	25^{y}	…	88^{y}	…	29^{y}	…	1 324^{y}	…	1.7^{y}
Marshall Islands	13.3	*9.5*^{y}	…	16^{x}	…	…	…	…	…	…	…	…
Micronesia	6.5	…	…	…	…	…	…	…	…	…	…	…
Myanmar	0.6	…	8	…	64	…	…	…	…	…	…	…
Nauru	…	…	…	…	…	…	…	…	…	…	…	…
New Zealand	7.2	6.1	…	15^{z}	*95*	100	*27*	24	*3 971*	4 831	*1.8*	1.5
Niue	…	…	…	…	100	…	32	…	…	…	…	…
Palau	…	…	…	…	…	…	…	…	…	…	…	…
Papua New Guinea	…	…	…	…	…	…	…	…	…	…	…	…
Philippines	…	2.3^{z}	…	15^{z}	…	93^{z}	…	54^{z}	…	418^{z}	…	1.2^{z}
Republic of Korea	3.8	4.6^{y}	13	16^{y}	*80*	88^{y}	*44*	34^{y}	*2 621*	3 379^{y}	*1.3*	1.4^{y}
Samoa	4.5	…	13	…	99	…	*32*	…	*443*	…	*1.4*	…
Singapore	…	…	…	…	…	…	…	…	…	…	…	…
Solomon Islands	*3.3*	…	…	…	…	…	…	…	…	…	…	…
Thailand	5.1	4.3^{z}	28	25^{z}	…	…	…	…	…	…	…	…
Timor-Leste	…	…	…	…	…	…	…	…	…	…	…	…
Tokelau	…	…	…	15^{x}	…	…	…	…	…	…	…	…
Tonga	*6.7*	4.9^{y}	…	13^{x}	…	…	…	…	…	…	…	…
Tuvalu	…	…	…	…	…	…	…	…	…	…	…	…
Vanuatu	6.7	10.0^{x}	17	…	84	…	39	…	409	…	2.2	…
Viet Nam	…	…	…	…	…	…	…	…	…	…	…	…
Latin America and the Caribbean												
Anguilla	…	4.0^{z}	…	14^{z}	…	90^{z}	…	30^{z}	…	…	…	1.1^{z}
Antigua and Barbuda	3.5	…	…	…	100	…	…	…	…	…	…	…
Argentina	4.6	4.0^{y}	13	13^{y}	94	99^{y}	37	37^{y}	1 637	1 703^{z}	1.6	1.5^{z}
Aruba	…	5.1^{z}	14	15^{z}	90	84^{z}	30	30^{z}	…	…	…	1.3^{z}
Bahamas	…	…	…	…	…	…	…	…	…	…	…	…
Barbados	5.3	7.2^{z}	15	16^{z}	92	96^{z}	*21*	*28*^{z}	…	…	*1.0*	*2.0*^{z}
Belize	*5.7*	5.8^{y}	*17*	18^{x}	…	88^{y}	…	47^{y}	…	846^{y}	…	2.4^{y}
Bermuda	…	1.2	…	…	…	97^{z}	…	*41*^{z}	…	…	…	*0.8*^{z}
Bolivia	5.8	6.6^{x}	16	18^{x}	84	96^{x}	*41*	46^{x}	*295*	435^{x}	*2.0*	2.9^{x}
Brazil	4.0	4.1^{y}	10	…	*95*	94^{y}	*33*	32^{y}	*788*	1 005^{y}	*1.3*	1.3^{y}
British Virgin Islands	…	4.0	…	12^{z}	…	95	…	27	…	…	…	1.0
Cayman Islands	…	2.9	…	…	…	…	…	…	…	…	…	…
Chile	4.0	3.6	16	16	88	95	45	36	1 256	1 287	1.5	1.2
Colombia	4.5	4.9	17	11^{z}	…	99	…	41	…	1 257	…	2.0
Costa Rica	5.5	4.9	…	21	100	79^{y}	47	56^{y}	1 469	1 623^{y}	2.6	2.3^{y}
Cuba	7.7	9.3	14	14	…	88	…	32	…	…	…	2.6
Dominica	*5.5*	…	…	…	…	…	…	…	…	…	…	…
Dominican Republic	…	3.9	…	17	…	96	…	…	…	*644*^{z}	…	*1.2*^{z}
Ecuador	2.0	…	10	…	93*	…	…	…	…	…	…	…
El Salvador	*2.4*	3.2	*17*	…	…	89	…	48	…	478	…	1.4
Grenada	…	6.0^{x}	…	13^{x}	…	*87*^{x}	…	*35*^{x}	…	*766*^{x}	…	*1.8*^{x}
Guatemala	…	2.6	…	…	…	92	…	66	…	390	…	1.6
Guyana	*9.3*	8.6	*18*	15	…	91	…	27	…	752^{z}	…	2.1
Haiti	…	…	…	…	…	…	…	…	…	…	…	…
Honduras	…	…	…	…	…	…	…	…	…	…	…	…
Jamaica	…	5.6^{z}	…	9^{z}	…	97^{z}	…	34^{z}	…	547^{z}	…	1.8^{z}
Mexico	4.5	5.6^{z}	23	26^{y}	95	97^{z}	41	39^{z}	1 114	1 604^{z}	1.8	2.2^{z}
Montserrat	…	…	*11*	…	47	65^{y}	…	…	…	…	…	…
Netherlands Antilles	…	…	14	…	94	…	…	…	…	…	…	…
Nicaragua	4.0	*3.3*^{x}	6	…	…	…	…	…	…	331	…	1.6
Panama	5.1	*4.1*^{y}	…	*9*^{y}	…	…	…	…	867	…	1.9	…
Paraguay	5.1	4.1^{y}	9	10^{y}	88	96^{y}	…	46^{y}	…	518^{y}	…	1.8^{y}
Peru	3.4	2.7	21	15	88	93	40	42	366	446	1.2	1.1
Saint Kitts and Nevis	*5.6*	10.8^{z}	*13*	13^{x}	…	37^{z}	…	…	…	…	…	…
Saint Lucia	8.0	7.1	21	19	79	74	*53*	39	*1 197*	949	*3.3*	2.0

Public current expenditure on primary education per pupil as % of GNP per capita		Public current expenditure on secondary education as % of public current expenditure on education		Public current expenditure on secondary education per pupil (unit cost) at PPP in constant 2005 US$		Public current expenditure on secondary education as % of GNP		Public current expenditure on secondary education per pupil as % of GNP per capita		Primary teachers' compensation as % of current expenditure on primary education, in public institutions		
1999	2006	1999	2006	1999	2006	1999	2006	1999	2006	1999	2006	**Country or territory**
…	19[y]	…	33[y]	…	1 060[y]	…	2.1[y]	…	17[y]	…	…	Fiji
…	…	…	…	…	…	…	…	…	…	…	…	Indonesia
…	…	…	…	…	…	…	…	…	…	…	…	Japan
…	…	…	…	…	…	…	…	…	…	…	…	Kiribati
…	3[z]	…	30[z]	…	91[z]	…	0.3[z]	…	5[z]	…	…	Lao PDR
…	…	…	…	…	…	…	…	…	…	…	…	Macao, China
…	13[y]	…	34[y]	…	1 923[y]	…	2.0[y]	…	19[y]	70	64[y]	Malaysia
…	…	…	…	…	…	…	…	…	…	…	…	Marshall Islands
…	…	…	…	…	…	…	…	…	…	…	…	Micronesia
…	…	…	…	…	…	…	…	…	…	…	…	Myanmar
…	…	…	…	…	…	…	…	…	…	…	…	Nauru
19	17	*40*	42	*4 947*	5 617	*2.7*	2.6	*24*	20	…	…	New Zealand
…	…	59	…	…	…	…	…	…	…	…	…	Niue
…	…	…	…	…	…	…	…	…	…	…	…	Palau
…	…	…	…	…	…	…	…	…	…	…	…	Papua New Guinea
…	7[z]	…	27[z]	…	435[z]	…	0.6[z]	…	8[z]	…	94[y]	Philippines
16	16[y]	*38*	43[y]	*2 177*	4 814[y]	*1.2*	1.7[y]	*13*	23[y]	78	64[y]	Republic of Korea
9	…	*27*	…	*468*	…	*1.2*	…	*10*	…	…	…	Samoa
…	…	…	…	…	…	…	…	…	…	…	…	Singapore
…	…	…	…	…	…	…	…	…	…	…	…	Solomon Islands
…	…	…	…	…	…	…	…	…	…	…	…	Thailand
…	…	…	…	…	…	…	…	…	…	…	…	Timor-Leste
…	…	…	…	…	…	…	…	…	…	…	…	Tokelau
…	…	…	…	…	…	…	…	…	…	…	…	Tonga
…	…	…	…	…	…	…	…	…	…	…	…	Tuvalu
12	…	52	…	2 081	…	2.9	…	61	…	94	…	Vanuatu
…	…	…	…	…	…	…	…	…	…	…	…	Viet Nam
												Latin America and the Caribbean
…	9[z]	…	17[x]	…	…	…	…	…	…	…	…	Anguilla
…	…	…	…	…	…	…	…	…	…	66	…	Antigua and Barbuda
12	12[z]	35	38[y]	2 044	2 789[z]	1.5	1.8[z]	15	20[z]	…	57[z]	Argentina
…	13[z]	32	32[z]	…	…	…	1.4[z]	…	20[z]	…	…	Aruba
…	…	…	…	…	…	…	…	…	…	…	…	Bahamas
11	*24*[z]	31	30[z]	…	…	1.5	2.1[z]	18	26[z]	…	…	Barbados
…	13[y]	…	44[y]	…	1 226[y]	…	2.2[y]	…	19[y]	…	86[y]	Belize
…	*11*[z]	…	*52*[z]	…	…	…	*1.0*[z]	…	*14*[z]	…	…	Bermuda
11	17[x]	*22*	25[x]	*278*	350[x]	*1.1*	1.6[x]	*11*	13[x]	…	…	Bolivia
10	12[y]	*36*	40[y]	*714*	926[y]	*1.4*	1.5[y]	*9*	11[y]	…	…	Brazil
…	8	…	36	…	…	…	1.4	…	15	…	81[z]	British Virgin Islands
…	…	…	…	…	…	…	…	…	…	…	89	Cayman Islands
13	12	36	38	1 424	1 435	1.3	1.3	15	13	…	85	Chile
…	17	…	29	…	1 052	…	1.4	…	14	91*	81	Colombia
18	17[y]	29	34[y]	2 127	1 632[y]	1.6	1.4[y]	26	17[y]	…	…	Costa Rica
…	33	…	36	…	…	…	3.0	…	36	…	69[z]	Cuba
…	…	…	…	…	…	…	…	…	…	…	…	Dominica
…	*9*[z]	…	…	…	*460*[z]	…	*0.5*[z]	…	*6*[z]	…	71[z]	Dominican Republic
…	…	…	…	…	…	…	…	…	…	…	…	Ecuador
…	9	…	24	…	457	…	0.7	…	9	…	73	El Salvador
…	*11*[x]	…	*35*[x]	…	*841*[x]	…	*1.8*[x]	…	*13*[x]	…	93[x]	Grenada
…	8	…	10	…	179	…	0.2	…	4	…	*88*[z]	Guatemala
…	18[z]	…	35	…	*1 327*	…	2.8	…	*29*	…	75[z]	Guyana
…	…	…	…	…	…	…	…	…	…	…	…	Haiti
…	…	…	…	…	…	…	…	…	…	…	…	Honduras
…	15[z]	…	38[z]	…	820[z]	…	2.0[z]	…	22[z]	…	87[z]	Jamaica
12	15[z]	…	30[z]	…	1 722[z]	…	1.7[z]	…	16[z]	86	84[z]	Mexico
…	…	…	…	…	…	…	…	…	…	…	…	Montserrat
…	…	…	…	…	…	…	…	…	…	…	…	Netherlands Antilles
…	9	…	…	…	146	…	0.3	…	4	…	88	Nicaragua
14	…	…	…	1 236	…	1.5	…	19	…	…	99[z]	Panama
…	11[y]	30	30[y]	816	600[y]	1.3	1.2[y]	16	13[y]	…	82[y]	Paraguay
7	8	28	36	491	554	0.9	0.9	10	9	88	66	Peru
…	…	…	…	…	…	…	…	…	…	…	68[z]	Saint Kitts and Nevis
20	14	*33*	30	1 601	1 231	*2.0*	1.6	*27*	18	88	79	Saint Lucia

Table 11 (continued)

Country or territory	Total public expenditure on education as % of GNP		Total public expenditure on education as % of total government expenditure		Public current expenditure on education as % of total public expenditure on education		Public current expenditure on primary education as % of public current expenditure on education		Public current expenditure on primary education per pupil (unit cost) at PPP in constant 2005 US$		Public current expenditure on primary education as % of GNP	
	1999	2006	1999	2006	1999	2006	1999	2006	1999	2006	1999	2006
Saint Vincent/Grenad.	*7.2*	8.8[z]	…	16[z]	…	68[z]	…	50[z]	…	1 227[z]	…	3.0[z]
Suriname	…	…	…	…	…	…	…	…	…	…	…	…
Trinidad and Tobago	3.9	…	*16*	…	96	…	40	…	1 012	…	1.5	…
Turks and Caicos Islands	…	…	17	12[z]	73	88[z]	30	*20[z]*	…	…	…	…
Uruguay	2.8	3.0	…	12	92	…	32	…	748	…	0.8	…
Venezuela, B. R.	…	3.7	…	…	…	92	…	30	…	583	…	1.0
North America and Western Europe												
Andorra	…	2.3	…	…	…	94	…	25	…	…	…	0.5
Austria	6.4	5.5[z]	12	11[z]	*94*	96[z]	*19*	19[z]	*7 112*	7 596[z]	*1.1*	1.0[z]
Belgium	…	6.0[y]	…	12[y]	…	98[y]	…	24[y]	…	6 303[y]	…	1.4[y]
Canada	6.0	5.1[z]	…	…	*98*	95[z]	…	…	…	…	…	…
Cyprus	5.4	6.5[y]	…	15[z]	86	87[z]	34	30[z]	…	…	1.6	1.7[y]
Denmark	8.2	8.3[z]	15	16[z]	…	95[z]	…	22[z]	*7 345*	7 949[z]	*1.6*	1.8[z]
Finland	6.3	6.4[z]	12	13[z]	*94*	94[z]	*21*	20[z]	*4 615*	5 373[z]	*1.2*	1.2[z]
France	5.7	5.7[z]	11	11[z]	*91*	91[z]	*20*	21[z]	*4 697*	5 224[z]	*1.1*	1.1[z]
Germany	4.5	4.6[y]	10	10[y]	…	98[y]	…	15[y]	…	4 837[y]	…	0.7[y]
Greece	3.5	4.4[z]	7	9[z]	*78*	78[z]	*25*	*26[z]*	*2 148*	*3 562[z]*	*0.7*	*0.9[z]*
Iceland	…	7.9[y]	…	17[y]	…	90[y]	…	34[y]	…	7 788[y]	…	2.4[y]
Ireland	4.9	5.6[z]	13	14[z]	*91*	92[z]	*32*	33[z]	*3 112*	5 100[z]	*1.4*	1.7[z]
Israel	7.5	7.1[y]	14	14[x]	*94*	95[y]	*34*	36[y]	*4 835*	5 135[y]	*2.4*	2.4[y]
Italy	4.7	4.5[z]	10	9[z]	94	94[z]	*26*	25[z]	*6 425*	6 347[z]	*1.2*	1.0[z]
Luxembourg	*3.7*	…	*8*	…	…	…	…	…	…	*9 953[z]*	…	*1.4[z]*
Malta	*4.9*	5.2[y]	…	11[y]	…	95[y]	…	22[y]	…	2 549[y]	…	1.1[y]
Monaco	…	…	5	…	92	91[y]	18	17[y]	…	…	…	…
Netherlands	4.5	5.2[z]	10	11[z]	*96*	94[z]	*26*	26[z]	*4 606*	5 572[z]	*1.1*	1.3[z]
Norway	7.2	7.1[z]	16	17[z]	90	92[z]	*25*	24[z]	*6 456*	7 072[z]	*1.6*	1.6[z]
Portugal	*5.4*	5.5[z]	*13*	11[z]	*93*	98[z]	*31*	31[z]	*3 872*	4 908[z]	*1.5*	1.7[z]
San Marino	…	…	…	…	…	…	…	…	…	…	…	…
Spain	4.4	4.3[z]	11	11[z]	*91*	91[z]	*28*	26[z]	*4 112*	4 800[z]	*1.1*	1.0[z]
Sweden	7.5	7.2[z]	14	13[y]	…	100[z]	…	26[z]	…	8 415[z]	…	1.9[z]
Switzerland	5.0	5.3[z]	15	13[x]	90	92[z]	32	29[z]	7 066	7 811[z]	1.4	1.4[z]
United Kingdom	4.6	5.5[z]	11	12[z]	…	93[z]	…	26[z]	…	5 596[z]	…	1.3[z]
United States	5.0	5.3[z]	…	14[z]	…	…	…	…	…	…	…	…
South and West Asia												
Afghanistan	…	…	…	…	…	…	…	…	…	…	…	…
Bangladesh	2.3	2.6[z]	15	14[z]	64	79[z]	39	*35[z]*	64	*115[z]*	0.6	*0.7[z]*
Bhutan	…	7.2[z]	…	17[z]	…	59[z]	…	27[z]	…	…	…	1.1[z]
India	4.5	3.3[z]	13	11[x]	*98*	…	*30*	…	*288*	…	*1.3*	…
Iran, Islamic Republic of	4.5	5.2	19	19	91	93	…	29	…	927	…	1.4
Maldives	…	8.3	…	15[z]	…	*81[z]*	…	*54[z]*	…	…	…	*3.5[z]*
Nepal	*2.9*	3.2[x]	*12*	15[x]	*74*	77[x]	*53*	*49[x]*	*97*	*119[x]*	*1.1*	*1.2[x]*
Pakistan	2.6	2.7	…	12	89	75	…	…	…	…	…	…
Sri Lanka	…	…	…	…	…	…	…	…	…	…	…	…
Sub-Saharan Africa												
Angola	*3.4*	2.7[z]	*6*	…	*89*	42[z]	…	20[z]	…	…	…	0.2[z]
Benin	3.0	4.4[y]	16	17[y]	88	82[y]	…	50[y]	…	*120[z]*	…	*1.7[z]*
Botswana	…	**9.3**	…	**21**	…	**75**	…	**19**	…	1 158[z]	…	**1.3**
Burkina Faso	…	4.2	…	15	…	95	…	66	…	328	…	2.6
Burundi	3.5	5.2[z]	…	18[z]	94	98[z]	39	52[z]	*85*	132[z]	1.3	2.7[z]
Cameroon	*2.1*	3.3	*10*	17	…	74	…	34	128	107	1.0	0.8
Cape Verde	…	6.6	…	16	…	74	…	58	…	1 052	…	2.8
Central African Republic	…	1.4	…	…	…	98	…	52	…	88	…	0.7
Chad	*1.7*	2.3[z]	…	10[z]	…	50[z]	…	48[z]	…	54[z]	…	0.6[z]
Comoros	…	…	…	…	…	…	…	…	…	…	…	…
Congo	6.0	2.5[z]	22	8[z]	93	91[z]	36	27[z]	191	39[z]	2.0	0.6[z]
Côte d'Ivoire	5.6	…	…	…	74	…	43	…	274	…	1.8	*0.1[z]*
D. R. Congo	…	…	…	…	…	…	…	…	…	…	…	…
Equatorial Guinea	…	*1.4[x]*	…	*4[x]*	…	*90[x]*	…	…	…	…	…	…
Eritrea	5.3	2.4	…	…	*70*	80	…	39	…	99	…	0.8
Ethiopia	*3.6*	6.0	…	18	…	65	…	51	…	130	…	2.0
Gabon	*3.5*	…	…	…	*87*	…	…	…	…	…	…	…

Public current expenditure on primary education per pupil as % of GNP per capita		Public current expenditure on secondary education as % of public current expenditure on education		Public current expenditure on secondary education per pupil (unit cost) at PPP in constant 2005 US$		Public current expenditure on secondary education as % of GNP		Public current expenditure on secondary education per pupil as % of GNP per capita		Primary teachers' compensation as % of current expenditure on primary education, in public institutions		Country or territory
1999	2006	1999	2006	1999	2006	1999	2006	1999	2006	1999	2006	
…	20[z]	…	30[z]	…	1 235[z]	…	1.8[z]	…	20[z]	…	85[z]	Saint Vincent/Grenad.
…	…	…	…	…	…	…	…	…	…	…	…	Suriname
11	…	31	…	1 163	…	1.2	…	13	…	78	…	Trinidad and Tobago
…	…	40	30[z]	…	…	…	…	…	…	*63*	…	Turks and Caicos Islands
8	…	37	…	1 100	…	1.0	…	11	…	71	52[y]	Uruguay
…	8	…	18	…	588	…	0.6	…	8	…	…	Venezuela, B. R.
												North America and Western Europe
…	9	…	22	…	…	…	0.5	…	9	…	50	Andorra
23	23[z]	*45*	47[z]	*8 768*	8 608[z]	*2.7*	2.5[z]	*29*	26[z]	71	55[z]	Austria
…	19[y]	…	43[y]	…	10 662[y]	…	2.5[y]	…	33[y]	…	66[y]	Belgium
…	…	…	…	…	…	…	…	…	…	…	…	Canada
17	21[y]	53	49[z]	…	…	2.4	2.9[y]	27	34[y]	…	78[z]	Cyprus
23	23[z]	…	36[z]	*11 578*	11 440[z]	*2.9*	2.9[z]	*37*	33[z]	49	51[z]	Denmark
17	17[z]	*39*	41[z]	*6 858*	9 755[z]	*2.3*	2.5[z]	*25*	30[z]	59	58[z]	Finland
16	16[z]	*50*	47[z]	*7 678*	7 774[z]	*2.6*	2.4[z]	*26*	24[z]	…	53[z]	France
…	16[y]	…	49[y]	…	6 427[y]	…	2.2[y]	…	22[y]	…	…	Germany
12	*16[z]*	*38*	37[z]	*2 674*	4 578[z]	*1.0*	1.3[z]	*14*	20[z]	…	*91[z]*	Greece
…	23[y]	…	35[y]	…	7 556[y]	…	2.5[y]	…	22[y]	…	…	Iceland
12	15[z]	*37*	35[z]	*4 685*	7 731[z]	*1.6*	1.8[z]	*18*	23[z]	83	76[z]	Ireland
20	21[y]	*30*	30[y]	*5 422*	5 429[y]	*2.1*	2.0[y]	*23*	22[y]	…	…	Israel
23	22[z]	*47*	47[z]	*7 398*	7 429[z]	*2.1*	2.0[z]	*26*	26[z]	…	65[z]	Italy
…	*18[z]*	…	…	…	12 142[z]	…	1.7[z]	…	22[z]	…	*74[z]*	Luxembourg
…	14[y]	…	42[y]	…	3 622[y]	…	2.0[y]	…	20[y]	…	58[y]	Malta
…	…	51	46[y]	…	…	…	…	…	…	…	…	Monaco
14	16[z]	*39*	40[z]	*6 619*	7 861[z]	*1.7*	2.0[z]	*20*	23[z]	…	…	Netherlands
17	17[z]	*32*	35[z]	*9 082*	11 072[z]	*2.1*	2.3[z]	*24*	27[z]	…	79[z]	Norway
19	24[z]	*44*	41[z]	*5 280*	7 224[z]	*2.2*	2.2[z]	*26*	35[z]	…	85[z]	Portugal
…	…	…	…	…	…	…	…	…	…	…	…	San Marino
17	18[z]	*47*	41[z]	*5 435*	5 909[z]	*1.9*	1.6[z]	*23*	22[z]	78	73[z]	Spain
…	26[z]	…	38[z]	…	10 973[z]	…	2.7[z]	…	34[z]	50	54[z]	Sweden
19	20[z]	40	38[z]	8 790	9 382[z]	1.8	1.9[z]	24	24[z]	72	72[z]	Switzerland
…	17[z]	…	35[z]	…	6 096[z]	…	1.8[z]	…	18[z]	52	53[z]	United Kingdom
…	…	…	…	…	…	…	…	…	…	56	55[z]	United States
												South and West Asia
…	…	…	…	…	…	…	…	…	…	…	…	Afghanistan
4	*6[z]*	*42*	47[z]	*140*	265[z]	*0.6*	1.0[z]	*8*	13[z]	…	…	Bangladesh
…	…	…	44[z]	…	…	…	1.9[z]	…	…	…	…	Bhutan
12	…	*38*	…	*600*	…	*1.7*	…	*24*	…	79	80[y]	India
…	13	…	47	…	720[z]	…	2.3	…	11[z]	…	…	Iran, Islamic Republic of
…	*20[z]*	…	…	…	…	…	…	…	…	…	…	Maldives
7	*8[x]*	*29*	28[x]	*151*	144[x]	*0.6*	0.7[x]	*11*	10[x]	…	…	Nepal
…	…	…	…	…	…	…	…	…	…	…	…	Pakistan
…	…	…	…	…	…	…	…	…	…	…	…	Sri Lanka
												Sub-Saharan Africa
…	…	…	66[z]	…	…	…	0.8[z]	…	…	…	…	Angola
…	*11[z]*	…	*28[y]*	…	*267[y]*	…	*1.0[y]*	…	*24[y]*	…	…	Benin
…	11[z]	…	***48***	…	*3 732[z]*	…	**3.4**	…	*37[z]*	…	…	Botswana
…	25	…	12	…	264	…	0.5	…	20	…	…	Burkina Faso
12	19[z]	37	33[z]	…	*506[z]*	1.2	1.7[z]	…	*74[z]*	…	…	Burundi
7	5	…	55	279	746	0.6	1.4	*15*	32	…	…	Cameroon
…	18	…	36	…	861	…	1.8	…	15	…	86	Cape Verde
…	7	…	24	…	…	…	0.3	…	…	…	…	Central African Republic
…	4[z]	…	29[z]	…	*177[z]*	…	0.3[z]	…	*14[z]*	…	…	Chad
…	…	…	…	…	…	…	…	…	…	…	…	Comoros
24	4[z]	24	41[z]	…	…	1.3	0.9[z]	…	…	…	…	Congo
16	…	36	…	*743*	…	1.5	0.5[z]	*42*	…	…	…	Côte d'Ivoire
…	…	…	…	…	…	…	…	…	…	…	…	D. R. Congo
…	…	…	…	…	…	…	…	…	…	…	…	Equatorial Guinea
…	9	…	13	…	52	…	0.2	…	5	…	…	Eritrea
…	13	…	10	…	95	…	0.4	…	9	…	…	Ethiopia
…	…	…	…	…	…	…	…	…	…	…	…	Gabon

Table 11 (continued)

Country or territory	Total public expenditure on education as % of GNP		Total public expenditure on education as % of total government expenditure		Public current expenditure on education as % of total public expenditure on education		Public current expenditure on primary education as % of public current expenditure on education		Public current expenditure on primary education per pupil (unit cost) at PPP in constant 2005 US$		Public current expenditure on primary education as % of GNP	
	1999	2006	1999	2006	1999	2006	1999	2006	1999	2006	1999	2006
Gambia	3.1	*2.1*[y]	14	…	87	*86*[x]	…	…	…	…	…	…
Ghana	*4.2*	5.5[z]	…	…	…	86[z]	…	34[z]	…	300[z]	…	1.6[z]
Guinea	*2.1*	1.7[z]	…	…	…	…	…	…	…	…	…	…
Guinea-Bissau	5.6	…	12	…	41	…	…	…	…	…	…	…
Kenya	5.4	6.9	…	18[z]	95	94	…	55	…	237	…	3.6
Lesotho	10.2	10.8	26	30[z]	74	91	43	38	566	663	3.2	3.8
Liberia	…	…	…	…	…	…	…	…	…	…	…	…
Madagascar	*2.5*	3.1	…	25[z]	…	84	…	46	…	57	…	1.2
Malawi	4.7	5.9[x]	25	…	82	82[x]	…	63[x]	…	90[x]	…	3.0[x]
Mali	*3.0*	4.4	…	17	*90*	73	*49*	60	*136*	183	*1.3*	1.9
Mauritius	4.2	3.9	18	13	91	88	32	28	1 067	1 205	1.2	1.0
Mozambique	*2.5*	5.3[z]	…	23[y]	…	77[z]	…	70[y]	…	156[y]	…	2.6[y]
Namibia	7.9	6.8[x]	…	…	94	…	59	…	1 416	944[x]	4.4	3.9[x]
Niger	…	3.3	…	18	…	81	…	64	…	178	…	1.7
Nigeria	…	…	…	…	…	…	…	…	…	…	…	…
Rwanda	…	3.8[z]	…	**19**	…	**94**	…	**45**	…	*109*[z]	…	1.9[z]
Sao Tome and Principe	…	…	…	…	…	…	…	…	…	…	…	…
Senegal	*3.5*	5.0	…	26	…	92	…	46[z]	…	299[z]	…	2.1[z]
Seychelles	5.5	6.8	…	13	…	88	…	21	…	*2 399*[y]	…	1.3
Sierra Leone	…	*3.9*[z]	…	…	…	*99*[z]	…	*52*[x]	…	…	…	*2.3*[x]
Somalia	…	…	…	…	…	…	…	…	…	…	…	…
South Africa	6.2	5.5	22	18	98	97	45	45	1 403*	1 383[z]	2.7	2.4
Swaziland	5.7	6.9[z]	…	…	100	100[y]	33	*38*[y]	437	*484*[y]	1.9	*2.3*[y]
Togo	4.3	…	26	…	97	…	*43*	…	*150*	…	*1.8*	…
Uganda	…	*5.3*[y]	…	*18*[y]	…	*75*[y]	…	*62*[y]	…	*110*[y]	…	*2.5*[y]
United Republic of Tanzania	*2.2*	…	…	…	…	…	…	…	…	…	…	…
Zambia	2.0	2.1[z]	…	15[y]	…	99[z]	…	59[z]	…	55[z]	…	1.3[z]
Zimbabwe	…	…	…	…	…	…	…	…	…	…	…	…
World[1]	4.5	4.9	…	15	…	92.1	…	33	…	1 005	…	1.4
Countries in transition	3.7	3.9	14	17	…	94.2	…	…	…	…	…	…
Developed countries	4.9	5.3	11	12	…	93.8	…	24	…	5 100	…	1.1
Developing countries	4.5	4.4	…	16	…	89.5	…	…	…	…	…	1.7
Arab States	…	4.6	…	21	…	…	…	…	…	…	…	1.7
Central and Eastern Europe	4.4	5.3	…	13	…	93.0	…	19	…	2 182	…	0.8
Central Asia	3.7	3.4	…	…	…	94.6	…	…	…	…	…	…
East Asia and the Pacific	4.7	…	…	…	…	…	…	…	…	…	…	…
East Asia	3.6	3.6	13	16	…	…	…	…	…	…	…	…
Pacific	6.5	…	…	…	…	…	…	…	…	…	…	…
Latin America/Caribbean	4.9	4.1	16	15	…	91.9	…	37	…	…	…	1.7
Caribbean	…	5.8	…	15	…	88.0	…	32	…	…	…	1.8
Latin America	4.5	4.0	15	15	93	94.5	…	41	…	614	…	1.6
N. America/W. Europe	5.0	5.5	12	12	92	93.6	26	25	4 697	5 584	1.3	1.3
South and West Asia	2.9	3.3	…	15	89	77.9	…	35	…	…	…	1.2
Sub-Saharan Africa	3.6	4.4	…	18	…	86.4	…	48	…	167	…	1.9

1. All regional values shown are medians.
Data in italic are UIS estimates.
Data in bold are for 2007.

(z) Data are for 2005.
(y) Data are for 2004.
(x) Data are for 2003.
(*) National estimate.

Public current expenditure on primary education per pupil as % of GNP per capita		Public current expenditure on secondary education as % of public current expenditure on education		Public current expenditure on secondary education per pupil (unit cost) at PPP in constant 2005 US$		Public current expenditure on secondary education as % of GNP		Public current expenditure on secondary education per pupil as % of GNP per capita		Primary teachers' compensation as % of current expenditure on primary education, in public institutions		Country or territory
1999	2006	1999	2006	1999	2006	1999	2006	1999	2006	1999	2006	
...	...	...	...	...	...	...	...	...	...	...	75[y]	Gambia
...	12[z]	...	37[z]	...	*707[z]*	...	1.8[z]	...	*29[z]*	...	...	Ghana
...	...	...	...	...	...	...	...	...	...	...	...	Guinea
...	...	...	...	...	...	...	...	...	...	...	...	Guinea-Bissau
...	20	...	23	...	*245*	...	1.5	...	*21*	...	...	Kenya
15	16	24	19	1 655	1 439	1.9	1.8	45	35	84	...	Lesotho
...	...	...	...	...	...	...	...	...	...	...	...	Liberia
...	6	...	21	...	134	...	0.6	...	14	...	...	Madagascar
...	13[x]	...	10[x]	...	*80[x]*	...	0.5[x]	...	*12[x]*	...	...	Malawi
16	17	*34*	27	*412*	291	*0.9*	0.9	*48*	27	...	...	Mali
11	10	37	43	1 576	*1 778*	1.4	1.5	16	*14*	...	...	Mauritius
...	14[y]	...	17[y]	...	538[y]	...	0.6[y]	...	49[y]	...	93[y]	Mozambique
21	19[x]	28	...	2 313	1 140[x]	2.1	1.6[x]	34	23[x]	...	...	Namibia
...	22	...	25	...	366	...	0.7	...	45	...	...	Niger
...	...	...	...	...	...	...	...	...	...	...	...	Nigeria
...	*9[z]*	...	**20**	...	*197[z]*	...	0.4[z]	...	*17[z]*	...	...	Rwanda
...	...	...	...	...	...	...	...	...	...	...	...	Sao Tome and Principe
...	17[z]	...	26[z]	...	590[z]	...	1.2[z]	...	34[z]	...	...	Senegal
...	*15[y]*	...	21	...	*2 828[y]*	...	1.3	...	*18[y]*	...	68	Seychelles
...	...	...	*27[x]*	...	...	...	*1.2[x]*	...	...	...	...	Sierra Leone
...	...	...	...	...	...	...	...	...	...	...	...	Somalia
14*	14[z]	34	31	1 973*	1 726[z]	2.0	1.6	20*	17[z]	...	78	South Africa
9	*12[y]*	27	*28[y]*	1 237	*1 203[y]*	1.5	*1.7[y]*	25	*31[y]*	...	...	Swaziland
10	...	34	...	484	...	1.4	...	31	...	79	...	Togo
...	*9[y]*	...	*20[y]*	...	*376[y]*	...	0.8[y]	...	*30[y]*	...	...	Uganda
...	...	...	...	...	...	...	...	...	...	...	...	United Republic of Tanzania
...	6[z]	...	15[z]	...	*84[z]*	...	0.3[z]	...	*9[z]*	...	93[y]	Zambia
...	...	...	...	...	...	...	...	...	...	...	...	Zimbabwe
...	14	...	36	...	...	...	1.6	...	20	...	...	World[1]
...	...	...	...	...	...	...	...	...	...	...	...	Countries in transition
...	17	...	42	...	6 427	...	2.2	...	23	...	...	Developed countries
...	13	...	...	...	...	...	1.4	...	...	...	...	Developing countries
...	12	...	...	...	...	...	...	...	...	...	...	Arab States
...	17	...	46	...	1 203	...	1.4	...	21	...	...	Central and Eastern Europe
...	...	...	...	...	...	...	...	...	...	...	...	Central Asia
...	...	...	...	...	...	...	...	...	...	...	...	East Asia and the Pacific
...	...	...	...	...	...	...	...	...	...	...	...	East Asia
...	...	...	...	...	...	...	...	...	...	...	...	Pacific
...	12	...	32	...	...	...	1.4	...	14	...	82	Latin America/Caribbean
...	13	...	33	...	...	...	...	...	...	...	...	Caribbean
...	12	...	30	...	594	...	1.3	...	13	...	81	Latin America
17	18	42	40	6 858	7 753	2.1	2.1	25	24	...	65	N. America/W. Europe
...	...	...	...	...	...	...	...	...	...	...	...	South and West Asia
...	13	...	26	...	376	...	1.0	...	20	...	...	Sub-Saharan Africa

Table 12

Trends in basic or proxy indicators to measure EFA goals 1, 2, 3, 4 and 5

	GOAL 1			GOAL 2						GOAL 3			
	Early childhood care and education			Universal primary education						Learning needs of all youth and adults			
	GROSS ENROLMENT RATIO (GER) IN PRE-PRIMARY EDUCATION (%)			NET ENROLMENT RATIO (NER) IN PRIMARY EDUCATION						YOUTH LITERACY RATE (15-24)			
	School year ending in			School year ending in									
	1991	1999	2006	1991		1999		2006		1985-1994[1]		2000-2006[1]	
Country or territory	Total (%)	Total (%)	Total (%)	Total (%)	GPI (F/M)	Total (%)	GPI (F/M)	Total (%)	GPI (F/M)	Total (%)	GPI (F/M)	Total (%)	GPI (F/M)
Arab States													
Algeria	…	3	15	89	0.88	91	0.96	95	0.98	74	0.72*	92	0.95
Bahrain	27	36	52	99	1.00	96	1.03	98[z]	1.00[z]	97	0.99*	100	1.00
Djibouti	0.6	0.4	2	29	0.72	27	0.73	38	0.82	…	…	…	…
Egypt	6	11	**17**	_86_	_0.84_	_94_	_0.93_	**_96_**	**_0.96_**	63	0.76*	85	0.89
Iraq	8	5	_6[z]_	_94_	_0.88_	85	0.85	_89[z]_	_0.86[z]_	…	…	85	0.91*
Jordan	21	29	32	94	1.01	91	1.01	90	1.02	…	…	99	1.00
Kuwait	33	78	75	_49_	_0.93_	87	1.01	83	0.99	87	0.93*	99	1.00*
Lebanon	…	61	64	_66_	_0.97_	_86_	_0.96_	82	0.99	…	…	…	…
Libyan Arab Jamahiriya	…	5	9	_93_	_0.96_	…	…	…	…	95	0.92	99	0.98
Mauritania	…	…	_2[z]_	_36_	_0.78_	64	0.99	79	1.05	…	…	66	0.88
Morocco	58	62	59	56	0.70	70	0.85	88	0.94	58	0.64*	74	0.78
Oman	3	6	8	69	0.95	81	1.00	74	1.02	…	…	98	0.99
Palestinian A. T.	21	39	30	…	…	97	1.00	76	1.00	…	…	99	1.00
Qatar	28	25	43	89	0.98	92	1.01	94	1.01	90	1.03*	97	1.01
Saudi Arabia	7	…	…	59	0.80	…	…	…	…	88	0.86*	97	0.98
Sudan[2]	18	19	24	_40_	_0.75_	…	…	…	…	…	…	77	0.84*
Syrian Arab Republic	6	8	11	91	0.91	_92_	_0.93_	…	…	…	…	93	0.96
Tunisia	8	14	…	93	0.93	93	0.98	96	1.01	…	…	95	0.97
United Arab Emirates	56	64	78	99	0.98	79	0.99	88	1.00	82	1.04*	97	0.98
Yemen	0.7	0.7	0.9[z]	_50_	_0.38_	56	0.59	75[z]	0.76[z]	60	0.43*	79	0.69
Central and Eastern Europe													
Albania	59	40	49[y]	_95_	_1.01_	_94_	_0.98_	94[y]	0.99[y]	…	…	99	1.00
Belarus	84	75	103	_85_	_0.96_	…	…	89	_0.98_	100	1.00*	100	1.00
Bosnia and Herzegovina	…	…	…	79	1.00	…	…	…	…	…	…	100	1.00*
Bulgaria	91	67	82	85	1.00	97	0.98	92	0.99	…	…	98	1.00
Croatia	28	40	50	79	1.00	85	0.98	90	0.99	100	1.00*	100	1.00
Czech Republic	95	90	114	_87_	_1.00_	_97_	_1.00_	_93[z]_	_1.03[z]_	…	…	…	…
Estonia	76	87	93	_100_	_0.99_	_96_	_0.98_	94	0.99	100	1.00*	100	1.00
Hungary	113	78	86	91	1.01	88	0.99	88	0.99	…	…	…	…
Latvia	47	53	89	_94_	_0.99_	_97_	_0.98_	_90[z]_	_1.03[z]_	100	1.00*	100	1.00
Lithuania	58	50	69	…	…	95	0.99	89	0.99	100	1.00*	100	1.00
Montenegro	…	…	…	…	…	…	…	…	…	…	…	…	…
Poland	47	50	57	97	1.00	96	1.00	96	1.01	…	…	…	…
Republic of Moldova[3,4]	70	48	71	_86_	_1.01_	_93_	…	88	1.00	100	1.00*	100	1.00
Romania	76	62	72	_81_	_1.00_	96	…	93	1.00	99	1.00*	98	1.00
Russian Federation[5]	74	68	87	_98_	_1.00_	…	…	91	1.00	100	1.00*	100	1.00
Serbia[3]	…	_54_	**59**	…	…	…	…	**95**	**1.00**	…	…	…	…
Slovakia	86	82	93	…	…	…	…	_92[z]_	_1.01[z]_	…	…	…	…
Slovenia	66	75	81	_96_	_1.01_	96	0.99	95	1.00	100	1.00*	100	1.00
TFYR Macedonia	…	27	33[z]	94	0.99	93	0.98	92[z]	1.00[z]	99	0.99*	99	1.00
Turkey	4	6	13	89	0.92	…	…	91	0.96	93	0.92*	96	0.96*
Ukraine	86	50	90	_81_	_1.00_	…	…	90	1.00*	…	…	100	1.00
Central Asia													
Armenia	37	26	36	…	…	…	…	82	1.05	100	1.00*	100	1.00
Azerbaijan	19	21	32	89	0.99	85	1.01	85	0.97	…	…	100	1.00
Georgia	59	36	55	_97_	_1.00_	77*	1.00*	89	1.03	…	…	…	…
Kazakhstan	73	14	**38**	_88_	_0.99_	…	…	**90**	**1.00**	100	1.00*	100	1.00
Kyrgyzstan	34	10	14	_92_	_1.00_	88*	0.99*	86	0.99	…	…	100	1.00
Mongolia	39	25	54	_90_	_1.02_	89	1.04	91	1.02	…	…	96	1.03
Tajikistan	16	8	9	_77_	_0.98_	…	…	97	0.96	100	1.00*	100	1.00
Turkmenistan	…	…	…	…	…	…	…	…	…	…	…	100	1.00
Uzbekistan	73	24	**27**	_78_	_0.99_	…	…	…	…	…	…	99	1.00*
East Asia and the Pacific													
Australia	71	…	104	99	1.00	94	1.01	96	1.01	…	…	…	…
Brunei Darussalam	48	50	51	92	0.98	…	…	94	1.00	98	1.00*	100	1.00
Cambodia	4	_5_	11	_72_	_0.84_	_83_	_0.91_	90	0.98	…	…	85	0.92

GOAL 4				GOAL 5												
Improving levels of adult literacy				Gender parity in primary education						Gender parity in secondary education						
ADULT LITERACY RATE (15 and over)				GROSS ENROLMENT RATIO (GER)						GROSS ENROLMENT RATIO (GER)						
				School year ending in						School year ending in						
1985-1994[1]		2000-2006[1]		1991		1999		2006		1991		1999		2006		
Total (%)	GPI (F/M)	Total (%)	GPI (F/M)	Total (%)	GPI (F/M)	Total (%)	GPI (F/M)	Total (%)	GPI (F/M)	Total (%)	GPI (F/M)	Total (%)	GPI (F/M)	Total (%)	GPI (F/M)	Country or territory
																Arab States
50	0.57*	75	0.78	96	0.85	105	0.91	110	0.93	60	0.80	…	…	*83*[z]	*1.08*[z]	Algeria
84	0.87*	88	0.95	110	1.00	107	1.01	120	1.00	100	1.04	95	1.08	102	1.04	Bahrain
…	…	…	…	34	0.72	33	0.71	44	0.81	11	0.66	14	0.72	22	0.67	Djibouti
44	0.55*	71	0.72	94	0.83	*102*	*0.91*	**105**	**0.95**	71	0.79	*82*	*0.92*	*88*[y]	*0.94*[y]	Egypt
…	…	74	0.76*	108	0.83	92	0.82	*99*[z]	*0.83*[z]	44	0.63	34	0.63	*45*[z]	*0.66*[z]	Iraq
…	…	93	0.92	101	1.01	98	1.00	97	1.02	63	1.04	89	1.02	89	1.03	Jordan
74	0.88*	93	0.96*	60	0.95	100	1.01	96	0.99	43	0.98	*98*	*1.02*	89	1.05	Kuwait
…	…	…	…	*97*	*0.97*	105	0.95	94	0.97	…	…	74	1.09	81	1.10	Lebanon
76	0.71	86	0.82	101	0.94	120	0.98	110	0.95	80	…	…	…	94	1.17	Libyan Arab Jamahiriya
…	…	55	0.76	52	0.77	89	0.99	102	1.05	14	0.49	*19*	*0.77*	25*	0.86*	Mauritania
42	0.52*	55	0.62	64	0.69	86	0.81	106	0.89	36	0.72	37	0.79	52	…	Morocco
…	…	84	0.86	85	0.92	91	0.97	82	1.01	45	0.81	75	1.00	89	0.96	Oman
…	…	92	0.91	…	…	105	1.01	83	1.00	…	…	80	1.04	94	1.06	Palestinian A. T.
76	0.94*	90	1.00	101	0.93	102	0.96	105	0.99	84	1.06	87	1.11	101	0.97	Qatar
71	0.72*	84	0.89	73	0.85	…	…	…	…	44	0.80	…	…	…	…	Saudi Arabia
…	…	61	0.73*	49	0.77	*49*	*0.85*	66	0.87	21	0.79	*26*	…	34	0.96	Sudan [2]
…	…	83	0.85	101	0.90	102	0.92	126	0.96	48	0.73	40	0.91	70	0.95	Syrian Arab Republic
…	…	77	0.79	113	0.90	113	0.95	108	0.97	45	0.79	72	1.02	85	*1.10*	Tunisia
71	0.95*	90	0.98	114	0.97	90	0.97	104	0.99	68	1.16	76	1.06	90	1.02	United Arab Emirates
37	0.30*	57	0.51	*63*	*0.35*	71	0.56	87[z]	0.74[z]	…	…	41	0.37	46[z]	0.49[z]	Yemen
																Central and Eastern Europe
…	…	99	0.99	100	1.00	103	0.98	105[y]	0.99[y]	78	0.86	71	0.98	77[y]	0.96[y]	Albania
98	0.97*	100	1.00	95	*0.96*	111	0.99	96	0.98	93	…	85	1.05	96	1.02	Belarus
…	…	97	0.95*	…	…	…	…	…	…	…	…	…	…	…	…	Bosnia and Herzegovina
…	…	98	0.99	97	0.98	106	0.98	100	0.99	75	1.04	91	0.98	106	0.96	Bulgaria
97	0.96*	99	0.98	85	0.99	92	0.98	99	1.00	76	1.10	84	1.02	91	1.03	Croatia
…	…	…	…	97	1.00	103	0.99	100	0.99	91	0.97	83	1.04	96	1.01	Czech Republic
100	1.00*	100	1.00	112	0.97	102	0.97	99	0.98	100	1.08	93	1.04	100	1.02	Estonia
…	…	…	…	95	1.00	102	0.98	97	0.98	79	1.01	94	1.02	96	0.99	Hungary
99	0.99*	100	1.00	98	1.00	100	0.98	95	0.96	92	1.02	88	1.04	99	1.00	Latvia
98	0.99*	100	1.00	92	0.95	102	0.98	95	0.99	92	…	95	1.01	99	1.00	Lithuania
…	…	…	…	…	…	…	…	…	…	…	…	…	…	…	…	Montenegro
…	…	…	…	98	0.99	98	0.98	98	1.00	81	1.05	99	0.99	100	0.99	Poland
96	0.96*	99	0.99	90	1.02	100	1.00	97	0.99	78	1.10	83	0.98	89	1.04	Republic of Moldova [3,4]
97	0.96*	98	0.98	91	1.00	105	0.98	105	0.99	92	0.99	79	1.01	86	1.00	Romania
98	0.97*	100	1.00	108	1.00	108	0.98	96	1.00	93	1.06	…	…	84	0.98	Russian Federation [5]
…	…	…	…	…	…	*112*	*0.99*	**97**	**1.00**	…	…	*93*	*1.01*	**88**	**1.03**	Serbia [3]
…	…	…	…	…	…	103	0.99	100	0.98	…	…	85	1.02	94	1.01	Slovakia
100	1.00*	100	1.00	100	…	100	0.99	100	0.99	89	…	100	1.03	95	1.00	Slovenia
94	0.94*	97	0.97	99	0.98	101	0.98	98[z]	1.00[z]	56	0.99	82	0.97	84[z]	0.98[z]	TFYR Macedonia
79	0.76*	88	0.84*	99	0.92	…	…	*94*	*0.95*	48	0.63	…	…	*79*	*0.83*	Turkey
…	…	100	1.00	89	1.00	109	0.99	102	1.00	94	…	98	1.03*	93	0.98*	Ukraine
																Central Asia
99	0.99*	99	1.00	…	…	100	…	98	1.04	…	…	91	…	90	1.04	Armenia
…	…	99	0.99	*111*	*0.99*	94	1.00	96	0.97	88	1.01	76	1.00	83	0.96	Azerbaijan
…	…	…	…	97	1.00	98	1.00	96	1.03	95	0.97	79	0.98	85	*1.04*	Georgia
98	0.97*	100	1.00	89	*0.99*	97	1.01	**105**	**1.00**	100	1.03	92	1.00	**93**	**0.99**	Kazakhstan
…	…	99	1.00	…	…	98	0.99	97	0.99	100	1.02	83	1.02	86	1.01	Kyrgyzstan
…	…	97	1.01	97	1.02	97	1.04	101	1.02	82	1.14	58	1.27	89	1.12	Mongolia
98	0.98*	100	1.00	91	0.98	98	0.95	100	0.95	102	…	74	0.86	83	0.83	Tajikistan
…	…	99	1.00	…	…	…	…	…	…	…	…	…	…	…	…	Turkmenistan
…	…	97	0.98*	81	0.98	98	1.00	**95**	**0.97**	99	0.91	86	0.98	**102**	**0.98**	Uzbekistan
																East Asia and the Pacific
…	…	…	…	108	0.99	100	1.00	105	1.00	83	1.03	157	1.00	150	0.95	Australia
88	0.89*	95	0.96	114	0.94	114	0.97	107	0.99	77	1.09	85	1.09	98	1.04	Brunei Darussalam
…	…	76	0.78	90	*0.81*	97	0.87	122	0.93	25	0.43	*17*	*0.53*	38	0.79	Cambodia

Table 12 (continued)

Country or territory	GOAL 1 Early childhood care and education GROSS ENROLMENT RATIO (GER) IN PRE-PRIMARY EDUCATION (%) School year ending in			GOAL 2 Universal primary education NET ENROLMENT RATIO (NER) IN PRIMARY EDUCATION School year ending in						GOAL 3 Learning needs of all youth and adults YOUTH LITERACY RATE (15-24)			
	1991	1999	2006	1991		1999		2006		1985-1994[1]		2000-2006[1]	
	Total (%)	Total (%)	Total (%)	Total (%)	GPI (F/M)	Total (%)	GPI (F/M)	Total (%)	GPI (F/M)	Total (%)	GPI (F/M)	Total (%)	GPI (F/M)
China[6]	22	38	39	98	0.96	…	…	…	…	94	0.94*	99	1.00
Cook Islands[3]	…	86	*94[z]*	…	…	85	0.96	*74[z]*	*1.03[z]*	…	…	…	…
DPR Korea	…	…	…	…	…	…	…	…	…	…	…	…	…
Fiji	14	16	16	…	…	99	1.01	91	1.00	…	…	…	…
Indonesia	18	*23*	37	96	0.96	…	…	96	…	96	0.98*	99	1.00
Japan	48	83	86	100	1.00	100	…	100	…	…	…	…	…
Kiribati[3]	…	…	*75[y]*	…	…	*97*	*1.01*	…	…	…	…	…	…
Lao PDR	7	8	11	*62*	*0.86*	76	0.92	84	0.94	…	…	82	0.93
Macao, China	89	87	87	*81*	*0.98*	85	1.01	91	0.98	…	…	100	1.00
Malaysia	37	108	125[z]	93	0.99	98	0.98	100[z]	…	96	0.99*	98	1.00
Marshall Islands[3]	…	*59*	**45**	…	…	…	…	**66**	**0.99**	…	…	…	…
Micronesia	…	37	…	98	1.04	…	…	…	…	…	…	…	…
Myanmar[7]	…	2	6	*99*	…	*92*	*0.99*	100	…	…	…	95	0.98*
Nauru	…	…	***89***	…	…	…	…	…	…	…	…	…	…
New Zealand	76	85	92	98	1.00	99	1.00	99	1.00	…	…	…	…
Niue[3]	…	154	119[z]	…	…	99	1.00	…	…	…	…	…	…
Palau[3]	…	63	*64[z]*	…	…	*97*	*0.94*	…	…	…	…	…	…
Papua New Guinea	0.3	…	…	66	0.86	…	…	…	…	…	…	64	1.03
Philippines	12	30	45	*96*	*0.99*	92	1.00	91	1.02	97	1.01*	94	1.02
Republic of Korea	55	80	**101**	100	1.01	94	0.97	**98**	…	…	…	…	…
Samoa	…	*53*	*48[y]*	…	…	92	0.99	*90[y]*	…	99	1.00*	99	1.00
Singapore	…	…	…	96	0.99	…	…	…	…	99	1.00*	100	1.00
Solomon Islands	36	*35*	…	84	0.86	…	…	62[z]	0.99[z]	…	…	…	…
Thailand	49	97	92	*88*	*0.99*	…	…	94	…	…	…	98	1.00
Timor-Leste	…	…	10[z]	…	…	…	…	*68[z]*	*0.96[z]*	…	…	…	…
Tokelau[3]	…	…	*125[y]*	…	…	…	…	…	…	…	…	…	…
Tonga	…	30	*23[z]*	97	0.97	88	0.96	96[z]	…	…	…	100	1.00
Tuvalu[3]	…	…	107	…	…	…	…	…	…	…	…	…	…
Vanuatu	…	…	**29**	71	1.01	91	0.99	**87**	**0.99**	…	…	…	…
Viet Nam	28	39	…	*90*	*0.92*	95	…	…	…	94	0.99*	94	0.99*
Latin America and the Caribbean													
Anguilla	…	…	*103*	…	…	…	…	*92*	*1.00*	…	…	…	…
Antigua and Barbuda	…	…	…	…	…	…	…	…	…	…	…	…	…
Argentina[8]	50	57	66[z]	94	1.00	99*	1.00*	99[z]	0.99[z]	98	1.00*	99	1.00
Aruba	…	99	99	…	…	98	1.03	100	1.00	…	…	99	1.00
Bahamas	…	12	…	*90*	*1.03*	89	0.99	88	1.03	…	…	…	…
Barbados	…	74	94	*79*	*0.98*	*94*	*0.99*	96	0.99	…	…	…	…
Belize	23	27	34	*94*	*0.99*	*94*	*0.99*	97	1.01	76	1.01*	…	…
Bermuda[3]	…	…	…	…	…	…	…	*92*	…	…	…	…	…
Bolivia	32	45	50	91	0.92	95	1.00	95	1.01	94	0.95*	98	0.99
Brazil	48	58	69[z]	85	0.95	91	…	94[z]	1.02[z]	…	…	98	1.02*
British Virgin Islands[3]	…	62	93	…	…	*96*	*1.02*	*95*	*1.00*	…	…	…	…
Cayman Islands[9]	…	…	…	…	…	…	…	…	…	…	…	…	…
Chile	72	77	55	89	0.98	…	…	…	…	98	1.01*	99	1.00
Colombia	13	37	40	68	1.15	89	*1.01*	88	1.00	91	1.03*	98	1.01*
Costa Rica	65	84	70	87	1.01	…	…	…	…	…	…	98	1.01
Cuba	102	109	113	94	1.00	97	…	97	1.01	…	…	100	1.00
Dominica[3]	…	80	77[z]	…	…	*94*	*0.98*	77	1.06	…	…	…	…
Dominican Republic	…	32	32	*56*	*2.15*	84	1.01	77	1.03	…	…	96	1.02
Ecuador	42	64	90	*98*	*1.01*	97	1.01	97	…	96	0.99*	96	1.01
El Salvador	21	43	51	75	1.01	…	…	94	1.00	85	1.00*	95	1.01*
Grenada[3]	…	93	*81[z]*	100	1.00	…	…	*84[z]*	*0.99[z]*	…	…	…	…
Guatemala	25	46	29	64	0.91	82	0.91	94	0.96	76	0.87*	85	0.94
Guyana	74	124	*99*	89	1.00	…	…	…	…	…	…	…	…
Haiti	33	…	…	21	1.05	…	…	…	…	…	…	…	…
Honduras	13	…	38	88	1.01	…	…	96	1.02	…	…	90	1.06
Jamaica	78	78	92[z]	96	1.00	*88*	*1.00*	*90[z]*	*1.00[z]*	…	…	94	1.08
Mexico	63	74	106	98	0.97	97	1.00	98	0.99	95	0.99*	98	1.00*
Montserrat	…	…	*91*	…	…	…	…	*99*	…	…	…	…	…
Netherlands Antilles	…	111	…	…	…	…	…	…	…	97	1.01*	98	1.00
Nicaragua	13	27	52	70	1.03	76	1.01	90	1.00	…	…	88	1.07

GOAL 4				GOAL 5														
Improving levels of adult literacy				Gender parity in primary education						Gender parity in secondary education								
ADULT LITERACY RATE (15 and over)				GROSS ENROLMENT RATIO (GER)						GROSS ENROLMENT RATIO (GER)								
				School year ending in						School year ending in								
1985-1994[1]		2000-2006[1]		1991		1999		2006		1991		1999		2006				
Total (%)	GPI (F/M)	Total (%)	GPI (F/M)	Total (%)	GPI (F/M)	Total (%)	GPI (F/M)	Total (%)	GPI (F/M)	Total (%)	GPI (F/M)	Total (%)	GPI (F/M)	Total (%)	GPI (F/M)			**Country or territory**
78	0.78*	93	0.93	126	0.93	…	…	111	0.99	49	0.75	62	…	76	1.01			China[6]
…	…	…	…	…	…	96	0.95	*80[z]*	*1.01[z]*	…	…	60	1.08	*72[z]*	*1.04[z]*			Cook Islands[3]
…	…	…	…	…	…	…	…	…	…	…	…	…	…	…	…			DPR Korea
…	…	…	…	133	1.00	109	0.99	100	0.98	64	0.95	80	1.11	84	1.10			Fiji
82	0.86*	91	0.92	114	0.98	…	…	114	0.96	45	0.83	…	…	64	1.00			Indonesia
…	…	…	…	100	1.00	101	1.00	100	1.00	97	1.02	102	1.01	101	1.00			Japan
…	…	…	…	…	…	104	1.01	113[z]	1.01[z]	…	…	84	1.18	88[z]	1.14[z]			Kiribati[3]
…	…	72	0.83	103	0.79	111	0.85	116	0.89	23*	0.62*	33	0.69	43	0.78			Lao PDR
…	…	93	0.94	99	0.96	100	0.96	106	0.94	65*	1.11*	76	1.08	98	1.00			Macao, China
83	0.87*	92	0.95	93	0.99	98	0.98	100[z]	1.00[z]	57	1.05	65	1.07	69[z]	1.10[z]			Malaysia
…	…	…	…	…	…	*101*	*0.98*	**93**	**0.97**	…	…	*72*	*1.06*	**66**	**1.02**			Marshall Islands
…	…	…	…	…	…	…	…	**110**	**1.01**	…	…	…	…	***91***	…			Micronesia
…	…	90	0.92*	114	0.97	100	0.99	114	1.01	23	0.99	36	1.01	49	1.00			Myanmar[7]
…	…	…	…	…	…	…	…	***79***	***1.03***	…	…	…	…	***46***	***1.19***			Nauru
…	…	…	…	102	0.99	100	1.00	102	1.00	90	1.02	113	1.05	120	1.05			New Zealand
…	…	…	…	…	…	99	1.00	105[z]	0.95[z]	…	…	98	1.10	99[z]	1.07[z]			Niue[3]
…	…	…	…	…	…	114	0.93	*104[z]*	*0.94[z]*	…	…	101	1.07	*102[z]*	…			Palau[3]
…	…	57	0.85	65	0.85	…	…	55	0.84	12	0.62	…	…	…	…			Papua New Guinea
94	0.99*	93	1.01	109	0.99	113	1.00	110	0.99	71	1.04	76	1.09	83	1.11			Philippines
…	…	…	…	105	1.01	95	0.97	**105**	**0.97**	90	0.97	100	1.01	**98**	**0.94**			Republic of Korea
98	0.99*	99	0.99	124	1.02	99	0.98	*100[z]*	*1.00[z]*	33	1.96	79	1.10	*81[z]*	*1.13[z]*			Samoa
89	0.87*	94	0.94	103	0.97	…	…	…	…	67	0.93	…	…	…	…			Singapore
…	…	…	…	88	0.87	88	0.94	101[z]	0.96[z]	15	0.61	25	0.76	30[z]	0.84[z]			Solomon Islands
…	…	94	0.96	113	0.98	106	0.99	108	1.00	33	0.96	…	…	78	1.09			Thailand
…	…	…	…	…	…	…	…	99[z]	0.92[z]	…	…	…	…	53[z]	1.00[z]			Timor-Leste
…	…	…	…	…	…	…	…	*93[y]*	*1.35[y]*	…	…	…	…	*101[y]*	*0.88[y]*			Tokelau[3]
…	…	99	1.00	112	0.98	108	0.96	113	0.95	98	1.04	102	1.11	94	1.04			Tonga
…	…	…	…	…	…	98	1.02	106	0.99	…	…	…	…	…	…			Tuvalu[3]
…	…	…	…	95	0.96	111	0.98	**108**	**0.97**	18	0.80	30	0.87	40[y]	0.86[y]			Vanuatu
88	0.89*	90	0.93*	107	*0.93*	108	0.93	…	…	32	…	62	0.90	…	…			Viet Nam
																		Latin America and the Caribbean
…	…	…	…	…	…	…	…	*93*	*0.99*	…	…	…	…	*83*	*1.02*			Anguilla
…	…	…	…	…	…	…	…	…	…	…	…	…	…	…	…			Antigua and Barbuda
96	1.00*	98	1.00	108	…	117	1.00	112[z]	0.99[z]	72	…	94	1.07	84[z]	1.11[z]			Argentina[8]
…	…	98	1.00	…	…	114	0.99	115	0.98	…	…	99	1.07	100	1.04			Aruba
…	…	…	…	96	*1.03*	95	0.98	98	1.00	…	…	79	0.99	91	1.01			Bahamas
…	…	…	…	92	1.00	98	0.98	103	0.98	…	…	100	1.05	102	1.04			Barbados
70	1.00*	…	…	112	0.98	118	0.97	123	0.97	44	1.15	64	1.08	79	1.06			Belize
…	…	…	…	…	…	…	…	100	0.85	…	…	…	…	84	1.06			Bermuda[3]
80	0.82*	90	0.89	97	0.92	113	0.98	109	1.00	…	…	78	0.93	82	0.96			Bolivia
…	…	90	1.01*	104	…	154	0.94	137[z]	0.94[z]	40	…	99	1.11	105[z]	1.10[z]			Brazil
…	…	…	…	…	…	112	0.97	112	0.97	…	…	99	0.91	107	1.13			British Virgin Islands[9]
…	…	…	…	…	…	…	…	…	…	…	…	…	…	…	…			Cayman Islands[7]
94	0.99*	96	1.00	101	0.98	101	0.97	104	0.95	73	1.07	79	1.04	91	1.02			Chile
81	1.00*	92	1.00*	103	1.02	114	1.00	116	0.99	50	1.19	70	1.11	82	1.11			Colombia
…	…	96	1.00	103	0.99	108	0.98	111	0.99	45	1.06	57	1.09	86	1.06			Costa Rica
…	…	100	1.00	100	0.97	111	0.97	101	0.97	94	1.15	77	1.07	94	1.02			Cuba
…	…	…	…	…	…	104	0.95	86	1.02	…	…	90	1.35	106	0.98			Dominica[3]
…	…	89	1.01	*91*	*1.00*	113	0.98	98	0.95	…	…	57	1.24	69	1.20			Dominican Republic
88	0.95*	92	0.98	116	*0.99*	114	1.00	117	1.00	55*	…	57	1.03	68	1.02			Ecuador
74	0.92*	84	0.93*	81	1.01	112	0.96	114	0.96	25	1.22	52	0.98	65	1.04			El Salvador
…	…	…	…	117	0.85	…	…	*93[z]*	*0.96[z]*	100	1.16	…	…	100[z]	1.03[z]			Grenada[3]
64	0.80*	72	0.86	81	0.87	101	0.87	114	0.93	23	…	33	0.84	53	0.92			Guatemala
…	…	…	…	94	0.99	121	0.98	124[z]	0.99[z]	79	1.06	82	1.02	*105*	*0.98*			Guyana
…	…	…	…	46	0.95	…	…	…	…	21*	0.94*	…	…	…	…			Haiti
…	…	83	1.01	107	1.04	…	…	118	0.99	33	1.23	…	…	76[z]	1.30[z]			Honduras
…	…	85	1.13	101	0.99	*92*	*1.00*	95[z]	1.00[z]	65	1.06	*88*	*1.02*	87[z]	1.03[z]			Jamaica
88	0.94*	92	0.96*	112	0.97	111	0.98	113	0.97	53	0.99	70	1.01	87	1.02			Mexico
…	…	…	…	…	…	…	…	*114*	*1.00*	…	…	…	…	*125*	*0.98*			Montserrat
95	1.00*	96	1.00	…	…	131	0.95	…	…	93	1.19	92	1.16	…	…			Netherlands Antilles
…	…	80	1.02	91	1.06	100	1.01	116	0.98	42	1.20	*52*	*1.19*	66	1.14			Nicaragua

Table 12 (continued)

Country or territory	GOAL 1 Early childhood care and education GROSS ENROLMENT RATIO (GER) IN PRE-PRIMARY EDUCATION (%) School year ending in			GOAL 2 Universal primary education NET ENROLMENT RATIO (NER) IN PRIMARY EDUCATION School year ending in						GOAL 3 Learning needs of all youth and adults YOUTH LITERACY RATE (15-24)			
	1991	1999	2006	1991		1999		2006		1985-1994[1]		2000-2006[1]	
	Total (%)	Total (%)	Total (%)	Total (%)	GPI (F/M)	Total (%)	GPI (F/M)	Total (%)	GPI (F/M)	Total (%)	GPI (F/M)	Total (%)	GPI (F/M)
Panama	57	39	67	92	1.00	96	0.99	98	0.99	95	0.99*	96	1.00
Paraguay	31	29	34[z]	94	0.99	96	1.00	94[z]	1.01[z]	96	0.99*	96	1.00
Peru	30	55	68	88	0.99	*98*	…	96	1.01	95	0.97*	98	0.98*
Saint Kitts and Nevis	…	…	***99***	99	0.99	…	…	***71***	***1.22***	…	…	…	…
Saint Lucia	51	*70*	69	*95*	*0.97*	*96*	*0.99*	98	0.98	…	…	…	…
Saint Vincent/Grenad.	45	…	*88*[z]	91	0.99	…	…	90[z]	0.96[z]	…	…	…	…
Suriname	79	…	84	*81*	*1.06*	…	…	96	1.03	…	…	95	0.99
Trinidad and Tobago	8	*58*	85*,[z]	89	1.00	87	1.01	85*,[z]	1.00*,[z]	99	1.00*	99	1.00
Turks and Caicos Islands	…	…	*118*[z]	…	…	…	…	*78*[z]	*1.07*[z]	…	…	…	…
Uruguay	43	60	79	91	1.01	…	…	100	…	99	1.01*	99	1.01*
Venezuela, B. R.	40	45	60	87	1.03	86	1.01	91	1.00	95	1.02*	97	1.02*
North America and Western Europe													
Andorra[3]	…	…	102	…	…	…	…	83	1.01	…	…	…	…
Austria	69	82	90	*88*	*1.02*	*97*	*1.01*	*97*	*1.01*	…	…	…	…
Belgium	105	111	121	96	1.02	99	1.00	97	1.00	…	…	…	…
Canada	61	64	*68*[y]	98	1.00	99	1.00	…	…	…	…	…	…
Cyprus[3]	48	60	79	87	1.00	95	1.00	99	1.00	100	1.00*	100	1.00
Denmark	99	90	95	98	1.00	97	1.00	96	1.01	…	…	…	…
Finland	34	48	62	*98*	*1.00*	99	1.00	97	1.00	…	…	…	…
France[10]	83	112	116	100	1.00	99	1.00	99	1.00	…	…	…	…
Germany	…	94	105	*84*	*1.03*	…	…	*98*	…	…	…	…	…
Greece	57	68	69	95	0.99	92	1.01	99	1.00	99	1.00*	99	1.00
Iceland	…	88	96	*100*	*0.99*	99	…	98	0.99	…	…	…	…
Ireland	101	…	…	90	1.02	94	1.01	95	1.01	…	…	…	…
Israel	85	105	91	*92*	*1.03*	98	1.00	97	1.01	…	…	…	…
Italy	94	95	104	*100*	*1.00*	99	…	99	0.99	…	…	100	1.00
Luxembourg	92	73	88	…	…	97	1.03	97	1.01	…	…	…	…
Malta	103	103	97[z]	97	0.99	95	1.02	91[z]	0.99[z]	98	1.02*	97	1.03
Monaco[9]	…	…	…	…	…	…	…	…	…	…	…	…	…
Netherlands	99	97	90	95	1.04	99	0.99	98	0.99	…	…	…	…
Norway	88	75	90	100	1.00	100	1.00	98	1.01	…	…	…	…
Portugal	51	69	79	98	1.00	…	…	98	0.99	99	1.00*	100	1.00
San Marino[9]	…	…	…	…	…	…	…	…	…	…	…	…	…
Spain	58	100	121	100	1.00	100	1.00	100	1.00	100	1.00*	100	1.00
Sweden	65	76	95	100	1.00	100	…	95	1.00	…	…	…	…
Switzerland	60	89	99	84	1.02	94	1.00	89	0.99	…	…	…	…
United Kingdom	52	77	72	98	1.00	100	1.00	98	1.01	…	…	…	…
United States	63	58	61	97	1.00	94	1.00	92	1.02	…	…	…	…
South and West Asia													
Afghanistan	…	…	*0.8*[y]	25	0.55	…	…	…	…	…	…	34	0.36*
Bangladesh	…	17	10[y]	76	0.87	83*	1.00*	89*,[y]	1.04*,[y]	45	0.73*	71	1.02
Bhutan	…	0.9	*2*	55	…	56	0.89	79	1.00	…	…	76	0.86
India[2]	3	18	39[z]	…	…	…	…	89	0.96	62	0.67*	81	0.88
Iran, Islamic Republic of[11]	12	13	53	*92*	*0.92*	*82*	*0.97*	*94*	…	87	0.88*	98	0.99
Maldives	…	54	82	87	1.00	98	1.01	97	1.00	98	1.00*	98	1.01
Nepal	…	*11*	27	63	0.50	65*	0.79*	*79*[y]	*0.87*[y]	50	0.48*	78	0.84
Pakistan	…	…	52[z]	*33*	…	…	…	*66*	*0.78*	…	…	69	0.74*
Sri Lanka[2]	…	…	…	84	0.95	…	…	*97*[y]	…	…	…	97	1.01*
Sub-Saharan Africa													
Angola	47	…	…	*50*	*0.95*	…	…	…	…	…	…	72	0.75*
Benin	2	4	6	*41*	*0.54*	50*	0.68*	80	0.84	40	0.48*	51	0.63
Botswana	…	…	15[z]	88	1.08	80	1.04	84[z]	1.03[z]	89	1.07*	94	1.03
Burkina Faso	0.8	2	2	27	0.65	35	0.70	47	0.82	20	0.53*	34	0.69
Burundi	…	0.8	2	*53*	*0.85*	…	…	75	0.97	54	0.81*	73	0.92*
Cameroon	12	11	19	*69*	*0.88*	…	…	…	…	…	…	…	…
Cape Verde	…	…	53	*91*	*0.95*	*99*	*0.98*	88	0.99	88	0.96*	97	1.01
Central African Republic	6	…	*2*[y]	52	0.66	…	…	46	0.72	48	0.56*	59	0.67*
Chad	…	…	*1*[z]	*34*	*0.45*	51	0.62	…	…	17	…	38	0.42*
Comoros	…	2	*3*[z]	*57*	*0.73*	49	0.85	…	…	…	…	…	…

GOAL 4				GOAL 5														
Improving levels of adult literacy				Gender parity in primary education						Gender parity in secondary education								
ADULT LITERACY RATE (15 and over)				GROSS ENROLMENT RATIO (GER)						GROSS ENROLMENT RATIO (GER)								
				School year ending in						School year ending in								
1985-1994[1]		2000-2006[1]		1991		1999		2006		1991		1999		2006				
Total (%)	GPI (F/M)	Total (%)	GPI (F/M)	Total (%)	GPI (F/M)	Total (%)	GPI (F/M)	Total (%)	GPI (F/M)	Total (%)	GPI (F/M)	Total (%)	GPI (F/M)	Total (%)	GPI (F/M)			Country or territory
89	0.99*	93	0.99	105	...	108	0.97	112	0.97	62	...	67	1.07	70	1.09			Panama
90	0.96*	94	0.98	106	0.97	*119*	*0.96*	111[z]	0.97[z]	31	1.05	58	1.04	66[z]	1.03[z]			Paraguay
87	0.88*	89	0.89*	118	0.97	122	0.99	116	1.01	67	0.94	84	0.94	94	1.03			Peru
...	...	...	...	119	1.02	...	...	***94***	***1.20***	85	1.11	...	...	***105***	***0.91***			Saint Kitts and Nevis
...	...	...	...	139	0.94	109	0.98	118	0.94	53	1.45	71	1.29	87	1.19			Saint Lucia
...	...	...	...	112	0.98	...	...	**97**	**1.06**	58	1.24	...	...	75[z]	1.24[z]			Saint Vincent/Grenad.
...	...	90	0.95	104	1.03	...	...	121	1.00	58	1.16	...	...	77	1.37			Suriname
97	0.98*	99	0.99	94	1.00	96	1.00	95*,[z]	0.98*,[z]	82	1.04	77	1.10	76*,[z]	1.05*,[z]			Trinidad and Tobago
...	...	...	...	...	...	...	...	*90[z]*	*1.04[z]*	...	...	...	...	*86[z]*	*0.94[z]*			Turks and Caicos Islands
95	1.01*	98	1.01*	108	0.99	111	0.99	115	0.97	84	...	92	1.17	101	1.16			Uruguay
90	0.98*	93	0.99*	95	1.03	100	0.98	104	0.98	34	1.38	56	1.22	77	1.12			Venezuela, B. R.
																		North America and Western Europe
...	...	...	...	...	...	...	...	90	1.00	...	...	...	...	85	1.04			Andorra[3]
...	...	...	...	101	1.00	103	0.99	102	0.99	102	0.93	99	0.96	102	0.96			Austria
...	...	...	...	100	1.01	105	0.99	102	0.99	101	1.01	143	1.07	110	0.97			Belgium
...	...	...	...	104	0.98	99	1.00	*100[y]*	*0.99[y]*	101	1.00	...	...	*117[y]*	*0.97[y]*			Canada
94	0.93*	98	0.97	90	1.00	97	1.00	102	1.00	72	1.02	93	1.03	97	1.02			Cyprus[3]
...	...	...	...	98	1.00	101	1.00	99	1.00	109	1.01	125	1.06	120	1.03			Denmark
...	...	...	...	99	0.99	99	1.00	98	1.00	116	1.19	121	1.09	112	1.04			Finland
...	...	...	...	108	0.99	107	0.99	110	0.99	98	1.05	111	1.00	114	1.00			France[10]
...	...	...	...	101	*1.01*	106	0.99	103	1.00	98	0.97	98	0.98	101	0.98			Germany
93	0.93*	97	0.98	98	0.99	94	1.00	102	1.00	94	0.98	90	1.04	103	0.97			Greece
...	...	...	...	101	0.99	99	0.98	98	0.99	100	0.96	110	1.06	110	1.03			Iceland
...	...	...	...	102	*1.00*	104	0.99	104	0.99	100	1.09	107	1.06	112	1.07			Ireland
...	...	...	...	98	1.03	112	0.99	110	1.02	88	1.08	90	1.00	92	0.99			Israel
...	...	99	0.99	104	1.00	103	0.99	103	0.99	83	1.00	92	0.99	100	0.99			Italy
...	...	...	...	91	1.08	101	1.02	102	1.01	75	...	98	1.04	96	1.04			Luxembourg
88	1.01*	91	1.04	108	0.96	107	1.01	100[z]	0.98[z]	83	0.94	...	...	99[z]	1.00[z]			Malta
...	...	...	...	...	...	...	...	...	...	...	...	...	...	...	...			Monaco[9]
...	...	...	...	102	1.03	108	0.98	107	0.98	120	0.92	124	0.96	118	0.98			Netherlands
...	...	...	...	100	1.00	101	1.00	98	1.01	103	1.03	120	1.02	113	0.99			Norway
88	0.92*	95	0.96	119	0.95	123	0.96	115	0.95	66	1.16	106	1.08	97	1.09			Portugal
...	...	...	...	...	...	...	...	...	...	...	...	...	...	...	...			San Marino[9]
96	0.97*	97	0.98	106	0.99	106	0.99	105	0.98	105	1.07	108	1.07	119	1.06			Spain
...	...	...	...	100	1.00	110	1.03	96	1.00	90	1.05	157	1.29	103	0.99			Sweden
...	...	...	...	90	1.01	102	1.00	97	0.99	99	0.95	94	0.92	93	0.95			Switzerland
...	...	...	...	105	1.01	101	1.00	105	1.01	87	1.04	101	1.00	98	1.03			United Kingdom
...	...	...	...	103	0.98	101	1.03	98	1.01	92	1.01	95	...	94	0.99			United States
																		South and West Asia
...	...	28	0.29*	29	0.55	28	0.08	101[z]	0.59[z]	16	0.51	...	...	19[z]	0.33[z]			Afghanistan
35	0.58*	52	0.81	...	...	102	0.99	103[y]	1.03[y]	...	...	45	1.01	44[y]	1.03[y]			Bangladesh
...	...	54	0.61	...	...	75	0.85	102	0.98	...	...	37	0.81	49	0.91			Bhutan
48	0.55*	65	0.70	94	0.77	93	0.84	112	0.96	42	0.60	44	0.71	54[z]	0.82[z]			India[2]
66	0.76*	84	0.88	109	0.90	96	0.95	118	1.27	57	0.75	78	0.93	81[z]	0.94[z]			Iran, Islamic Republic of[11]
96	1.00*	97	1.00	...	...	134	1.01	116	0.97	...	...	43	1.07	*83*	*1.07*			Maldives
33	0.35*	55	0.61	110	0.63	114	0.77	126	0.95	34	0.46	34	0.70	*43*	*0.89*			Nepal
...	...	54	0.59*	...	...	...	...	84	0.78	25	0.48	...	...	30	0.78			Pakistan
...	...	91	0.96*	115	0.96	...	...	*108[z]*	*1.00[z]*	71	1.09	...	...	*87[y]*	*1.02[y]*			Sri Lanka[2]
																		Sub-Saharan Africa
...	...	67	0.65*	80	0.92*	*64*	*0.86*	...	...	11	...	13	0.76	...	...			Angola
27	0.42*	40	0.52	54	0.51	74	0.67	96	0.83	10	0.42	19	0.47	*32[z]*	*0.57[z]*			Benin
69	1.09*	82	1.00	107	1.07	104	1.00	107[z]	0.99[z]	48	1.18	74	1.07	76[z]	1.05[z]			Botswana
14	0.42*	26	0.52	33	0.64	43	0.70	60	0.82	7	0.54	10	0.62	15	0.72			Burkina Faso
37	0.57*	59	0.78*	71	0.84	*60*	*0.80*	103	0.91	5	0.58	...	...	*14*	*0.74*			Burundi
...	...	68	0.78*	94	0.86	84	0.82	107	0.84	26	0.71	*25*	*0.83*	24	0.79			Cameroon
63	0.71*	83	0.88	111	*0.94*	119	0.96	106	0.95	21*	...	...	...	80	1.15			Cape Verde
34	0.42*	49	0.52*	63	0.64	...	...	61	0.69	11	0.40	...	...	...	...			Central African Republic
12*	...	26	0.31*	51	0.45	63	0.58	76[z]	0.68[z]	7	0.20	10	0.26	*15[z]*	*0.33[z]*			Chad
...	...	...	...	75	0.73	76	0.85	*85[z]*	*0.88[z]*	18	0.65	25	0.81	*35[z]*	*0.76[z]*			Comoros

Table 12 (continued)

Country or territory	GOAL 1 Early childhood care and education GROSS ENROLMENT RATIO (GER) IN PRE-PRIMARY EDUCATION (%)			GOAL 2 Universal primary education NET ENROLMENT RATIO (NER) IN PRIMARY EDUCATION						GOAL 3 Learning needs of all youth and adults YOUTH LITERACY RATE (15-24)			
	School year ending in			School year ending in									
	1991	1999	2006	1991		1999		2006		1985-1994[1]		2000-2006[1]	
	Total (%)	Total (%)	Total (%)	Total (%)	GPI (F/M)	Total (%)	GPI (F/M)	Total (%)	GPI (F/M)	Total (%)	GPI (F/M)	Total (%)	GPI (F/M)
Congo	3	2	9	*82*	*0.94*	…	…	55	0.90	94	0.95	98	0.99
Côte d'Ivoire	0.9	2	3	45	0.71	52	0.75	…	…	49	0.63*	61	0.74*
D. R. Congo	…	…	…	54	0.78	…	…	…	…	…	…	70	0.81*
Equatorial Guinea	…	34	44[z]	*96*	*0.97*	89	…	…	…	…	…	95	1.00*
Eritrea	…	5	14	*15*	*1.00*	33	0.86	47	0.87	…	…	…	…
Ethiopia	1	1	**3**	*22*	*0.75*	34	0.69	**71**	**0.92**	34	0.71*	50	0.62*
Gabon	…	…	…	*94*	*1.00*	…	…	…	…	93	0.98*	97	0.98
Gambia	…	18	*17*[y]	*46*	*0.72*	64	0.89	62	1.09	…	…	…	…
Ghana	…	*39*	**60**	*54*	*0.89*	*57*	*0.96*	**72**	**0.97**	…	…	77	0.94
Guinea	…	…	7	*27*	*0.52*	45	0.69	72	0.86	…	…	47	0.57*
Guinea-Bissau	…	*3*	…	*38*	*0.56*	*45*	*0.71*	…	…	…	…	…	…
Kenya	35	44	49	76	1.01	63	1.01	75	1.02	…	…	80	1.01*
Lesotho	…	*21*	18	72	1.24	57	1.12	72	1.04	…	…	…	…
Liberia	…	41	100	…	…	42	0.77	39	0.97	51	0.84	70	1.10
Madagascar	…	*3*	8	*64*	*1.00*	63	1.01	96	1.00	…	…	70	0.94*
Malawi	…	…	…	49	0.93	98	…	91	1.06	59	0.70*	82	0.98
Mali	…	2	3	25	0.60	*46*	*0.70*	61	0.79	…	…	29	0.61
Mauritius	…	96	101	91	1.00	91	1.01	95	1.02	91	1.01*	96	1.02
Mozambique	…	…	…	42	0.79	52	0.79	76	0.93	…	…	52	0.79
Namibia	13	21	22	86	1.08	73	1.07	76	1.06	88	1.06*	93	1.04
Niger	1	1	2	24	0.61	26	0.68	43	0.73	…	…	38	0.46
Nigeria[12]	…	…	14[y]	*55*	*0.77*	*58*	*0.82*	*63*[z]	*0.86*[z]	71	0.77*	86	0.95
Rwanda	…	…	…	67	0.94	…	…	*79*[z]	*1.06*[z]	75	…	78	0.98*
Sao Tome and Principe	…	25	**34**	96	0.94	86	0.99	**98**	**1.01**	94	0.96*	95	1.00
Senegal	2	3	9	*45*	*0.75*	54	*0.88*	71	0.98	38	0.57*	51	0.74
Seychelles[3]	…	109	**109**	…	…	…	…	99[y]	…	99	1.01*	99	1.01*
Sierra Leone	…	…	**5**	*43*	*0.73*	…	…	…	…	…	…	52	0.66
Somalia	…	…	…	*9*	*0.55*	…	…	…	…	…	…	…	…
South Africa	21	21	38[y]	90	1.03	94	1.01	88[y]	1.00[y]	…	…	95	1.02
Swaziland	…	…	*17*[z]	75	1.05	74	1.02	78[z]	1.01[z]	84	1.01*	88	1.03*
Togo	3	2	*2*[y]	64	0.71	79	0.79	80	0.87	…	…	74	0.76*
Uganda	…	*4*	3	51	0.83	…	…	…	…	70	0.82*	85	0.94
United Republic of Tanzania	…	…	**32**	51	1.02	50	1.04	98	0.99	82	0.90*	78	0.96
Zambia	…	…	…	78	0.96	68	0.96	92	1.03	66	0.97*	69	0.91*
Zimbabwe	…	*41*	…	84	1.00	83	1.01	88	1.01	95	0.98*	98	1.01
	Weighted average			Weighted average						Weighted average			
World	…	33	41	81	0.88	82	0.93	86	0.97	84	0.90	89	0.95
Countries in transition	…	46	62	89	0.99	88	0.99	90	0.99	100	1.00	100	1.00
Developed countries	…	73	79	96	1.00	97	1.00	95	1.01	99	1.00	99	1.00
Developing countries	…	27	36	78	0.86	81	0.92	85	0.96	80	0.88	87	0.94
Arab States	…	15	18	73	0.81	78	0.90	84	0.93	76	0.80	86	0.89
Central and Eastern Europe	…	49	62	91	0.98	91	0.97	92	0.98	98	0.98	99	0.99
Central Asia	…	21	28	84	0.99	87	0.99	89	0.98	100	1.00	99	1.00
East Asia and the Pacific	…	40	45	97	0.97	96	1.00	93	1.00	95	0.96	98	1.00
East Asia	…	40	44	97	0.97	96	1.00	94	1.00	95	0.96	98	1.00
Pacific	…	61	74	91	0.97	90	0.98	84	0.97	92	0.98	91	1.00
Latin America/Caribbean	…	56	65	86	0.99	92	0.98	94	1.00	94	1.01	97	1.01
Caribbean	…	65	79	51	1.02	75	0.97	72	0.97	78	1.07	86	1.09
Latin America	…	55	64	87	0.99	93	0.98	95	1.00	94	1.01	97	1.01
N. America/W. Europe	…	75	81	96	1.00	97	1.00	95	1.01	99	1.00	99	1.00
South and West Asia	…	21	39	70	0.67	75	0.84	86	0.95	61	0.69	79	0.88
Sub-Saharan Africa	…	9	14	54	0.86	56	0.89	70	0.92	64	0.83	71	0.87

1. Data are for the most recent year available during the period specified. See the web version of the introduction to the statistical tables for a broader explanation of national literacy definitions, assessment methods, and sources and years of data. For countries indicated with (*), national observed literacy data are used. For all others, UIS literacy estimates are used. The estimates were generated using the UIS Global Age-specific Literacy Projections model. Those in the most recent period refer to 2006 and are based on the most recent observed data available for each country.
2. Literacy data for the most recent year do not include some geographic regions.
3. National population data were used to calculate enrolment ratios.
4. Enrolment and population data used to calculate enrolment rates exclude Transnistria.
5. In the Russian Federation two education structures existed in the past, both starting at age 7. The most common or widespread one lasted three years and was used to calculate indicators; the second one, in which about one-third of primary pupils were enrolled, had four grades. Since 2004, the four-grade structure has been extended all over the country.
6. Children enter primary school at age 6 or 7. Since 7 is the most common entrance age, enrolment ratios were calculated using the 7-11 age group for both enrolment and population.

GOAL 4				GOAL 5														
Improving levels of adult literacy				Gender parity in primary education						Gender parity in secondary education								
ADULT LITERACY RATE (15 and over)				GROSS ENROLMENT RATIO (GER)						GROSS ENROLMENT RATIO (GER)								
				School year ending in						School year ending in								
1985-1994[1]		2000-2006[1]		1991		1999		2006		1991		1999		2006				
Total (%)	GPI (F/M)	Total (%)	GPI (F/M)	Total (%)	GPI (F/M)	Total (%)	GPI (F/M)	Total (%)	GPI (F/M)	Total (%)	GPI (F/M)	Total (%)	GPI (F/M)	Total (%)	GPI (F/M)			Country or territory
74	0.79	86	0.88	121	0.90	56	0.95	108	0.90	46	0.72	…	…	*43[y]*	*0.84[y]*			Congo
34	0.53*	49	0.63*	64	0.71	69	0.74	71	0.79	21*	0.48	*22*	*0.54*	…	…			Côte d'Ivoire
…	…	67	0.67*	70	0.75	48	0.90	…	…	…	…	18	0.52	…	…			D. R. Congo
…	…	87	0.86*	*173*	*0.96*	142	0.79	122[z]	0.95[z]	…	…	33	0.37	…	…			Equatorial Guinea
…	…	…	…	20	0.95	52	0.82	62	0.81	…	…	21	0.69	31	0.60			Eritrea
27	0.51*	36	0.46*	30	0.66	48	0.61	**91**	**0.88**	13	0.75	12	0.68	**30**	**0.67**			Ethiopia
72	0.82*	85	0.91	*155*	*0.98*	148	1.00	*152[y]*	*0.99[y]*	…	…	49	0.86	…	…			Gabon
…	…	…	…	59	0.70	77	0.87	74	1.08	17	0.50	32	0.66	45	0.90			Gambia
…	…	64	0.80	74	0.85	75	0.92	**98**	**0.99**	34	0.65	37	0.80	***49***	***0.88***			Ghana
…	…	29	0.43*	37	0.48	57	0.64	88	0.84	10	0.34	*14*	*0.37*	35	0.53			Guinea
…	…	…	…	*50*	*0.55*	*70*	*0.67*	…	…	…	…	…	…	…	…			Guinea-Bissau
…	…	74	0.90*	94	0.96	93	0.97	106	0.97	28	0.77	38	0.96	50	0.93			Kenya
…	…	82	1.23*	109	1.22	102	1.08	114	1.00	24	1.42	31	1.35	37	1.27			Lesotho
41	0.57	54	0.83	…	…	85	0.74	91	0.90	…	…	29	0.65	…	…			Liberia
…	…	71	0.85*	93	0.98	93	0.97	139	0.96	17	0.97	…	…	24	0.95			Madagascar
49	0.51*	71	0.80	66	0.84	137	0.96	119	1.04	8	0.46	36	0.70	29	0.84			Malawi
…	…	23	0.50	30	0.59	59	0.70	80	0.79	8	0.50	16	0.52	28	0.61			Mali
80	0.88*	87	0.94	109	1.00	105	1.00	102	1.00	55	1.04	76	0.98	*88[z]*	*0.99[z]*			Mauritius
…	…	44	0.56	60	0.74	70	0.74	105	0.86	7	0.57	5	0.69	16	0.72			Mozambique
76	0.95*	88	0.98	128	1.03	104	1.01	107	1.00	45	1.22	55	1.12	57	1.15			Namibia
…	…	30	0.36	28	0.61	31	0.68	51	0.73	7	0.37	7	0.60	11	0.63			Niger
55	0.65*	71	0.79	83	0.79	88	0.79	96[z]	0.83[z]	24	0.72	23	0.89	32[z]	0.82[z]			Nigeria[12]
58	…*	65	0.84*	71	0.93	92	0.98	140	1.04	9	0.73	9	0.99	*13[z]*	*0.89[z]*			Rwanda
73	0.73*	87	0.88	…	…	108	0.97	**127**	**1.00**	…	…	…	…	*46*	*1.07*			Sao Tome and Principe
27	0.48*	42	0.60	55	0.73	64	*0.86*	80	0.98	15	0.53	15	0.64	*24*	*0.76*			Senegal
88	1.02*	92	1.01*	…	…	116	0.99	**125**	**0.99**	…	…	113	1.04	**112**	**1.13**			Seychelles[3]
…	…	37	0.52	53	0.70	…	…	**147**	**0.90**	17	0.57	…	…	**32**	**0.69**			Sierra Leone
…	…	…	…	…	…	…	…	…	…	…	…	…	…	…	…			Somalia
…	…	88	0.98	109	0.99	116	0.97	106[y]	0.96[y]	69	1.18	89	1.13	95[y]	1.07[y]			South Africa
67	0.94*	80	0.97*	94	0.99	100	0.95	106[z]	0.93[z]	42	0.96	45	1.00	47[z]	1.00[z]			Swaziland
…	…	53	0.56*	94	0.65	112	0.75	102	0.86	20	0.34	28	0.40	*40[z]*	*0.51[z]*			Togo
56	0.66*	73	0.79	70	0.84	125	0.92	117	1.01	11	0.59	*10*	*0.66*	*18[z]*	*0.81[z]*			Uganda
59	0.67*	72	0.83	70	0.98	67	1.00	**112**	**0.98**	5	0.77	*6*	*0.82*	…	…			United Republic of Tanzania
65	0.79*	68	0.78*	95	…	80	0.92	117	0.98	23	…	20	*0.77*	*30[z]*	*0.82[z]*			Zambia
84	0.88*	91	0.94	106	0.97	100	0.97	101	0.99	49	0.79	43	0.88	40	0.93			Zimbabwe
Weighted average				Weighted average						Weighted average								
76	0.85	84	0.89	98	0.89	99	0.92	105	0.95	51	0.83	60	0.92	66	0.95			World
98	0.98	99	1.00	97	0.99	104	0.99	99	0.99	95	1.03	90	1.01	89	0.97			Countries in transition
99	0.99	99	1.00	102	0.99	102	1.00	101	1.00	93	1.01	100	1.00	101	1.00			Developed countries
68	0.77	79	0.85	97	0.87	99	0.91	106	0.94	42	0.75	52	0.89	60	0.94			Developing countries
58	0.66	72	0.75	84	0.80	90	0.87	97	0.90	51	0.76	60	0.89	68	0.92			Arab States
96	0.96	97	0.97	98	0.98	102	0.96	97	0.98	82	0.98	87	0.98	88	0.96			Central and Eastern Europe
98	0.98	99	0.99	90	0.99	98	0.99	100	0.98	98	0.99	83	0.98	91	0.96			Central Asia
82	0.84	93	0.94	118	0.95	112	0.99	109	0.99	52	0.83	65	0.96	75	1.01			East Asia and the Pacific
82	0.84	93	0.94	118	0.95	113	0.99	110	0.99	51	0.83	64	0.96	75	1.01			East Asia
94	0.99	93	0.99	98	0.97	95	0.97	91	0.97	66	1.00	111	0.99	107	0.96			Pacific
87	0.98	91	0.98	103	0.97	121	0.97	118	0.97	51	1.09	80	1.07	89	1.07			Latin America/Caribbean
66	1.02	74	1.05	70	0.98	112	0.98	108	0.99	44	1.03	53	1.03	57	1.03			Caribbean
87	0.97	91	0.98	104	0.97	122	0.97	118	0.97	52	1.09	81	1.07	91	1.07			Latin America
99	0.99	99	1.00	104	0.99	103	1.01	101	1.00	94	1.02	100	0.99	101	1.00			N. America/W. Europe
48	0.57	64	0.71	89	0.77	90	0.84	108	0.95	39	0.60	45	0.75	51	0.85			South and West Asia
53	0.71	62	0.75	72	0.84	78	0.85	95	0.89	21	0.75	24	0.82	32	0.80			Sub-Saharan Africa

7. The dramatic increase in primary education NER from 90% in 2005 (figure published in the 2008 GMR) to the nearly 100% figure for 2006 published in this year Report is essentially due to the use of the latest UN population estimates (2006 revision) that indicate a lower primary school age population as compared with the previous estimates (2004 revision). The reported change should not be interpreted as an accurate representation of progress towards UPE as the country own data show.

8. The apparent decrease in total secondary education enrolment between 1999 and 2005 is essentially due to a change in data reporting. Since 2003, programmes designed for people beyond the regular school age (e.g. adult education) have been excluded from the figures for secondary enrolment, leading to a reported decline in the GER. The secondary NER has increased over the period in question.

9. Enrolment ratios were not calculated due to lack of United Nations population data by age.

10. Data include French overseas departments and territories (DOM-TOM).

11. The apparent increase in the gender parity index (GPI) of primary education GER is due to the recent inclusion in enrolment statistics of literacy programmes in which 80% of participants are women.

12. Due to the continuing discrepancy in enrolment by single age, the net enrolment ratio in primary education is estimated using the age distribution of the 2004 DHS data.

Data in italic are UIS estimates.

Data in bold are for the school year ending in 2007.

(z) Data are for the school year ending in 2005.

(y) Data are for the school year ending in 2004.

(*) National estimate.

Table 13
Trends in basic or proxy indicators to measure EFA goal 6

	Country or territory	GOAL 6 Educational quality								
		SURVIVAL RATE TO GRADE 5						PUPIL/TEACHER RATIO IN PRIMARY EDUCATION[1]		
		School year ending in						School year ending in		
		1991		1999		2005		1991	1999	2006
		Total (%)	GPI (F/M)	Total (%)	GPI (F/M)	Total (%)	GPI (F/M)			
	Arab States									
1	Algeria	95	0.99	95	1.02	95	1.01	28	28	24
2	Bahrain	89	1.01	*97*	*1.01*	99[y]	0.98[y]	19	…	…
3	Djibouti	87	1.81	77	1.19	90	0.94	43	40	34
4	Egypt	…	…	*99*	*1.01*	…	…	24	*23*	***27***
5	Iraq	…	…	*66*	*0.94*	*81[y]*	*0.84[y]*	25	25	*21[z]*
6	Jordan	…	…	98	0.99	…	…	25	…	…
7	Kuwait	…	…	…	…	96	1.02	18	13	10
8	Lebanon	…	…	91	1.07	91	1.06	…	14	14
9	Libyan Arab Jamahiriya	…	…	…	…	…	…	14	…	…
10	Mauritania	75	0.99	*68*	*0.94*	57	0.96	45	47	41
11	Morocco	75	1.02	82	1.00	80	0.97	27	28	27
12	Oman	97	0.99	94	1.00	100	1.00	28	25	*14*
13	Palestinian A. T.	…	…	…	…	…	…	…	38	32
14	Qatar	64	1.02	…	…	…	…	11	13	11
15	Saudi Arabia	83	1.03	…	…	…	…	16	…	…
16	Sudan	94	1.09	*84*	*1.10*	79[y]	1.02[y]	34	…	34
17	Syrian Arab Republic	96	0.98	92	0.99	…	…	25	25	…
18	Tunisia	86	0.83	92	1.02	97	1.01	28	24	19
19	United Arab Emirates	80	0.99	92	0.99	99	1.02	18	16	15
20	Yemen	…	…	*87*	…	66[y]	0.96[y]	…	*22*	…
	Central and Eastern Europe									
21	Albania	…	…	…	…	…	…	19	*23*	*21[y]*
22	Belarus	…	…	…	…	…	…	…	20	16
23	Bosnia and Herzegovina	…	…	…	…	…	…	…	…	…
24	Bulgaria	91	0.99	…	…	…	…	15	18	16
25	Croatia	…	…	…	…	…	…	19	19	17
26	Czech Republic	…	…	98	1.01	100	1.00	23	18	16
27	Estonia	…	…	99	1.01	97	1.00	…	16	11
28	Hungary	98	1.26	…	…	…	…	12	11	10
29	Latvia	…	…	…	…	…	…	15	15	12
30	Lithuania	…	…	…	…	…	…	18	17	14
31	Montenegro	…	…	…	…	…	…	…	…	…
32	Poland	98	1.08	99	…	99	…	16	…	11
33	Republic of Moldova	…	…	…	…	…	…	23	21	17
34	Romania	…	…	…	…	…	…	22	19	17
35	Russian Federation	…	…	…	…	…	…	22	18	17
36	Serbia	…	…	…	…	…	…	…	*17*	***13***
37	Slovakia	…	…	…	…	…	…	…	19	17
38	Slovenia	…	…	…	…	…	…	…	14	*15*
39	TFYR Macedonia	…	…	…	…	…	…	21	22	19[z]
40	Turkey	98	0.99	…	…	97[y]	0.99[y]	30	…	…
41	Ukraine	…	…	…	…	…	…	22	20	17
	Central Asia									
42	Armenia	…	…	…	…	…	…	…	…	21
43	Azerbaijan	…	…	…	…	…	…	…	19	13
44	Georgia	…	…	…	…	100	…	17	17	*15[y]*
45	Kazakhstan	…	…	…	…	…	…	21	…	**17**
46	Kyrgyzstan	…	…	…	…	…	…	…	24	24
47	Mongolia	…	…	…	…	…	…	28	32	33
48	Tajikistan	…	…	…	…	…	…	21	22	22
49	Turkmenistan	…	…	…	…	…	…	…	…	…
50	Uzbekistan	…	…	…	…	…	…	24	21	**18**
	East Asia and the Pacific									
51	Australia	99	1.01	…	…	…	…	17	*18*	…
52	Brunei Darussalam	…	…	…	…	100	1.00	15	14*	13
53	Cambodia	…	…	*56*	*0.93*	62	1.05	33	*48*	50

GOAL 6
Educational quality

% FEMALE TEACHERS IN PRIMARY EDUCATION			TRAINED PRIMARY-SCHOOL TEACHERS[2] as % of total		PUBLIC CURRENT EXPENDITURE ON PRIMARY EDUCATION as % of GNP			PUBLIC CURRENT EXPENDITURE ON PRIMARY EDUCATION PER PUPIL (unit cost) at PPP in constant 2005 US$			
School year ending in			School year ending in		School year ending in			School year ending in			
1991	1999	2006	1999	2006	1991	1999	2006	1991	1999	2006	
										Arab States	
39	46	52	94	99	4.5	…	*1.6[x]*	1 560	…	*692[x]*	1
54	…	…	…	…	…	…	…	…	…	…	2
37	28	27	…	79	1.8	…	…	1 006	…	…	3
52	*52*	***56***	…	…	…	…	…	…	…	…	4
70	72	*72[z]*	…	100[y]	…	…	…	…	…	…	5
62	…	…	…	…	…	1.9	1.8[z]	…	568	695[z]	6
61	73	87	100	100	1.5	…	0.7	…	…	2 204[z]	7
…	82	85	15	13	…	…	*0.9[z]*	…	…	*402[z]*	8
…	…	…	…	…	…	…	…	…	…	…	9
18	26	32	…	100	…	…	*1.4[z]*	…	…	*224[z]*	10
37	39	47	…	100[z]	1.6	2.2	2.9[z]	607	697	1 005[z]	11
47	52	*65*	100	*100*	1.5	1.4	1.8[y]	…	…	…	12
…	54	67	100	100[z]	…	…	…	…	…	…	13
72	75	85	…	52	…	…	…	…	…	…	14
48	…	…	…	…	…	…	…	…	…	…	15
51	…	68	…	59	…	…	…	…	…	…	16
64	*65*	…	81	…	…	1.7	1.9	…	349	611	17
45	50	52	…	…	…	…	*2.4[z]*	…	…	*1 581[z]*	18
64	73	84	…	60[z]	…	0.7	0.4[y]	…	1 997	1 636[y]	19
…	*20*	…	…	…	…	…	…	…	…	…	20
										Central and Eastern Europe	
55	*75*	*76[y]*	…	…	…	…	…	…	…	…	21
…	99	99	…	100	1.8	…	*0.5*	…	…	*1 196*	22
…	…	…	…	…	…	…	…	…	…	…	23
77	*91*	93	…	…	2.8	…	0.8[z]	…	…	2 045[z]	24
75	89	90	100	…	…	…	*0.8[y]*	…	…	*2 197[x]*	25
…	85	95	…	…	…	*0.7*	0.6[y]	…	*1 688*	2 242[y]	26
…	*86*	89	…	…	…	…	1.3[y]	…	…	2 511[y]	27
84	85	96	…	…	2.4	*0.9*	1.1[z]	2 480	*2 339*	4 479[z]	28
…	97	97	…	…	…	…	…	…	…	…	29
94	98	98	…	…	…	…	0.7[z]	…	…	2 166[z]	30
…	…	…	…	…	…	…	…	…	…	…	31
…	…	84	…	…	1.8	…	1.7[z]	1 011	…	3 155[z]	32
97	96	97	…	…	…	…	…	…	…	…	33
84	86	87	…	…	…	…	*0.5[z]*	…	…	*941[z]*	34
99	98	98	…	…	…	…	…	…	…	…	35
…	…	…	…	…	…	…	…	…	…	…	36
…	93	89	…	…	…	*0.6*	0.6[z]	…	*1 245*	2 149[z]	37
…	96	*97*	…	…	1.0	…	*1.1[z]*	2 487	…	*5 206[z]*	38
…	66	70[z]	…	…	…	…	…	…	…	…	39
43	…	…	…	…	1.3	…	*1.5[y]*	657	…	*1 059[y]*	40
98	98	99	…	100	…	…	…	…	…	…	41
										Central Asia	
…	…	99	…	77[z]	…	…	…	…	…	…	42
…	83	86	100	100	…	…	*0.4*	…	…	*356*	43
92	92	*95[y]*	…	…	…	…	…	…	…	…	44
96	…	**98**	…	…	…	…	…	…	…	…	45
81	95	97	48	61	…	…	…	…	…	…	46
90	93	95	…	…	…	…	1.2[y]	…	…	261[y]	47
49	56	65	…	93	…	…	*0.9[z]*	…	…	*106[z]*	48
…	…	…	…	…	…	…	…	…	…	…	49
79	84	**85**	…	**100**	…	…	…	…	…	…	50
										East Asia and the Pacific	
72	…	…	…	…	…	*1.6*	1.5[z]	…	*4 637*	5 181[z]	51
57	66*	73	…	85	0.5	…	…	…	…	…	52
31	*37*	42	…	98	…	…	…	…	…	…	53

Table 13 (continued)

		GOAL 6 Educational quality								
		SURVIVAL RATE TO GRADE 5						PUPIL/TEACHER RATIO IN PRIMARY EDUCATION[1]		
		School year ending in						School year ending in		
		1991		1999		2005		1991	1999	2006
	Country or territory	Total (%)	GPI (F/M)	Total (%)	GPI (F/M)	Total (%)	GPI (F/M)			
54	China	86	1.36	…	…	…	…	22	…	18
55	Cook Islands	…	…	…	…	…	…	…	18	16[z]
56	DPR Korea	…	…	…	…	…	…	…	…	…
57	Fiji	87	0.97	87	0.96	*86*	*1.02*	31	…	*28[z]*
58	Indonesia	84	2.27	…	…	*84*	*1.04*	23	…	*20*
59	Japan	100	1.00	…	…	…	…	21	21	19
60	Kiribati	92	…	…	…	82[x]	1.16[x]	29	25	25[z]
61	Lao PDR	…	…	54	0.98	62	0.99	27	31	31
62	Macao, China	…	…	…	…	…	…	…	31	21
63	Malaysia	97	1.00	…	…	99[y]	1.01[y]	20	21	17[z]
64	Marshall Islands	…	…	…	…	…	…	…	15	…
65	Micronesia	…	…	…	…	…	…	…	…	***17***
66	Myanmar	…	…	…	…	72	1.01	48	31	30
67	Nauru	…	…	…	…	…	…	…	…	**23**
68	New Zealand	…	…	…	…	…	…	17	18	16
69	Niue	…	…	…	…	…	…	20	16	*12[z]*
70	Palau	…	…	…	…	…	…	…	15	*13[z]*
71	Papua New Guinea	69	0.97	…	…	…	…	31	…	*36*
72	Philippines	…	…	…	…	74	1.11	33	35	35
73	Republic of Korea	99	1.00	100	1.00	**99**	1.00	36	31	**27**
74	Samoa	…	…	94	1.05*	…	…	26	*24*	*25[y]*
75	Singapore	…	…	…	…	…	…	26	27	23
76	Solomon Islands	88	1.28	…	…	…	…	21	19	…
77	Thailand	…	…	…	…	…	…	22	21	18
78	Timor-Leste	…	…	…	…	…	…	…	…	34[z]
79	Tokelau	…	…	…	…	…	…	…	…	*6[y]*
80	Tonga	…	…	…	…	92	1.00	23	21	22
81	Tuvalu	…	…	…	…	…	…	…	19	19[y]
82	Vanuatu	…	…	72	0.99	…	…	29	24	20[y]
83	Viet Nam	…	…	83	1.08	*92*	…	35	30	21
	Latin America and the Caribbean									
84	Anguilla	…	…	…	…	97[y]	1.06[y]	…	22	17
85	Antigua and Barbuda	…	…	…	…	…	…	…	…	…
86	Argentina	…	…	90	1.00	90[y]	1.03[y]	…	22	17[z]
87	Aruba	…	…	…	…	97	…	…	19	18
88	Bahamas	84	…	…	…	85	1.07	…	14	15
89	Barbados	…	…	…	…	…	…	18	*18*	*15*
90	Belize	67	0.96	78	…	92	…	26	*24*	23
91	Bermuda	…	…	…	…	90	…	…	…	8
92	Bolivia	…	…	82	0.97	*85[x]*	*1.00[x]*	24	*25*	*24[y]*
93	Brazil	73	…	…	…	…	…	23	26	21[z]
94	British Virgin Islands	…	…	…	…	…	…	19	18	15
95	Cayman Islands	…	…	*74*	…	…	…	…	15	12
96	Chile	92	0.97	100	1.00	99[x]	1.00[x]	25	32	26
97	Colombia	76	…	67	1.08	82	1.10	30	24	28
98	Costa Rica	84	1.02	91	1.03	94	1.02	32	27	20
99	Cuba	92	…	94	1.00	97	1.02	13	12	10
100	Dominica	75	…	*91*	…	92	…	29	20	17
101	Dominican Republic	…	…	75	1.11	68	1.09	…	…	23
102	Ecuador	…	…	77	1.01	77	1.02	30	27	23
103	El Salvador	58	1.08	*65*	*1.02*	72	1.06	…	…	40*
104	Grenada	…	…	…	…	…	…	…	…	*18[z]*
105	Guatemala	…	…	56	1.06	69	0.96	34	38	31*
106	Guyana	…	…	95	…	…	…	30	27	28[z]
107	Haiti	…	…	…	…	…	…	23	…	…
108	Honduras	…	…	…	…	83	1.08	38	…	28
109	Jamaica	…	…	…	…	…	…	34	…	*28[z]*
110	Mexico	80	2.06	89	1.02	94	1.02	31	27	28
111	Montserrat	…	…	…	…	…	…	…	21	17
112	Netherlands Antilles	…	…	…	…	…	…	…	20	…
113	Nicaragua	44	3.33	48	1.19	54	1.14	36	34	33

GOAL 6
Educational quality

% FEMALE TEACHERS IN PRIMARY EDUCATION			TRAINED PRIMARY-SCHOOL TEACHERS[2] as % of total		PUBLIC CURRENT EXPENDITURE ON PRIMARY EDUCATION as % of GNP			PUBLIC CURRENT EXPENDITURE ON PRIMARY EDUCATION PER PUPIL (unit cost) at PPP in constant 2005 US$			
School year ending in			School year ending in		School year ending in			School year ending in			
1991	1999	2006	1999	2006	1991	1999	2006	1991	1999	2006	
43	…	55	…	…	…	*0.6*	…	…	…	…	*54*
…	86	77[z]	…	95[z]	…	0.2	…	…	…	…	*55*
…	…	…	…	…	…	…	…	…	…	…	*56*
57	…	*57[z]*	…	…	…	…	2.5[y]	…	…	1 143[y]	*57*
51	…	…	…	…	…	…	…	…	…	…	*58*
58	…	*65*	…	…	…	…	…	…	…	…	*59*
58	62	75[z]	…	…	…	…	…	…	…	…	*60*
38	43	46	76	86	…	…	0.5[z]	…	…	61[z]	*61*
…	87	87	81	89	…	…	…	…	…	…	*62*
57	66	66[z]	…	…	1.5	…	1.7[y]	671	…	1 324[y]	*63*
…	…	…	…	…	…	…	…	…	…	…	*64*
…	…	…	…	…	…	…	…	…	…	…	*65*
62	73	82	60	98	…	…	…	…	…	…	*66*
…	…	**91**	…	…	…	…	…	…	…	…	*67*
80	82	83	…	…	1.7	*1.8*	1.5	3 255	*3 971*	4 831	*68*
…	100	*100[z]*	…	…	…	…	…	…	…	…	*69*
…	82	…	…	…	…	…	…	…	…	…	*70*
34	…	*43*	…	…	…	…	…	…	…	…	*71*
…	87	87	*100*	…	…	…	1.2[z]	…	…	418[z]	*72*
50	64	**76**	…	…	1.3	*1.3*	1.4[y]	1 379	*2 621*	3 379[y]	*73*
72	*71*	*73[y]*	…	…	…	*1.4*	…	…	*443*	…	*74*
…	80	83	…	…	…	…	…	…	…	…	*75*
…	41	…	…	…	2.2	…	…	349	…	…	*76*
…	63	60	…	…	1.5	…	…	637	…	…	*77*
…	…	31[z]	…	…	…	…	…	…	…	…	*78*
…	…	*69[y]*	…	…	…	…	…	…	…	…	*79*
67	67	…	…	…	…	…	…	…	…	…	*80*
…	…	…	…	…	…	…	…	…	…	…	*81*
40	49	54[y]	…	…	…	2.2	…	…	409	…	*82*
…	78	78	78	96	…	…	…	…	…	…	*83*
Latin America and the Caribbean											
…	87	93	76	64	…	…	1.1[z]	…	…	…	*84*
…	…	…	…	…	…	…	…	…	…	…	*85*
…	88	88[z]	…	…	…	1.6	1.5[z]	…	1 637	1 703[z]	*86*
…	78	82	100	99	…	…	1.3[z]	…	…	…	*87*
…	63	81	58	89	…	…	…	…	…	…	*88*
72	*76*	*78*	…	73[z]	…	*1.0*	*2.0[z]*	…	…	…	*89*
70	*64*	71	…	39	2.7	…	2.4[y]	528	…	846[y]	*90*
…	…	89	…	100	1.1	…	*0.8[z]*	…	…	…	*91*
59	*61*	*61[y]*	…	…	…	*2.0*	2.9[x]	…	*295*	435[x]	*92*
…	93	88[z]	…	…	…	*1.3*	1.3[y]	…	*788*	1 005[y]	*93*
…	86	88	72	74	…	…	1.0	…	…	…	*94*
…	89	88	98	97	…	…	…	…	…	…	*95*
73	77	78	…	…	…	1.5	1.2	…	1 256	1 287	*96*
…	77	76	…	…	…	…	2.0	…	…	1 257	*97*
80	80	80	93	88	1.2	2.6	2.3[y]	552	1 469	1 623[y]	*98*
79	79	77	100	100	…	…	2.6	…	…	…	*99*
81	75	84	64	64	…	…	…	…	…	…	*100*
…	…	76	…	88	…	…	*1.2[z]*	…	…	*644[z]*	*101*
…	68	70	…	71	…	…	…	…	…	…	*102*
…	…	70*	…	94*	…	…	1.4	…	…	478	*103*
…	…	*76[z]*	…	*67[z]*	…	…	*1.8[x]*	…	…	*766[x]*	*104*
…	…	64*	…	…	…	…	1.6	…	…	390	*105*
76	86	86[z]	52	57[z]	…	…	2.1	…	…	752[z]	*106*
45	…	…	…	…	0.7	…	…	194	…	…	*107*
74	…	…	…	87[y]	…	…	…	…	…	…	*108*
…	…	*89[z]*	…	…	1.5	…	1.8[z]	421	…	547[z]	*109*
…	62	67	…	…	0.8	1.8	2.2[z]	431	1 114	1 604[z]	*110*
…	84	100	100	77	…	…	…	…	…	…	*111*
…	86	…	100	…	…	…	…	…	…	…	*112*
86	83	74	79	74	…	…	1.6	…	…	331	*113*

Table 13 (continued)

	Country or territory	GOAL 6 Educational quality								
		SURVIVAL RATE TO GRADE 5						PUPIL/TEACHER RATIO IN PRIMARY EDUCATION[1]		
		School year ending in						School year ending in		
		1991		1999		2005		1991	1999	2006
		Total (%)	GPI (F/M)	Total (%)	GPI (F/M)	Total (%)	GPI (F/M)			
114	Panama	…	…	92	1.01	88	1.03	…	26	25
115	Paraguay	74	1.02	*78*	*1.05*	88[y]	1.05[y]	25	…	*28[y]*
116	Peru	…	…	87	0.98	89	0.98	29	…	22
117	Saint Kitts and Nevis	…	…	…	…	…	…	22	…	**15**
118	Saint Lucia	96	…	*90*	…	…	…	29	22	24
119	Saint Vincent/Grenad.	…	…	…	…	…	…	20	…	*18[z]*
120	Suriname	…	…	…	…	…	…	22	…	16
121	Trinidad and Tobago	…	…	…	…	91[*,y]	1.03[*,y]	26	21	17[*,z]
122	Turks and Caicos Islands	…	…	…	…	…	…	…	*18*	*15[z]*
123	Uruguay	97	1.03	…	…	93	1.03	22	20	20
124	Venezuela, Bolivarian Rep. of	86	1.09	91	1.08	92	1.05	23	…	19[z]
	North America and Western Europe									
125	Andorra	…	…	…	…	…	…	…	…	10
126	Austria	…	…	…	…	…	…	11	13	12
127	Belgium	91	1.02	…	…	96	1.01	…	…	11
128	Canada	97	1.04	…	…	…	…	15	17	…
129	Cyprus	100	1.00	96	1.03	99	1.02	21	18	16
130	Denmark	94	1.00	…	…	93[y]	1.00[y]	…	10	…
131	Finland	100	1.00	…	…	99	1.01	…	17	*16*
132	France	96	1.37	98	*0.99*	…	…	…	19	*19*
133	Germany	…	…	…	…	…	…	…	17	14
134	Greece	100	1.00	…	…	99	1.03	19	14	11
135	Iceland	…	…	…	…	99	1.02	…	*11*	*10*
136	Ireland	100	1.01	95	1.03	*99*	*1.03*	27	22	17
137	Israel	…	…	…	…	…	…	15	13	13
138	Italy	…	…	97	…	100	1.01	12	11	11
139	Luxembourg	…	…	*96*	*1.08*	100	1.01	13	…	11
140	Malta	99	1.01	99	0.99	…	…	21	20	12[z]
141	Monaco	83	0.81	…	…	…	…	…	*16*	*14[y]*
142	Netherlands	…	…	100	1.00	…	…	17	…	…
143	Norway	100	1.01	…	…	100	1.00	…	…	*11[y]*
144	Portugal	…	…	…	…	…	…	14	…	11
145	San Marino	88	…	…	…	…	…	6	…	6[y]
146	Spain	…	…	…	…	*100[y]*	*1.00[y]*	22	15	14
147	Sweden	100	1.00	…	…	…	…	10	12	10
148	Switzerland	…	…	…	…	…	…	…	…	13
149	United Kingdom	…	…	…	…	…	…	20	19	18
150	United States	…	…	94	…	97	1.03	…	15	14
	South and West Asia									
151	Afghanistan	…	…	…	…	…	…	…	36	83[z]
152	Bangladesh	…	…	65	1.16	65[x]	1.07[x]	…	56	51[y]
153	Bhutan	…	…	90	1.04	93	1.04	…	42	29
154	India	…	…	62	0.95	73[y]	1.00[y]	47	35*	*40[y]*
155	Iran, Islamic Republic of	90	0.98	…	…	…	…	31	27	19
156	Maldives	…	…	…	…	…	…	…	24	16
157	Nepal	51	0.99	58	1.10	79	1.10*	39	39	*40*
158	Pakistan	…	…	…	…	70[y]	1.07[y]	…	…	39
159	Sri Lanka	92	1.01	…	…	…	…	31	…	*22[z]*
	Sub-Saharan Africa									
160	Angola	…	…	…	…	…	…	32	…	…
161	Benin	55	1.02	…	…	72	0.98	36	53	44
162	Botswana	84	1.06	87	1.06	83[y]	1.05[y]	30	27	24[z]
163	Burkina Faso	70	0.96	68	1.05	72	1.03	57	49	46
164	Burundi	62	0.89	…	…	88	1.09	67	*57*	54
165	Cameroon	…	…	*81*	…	…	…	51	52	45
166	Cape Verde	…	…	…	…	92	1.06	…	*29*	25
167	Central African Republic	23	0.90	…	…	50	0.86	77	…	…
168	Chad	51	0.74	55	0.86	33[y]	0.94[y]	66	68	63[z]
169	Comoros	…	…	…	…	*80[y]*	*1.02[y]*	37	35	*35[z]*

GOAL 6
Educational quality

% FEMALE TEACHERS IN PRIMARY EDUCATION			TRAINED PRIMARY-SCHOOL TEACHERS[2] as % of total		PUBLIC CURRENT EXPENDITURE ON PRIMARY EDUCATION as % of GNP			PUBLIC CURRENT EXPENDITURE ON PRIMARY EDUCATION PER PUPIL (unit cost) at PPP in constant 2005 US$			
School year ending in			School year ending in		School year ending in			School year ending in			
1991	1999	2006	1999	2006	1991	1999	2006	1991	1999	2006	
…	75	76	79	91	1.7	1.9	…	615	867	…	114
…	…	*72[y]*	…	…	…	…	1.8[y]	…	…	518[y]	115
…	…	64	…	…	…	1.2	1.1	…	366	446	116
74	…	**87**	…	**64**	1.1	…	…	…	…	…	117
83	*84*	86	…	80	2.5	*3.3*	2.0	536	*1 197*	949	118
67	…	*73[z]*	…	*74[z]*	3.0	…	3.0[z]	724	…	1 227[z]	119
84	…	91	…	…	…	…	…	…	…	…	120
70	76	72[*,z]	71	81[*,y]	…	1.5	…	…	1 012	…	121
…	*92*	*89[z]*	*81*	*82[z]*	…	…	…	…	…	…	122
…	*92*	…	…	…	0.9	0.8	…	634	748	…	123
74	…	81[z]	…	84[z]	…	…	1.0	…	…	583	124
North America and Western Europe											
…	…	76	…	100	…	…	0.5	…	…	…	125
82	89	89	…	…	0.9	*1.1*	1.0[z]	4 812	*7 112*	7 596[z]	126
…	…	79	…	…	1.1	…	1.4[y]	4 158	…	6 303[y]	127
69	*68*	…	…	…	…	…	…	…	…	…	128
60	67	83	…	…	1.2	1.6	1.7[y]	…	…	…	129
…	63	…	…	…	…	*1.6*	1.8[z]	…	*7 345*	7 949[z]	130
…	71	*76*	…	…	1.7	*1.2*	1.2[z]	5 132	*4 615*	5 373[z]	131
…	78	*82*	…	…	0.9	*1.1*	1.1[z]	3 099	*4 697*	5 224[z]	132
…	82	84	…	…	…	…	0.7[y]	…	…	4 837[y]	133
52	*57*	64	…	…	0.6	*0.7*	*0.9[z]*	1 248	*2 148*	*3 562[z]*	134
…	*76*	*80*	…	…	…	…	2.4[y]	…	…	7 788[y]	135
77	85	85	…	…	1.5	*1.4*	1.7[z]	2 082	*3 112*	5 100[z]	136
82	…	86	…	…	1.9	*2.4*	2.4[y]	2 609	*4 835*	5 135[y]	137
91	95	96	…	…	0.8	*1.2*	1.0[z]	3 770	*6 425*	6 347[z]	138
51	…	72	…	…	…	…	*1.4[z]*	…	…	*9 953[z]*	139
79	87	86[z]	…	…	0.9	…	1.1[y]	1 306	…	2 549[y]	140
…	*87*	*80[y]*	…	…	…	…	…	…	…	…	141
53	…	…	…	…	0.9	*1.1*	1.3[z]	3 315	*4 606*	5 572[z]	142
…	…	*73[y]*	…	…	2.5	*1.6*	1.6[z]	9 534	*6 456*	7 072[z]	143
81	…	81	…	…	1.7	*1.5*	1.7[z]	2 779	*3 872*	4 908[z]	144
89	…	…	…	…	…	…	…	…	…	…	145
73	68	70	…	…	0.8	*1.1*	1.0[z]	2 253	*4 112*	4 800[z]	146
77	80	81	…	…	3.1	…	1.9[z]	10 960	…	8 415[z]	147
…	…	79	…	…	2.1	1.4	1.4[z]	12 056	7 066	7 811[z]	148
78	76	81	…	…	1.2	…	1.3[z]	3 440	…	5 596[z]	149
…	86	89	…	…	…	…	…	…	…	…	150
South and West Asia											
…	–	*34[z]*	…	36[z]	…	…	…	…	…	…	151
…	33	34[y]	64	48[y]	…	0.6	*0.7[z]*	…	64	*115[z]*	152
…	32	50	100	92	…	…	1.1[z]	…	…	…	153
28	33*	*44[y]*	…	…	…	*1.3*	…	…	*288*	…	154
53	53	62	…	100[z]	…	…	1.4	…	…	927	155
…	60	70	67	68	…	…	*3.5[z]*	…	…	…	156
14	23	*30*	46	31[z]	…	*1.1*	*1.2[x]*	…	*97*	*119[x]*	157
27	…	45	…	85	…	…	…	…	…	…	158
…	…	*79[z]*	…	…	…	…	…	…	…	…	159
Sub-Saharan Africa											
…	…	…	…	…	…	…	0.2[z]	…	…	…	160
25	23	17	58	72	…	…	*1.7[z]*	…	…	*120[z]*	161
78	81	78[z]	90	87[z]	…	…	**1.3**	…	…	1 158[z]	162
27	25	30	…	87	…	…	2.6	…	…	328	163
46	*54*	55	…	88[z]	1.5	1.3	2.7[z]	140	*85*	132[z]	164
30	36	40	…	62*	…	1.0	0.8	…	128	107	165
…	*62*	66	…	81	…	…	2.8	…	…	1 052	166
25	…	…	…	…	1.2	…	0.7	167	…	88	167
6	9	12[z]	…	27[z]	0.7	…	0.6[z]	82	…	54[z]	168
…	26	*33[z]*	…	…	…	…	…	…	…	…	169

Table 13 (continued)

		GOAL 6 Educational quality								
		SURVIVAL RATE TO GRADE 5						PUPIL/TEACHER RATIO IN PRIMARY EDUCATION[1]		
		School year ending in						School year ending in		
		1991		1999		2005		1991	1999	2006
	Country or territory	Total (%)	GPI (F/M)	Total (%)	GPI (F/M)	Total (%)	GPI (F/M)			
170	Congo	60	1.16	...	...	...	...	65	61	55
171	Côte d'Ivoire	73	0.93	69	0.89	...	...	37	43	46
172	D. R. Congo	55	0.86	...	...	...	...	40	26	...
173	Equatorial Guinea	...	...	...	...	...	...	...	57	...
174	Eritrea	...	...	95	0.95	74	0.90	38	47	47
175	Ethiopia	18	1.47	56	1.06	**64**	1.03	36	46	...
176	Gabon	...	...	...	...	...	...	...	44	*36*[y]
177	Gambia	...	...	...	...	...	...	31	33	35*
178	Ghana	80	0.98	...	...	...	...	29	30	**35**
179	Guinea	59	0.76	...	...	81	0.94	40	47	44
180	Guinea-Bissau	...	...	...	...	...	...	...	*44*	...
181	Kenya	77	1.04	...	...	...	...	32	32	*40*[z]
182	Lesotho	66	1.26	74	1.20	74	1.18	54	44	40
183	Liberia	...	...	...	...	...	...	...	39	19
184	Madagascar	21	0.96	51	1.02	36	1.05	40	47	48
185	Malawi	64	0.80	49	0.77	44	1.00	61	...	...
186	Mali	70	0.95	*78*	*0.97*	81	0.96	47	62*	56
187	Mauritius	97	1.01	99	0.99	99	1.02	21	26	22
188	Mozambique	34	0.87	43	0.79	58	0.93	55	61	67
189	Namibia	62	1.08	92	1.02	87	1.07	...	32	*31*
190	Niger	62	1.06	...	...	56	0.92	42	41	40
191	Nigeria	89	...	...	...	*73*[x]	*1.05*[x]	39	*41*	37[z]
192	Rwanda	60	0.97	45	...	46[x]	1.13[x]	57	54	66
193	Sao Tome and Principe	...	...	...	...	**64**	1.22	...	36	*31*
194	Senegal	85	...	...	...	65	1.00	53	49	39
195	Seychelles	93	1.03	...	...	...	...	...	15	**12**
196	Sierra Leone	...	...	...	...	...	...	35	...	**44**
197	Somalia	...	...	...	...	...	...	...	...	...
198	South Africa	...	...	65	0.99	82[x]	1.02[x]	27	35	*36*[y]
199	Swaziland	77	1.09	80	1.22	84[y]	1.08[y]	32	33	33[z]
200	Togo	48	0.80	...	...	75[y]	0.89[y]	58	41	38
201	Uganda	36	...	...	...	*49*[y]	*0.99*[y]	33	57	49
202	United Republic of Tanzania	81	1.02	...	...	***87***	*1.05*	36	40	**53**
203	Zambia	...	...	81	0.94	89	0.95	...	47	51
204	Zimbabwe	76	1.12	...	...	...	...	39	41	38

		Median						Weighted average		
I	World	...	...	...	...	...	...	26	25	25
II	Countries in transition	...	...	...	...	...	...	22	20	18
III	Developed countries	...	...	...	...	...	...	17	16	14
IV	Developing countries	...	...	...	...	83	1.08	29	27	28
V	Arab States	86.9	1.00	92	1.03	...	...	25	23	22
VI	Central and Eastern Europe	...	...	...	...	...	...	21	19	18
VII	Central Asia	...	...	...	...	...	...	21	21	19
VIII	East Asia and the Pacific	...	...	...	...	...	...	23	22	20
IX	East Asia	...	...	...	...	84	1.04	23	22	20
X	Pacific	...	...	...	...	...	...	19	20	19
XI	Latin America and the Caribbean	...	...	87	...	90	1.03	25	26	23
XII	Caribbean	...	...	...	...	...	...	25	24	22
XIII	Latin America	79.5	...	85	0.98	88	1.04	25	26	23
XIV	North America and Western Europe	...	...	...	...	...	...	16	15	14
XV	South and West Asia	...	...	...	...	73	1.00	45	37	40
XVI	Sub-Saharan Africa	63.4	0.93	...	...	74	0.90	37	41	45

1. Based on headcounts of pupils and teachers.

2. Data on trained teachers (defined according to national standards) are not collected for countries whose education statistics are gathered through the OECD, Eurostat or the World Education Indicators questionnaires.

GOAL 6
Educational quality

% FEMALE TEACHERS IN PRIMARY EDUCATION			TRAINED PRIMARY-SCHOOL TEACHERS[2] as % of total		PUBLIC CURRENT EXPENDITURE ON PRIMARY EDUCATION as % of GNP			PUBLIC CURRENT EXPENDITURE ON PRIMARY EDUCATION PER PUPIL (unit cost) at PPP in constant 2005 US$			
School year ending in			School year ending in		School year ending in			School year ending in			
1991	1999	2006	1999	2006	1991	1999	2006	1991	1999	2006	
32	42	47	…	89	…	2.0	0.6[z]	…	191	39[z]	*170*
18	20	23	…	…	…	1.8	*0.1*[z]	…	274	…	*171*
24	21	…	…	…	…	…	…	…	…	…	*172*
…	28	…	…	…	…	…	…	…	…	…	*173*
45	35	43	73	88	…	…	0.8	…	…	99	*174*
24	28	…	…	…	1.1	…	2.0	168	…	130	*175*
…	42	*45*[y]	…	…	…	…	…	…	…	…	*176*
31	29	34*	72	76*	1.3	…	…	254	…	…	*177*
36	32	**37**	72	**59**	…	…	1.6[z]	…	…	300[z]	*178*
22	25	25	…	68	…	…	…	…	…	…	*179*
…	*20*	…	…	…	…	…	…	…	…	…	*180*
38	42	*45*[z]	…	99[y]	3.1	…	3.6	172	…	237	*181*
80	80	78	78	66	…	3.2	3.8	…	566	663	*182*
…	19	27	…	…	…	…	…	…	…	…	*183*
…	58	57	…	36[z]	…	…	1.2	…	…	57	*184*
31	…	…	…	…	1.1	…	3.0[x]	38	…	90[x]	*185*
25	23*	30	…	…	…	*1.3*	1.9	…	*136*	183	*186*
45	54	64	100	100	1.3	1.2	1.0	696	1 067	1 205	*187*
23	25	26	…	65	…	…	2.6[y]	…	…	156[y]	*188*
…	67	*67*	29	92[z]	…	4.4	3.9[x]	…	1 416	944[x]	*189*
33	31	40	98	92	…	…	1.7	…	…	178	*190*
43	*47*	51[z]	…	50[z]	…	…	…	…	…	…	*191*
46	55	53	49	98	…	…	1.9[z]	…	…	*109*[z]	*192*
…	…	*55*	…	…	…	…	…	…	…	…	*193*
27	*23*	*25*	…	100[z]	1.7	…	2.1[z]	303	…	299[z]	*194*
…	85	**85**	82	…	…	…	1.3	…	…	*2 399*[y]	*195*
…	…	**26**	…	**49**	…	…	*2.3*[x]	…	…	…	*196*
…	…	…	…	…	…	…	…	…	…	…	*197*
58	78	*76*[y]	62	…	…	2.7	2.4	1 843	1 403*	1 383[z]	*198*
78	75	73[z]	91	91[z]	1.4	1.9	*2.3*[y]	301	437	*484*[y]	*199*
19	13	12	…	37[z]	…	*1.8*	…	…	*150*	…	*200*
…	33	*39*	…	85[z]	…	…	*2.5*[y]	…	…	*110*[y]	*201*
40	45	**49**	…	**100**	…	…	…	…	…	…	*202*
…	49	48	94	…	…	…	1.3[z]	…	…	55[z]	*203*
40	47	…	…	…	4.3	…	…	625	…	…	*204*

Weighted average			Median		Median			Median			
56	58	62	…	…	…	…	1.4	…	…	1 005	*I*
93	93	94	…	100	…	…	…	…	…	…	*II*
78	81	83	…	…	…	…	1.1	…	…	5 100	*III*
49	52	57	…	85	…	…	1.7	…	…	…	*IV*
52	52	58	…	100	…	…	1.7	…	…	…	*V*
81	82	81	…	…	…	…	0.8	…	…	2 182	*VI*
85	84	87	…	93	…	…	…	…	…	…	*VII*
48	55	60	…	…	…	…	…	…	…	…	*VIII*
48	55	60	…	…	…	…	…	…	…	…	*IX*
67	71	75	…	…	…	…	…	…	…	…	*X*
77	76	77	…	80	…	…	1.7	…	…	…	*XI*
65	50	57	76	74	…	…	1.8	…	…	…	*XII*
77	77	78	…	88	…	…	1.6	…	…	614	*XIII*
80	81	85	…	…	1.2	1.3	1.3	3 378	4 697	5 584	*XIV*
31	35	45	…	68	…	…	1.2	…	…	…	*XV*
40	43	45	…	85	…	…	1.9	…	…	167	*XVI*

Data in italic are UIS estimates.
Data in bold are for the school year ending in 2006 for survival rates to grade 5, and the school year ending in 2007 for the remaining indicators.

(z) Data are for the school year ending in 2005.
(y) Data are for the school year ending in 2004.

(x) Data are for the school year ending in 2003.
(*) National estimate.

Aid tables

Introduction

Most of the data on aid used in this Report are derived from the OECD's International Development Statistics (IDS) database, which records information provided annually by all member countries of the OECD Development Assistance Committee (DAC). The IDS comprises the DAC database, which provides aggregate data, and the Creditor Reporting System, which provides project- and activity-level data. The IDS is available online at www.oecd.org/dac/stats/idsonline. It is updated frequently. The data presented in this Report were downloaded between March and June 2008.

The focus of this section of the annex on aid data is official development assistance. This term and others used in describing aid data are explained below to help in understanding the tables in this section and the data presented in Chapter 4. Private funds are not included.

Aid recipients and donors

Official development assistance (ODA) is public funds provided to developing countries to promote their economic and social development. It is concessional: that is, it takes the form either of a grant or of a loan carrying a lower rate of interest than is available in the market and, usually, a longer than normal repayment period. ODA may be provided directly by a government (bilateral ODA) or through an international agency (multilateral ODA). ODA can include technical cooperation (see below).

Developing countries are those in Part I of the DAC List of Aid Recipients, which essentially comprises all low- and middle-income countries. Twelve central and eastern European countries, including new independent states of the former Soviet Union, plus a set of more advanced developing countries are in Part II of the list, and aid to them is referred to as official aid (OA). The data presented in this Report do not include OA unless indicated.

Bilateral donors are countries that provide development assistance directly to recipient countries. The majority (Australia, Austria, Belgium, Canada, Denmark, Finland, France, Germany, Greece, Ireland, Italy, Japan, Luxembourg, the Netherlands, New Zealand, Norway, Portugal, Spain, Sweden, Switzerland, the United Kingdom and the United States) are members of the DAC, a forum of major bilateral donors established to promote the volume and effectiveness of aid. Non-DAC bilateral donors include the Republic of Korea and some Arab states. Bilateral donors also contribute substantially to the financing of multilateral donors through contributions recorded as multilateral ODA. The financial flows from multilateral donors to recipient countries are also recorded as ODA receipts.

Multilateral donors are international institutions with government membership that conduct all or a significant part of their activities in favour of developing countries. They include multilateral development banks (e.g. the World Bank and the Inter-American Development Bank), United Nations agencies (e.g. UNDP and UNICEF) and regional groupings (e.g. the European Commission and Arab agencies). The development banks also make non-concessional loans to several middle- and higher-income countries, and these are not counted as part of ODA.

Types of aid

Unallocated aid: some contributions are not susceptible to allocation by sector and are reported as non-sector-allocable aid. Examples are aid for general development purposes (direct budget support), balance-of-payments support, action relating to debt (including debt relief) and emergency assistance.

Basic education: the definition of basic education varies by agency. The DAC defines it as covering primary education, basic life skills for youth and adults, and early childhood education.

Education, level unspecified: the aid to education reported in the DAC database includes basic, secondary and post-secondary education, and a subcategory called 'education, level unspecified'. This subcategory covers aid related to any activity that cannot be attributed solely to the development of a single level of education.

Sector budget funding: funds contributed directly to the budget of a ministry of education are often reported by donors in this subcategory. Although in practice this aid will mainly be used for specific levels of education, such information is not available in the DAC database. This reduces accuracy in assessing the amount of resources made available for each specific level of education.

Technical cooperation (sometimes referred to as technical assistance): according to the DAC Directives, technical cooperation is the provision of know-how in the form of personnel, training, research and associated costs. It includes (a) grants to nationals of aid recipient countries receiving education or training at home or abroad; and (b) payments to consultants, advisers and similar personnel as well as teachers and administrators serving in recipient countries (including the cost of associated equipment). Where such assistance is related specifically to a capital project, it is included with project and programme expenditure, and is not separately reported as technical cooperation. The aid activities reported in this category vary by donor, as interpretations of the definition are broad.

Debt relief: this includes debt forgiveness, i.e. the extinction of a loan by agreement between the creditor (donor) and the debtor (aid recipient), and other action on debt, including debt swaps, buy-backs and refinancing. In the DAC database, debt forgiveness is reported as a grant. It raises gross ODA but not necessarily net ODA (see below).

Commitments and disbursements: a commitment is a firm obligation by a donor, expressed in writing and backed by the necessary funds, to provide specified assistance to a country or multilateral organization. The amount specified is recorded as a commitment. Disbursement is the release of funds to, or purchase of goods or services for, a recipient; in other words, the amount spent. Disbursements record the actual international transfer of financial resources or of goods or services valued by the donor. As the aid committed in a given year can be disbursed later, sometimes over several years, the annual aid figures based on commitments differ from those based on disbursements.

Gross and net disbursements: gross disbursements are the total aid extended. Net disbursements are the total aid extended minus amounts of loan principal repaid by recipients or cancelled through debt forgiveness.

Current and constant prices: aid figures in the DAC database are expressed in US$. When other currencies are converted into dollars at the exchange rates prevailing at the time, the resulting amounts are at current prices and exchange rates. When comparing aid figures between different years, adjustment is required to compensate for inflation and changes in exchange rates. Such adjustments result in aid being expressed in constant dollars, i.e. in dollars fixed at the value they held in a given reference year, including their external value in terms of other currencies. Thus, amounts of aid for any year and in any currency expressed in 2006 constant dollars reflect the value of that aid in terms of the purchasing power of dollars in 2006. In this Report, most aid data are presented in 2006 constant dollars. The indices used for adjusting currencies and years (called deflators) are derived from Table 36 of the statistical annex of the 2007 DAC Annual Report (OECD-DAC, 2008*b*). In previous editions of the *EFA Global Monitoring Report*, amounts of aid were based on the constant prices of different years (the 2007 Report used 2003 constant prices), so amounts for a given country for a given year in these editions differ from the amounts presented in this Report for the same year.

For more detailed and precise definitions of terms used in the DAC database, see the DAC Directives, available at www.oecd.org/dac/stats/dac/directives.

Source: OECD-DAC (2008*c*).

Table 1: Bilateral and multilateral ODA

	Total ODA			Net disbursements as % of GNI				Sector-allocable ODA			Debt relief and other actions relating to debt		
	Constant 2006 US$ millions							Constant 2006 US$ millions			Constant 2006 US$ millions		
	1999–2000 annual average	2005	2006	1999–2000 annual average	2005	2006	2007	1999–2000 annual average	2005	2006	1999–2000 annual average	2005	2006
Australia	1 576	1 476	1 796	0.27	0.25	0.30	0.30	1 170	1 083	1 317	10	7	380
Austria	708	1 289	1 083	0.24	0.52	0.47	0.49	366	249	264	219	895	718
Belgium	696	1 625	1 545	0.33	0.53	0.50	0.43	452	830	855	64	516	403
Canada	1 971	3 065	2 678	0.27	0.34	0.29	0.28	864	1 487	1 323	55	511	245
Denmark	1 271	1 652	1 369	1.04	0.81	0.80	0.81	970	1 329	742	14	68	256
Finland	314	705	606	0.32	0.46	0.40	0.40	184	486	394	24	1	2
France	5 965	9 110	9 944	0.34	0.47	0.47	0.39	3 718	3 796	4 705	1 403	3 867	3 897
Germany	4 879	9 396	9 477	0.27	0.36	0.36	0.37	3 719	4 694	5 677	327	4 015	3 034
Greece	136	215	189	0.18	0.17	0.17	0.16	0	144	149	0	0	0
Ireland	243	501	632	0.30	0.42	0.54	0.54	67	327	413	7	0	0
Italy	1 019	2 768	2 508	0.14	0.29	0.20	0.19	457	458	0	248	1 828	0
Japan	11 981	16 169	13 612	0.28	0.28	0.25	0.17	8 325	8 779	8 105	899	5 327	3 781
Luxembourg	147	202	205	0.69	0.86	0.89	0.90	0	134	128	0	0	0
Netherlands	3 536	3 610	10 831	0.82	0.82	0.81	0.81	1 350	2 359	5 011	243	0	1 478
New Zealand	142	296	297	0.26	0.27	0.27	0.27	0	165	204	0	0	0
Norway	1 713	2 247	2 648	0.82	0.94	0.89	0.95	1 095	1 506	1 702	29	3	226
Portugal	468	231	217	0.26	0.21	0.21	0.19	220	234	160	190	3	0
Spain	1 446	2 473	2 438	0.23	0.27	0.32	0.41	1 113	1 147	1 644	105	653	526
Sweden	1 806	2 592	3 103	0.75	0.94	1.02	0.93	718	1 761	1 920	0	54	292
Switzerland	995	1 378	1 243	0.35	0.44	0.39	0.37	607	652	712	0	225	98
United Kingdom	3 467	8 809	9 274	0.28	0.47	0.51	0.36	3 578	3 722	4 832	160	4 746	2 557
United States	11 830	28 564	24 293	0.10	0.23	0.18	0.16	7 316	17 391	16 860	119	4 221	1 686
Total DAC	**56 308**	**98 374**	**99 990**	**0.22**	**0.33**	**0.31**	**0.20**	**36 289**	**52 734**	**57 117**	**4 116**	**26 941**	**19 577**
African Development Fund	818	1 563	1 670	...	...	...	...	670	1 201	1 374	...	...	...
Asian Development Fund	1 282	1 450	1 175	...	...	...	...	1 225	1 243	1 175	...	...	...
European Commission	8 908	11 670	12 311	...	...	...	...	5 666	8 056	9 185	...	...	...
Fast Track Initiative	0	52	85	...	...	...	...	0	52	85	...	...	...
International Development Association	6 824	8 957	8 716	...	...	...	...	5 542	4 317	7 151	...	...	...
Inter-American Development Bank Special Fund	350	508	362	...	...	...	...	350	498	362	...	...	...
UNICEF	199	760	775	...	...	...	...	175	495	531	...	...	...
Total multilaterals	**19 102**	**26 613**	**27 394**	**...**	**...**	**...**	**...**	**14 299**	**17 515**	**22 137**	**...**	**...**	**...**
Total	**75 410**	**124 987**	**127 384**	**...**	**...**	**...**	**...**	**50 588**	**70 248**	**79 254**	**...**	**...**	**...**

Notes:
(...) indicates that data are not available.
All data represent commitments unless otherwise specified.
Source: OECD-DAC (2008*c*).

Table 2: Bilateral and multilateral aid to education

	Total aid to education			Total aid to basic education			Direct aid to education			Direct aid to basic education			Direct aid to secondary education		
	Constant 2006 US$ millions			Constant 2006 US$ millions			Constant 2006 US$ millions			Constant 2006 US$ millions			Constant 2006 US$ millions		
	1999–2000 annual average	2005	2006	1999–2000 annual average	2005	2006	1999–2000 annual average	2005	2006	1999–2000 annual average	2005	2006	1999–2000 annual average	2005	2006
Australia	248	143	155	77	38	74	248	142	155	64	21	33	22	15	4
Austria	126	97	104	6	4	5	126	97	104	4	3	3	41	1	5
Belgium	93	150	164	16	37	42	90	148	161	5	23	29	11	18	11
Canada	104	269	270	52	206	213	103	254	266	30	159	196	18	3	20
Denmark	73	133	44	44	73	27	66	129	16	36	34	12	19	21	0
Finland	26	54	46	12	29	19	25	51	33	3	10	5	1	1	3
France	1 607	1 537	1 862	364	240	308	1 584	1 509	1 790	95	203	105	297	154	72
Germany	847	419	1 388	122	162	155	844	411	1 367	99	117	108	99	84	214
Greece	0	40	24	0	6	3	0	40	23	0	0	0	0	0	0
Ireland	18	65	68	9	40	45	18	60	64	4	23	37	1	3	9
Italy	54	0	0	15	0	0	51	0	0	1	0	0	12	0	0
Japan	327	815	920	122	254	243	307	788	899	43	145	101	34	46	61
Luxembourg	0	31	30	0	14	11	0	31	30	0	3	5	0	6	13
Netherlands	280	600	1 357	181	396	1 129	242	512	1 296	131	299	1 083	10	9	40
New Zealand	0	63	60	0	46	20	0	58	58	0	42	17	0	3	3
Norway	153	224	266	94	126	135	149	200	234	80	85	101	9	6	8
Portugal	38	67	66	10	11	9	36	67	66	4	4	6	4	6	9
Spain	238	229	233	72	86	88	238	227	231	22	59	42	32	45	42
Sweden	70	178	211	45	65	153	45	148	178	24	1	107	1	5	2
Switzerland	45	24	69	19	5	28	45	24	60	14	3	18	20	7	18
United Kingdom	456	352	1 170	335	261	834	331	267	906	245	170	526	16	1	1
United States	366	732	553	200	565	403	344	639	477	181	458	275	45	40	0
Total DAC	**5 167**	**6 223**	**9 058**	**1 795**	**2 662**	**3 944**	**4 892**	**5 802**	**8 416**	**1 083**	**1 862**	**2 811**	**693**	**475**	**535**
African Development Fund	77	127	206	48	64	70	70	68	147	19	0	29	0	0	66
Asian Development Fund	130	321	190	9	34	26	130	291	190	0	19	0	108	272	138
European Commission	725	975	683	463	487	302	521	741	590	344	319	197	62	63	105
Fast Track Initiative	0	52	85	0	52	85	0	52	85	0	52	85	0	0	0
International Development Association	818	674	1 026	422	321	597	633	290	721	149	74	216	55	20	48
Inter-American Development Bank Special Fund	6	23	0	3	0	0	6	23	0	0	0	0	0	23	0
UNICEF	29	70	40	29	69	39	29	70	40	29	69	38	0	1	0
Total multilaterals	**1 791**	**2 241**	**2 231**	**976**	**1 027**	**1 119**	**1 395**	**1 535**	**1 774**	**541**	**532**	**565**	**226**	**379**	**358**
Total	**6 958**	**8 464**	**11 289**	**2 771**	**3 689**	**5 063**	**6 287**	**7 337**	**10 190**	**1 624**	**2 395**	**3 376**	**919**	**854**	**893**

Notes:
(…) indicates that data are not available.
Data for sector-allocable aid include general budget support.
All data represent commitments unless otherwise specified.
Source: OECD-DAC (2008*c*).

Direct aid to post-secondary education (Constant 2006 US$ millions)			Education, level unspecified (Constant 2006 US$ millions)			Share of education in total ODA (%)			Share of education in total sector-allocable ODA (%)			Share of basic education in total aid to education (%)			
1999–2000 annual average	2005	2006	1999–2000 annual average	2005	2006	1999–2000 annual average	2005	2006	1999–2000 annual average	2005	2006	1999–2000 annual average	2005	2006	
136	73	37	25	32	81	16	10	9	21	13	12	31	26	48	Australia
77	91	93	4	2	4	18	8	10	34	39	39	4	4	5	Austria
55	82	99	20	24	21	13	9	11	21	18	19	17	25	25	Belgium
11	13	19	44	78	31	5	9	10	12	18	20	50	77	79	Canada
0	1	2	10	74	1	6	8	3	7	10	6	61	55	62	Denmark
4	4	9	17	36	16	8	8	8	14	11	12	44	54	41	Finland
677	1 105	1 280	515	47	333	27	17	19	43	40	40	23	16	17	France
603	129	972	43	82	73	17	4	15	23	9	24	14	39	11	Germany
0	27	18	0	12	5	0	18	13	…	27	16	…	15	12	Greece
2	4	6	11	30	13	7	13	11	27	20	17	51	62	66	Ireland
13	0	0	25	0	0	5	0	0	12	0	…	28	…	…	Italy
93	406	474	139	191	263	3	5	7	4	9	11	37	31	26	Japan
0	0	0	0	21	11	0	15	14	…	23	23	…	44	36	Luxembourg
38	98	142	63	106	32	8	17	13	21	25	27	65	66	83	Netherlands
0	11	34	0	3	4	0	21	20	…	38	30	…	73	33	New Zealand
36	51	88	25	58	36	9	10	10	14	15	16	62	56	51	Norway
19	44	44	9	12	6	8	29	30	17	29	41	26	16	14	Portugal
84	70	57	100	53	89	16	9	10	21	20	14	30	38	38	Spain
2	44	9	17	97	60	4	7	7	10	10	11	65	37	73	Sweden
1	9	13	10	5	12	5	2	6	7	4	10	43	21	41	Switzerland
14	0	28	57	96	352	13	4	13	13	9	24	74	74	71	United Kingdom
101	21	22	16	119	179	3	3	2	5	4	3	55	77	73	United States
1 968	**2 286**	**3 447**	**1 148**	**1 178**	**1 623**	**9**	**6**	**9**	**14**	**12**	**16**	**35**	**43**	**44**	**Total DAC**
0	0	29	51	68	22	9	8	12	12	11	15	62	50	34	African Development Fund
4	0	0	18	0	52	10	22	16	11	26	16	7	10	14	Asian Development Fund
82	256	171	33	103	117	8	8	6	13	12	7	64	50	44	European Commission
0	0	0	0	0	0	…	100	100	…	100	100	…	100	100	Fast Track Initiative
68	85	0	362	112	457	12	8	12	15	16	14	52	48	58	International Development Association
0	0	0	6	0	0	2	4	0	2	5	0	50	0	…	Inter-American Development Bank Special Fund
0	0	0	0	0	3	14	9	5	16	14	8	100	99	97	UNICEF
154	**341**	**200**	**474**	**283**	**651**	**9**	**8**	**8**	**13**	**13**	**10**	**55**	**46**	**50**	**Total multilaterals**
2 121	**2 627**	**3 647**	**1 622**	**1 462**	**2 274**	**9**	**7**	**9**	**14**	**12**	**14**	**40**	**44**	**45**	**Total**

Table 3: ODA recipients

	Total ODA (Constant 2006 US$ millions)			Per capita ODA (Constant 2006 US$)			Sector-allocable ODA (Constant 2006 US$ millions)			Debt relief and other actions relating to debt (Constant 2006 US$ millions)		
	1999–2000 annual average	2005	2006	1999–2000 annual average	2005	2006	1999–2000 annual average	2005	2006	1999–2000 annual average	2005	2006
Arab States	**6 706**	**29 567**	**16 653**	**25**	**97**	**54**	**5 344**	**11 549**	**10 913**	**501**	**14 168**	**3 063**
Algeria	258	573	491	9	17	15	232	479	449	0	39	20
Bahrain	1	0	0	1	0	0	1	0	0	0	0	0
Djibouti	105	99	83	166	124	102	85	85	75	2	0	0
Egypt	1 753	958	1 598	26	13	22	1 447	808	1 259	304	133	134
Iraq	124	20 687	7 295	5	718	256	18	5 905	4 293	0	13 856	2 875
Jordan	612	592	529	125	104	92	449	370	337	84	12	17
Lebanon	148	254	626	42	71	154	131	225	236	0	0	0
Libyan Arab Jamahiriya	2	5	34	0	1	6	2	5	34	0	0	0
Mauritania	263	257	302	99	84	99	182	138	273	21	43	3
Morocco	954	930	1 185	32	30	38	865	884	1 158	66	0	2
Oman	7	10	7	3	4	3	7	9	6	0	0	0
Palestinian A. T.	603	997	1 064	189	269	273	523	644	762	0	0	0
Saudi Arabia	4	7	11	0	0	0	4	7	10	0	0	0
Sudan	312	2 755	2 049	10	76	54	65	964	816	5	7	3
Syrian Arab Republic	128	105	129	8	6	7	125	99	123	0	0	0
Tunisia	670	469	475	71	46	47	655	352	420	0	2	0
Yemen	475	348	314	26	17	14	356	253	270	19	76	10
Central and Eastern Europe	**6 056**	**5 492**	**5 604**	**39**	**34**	**38**	**3 376**	**4 638**	**4 567**	**297**	**200**	**466**
Albania	615	332	251	196	106	79	413	315	248	2	0	0
Belarus	0	58	63	…	6	6	0	53	57	0	0	0
Bosnia and Herzegovina	1 239	442	484	311	113	123	645	379	471	295	0	0
Croatia	98	211	232	21	46	51	82	202	228	0	0	0
Republic of Moldova	164	204	190	38	48	50	119	162	159	0	0	0
TFYR Macedoniao	384	184	198	189	91	97	223	159	196	0	0	0
Turkey	822	1 580	1 124	12	22	15	624	1 486	1 066	0	0	0
Ukraine	0	592	500	0	13	11	0	580	496	0	0	0
Central Asia	**1 970**	**2 073**	**2 596**	**26**	**27**	**33**	**1 484**	**1 715**	**2 310**	**1**	**41**	**18**
Armenia	272	384	479	72	127	159	229	301	427	0	24	1
Azerbaijan	292	453	262	36	54	31	245	404	254	0	0	0
Georgia	317	306	681	60	68	154	236	225	575	0	0	5
Kazakhstan	209	143	131	13	10	9	206	129	117	1	0	0
Kyrgyzstan	262	194	233	53	37	44	167	168	208	0	8	11
Mongolia	276	143	239	109	54	92	146	108	228	0	8	0
Tajikistan	155	246	256	25	38	39	84	186	202	0	0	0
Turkmenistan	25	22	16	5	4	3	21	21	15	0	0	0
Uzbekistan	162	145	124	7	5	5	150	139	120	0	0	0
East Asia and the Pacific	**13 659**	**13 486**	**11 706**	**7**	**7**	**6**	**11 506**	**10 588**	**10 398**	**146**	**559**	**156**
Cambodia	521	555	584	40	39	41	410	515	549	0	0	0
China	2 673	1 978	2 471	2	2	2	2 538	1 861	2 383	0	0	0
Cook Islands	3	14	13	140	783	924	3	12	6	0	0	0
DPR Korea	204	67	46	9	3	2	7	17	11	0	0	0
Fiji	23	43	54	28	50	65	21	41	50	0	0	0
Indonesia	2 060	4 073	3 153	10	18	14	1 100	2 259	2 542	100	451	98
Kiribati	23	27	15	281	273	166	23	27	15	0	0	0
Korea, Rep.	0	0	0	0	0	0	0	0	0	0	0	0
Lao PDR	219	327	249	41	55	43	193	289	226	3	4	0
Malaysia	1 163	745	115	52	29	4	1 163	742	112	0	0	0
Marshall Islands	61	53	56	1 193	862	972	27	52	52	0	0	0
Micronesia	0	0	0	0	0	0	0	0	0	0	0	0
Myanmar	60	141	142	1	3	3	36	73	103	12	4	4
Nauru	0	17	19	12	1 219	1 902	0	14	18	0	0	0
Niue	1	31	8	519	21 618	4 789	1	14	8	0	0	0

Table 3 (continued)

	Total ODA Constant 2006 US$ millions			Per capita ODA Constant 2006 US$			Sector-allocable ODA Constant 2006 US$ millions			Debt relief and other actions relating to debt Constant 2006 US$ millions		
	1999–2000 annual average	2005	2006	1999–2000 annual average	2005	2006	1999–2000 annual average	2005	2006	1999–2000 annual average	2005	2006
Palau	36	28	33	1 887	1 426	1 636	23	18	22	0	0	0
Papua New Guinea	516	264	304	107	45	49	479	257	294	0	0	0
Philippines	1 601	522	448	21	6	5	1 521	489	391	0	0	0
Samoa	32	67	43	202	364	230	32	66	40	0	0	0
Solomon Islands	118	171	201	264	357	415	84	164	198	0	4	0
Thailand	1 475	597	348	23	9	5	1 338	521	299	0	0	0
Timor-Leste	322	193	205	437	203	184	214	166	175	0	0	0
Tokelau	0	14	11	…	10 195	8 069	0	2	5	0	0	0
Tonga	17	18	27	174	176	270	17	16	25	0	0	0
Tuvalu	7	18	6	710	1 714	545	7	17	5	0	0	0
Vanuatu	44	76	112	221	359	509	40	74	109	1	0	0
Viet Nam	2 227	2 816	2 596	29	33	30	2 063	2 491	2 367	31	96	54
Latin America and the Caribbean	**9 194**	**8 751**	**9 080**	**18**	**16**	**16**	**7 079**	**6 462**	**7 707**	**562**	**1 088**	**424**
Anguilla	6	2	10	542	172	838	6	2	10	0	0	0
Antigua and Barbuda	8	3	0	124	39	3	8	3	0	0	0	0
Argentina	119	109	77	3	3	2	64	100	74	0	0	0
Aruba	0	0	0	2	0	0	0	0	0	0	0	0
Barbados	2	3	7	8	9	22	2	2	6	0	0	0
Belize	39	21	17	171	78	59	37	18	16	0	2	0
Bolivia	1 055	700	706	127	76	75	702	552	574	248	77	68
Brazil	257	331	288	2	2	2	246	300	274	0	0	0
Chile	73	69	48	5	4	3	68	59	44	1	0	0
Colombia	956	989	1 584	23	22	35	924	857	1 463	3	0	0
Costa Rica	57	88	199	14	20	45	46	81	194	9	0	0
Cuba	76	66	52	7	6	5	52	52	46	0	0	0
Dominica	20	35	7	279	441	99	15	33	7	0	1	0
Dominican Republic	373	119	258	45	13	27	295	111	174	1	1	14
Ecuador	194	234	234	15	18	18	148	203	208	0	8	3
El Salvador	218	237	182	35	34	27	172	206	162	2	1	1
Grenada	14	26	11	153	250	100	11	23	10	0	0	0
Guatemala	385	352	575	34	28	44	316	276	308	0	0	179
Guyana	169	123	63	222	164	85	128	107	52	21	9	1
Haiti	273	960	575	34	113	61	193	621	495	4	17	1
Honduras	978	1 415	473	152	196	68	654	577	275	89	694	141
Jamaica	125	72	73	49	27	27	80	44	66	5	16	0
Mexico	218	297	455	2	3	4	209	285	449	0	0	0
Montserrat	43	5	24	10 806	1 021	4 131	30	5	24	0	0	0
Nicaragua	778	751	1 023	153	137	185	545	490	884	62	177	13
Panama	36	47	57	13	14	17	36	41	51	0	0	0
Paraguay	205	64	322	37	10	54	49	60	288	0	0	0
Peru	1 099	484	700	43	17	25	882	379	644	118	81	1
Saint Kitts and Nevis	5	6	4	144	131	74	5	6	4	0	0	0
Saint Lucia	28	45	11	192	282	68	20	43	10	0	0	0
St Vincent/Grenad.	13	7	11	117	62	95	10	7	11	0	0	0
Suriname	39	51	40	94	113	88	37	51	36	0	0	0
Trinidad and Tobago	9	40	38	7	31	29	8	38	38	0	0	0
Turks and Caicos Islands	5	1	13	282	38	532	5	1	0	0	0	0
Uruguay	19	65	23	6	19	7	19	59	21	0	2	0
Venezuela, B. R.	143	42	36	6	2	1	113	36	34	0	0	0
North America and Western Europe	**76**	**176**	**28**	**194**	**439**	**68**	**75**	**169**	**27**	**0**	**0**	**0**
Malta	2	0	0	4	…	…	2	0	0	0	0	0
South and West Asia	**6 764**	**14 476**	**13 893**	**5**	**9**	**9**	**5 378**	**9 641**	**11 433**	**590**	**179**	**346**
Afghanistan	187	3 476	3 257	9	116	125	55	2 647	2 770	0	0	0
Bangladesh	2 059	2 038	2 374	15	14	15	1 660	1 660	1 898	156	39	245

Table 3 (continued)

	Total ODA			Per capita ODA			Sector-allocable ODA			Debt relief and other actions relating to debt		
	Constant 2006 US$ millions			Constant 2006 US$			Constant 2006 US$ millions			Constant 2006 US$ millions		
	1999–2000 annual average	2005	2006	1999–2000 annual average	2005	2006	1999–2000 annual average	2005	2006	1999–2000 annual average	2005	2006
Bhutan	73	80	69	35	37	107	72	78	53	0	0	0
India	2 314	3 656	4 518	2	3	4	2 032	2 993	4 446	1	0	0
Iran, Islamic Republic of	150	62	117	2	1	2	126	46	69	0	0	0
Maldives	33	76	56	113	230	188	32	16	18	0	0	0
Nepal	495	517	481	21	19	17	467	433	405	17	32	31
Pakistan	857	2 928	2 205	6	19	14	384	1 009	1 193	416	0	5
Sri Lanka	598	1 608	769	32	78	40	551	756	544	0	108	65
Sub-Saharan Africa	**20 023**	**35 882**	**37 772**	**33**	**51**	**51**	**13 082**	**17 321**	**19 635**	**1 978**	**11 240**	**10 821**
Angola	368	442	249	28	28	15	202	270	209	1	0	0
Benin	427	556	810	68	66	92	325	441	697	32	55	11
Botswana	46	116	78	30	66	42	40	109	71	3	5	5
Burkina Faso	610	961	728	53	73	51	465	448	521	40	55	17
Burundi	187	320	565	29	42	69	100	105	354	9	22	9
Cameroon	669	465	1 884	45	28	104	370	197	566	153	235	1 121
Cape Verde	151	345	140	353	681	270	109	297	110	1	1	1
C. A. R.	154	112	252	42	28	59	96	77	134	21	7	12
Chad	376	443	267	48	45	26	313	289	113	12	14	7
Comoros	30	66	36	42	82	44	20	53	30	3	2	2
Congo	138	1 600	361	46	400	98	42	105	89	77	1 421	233
Côte d'Ivoire	687	268	418	43	15	22	325	115	185	252	54	60
D. R. Congo	190	2 044	2 037	4	36	34	111	882	753	16	532	869
Equatorial Guinea	33	42	38	72	84	77	28	25	35	3	13	2
Eritrea	267	332	104	73	75	22	152	148	63	0	0	0
Ethiopia	906	2 144	2 212	14	28	27	426	1 022	1 833	3	207	32
Gabon	115	67	162	94	49	123	87	49	159	28	10	0
Gambia	64	94	71	49	62	43	52	90	65	1	1	0
Ghana	1 054	1 438	1 369	55	65	59	739	550	865	7	547	7
Guinea	288	216	223	35	23	24	242	142	182	27	29	16
Guinea-Bissau	99	80	77	83	50	47	48	40	59	11	6	7
Kenya	933	1 146	1 576	30	33	43	699	1 014	1 211	17	26	69
Lesotho	93	94	119	46	52	60	89	86	115	0	0	0
Liberia	45	226	350	15	69	98	23	106	192	0	0	0
Madagascar	655	1 372	636	41	74	33	339	626	454	90	537	28
Malawi	696	1 033	651	62	80	48	456	692	471	29	46	17
Mali	609	984	757	54	73	63	482	675	594	37	97	26
Mauritius	48	48	79	42	39	63	48	46	78	0	0	0
Mozambique	1 723	1 466	1 317	94	74	63	1 021	929	939	272	83	83
Namibia	127	113	209	72	56	102	120	107	204	0	0	0
Niger	302	667	541	28	48	39	186	319	361	34	65	13
Nigeria	600	6 573	8 509	5	50	59	581	953	1 171	0	5 586	7 330
Rwanda	513	539	734	67	60	78	230	316	421	20	55	59
Sao Tome and Principe	48	22	26	347	140	167	42	17	22	2	1	2
Senegal	923	974	1 001	98	84	83	637	702	781	204	243	166
Seychelles	7	13	14	84	161	160	7	8	11	0	0	2
Sierra Leone	313	398	252	71	72	44	108	245	120	0	12	53
Somalia	129	176	427	15	21	51	45	54	91	3	1	1
South Africa	547	977	890	13	21	18	522	932	877	0	0	0
Swaziland	28	67	41	30	65	37	22	64	40	0	0	0
Togo	106	72	60	23	12	9	78	56	46	18	6	6
Uganda	1 150	1 437	1 216	49	50	41	761	936	801	99	129	6
U. R. Tanzania	1 354	1 883	2 656	39	49	67	840	1 214	1 036	185	149	3
Zambia	1 179	1 949	1 543	113	167	132	573	724	853	265	987	544
Zimbabwe	239	225	338	19	17	26	213	137	265	0	0	0
Unallocated by countries	*9 257*	*14 777*	*24 235*	…	…	…	*3 482*	*8 264*	*12 307*	*57*	*73*	*1 779*
Total	73 705	124 681	121 566	15	24	22	50 807	70 347	79 296	4 132	27 548	17 072

Table 3 (continued)

	Total ODA			Per capita ODA			Sector-allocable ODA			Debt relief and other actions relating to debt		
	Constant 2006 US$ millions			Constant 2006 US$			Constant 2006 US$ millions			Constant 2006 US$ millions		
	1999–2000 annual average	2005	2006	1999–2000 annual average	2005	2006	1999–2000 annual average	2005	2006	1999–2000 annual average	2005	2006
Upper middle income countries	3 915	5 177	4 514	11	13	11	3 465	4 871	3 964	41	20	7
Low middle income countries	25 893	44 189	30 766	11	18	13	19 726	23 236	23 933	1 338	15 714	4 092
High income countries	140	0	0	3	0	0	132	0	0	0	0	0
Unallocated by income	11 914	18 518	28 883	...	...	...	5 535	10 833	15 983	58	74	1 780
Least developed countries	**19 607**	**33 667**	**31 214**	**29**	**44**	**40**	**12 804**	**20 315**	**20 950**	**1 676**	**3 581**	**2 289**
Low income countries	**31 843**	**56 797**	**57 403**	**15**	**23**	**23**	**21 948**	**31 407**	**35 416**	**2 694**	**11 740**	**11 193**
Middle income countries	**29 808**	**49 365**	**35 280**	**11**	**17**	**12**	**23 191**	**28 107**	**27 897**	**1 379**	**15 734**	**4 099**
Total	**73 705**	**124 681**	**121 566**	**15**	**24**	**22**	**50 807**	**70 347**	**79 296**	**4 132**	**27 548**	**17 072**

	Total ODA 1999–2000	2005	2006	Per capita ODA 1999–2000	2005	2006	Sector-allocable ODA 1999–2000	2005	2006	Debt relief 1999–2000	2005	2006
Arab States	6 706	29 567	16 653	25	97	54	5 344	11 549	10 913	501	14 168	3 063
Central and Eastern Europe	6 056	5 492	5 604	39	34	38	3 376	4 638	4 567	297	200	466
Central Asia	1 970	2 073	2 596	26	27	33	1 484	1 715	2 310	1	41	18
East Asia and the Pacific	13 659	13 486	11 706	7	7	6	11 506	10 588	10 398	146	559	156
Latin America and the Caribbean	9 194	8 751	9 080	18	16	16	7 079	6 462	7 707	562	1 088	424
North America and Western Europe	76	176	28	194	439	68	75	169	27	0	0	0
South and West Asia	6 764	14 476	13 893	5	9	9	5 378	9 641	11 433	590	179	346
Sub-Saharan Africa	20 023	35 882	37 772	33	51	51	13 082	17 321	19 635	1 978	11 240	10 821
Unallocated by region	*9 257*	*14 777*	*24 235*	...	...	...	*3 482*	*8 264*	*12 307*	*57*	*73*	*1 779*
Total	**73 705**	**124 681**	**121 566**	**15**	**24**	**22**	**50 807**	**70 347**	**79 296**	**4 132**	**27 548**	**17 072**

Notes:
(...) indicates that data are not available.
All data represent commitments unless otherwise specified.
Totals may not match those presented in Table 1 due to the use of different databases.
Source: OECD-DAC (2008c).

Table 4: Recipients of aid to education

	Total aid to education (Constant 2006 US$ millions)			Total aid to basic education (Constant 2006 US$ millions)			Total aid to basic education per primary school-age child (Constant 2006 US$)			Direct aid to education (Constant 2006 US$ millions)			Direct aid to basic education (Constant 2006 US$ millions)		
	1999–2000 annual average	2005	2006	1999–2000 annual average	2005	2006	1999–2000 annual average	2005	2006	1999–2000 annual average	2005	2006	1999–2000 annual average	2005	2006
Arab States	**1 094**	**1 310**	**1 672**	**319**	**479**	**549**	**8**	**12**	**13**	**1 073**	**1 215**	**1 625**	**146**	**375**	**318**
Algeria	125	183	197	38	26	19	8	7	5	125	183	197	0	25	0
Bahrain	1	0	0	0	0	0	0	0	0	1	0	0	0	0	0
Djibouti	48	55	41	14	33	16	118	271	128	45	55	41	1	31	13
Egypt	149	99	154	40	79	120	5	8	13	149	99	154	37	74	119
Iraq	8	135	61	1	93	26	0	21	6	8	135	61	0	92	2
Jordan	23	58	104	1	34	70	1	41	85	23	19	70	0	13	53
Lebanon	43	50	65	9	5	5	23	10	11	43	50	65	1	1	5
Libyan Arab Jamahiriya	2	3	6	0	0	0	0	0	0	2	3	6	0	0	0
Mauritania	41	36	93	12	28	42	29	63	93	33	36	92	1	28	13
Morocco	266	243	315	65	36	34	16	9	9	265	243	315	11	32	13
Oman	1	1	1	0	0	0	0	0	1	1	1	1	0	0	0
Palestinian A. T.	56	108	93	29	53	52	81	119	112	55	73	92	18	21	28
Saudi Arabia	2	4	7	0	1	2	0	0	1	2	4	7	0	0	2
Sudan	21	38	174	5	21	88	1	4	15	13	37	173	1	7	11
Syrian Arab Republic	39	23	66	4	1	2	2	1	1	39	23	66	0	0	1
Tunisia	180	210	162	45	16	7	36	15	7	179	190	152	29	4	1
Yemen	66	42	65	50	40	57	15	11	15	66	42	64	41	39	55
Central and Eastern Europe	**409**	**312**	**427**	**131**	**33**	**49**	**11**	**3**	**4**	**372**	**297**	**412**	**87**	**12**	**28**
Albania	32	21	42	11	4	10	38	17	45	25	21	42	2	2	7
Belarus	0	8	23	0	1	0	0	1	0	0	8	23	0	0	0
Bosnia and Herzegovina	37	34	31	11	3	2	61	14	9	28	34	31	2	1	1
Croatia	20	13	19	0	0	0	2	2	1	20	13	19	0	0	0
Republic of Moldova	10	10	30	4	1	12	13	3	64	3	10	28	0	0	11
TFYR Macedoniao	25	16	19	11	4	5	86	37	50	13	12	19	4	2	5
Turkey	222	104	107	84	5	2	10	1	0	222	104	107	78	1	1
Ukraine	0	31	66	0	0	1	0	0	0	0	31	66	0	0	0
Central Asia	**102**	**115**	**211**	**24**	**55**	**73**	**3**	**9**	**12**	**86**	**101**	**190**	**9**	**40**	**43**
Armenia	11	7	38	2	1	6	7	9	47	9	6	33	0	0	0
Azerbaijan	7	9	6	2	5	0	3	8	0	6	5	6	0	2	0
Georgia	21	11	46	5	4	12	15	11	35	13	6	32	0	1	4
Kazakhstan	16	10	11	2	3	1	1	3	1	16	10	11	2	0	0
Kyrgyzstan	8	19	21	3	13	11	6	29	25	3	19	21	0	11	6
Mongolia	13	27	43	5	17	19	18	65	78	13	26	43	4	15	11
Tajikistan	8	15	18	3	10	12	5	14	18	7	14	16	1	8	11
Turkmenistan	4	3	1	0	0	0	1	1	1	4	3	1	0	0	0
Uzbekistan	14	13	26	2	2	12	1	1	5	14	13	26	1	1	10
East Asia and the Pacific	**1 113**	**1 244**	**1 948**	**300**	**439**	**634**	**2**	**3**	**4**	**1 069**	**1 153**	**1 892**	**155**	**264**	**414**
Cambodia	38	56	61	14	27	47	6	13	22	33	56	61	7	10	45
China	169	318	854	27	11	131	0	0	1	169	318	854	17	4	64
Cook Islands	0	2	3	0	1	2	0	284	574	0	2	3	0	0	1
DPR Korea	1	1	2	0	0	0	0	0	0	1	1	2	0	0	0
Fiji	7	6	9	1	1	3	9	13	31	7	6	9	1	1	0
Indonesia	208	205	423	73	77	280	3	3	11	197	166	403	56	40	218
Kiribati	7	1	2	3	0	1	218	13	65	7	1	2	0	0	0
Korea, Rep.	0	0	0	0	0	0	0	0	0	0	0	0	0	0	0
Lao PDR	30	22	19	4	8	5	5	11	6	30	20	17	2	4	1
Malaysia	85	18	86	1	3	2	0	1	1	85	18	86	0	0	0
Marshall Islands	4	13	13	2	7	7	227	808	750	0	13	13	0	0	0
Micronesia	0	0	0	0	0	0	0	0	0	0	0	0	0	0	0
Myanmar	3	14	20	2	7	16	0	2	4	3	14	20	1	3	15
Nauru	0	1	2	0	0	1	0	220	548	0	1	2	0	0	0
Niue	0	4	0	0	2	0	0	12 091	183	0	1	0	0	0	0

Direct aid to secondary education			Direct aid to post-secondary education			Education, level unspecified			Share of education in total ODA			Share of education in total sector-allocable ODA			Share of basic education in total aid to education		
Constant 2006 US$ millions			Constant 2006 US$ millions			Constant 2006 US$ millions			(%)			(%)			(%)		
1999–2000 annual average	2005	2006	1999–2000 annual average	2005	2006	1999–2000 annual average	2005	2006	1999–2000 annual average	2005	2006	1999–2000 annual average	2005	2006	1999–2000 annual average	2005	2006
210	**112**	**118**	**393**	**615**	**775**	**325**	**113**	**414**	**16**	**4**	**10**	**20**	**11**	**15**	**29**	**37**	**33**
5	1	7	44	155	153	76	2	38	48	32	40	54	38	44	31	14	10
0	0	0	0	0	0	0	0	0	97	…	…	97	…	…	2	…	…
13	4	0	9	17	22	22	3	6	46	56	50	57	64	55	28	60	38
46	1	12	60	13	22	6	10	2	9	10	10	10	12	12	27	80	77
0	37	1	7	4	10	1	1	48	7	1	1	46	2	1	8	69	42
4	0	1	18	4	15	1	2	1	4	10	20	5	16	31	4	58	68
10	7	10	17	34	49	15	9	1	29	20	10	33	22	28	20	10	8
0	0	0	1	2	6	0	0	0	87	48	18	93	54	18	11	3	5
6	0	10	14	8	12	12	0	58	16	14	31	23	26	34	28	78	46
61	11	20	86	193	238	108	7	44	28	26	27	31	28	27	24	15	11
0	0	0	1	0	0	0	0	0	8	7	12	9	7	13	12	6	22
10	5	2	7	18	14	21	29	47	9	11	9	11	17	12	51	49	56
0	1	2	1	1	2	1	1	1	55	58	62	55	60	67	13	19	29
1	1	1	10	2	8	1	27	152	7	1	8	32	4	21	26	56	51
1	0	1	31	21	61	8	1	3	30	21	51	31	23	53	10	5	4
51	43	45	67	139	105	31	4	1	27	45	34	27	60	39	25	8	4
1	1	0	7	1	7	17	2	2	14	12	21	18	17	24	76	94	87
49	**27**	**36**	**186**	**230**	**321**	**50**	**28**	**28**	**7**	**6**	**8**	**12**	**7**	**9**	**32**	**11**	**11**
3	0	12	9	15	17	11	3	5	5	6	17	8	7	17	34	19	23
0	0	0	0	7	23	0	1	0	…	13	36	…	15	40	…	7	1
0	12	3	16	19	26	9	2	2	3	8	6	6	9	7	30	8	5
0	1	0	19	11	18	1	1	0	20	6	8	25	6	8	2	2	1
0	0	6	3	9	10	0	1	0	6	5	16	8	6	19	37	7	40
2	0	1	5	10	12	2	0	1	7	9	10	11	10	10	43	26	28
41	1	1	91	94	102	11	8	3	27	7	10	36	7	10	38	4	2
0	0	0	0	30	65	0	1	1	…	5	13	…	5	13	…	1	1
24	**7**	**25**	**39**	**36**	**82**	**14**	**18**	**39**	**5**	**6**	**8**	**7**	**7**	**9**	**23**	**48**	**35**
0	1	9	8	4	17	1	1	6	4	2	8	5	2	9	15	17	16
0	0	0	3	2	6	3	0	0	2	2	2	3	2	3	32	52	2
0	0	3	12	4	23	0	1	2	7	4	7	9	5	8	22	37	26
10	0	1	5	5	8	1	5	2	8	7	8	8	8	9	11	28	8
1	0	0	1	4	5	0	3	10	3	10	9	5	11	10	35	69	53
1	0	0	7	7	15	2	4	16	5	19	18	9	25	19	36	64	45
3	1	4	0	3	1	3	1	1	5	6	7	10	8	9	40	62	67
3	0	0	0	3	1	0	0	0	14	15	8	17	16	9	10	11	16
7	4	7	3	5	7	3	2	3	9	9	21	10	9	22	16	19	44
212	**103**	**63**	**456**	**527**	**1 030**	**246**	**259**	**386**	**8**	**9**	**17**	**10**	**12**	**19**	**27**	**35**	**33**
3	1	1	14	10	11	9	35	5	7	10	11	9	11	11	38	49	77
10	4	11	122	295	644	20	14	134	6	16	35	7	17	36	16	3	15
0	0	0	0	0	1	0	2	1	3	15	27	3	18	57	0	37	47
0	0	0	1	1	1	0	0	0	1	1	3	16	4	14	4	8	11
0	1	0	5	3	2	0	2	7	29	15	17	30	15	18	15	23	38
56	8	19	62	82	62	24	36	105	10	5	13	19	9	17	35	38	66
0	0	0	1	1	0	6	0	1	29	4	15	30	4	15	43	17	41
0	0	0	0	0	0	0	0	0	…	…	…	…	…	…	…	…	…
3	2	7	20	7	4	4	6	5	14	7	8	15	7	8	14	39	24
2	1	1	81	12	82	2	5	3	7	2	75	7	2	77	1	14	2
0	0	0	0	0	0	0	12	12	7	25	23	16	26	25	45	49	51
0	0	0	0	0	0	0	0	0	…	…	…	…	…	…	…	…	…
0	0	0	1	4	4	1	6	0	5	10	14	8	19	19	58	47	80
0	0	0	0	0	0	0	1	2	52	8	9	52	9	10	0	27	50
0	0	0	0	1	0	0	0	0	32	14	4	35	30	4	0	48	10

Table 4 (continued)

	Total aid to education			Total aid to basic education			Total aid to basic education per primary school-age child			Direct aid to education			Direct aid to basic education		
	Constant 2006 US$ millions			Constant 2006 US$ millions			Constant 2006 US$			Constant 2006 US$ millions			Constant 2006 US$ millions		
	1999–2000 annual average	2005	2006	1999–2000 annual average	2005	2006	1999–2000 annual average	2005	2006	1999–2000 annual average	2005	2006	1999–2000 annual average	2005	2006
Palau	2	3	3	1	2	2	376	931	988	0	1	1	0	0	0
Papua New Guinea	92	69	34	60	59	21	74	63	22	90	69	34	53	52	14
Philippines	166	57	43	58	36	21	5	3	2	166	57	43	5	31	13
Samoa	7	11	21	3	9	6	122	291	192	7	11	21	1	9	0
Solomon Islands	13	22	4	4	20	1	56	264	17	7	22	4	0	20	1
Thailand	27	36	34	3	4	2	0	1	0	25	36	34	0	0	0
Timor-Leste	8	16	31	2	4	20	17	23	107	8	14	30	1	1	15
Tokelau	0	2	1	0	1	1	0	4 748	2 777	0	0	0	0	0	0
Tonga	2	5	15	0	3	10	19	183	692	2	5	15	0	2	9
Tuvalu	1	2	0	0	1	0	271	484	29	1	2	0	0	0	0
Vanuatu	12	17	11	1	4	5	17	109	144	12	17	11	0	3	2
Viet Nam	177	302	220	28	134	35	3	16	4	175	261	191	6	78	12
Latin America and the Caribbean	**592**	**703**	**785**	**266**	**279**	**280**	**5**	**5**	**5**	**571**	**660**	**741**	**182**	**168**	**155**
Anguilla	3	0	0	0	0	0	260	0	0	3	0	0	0	0	0
Antigua and Barbuda	2	3	0	1	0	0	...	0	0	2	3	0	0	0	0
Argentina	16	30	17	3	15	2	1	4	1	16	30	17	0	14	1
Aruba	0	0	0	0	0	0	0	0	0	0	0	0	0	0	0
Barbados	0	0	0	0	0	0	1	1	0	0	0	0	0	0	0
Belize	1	1	1	1	0	0	20	10	7	1	1	1	1	0	0
Bolivia	41	86	42	30	39	17	23	28	12	39	83	40	26	5	12
Brazil	46	39	62	11	8	12	1	1	1	46	39	62	5	3	8
Chile	20	12	18	3	2	3	1	1	2	20	12	18	1	1	2
Colombia	35	30	46	12	5	8	3	1	2	35	30	46	4	5	7
Costa Rica	4	3	6	0	1	1	1	2	2	4	3	6	0	1	1
Cuba	8	4	4	1	0	1	1	1	1	8	4	4	0	0	0
Dominica	1	1	0	0	0	0	41	13	2	0	1	0	0	0	0
Dominican Republic	22	13	88	7	6	41	6	5	32	22	13	79	7	3	5
Ecuador	10	15	36	2	3	12	1	2	7	10	15	36	1	2	3
El Salvador	14	11	19	7	5	8	9	6	9	14	11	19	5	3	2
Grenada	0	12	0	0	12	0	4	692	1	0	12	0	0	12	0
Guatemala	31	41	23	20	30	9	11	15	4	31	41	23	18	27	8
Guyana	7	1	6	1	0	5	8	2	52	6	1	4	0	0	4
Haiti	32	67	53	19	22	12	14	16	9	28	54	51	11	8	5
Honduras	22	62	22	13	42	17	12	39	16	21	43	22	5	28	15
Jamaica	22	6	6	18	4	5	52	13	14	16	6	6	15	3	4
Mexico	22	23	47	4	3	4	0	0	0	22	23	47	1	2	4
Montserrat	2	0	0	1	0	0	3 466	0	0	0	0	0	0	0	0
Nicaragua	75	48	113	61	35	81	74	41	97	75	41	96	54	30	59
Panama	14	4	3	1	0	1	3	1	2	14	4	3	1	0	0
Paraguay	4	14	15	2	5	7	3	5	8	4	14	8	2	3	2
Peru	28	31	66	9	11	13	3	3	4	28	31	63	6	7	8
Saint Kitts and Nevis	0	0	0	0	0	0	0	0	0	0	0	0	0	0	0
Saint Lucia	2	1	1	1	0	1	59	22	27	1	1	1	0	0	0
St Vincent/Grenad.	1	0	0	1	0	0	31	11	6	1	0	0	0	0	0
Suriname	1	15	2	0	7	0	1	120	0	1	15	2	0	0	0
Trinidad and Tobago	1	0	35	0	0	0	0	0	0	1	0	35	0	0	0
Turks and Caicos Islands	2	0	3	2	0	1	...	149	...	2	0	0	2	0	0
Uruguay	5	3	4	1	0	1	3	1	3	5	3	4	0	0	1
Venezuela, B. R.	23	7	10	2	0	1	1	0	0	23	7	10	0	0	1
North America and Western Europe	**3**	**0**	**0**	**0**	**0**	**0**	**5**	**8**	**0**	**3**	**0**	**0**	**0**	**0**	**0**
Malta	1	0	0	0	0	0	1	0	0	1	0	0	0	0	0
South and West Asia	**842**	**1 175**	**986**	**448**	**575**	**478**	**3**	**3**	**3**	**827**	**949**	**839**	**342**	**374**	**326**
Afghanistan	8	253	143	2	180	105	0	42	24	8	221	140	1	156	82
Bangladesh	134	360	237	82	126	75	5	7	4	134	319	209	77	80	59

Direct aid to secondary education (Constant 2006 US$ millions)			Direct aid to post-secondary education (Constant 2006 US$ millions)			Aid to education, level unspecified (Constant 2006 US$ millions)			Share of education in total ODA (%)			Share of education in total sector-allocable ODA (%)			Share of basic education in total aid to education (%)		
1999–2000 annual average	2005	2006	1999–2000 annual average	2005	2006	1999–2000 annual average	2005	2006	1999–2000 annual average	2005	2006	1999–2000 annual average	2005	2006	1999–2000 annual average	2005	2006
0	0	0	0	0	0	0	1	0	4	11	8	7	18	13	40	54	57
9	1	2	17	1	4	12	14	14	18	26	11	19	27	11	65	86	62
31	6	5	23	11	8	107	9	16	10	11	9	11	12	11	35	62	50
1	1	1	1	1	8	4	1	11	23	17	49	23	17	52	46	81	29
2	0	0	4	2	3	1	0	0	11	13	2	16	14	2	29	88	30
5	1	1	18	29	30	2	7	3	2	6	10	2	7	11	9	10	5
0	4	1	5	5	5	1	5	10	3	8	15	4	9	17	29	27	65
0	0	0	0	0	0	0	0	0	93	18	13	93	109	31	0	44	43
0	0	1	2	1	2	0	2	3	12	28	57	12	33	62	14	54	68
0	0	0	0	1	0	1	1	0	16	11	1	16	11	2	34	35	50
5	10	0	5	2	3	1	1	5	28	22	10	30	23	10	4	22	44
83	60	11	44	51	151	42	72	17	8	11	8	9	12	9	16	44	16
59	**87**	**96**	**183**	**226**	**283**	**148**	**180**	**206**	**6**	**8**	**9**	**8**	**11**	**10**	**45**	**40**	**36**
2	0	0	0	0	0	1	0	0	52	1	0	54	1	0	12	…	…
0	3	0	0	0	0	2	0	0	21	96	4	21	98	5	50	0	0
3	3	1	9	11	12	4	2	2	14	28	22	26	30	23	15	50	14
0	0	0	0	0	0	0	0	0	…	…	…	…	…	…	…	…	…
0	0	0	0	0	0	0	0	0	4	3	2	4	4	2	23	25	0
0	0	0	0	0	0	0	0	0	3	3	3	3	4	3	77	63	55
1	7	13	7	6	7	5	65	8	4	12	6	6	16	7	73	45	40
4	2	4	25	24	41	12	10	9	18	12	21	19	13	23	24	21	20
3	1	1	13	9	13	4	2	1	27	18	36	29	21	40	13	17	15
2	5	6	12	18	30	16	2	3	4	3	3	4	3	3	35	18	18
1	0	1	2	2	4	0	1	1	6	3	3	8	4	3	11	29	20
2	1	0	4	3	4	1	0	0	11	6	8	16	8	9	10	12	12
0	0	0	0	0	0	0	0	0	5	2	4	7	2	5	48	20	7
11	3	3	3	1	9	1	7	62	6	11	34	7	12	51	33	46	46
2	6	6	5	5	10	2	2	18	5	7	15	7	8	17	19	21	32
2	1	2	3	2	3	4	5	13	7	5	10	8	5	12	51	49	44
0	0	0	0	0	0	0	0	0	1	47	1	1	53	1	47	99	29
2	2	2	7	6	9	4	6	4	8	12	4	10	15	7	65	73	41
5	0	0	0	0	0	0	0	0	4	0	10	5	0	12	10	29	79
2	23	8	4	7	26	11	16	11	12	7	9	16	11	11	59	33	23
1	2	1	2	3	1	14	11	5	2	4	5	3	11	8	56	68	78
0	0	0	1	0	0	0	2	1	18	8	8	28	13	9	81	78	81
1	1	4	15	18	38	5	2	1	10	8	10	10	8	10	17	14	9
0	0	0	0	0	0	0	0	0	4	…	…	6	…	…	54	…	…
3	6	7	3	2	2	14	3	28	10	6	11	14	10	13	82	73	72
1	2	1	11	1	1	0	1	1	38	8	5	38	9	6	7	10	22
0	7	2	1	2	2	2	3	3	2	22	5	9	24	5	56	32	47
5	8	30	11	9	16	6	7	9	3	6	9	3	8	10	33	34	20
0	0	0	0	0	0	0	0	0	0	0	1	0	0	1	5	0	0
0	0	0	0	0	0	0	0	0	8	2	10	12	2	11	58	60	50
0	0	0	0	0	0	1	0	0	9	6	3	12	7	3	50	40	28
0	0	0	1	2	2	0	13	0	3	29	5	3	29	6	6	44	1
0	0	0	1	0	35	0	0	0	9	1	91	11	1	92	9	4	0
0	0	0	0	0	0	0	0	0	35	36	20	35	36	…	100	100	…
1	1	1	3	2	2	2	0	0	28	4	16	28	4	17	16	11	27
1	1	2	18	5	7	3	1	1	16	17	29	20	20	31	8	6	11
0	**0**	**0**	**2**	**0**	**0**	**0**	**0**	**0**	**4**	**0**	**0**	**4**	**0**	**0**	**6**	**50**	**0**
0	0	0	1	0	0	0	0	0	39	…	…	40	…	…	7	…	…
114	**254**	**196**	**174**	**145**	**159**	**197**	**176**	**158**	**12**	**8**	**7**	**16**	**12**	**9**	**53**	**49**	**49**
0	5	9	5	43	7	1	16	42	4	7	4	14	10	5	22	71	73
39	177	136	8	11	11	9	51	3	6	18	10	8	22	13	61	35	32

Table 4 (continued)

	Total aid to education			Total aid to basic education			Total aid to basic education per primary school-age child			Direct aid to education			Direct aid to basic education		
	Constant 2006 US$ millions			Constant 2006 US$ millions			Constant 2006 US$			Constant 2006 US$ millions			Constant 2006 US$ millions		
	1999–2000 annual average	2005	2006	1999–2000 annual average	2005	2006	1999–2000 annual average	2005	2006	1999–2000 annual average	2005	2006	1999–2000 annual average	2005	2006
Bhutan	5	7	9	1	1	3	10	9	33	5	7	6	0	0	0
India	462	82	160	295	18	76	2	0	1	448	82	160	205	16	50
Iran, Islamic Republic of	79	19	50	4	1	1	0	0	0	79	19	50	0	0	1
Maldives	15	8	5	0	1	2	6	22	41	15	8	5	0	0	1
Nepal	60	19	56	50	10	27	16	3	7	60	16	56	49	7	10
Pakistan	27	287	276	10	195	185	0	10	9	27	141	164	5	107	120
Sri Lanka	52	139	48	4	43	5	3	28	3	52	136	48	4	6	3
Sub-Saharan Africa	**2 352**	**2 840**	**3 811**	**1 186**	**1 474**	**2 070**	**11**	**12**	**17**	**1 842**	**2 207**	**3 051**	**658**	**891**	**1 205**
Angola	22	67	38	8	57	22	5	31	12	22	67	38	3	54	20
Benin	38	71	80	18	26	44	15	19	31	29	63	62	9	8	33
Botswana	14	66	2	0	33	0	1	107	2	14	66	2	0	0	0
Burkina Faso	68	166	194	36	98	137	19	44	59	54	84	165	25	54	114
Burundi	6	22	45	2	11	26	2	9	20	5	11	26	0	2	13
Cameroon	113	72	153	29	28	32	11	10	11	95	72	116	6	19	12
Cape Verde	27	47	32	7	10	2	91	127	30	22	39	29	2	1	1
C. A. R.	28	17	24	7	10	10	11	15	14	22	15	6	2	9	1
Chad	32	20	7	11	12	2	8	7	1	23	14	7	6	9	2
Comoros	7	28	11	3	11	1	29	85	9	6	28	10	0	0	0
Congo	16	31	21	7	8	1	15	13	1	16	23	21	0	3	1
Côte d'Ivoire	129	39	35	46	10	8	16	4	3	115	38	35	23	10	7
D. R. Congo	15	59	32	7	26	13	1	3	1	15	38	31	3	13	11
Equatorial Guinea	10	9	8	4	5	3	84	83	54	10	9	8	3	3	0
Eritrea	35	98	2	28	83	0	55	145	0	35	98	2	26	68	0
Ethiopia	54	61	402	26	33	306	2	3	23	53	42	400	19	18	233
Gabon	52	25	34	16	4	4	86	20	20	52	25	34	11	4	0
Gambia	11	1	13	10	1	9	48	3	38	10	1	13	8	1	9
Ghana	120	110	345	88	60	181	28	18	53	92	56	253	73	30	35
Guinea	43	47	33	20	25	9	15	18	6	43	47	33	16	14	9
Guinea-Bissau	14	18	6	5	7	2	24	29	6	8	16	6	2	1	1
Kenya	66	66	207	40	51	111	8	9	19	35	66	207	23	46	50
Lesotho	16	3	9	2	1	9	5	4	25	16	2	9	1	1	9
Liberia	2	3	17	1	3	9	3	5	15	2	3	17	1	3	1
Madagascar	75	132	103	26	74	59	12	29	22	43	101	83	1	44	47
Malawi	142	98	56	98	51	21	51	21	9	109	63	38	71	22	11
Mali	87	77	308	45	39	256	27	20	127	75	50	289	21	14	221
Mauritius	25	17	19	3	2	1	26	15	11	25	17	19	0	2	1
Mozambique	155	285	182	84	193	113	25	50	28	113	207	131	34	114	74
Namibia	25	6	6	17	4	4	46	10	10	25	6	6	14	3	3
Niger	32	85	47	13	52	24	8	24	11	19	45	35	3	31	9
Nigeria	73	12	80	42	7	18	2	0	1	72	12	80	24	7	10
Rwanda	78	42	121	38	17	59	26	12	41	41	16	76	5	3	12
Sao Tome and Principe	6	5	12	1	1	4	53	23	148	5	5	12	0	0	0
Senegal	143	247	309	77	27	129	47	15	70	135	247	303	42	21	39
Seychelles	1	1	0	1	0	0	65	31	16	1	1	0	0	0	0
Sierra Leone	24	31	12	12	17	8	17	20	9	2	9	7	0	3	5
Somalia	5	6	15	3	5	13	2	3	9	5	6	15	0	4	13
South Africa	86	131	80	40	88	32	6	12	4	86	131	80	35	70	20
Swaziland	1	26	0	0	26	0	0	123	1	1	26	0	0	26	0
Togo	13	18	19	5	6	3	6	6	3	12	18	18	2	6	3
Uganda	154	103	158	92	37	91	18	6	14	104	74	125	49	18	61
U. R. Tanzania	83	128	387	42	53	213	7	8	30	33	42	79	16	6	56
Zambia	138	190	91	93	153	70	48	68	30	76	152	71	56	124	58
Zimbabwe	24	5	6	8	1	2	3	1	1	23	5	6	1	1	2
Unallocated by countries	*452*	*564*	*679*	*98*	*153*	*158*	…	…	…	*444*	*554*	*669*	*46*	*71*	*116*
Total	**6 958**	**8 464**	**11 289**	**2 771**	**3 689**	**5 063**	**5**	**6**	**9**	**6 287**	**7 337**	**10 190**	**1 624**	**2 395**	**3 376**

Direct aid to secondary education Constant 2006 US$ millions			Direct aid to post-secondary education Constant 2006 US$ millions			Aid to education, level unspecified Constant 2006 US$ millions			Share of education in total ODA (%)			Share of education in total sector-allocable ODA (%)			Share of basic education in total aid to education (%)		
1999–2000 annual average	2005	2006	1999–2000 annual average	2005	2006	1999–2000 annual average	2005	2006	1999–2000 annual average	2005	2006	1999–2000 annual average	2005	2006	1999–2000 annual average	2005	2006
2	4	0	1	1	2	2	1	3	7	9	13	8	9	17	21	13	36
12	7	5	65	56	53	166	4	52	20	2	4	23	3	4	64	22	47
0	1	1	70	17	48	8	1	0	53	31	43	63	42	72	6	4	2
10	6	1	5	0	0	0	1	3	47	11	9	49	50	28	2	14	38
4	0	1	5	5	12	1	3	33	12	4	12	13	4	14	83	53	48
1	0	9	12	5	18	9	28	16	3	10	13	7	28	23	35	68	67
45	53	33	2	6	7	1	72	4	9	9	6	9	18	9	9	31	10
224	**242**	**229**	**413**	**542**	**647**	**546**	**532**	**970**	**12**	**8**	**10**	**18**	**16**	**19**	**50**	**52**	**54**
1	0	4	7	7	9	10	6	5	6	15	15	11	25	18	38	85	59
5	6	1	6	20	24	10	29	4	9	13	10	12	16	12	47	37	55
2	0	1	12	0	0	0	65	1	30	57	2	35	60	2	3	50	26
10	2	20	12	21	14	7	7	17	11	17	27	15	37	37	53	59	71
0	0	0	2	3	6	2	6	7	3	7	8	6	21	13	32	50	57
4	1	3	56	35	99	30	17	3	17	16	8	30	37	27	26	38	21
3	1	2	11	27	26	5	11	0	18	14	23	25	16	29	26	21	7
10	0	0	8	6	5	2	0	0	18	15	10	30	22	18	23	59	40
2	0	0	13	5	4	2	0	0	8	4	2	10	7	6	36	60	26
1	0	0	0	7	9	5	20	1	23	43	30	34	53	36	45	37	11
0	0	1	2	19	20	14	0	0	12	2	6	39	30	24	44	24	3
23	0	1	37	28	27	32	0	0	19	14	8	40	34	19	35	27	22
1	8	2	4	12	14	7	5	5	8	3	2	13	7	4	46	44	42
2	0	0	1	1	1	3	5	6	29	21	21	34	35	23	47	58	42
3	0	1	2	0	1	3	29	0	13	30	2	23	66	3	80	85	13
4	3	4	17	10	19	13	12	144	6	3	18	13	6	22	48	54	76
18	0	1	14	21	25	9	0	7	45	36	21	60	50	21	30	15	11
0	0	2	0	0	1	1	0	2	18	1	18	22	1	20	84	62	72
11	4	4	7	16	14	1	6	199	11	8	25	16	20	40	73	55	53
8	0	0	12	11	23	6	21	1	15	22	15	18	33	18	45	54	27
1	1	1	4	4	4	1	11	0	14	22	8	28	45	11	37	41	24
2	5	22	6	7	13	4	9	122	7	6	13	9	7	17	62	77	54
13	0	0	1	0	0	1	2	0	18	3	8	18	3	8	12	56	98
0	1	0	0	0	0	1	0	15	4	1	5	8	3	9	67	81	51
8	0	3	15	27	29	18	30	4	11	10	16	22	21	23	35	57	57
15	6	24	1	13	1	22	22	4	20	10	9	31	14	12	69	52	38
11	0	2	7	13	16	36	23	50	14	8	41	18	11	52	52	51	83
0	0	2	18	15	16	6	0	0	51	36	24	51	37	24	13	11	7
8	4	19	13	9	10	58	81	28	9	19	14	15	31	19	54	68	63
3	1	2	3	1	1	5	1	0	20	5	3	21	5	3	67	68	56
6	7	1	3	6	8	7	2	17	11	13	9	17	27	13	42	60	51
3	1	46	10	4	10	34	1	14	12	0	1	13	1	7	57	58	22
4	1	1	4	10	15	28	3	49	15	8	16	34	13	29	48	41	48
1	0	1	2	4	4	1	0	7	12	21	48	14	27	56	21	12	29
9	154	19	22	61	70	61	11	175	16	25	31	23	35	40	54	11	42
0	0	0	0	0	0	1	0	0	18	5	3	18	8	4	47	36	28
0	0	0	1	0	1	0	5	1	8	8	5	22	12	10	49	55	64
0	0	1	0	0	0	4	2	1	4	4	4	11	12	16	51	76	90
11	17	12	29	8	25	11	36	23	16	13	9	17	14	9	46	67	39
1	0	0	0	0	0	0	1	0	5	39	1	7	41	1	7	99	47
0	0	1	3	12	15	7	0	1	12	24	32	17	32	41	41	34	17
3	6	22	16	42	15	36	8	27	13	7	13	20	11	20	60	35	58
6	6	3	8	22	14	3	7	6	6	7	15	10	11	37	51	41	55
4	4	2	4	5	7	13	19	3	12	10	6	24	26	11	67	80	77
3	0	0	5	3	4	13	1	1	10	2	2	11	4	2	35	27	28
27	*22*	*130*	*275*	*306*	*349*	*96*	*156*	*75*	*5*	*4*	*3*	*13*	*7*	*6*	*22*	*27*	*23*
919	**854**	**893**	**2 121**	**2 627**	**3 647**	**1 622**	**1 462**	**2 274**	**9**	**7**	**9**	**14**	**12**	**14**	**40**	**44**	**45**

Table 4 (continued)

	Total aid to education			Total aid to basic education			Total aid to basic education per primary school-age child			Direct aid to education			Direct aid to basic education		
	Constant 2006 US$ millions			Constant 2006 US$ millions			Constant 2006 US$			Constant 2006 US$ millions			Constant 2006 US$ millions		
	1999–2000 annual average	2005	2006	1999–2000 annual average	2005	2006	1999–2000 annual average	2005	2006	1999–2000 annual average	2005	2006	1999–2000 annual average	2005	2006
Upper middle income countries	673	539	578	175	179	69	4	4	1	667	536	573	132	108	41
Low middle income countries	2 081	2 500	3 460	601	772	1 013	3	4	5	2 002	2 310	3 340	299	480	626
High income countries	39	0	0	4	0	0	1	0	0	39	0	0	0	0	0
Unallocated by income	626	787	866	168	203	199	...	...	...	613	777	856	88	93	124
Least developed countries	**2 111**	**3 228**	**3 821**	**1 092**	**1 685**	**2 195**	**11**	**15**	**19**	**1 658**	**2 565**	**3 149**	**626**	**1 078**	**1 392**
Low income countries	**3 540**	**4 638**	**6 385**	**1 822**	**2 535**	**3 783**	**6**	**8**	**12**	**2 965**	**3 714**	**5 420**	**1 105**	**1 714**	**2 585**
Middle income countries	**2 754**	**3 039**	**4 038**	**776**	**951**	**1 081**	**3**	**4**	**4**	**2 669**	**2 846**	**3 914**	**431**	**587**	**667**
Total	6 958	8 464	11 289	2 771	3 689	5 063	5	6	9	6 287	7 337	10 190	1 624	2 395	3 376
Arab States	1 094	1 310	1 672	319	479	549	8	12	13	1 073	1 215	1 625	146	375	318
Central and Eastern Europe	409	312	427	131	33	49	11	3	4	372	297	412	87	12	28
Central Asia	102	115	211	24	55	73	3	9	12	86	101	190	9	40	43
East Asia and the Pacific	1 113	1 244	1 948	300	439	634	2	3	4	1 069	1 153	1 892	155	264	414
Latin America and the Caribbean	592	703	785	266	279	280	5	5	5	571	660	741	182	168	155
North America and Western Europe	3	0	0	0	0	0	5	8	0	3	0	0	0	0	0
South and West Asia	842	1 175	986	448	575	478	3	3	3	827	949	839	342	374	326
Sub-Saharan Africa	2 352	2 840	3 811	1 186	1 474	2 070	11	12	17	1 842	2 207	3 051	658	891	1 205
Unallocated by region	*452*	*765*	*1 451*	*98*	*354*	*930*	...	...	...	*444*	*755*	*1 441*	*46*	*271*	*888*
Total	6 958	8 464	11 289	2 771	3 689	5 063	5	6	9	6 287	7 337	10 190	1 624	2 395	3 376

Notes:
(...) indicates that data are not available.
All data represent commitments unless otherwise specified.
Source: OECD-DAC (2008*c*).

Direct aid to secondary education Constant 2006 US$ millions			Direct aid to post-secondary education Constant 2006 US$ millions			Aid to education, level unspecified Constant 2006 US$ millions			Share of education in total ODA (%)			Share of education in total sector-allocable ODA (%)			Share of basic education in total aid to education (%)		
1999–2000 annual average	2005	2006	1999–2000 annual average	2005	2006	1999–2000 annual average	2005	2006	1999–2000 annual average	2005	2006	1999–2000 annual average	2005	2006	1999–2000 annual average	2005	2006
98	42	43	356	248	439	80	139	50	17	10	13	19	11	15	26	33	12
385	240	269	793	1 195	1 792	526	396	654	8	6	11	11	11	14	29	31	29
0	0	0	30	0	0	9	0	0	28	...	...	29	...	...	11	...	...
38	30	139	340	444	453	148	210	140	5	4	3	11	7	5	27	26	23
231	**451**	**314**	**322**	**484**	**509**	**479**	**552**	**933**	**11**	**10**	**12**	**16**	**16**	**18**	**52**	**52**	**57**
399	**542**	**442**	**602**	**740**	**963**	**859**	**718**	**1 430**	**11**	**8**	**11**	**16**	**15**	**18**	**51**	**55**	**59**
483	**281**	**312**	**1 150**	**1 443**	**2 231**	**606**	**534**	**703**	**9**	**6**	**11**	**12**	**11**	**14**	**28**	**31**	**27**
919	**854**	**893**	**2 121**	**2 627**	**3 647**	**1 622**	**1 462**	**2 274**	**9**	**7**	**9**	**14**	**12**	**14**	**40**	**44**	**45**
10	112	118	393	615	775	325	113	414	16	4	10	20	11	15	29	37	33
49	27	36	186	230	321	50	28	28	7	6	8	12	7	9	32	11	11
24	7	25	39	36	82	14	18	39	5	6	8	7	7	9	23	48	35
212	103	63	456	527	1 030	246	259	386	8	9	17	10	12	19	27	35	33
59	87	96	183	226	283	148	180	206	6	8	9	8	11	10	45	40	36
0	0	0	2	0	0	0	0	0	4	0	0	4	0	0	6	50	0
114	254	196	174	145	159	197	176	158	12	8	7	16	12	9	53	49	49
224	242	229	413	542	647	546	532	970	12	8	10	18	16	19	50	52	54
27	*22*	*130*	*275*	*306*	*349*	*96*	*156*	*75*	*5*	*5*	*6*	*13*	*9*	*12*	*22*	*46*	*64*
919	**854**	**893**	**2 121**	**2 627**	**3 647**	**1 622**	**1 462**	**2 274**	**9**	**7**	**9**	**14**	**12**	**14**	**40**	**44**	**45**

© Keith Dannemiller/CORBIS

Mexico's Oportunidades programme reaches out to poor and indigenous households

Glossary

Achievement. Performance on standardized tests or examinations that measure knowledge or competence in a specific subject area. The term is sometimes used as an indication of education quality within an education system or when comparing a group of schools.

Adult education. Educational activities, offered through formal, non-formal or informal frameworks, targeted at adults and aimed at advancing, or substituting for, initial education and training. The purpose may be to (a) complete a given level of formal education or professional qualification; (b) acquire knowledge and skills in a new field (not necessarily for a qualification); and/or (c) refresh or update knowledge and skills. See also **Basic education** and **Continuing education.**

Adult literacy rate. Number of literate persons aged 15 and above, expressed as a percentage of the total population in that age group. Different ways of defining and assessing literacy yield different results regarding the number of persons designated as literate.

Age-specific enrolment ratio (ASER). Enrolment of a given age or age group, regardless of the level of education in which pupils or students are enrolled, expressed as a percentage of the population of the same age or age group.

Basic education. The whole range of educational activities taking place in various settings (formal, non-formal and informal) that aim to meet **basic learning needs;** in the Dakar Framework the term is synonymous with the broad EFA agenda. Similarly, the OECD-DAC and standard aid classifications use a definition that includes early childhood education, primary education, and basic life skills for youths and adults, including literacy. According to the **International Standard Classification of Education (ISCED)**, basic education comprises primary education (first stage of basic education) and lower secondary education (second stage).

Basic learning needs. As defined in the World Declaration on Education for All (Jomtien, Thailand, 1990): essential learning tools (literacy, oral expression, numeracy, problem-solving) and basic learning content (knowledge, skills, values, attitudes) required by human beings to survive, develop their full capacities, live and work in dignity, participate fully in development, improve the quality of their lives, make informed decisions and continue learning. The scope of basic learning needs and how they should be met varies by country and culture, and changes over time.

Charter school. A public school that is not subject to some of the local and state regulations applied to conventional public schools, allowing parents, community leaders, educational entrepreneurs or others greater autonomy over decisions in defined areas. Charter schools are sponsored by local, state or other organizations, which monitor their quality and hold them accountable for academic results and good financial practice as specified in their charters.

Child labour. A term often defined as work that deprives children of their childhood, their potential and their dignity, and that is harmful to their physical and mental development. The term refers to work that is mentally, physically, socially or morally dangerous, that harms children and that interferes with their schooling by depriving them of the opportunity to attend school, obliging them to leave school prematurely or requiring them to try to combine school attendance with excessively long and heavy work hours.

Child- or under-5 mortality rate. Probability of dying between birth and the fifth birthday, expressed per 1,000 live births.

Cognitive development. Development of the mental action or process of acquiring knowledge through thought, experience and senses.

Compulsory education or attendance. Educational programmes that children and young people are legally obliged to attend, usually defined in terms of a number of grades or an age range, or both.

Constant prices. A way to express financial values in real terms, that enables comparisons over time. To measure changes in real national income or product, economists calculate the value of total production in each year at constant prices using a set of prices that are applied in a chosen base year.

Continuing or further education. A general term referring to a wide range of educational activities designed to meet the learning needs of adults. See also **Adult education.**

Disability. A temporary or permanent physical or mental condition that may limit a person's opportunities to take part in the community on an equal level with others.

Dropout rate by grade. Percentage of pupils or students who drop out of a given grade in a given school year. It is the difference between 100% and the sum of the promotion and repetition rates.

Early childhood. The period of a child's life from birth to age 8.

Early childhood care and education (ECCE). Programmes that, in addition to providing children with care, offer a structured and purposeful set of learning activities either in a formal institution (pre-primary or ISCED 0) or as part of a non-formal child development programme. ECCE programmes are normally designed for children from age 3 and include organized learning activities that constitute, on average, the equivalent of at least 2 hours per day and 100 days per year.

Education attainment rate. The percentage of a population belonging to a particular age group that has attained or completed a specified education level (typically primary, secondary or tertiary) or grade in school.

EFA Development Index (EDI). Composite index aimed at measuring overall progress towards EFA. At present, the EDI incorporates four of the most easily quantifiable EFA goals – universal primary education as measured by the total primary net enrolment ratio, adult literacy as measured by the adult literacy rate, gender parity as measured by the **gender-specific EFA index** and quality of education as measured by the survival rate to grade 5. Its value is the arithmetic mean of the observed values of these four indicators.

EFA Inequality Index for Income Groups (EIIIG). A composite index measuring inequality in overall EFA achievement across different population groups. The EIIIG measures the (unequal) distribution of overall EFA achievement within countries according to household wealth and other socio-demographic markers, using a set of indicators from household surveys that differs from those in the **EDI**.

Elementary education. See **primary education.**

Enrolment. Number of pupils or students enrolled at a given level of education, regardless of age. See also **Gross enrolment ratio** and **Net enrolment ratio.**

Entrance age (official). Age at which pupils or students would enter a given programme or level of education, assuming they had started at the official entrance age for the lowest level, studied full time throughout and progressed through the system without repeating or skipping a grade. The theoretical entrance age for a given programme or level may be very different from the actual or even the most common entrance age.

Equity. As used in the report, the term describes fairness in the distribution of opportunities for education. Enhanced equity implies a reduction in disparities based on gender, poverty, residence, ethnicity, language or other characteristics and circumstances that should not influence education outcomes.

Equivalency education. Programmes primarily organized for children and youth who did not have access to, or who dropped out of, formal primary/basic education. Typically, these programmes aim at providing equivalency to formal primary/basic education and at mainstreaming the target groups into the formal system upon successful completion of the programme.

Fields of study in tertiary or higher education.

Education: teacher training and education science.

Humanities and arts: humanities, religion and theology, fine and applied arts.

Social sciences, business and law: social and behavioural sciences, journalism and information, business and administration, law.

Science: life and physical sciences, mathematics, statistics and computer sciences.

Engineering, manufacturing and construction: engineering and engineering trades, manufacturing and processing, architecture and building.

Agriculture: agriculture, forestry and fishery, veterinary studies.

Health and welfare: medical sciences and health-related sciences, social services.

Services: personal services, transport services, environmental protection, security services.

Foreign students. Students enrolled in an education programme in a country of which they are not permanent residents.

Gender parity index (GPI). Ratio of female to male values (or male to female, in certain cases) of a given indicator. A GPI of 1 indicates parity between sexes; a GPI above or below 1 indicates a disparity in favour of one sex over the other.

Gender-specific EFA index (GEI). A composite index measuring gender parity in total participation in primary and secondary education, and in adult literacy. The GEI is calculated as the arithmetic mean of the gender parity indices of the primary and secondary gross enrolment ratios and of the adult literacy rate.

General education. Programmes designed to lead students to a deeper understanding of a subject or group of subjects, especially, but not necessarily, with a view to preparing them for further education at the same or a higher level. These programmes are typically school-based and may or may not contain vocational elements. Their successful completion may or may not provide students with a labour-market-relevant qualification.

Grade. Stage of instruction usually equivalent to one complete school year.

Graduate. A person who has successfully completed the final year of a level or sub-level of education. In some countries completion occurs as a result of passing an examination or a series of examinations. In other countries it occurs after a requisite number of course hours have been accumulated. Sometimes both types of completion occur within a country.

Gross enrolment ratio (GER). Total enrolment in a specific level of education, regardless of age, expressed as a percentage of the population in the official age group corresponding to this level of education. For the tertiary level, the population used is that of the five-year age group following on from the secondary school leaving age. The GER can exceed 100% due to early or late entry and/or grade repetition.

Gross intake rate (GIR). Total number of new entrants to a given grade of primary education, regardless of age, expressed as a percentage of the population at the official school entrance age for that grade.

Gross domestic product (GDP). The value of all final goods and services produced in a country in one year (see also **Gross national product**). GDP can be measured by aggregating an economy's (a) income (wages, interest, profits, rents) or (b) expenditure (consumption, investment, government purchases), plus net exports (exports minus imports). The results should be the same because one person's expenditure is always another person's income; the sum of all income must equal the sum of all expenditure.

Gross domestic product per capita. GDP divided by the total population at mid-year.

Gross national product (GNP). The value of all final goods and services produced in a country in one year (gross domestic product) plus income that residents have received from abroad, minus income claimed by non-residents. GNP may be much less than GDP if much of the income from a country's production flows to foreign persons or firms. But if the people or firms of a country hold large amounts of the stocks and bonds of firms or governments of other countries, and receive income from them, GNP may be greater than GDP.

Gross national product per capita. GNP divided by the total population at mid-year.

HIV prevalence rate. Estimated number of people of a given age group living with HIV/AIDS at the end of a given year, expressed as a percentage of the total population of the corresponding age group.

Household survey. Survey whose purpose is to compile socio-economic and demographic information on households and individual household members in such areas as education, health, income, employment, mortality and fertility. In the area of education, large-scale household surveys supplement information derived from administrative sources, censuses and school surveys. They are conducted using standard sampling procedures.

Illiterate. See **Literate**.

Indigenous language. A language that originated in a specified territory or community and was not brought in from elsewhere.

Infant mortality rate. Probability of dying between birth and the first birthday, expressed as deaths per 1,000 live births.

Infectious diseases. Diseases that are caused by pathogenic micro-organisms, such as bacteria, fungi, parasites or viruses, and that can be spread directly or indirectly from one person to another. They include influenza, dengue, hepatitis, malaria, measles, tuberculosis and yellow fever.

Informal education. Learning that takes place in daily life without clearly stated objectives. The term refers to a lifelong process whereby all individuals acquire attitudes, values, skills and knowledge from daily experience, and from the educative influence and resources in their environment.

International Standard Classification of Education (ISCED). Classification system designed to serve as an instrument for assembling, compiling and presenting comparable indicators and statistics of education both within countries and internationally. The system, introduced in 1976, was revised in 1997 (ISCED97).

Labour force participation rate. The share of employed plus unemployed people in comparison with the working age population.

Least developed countries (LDCs). Low-income countries that, according to the United Nations, have human resource weaknesses (based on indicators of nutrition, health, education and adult literacy) and are economically vulnerable. The category is used to guide donors and countries in allocating foreign assistance.

Life expectancy at birth. Approximate number of years a newborn infant would live if prevailing patterns of age-specific mortality rates in the year of birth were to stay the same throughout the child's life.

Literacy. According to UNESCO's 1958 definition, the term refers to the ability of an individual to read and write with understanding a simple short statement related to his/her everyday life. The concept of literacy has since evolved to embrace multiple skill domains, each conceived on a scale of different mastery levels and serving different purposes. Many today view literacy as the ability to identify, interpret, create, communicate and compute, using printed and written materials in various contexts. Literacy is a process of learning that enables individuals to achieve personal goals, develop their knowledge and potential, and participate fully in the community and wider society.

Literate/illiterate. As used in the statistical tables, the term refers to a person who can/cannot read and write with understanding a simple statement related to his/her everyday life.

Literate environment. The term can have at least two meanings: (a) the availability of written, printed and visual materials in learners' surrounding environment, enabling them to make use of their basic reading and writing skills; and/or (b) the prevalence of literacy in households and communities, enhancing the prospects of successful literacy acquisition by learners.

Lower-secondary education (ISCED level 2). See **Secondary education**.

Net attendance rate (NAR). Number of pupils in the official age group for a given level of education who attend school in that level, expressed as a percentage of the population in that age group.

Net enrolment ratio (NER). Enrolment of the official age group for a given level of education, expressed as a percentage of the population in that age group.

Net intake rate (NIR). New entrants to the first grade of primary education who are of the official primary school entrance age, expressed as a percentage of the population of that age.

New entrants. Pupils entering a given level of education for the first time; the difference between enrolment and repeaters in the first grade of the level.

New entrants to the first grade of primary education with ECCE experience. Number of new entrants to the first grade of primary school who have attended the equivalent of at least 200 hours of organized ECCE programmes, expressed as a percentage of the total number of new entrants to the first grade.

Non-formal education. Learning activities typically organized outside the formal education system. The term is generally contrasted with formal and informal education. In different contexts, non-formal education covers educational activities aimed at imparting adult literacy, basic education for out-of-school children and youth, life skills, work skills and general culture. Such activities usually have clear learning objectives, but vary in duration, in organizational structure and in conferring certification for acquired learning.

Out-of-school children. Children in the official primary school age range who are not enrolled in either primary or secondary school.

Post-secondary non-tertiary education (ISCED level 4). Programmes that lie between the upper secondary and tertiary levels from an international point of view, even though they might clearly be considered upper secondary or tertiary programmes in a national context. They are often not significantly more advanced than programmes at ISCED level 3 (upper secondary) but they serve to broaden the knowledge of students who have completed a programme at that level. The students are usually older than those at ISCED level 3. ISCED 4 programmes typically last between six months and two years.

Pre-primary education (ISCED level 0). Programmes at the initial stage of organized instruction, primarily designed to introduce very young children, aged at least 3 years, to a school-type environment and provide a bridge between home and school. Variously referred to as infant education, nursery education, pre-school education, kindergarten or early childhood education, such programmes are the more formal component of ECCE. Upon completion of these programmes, children continue their education at ISCED 1 (primary education).

Primary cohort completion rate. The number of pupils who complete the final year of primary school, expressed as a percentage of the number who entered the first year.

Primary education (ISCED level 1). Programmes normally designed on a unit or project basis to give pupils a sound basic education in reading, writing and mathematics, and an elementary understanding of subjects such as history, geography, natural sciences, social sciences, art and music. Religious instruction may also be featured. These subjects serve to develop pupils' ability to obtain and use information they need about their home, community or country. Also known as elementary education.

Private enrolment/institutions. Number of pupils/students enrolled in private institutions, that is, in institutions that are not operated by public authorities but are controlled and managed, whether for profit or not, by private bodies such as non-government organizations, religious bodies, special interest groups, foundations or business enterprises.

Public enrolment/institutions. Number of students enrolled in public institutions, that is, institutions controlled and managed by public authorities or agencies (national/federal, state/provincial or local), whatever the origins of their financial resources.

Public expenditure on education. Total current and capital expenditure on education by local, regional and national governments, including municipalities. Household contributions are excluded. The term covers public expenditure for both public and private institutions. Current expenditure includes expenditure for goods and services that are consumed within a given year and have to be renewed the following year, such as staff salaries and benefits; contracted or purchased services; other resources, including books and teaching materials; welfare services and items such as furniture and equipment, minor repairs, fuel, telecommunications, travel, insurance and rent. Capital expenditure includes expenditure for construction, renovation and major repairs of buildings, and the purchase of heavy equipment or vehicles.

Pupil. A child enrolled in pre-primary or primary education. Youth and adults enrolled at more advanced levels are often referred to as students.

Pupil/teacher ratio (PTR). Average number of pupils per teacher at a specific level of education, based on headcounts for both pupils and teachers.

Pupil/trained-teacher ratio. Average number of pupils per trained teacher at a specific level of education, based on headcounts for both pupils and trained teachers. See also **Trained teacher**.

Purchasing power parity (PPP). An exchange rate that accounts for price differences among countries, allowing international comparisons of real output and incomes.

Quintile. In statistics, any of five equal groups into which a population can be divided according to the distribution of values of a variable.

Repeaters. Number of pupils enrolled in the same grade or level as the previous year, expressed as a percentage of the total enrolment in that grade or level.

Repetition rate by grade. Number of repeaters in a given grade in a given school year, expressed as a percentage of enrolment in that grade the previous school year.

School-age population. Population of the age group officially corresponding to a given level of education, whether enrolled in school or not.

School life expectancy (SLE). Number of years a child of school entrance age is expected to spend in school or university, including years spent on repetition. It is the sum of the age-specific enrolment ratios for primary, secondary, post-secondary non-tertiary and tertiary education.

Secondary education (ISCED levels 2 and 3). Programme made up of two stages: lower and upper secondary. Lower secondary education (ISCED 2) is generally designed to continue the basic programmes of the primary level but the teaching is typically more subject-focused, requiring more specialized teachers for each subject area. The end of this level often coincides with the end of compulsory education. In upper secondary education (ISCED 3), the final stage of secondary education in most countries, instruction is often organized even more along subject lines and teachers typically need a higher or more subject-specific qualification than at ISCED level 2.

Sector-wide approach (SWAp). A development approach in which all significant donor funding for a given sector supports a single sector policy and expenditure programme, under the leadership of the recipient government. Donor support for a SWAp may take the form of project aid, technical assistance, basket/pooled funding or budget support. There is commonly a commitment to progress towards reliance on government procedures to disburse and account for donor funds.

Stunting rate. Proportion of children in a given age group whose height for their age is between two and three standard deviations (moderate stunting) or three or more standard deviations (severe stunting) below the reference median established by the National Center for Health Statistics and the World Health Organization. Low height for age is a basic indicator of malnutrition.

Survival rate by grade. Percentage of a cohort of students who are enrolled in the first grade of an education cycle in a given school year and are expected to reach a specified grade, regardless of repetition.

Teacher compensation. A base teaching salary plus bonuses. Base salary refers to the minimum scheduled gross annual salary for a full-time teacher with the minimum training necessary to be qualified at the beginning of his or her teaching career. Reported base salaries are defined as the total sum of money paid by the employer for the labour supplied, minus the employer contribution to social and pension funding. Bonuses that are a regular part of the annual salary, like a thirteenth month or holiday bonus, are usually included in the base salary.

Teachers/teaching staff. Number of persons employed full time or part time in an official capacity to guide and direct the learning experience of pupils and students, irrespective of their qualifications or the delivery mechanism (i.e. face to face and/or at a distance). Excludes education personnel who have no active teaching duties (e.g. headmasters, headmistresses or principals who do not teach) and persons who work occasionally or in a voluntary capacity.

Technical and vocational education and training (TVET). Programmes designed mainly to prepare students for direct entry into a particular occupation or trade (or class of occupations or trades). Successful completion of such programmes normally leads to a labour-market-relevant vocational qualification recognized by the education ministry, employers' associations or other authorities in the country in which it is obtained.

Tertiary or higher education (ISCED levels 5 and 6). Programmes with an educational content more advanced than what is offered at ISCED levels 3 and 4. The first stage of tertiary education, ISCED level 5, includes level 5A, composed of largely theoretically based programmes intended to provide sufficient qualifications for gaining entry to advanced research programmes and professions with high skill requirements; and level 5B, where programmes are generally more practical, technical and/or occupationally specific. The second stage of tertiary education, ISCED level 6, comprises programmes devoted to advanced study and original research and leading to the award of an advanced research qualification.

Total debt service. Sum of principal repayments and interest paid in foreign currency, goods or services on long-term debt, or interest paid on short-term debt, as well as repayments (repurchases and charges) to the International Monetary Fund.

Total fertility rate. Average number of children that would be born to a woman if she were to live to the end of her childbearing years (15 to 49) and bear children at each age in accordance with prevailing age-specific fertility rates.

Total primary net attendance rate (TNAR). Number of pupils of the official primary school age group who attend school in either primary or secondary education, expressed as a percentage of the population in that age group.

Total primary net enrolment ratio (TNER). Enrolment of children of the official primary school age group in either primary or secondary schools, expressed as a percentage of the population in that age group.

Trained teacher. Teacher who has received the minimum organized teacher training normally required for teaching at the relevant level in a given country.

Transition rate to secondary education. New entrants to the first grade of secondary education in a given year, expressed as a percentage of the number of pupils enrolled in the final grade of primary education in the previous year.

Undernutrition/malnutrition. The condition of people whose dietary energy intake is below that needed to maintain a healthy life and carry out light physical activity. Malnutrition refers to food deficiencies either in terms of quantity or quality (lack of specific nutrients or vitamins).

Upper-secondary education (ISCED level 3). See **Secondary education**.

Variance. A measure of dispersion of a given distribution.

Youth literacy rate. Number of literate persons aged 15 to 24, expressed as a percentage of the total population in that age group.

References*

Abadzi, H. 2006. *Efficient Learning for the Poor: Insights from the Frontier of Cognitive Neuroscience.* Washington, DC, World Bank. (Directions in Development.)

— 2007. *Absenteeism and Beyond: Instructional Time Loss and Consequences.* Washington, DC, World Bank, Independent Evaluation Group Sector, Thematic and Global Evaluation Division. (Policy Research Working Paper, 4376.)

Abkula, D. T. 2002. Jumping on the train: the pastoralist experience in Kenya's PRSP. *PPLA Notes,* Vol. 43, pp. 31–3.

Abu-Duhou, I. 1999. *School-Based Management.* Paris, UNESCO International Institute for Educational Planning. (Fundamentals of Educational Planning, 62.)

Academy for Education Development and USAID Ethiopia. 2004. *Ethiopian Second National Learning Assessment of Grade 4 Students.* Addis Ababa, National Organization for Examination.

Acharya, S. 2007. *Social Inclusion: Gender and Equity in Education SWAps in South Asia – Nepal Case Study.* Kathmandu, UNICEF Regional Office for South Asia.

Ackers, J., Migoli, J. and Nzomo, J. 2001. Identifying and addressing the causes of declining participation rates in Kenyan primary schools. *International Journal of Educational Development,* Vol. 21, No. 4, pp. 361–74.

Adams, S. J. 2005. *Vietnam's Health Care System: A Macroeconomic Perspective.* International Symposium on Health Care Systems in Asia, Hitotsubashi University, Tokyo, International Monetary Fund, 21–22 January.

Adediran, S., Anyanwu, S., Foot, S., Maiyashi, T., Nwobodo, E. and Umar, A. 2008. *Study of States Access to and Utilisation of Universal Basic Education Intervention Funds.* Abuja, Universal Basic Education Commission, Capacity for Universal Basic Education.

Advisory Board for Irish Aid. 2008. *Final Synthesis Report. Good Governance, Aid Modalities and Poverty Reduction: From Better Theory to Better Practice.* Dublin, Advisory Board for Irish Aid. (Good Governance, Aid Modalities and Poverty Reduction: Linkages to the Millennium Development Goals and Implications for Irish Aid, Research project [RP-05-GG] of the Advisory Board for Irish Aid.)

Agüero, J. M., Carter, M. R. and Woolard, I. 2006. *The Impact of Unconditional Cash Transfers on Nutrition: The South African Child Support Grant.* Washington, DC, Center for Global Development.

Ahmed, M., Ahmed, K. S., Islam Khan, N. and Ahmed, R. 2007. *Access to Education in Bangladesh: Country Analytic Review of Primary and Secondary Education.* Brighton, UK/Dhaka, University of Sussex, Sussex School of Education, Centre for International Education, Consortium for Research on Educational Access, Transitions & Equity/BRAC University, Institute of Educational Development.

Aide et Action. 2008. *Back 2 Basics – Study Report.* Paris, Aide et Action.

Akyeampong, K. 2008. *Public Private Partnership in the Provision of Basic Education for Poor and Disadvantaged Groups in Ghana and Rwanda: Possibilities and Constraints.* Brighton, UK, University of Sussex, Sussex School of Education, Centre for International Education. (Unpublished paper.)

Akyeampong, K., Djangmah, J., Oduro, A., Seidu, A. and Hunt, F. 2007. *Access to Basic Education in Ghana: The Evidence and the Issues. Country Analytic Report.* Brighton, UK/Winneba, Ghana, University of Sussex, Sussex School of Education, Centre for International Education, Consortium for Research on Educational Access, Transitions & Equity/Ghana University of Education.

Al-Samarrai, S. 2007. *Changes in Employment in Bangladesh, 2000–2005: The Impacts on Poverty and Gender Equity.* Washington, DC, World Bank, South Asia Region. (Background paper for the Bangladesh Poverty Assessment. Draft for comments.)

Albó, X. and Anaya, A. 2003. *Niños Alegres, Libres, Expresivos: La Audacia de la Educación Intercultural Bilingüe en Bolivia* [Children, Free, Expressive Children: The Audacity of Intercultural Bilingual Education in Bolivia]. La Paz, Centro de Investigación y Promoción del Campesinado. (Cuadernos de investigación, 59.) (In Spanish.)

Alderman, H. and King, E. M. 1998. Gender differences in parental investment in education. *Structural Change and Economic Dynamics,* Vol. 9, No. 4, pp. 453–68.

Alexander, R. J. 2008. *Education for All, the Quality Imperative and the Problem of Pedagogy.* Brighton, UK/London, University of Sussex, Sussex School of Education, Centre for International Education, Consortium for Research on Educational Access, Transitions & Equity/University of London, Institute of Education. (CREATE Pathways to Access Research Monograph, 20.)

Alsop, R. and Kurey, B. 2005. *Local Organizations in Decentralized Development: Their Functions and Performance in India.* Washington, DC, World Bank.

* All background papers for *EFA Global Monitoring Report 2009* are available at www.efareport.unesco.org

Altinok, N. 2008. An international perspective on trends in the quality of learning achievement (1965–2007). Background paper for *EFA Global Monitoring Report 2009.*

Anderson, L. W., Ryan, D. W. and Shapiro, B. J. (eds). 1989. *The IEA Classroom Environmental Study.* Oxford, UK, Pergamon Press.

Andrabi, T., Das, J. and Khwaja, A. I. 2006. *A Dime a Day: The Possibilities and Limits of Private Schooling in Pakistan.* Washington, DC, World Bank. (Policy Research Working Paper, 4066.)

Andrabi, T., Das, J., Khwaja, A. I., Vishwanath, T., Zajonc, T. and The LEAPS Team. 2008. *Pakistan. Learning and Educational Achievements in Punjab Schools (LEAPS): Insights to Inform the Education Policy Debate.* Washington, DC, World Bank.

Appleton, S. and Balihuta, A. 1996. Education and agricultural productivity: evidence from Uganda. *Journal of International Development,* Vol. 8, No. 3, pp. 415–44.

Armecin, G., Behrman, J. R., Duazo, P., Ghuman, S., Gualtiano, S., King, E. M. and Lee, N. 2006. *Early Childhood Development through an Integrated Program: Evidence from the Philippines.* Washington, DC, World Bank. (Policy Research Working Paper, WPS3922-IE.)

Arsen, D. and Ni, Y. 2008. *The Competitive Effect of School Choice Policies on Performance in Traditional Public Schools.* Tempe, Ariz./Boulder, Colo., Arizona State University, College of Education, Division of Educational Leadership and Policy Studies, Education Policy Research Unit/University of Colorado, School of Education, Education and the Public Interest Center.

Arze del Granado, F. J., Fengler, W., Ragatz, A. and Yavuz, E. 2007. *Investing in Indonesia's Education: Allocation, Equity and Efficiency of Public Expenditures.* Washington, DC, World Bank, Poverty Reduction and Economic Management and Human Development of the East Asia and Pacific Region. (Policy Research Working Paper, WPS4329.)

Asian Development Bank. 2007. *Key Indicators 2007: Inequality in Asia.* Manila, Asian Development Bank.

Aslam, M. 2007. *The Relative Effectiveness of Government and Private Schools in Pakistan: Are Girls Worse Off?* Cambridge, UK, University of Cambridge, Faculty of Education, Research Consortium on Education Outcomes and Poverty. (RECOUP Working Paper, WP07/04.)

Aslam, M., Kingdon, G. and Söderbom, M. Forthcoming. Is education a path to gender equality in the labor market? Evidence from Pakistan. World Bank (ed.), *Education as a Path to Gender Equality.* Washington, DC, World Bank.

Ayyar, R. V. V. 2008. Country-agency relationship in development cooperation: an Indian experience. Background paper for *EFA Global Monitoring Report 2009.*

Azevedo de Aguiar, G., Barker, G., Nascimento, M. and Segundo, M. 2007. *Early Childhood in Brazil: General Overview and Current Issues.* The Hague, Bernard van Leer Foundation. (Working Papers in Early Childhood Development, 44.)

Baines, S. 2005. *Controlling Corruption: Lessons from the School Improvement Grants Program in Indonesia.* International Conference 'Education Finance and Decentralization', Washington, DC, World Bank, 13–14 January.

Baker, D. P., Goesling, B. and LeTendre, G. K. 2002. Socioeconomic status, school quality and national economic development: a cross-national analysis of the 'Heyneman-Loxley effect' on mathematics and science achievement. *Comparative Education Review,* Vol. 46, No. 3, pp. 291–312.

Baker, D. P. and Jones, D. P. 1993. Creating gender equality: cross-national gender stratification and mathematic performance. *Sociology of Education,* Vol. 66, No. 2, pp. 91–103.

Banerjee, A. V., Banerji, R., Duflo, E., Glennerster, R. and Khemani, S. 2006. *Can Information Campaigns Spark Local Participation and Improve Outcomes? A Study of Primary Education in Uttar Pradesh, India.* Washington, DC, World Bank. (Policy Research Working Paper, 3967.)

— 2008. *Pitfalls of Participatory Programs: Evidence from a Randomized Evaluation in Education in India.* Washington, DC, World Bank, Development Research Group, Human Development and Public Services Team. (Impact Evaluation Series, 21. Policy Research Working Paper, 4584.)

Bangladesh Bureau of Educational Information and Statistics. 2006. *Key Educational Indicators.* Dhaka, Bureau of Educational Information and Statistics. http://www.banbeis.gov.bd/db_bb.htm (Accessed 19 September 2008.)

Bangladesh Bureau of Statistics and UNICEF. 2007. *Bangladesh Multiple Indicator Cluster Survey: Progotir Pathey 2006. Volume I: Technical Report.* Dhaka, Ministry of Planning, Planning Division, Bangladesh Bureau of Statistics/UNICEF. (Monitoring the Situation of Children and Women.)

Bano, M. 2007. Pakistan country case study. Background paper for *EFA Global Monitoring Report 2008.*

— 2008. Public Private Partnerships (PPPs) as 'anchor' of educational reforms: lessons from Pakistan. Background paper for *EFA Global Monitoring Report 2009.*

Barber, N. 2006. Is the effect of national wealth on academic achievement mediated by mass media and computers? *Cross-Cultural Research,* Vol. 40, No. 2, pp. 130–51.

Barro, R. J. and Lee, J.-W. 2000. *International Data on Educational Attainment Updates and Implications.* Cambridge, Mass., National Bureau of Economic Research. (Working Paper, 7911.)

Bedard, K. and Cho, I. 2007. *The Gender Test Score Gap Across OECD Countries*. Santa Barbara, Calif., University of California, Santa Barbara, Department of Economics.

Behrman, J. R., Birdsall, N. and Szekely, M. 2003. *Economic Policy and Wage Differentials in Latin America*. Washington, DC, Center for Global Development. (Working Paper, 29.)

Behrman, J. R. and Hoddinott, J. 2005. Programme evaluation with unobserved heterogeneity and selective implementation: the Mexican Progresa impact on child nutrition. *Oxford Bulletin of Economics and Statistics*, Vol. 67, No. 4, pp. 547–69.

Behrman, J. R., Parker, S. W. and Todd, P. E. 2004. *Medium-Term Effects of the Oportunidades Program Package, Including Nutrition, on Education of Rural Children Age 0–8 in 1997*. Philadelphia, Penn., University of Pennsylvania. (Technical Document Number 9 on the Evaluation of Oportunidades 2004.)

Belfield, C. R. 2007. Introduction to the special issue 'The Economics of Early Childhood Education'. *Economics of Education Review*, Vol. 26, No. 1, pp. 1–2.

Bellei, C. 2005. *The Private-Public School Controversy: The Case of Chile*. Conference on 'Mobilizing the Private Sector for Public Education', Cambridge, Mass., Harvard University, Kennedy School of Government, Program on Education Policy and Governance/World Bank, 5–6 October.

Benavot, A. and Tanner, E. 2007. The growth of national learning assessments in the world, 1995–2006. Background paper for *EFA Global Monitoring Report 2008*.

Bennell, P. 1998. Rates of return to education in Asia: a review of the evidence. *Education Economics*, Vol. 6, No. 2, pp. 107–20.

— 2005*a*. The impact of the AIDS epidemic on the schooling of orphans and other directly affected children in sub-Saharan Africa. *Journal of Development Studies*, Vol. 41, No. 3, pp. 467-88.

— 2005*b*. *Teacher Mortality in sub-Saharan Africa: An Update*. Brighton, UK, Knowledge and Skills for Development.

— 2006. *Anti-Retroviral Drugs are Driving Down Teacher Mortality in sub-Saharan Africa*. Brighton, UK, Knowledge and Skills for Development.

Bennell, P. and Akyeampong, K. 2007. *Teacher Motivation in sub-Saharan Africa and South Asia*. London, UK Department for International Development, Central Research Department. (Educational Papers. Researching the Issues, 71.)

Bennell, P., Anyanwu, S., Ayara, N., Ayuba, A., Aigbokhan, B., Bashir, Y., Chete, L., Dandago, K., Jimoh, A., Muhammed, M., Oladeji, S., Onyukwu, O., Sagagi, M. and Tella, S. 2007. *Nigeria: Education Public Expenditure Review. A Synthesis of the Main Findings and Recommendations from Nine State Reports*. Brighton, UK, University of Sussex, Sussex School of Education, Centre for International Education. (First draft.)

Benson, T. 2004. *Africa's Food and Nutrition Security Situation: Where Are We and How Did We Get Here?* Washington, DC, International Food Policy Research Institute. (2020 Discussion Paper, 37.)

Bentaouet-Kattan, R. 2005. Primary school fees: an update. Background paper for *EFA Global Monitoring Report* 2006.

Benveniste, L. 2002. The political structuration of assessment: negotiating state power and legitimacy. *Comparative Education Review*, Vol. 46, No. 1, pp. 89–118.

Benveniste, L., Marshall, J. and Santibañez, L. 2008. *Teaching in Lao PDR*. Washington, DC/Vientiane, World Bank, East Asia and the Pacific Region, Human Development Sector/Lao People's Democratic Republic Ministry of Education.

Berlinski, S., Galiani, S. and Gertler, P. J. 2006. *The Effect of Pre-Primary Education on Primary School Performance*. London, Institute for Fiscal Studies. (Working Paper, 06/04.)

Bernard, J. M. and Michaelowa, K. 2006. How can countries use cross-national research results to address 'the big policy issues'? Ross, K. N. and Genevois, I. J. (eds), *Cross-National Studies of the Quality of Education: Planning Their Design and Managing Their Impact*. Paris, UNESCO International Institute for Educational Planning.

Berry, C. 2007. *Education Aid in Fragile States: Delivering It Effectively*. London, Overseas Development Institute, Strategic Policy Impact and Research Unit. (Briefing Paper, 1.)

Bicego, G. T., Rutstein, S. and Johnson, K. 2003. Dimensions of the emerging orphan crisis in sub-Saharan Africa. *Social Science & Medicine*, Vol. 56, No. 6, pp. 1235–47.

Bird, R. M. and Smart, M. 2001. *Intergovernmental Fiscal Transfers: Some Lessons from International Experience*. Toronto, Ont., University of Toronto, Rotman School of Management, International Tax Program.

Bjork, C. 2004. Decentralisation in education, institutional culture and teacher autonomy in Indonesia. *International Review of Education*, Vol. 50, No. 3-4, pp. 245–62.

Björklund, A., Edin, P.-A., Fredriksson, P. and Krueger, A. 2004. *Education, Equality and Efficiency – An Analysis of Swedish School Reforms During the 1990s*. Uppsala, Sweden, Institute for Labour Market Policy Evaluation.

Black, R. 2004. *Migration and Pro-Poor Policy in Africa*. Brighton, UK, University of Sussex, Development Research Centre on Migration, Globalisation and Policy. (Working Paper, C6.)

Black, R. E., Allen, L. H., Bhutta, Z. A., Caulfield, L. E., de Onis, M., Ezzati, M., Mathers, C. and Rivera, J. 2008. Maternal and child undernutrition: global and regional exposures and health consequences. *The Lancet*, Vol. 371, No. 9608, pp. 243–60. (Maternal and Child Undernutrition 1)

Blondiaux, M., Diallo, A., Diallo, M. K., Diallo, F. K., Dramé, M. B., Fernandez, S., Sow, A., Tinguiano, J. S. and Traoré, G. 2006. *Les Compétences des Elèves de 4A en Compréhension des Textes Ecrits* [Grade 4A Pupils' Competencies in Comprehension of Written Texts]. Conakry, Guinea Ministry of Education, National Education Systems Coordination Unit. (In French.)

Bloom, D. E. 2006. Measuring global educational progress. Cohen, J. E., Bloom, D. E. and Malin, M. B. (eds), *Educating All Children: A Global Agenda.* Cambridge, Mass., American Academy of Arts and Sciences/MIT Press, pp. 33–120.

Blumberg, R. L. 2007. Gender bias in textbooks: a hidden obstacle on the road to equality in education. Background paper for *EFA Global Monitoring Report 2008.*

Böhlmark, A. and Lindahl, M. 2007. *The Impact of School Choice on Pupil Achievement, Segregation and Costs: Swedish Evidence.* Bonn, Germany, Institute for the Study of Labor. (IZA Discussion Paper, 2786.)

Bonnet, G. 2007. What do recent evaluations tell us about the state of teachers in sub-Saharan countries? Background paper for *EFA Global Monitoring Report 2008.*

Booth, D. and Curran, Z. 2005. *Developing the Empirical Evidence for DFID's Strategy on Exclusion: Aid Instruments and Exclusion.* London, Overseas Development Institute.

Bosnia and Herzegovina Directorate for Economic Planning, Republika Srpska Ministry of Health and Social Welfare, Bosnia and Herzegovina Ministry of Health, UNICEF and DFID. 2007. *Bosnia and Herzegovina: Multiple Indicator Cluster Survey 2006.* Sarajevo, Directorate for Economic Planning/Ministry of Health and Social Welfare/Ministry of Health/UNICEF/DFID. (Monitoring the Situation of Children and Women.)

Bossert, T. J., Larrañaga, O., Giedion, U., Arbelaez, J. J. and Bowser, D. M. 2003. Decentralisation and equity of resource allocation: evidence from Colombia and Chile. *Bulletin of the World Health Organization,* Vol. 81, No. 2, pp. 95–100.

Bourguignon, F. 2000. *Can Redistribution Accelerate Growth and Development?* ABCDE Europe, Paris, 26–28 June.

Bracho, T. 2006. *Evaluación Externa del Programa Escuelas de Calidad (PEC) 2006–2007* [External Evaluation of the Quality Schools Programme (PEC) 2006–2007]. México, DF, Centro de Investigación y Docencia Económicas, División de Administración Pública. (In Spanish.)

Bradshaw, J. and Finch, N. 2002. *A Comparison of Child Benefit Packages in 22 Countries.* Huddersfield, UK, UK Department for Work and Pensions. (Research Report, 174.)

Bray, M. 2003. *Adverse Effects of Private Supplementary Tutoring: Dimensions, Implications and Government Responses.* Paris, UNESCO International Institute for Educational Planning.

Breman, J. G., Mills, A., Snow, R. W., Mulligan, J.-A., Lengeler, C., Mendis, K., Sharp, B., Morel, C., Marchesini, P., White, N. J., Steketee, R. W. and Doumbo, O. K. 2006. Conquering malaria. Jamison, D. T., Breman, J. G., Measham, A. R., Alleyne, G., Claeson, M., Evans, D. B., Jha, P., Mills, A. and Musgrove, P. (eds), *Disease Control Priorities in Developing Countries,* 2nd edn. Washington, DC/New York, World Bank/Oxford University Press, pp. 413–21.

Briggs, K. L. and Wohlstetter, P. 2003. Key elements of a successful school-based management strategy. *School Effectiveness and School Improvement,* Vol. 14, No. 3, pp. 351–72.

Bruneforth, M. 2008. Interpreting the distribution of out-of-school children by past and expected future school enrolment. Background paper for *EFA Global Monitoring Report 2009.*

Bruns, B., Mingat, A. and Rakotomalala, R. 2003. *Achieving Universal Primary Education by 2015: A Chance for Every Child.* Washington, DC, World Bank.

Burd-Sharps, S., Lewis, K. and Borges Martins, E. 2008. *The Measure of America: American Human Development Report, 2008–2009.* New York, Columbia University Press.

Burkina Faso Ministry of Economy and Development. 2004. *Poverty Reduction Strategy Paper.* Ouagadougou, Ministry of Economy and Development.

Burkina Faso Ministry of Economy and Finance. 2000. *Poverty Reduction Strategy Paper.* Ouagadougou, Ministry of Economy and Finance.

Caillods, F. and Hallak, J. 2004. *Education and PRSPs: A Review of Experiences.* Paris, UNESCO International Institute for Educational Planning.

Caldwell, B. J. 2005. *School-Based Management.* Brussels/Paris, International Academy of Education/UNESCO International Institute for Educational Planning. (Education Policy Series, 3.)

Cambodia Council for Social Development. 2002. *National Poverty Reduction Strategy 2003–2005.* Phnom Penh, Council for Social Development.

Cambodia Education Sector Support Project. 2006. *Student Achievement and Education Policy: Results from the Grade Three Assessment.* Phnom Penh, Ministry of Education.

Cambodia Government. 2005. *National Strategic Development Plan 2006–2010.* Phnom Penh, Government of Cambodia.

Cambodia Ministry of Education, Youth and Sports and Interdepartmental Committee on HIV/AIDS. 2007. *HIV/AIDS in the Education Sector in Cambodia: Fact Sheet 1.* Phnom Penh, Ministry of Education, Youth and Sports/Interdepartmental Committee on HIV/AIDS.

Cárdenas, S. 2008. School based management in Latin America. Background paper for *EFA Global Monitoring Report 2009.*

Carnoy, M., Brodziak, I., Molina, A. and Socias, M. 2007. The limitations of teacher pay incentive programs based on inter-cohort comparisons: the case of Chile's SNED. *Education Finance and Policy,* Vol. 2, No. 3, pp. 189–227.

Carnoy, M., Gove, A. K., Loeb, S., Marshall, J. H. and Socias, M. 2008. How schools and students respond to school improvement programs: the case of Brazil's PDE. *Economics of Education Review,* Vol. 27, No. 1, pp. 22–38.

Carnoy, M., Jacobsen, R., Mishel, L. and Rothstein, R. 2005. *The Charter School Dust-Up: Examining the Evidence on Enrollment and Achievement.* Washington, DC/New York, Economic Policy Institute/Teachers College Press.

Carr, M., Jessup, D. L. and Fuller, D. 1999. Gender differences in first-grade mathematic strategy use: parent and teacher contributions. *Journal for Research in Mathematics Education,* Vol. 30, No. 1, pp. 28–57.

Carr-Hill, R. 2005. Analyses of literacy data. Background paper for *EFA Global Monitoring Report 2006.*

Carroli, G., Rooney, C. and Villar, J. 2001. How effective is antenatal care in preventing maternal mortality and serious morbidity? An overview of the evidence. *Paediatric & Perinatal Epidemiology,* Vol. 15, Supplement 1, pp. 1–42.

Case, A., Hosegood, V. and Lund, F. 2005. The reach and impact of child support grants: evidence from KwaZulu-Natal. *Development Southern Africa,* Vol. 22, No. 4, pp. 467–82.

Castello-Climent, A. 2006. *On the Distribution of Education and Democracy.* Valencia, Spain, University of Valencia, International Economics Institute.

Center on Education Policy. 2007. *Answering the Question That Matters Most: Has Student Achievement Increased Since No Child Left Behind?* Washington, DC, Center on Education Policy.

Chakrabarti, R. 2007. *Can Increasing Private School Participation and Monetary Loss in a Voucher Program Affect Public School Performance? Evidence from Milwaukee.* New York, Federal Reserve Bank of New York. (FRBNY Staff Reports, 300.)

Chandani, T., Balan, J., Smith, M. and Donahue, M. 2007. *Strengthening the Private Basic Education Sector: A Case for USAID Support and Financing through the Development Credit Authority.* New York, Banyan Global.

Chapman, D. W., Weidman, J., Cohen, M. and Mercer, M. 2005. The search for quality: a five country study of national strategies to improve educational quality in Central Asia. *International Journal of Educational Development,* Vol. 25, No. 5, pp. 514–30.

Chaudhury, N., Hammer, J., Kremer, M., Muralidharan, K. and Rogers, F. H. 2006. Missing in action: teacher and health worker absence in developing countries. *Journal of Economic Perspectives,* Vol. 20, No. 1, pp. 91–116.

Chinyama, V. 2006. *Kenya's Abolition of School Fees Offers Lessons for Rest of Africa.* Nairobi, UNICEF Kenya. http://www.unicef.org/infobycountry/kenya_33391.html

Choudhry, M. A. 2005. Pakistan: where and who are the world's illiterates? Background paper for *EFA Global Monitoring Report 2006.*

Chronic Poverty Research Centre. 2008. *The Chronic Poverty Report 2008-09: Escaping Poverty Traps.* Manchester, UK, University of Manchester, School of Environment and Development, Institute for Development Policy and Management, Chronic Poverty Research Centre.

Clark, D. and Bundy, D. 2004. *The EFA Fast-Track Initiative: Responding to the Challenge of HIV and AIDS to the Education Sector.* London/Washington, DC, UK Department for International Development/World Bank.

— 2006. *The EFA Fast Track Initiative: An Assessment of the Responsiveness of Endorsed Education Sector Plans to HIV and AIDS.* New York, UNICEF Inter-Agency Task Team on Children and HIV and AIDS.

Colclough, C. 2007. *Global Gender Goals and the Construction of Equality: Conceptual Dilemmas and Policy Practice.* Cambridge, UK/London, University of Cambridge, Faculty of Education, Research Consortium on Educational Outcomes and Poverty/UK Department for International Development. (RECOUP Working Paper, WP07/02.)

Commonwealth Education Fund. 2007. *Funding Change: Sustaining Civil Society Advocacy in Education.* London, Commonwealth Education Fund.

Contreras, D. 2001. *Evaluating a Voucher System in Chile: Individual, Family and School Characteristics.* Santiago, Universidad de Chile, Departamento de Economía. (Documento de Trabajo, 175.)

Côte d'Ivoire National Institute of Statistics. 2007. *Enquête à indicateurs multiples, Côte d'Ivoire 2006, Rapport final* [Multiple Indicator Cluster Survey, Côte d'Ivoire 2006, Final Report]. Abidjan, Côte d'Ivoire, Ministry of State, Ministry of Planning and of Development, National Institute of Statistics. (In French.)

Council of the European Union. 2008. *The EU as a Global Partner for Pro-Poor and Pro-Growth Development: EU Agenda for Action on MDGs.* Brussels, Council of the European Union. (11096/08.)

Creemers, B. 1997. *Effective Schools and Effective Teachers: An International Perspective.* Coventry, UK, University of Warwick, Centre for Cultural Policy Studies, Centre for Research in Elementary and Primary Education. (CREPE Occasional Papers, 4.)

Crouch, L. 2006. Education sector: standards, accountability and support. Cotlear, D. (ed.), *A New Social Contract for Peru: An Agenda for Improving Education, Health Care and the Social Safety Net.* Washington, DC, World Bank, pp. 71–105. (A World Bank Country Study.)

Crouch, L. and Winkler, D. 2007. Governance, management and financing of Education for All: basic frameworks and case studies. Background paper for *EFA Global Monitoring Report 2009* (through Research Triangle Institute).

Das, J., Pandey, P. and Zajonc, T. 2006. *Learning Levels and Gaps in Pakistan.* Washington, DC, World Bank. (Policy Research Working Paper, WPS4067.)

Das, J. and Zajonc, T. 2008. *India Shining and Bharat Drowning: Comparing Two Indian States to the Worldwide Distribution in Mathematics Achievement.* Washington, DC, World Bank, Development Research Group, Human Development and Public Services Team. (Policy Research Working Paper, WPS4644.)

De Grauwe, A. 2008. The role of monitoring and evaluation systems for education quality improvements for all. Background paper for *EFA Global Monitoring Report 2009.*

De Grauwe, A., Lugaz, C., Baldé, D., Diakhaté, C., Dougnon, D., Moustapha, M. and Odushina, D. 2005. Does decentralization lead to school improvement? Findings and lessons from research in West-Africa. *Journal of Education for International Development* Vol. 1, No. 1. http://www.equip123.net/JEID/articles/1/1-1.pdf (Accessed 4 August 2008.)

de Heus, M., Dronkers, J. and Levels, M. 2008. *Educational Systems as a Resource or Hindrance for Immigrants? The Effects of Educational System Characteristics of Both Countries of Origin and Destination on the Scientific Literacy of Immigrant Children in Western Countries.* RC28 Spring Meeting 2008 'Social Stratification and Insiders/Outsiders: Cross-National Comparisons within and between Continents' and 'Dutch-Fleming Meeting of Sociology 2008', Florence, Italy/Leuven, Belgium, European University Institute, 15–18 May/29 May.

de Janvry, A., Finan, F., Sadoulet, E. and Vakis, R. 2006*a*. Can conditional cash transfer programs serve as safety nets in keeping children at school and from working when exposed to shocks? *Journal of Development Economics,* Vol. 79, No. 2, pp. 349–73.

de Janvry, A., Sadoulet, E., Solomon, P. and Vakis, R. 2006*b*. *Uninsured Risk and Asset Protection: Can Conditional Cash Transfer Programs Serve as Safety Nets?* Washington, DC, World Bank. (Social Protection Discussion Paper, 0604.)

de Mello, L. and Hoppe, M. 2005. *Education Attainment in Brazil: The Experience of FUNDEF.* Paris, Organisation for Economic Co-operation and Development. (OECD Economics Department Working Paper, ECO/WKP[2005]11.)

De Renzio, P., Booth, D., Rogerson, A. and Curran, Z. 2005. *Incentives for Harmonisation and Alignment in Aid Agencies.* London, Overseas Development Institute.

Deaton, A. and Drèze, J. 2008. *Nutrition in India: Facts and Interpretations.* Princeton, NJ/Allahabad, India, Princeton University, Research Program in Development Studies, Center for Health and Wellbeing/Allahabad University, Department of Economics.

Denny, K., Harmon, C. and O'Sullivan, V. 2003. *Education, Earnings and Skills: A Multi-Country Comparison.* London, Institute for Fiscal Studies. (WP04/08.)

DFID. 2006. *Eliminating World Poverty. Making Governance Work for the Poor.* London, UK Department for International Development.

DFID and VSO. 2008. *Listening to Teachers: The Motivation and Morale of Education Workers in Mozambique.* London, UK Department for International Development/Voluntary Service Overseas.

Di Gropello, E. 2006. *A Comparative Analysis of School-Based Management in Central America.* Washington, DC, World Bank. (Working Paper, 72.)

Di Gropello, E. and Marshall, J. H. 2005. Teacher effort and schooling outcomes in rural Honduras. Vega, E. (ed.), *Incentives to Improve Teaching: Lessons from Latin America.* Washington, DC, World Bank, pp. 307–59. (Directions in Development.)

Diagne, A. W. 2008. *Préparation du Document de Politique de Formation des Enseignants de l'Education Non Formelle: Analyse de la Situation de la Formation des Enseignants du Non Formel dans les Pays LIFE* [Preparation of the Non-Formal Education Teachers Policy Document: Analysis of the Situation Regarding Trainning of Non-Formal Education Teachers in LIFE Countries]. Dakar, UNESCO Teacher Training Initiative for Sub-Saharan Africa. (In French.)

Dikhanov, Y. 2005. *Human Development Report 2005: Trends in Global Income Distribution, 1970–2000, and Scenarios for 2015.* New York, United Nations Development Program, Human Development Report Office. (Occasional Paper, 2005/8.)

Dominican Republic Secretary of State for Economy Planning and Development. 2008. *Encuesta Nacional de Hogares de Propósitos Múltiples (ENHOGAR 2006): Informe General* [National Household Multiple Indicator Cluster Survey (ENHOGAR 2006): General Findings]. Santo Domingo, Secretary of State for Economy Planning and Development, National Statistics Office, Census and Surveys Manager's Office, Department of Surveys/UNICEF. (In Spanish.)

Downey, D. B. 1994. The school performance of children from single-mother and single-father families: economic or interpersonal deprivation? *Journal of Family Issues,* Vol. 15, No. 1, pp. 129–47.

Dronkers, J. and Robert, P. 2008. Differences in scholastic achievement of public, private government-dependent and private independent schools: a cross-national analysis. *Educational Policy,* Vol. 22, No. 4, pp. 541–77.

Duflo, E., Hanna, R. and Ryan, S. 2007. *Monitoring Works: Getting Teachers to Come to School.* Boston, Mass./Paris/New York, Department of Economics and Poverty Action Lab, Massachusetts Institute of Technology/Wagner School of Public Service, New York University and Poverty Action Lab.

Dumay, X. and Dupriez, V. 2007. Accounting for class effect using the TIMSS 2003 8th grade database: net effect of group composition, net effect of class processes and joint effect. *School Effectiveness and School Improvement,* Vol. 18, No. 4, pp. 383–408.

Duncan, G. J. and Brooks-Gunn, J. (eds). 1997. *Consequences of Growing Up Poor.* New York, Russell Sage Foundation.

Dunne, M., Akyeampong, K. and Humphreys, S. 2007. *School Processes, Local Governance and Community Participation: Understanding Access.* Brighton, UK, University of Sussex, Sussex School of Education, Centre for International Education, Consortium for Research on Educational Access, Transitions & Equity. (CREATE Pathways to Access Research Monograph, 6.)

Dutch Coalition on Disability and Development. 2006. *All Equal, All Different. Inclusive Education: A DCDD Publication about Education for All.* Utrecht, Netherlands, Dutch Coalition on Disability and Development. (Towards an Inclusive Policy. A DCDD Publication Series on Integrating Disability in Policy and Practice.)

Duthilleul, Y. 2005. *Lessons Learnt in the Use of 'Contract' Teachers.* Paris, UNESCO International Institute for Educational Planning.

Education Commission of the States. 2008. *ECS State Policies for Charter Schools Database.* Denver, Colo., Education Commission of the States. http://www.ecs.org/html/educationIssues/CharterSchools/CHDB_intro.asp

Education Policy and Data Center. 2008*a*. 2008 series of education projections to 2015 and 2025. Background paper for *EFA Global Monitoring Report 2009.*

—— 2008*b*. Efficiency: pupil performance and age. A study of promotion-, repetition-, and dropout rates among pupils in four age-groups in 35 developing countries. Background paper for *EFA Global Monitoring Report 2009.*

Education Support Program. 2006. *Education in a Hidden Marketplace: Monitoring of Private Tutoring.* Budapest, Open Society Institute, Education Support Program.

Educational Research Network for West and Central Africa and USAID. 2002. *A Transnational View of Basic Education: Issues of Access, Quality, and Community Participation in West and Central Africa.* Washington, DC, ERNWACA/USAID, Office of Sustainable Development, Support for Analysis and Research in Africa (SARA) Project.

Edward, M. and Michael, K. 2004. Worms: identifying impacts on education and health in the presence of treatment externalities. *Econometrica,* Vol. 72, No. 1, pp. 159–217.

Egypt Ministry of Education. 2006. *Critical Thinking Achievement and Problem-Solving (CAPS) Test: Baseline 2006 Report.* Cairo, Ministry of Education, National Center for Examinations and Educational Evaluation, Education Reform Programme/USAID.

Ekwè, D. 2007. Vincent Bikono: Contract Worker and Not Proud of It. *UNESCO Courier,* No. 10. http://portal.unesco.org/en/ev.php-URL_ID=41199&URL_DO=DO_TOPIC&URL_SECTION=201.html (Accessed 11 August 2008.)

El-Zanaty, F. and Gorin, S. 2007. *Egypt Household Education Survey 2005–06.* Cairo, El-Zanaty and Associates/Macro International Inc.

Elacqua, G. 2004. *School Choice in Chile: An Analysis of Parental Preferences and Search Behavior.* New York, Columbia University, National Center for the Study of Privatization in Education.

Ellis, S. 2006. EFA Goal 3: some initial concepts. Background paper for *EFA Global Monitoring Report 2006.*

Epple, D., Figlio, D. and Romano, R. 2004. Competition between private and public schools: testing stratification and pricing predictions. *Journal of Public Economics,* Vol. 88, No. 7-8, pp. 1215–45.

Espínola, V. 2000. *Regional. Autonomía Escolar: Factores que Contribuyen a una Escuela Más Efectiva* [Regional. School Autonomy: Contributing Factors for a More Effective School]. Washington, DC, Banco Interamericano de Desarrollo, Departamento Regional de Operaciones, División de Programas Sociales. (In Spanish.)

Ethiopia Ministry of Finance and Economic Development. 2002. *Ethiopia: Sustainable Development and Poverty Reduction Program (SDPRP).* Addis Ababa, Ministry of Finance and Economic Development.

—— 2006. *Ethiopia: Building on Progress. A Plan for Accelerated and Sustained Development to End Poverty (PASDEP) 2005/6–2009/10.* Addis Ababa, Ministry of Finance and Economic Development.

—— 2007. *Ethiopia: Building on Progress. A Plan for Accelerated and Sustained Development to End Poverty (PASDEP). Annual Progress Report 2006/07.* Addis Ababa, Ministry of Finance and Economic Development.

European Commission. 2007*a*. *The European Labor Force Survey 2006.* Brussels, European Commission. http://circa.europa.eu/irc/dsis/employment/info/data/eu_lfs/index.htm (Accessed 27 September 2008.)

—— 2007*b*. *More and Better Aid to Education.* A Discussion Paper for the Meeting of the European Experts of the EU Member States, Norway and Switzerland, Brussels, European Commission, 7 November.

Evans, G. and Rose, P. 2007*a*. *Education and Support for Democracy in sub-Saharan Africa: Testing Mechanisms of Influence.* Paper presented at 'The Micro-Foundations of Mass Politics in Africa', East Lansing, Mich., Michigan State University, 12–13 May.

—— 2007*b*. Support for democracy in Malawi: does schooling matter? *World Development,* Vol. 35, No. 5, pp. 904–19.

Ezeamama, A. E., Friedman, J. F., Acosta, L. P., Bellinger, D. C., Langdon, G. C., Manalo, D. L., Olveda, R. M., Kurtis, J. D. and McGarvey, S. T. 2005. Helminth infection and cognitive impairment among Filipino children. *The American Journal of Tropical Medicine and Hygiene,* Vol. 72, No. 5, pp. 540–8.

Farah, M. J., Noble, K. G. and Hurt, H. 2005. Poverty, privilege and brain development: empirical findings and ethical implications. Illes, J. (ed.), *Neuroethics: Defining the Issues in Theory, Practice and Policy.* New York, Oxford University Press.

Fernald, L. C., Gertler, P. J. and Neufeld, L. M. 2008. Role of cash in conditional cash transfer programmes for child health, growth, and development: an analysis of Mexico's Oportunidades. *The Lancet,* Vol. 371, No. 9615, pp. 828–37.

Fernando, S. D., Gunawardena, D. M., Bandara, M. R. S. S., De Silva, D., Carter, R., Mendis, K. N. and Wickremasinghe, A. R. 2003. The impact of repeated malaria attacks on the school performance of children. *American Journal of Tropical Medicine and Hygiene,* Vol. 69, No. 6, pp. 582–8.

Filmer, D. 2008. Disability, poverty, and schooling in developing countries: results from 14 household surveys. *Economic Review,* Vol. 22, No. 1, pp. 141–63.

Filmer, D., Hasan, A. and Pritchett, L. 2006. *A Millennium Learning Goal: Measuring Real Progress in Education.* Washington, DC, Center for Global Development. (Working Paper, 97.)

Filmer, D. and Pritchett, L. 1999. The effect of household wealth on educational attainment: evidence from 35 countries. *Population and Development Review,* Vol. 25, No. 1, pp. 85–120.

Financial Management Reform Programme. 2005. *Social Sector Performance Surveys. Secondary Education in Bangladesh: Assessing Service Delivery.* Oxford, UK, Oxford Policy Management.

— 2006*a*. *Primary Education in Bangladesh: Assessing Service Delivery.* Dhaka, Oxford Policy Management. (Final report.)

— 2006*b*. *Social Sector Performance Surveys: Primary Education in Bangladesh: Assessing Service Delivery.* Dhaka, Oxford Policy Management.

Flores-Crespo, P. 2007. Ethnicity, identity and educational achievement in Mexico. *International Journal of Educational Development,* Vol. 27, No. 3, pp. 331–9.

Fomba, C. O. 2006. *Evaluation du Niveau d'acquisition en Français, en Mathématiques et en Sciences des Elèves des Ecoles Traditionnelles du Cycle de Base 1* [Evaluation of Achievement Level in French, Mathematics and Sciences of Students in Traditional Basic Cycle 1 Schools]. Niamey, Niger Ministry of Basic Education and Literacy, Exams and Examinations Evaluation Direction, Division of Evaluation and Monitoring of Student Achievement. (In French.)

Forum on China-Africa Cooperation. 2006. Action plan adopted at China-Africa summit, mapping cooperation course. *Beijing Summit & Third Ministerial Conference of Forum on China-Africa Cooperation.* http://english.focacsummit.org/2006-11/05/content_5167.htm (Accessed 17 July 2008.)

Forum on Educational Accountability. 2004. *Joint Organizational Statement on No Child Left Behind (NCLB) Act. October 21, 2004 (List of 144 Signers Updated April 8, 2008),* Forum on Educational Accountability. http://www.edaccountability.org/Joint_Statement.html (Accessed 19 September 2008.)

Foster, M. 2008. *Achieving Quality Primary Education For All By 2015: What More Could the UK Government Do? A study for the Global Campaign for Education UK.* Chelmsford, UK, Mick Foster Economics Ltd.

France Ministry of External and European Affairs. 2008. Déclarations Officielles de politique étrangère. Sommet Franco-Britannique: Declaration Finale [Official External Policy Statement. Anglo French Summit: Final Declaration]. *Bulletin of Current Affairs,* No. 1 April. https://pastel.diplomatie.gouv.fr/editorial/actual/ael2/bulletin.asp?liste=20080401.html&xtor=EPR-7#Chapitre1 (Accessed 16 July 2008.) (In French)

Fraser, A. 2006. *Aid-Recipient Sovereignty in Historical Perspective.* Oxford, UK, The University of Oxford & University College, The Global Economic Governance Programme.

Fredriksen, B. 2007. *School Grants: One Efficient Instrument to Address Key Barriers to Attaining Education for All.* Capacity Development Workshop 'Country Leadership and Implementation for Results in the EFA FTI Partnership', Cape Town, South Africa, 16–19 July.

FTI Secretariat. 2006. *Education For All Fast Track Initiative: Analysis of Official Development Assistance.* Washington, DC, Fast Track Initiative Secretariat.

— 2007*a*. *Catalytic Fund Beneficiary Countries Implementation Progress Report. An Update.* Washington, DC, Fast Track Initiative Secretariat.

— 2007*b*. *Quality Assurance in the Fast Track Initiative.* Washington, DC, Fast Track Initiative Secretariat.

— 2008. *Education Sector Survey 2008. Synthesis Report – Final Draft August 2008.* Washington, DC, Fast Track Initiative Secretariat.

Fuchs, T. and Wößmann, L. Forthcoming. What accounts for international differences in student performance? A re-examination using PISA data. *Empirical Economics,* Vol. 32, No. 3, pp. 433–64.

Fuller, B. 1987. What school factors raise achievement in the third world? *Review of Educational Research,* Vol. 57, No. 3, pp. 255–92.

Fuller, B. and Clarke, P. 1994. Raising school effects while ignoring culture? Local conditions and the influence of classroom tools, rules and pedagogy. *Review of Educational Research,* Vol. 64, No. 1, pp. 119–57.

Fuller, B. and Rivarola, M. 1998. *Nicaragua's Experiment to Decentralize Schools: Views of Parents, Teachers and Directors.* Washington, DC, World Bank, Development Economics Research Group. (Working Paper Series on Impact Evaluation of Education Reforms, 5.)

Galiani, S., Gertler, P. and Schargrodsky, E. Forthcoming. School decentralization: helping the good get better, but leaving the poor behind. *Journal of Public Economics.*

Gambia Bureau of Statistics. 2007. *The Gambia Multiple Indicator Cluster Survey 2005/2006 Report.* Banjul, Bureau of Statistics/UNICEF/World Bank.

Gambia Department of State for Finance and Economic Affairs. 2002. *Strategy for Poverty Alleviation (SPAII) (PRSP).* Banjul, Department of State for Finance and Economic Affairs, Strategy for Poverty Alleviation Co-ordinating Office.

— 2006. *Poverty Reduction Strategy: 2007–2011.* Banjul, Department of State for Finance and Economic Affairs. (Approved copy.)

GAVI Alliance. 2008. *Successes in Global Immunisation Boosts Progress Towards MDGs.* Geneva, Switzerland, GAVI Alliance. http://www.gavialliance.org/media_centre/press_releases/2008_06_20_annual_report.php (Accessed 27 September 2008.)

Gershberg, A. I. and Maikish, A. 2008. Targeting education funding to the poor: universal primary education, education decentralization and local level outcomes in Ghana. Background paper for *EFA Global Monitoring Report 2009.*

Gershberg, A. I. and Winkler, D. R. 2003. *Education Decentralisation in Africa: A Review of Recent Policy and Practice.* Washington, DC, World Bank.

Gertler, P. 2004. Do conditional cash transfers improve child health? Evidence from Progresa's control randomized experiment. *American Economic Review,* Vol. 94, No. 2, pp. 336–41.

Gertler, P., Patrinos, H. and Rubio-Codina, M. 2006. *Empowering Parents to Improve Education: Evidence from Rural Mexico.* Washington, DC, World Bank. (Policy Research Working Papers, 3935, Impact Evaluation Series, 4.)

Ghana National Development Planning Commission. 2003. *Ghana Poverty Reduction Strategy 2003–2005: An Agenda for Growth and Prosperity. Volume I: Analysis and Policy Statement.* Accra, National Development Planning Commission.

— 2005. *Growth and Poverty Reduction Strategy (GPRSII) (2006–2009): Economic Development and Poverty Reduction in Ghana.* Accra, National Development Planning Commission.

Gibbons, S., Machin, S. and Silva, O. 2006. *Competition, Choice and Student Achievement.* London, London School of Economics, Centre for the Economics of Education.

Giffard-Lindsay, K. 2008. Poverty reduction strategies and governance with equity for education. Four case studies: Cambodia, Ethiopia, Ghana and Nepal. Background paper for *EFA Global Monitoring Report 2009.*

Gilmore, A. 2005. *The Impact of PIRLS (2001) and TIMSS (2003) in Low-Income and Middle-Income Countries: An Evaluation of the Value of World Bank Support for International Surveys of Reading Literacy (PIRLS) and Mathematics and Science (TIMSS).* Amsterdam, International Association for the Evaluation of Educational Achievement.

Giordano, E. A. 2008. *School Clusters and Teacher Resource Centres.* Paris, UNESCO International Institute for Educational Planning. (Fundamentals of Educational Planning, 86.)

Glaeser, E. L., Ponzetto, G. and Shleifer, A. 2006. *Why Does Democracy Need Education?* Cambridge, Mass., National Bureau of Economic Research. (Working Paper, 12128.)

Glewwe, P., Ilias, N. and Kremer, M. 2003. *Teacher Incentives.* Cambridge, Mass., National Bureau of Economic Research. (Working Paper, 9671.)

Glewwe, P., Jacoby, H. G. and King, E. M. 2001. Early childhood nutrition and academic achievement: a longitudinal analysis. *Journal of Public Economics,* Vol. 81, No. 3, pp. 345–68.

Global Fund to Fight AIDS, Tuberculosis and Malaria. 2008. *Global Fund Investments Support AIDS Treatment for 1.75 Million People.* Geneva, Switzerland, Global Fund to Fight AIDS, Tuberculosis and Malaria. http://www.theglobalfund.org/en/media_center/press/pr_080609.asp (Accessed 27 September 2008.)

Global March Against Child Labour and International Center on Child Labor and Education. 2006. *Review of Child Labour, Education and Poverty Agenda: India Country Report.* New Delhi/Washington, DC, Global March Against Child Labour/International Center on Child Labor and Education.

Goetz, A.-M. and Jenkins, R. 2005. *Reinventing Accountability: Making Democracy Work for Human Development.* Basingstoke, UK, Palgrave Macmillan.

Goldring, E. and Rowley, K. J. 2006. *Parent Preferences and Parent Choices: The Public-Private Decision about School Choice.* Paper presented at the Annual Meeting of the American Educational Research Association, San Francisco, Calif., 8 April.

González, P. 2008. Governance, management and financing of educational equity-focused policies in Chile. Background paper for *EFA Global Monitoring Report 2009.*

Gordon, N. and Vegas, E. 2005. Educational finance equalization, spending, teacher quality, and student outcomes: The case of Brazil's FUNDEF. Vegas, E. (ed.), *Incentives to Improve Teaching: Lessons from Latin America.* Washington, DC, World Bank, pp. 151–86.

Göttelmann-Duret, G. and Tournier, B. 2008. Crucial management aspects of equitable teacher provision. Background paper for *EFA Global Monitoring Report 2009.*

Govinda, R. and Bandyopadhyay, M. 2008. *Access to Elementary Education in India: Country Analytical Review.* Brighton, UK/New Delhi, University of Sussex, Sussex School of Education, Centre for International Education, Consortium for Research on Educational Access, Transitions & Equity/National University of Educational Planning and Administration.

Govinda, R. and Josephine, Y. 2004. *Para Teachers in India: A Review.* Paris, UNESCO International Institute for Educational Planning. (Draft, IIEP/Prg.YD/04.XX.)

Gragnolati, M., Shekar, M., Das Gupta, M., Bredenkamp, C. and Lee, Y.-K. 2006. *India's Undernourished Children: A Call for Reform and Action.* Washington, DC, World Bank. (Health, Nutrition and Population Series.)

Grant, U. and Marcus, R. 2006. *Chronic Poverty and PRSs – A Desk Study.* Manchester, UK, University of Manchester, School of Environment and Development, Institute for Development Policy and Management, Chronic Poverty Research Centre. (Mimeo.)

Grantham-McGregor, S. 1995. A review of studies of the effects of severe malnutrition on mental development. *Journal of Nutrition,* Vol. 125, No. 8, pp. 2233–8.

Grantham-McGregor, S. and Baker-Henningham, H. 2005. Review of the evidence linking protein and energy to mental development. *Public Health Nutrition,* Vol. 8, No. 7A, pp. 1191–201.

Grantham-McGregor, S., Cheung, Y. B., Cueto, S., Glewwe, P., Richter, L., Strupp, B. and International Child Development Steering Group. 2007. Developmental potential in the first 5 years for children in developing countries. *The Lancet,* Vol. 369, No. 9555, pp. 60–70.

Greaney, V. and Kellaghan, T. 2008. *Assessing National Achievement Levels in Education.* Washington, DC, World Bank.

Greeley, M. 2007*a*. *Financing Primary Education in Afghanistan.* London, International Save the Children Alliance.

— 2007*b*. *Financing Primary Education in the Democratic Republic of the Congo.* London, International Save the Children Alliance.

Grenier, S., Jones, S., Strucker, J., Murray, T. S., Gervais, G. and Brink, S. 2008. *International Adult Literacy Survey. Learning Literacy in Canada: Evidence from the International Survey of Reading Skills.* Ottawa, Minister of Industry, Statistics Canada, Human Resources and Social Development Canada.

Grindle, M. S. 2004. Good enough governance: poverty reduction and reform in developing countries. *Governance: An International Journal of Policy, Administration and Institutions,* Vol. 17, No. 4, pp. 525–48.

Group of 8. 2005. *Africa.* G8 Summit 2005, Gleneagles, UK, Group of 8, 6–8 July.

— 2007. *Growth and Responsibility in Africa: Summit Declaration.* G8 Summit 2007, Heiligendamm, Germany, Group of G8, 8 June.

Guarcello, L., Lyon, S. and Rosati, F. C. 2006. *Child Labour and Education For All: An Issue Paper.* Rome, ILO/UNICEF/World Bank, Understanding Children's Work Project/University of Rome Tor Vergata, Faculty of Economics. (Working Paper.)

Guinea Government. 2002. *Poverty Reduction Strategy Paper: Republic of Guinea.* Conakry, Government of the Republic of Guinea.

Guinea Ministry of the Economy, Finances and Planning. 2007. *Poverty Reduction Strategy Paper PRSP-2 (2007–2010).* Conakry, Ministry of the Economy, Finances and Planning.

Guinea-Bissau Ministry of Economy. 2006. *Enquête par Grappes à Indicateurs Multiples, Guinée-Bissau, 2006, Rapport Final* [Multiple Indicator Cluster Survey, Guinea-Bissau, 2006, Final Report]. Bissau, Ministry of Economy, Secretary of State for Planning and Regional Integration. (In French.)

Guiso, L., Monte, F., Sapienza, P. and Zingales, L. 2008. Diversity: culture, gender and math. *Science,* Vol. 320, No. 5880, pp. 1164–5.

Gunnarsson, L. V., Orazem, P., Sanchez, M. and Verdisco, A. 2004. *Does Local School Control Raise Student Outcomes? Theory and Evidence on the Roles of School Autonomy and Community Participation.* Ames, Iowa, Iowa State University, Department of Economics. (Staff General Research Papers, 11417.)

Gwatkin, D. R., Rutstein, S., Johnson, K., Suliman, E., Wagstaff, A. and Amouzou, A. 2007*a*. *Socio-Economic Differences in Health, Nutrition and Population within Developing Countries: An Overview.* Washington, DC, World Bank, Human Development Network, Health, Nutrition and Population/Government of the Netherlands/Swedish International Development Cooperation Agency. (Country Reports on HNP and Poverty.)

— 2007*b*. *Socio-Economic Differences in Health, Nutrition and Population. Bangladesh: 1996/97, 1999/2000, 2004.* Washington, DC, World Bank, Human Development Network, Health, Nutrition and Population. (Country Reports on HNP and Poverty.)

— 2007*c*. *Socio-Economic Differences in Health, Nutrition and Population. Bolivia: 1998, 2003*. Washington, DC, World Bank, Human Development Network, Health, Nutrition and Population. (Country Reports on HNP and Poverty.)

— 2007*d*. *Socio-Economic Differences in Health, Nutrition and Population. Chad: 1997/97, 2004*. Washington, DC, World Bank, Human Development Network, Health, Nutrition and Population. (Country Reports on HNP and Poverty.)

— 2007*e*. *Socio-Economic Differences in Health, Nutrition and Population. Colombia: 1995, 2000, 2005*. Washington, DC, World Bank, Human Development Network, Health, Nutrition and Population. (Country Reports on HNP and Poverty.)

— 2007*f*. *Socio-Economic Differences in Health, Nutrition and Population. Dominican Republic: 1996, 2002*. Washington, DC, World Bank, Human Development Network, Health, Nutrition and Population. (Country Reports on HNP and Poverty.)

— 2007*g*. *Socio-Economic Differences in Health, Nutrition and Population. Ethiopia: 2000*. Washington, DC, World Bank, Human Development Network, Health, Nutrition and Population. (Country Reports on HNP and Poverty.)

— 2007*h*. *Socio-Economic Differences in Health, Nutrition and Population. Indonesia: 1997, 2002/03*. Washington, DC, World Bank, Human Development Network, Health, Nutrition and Population. (Country Reports on HNP and Poverty.)

— 2007*i*. *Socio-Economic Differences in Health, Nutrition and Population. Morocco: 1992, 2003/04*. Washington, DC, World Bank, Human Development Network, Health, Nutrition and Population. (Country Reports on HNP and Poverty.)

— 2007*j*. *Socio-Economic Differences in Health, Nutrition and Population. Nepal: 1996, 2001*. Washington, DC, World Bank, Human Development Network, Health, Nutrition and Population. (Country Reports on HNP and Poverty.)

— 2007*k*. *Socio-Economic Differences in Health, Nutrition and Population. Nicaragua: 1997/97, 2001*. Washington, DC, World Bank, Human Development Network, Health, Nutrition and Population. (Country Reports on HNP and Poverty.)

— 2007*l*. *Socio-Economic Differences in Health, Nutrition and Population. Nigeria: 1990, 2003*. Washington, DC, World Bank, Human Development Network, Health, Nutrition and Population. (Country Reports on HNP and Poverty.)

— 2007*m*. *Socio-Economic Differences in Health, Nutrition and Population. Philippines: 1998, 2003*. Washington, DC, World Bank, Human Development Network, Health, Nutrition and Population. (Country Reports on HNP and Poverty.)

— 2007*n*. *Socio-Economic Differences in Health, Nutrition and Population. Tanzania: 1996, 1999, 2004*. Washington, DC, World Bank, Human Development Network, Health, Nutrition and Population. (Country Reports on HNP and Poverty.)

HakiElimu. 2005. *Three Years (2002–2004) of PEDP Implementation: Key Findings from Official Reviews July 2005*. Dar es Salaam, HakiElimu.

Hallak, J. and Poisson, M. 2004. Presentation of the series. Levačiç, R. and Downes, P. (eds), *Formula Funding of Schools, Decentralization and Corruption: A Comparative Analysis*. Paris, UNESCO International Institute for Educational Planning, pp. 5–7.

— 2007. *Corrupt Schools, Corrupt Universities: What Can Be Done?* Paris, UNESCO International Institute for Educational Planning. (Ethics and Corruption in Education.)

Hallman, K., Peracca, S., Catino, J. and Ruiz, M. J. 2007. Indigenous girls in Guatemala: poverty and location. Lewis, M. and Lockheed, M. (eds), *Exclusion, Gender and Education: Case Studies from the Developing World*. Washington, DC, Center for Global Development, pp. 145–75.

Hampden-Thompson, G. and Johnston, J. S. 2006. *Variation in the Relationship Between Non-School Factors and Student Achievement on International Assessments*. Washington, DC, US Department of Education, Institute of Education Science, National Center for Education Statistics. (Statistics in Brief. NCES 2006014.)

Hampden-Thompson, G. and Pong, S.-L. 2005. Does family policy environment moderate the effect of single-parenthood on children's academic achievement? A study of 14 European countries. *Journal of Comparative Family Studies*, Vol. 36, No. 2, pp. 227–48.

Hanushek, E. A. 2003. The failure of input-based schooling policies. *Economic Journal*, Vol. 113, No. 485, pp. 64–98.

Hanushek, E. A., Jamison, D. T., Jamison, E. A. and Wößmann, L. 2008. Education and economic growth: it's not just going to school but learning that matters. *Education Next*, Vol. 8, No. 2, pp. 62–70.

Hanushek, E. A. and Luque, J. A. 2003. Efficiency and equity in schools around the world. *Economics of Education Review*, Vol. 22, No. 5, pp. 481–502.

Hanushek, E. A. and Wößmann, L. 2007. *The Role of Education Quality for Economic Growth*. Washington, DC, World Bank, Human Development Network. (Policy Research Working Paper, 4122.)

Hargreaves, A. and Shaw, P. 2006. *Knowledge and Skill Development in Developing and Transitional Economies: An Analysis of World Bank/DfID Knowledge and Skills for the Modern Economy Project*. Boston/Victoria, BC, Boston College/University of Victoria.

Harlen, W. 2007. *The Quality of Learning: Assessment Alternatives for Primary Education*. Cambridge, UK, University of Cambridge. (Interim Reports. The Primary Review. Research Survey 3/4.)

Härmä, J. 2008. *Can Choice in Primary Schooling Promote Education for All? Evidence from Private School Growth in Rural Uttar Pradesh, India*. Brighton, UK, University of Sussex, Sussex School of Education, Centre for International Education. (Unpublished.)

Harttgen, K., Klasen, S. and Misselhorn, M. 2008. Education for All? Measuring pro-poor educational outcomes in developing countries. Background paper for *EFA Global Monitoring Report 2009*.

Harvard University Center on the Developing Child. 2007. *A Science-Based Framework for Early Childhood Policy: Using Evidence to Improve Outcomes in Learning, Behavior and Health for Vulnerable Children.* Cambridge, Mass., Harvard University, Center on the Developing Child, National Scientific Council on the Developing Child, National Forum on Early Childhood Program Evaluation.

Haskins, R. 2008. *Testimony, House Committee on Education and Labor. Investing in Early Education: Paths to Improving Children's Success.* Washington, DC, Brookings Institution. (Testimony to the House Committee on Education and Labor, 23 January 2008.)

Haveman, R., Wolfe, B. and Spaulding, J. 1991. Childhood events and circumstances influencing high school completion. *Demography,* Vol. 28, No. 1, pp. 133–57.

Hayman, R. 2007. Are the MDGs enough? Donor perspectives and recipient visions of education and poverty reduction in Rwanda. *International Journal of Educational Development,* Vol. 27, No. 4, pp. 371–82.

Heckman, J. J. 2008. Schools, skills and synapses. *Economic Inquiry,* Vol. 46, No. 3, pp. 289–324.

Heckman, J. J. and Masterov, D. V. 2004. *The Productivity Argument for Investing in Young Children.* Invest in Kids Working Group, Washington, DC, Committee on Economic Development, 4 December.

Herz, B. and Sperling, G. B. 2004. *What Works in Girls' Education: Evidence and Policies from the Developing World.* New York, Council on Foreign Relations Press.

Heyneman, S. P. and Loxley, W. A. 1983. The effect of primary-school quality on academic achievement across twenty-nine high- and low-income countries. *The American Journal of Sociology,* Vol. 88, No. 6, pp. 1162–94.

Hirschman, A. O. 1970. *Exit, Voice and Loyalty: Responses to Decline in Firms, Organizations and States.* Cambridge, Mass./London, Harvard University Press.

Hoffmann, A. M. and Olson, R. 2006. *Freedom as Learning: Life Skills Education and Sustainable Human Development in a World with HIV and AIDS.* New York, UNICEF.

Hoppers, W. 2007. Meeting the learning needs of all young people and adults: an exploration of successful policies and strategies in non-formal education. Background paper for *EFA Global Monitoring Report 2008*.

Hossain, N. 2007. Expanding access to education in Bangladesh. Narayan, D. and Glinskaya, E. (eds), *Ending Poverty in South Asia: Ideas that Work.* Washington, DC, World Bank, pp. 304–25.

Hoxby, C. M. 2003. School choice and school productivity: could school choice be a tide that lifts all boats? Hoxby, C. M. (ed.), *The Economics of School Choice.* Chicago, Ill., University of Chicago Press, pp. 287–342. (A National Bureau of Economic Research Conference Report.)

Hoxby, C. M. and Murarka, S. 2008. New York charter schools: how well are they teaching their students? *Education Next,* Vol. 8, No. 3, pp. 54–61.

Hubbard, P. 2007. *Putting the Power of Transparency in Context: Information's Role in Reducing Corruption in Uganda's Education Sector.* Washington, DC, Center for Global Development. (Working Paper, 135.)

Huong, P. L. 2006. *Fiscal Decentralisation from Central to sub-National Government in Viet Nam.* Paper presented at the Seventh Annual Global Development Conference, Institutions and Development: At the Nexus of Global Change, St Petersburg, Russian Federation, 20 January.

Huq, M. N. and Tasnim, T. 2008. Maternal education and child healthcare in Bangladesh. *Maternal and Child Health Journal,* Vol. 12, No. 1, pp. 43–51.

ILO. 2006. *Report of the Director-General. The End of Child Labour: Within Reach. Global Report under the Follow-Up to the ILO Declaration on Fundamental Principles and Rights at Work. Report I (B).* International Labour Conference, 95th Session 2006, Geneva, Switzerland, International Labour Organization.

—— 2008. *LABORSTAT Internet. Statistics: Total and Economically Active Population. Economically Active Population Estimates and Projections 1980-2020 (EAPEP).* Geneva, International Labour Organization. http://laborsta.ilo.org/ (Accessed 27 September 2008.)

IMF. 2006. *Senegal: Poverty Reduction Strategy Paper.* Washington, DC, International Monetary Fund. (IMF Country Report, 07/316.)

International Development Association and IMF. 2006. *Nepal: Poverty Reduction Strategy Paper Annual Progress Report – Joint Staff Advisory Note.* Washington, DC, International Monetary Fund. (IMF Country Report, 06/443.)

International Institute for Population Sciences and Macro International Inc. 2007. *National Family Health Survey (NFHS-3), 2005–06. India: Volume 1.* Mumbai, India, International Institute for Population Sciences.

International Organization for Migration. 2005. *World Migration 2005: Costs and Benefits of International Migration.* Geneva, Switzerland, International Organization for Migration; Migration Policy, Research and Communication Department.

International Telecommunication Union. 2008. *World Telecommunication/ICT Indicators Database 2007 (11th Edition).* Geneva, Switzerland, International Telecommunication Union. http://www.itu.int/ITU-D/ict/publications/world/world.html (Accessed 27 September 2008.)

Jack, A. 2008. Incentives nudge Mexico's poor in right direction. *Financial Times.* http://www.ft.com/cms/s/0/f02a781e-670d-11dd-808f-0000779fd18c.html?nclick_check=1 (Accessed 16 September 2008.)

Jaramillo, A. and Mingat, A. 2008. Early childhood care and education in sub-Saharan Africa: what would it take to meet the Millennium Development Goals? Garcia, M., Pence, A. and Evans, J. L. (eds), *Africa's Future, Africa's Challenge: Early Childhood Care and Development in sub-Saharan Africa.* Washington, DC, World Bank, Human Development, pp. 51–70. (Directions in Development, 42700.)

Jayasuriya, R. and Wodon, Q. T. 2007. Efficiency in improving health and education outcomes: provincial and state-level estimates for Argentina and Mexico. *Estudios Económicos,* Vol. 22, No. 1, pp. 57–97.

Jayaweera, S. and Gunawardena, C. 2007. *Social Inclusion: Gender and Equity in Education SWAps in South Asia – Sri Lanka Case Study.* Kathmandu, UNICEF Regional Office for South Asia.

Jimenez, E. and Sawada, Y. 1999. Do community-managed schools work? An evaluation of El Salvador's EDUCO program. *The World Bank Economic Review,* Vol. 13, No. 3, pp. 415–41.

—— 2003. *Does Community Management Help Keep Kids in Schools? Evidence Using Panel Data from El Salvador's EDUCO Program.* Tokyo, University of Tokyo, Faculty of Economics. (CIRJE Discussion Papers, CIRJE-F-236.)

Jukes, M. C., Nokes, C. A., Alcock, K. J., Lambo, J. K., Kihamia, C., Ngorosho, N., Mbise, A., Lorri, W., Yona, E., Mwanri, L., Baddeley, A. D., Hall, A., Bundy, D. A. and Partnership for Child Development. 2002. Heavy schistosomiasis associated with poor short-term memory and slower reaction times in Tanzanian schoolchildren. *Tropical Medicine and International Health,* Vol. 7, No. 2, pp. 104–17.

Kadzamira, E. C. 2006. *Teacher Motivation and Incentives in Malawi.* Zomba, Malawi, University of Malawi, Centre for Educational Research and Training.

Kadzamira, E. C., Moran, D., Mulligan, J., Ndirenda, N., Nthara, K., Reed, B. and Rose, P. 2004. *Country Studies. Malawi: Study of Non-State Providers of Basic Services.* Birmingham, UK, University of Birmingham, School of Public Policy, International Development Department. (Commissioned by UK Department for International Development, Policy Division.)

Kanjee, A. Forthcoming. Supporting teachers improve classroom assessment practices in rural schools: evaluation of the assessment resources banks in South Africa. *Education as Change.*

Kano State Ministry of Education. 2008. *Education Sector Analysis.* Kano, Nigeria, Kano State Ministry of Education.

Kapur, D. and Crowley, M. 2008. *Beyond the ABCs: Higher Education and Developing Countries.* Washington, DC, Center for Global Development. (Working Paper, 139.)

Kaufmann, D., Kraay, A. and Mastruzzi, M. 2007. *Governance Matters VI: Aggregate and Individual Governance Indicators 1996–2006.* Washington, DC, World Bank. (Policy Research Working Paper, 4280.)

Keeves, J. P. 1995. *The World of School Learning: Selected Key Findings from 35 Years of IEA Research.* The Hague, International Association for the Evaluation of Educational Achievement.

Kellaghan, T. and Greaney, V. 2004. *Assessing Student Learning in Africa.* Washington, DC, World Bank. (Directions in Development.)

Kelly, M. J. 2004. Preventing HIV transmission through education. Coombe, C. (ed.), *The HIV Challenge to Education: A Collection of Essays.* Paris, UNESCO International Institute for Educational Planning. (Education in the Context of HIV/AIDS.)

Khan, F. 2007. School management councils: a lever for mobilizing social capital in rural Punjab, Pakistan? *Prospects: Quarterly Review of Comparative Education,* Vol. 37, No. 1, pp. 57–79.

King, E. M. and Cordeiro Guerra, S. 2005. Education reforms in East Asia: policy, process and impact. World Bank (ed.), *East Asia Decentralizes: Making Local Government Work.* Washington, DC, World Bank, pp. 179–207.

King, E. M. and Ozler, B. 1988. *What's Decentralization Got to Do With Learning? The Case of Nicaragua's School Autonomy Reform.* Washington, DC, World Bank. (Working Paper Series on Impact Evaluation of Education Reforms, 9.)

King, E. M. and van de Walle, D. 2007. Girls in Lao PDR: ethnic affiliation, poverty and location. Lewis, M. and Lockheed, M. (eds), *Exclusion, Gender and Education: Case Studies from the Developing World.* Washington, DC, Center for Global Development, pp. 31–70.

King, K. and Palmer, R. 2008. *Skills for Work, Growth and Poverty Reduction: Challenges and Opportunities in the Global Analysis and Monitoring of Skills in Relation to Dakar Goal 3 and Beyond.* Edinburgh, UK, University of Edinburgh, Centre of African Studies. (Draft paper submitted to the UK National Commission for UNESCO's Education Committee [Education for All Working Group] and the British Council.)

Kingdon, G. G. 2006. *The Progress of School Education in India.* Oxford, UK, University of Oxford, Global Poverty Research Group, an Economics & Social Research Council Research Group. (Working Papers Series, GPRG-WPS-071.)

Kirk, J. 2008. Teacher management issues in fragile states: illustrative examples from Afghanistan and Southern Sudan. Background paper for *EFA Global Monitoring Report 2009.*

Kremer, M., Chaudhury, N., Rogers, F. H., Muralidharan, K. and Hammer, J. 2005. Teacher absence in India: a snapshot. *Journal of the European Economic Association,* Vol. 3, No. 2–3, pp. 658–67.

Kremer, M. and Miguel, E. 2007. The illusion of sustainability. *The Quarterly Journal of Economics,* Vol. 122, No. 3, pp. 1007–136.

Kyrgyz Republic National Statistical Committee and UNICEF. 2007. *Multiple Indicator Cluster Survey 2006, Kyrgyz Republic. Final Report.* Bishkek, National Statistical Committee/UNICEF.

Lacireno-Paquet, N. and Brantley, C. 2008. *Who Chooses Schools, And Why?* Tempe, Ariz./Boulder, Colo., Arizona State University, College of Education, Division of Educational Leadership and Policy Studies, Education Policy Research Unit/University of Colorado, School of Education, Education and the Public Interest Center.

Levels, M., Dronkers, J. and Kraaykamp, G. 2007. *Educational Achievement of Immigrants in Western Countries: Origin, Destination and Community Effects on Mathematical Performance.* San Domenico di Fiesole, Italy, European University Institute. (SPS Working Papers, 2007/05.)

Lewis, M. and Lockheed, M. 2006. *Inexcusable Absence: Why 60 Million Girls Still Aren't in School and What To Do about It.* Washington, DC, Center for Global Development.

— 2008. *Social Exclusion and the Gender Gap in Education.* Washington, DC, World Bank, Human Development Network, Chief Economist's Office. (Policy Research Working Paper, 4562.)

Lindert, K., Linder, A., Hobbs, J. and de la Brière, B. 2007. *The Nuts and Bolts of Brazil's Bolsa Família Program: Implementing Conditional Cash Transfers in a Decentralized Context.* Washington, DC, World Bank. (Social Protection Discussion Paper, 0709.)

Lloyd, C. B., Mete, C. and Grant, M. 2007. Rural girls in Pakistan: constraints of policy and culture. Lewis, M. and Lockheed, M. (eds), *Exclusion, Gender and Education: Case Studies from the Developing World.* Washington, DC, Center for Global Development, pp. 99–118.

Lockheed, M. 2008. *Measuring Progress with Tests of Learning: Pros and Cons for 'Cash on Delivery Aid' in Education.* Washington, DC, Center for Global Development. (Working Paper, 147.)

Lockheed, M. and Verspoor, A. 1991. *Improving Primary Education in Developing Countries.* Oxford, UK, Oxford University Press.

Lubienski, C. 2008. School choice research in the United States and why it doesn't matter: the evolving economy of knowledge production in a contested policy domain. Forsey, M., Davies, S. and Walford, G. (eds), *The Globalisation of School Choice?* Oxford, UK, Symposium Books, pp. 27–54.

Lugaz, C. and De Grauwe, A. 2006. *École et Décentralisation: Résultats d'une Recherche en Afrique Francophone de l'Ouest* [School and Decentralization: Results of Research in Francophone West Africa]. Paris, UNESCO International Institute for Educational Planning. (In French.)

Ma, X. 2007. Gender differences in learning outcomes. Background paper for *EFA Global Monitoring Report 2008.*

— 2008. A global perspective on socioeconomic differences in learning outcomes. Background paper for *EFA Global Monitoring Report 2009.*

Macedonia State Statistical Office. 2007. *Multiple Indicator Cluster Survey: 2005–2006. Final Report.* Skopje, State Statistical Office.

Macro International Inc. 2008. *STATcompiler.* Calverton, Md., Macro International Inc., MEASURE DHS. http://www.statcompiler.com/ (Accessed 27 September 2008.)

Madagascar Government. 2003. *Poverty Reduction Strategy Paper.* Antananarivo, Government of the Republic of Madagascar.

— 2007. *Madagascar Action Plan 2007–2012: A Bold and Exciting Plan for Rapid Development.* Antananarivo, Government of the Republic of Madagascar.

Madagascar Ministry of National Education & Scientific Research and UNESCO. 2004. *Education de Qualité pour Tous. Enquête sur les Acquis Scolaires des Élèves de la 8eme Année en Mathématiques et en Sciences Liées à la Vie Courante, MLA II: Rapport National* [Quality Education for All. Survey of 8th Year Student Achievement in Mathematics and Sciences Related to Everyday Life, MLA II, National Report]. Antananarivo/Paris, Ministry of National Education & Scientific Research/UNESCO. (In French.)

Magnuson, K. A. and Waldfogel, J. 2005. Early childhood care and education: effects on ethnic and racial gaps in school readiness. *The Future of Children,* Vol. 15, No. 1, pp. 169–96.

Malawi Government. 2002. *Malawi Poverty Reduction Strategy Paper.* Lilongwe, Government of Malawi. (Final Draft.)

— 2006. *Malawi Growth and Development Strategy: From Poverty to Prosperity 2006–2011.* Lilongwe, Government of Malawi.

Malhotra, A. and Schuler, S. R. 2005. Women's empowerment as a variable in international development. Narayan, D. (ed.), *Measuring Empowerment: Cross-disciplinary Perspectives.* Washington, DC, World Bank, pp. 71–88.

Mali Government. 2006. *Growth and Poverty Reduction Strategy Paper.* Bamako, Government of the Republic of Mali.

Mali Ministry of Economy and Finance. 2002. *Poverty Reduction Strategy Paper.* Bamako, Ministry of Economy and Finance. (Final Draft.)

Maluccio, J. A. and Flores, R. 2004. *Impact Evaluation of a Conditional Cash Transfer Program: The Nicaraguan Red de Protección Social.* Washington, DC, International Food Policy Research Institute, Food Consumption and Nutrition Division. (FCND Discussion Paper, 184.)

Maluccio, J. A., Hoddinott, J., Behrman, J. R., Martorell, R., Quisumbing, A. R. and Stein, A. D. 2006. *The Impact of Nutrition during Early Childhood on Education among Guatemalan Adults.* Philadelphia, Penn., University of Pennsylvania, Department of Economics, Penn Institute for Economic Research. (Working Paper, 06-026.)

Marcus, R. 2007. *Social Protection Transfers for Chronically Poor People.* Manchester, UK, University of Manchester, School of Environment and Development, Institute for Development Policy and Management, Chronic Poverty Research Centre. (Policy Brief, 2.)

Marks, G. N. 2008. Accounting for the gender gaps in student performance in reading and mathematics: evidence from 31 countries. *Oxford Review of Education,* Vol. 34, No. 1, pp. 89–109.

Maurer, M. 2005. An exploratory study of conceptualisations of literacy, numeracy and life skills based on the 2004 series of national reports. Background paper prepared for *EFA Global Monitoring Report 2005.*

Mauritania Government. 2000. *Poverty Reduction Strategy Paper.* Nouakchott, Government of the Islamic Republic of Mauritania.

— 2006. *Poverty Reduction Strategy Paper Action Plan 2006–2010.* Nouakchott, Government of the Islamic Republic of Mauritania.

McEwan, P. 2004. The indigenous test score gap in Bolivia and Chile. *Economic Development and Cultural Change,* Vol. 53, No. 1, pp. 157–90.

— Forthcoming. Can schools reduce the indigenous test score gap? Evidence from Chile. *Journal of Development Studies.*

McEwan, P. and Trowbridge, M. 2007. The achievement of indigenous students in Guatemalan primary schools. *International Journal of Educational Development,* Vol. 27, No. 1, pp. 61–76.

McLanahan, S. and Sandefur, G. 1994. *Growing Up With a Single Parent: What Hurts, What Helps.* Cambridge, Mass., Harvard University Press.

MDRC. 2007. *MDRC to Help Design and Evaluate Mayor Bloomberg's 'Opportunity NYC' Initiative.* New York, MDRC. http://www.mdrc.org/announcement_hp_122.html (Accessed 27 September 2008.)

Meade, B. and Gershberg, A. 2008. Restructuring towards equity? Examining recent efforts to better target education resources to the poor in Colombia. Background paper for *EFA Global Monitoring Report 2009.*

Mehrotra, S. and Panchamukhi, P. R. 2007. Universalising elementary education in India: is the private sector the answer? Srivastava, P. and Walford, G. (eds), *Private Schooling in Less Economically Developed Countries: Asian and African Perspectives.* Oxford, UK, Symposium Books, pp. 129–52.

Merle, V. 2004. *Draft: Developing an International Survey on Adult Skills and Competencies – Aims and Methodological Issues.* Programme for International Assessment of Adult Competencies (PIAAC), Paris, OECD, 26–27 April.

Meza, D., Guzmán, J. L. and de Varela, L. 2006. *EDUCO: Schools Managed by the Community in Rural Areas of El Salvador (1991–2005).* Latin American Lessons in Promoting Education for All, Cartagena de Indias, Colombia, World Bank/Inter-American Development Bank, 9–11 October.

Michaelowa, K. 2004*a*. *Aid Effectiveness Reconsidered: Panel Data Evidence for the Education Sector.* Hamburg, Germany, Hamburg Institute of International Economics. (HWWA Discussion Paper, 264.)

— 2004*b*. *Quality and Equity of Learning Outcomes in Francophone Africa.* Montreal, Que, UNESCO Institute for Statistics. (Processed.)

Miguel, E. and Kremer, M. 2004. Worms: identifying impacts on education and health in the presence of treatment externalities. *Econometrica,* Vol. 72, No. 1, pp. 159–217.

Minot, N. 2008. *The Food Crisis and its Implications for Agricultural Development.* Washington, DC, International Food Policy Research Institute. (Testimony presented to the US House Agriculture Committee, Subcommittee on Specialty Crops, Rural Development and Foreign Agriculture, 16 July 2008.)

Miron, G., Evergreen, S. and Urschel, J. 2008. *The Impact of School Choice Reforms on Student Achievement.* Tempe, Ariz./Boulder, Colo., Arizona State University, College of Education, Division of Educational Leadership and Policy Studies, Education Policy Research Unit/University of Colorado, School of Education, Education and the Public Interest Center. (School Choice: Evidence and Recommendations.)

Mizala, A. and Romaguera, P. 2000. *Determinación de Factores Explicativos de los Resultados Escolares en Educación Media en Chile* [Identification of Explanatory Factors of School Outcomes in Middle Education in Chile]. Santiago, Universidad de Chile, Centro de Economía Aplicada. (Documentos de trabajo, 85.) (In Spanish.)

Mizala, A., Romaguera, P. and Farren, D. 1998. *Eficiencia Técnica de los Establecimientos Educacionales en Chile* [Technical Efficiency of Educational Establishments in Chile]. Santiago, Universidad de Chile, Centro de Economía Aplicada. (Documentos de trabajo, 38.) (In Spanish.)

Molnar, A. 1999. *Educational Vouchers: A Review of the Research.* Milwaukee, Wis., University of Wisconsin-Milwaukee School of Education, Center for Education Research, Analysis and Innovation. (CERAI-99-21.)

Momoniat, I. 2003. *Fiscal Decentralisation in South Africa: A Practitioner's Perspective.* Washington, DC, World Bank.

Mongolia Ministry of Education, Culture and Science and UNICEF. 2008. *Basic Education Learning Achievement Study–2007.* Ulaanbaatar, Ministry of Education, Culture and Science/UNICEF.

Mongolia National Statistical Office and UNICEF. 2007. *The Mongolia Child and Development 2005 Survey (MICS-3), Final Report.* Ulaanbaatar, National Statistical Office/UNICEF.

Montenegro Statistical Office and Strategic Marketing Research Agency. 2006. *Montenegro Multiple Indicator Cluster Survey 2005, Final Report.* Podgorica, Statistical Office/Strategic Marketing Research Agency.

Morduchowicz, A. and Duro, L. 2007. *La Inversión Educativa en América Latina y el Caribe: Las Demandas de Financiamiento y Asignación de Recursos* [Education Investment in Latin America and the Caribbean: Financing Demands and Resource Allocation]. Buenos Aires, UNESCO International Institute for Educational Planning, Sede Regional Buenos Aires. (Contribución preparada a solicitud de la Oficina Regional de Educación para América Latina y el Caribe en el marco de la II Reunión Intergubernamental del Proyecto Regional de Educación para América Latina y el Caribe, 29 y 30 de marzo de 2007, Buenos Aires, Argentina.) (In Spanish.)

Morley, L. 2005. *Gender Equity in Commonwealth Higher Education: Research Findings.* London, University of London, Institute of Education, Centre for Higher Education Studies. (Working Paper, 6.)

Mosse, D. 2004. Power relations and poverty reduction. Alsop, R. (ed.), *Power, Rights and Poverty: Concepts and Connections.* Washington, DC, World Bank, pp. 51–67.

Mozambique Government. 2001. *Action Plan for the Reduction of Absolute Poverty (2001–2005) (PARPA).* Maputo, Government of the Republic of Mozambique. (Final Draft.)

— 2006. *Action Plan for the Reduction of Absolute Poverty 2006–2009 (PARPA II).* Maputo, Government of the Republic of Mozambique.

Mugisha, F. 2008. *School Choice among Slum and Non-Slum Communities in Nairobi, Kenya: The Realities After Free Primary Education.* Nairobi, African Population and Health Research Center.

Mullis, I. V. S., Martin, M. O., Fierros, E. G., Goldberg, A. L. and Stemler, S. E. 2000. *Gender Differences in Achievement: IEA's Third International Mathematics and Science Study.* Chestnut Hill, Mass., Boston College, Lynch School of Education, International Study Center/International Association for the Evaluation of Educational Achievement.

Mullis, I. V. S., Martin, M. O., Gonzalez, E. J. and Kennedy, A. M. 2003. *PIRLS 2001 International Report: IEA's Study of Reading Literacy Achievement in Primary Schools in 35 Countries.* Chestnut Hill, Mass., Boston College, Lynch School of Education, International Study Center/International Association for the Evaluation of Educational Achievement.

Mullis, I. V. S., Martin, M. O., Kennedy, A. M. and Foy, P. 2007. *PIRLS 2006 International Report: IEA's Progress in International Reading Literacy Study in Primary School in 40 Countries.* Chestnut Hill, Mass., Boston College, Lynch School of Education, TIMSS & PIRLS International Study Center/International Association for the Evaluation of Educational Achievement.

Mundy, K., Cherry, S., Haggerty, M., Maclure, R. and Sivasubramaniam, M. 2007. *Basic Education, Civil Society Participation and the New Aid Architecture: Lessons from Burkina Faso, Kenya, Mali and Tanzania.* Toronto, University of Toronto, Ontario Institute for Studies in Education.

Muralidharan, K. and Kremer, M. 2006. *Public and Private Schools in Rural India.* Cambridge, Mass., Harvard University, Department of Economics.

Muralidharan, K. and Sundararaman, V. 2006. *Teacher Incentives in Developing Countries: Experimental Evidence from India.* Boston, Mass., Harvard University, Department of Economics. (Job Market Paper.)

Murnane, R. J., Willet, J. B. and Cárdenas, S. 2006. *Did Participation of Schools in Programa Escuelas de Calidad (PEC) Influence Student Outcomes?* Cambridge, Mass., Harvard University, Graduate School of Education. (Mimeo.)

N'tchougan-Sonou, C. H. 2001. Automatic promotion or large-scale repetition – which path to quality? *International Journal of Educational Development,* Vol. 21, No. 2, pp. 149–62.

Naidoo, J. P. 2005. *Educational Decentralization and School Governance in South Africa: From Policy to Practice.* Paris, UNESCO International Institute for Educational Planning.

National Agency to Fight Illiteracy. 2007. *Illiteracy: The Statistics. Analysis by the National Survey to Fight Illiteracy of the IVQ Survey Conducted in 2004-2005 by INSEE.* Lyon, France, National Agency to Fight Illiteracy.

National Scientific Council on the Developing Child. 2007. *Science Briefs: How Early Child Care Affects Later Development.* Cambridge, Mass., Harvard University, Center on the Developing Child. http://www.developingchild.net/pubs/sb/pdf/Early_Child_Care.pdf (Accessed 27 September 2008.)

Nepal Ministry of Education and Sports. 2006. *Flash I Report 2064 (2007–08).* Sanothimi, Bhaktapur, Nepal, Ministry of Education and Sports, Department of Education.

Nepal National Planning Commission. 2005. *An Assessment of the Implementation of the Tenth Plan (PRSP). Second Progress Report: On the Road to Freedom from Poverty.* Kathmandu, National Planning Commission.

Netherlands Ministry of Foreign Affairs. 2006. *Dutch Humanitarian Assistance: An Evaluation.* The Hague, Ministry of Foreign Affairs, Policy and Operations Evaluation Department. (IOB Evaluations, 33.)

Ni, Y. 2007. *Do Traditional Public Schools Benefit from Charter School Competition? Evidence from Michigan.* New York, Columbia University, National Center for the Study of Privatization in Education. (145.)

Nicaragua Government. 2001. *A Strengthened Growth and Poverty Reduction Strategy.* Managua, Government of the Republic of Nicaragua.

— 2005. *National Development Plan.* Managua, Government of the Republic of Nicaragua.

Nielsen, H. D. 2007. Empowering communities for improved educational outcomes: some evaluation findings from the World Bank. *Prospects: Quarterly Review of Comparative Education,* Vol. 37, No. 1, pp. 81–93.

Nigeria Federal Ministry of Education, UNICEF and UNESCO. 2005. *Monitoring of Learning Achievement Project 2003: Assessment of Learning Achievement of Primary Four & Primary Six Pupils. National Report.* Abuja, Federal Ministry of Education, Education Sector Analysis/UNICEF/UNESCO.

Nigeria National Bureau of Statistics. 2006*a*. *Core Welfare Indicator Questionnaire Survey 2006.* Abuja, National Bureau of Statistics.

— 2006*b*. *Draft Report on Nigeria Living Standard Survey 2003/2004.* Abuja, National Bureau of Statistics.

Nigeria National Population Commission and ORC Macro. 2004. *Nigeria DHS EdData Survey 2004: Education Data for Decision-Making.* Abuja/Calverton, Md., National Population Commission/ORC Macro.

Noble, K. G., McCandliss, B. D. and Farah, M. J. 2007. Socioeconomic gradients predict individual differences in neurocognitive abilities. *Developmental Science,* Vol. 10, No. 4, pp. 464–80.

Nores, M., Belfield, C. R., Barnett, W. S. and Schweinhart, L. 2005. Updating the economic impacts of the High/Scope Perry Preschool Program. *Educational Evaluation and Policy Analysis,* Vol. 27, No. 3, pp. 245–61.

Nzomo, J. and Makuwa, D. 2006. How can countries move from cross-national research results to dissemination and then to policy reform? (Case studies from Kenya and Namibia). Ross, K. N. and Genevois, I. J. (eds), *Cross-National Studies of the Quality of Education: Planning Their Design and Managing Their Impact.* Paris, UNESCO International Institute for Educational Planning.

Obwona, M., Steffensen, J., Trollegaad, S., Mwanga, Y., Luwangwa, F., Twodo, B., Ojoo, A. and Seguya, F. 2000. *Fiscal Decentralisation and sub-National Government Finance in Relation to Infrastructure and Service Provision in Uganda.* Copenhagen/Kampala, National Association of Local Authorities in Denmark/Economic Policy Research Centre. (Fiscal Decentralisation and sub-National Finance in Africa, Main Report.)

OECD. 2006*a*. *Demand-Sensitive Schooling? Evidence and Issues.* Paris, Organisation for Economic Co-operation and Development, Centre for Educational Research and Innovation. (Education & Skills.)

— 2006*b*. *Where Immigrant Students Succeed: A Comparative Review of Performance and Engagement in PISA 2003.* Paris, Organisation for Economic Co-operation and Development, Programme for International Student Assessment.

— 2007*a*. *Education at a Glance 2007: OECD Indicators.* Paris, Organisation for Economic and Development Co-operation.

— 2007*b*. *PISA 2006: Science Competencies for Tomorrow's World. Volume 1 – Analysis.* Paris, Organisation for Economic Co-operation and Development, Programme for International Student Assessment.

— 2007*c*. *PISA 2006: Science Competencies for Tomorrow's World. Volume 2 – Data.* Paris, Organisation for Economic Co-operation and Development, Programme for International Student Assessment.

— 2008*a*. *OECD Family Database.* Paris, Organisation for Economic Co-operation and Development; Directorate for Employment, Labour and Social Affairs. http://www.oecd.org/document/4/0,3343,en_2649_34819_37836996_1_1_1_1,00.html (Accessed 27 September 2008.)

— 2008*b*. *OECD.Stat.* Paris, Organisation for Economic Co-operation and Development. http://stats.oecd.org/wbos/Index.aspx?usercontext=sourceoecd (Beta Version.) (Accessed 22 September 2008.)

OECD-DAC. 2005. *Paris Declaration on Aid Effectiveness: Harmonization, Alignment, Results and Mutual Accountability.* High Level Forum on Aid Effectiveness, Paris, Organisation for Economic Co-operation and Development, Development Co-operation Directorate, Development Assistance Committee, 28 February–2 March.

— 2007*a*. *DAC List of ODA Recipients: Effective from 2006 for Reporting on Flows in 2005, 2006 and 2007.* Paris, Organisation for Economic Co-operation and Development, Development Co-operation Directorate, Development Assistance Committee. www.oecd.org/dac/stats/daclist (Accessed 5 October 2007.)

— 2007*b*. *Summary of Partner Country Consultation on the Preparation of the Accra High Level Forum on Aid Effectiveness.* Prepared for Third High Level Forum on Aid Effectiveness, Accra, OECD-DAC, 2–4 September 2008.

— 2008*a*. *2008 Survey on Monitoring the Paris Declaration. Effective Aid by 2010? What It Will Take? Vol. 1: Overview.* Prepared for Third High Level Forum on Aid Effectiveness, Accra, OECD-DAC, 2–4 September.

— 2008*b*. *Development Co-operation Report 2007.* Paris, Organisation for Economic Co-operation and Development, Development Co-operation Directorate, Development Assistance Committee.

— 2008*c*. *International Development Statistics: Online Databases on Aid and Other Resource Flows.* Paris, Organisation for Economic Co-operation and Development, Development Co-operation Directorate, Development Assistance Committee. www.oecd.org/dac/stats/idsonline (Accessed 17 July 2008.)

— 2008d. *Scaling Up: Aid Fragmentation, Aid Allocation and Aid Predictability. Report of 2008 Survey of Aid Allocation Policies and Indicative Forward Spending Plans.* Paris, Organisation for Economic Co-operation and Development, Development Co-operation Directorate, Development Assistance Committee. (OECD Journal on Development.)

O'Malley, B. 2007. *Education under Attack: A Global Study on Targeted Political and Military Violence against Education Staff, Students, Teachers, Union and Government Officials and Institutions.* Paris, UNESCO.

Oosterbeek, H., Ponce, J. and Schady, N. 2008. *The Impact of Cash Transfers on School Enrollment: Evidence from Ecuador.* Washington, DC, World Bank, Development Research Group, Human Development and Public Services Team. (Impact Evaluation Series, 22. Policy Research Working Paper, 4645.)

Osungbade, K., Oginni, S. and Olumide, A. 2008. Content of antenatal care services in secondary health care facilities in Nigeria: implications for quality of maternal health care. *International Journal for Quality in Health Care,* Vol. 20, No. 5, pp. 346–51.

Oxfam International. 2004. *From 'Donorship' to Ownership? Moving towards PRSP, Round Two.* Washington, DC, Oxfam International. (Oxfam Briefing Paper, 51.)

Paes de Barros, R. and Mendonça, R. 1998. The impact of three institutional innovations in Brazilian education. Savedoff, W. D. (ed.), *Organization Matters: Agency Problems in Health and Education in Latin America.* Washington, DC, Inter-American Development Bank, pp. 75–130.

Paixão, M. and Carvano, L. (eds). 2008. *Relatório Anual das Desigualdades Raciais no Brasil* [Annual Report on Racial Inequalities in Brazil]. Rio de Janeiro, Brazil, Garamont.

Pakistan Ministry of Education. 2006. *National Education Census: District Education Statistics.* Islamabad, Ministry of Education.

Pandey, S. 2006. Para-teacher scheme and quality education for all in India: policy perspectives and challenges for school effectiveness. *Journal of Education for Teaching,* Vol. 32, No. 3, p. 319.

Park, H. 2008. The varied educational effects of parent-child communication: a comparative study of fourteen countries. *Comparative Education Review,* Vol. 52, No. 2, pp. 219–43.

Parker, C. E. 2005. Teacher incentives and student achievement in Nicaraguan Autonomous Schools. Vegas, E. (ed.), *Incentives to Improve Teaching: Lessons from Latin America.* Washington, DC, World Bank, pp. 359–88.

Patrinos, H. A. 2007. *The Living Conditions of Children.* Washington, DC, World Bank. (Policy Research Working Paper, 4251.)

Patrinos, H. A. and Kagia, R. 2007. Maximizing the performance of education systems: the case of teacher absenteeism. Campos, J. E. and Pradhan, S. (eds), *The Many Faces of Corruption: Tracking Vulnerabilities at the State Sector.* Washington, DC, World Bank, pp. 63–87.

Patrinos, H. A. and Sosale, S. 2007. Public-private partnerships in education. Patrinos, H. A. and Sosale, S. (eds), *Mobilizing the Private Sector for Public Education: A View from the Trenches.* Washington, DC, World Bank, pp. 1–10.

Paxson, C. and Schady, N. 2005. *Cognitive Development among Young Children in Ecuador: The Roles of Wealth, Health and Parenting.* Washington, DC, World Bank. (Policy Research Working Paper, 3605.)

— 2007. *Does Money Matter? The Effects of Cash Transfers on Child Health and Development in Rural Ecuador.* Washington, DC, World Bank. (Impact Evaluation Series, 15. Policy Research Working Paper, 4226.)

Penny, A., Ward, M., Read, T. and Bines, H. 2008. Education sector reform: the Ugandan experience. *International Journal of Educational Development,* Vol. 28, No. 3, pp. 268–85.

Peterson, P. E. and Howell, W. G. 2006. *The Education Gap: Vouchers and Urban Schools,* Rev. edn. Washington, DC, Brookings Institution Press.

Pirnay, E. 2007. *Increasing Aid Effectiveness in the Cambodian Education Sector: Analysis and Recommendations.* Phnom Penh, European Commission.

Pong, S.-L., Dronkers, J. and Hampden-Thompson, G. 2003. Family policies and children's school achievement in single- versus two-parent families. *Journal of Marriage and the Family,* Vol. 65, No. 3, pp. 681–99.

Porta Pallais, E. and Laguna, J. R. 2007. *Educational Equity in Central America: A Pending Issue for the Public Agenda.* Washington, DC, USAID/Academy for Educational Development, EQUIP2: Educational Policy, Systems Development and Management.

Postlethwaite, T. N. 2004. *Monitoring Educational Achievement.* Paris, UNESCO International Institute for Educational Planning. (Fundamentals of Educational Planning, 81.)

Postlethwaite, T. N. and Kellaghan, T. Forthcoming. *National Assessment of Education.* Paris, UNESCO International Institute for Educational Planning.

Prasertsri, S. S. 2008. Cambodia case study of government and donor efforts for improved aid effectiveness in the education sector. Background paper for *EFA Global Monitoring Report 2009.*

Pratham Resource Center. 2008. *Annual Status of Education Report (Rural) 2007: Provisional.* Mumbai, India, Pratham Resource Centre.

PREAL and Foro Educativo Nicaragüense EDUQUEMOS. 2008. *Apostar por la Educación: Informe de Progreso Educativo de Nicaragua 2007* [Bet on Education: Nicaragua Education Progress Report 2007]. Washington, DC/Managua, Programa de Promoción de la Reforma Educativa de América Latina y el Caribe/Foro Educativo Nicaragüense EDUQUEMOS. (In Spanish.)

Pridmore, P. 2007. *Impact of Health on Education Access and Achievement: A Cross-National Review of the Research Evidence.* Brighton, UK/London, University of Sussex, Sussex School of Education, Centre for International Education, Consortium for Research on Educational Access, Transitions & Equity/University of London, Institute of Education. (CREATE Pathways to Access, Research Monograph, 2.)

Pridmore, P. and Yates, C. 2006. *The Role of Open, Distance and Flexible Learning (ODFL) in HIV/AIDS Prevention and Mitigation for Affected Youth in South Africa and Mozambique.* London, UK Department for International Development. (Researching the Issues, 61.)

Pritchett, L. 2004*a*. Access to education. Lomborg, B. (ed.), *Global Crises, Global Solutions.* Cambridge, UK, Cambridge University Press, pp. 175–234.

— 2004*b*. *Towards a New Consensus for Addressing the Global Challenge of the Lack of Education.* Washington, DC, Center for Global Development. (Working Paper, 43.)

Pritchett, L. and Pande, V. 2006. *Making Primary Education Work for India's Rural Poor: A Proposal for Effective Decentralization.* Washington, DC, World Bank. (Social Development Papers, South Asia Series, 95.)

Psacharopoulos, G. and Patrinos, H. A. 2004. Returns to investment in education: a further update. *Education Economics,* Vol. 12, No. 2, pp. 111–34.

Punjab Education Foundation. 2008. *Education Foundation: Briefing Document.* Garden Town Lahore, Pakistan, Punjab Education Foundation.

Quisumbing, A. R. 1996. Male-female differences in agricultural productivity: Methodological issues and empirical evidence. *World Development,* Vol. 24, No. 10, pp. 1579–95.

Rajkumar, A. S. and Swaroop, V. 2008. Public spending and outcomes: does governance matter? *Journal of Development Economics,* Vol. 86, No. 1, pp. 96–111.

Ram, F. and Singh, A. 2006. Is antenatal care effective in improving maternal health in rural Uttar Pradesh? Evidence from a district level household survey. *Journal of Biosocial Science,* Vol. 38, No. 4, pp. 433–49.

Ramachandran, V., Pal, M., Jain, S., Shekar, S. and Sharma, J. 2005. *Teacher Motivation in India.* New Delhi, UK Department for International Development.

Ravela, P. 2005. A formative approach to national assessments: the case of Uruguay. *Prospects: Quarterly Review of Comparative Education,* Vol. 35, No. 1, pp. 21–43.

Reading and Writing Foundation. 2008. *Scope of the Problem.* The Hague, Stichting Lezen & Schrijven (Reading and Writing Foundation). http://www.lezenenschrijven.nl/en/illiteracy/scope-of-problem/ (Accessed 27 September 2008.)

Regalsky, P. and Laurie, N. 2007. 'The school, whose place is this'? The deep structures of the hidden curriculum in indigenous education in Bolivia. *Comparative Education,* Vol. 43, No. 2, pp. 231–51.

Reimers, F. and Cárdenas, S. 2007. Who benefits from school-based management in Mexico? *Prospects: Quarterly Review of Comparative Education,* Vol. 37, No. 1, pp. 37–56.

Reinikka, R. and Smith, N. 2004. *Public Expenditure Tracking Surveys in Education.* Paris, UNESCO International Institute for Educational Planning.

Reuters. 2007. *AIDS leaves Mozambique pupils without teachers.* Maputo. http://africa.reuters.com/top/news/usnBAN248950.html (Accessed 30 November 2007.)

Reynolds, D., Creemers, B., Bellin, W., Stringfield, S., Teddlie, C. and Schaffer, G. (eds). 2002. *World Class Schools: International Perspectives on School Effectiveness.* London, RoutledgeFalmer.

Rhoten, D. 2000. Education decentralization in Argentina: a 'global-local conditions of possibility' approach to state, market and society change. *Journal of Education Policy,* Vol. 15, No. 1, pp. 593–619.

Riddell, A. 2008. *Factors Influencing Educational Quality and Effectiveness in Developing Countries: A Review of Research.* Eschborn, Germany, Deutsche Gesellschaft für Technische Zusammenarbeit.

Robinson-Pant, A. 2008. *Literacy in the World Today.* Paris, UNESCO. (Background paper for the Report of the Director-General of UNESCO on the Implementation of the International Plan of Action for the United Nations Literacy Decade.)

Rocha Menocal, A. and Mulley, S. 2006. *Learning from Experience? A Review of Recipient-Government Efforts to Manage Donor Relations and Improve the Quality of Aid.* London, Overseas Development Institute. (ODI Working Paper, 268.)

Rodrik, D. 2008. Thinking about governance. North, D., Acemoglu, D., Fukuyama, F. and Rodrik, D., *Governance, Growth and Development Decision-Making.* Washington, DC, World Bank, pp. 17–24.

Roebuck, M. 2007. *The Relationship between Inspection and School Improvement.* Paper presented at South Asia Regional Conference on Education Quality, New Delhi, World Bank, 24–26 October.

Rose, P. 2006. Collaborating in Education for All? Experiences of government support for non-state provision of basic education in South Asia and sub-Saharan Africa. *Public Administration and Development,* Vol. 26, No. 3, pp. 219–30.

Rose, P. and Adelabu, M. 2007. Private sector contributions to Education for All in Nigeria. Srivastava, P. and Walford, G. (eds), *Private Schooling in Less Economically Developed Countries: Asian and African Perspectives.* Oxford, UK, Symposium Books, pp. 67–88.

Rose, P. and Brown, T. 2004. *Political Will and Capacity for Attaining the Gender MDG.* London, UK Department for International Development.

Rose, P. and Dyer, C. 2006. *Chronic Poverty and Education: A Review of the Literature.* Manchester, University of Manchester, School of Environment and Development, Institute for Development Policy and Management, Chronic Poverty Research Centre.

Rouse, C. E. 1998. Schools and student achievement: more evidence from the Milwaukee Parental Choice Program. *FRBNY Economic Policy Review,* Vol. 4, No. 1, pp. 61–76.

Rustemier, S. 2002. Inclusive education: a worldwide movement. *Inclusion Week.* http://inclusion.uwe.ac.uk/inclusionweek/articles/worldwide.htm (Accessed 20 August 2008.)

Rwanda Ministry of Finance and Economic Planning. 2002. *Poverty Reduction Strategy Paper.* Kigali, Ministry of Finance and Economic Planning, National Poverty Reduction Program.

— 2007. *Economic Development and Poverty Reduction Strategy, 2008–2012.* Kigali, Ministry of Finance and Economic Planning.

Sander, W. 2008. Teacher quality and earnings. *Economics Letters,* Vol. 99, No. 2, p. 307.

Sandström, F. M. and Bergström, F. 2005. School vouchers in practice: competition will not hurt you. *Journal of Public Economics,* Vol. 89, No. 2–3, pp. 351–80.

Sapelli, C. and Vial, B. 2002. The performance of private and public schools in the Chilean voucher system. *Cuadernos de Economía,* Vol. 39, No. 118, pp. 423–54.

Sauvageot, C. 2008. Reconstruction of the statistical information system in the Democratic Republic of the Congo. Background paper for *EFA Global Monitoring Report 2009.*

Save the Children. 2008*a*. *Dubai Cares Provides Multimillion Dollar Grant for Save the Children's Sudan Education Programs.* Westport, Conn., Save the Children. http://www.savethechildren.org/newsroom/2008/dubai-cares-grant.html (Accessed 27 September 2008.)

— 2008*b*. *Last in Line, Last in School 2008: How Donors are Failing Children in Conflict-Affected Fragile States.* London, International Save the Children Alliance.

Sawada, Y. and Ragatz, A. B. 2005. Decentralization of education, teacher behavior and outcomes. Vega, E. (ed.), *Incentives to Improve Teaching: Lessons from Latin America.* Washington, DC, World Bank, pp. 255–306.

Schady, N. 2006. *Early Childhood Development in Latin America and the Caribbean.* Washington, DC, World Bank. (Policy Research Working Paper, 3869.)

Schady, N. and Araujo, M. C. 2006. *Cash Transfers, Conditions, School Enrollment and Child Work: Evidence from a Randomized Experiment in Ecuador.* Washington, DC, World Bank. (Impact Evaluation Series, 3. Policy Research Working Paper, 3930.)

Schagen, I. and Shamsen, Y. 2007. *Analysis of International Data on the Impact of Private Schooling: Hyderabad, India.* Slough, UK, National Foundation for Educational Research, Statistics Research and Analysis Group.

Scheerens, J. 2004. Review of school and instructional effectiveness research. Background paper for *EFA Global Monitoring Report 2005.*

Schistosomiasis Control Initiative. 2008. *Schistosomiasis & NTD Control: Five Million School Children Receive Treatment on Mainland Tanzania Nov–Dec 2005.* London, Imperial College, Department of Infectious Disease Epidemiology. http://www.schisto.org/Tanzania/SchoolchildTreatment.htm (Accessed 27 September 2008.)

Schnepf, S. V. 2008. *Inequality of Learning amongst Immigrant Children in Industrialised Countries.* Bonn, Germany, Institute for the Study of Labor. (Discussion Paper, 3337.)

Schollar, E. 2006. *Integrated Education Program: Analysis of the Impact on Pupil Performance of the District Development Support Programme (DDSP).* Research Triangle Park, NC, RTI International.

Schuh Moore, A.-M., Destefano, J., Terway, A. and Balwanz, D. 2008. *Expanding Secondary Education for sub-Saharan Africa: Where are the Teachers?* Biennale on Education in Africa. Beyond Primary Education: Challenges and Approaches to Expanding Learning Opportunities in Africa, Maputo, Association for the Development of Education in Africa, 5–9 May.

Schuler, S. R. 2007. Rural Bangladesh: sound policies, evolving gender norms and family strategies. Lewis, M. and Lockheed, M. (eds), *Exclusion, Gender and Education: Case Studies from the Developing World.* Washington, DC, Center for Global Development, pp. 179–203.

Schütz, G., Ursprung, H. W. and Wößmann, L. 2005. *Education Policy and Equality of Opportunity.* Munich, Germany, CESifo. (Working Paper, 1518.)

Schütz, G., West, M. R. and Wößmann, L. 2007. *School Accountability, Autonomy, Choice and the Equity of Student Achievement: International Evidence from PISA 2003*. Paris, Organisation for Economic Co-operation and Development. (Education Working Papers, 14.)

Schweinhart, L. J., Montie, J., Xiang, Z., Barnett, W. S., Belfield, C. R. and Nores, M. 2005. *Lifetime Effects: The High/Scope Perry Preschool Study through Age 40*. Ypsilanti, Mich., High/Scope Press.

Seedco. 2007. *Mayor Bloomberg and Major Philanthropic Foundations Unveil Size, Scope and Schedule of Opportunity NYC, the Nation's First-Ever Conditional Cash Transfer Program*. New York, Seedco. http://www.seedco.org/pressreleases/newsrelease.php?id=46 (Accessed 27 September 2008.)

Semba, R. D., de Pee, S., Sun, K., Sari, M., Akhter, N. and Bloem, M. W. 2008. Effect of parental formal education on risk of child stunting in Indonesia and Bangladesh: a cross-sectional study. *The Lancet*, Vol. 371, No. 9609, pp. 322–28.

Sen, A. 1999. *Development as Freedom*. Oxford, UK, Oxford University Press.

Senegal Government. 2002. *Poverty Reduction Strategy Paper*. Dakar, Government of the Republic of Senegal.

— 2006. *Poverty Reduction Strategy Paper II*. Dakar, Government of the Republic of Senegal.

Serbia Statistical Office and Strategic Marketing Research Agency. 2007. *Republic of Serbia Multiple Indicator Cluster Survey 2005, Final Report*. Belgrade, Statistical Office of the Republic of Serbia/Strategic Marketing Research Agency.

Shekar, M. and Lee, Y.-K. 2006. *Mainstreaming Nutrition in Poverty Reduction Strategies: What Does it Take? A Review of the Early Experience*. Washington, DC, World Bank. (Health, Nutrition and Population Discussion Paper.)

Shenkut, M. K. 2005. *Ethiopia: where and who are the world's illiterates?* Background Paper for *EFA Global Monitoring Report 2006*.

Sherman, J. D. and Poirier, J. M. 2007. Sub-national disparities in participation in quality primary education: draft report. Background paper for *EFA Global Monitoring Report 2008*. (Through the American Institutes for Research.).

Sherry, H. 2008. *Teachers' Voice: A Policy Research Report on Teachers' Motivation and Perceptions of their Profession in Nigeria*. London, Voluntary Service Overseas .

Shoraku, A. 2008. Educational movement toward school-based management in East Asia: Cambodia, Indonesia and Thailand. Background paper for *EFA Global Monitoring Report 2009*.

Siaens, C., Subbarao, K. and Wodon, Q. T. 2003. *Are Orphans Especially Vulnerable? Evidence from Rwanda*. Washington, DC, World Bank.

Sierra Leone Statistics and UNICEF. 2007. *Sierra Leone Multiple Indicator Cluster Survey 2005, Final Report*. Freetown, Statistics Sierra Leone/UNICEF.

Simoes, E. A. F., Cherian, T., Chow, J., Shahid-Salles, S. A., Laxminarayan, R. and John, T. J. 2006. Acute respiratory infections in children. Jamison, D. T., Breman, J. G., Measham, A. R., Alleyne, G., Claeson, M., Evans, D. B., Jha, P., Mills, A. and Musgrove, P. (eds), *Disease Control Priorities in Developing Countries*. New York/Washington, DC, Oxford University Press/World Bank, pp. 483–97.

Sinyolo, D. 2007. *Teacher Supply, Recruitment and Retention in Six Anglophone sub-Saharan African Countries: A Report on a Survey Conducted by Education International in the Gambia, Kenya, Lesotho, Tanzania, Uganda and Zambia*. Brussels, Education International.

Skoufias, E. and Shapiro, J. 2006. *Evaluating the Impact of Mexico's Quality Schools Program: The Pitfalls of Using Nonexperimental Data*. Washington, DC, World Bank. (Impact Evaluation Series, 8. Policy Research Working Paper, 4036.)

Smits, J., Huisman, J. and Kruijff, K. 2008. Home language and education in the developing world. Background paper for *EFA Global Monitoring Report 2009*.

Soares, S., Osório, G., Soares, R., Veras, F., Medeiros, M. and Zepeda, E. 2007. *Conditional Cash Transfers in Brazil, Chile and Mexico: Impacts upon Inequality*. New York, United Nations Development Program. (International Poverty Centre Working Paper, 35.)

Sridhar, D. 2008. Linkages between nutrition, ill-health and education. Background paper for *EFA Global Monitoring Report 2009*.

Srivastava, P. 2006. Private schooling and mental models about girls' schooling in India. *Compare*, Vol. 36, No. 4, pp. 497–514.

— 2007. For philanthropy or profit? The management and operation of low-fee private schools in India. Srivastava, P. and Walford, G. (eds), *Private Schooling in Less Economically Developed Countries: Asian and African Perspectives*. Oxford, UK, Symposium Books, pp. 153–86.

— 2008. School choice in India: disadvantaged groups and low-fee private schools. Forsey, M., Davies, S. and Walford, G. (eds), *The Globalisation of School Choice?* Oxford, UK, Symposium Books, pp. 185–208.

Steiner-Khamsi, G., Harris-van Keuren, C., Silova, I. and Chachkhiani, K. 2008. Decentralization and recentralization reforms: their impact on teacher salaries in the Caucasus, Central Asia and Mongolia. Background paper for *EFA Global Monitoring Report 2009*.

Steiner, S. 2006. *Decentralisation in Uganda: Exploring the Constraints for Poverty Reduction*. Hamburg, Germany, German Institute of Global and Area Studies. (GIGA Working Paper, 31.)

Strategic Partnership with Africa. 2008. *Strategic Partnership with Africa: Survey of Budget Support, 2007. Volume I – Main Findings.* Prepared for SPA Annual Plenary Meeting, Tunis, 21–22 February.

Sumra, S. 2006. *The Living and Working Conditions of Teachers in Tanzania. A Research Report.* Dar es Salaam, HakiElimu.

Swedish National Agency for Education. 2008. *Barn, Elever Och Personal: Riksnivå: Sveriges Officiella Statistik om Förskolverksamhet, Skolbarnomsorg, Skola Och Vuxenutbildning. Del 2.* [Official Statistics for Pre-School Activities, School-Age Childcare, Schools and Adult Education]. Stockholm, National Agency for Education. (In Swedish.)

Swinkels, R. and Turk, C. 2006. *Explaining Ethnic Minority Poverty in Vietnam: A Summary of Recent Trends and Current Challenges.* Presented at MPI Meeting on Ethnic Minority Poverty, Hanoi, Committee for Ethnic Minorities, 28 September.

Syrian Arab Republic Central Bureau of Statistics. 2008. *The Syrian Arab Republic Multiple Indicator Cluster Survey (MICS) 2006.* Damascus, Central Bureau of Statistics.

Takala, T. 2008. Government and donor efforts for improved aid effectiveness in the education sector: a case study of Mozambique. Background paper for *EFA Global Monitoring Report 2009.*

Thailand National Statistical Office. 2006. *Thailand Multiple Indicator Cluster Survey, December 2005–February 2006, Final Report.* Bangkok, National Statistical Office.

The Communication Initiative Network. 2002. *Speaking Up on Disability. Country: Uganda.* Victoria, BC, The Communication Initiative Network. http://www.comminit.com/en/node/118065 (Accessed 27 September 2008.)

The Lancet. 2008. Maternal and child undernutrition series launched. *The Lancet,* Vol. 371, No. 9608.

Thirumurthy, H., Graff Zivin, J. and Goldstein, M. 2007. *AIDS Treatment and Intrahousehold Resource Allocations: Children's Nutrition and Schooling in Kenya.* Washington, DC, Center for Global Development. (Working Paper, 106.)

Thuilliez, J. 2007. *Malaria and Primary Education: A Cross-Country Analysis on Primary Repetition and Completion Rates.* Paris, University of Paris 1 Pantheon-Sorbonne, Sorbonne Economics Centre/National Centre for Scientific Research. (CES Working Papers, 2007.13.)

Tiedemann, J. 2000. Parents' gender stereotypes and teachers' beliefs as predictors of children's concept of their mathematical ability in elementary school. *Journal of Educational Psychology,* Vol. 92, No. 1, pp. 144–51.

Tokman Ramos, A. 2002. *Is Private Education Better? Evidence from Chile.* Santiago, Central Bank of Chile. (Working Papers, 147.)

Tomasevski, K. 2006. *The State of the Right to Education Worldwide. Free or Fee: 2006 Global Report.* Copenhagen.

Tooley, J. 2007. Could for-profit private education benefit the poor? Some a priori considerations arising from case study research in India. *Journal of Education Policy,* Vol. 22, No. 3, pp. 321–42.

Tooley, J. and Dixon, P. 2007. Private education for low-income families: results from a global research project. Srivastava, P. and Walford, G. (eds), *Private Schooling in Less Economically Developed Countries: Asian and African Perspectives.* Oxford, UK, Symposium Books, pp. 15–40.

Transparency International. 2005. *Stealing the Future: Corruption in the Classroom. Ten Real World Experiences.* Berlin, Transparency International.

Tsang, M. 2002. Establishing a substantial and regularized scheme of intergovernmental grants in compulsory education. *Harvard China Review,* Vol. 3, No. 2, pp. 15–20.

Uganda Local Government Finance Commission. 2000. *Equalisation Grant for Urban Local Governments: Analysis and Recommendations.* Kampala, Local Government Finance Commission.

Uganda Ministry of Finance Planning and Economic Development. 2000. *Poverty Reduction Strategy Plan: Uganda Poverty Eradication Action Plan Summary and Main Objectives.* Kampala, Ministry of Finance, Planning and Economic Development.

— 2004. *Poverty Eradication Action Plan (2004/5–2007/8).* Kampala, Ministry of Finance, Planning and Economic Development.

UIS. 2005. *Global Education Digest 2005: Comparing Education Statistics across the World.* Montreal, Que, UNESCO Institute for Statistics.

— 2006*a*. *Global Education Digest 2006: Comparing Education Statistics across the World.* Montreal, Que, UNESCO Institute for Statistics.

— 2006*b*. *Teachers and Educational Quality: Monitoring Global Needs for 2015.* Montreal, Que, UNESCO Institute for Statistics.

— 2007. *Global Education Digest 2007: Comparing Education Statistics across the World.* Montreal, Que, UNESCO Institute for Statistics.

— 2008. *Data Centre: Culture and Communication.* Montreal, Que, UNESCO Institute for Statistics. http://stats.uis.unesco.org/unesco/tableviewer/document.aspx?FileId=50 (Accessed 27 September 2008.)

Umansky, I. 2005. A literature review of teacher quality and incentives: theory and evidence. Vegas, E. (ed.), *Incentives to Improve Teaching: Lessons from Latin America.* Washington, DC, World Bank, pp. 21–62.

UN-HABITAT. 2006. *The State of the World's Cities Report 2006/7: The Millennium Development Goals and Urban Sustainability. 30 Years of Shaping the Habitat Agenda.* Nairobi, United Nations Human Settlements Programme.

UN Economic Commission for Latin America and the Caribbean. 2007. *Social Panorama of Latin America 2007.* Santiago, United Nations Economic Commission for Latin America and the Caribbean.

UN Millennium Project. 2005*a*. *Taking Action: Achieving Gender Equality and Empowering Women. Achieving the Millennium Development Goals.* London, United Nations Development Programme, UN Millennium Project, Task Force on Education and Gender Equality.

— 2005*b*. *Towards Universal Primary Education: Investments, Incentives and Institutions.* London, United Nations Development Programme, UN Millennium Project, Task Force on Education and Gender Equality.

UN Population Division. 2007. *World Population Prospects: The 2006 Revision Population Database.* New York, United Nations, Department of Economic and Social Affairs, Population Division. (ESA/P/WP.202.)

UNAIDS. 2008. *Report on the Global AIDS Epidemic 2008.* Geneva, Switzerland, Joint United Nations Programme on HIV/AIDS. (UNAIDS/08.25E / JC1510E.)

UNDP. 2006. *Human Development Report 2006. Beyond Scarcity: Power, Poverty and the Global Water Crisis.* New York, United Nations Development Programme.

— 2007. *Human Development Report 2007/2008. Fighting Climate Change: Human Solidarity in a Divided World.* New York, United Nations Development Programme.

UNDP Arab TIMSS Regional Office. 2003. *Achievements of Arab Countries that Participated in the Trends in International Mathematics and Science Study.* Amman, United Nations Development Programme, Arab TIMSS Regional Office.

UNESCO. 1997. *International Standard Classification of Education (ISCED) 1997.* Paris, UNESCO. (BPE.98/WS/1.)

— 2000. *The Dakar Framework for Action: Education for All – Meeting our Collective Commitments.* World Education Forum, Dakar, UNESCO.

— 2003. *EFA Global Monitoring Report 2003/4. Gender and Education for All: The Leap to Equality.* Paris, UNESCO.

— 2004. *EFA Global Monitoring Report 2005. Education for All: The Quality Imperative.* Paris, UNESCO.

— 2005. *EFA Global Monitoring Report 2006. Education for All: Literacy for Life.* Paris, UNESCO.

— 2006. *EFA Global Monitoring Report 2007. Strong Foundations: Early Childhood Care and Education.* Paris, UNESCO.

— 2007*a*. *EFA Global Monitoring Report 2008. Education for All by 2015: Will We Make It?* Paris, UNESCO/Oxford University Press.

— 2007*b*. *Supporting HIV-Positive Teachers in East and Southern Africa: Technical Consultation Report. 30 November–1 December 2006.* Nairobi, UNESCO.

UNESCO-IBE. 2007. Recent estimates of intended instructional time over the first nine years of schooling (prepared by Massimo Amadio). Background paper for *EFA Global Monitoring Report 2008.*

— 2008*a*. A compilation of background information about educational legislation, governance, management and financing structures and processes: Arab States. Background paper for *EFA Global Monitoring Report 2009.*

— 2008*b*. A compilation of background information about educational legislation, governance, management and financing structures and processes: Central and Eastern Europe. Background paper for *EFA Global Monitoring Report 2009.*

— 2008*c*. A compilation of background information about educational legislation, governance, management and financing structures and processes: Central Asia. Background paper for *EFA Global Monitoring Report 2009.*

— 2008*d*. A compilation of background information about educational legislation, governance, management and financing structures and processes: East Asia and the Pacific. Background paper for *EFA Global Monitoring Report 2009.*

— 2008*e*. A compilation of background information about educational legislation, governance, management and financing structures and processes: Latin America and the Caribbean. Background paper for *EFA Global Monitoring Report 2009.*

— 2008*f*. A compilation of background information about educational legislation, governance, management and financing structures and processes: North America and Western Europe. Background paper for *EFA Global Monitoring Report 2009.*

— 2008*g*. A compilation of background information about educational legislation, governance, management and financing structures and processes: South and West Asia. Background paper for *EFA Global Monitoring Report 2009.*

— 2008*h*. A compilation of background information about educational legislation, governance, management and financing structures and processes: sub-Saharan Africa. Background paper for *EFA Global Monitoring Report 2009.*

UNESCO-IIEP. 2006. Review of national education planning documents in 45 countries. Background paper for the *EFA Global Monitoring Report 2006.*

UNESCO-OREALC. 2008. *Los Aprendizajes de los Estudiantes de América Latina y el Caribe: Primer Reporte de los Resultados del Segundo Estudio Regional Comparativo y Explicativo* [Student Achievement in Latin America and the Caribbean: Results of the Second Regional Comparative and Explanatory Study]. Santiago, UNESCO Regional Bureau for Education in Latin America and the Caribbean, Latin American Laboratory for Assessment of the Quality of Education. (In Spanish.)

UNESCO-UNEVOC/UIS. 2006. *Participation in Formal and Vocational Education and Training Programmes Worldwide. An Initial Statistical Study.* Bonn, Germany/Montreal, Que, UNESCO-UNEVOC International Centre for Technical and Vocational Education and Training/UNESCO Institute for Statistics.

UNICEF. 2007. *The State of the World's Children 2008: Child Survival.* New York, UNICEF.

— 2008. *At a Glance: United Arab Emirates: UNICEF and Dubai Cares Support Quality Education to Break the Cycle of Poverty.* New York, UNICEF. http://www.unicef.org/infobycountry/uae_42888.html (Accessed 27 September 2008.)

UNICEF and Agency of the Republic of Kazakhstan on Statistics. 2007. *Kazakhstan Multiple Indicator Cluster Survey 2006: Final Report.* Astana, UNICEF Kazakhstan/Agency of the Republic of Kazakhstan on Statistics.

UNICEF and State Statistical Committee of the Republic of Uzbekistan. 2007. *Uzbekistan Multiple Indicator Cluster Survey 2006, Final Report.* Tashkent, UNICEF.

United Nations. 2006. *Convention on the Rights of Persons with Disabilities.* New York, United Nations. (Adopted by the Sixty-First Session Item 67 (b). Human Rights Questions: Human Rights Questions, Including Alternative Approaches for Improving the Effective Enjoyment of Human Rights and Fundamental Freedoms.)

United Republic of Tanzania Government. 2000. *Poverty Reduction Strategy Paper (PRSP).* Dar es Salaam, Government of the United Republic of Tanzania.

— 2005. *National Strategy for Growth and Reduction of Poverty (NSGRP).* Dar es Salaam, Government of the United Republic of Tanzania.

United Republic of Tanzania Ministry of Education and Vocational Training. 2007. *Basic Education Statistics in Tanzania (BEST) 2003–2007 National Data.* Dar es Salaam, Ministry of Education and Vocational Training.

United Republic of Tanzania Research and Analysis Working Group. 2007. *Poverty and Human Development Report (PHDR) 2007.* Dar es Salaam, Ministry of Planning, Economy and Empowerment, Research and Analysis Working Group, MKUKUTA Monitoring System.

United Republic of Tanzania Vice President's Office. 2005. *National Strategy for Growth and Reduction of Poverty (NSGRP).* Dar es Salaam, Vice President's Office.

US Department of Education, National Center for Education Statistics. 2007. *The Condition of Education 2007.* Washington, DC, Government Printing Office. (NCES 2007-064.)

US Social Security Administration. 2006. *Social Security Programs Throughout the World: Europe, 2006.* Washington, DC, Office of Policy, Office of Research, Evaluation and Statistics. (SSA Publication, 13-11801.)

— 2007*a*. *Social Security Programs Throughout the World: Africa, 2007.* Washington, DC, Office of Policy, Office of Research, Evaluation and Statistics. (SSA Publication, 13-11803.)

— 2007*b*. *Social Security Programs Throughout the World: Asia and the Pacific, 2006.* Washington, DC, Office of Policy, Office of Research, Evaluation and Statistics. (SSA Publication, 13-11802.)

— 2008. *Social Security Programs Throughout the World: The Americas, 2007.* Washington, DC, Office of Retirement and Disability Policy, Office of Research, Evaluation and Statistics. (SSA Publication, 13-11804.)

Vachon, P. 2007. Country case studies: Burkina Faso. Background paper for *EFA global Monitoring Report 2008.*

van der Berg, S. and Louw, M. 2007. *Lessons Learnt from SACMEQ II: South African Student Performance in Regional Context.* Metieland, South Africa, University of Stellenbosch, Department of Economics and Bureau for Economic Research. (Working paper, 16/07.)

Vandemoortele, J. and Delamonica, E. 2000. The 'education vaccine' against HIV. *Current Issues in Comparative Education,* Vol. 3, No. 1, pp. 6–13.

Vaux, T., Smith, A. and Subba, S. 2006. *Education for All – Nepal: Review From a Conflict Perspective.* London, International Alert.

Vegas, E. and De Laat, J. 2003. *Do Differences in Teacher Contracts Affect Student Performance? Evidence from Togo.* Washington, DC, World Bank.

Vegas, E. and Petrow, J. 2007. *Raising Student Learning in Latin America: The Challenge for the 21st Century.* Washington, DC, World Bank.

Viet Nam General Statistics Office. 2006. *Viet Nam Multiple Indicator Cluster Survey 2006, Final Report.* Hanoi, General Statistics Office.

Viet Nam Government. 2003. *The Comprehensive Poverty Reduction and Growth Strategy.* Hanoi, Government of the Socialist Republic of Vietnam.

— 2006. *The Five Year Socio-Economic Development Plan 2006–2010.* Hanoi, Government of the Socialist Republic of Vietnam.

VSO. 2007. *Teachers Speak Out: A Policy Research Report on Teachers' Motivation and Perceptions of their Profession in the Gambia.* London, Voluntary Service Overseas.

Wang, Y. 2004. *Governance of Basic Education: Service Provision and Quality Assurance in China.* Washington, DC, World Bank.

Ward, M., Penny, A. and Read, T. 2006. *Education Reform in Uganda – 1997 to 2004. Reflections on Policy, Partnership, Strategy and Implementation.* London, UK Department for International Development. (Researching the Issues, 60.)

Watkins, K. 2004. Private education and 'Education For All' – or how not to construct an evidence-based argument: a reply to Tooley. *Economic Affairs,* Vol. 24, No. 4, pp. 8–11.

Wedgwood, R. 2007. Education and poverty reduction in Tanzania. *International Journal of Educational Development,* Vol. 27, No. 4, pp. 383–96.

WHO. 2008. *World Health Statistics 2008.* Geneva, Switzerland, World Health Organization.

WHO, UNICEF, UNFPA and World Bank. 2007. *Maternal Mortality in 2005: Estimates Developed by WHO, UNICEF, UNFPA and the World Bank.* Geneva, Switzerland, World Health Organization.

William and Flora Hewlett Foundation. 2006. *Gates and Hewlett Foundations Join to Improve the Quality of Education in Developing Nations.* Menlo Park, Calif., William and Flora Hewlett Foundation. http://www.hewlett.org/Programs/GlobalAffairs/News/Gates+and+Hewlett+Foundations+Join+to+Improve+the+Quality+of+Education+in+Developing+Nations.htm (Accessed 27 September 2008.)

— 2007. *The Hewlett and Gates Foundations Award $9 million to Pratham's Read India Campaign.* Santa Clara, Calif., William and Flora Hewlett Foundation. http://www.pratham.org/documents/Pratham%20Hewlett%20Gates%20Grant%20Release%20Final%20July%205%202007.pdf (Accessed 27 September 2008.)

Willms, J. D. 2006. *Learning Divides: Ten Key Policy Questions about the Performance and Equity of Schools and Schooling Systems.* Montreal, Que, UNESCO Institute for Statistics. (UIS Working Paper, 5.)

Winkler, D. 2005. *Public Expenditure Tracking in Education.* Washington, DC, USAID/Academy for Educational Development, EQUIP2: Educational Policy, Systems Development and Management. (Policy Brief.)

Winters, M. A. and Greene, J. P. 2007. *Second Year Evaluation of the Systemic Effects of the DC Voucher Program.* Fayetteville, Ark., University of Arkansas. (School Choice Demonstration Project.)

Wodon, Q. T., Tsimpo, C., Backiny-Yetna, P., Joseph, G., Adoho, F. and Coulombe, H. 2008. *Measuring the Potential Impact of Higher Food Prices on Poverty: Summary Evidence from West and Central Africa.* Washington, DC, World Bank. (Mimeo.)

World Bank. 2002. *User Fees in Primary Education.* Washington, DC, World Bank. (Mimeo, review draft.)

— 2003. *World Development Report 2004: Making Services Work For Poor People.* Washington, DC, World Bank/Oxford University Press.

— 2004. *Books, Buildings and Learning Outcomes: An Impact Evaluation of World Bank Support to Basic Education in Ghana.* Washington, DC, World Bank, Operation Evaluation Department.

— 2005*a*. *Cambodia – Public Expenditure Tracking Survey (PETS) in Primary Education.* Washington, DC, World Bank, East Asia and Pacific Region, Human Development Sector Unit. (Human Development Sector Reports, 34911-KH.)

— 2005*b*. *Education Sector Strategy Update. Achieving Education For All, Broadening Our Perspective, Maximizing Our Effectiveness.* Washington, DC, World Bank. (Final Draft. Copyedited version of document presented to the Board of Directors on 7 November 2005.)

— 2005*c*. *Expanding Opportunities and Building Competencies for Young People: A New Agenda for Secondary Education.* Washington, DC, World Bank.

— 2005*d*. *Going to School/Going to Work: A Report on Child Labor and EFA in World Bank Projects and Policy Documents.* Third Roundtable on Child Labor and Education for All (EFA), Beijing, Global Task Force on Child Labour and Education, 28 November.

— 2005*e*. *Implementation Completion Report (IDA-35700 TF-50588) on a Credit in the Amount of SDR 119.1 Million (US$150 Equivalent) and a Grant in the Amount of US$50 Million to the United Republic of Tanzania for the Primary Education Development Program.* Washington, DC, World Bank, Africa Region, Human Development, Country Department. (32071.)

— 2005*f*. *Project Appraisal Document Vietnam. Targeted Budget Support for National Education for All Plan Implementation Program.* Washington, DC, World Bank.

— 2005*g*. *World Development Report 2006: Equity and Development.* Washington, DC, World Bank.

— 2006*a*. *Bolivia. Basic Education in Bolivia: Challenges for 2006–2010.* Washington, DC, World Bank; Latin America and the Caribbean Region; Bolivia, Ecuador, Peru and Venezuela Country Management Unit; Human Development Department. (35073-BO.)

— 2006*b*. *Repositioning Nutrition as Central to Development: A Strategy for Large-Scale Action. Overview.* Washington, DC, World Bank. (Directions in Development.)

— 2007*a*. *Chile: Institutional Design for an Effective Education Quality Assurance.* Washington, DC, World Bank; Latin America and the Caribbean Regional Office; Argentina, Chile, Paraguay and Uruguay Country Management Unit; Human Development. (39830-CL.)

— 2007*b*. *Ethiopia: Enhancing Human Development Outcomes through Decentralized Service Delivery.* Washington, DC, World Bank, AFTH3, Human Development Department, Africa Region. (32 675-ET.)

—— 2007*c*. *Pakistan. Social Protection in Pakistan: Managing Household Risks and Vulnerability.* Washington, DC, World Bank, Human Development Unit, South Asia Region. (35472-PK.)

—— 2007*d*. *Project Paper on a Proposed Additional Financing (Grant) in the Amount of SDR 38.7 Million (US$60,0 Million Equivalent) to Nepal for the Education For All Project*, World Bank, Human Development Unit, South Asia Regional Office. (41346-NP.)

—— 2007*e*. *What Do We Know About School-Based Management?* Washington, DC, World Bank, Education, Human Development Network.

—— 2007*f*. *What Is School-Based Management?* Washington, DC, World Bank, Education, Human Development Network.

—— 2008*a*. *Addressing the Food Crisis: The Need for Rapid and Coordinated Action.* Group of Eight: Meeting of Finance Ministers, Osaka, Japan, World Bank, 13–14 June.

—— 2008*b*. *Educational Attainment.* Washington, DC, World Bank. http://www.worldbank.org/research/projects/edattain/ (Accessed 27 September 2008.)

—— 2008*c*. *FYR Macedonia: Public Expenditure Review.* Washington, DC, World Bank, Poverty Reduction and Economic Management Unit, Europe and Central Asia Region. (42155-MK.)

—— 2008*d*. *MENA Development Report. The Road Not Travelled: Education Reform in the Middle East and North Africa.* Washington, DC, World Bank.

—— 2008*e*. *Nigeria: A Review of the Costs and Financing of Public Education. Volume 1: Executive Summary.* Washington, DC, World Bank, Human Development Unit, Africa Region. (42418-NG.)

—— 2008*f*. *Nigeria: A Review of the Costs and Financing of Public Education. Volume 2: Main Report.* Washington, DC, World Bank, Human Development Unit, Africa Region. (42418-NG.)

—— 2008*g*. *World Development Indicators.* Washington, DC, World Bank.

World Bank and IMF. 2005. *2005 PRS Review: Balancing Accountabilities and Scaling Up Results.* Washington, DC, World Bank/International Monetary Fund.

World Vision. 2007. *Education's Missing Millions: Including Disabled Children in Education through EFA FTI Processes and National Sector Plans. Main report of Study Findings.* Milton Keynes, UK, World Vision.

Wößmann, L. 2003. Schooling resources, educational institutions and student performance: the international evidence. *Oxford Bulletin of Economics and Statistics*, Vol. 65, No. 2, pp. 117–70.

—— 2006. *Public-Private Partnerships and Schooling Outcomes across Countries.* Paper prepared for the conference Mobilizing the Private Sector for Public Education, Cambridge, Mass., Harvard University, Kennedy School of Government, Program on Education Policy and Governance/World Bank, 5–6 October.

Wu, K. B., Goldschmidt, P., Boscardin, C. K. and Azam, M. 2007. Girls in India: poverty, location and social disparities. Lewis, M. and Lockheed, M. (eds), *Exclusion, Gender and Education: Case Studies from the Developing World.* Washington, DC, Center for Global Development, pp. 119–43.

Wyse, D., McCreery, E. and Torrance, H. 2008. *The Trajectory and Impact of National Reform: Curriculum and Assessment in English Primary Schools.* Cambridge, UK, University of Cambridge. (Interim Reports. The Primary Review. Research Survey, 3/2.)

Yoshikawa, H., McCartney, K., Myers, R., Bub, K. L., Lugo-Gil, J., Ramos, M. A. and Knaul, F. 2007. *Early Childhood Education in Mexico: Expansion, Quality Improvement and Curricular Reform.* Florence, Italy, UNICEF Innocenti Research Centre. (Innocenti Working Paper, IWP-2007-03.)

Young, M. E. and Richardson, L. M. (eds). 2007. *Early Child Development from Measurement to Action: A Priority for Growth and Equity.* Washington, DC, World Bank, Children and Youth Unit, Human Development Network.

Zambia Government. 2006. *Fifth National Development Plan 2006–2010.* Lusaka, Government of the Republic of Zambia.

Zambia Ministry of Finance and National Planning. 2002. *Zambia Poverty Reduction Strategy Paper 2002–2004.* Lusaka, Ministry of Finance and National Planning.

Zhang, Y., Postlethwaite, T. N. and Grisay, A. 2008. *A View Inside Primary Schools: A World Education Indicators (WEI) Cross-National Study.* Montreal, Que, UNESCO Institute for Statistics.

Zimmer, R., Gill, B., Razquin, P., Booker, K. and Lockwood III, J. R. 2007. *State and Local Implementation of the No Child Left Behind Act. Volume I – Title I School Choice, Supplemental Educational Services, and Student Achievement.* Washington, DC, US Department of Education, Office of Planning, Evaluation and Policy Development, Policy and Program Studies Service.

Abbreviations

ADB	Asian Development Bank
AfDF	African Development Fund
ARTF	Afghanistan Reconstruction Trust Fund
AsDF	Asian Development Fund
CONFEMEN	Conférence des Ministres de l'Éducation des pays ayant le français en partage
DAC	Development Assistance Committee (OECD)
DPT	Diphtheria Pertussis Tetanus vaccine
DFID	Department for International Development (United Kingdom)
DPEP	District Primary Education Programme (India)
E-9	Nine high-population countries (Bangladesh, Brazil, China, Egypt, India, Indonesia, Mexico, Nigeria, Pakistan)
EC	European Commission
ECCE	Early childhood care and education
EDI	EFA Development Index
EDUCO	Educación con Participación de la Comunidad (El Salvador)
EIIIG	EFA Inequality Index for Income Groups
EFA	Education for All
EMIS	Education Management Information System(s)
ESDP	Education Sector Development Programme (Ethiopia)
EU	European Union
FTI	Fast Track Initiative
FUNDEB	Fundo de Manutenção e Desenvolvimento da Educação Básica e de Valorizaçãodos Profissionais da Educação (Brazil) (formerly FUNDEF)
FUNDEF	Fundo de Manutenção e Desenvolvimento do Ensino Fundamental e de Valorização do Magistério (Brazil) (renamed FUNDEB in 2007)
FUNDESCOLA	Fundo de Fortalecimento da Escola (Brazil)
G8	Group of Eight (Canada, France, Germany, Italy, Japan, Russian Federation, United Kingdom and United States, plus EU representatives)
GDP	Gross domestic product
GEI	Gender-specific EFA index
GER	Gross enrolment ratio
GIR	Gross intake rate
GNI	Gross national income
GNP	Gross national product
GPI	Gender parity index
HIV/AIDS	Human immuno-deficiency virus/acquired immune deficiency syndrome
IBE	International Bureau of Education (UNESCO)
ICT	Information and communication technology
IDA	International Development Association (World Bank)
IDB	Inter-American Development Bank
IEA	International Association for the Evaluation of Educational Achievement
IIEP	International Institute for Educational Planning (UNESCO)
ILO	International Labour Organization
IMF	International Monetary Fund
ISCED	International Standard Classification of Education
LAMP	Literacy Assessment and Monitoring Programme

LDCs Least developed countries
LGA Local Government Area (Nigeria)
LLECE Laboratorio Latinamericano de Evaluación de la Calidad de la Educación
MDG Millennium Development Goal
MICS Multiple Indicator Cluster Surveys (UNICEF)
MOEYS Ministry of Education, Youth and Sports (Cambodia)
NAR Net attendance rate
NER Net enrolment ratio
NGO Non-government organization
NIR Net intake rate
ODA Official development assistance
OECD Organisation for Economic Co-operation and Development
OREALC UNESCO Regional Bureau for Education in Latin America and the Caribbean
PASEC Programme d'analyse des systèmes éducatifs de la CONFEMEN
PEC Programa Escuelas de Calidad (Mexico)
PETS Public Expenditure Tracking Survey
PIRLS Progress in Reading Literacy Study
PISA Programme for International Student Assessment (OECD)
PPP Purchasing power parity
PREAL Programa de Promoción de la Reforma Educativa de América Latina y el Caribe
PROHECO Programa Hondureño de Educación Comunitaria (Honduras)
PRSP Poverty reduction strategy paper
PTA Parent-teacher association
PTR Pupil/teacher ratio
SACMEQ Southern and Eastern Africa Consortium for Monitoring Educational Quality
SERCE Segundo Estudio Regional Comparativo y Explicativo
SIMECAL Sistema de Medición y Evaluación de la Calidad de la Educación (Bolivia)
SSA Sarva Shiksa Abhiyan (India)
SWAp Sector-wide approach
TIMSS Trends in International Mathematics and Science Study
TNER Total primary net enrolment ratio
TRC Teacher resource centre
TVET Technical and vocational education and training
UIL UNESCO Institute for Lifelong Learning
UIS UNESCO Institute for Statistics
UN United Nations
UN-HABITAT United Nations Human Settlements Programme
UNAIDS Joint United Nations Programme on HIV/AIDS
UNDP United Nations Development Programme
UNESCO United Nations Educational, Scientific and Cultural Organization
UNEVOC International Centre for Technical and Vocational Training (UNESCO)
UNFPA United Nations Population Fund
UNICEF United Nations Children's Fund
UNPD United Nations Population Division
UPE Universal primary education
USAID United States Agency for International Development
WEI World Education Indicators
WHO World Health Organization

Index

This index is in word-by-word order and covers chapters 1 to 5. Page numbers in *italics* indicate figures and tables; those in **bold** refer to material in boxes; ***bold italics*** indicates a figure or table in a box. The letter 'n' following a page number indicates information in a note at the side of the page; the letter 'm' indicates a map. Page numbers in superscript, e.g. 133^{2}, indicate the number of references to the topic on that page. Definitions of terms can be found in the glossary, and additional information on countries can be found in the statistical annex.

C

D

F

G

H

I

J

K

L

U

V

W

Y

Z